A NEW HISTORY OF IRELAND

UNDER THE AUSPICES OF THE ROYAL IRISH ACADEMY
PLANNED AND ESTABLISHED BY THE LATE T. W. MOODY

BOARD OF EDITORS

F. J. BYRNE   W. E. VAUGHAN

ART COSGROVE   J. R. HILL

DÁIBHÍ Ó CRÓINÍN

V

IRELAND UNDER THE UNION, I
1801–70

A NEW HISTORY OF
IRELAND

V

IRELAND UNDER THE UNION, I
1801–70

EDITED BY

W. E. VAUGHAN

OXFORD
UNIVERSITY PRESS

OXFORD

UNIVERSITY PRESS

Great Clarendon Street, Oxford OX2 6DP

Oxford University Press is a department of the University of Oxford.
It furthers the University's objective of excellence in research, scholarship,
and education by publishing worldwide in

Oxford New York

Auckland Cape Town Dar es Salaam Hong Kong Karachi
Kuala Lumpur Madrid Melbourne Mexico City Nairobi
New Delhi Shanghai Taipei Toronto

With offices in

Argentina Austria Brazil Chile Czech Republic France Greece
Guatemala Hungary Italy Japan Poland Portugal Singapore
South Korea Switzerland Thailand Turkey Ukraine Vietnam

Oxford is a registered trade mark of Oxford University Press
in the UK and in certain other countries

Published in the United States
by Oxford University Press Inc., New York

British Library Cataloguing in Publication Data

Data available

Library of Congress Cataloging in Publication Data

Data available

Typeset by SPI Publisher Services, Pondicherry, India
Printed in Great Britain
on acid-free paper by
CPI Antony Rowe, Chippenham, Wiltshire

ISBN 978-0-19-821743-5 (Hbk.)
978-0-19-957867-2 (Pbk.)

2 4 6 8 10 9 7 5 3 1

PREFACE

THE period of the parliamentary union of Ireland and Britain is covered by two companion volumes of the *New history*, of which the present volume is concerned with the period 1801–70, and its successor, volume VI, with 1870–1921. The arrangement of chapters has, to some extent, been determined by this division of the nineteenth century between two volumes: chapters on the Irish economy from 1850 to 1921 and on university education from 1793 to 1908, for example, will appear in volume VI, as will a bibliography for the whole period of the union.

Once again we thank Dr John A. Mulcahy, of New York, and the directors of the American Irish Foundation, for the generous financial help that enabled us to carry out much-needed research in the early stages of work on the *New history*.

We acknowledge the help received from the National Library of Ireland and the libraries of Trinity College, Dublin, and of the Royal Irish Academy. In compiling the illustrations we were greatly assisted by Charles Benson and Vincent Kinane of the department of early printed books in the library of Trinity College; by E. J. McParland, our adviser on jacket design; by Eileen Black of the Ulster Museum; by Anne Neary of the National Archives; by Peadar Slattery, F.R.P.S.; and by J. L. Desmond of the Irish Coursing Club and R. J. K. Sinclair and the members of the Royal Ulster Constabulary Historical Society, who provided information on two of the plates. We have pleasure in acknowledging the generosity of Nicholas Robinson, who put at our disposal his magnificent collection of early nineteenth-century caricatures.

Since the death of T. W. Moody in 1984, our chief concerns have been to maintain the standard of editing that he had established, and the continuity and concentration of aim that are indispensable in a cooperative project of this size. We take this opportunity of recording our debt in this endeavour to Colm Croker for his unstinting assistance with all aspects of the task of copy-editing; to our typist, Peggy Morgan, for her distinguished and devoted work; and to our secretary, Richard Hawkins, who in addition to his normal assistance with organising a large and complex text has applied in this volume his knowledge of police and law enforcement in nineteenth-century Ireland.

We record with sorrow the death on 12 March 1988 of Thomas Walter Freeman, whose *Pre-famine Ireland* (Manchester, 1957) is a classic of Irish

historical geography, and whose exemplary contribution appears below as
chapter XI.

F. X. MARTIN
F. J. BYRNE
W. E. VAUGHAN
ART COSGROVE
J. R. HILL

Royal Irish Academy
29 March 1989

CONTENTS

XII FAMINE AND GOVERNMENT RESPONSE, 1845–6
by James S. Donnelly, jr

XIII PRODUCTION, PRICES, AND EXPORTS, 1846–51
by James S. Donnelly, jr

XXI CHURCHMEN, TENANTS, AND INDEPENDENT OPPOSITION, 1850–56   by R. V. Comerford

XXV LITERATURE IN ENGLISH, 1801–91
by Thomas Flanagan

XXVI PRE-UNIVERSITY EDUCATION, 1782–1870
by D. H. Akenson

CONTRIBUTORS

Donald Harman Akenson

B.A. (Yale), M.Ed., Ph.D. (Harvard); F.R.S. (Can.); professor of history, Queen's University, Kingston, Ontario

James Christopher Brady

B.C.L., LL.B., Ph.D. (Q.U.B.); professor of the law of property and equity, University College, Dublin

Richard Vincent Comerford

M.A. (N.U.I.), Ph.D. (Dubl.); senior lecturer in modern history, St Patrick's College, Maynooth

Sean Joseph Connolly

B.A. (N.U.I.), D.Phil. (Ulster); lecturer in history, University of Ulster

James Stephen Donnelly, jr

B.A. (Fordham), Ph.D. (Harvard); professor of history, University of Wisconsin-Madison

David Noel Doyle

M.A. (Marquette), Ph.D. (Iowa); college lecturer in modern history, University College, Dublin

David Patrick Brian Fitzpatrick

B.A. (Melb.), Ph.D. (Cantab.); fellow, and lecturer in modern history, Trinity College, Dublin

Thomas James Bonner Flanagan

B.A. (Amherst), M.A., Ph.D. (Columbia); professor of English, State University of New York at Stony Brook

Thomas Walter Freeman

B.A., Dip.Ed. (Leeds), M.A. (Leeds, Dubl.); F.R.G.S.; emeritus professor of geography, University of Manchester (died 12 March 1988)

Oliver Ormond Gerard MacDonagh

M.A. (N.U.I.), M.A., Ph.D. (Cantab.); F.R. Hist. Soc., F.A.S.S.A., F.A.H.A.; professor of history, Australian National University

Robert Brendan McDowell

M.A., Ph.D., Litt.D. (Dubl.); M.R.I.A.; fellow emeritus, Trinity College, Dublin

Patrick James O'Farrell

M.A. (N.Z.), Ph.D. (A.N.U.); F.A.H.A.; professor of history, University of New South Wales

Cormac Ó Gráda

M.A., Ph.D. (Columbia), Dip. European Studies (Amsterdam); statutory lecturer in political economy and national economics of Ireland, University College, Dublin

William Edward Vaughan

M.A., Ph.D. (Dubl.); senior lecturer in modern history, Trinity College, Dublin

The maps have been drawn by Valerie Keegan, B.Sc., and Diana Large, B.A., under the direction of Mary Davies, B.A., cartographical adviser to this history, from material supplied by contributors. The index is the work of Helen Litton, M.A.

MAPS

FIGURES

ILLUSTRATIONS

The originals of these illustrations were made available through the courtesy of the
following, and are published by their permission; Mr Nicholas Robinson, plates 1a, 1b,
2a, 2b, 4a, 5a, 5b, 6a, 6b, 13a, 22a, 38a; the Board of Trinity College, Dublin, plates 3a, 3b,
4b, 7a, 8a, 8b, 10a, 11a, 11b, 12, 13b, 15a, 15b, 17a, 17b, 19, 20, 21, 23b, 24a, 24b, 25a, 25b,
26b, 27a, 28, 30a, 30b, 30c, 34, 35; the proprietors of *Punch*, plates 7b, 18b, 37a, 37b; the
Ulster Museum, plates 9a, 14a; the National Library of Ireland, plates 9b, 18a, 23a, 26a,
27b, 29b, 31a, 31b, 36; the Irish Architectural Archive and Dr Alastair Rowan, plates 10b,
30d; Mr F. J. Meagher, plate 14b; private owners, plate 16 and jacket illustration; the
Royal Irish Academy, plate 22b; the Hulton-Deutsch Collection, plate 29a; the director
of the National Archives of Ireland, plates 32, 33, 38b, 38c.

Other copies of the prints from the collection of Mr Nicholas Robinson are to be
found in the British Library collection: plate 1a, B.L. 9696; plate 1b, B.L. 10405; plate 2a,
B.L. 13420; plate 5b, B.L. 15681; plate 6a, B.L. 15684; plate 6b, B.L. 15539; plate 13a, B.L.
15440; plate 38a, B.L. 146675. Further details of plates 9b, 18a, 23a, 26a, 27b, 29b, and 36
are to be found in Rosalind M. Elmes (ed.), *National Library of Ireland. Catalogue of Irish
topographical prints and original drawings* (new ed., revised and enlarged by Michael
Hewson, Dublin, 1975).

ABBREVIATIONS AND CONVENTIONS

Abbreviations and conventions used in this volume are listed below. They consist of (a) the relevant items from the list in *Irish Historical Studies*, supplement I (Jan. 1968) and (b) abbreviations, on the same model, not included in the *Irish Historical Studies* list. Articles have not been given standardised abbreviations. Where an article is cited more than once in a chapter, an abbreviated form is used after the first full reference. Occasionally, however, the full reference is repeated for the convenience of the reader. A similar convention is used in chapters XII–XVI for titles of parliamentary papers. Special abbreviations used in references to law reports are listed separately below, p. 481.

A.H.R.	*American Historical Review* (New York, 1895–)
Adams, *Ir. emigration to New World*	William Forbes Adams, *Ireland and the Irish emigration to the New World* (New Haven, 1932)
Akenson, *Ir. education experiment*	D. H. Akenson, *The Irish education experiment: the national system of education in the nineteenth century* (London, 1970)
Anal. Hib.	*Analecta Hibernica, including the reports of the Irish Manuscripts Commission* (Dublin, 1930–)
Annual Reg., 1758 [etc.]	*The Annual Register, ... 1758* [etc.] (London, [1759]–)
Archiv. Hib.	*Archivium Hibernicum: or Irish historical records* (Catholic Record Society of Ireland, Maynooth, 1912–)
B.L., Add. MSS	British Library, Additional MSS
Ball, *Judges*	F. E. Ball, *The judges in Ireland, 1221–1921* (2 vols, London, 1926)
Bessborough comm. rep.	*Report of her majesty's commissioners of inquiry into the working of the Landlord and Tenant (Ireland) Act, 1870, and the acts amending the same* [earl of Bessborough, chairman], [C2779], H.C. 1881, xviii, 1–72
Black, *Econ. thought & Ir. question*	R. D. C. Black, *Economic thought and the Irish question, 1817–1870* (Cambridge, 1960)
Bolton, *Ir. act of union*	G. C. Bolton, *The passing of the Irish act of union: a study in parliamentary politics* (London, 1966)
Bowen, *Protestant crusade*	Desmond Bowen, *The protestant crusade in Ireland, 1800–1870: a study of protestant–catholic relations between the act of union and disestablishment* (Dublin, 1978)
Castlereagh corr.	*Memoirs and correspondence of Viscount Castlereagh, second marquess of Londonderry, edited by his brother, Charles* [William Stewart] *Vane,* [third] *marquess of Londonderry* (12 vols, London, 1848–53)

Census Ire., 1841	*Report of the commissioners appointed to take the census of Ireland for the year 1841* [504], H.C. 1843, xxiv
Census Ire., 1851, I, I [etc.]	*The census of Ireland for the year 1851: part I, showing the area, population and number of houses by townlands and electoral divisions*, vol. i, province of Leinster, H.C. 1852–3, xci [etc.]
Clark & Donnelly, *Ir. peasants*	Samuel Clark and J. S. Donnelly, jr (ed.), *Irish peasants: violence and political unrest, 1780–1914* (Madison, Wis., and Manchester, 1983)
Clogher Rec.	*Clogher Record* (Monaghan, 1953–)
Colchester corr.	*The diary and correspondence of Charles Abbot, Lord Colchester, speaker of the house of commons 1802–1817, edited by his son Charles,* [second] *Lord Colchester* (3 vols, London, 1861)
Connell, *Population*	K. H. Connell, *The population of Ireland, 1750–1845* (Oxford, 1950)
Connolly, *Priests & people in Ire.*	S. J. Connolly, *Priests and people in pre-famine Ireland 1780–1845* (Dublin, 1984)
Corish, *Ir. catholicism*	Patrick J. Corish (ed.), *A history of Irish catholicism* (16 fascs, Dublin and Melbourne, 1967–72)
Cork Hist. Soc. Jn.	*Journal of the Cork Historical and Archaeological Society* (Cork, 1892–)
Croker papers	*The Croker papers: the correspondence and diaries of the late Rt Hon. John Wilson Croker*, ed. Louis Jennings (3 vols, London, 1884)
Cullen, *Life in Ire.*	L. M. Cullen, *Life in Ireland* (London, 1968)
Devon comm. digest	*Digest of evidence taken before her majesty's commissioners of inquiry into the state of the law and practice in respect to the occupation of land in Ireland*, by J. P. Kennedy [secretary of the commission] (2 vols, London and Dublin, 1847–8)
Devon comm. rep.	*Report from her majesty's commissioners of inquiry into the state of the law and practice in respect to the occupation of land in Ireland* [earl of Devon, chairman], [605] H.C. 1845, xix, 1–56
Devoy's post bag	*Devoy's post bag, 1871–1928*, ed. William O'Brien and Desmond Ryan (2 vols, Dublin, 1948, 1953)
Donnelly, *Land & people of Cork*	J. S Donnelly, jr, *The land and people of nineteenth-century Cork* (London, 1973)
Dublin Hist. Rec.	*Dublin Historical Record* (Dublin, 1938–)
Econ. Hist. Rev.	*Economic History Review* (London, 1927–)
ed.	edited by, edition, editor(s)
Edwards & Williams, *Great famine*	R. Dudley Edwards and T. Desmond Williams (ed.), *The great famine: studies in Irish history, 1845–52* (Dublin, 1956)

Elliott, *Partners in revolution*	Marianne Elliott, *Partners in revolution: the United Irishmen and France* (New Haven and London, 1982)
F.J.	*Freeman's Journal* (Dublin, 1763–1924)
Fagan, *O'Connell*	William Fagan, *The life and times of Daniel O'Connell* (2 vols, Cork, 1847–8)
Fortescue MSS	*The manuscripts of J. B. Fortescue, Esq., preserved at Dropmore* (H.M.C., 10 vols, London, 1892–1927)
Galway Arch. Soc. Jn.	*Journal of the Galway Archaeological and Historical Society* (Galway, 1900–)
Gash, *Mr Secretary Peel*	Norman Gash, *Mr Secretary Peel: the life and times of Sir Robert Peel to 1830* (London, 1961)
Grattan, *Life*	*Memoirs of the life and times of the Rt Hon. Henry Grattan*, ed. Henry Grattan, jr (5 vols, London, 1839–46)
Green, *Lagan valley*	E. R. R. Green, *The Lagan valley, 1800–50: a local history of the industrial revolution* (London, 1949)
H.M.C.	Historical Manuscripts Commission
Hall, *Ire.*	Mr and Mrs S. C. Hall, *Ireland: its scenery, character, etc.* (3 vols, London, 1841–3)
Hansard 1, i [etc.]	*Cobbett's parliamentary debates*, 1803–12 (vols i–xxii, London, 1804–12); continued as *The parliamentary debates from the year 1803 to the present time*, 1812–20 (vols xxiii–xli, London, 1812–20; from vol. xxvii, 1813–14, the title includes: *published under the superintendence of T. C. Hansard*)
Hansard 2, i [etc.]	*The parliamentary debates . . ., published under the superintendence of T. C. Hansard*, new series, 1820–29 (vols i–xx, London, 1820–29; continued as *Hansard's parliamentary debates*, 1829–30 (vols xxi–xxv, London, 1829–30)
Hansard 3, i [etc.]	*Hansard's parliamentary debates*, third series, 1830–91 (vols i–ccclvi, London, 1831–91)
Hist. Jn.	*The Historical Journal* (Cambridge, 1958–)
Hist. Studies	*Historical studies: papers read before the Irish Conference of Historians* (vols i–vii, London, 1958–69; viii, Dublin, 1971; ix, Belfast, 1974; x, Indreabhan (Co. na Gaillimhe), 1976; xi, Belfast, 1978; xii, London, 1978; xiii–xv, Belfast, 1981–5; in progress)
Historical Studies	*Historical Studies, Australia and New Zealand* (Melbourne, 1940– ; from 1967, title *Historical Studies*)
I.E.R.	*Irish Ecclesiastical Record* (171 vols, Dublin, 1864–1968)
I.H.S.	*Irish Historical Studies: the joint journal of the Irish Historical Society and the Ulster Society for Irish Historical Studies* (Dublin, 1938–)

Ir. Ancestor	*The Irish Ancestor* ([Dublin], 1969–)
Ir. Econ. & Soc. Hist.	*Irish Economic and Social History: the journal of the Economic and Social History Society of Ireland* ([Dublin and Belfast], 1974–)
Ir. Geography	*Irish Geography (bulletin of the Geographical Society of Ireland)* (vols i–iv, Dublin, 1944–63); continued as *The Geographical Society of Ireland, Irish Geography* (vol. v, Dublin, 1964–)
Jn. Ecc. Hist.	*Journal of Ecclesiastical History* (London, 1950–)
Jn. Econ. Hist.	*Journal of Economic History* (New York, 1941–)
Jn. Relig. Hist.	*Journal of Religious History* (Sydney, 1960–)
Kane, *Industrial resources*	Sir Robert Kane, *The industrial resources of Ireland* (Dublin, 1844; 2nd ed., 1845; reprint of 2nd ed., Shannon, 1971)
Kerr, *Peel, priests, & politics*	Donal A. Kerr, *Peel, priests, and politics: Sir Robert Peel's administration and the Roman Catholic church in Ireland, 1841–6* (Oxford, 1982)
Kerry Arch. Soc. Jn.	*Journal of the Kerry Archaeological and Historical Society* ([Tralee], 1968–)
Lewis, *Topog. Dict. Ire.*	Samuel Lewis, *A topographical dictionary of Ireland* (2 vols + atlas, London, 1837)
Lowe, 'Irish in Lancashire'	W. J. Lowe, 'The Irish in Lancashire, 1846–71: a social history' (Ph.D. thesis, Dublin, 1975)
MacDonagh, *Post-bag*	Michael MacDonagh (ed.), *The viceroy's post-bag: correspondence hitherto unpublished of the earl of Hardwicke, first lord lieutenant of Ireland after the union* (London, 1904)
MacDonagh, *Pattern of govt growth*	Oliver MacDonagh, *A pattern of government growth, 1800–60: the passenger acts and their enforcement* (London, 1961)
McDowell, *Ir. administration*	R. B. McDowell, *The Irish administration, 1801–1914* (London, 1964)
McDowell, *Public opinion & govt policy*	R. B. McDowell, *Public opinion and government policy in Ireland, 1801–1846* (London, 1952)
MacIntyre, *Liberator*	Angus MacIntyre, *The Liberator: Daniel O'Connell and the Irish party, 1830–1847* (London, 1965)
Madden, *Emmet*	R. R. Madden, *The life and times of Robert Emmet, Esq.* (Dublin, 1847; many later eds)
Malcomson, *Foster*	A. P. W. Malcomson, *John Foster: the politics of Anglo-Irish ascendancy* (Oxford, 1978)
Memoirs of Myles Byrne	*Memoirs of Myles Byrne, edited by his widow* [Fanny Byrne] (2 vols, Paris and New York, 1863; reprint, with introduction by R. B. McDowell, Shannon, 1972)

Mokyr, *Why Ire. starved*	Joel Mokyr, *Why Ireland starved: a quantitative and analytical history of the Irish economy, 1800–1850* (London, 1982)
Moody & Beckett, *Queen's, Belfast*	T. W. Moody and J. C. Beckett, *Queen's, Belfast, 1845–1949: the history of a university* (2 vols, London, 1959)
N.I. Legal Quart.	*Northern Ireland Legal Quarterly* [*the journal of the Incorporated Law Society of Northern Ireland*] (Belfast, 1936–)
N.L.I.	National Library of Ireland
New Camb. mod. hist.	*The new Cambridge modern history* (13 vols + atlas, Cambridge, 1957–70)
Nicholls, *Ir. poor law*	George Nicholls, *History of the Irish poor law in connexion with the condition of the people* (London, 1856)
Nowlan, *Politics of repeal*	Kevin B. Nowlan, *The politics of repeal: a study in the relations between Great Briitain and Ireland, 1841–1850* (London, 1965)
O'Brien, *Econ. hist. Ire., union to famine*	George O'Brien, *The economic history of Ireland from the union to the famine* (Dublin, 1921)
O'Connell corr.	M. R. O'Connell (ed.), *The correspondence of Daniel O'Connell* (8 vols: vols i–ii, Shannon, 1972; vols iii–viii, Dublin, 1974–80)
O'Donovan, *Econ. hist.*	John O'Donovan, *The economic history of live stock in Ireland* (Cork, 1940)
O'Farrell, *Letters from Ir. Australia*	Patrick O'Farrell, *Letters from Irish Australia, 1825–1929* (Sydney and Belfast, 1984)
Ó Tuathaigh, *Ire. before the famine*	Gearóid Ó Tuathaigh, *Ireland before the famine* (Dublin, 1972)
P.R.O.	Public Record Office of England
P.R.O.I.	Public Record Office of Ireland
P.R.O.N.I.	Public Record Office of Northern Ireland
Past & Present	*Past and Present: a journal of scientific history* (London, 1952–)
Parker, *Peel*	*Sir Robert Peel from his private papers*, ed. C. S. Parker (3 vols, London, 1891–9)
Plowden, *Hist. Ire., 1801–10*	Francis Plowden, *The history of Ireland from its union with Great Britain, in January 1801, to October 1810* (3 vols, Dublin, 1811)
Poor inquiry, rep. 1	*First report from commissioners for inquiring into the condition of the poor in Ireland, with appendix (A.) and supplement*, H.C. 1835 (369), xxxii, pt 1, pp 1–14
Poor inquiry app. A [supp.]	Ibid., pp 15–810 [supplement, pp 811–1220]
Poor inquiry, app. B [supp.]	*Poor inquiry (Ireland), Appendix (B.) containing general reports upon the existing system of public medical relief ... local reports upon dispensaries, fever hospitals,*

county infirmaries and lunatic asylums, with supplement, parts I and II, H.C. 1835 (369), xxxii, pt 2

Poor inquiry, app. C, pt I [etc.]　　*Poor inquiry (Ireland), Appendix (C.). . . Part I: reports on the state of the poor, and on the charitable institutions in some of the principal towns; with supplement . . . Part II: report on the city of Dublin, and supplement . . . with addenda to appendix (A.) and communications* [35], H.C. 1836, xxx (pt I, pp 37–158; supplement, pp 159–220; pt II, pp 221–602)

Poor inquiry, app. D [*supp.*]　　*Poor inquiry (Ireland). Appendix (D.), containing baronial examinations relative to earnings . . . and supplement* . . . [36], H.C. 1836, xxxi, 1–116; supplement, pp 117–510

Poor inquiry, app. E [*supp.*]　　*Poor inquiry (Ireland). Appendix (E.), containing baronial examinations relative to food . . . and supplement* . . . [37], H.C. 1836, xxxii, 1–112; supplement, pp 113–506

Poor inquiry, app. F [*supp.*]　　*Poor inquiry (Ireland). Appendix (F.), containing baronial examinations relative to . . . landlord and tenant . . . and supplement* [38], H.C. 1836, xxxiii, 1–426; supplement, pp 427–820

Poor inquiry, app. D, E, F, supp. II　　*Poor inquiry (Ireland). Supplement II to appendices (D.) (E.) (F.), containing returns of civil bill ejectments from 1827 to 1833 . . .* [39], H.C. 1836, xxxiv, 1–426

Poor inquiry, app. G　　*Poor inquiry.—(Ireland.) Appendix G. Report on the state of the Irish poor in Great Britain* [40], H.C. 1836, xxxiv, 427–642

Poor inquiry, app. H, pt I　　*Poor inquiry (Ireland). Appendix (H.)—part I, containing reasons for recommending voluntary associations for the relief of the poor . . .* [41], H.C. 1836, xxxiv, 643–56

Poor inquiry, app. H, pt II　　*Poor inquiry (Ireland). Appendix (H.)—part II, remarks* [by J. E. Bicheno] *on the evidence . . . contained in the appendices (D.) (E.) (F.)* [42], H.C. 1836, xxxiv, 657–98

Poor inquiry, rep. 2　　*Second report of the commissioners for inquiring into the condition of the poorer classes in Ireland* [68], H.C. 1837, xxxi, 587–604

Poor inquiry, rep. 3　　*Third report of the commissioners for inquiring into the condition of the poorer classes in Ireland* [43], H.C. 1836, xxx, 1–34

Poor inquiry, Nicholls rep. 1*　　*Report of Geo. Nicholls . . . on poor laws, Ireland* [69], H.C. 1837, li, 201–42

Poor inquiry, Nicholls rep. 2*　　*Second report of Geo. Nicholls . . . on poor laws, Ireland* [104], H.C. 1837–8, xxxviii, 657–712

* These papers are not designated on their title pages as part of the poor inquiry, but are included here because of their close connection with it.

Poor inquiry, Nicholls rep. 3 *	*Poor laws—Ireland, Third report of Geo. Nicholls . . . containing the result of an inquiry into the condition of the labouring classes and the provision for the relief of the poor in Holland and Belgium* [126], H.C. 1837–8, xxxviii, 713–26
Poor inquiry, Senior letter *	*Poor law, Ireland. Letter from Nassau W. Senior . . . on the third report from the commissioners for inquiring into the condition of the poor in Ireland* [90], H.C. 1837, li, 243–54
Poor inquiry, Lewis remarks *	*Remarks on the third report of the Irish poor inquiry commissioners . . . by George Cornewall Lewis* [91], H.C. 1837, li, 255–92
R. Hist. Soc. Trans.	*Transactions of the Royal Historical Society* (London, 1872–)
R.I.A.	Royal Irish Academy
R.S.A.I. Jn.	*Journal of the Royal Society of Antiquaries of Ireland* (Dublin, 1892–)
Reynolds, *Catholic emancipation crisis*	J. A. Reynolds, *The catholic emancipation crisis in Ireland, 1823–29* (New Haven, 1954)
Richey, *Ir. land laws*	A. G. Richey, *The Irish land laws* (London, 1880)
Roberts, *Whig party*	Michael Roberts, *The whig party, 1807–12* (London, 1939; 2nd ed., 1965)
S.P.O.	State Paper Office of Ireland, Dublin castle
Stat. Soc. Ire. Jn.	*Journal of the Statistical and Social Inquiry Society of Ireland* (Dublin, 1861–)
Studia Hib.	*Studia Hibernica* (Dublin, 1961–)
T.C.D.	Trinity College, Dublin
U.C.C.	University College, Cork
U.C.D.	University College, Dublin
U.C.G.	University College, Galway
U.J.A.	*Ulster Journal of Archaeology* (Belfast, 3 series: 1853–62, 9 vols; 1895–1911, 17 vols; 1938–)
Vaughan & Fitzpatrick, *Ir. hist. statistics*	W. E. Vaughan and A. J. Fitzpatrick, *Irish historical statistics: population, 1821–1971* (Dublin, 1978)
Wakefield, *Account of Ire.*	Edward Wakefield, *An account of Ireland, statistical and political* (2 vols, London, 1812)
Waldersee, *Catholic society*	James Waldersee, *Catholic society in New South Wales, 1788–1860* (Sydney, 1974)
Whyte, *Indep. Ir. party*	J. H. Whyte, *The independent Irish party, 1850–59* (Oxford, 1958)
William & Mary Quart.	*William and Mary Quarterly: a magazine of early American history, institutions, and culture* (Williamsburg,

* For note see p. xliii.

Va., 1st series, 1892–1919; 2nd series, 1921–43; 3rd series, 1944–)

Woodham-Smith, *Great hunger*   Cecil Woodham-Smith, *The great hunger: Ireland 1845–9* (London, 1962)

Wylie, *Ir. land law*   J. C. W. Wylie, *Irish land law* (London, 1975)

Wyse, *Catholic Association*   Thomas Wyse, *Historical sketch of the late Catholic Association of Ireland* (2 vols, London, 1829)

Ireland and the union, 1801–70

OLIVER MACDONAGH

THIS volume is dominated, politically, by the act of union, which came into force on 1 January 1801. By the end of 1870 the land act of that year, the church act of the previous year, and the foundation of the Home Government Association had begun to undermine it.

The union, in British terms, represented a change from indirect to direct rule of Ireland. The constitutional settlement of 1782–3 had rendered indirect rule more difficult, but it had not destroyed it. The Irish executive remained in substantial control not only of government but also of legislation; and the British cabinet remained in substantial control of the Irish executive. In normal circumstances Dublin Castle was assured of majorities in both houses of parliament because crown patronage was at its disposal, and patronage still sufficed to gain the necessary numbers. During 1782–1800 the crown was losing both patronage and power *vis-à-vis* the house of commons in Great Britain. But in Ireland the crown was losing power, not to the Irish house of commons, but to the British cabinet, while its patronage, so far from diminishing, tended to grow. In short, the British cabinet was still in effect appointing, directing, and dismissing the chief Irish officers of state, while the chief Irish officers of state were still using the resources of patronage—if anything, augmented resources—to further British policy.

Naturally such a system fell short of minute, absolute, and constant control from London. With communication time often a week, the Irish executive had to be given a great deal of discretion. With the intricacies of Anglo-Irish family connections and contentions, the people on the spot alone could make the more personal judgements. With the channels so circuitous and so much of the activity vicarious, the British impact was bound to be muffled or blunted, to a degree. None the less, when it really mattered, it was Westminster that called the tune.

An important limitation on British power was, however, potential or actual Irish discontent. An increasing tendency in eighteenth-century British politics was to concede something to sustained and large-scale pressures from whatever quarter; and the North American revolution had demonstrated recently the deplorable consequence of failing to extend this habit far or fast enough even to colonies. The events of 1782–3 were themselves proof sufficient that Ireland too could exact 'conciliation'. Thereafter, however, British concessions were made more and more to the unfranchised and formally powerless body of the Irish, the catholics, rather than to the protestant ascendancy. The explanation of the paradox is complex. In part it was the fruit of enlightenment, in particular of the religious indifferentism of the *Aufklärung*, and the growing emphasis upon the homogeneity of similar economic and social classes, of whatever confession. In part it was the fruit of fear, fear of such premonitory manifestations of mass disorders as Whiteboyism and its offspring, and the vaguer but no less potent fears inculcated by the new British practice of historical and political reflection on cycles of past events, remote and close. In part it was the fruit of calculation, especially the calculation that 1782–3 represented the high-water mark of serious protestant challenge to the British monopoly of ultimate power in Ireland; henceforward, Irish protestants would probably acquiesce in their role as garrison rather than imperil their privileges, petty sway, and property.

At any rate, from 1783 to 1795 British policy in Ireland generally favoured the conciliation of catholicism, and its gradual absorption into, instead of legal outlawry from, political society. For various reasons, the outbreak of war with revolutionary France early in 1793 rendered this a more decided and urgent tendency; but in 1795 the entire process came to an abrupt end. When the new coalition government in Great Britain seemed on the brink of compelling the Irish parliament to pass a measure of catholic emancipation substantially like that of 1829, Pitt at the very last drew back. When the final calculations had to be made—and they could not be made coolly in the crisis precipitated by Fitzwilliam—the risks appeared too great. It was impossible for any British statesman of foresight in the mid-1790s to suppose that indirect rule through parliamentary corruption could be maintained indefinitely. This being so, emancipation might open a door that could not be closed at convenience, or perhaps at all. Again, there was a British dimension to be considered. Antipopery was already a rising force. Finally, the Irish executive, dominated by Fitzgibbon, was fiercely opposed to the concession.

British policy, therefore, reached a turning-point in 1795. At least, the strategic end of that policy—political control—was henceforward sought by other means. Immediately the moves towards parity for catholics were halted. Later in the year the failure to deal equally with Defender and Orange disturbances, capping Fitzwilliam's recall, precipitated the cycle of violence and repression, of presbyterian and catholic conflict, of presbyterian and Church of Ireland *rapport*, and of the change in the mass support of the United Irish movement, which ended in the outbreak of 1798. This did not mean that the British government had determined in 1795 *permanently* to throw its weight behind total protestant ascendancy, catholic abasement, and a pocket parliament. None of these seemed durable in the long run. But a union that converted a large catholic majority in Ireland into a United Kingdom minority of 20 per cent at most, and obviated the necessity for a scandalous and precarious parliamentary order, seemed an increasingly attractive alternative. The rebellion of 1798 clinched the argument. A protestant front had now clearly emerged, with security for protestant lives and interests as its overriding object. At the same time, it would be as dangerous (from Britain's standpoint) to endorse blindly and for the indefinite future the actions of this alarmed minority as to crush every hope in catholic breasts of further amelioration. So the die was cast. Union, coupled with emancipation and supra-factional government, was determined on. But union, when it came, was coupled with the opposite things: the maintenance of the old ascendancy and the retention of the Irish executive, unrepentant.[1]

IN many ways the act of union was a leap in the dark. It was several years before it was clear whether or not a separate Irish executive would remain. No one appears seriously to have considered the effect that the addition of a hundred Irish members would have on the British house of commons; it was probably assumed that one or two Irish Dundases would emerge to round up the Irish representation and shepherd it into the English party and group system, as with contemporary Scotland. Two apparently likely problems rapidly evaporated. Emmet's 'rebellion' of 1803 proved to be the dying spasm of United Irishism, while the considerable Irish protestant opposition to the union dwindled rapidly to a small and collectively harmless body. On the other hand, the great piece of 'unfinished business' of 1800, catholic emancipation, remained unachieved in the event. This was gradually to shape the character of Anglo-Irish political relations under the new order. In the first place it tended to divide the protestant communities from the catholic, since after 1798 protestant support for emancipation diminished rapidly. Later it tended to divide the catholic upper from the catholic middle classes and still more from the catholic masses, wherever they had become politically aroused. A generational cleavage was later added to that of class: the younger catholics were free from the subserviency and timidity of the *ancien régime*. But the most striking development of all was the growing involvement of the hierarchy and priests in what was becoming a positive agitation. In the veto controversies of 1808 and 1813–16, this was especially marked; and another manifestation of the same phenomenon was the intervention of the catholic clergy in several constituencies in the general elections of 1818 and 1820.

All this presaged the reordering of Anglo-Irish parliamentary politics in 1826–8. The Catholic Association, although non-sectarian in its own eyes, represented in fact the mobilisation of catholic power at all levels; and willy-nilly it was directed against the entire Westminster system of politics as well as

---

[1] Oliver MacDonagh, *Ireland: the union and its aftermath* (London, 1977), pp 162–4.

specific pieces of repressive legislation. Moreover, in the course of the struggle, great numbers in every stratum of the catholic community were indoctrinated in an ideology of resistance and civil rights and taught the tactics of demonstration and intimidation. The lessons proved lasting. The catholic relief act of 1829 did not bring to an end the type of political behaviour, organisation, and alignment that its long denial had called into existence.

By 1830 the lineaments of a new political system for Ireland were becoming clearly apparent. Over most of Connacht, Leinster, and Munster, the county and larger borough seats belonged potentially to the 'popular' party. That is to say, had the necessary determination and financial and organisational resources been applied, and suitable candidates been available, about two-thirds of the Irish seats might have been won. They never were before 1870; two-fifths, or less, was the normal harvest.[1] This was not because the task was intrinsically impossible, but because the 'popular' energies were never sufficiently concentrated on mere parliamentary representation. Moreover, the constituencies not won or not contested usually went to whigs or liberals; and at most stages in 1830–70 these were in tacit or open alliance with the 'independent' Irish members, and to some extent susceptible to the same popular pressures in Ireland. Thus after 1830 the three 'catholic' provinces played a new role in the political system of the United Kingdom. In terms of the British national parties, they added significantly to liberal strength. Yet because they were potentially independent they influenced liberal—and therefore usually government—policy towards Ireland. In addition, they probably strengthened, in a modest way, radical influences generally in the house of commons.

The *modus operandi* of the new politics of the 1830s was as important as the result. First, the catholic clergy were permanently involved in the political system. This had not been expected when they were first drawn into the struggle for a catholic relief act. But so it proved. They provided essential organisational and directional services in the localities, and in return exercised considerable influence over the choice of candidates and the character of the programme and tactics. Of course, the extent and intensity of their participation varied from time to time and issue to issue. But they formed an integral part of the popular movements down to and well after 1870. In fact it is arguable that clerical politics reached its apogee in the Parnellite party and the Land League. Secondly, alternative forms of political behaviour tended to be squeezed out. In 1830–70 there was a sort of antithetical relationship between the parliamentary method and the rest: as the former flourished, the latter were of comparatively small dimensions; when it was in desuetude, electoral corruption, social division, and violence and conspiracy tended to wax and swell. But normally it was the moderate and constitutional form of disaffection that predominated. Thirdly, the character of the new Irish agitations was such that a very high proportion of the population received an extensive education in

[1] Below, ix, 637–8.

political organisation and management. It was not merely the voters who were marshalled in the emancipation and repeal campaigns. The masses played a critical part and performed a continuous role in assemblages, demonstrations, and money-gathering. Moreover, it was not merely the central committees and the parish clergy who exercised leadership. Below them, considerable numbers were involved as wardens, marshals, collectors, readers, and 'constables'. In short, a sort of general political mobilisation or conscription was imposed for quite lengthy periods during the two decades 1825–45; and because of these the level of political experience in the country was remarkably high. Perhaps the United States alone surpassed Ireland in this respect in the second quarter of the century.

Thus a politicised church, electorate, and commonalty developed, with a bias against revolution, violence, extremism or absoluteness of objective, and conspiracy. This impress was lasting. Although constitutionalism and pragmatism might be temporarily displaced under particular stresses or concatenations, sooner or later opinion would swing back to the accustomed and ingrained courses. Yet if parliamentarianism were established, it was parliamentarianism of a peculiar order. It was, in the nature of things, most vigorous in opposition, and to operate effectively it required the support of an extra-parliamentary wing. Moreover, it often stood to gain from the threat that anti-parliamentarian elements would capitalise on every long frustration of the orthodox movement. The triumph of constitutionalism in 'popular' Irish politics was, therefore, modified severely by the particular circumstances of the case. While on one hand it had to extend itself to keep actual agrarian disturbances and incipient revolutionary violence within limits or at bay, on the other hand it was dependent on extra-constitutional allies and devices for its vigour.

The word 'popular' has been used several times above to describe this type of politics; 'national' and 'radical' are perhaps too narrow. It is true that the forces mobilised even in the catholic emancipation campaign were, broadly speaking, 'nationalist' also; and *a fortiori* this applies to the succeeding movements. But the choice before electors in the 'catholic' provinces was rarely one between a repealer and an anti-repealer, or whatever the equivalent antithesis might have been from time to time. Nor was the successful candidate's platform a sure guide to his subsequent vote in the house of commons. Moreover, his 'nationalism', whatever its degree, was rarely critical in determining his parliamentary choices.

Correspondingly, apart from education in the middle and the land question in the last twenty years of the period, the 'popular' interest in Ireland was little concerned with radicalism in the sense of social reform. Here the contrast with Britain is striking. It is true that some of the British agitation for social or economic change was masked as political demands—the People's Charter is an obvious case in point. Similarly, some—perhaps much—of the nationalistic programmes may have been calls for social reordering in disguise. None the less, there were no real Irish counterparts, except possibly the temperance movements, to the multitude of British movements, ranging from anti-vaccinationism to the Anti-Corn Law League and from the civil service reformers to the Law Amendment Society, which ultimately registered some success in, or at least some mark on, the statute book. More important still, there was no true Irish counterpart to the British struggles for social amelioration through local government and civic agencies. The battleground of some of the greatest issues in early and mid-nineteenth-century Britain—pollution, sanitation, contagion, working-class dwellings, and the neglect of juveniles, for example—was the local rather than the national arena. But in Ireland the case was different. Local government, however 'popularised', and local pressure groups and associations did not concern themselves much with such affairs. They may have had less need to. Many of these problems, in the acutest form at least, sprang from vast and rapid urbanisation. But none of them was absent in Ireland. What was absent was a strongly rooted tradition of social inquiry and action. Instead 'politics' was ordinarily penned within the triangle of nationalism, religion, and land.

Part cause and part effect of this constriction was a disjunction between politics and power in Ireland. From what has gone before it will be clear that, for a people supposedly enjoying representative and responsible government, the Irish stood in a very unusual relationship to both the central and local administration. The catholic majority lacked anything like a proportionate influence in or membership of the controlling bodies. Despite some advances, especially in 1831–41, this was still true in 1870. But the protestant communities also suffered, although in a different fashion. They predominated numerically in most branches of the civil administration and most organs of local government. But the state, as represented now by Whitehall as well as Dublin Castle, increasingly expressed British rather than Irish protestant—let alone Church of Ireland—policy, and it was steadily encroaching on the preserves of local government. We must guard against exaggeration. On some matters official British and self-interested Irish protestant attitudes were practically indistinguishable. Protestants retained a near-monopoly of the grand juries, whose powers remained considerable, down to 1898; and they dominated the magistracy for even longer. None the less, partly by dilution in appointments, partly by the loss of power of the traditional agencies of local government, and partly by the growth of new state activity centred in and controlled from London, even the Irish protestants were ceasing to enjoy self-rule in the old pre-1801 style.

THUS in certain respects Ireland in 1801–70 was dwindling into a colonial condition. But she differed from the British colonies of white settlement in two important respects. First, they were attaining responsible government; and in

British eyes this was both an inevitable and a desirable tendency. The case of Ireland in 1801–70 was different at every point. Secondly, Ireland was represented at Westminster, and Irish members could exercise some measure of power, even if 'irresponsibly', when the major British parties competed for office on nearly equal numerical terms in the house of commons. O'Connell in 1835–9, and the Irish tories in 1841–3, possessed a species of indirect control over Irish appointments, the conduct of the Irish executive, and the content of Irish legislation. Even in the 1860s men of the meagre calibre of John Francis Maguire and the O'Donoghue coloured the Irish policy of the liberal governments. At best, such an influence was akin to that of Victorian women over husbands and fathers—not indeed in terms of affection or compassion, but in terms of domestic miseries that might ensue were they wholly thwarted, maltreated, or abandoned. Correspondingly, the role of importunate irritant was morally debilitating for the Irish. Only when Parnell laboriously constructed a national front and a disciplined sectional party, or when Carson seized the initiative in unionism in 1912–14, were the tables turned. But both lie beyond 1870, and both were short-lived—perhaps doomed to be ephemeral once the British parliamentary system had recovered from the initial shock and found means of defusing the unfamiliar outbursts.

If, moreover, economic 'exploitation' is conceived of as a necessary element in colonialism, it is difficult to see what Britain gained from her Irish 'possession' in the nineteenth century. Particular gains can, of course, be enumerated, and they range from markets for ironware to breeding-grounds of unskilled, clerical, domestic, and other labour. But no matter what kind of balance-sheet we contrive, it would hardly show Ireland to have been profitable; nor is there any evidence that British contemporaries so regarded it. Still less was it plausible to think of Ireland as being in a state of tutelage. Before 1850 there were many vague aspirations to reproduce British social and economic structures there, after the style of the ancient colonies of Greece so admiringly canvassed in the 1830s. But these were empty and ignorant phantoms. Even the so-called English and Scottish colonies in Ireland had long since grown apart from their mother countries. They might well have gone the way of the Dutch colonies in South Africa a century before had it not been for the geographical contiguity of Britain and Ireland, and the rising influence of the 'native' population by whom they were so heavily outnumbered.

This returns us to our starting-point: the ultimate explanations of the union were geographical contiguity and the numerical disproportion of the Irish catholic and protestant populations. These remained the governing factors, although their forms and emphasis changed during the course of the period. In 1801 contiguity carried weight in British minds mainly because of its military and strategic implications. But as the Bonapartist threat receded, and Britain's naval supremacy and independence of continental Europe seemed permanently established, so too did the need (in Salisbury's later phrase) to keep Ireland 'at all hazards'[1] cease to occupy the forefront of British policy.

On the other hand, contiguity took on a new meaning during the decades between Waterloo and Sedan. In 1815 the journey from London to Dublin might still take three or four days, depending on wind and weather. In extraordinarily bad conditions a week might elapse. Steam transport and the telegraph changed this dramatically. In 1870 a man might leave Dublin at night and reach London on the following morning; people in Dublin might know of some happening in London within the hour; and the increasing cheapness of communication of all kinds was of almost equal significance in diminishing distance. These developments had many and various implications, and two of them are of peculiar importance. First, the increased speed and ease of communications tended to make Ireland dependent on a wide range of British skills and British examples. Admittedly, Britain imported some Irish manufactures and a vast number of Irish cattle, sheep, and pigs; but in diversity and pervasiveness Britain's goods and services had the advantage, and this applied not merely to produce and manufactures but also to a wide range of economic institutions, from central banking and insurance companies to stock markets and trade unions. Secondly, the new communications opened new doors to anglicisation, especially in the more modern fields of cultural formation, from popular literature to music-hall entertainment or the 'turf'. The general effect was this: geographical contiguity was taking on sharper meaning, rendering it more difficult for British people to see Ireland as a foreign, or even a markedly distinct, country, and for Irish people to specify or maintain a counter-culture.

Correspondingly, in several ways, the numerical disproportion of the catholic and protestant populations in Ireland increased rather than diminished in significance after 1800. For one thing, the battle between the numerical principle and the principle of interests in British politics was slowly but surely moving in favour of the former. Even in the reform act of 1832, whose authors specifically claimed to be reorganising the franchise and constituency boundaries on the basis of interest, the actual changes made were almost invariably based on greater approximation to numerical equality. Thus, for quite extraneous reasons, the marked numerical superiority of catholics in Ireland (between 75 and 80 per cent of the total population throughout the century) grew in political importance. Decade by decade it became more difficult to justify publicly their lack of power and weight in Irish society. Again, the remarkable religious toleration and indifferentism of *c.*1770–95 (characteristic of the European enlightenment, at last manifesting itself in Ireland) proved to be ephemeral. First, the events of 1795–8 redrew the political boundary lines in more or less sectarian terms, and the promise of security for protestants largely explains the Anglo-Irish acquiescence in the act of union. Secondly, the first

---

[1] [Lord Salisbury], 'The position of parties' in *Quarterly Review*, cxxxiii, no. 266 (Oct. 1872), p. 572.

quarter of the nineteenth century saw the emergence of various exacerbating forces. Evangelicalism awoke among Irish protestants a new missionary and proselytising zeal. Catholicism, emerging from the mouseholes of compliancy, responded with equal combativeness and counter-aggression, while lay pressure hurried catholic ecclesiastics along the road towards conflict in place of consensus and forced them into extra-religious fields. The dominant theme of Irish politics in 1820–40 was the sectarian contest for the diminution or retention of the protestant ascendancy, material and symbolic alike.

By 1840 the main lines and characteristics of religion in Ireland for the remainder of the period—and in fact for much longer—were becoming clear. Catholicism had completed its basic ecclesiastical reorganisation and had begun to move into outer fields—into education and the social services, into the fostering of regular clergy, and into the overseas 'missions' in Great Britain, the United States, and the areas of white settlement within the empire. Correspondingly, its spirit was by now decidedly confident, not to say truculent and triumphalist. In the countryside particularly, the church dominated much of the everyday organisation of society. The Church of Ireland, by contrast, had ceased to see itself as an evangelising agency, and its attitude had become essentially defensive; for it had long since tended to identify the preservation of its own standing and advantages with the preservation of the British connection. At the same time, it was 'lower' and more 'biblical' than its English counterpart in the mid-century. This rendered easier another striking development, its increasingly warm relations with the third major Irish church, the presbyterian. Once again Irish circumstances were producing a deviation from the contemporary British pattern. It is true that devotional and social conflict of the English kind, between dissenter and churchman, was also apparent in Ireland. But it was much more muted, and quite outweighed in time of crisis, by the need to present a common protestant front in the face of popery. The consequent conversion, over time, of the great bulk of Irish protestants to tory-unionism, and the decline of liberalism and radicalism in their ranks, were among the more significant developments of the period. Finally, it was important in Irish no less than British history that protestant evangelicalism should have enjoyed its English heyday in 1801–70. This limited the extent and type of the concessions that governments could make in Ireland, and at the same time helped to keep the Irish catholic church in a more or less disaffected and counter-aggressive condition. The great Irish innovations of the early and mid-nineteenth century were not always autogenic, but sometimes, as in this case, to no inconsiderable degree responsive.

IN one area, however, the initiating role of Britain was readily apparent as early as 1825. In 1801 the disparity between the British and the Irish economies had not seemed extraordinarily marked, and Ireland appeared to be following Britain's industrial advance. There were even grounds for believing that she was following, albeit modestly, Britain's manufacturing lead. After all, the industrial revolution was still mainly confined to textiles, and Irish textile production was increasing steadily. At any rate, Ireland was certainly gaining from the new markets that the growth in, and growing urbanisation of, Britain's population was creating. During the 1780s and 1790s both food prices and the demand for agricultural produce had been rising. In response, Irish agriculture had turned as never before to tillage and the export of cereals. At the same time the 'agricultural' industries of brewing, distilling, and linen were in a comparatively flourishing condition, and the provisions and butter trades seemed securely lodged within the British imperial economy. In several of these cases, the onset of war in 1793 meant greatly increased production and profits; and despite occasional crises and collapses, high prices and high demand prevailed until 1815.

But the era of comparative prosperity had been built on insecure foundations. Tillage was labour-intensive, and the necessary labour had been supplied by early marriages and high birth rates. Cereal production also favoured (for technical reasons) the widespread cultivation of potatoes, and potatoes were a very cheap and easily produced food, taking up comparatively little land. Thus the stage was set for a population explosion—or rather a sustaining of the mid-eighteenth-century explosion—with more and more of the demographic increase taking place within the ranks of the landless labourers, the cottiers, and the conacre men, whose dependence on a single root crop for food became ever more complete as their numbers expanded. Furthermore, the structure of Irish farming was weak, not to say iniquitous. Tenure was precarious, and was steadily becoming more so; middlemen intervened between landlord and the occupying tenants; tenants sublet, and found it more and more profitable, or necessary, to do so as it provided them with cheap labour at the cost of a potato patch or cabin and garden. Landlords were rarely obliged, or inclined, to maintain farms in good order; middlemen neglected their obligations to do so; and if tenants tried to supply their superiors' deficiencies, they feared increased rents. In short, reinvestment was low in Irish agriculture, and the entire system favoured the grasping of short-term advantages by each party at the expense of all the others who might be involved.

'And the day on which peace was signed . . . [the] great customer of the producers died.'[1] Between 1815 and 1825 cereal prices declined by one-third,[2] and, with periodic variations, they remained depressed over the next quarter of a century. But the fall in livestock prices was much less, and they recovered steadily between 1825 and 1845. The response of the Irish agricultural economy to these changes, and to the new export prospects for live cattle, sheep, and pigs, opened up by steam transport, was, of course, to move into pasture, so far as practicable. But it was practicable only to a limited degree. For the most part

[1] Robert Owen, *The life of Robert Owen* (2 vols, London, 1857–8), i, 124.
[2] Cf. below, p. 57.

the ultimate controllers of agriculture—landlords, middlemen, and farmers—sought to maintain their incomes by a less laborious and perilous path. They exploited the pressure of demand for land as the population swelled; they raised rents and broadcast tenancies-at-will. The alternative courses, evictions and clearances, were difficult and dangerous. Thus, although livestock production and pasturage increased during 1815–45, so too did tillage and potato farming. But these last now indicated desperation rather than achievement. The new intensity of cultivation and the bringing into use of more and more bog and mountain land represented the final effort to keep sustenance abreast of population. By 1845 one-third of the people depended almost solely on the potato for their food, and practically as many depended on it partially.

Thus, when the potato failed to some degree or other in seven successive seasons, 1845–51, it was inevitable that the old form of rural society should collapse. Population fell by one-fifth; over two million persons either died from hunger and hunger-induced diseases, or emigrated overseas. Of course, the effects were not uniform. It was the labouring and cottier classes that suffered most in the country as a whole, yet in some areas the small tenant farmers accounted for an absolute majority of the emigration. Many of the landlords who were driven into bankruptcy at last were replaced by Irish entrepreneurs or large farmers. In the poorest western and south-western regions the pre-famine patterns of agricultural subdivision and smallholdings survived somehow for another generation. None the less, Irish farming and Irish rural society had been revolutionised overall.

Although not immediately, tillage gradually gave way to pasturage, farm sizes increased, the cottier class disappeared, and the proportion of labourers to tenant farmers fell continuously. The potato ceased to be necessary for survival. A trend towards consolidation of holdings replaced the earlier incessant subdivision, and very late marriages became common. The 1850s were the critical decade in the initiation of all these changes, primarily because of the great resettlement of values, practices, and institutions that had followed the upheaval of 1845–51. But three other contemporary, and more or less independent, factors contributed to the same end. The first was the railway-building that transformed communications in the Irish interior; the second, the return of substantially full employment and rising real wages in Britain, which meant an assured market and improving prices for Irish livestock and dairy produce; and the third, the cheapening of and greater security in emigration, now that the passenger trade had become an important element in the Atlantic traffic in its own right, and the famine emigrants had painfully blazed the trail in all the great cities of the eastern United States.

By 1870 the Irish economy and social structure differed markedly from that of 1801. The economy was much more closely interwoven with Great Britain's; in fact it might be better described as a regional element of the British. Its leading feature was the supply of livestock and livestock products to Britain. Apart from the single industrial region of the Lagan valley, and a handful of large-scale 'agricultural' industries such as brewing and distilling, manufacturing had not developed. The three vital elements of early nineteenth-century industrialisation—coal, iron, and speculative capital—had all been missing. The domestic market had shrunk, and was now settled into a process of continuous shrinkage. Textiles offer a supreme example of the consequences of British competition and domestic insufficiencies combined for the survival of small-scale, unmechanised production. Woollen and to an even greater extent cotton manufacturing had gone to the wall when faced with cheap mass-produced and standardised British cloth, now readily transported, advertised, distributed, and sold.

The other side of the coin was rising real incomes, markedly higher standards of life, and a greater choice of and cheapness in consumer goods for the Irish community as a whole. In part this derived from the better and steadier prices prevailing in the British food markets from the early 1850s; in part, from the fact that the rise in rents generally fell below the rise in farm incomes; and in part, from the falling pressure on resources of all kinds as population declined.

Between 1841 and 1870 cattle and sheep more than doubled in numbers. Conversely, cereal production was halved, although the falls were uneven, wheat being the worst sufferer. Curiously, both the number of pigs and acreage (but not the quantity) of potatoes—the two 'crops' peculiarly associated with pre-famine poverty—increased slightly; but these were now being produced more for cash income than for, respectively, rents and survival. Thus the value of agricultural production did not decline after 1845; instead it rose steadily between the famine and the 1870s, apart from the distressed years of 1859–64. Furthermore, the numbers it supported were falling steadily. Nor was this relative improvement to be expressed merely in monetary terms. The whole socio-economic infrastructure, from hospitals to housing and from public dispensaries to public works, was carrying a lesser load, and was correspondingly more effective.

But the social and psychological price exacted for the improvement was grievous. The great famine destroyed much more than patterns of husbandry or cultural forms. Anglo-Irish relations were permanently embittered, and the Irish self-picture deeply suffused with shame, resentment, and a sense of loss. The new dispensation depended on marriage postponement on a vast scale, with all its attendant ills and distortions. It also depended on an incessant haemorrhage of people, mostly young. The post-famine 'equilibrium' rested on an annual average emigration of some 65,000 persons, and an annual average net loss of population of some 35,000. The other side of the coin was the development of very large Irish communities abroad. By 1870 the number of Irish-born living permanently overseas was more than half the number still living in Ireland itself. But there was—as yet, at any rate—no widespread pride in this species of 'empire', either at home or abroad. Rather was it regarded as both a mark of national failure and a consequence of Britain's power-lust and exploitation.

As if in sympathy, the years 1845–70 were among the most barren culturally in modern Irish history. Indeed, the crop of the entire period was very sparse. At first there was a faint afterglow of the great burst of creativity in the late eighteenth century. The 'Georgian' squares of Dublin were still being built in the 1820s; and the new public buildings and churches, the General Post Office and the King's Inns, St Andrew's catholic church, Westland Row, and St Patrick's catholic church, Cork, were respectable representatives of neo-classicism. The forensic rhetoric of Curran, Grattan, and their kind continued for a few years after the act of union. The age of improvement, of practical invention, of the universal 'philosopher' and the polymath, was still embodied in Ireland so long as Richard Lovell Edgeworth survived. His daughter's *Castle Rackrent*, Swiftian or Sternean in vein, was published in 1800.

But Maria Edgeworth's own subsequent descent from patrician irony to sentimentality and finally partisan spite is an index of the early nineteenth-century degeneration. Gaelic poetry, which had flowered autumnally as late as the 1780s, was now quite withered. Verse in English, when it revived in the later 1830s and 1840s, was polemical in purpose, and generally showed no more than facility in the pseudo-balladic form. The exception here was Mangan, whose inherent poetic powers often rose above the flaccidity of his medium. By 1830 the Irish novelists were writing primarily for the growing 'mass' market for fiction in Britain. This was true not only of the comic or picaresque work of Lever and Lover, but also of the most substantial and penetrative Irish novels of the period, William Carleton's. The consequent strain of stage Irishry (tragic as well as light) by no means destroyed all value or merit in these books, but it certainly reduced them sadly. Even when, in Carleton's famine and post-famine novels, new depths of realism were attempted, the result was often mere pamphleteering—and ill-organised at that. We have to wait to the close of the period, until the publication of Kickham's *Knocknagow*, for a fresh departure in Irish fiction. With *Knocknagow*, it was an Irish audience that was being addressed at last, and in the exclusive tones of native sympathies and anti-pathies.

The most infertile period of all in Irish letters, 1850–65, was prolific in anti-quarian studies, as O'Curry and O'Donovan laid the foundations for modern scholarship in this field. At the same time, so far as Gaelic culture was concerned, this was the painstaking labour of obituary writers rather than the first steps towards revival. The Irish language had been forsaken by the catholic gentry, middle classes, and clergy by 1801. It was still spoken then by one-half of the population, but this probably coincided closely with the poorest half of the population and of the countryside. The links between poverty and

Irish-speaking continued, with the corollary (for contemporaries) that the abandonment of the latter was a necessary first step towards escaping from the former. Gaelic culture was interwoven not merely with the language itself but also with patronage by the wealthy, so that it was already in its death-throes at the time of the union. By 1851 the drive towards social advancement, and the general use of English in politics, religion, the conduct of the state, and the national system of primary education established in 1831 had between them reduced the number of Irish-speakers to less than one-quarter of the population, and the number of those who spoke only Irish to one-twentieth. By 1871 the proportions were respectively about 15 and 2 per cent.

Yet if the period begins with the traditional culture fast disintegrating, well before 1870 an attempt to restore it and to use it as a political arsenal had achieved some success. If the contribution of romanticism to Irish literature, painting, and architecture was small and undistinguished, it was otherwise with political ideology. There were occasional gleams of 'sensibility' in O'Connell's expressions, such as, for instance, 'In my day-dreams I revise the brighter period of Irish history when Erin was the hotbed of saints and science.'[1] But generally O'Connell belonged to the pragmatic, as Tone had belonged to the dogmatic, branch of eighteenth-century rationalism and universalism in politics. From 1840 onwards, however, German romanticism had its Irish counterpart. It had a founder of talent and personal magnetism in Thomas Davis, a body of able propagandists in the group of young versifiers and journalists whom he attracted, a powerful organ in the *Nation*, and a favourable climate for growth in the repeal agitation, and still more in that movement's degeneration and collapse. Young Ireland itself fell apart as an organised body in 1848. But by then it had not only sown the seeds of fenianism, but also changed the tone of Irish nationalism generally. The principal political fruit of romanticism in Ireland was the separatist idea—not in its old form of breaking the constitutional connection with Great Britain, but in its new form of creating (or re-creating) a distinct cultural, linguistic, and racial entity in Ireland. Whether necessarily or not, this had portentous further implications. Violence was legitimised, religion and class were relegated to insignificance as determinants of group identity, and the entire island was assumed to be coterminous with Irish nationality.

By 1870 the new separatist politics—anti-collaborationist in method and spirit as well as object—had completed their first cycle; had risen, waxed, and waned within a decade. Three freshets of the early 1860s had swelled them suddenly. First, the independent Irish party broke up finally in 1859, and Irish members were practically absorbed in the British parliamentary groupings during the next decade. Secondly, the famine immigrants in the United States had at last gained sufficient confidence, resources, and organisation to throw up an anti-British movement of considerable power; while the American civil

[1] O'Connell to Bp Doyle, 6 Aug. 1829 (*O'Connell corr.*, iv, 88).

war had habituated or rehabituated many, even on the eastern shores of the Atlantic, to the ideas of arms and violence, and to the concept of moral and popular war. Finally, the reformation of the Irish social structure after the dislocations of the famine years had produced a considerable body of uprooted, aspiring, and frustrated young men to form the *corps d'armée* of fenianism. At any rate, the circumstances of the early 1860s were most propitious for militant republicanism.[1] The catastrophic failure of fenianism in arms in 1867, however, represented as dizzy a fall as the earlier outspread had been astonishing in its velocity.

Yet, as Gladstone owned in 1869, 'the fenian conspiracy has had an important influence with respect to Irish policy';[2] it precipitated or facilitated a new campaign of reform—or rather it did both together. Later the 'conspiracy' was of a still greater importance in re-creating an independent Irish parliamentary party and a supporting quasi-violent agitation. But these were not matters of simple causation. Even the concessions of 1869–70 make this clear. The Irish church issue knit the British nonconformists to the liberal government. The Irish land issue knit the new British radicalism to it in a similar fashion. The general course of Irish conciliation on which Gladstone had determined implied amnesty—not to say amnesia—in dealing with the remnants of fenianism. Moreover, Gladstone's celebrated metaphor, that fenianism served Irish reform in much the same way as the tolling of the summoning-bell served church worship, had its point: men were being reminded, not that it was their duty to worship, but that the time had come for them to move. In short, violent separatism was only one element in the explosive compound, and perhaps as much a symptom as a cause of change.

Similarly, the legislative changes of 1869–70 presaged further and much greater change. They signalled the contraction of the act of union; two of its Irish pillars, the Anglican establishment and the absolute legal rights of landownership, were knocked away. They also signalled the limit of British concession for a generation, unless some great new force, parliamentary and extra-parliamentary together, were organised and applied at Westminster and in Ireland; but this would come. In 1868–70 Anglo-Irish relations clearly altered course. At the same time the materials of the revolutionary decade of the 1880s were being silently assembled.

THE introduction to volume III of *A new history of Ireland*, after noting that the seventeenth century saw the first Irish examples of modern historical scholarship based on critical use of primary sources, goes on to observe that it 'was not till the nineteenth century that Irish scholars of similar calibre—Petrie, O'Donovan, O'Curry, Todd, Reeves, and others—were to resume work on the

[1] Below, pp 423–6.
[2] *Hansard 3*, cxcvi, 1062 (31 May 1869).

foundations thus laid'.[1] This indicates clearly the area of Irish historiography in which the main advances were made during 1801–70. The establishment of authentic sources for the earlier periods of Irish history and the beginnings of historical reconstruction on this base were probably the major achievement of early and mid-nineteenth-century Irish historians.

In so far as this development had a single 'father', it was probably Rev. Edward Ledwich, whose *Antiquities of Ireland* (1790), partly by its strain of 'enlightened' rejection of what he called 'bardic fictions', and partly because of his cavalier use of texts, opened a protracted period of controversy from which it came gradually to be 'recognised that the document treated critically was to be the basis of historical writing on early Ireland'.[2] But institutional developments also contributed to this outcome. Among these was the setting up of the Irish record commission in 1810 and the establishment of the ordnance survey in 1824. The record commission (despite the lack of direction and method that was to bring about its disbandment within twenty years)[3] was to furnish some training in original sources for several of the next generation of historical scholars, while from the start the ordnance survey was led into antiquarian and linguistic studies. But the Royal Irish Academy, the Gaelic Society and the short-lived Iberno-Celtic Society (whose sole publication was important, a descriptive catalogue of nearly 400 Irish writers) were also significant agencies in the work of authentification and translation of early documents. Finally, some scholars had been bred in continental scholarly methods. Rev. John Lanigan, whose *Ecclesiastical history of Ireland* was published in 1822, had earlier been a professor at the University of Pavia. In all, the pioneering work of 1800–40 prepared the way for the great flowering in topographical, legal, and general early Irish history at and immediately after the mid-century.[4]

To some extent these developments in early Irish history had been spurred on, particularly at first, by political partisanship. Initially, protestant and unionist historians were striving to dissipate romantic notions of a glorious pre-Norman or pre-Danish past in Ireland; catholics and nationalists were striving to sustain them. The very ardour of the collisions, however, helped in the long run to promote the work of establishing, editing, cataloguing, and scrutinising accurate texts: this was the most effective way in which to undermine an opponent's case. But by the second quarter of the century what had often begun as a polemical exercise had produced an historical method that was anti-polemical in tendency, and a disinterested and scientific cast of mind.

[1] Above, iii, p. lxi.

[2] Donald MacCartney [*recte* Donal McCartney], 'The writing of history in Ireland, 1800–30' in *I.H.S.*, x, no. 40 (Sept. 1957), p. 351. I am much indebted to this paper. The second edition of Ledwich's *Antiquities* was published in 1804.

[3] Margaret Griffith, 'The Irish record commission, 1810–30' in *I.H.S.*, vii, no. 25 (Mar. 1950), pp 22–8.

[4] Numerous translations of Gaelic works by John O'Donovan were published from 1842 onwards by the Irish Archaeological Society, the Commission for Publishing the Ancient Laws and Institutes of Ireland, and other bodies.

The same, however, could not be said of the equivalent work on the more modern periods of Irish history. Here subjects tended to attract historical attention much more strictly in tune with current controversy, and partisanship did not yield nearly so fast or so far to scholarly findings. In the first decade of the century the main arena of modern historical combat was the rising of 1641. The rebellion of 1798 had revived such questions as whether catholics were inherently disloyal, whether a course of concession to them merely invited revolt, and whether the 1641 and 1798 outbursts were essentially similar in character and aims. As catholic emancipation came to the forefront after 1810 the battleground changed to the 'treaty' of Limerick of 1691 and the further issues of the nature of the royal prerogative and the natural rights of catholics. Two decades later historical controversy moved on, in step with the burgeoning campaign for repeal of the act of union, to the events of 1799–1800, and behind them the events of 1782–3.

This historicisation of contemporary politics was in itself an important constituent of the history of Ireland in the nineteenth century. But although it led incidentally to some clarifications and corrections, and to the enlargement of the body of documentary information, it generally worked against the development of modern historical science. The critical use of primary sources was still a distant thing in Irish history so far as the more recent centuries were concerned. It was only in the last decade of this period that this particular situation began to change. One harbinger of a more scholarly and dispassionate future was W. E. H. Lecky's *Leaders of public opinion in Ireland*, published anonymously in 1861. Lecky was only twenty-three when this work appeared; it attracted little notice immediately; and he was to revise it very substantially in two later editions (1871 and 1903). But before the 1860s had run their course, Lecky, with both *The history of the rise and influence of the spirit of rationalism in Europe* (1865) and *The history of European morals* (1869) to his credit, was established as one of the leading historians of his day; and in the next decade he began his monumental work on the history of England in the eighteenth century, five of whose twelve volumes constituted a history of Ireland in the same period. Meanwhile his *Leaders of public opinion*, even in its original form, marked a new departure in Irish historiography.

Lecky was a representative of an intermediate stage in the development of historiography; and *Leaders of public opinion* in all its versions was arguing a particular political brief. None the less, such was the power and sweep of Lecky's mind, and the range of his historical knowledge, that even in his earliest work— in effect an historical tract—he was setting modern Irish historiography on a new level of sophistication and generality. Meanwhile Lecky's friend J. P. Prendergast, with the publication of *The Cromwellian settlement in Ireland* (1865), made his first contribution to modern Irish history within the period—a second indication that the subject had reached a more scholarly and critical plane.

To the work in the more modern fields of Irish history should be added the body of 'contemporary history', in all its varieties, written between 1801 and 1870. During the first half of this period many participants in, or immediate observers of, the 'independent' Irish parliament of 1782–1800, the United Irish conspiracy, and the 1798 rebellion published works of reminiscence or description. In aggregate these constitute important sources for the various topics and phases, all the more so because they represent between them a large spread of experience and points of view. A leading example of the genre, although its subject-matter is different, is Thomas Wyse's *Historical sketch of the late Catholic Association of Ireland* (1829), hot on the heels of the legislative triumph. Wyse's volumes not merely record many of the administrative procedures and changes in tactics of the catholic movement of the 1820s, but also evaluate its significance and success most shrewdly. Another type of 'contemporary history' is exemplified by Sir George Nicholls's *History of the Irish poor law in connexion with the condition of the people* (1856). Although the work is in part the apologia of a much abused public servant, it also serves as an indispensable source for the formation of the first general social service system in Ireland. The same may be said of Sir Charles Trevelyan's *The Irish crisis* (1848) and the earlier years of the great famine. Yet another form of 'contemporary history' was the attempted historical description of some current or very recent social phenomenon. John Francis Maguire's *The Irish in America* (1868), modestly described as 'impressions' of a visit to North America but in its way a pioneering work of historical survey, is a member of this category. Curiously, no attempt was made before the 1870s to depict the great famine as an historical event, even at this level; it was not until 1875 that the pioneering work of Rev. John O'Rourke, *The history of the great Irish famine of 1847, with notices of earlier famines*, was published.

Comparatively few of the 'life and letters' memorials of the leading figures in Irish history between 1780 and 1870 were published until after 1870. 'Standard' biographies of even such men as O'Connell, MacHale, Davis, Peel, Thomas Drummond, or Henry Cooke did not appear until the late nineteenth century. A few contributions were made in this field before 1871. Grattan's *Memoirs* (1839–48), *The life, times, and correspondence of the Rt Rev. Dr Doyle* (1861), and the *Life and correspondence of Richard Whately* (1866) are examples. Moreover, some slighter biographical memoirs such as W. J. O'Neill Daunt's *Personal recollections of the late Daniel O'Connell* (1849) also belong to the period; and although most of the writings on Young Ireland by contemporaries were published in the 1880s and 1890s, a little, including John Mitchel's *Jail journal* (1854), appeared soon after 1848. Overall, the amount of Irish historical biography and memoirs published between 1801 and 1870 was considerably smaller than that published in the next three decades. By 1870 we are still on or barely over the threshold of the age of standard lives and marshalled recollections.

Thus, with the exception to some extent of early Irish history, the years 1801–70 were comparatively infertile, historiographically, in Ireland. The immense advances in the historical sciences in continental Europe in this period were as yet unreflected in most areas of Irish history and ignored by or unknown to most practitioners therein. It is true that there were abundant signs of better things in the 1860s. Both the establishment of the Irish public record office (1868) and the publication of Eugene O'Curry's *Collection of early Irish law tracts* (1860), *Lectures on the manuscript materials of ancient Irish history* (1861), and (with John O'Donovan) the first two volumes of *Ancient laws of Ireland* (1865, 1869) belong to this decade; and during it, as we have seen, Lecky and Prendergast were changing the tone and level of seventeenth- and eighteenth-century historical studies. None the less, the seventy years, taken as a single span, ill bear comparison, historiographically, with the achievements of many other European nations. This forms an odd contrast to the assembling of materials for future generations of historians—to say nothing of other social scientists— to work on. The Irish experience of 1801–70 ran much of the gamut of minority political organisation and action familiar in the present century. It formed an especially interesting case in a phase of religious revival, of democratic beginnings, of cultural fissipation, and of nationalistic ferment. It rang the changes in modern demographic patterns. Above all, in the precarious economic balance of 1815–45 and the final economic catastrophe of the famine, it prefigures the most pressing concerns of the whole world a century and a half ahead. However meagre the historiographical crops of 1801–70 may have been, the seed for later reaping was being broadcast thickly.

CHAPTER I

Aftermath and adjustment

S. J. CONNOLLY

THE 1790s were a decade of high drama, culminating in localised but bloody civil war and in a drastic redefinition of Ireland's constitutional position. In comparison, the years immediately following the union must inevitably seem somewhat tame, an interlude of quiet interrupted only by a brief flurry of excitement—itself ultimately anticlimactic—in July 1803. Yet it was during these years that the long-term consequences of the upheavals of the 1790s worked themselves out. As the dust of the twin crises of union and rebellion settled it became possible to discern the outlines of a new landscape, in some respects transformed forever, in others oddly unchanged.

The acts for the union of Great Britain and Ireland came into effect on 1 January 1801.[1] On that day, 'and for ever', the two formerly separate kingdoms were joined in 'the United Kingdom of Great Britain and Ireland'. The first Irish peers and M.P.s took their seats at Westminster on 22 January. In Dublin the former Parliament House in College Green found a temporary use as the venue for art exhibitions and, in the aftermath of Emmet's rebellion, as quarters for two companies of yeomanry, before being sold to the Bank of Ireland in August 1803. The implementation of the union was rapidly followed by the withdrawal from office of the men who had been its chief architects. Pitt resigned as prime minister on 3 February 1801, after the king had made it clear that he would not consent to any proposal to follow the union with the removal of the remaining legal disabilities affecting catholics. In May Cornwallis, who had been closely associated with Pitt's plan for catholic relief, was withdrawn as lord lieutenant and replaced by Philip Yorke, earl of Hardwicke, who was to remain in office until March 1806.

As the first lord lieutenant to take office after the union, Hardwicke encountered a variety of special problems. Some of these concerned the scope of his authority. There had been suggestions that Ireland, now a province rather than a separate kingdom, no longer needed a lord lieutenant at all, and although it had been decided to retain the office for the time being, there was general agreement that the powers attached to it should be more limited than in the past. Hardwicke himself accepted that there should be some reduction in

[1] 39 & 40 Geo. III, c. 67 [G.B.] (2 July 1800); 40 Geo. III, c. 38 [Ire.] (1 Aug. 1800).

the scope of his new office, but before he had been long in Ireland he found himself fighting to prevent what he saw as unwarranted encroachments on his authority. There were disputes over claims that the disposal of Irish patronage should now be decided in London rather than in Dublin, and over the extent to which the lord lieutenant could act independently in regulating the export of food from Ireland. Further problems arose when a newly appointed commander-in-chief was found to have been issued with instructions that implied that he would act under the direct control of the Horse Guards, without reference to the lord lieutenant. The most serious of these clashes were between Hardwicke and the home secretary, Lord Pelham, who had from the start made clear his belief that the greater part of the lord lieutenant's powers, particularly those relating to patronage, should be transferred to his own department. Constitutional disagreements became increasingly involved with personal quarrels, and much of the tension was relieved when Pelham resigned in August 1803, particularly since his successor as home secretary was Charles Yorke, Hardwicke's brother. However, in 1805 there was a further clash when Pitt, back in office as prime minister since May 1804, allocated Irish patronage without consulting Hardwicke.

In addition to these tensions, the new lord lieutenant found himself burdened by the necessity of meeting the long list of political debts incurred by his predecessor in the course of carrying the union through the Irish parliament. The majority vote in favour of the union on 6 February 1800, which had reversed an earlier anti-union majority, had been achieved by means of a lavish distribution of favours. Some supporters of the union were promised specific rewards: places or promotions, for themselves or their dependants, within the peerage, the church, the law, the army, or the government service. Others had been allocated what Hardwicke delicately referred to as 'salaries without office, or money payments',[1] which were to continue until some regular provision was made for them. Some of these debts had been paid off before Cornwallis left office, but the rest remained in a list of 'union engagements' that the new ministry of Henry Addington (17 Mar. 1801–30 Apr. 1804) regarded itself as bound to honour. The result, Hardwicke complained, was that the patronage of the crown remained for much of his term of office under a 'heavy mortgage'.[2] Repeatedly his requests that something be done, either for a personal friend or for a useful political ally, were turned down on the ground that union engagements must take precedence over all other requests. As late as 1804 he complained that he had not during his period in office been able to dispose of a single living within the patronage of the crown worth more than £100 a year, and that he still had two or three engagements for church patronage unsatisfied.[3] Hardwicke's difficulties were compounded by his desire to combine the settlement of the government's debts with some degree of selectivity in appointments. He had begun, he explained in 1804, by choosing from the list of

[1] MacDonagh, *Post-bag*, p. 71.   [2] *Colchester corr.*, i, 325.   [3] MacDonagh, op. cit., pp 38–9.

union engagements 'those who appeared most proper for the situations in which openings occurred'. The result was that all those who were qualified for any office of trust or responsibility were now provided for, leaving a rump who were fit only for sinecures, 'which are not very easily found'.[1]

The obsession with patronage that was thus forced on Hardwicke and his colleagues was all the more galling because the members of the Irish executive in the first years after the union saw themselves as having come to Ireland with the specific mission of rescuing it from the rampant corruption that had up to then dominated its politics. This perception of pre-union Irish political morality, as a recent authoritative study[2] makes clear, largely missed the point. The prominence of patronage before 1801 was the result not of any exceptional tendency to corruption among politicians but rather of the nature of the 'constitution of 1782', which provided no other means of ensuring that the executive would have the parliamentary majority necessary for the discharge of its normal functions. (The same study points out that the members of Hardwicke's cabinet, despite their stern condemnations of Irish jobbery, did not themselves do at all badly out of Irish office.) But the sense that the union should mark the start of a new era was nevertheless a strong one. The new lord lieutenant, as George III told Addington in February 1801, must 'clearly understand that the union has closed the reign of Irish jobs'.[3] Hardwicke's first chief secretary, Charles Abbot (1801–2), launched a whirlwind campaign to reform government departments, while his successor, William Wickham, wrote of the need 'to be without ceasing on our guard against everybody and everything that is Irish'.[4] The lord chancellor, Lord Redesdale, argued confidently that the Irish themselves looked to the union to put an end to the corruption that had ruined their country: 'Every job weighs against the union; everything which shows a disposition to put an end to job weighs for it.' At the same time he expressed his fear that the spirit of 'Irish job' might be permitted to infect British political life, in which case 'the union will ruin England'.[5]

In addition to this general suspicion of Irish jobbery, Hardwicke and his colleagues believed that there was a real danger that leading local politicians might somehow manage to turn the union to their own advantage. Hardwicke complained in 1801 to Addington of the existence of cabals made up of those 'who imagined that one consequence of the union would be the governing of Ireland by means of some of its leading men, formerly known by the name of undertakers'.[6] At this point the leader of such cabals was identified as the lord

---

[1] Ibid., p. 42.

[2] Malcomson, *Foster*, pp 236–45. The sanctimonious comments of the duke of York on the need to end jobbery in the Irish army (MacDonagh, op. cit., p. 71) are particularly ironic. In 1809 the duke was forced to resign as commander-in-chief following allegations that his mistress had accepted money in exchange for her influence in securing commissions and promotions in the army.

[3] MacDonagh, op. cit., p. 3.   [4] Malcomson, op. cit., p. 86.

[5] *Colchester corr.*, i, 406–8; E. B. Mitford, *Life of Lord Redesdale* (London, 1939), p. 56.

[6] MacDonagh, op. cit., p. 62.

chancellor, John Fitzgibbon, now earl of Clare. Clare died in January 1802, but suspicion was soon transferred to John Foster, the former speaker of the Irish house of commons, who now sat at Westminster as M.P. for County Louth. According to Redesdale, writing in 1805, Foster was the head of 'the junto who are always endeavouring to govern Ireland in England', his aim being 'to degrade the office of lord lieutenant and to draw to himself all the power and influence of the country'.[1] Such charges, though exaggerated, had a basis in fact. In 1804, after Pitt's return to office, Foster became chancellor of the Irish exchequer and in addition first lord of the Irish treasury. He soon made it clear that he intended to use this combination of offices to build the treasury into an independent political fief, outside the control of the lord lieutenant. Foster went out of office after Pitt's death in January 1806, and when he returned as chancellor in 1807 under the duke of Portland he was not permitted to combine that office with the first lordship of the treasury. This greatly reduced his opportunities for the sort of self-aggrandisement he had attempted in 1804–6, but he nevertheless remained a troublesome colleague right up to his final withdrawal from office in 1811.[2]

Hardwicke's clashes with Pelham over the scope of his authority, the spirit of reforming zeal in which members of his administration approached the task of governing Ireland, the fear that wily local politicians would somehow turn the union to their own advantage: all these were natural responses at a time when the implications of major constitutional change had still to be worked out. By degrees, however, as the shape of the new political system became apparent, it was clear that change, though real, was not to be as far-reaching as many had hoped or feared. One major issue, of both symbolic and practical importance, was the continuation of the lord lieutenancy. Given that Ireland was now to be fully integrated into the United Kingdom, it could be argued that a viceregal court was no more justified in Dublin than in Edinburgh or Cardiff. Yet in practice it was clear that Ireland needed a degree of direct political control that could not be provided by a secretary of state based in London. The issue was never definitively resolved. Suggestions that the office of lord lieutenant should be abolished were put forward at intervals, not only in the years immediately after the union, but well into the second half of the nineteenth century. The issue was openly debated in parliament on three separate occasions, in 1823, 1830, and 1844, and in 1830 there were indications that the incoming whig government had actually decided on abolition. All such plans, however, came to nothing, and once the office had survived the early years of the union it acquired a familiarity that in itself constituted a powerful argument against change.

After as before the union, then, the effective head of government in Ireland was the lord lieutenant, working within the limits of policies agreed in cabinet

---

[1] Mitford, *Redesdale*, pp 171, 172.
[2] For this phase in Foster's career see Malcomson, *Foster*, pp 88–109.

but enjoying extensive personal discretion. At the same time the scope of the office was inevitably somewhat changed. After 1800 the powers of the lord lieutenant could never be quite what they had been when he had represented the link between the cabinet in London and an independent parliament. In addition, it was now necessary that the parliamentary business connected with Irish government should be conducted in London. This task fell to the chief secretary, an office that had already been increasing in importance in the last years before the union. Charles Abbot, the first chief secretary appointed after the union, was told 'that I must be in England during the session, and do the parliamentary business of Ireland; that I should have an office for the purpose to attend to; and after each session I should go over to Ireland and make that my country house'.[1] The casual bucolic image concealed what was in fact to be an exceedingly onerous dual role. At the same time the chief secretary's status as the government's main spokesman on Irish affairs, in direct contact with members of the cabinet, and far enough away from his nominal superior to be guaranteed a considerable degree of practical independence, inevitably enhanced his prestige relative to that of the lord lieutenant.

A crucial determinant of the shape that Irish politics assumed in the years following the union was, of course, the character and outlook of the 100 M.P.s who now represented Ireland at Westminster. In its effects on the basis of parliamentary representation in Ireland, the act of union could fairly be said to have represented the most sweeping constitutional innovation to be seen either in Ireland or in Great Britain since the restoration of Charles II. The Irish parliament had been stigmatised by Grattan as a 'borough parliament'. Of its 300 members, more than two-thirds had represented 'close' boroughs, in which the return of M.P.s was generally under the complete control of one or two patrons. Only the 64 county M.P.s and the 20 representatives of 'open' boroughs, in which the electorate was too large to be under the control of any single patron, had faced even the possibility of a genuine contest for their seats. The union reversed this balance. Of the 100 Irish M.P.s at Westminster, 64 sat for the counties, one for Dublin University, and the remaining 35 for 33 boroughs, of which 14 could be considered as in some degree 'open'. Representatives of 'close' constituencies, in other words, had been reduced to no more than a fifth of the entire parliamentary representation.[2] This, along with the fact that seats were now in shorter supply, undoubtedly made Irish electoral politics more competitive than they had been before 1801. But it did not result in any dramatic change in the social composition of the M.P.s elected. Of the 256 Irish members who sat at Westminster in the period

---

[1] *Colchester corr.*, i, 237.
[2] This analysis takes as 'open' the 5 boroughs where the vote was based on a property qualification, the 8 boroughs in which forty-shilling freeholders could vote along with burgesses and freemen, and also Derry, with its large freeman electorate. For a full account see P. J. Jupp, 'Urban politics in Ireland 1801–31' in *Hist. Studies*, xii (1981), pp 103–23.

1801–20, one-third were of aristocratic parentage and two-thirds came from substantial landowning families. Only fifteen came from families that had not sent representatives to the Irish parliament.[1]

The failure of the union to bring about any striking change in the social background—or even in the family names—of Ireland's elected representatives is not as surprising as might at first sight appear. The county electorates who now returned two-thirds of all Irish M.P.s may have been too large for any single patron to control; for that very reason, however, seats were expensive to contest, and a large personal following remained a vital electoral advantage. But it is in any case a mistake to assume that a restructuring of the electoral system would automatically produce dramatic changes in representation. For this to happen it was necessary not just that the system be changed but that some alternative political elite should take the opportunity to challenge the existing holders of political power. In Ireland no such alternative elite yet existed. The return of landed gentlemen to the Irish parliament before 1801 had depended not just on an electoral system biased in their favour but also on a widespread acceptance of their claim to be the natural representatives of their communities. Such deference continued after the union and largely neutralised, for two decades at least, what had been in its practical effects a substantial measure of parliamentary reform.[2]

The Irish M.P.s who sat at Westminster in the first twenty years after the union have achieved the remarkable feat of failing to excite the enthusiasm even of their closest student.[3] A minority stood out as significant figures. John Foster, as already mentioned, awakened fears in the administration that he intended to govern Ireland from England; George Ponsonby was leader of the whig party in the commons from 1808 until 1817, although he achieved this position as a compromise candidate rather than for any outstanding abilities he displayed;[4] Henry Grattan, Sir John Newport, and Sir Henry Parnell were effective speakers on a variety of Irish issues; Richard Martin, M.P. for County Galway, won a lasting reputation and the nickname 'Humanity Dick' for his work in promoting legislation to outlaw cruelty to animals. But these were the exceptions. Fully half of the Irish M.P.s who sat at Westminster in the period 1801–20 made no recorded speech in the house, and the contributions of most of the remainder appear to have been insignificant.

The importance of parliamentary oratory can, of course, be overestimated. But in other ways too the Irish members, as a political group, had only a limited

---

[1] P. J. Jupp, 'Irish M.P.s at Westminster in the early nineteenth century' in *Hist. Studies*, vii (1969), pp 66–7.
[2] For the importance of deference in Irish elections at this period see Malcomson, *Foster*, pp xxiv–xxvii, 336–49.
[3] Jupp, 'Irish M.P.s', pp 68, 80.
[4] Roberts, *Whig party*, pp 307–29. See also the comments of Henry Grattan in 1803: '... with excellent understanding and great powers (this is confidential) Ponsonby is lazy ... he loves his ease, his bed, and is tired of the parliamentary battle' (Grattan, *Life*, v, 240).

impact. At no time did they attempt to form a cohesive party, or even to act together consistently on matters of specifically Irish interest. Some were consistent supporters of the whigs, or of one of the other political groupings of the period: Grenvillites, Canningites, or friends of the prince of Wales. A few were genuine independents, voting on issues purely on what seemed to be their merits. But a high proportion were content simply to be passive supporters of the government of the day. In this, of course, they were not very different from a large body of English, Scottish, and Welsh M.P.s, who saw it as their duty to vote, in normal circumstances, in support of the king's ministers. In addition, it has been pointed out, the considerable degree of continuity between successive governments in the period between 1801 and 1827 made such a policy relatively easy to maintain. But where changes in government did involve a change in political complexion the adaptability of the Irish was striking. Thus in 1806–7 no less than fifty Irish members—half the total number—appear to have given their support, in quick succession, to Pitt, to the 'ministry of all the talents', and to the duke of Portland.[1]

Several reasons can be suggested for the unimpressive performance of Irish M.P.s at Westminster during the early years of the union. The reduction in their numbers from 300 to 100 meant that there was from the start a smaller pool of potential talent to draw from. Increased competition for the reduced number of seats would have meant that fewer openings existed for talent not backed by adequate electoral influence. In addition, it has been pointed out that the settlement of union engagements meant that a large proportion of the politicians active at the end of the 1790s ended up with peerages or alternatively with offices that either required residence in Dublin or disqualified the holder from sitting in parliament. The result was that a generation of political talent was 'buried in the Irish peerage, the Irish bureaucracy, and the seatless wilderness',[2] while their places were taken by men whose conventional outlook and lack of ambition left them happy to support whatever government was in power. They were encouraged in this by a liberal distribution of patronage. The enthusiasm for eliminating jobbery expressed by Hardwicke and his colleagues faded quietly away as a succession of governments found Irish votes in the commons too valuable to be dispensed with. Instead, as the union engagements were paid off, a succession of lesser parliamentary bargains took their place. The management of Irish M.P.s became one of the main duties of the chief secretary. It was for the most part a thankless task. Irishmen were notorious for their irregular attendance, and Robert Peel, writing in 1813, commented bitterly on those who, 'receiving ten times as many favours as the English members . . . do not give us one-tenth of their support'.[3]

---

[1] P. J. Jupp, 'Irish parliamentary representation, 1801–20' (Ph.D. thesis, Reading, 1966), pp 174, 181. For the circumstances of these changes of government see below, pp 30–36.

[2] Malcomson, *Foster*, p. 447.

[3] Gash, *Mr Secretary Peel*, p. 119.

Hardwicke's position as the first lord lieutenant appointed after the union thus required him to cope with the legacy (or—in the case of his dread of 'undertakers'—the ghosts) of the eighteenth century. But the most threatening legacy of all lay not in the sphere of establishment politics but outside it. The defeat of the French invasion force and its Irish allies in September 1798 had not marked the end of violence, terror, and counter-terror in Ireland. In several parts of the country groups of former rebels remained at large, harassing the authorities and living off the surrounding countryside, the most important being the band in County Wicklow led by Michael Dwyer. The winter of 1798–9 saw a widespread outbreak of cattle-houghing and other forms of agrarian crime, as well as raids for arms. All the evidence indicated that the motives for these outbreaks were purely economic, but inevitably there were suggestions of an underlying treasonable purpose.[1] Violence also came from the victorious loyalist side. As late as August 1800 the catholic archbishop of Dublin, John Thomas Troy, complained to the chief secretary of continued attacks on chapels in County Wexford and intimidation of catholic clergymen,[2] while Orange attacks on catholics were also reported from Ulster. Meanwhile a new group of United Irish leaders were known to be rebuilding their organisation in both Ireland and Britain, and in the summer of 1800 there were fears that a new French invasion was imminent.

Emergency legislation introduced during the crisis of the late 1790s, the act for the suppression of rebellion in Ireland and the suspension of habeas corpus, was still in force when the act of union came into effect.[3] Between 10 November 1800 and 24 February 1801 a total of 63 men were convicted under the former act, of whom 34 were sentenced to death and 21 actually executed,[4] and in March and June 1801 the government secured the continuation of both measures. By the time this renewal had been secured, however, a degree of peace had at last been restored. Already in February Cornwallis had reported to Castlereagh that, despite the hardship caused by a poor harvest and the resulting high price of food, 'I hear nowhere of any symptoms of ill-humour.'[5] Tension was further reduced when preliminary articles of peace between France and Great Britain were signed in August 1801. In November the government decided that a number of persons in the counties of Wicklow and Kildare charged with 'acts connected with rebellion' should be tried by jury, without invoking the emergency legislation. This was done 'to try the disposition of juries and witnesses, and to accustom the country to the ordinary course of law and regular administration of justice'. The experiment, it was judged,

---

[1] Cf. below, pp 56–8.

[2] Troy to Castlereagh, 5 Aug. 1800 (S.P.O., Rebellion papers, 650/58/100).

[3] The suppression of rebellion act (39 Geo. III, c. 11 (25 Mar. 1799)) was kept in force by three continuing and amending acts until 1802. The suspension of habeas corpus (initiated by 37 Geo. III, c. 1 (26 Oct. 1796)) was similarly continued until June 1801, with a short break between June 1799 and Apr. 1800. See also below, p. 16.

[4] *Castlereagh corr.*, iv, 214.   [5] Ibid., p. 25.

'answered the most sanguine expectations of the government'. When a definitive peace treaty was concluded in March 1802, the government felt secure enough to reduce the military establishment of regular troops, yeomanry, and militia from nearly 60,000 to less than 20,000.[1] The coming of peace also permitted the government to complete its bargain with the United Irish leaders who had been arrested before the outbreak of rebellion, the so-called 'state prisoners'.[2] In June 1802 they were taken from Fort George in Scotland, where they had been held since April 1799, shipped to Hamburg, and released.

The anxiety of the Irish administration to dispense as rapidly as possible with emergency legislation was part of Hardwicke's declared aim, announced when he had accepted the position of lord lieutenant, of 'pursuing the same system with Lord Cornwallis of general conciliation'.[3] The extent of his commitment to this principle was made clear at the beginning of 1803, when the military commander at Limerick, Major-general Edward Morrison, forwarded a series of alarming reports on the state of his district. Large bodies of armed men were said to have assembled; houses had been raided for guns; a blacksmith had been caught manufacturing pikes; anonymous letters spoke of a planned attack on Limerick city. Hardwicke was sceptical from the start, suggesting that Morrison had been imposed on by local gentlemen whose main interest was in having their yeomanry corps put on permanent duty, or in having themselves restored to the positions of authority or profit that they had held during the rebellion. The chief secretary, William Wickham, and the solicitor general, James McClelland, travelled to Limerick to investigate, and their report bore out Hardwicke's scepticism. The total number of violent outrages was found to amount to only six, and in five of these some of those responsible had already been apprehended. None of the outrages, furthermore, had had any political purpose. Instead they had arisen solely out of economic grievances, 'the prejudice which has existed in the southern counties for nearly a century, of the lowest labourers, against farmers and stewards who endeavour to introduce task work, and against labourers from other counties who offer to work at lower wages than the Limerick people wished to establish'. The request for extraordinary security measures was refused, and Hardwicke suggested that Morrison should be replaced by an officer who would be equally ready to support the civil authorities 'without giving credit to partial reports from interested persons'.[4]

---

[1] These particulars are taken from an account compiled by the chief secretary, William Wickham, after Emmet's rebellion in 1803. The document (B.L., Add. MS 35744, ff 195–210) is reprinted in Geraldine Hume and Anthony Malcomson, *Robert Emmet—the insurrection of 1803* (Belfast, 1976), pp 5–21.

[2] For this bargain see above, iv, 361.

[3] Cooke to Castlereagh, 27 Feb. 1801 (*Castlereagh corr.*, iv, 63).

[4] Morrison to Wickham, 6 Jan. 1803, with enclosures (P.R.O., H.O. 100/112/16r–29r); Hardwicke to Pelham, 9, 15 Jan. 1803 (5r–6v, 424–48v).

If the coming of peace allowed the government in Ireland to relax its vigil-
ance and experiment with a return to the normal processes of law, for the
United Irishmen it meant at least the postponement of their hopes for future
action. The rebuilding of a secret organisation in Ireland had begun early in
1799. In contrast to the mass following that the United Irishmen had recruited
before 1798, the new society was confined to a relatively small group who were
to be the officers in the planned rebellion. The rank and file, it was assumed,
would come forward spontaneously once the signal for action was given. At the
same time it was taken for granted that nothing could be attempted without
French assistance. At first the prospects for a new French expedition seemed
good, and at the beginning of 1801 United Irish emissaries in France were led
to believe that an invasion force was actually being assembled at Brest. But this
turned out to be a manoeuvre by Bonaparte, partly to put pressure on Britain to
begin peace negotiations, partly to distract attention from other naval projects.
After the peace preliminaries had been signed in August 1801, Bonaparte
considered expelling the United Irish leaders from France in exchange for the
expulsion of royalist *émigrés* from Britain. The British government did not
respond to his overtures, and no expulsions took place. But it was clear that for
the moment there was no prospect that the French would support a further
rebellion in Ireland.[1]

In England as in Ireland some elements of a revolutionary organisation
survived the disasters of 1798.[2] In London, English radicals and immigrant
Irish continued to be organised separately in the United Englishmen and the
United Irishmen, the latter greatly strengthened during the winter of 1798–9 by
an influx of fugitives from Ireland. In the north of England there were surviving
cells of United Englishmen, in this case involving both English and Irish
members. After a flurry of excitement in the spring of 1799, however, these
organisations largely faded from sight for almost two years. From the summer
of 1800 rising food prices combined with industrial depression produced
widespread discontent in many parts of England. Much of this took the form of
food riots and combinations of workers, popular action solely concerned with
economic as opposed to political objectives. But from early 1801 the government also began to receive reports of a revival of clandestine radical organisation. In March there were reports that a new society, taking the name United
Britons, had been created in London, and by the summer a similar organisation, having some links with the capital, was spreading through Lancashire and
Yorkshire. Once again it is clear that this underground activity involved close
cooperation between disaffected English and Irish, possibly through a com-

[1] For a detailed account of these transactions see Elliott, *Partners in revolution*, pp 276–81.
[2] The history of popular revolutionary organisation in England during this period remains
obscure and, at some points, controversial. The most recent study, which is followed here, is Roger
Wells, *Insurrection: the British experience* (Gloucester, 1983).

mittee linking the two or possibly through an actual incorporation of United Irish groups into the remodelled United Britons.[1]

Radical activity fell off in the autumn of 1801 as economic conditions improved and war with France came to an end, but from early in 1802 it had resumed with a new vigour. Reports reaching the authorities spoke not only of secret meetings and oath-taking, but also of military drill and the manufacture of pikes. On 16 November 1802 Bow Street Runners raided the Oakley Arms, a public house in Lambeth, where they arrested some thirty men, many of them Irish. Prominent among them was Colonel Edward Marcus Despard, a former army officer, himself of Irish extraction, who had been one of the leading militants in the London Corresponding Society and who had taken a prominent part in attempts to form a union of English radicals and United Irishmen in London in 1797–8. Despard and six others were tried for treason, convicted, and hanged in February 1803. Prosecution witnesses at the trial claimed that the accused men had planned a rising in London, to take place on 23 November, involving the assassination of the king and the seizure of key buildings. Their action was to be supported by risings in the north, for which the signal was to be the failure of the mail coaches to arrive from London. Some historians, while rejecting the wilder elements of the alleged conspiracy, have accepted that some sort of rising was in fact being prepared. An alternative analysis, however, suggests that the prosecution evidence was a fabrication and that Despard's real mission at the time of his arrest was to restrain a rank and file impatient for immediate action, and to persuade them to wait until an English rising could be combined with a French expedition and a rebellion in Ireland.[2]

Whatever the true nature of Despard's conspiracy, by the time of his execution a genuine plot to bring about immediate revolution in Ireland was under way. The central figure in the project was Robert Emmet, younger brother of the Thomas Addis Emmet who had been from an early stage one of the principal leaders of the United Irish society. Robert Emmet had been expelled from Trinity College, Dublin, in June 1798, during a visitorial purge of students known to have been active in the United movement. He had played a leading part in the reconstruction of the underground movement after the rebellion, and in April 1799 had fled to the Continent to avoid arrest. However, no formal charge had been laid against him, and he had returned openly to Ireland in October 1802. His return appears to have been primarily for family and personal reasons, but by the beginning of 1803 he was involved in preparations for another rising. Large numbers of those who had participated in the 1798 rebellion, particularly in the counties of Kildare, Wicklow, and Wexford, had

---

[1] For different views on this point see Marianne Elliott, 'The "Despard conspiracy" reconsidered' in Past & Present, no. 75 (May 1977), p. 52; Wells, op. cit., p. 240.

[2] Elliott, Partners in revolution, pp 282–97; Elliott, 'The "Despard conspiracy"', pp 57–60.

subsequently taken refuge in Dublin, and many of them still remained there, working quietly in a variety of occupations. It was with these men that Emmet now began to establish contact. By confiding only in men who had already proved themselves, as one of his lieutenants later recorded, Emmet could be confident of total secrecy, and his organisation proceeded without the oaths and tests on which the original United Irishmen had relied with such limited success.[1] As well as recruiting, Emmet set about building up a supply of weapons. Houses were rented to act as depots for the preparation and storage of firearms, ammunition, pikes, and explosives, the principal depots being in Patrick Street, Thomas Street, and Marshalsea Lane. In March and April 1803 Emmet was joined in Dublin by two of the men who had been deported to the Continent at the conclusion of the war with France: Michael Quigley, a brick-layer from County Kildare, and Thomas Russell, one of the founders of the United Irishmen.

Emmet's plan was for a seizure of certain strategic sites in Dublin city, carried out by his elite of tried revolutionaries, which would act as the signal for a wider popular rising. The places to be seized were the castle, the Pigeon House fort, and the artillery barracks at Islandbridge; other groups would take up positions outside the old Custom House and the barracks at Mary Street, pinning down the soldiers stationed there, while barricades of chains and com-mandeered vehicles were to be erected in the streets west of the castle.[2] All this was to be accomplished by the men Emmet had recruited in Dublin, aided by others who would come in on the appointed day from the counties of Dublin, Kildare, Wexford, and Wicklow. Emmet was confident that once the provisional government had been proclaimed from Dublin castle the inhabitants of the city would come forward in large numbers to reinforce the insurgents. In addition, the seizure of the capital would be the signal for risings in the provinces. These were to be largely spontaneous. Emmet claimed to have been in communica-tion with selected leaders, once again veterans of the rebellion, in a total of nineteen counties. But for the most part contact appears to have been confined to vague injunctions to these men to hold themselves in readiness, along with details of the characteristically elaborate system by which they would receive the instructions of the provisional government.[3] Even in the counties of Kildare, Wexford, and Wicklow, where Emmet's contacts were most devel-oped, attention was concentrated on the plan for seizing the capital.

The action envisaged in these plans was to be timed to coincide with a French invasion. However, Emmet's attitude to France was from the start ambivalent. Like other leading United Irishmen he had little respect for Bona-parte's regime, particularly in view of the way in which the United Irishmen

[1] *Memoirs of Myles Byrne*, i, 252.

[2] Emmet's account of his plan, drawn up while in prison for the information of his brother, Thomas Addis Emmet, but retained by the authorities, is reprinted in Madden, *Emmet*, pp 104–110.

[3] *Memoirs of Myles Byrne*, i, 263–4, 266.

themselves had been used in the manoeuvrings that had accompanied the conclusion of the peace of Amiens. More important, there now seemed a real danger that if the French did invade Ireland they might do so as conquerors rather than as allies. In one of his first conversations with Myles Byrne, Emmet had raised the question of whether Bonaparte could be trusted 'to deal fairly with the Irish nation',[1] and he returned to these doubts at the time of his trial, proclaiming in his speech from the dock that if the French came to Ireland as enemies they should be received 'with all the destruction of war'.[2] Leonard McNally, who interviewed Emmet in prison, later reported to the government that he had acted from 'a hope of being able to head an Irish army and render the aid of France unnecessary'.[3] However, it is unlikely that Emmet did in fact ever contemplate dispensing with French aid entirely. Instead his purpose appears to have been to ensure that the forces of revolution within Ireland should be able to act independently to secure for themselves a position of strength from which they would be able to negotiate with their dubious liberators as something approaching equals.

Emmet's preparations continued throughout the first half of 1803 almost completely unknown to the government. Occasional whispers were heard. In March it was learned that Michael Quigley had been on a mission to County Kildare, while at the end of May an informant in Belfast reported that word had come from Dublin of 'an immediate business'.[4] But none of this was sufficient to cause alarm, especially in a government consciously seeking to promote a return to normality. On Saturday 16 July, however, there was a small explosion of loose gunpowder at the depot in Patrick Street. When the occupants refused to admit the fire brigade, police were called. From Emmet's point of view this was not in fact the disaster it might have been. A search of the house turned up some ammunition and gunpowder, but the bulk of Emmet's arsenal remained undiscovered behind a false wall, and his men were able to return that night and carry the weapons away.[5] Meanwhile the one man taken into custody after the explosion had refused to reveal anything to the authorities. Nevertheless, Emmet concluded that it was now only a matter of time before his preparations were discovered. The only hope seemed to lie in immediate action, and accordingly it was decided that the rising should go ahead on the following Saturday, 23 July.[6] The original plan for concerted attacks on five strategic points was scaled down, with all resources to be concentrated instead on an attempt to seize Dublin castle.

[1] Ibid., p. 250.
[2] Elliott, *Partners in revolution*, pp 303–15.
[3] MacDonagh, *Post-bag*, p. 442.
[4] Ibid., p. 274.
[5] *Memoirs of Myles Byrne*, i, 272–3. This contradicts Emmet's own account, which claims that because of the explosion he lost the pikes deposited in Patrick Street (Madden, *Emmet*, p. 109).
[6] This is the generally accepted version, confirmed by *Memoirs of Myles Byrne*, i, 270. However, Emmet himself later claimed that 'the day of action was fixed on before this and could not be changed' (Madden, *Emmet*, p. 109).

From this point, whether because of the need to act prematurely or because of their inherent weaknesses, Emmet's elaborate plans began to fall apart. Several thousand pikes had been manufactured, but his men had practically no firearms. The elaborate explosive devices on which he had expended much time and resources were not prepared, partly through lack of time, but partly— as his own account makes clear—through inefficiency:

> The man who was to turn the fuses and rammers for the beams forgot them and went off to Kildare to bring men, and did not return till the very day. . . . The person who had the management of the depot mixed, by accident, the slow matches that were prepared with what were not, and all our labour went for nothing. The fuses for the grenades he had also laid by, where he forgot them, and could not find in the crowd.[1]

Men from County Kildare came into the city as arranged on Friday night and during Saturday, but when their leaders learned that Emmet had no firearms to distribute, 'the whole of them returned to their respective homes, sending back their followers whom they met on the road'.[2] The expected supporters from County Wicklow also failed to appear, either because Emmet's message did not reach them in time or because they too had lost faith in his enterprise. In Dublin itself some of those who had promised to take part held back, while others were put off by a false report that the rising had been postponed. The result was that Emmet was joined in his Thomas Street depot on Saturday evening by about eighty men, instead of the 2,000 he claimed to have expected. At this point his plan required that an advance party should drive into the castle yard, emerge, and overpower the sentries. For this purpose Emmet sent one of his men to hire six hackney coaches. Not surprisingly, this makeshift arrangement also went wrong: the sight of one man with six coaches aroused the suspicions of a passing army officer, a shot was fired, and the coachmen fled with their vehicles.

If the rebels' final preparations had been confused and inadequate, those of the authorities had been little better. The evidence of preparations for some sort of action, which had been provided by the Patrick Street explosion, was confirmed by an incident on Sunday 17 July, when watchmen encountered a party of Emmet's men as they were transporting a barrel of ammunition to a new hiding place. On 20 July Hardwicke wrote to London recommending that habeas corpus should be suspended, so that the government could detain suspected persons. On Saturday 23 July the signs of danger became more urgent. Reports received from a priest in Dublin and from a manufacturer on the outskirts of the city both suggested that a rising was imminent, and it was also noted that large bodies of men had been entering the city by the different roads from County Kildare. However, the commander-in-chief, Lieutenant-general Henry Fox, chose to take no immediate action, simply ordering three of

[1] Madden, *Emmet*, p. 109.
[2] Wickham's account, in Geraldine Hume and Anthony Malcomson, *Robert Emmet—the insurrection of 1803* (Belfast, 1976), p. 21.

his senior officers to meet him at 9.15 that evening. By that time Emmet's men were already on the streets, finally driven to break cover by a false report that soldiers had begun to surround their hiding place. Emmet himself had by this time given up the attempt as hopeless. He withdrew along with nine followers, first to Rathfarnham and then to the Wicklow mountains, arriving, according to his own account, in time to call off supporting actions in the countryside. However, the men from the Thomas Street depot were joined by others, and a group of around 300 armed men remained in possession of James's Street and Thomas Street. In Thomas Street they surrounded the coach of the lord chief justice, Lord Kilwarden, who was attempting to make his way to the castle, and killed him along with his nephew, Rev. Richard Wolfe. They also killed an army officer, a dragoon, and one or two others who were unfortunate enough to come across them. However, an attack on James's Street barracks was easily beaten off, and after about two hours the rebels were dispersed by soldiers, leaving about thirty dead behind them. Meanwhile a further detachment, led by Myles Byrne, had been waiting on the quays, ready to fall in behind Emmet's party as they passed in their coaches on their way to the castle. When it became clear that something had gone wrong, Byrne and his men marched back and forth through the Liberties for several hours, hoping to come across Emmet and his group, and then dispersed without having struck a blow. The only action to have taken place outside Dublin was at Maynooth, County Kildare, where a party of armed men assembled and tried unsuccessfully to stop the mail coach as it passed through on its way from Dublin.

Emmet's rebellion was over in a matter of hours. All that remained was the mopping up. A special commission tried those who had been involved. These included Emmet, who was arrested on 25 August, at the house where he was living under an assumed name, and executed on 20 September. Thomas Russell, who at the time of the Dublin rising had been in Ulster attempting to find support for an insurrection there, returned to Dublin in the hope of being able to rescue Emmet. He was arrested on 9 September, and later transferred to Downpatrick, where he was hanged on 21 October. Meanwhile the government was forced to defend itself against charges, both in Ireland and at Westminster, that it had allowed itself to be taken culpably unawares. Such criticisms were unfair. The failure to act on the reasonably clear-cut danger signals received on Saturday 23 July had been the fault of Lieutenant-general Fox, not of the civilian administration. Before that day there had been little concrete evidence to go on, and the danger of ignoring vague or suspect warnings that did in fact relate to a genuine conspiracy had always been inherent in the policy of restoring normal processes of law and refusing to be panicked into overreaction. The extent to which this policy of conscious moderation survived the crisis of Emmet's rebellion is not clear. Twenty-two men, including Emmet himself, were executed in the weeks following the rebellion. Others were detained under an act for the suspension of habeas corpus rushed through parliament after the insurrection, many of them remaining in prison until the measure lapsed in March 1806.[1] The rough treatment inflicted on one of those detained, Emmet's servant Anne Devlin, is well known, but it is not clear whether this was in any way typical. The catholic polemicist Francis Plowden later claimed that the government had sought to compensate for its earlier errors of judgement by a policy of conspicuous harshness, and that over 2,000 persons were detained, many of them on flimsy grounds, in conditions of un-necessary severity.[2] Against this must be put the praise that the government's handling of the crisis drew from some extremely unlikely quarters. Thomas Russell, awaiting execution in Downpatrick, was quoted as saying that Wickham and Redesdale were 'quieting the country by such means as have not been adopted by any other administration'.[3] Grattan went even further: 'From the manner in which this last rebellion was put down, I incline to think that if Lord Hardwicke had been viceroy, and Lord Redesdale chancellor, in '98, the former rebellion had never existed.'[4]

Emmet's rebellion remains difficult to assess. There is little doubt that Emmet himself was an exceptional personality. Patriotic eulogies on his extreme youth are misplaced: in July 1803 he was twenty-five, older than Pitt had been when he first became prime minister, or Robert Peel when he arrived in Ireland as chief secretary in 1812. Nevertheless, the degree of trust placed in him by older and experienced men like Russell and Quigley remains striking. Myles Byrne (two years younger than Emmet, but a veteran of 1798) paid tribute to his powers of persuasion.[5] Even more striking was the response of William Wickham, whose encounter with Emmet shook him so deeply that it played a major part in his decision shortly afterwards to withdraw from office.[6] But none of this tells us how seriously we should take Emmet's attempt at rebellion. The elaborate and detailed nature of his plans has led some to conclude that his project constituted a more serious threat than the government—anxious to conceal the narrowness of their escape—were willing to admit. But a close attention to points of detail can be equally the mark of a genius or of a crank; what matters is whether the overall enterprise is a practical one. The problem in Emmet's case is that he was forced to act prematurely, so that the feasibility of his scheme was never fairly tested. At the same time it is impossible not to be struck by the contrast between the neatness of his plans and the not merely

---

[1] 43 Geo. III, c. 116 (29 July 1803), continued by 44 Geo. III, c. 8 (15 Dec. 1803) and 45 Geo. III, c. 4 (22 Feb. 1805). The powers of the suppression of rebellion act (above, p. 8) were revived by 43 Geo. III, c. 117 (29 July 1803) and continued by 44 Geo. III, c. 9 (15 Dec. 1803).

[2] Plowden, *Hist. Ire., 1801–10*, i, 186–7, nn 226–7; ii, 75. A return in Mar. 1805 listed almost 1,000 political prisoners held in different jails, but this was clearly incomplete. See Helen Landreth, *The pursuit of Robert Emmet* (Dublin, 1949), pp 395–7, which estimates that the total number detained was about 3,000.

[3] MacDonagh, *Post-bag*, p. 424.

[4] Grattan to Fox, 12 Dec. 1803 (Grattan, *Life*, v, 241–3).

[5] *Memoirs of Myles Byrne*, i, 260–63.

[6] Elliott, *Partners in revolution*, pp 321–2.

hurried but often muddled nature of their execution. The sense of priorities is also suggestive. There had been no time or money to procure guns. But the proclamation of the provisional government was written and printed, and complete outfits were prepared for its senior officers—an elaborate general's uniform for Emmet, others for his colonels, 'laced also, but not so richly, and several without lace for persons of inferior class'.[1] As for the underlying assumption, on which all else depended, that a successful seizure of the castle would spark off spontaneous revolts in both Dublin and the provinces—this too was never tested. But it remains, at the very least, a huge assumption on which to have staked so much.

Emmet's failure meant the end of the United Irishmen as a serious revolutionary force. The principal leaders remained in France, but by now their movement was breaking up. There were bitter internal feuds between supporters of Thomas Addis Emmet and of Arthur O'Connor, who had succeeded in establishing himself, in the eyes of the French government, as the sole spokesman for the forces of Irish revolution. Emmet left France for America in October 1805, and he was followed over the next year or so by a number of others. An Irish legion had been created in August 1803, but with the passage of time this came increasingly to be seen as a unit of the French army, rather than a force dedicated specifically to the liberation of Ireland, and the legion was disbanded in 1815 after the second Bourbon restoration.[2] Plans for a new French expedition to Ireland were considered in 1804 and again in 1811, but in each case they came to nothing.[3] In Ireland itself there was no attempt to rebuild a United movement after the arrest or dispersal of Emmet's followers. The end of armed resistance was symbolised by the surrender of Michael Dwyer, who gave himself up in December 1803. He was transported to Australia, where he later joined the police force and rose to the position of high constable of Sydney.

What legacy, in terms of popular political consciousness, did the United Irishmen leave behind them? The evidence is for the most part fragmentary and elusive. Rural Ireland in the first half of the nineteenth century was to see a great deal of popular discontent, expressed in organised and often violent protest. The greater part of this protest, however, was to be limited in its aims, concerned solely with economic grievances and seeking to defend what were seen as existing rights rather than to overthrow the social order. Thus the first major movement of popular protest to emerge after the failure of Emmet's rebellion, the Threshers in Connacht in 1806–7, was a quite formidable but entirely non-political agitation on the issues of tithes, priests' fees, wages, and the price of land. In some cases, indeed, those involved took care to advertise their loyalty to the state, ending the administration of their oath with the words

[1] Wickham's account, quoted in MacDonagh, *Post-bag*, p. 283.
[2] Above, iv, 635–6.
[3] For a full account of these developments see Elliott, *Partners in revolution*, pp 323–64.

'God save the king'.[1] The proceedings of later agrarian campaigns in Munster and Leinster[2] made clear that these too looked back to the Whiteboys of the 1760s, 1770s, and 1780s rather than to the Defenders or United Irishmen. Attempts were, of course, made to invest rural protest with an ulterior political motive, or to see it as part of a grand revolutionary conspiracy. For the most part, however, these reflected only the gullibility and paranoia of sections of the Irish establishment and the dangers of reliance on the word of paid informers. For real evidence that the events of the 1790s had not been entirely forgotten it is necessary to turn to other, less dramatic reports. In March 1805, for example, an official sent to disperse a crowd that had assembled at Stoneybatter in Dublin to watch football and wrestling matches reported that he had heard cries of 'Success to Ballanamuck, Vinegar Hill, Killala, and Taragh.'[3] When Tone's father was buried in Naas, County Kildare, in August of the same year, 'great numbers of the peasantry assembled, and lamented the sufferings of that family'.[4] On 12 July 1810 a 'tree of liberty' was planted in a remote part of the town of Wexford, accompanied by three white flags 'and the same sort of horrid yells that were used in 1798'.[5] The image of the French as potential liberators also lingered on. References to the possibility of another French invasion occurred regularly in popular songs of the early nineteenth century. News of Napoleon's escape from Elba was greeted with considerable excitement, while on the night that Dublin celebrated the news of Waterloo the lord lieutenant reported the arrest of some 'blackguards running about the streets . . . denying the victory and asserting that Bonaparte was the conqueror'.[6]

The survival in popular memory of the grievances and antagonisms of the 1790s was also reflected, and to some degree encouraged, by the appearance in 1807 of a new journal, the *Irish Magazine*, published by a disreputable survivor of that decade, Walter (Watty) Cox. Peel, writing just after the journal had ceased publication in 1815, claimed that its object had been 'to ferment a bitter hatred against England. . . . Many parts are only suited for and only intelligible to the lower orders. They relate to the character of constables, police magistrates, and persons flogging or flogged in the rebellion.'[7] It was the *Irish Magazine*, for example, which produced in 1810 the lurid drawings of pitch-cappings and floggings that continue down to the present day to adorn narratives of the events of 1798.[8] 'The work', Peel added, 'was distributed

---

[1] Col. Harcourt to ——, 28 Nov. 1806 (S.P.O., State of the country papers, 1092/3).

[2] See below, pp 56–9, 70–71, 80–83, 93.

[3] Luke Brien to Major Sirr, 10 Mar. [1805] (S.P.O., State of the country papers, 1031/16).

[4] William Corbet to ——, 22 Aug. 1805 (ibid., 1031/36).

[5] Charles Tottenham to Sir Charles Saxton, 24 July 1810 (ibid., 1275/33).

[6] Gash, *Mr Secretary Peel*, p. 136; Elliott, *Partners in revolution*, pp 340–44, 353–7. See also G.-D. Zimmerman, *Songs of Irish rebellion: political street ballads and rebel songs, 1780–1900* (Dublin, 1967); and note O'Connell's reaction, below, p. 198.   [7] *Croker papers*, i, 89–90.

[8] *Cox's Irish Magazine and Monthly Asylum for Neglected Biography* (Jan. 1810), pp 1–2; (Feb. 1810), pp 49–50; (Apr. 1810), pp 147–8; (July 1810), pp 291–2. See also ibid., (Nov. 1807), p. 6; (Jan. 1808), pp 24–5; (Aug. 1808), pp 389–92; (May 1809), pp 238–8; (Dec. 1809), pp 545–6.

occasionally gratis, and generally sold at a price which could not defray the expense of printing. It was greatly admired by the common people.' A Church of Ireland clergyman in County Kilkenny confirmed the popularity of the paper, noting that he had 'often known Cox's magazine to be read to a crowd of villagers on a Sunday evening, while the people swallowed down every word, and imbibed every principle'.[1]

What this sort of evidence suggests is the continuation from the 1790s not so much of a political ideology as of something more vague: a sense of grievance and a set of symbols of opposition to the political and social establishment. Evidence of a more concrete legacy from that period is provided by the appearance around 1811 of a new type of secret society, the Ribbonmen. Contemporaries often used the term 'Ribbonism' indiscriminately to refer to all types of lower-class combination in early and mid-nineteenth-century Ireland, including the numerous agrarian secret societies of the period. This was quite misleading. Ribbonism and the main movements of agrarian protest differed from one another in their geographical base, in their social composition, in forms of organisation, and in content. Whereas agrarian protest was most violent and most frequent in the southern half of Ireland, in Munster and south Leinster, Ribbonism was mainly found in the northern half of the country, more especially in Dublin, in the northern counties of Leinster, in north Connacht, and in south and central Ulster. Whereas agrarian crime at this period was overwhelmingly the work of the rural poor, of labourers, cottiers, and small occupiers, Ribbonism found its strongest support among tradesmen and had a strong urban bias. Some farmers were found in its lodges, but few labourers or cottiers; its tone was artisan and lower-middle-class, rather than peasant or proletarian. While agrarian crime was generally the work of individuals or of small, localised groups, Ribbonism had—on paper at least—a sophisticated organisation, extending not only to different parts of Ireland, but also to Irish communities in some of the major urban centres of Great Britain. Finally, and most important, agrarian protest in this period was, as already mentioned, concerned exclusively with limited and pragmatic goals connected with the preservation of what were seen as existing rights within the land system. Ribbonism, on the other hand, embodied at least some elements of a political ideology.

What exactly this ideology consisted of is difficult to determine. Ribbonmen devoted a great deal of their time and energy to the externals of clandestine association, secret signs, passwords, and ritual, as well as to recurrent and often violent internal feuding, and there is some reason to believe that for many these became almost an end in themselves. At the same time the areas in which the Ribbonmen were strongest were also the areas in which the Defenders had earlier been most active, and it seems clear that they carried forward some

[1] William Shaw Mason (ed.), *A statistical account or parochial survey of Ireland, drawn up from the communications of the clergy* (3 vols, Dublin, 1814–19), iii, 639.

elements of the latter's revolutionary and nationalist sentiments. As with the
Defenders themselves, these did not always take a very coherent form. The
testimony of an informer who, towards the end of 1821, succeeded in penetrating Dublin Ribbon circles provides an indication of the type of unfocused
aspirations and animosities that, at this level, made up of the legacy of the
1790s. Giving evidence at the trial of a number of members of the society he had
joined, he was asked whether he had heard at any meeting what the object of
their movement was:

> I have heard different discourses concerning prophecies, respecting the destruction
> of the protestant religion and the British government.
> What was said of that?
> They seemed to be waiting for the day when these prophecies would be accom-
> plished.
> Did you ever hear any thing said as to what the members were to do?
> The same as all the other societies of the same nature.
> What was that?
> I heard different sentiments about it on different Sundays.
> Tell any that you recollect.
> They spoke of a prophecy to be fulfilled in the year 1825, for the overthrow of the
> tyranny of Orangemen and government, and that there will be but one religion.[1]

Yet despite the vague nature of their political ideas and their failure at any
point to translate them into effective action, the Ribbonmen can be seen as
having provided an important vehicle for the perpetuation of the tradition of
popular disaffection and conspiracy established by the Defenders and United
Irishmen.[2]

There was, of course, one group whose political attitudes during this period
were moving in a very different direction. The presbyterians of eastern Ulster,
who had been the main supporters of the United Irish society in its first years as
a popular movement, rapidly withdrew from any significant involvement in
revolutionary politics. Loyalties did not, of course, change overnight. When the
government in 1802 increased the grant paid to the presbyterian clergy, the
regium donum, at the same time introducing a tripartite hierarchy of ministers
paid at different rates, this was a deliberate attempt to increase the control of
the state over what was still seen as a potentially dangerous group. Nor were
such suspicions entirely unfounded. It is true that when Thomas Russell
attempted to stage an Ulster rising in support of Emmet's attempted seizure of

---

[1] *A report of the trial of Michael Keenan for administering an unlawful oath* [*and*] *a report of the trial of Edward Browne and others for administering and of Laurence Woods for taking an unlawful oath* (Dublin, 1822), pp 80–81. Cf. below, pp 80–83.
[2] Tom Garvin, 'Defenders, Ribbonmen and others: underground political networks in pre-famine Ireland' in *Past & Present*, no. 96 (1982), pp 133–55; M. R. Beames, 'The Ribbon societies: lower-class nationalism in pre-famine Ireland' in *Past & Present*, no. 97 (1982), pp 157–71. See also S. J. Connolly, 'Catholicism in Ulster, 1800–1850' in Peter Roebuck (ed.), *Plantation to partition: essays in Ulster history in honour of J. L. McCracken* (Belfast, 1981), pp 168–70; and below, p. 390.

Dublin in July 1803, he was turned away by former United Irishmen. But there is evidence to suggest that this was due not to the absence of revolutionary sentiment but rather to a lack of faith in what was so obviously a desperate attempt to retrieve a hopeless situation, and to the lack of prior organisation. 'Although in many parts anxious for a rising,' an informer reported from Belfast, 'yet they can't see how it is to be effected, having no system amongst them. Arms they have but few.'[1] Even after 1803 reports of clandestine organisation among former United Irishmen in eastern Ulster continued from time to time to reach the government. As late as 1814 it was claimed that 'a few protestant traitors, a remnant of the views and projects of 1798', continued to associate, under the label of 'Defenders', in Belfast and in parts of the surrounding countryside, and to cooperate with the exclusively catholic Ribbonmen.[2] By this time, however, such 'protestant traitors' were a tiny and unrepresentative minority, and as memories of the 1790s faded the loyalty of Ulster presbyterians came increasingly to be taken for granted. By 1835 a reporter for the ordnance survey could note with detachment that the inhabitants of the parish of Connor in County Antrim 'were almost to a man engaged in the rebellion of 1798. . . . However, since that time their politics have changed, and they now seem indifferent and careless on the subject.'[3]

The reasons for this change in the political outlook of Ulster presbyterians are clear enough. Military repression during the disarming of Ulster in 1797, and after the rebellion of June 1798, had provided a brutal lesson in the realities of revolution. More important, perhaps, events in the south over the same period had given Ulster presbyterians a new appreciation of the particular dangers they faced as part of a protestant minority in a predominantly catholic Ireland. It was thus not the political or social attitudes of Ulster presbyterians that were transformed in the aftermath of 1798, but rather their appreciation of the risks of translating those attitudes into action. Edward Wakefield, writing in 1812, complained that the presbyterians remained 'republicans in principle', their quietness being 'the quietness of expediency alone'; and accounts compiled for the ordnance survey in the mid-1830s confirmed that the presbyterian farmers and weavers of County Antrim continued to be conspicuous for their independent and egalitarian social attitudes, their 'notion that they have no superiors, and that courtesy is but another term for servility'.[4] Such attitudes, furthermore, continued to find a political expression. In Belfast in particular there remained a recognisable body of protestant radical opinion, surfacing regularly in support of such causes as parliamentary reform, the exposure of official corruption, and the claims of the disgraced Queen Caroline, while a much larger group continued to give electoral support,

[1] MacDonagh, Post-bag, p. 415. See also Elliott, Partners in revolution, pp 312–13.
[2] Sir George Hill to Peel, 9 Mar. 1814 (S.P.O., State of the country papers, 1567/10).
[3] R.I.A., ordnance survey memoirs, 8/II/1, p. 22.
[4] Wakefield, Account of Ire., ii, 547; Memoir of Doagh, 1839 (R.I.A., ordnance survey memoirs, 9/III/3, p. 56).

through whig and liberal candidates, to the cause of moderate reform. There was thus no question of Ulster presbyterians passing directly from the radicalism of the 1790s to a tame acceptance of the established order. What survived into the early nineteenth century, however, was a much modified radicalism, purged of all associations with physical force, republicanism, and separatism. As such it represented a middle ground that was increasingly to come under pressure as Irish public life became the exclusive preserve of competing extremes.

The transformation of presbyterian political attitudes in the years after 1801 is well known. But outside Ulster too—though in a less dramatic manner—protestants found it necessary to adjust their thinking to new conditions. This was particularly so in relation to the union. There was, initially at least, no reason to assume that the strong hostility the proposal for a union had encountered among many protestants would automatically disappear once the measure had become law. The government certainly made no such assumption. Their anxiety on this score was made clear in 1803 when the sale to the Bank of Ireland of the former Parliament House on College Green was accompanied by a confidential stipulation that the lords and commons chambers should be adapted in such a way as completely to alter their former appearance and to ensure that they would never again be used as public debating rooms. Nor was such concern entirely misplaced: there were indeed those for whom the union remained a live political issue. When a proposal to erect a monument to the recently deceased Cornwallis was discussed at Westminster in 1806, Charles O'Hara, M.P. for County Sligo, objected on the grounds that Cornwallis had been the author of the union, a measure that he hoped to see parliament at some stage rescind.[1] His speech, along with some apparently sympathetic remarks by Fox, encouraged several of the Dublin guilds to discuss the possibility of petitioning for a repeal of the union. In 1808 a motion calling for such a petition was carried in the quarter assembly of Dublin corporation. Similar resolutions were carried in 1810, and seconded at a general meeting of the citizens, freemen, and freeholders of the city.

In the long run, of course, this support for repeal by the protestant-dominated guilds and corporation of Dublin, and by Irish protestants generally, was to give way to a determination to maintain the union at all costs. The principal reason for this change of attitude, as for the decline of presbyterian radicalism in the north, was the growing aggressiveness of catholics. A restoration of the Irish parliament as it had been before 1801 was one thing; the creation of an independent parliament in the wake of catholic emancipation and a possible reform of the electoral system was quite another. In the debates on the catholic petition in May 1805[2] John Foster set out with remorseless logic the realities of a new political world. Because the union had swept away the majority of the boroughs, he pointed out, catholic emancipation would mean

[1] *Hansard 1*, vi, 126–8 (3 Feb 1806).   [2] Below, pp 28–30.

that the majority of the M.P.s returned for Irish seats would be catholics. However, they would soon find that fifty, or sixty, or even a hundred M.P.s counted for little in a parliament of 658 members.

Possessed, then, of this reform [the destruction of the boroughs] and of their power of sitting, it might be natural for them to look to a restoration of the Irish legislature. . . . They would call for three hundred members to assume their functions in an Irish parliament; and the two hundred seats added in the room of the one hundred protestant boroughs, which we have demolished, would all be filled by popular elections, where numbers, in which their strength consists, would decide. What would not a majority, so constituted, look to? They would see their own aggrandisement, the maintenance and dignity of their clergy, and the consequent superiority of their church, all within their view. . . . The seeds of separation would be sown, and Ireland might be torn from her connection with Britain, without which she is and must be incapable of enjoying wealth, tranquillity, happiness, or any of the blessings of human life.[1]

Thus, within a space of less than five years, the union had come to be accepted by one of its leading opponents as an essential guarantee of the survival of Irish protestants. Foster had not made sufficient allowance for the continuing power of deference and landlord influence, but in the long term his analysis was incontrovertible. Not all Irish protestants, however, could adjust as quickly to the logic of a changed situation. Right up to the early 1830s Dublin protestants intermittently raised the question of the union and called for its repeal.[2] In retrospect such demands can be seen as one of the cul-de-sacs of history. But in this respect, as in others, the assumptions and loyalties of the later eighteenth century refused to be tidied away with anything like the neatness or finality that logic and hindsight would seek to impose.

[1] *Hansard 1*, iv, 1003-4 (14 May 1805).
[2] For a brief account see Jacqueline Hill, 'The politics of privilege: Dublin corporation and the catholic question, 1792-1823' in *Maynooth Review*, vii (1982), p. 36 and n. 81.

CHAPTER II

The catholic question, 1801–12

S. J. CONNOLLY

ONE further consequence of Emmet's rebellion was to bring to new prominence debates that had been going on for some time about the possible involvement of the catholic clergy in treasonable conspiracy. The controversy had begun with a cluster of pamphlets in 1798 and 1799 arising out of allegations that James Caulfield, catholic bishop of Ferns (1786–1814), along with some of his priests, had cooperated with the rebel army in the south-east and had failed to prevent the murder of protestant prisoners. In 1801 these and other charges were restated in Sir Richard Musgrave's *Memoirs of the different rebellions in Ireland*. The catholic bishops, Musgrave alleged, could have warned the government as early as 1793 that a treasonable conspiracy was in progress, but they had failed to do so. As for Caulfield, he had not only refused to intervene to prevent the massacre of protestant prisoners in Wexford town, but had given his blessing immediately beforehand to the pikemen concerned.[1] The attack was renewed after Emmet's rebellion, this time directed at the clergy of Dublin, and in particular at their archbishop, John Thomas Troy. On the day following the outbreak, Sunday 24 July, Troy had issued a pastoral letter repeating his many earlier statements on the doctrine of absolute obedience to established civil authority, condemning French revolutionary principles, and praising Hardwicke's 'mild administration'.[2] Despite this, allegations were soon in circulation that Troy and his clergy had known in advance of the conspiracy but had made no attempt to warn the government. Even Troy's pastoral letter became evidence against him, its prompt appearance the day after the rebellion being presented as proof that his response had been prepared in advance. In July 1804 these charges were finally stated in print in the London-based journal, the *Anti-Jacobin*. Troy successfully sued the editor, Henry Symonds, for libel, being awarded damages of £50.

None of these allegations against the catholic clergy had more than the most slender foundation in fact. The catholic bishops of the late eighteenth and early

[1] Sir Richard Musgrave, *Memoirs of the different rebellions in Ireland* (Dublin, 1801), pp 290–93, 489–96.
[2] Troy's pastoral letter is printed in M. V. Ronan (ed.), 'Archbishop Troy's correspondence with Dublin Castle' in *Archiv. Hib.*, xi (1944), pp 28–30.

nineteenth centuries were men of conservative social outlook, firmly opposed to revolutionary activity of any kind. Among the lower clergy, a small number had sympathised with the cause of the United Irishmen, but the great majority appear to have shared in the loyalism, or at least the passivity, of their ecclesiastical superiors.[1] It might be assumed, in consequence, that suspicions of the kind voiced by Musgrave and others were to be found only among a lunatic fringe of protestant extremists. But in fact they were widely shared by otherwise responsible observers, including senior members of the Irish government. In August and September 1803 the lord chancellor, Redesdale, engaged in a superficially polite but increasingly acrimonious exchange of letters with the catholic peer Lord Fingall, in which Redesdale openly stated his belief that the conduct of some senior members of the Irish catholic clergy 'is calculated to excite in the minds of those under their care hatred of their protestant fellow subjects and disloyalty to their government'. For the most part Redesdale confined himself to relatively harmless allegations, in particular the claim that the catholic clergy encouraged the doctrine that only those who submitted to the authority of the pope were to be considered Christians. But he also maintained that in at least one diocese priests who had saved the lives of loyalists in 1798 had been 'universally discountenanced' by their bishop, while a priest who had taken part in the rebellion had been triumphantly reinstated in his parish on his return from transportation.[2] When Redesdale's letters to Fingall were published in 1804, they caused great offence among catholics, as well as some embarrassment on the government side. Yet in private the chancellor had gone much further, condemning what he called the 'canting hypocrisy' of Troy's response to Emmet's rebellion, and arguing that the catholic clergy could not all have been entirely ignorant of what was being planned.[3] Hardwicke, writing to the home secretary, was equally vehement: 'I think Dr Troy's pastoral letter to the popish clergy of the archdiocese of Dublin is the greatest piece of craft, dissimulation, and hypocrisy that I ever read. ... Nobody can give the least credit to his total ignorance of the conspiracy.'[4] Just after the rebellion an official emissary was sent to examine the papers of Thomas Hussey, catholic bishop of Waterford and Lismore, who had

---

[1] For a discussion of the political loyalties of priests and bishops during the 1790s see Connolly, *Priests & people in Ire.*, pp 226–9. The only catholic bishop to whom any genuine suspicion can be attached would seem to be Dominic Bellew, bishop of Killala. See Patrick Hogan, 'Some observations on contemporary allegations as to Bishop Dominick Bellew's (1745–1813) sympathies during the 1798 rebellion in Connaught' in *Seanchas Ardmhacha*, x, no. 2 (1982), pp 417–25.

[2] The correspondence is printed in *Castlereagh corr.*, iv, 298–313. Its content appears to have become general knowledge almost at once. On 17 Sept., a month after Redesdale's first letter to Fingall, the marquis of Buckingham wrote to Lord Grenville that Redesdale 'has been writing *ostensibly* to Lord Fingall [i.e. intending the letter to be widely circulated] in the style of a fanatic of 1640, and these documents have run like wildfire through all Ireland' (*Fortescue MSS*, vii, 188).

[3] *Colchester corr.*, i, 436. Redesdale had held similar views even before Emmet's rebellion, but at that stage he had been able to express them with a sardonic detachment missing from his exchange with Fingall. See his letter to Charles Abbot, 15 Aug. 1802 (ibid., p. 408).

[4] MacDonagh, *Post-bag*, p. 326.

died on 11 July 1803—ostensibly in case they contained confidential communications from the government, but in reality to search for evidence of any treasonable correspondence in which the bishop might have been engaged.

This belief that leading catholic clergymen had connived at treasonable conspiracy, privately shared even by senior and well informed official observers, forms an essential part of the background to what was to be the single most important issue in the politics of early nineteenth-century Ireland, the question of catholic emancipation. Positively penal legislation directed against catholics—the outlawing of bishops and regular clergy, the prohibition of catholic schools, the restrictions on ownership of landed property—had been abolished by a series of relief acts passed between 1772 and 1782. A further act of 1793[1] had restored to catholics the right to vote in parliamentary elections and to become members of municipal corporations. The same act had admitted catholics to civil and military office, but it had done so only subject to a series of vital exceptions. Catholics were excluded from the offices of lord lieutenant, chief secretary, chancellor of the exchequer, attorney general, and solicitor general, from membership of the privy council, and from most other senior positions in the administration. They could not be generals on the staff, judges, or king's counsel, or governors, sheriffs, or sub-sheriffs. Most important of all, they could not sit in parliament.

Catholic emancipation, therefore, meant first and foremost the admission of catholics to those offices from which they were still excluded by law, and the granting of the right to sit in parliament. The grievances of Irish catholics, however, were not confined to these formal legal disabilities. They also complained that they were still, in practice, excluded from the offices for which they were now theoretically eligible. To some extent, of course, this could be attributed to the fact that catholics, though making up more than 80 per cent of the total population, were seriously underrepresented among the middle classes—and even more the landed classes—from whom the majority of holders of the offices in question would be drawn. At the same time figures compiled for the Catholic Association in 1828 leave little doubt that there was also systematic discrimination. Of 1,314 offices connected with the administration of justice to which catholics could legally be appointed, only 39 were in fact held by catholics. On another list of 3,033 offices that were either under the direct control of the crown or else connected with societies or institutions supported out of public funds, catholics held 134 posts.[2] A further grievance concerned the administration of the law, and in particular charges that local magistrates turned a blind eye to cases of Orange violence against catholics. The polemical history of the first decade of the union written by Francis Plowden (1811) returns repeatedly to instances of this kind of partiality, and a

[1] 33 Geo. III, c. 21 (9 Apr. 1793).
[2] Wyse, *Catholic Association*, ii, appendix, pp cclxxxii–ccxc.

purge of partisan magistrates—along with the appointment of more catholics to the bench—was prominent among catholic demands.[1]

The formal exclusion of catholics from the highest levels of the administration and the legal profession was thus part of a much wider set of grievances. Some of these arose out of the way in which the political and legal system operated in practice; others lay outside the sphere of law and politics altogether. Wakefield, writing in 1812, emphasised that there were catholic disabilities that could not be removed by an alteration in the law, but only by a change in public opinion:

> Among them are militia regiments without a Roman Catholic officer; Roman Catholic chapels without steeples, while the board of first-fruits is erecting those marks of distinction on all churches for the established religion; and country gentlemen, to use their own expression, making 'pets' of protestant yeomen, or in common language giving them the preference in every occurrence of life.[2]

As catholic discontent came to be organised in a national political movement, attention inevitably focused on the concrete and straightforward demand for the removal of the remaining legal disabilities. But it is impossible to understand the character that the movement assumed—and in particular the support it came to attract among those to whom the achievement of its explicit political aims could make no conceivable difference—unless it is seen as also expressing the sense of a much wider exclusion and injustice.

It had at one time seemed likely that most of the remaining legal disabilities affecting catholics would be removed at the time of the union. Pitt's plans for Ireland had envisaged a comprehensive settlement, in which the union would be accompanied and cemented by a series of measures designed to put an end to religious antagonisms in Ireland: payment of the catholic clergy by the state, reform of the tithe system, and a catholic relief act. The principal obstacle to this wider plan was George III. When proposals for the union were first laid before him in June 1798, he had made clear that the project must not involve any further concessions to the catholics. Pitt had nevertheless gone ahead— apparently in the hope that when the time came the king could be pressed into giving his assent. However, he was forestalled by members of his own cabinet, themselves opponents of catholic emancipation, who warned the king at the beginning of 1801 of what Pitt was planning. At a levee held on 28 January the king went on the offensive, informing a member of Pitt's cabinet that he would in future consider any man who proposed further concessions to catholics as a personal enemy. Pitt submitted a memorandum setting out the case for catholic relief, and offering his resignation if his advice was not accepted. The king was immovable, and Pitt resigned. What happened next can only be understood in

---

[1] Plowden, *Hist. Ire., 1801–10*, i, 25–30, 41–2, 73–6; ii, 347–73, 444–51; iii, 634–5, 711–16, 749–63, 760n, 887–90.

[2] Wakefield, *Account of Ire.*, ii, 589–90.

terms of the close relationship that had been built up over a long period between the two men. Two weeks after Pitt's resignation the king suffered a short period of mental disturbance, and on his recovery blamed the attack on the agitation Pitt had caused him. When Pitt learned of this, he sent a promise that he would never again raise with the king the question of catholic emancipation, and that he would resist all attempts by others to bring forward any measure of that kind. He also agreed not to oppose the new government, which had by this time been put together under Henry Addington. The members of this new administration were not required to make any pledge of opposition to emancipation in principle, but they were required to agree that the question should not be raised for the moment. Thus Hardwicke, a supporter of the principle of emancipation, accepted the post of lord lieutenant of Ireland, on the understanding 'that he was against *now* agitating the question, reserving himself for other times and circumstances upon the principle'.[1]

Throughout these transactions Pitt and his associates insisted that they had made no explicit promise to the Irish catholics that their support for the union would be rewarded by further concessions. This was strictly true, but the leaders of catholic opinion had certainly been encouraged to believe that if the union were carried a further measure of catholic relief would be possible and even likely. There was thus some concern about how catholics might react to the news that their expectations were not to be fulfilled. Before leaving office, Cornwallis wrote two letters for circulation among leading catholics, warning against any unconstitutional or imprudent action, and reminding them 'of the benefit they possess by having so many characters of eminence pledged not to embark in the service of government, except on the terms of the catholic privileges being obtained'.[2] In fact the catholic leaders offered no public response to their disappointment, and they remained almost entirely quiet during the succeeding three years. When Pitt returned to office in May 1804, however, it soon became clear that Cornwallis's incautious references to a 'pledge' would be put to the test. A series of catholic meetings held in Dublin during the autumn of 1804 showed that there was substantial support for a petition to parliament calling for the removal of catholic disabilities. The government responded by seeking to persuade the more amenable of the catholic leaders, in a series of confidential meetings, that such a step at this time would only damage their cause. For a while it seemed as if these tactics might succeed, but at a meeting on 16 February 1805 the moderate party gave way and it was agreed to present the petition. A catholic delegation called on Pitt on 12 March and asked him to present the petition in parliament. When he refused, the delegation turned to the opposition. The whig leaders, and in

---

[1] *Colchester corr.*, i, 241.

[2] *Correspondence of Charles, first Marquis Cornwallis*, ed. Charles Ross (3 vols, London, 1859), iii, 348. Cornwallis was later forced to admit that he had had no explicit authority to use the word 'pledge' in this context. See his letters to Plowden, 7, 9 Apr. 1805 (*Castlereagh corr.*, iv, 373–4).

particular Charles James Fox, were long-standing supporters of catholic relief and of a general policy of conciliation and reform in Ireland. Lord Grenville, formerly Pitt's foreign secretary, was a more conservative figure, but he had resigned along with Pitt in 1801, and in the debates that followed had identified himself strongly with the cause of catholic relief. Moreover he had not returned to office in 1804, but had remained in opposition, allied to the whigs. Accordingly it was agreed that the catholic petition would be presented by Fox in the commons and Grenville in the lords. The petition also provided the occasion for the return to politics of Henry Grattan, who had withdrawn from public life after the union, but who was now returned for an English pocket borough controlled by the whig magnate Earl Fitzwilliam, to enable him to contribute to the debate. The petition was debated in May 1805, and was rejected by votes of 178 to 49 in the lords and 336 to 124 in the commons.[1]

These huge majorities could be attributed partly to the influence of Pitt, who had spoken against the petition, and to a recognition by some who were prepared to agree to a measure of catholic relief that the king's attitude made a vote in support on this occasion pointless. But the voting was also clear evidence of the strength of the opposition to catholic emancipation that existed in British political circles. This opposition derived from several sources. Some opponents of catholic emancipation rested their case on the principle that the existence of a single national church, supporting and supported by the state, was essential to social and political stability. This was the view put forward by George III in June 1798:

... no country can be governed where there is more than one established religion; the others may be tolerated, but that cannot extend further than leave to perform their religious duties according to the tenets of their church, for which indulgence they cannot have any share in the government of the state.[2]

Others argued that it was the particular character of catholicism that made it impossible to admit its adherents to full political rights. Catholics were required to put obedience to their spiritual superiors before obedience to their temporal rulers; their ultimate loyalty was to a foreign temporal power, the papacy; and they could never be trusted, since their religion taught them that they were under no obligation to keep faith with heretics. Other charges were aimed specifically at Irish catholics. If admitted to political rights, it was claimed, they would seek to use their new power to seize the endowments of the Church of Ireland, to oppress the protestant minority, and ultimately to seek the separation of Ireland from Britain. Two speakers in the debate of May 1805 went so far as to bring up the old charge that catholic families in Ireland kept

[1] The voting of the Irish M.P.s, 27 for and 47 against, closely reflected that of parliament as a whole (P. J. Jupp, 'Irish parliamentary representation, 1801-20' (Ph.D. thesis, Reading, 1966), p. 172).
[2] Bolton, *Ir. act of union*, p. 56.

maps, handed down from generation to generation, showing the location of the lands once owned by their ancestors, in anticipation of the day when they would be able to reverse the seventeenth-century forfeitures. This, of course, was precisely the sort of objection that Pitt had argued would cease to carry weight once Ireland and Great Britain had been united into one predominantly protestant kingdom. But the truth was that much of the opposition to catholic claims rested not on practical political considerations but on emotion. In part this was a matter of cultural distance: to most British protestants of the early nineteenth century, catholicism, with its authoritarian ethos, its incomprehensible Latin rites, its celibate clergy, and its mysterious and degrading ceremony of confession, was both alien and profoundly distasteful. Antipathy and suspicion, furthermore, were reinforced by a strong sense of history and tradition. The great debate over emancipation, Edward Cooke had warned Castlereagh in January 1801, would not rest on practical arguments over policy,

but upon the wisdom, policy, beneficial experience of the test laws, the free principles of the reformation, the freer principles of the revolution; and the conduct and prejudices of two hundred years will be appealed to, and a constitution purchased by the blood of martyrs and patriots, who perished at the stake in Smithfield, and fell upon the banks of the Boyne, and on the plains of Aughrim.[1]

When the catholic delegation returned to Ireland after the rejection of their petition, the committee established in February 1805 was dissolved and a new one elected, but this body appears not to have held any further meetings. Then, at the beginning of 1806, the prospects of the catholics seemed to be transformed with the death of Pitt on 23 January and the accession on 11 February of a new ministry. Hailed as constituting a 'ministry of all the talents', this was in fact a coalition of whigs, Grenvillites, and followers of Addington (now raised to the peerage as Lord Sidmouth), with Grenville as prime minister and Fox as foreign secretary. Hardwicke was withdrawn and replaced as lord lieutenant by the duke of Bedford, a whig magnate of liberal principles. The new ministry won immediate favour with Irish catholics by two measures: the lord chancellor, Redesdale, whose hostility had been advertised both in his letters to Fingall and in the debate on the catholic petition, was dismissed and replaced by George Ponsonby, while the act for the suspension of habeas corpus, introduced after Emmet's rebellion, was allowed to lapse on 7 March. The new government, however, held out no hope of an immediate measure for the removal of catholic disabilities. If the catholics presented another petition to parliament, Fox wrote in February 1806, he would support it, but it would not be in their own interest for them to do so. They would achieve nothing except to bring down a government favourable to their interests. If, on the other hand, they refrained from pressing for formal legislation in their favour, they would receive the practical benefits of more equitable administration. The govern-

[1] *Castlereagh corr.*, iv, 17.

ment would do for them 'all that is consistent with existing bad laws, by giving them in substance what they have now only in words, a right to be in the army, to be corporators, etc. etc.; by a change of justices of peace, whose conduct has been notoriously oppressive; I hope too, by some arrangement about tithes'.[1]

Fox's correspondent on this occasion was James Ryan, a Dublin merchant, who had come to prominence during the revival of the catholic agitation in 1804–5. Most of the catholic meetings held during that period had in fact taken place at Ryan's house in Marlborough Street, Dublin, and he had also been one of the delegates elected to accompany the catholic petition to London, where he had first met Fox. Ryan now proceeded to organise a further set of meetings, the first taking place once again in his house, at which he and his associates brought forward proposals to implement Fox's advice. These involved postponing all plans for a further petition to parliament, and instead presenting a declaration of unlimited confidence in the new ministry. Ryan's activities, however, almost immediately came under attack. Other catholic spokesmen, notably John Keogh, the veteran leader of the 1790s, and Lord Ffrench, an eccentric peer with banking interests, came forward to charge him with assuming an authority he did not possess, first in writing to Fox in the manner of an official representative of the catholic body, and then in organising what were denounced as unrepresentative meetings. Hostility to Ryan was further sharpened by the discovery that he had applied to the new ministry for a lucrative appointment for himself. The conflict came to a head at an acrimonious general meeting of catholics on 13–14 March 1806. A resolution condemning the holding of meetings in private houses as 'unfavourable to the freedom of discussion, and inadequate to the collection of public sentiment' was passed unanimously, but Ryan's critics failed to carry a second resolution explicitly condemning his recent actions. Ryan, according to a protestant onlooker, 'collected all the grocers' apprentices to beat Lord Ffrench on a division'.[2] However, by the following month the same observer reported that Ryan's influence among the catholics was in decline, while that of Keogh and Ffrench was increasing.[3]

This repudiation of Ryan's activities was not followed by any drastic new departure. A meeting of catholic gentlemen in Dublin on 3 April resolved to form an association that would be 'representative of the full respectability of the catholic body', in order to provide a medium of communication with the government. This was abandoned after a few weeks, when the chief secretary made it clear that Bedford would not receive any communication from a body claiming representative status contrary to the convention act of 1793.[4] A loyal

[1] Plowden, *Hist. Ire., 1801–10*, ii, 304–7.
[2] Ibid., pp 293–316; J. S. Rochfort to John Foster, 14 Mar. 1806 (P.R.O.N.I., D207/33/79).
[3] Rochfort to Foster, 17 Apr. 1806 (P.R.O.N.I., D207/33/89). In December 1809 Ryan was reported to have again tried, without success, to supplant Keogh and his associates and assume the leadership of the Irish catholics (*Fortescue MSS*, ix, 161–2).
[4] 33 Geo. III, c. 29 (16 Aug. 1793). Plowden, *Hist. Ire., 1801–10*, ii, 328–9n; Rochfort to Foster,

address presented to Bedford in the name of the catholics of Dublin and elsewhere on 29 April referred only in the most indirect terms to their 'hope' of
future benefits from 'the wise generosity of our lawgivers'.[1] During the months
that followed, dissatisfaction with the 'talents' increased. Francis Plowden was
to claim in 1811 that the government made no attempt whatever to direct a
share of patronage towards catholics or to check the partiality of Orange
magistrates.[2] These allegations, made after Grenville and the whigs had fallen
out with the Irish catholics on the question of the veto on episcopal appointments, are not necessarily to be trusted. The ministers did make some effort to
fulfil Fox's promise of better government within the limits of existing laws.
When six vacancies occurred on the Irish revenue boards, both Grenville and
Bedford insisted that those appointed must include a catholic, and John
Therry was duly nominated as 'the fittest Roman Catholic for that situation'.[3]
In the counties of Carlow and Wexford magistrates held to have abused their
authority were removed, and in Wexford six catholic gentlemen were put into
the commission of the peace. The parliamentary grant to the catholic seminary
at Maynooth was increased from £8,000 to £13,000 a year, although the ministry
went out of office before this could be implemented. Grenville pressed Bedford
to bring forward proposals for a reform of the tithe system. It became increasingly clear, however, that none of this was sufficient. The government's three
major Irish appointments, Lord Holland later conceded, all failed in different
ways to win the confidence of the catholics. Bedford was too reticent; his chief
secretary, William Elliot, was cold and stiff in manner, and was compromised
in the eyes of many by his earlier service as under-secretary in the military
department (1796–1801). Ponsonby 'became somewhat pompous upon his
elevation to the seals' and kept aloof from former political friends. His changes
in the magistracy in Carlow and Wexford earned the administration less credit
than they might have done, because of a widespread belief that in some cases
reform had been sacrificed to the maintenance of electoral interests.[4] The
government's failings in this crucial area were further emphasised when
Richard Wilson, a protestant magistrate in County Tyrone, published details
of his unsuccessful attempts to have action taken against some of his colleagues
in County Armagh who had blatantly connived at Orange outrages. The gap

29 Apr. 1806 (P.R.O.N.I., D207/33/93). Wyse presents the meeting of April 1806 as inaugurating a
new attempt to create a catholic organisation, which continued until April 1807 (*Catholic Association*, i, 141). However, Plowden's account of the first of the meetings that marked the renewal of
catholic pressure on the government in January 1807 seems to suggest that there was no such direct
continuity (*Hist. Ire., 1801–10*, ii, 423).

[1] Plowden, *Hist. Ire., 1801–10*, ii, 323–5.
[2] Ibid., pp 334–73.
[3] *Fortescue MSS*, viii, 215, 227.
[4] Henry, Lord Holland, *Memoirs of the whig party during my time*, ed. Henry Edward, Lord Holland
(2 vols, London, 1852–4), ii, 163–8. There were also complaints that the duchess of Bedford
extended invitations only to those she particularly liked, and that two of her friends had publicly
made fun of the local accent (Rochfort to Foster, 5 May 1806 (P.R.O.N.I., D207/33/94)).

between the expectations that the 'talents' had awakened and their ability or willingness to satisfy them was also embarrassingly highlighted when reports from Connacht revealed that the Threshers claimed to act in the belief that the government tacitly approved of their attempts to reduce the level of tithe payments.[1] Meanwhile the death of Fox in September 1806 had been seen by many catholics as removing their most sincere supporter within the ministry.

At the beginning of February 1807 the cabinet received a letter from Bedford warning that affairs in Ireland were approaching a crisis. During the previous month there had been a series of catholic meetings in Dublin, and a delegation had waited on Elliot to ask whether the government intended to bring in a catholic relief bill. When Elliot and Bedford replied that they would have to consult the cabinet, the catholics appointed a committee to draw up a new petition, to be presented to parliament in the event of an unfavourable reply being received from London. The majority of the catholic aristocracy and gentry, led by Lord Fingall and Sir Edward Bellew, had at first declined to take part in these proceedings, despite insistent appeals to them to do so. Now, however, they too had joined in the agitation—not out of any enthusiasm for an immediate assertion of catholic claims, but rather because they were reluctant to cut themselves off from their fellow catholics. Despite these ominous signs, however, Bedford believed that it might still be possible to prevent the catholics from going ahead with their petition, by offering them some concessions of immediate practical value. He suggested three measures: that catholics should become eligible to serve as sheriffs; that they should be enabled to enter municipal corporations; and that all restrictions on service by catholics in the army be removed.

The anxiety of Grenville and the whigs to forestall a catholic petition did not mean that their earlier support for catholic emancipation had been insincere. They had, however, no taste for pointless sacrifice. The debate of 1805 had made clear that there was a strong majority in parliament opposed to any further relaxation of catholic disabilities, so that any petition, or any actual measure for catholic emancipation, would inevitably be rejected. At the same time a petition would be at the very least embarrassing, while at worst, by forcing ministers to speak and vote once again in support of emancipation, it might provoke a confrontation with the king and the fall of the government. Accordingly the cabinet moved quickly to take up Bedford's suggestion of immediate, practical concessions. To seek to make catholics eligible for appointment as sheriffs would require legislation, and thus would be as pointless and probably disastrous as to introduce a full-scale relief act. The exclusion of catholics from corporations was outside the control of parliament in any case, since it arose not from legislation but from the refusal of protestant corporations to admit catholics as burgesses or freemen. There remained the

[1] *Fortescue MSS*, viii, 475–6; Col. Harcourt to ——, 28 Nov. 1806 (S.P.O., State of the country papers, 1092/3).

third concession mentioned by Bedford: service in the army. Under the terms of the relief act of 1793 catholics could serve in the ranks and hold commissions, but they remained excluded from positions on the staff. The act of 1793, furthermore, passed by the Irish parliament, had applied only to Ireland. This meant that when Irish troops were transferred to Great Britain, catholic officers' commissions became invalid, while private soldiers could be required to attend the religious services of the established church. It was these deficiencies in the existing legislation that the government now proposed to remedy. In doing so they were hardly addressing the most pressing of the grievances felt by catholics, and indeed the reaction in Ireland to their proposals seems to have been fairly cool.

From the government's point of view, however, the idea was an attractive one, not only because there seemed a reasonable chance of securing the consent of king and parliament, but also because the measure they proposed promised to relieve another, quite separate problem. Britain was suffering from a chronic shortage of manpower with which to carry on the war with France. Recruiting in Ireland, which held one-third of the population of the newly created United Kingdom, had never reached satisfactory levels—largely, it was felt, because of fears that the religion of catholic soldiers would be interfered with. Already in 1806 Grenville had proposed one solution to this problem: the recruitment of specifically catholic regiments for service in catholic countries overseas. A bill to remedy the defects of the act of 1793 promised to be a more satisfactory solution to the same problem, while at the same time possibly placating the catholics.

On 4 March 1807 the government introduced the catholic militia bill, which opened all commissions in the army and navy to any subject of the king who took a prescribed oath, and which guaranteed to all soldiers and sailors the undisturbed exercise of their religion. Six days later the king informed Grenville that he intended to declare his opposition to the measure. Exactly what had happened remains unclear. The central issue was the difference between the Irish catholic relief act of 1793, which admitted catholics to the army but excluded them from posts on the staff, and the militia bill of 1807, which would have made catholics eligible for all commissions, in both the army and the navy. The whigs maintained that the king had led them to believe that he had given his consent, however reluctantly, to these additional concessions. By declaring his opposition only after they had committed themselves irrevocably to the measure, they claimed, the king had sought to manoeuvre them into a position in which they would feel obliged to resign. The most detailed modern study, on the other hand, accepts the king's claim that what he had consented to was only the extension to Britain of the concessions already granted in Ireland by the act of 1793. According to this interpretation, it was the 'talents' who had been guilty of sharp practice, by attempting to smuggle past the king, as part of a mere extension to Britain of the 1793 act, something that was in fact an important further concession.[1] A third theory is that the ministers did not themselves realise at first that they were proposing concessions that went beyond those contained in the act of 1793, and that they blundered rather than schemed their way into the crisis that followed.[2] But whatever the explanation, the sequel was clear enough. The 'talents' offered to compromise by modifying the offending bill, but the king refused to agree. Next they agreed to drop the measure altogether, but they added a demand that they should be free to express their opinions on the catholic question and to raise the subject with the king again. The king took up the implied challenge, demanding from his ministers a pledge that they would not trouble him again with proposals for further concessions. The ministers refused and on 24 March 1807 they resigned, being replaced by a new ministry under the duke of Portland.

The dissatisfaction among Irish catholics with the performance of the 'ministry of all the talents' was cancelled by the circumstances of its fall. In April 1807 a general meeting in Dublin considered whether to go ahead with the proposed petition. At this point it still seemed possible that Portland's government might fail to secure a stable majority, and a letter from Henry Grattan was read to the meeting advising the catholics not to embarrass their parliamentary supporters at such a delicate moment. There was some opposition to the abandonment of the petition, but John Keogh and Daniel O'Connell, both formerly supporters of firm action, came forward to argue that in view of the sacrifice the whigs had made on behalf of the catholics their advice should be accepted, and the petition was accordingly postponed. (In the event Portland's government remained in office, and in June 1807 confirmed its position in a general election during which the theme 'no popery' played a prominent part.) Appreciation of the merits of the whigs was further enhanced by the policies adopted by the new government. The lord lieutenant, the duke of Richmond, was a strong opponent of catholic emancipation. It is true that, in a tour of Ireland undertaken in 1809, he was to make a deliberate attempt to advertise his willingness to deal fairly with all groups, going so far as to object on one occasion when a toast was proposed to 'the protestant ascendancy'. At the same time there was much to support the charge that Richmond was the first lord lieutenant since the union 'to commence a system of governing by a party and for a party'.[3] John Giffard, whom Hardwicke had dismissed from his post in the customs administration for having organised a protest against the catholic petition in 1805, was given a new office of profit. Patrick Duigenan, the secretary of the Grand Orange Lodge of Ireland and one of the leading parliamentary opponents of catholic emancipation, became a privy councillor. William Saurin, another prominent opponent of catholic claims, became attorney

[1] Roberts, *Whig party*, pp 18–34.
[2] Philip Ziegler, *Addington: a life of Henry Addington, first Viscount Sidmouth* (London, 1965), pp 263–8. Ziegler quotes Howick's admission to the commons: 'I must confess that I have not myself sufficiently attended to the distinction between [the militia bill] and the Irish act' (p. 264).
[3] Fagan, *O'Connell*, i, 63.

general. The parliamentary grant to Maynooth college, which the 'talents' had decided to increase to £13,000, was fixed instead at £9,250.[1] Several of the magistrates removed by Ponsonby were restored. The feeling among militant protestants that they now had a government more favourable to their interests was reflected in an apparent increase in the frequency of Orange outrages against catholics, including the murder of a priest in King's County on 12 July 1808 and the wounding of another in County Cavan in the following year.[2]

This greater degree of harmony between the Irish catholics and their parliamentary friends was not to last. The issue on which it fractured was the question of the veto. The idea that a complete or partial removal of the legal disabilities of Irish catholics should be accompanied by other measures, designed to ensure that the clergy of the church thus freed from restrictions would be loyal to the state, was not new. In 1782 Irish M.P.s sympathetic to catholic relief had first raised the possibility of giving the king the right to veto the appointment of unacceptable individuals to catholic bishoprics—a power already enjoyed by most European monarchs ruling over substantial catholic populations. Pitt's plans for a comprehensive settlement of the Irish question at the time of the act of union involved vesting in the king a similar power of veto. In addition, Pitt proposed to make the lower ranks of the catholic clergy less dependent on their flocks and to attach them more securely to the state by granting them salaries out of public funds. These proposals were laid before the catholic hierarchy at the end of 1798. In January 1799 the four catholic archbishops and six of the bishops, meeting in Dublin in their capacity as trustees of Maynooth college, passed resolutions accepting the suggestion of a royal veto, although warning that any such scheme would require the consent of the pope. In addition, they resolved that a state provision for the catholic clergy ought to be 'thankfully accepted'.[3] Both these proposals were allowed to lapse when it became clear that there was to be no catholic emancipation act accompanying the union, but they did not disappear completely. Speakers in the debate on the catholic petition in May 1805 referred to the possibility both of a veto and of state payment of the catholic clergy, although at this stage neither idea appears to have attracted much attention.

The person chiefly responsible for removing the veto from the margins of the emancipation debate and making it the centre of a major controversy appears to have been Lord Fingall, who brought up the question when discussions on a new petition began early in 1808. In May Fingall was appointed to carry the petition to London and arrange for it to be laid before parliament. During his discussions with the whigs he arranged for George Ponsonby to meet John Milner, vicar apostolic of the midlands district of England and London agent of the Irish hierarchy, to be briefed on what sort of veto arrangements would be

---

[1] Above, p. 32.
[2] Plowden, *Hist. Ire., 1801-10*, iii, 711–16, 759–63.
[3] The bishops' resolutions are printed in ibid., appendix, pp 9–10.

acceptable to the catholic church. On 25 May Grattan, who had been informed of the substance of Ponsonby's discussions with Milner, introduced the catholic petition in the house of commons. During his speech he announced that he was authorised by the catholics to bring forward a scheme whereby all future appointments to vacant bishoprics would require the approval of the king. Ponsonby, speaking in support of Grattan's motion, described in more detail how the names of candidates would be submitted to the lord lieutenant before being transmitted to Rome. Both men made large claims for the system they proposed. 'The proposition', Grattan maintained, 'will make a double connection—the two churches will be as one, and the king at the head.'[1] The right of the lord lieutenant to go on rejecting successive nominees until a wholly satisfactory name was brought forward would mean, according to Ponsonby, that 'the real and effectual nomination' of catholic bishops lay with the crown.[2] Despite these assurances, however, the petition was again rejected, by 281 votes to 128. Meanwhile Milner had almost immediately disowned Ponsonby's suggestion that the king should have any positive voice in the selection process; his proposal, he insisted, had been that names would be presented one at a time, and that only a reasonable number of rejections would be entertained. Such fine distinctions, however, were soon submerged in a much broader controversy. As the details of what Grattan and Ponsonby had proposed became generally known, sections of the Irish catholic laity began a mounting chorus of protest against any suggestion of government involvement in the appointment of their bishops. On 14–16 September 1808 the bishops met in Dublin and agreed to resolutions stating that it would be 'inexpedient' to make any change in the existing method of appointment.

After two decisive parliamentary defeats in a space of three years the catholics now faced the problem of what to do next. Keogh argued that further petitions would be pointless and possibly damaging; having had their appeals for political equality unreasonably refused, catholics should opt for a policy of dignified silence. Others, however, believed that they should refuse to be ignored, continuing to present their case in regular petitions, no matter how often they were rejected. The issue was resolved, in a somewhat indirect way, at a general meeting held on 24 May 1809. This began by accepting a resolution, proposed by Keogh, stating that the catholics were unwilling to press their claims in further petitions to parliament, but it went on to pass a whole series of directly contradictory resolutions, establishing a committee to prepare a new petition for presentation to parliament. Before this petition could be presented the question of the veto, apparently laid to rest by the bishops' declaration of September 1808, had been reopened. The first steps towards its revival came in

[1] *Hansard 1*, xi, 556–7.

[2] Ibid., col. 608–9. In his main speech Ponsonby presented the lord lieutenant as choosing from three names presented to him, with further names being brought forward if all three proved unacceptable. At a later point he seemed to envisage names being suggested singly, but still maintained that 'the appointment should finally rest with the king' (ibid., col. 619).

1809, when Sir John Coxe Hippisley, an English M.P. and self-appointed expert on catholic affairs, circulated details of a new scheme whereby the names of candidates for vacant sees would be submitted to the government for approval. Next, in January 1810, Grenville published an open letter addressed to Fingall, in which he restated his belief that catholics must offer some securities against foreign interference in their ecclesiastical affairs.[1] He also announced that although he would agree to lay the latest catholic petition on the table of the house of lords, and would speak in its support in any debate that followed, he would not himself be prepared to introduce any motion regarding it. When Grenville was approached soon after by representatives of the English catholics, he insisted as the price of future support that they should accept a declaration, drafted by the whig leader Lord Grey, 'that they are firmly persuaded that adequate provision for the maintenance of the civil and religious establishments of this kingdom may be made consistently with the strictest adherence on their part to the tenets and discipline of the Roman Catholic religion'.[2] This declaration, published as the fifth resolution adopted at a meeting of English catholics on 1 February 1810, was immediately condemned in Ireland as granting the veto in all but name.

The sudden resurrection of the veto issue at the beginning of 1810 provoked a new flurry of pamphlets, meetings, and resolutions. On 26 February a meeting of the catholic bishops reaffirmed the earlier rejection of the veto. On 2 March the General Committee of the Catholics of Ireland, the body established in the previous May, voted its thanks to the bishops for their decision. On 7 May, however, the committee went on to introduce its own solution to the problem of episcopal appointments—a system of domestic nomination, whereby the church in Ireland would appoint and consecrate its own bishops without reference to Rome. The revived controversy, dividing as it did the Irish catholics from some of their principal parliamentary supporters, inevitably cast its shadow over the debate on the new catholic petition. In the house of lords the petition was presented by Lord Donoughmore, and Grenville did not appear for the debate. Grattan, introducing the petition in the commons on 27 February 1810, made a brave attempt to avoid recriminations over the events of 1808: 'Whether he had misinformed the house, or the catholics had been guilty of retraction, was a question which he should never agitate, it being his fixed principle never to defend himself at the expense of his country.' He went on, nevertheless, to argue that some measures were needed to secure the appointment of 'the spiritual magistrates of so great a portion of the community' from foreign interference, and to propose a system of domestic nomination.[3] When the petition was debated in May, Hippisley and Ponsonby both made long speeches discussing in detail the events of the past two years and criticising the Irish catholics for their attacks on the veto and its supporters. These divisions, Plowden claimed, weakened the catholic case and

[1] Below, p. 40.   [2] Roberts, *Whig party*, p. 74.   [3] *Hansard 1*, xv, 634–5; xvii, 17.

ensured an easy victory for the opponents of emancipation.[1] In fact it is unlikely that they had any very significant effect on a body where minds were for the most part already made up. Grattan's motion to go into committee to discuss the petition was rejected by 213 votes to 109, almost exactly the same proportion as in 1808.

The importance that the veto was permitted to assume in the debate on catholic emancipation is at first sight surprising. The original purpose of the proposal had been to reassure those who believed that catholics could not safely be admitted to full political rights because the clergy of their church were under the ultimate control of a foreign power. Yet it soon became clear that the opponents of emancipation had little or no interest in the guarantees so enthusiastically outlined by Grattan and Ponsonby. Instead it was the existing supporters of catholic claims who now insisted that the veto must form part of any future relief measure. This paradoxical outcome can be attributed partly to the unfortunate and confused circumstances in which the question had been brought forward. Having publicly admitted that some guarantee of catholic loyalty to a protestant state was desirable, Grenville and the whigs were understandably reluctant to expose themselves to the charge of inconsistency by returning to their earlier support for unqualified emancipation. They were also influenced by two other considerations. The first was their belief that they had been shabbily treated in 1808, when the catholics had retracted an offer made by their representatives. Secondly, they were resentful of any suggestion that they should act under the directions of the catholics, or be answerable to them for their conduct. 'I am not surprised at your alarm', Ponsonby was said to have told Milner after the debate in 1808; 'I do not pretend that you authorised me to say all that I did say; but I was at liberty to argue as best suited my cause.'[2]

In addition to these personal and political considerations, however, it seems clear that the Grenvillites and whigs insisted so strongly on the veto because they regarded it as a desirable measure in itself. In this respect the result of the veto debate was to highlight what had always been a somewhat uneasy relationship between the Irish catholics and their parliamentary friends. The support of the latter for catholic emancipation did not necessarily reflect any sympathy for catholicism itself. On the contrary, many who voted in favour of successive catholic petitions shared the educated Englishman's distaste for popery in all its forms and regarded at least some sections of the catholic population of Ireland as politically suspect. They advocated emancipation as a means of making Ireland more secure, by attaching the catholic propertied classes more firmly to the constitution and limiting the scope for sedition among the common people; they did not mean to imply that Irish catholics were to be either liked or trusted. Furthermore, even for those who did not share this widespread distaste and suspicion, the demand for a royal veto appeared fully

---

[1] Plowden, *Hist. Ire., 1801–10*, iii, 868–9.
[2] Roberts, *Whig party*, p. 52.

justified. The passionate denunciations in Ireland of possible political interference in the choice of the catholic hierarchy tended to conceal the fact that, in
the political conditions of early nineteenth-century Europe, the unfettered
nomination of bishops from Rome posed a real problem. The extent to which
this was so was driven home in July 1809, when the pope became formally the
prisoner of France. When the catholic committee shortly afterwards took up
the possibility of domestic nomination, they too implicitly conceded that there
was a genuine difficulty to be resolved.

Among the catholics themselves, the result of the veto debate was to reopen
long-standing internal divisions. The revived agitation of the years after 1804
had at all times sought to give a prominent place to the catholic nobility and
gentry. Three of the five delegates sent to London in 1805 had been peers or
landed gentlemen. The peers and baronets were automatically included as
members of the body appointed to draw up a petition in 1807, and of the committee set up in 1809. Catholic meetings throughout the whole period were
almost invariably chaired by a peer, most frequently by Lord Fingall. The
prominence thus accorded to the small catholic landed class can be attributed
partly to genuine deference, and partly to an appreciation of the realities of
early nineteenth-century politics. The request of a County Galway gentleman,
John Ignatius Burke, to be nominated to the delegation sent to London in 1811
is revealing, not only for the social assumptions it reveals, but also for the
practical arguments it advances:

A person like me, already acquainted with the prince [of Wales] and most of the
members of the opposition, might be of some service and who would not degrade the
people that sent me by living in coffee-houses in a shabby manner. I conceive that
persons sent over on occasions of this kind should have both the ability and inclination
to keep up the respect of our body by living in a splendid manner.[1]

Yet this thrusting of leadership on the catholic landed class, however strong the
arguments in its favour, created recurrent problems. An instinctive conservatism, long-standing habits of political passivity, and the natural caution of those
who had most to lose, all combined to make the peers and landed gentry favour
a moderate and even deferential style of political agitation. This brought them
into conflict with sections of the professional and mercantile classes who
sought a more aggressive policy. The first split along these lines had come in
1791–2, when the conservatives, led by Lord Kenmare and other landed gentlemen, had seceded from the Catholic Committee.[2] The same divisions
reappeared after 1800, most notably in 1807, when the catholic peers pointedly
held aloof from the early stages of the revived campaign for a relief bill.
Ponsonby, writing in March 1807, saw the catholics as divided into 'the people

---

[1] *O'Connell corr.*, i, 243–4. Burke did in fact go to London as part of the delegation in 1811, and he
was again included in a catholic delegation in January 1813 (ibid., pp 258, 319).
[2] Above, iv, 303–6.

of property and education, who are contented to postpone their claims', and 'the people of the middling orders, in this and in the country towns, who wish to urge them in a vain hope of carrying them'.[1] The conflict over the veto, which continued intermittently from 1808 until 1815, marked a further stage in the same division between conservative and militant elements within the catholic body.

It would, of course, be an oversimplification to see either the veto debate or the earlier divisions solely in terms of social class. In 1806, for example, the main supporter of a policy of moderation was James Ryan, a Dublin merchant, while his leading opponents had included a landed gentleman, Lord Ffrench. William Fagan, O'Connell's first biographer, confirmed that the supporters of the veto included not just the aristocracy but also 'a large portion of the mercantile class'.[2] Nevertheless, it seems clear that those who took part in the conflict interpreted it partly in terms of social divisions. Cox's *Irish Magazine*, strongly hostile to the veto, presented the scheme as a betrayal of the catholic religion by the privileged minority who stood to gain immediately from emancipation: 'These great catholic folks, it seems, will give up anything to get into parliament, and to be made judges and generals.'[3] In the same way supporters of the veto, outvoted at a meeting in Cork in 1813, contested the result by appealing to 'the wise principle of the constitution, by which property is made the standard of opinion'.[4] Furthermore, even if the catholic aristocracy were not the sole supporters of the veto, they were the group most closely identified with it. The result was that the decisive rejection of the veto also meant the end of their somewhat uneasy leadership of the catholic agitation. This did not happen overnight: in 1810 the controversy was for the moment suspended, and Lord Fingall was soon back in the chair at meetings of the Catholic Committee. But taken as a whole the veto debate was to mark the final stage in the transfer of power from the catholic landed gentry to a more militant and aggressive section of the catholic professional and business classes.

What part did the catholic clergy play in all this? It is clear that some senior clergymen were, initially at least, prepared to accept the scheme outlined by Grattan and Ponsonby. In January 1799, as already mentioned, the four archbishops and six of the bishops had passed resolutions accepting the idea of a veto. Following the debate in May 1808, Archbishop Dillon of Tuam, Archbishop Troy of Dublin, and all three of Troy's suffragans expressed support for the proposal, and even after the bishops' meeting in September 1808 Troy voiced private regrets that their rejection of the veto had not been qualified by inserting the word 'now' in front of 'inexpedient'. Archbishop O'Reilly of Armagh also caused renewed dissension after the meeting by declaring his opinion that the dangers inherent in the scheme were of a temporary nature. This evidence has led both contemporaries and historians to argue that the

---

[1] Grattan, *Life*, v, 338.   [2] Fagan, *O'Connell*, i, 71.
[3] *Irish Magazine* (July 1808), p. 346.   [4] Fagan, *O'Connell*, i, 110–11.

bishops were frightened into changing their stance by the strength of lay opposition to the veto. It is certainly true that opponents of the scheme had no hesitation about openly attacking clergymen whom they believed to be favourable to it. The *Irish Magazine* in July 1808 had a County Wexford catholic explaining to a less well informed friend that

Doctor Troy had a nephew that the government *did for*, and that he does be at the castle, and that he is a freeman of the corporation to which Giffard belongs, and that he is all and all with the lord lieutenant who goes to shoot sometimes to his brother Watts. . . . Father Murphy says he is a complete government man, and fond of high life, and does not care about any person but the great ones.[1]

In October 1808, despite the hierarchy's statement of the previous month, a placard appeared on the streets of Dublin:

To be sold to the highest bidder, an antient hierarchy, very little the worse for the wear, which has stood many storms, but cannot endure fair weather. Apply to Messrs Troy, Moylan, & Co., on the premises; to Randall McDonnell, broker to the concern; or to Dr Milner, travelling agent.[2]

On the other hand, one recent study has dissented from the view that the hierarchy were frightened into line by the violence of public opinion, arguing that the bishops' rejection of the measure came before the full strength of popular opposition to the veto had become clear.[3] The truth is probably that the majority of bishops were flexible in their attitude. None of them is likely to have favoured the veto in itself, but if the pressure to accept the scheme had been strong enough they would most likely have acquiesced. That, after all, was what had happened in 1799, when the government had put forward a definite scheme—one which, in the aftermath of the rebellion, it might have been dangerous to reject.[4] In 1808, on the other hand, the government was clearly indifferent to the whole business, while at least a section of the laity was decidedly hostile. For Bishop Young of Limerick, who wrote to Archbishop Bray of Cashel in August 1808 to argue that the hierarchy should make no comment whatever on the question, the attitude of government was the crucial consideration. 'The only effectual remedy that remains to dismiss this unpleasant subject, for the present', he wrote, 'would be in my mind, to quit off the intended subject till the subject is pressed on us by government.'[5] The bishops as a whole rejected Young's view that they should avoid committing

---

[1] *Irish Magazine* (July 1808), p. 347. The allegation that Troy had used his contacts with the Castle to obtain preferment for his nephew was in fact true. See M. V. Ronan (ed.), 'Archbishop Troy's correspondence with Dublin Castle' in *Archiv. Hib.*, xi (1944), pp 3–4, 13–14, 22; Mac-Donagh, *Post-bag*, pp 177–9.

[2] Roberts, *Whig party*, p. 44.

[3] V. J. C. McNally, 'Archbishop John Thomas Troy and the catholic church in Ireland, 1787–1817' (Ph.D. thesis, Dublin, 1976), pp 321, 368, 415–16.

[4] Above, p. 36.

[5] Young to Thomas Bray, archbishop of Cashel, 15 Aug. 1808 (Bray papers, 1808/13, Cashel diocesan records; N.L.I., microfilm P.6999).

themselves. But it was probably a similar calculation of the balance of political pressures, rather than a simple surrender to intimidation, that led them to override the doubts of Troy and others and reverse their earlier endorsement of the veto.

If the government showed little interest in the question of the veto, it watched the wider proceedings of the catholic organisation with suspicion. This suspicion intensified in the summer of 1810, a period that also saw widespread agrarian disturbances in several counties of the south, as well as a crop of informers' reports concerning a supposed renewal of treasonable conspiracies and of contact between dissidents in Ireland and Napoleon's France. On 23 July the chief secretary, William Wellesley-Pole, wrote to London drawing attention to the inflammatory and threatening nature of the speeches made at a meeting of the Catholic Committee ten days earlier. The most dramatic (and most frequently quoted) item in Wellesley-Pole's report was the claim that John Keogh had deliberately invoked the name of Wolfe Tone and had spoken meaningfully of the possibility of a French invasion. On both these points Wellesley-Pole's allegations seem to have been based on quite innocent remarks that he had wrenched, consciously or unconsciously, from their original context.[1] His report was in any case wide of the mark, in that it was apparently this meeting that marked the final withdrawal of Keogh from the management of catholic affairs, after his call for a policy of 'dignified silence' had once again been rejected.[2] Yet Wellesley-Pole's suspicions regarding developments within the catholic body were not entirely without foundation. When a French agent, Luke Lawless of the Irish legion, visited Ireland in September 1811, he had contact with a number of individuals active in catholic politics and was told that there would be considerable support among Irish catholics for a French invasion. The full significance of Lawless's mission is difficult to assess. Earlier events had made all too clear the extent to which the existence and strength of revolutionary sentiment could be the subject of self-preserving or self-deluding exaggeration, and in this case the credibility of Lawless's report is not enhanced by the discovery that one of his principal contacts was James Ryan, the dubious moderate of 1806 turned equally dubious revolutionary conspirator five years later.[3] At the same time the episode makes

[1] Wellesley-Pole to Ryder, 23 July 1810 (P.R.O., H.O. 100/158/461 ff). The speeches to which Wellesley-Pole referred were reported in *Dublin Evening Post*, 17, 19 July 1810, copies of which he included with his letter. Keogh's mention of Wolfe Tone was made in the course of a review of his own political career, offered in response to an attack by an anonymous critic, who had accused him of failing, for corrupt motives, to push the catholic cause with sufficient vigour. His reference to a possible French invasion was a rhetorical flourish, used to reinforce his argument that catholics should not at this point bind themselves to a fixed course of action to be followed in the next year, when circumstances might have changed dramatically. Neither comment seems to have had the ulterior purpose Wellesley-Pole alleged.

[2] Keogh's withdrawal is discussed in Fagan, *O'Connell*, i, 215–16. He does not specify the date, but his description seems to fit the meeting of 13 July 1810.

[3] Elliot, *Partners in revolution*, pp 359–60.

clear that some of those active in the catholic agitation were prepared at least to dabble in French-inspired conspiracy. Although the majority of those so active almost certainly kept well clear of such dangerous entanglements, Wellesley-Pole was nevertheless correct in claiming that their proceedings had begun to reveal a new spirit of self-assertion and militancy. Thus one of the resolutions considered at the meeting of 13 July 1810 had expressed not just regret but also 'indignation' at the rejection of the catholic petition two months earlier, while Daniel O'Connell had wondered aloud what would be the result if the catholic clergy of Ireland were to instruct their flocks to cease enlisting in the army and navy. This adoption of a more aggressive tone can be partly attributed to the veto debate, which had seen the advocates of moderation and compromise fatally weaken their authority, while supporters of a stronger policy had correspondingly enhanced their prestige. But it also reflected a deep resentment at the way in which yet another petition had been rejected out of hand, and a growing belief that reasoned argument and responsible agitation could not in themselves make headway against prejudice and vested interest. It was in this spirit that members of the Catholic Committee began to move beyond the politics of persuasion and petition towards an open confrontation with the government.

The issue on which this confrontation was to develop was representation. At the end of 1792 a catholic convention made up of elected delegates from all parts of Ireland had assembled in Dublin to petition for a relief act.[1] This summoning of an elected assembly to overawe a hostile parliament and to add moral force to a political demand was, of course, a tactic borrowed from earlier agitations for free trade and constitutional reform. The relief act was passed in 1793, but the government—determined not to be similarly coerced in the future—followed it with the convention act, which declared illegal any future assembly claiming a representative character and seeking to bring about an alteration in the law regarding church or state.[2] As a result, the renewed catholic agitation of the years after 1804 was at first conducted by committees of persons nominated at public meetings but making no formal claim to represent the catholic population as a whole. Before long, however, attempts were made to move beyond this cautious starting-point. The Catholic Committee established in May 1809 managed to smuggle into its composition two elected elements by including among its members the surviving delegates to the 1792 convention and the individuals elected by the citizens of Dublin to prepare a petition to Bedford in 1806. At the same time it carefully declared that its members 'are not representative of the catholic body, or any portion thereof'.[3] Next, at the end of June 1810, a circular sent to leading catholics throughout the country recommended that the demand for catholic emancipation should be

[1] Above, iv, 315–16.
[2] Cf. above, p. 31.
[3] Wyse, *Catholic Association*, ii, appendix, p. xxix.

pressed home by regular local meetings, and also pointed out that 'the establishment of permanent boards, holding communication with the general committee in Dublin, has been deemed in several counties highly useful to the interests of the catholic cause'.[1] This was clearly an attempt to give the committee a broader base within the catholic population, but it still stopped short of seeking the sort of direct representation prohibited by the convention act. On 1 January 1811, however, the secretary of the Catholic Committee, Edward Hay, sent out another circular, this time calling for the election of ten delegates from each county to join the Catholic Committee in Dublin. This was permissible, the committee claimed, because the working of the convention act, although prohibiting any assembly that sought to challenge parliament as the sole representative of public opinion, made an exception for bodies whose purpose was to draw up a petition to parliament. The government responded on 12 February 1811 with a letter to sheriffs and magistrates throughout the country, ordering them to arrest any person involved in the election of delegates to the Catholic Committee.

In issuing this circular Wellesley-Pole had acted on his own initiative, without first consulting the cabinet. The result was a serious political crisis. Towards the end of 1810 the king had suffered another mental breakdown, and on 5 February 1811 the prince of Wales had assumed the powers of regent. The prince had long been regarded as sympathetic towards catholic emancipation, and he was known to have little liking for his father's ministers, so that there was already the possibility that he might at any time dismiss Spencer Perceval, who had replaced Portland as prime minister in 1809, and turn instead either to the whigs and Grenvillites or to his own supporters in both houses of parliament. Wellesley-Pole's circular seemed greatly to increase the likelihood of this happening. In the event, however, Perceval persuaded the regent to approve Wellesley-Pole's policy. On 26 February 1811 police raided a meeting of the Catholic Committee, with inconclusive results. The catholics responded by petitioning for the removal of Wellesley-Pole and Richmond, but the plan for an election of delegates appears to have been temporarily dropped. On 9 July it was again resolved to elect a committee, made up of ten persons appointed by the catholics of each county, and five persons elected by the catholic inhabitants of each parish in Dublin, to frame petitions to parliament. Richmond responded with a proclamation declaring the proposed assembly illegal, and in August six middle-class catholics who had taken part in the election of delegates for the Dublin parishes were arrested and charged with a breach of the convention act. On 19 October police raided a meeting of the newly expanded Catholic Committee, but arrived after its business had been concluded. On 23 December, however, a further meeting was forcibly dispersed. Edward Sheridan, the first of the six men arrested in August, was tried in November and acquitted, but in February 1812 a second man, Thomas

[1] Plowden, *Hist. Ire., 1801–10*, iii, 885.

Kirwan, was found guilty. The government, declaring itself satisfied that the law had been made clear to all, dropped the prosecutions against the other four, and Kirwan was let off with a nominal fine.

This confrontation with the government on the issue of the convention act was welcomed by the catholic leaders for its effect on morale. Richmond's proclamation, O'Connell told his wife in August 1811, 'is precisely what will secure our unanimity and raise a spirit amongst us that will put success beyond a doubt'.[1] The conviction of Kirwan, on charges almost identical to those of which Sheridan had earlier been acquitted, caused considerable indignation, with allegations that the jury in the second case had not been properly selected, but it did not stop the agitation. A meeting on 28 February 1812 accepted the judgement of the court, resolving that the committee elected in accordance with the resolutions of the previous July should not meet 'until the question lately raised on the convention act be decided'.[2] However, a new catholic organisation was immediately created, in the form of a Catholic Board made up of named individuals and thereby avoiding all formal claims to representative status. For larger and more public assemblies the catholics adopted the device of 'aggregate meetings', a term once again chosen to exclude any charges of a claim to delegate status. The continued determination of the catholics to press their claims by all possible means was made clear in a series of meetings at which the catholics of different counties pledged themselves to vote only for parliamentary candidates who would oppose the existing ministry and support catholic emancipation. 'The spirit is got abroad', O'Connell wrote to his wife after one such meeting in Clare in March 1812, 'and it would be impossible to allay it without full emancipation. You cannot conceive how anxious everybody is to press forward.'[3]

The mood of confidence that O'Connell proclaimed appeared to be fully justified by the events of the months that followed. The catholic petition of May 1811 had been rejected by 146 votes to 83, the defeat being of less significance than the fact that only just over one-third of M.P.s had bothered to vote at all. In April 1812, however, a new catholic petition attracted a much fuller house, and was rejected by a greatly reduced majority of 300 to 215. On 11 May Perceval, the committed evangelical whom catholics had come to see as one of the major obstacles to further progress, was removed from the scene when he was shot dead in the lobby of the house of commons. The new ministry formed under Lord Liverpool in June included a number of known supporters of emancipation. Liverpool himself was opposed to any early measure of catholic relief, but it was announced that emancipation would in future be an 'open question', with ministers and government supporters free to vote according to their own judgement. On 22 June a motion proposed by

---

[1] *O'Connell corr.*, i, 264.
[2] Ibid., p. 282.
[3] Ibid., p. 285. For similar meetings elsewhere see Grattan, *Life*, v, 483.

George Canning calling for an inquiry into catholic claims was carried in the commons by 235 votes to 106, and lost by only one vote in the house of lords. All the signs were that opinion within parliament had at last begun to move in the direction of emancipation, and that the legal defeat suffered over the convention act would shortly become irrelevant. At the end of 1812 Grattan summoned his closest associates to his country house at Tinnehinch, County Wicklow, to draw up the relief bill that he would introduce in the next session of parliament.

CHAPTER III

Union government, 1812–23

S. J. CONNOLLY

In September 1812 a new chief secretary arrived in Dublin. Robert Peel (son of a Lancashire cotton manufacturer who had risen to be a landlord, an M.P., and a baronet) had entered parliament in 1809 and had already served as under-secretary to Lord Liverpool at the department of war and colonies. His appointment as chief secretary, at the age of twenty-four, was in a number of ways a significant one. Previous holders of the office had included men of considerable ability, as well as others who had been less than satisfactory. None of them, however, had stayed long enough to leave any real mark: by 1812 there had been no fewer than ten chief secretaries since the union. Peel, by contrast, was to remain in office continuously until 1818. During these six years Irish affairs were to receive the undivided attention of the man who was to prove the most able and forceful politician of his generation. At the same time, the importance of Peel's chief-secretaryship did not lie solely in the man, or in the length of time that he held office. By 1812 Ireland had been part of the United Kingdom for eleven years. The issues that had largely preoccupied the government during that period—the threat, both real and imagined, of popular disaffection, and the militancy of a succession of catholic organisations—showed no signs of going away. But in the second decade of the union the British and Irish administrations were also forced increasingly to take account of other long-term problems that contributed to the difficulties of governing Ireland. In their response to these problems they gave the first indications of how post-union government might itself take shape.

There was nothing new, however, about the first of the issues that confronted Peel. The success of Canning's motion in June 1812[1] had made an early parliamentary confrontation on the issue of catholic emancipation inevitable. Lord Liverpool's ministry had agreed to treat emancipation as an open question, but this, in an anomaly that was to continue for several years, was not seen as extending to the Irish executive. Instead it seems to have been taken for granted that Peel, in his capacity as chief secretary, would play a leading part on the anti-emancipationist side. It was at first a losing battle. When parliament assembled in February 1813, Grattan's motion for a committee of the

[1] Above, p. 47.

whole house to consider the catholic question was carried by 264 votes to 224. His resolution in committee declaring the desirability of removing the civil and military disabilities affecting catholics was carried by 186 votes to 119, while on 11 May a draft relief bill received its second reading, passing by 245 votes to 203. So far, however, all votes had been on the *principle* of a relief measure. Peel, writing to Richmond on 13 May, pointed out that the best opportunity for defeating the project would come when a detailed bill emerged from committee. Peel was not in fact very optimistic. 'We have been so often beaten,' he told the lord lieutenant, 'and to say the truth, we make so poor a fight in argument, that I am not very sanguine in my hopes of ultimate success.'[1] Nevertheless, his prophecy proved correct. When the bill was next considered, on 24 May, the speaker, Charles Abbot, the former chief secretary (1801-2), proposed an amendment deleting the clause that permitted catholics to sit in parliament. Two hundred and forty-seven members voted against Abbot's amendment, two more than had supported the bill on its second reading. However, the anti-emancipationists, shaking off the apathy of which Peel had earlier complained, turned out in greater numbers than in any previous division, and the amendment was carried by four votes. Without the deleted clause the bill was largely pointless, and it was withdrawn by its supporters.

Although the demand for catholic emancipation had for the moment been pushed back, there was, at first sight at least, no reason to assume that its supporters had suffered anything more than a temporary reverse. Certainly the Catholic Board showed no signs of giving up the struggle, and the Irish executive, for its part, continued to regard the activities of the board with intense hostility. Richmond, writing while Grattan's bill was still being debated, seemed almost to relish the prospect that its rejection might lead to violence. 'Please God, if we are obliged to draw the sword', he promised Peel, 'the committee gentlemen shall have their full share of it, if I can catch them.'[2] Peel, if less homicidal in his rhetoric, was equally decided in his hostility. 'I believe most firmly', he wrote in June 1813, 'that sooner or later we must interfere—that we must not only crush the board, but must destroy the seeds of future boards, committees, and conventions.'[3] However, there seemed no immediate prospect of achieving this. The board, the Irish executive was advised, could not be suppressed under the existing laws, and to introduce special legislation at this point would smack too much of elation at the recent parliamentary victory. For the moment, therefore, the authorities confined themselves to indirect action. Already, in February 1813, Hugh Fitzpatrick, who had printed a pamphlet on the penal laws published anonymously by Denys Scully of the Catholic Board, had been prosecuted for libel, being fined £200 and sentenced to eighteen months' imprisonment. Now, in July 1813, John Magee, proprietor of the *Dublin Evening Post*, was prosecuted for having

---

[1] Parker, *Peel*, i, 84.　　[2] Ibid., p. 79.　　[3] Ibid., p. 119.

published an extremely critical review of the duke of Richmond's administration. The *Evening Post*, though not an official organ of the Catholic Board, was one of its most important channels of communication with a wider public. Magee was convicted of criminal libel, sentenced to two years' imprisonment, and fined £500. When the *Evening Post* published a series of resolutions, passed by the catholics of Kilkenny city and county, condemning the prosecution, Magee was prosecuted again, fined a further £1,000, and sentenced to an additional six months' imprisonment. Shortly afterwards his brother James, to whom he had by then transferred control of the paper, was also prosecuted, this time for printing a speech by O'Connell claiming that the authorities failed to protect catholics from attacks by Orangemen.

The outcome of these prosecutions was, from the point of view of the Irish executive, highly satisfactory. They did not succeed, as they had hoped, in bringing any members of the Catholic Board itself to account for their public utterances. But this was only because, in both of the later prosecutions, those whose resolutions and speeches the *Evening Post* had reported had refused to accept their share of the legal responsiblity for the contents. As a result, the Magee brothers withdrew their support from the board and shortly afterwards made their peace with the government. In February 1814 Peel expressed the hope that the board, deprived of an outlet for its 'infamous and inflammatory libels', would simply fade away.[1] When this did not happen, he returned to the idea of strengthening the convention act in such a way as to permit the suppression of the board and any similar bodies in the future. Liverpool, however, was reluctant to provoke what would in effect be another parliamentary debate on the catholic question, and refused to sanction fresh legislation. Instead the government proceeded under the provisions of the existing law. A proclamation signed by the lord lieutenant and issued on 3 June 1814 declared that the board was an illegal body under the terms of the convention act, and warned that anyone attending future meetings would be liable to prosecution. The claim was, to say the least, a dubious one. The board was composed entirely of named individuals, with none of the provision for election of delegates that had left the Catholic Committee open to successful legal action in 1811–12. In suppressing the board, the executive were in fact acting contrary to the earlier opinions of their own legal advisers. To the obvious question of why, if the board were a violation of the convention act, no action had been taken against it sooner, the proclamation could only reply feebly that it had been hoped that those involved would see for themselves the error of their ways. Despite the weakness of the government's case, however, the catholic leaders agreed to submit to the ban and the board was dissolved in June 1814.

The suppression of the Catholic Board did not put an end to the campaign for catholic emancipation. The former members of the board continued to meet informally and to communicate with their followers through the old device of

[1] Parker, *Peel*, i, 134–5.

aggregate meetings. Yet even before the government had taken action there had been signs that the tide had begun to run against the catholic cause. One reason for this was that the high hopes that the catholics and their allies had held at the beginning of 1813 had from the start been based on a false premise: the belief that the regent was sympathetic to their aspirations. It was true that the prince had in the past repeatedly declared himself a supporter of catholic emancipation. But the reasons for this had been largely personal. Such declarations had been in part an act of youthful rebellion against George III, and in part a product of his friendship with certain prominent supporters of emancipation, most notably Charles James Fox. By 1813, however, the prince had turned fifty, and, for the moment at least, had replaced his father as head of state. Fox, moreover, was dead, and his place as the prince's confidant had been taken by others, in particular the strongly anti-catholic Seymour family. In public the regent, reluctant to be seen to go back on his word, maintained that he could take no action on the catholic question while his father was still alive. In private, however, he actively opposed any attempt to promote further measures of catholic relief. At the same time support for the catholic cause was also being undermined by the changing international situation. Many M.P.s who supported, or were prepared to tolerate, the removal of catholic disabilities were so inclined principally for reasons of expediency, believing that such concessions were necessary to ensure the loyalty or at least the tranquillity of Ireland during a lengthy and hard-fought foreign war. But from early in 1813 the French, weakened by the disastrous Russian campaign of the winter, began to lose ground on the Continent, and by the end of the year Britain and her allies had carried the war inside the boundaries of France itself. As the final defeat of Napoleon became imminent, the need to conciliate Irish catholics seemed less urgent, and traditional doubts and prejudices began to reassert themselves.

Just as events in London and abroad were beginning to weaken the catholic case, the agitation itself began to lose something of its former confidence and energy. The disappointing outcome of the parliamentary session of 1813, coming after such high hopes, inevitably produced disillusionment. More important, the catholics were again divided among themselves on the question of the veto, which had arisen in a new form during the debates on Grattan's relief bill. Grattan himself had by this time abandoned the idea of linking catholic emancipation to any attempt to guarantee the loyalty of catholic bishops, and the bill he brought forward had been a simple measure that would have admitted catholics to parliament and to all offices other than those of lord lieutenant of Ireland and lord chancellor of Great Britain. When his proposals were discussed in committee, however, Canning and Castlereagh, both leading supporters of emancipation, reintroduced the question of securities. Grattan, anxious to maximise support for his bill, accepted the addition of clauses providing for a commission, made up mainly of catholic peers, that would certify the loyalty of all candidates for sees and scrutinise all documents received from Rome in connection with their appointment. In Ireland, news of these amendments was greeted with widespread hostility among both clergy and laity. On 26 May 1813, two days after the bill had been sabotaged by Abbot,[1] the Irish bishops issued a joint pastoral letter rejecting its proposals as unacceptable. Their unanimity, in sharp contrast to the imperfectly concealed divisions that had existed in 1808, was evidence of the change that had since taken place both in the political climate and in the attitudes of the bishops themselves. Even more striking testimony to the extent of change was provided in the following year, when Mgr Giovanni Quarantotti, secretary to the Congregation of Propaganda, to whom the provisions of Grattan's bill had been referred by the agent of the English and Scottish bishops, issued a rescript stating that the arrangements it proposed were acceptable. Archbishop Troy's first reaction was to accept the rescript as a final judgement, but he found himself overruled by his colleagues. At a meeting in May 1814 the bishops agreed to declare that the rescript was not mandatory, and to send Troy's coadjutor, Daniel Murray, to Rome to present the case against the veto. They were all the more easily able to take this attitude, of course, because Quarantotti had acted on his own initiative, the pope being still a prisoner of the French. At the same time the bishops' determination to resist all proposals for a veto, from whatever source, was striking. Even Archbishop O'Reilly of Armagh, one of those who in 1808 had been prepared to find the veto acceptable, was now reported to have said that if he were required to participate in the consecration of a bishop elected under any such arrangement, he would resign his see.[2] And when Pius VII, in a formal letter issued in February 1816, confirmed the acceptability of a limited veto, the bishops immediately replied with a decorously worded but firm expression of dissent.

Whatever the private doubts of individuals, therefore, the catholic bishops displayed a remarkable unity in their response to the revival of the veto question. Among the laity, on the other hand, its reappearance produced what became a permanent schism. At a meeting of the Catholic Board on 29 May 1813 the chairman, Lord Trimleston, lamented the loss of Grattan's bill, only to be opposed by cries of 'No, no!' from the floor. When O'Connell proposed a motion thanking the bishops for their rejection of the bill, he was opposed by a group led by Sir Edward Bellew, head of the County Louth landowning family. The motion was carried by a majority of 61 votes to 20, but the defeated group withdrew from further meetings of the board. As in 1808, the defenders of some form of veto, though in a minority, included many of the leading catholic nobility and landed gentry. There was a last attempt to heal the split in January 1815, when Lord Fingall and others attended an aggregate catholic meeting to discuss future action. Arthur James Plunkett, earl of Fingall, representative of

---

[1] Above, p. 49.
[2] John Power, bishop of Waterford and Lismore, to Archbishop Bray of Cashel, 9 Sept. 1815 (Bray papers, 1815/7, Cashel diocesan records).

an ancient catholic family in County Meath, has often been presented as a typical example of the conservative and socially aloof catholic nobility whose withdrawal from the mainstream of the catholic agitation was precipitated by the veto debate. Yet this is quite unfair. The real leaders of a conservative alternative party within the catholic ranks appear to have been other men: the Bellews and Lord Trimleston (later depicted by Thomas Wyse as having represented the feudal traditions of pre-revolutionary France, where he had received his education). Fingall, by contrast, appears to have been, of all the catholic nobility, the one most willing to seek agreement with the middle-class leaders who now dominated catholic affairs. Indeed it was precisely this willingness to seek common ground that led him to figure so prominently in debates on the veto, and so accounts for his unmerited posthumous reputation as the epitome of aristocratic reaction.[1] Despite this, however, the meeting of 24 January 1815 ended in failure. When the organisers insisted on putting forward resolutions calling on catholics to go on petitioning for unqualified emancipation, Fingall and his supporters withdrew, and the split between vetoist and anti-vetoist became permanent.

Why did the majority of Irish catholics reject the veto with such vehemence? Later historical writing has for the most part taken it as axiomatic that they should have done so. But this reflects only the extent to which it was the anti-vetoists who won the contemporary debate. The truth was that arrangements of the kind proposed in the different schemes for a veto were perfectly compatible with the doctrines of the catholic church. This was clear not only from the pope's letter of February 1816 but from actual practice throughout catholic Europe. Irish catholics, Peel rightly pointed out in 1813, wished to deny their government 'that security which every despotic sovereign in Europe has by the concession of the pope himself'.[2] Their reason for doing so clearly lay not in religious principle but in their attitude to the state. Where the Irish executive was concerned, this was perhaps understandable: O'Connell, introducing his resolution of thanks to the Irish bishops in May 1813, was able to point to the absurdity of declared opponents of catholic emancipation such as Peel and the attorney general, William Saurin, being permitted to interfere in the internal management of the catholic church in Ireland. At the same time there is nothing to indicate that the vesting of control in a more distant or neutral representative of the state would have been any more acceptable. Irish catholics might loudly protest their loyalty to the king and to the existing political order. But that loyalty, unconsciously at least, was qualified by certain reservations. In the obscure prehistory of modern Irish nationalism, the episode of the veto is

---

[1] Compare Wyse's portrayal of Fingall (*Catholic Association*, i, 147–8) with his portrayal of Trimleston (ibid., pp 150–51). See also O'Connell's comments in 1818 (*O'Connell corr.*, ii, 184). Fingall himself was reported to have observed before his death that he 'went forward to an extent that caused me to be sometimes snubbed by those of my own order' (Fagan, *O'Connell*, i, 162).

[2] Parker, *Peel*, i, 76.

important in showing how, even at the beginning of the nineteenth century, the majority of politically aware catholics withheld from the state a last, but possibly crucial, degree of legitimacy.

As well as dividing catholics among themselves, renewed dissension over the question of securities helped to alienate Grattan, who up to now had been their principal parliamentary spokesman. In November 1813 the Catholic Board wrote to Grattan and Lord Donoughmore about the content of any future relief bill. Both objected to the tone of the letter, arguing that it sought to dictate to them how they should behave in their capacity as members of parliament. The dispute was eventually patched up, and Grattan duly presented the catholic petition in May 1814, although he announced that he would not initiate any debate on the subject, on the ground that to do so at this point would lose rather than gain support. In 1815, however, when the former members of the Catholic Board produced a petition calling for unqualified emancipation, Grattan refused to present it, arguing that it was necessary for catholics to show some willingness to allay protestant anxieties about the effects of emancipation. The petition was eventually entrusted to Sir Henry Parnell. In 1816 two separate catholic petitions were presented. The first, drawn up by Trimleston and others, and worded so as to leave the way open for some sort of securities to accompany a measure of catholic relief, was presented by Grattan. The second, drawn up by former members of the Catholic Board and calling for unqualified emancipation, was presented by Parnell.

One further result of the events of 1813–15 was to confirm the leading position, within the mainstream of the catholic agitation, of Daniel O'Connell. O'Connell, nephew and eventual heir to a substantial County Kerry landowner, was born in 1775, studied in France and London, and was called to the Irish bar in 1798. He had made his first important political appearance in January 1800, as one of the minority of catholics actively opposing the union. When the campaign for catholic emancipation resumed in 1804, O'Connell quickly rose to prominence. There is unfortunately no satisfactory modern account of O'Connell's early career as a catholic agitator, and there is an obvious danger in relying too heavily on accounts that, though nearly contemporary, were written after he had become the acknowledged political leader of Ireland's catholics. Nevertheless, it seems to be true that he was from the start one of the advocates of an aggressive stance, criticising the excessively deferential attitude of the majority towards the 'ministry of all the talents' in 1807, calling for a policy of continuous petitioning in opposition to the still influential Keogh, and pressing for a confrontation with the government on the issue of the convention act. Up to this point, however, O'Connell was still only one of several able and energetic men active in catholic affairs and, to some extent, competing with one another for leadership. It appears to have been the renewal of the veto controversy between 1813 and 1815, and O'Connell's forceful articulation of the general hostility that now existed towards any such arrangement, that confirmed his position as the most important single figure in the catholic agitation. Thus it was O'Connell who proposed the motion of thanks to the bishops that precipitated the first clash with supporters of the veto in May 1813. When the final attempt at reconciliation broke down in January 1815, it was again O'Connell who acted as spokesman for the intransigent majority, arguing that the pope had no authority to impose the veto on the Irish catholic church and warning that, if the bishops did by any chance agree to become 'the vile slaves of the clerks of the Castle', they would be deserted by their flocks, 'and the Castle clergy would preach to still thinner numbers than attend in Munster or in Connacht the reverend gentlemen of the *present* established church'.[1]

O'Connell's emergence as the dominant figure within the catholic agitation was partly a matter of ability, reflecting his exceptional energy, oratorical skill, and political judgement. Also important, however, was his distinctive political style, characterised by a flamboyance and a capacity for brinkmanship that accorded well with the militant mood of a substantial section of catholic opinion. Thus, when O'Connell acted as John Magee's defence counsel in July 1813, he decided from the start that a conviction was inevitable, and so chose to turn the occasion into a major piece of political theatre. His speech for the defence took the form of a lengthy attempt to show that Magee's criticisms of Richmond's administration, and of those of his predecessors, could not be libellous because they were true. It was a deliberately provocative performance: O'Connell claimed later that one of his aims had been to provoke the attorney general, William Saurin, into challenging him to a duel.[2] As such it had the unfortunate effect of earning Magee a heavier sentence than he might other-wise have received, and so began the alienation of the Magee brothers from O'Connell and the Catholic Board. But it also contributed greatly to O'Connell's popular reputation. His stature was further increased in January 1815 when he was called to account by John Norcot D'Esterre for his descrip-tion of the corporation of Dublin, of which D'Esterre was a member, as 'beggarly'. O'Connell refused to withdraw his words, the two men fought, and D'Esterre was killed. A second political duel, this time with no less a person than Peel, almost followed in August of the same year, being prevented only by the arrest of O'Connell in London, on his way to the agreed meeting place on the Continent. Both sides, of course, interpreted this outcome in their own way. When O'Connell shortly afterwards pleaded a case before Lord Norbury, he expressed the fear that he was not making himself understood on a certain point, only to be jovially assured that no man was more easily *apprehended* when he wanted to be.[3] Among his own followers, on the other hand, O'Connell's status as a popular champion was confirmed.

If O'Connell had by now established his primacy in the catholic agitation,

[1] *Life and speeches of Daniel O'Connell*, ed. John O'Connell (2 vols, Dublin, 1846), ii, 178.
[2] *O'Connell corr.*, i, 349–50.
[3] *Croker papers*, i, 130.

however, it was as leader of a much diminished movement. In the years after 1815 he and others attempted to keep the campaign for catholic emancipation going. The association created to prepare the petitions of 1815 and 1816 was succeeded in 1817 by a new Catholic Board, but this suspended its meetings at the end of the year, at least partly, it appears, on account of financial difficulties.[1] The authorities continued to use the wide powers that the law provided for the suppression of hostile newspaper comment. The catholic leaders responded to the loss of the *Evening Post*, and the growing unwillingness of other newspapers to carry material that might expose them to prosecution, by launching their own newspaper, the *Dublin Chronicle*, in the summer of 1815. However, the nominal proprietor, Aeneas McDonnell, was successfully prosecuted in 1816, and the paper ceased publication the following year. Also in 1816 the printer of the *Cork Mercantile Chronicle* was jailed for two years and fined £300 for publishing a speech by O'Connell alleging corrupt practices in the courts.

O'Connell continued to show a remarkable flair for publicity and self-advertisement. In 1820, for example, he sought to take advantage of the estrangement of the new king, George IV, from his wife Caroline, arguing that, as queen, Caroline was entitled to appoint her own law officers in Ireland, that these positions had not been included in the laws that had barred catholics from holding high legal office, and that he himself could thus be appointed her attorney general for Ireland.[2] But antics of this kind could not conceal the fact that the campaign for catholic emancipation had lost much of its impetus. Deprived of the special circumstances that in 1812–13 had briefly made its triumph seem inevitable, discouraged by defeat, weakened by internal divisions, and faced by a hostile and determined Irish executive, the movement receded for several years into relative unimportance.

As the challenge presented by organised catholic discontent was becoming less formidable, other problems were assuming new proportions. The first of these to force itself upon the attention of the Irish executive was agrarian crime. Violent protest had been a familiar feature of rural life for over half a century, and the years since the rebellion of 1798 had already seen a number of serious episodes. Widely dispersed outbreaks of crime in the winter of 1798–9 had been followed by the lesser disturbances in County Limerick in 1802–3 and the Thresher movement in several north-western counties in 1806–7. In 1809–11 parts of Leinster and Munster were disturbed by the activities of the Caravats and the Shanavests, two groups that appeared to most contemporary observers to be no more than warring factions but which, it has been suggested, also embodied elements of a social conflict, involving farmers and shopkeepers on

[1] *O'Connell corr.*, ii, 184–5.
[2] Ibid., pp 287–307, 322.

the one hand and labourers and cottiers on the other.[1] In the winter of 1812–13 there had been further disturbances, this time in the midland counties of King's County, Longford, Roscommon, and Westmeath, arising out of grievances over food prices, conacre rents, and the eviction of smaller occupiers. All these outbreaks had occurred while rural Ireland was still enjoying the benefits of the long period of prosperity that had begun in the early 1790s, when wartime conditions had boosted the demand for Irish agricultural products while at the same time largely excluding rival suppliers from the British market. Now, however, the long period of boom came suddenly to an end. Grain prices fell sharply after a bumper harvest in the autumn of 1813,[2] while in the following year there was an equally catastrophic fall in the price of livestock as high wartime demand for provisions disappeared. By 1816 the prices of oats, barley, beef, and pork had all fallen by more than a half, and wheat and butter prices were also severely depressed. The results of this general collapse of prices were seen in an immediate intensification of agrarian violence, with disturbances continuing in the midlands and at the same time spreading to the Munster counties of Clare, Limerick, Tipperary, and Waterford, as well as to parts of south Leinster. Throughout these regions violence rose to a level not seen since the 1790s: livestock were mutilated, houses burned, arms seized, and offending individuals threatened, assaulted, and sometimes killed, in an outbreak of agrarian terror that continued from 1813 to 1816.

The more or less permanent presence in early nineteenth-century Ireland of some level of agrarian crime, erupting at intervals into major outbreaks such as that of 1813–16, seemed to most contemporaries to mark the country out as peculiarly violent and lawless. 'In a large part of Ireland', it was claimed in 1836, 'there is still less security of person and property than in any other part of Europe, except perhaps the wildest districts of Calabria or Greece.'[3] The precise character of the agrarian protest that gave rise to such comment has been the subject of much debate. The principal aim behind outrage and intimidation has most commonly been seen as the defence of the occupiers of land from excessive rents and eviction. This was the view taken by the most perceptive contemporary analyst of Irish agrarian crime:

The Whiteboy association may be considered as a vast trades' union for the protection of the Irish peasantry: the object being, not to regulate the rate of wages, or the hours of work, but to keep the actual occupant in possession of his land, and in general to regulate the relation of landlord and tenant for the benefit of the latter.[4]

---

[1] P. E. W. Roberts, 'Caravats and Shanavests: Whiteboyism and faction fighting in east Munster, 1802–11' in Clark & Donnelly, *Ir. peasants*, pp 64–101.

[2] Below, pp 132–3.

[3] George Cornewall Lewis, *On local disturbances in Ireland, and on the Irish church question* (London, 1836), p. 1.

[4] Ibid., p. 99. Lewis is here using 'Whiteboy' as a generic term for all agrarian societies, in the same way that other contemporaries used the term 'Ribbonism'.

A more recent analysis adds the suggestion that such attempts at self-defence on the part of tenants were most likely to take place in cases where an improving landlord attempted to revise existing tenurial arrangements in the interests of greater efficiency.[1] Other accounts, however, have sought to shift the emphasis away from tenant issues to conflict between farmers on the one hand and labourers and cottiers on the other, particularly in relation to the attempted transfer of land from tillage to pasture.[2] The true explanation is almost certainly that the precise character of rural conflict varied from region to region, depending on variations both in the pattern of agriculture and in local social structure.[3] The rents paid by farmers; landlord attempts at reorganisation; conacre rents; labourers' wages; the abandonment of tillage for pasture; the employment of 'strangers' from outside the immediate locality; tithes, taxes, and tolls at fairs: any of these could become the cause of violence and intimidation in a society where the rural poor sought desperately to maintain a foothold in an increasingly overcrowded agrarian system.

From the point of view of the government, of course, the most important question was not the social basis of agrarian protest, but rather the means by which it could be suppressed or contained. The resources available to cope with violence on the scale now becoming commonplace in large parts of the south and midlands were wholly inadequate. Law enforcement in early nineteenth-century Ireland was still the responsibility of the landed gentry and the rural middle classes, in their capacity as justices of the peace and grand jurors, with no official backing other than that of a thinly spread network of parish constables and watchmen. This system, relying essentially on deference and on the natural authority of the gentry, was the same as that which operated in most parts of contemporary Britain, and for most of the eighteenth century it had succeeded in maintaining a tolerable level of order. By the end of the century, however, the strains imposed by mounting political, sectarian, and economic tension had stretched the traditional system past breaking-point. Acts passed by the Irish parliament in 1787 and 1792,[4] when the inadequacy of existing resources was first becoming clear, had created a new force of baronial constables; but these, untrained, underpaid, and recruited with little regard to their fitness for the task of law enforcement, were for the most part ineffective.

---

[1] M. R. Beames, 'Rural conflict in pre-famine Ireland: peasant assassinations in Tipperary, 1837-47' in *Past & Present*, no. 81 (1978), pp 78-9, 89. See below, pp 128-32.

[2] J. J. Lee, 'The Ribbonmen' in T. D. Williams (ed.), *Secret societies in Ireland* (Dublin, 1973); J. J. Lee, 'Patterns of rural unrest in nineteenth-century Ireland: a preliminary survey' in L. M. Cullen and François Furet (ed.), *Ireland and France, 17th-20th centuries: towards a comparative study of rural history* (Paris, 1980), pp 223-37; Samuel Clark, 'The importance of agrarian classes: agrarian class structure and collective action in nineteenth-century Ireland' in *British Journal of Sociology*, xxix (1978), pp 22-40.

[3] For a detailed demonstration of the extent to which this was so see J. S. Donnelly, jr, 'The social composition of agrarian rebellions in early nineteenth-century Ireland: the case of the Carders and Caravats' in P. J. Corish (ed.), *Radicals, rebels, and establishments* (Belfast, 1985), pp 151-69.

[4] 27 Geo. III, c. 40 (21 May 1787); 32 Geo. III, c. 16 (18 Apr. 1792).

Instead the growing burden of maintaining public order fell heavily on the army, made up partly of regular troops and partly of units of British and Irish militia. But such a system, which involved troops being used for routine police functions, often dispersed round the countryside in small units, was never entirely satisfactory, either to army officers or to civilian administrators. As the end of the French war came in sight, furthermore, it was clear that the large Irish military establishment—some 35,000 men in 1813—could not be maintained indefinitely. An additional problem was that the legislation that had created the baronial constabulary was due to expire on 1 March 1814.

These circumstances, along with the upsurge in agrarian violence that began in 1813, provided the background to what was to be Peel's most distinctive contribution, during his chief-secretaryship, to the government of Ireland. As a short-term solution Peel suggested that the government should reintroduce the insurrection act, a draconian measure providing for the suspension of trial by jury in disturbed districts and the imposition of a sunset-to-sunrise curfew, which had been introduced in 1807, but repealed, without ever having been applied, three years later.[1] To this he added a more original proposal: that the lord lieutenant should be empowered to appoint a specialist force of police to be sent into particularly disturbed districts to assist in the maintenance of law and order. Both suggestions were initially resisted in London. The police act, as Peel himself called it, touched off a prejudice, firmly rooted in the minds of the British governing class, against centralised law enforcement of the kind associated with the worst traditions of continental despotism; Peel's proposal, Lord Liverpool complained, was 'not English'.[2] A measure as extreme as the insurrection act, meanwhile, was likely to be contentious at home and damaging to Britain's image abroad. In the end, however, Peel's superiors gave their approval, and both measures passed through parliament, with surprisingly little opposition, in the summer of 1814.[3]

The new peace preservation act permitted the lord lieutenant, acting either on his own initiative or on an application from local magistrates, to proclaim a district as being in a state of disturbance. He was then empowered to appoint a force of special constables, under the command of a superintending magistrate, to assist in policing the proclaimed area. The act was applied for the first time in September 1814, when a force of twenty constables was sent to the barony of Middlethird in County Tipperary. The new system did not prove uniformly popular or successful. Because the cost of maintaining the force was levied on the district to which it was sent, local magistrates tended to oppose its introduction, pressing instead for troops and for the application of the insurrection act. Where the peace preservation force was deployed, furthermore, it

[1] 47 Geo. III, sess. 2, c. 13 (1 Aug. 1807). This was a refined version of the original insurrection act (36 Geo. III, c. 20 [Ire.] (24 Mar. 1796)), incorporating many amendments.
[2] Galen Broeker, *Rural disorder and police reform in Ireland, 1812-36* (London, 1970), p. 60.
[3] Peace preservation act, 54 Geo. III c. 131 (25 July 1814); insurrection act, 54 Geo. III, c. 180 (30 July 1814).

generally proved necessary to supplement it heavily with the use of these older resources. When a superintending magistrate and special constables were again sent into parts of County Tipperary in the autumn of 1815, for example, they were accompanied by the application of the insurrection act and the deployment, according to one account, of more than 12,000 soldiers. When backed up in this way, however, the peace preservation force established its usefulness as a specialist body, supplementing more traditional forms of law enforcement at the points where they were most obviously unable to cope. Over the next two years (1816–17) the force was deployed on a further six occasions, being introduced twice into different parts of County Clare and also into parts of Counties Cavan, Donegal, Kildare, and Louth. An amending act in 1817, permitting the exchequer to bear up to two-thirds of the cost of maintaining the peace preservation force in a proclaimed area, removed one significant obstacle to its widespread acceptance.[1]

THE upsurge of violent protest to which the peace preservation act was a response was only one symptom of wider social problems. Even during the period of high wartime prices there had been signs of mounting difficulties in the Irish economy.[2] The cotton industry was no longer growing as it had done in the 1780s and 1790s, the longer-established woollen industry was already failing to compete with imported goods, while the linen industry was suffering from the competition of a partly mechanised cotton manufacture in Great Britain. In the countryside, meanwhile, the consequences of rapid population growth combined with a limited industrial sector were already becoming apparent. Edward Wakefield, writing in 1812, noted that the prosperity that high prices had brought to tenant farmers was not being shared with the labourer and cottier classes,[3] and the recurrence during these years of agrarian protest confirms the existence of serious underemployment and growing competition for land. Such problems were intensified when the long period of widespread, if unequally distributed, prosperity came to an end. For the farming population the consequences of the collapse of agricultural prices that began in 1813 were serious enough. Rents agreed in the years of high prices now proved far more burdensome than had been anticipated, arrears mounted, and living standards fell. But it was among those below the level of farmer that the impact of depression was inevitably most severe. Households that had formerly just been able to make ends meet now found that they could no longer do so—here the fall in the price of pigs, the major source of cash earnings for a large proportion of cottier and labourer households, was particularly important. Labourers found it harder to obtain work, partly because the farmers who might have employed them were themselves less affluent than before, but also

[1] 57 Geo. III, c. 22 (29 Apr. 1817).
[2] Below, pp 137–57.
[3] Wakefield, *Account of Ire.*, ii, 233–4.

because the new pattern of agricultural prices made it increasingly attractive for many farmers to use land for grazing sheep and cattle, rather than tilling it themselves with the aid of hired labour or letting it out in small units to cottier tenants or in conacre. At around the same time another vital element in the economy of some sections of the rural lower classes began to be eroded as the domestic spinning and weaving of linen, formerly fairly widely diffused, became increasingly concentrated in a few counties of eastern Ulster. This general curtailment in the availability of both land and employment, further-more, took place at a time when the population was still rising rapidly. For the labourer, the cottier, and the small farmer—what may be collectively described as the rural poor—the post-war depression was thus only the beginning of a prolonged crisis, marked by underemployment, land hunger, and growing physical deprivation, which was to culminate in the great famine.

Already by the second decade of the union, then, Ireland, and more particu-larly rural Ireland, was beginning to exhibit what even by the standards of the time were recognised as appalling social problems, of which the most obvious manifestations were the miserable cabins that lined the sides of roads, and the hordes of beggars travelling round the countryside or thronging the streets of the towns, features that attracted the attention of virtually every tourist and visitor. But these, even if more extensive and conspicuous than before, had always been features of Irish life. More serious was the way in which the growth of population, concentrated among the rural poor, had left that expanding social group increasingly vulnerable to fluctuations in the supply of food, and more particularly to any shortfall in the potato crop, on which the greater part of their diet depended. It was this problem that from the end of 1816 forced itself on the attention of the Irish executive. The summer and autumn of 1816 had been unusually cold and wet: a report from Drogheda in October spoke of ducks swimming among the oats and potatoes in the flooded fields.[1] Both grain and potato crops suffered serious damage, and by early 1817 there were reports of acute distress among the poor, as well as outbreaks of rioting against the removal of food from one district to another. The crisis continued until the first crops of the unusually good harvest of 1817 became available. But by then hunger had been joined by fever. An epidemic of typhus, first appearing in the spring and summer of 1817, spread to all parts of the country and continued until 1819. Contemporary estimates, generally regarded as moderate, put the total number of deaths from fever at 65,000.

There have been conflicting verdicts on the government's response to this crisis. To Peel's biographer, the distress of 1816–17 showed him 'at the height of his powers', coming 'nearer to grasping the realities of the Irish problem than perhaps any other man in public life'.[2] On the other hand, the most

---

[1] Maurice A. Trant, 'Government policy and Irish distress, 1816–19' (M.A. thesis, N.U.I. (U.C.D.), 1965), p. 1.
[2] Gash, *Mr Secretary Peel*, p. 225.

detailed study of the crisis of these years emphasises the limited nature of the government's relief measures, and the extent to which it seemed to be moved to action more by fear of public disorder than by concern over distress.[1] In reality the government's response, though not beyond criticism, appears to have been creditable enough. The most serious charge against Peel is that he should have taken more positive action when the threat of food shortages first became clear, in the autumn of 1816, rather than waiting until the following spring. Such criticism, however, is not altogether justified. With the exception of the partial crop failures of 1799–1801, in the troubled aftermath of the rebellion, the food shortages of 1816–17 represented the first emergency of this kind to have arisen for several decades. One should not, therefore, exaggerate the extent to which the practical consequences of the bad harvest could have been provided against in advance. It is also important to remember that the Irish executive could act only with the approval of a cabinet inevitably less informed and less concerned about Irish problems than it was itself. Once concrete evidence of distress became available in the spring of 1817, giving Peel both an indication of the scale of the problem to be faced and the necessary evidence to lay before the prime minister and home secretary, he took immediate action. The first attempt at relief, the importation of seed oats in March and April, was unsuccessful, the imported seeds being of poor quality and the prices at which they were sold too high. In June, however, Peel obtained from the government extensive discretionary powers to draw on the treasury for relief measures. A central committee was appointed to supervise the administration of relief, making grants to local voluntary relief committees. The total sum disbursed amounted to £37,000. A similar committee was set up to supervise the distribution of funds to localities for the containment of the typhus epidemic, eventually distributing more than £18,000. In addition, a select committee appointed in April 1818 examined the problem of contagious fever in Ireland. Its recommendations led to an act that provided for the appointment of local boards of health and permitted grand juries to make presentments for the building of fever hospitals of up to twice the amount raised by local subscriptions.[2]

The mounting economic problems of early nineteenth-century Ireland had other implications. The act of union had provided that Ireland and Great Britain should each retain separate treasuries, with Ireland contributing two-seventeenths of the common expenditure of the United Kingdom. Each country was to retain and service its own national debt. However, when the two debts could be brought into the same proportion to one another as that agreed for United Kingdom expenditure, two to fifteen, the separate exchequers would be amalgamated. At the time it was assumed that this would be achieved by means of a reduction of the British debt, once the war with France was over. In fact the wars dragged on for another fifteen years, and total United Kingdom expenditure, of which Ireland now had to pay two-seventeenths, continued to

---

[1] Trant, op. cit., pp 4–5.   [2] 58 Geo. III, c. 47 (30 May 1818).

rise. The result was that chancellors of the Irish exchequer found themselves forced to introduce steadily more stringent financial measures in an effort to support an impossible burden. It was this desperate need to raise revenue, for example, that led to a steady increase in the tax on spirits, and with it the enactment of draconian measures against illicit distillation. Such measures, however, proved impossible to enforce, partly because of inadequate law-enforcement resources, and because so much of lower-class social life revolved around cheap drink, but also because there were areas of the country, notably in Connacht and the north-west, where cash earnings from illicit distillation were a vital part of the economy of large sections of the population.[1] Thus, when the peace preservation force was sent into Inishowen, County Donegal, in July 1817, its task was to suppress illicit distillation, not agrarian crime. But not even the most stringent measures could balance the national books. Between 1801 and 1817 revenue from Irish taxation more than doubled. Over the same period, however, the national debt rose fourfold, with the result that Ireland's debt became two-seventeenths of the total, the proportion specified in the act of union. By this time also it had become clear that the problems of allocating power between the chief secretary and the chancellor of the Irish exchequer that had first appeared with John Foster had not been solved by his departure from the political scene. A new chancellor, William Vesey Fitzgerald, was threatening to resign on the grounds that he was not being permitted to exercise real control over financial affairs. One obvious solution, that the chief secretary should also act as chancellor of the exchequer, was rejected as too burdensome for the individual concerned. Instead a committee of inquiry set up in 1815 recommended that the Irish exchequer should be abolished, and this was done with effect from 5 January 1817,[2] thus eliminating one at least of the administrative anomalies inherited from the union.

PEEL left Ireland in August 1818. During his six years as chief secretary the government had been faced with a succession of crises: the catholic agitation, the upsurge of rural violence, and the partial famine of 1816–17. Peel's response to all three had been vigorous and, in the last two, innovative. He had also sought to improve the general level of efficiency in those parts of the administration that came under his control, and in his service under three lords lieutenant he is generally credited with having brought about a permanent enhancement in the status of the chief-secretaryship. But the events of Peel's period in office, while important in themselves, also had a wider significance. The two major achievements of his secretaryship, the peace preservation act of 1814 and the handling of the crisis of 1816–17, had each involved government

---

[1] For a survey of illicit distillation in early nineteenth-century Ireland see Elizabeth Malcolm, 'Ireland sober, Ireland free' (Dublin, 1986), pp 33–8.
[2] 56 Geo. III, c. 98 (1 July 1816).

taking on new functions and a style of administration that diverged sharply from that in contemporary Britain. The peace preservation act was in itself a limited measure, permitting the calling into temporary existence of a small force in order to deal with a specific crisis. At the same time the nature of that force, with its uniformed special constables operating under the command of a salaried official directly responsible to Dublin Castle, marked a definite break with the tradition of the self-policing community. In the crisis of 1816–17, likewise, the government had, however reluctantly, acknowledged new responsiblities, organising and paying for a major relief scheme and even, in its importation of seed oats, intervening directly to regulate the operation of the market. The crisis also left a more tangible legacy in the form of the act permitting grand juries to make grants to fever hospitals, as well as another measure empowering the central government to provide funds for public works.[1] In both these areas there was a clear indication of the trend towards an interventionist state and towards centralised control over local agencies, which was to be one of the most striking features of the development of government in post-union Ireland.[2]

A second feature of Peel's chief-secretaryship that had an important wider significance was his attitude to patronage. Like his predecessors in the earliest years of the union, Peel was appalled by what he saw as the shamelessness and excess of the Irish appetite for jobbery. The majority of the inhabitants, he wrote in 1815, seemed to have 'the same idea of the government which the natives are said to have of the East India Company. They attach to the government all the attributes of omnipotence, which it is peculiarly disposed to exert in every species of job and fraud and peculation.'[3] Peel's acid language should not, of course, be taken entirely at face value. His comment on his situation in London during the parliamentary session—'I am in the midst of all the vultures and must throw a little food among them occasionally'[4]—may reflect his deep distaste for the system of official patronage that kept the majority of Irish M.P.s loyal to the government of the day, but it is also a reminder that it was Peel, in his capacity as chief secretary, who was primarily responsible for keeping this and other parts of the machine in smooth working order. Where he did intervene to curb particularly outrageous abuses, it has been pointed out, his motive was at least partly to avoid giving a pretext for attacks by unfriendly parties on the system as a whole.[5] Nevertheless, where important issues were concerned, Peel was prepared to insist that the solicitations of personal and political interest should be controlled or ignored. In the case of the peace preservation force

---

[1] Fever hospitals act, 58 Geo. III, c. 47 (30 May 1818); grand jury presentments act, 57 Geo. III, c. 107 (11 July 1817); below, pp 547–8.

[2] Below, pp 206–7, 538–61.

[3] Gash, *Mr Secretary Peel*, p. 120.

[4] Parker, *Peel*, i, 161.

[5] Robert Shipkey, 'Problems of Irish patronage during the chief secretaryship of Robert Peel, 1812–18' in *Hist. Jn.*, x, no. 1 (1967), p. 56.

in particular he took a strong stand. 'If the present or any government make a job of it,' he told the attorney general, 'they will most grossly betray the confidence which parliament has placed in them, and shamefully sacrifice the best interests of the country to the worst.'[1] To another correspondent he was even more blunt: 'We ought to be crucified if we make the measure a job, and select our constables from the servants of our parliamentary friends.'[2]

Peel's antipathy to patronage and his unwillingness to allow it to jeopardise important policy initiatives were sharpened by his personal concern with efficiency. At the same time they also reflected the new ideas of administrative impartiality and bureaucratic rationality that by the early years of the nineteenth century were rapidly gaining ground in British public life. In Britain these ideas were to lead to the progressive dismantling, particularly after 1832, of the gigantic complex of patronage and vested interest that the radical William Cobbett had dubbed 'Old Corruption'.[3] When similar ideas were applied to Ireland, however, the results were at once more complex and more important. For the same outlook and procedures that allocated places and profits to those with personal or political connections also operated to exclude catholics from their fair share even of those posts and privileges to which they were legally entitled. The reign of 'Old Corruption' was inextricably bound up with the privileged position of a religious minority, and any attempt to do away with the first, by applying the new standards that were gaining ground in British public life, would inevitably affect the second as well. For the same reason, of course, the dangers of not applying those standards, of allowing the state to remain the exclusive preserve of a privileged minority, were all the greater. The religious aspect of the patronage issue emerges in Peel's advice to the lord lieutenant at the time that the central relief committee was set up in 1817: 'Let the commissioners be above all exception. Put a quaker or two, a catholic or two, and let it be quite clear that there is no party, no government view in the appointment.'[4] But it was inevitably in the area of law and order that the question of impartiality between different religious groups was most prominent. Writing to the prime minister in 1813 about the recent increase in sectarian violence in Ulster, Peel was careful to point out that 'the administration of justice (so far at least as the exercise of mercy by the lord lieutenant is concerned) has not been impeached, and that there is no impression whatever on the mind of the catholic that the case of each party has not been viewed through a medium perfectly impartial'.[5] The Orange Order, as Peel frankly admitted, presented the government with acute problems: 'We find it, I assure

[1] Parker, *Peel*, i, 151–2.

[2] Ibid., p. 152.

[3] For a recent analysis see W. D. Rubinstein, 'The end of "Old Corruption" in Britain, 1780–1860' in *Past & Present*, no. 101 (Nov. 1983), pp 55–86.

[4] Maurice A. Trant, 'Government policy and Irish distress, 1816–19' (M.A. thesis, N.U.I. (U.C.D.), 1965), p. 30.

[5] Parker, *Peel*, i, 123.

you, a most difficult task when anti-catholicism . . . and loyalty are so much united . . . to appease the one without discouraging the other.'¹ At the same time he argued strongly that members of the yeomanry should not be permitted to appear in uniform or with their bands at Orange processions. 'If they meet as yeomen, and offer just cause of offence to their catholic brethren, and we do not interfere to prevent it, we are in fact little less than a party to it.'²

Comments of this kind can be seen as representing the beginning of what was to be a second major distinguishing feature of the development of Irish government in the decades following the union: the emergence of the state as a neutral body, holding itself aloof from exclusive identification with any of the competing parties within Irish society.³ At this stage, of course, such beginnings were, to say the least, muted ones. The administration of which Peel was part was one in which catholics were excluded, by both law and practice, from the great majority of positions of influence and profit. In addition, the Irish executive remained throughout this period a centre of resistance to pressures for a removal of catholic legal disabilities; Peel himself had in fact emerged, in a succession of debates, as the leading parliamentary champion of the 'protestant' party. Yet despite all this, the first steps had been taken towards a recognition that government in Ireland could not be effective or generally accepted as long as it remained the exclusive preserve of a single group. Peel's departure in 1818, furthermore, marked the end of the Irish executive's role as a centre of uncompromising protestantism. The new chief secretary, Charles Grant, was a known supporter of catholic emancipation, and although this was not in any sense the reason for his selection, the appointment marked the belated extension to Ireland of the principle, accepted within the cabinet since 1812,⁴ that the catholic question was to be considered an open one.

Grant's declared commitment to catholic emancipation was no empty formula. Although the agitation among Irish catholics was in eclipse, the parliamentary advocates of emancipation had by this time recovered from the defeat of 1813 and were pressing their case with growing success. In 1815 a motion by Sir Henry Parnell for a committee to inquire into catholic claims had been heavily defeated, by 228 votes to 147, while the following year a motion by Grattan had attracted only a thin house and was lost by 172 votes to 141. In 1817, however, Grattan had once more moved for a committee. His motion was again defeated, by 245 votes to 221, but the larger attendance suggested that interest in the question was reviving, and the majority against was by no means prohibitive. On the next occasion, in 1819, Grattan's motion for a committee was lost by only two votes, 243 to 241. Grattan died in June 1820, but in the following year William Conyngham Plunket, the member for

---

¹ Parker, *Peel*, i, 122.
² Ibid., p. 158.
³ See Oliver MacDonagh, *Ireland* (Englewood Cliffs, N.J., 1968), pp 7–9, and below, p. 158.
⁴ Above, pp 46–7.

Dublin University, introduced what was by now the standard resolution calling for a committee, and this time the motion was carried by 227 votes to 221. Plunket, taken somewhat by surprise, now hurried to prepare a draft relief bill. The measure that finally emerged from committee returned yet again to the question of securities. It revived the idea of government-appointed commissions that would certify the loyalty of candidates for vacant catholic sees and examine correspondence with Rome, and at the same time proposed a new device, a legislative explanation of the oath of supremacy that would permit catholics to take it without compromising their religious beliefs. In this form the bill passed its third reading in the commons by a majority of 19, but was defeated in the house of lords, on 17 April 1821, by 159 votes to 120.

This renewal of proposals for securities to accompany catholic emancipation met with a predictable reaction in Ireland. The bill was welcomed by Richard Lalor Sheil, the chief spokesman for the catholic supporters of some form of veto, but was strongly attacked by O'Connell and several catholic bishops. This open hostility from the representatives of majority catholic opinion may have contributed to the eventual defeat of the bill in the house of lords. For the most part, however, what the progress of Plunket's bill demonstrated was the irrelevance of the catholic agitation to the parliamentary debate on catholic emancipation. That debate, conducted on grounds both of expediency and of principle, had continued for almost twenty years. Throughout this period the supporters of emancipation, though generally recognised as including the majority of men of ability, had been outnumbered by its opponents. But by 1821, at a time when organised catholic agitation was at its lowest ebb, the emancipationists had at last won the protracted argument. The house of commons had given majority support not merely to a declaration of principle, as in 1813, but to an actual measure of catholic relief. From this point on, the real obstacle to the achievement of catholic emancipation was to lie in the exercise of purely hereditary power, represented first by the house of lords and secondly by the king.

Even in 1821, however, there seems to have been at least some doubt about the role that royal power might play. George III had died in January 1820. In August 1821, a few weeks after his coronation, George IV visited Ireland. The visit had no direct connection with Irish policy. The new king, despite his somewhat battered personal image, brought to the throne a novel concern with the public face of monarchy. He had taken a close interest in the details of his elaborate and expensive coronation, and followed it with royal visits, not just to Ireland, but also to Hanover and Scotland. The Irish visit began with the sea crossing on 12 August 1821. It was the king's fifty-ninth birthday, and he had been upset by news of the death, four days earlier, of his estranged wife, Caroline. His unsteady condition by the time he disembarked at Howth was the subject of much comment, both scandalised and amused, and the alcoholic excesses that reportedly accompanied the tour as a whole were to pass into popular legend. Despite this, however, the visit was a great success. The king's public entry into Dublin on 17 August, passing up Sackville Street under a triumphal arch inscribed '*"An hundred thousand welcomes"*' in Irish,[1] was attended by a procession of carriages and horsemen estimated at a mile in length. The occasion, Castlereagh reported, 'beat the coronation, not in splendour of dresses, but in crowd and in the enthusiasm of the people'.[2] When the king attended a dinner given by the lord mayor and corporation on 23 August, 'the distant cheering of the people from the surrounding streets' could be heard through the windows of the banqueting hall.[3] His departure from Dunleary (shortly afterwards renamed Kingstown in his honour) on 3 September was the occasion for further display, as spectators lined the shore, some following the royal barge until they stood up to their necks in the water. Contemporaries were struck by the contrast between the enthusiasm thus displayed and the reports of popular disaffection that normally dominated the news from Ireland. The king, for his part, responded warmly, announcing to the cheering crowds on his arrival that his heart had always been Irish, decorating his hat with shamrock for the entry into Dublin, and generally behaving, in the words of one disapproving observer, 'like a popular candidate come down on an electioneering trip'.[4]

For many contemporaries, however, the chief interest of the royal visit lay less in its novel element of showmanship than in what might be revealed of the new king's intentions towards the catholics. In some ways it is difficult to see how there could have been any continuing doubts regarding George IV's firm opposition to catholic political claims. His change of heart while still regent had been widely publicised by his former political associates, and in particular Lord Donoughmore, in 1812. As far as the Irish catholics were concerned, an irreparable breach would seem to have taken place in June 1812, when an aggregate meeting had passed resolutions lamenting the way in which the promised granting of emancipation had been prevented by 'the fatal witchery of an unworthy secret influence'.[5] As recently as 1819, when an attempt had been made to shift to members of the parliamentary opposition the blame for this highly offensive reference to the regent's relationship with Lady Hertford, O'Connell had come forward to admit that it was in fact he who had sponsored the resolution.[6] In 1821, however, all this appeared to have been forgotten on both sides. When the catholic bishops came forward to present a loyal address, wearing their full ecclesiastical dress, they were graciously received, and the

---

[1] *Croker papers*, i, 203.

[2] *The journal of Mrs Arbuthnot, 1820–32*, ed. Francis Bamford and the seventh duke of Wellington (2 vols, London, 1950), i, 115.

[3] *Croker papers*, i, 205.

[4] Viscount Dudley, quoted in Christopher Hibbert, *George IV, regent and king, 1811–30* (London, 1973), p. 213.

[5] *Life and speeches of Daniel O'Connell*, ed. John O'Connell (2 vols, Dublin, 1846), i, 171.

[6] *O'Connell corr.*, ii, 209.

king presided over the installation of the earl of Fingall, Ireland's premier catholic layman, as a knight of the Order of Saint Patrick. Although gestures of this kind reflected only the king's desire to create a general atmosphere of benevolence and goodwill, they were widely interpreted as implying something more. In later life, it is true, O'Connell was to speak very dismissively of the royal visit: 'He came to Ireland to humbug the catholics, who, he thought, would take sweet words instead of useful deeds. Ah! We were not to be humbugged.'[1] At the time, however, he showed no such reservations, coming forward on the day of the king's departure to present him with a laurel crown, and continuing for some time after to make extravagant professions of devotion to the new king.

Continuing belief among catholics that the king was sympathetic to their claims may have been encouraged by a major restructuring, shortly after his visit, of the Irish executive. There was in fact no connection between the two events. Peel's successor as chief secretary, Charles Grant, had never been regarded as a successful administrator, and his relations with the lord lieutenant, Earl Talbot, and other members of the executive were poor. Long-standing disagreements came to a head in 1821, when Talbot asked for the chief secretary's recall. By this time, however, negotiations were in progress to bring Lord Grenville and his followers, who had by now broken with the whigs, into the government. Their adhesion was to be under the existing arrangement whereby emancipation was to be treated as an open question, but some adjustment of policy would obviously help to make final agreement easier. Accordingly Liverpool chose to solve the problem of a disunited Irish executive by recalling both Talbot and Grant. Talbot was replaced by Marquis Wellesley, elder brother of the duke of Wellington, a man who for a brief period in 1812 had actually seemed a potential prime minister, but who had since receded into political obscurity. The choice of Wellesley, a supporter of catholic emancipation, was balanced by the appointment of an anti-emancipationist, Henry Goulburn, as chief secretary. In addition, in what was widely seen as a significant move, the notoriously anti-catholic William Saurin was replaced as attorney general by William Conyngham Plunket, author of the relief bill of 1821.

These changes created high expectations. To O'Connell, writing in January 1822, Wellesley was 'the harbinger of emancipation'.[2] Such hopes were quite unrealistic. What Wellesley offered was what Bedford and the 'ministry of all the talents' had offered fifteen years before: liberal and, from the point of view of catholics, conciliatory government within the framework of the existing laws. Bishops and other prominent catholics were invited to attend viceregal levees, and the new executive embarked on a number of practical reforms, the first of

[1] W. J. O'Neill Daunt, *Personal recollections of the late Daniel O'Connell M.P.* (2 vols, London 1848), i, 131.
[2] *O'Connell corr.*, ii, 347.

which was a revision of the magistracy. It had long been recognised that magistrates were in many cases far from suitable for the functions entrusted to them: some were unwilling, either through idleness or timidity, to perform their duties properly; others were blatantly partisan; a few were openly corrupt. The accession of a new king provided the occasion for drawing up during 1822 and 1823 an entirely new commission of the peace for every county. The revision was not in the end as thorough or as far-reaching as had originally been hoped, but the opportunity was nevertheless taken to remove some of the most notoriously incapable or unfit magistrates, while adding other, more suitable names. A second reform concerned the long-standing grievances associated with tithes. The tithe composition act of July 1823[1] provided for the commutation of tithes to a fixed charge on land: commissioners appointed by the incumbent and his parishioners calculated the amount of tithe that should be paid by the parish, and then apportioned this charge among the different occupiers of land on the basis of an examination of the amount and quality of land held. The amounts thus arrived at would stand for a period of twenty-one years, after which there would be a new applotment. The act did nothing to remove the essential anomaly of a tax intended for the support of the Church of Ireland being levied on a predominantly catholic population, but it did make the actual collection of tithes less aggravating. Instead of a range of fluctuating levies, the occupier now faced a single fixed charge, and it was no longer necessary for his crop to be inspected and valued each year by the hated tithe proctor. An amending act of 1824[2] allowed the lord lieutenant to impose a settlement in cases where a clergyman and the tithe-payers could not agree, and by 1832 a composition had been effected in half the parishes of Ireland. A third reform, attempting to resolve the contentious question of access to grave-yards, was less successful. A burial act in 1824 permitted the interment of catholics and dissenters in cemeteries belonging to the Church of Ireland, but prohibited their clergy from officiating at the graveside.[3] The Catholic Association preferred to go ahead with plans already agreed for the purchase of sites for exclusively catholic cemeteries. The first such site, at Golden Bridge outside Dublin, was opened in 1829, and a second, at Glasnevin, three years later.

Of greater long-term importance than these worthy but limited reforms was the new executive's response to two related crises that occurred within months of its formation. The first of these was a crisis of law and order. Among the issues that had led to the final breakdown in relations between Talbot and Grant had been disagreements over how best to respond to serious disturbances, affecting parts of all three southern provinces, which had begun in the autumn of 1819. These had died out in the spring of 1820, but from autumn of the following year they were succeeded by fresh outbreaks, the most grave since

---

[1] 4 Geo. IV, c. 99 (19 July 1823).
[2] 5 Geo. IV, c. 63 (17 June 1824).
[3] 5 Geo. IV, c. 25 (15 Apr. 1824).

the union, which continued until the spring of 1823.[1] This wave of protest, like its predecessor in 1813–16, was in direct response to a drop in agricultural prices, corn prices in particular falling drastically in the years 1818–22.[2] The disturbances were most intense in Munster, but also extended to parts of the three other provinces. A new and, from the point of view of the authorities, particularly alarming development was reported in parts of County Cork, where large numbers of men were said to have left their homes and withdrawn to strongholds in the mountains. The spectre thus created, of scattered protest giving place to the mobilisation of peasant armies in a full-scale insurrection, gained added substance from several incidents in which police and troops came under attack from parties several hundred strong. At the same time the more normal pattern of threats, cattle-maiming, assaults, arson, and the occasional killing continued throughout the affected areas.

As an immediate response to these developments the government in February 1822 reintroduced the insurrection act, which had been repealed four years earlier, and at the same time brought in a second measure, never in fact applied, providing for the temporary suspension of habeas corpus in disturbed areas.[3] As in 1814, however, the pressures of a renewed crisis of law and order also provided the impetus for a more significant development. Early in 1822 work began on plans for a new police bill. The proposed measure went far beyond Peel's peace preservation act, envisaging nothing less than a permanent police establishment, consisting of constables and sub-constables, with a chief constable for each county and an inspector general for each province. On the important issue of central as opposed to local control, the government compromised. Where the peace preservation force had been appointed by and answerable solely to Dublin Castle, the new constables and sub-constables (though not the higher ranks) could be appointed by the magistrates of the county in which they were to serve, and they were to operate under the direction of those magistrates. At the same time the importance of the precedent set by Peel's bill can be seen in the ease with which, this compromise having been made, the constabulary act passed through parliament.[4] The new force took some time to organise and recruit, and it made no appreciable impact on the immediate crisis that had inspired its creation, the decline in agrarian crime from early 1823 being due mainly to an improvement in economic conditions. By the beginning of 1825, however, Ireland had a fully fledged professional police force, consisting of some 4,500 men distributed across the whole country.

The second emergency that confronted the new executive was the reappearance of serious food shortages and threatened famine. The same fall in

---

[1] Below, pp 80–82. 　　[2] Below, pp 132–3. 　　[3] 3 Geo. IV, cc 1, 2 (11 Feb. 1822).
[4] 3 Geo. IV, c. 103 (1 Aug. 1822); see also Galen Broeker, *Rural disorder and police reform in Ireland, 1812–36* (London, 1970), pp 141–9; Stanley H. Palmer, *Police and protest in England and Ireland 1780–1850* (Cambridge, 1988), pp 198–203.

agricultural prices that had triggered off renewed agrarian protest had also struck further blows at the living standards of the rural population. But the real crisis began when heavy rains in the autumn of 1821 inflicted severe damage on the potato crop. By the summer of 1822 most of Connacht and the western counties of Munster faced the threat of widespread starvation. At the height of the crisis an estimated one million people, more than half the population of the areas affected, were dependent on relief schemes for their survival. The government response drew on the example of the measures adopted to cope with the dearth of 1816–17. Once again a central relief committee was set up to allocate funds to local relief committees applying for assistance. During the summer of 1822 the central committee distributed a total of £175,000, the funds being used both to purchase food, either for free distribution or for sale at reduced prices, and also to organise local relief works. At the same time the government organised its own public works scheme, providing employment on road-building, the construction of harbours, and a range of other projects, as well as sending provisions, in the form of potatoes, wheatmeal, and oatmeal, to the distressed areas. The success of these different measures in preventing or reducing deaths from fever and starvation awaits detailed evaluation. The effectiveness of relief measures was almost certainly reduced by continued uneasiness at the implications of any interference with the free workings of the market. Yet despite such scruples the government had in practice been forced to intervene on a scale far exceeding that seen in 1816–17, confirming the trend towards a more interventionist approach to Irish social problems that had already become apparent in the preceding decade.

Wellesley's known support for catholic emancipation, and his policies of reform and conciliation, were hardly calculated to make him popular among Irish protestants. What brought him into open conflict with protestant opinion, however, was his espousal of one particularly contentious form of conciliation: an attempt to interfere with the ceremonies carried out on certain days at the statue of William III in College Green, Dublin. The customary decoration of the statue on 12 July had in fact first been discouraged in 1821 as part of the attempt to damp down sectarian animosities in the period before the king's visit. When the lord mayor, acting on Wellesley's instructions, attempted to renew the prohibition in July 1822, Dublin Orangemen defied the ban and the ceremony was followed by fighting with catholic counterdemonstrators. On the next occasion that the statue was due to be decorated, King William's birthday on 4 November, Orangemen who attended were forcibly dispersed by troops and police. A few weeks later, as Wellesley attended a performance at the New Theatre Royal, he was hissed by members of the audience and two missiles, a quart bottle and part of a watchman's rattle, were thrown at the viceregal box. The incident, despite the lord lieutenant's insistence that he had been the target of a full-scale murder attempt, was in itself fairly trivial. What was significant was the legal aftermath. When Plunket, as attorney general, brought charges of riot and conspiracy against some of those involved, he succeeded only in provoking a display of protestant solidarity and hostility to the government. The charges were thrown out by the grand jury, and when Plunket nevertheless proceeded to a trial, the accused were acquitted.

O'Connell received the news of the 'bottle riot' of December 1822 with jubilation. He welcomed the spectacle of Orangemen and government at daggers drawn, and wrote offering to raise a force of a thousand men to help restore order. 'How *my* poor troops would be delighted to be hunting Orangemen,' he told his wife. 'I confess it would amuse me to have one good day's running after the rascals.'[1] At this point O'Connell was still convinced that a catholic relief bill would pass through parliament in the forthcoming session. In April 1823 Plunket did in fact bring forward a fresh resolution calling for a committee to inquire into catholic claims, but this was a private venture rather than a government-sponsored resolution, and the motion was lost after unedifying squabbles between the emancipationists still in opposition and those who had recently accepted office. By now O'Connell had abandoned his former high hopes. 'Lord Wellesley', he lamented on 18 April, 'is, I think, yielding to the Orange scoundrels.'[2] Such a charge, directed at a lord lieutenant who had aroused unparalleled hostility among protestants, was hardly justified. But O'Connell's reaction only reflected the prevailing political climate. Already by 1823 divisions between catholics and protestants had reached a point where the idea of conciliation had become largely irrelevant. This was as true of practical reforms of the kind offered by Wellesley as it was of such purely cosmetic exercises as the king's visit. Attempts to steer a middle course between the two parties succeeded only in alienating one without satisfying the other. All this, furthermore, was at a time when organised catholic agitation was at a low ebb. In the next few years sectarian divisions were to be widened still further as catholic self-assertion reemerged in a new and much more threatening form.

[1] *O'Connell corr.*, ii, 427.   [2] Ibid., p. 462.

EDITOR'S NOTE

Since this volume went to press, the need for a modern account of O'Connell's early career (mentioned above, p. 54) has been satisfied by Oliver MacDonagh, *The hereditary bondsman: Daniel O'Connell 1775–1829* (London, 1988).

CHAPTER IV

Mass politics and sectarian conflict, 1823–30

S. J. CONNOLLY

RELATIONS between catholics and protestants in the first two decades of the nineteenth century were strangely mixed in character. On the one hand the events of the 1790s had revived and strengthened long-standing fears and suspicions; in particular, the rebellion and its aftermath had left both sides with a replenished treasury of grievances and remembered atrocities. At the same time the tradition of sectarian recrimination and hostility, represented in the writings of polemicists such as Watty Cox and Sir Richard Musgrave, existed side by side with a considerable degree of tolerance and practical cooperation. Members of the different denominations took part in each other's major public ceremonies. In 1818, for example, the consecration of Edward Kernan, co-adjutor to the catholic bishop of Clogher, was attended by prominent local protestants, while a few years later the catholic clergy of the city of Limerick, led by their bishop, joined in the funeral procession for the protestant vicar general of the diocese.[1] In addition, both clergy and laity of the different churches worked together in a wide range of voluntary charitable ventures. The same spirit of cooperation was seen in the early years of the Society for Promoting the Education of the Poor in Ireland, more commonly known as the Kildare Place Society, which had been founded in 1811 with the explicit aim of providing schools for the lower classes 'divested of all sectarian distinctions in Christianity'.[2] A number of prominent catholics, including Daniel O'Connell, served on the society's board of managers, and it received widespread support from both catholic laity and catholic clergy. After 1820, however, this continuing spirit of mutual accommodation and cooperation was to be undermined by a sharp resurgence of sectarian hostility, affecting all levels of Irish society.

This revival of religious animosities had several causes; undoubtedly the

[1] Seosamh Ó Dufaigh, 'James Murphy, bishop of Clogher, 1801–24' in *Clogher Rec.*, vi, no. 3 (1968), p. 448; Ignatius Murphy, 'Some attitudes to religious freedom and ecumenism in pre-emancipation Ireland' in *I.E.R.*, cv (1966), pp 97–8. In the same way the funeral in 1816 of John Power, catholic bishop of Waterford, was attended by the Church of Ireland bishop and several of his clergy.

[2] Akenson, *Ir. education experiment*, p. 86.

most striking was a general revival of religious enthusiasm, challenging the more relaxed and rationalistic approach to spiritual matters that had prevailed for most of the eighteenth century. The religious revival of the early nineteenth century was a broadly based movement, affecting both Great Britain and Ireland. Its effects were felt by all the major Irish denominations. The Church of Ireland at the beginning of the nineteenth century exhibited all the classic symptoms of lax internal discipline combined with a low overall level of religious zeal. Bishops and clergy frequently failed to reside in their dioceses or parishes; benefices were too large or held in plurality; churches and glebe houses were inadequate or in poor repair; appointments at all levels were often made on grounds of patronage rather than merit. The decades following the union, however, saw a general improvement in ecclesiastical discipline, curbing if not eliminating the most serious abuses. Between 1806 and 1832 the proportion of incumbents resident in their parishes rose from 46 per cent to 75 per cent. Pluralism was reduced, large benefices were divided, and a reformed board of first-fruits and tenths promoted the widespread building and repair of churches and glebe houses. These developments can in part be attributed to the growing influence within the Church of Ireland of the evangelical movement, encouraging a new spirit of commitment and devotion among clergy and laity alike. At the same time it is important to remember that evangelicals, throughout the first half of the nineteenth century, remained a minority group within the established church.[1] As such they are perhaps best seen as representing only the most extreme wing of a much broader shift in attitudes and ideas within the Church of Ireland. Most of the major changes seen in the Church of Ireland during this period were in fact the work of conservative reformers, high-ranking churchmen such as Lord John George Beresford (archbishop of Armagh 1822–62), who were in no sense evangelicals but were nevertheless committed to the introduction of higher standards within the church.

The catholic church of the early nineteenth century suffered from problems very similar to those that afflicted its established rival. There were frequent complaints that the parish clergy neglected basic pastoral duties, such as those of preaching regularly and providing for the religious instruction of the young; that they extorted exorbitant fees from their parishioners, sometimes withholding the sacraments to enforce their demands; and that they participated too freely in the social life of the laity. The general weakness of ecclesiastical discipline was also reflected in the frequent and unrestrained factional disputes that divided the clergy of different dioceses. Such problems can in part be attributed to the practical difficulties under which the catholic church of this period operated: the disruptive effects of the penal restrictions imposed for

---

[1] See D. H. Akenson, *The church of Ireland: ecclesiastical reform and revolution, 1800–1885* (New Haven and London, 1971), p. 132. Bowen, *Protestant crusade*, p. 45, makes larger claims for specifically evangelical influences as the main force behind reform within the Church of Ireland.

most of the eighteenth century, the continued shortage of money, the back-wardness and isolation of many of the communities to which the church's mission extended. At the same time it seems clear that the catholic church, like the Church of Ireland, was affected by a certain lack of zeal and commitment on the part of many of its servants. Also as in the Church of Ireland, however, the late eighteenth and early nineteenth centuries saw the beginnings of a general movement for change. Bishops in different dioceses sought to impose new standards of behaviour and performance on their clergy, regulating their financial demands, supervising their pastoral work more carefully than before, and restricting their participation in popular social life. These efforts to tighten internal discipline were accompanied by an attempt to improve the level of religious services provided for the laity. Preaching and cathechising became more frequent, higher standards of external display were introduced in public worship, and the 1820s and 1830s in particular saw a major programme of church-building. The early decades of the nineteenth century also brought the first signs of a religious revival among the catholic laity, with the spread of sodalities and confraternities and the introduction or increased use of supplementary devotional practices such as benediction or the forty hours' devotion. Such developments, however, were largely confined to the better-off. It was not until after the famine that the mass of the catholic population were introduced to the elaborate range of religious practices that has continued to characterise Irish catholicism down to the present day.[1]

The effects of changing religious attitudes were also apparent among Irish presbyterians in the early nineteenth century. Indeed, it was here that the religious revival of the period had its most dramatic effects. The issue in the case of presbyterianism was not primarily one of ecclesiastical discipline, but rather of theological orthodoxy. The synod of Ulster, the largest presbyterian body, had long accepted a division within its ranks between an 'old light' party, committed to support for a clearly defined body of religious doctrine, and a 'new light' party, prepared to accept a looser definition of belief. Although all clergy of the synod were technically required to subscribe to the Westminster confession, the touchstone of presbyterian orthodoxy, many in practice never did so. When the Belfast Academical Institution was opened in 1814 to train candidates for the presbyterian ministry, the teaching staff included several known theological liberals. Within a few years, however, the growing influence within the synod of evangelicalism had led to the emergence of a movement for greater theological orthodoxy, led by Henry Cooke, minister of Killyleagh, County Down. An initial demand for guarantees concerning the doctrinal soundness of teachers at the institution developed into a campaign for scrutiny

---

[1] For a fuller discussion of these points see Connolly, *Priests & people in Ire.* For an alternative view of pre-famine Irish catholicism see Desmond Keenan, *The catholic church in nineteenth-century Ireland: a sociological study* (Dublin, 1983). See also Emmet Larkin, 'The devotional revolution in Ireland, 1850–75' in *A.H.R.*, lxxvii (1972), pp 625–52.

of the theological views of all new ministers. In 1829, after the synod had introduced new regulations providing for such a scrutiny, the latitudinarians seceded, forming in 1830 their own body, the remonstrant synod. Their departure cleared the way for the unification in 1840 of the synod of Ulster and the severely orthodox secession synod, which came together to form the General Assembly of the Presbyterian Church in Ireland. These theological controversies and realignments, meanwhile, were accompanied by the same popular religious revival seen in the Church of Ireland and the Roman Catholic church. Reports from predominantly presbyterian districts of east Ulster in the 1830s noted a general improvement in observance of the sabbath and the spread of temperance societies, as well as the decline of traditional amusements such as dancing and cockfighting and their replacement by more restrained and respectable forms of entertainment.

The growing influence of evangelicalism among Ulster presbyterians is sometimes seen as having had a political as well as a theological significance, contributing to the decline of earlier radical allegiances.[1] In fact it is doubtful whether there was any such connection. It is true that the opening decades of the nineteenth century saw a marked change in their political outlook, which included a hardening of attitudes on the subject of catholic emancipation. In 1813 the general synod of Ulster had passed a resolution supporting the abolition of all political distinctions founded on religious profession. Twelve years later, however, Cooke, at that time moderator of the synod, told a parliamentary inquiry that opposition to catholic emancipation among Ulster presbyterians had grown, particularly among the less informed. Although Cooke's comments were condemned by his liberal opponents within the synod, others came forward to support his view, and by 1829 even the *Northern Whig* was prepared to admit that 'an inveterate and determined hostility exists among the ignorant mass of the presbyterian body against the catholic claims'.[2] Whether the growth of evangelicalism contributed significantly to these changes in political outlook, however, remains open to question. Although Cooke himself had close personal associations with tory political circles, it does not seem to have been the case that 'old light' theological views were necessarily linked to a conservative political outlook, or 'new light' theology to a liberal one.[3] The movement of the great majority of Ulster presbyterians away from the radicalism of the 1790s had in any case begun well before the great theological controversies of the 1820s, and it can be more convincingly related to the increasing self-assertion of Irish catholics than to any doctrinal influences.

Although the specific connection between the growth of evangelicalism and

---

[1] Above, pp 20–22; cf. below, pp 166, 200, 236–7.
[2] Finlay Holmes, *Henry Cooke* (Belfast, 1981), pp 35, 64–5.
[3] David Miller, 'Presbyterianism and "modernisation" in Ulster' in *Past & Present*, no. 80 (1978), pp 76–80.

the political realignment of Ulster presbyterians has almost certainly been overstated, there seems little doubt that the religious revival of the early nineteenth century helped to intensify denominational divisions, encouraging all parties to adopt more rigid and combative attitudes. One reflection of this was the development during the 1820s of a new spectator sport, in the form of public theological controversy. Large numbers attended venues throughout the country to hear protestant and catholic orators engage in lengthy debates, in which arcane points of church history and theology were combined with polemical comment on contemporary issues. One such encounter, between Rev. Richard Pope and Fr Thomas Maguire, held in Dublin in 1827, went on for a total of six days. These verbal confrontations were accompanied by a voluminous and equally inflammatory pamphlet literature. By far the most serious consequence of the religious revival of the early nineteenth century, however, was the appearance among British and Irish protestants of a new enthusiasm for missionary efforts, directed not only to heathens in far-off places, but also to Christians nearer home, notably in the form of efforts to bring about a mass conversion of the catholic Irish. The first moves in this direction came from the Irish methodists, who in 1799 sent out their first three Irish-speaking missionaries to work among the catholic population. By 1816 there were twenty-one methodist missionaries operating from fourteen stations in different parts of the country. Meanwhile, the missionary urge had spread to other denominations. The Hibernian Bible Society was founded in 1806, the Sunday School Society in 1809, and the Religious Tract and Book Society in 1810. These were followed in 1818 by the expressively named Irish Society for Promoting the Education of the Native Irish through the Medium of their own Language. In addition to these anglican bodies, there was an interdenominational Irish Evangelical Society, founded in 1814, as well as separate missionary organisations maintained by presbyterians and baptists.

If the pursuit of a mass conversion of catholics appears in retrospect as a hopelessly unrealistic venture, it did not seem so to those involved. It was not until 1835 that the commissioners of public instruction provided the first imperfect census of religious affiliations in Ireland; before that, although it was recognised that catholics made up a majority of the population, the extent of their numerical superiority was widely underestimated. More important, the supporters of the 'second reformation' acted from an absolute conviction of the truth and value of their message. Properly communicated, God's word could not fail to triumph over ignorance and superstition. To some extent, it has been suggested, missionary enthusiasm was also strengthened by the millenarian ideas that circulated widely among British and Irish protestants at this time.[1] Certainly there is no doubting the enormous investment, in money and human effort, that the 'second reformation' represented. The missionary drive took three main forms. Itinerant missionaries, many of them trained in the use of

[1] Bowen, *Protestant crusade*, pp 64–7.

Irish, were dispatched through the countryside, preaching and organising meetings. Secondly, bibles and religious tracts, again often printed in Irish, were circulated in huge numbers. The Religious Tract and Book Society alone distributed a total of 4.4 million tracts over a period of ten years. Finally, and most important, the different missionary societies established schools, in which an elementary education was available free of charge to those who were prepared to accept the scriptural and religious instruction that went with it. Such an offer, at a time of strong popular demand for schooling, was not easily ignored. In the mid-1820s, when growing opposition from the catholic clergy had already led to the withdrawal of large numbers of pupils from the schools run by the protestant missionary societies, there were still over 17,000 catholic children attending schools connected with the London Hibernian Society, as well as smaller numbers in the schools of other missionary bodies.

The launching of the 'second reformation' inevitably damaged relations between catholics and protestants. The considerable degree of mutual tolerance and accommodation that had existed up to the 1820s had depended, among other things, on the absence of any attempt by the different churches to meddle with one another's congregations. Now, for the first time in over a century, protestants were making serious efforts to win converts among the catholic population. They were doing so, furthermore, at a time when the catholic church itself was becoming more rigid in its attitudes, more tightly organised, and more assertive. One notable victim of the changed religious climate was the Kildare Place Society, whose initial commitment to non-denominational education had given way by 1820 to what catholic spokesmen denounced as naked proselytism. As a result, O'Connell and other catholic representatives severed their connection with the society, and the catholic clergy increasingly sought to keep their parishioners' children away from its schools. The deterioration in relations was probably most serious among the clergy, as priests and parsons who had formerly found it possible to cooperate on matters of mutual concern now came to regard one another as rivals or potential aggressors. But among the laity, too, sectarian tensions were heightened by the inflammatory rhetoric of the new style of religious controversy and by the resentment of catholics at attempts, real or imagined, to tamper with their religious beliefs and those of their children. In the western diocese of Killaloe the catholic bishop complained in 1824 that the setting up of bible schools had been 'the cause of diminishing considerably that mutual harmony and friendship between catholics and protestants that had subsisted till the unfortunate period of their existence'.[1] Elsewhere too the activities of itinerant preachers and protestant education societies were the cause of bitter local quarrels, in some cases erupting into violence.

Although the protestant missionary crusade undoubtedly contributed to the

[1] Ignatius Murphy, 'Some attitudes to religious freedom and ecumenism in pre-emancipation Ireland' in *I.E.R.*, cv (1966), p. 102.

deterioration of relations between catholics and protestants in the 1820s and after, it would be wrong to suggest that it was the sole or even the main cause of that deterioration. In the first place, it is by no means clear that the amicable relations that had existed up to the 1820s among many of the clergy and the middle classes were also to be seen lower down the social scale. Certainly there had remained ever since the 1790s a tradition of mutual hostility between protestants and catholics, periodically breaking out in violence. Conflict was inevitably most serious in Ulster, where random sectarian brawling, and more organised feuding between Orangemen and their catholic counterparts, the Defenders and later the Ribbonmen, were a regular occurrence. In Garvagh, County Londonderry, for example, there were confrontations between catholics and protestants on three successive fair-days in 1813, culminating in a pitched battle in which one man was shot dead and several others wounded. In Belfast in the same year two men died in rioting following the celebration of 12 July, although sectarian fighting was not to become commonplace in the town until after the 1830s, when the rapid increase in the size of the catholic population threatened for a time to make Belfast a predominantly catholic town. At the same time sectarian tension and occasional violence were by no means confined to Ulster. Even in County Kerry, which had few protestants and had been virtually untouched by the events of 1798, displays of Orange insignia by members of the Meath militia stationed in Tralee in 1805 led to an exchange of insults and an affray.[1] In Carlow town a protestant tradesman told Edward Wakefield in the summer of 1809 that no catholic in the district would have dealings with him. Four years later, notices posted up in the counties of Longford, Mayo, Roscommon, and Sligo called on catholics to have no deal-ings with Orangemen or (in one case) with any protestants other than a few named individuals.[2]

Even in the first two decades of the nineteenth century, then, a degree of anti-protestant sentiment existed among catholics, not only in Ulster but also in other parts of Ireland. In the early 1820s this animosity came suddenly and violently to the surface. The form that it assumed was a wave of millenarian excitement, accompanying the major agrarian disturbances that took place in large parts of Leinster and Munster between 1821 and 1824. This derived its inspiration from the *General history of the Christian church*, an elaborate analysis of the Book of Revelation in which an English catholic bishop, Charles Walmesley, writing under the pseudonym 'Pastorini', had claimed to demon-strate that the year 1825 would see the violent destruction of the protestant churches—the locusts from the bottomless pit that had been permitted to torment the faithful for the three centuries since the reformation. Walmesley's book was first published in 1771, but it was only as the upheavals he had

---

[1] Brigade-major Daniel Mahony to ——, 18 July 1805 (S.P.O., State of the country papers, 1031/30).
[2] Wakefield, *Account of Ire.*, ii, 598; S.P.O., State of the country papers, 1544/49, 64, 84, 95.

predicted drew near that it acquired a mass following. The first references to Pastorini among persons involved in agrarian disturbances were noted in parts of the west midlands around 1817; by 1822 the name was familiar throughout the disturbed districts of Munster and Leinster.[1] The circulation of cheap, mass-produced copies of the *General history* was supplemented by the production of handbills and pamphlets containing more easily accessible digests of the work and extracts of selected passages, while knowledge of the prophecies was further disseminated through ballads and by word of mouth. Observers in different parts of the country spoke anxiously of the stimulus that the expectation of a coming upheaval had given to popular disaffection: Pastorini, one County Limerick correspondent maintained in January 1822, 'has done more towards the subversion of the British empire than Bonaparte with all his legions'.[2] Convicts awaiting transportation in Cork were said to have declared that they were glad to be leaving Ireland, since they would not have to witness the bloody scenes that were to be enacted there. A king's counsel in County Limerick, who had systematically examined all the threatening notices ånd other documents circulated in the county, reported that he did not recall a single one in which there was not some reference to Pastorini and his prophecies.[3]

Although the currency and apparent credence achieved by Pastorini's prophecies was undoubtedly spectacular, the practical influence of such ideas on the agrarian disturbances of the early 1820s must be assessed with caution. Despite the millenarian rhetoric that accompanied it, the Rockite movement of 1821–4 was not radically different from other agrarian protests of the early nineteenth century. Like them, it was primarily a pragmatic, even conservative, movement, concerned with limited and specific goals: the regulation of rents, wages, and tithes; protection of tenants threatened with eviction; and wider access to land, particularly for tillage. Where millenarianism was important was less in influencing the content of the Rockite movement than in giving it added energy and cohesion. The widespread conviction that a major social and political upheaval was shortly to take place gave greater confidence to all those tempted to take direct action to remedy economic or other grievances. Moreover, this particular brand of millenarianism, with its emphasis on an imminent cataclysm in which all catholics would share a common destiny, helped to induce farmers, cottiers, and labourers to forget the very real economic conflicts that divided them and to unite in support of the Rockite movement.

[1] For the origins and spread of popular millenarianism in this period see J. S. Donnelly, jr, 'Pastorini and Captain Rock: millenarianism and sectarianism in the Rockite movement of 1821–4' in Clark & Donnelly, *Ir. peasants*, pp 102–39.

[2] Anonymous letter, signed 'Indignator', Adare, 22 Jan. 1822 (S.P.O., State of the country papers, 2350/30).

[3] *Minutes of evidence taken before the select committee appointed to inquire into the disturbances in Ireland . . .*, p. 145, H. C. 1825 (20), vii; *Minutes of evidence taken before the select committee of the house of lords appointed to examine into the nature and extent of the disturbances which have prevailed in those districts of Ireland, which are now subject to the provisions of the insurrection act . . .*, p. 7, H.C. 1825 (200), vii.

In both of these respects the influence of popular millenarianism might help to explain why the agrarian disturbances of the early 1820s were the most extensive and formidable of the whole pre-famine period. However, while the greater part of Rockite activity was confined to the pursuit of practical economic grievances, there were also a number of incidents in which expressions of anti-protestant sentiment went beyond mere rhetoric. Thus in April 1823 a band of over a hundred men attacked the village of Glenosheen in County Limerick, a distinctively protestant settlement inhabited by descendants of eighteenth-century refugees from the German Palatinate, destroying three houses and damaging four others. In addition, some six protestant churches were burnt down in different Munster counties in the course of the disturbances. It is, of course, often difficult to distinguish between expressions of animosity towards protestants in general and a more specific hostility towards Orangeism or towards the financial demands of the established church: the Palatines, for example, were noted for their ultra-protestant sympathies. At the same time there seems little doubt that specific grievances were reinforced by a widespread hostility towards protestants as such. Irish protestants themselves had few doubts on the matter. 'If strong measures are not resorted to by government', Adam Clarke, the president of the Irish Methodist Conference, wrote in June 1823, 'I have no doubt that a general massacre of the protestants is at the door.'[1] Fears of rebellion and massacre reached a particular peak in the last weeks of 1824, when many protestant families barricaded themselves in their homes, fearing even to attend church on Christmas day.[2]

Why did the agrarian disturbances of the early 1820s assume this marked sectarian character? One reason, already mentioned, is the increasing antagonism aroused by the activities of preachers and other representatives of the 'second reformation'. In addition, it has been pointed out, the forces being employed to suppress the agrarian disturbances of this period—the police, the army, and the yeomanry—were all seen by large sections of the population as essentially protestant bodies, and the first two were in fact widely penetrated by Orangemen. The inevitable tensions associated with the administration of large-scale repressive measures were thus easily translated into sectarian terms.[3] The prominence of tithes among the grievances that inspired the Rockite agitation also encouraged both sides to think in terms of a religious as well as an economic conflict. There was also the impact of the economic crisis of the early 1820s. The agrarian disturbances of these years were the direct result of a further sharp fall in agricultural prices, severely affecting the living standards of large sections of the rural population. More serious still was the

[1] *The early correspondence of Jabez Bunting*, 1820–29, ed. W. R. Ward (Camden Society, 4th ser., vol. ii, London, 1972), p. 90.

[2] Reynolds, *Catholic emancipation crisis*, pp 141–3.

[3] For a detailed discussion see Donnelly, 'Pastorini and Captain Rock', in Clark & Donnelly, *Ir. peasants*, pp 127–35.

bad harvest of the autumn of 1821; the threat now was not just of increased poverty but of actual starvation.[1] Millenarianism, focusing on the prospect of a divinely ordained overthrow of the entire social and political order, is one classic response of the poor and helpless to such catastrophes as famine, war, or epidemic disease. Thus it is probably no accident that Pastorini's prophecies first began to acquire a popular following at the time of the typhus epidemic of 1816–17, and their remarkable spread through Munster and Leinster in the early 1820s can likewise be seen as a response to the desperate social conditions of those years. That popular millenarianism should have taken the precise form it did, focusing on a coming conflict between catholic and protestant in which the latter would be totally destroyed, is, of course, another matter. It is at this point that it seems most realistic to see hostility towards a supposed protestant oppressor as a permanent feature of popular attitudes in early nineteenth-century Ireland, brought to the surface rather than created by the crisis of the early 1820s.

Finally, the intensification of sectarian animosities also owed much to the revival of the campaign for catholic emancipation. Even before the appearance of a renewed catholic campaign in 1823–4, Irish protestants were being placed increasingly on the defensive by the growth of support for emancipation in British political circles and the ever more equivocal stance of the government on the catholic question. Their resentment and anxiety found expression in the appearance of a militantly protestant press. Up to the 1820s, it has been pointed out, the most successful Irish newspapers had all been favourable to catholic emancipation. Now, however, the violently anti-catholic *Dublin Evening Mail*, launched in 1823, quickly achieved a circulation three times that of any other Dublin newspaper, while the early 1820s also saw the establishment of several other militantly protestant publications.[2] At first the main targets for protestant hostility were Wellesley and Plunket, visible symbols of the government's betrayal of its Irish protestant supporters. Feeling against Wellesley, already strong at the time of the 'bottle riot' of December 1822, reached new peaks of outrage when in October 1825 he married an American catholic widow, Marianne Paterson, in a private ceremony at the viceregal lodge that was solemnised not only by the protestant archbishop of Armagh but also, subsequently, by the catholic archbishop of Dublin. A notice in the *Dublin Evening Mail* a few months later reflected the mixture of detestation and paranoia with which the Irish executive, and more particularly the lord lieutenant, had come to be regarded:

Private chaplain's office, Phoenix Park; Feb. 17, 1826. There will be a rosary at the Lodge on the evening of Monday the 20th inst. The ladies and gentlemen who attend are requested to bring their own beads.[3]

---

[1] Above, pp 71–2.
[2] Brian Inglis, *The freedom of the press in Ireland, 1784–1841* (London, 1954), pp 170–71.
[3] Ibid., p. 172.

Hostility to Wellesley continued until he left Ireland in 1828. Long before this, however, protestant anxieties had found another, even more powerful focus in the emergence of a new and unprecedentedly effective campaign for catholic emancipation.

The first step towards the revival of a catholic agitation in Ireland came in February 1823 in the form of a reconciliation between Daniel O'Connell and Richard Lalor Sheil, the chief spokesmen for the two factions into which politically minded catholics had been divided since the veto controversy had reached its climax eight years before.[1] Meeting in the house of a mutual friend, the two men agreed to put their differences behind them and to join in setting up a new political association. A preliminary meeting on 25 April was followed on 12 May by the launching of the Catholic Association of Ireland, its aim being 'to adopt all such legal and constitutional measures as may be most useful to obtain catholic emancipation'.[2] The progress of the new movement was at first unspectacular. Its membership, like that of earlier catholic bodies, was drawn exclusively from the middle and upper classes: of the 62 members enrolled at its foundation, 15 were of aristocratic or landowning families, 31 were barristers or attorneys, and 11 were merchants.[3] This small initial membership, furthermore, rose only slowly, and interest in the new society was slight; at times during the first year, it proved impossible even to find a quorum of ten for the regular Saturday-afternoon meetings. All in all, there was nothing to indicate that the new catholic body would be any more effective or formidable than its various predecessors over the last twenty years.

The turning-point in the history of the Catholic Association came in January 1824, when O'Connell introduced a new set of proposals regarding membership and finance. The original constitution had fixed a membership fee of one guinea a year. What O'Connell now proposed was the creation of a new category of associate member, for whom contributions to the association's funds could be as little as a penny a month. Such a step, he argued, would bring in much-needed money, but it would also have other advantages. By making such small but regular contributions, ordinary catholics would come to identify more closely with the association and its struggle, while the existence of a mass membership would serve to demonstrate 'that the catholic millions felt a deep interest in the cause, and that it was not confined, as is supposed, to those styled "agitators"'.[4] Both types of aim were fully realised. By June 1824 the association had issued 4,000 collector's books to agents in different parts of the country. By March 1825 the 'catholic rent', as it came to be called, had brought in £16,836, and over the period 1824–9 it was to raise over £51,000. At the same time its introduction changed the whole character of the catholic agitation.

---

[1] Above, pp 51–3, 67.
[2] Wyse, *Catholic Association*, ii, p. xxxvii.
[3] The remainder consisted of three newspaper editors, a surgeon, and a Carmelite friar.
[4] Reynolds, *Catholic emancipation crisis*, p. 16.

Throughout the country thousands of associate members were involved, by means of their regular subscriptions, in the affairs of the association; in addition, the collection of the 'rent', in small, regular payments from large numbers of individuals, made necessary the creation of local administrative machinery of a type never before developed by an Irish political organisation. In parishes everywhere, local committees were formed and officials elected to collect the rent and to forward money and accounts to the central body in Dublin. From being a caucus of Dublin-based members of the professional, commercial, and landed elites, the Catholic Association now became the focus of a popular political agitation extending across the greater part of Ireland.

The institution of the 'catholic rent' is rightly seen as a masterstroke of political strategy. Such a system of small, regular contributions was, as the under-secretary, William Gregory, observed in April 1824, 'the most efficient mode that could be devised for opening direct communication between the popish parliament and the whole mass of the catholic population'.[1] Yet the success of the Catholic Association did not depend on the rent alone. The initial period of rent collection was in fact rather short, lasting from January 1824 until the suppression of the association in March 1825: during this period one-third of the total collected between 1824 and 1829 was received. When collections resumed in 1826, receipts remained at less than a quarter of the level achieved in 1824–5, until the climax of the agitation brought subscriptions to a new peak in 1828. The institution of the catholic rent, however, was only the first of a number of strategies developed over the succeeding five years, all of them directed towards the same object, 'the improving into a more complete system of organisation the spirit which now had been so universally roused in the catholic body'.[2] In 1825 the association called on its supporters throughout the country to carry out a religious census of their parishes. The census project had the same virtues as the catholic rent: the end product, a series of figures that could be used to emphasise the disparity between the numerical superiority of Irish catholics and their very limited share of power and privilege, was valuable in itself, while the compilation of the census gave local activists a sense of unity and purpose, as well as a further stimulus to activity and organisation. In many districts, meanwhile, the launching of the catholic rent had given rise to a wider system of local organisation as the committees formed to manage its collection took on a range of other functions, organising public meetings, drawing up petitions, corresponding with the association's headquarters on a variety of local issues and grievances. In 1828 the association introduced a new and more elaborate system of local organisation, based on the selection in each parish of two churchwardens, one chosen by the parish priest, the other by the local inhabitants. These churchwardens were to be the main link between the national leadership and their local area—on the one hand, forwarding regular monthly reports to Dublin, on the other, publicising the

[1] Gash, *Mr Secretary Peel*, p. 387.   [2] Wyse, *Catholic Association*, i, 335–6.

activities of the association among their fellow parishioners. A more elaborate stage in the emergence of a new type of local political organisation was the liberal clubs that were established in some eighteen counties following the general election of 1826. In its most developed form this system, providing for county clubs that would maintain and oversee a network of local branches while themselves communicating with the central body in Dublin, provided the model for a permanent institutional link between the leaders of the Catholic Association and local supporters and activists.[1]

In practice none of the organisational innovations of the association were developed to their full potential. Thomas Wyse's account, although written in the immediate aftermath of victory, nevertheless makes clear that, right up to the end of the agitation, he and others were preoccupied by the same set of problems: the uneven progress of the agitation in different areas, its excessive dependence on the energies and ability of particular individuals, and the difficulty of maintaining in quieter times the enthusiasm evoked at moments of crisis. Yet these deficiencies are hardly surprising, given the lack of precedent for the sort of agitation that the Catholic Association was attempting to mount, and the social background against which it had to operate. The level of organisation that it did manage to achieve, moreover, in the short period of five years, marks a major step forward in the evolution of Irish popular politics.

In addition to creating an increasingly sophisticated political organisation, the Catholic Association developed other techniques to reach the mass audience that the rent scheme had first opened up to it. In particular, it devoted considerable effort—and money—to ensuring that its proceedings were fully reported in national and provincial newspapers, as well as producing its own pamphlets, handbills, and other publications. Among the duties of the church-wardens was to receive copies of the *Weekly Register*, containing detailed reports of the proceedings of the Catholic Association in Dublin, which they were to make available to their fellow parishioners and to read aloud outside catholic churches on Sunday mornings. At the peak of the agitation 6,000 copies of the *Register* were being distributed in this manner each week.[2] The association also staged regular political meetings at every level from the parish to the province, boosting the morale of local supporters and activists and helping to maintain links between the association and its mass following. By the end of the emancipation campaign, it has been estimated, at least half the parishes in Ireland had had at least one political meeting.[3] Leading figures in the agitation toured the country regularly, speaking to huge crowds in carefully orchestrated displays of unity and commitment. O'Connell in particular, already a well known orator and public figure, now established himself as the

[1] For a detailed examination of the new style of political agitation pioneered by the Catholic Association, see Fergus O'Ferrall, *Catholic emancipation: Daniel O'Connell and the birth of Irish democracy, 1820–30* (Dublin, 1985).

[2] Wyse, *Catholic Association*, i, 340.

[3] Fergus O'Ferrall, *Daniel O'Connell* (Dublin, 1981), p. 54.

undisputed leader of militant catholicism, a figure of charisma whose public appearances were major events.

A further important device adopted by the new agitation was the widespread use of the catholic clergy as local agents and organisers. The constitution of the Catholic Association had from the start included the clergy as *ex officio* members, without the need to pay the annual subscription, but few priests had in fact taken an active part in its proceedings. When the scheme for a catholic rent was first put forward early in 1824, however, O'Connell proposed that the local clergy should be asked to supervise the workings of the scheme, both as a safeguard against fraud and in order to ensure that the funds collected were not diverted to illegal or seditious organisations. Several bishops immediately endorsed the rent scheme and provided the association with lists of their parish clergy. Others had reservations about the wisdom of undertaking a mass agitation of the kind proposed, but as the popularity of the new tactics became clear they chose to keep any continuing doubts to themselves, and the association was eventually to receive at least the formal backing of the entire catholic hierarchy. The lower clergy, meanwhile, responded with enthusiasm to the request for their support. Throughout the country parish priests and curates publicised the rent scheme from their pulpits, helped to set up the committees that would organise its collection, and carried on much of the correspondence with the central body in Dublin. When the Catholic Association began to exert its influence in electoral politics, in 1826 and again in 1828, the role of the clergy was even more prominent as priests preached and spoke in support of candidates favoured by the association, directed the canvass of prospective voters, and appeared on election day itself to lead processions of their parishioners to the polling booths.

This new role as political activists was in sharp contrast to the stance adopted by the catholic clergy before the 1820s, when the political utterances of the great majority of bishops and priests had been confined to regular exhortations to their congregations to loyalty, obedience, and the avoidance of illegal associations. Many contemporaries attributed the change to the foundation in 1795 of the catholic seminary at Maynooth. Before 1795, it was claimed, the need for priests to travel to the Continent for their education had ensured both that the catholic clergy was recruited from a reasonably respectable level of society and that its members benefited from the liberalising effects of foreign residence and a university education. The Maynooth priests, by contrast, were said to be drawn from the very lowest levels of catholic society and to have been trained in an environment that reinforced rather than diluted the prejudices of their home background. Such arguments, however, were quite unfounded. Among the priests who took an active part in politics in the 1820s, as among the catholic clergy as a whole, only a minority had in fact been trained at Maynooth. In so far as there was a clear line of division, it related not to training but to age, which divided bishops and priests who retained the attitudes of a period when official toleration could not yet be taken for granted from a younger generation that had no such memories.[1] Contemporary allegations that the new breed of political priest, wielding an almost limitless tyranny over his ignorant and superstitious parishioners, was in fact the real power behind the catholic campaign were equally wide of the mark. The assistance of so many priests undoubtedly contributed significantly to the successful launching of this new form of mass agitation. The catholic clergy, after all, were not only men of considerable local influence; in addition, they were familiar through their own work with basic organisational procedures; they were more or less evenly distributed across the country; and they could, through the medium of their bishops, be more easily communicated with and mobilised than any comparable group within Irish society. Nevertheless, the most recent study has emphasised the essentially secondary role of the clergy, as assistants rather than leaders in the emancipation campaign.[2] In those cases where priests declined to take the part expected of them as local agents of the Catholic Association, furthermore, they could find themselves abused, boycotted, and in some cases even threatened with physical violence. 'The priest', Thomas Wyse observed, 'after a little time was hurried along by the torrent, and had only to decide whether he should ride on its surface or be buried altogether beneath the stream.'[3]

The achievement of the Catholic Association in mobilising the mass of the population behind its demands should not, of course, be seen in isolation. The association's campaign in 1824–9 was part of a much longer process by which, over a period of a century or more, traditional political structures were gradually undermined by the growth of popular awareness and participation. The origins of this process can be traced back to the mid-eighteenth century, when conservative politicians had first begun to complain of the growth of 'out of doors' opinion; its conclusion is probably best placed in the 1870s and 1880s.[4] Long before 1824 campaigners for catholic emancipation had sought to exploit this increasing political awareness. In particular, the summoning of the catholic convention in 1792,[5] with its delegates chosen by county electors,

---

[1] For a fuller discussion of these points see Connolly, *Priests & people in Ire.*, pp 37–47; Fergus O'Ferrall, '"The only lever . . .?": the catholic priest in Irish politics, 1823–29' in *Studies*, lxx (1981), pp 313–16, 319–20.

[2] O'Ferrall, loc. cit., pp 308–13.

[3] Wyse, *Catholic Association*, i, 283.

[4] For the growth of 'out-of-doors' opinion in the mid-eighteenth century see R. B. McDowell, *Ireland in the age of imperialism and revolution, 1760–1801* (Oxford, 1979), pp 209–10, 213. For the survival of traditional styles of political behaviour into the second half of the nineteenth century, and the case for seeing the 1870s and 1880s as marking the final stage in their decline, see K. T. Hoppen, 'Landlords, society and electoral politics in mid-nineteenth-century Ireland' in *Past & Present*, no. 75 (1977), pp 62–93; K. T. Hoppen, 'National politics and local realities in mid-nineteenth-century Ireland' in Art Cosgrove and Donal McCartney (ed.), *Studies in Irish history* (Dublin, 1979), pp 190–227; and K. T. Hoppen, *Elections, politics, and society in Ireland 1832–1885* (Oxford, 1984).

[5] Above, iv, 315–17.

themselves elected at parish meetings, had been a conscious attempt to give catholic demands the backing of a nation-wide popular movement. Even in the quieter years following the union, interest in the issue of emancipation extended beyond the catholic middle and upper classes. After the rejection of the catholic petition in 1805[1] it was noted that Grattan's speech in the commons, 'with a good likeness of him well engraved, is now printed in a sheet and sold for 6*d*.'. The same observer noted that there was also 'a good deal of discontent among the lower orders, though the decision of the house cannot affect them'.[2] By 1811–12 the catholic leaders were again thinking of bringing the pressures of mass opinion to bear on the political establishment. In January 1811 Aeneas McDonnell wrote to O'Connell from County Mayo to stress the importance of collecting the maximum number of signatures on copies of the latest catholic petition, '*particularly in the country* for ... it generates a very strong feeling of independence among the peasantry, I assure you it is scarcely credible how much it has diminished the terror of the petty tyrant in this wretched county'.[3] A few months later an attempt to repeat the tactics of 1792 by organising a nation-wide election of delegates was prevented only by the vigorous action of government.[4] When a catholic bill seemed imminent in 1813, popular feeling again ran high. Soon after news of one of the early divisions in favour of Grattan's bill reached Dublin, the lord lieutenant told Peel, 'people were employed in the streets to declare bread would be sold for almost nothing now the catholics had triumphed'.[5] Seen in this light, the mass agitation of 1824–9 was not an entirely new development, but an extension of tactics that had been at least intermittently employed over the preceding thirty years.

To say this is not to deny that the Catholic Association of the 1820s achieved a degree and extent of popular political mobilisation unequalled by any previous agitation, either for emancipation or for any other cause. Part of the credit for this must clearly go to O'Connell, whose skilful leadership and personal stature contributed greatly to the association's success. Yet skilful and even charismatic leadership would have been of little effect had not other circumstances also been favourable. In the years before 1824 a whole range of social changes had prepared the way for the introduction of the new style of mass politics represented by the emancipation campaign. The first of these was the rapid expansion of elementary education in the late eighteenth and early nineteenth centuries. Between 1806 and 1824 the number of children attending schools of different types rose from around 200,000 to over 560,000, representing 40 per cent of all children of school age. The 1841 census showed that, of the generation of school age between 1791 and 1810, 57 per cent of men and 36 per cent of women claimed to be able to read. Such a growth of a substantial literate population was important both in increasing popular awareness of political issues and in allowing the Catholic Association to make systematic use

[1] Above, pp 28–30.   [2] P.R.O.N.I., D207/33/35.
[3] *O'Connell corr.*, i, 246.   [4] Above, p. 45.   [5] Parker, *Peel*, i, 78.

of the written word—newspapers, pamphlets, and other publications—in order to keep its supporters active and informed. The progressive extension in the early nineteenth century of the knowledge and use of English was also a crucial development if large numbers of the catholic lower classes were to be induced to take a more active part in the affairs of an English-speaking political world. In other ways too the early years of the nineteenth century were a period of rapid change in Irish popular culture. By the 1820s and 1830s observers were beginning to note the disappearance or declining importance of a whole range of traditional beliefs and customs. Patterns and festivals, wake-games, belief in fairies, forms of magical healing: all were being undermined as society became more commercialised, better educated, more open to outside influences. The same social changes affected political life, steadily weakening the influence of deference, localism, and passivity. The link between the decline of traditional culture and the spread of a new style of popular politics was clear to the antiquarian John O'Donovan. Visiting County Longford in 1837, he found that the local inhabitants could no longer tell him the ancient names of the islands on Lough Ree. 'The people on this side of the lake', he commented sourly, 'know more about elections than hagiology.'[1]

The spectacular success of the Catholic Association in pioneering new techniques of mass agitation thus depended heavily on the far-reaching changes that had been taking place in the character of society. It is hardly surprising, therefore, that the impact of such techniques should have been greatest in those areas, and among those social groups, in which the processes of social change were most advanced. Support for the Catholic Association was at all times stronger in Leinster and in Munster than in Ulster or Connacht. In the period between the launching of the catholic rent and the suppression of the association in March 1825, for example, Connacht, containing about 20 per cent of the catholics of Ireland, contributed £1,408, while Munster and Leinster, with about 30 per cent each, contributed £6,571 and £7,043 respectively. A similar pattern was recorded in later years.[2] Such contrasts reflected differences in levels of literacy, in commercial development, in the extent of cultural change, and in living standards: a population living close to subsistence level, preoccupied with the struggle to survive, had neither the time nor the resources to devote to political agitation, even if they understood its language or read its propaganda. The most important difference of all, however, was in social structure. In all parts of the country it was the better-off sections of the catholic population that were the backbone of the new agitation, and whose relative strength or weakness largely dictated the extent of its success. The original concept of the very poor contributing their individual pennies to the associa-

[1] R.I.A., ordnance survey letters, County Longford, 22 May 1837. For a more detailed discussion of changes in Irish popular culture during this period see Connolly, *Priests & people in Ire.*, pp 100–20.

[2] Reynolds, *Catholic emancipation crisis*, p. 62; Fergus O'Ferrall, *Catholic emancipation: Daniel O'Connell and the birth of Irish democracy, 1820-30* (Dublin, 1985), pp 67, 317.

tion's funds has been shown by a recent analysis to have existed more often in political rhetoric and in later myth than in reality.[1] The great bulk of contributions to the catholic rent came not in pennies but in shillings, and often in pounds. The contributors, in other words, were not the labourers, cottiers, and smallholders who made up the majority of the catholic population, but rather the artisans, shopkeepers, businessmen, and professional people of the towns, and the more comfortable farmers. Of these two groups, furthermore, it was the former, the townsmen, who predominated. According to Thomas Wyse, the rent received from the towns, right up to the completion of the agitation in 1829, was double that received from the rural areas in which seven out of eight of the inhabitants of Ireland lived.[2]

These conclusions concerning the distribution of support for the Catholic Association are further borne out by the case of Ulster, where in 1824–5 contributions to the catholic rent were £1,837, a little higher than those for Connacht, but far below Leinster or Munster. In 1827, a year of lower receipts generally, Ulster contributed only £204 out of a total of £2,899. To many later writers, the failure of Ulster to contribute more substantially to the emancipation campaign has been self-explanatory: 'protestant Ulster' could hardly have been expected to warm to the Catholic Association. But this is quite misleading. More than half the population of Ulster in the first half of the nineteenth century was catholic, and the province contained around 20 per cent of the catholics of Ireland. Protestants made up a majority of the population only in four of the nine Ulster counties, Antrim, Armagh, Down, and Londonderry. Even in the latter two, furthermore, the imbalance between catholic and protestant was fairly small, and elsewhere in Ulster the relative inactivity of a majority catholic population requires some other explanation. The history of Defenderism and later of Ribbonism further confirms that the presence in Ulster of a large and hostile protestant population was not in itself sufficient to prevent catholics in the province from developing forms of collective action. A better explanation is that the catholic population of Ulster was heavily concentrated at the bottom of the social scale, among the labourers, cottiers, and small occupiers of the countryside, and the unskilled workers of the towns. In 1861 only 29 per cent of Ulster catholics were able to read and write, compared to 50 per cent of members of the Church of Ireland and 59 per cent of presbyterians. As in Connacht, the weakness of the Catholic Association reflected the depressed circumstances of the majority of its potential supporters, and the absence of those social groups—middle-class townsmen and larger farmers— that elsewhere in Ireland made up the backbone of the agitation.[3] One of the few exceptions to the general picture was the town of Newry, which even before

---

[1] O'Ferrall, op. cit., pp 65–75.

[2] Wyse, *Catholic Association*, i, 209 n.

[3] For a fuller discussion of the political development of Ulster catholics see S. J. Connolly, 'Catholicism in Ulster, 1800–1850' in Peter Roebuck (ed.), *Plantation to partition* (Belfast, 1981), pp 157–71.

the 1820s was noted as a major centre of catholic political activity. The catholics of the town were aware of their own distinctiveness: 'from their numbers, being three-fourths of the inhabitants, and from their respectability and property, [they] are the most important body of that persuasion in any town of Ulster, and therefore assumed to speak without impropriety in some degree for that province'.[1]

To say that the Catholic Association was overwhelmingly a movement of the middle and lower-middle classes, and predominantly a movement of townsmen, is not to deny that other social groups also responded to the association's campaign. A wide range of contemporary observers testified to the degree of excitement that the association generated even among the rural poor. In Connacht, where the association's formal structure was very much weaker than elsewhere, O'Connell nevertheless had a status as a popular hero possibly greater than that he enjoyed among the more politicised and sophisticated catholics of the south and east. The emancipation campaign can best be seen as having existed simultaneously at two levels. On the one hand there was the formal political machine, represented by the systematic collection of funds, the enrolment of members, the regular meetings of local activists, all dominated by the middle and lower-middle classes in alliance with the clergy. On the other there was the majority of the catholic population, only intermittently involved in the regular business of the party machine, but nevertheless fervent supporters, who could be called on as needed for meetings and demonstrations. The distinction between these two levels was neatly summed up in Thomas Wyse's observation that the collectors of the catholic rent 'became the disciplined, as the rent contributors were the irregular, troops of the association'.[2] A similar division was recognised later in the campaign. One of the duties of churchwardens, as already mentioned, was to read aloud newspaper accounts of the association's proceedings for the benefit of those who could not read them for themselves. But in the liberal clubs, the final stage in the creation of a local political organisation, membership was made up of 'the gentry, the clergymen, the reading farmers (for reading was a necessary condition for admission)'.[3]

The existence of two separate levels within the emancipation campaign, however, was not solely a matter of differences in literacy or in the degree of involvement in the details of local political organisation. The vision of emancipation that moved the mass of the catholic population was in many cases radically different from that held by the small-town notables and strong farmers who dominated the local rent committees and liberal clubs. Reports from different parts of the country spoke of the expectations that the launching

---

[1] Plowden, *History*, ii, 449. Plowden is here paraphrasing an affidavit made on behalf of the catholics of Newry in 1806.

[2] Wyse, *Catholic Association*, i, 209.

[3] Ibid., pp 343–4.

of the new agitation had raised among the rural poor: that the Catholic Association was in fact preparing the way for a new rebellion, that the 'rent' was to be
used to purchase arms, that after emancipation had been granted the land was
to be redivided.[1] Reports of this kind, some emanating from paid informers,
others from nervous officials or resident gentry, others again from politically
motivated observers who had every reason to present the association in a
sinister light, must be treated with a certain caution. But a broadly similar
picture emerges from the evidence of popular poetry and song. There emancipation was presented as the key to much wider changes in the structure of
society. The Catholic Association and its leaders were presented not as the
exemplars of a new style of democratic and constitutional agitation, but as the
champions of an oppressed Irish catholicism, who would strike down the traditional protestant enemy.[2] The growth of popular support for the Catholic Association in the second half of 1824, it has been pointed out, coincided with the
decline of the Rockite disturbances, and it is likely that for many of the rural
poor the association became the focus for energies and aspirations—and a
sense of millenarian expectancy—that had earlier been channelled into
agrarian protest.[3]

An identification of the objects of the emancipation campaign with the
practical grievances of ordinary catholics was encouraged by the association
itself. Indeed, one of the great achievements of the association's leaders was
precisely this elevation of the remaining legal and political disabilities of
catholics, matters that directly affected only the relatively small catholic middle
class and the even smaller catholic gentry, into a major popular grievance.
Where earlier agitations had confined themselves to the single issue of emancipation, the association from the start took up a much wider range of grievances.
The privileged position of the Church of Ireland; the authorities' toleration of
Orange excesses; the misuse of patronage; interference with the education of
catholic children—all became subjects of protest and propaganda. The
unequal administration of justice as between catholic and protestant was a
long-standing grievance. The Catholic Association made it a major issue,
denouncing instances of partiality on the part of magistrates and other officials,
instituting its own prosecutions against Orangemen alleged to have committed
outrages against catholics, and at one point setting up a special committee to
keep watch on the activities of the police. Such attacks on the partiality of the
legal system linked the grievances of an ambitious professional man like
O'Connell, excluded from advancement by the remnants of the penal laws, and
the problems of the lower-class catholic exposed to discrimination and harass-
ment in his daily life. In the same way attacks on the exorbitant amounts of

[1] Reynolds, *Catholic emancipation crisis*, pp 74 (n. 34), 138–9; Donnelly, 'Pastorini and Captain
Rock', in Clark & Donnelly, *Ir. peasants*, pp 135–7.
[2] Gearóid Ó Tuathaigh, 'Gaelic Ireland, popular politics, and Daniel O'Connell' in *Galway
Arch. Soc. Jn.*, xxxiv (1974–5), pp 21–34.
[3] Donnelly, 'Pastorini and Captain Rock', pp 135–7.

money extracted in tithes linked the privileged position of the Church of Ireland to the concrete economic grievances of the catholic farmer and small occupier. By these means the mass of the population was encouraged to give the removal of the remaining legal disabilities affecting catholics an importance far greater than its likely practical effects, translating emancipation into a symbol of their aspirations for an escape from poverty and subordination.

In thus exploiting the potentially explosive economic and social grievances of the catholic lower classes, the leaders of the Catholic Association were playing a dangerous game. O'Connell was not, as is often assumed, opposed in principle to the use of violence for political ends. He had, after all, fought one political duel and had sought to provoke at least one other. He had sent his son Morgan to join Simon Bolivar in the fight against Spanish rule in Venezuela, and he welcomed the news of revolt in Spain itself in 1820. Where Ireland was concerned, however, he had no doubt that any resort to force was doomed to failure. The great crime of the United Irishmen, as far as O'Connell was concerned, was that they had induced lesser men to bring disaster on themselves in a hopeless venture. In addition, propertied catholic families like the O'Connells had their own reasons to fear the likely consequences of a popular revolt. In 1803 Mary O'Connell, distressed by reports of an expected French invasion, consoled herself with the thought that Kerry was the last place an invading force would reach, and that 'the yeomanry, I trust in God, will be able to keep down the common people'.[1] A successful French invasion, O'Connell himself had noted six years earlier, would 'have shook the foundations of all property'.[2] Yet if O'Connell and the other catholic leaders were not themselves prepared to resort to violence, they were willing to make free use of the argument that violence would inevitably follow if their demands were not met. The claim that only the granting of catholic emancipation could prevent Ireland from erupting into revolt, or succumbing to foreign invasion, was a constant element in the rhetoric of the Catholic Association. At times, furthermore, such warnings became indistinguishable from threats. The classic example of the equivocal stance adopted by the catholic leaders was O'Connell's famous speech of December 1824, beginning with the hope that Ireland would never have to resort to the methods used by the Greeks and South Americans to obtain their rights, but going on to declare his wish that if Ireland were ever driven to such a revolt 'a new Bolivar' would arise to lead it. In adopting this tone, the catholic leaders took up the characteristic stance of bourgeois politicians throughout early nineteenth-century Europe, seeking to use popular discontent to further their own political aims, while at the same time holding back from the point at which that discontent would erupt into uncontrollable violence.

Although the threat represented by the new style of catholic agitation was

[1] *O'Connell corr.*, i, 102.
[2] Ibid., p. 30. See also, however, O'Connell's reaction to the battle of Waterloo (below, p. 198).

recognised from the start, the government was slow to find an effective response. Legal advice suggested that the Catholic Association did not contravene the convention act or any other existing law. To suppress the association it would thus be necessary to introduce special legislation, and this might provide the occasion for a further unwelcome debate on the wider issues of emancipation. The difficulty was compounded by the lack of sympathy and trust between Peel, now back in office as home secretary, and Wellesley. Throughout 1824 the question of whether or not the association should be suppressed was batted back and forth between Dublin and London, accompanied by veiled recriminations as each side sought to transfer to the other responsibility for the delay in acting. At the end of the year the Irish executive, acting on its own initiative, launched two simultaneous prosecutions, the first against O'Connell for his 'Bolivar' speech, the second against Sir Harcourt Lees, a prominent Orange spokesman, for a speech in which he had called on the protestants of Ulster to take up arms against the catholics. As in the past, such a policy of conspicuous even-handedness won the government no credit with any party, especially since both prosecutions ultimately failed. By this time, however, the cabinet had at length made its own decision. In February 1825 Goulburn, the chief secretary, introduced a bill declaring unlawful any body that remained in existence for more than fourteen days to seek a redress of grievances in church or state. Goulburn's bill, in effect a ban on political societies, became law on 9 March,[1] and the Catholic Association dissolved itself nine days later.

The successful passage of Goulburn's act did not, however, mean that the government could now forget the issue of catholic emancipation. Although the bill had passed the commons with a comfortable majority, this had included a number of M.P.s, in particular liberal tories, who continued to favour catholic emancipation while strongly disapproving of the methods by which the Catholic Association pursued it. The extent of continued parliamentary support for emancipation was made clear on 1 March 1825, when a motion by the veteran English radical Sir Francis Burdett, calling for a committee of the whole house to inquire into catholic claims, was carried by thirteen votes. When Burdett went on to introduce on 25 March a relief bill, the general feeling among supporters of emancipation was that this time there was a real chance of success. At the same time the emancipationists were taking no chances. In its final form, Burdett's bill, proposing the removal of the great majority of the remaining legal disabilities affecting Irish catholics, was accompanied by two important supplementary measures, which came to be known as the 'wings'. The first provided for the payment out of public funds of salaries to the catholic clergy, while the second proposed the abolition of the forty-shilling freehold franchise in county constituencies. The purpose in each case was to minimise opposition to the relief proposal; a state salary, it was argued,

[1] 6 Geo. IV, c. 4 (9 Mar. 1825).

would leave the catholic clergy both more attached to the state and less sub-servient to their congregations in political matters, while the abolition of the forty-shilling freehold franchise, the least demanding and by far the most common of the qualifications under which catholics obtained the right to vote, would create a smaller, more respectable, and more trustworthy electorate. Similar offers of 'securities' to accompany measures of catholic relief had in the past met with violent opposition from those they were supposed to benefit. In this case, however, O'Connell, who had come to London to lobby against Goulburn's bill and in support of catholic claims, announced that the 'wings' were entirely acceptable and gave Burdett's bill his full support.

The precise reasons why O'Connell accepted the 'wings' in this manner remain a matter for debate. He himself defended his decision with the claim that the proposed bill required Irish catholics to give up nothing of value. It was true that the abolition of the forty-shilling freehold franchise would reduce the electorate to a fraction of its former size: when that franchise was in fact abol-ished four years later, the number of voters fell from about 216,000 to about 37,000. O'Connell, however, argued that the forty-shilling freeholders, the poorest and least independent section of the electorate, were an impediment rather than an aid to political progress, their existence serving only to strengthen the power of the landlords who controlled their votes. As for the state payment of the catholic clergy, this would not only benefit the church but in addition 'will actually inundate Ireland with English capital'.[1] On the first of these issues, O'Connell was probably expressing a genuinely held view, one to which he was to cling until the general election of 1826 conclusively proved him wrong. Where the catholic clergy was concerned, O'Connell could correctly claim that the proposal for state salaries did not itself give the crown any power to interfere in ecclesiastical affairs. At the same time it is difficult to see how the man who had so vehemently opposed the veto fifteen years before could not have had some qualms at the possibilities thus created for future intervention by the state in church affairs. One reason why O'Connell was now prepared to compromise in exchange for a quick settlement may have been his awareness that the mass movement he had created could not be sustained indefinitely without popular excitement either fading or spilling over into violence. In addition, it should be remembered, O'Connell was at this time in London, fêted by English supporters of emancipation but cut off from his own supporters. The most straightforward explanation of O'Connell's decision, however, lies in the temptations held out by Burdett's relief bill itself. In 1825 O'Connell was fifty years old, barred by the penal laws from further advance-ment in his profession, and burdened by heavy debts. The passage of Burdett's bill would have meant a successful culmination to twenty years of political labour, and at the same time opened the way to a transformation of his personal circumstances. But whatever his precise motives, O'Connell's acceptance of

[1] *O'Connell corr.*, iii, 135.

the 'wings' was to prove a rare lapse of political judgement. This was so on two counts. In the first place, the bill, although it passed through the commons with a majority on the third reading of 248 votes to 227, was defeated in the lords by 178 votes to 130—an unexpectedly large margin, and one that allowed the government to go on ignoring the contrary verdict of the lower house. By this time, furthermore, it had become clear that O'Connell's endorsement of the 'wings' threatened seriously to damage his political standing, exposing him to bitter attacks not only in English radical circles but also among his supporters and allies in Ireland.

The passage of the unlawful societies act and the loss of Burdett's bill did not put an end to the catholic agitation. On 13 July 1825 the leaders of the movement launched the new Catholic Association, with a set of declared objects ranging from a census of the catholic population and the encouragement of a liberal education system to the promotion of public peace and harmony and the pursuit of public charity. All explicitly political business of the type prohibited in Goulburn's act was carefully excluded from its proceedings, being reserved instead for a series of aggregate meetings nominally unconnected with the association. Although the catholic leaders were able to make some political capital out of the skill and inventiveness with which a repressive measure had been circumvented, the new association was considerably more restrained than its predecessor. The collection of the catholic rent was not resumed immediately, and the proceedings in general were cautious to the point of timidity. The agitation was further weakened by the sense of anticlimax that inevitably followed the excitement of the previous twelve months, and also by the serious internal divisions that O'Connell's acceptance of the 'wings' had opened up. Eventually, drawing on his demagogic skills and on the reserves of popularity he had built up in preceding years, O'Connell was able to silence his critics and reassert his own ascendancy. Internal dissensions, however, continued throughout the rest of 1825, and even when these had subsided the agitation did not succeed in regaining its earlier momentum.

It was against this background that all parties looked forward to the general election that was expected some time in 1826. Long before the rise of the Catholic Association it had been recognised that the voting power of catholic electors was a significant force in political life. Already in 1812 the duke of Richmond found his sense of political decorum outraged by the willingness of Irish M.P.s to pander to catholic voters by supporting emancipation: 'In most English counties people are a little afraid of their constituents but here it is quite ridiculous and I must say disgraceful.'[1] On some occasions, furthermore, this catholic vote had been systematically mobilised by clergy and lay activists in support of pro-emancipation candidates. Indeed, it was one such occasion, the County Dublin by-election of February 1823, that provided part of the

[1] P. J. Jupp, 'Irish parliamentary elections and the influence of the catholic vote' in *Hist. Jn.*, x (1967), p. 193.

impetus for the launching three months later of the Catholic Association. In September 1825, despite the diminished strength of the catholic agitation, Goulburn still warned that the next election would see serious challenges to the protestant interest in Irish constituencies. The catholic leaders themselves, however, were more pessimistic. O'Connell—fortified, no doubt, by his recent clashes with critics of the 'wings'—held firmly to his view that little could be expected of the majority of catholic freeholders. As the election approached, the association issued a number of public and private letters commending some candidates to catholic voters and attacking others, but it made no plans for any more direct intervention. Instead the initiative for most of the really effective action came at local level, and even there events appear to have outstripped what was originally envisaged.

The pre-history of the electoral upheavals of 1826 is normally dated from July of the previous year, when a group of County Waterford liberals agreed to challenge the long-standing political dominance of the Beresford family in the county. Their candidate was to be Henry Villiers Stuart of Dromana, a wealthy young landowner. At this stage Stuart's supporters believed that their candidate could count on the support of a majority of the county's freeholders. Thomas Wyse, who played a prominent part in organising the campaign, later admitted that if the election had been held as originally expected in October 1825 it would have been an aristocratic contest of the traditional type, in which Stuart would have defeated the Beresford candidate 'in fair feudal lists'.[1] In fact the election did not come until the summer of 1826, and in the interval the appearance and disappearance of freeholders had transferred the advantage to the Beresfords. By this time, however, it was becoming clear that what was about to take place was not after all to be a routine clash of proprietorial interests. As the canvass progressed, freeholders who would normally have been expected to support Lord George Beresford openly declared their willingness to defy their landlords and vote for Stuart. The surge of popular enthusiasm was supported and maintained by an efficient local organisation, as Wyse transformed local branches of the Catholic Association into election committees that kept in regular touch with the central committee in Waterford city. By mid-June the progress of Stuart's campaign had impressed even O'Connell. Having earlier refused a request for financial aid, he now travelled to Waterford to lend his personal support. Once there he was left in no doubt as to the state of popular feeling. On 19 June, four days before the poll, he reported to his wife:

We breakfasted at Kilmacthomas, a town belonging to the Beresfords, but the people belong to us. They came out to meet us with green boughs and such shouting you can have no idea of. I harangued them from the window of the inn, and we had a good deal of laughing at the bloody Beresfords. Judge what the popular feeling

[1] Wyse, *Catholic Association*, i, 270.

must be when in this, a Beresford town, every man their tenant, we had such a reception.[1]

When polling began, these pledges of support were fully redeemed. Richard Power, one of the sitting M.P.s and a supporter of catholic emancipation, headed the poll with 1,426 votes. However, he was closely followed by Stuart, with 1,357 votes, while Beresford came a humiliating third, withdrawing from the contest with only 527 votes.

The Waterford campaign has been the best remembered of the contests in the 1826 general election. This was partly because the particular interest that the Catholic Association set out to challenge was such a powerful one, and partly, one suspects, because of the personal involvement of O'Connell and of the future historian of the emancipation struggle, Thomas Wyse. Election results in other counties demonstrated that County Waterford was in fact only the most dramatic example of a wider movement among catholic voters. In County Louth Alexander Dawson, introduced at the last moment as an emancipationist, defeated one of the sitting members and beat the other into second place, being enabled to do so by a widespread revolt of the county's freeholders against proprietorial control. In County Monaghan Henry Westenra defeated the strongly anti-emancipationist Charles Powell Leslie, again with the votes of large numbers of rebellious freeholders. In County Cavan an estimated 800 catholic tenants defied landlords' instructions, enabling two emancipationist candidates to mount a serious though unsuccessful challenge to the established interests. There were also victories for emancipationist candidates in the counties of Armagh, Dublin, and Westmeath, and an unsuccessful but credible challenge in County Kilkenny, although of these only the Westmeath contest appears to have involved a substantial revolt by normally obedient freeholders.

The general election of 1826 was a turning-point in Irish political history. Deference and proprietorial control were to go on playing a major role in elections for more than half a century longer, but the era of their automatic and unquestioned dominance was gone forever. In the short term, it was true, landlords in the counties affected by the freeholders' revolt could use economic sanctions to punish those who had flouted their authority. But this merely showed up even more clearly the limits of their power. The characteristic form of landlord reprisal was not, as is sometimes imagined, the wholesale eviction of disobedient tenants: since those who voted under the forty-shilling freehold qualification were by definition leaseholders, they could not in fact be evicted at will. What landlords could do was to threaten that leases would not be renewed, to withdraw privileges, and to insist on a strict performance of all covenants in a lease. Most important of all, they could unilaterally abandon the generally accepted practice by which all rents were paid six months in arrears,

---

[1] *O'Connell corr.*, iii, 248.

and instead demand immediate payment. Such a demand, while entirely legal, could cripple a small tenant. When this and other forms of reprisal were employed in the aftermath of the 1826 election, however, it soon became clear that methods more than sufficient to crush individual rebels were inadequate to deal with a general revolt. This was partly because the Catholic Association, revived by these unexpected victories, launched a new catholic rent, the proceeds of which were devoted to paying off arrears of rent suddenly demanded by vengeful landlords and giving financial aid to those otherwise penalised. But even without such intervention, landlord reprisals were not always successful. A County Monaghan landlord who distrained the cattle of tenants in arrears was eventually forced to return the animals because no one would purchase them.[1] In addition, a landlord who set out to turn the tenants on whose rents he depended into economic cripples damaged himself as well as them: it was on these grounds that the trustee of the heavily indebted Foster estates in County Louth successfully opposed proposals to call in the arrears of tenants who had voted for Dawson.[2] There was also, of course, the risk that widespread evictions and seizures of goods or livestock would lead to an upsurge of social disorder. At the same time it was not only practical considerations that made the use of economic sanctions against an entire tenant population, as opposed to isolated offenders, impracticable. Coercion on the scale seen in 1826 also undermined the paternalist notion of a set of mutually acknowledged obligations and duties, linking landlord and tenant, on which the entire political system rested. For this reason alone, coercion could never be acceptable as a long-term solution.

The electoral successes of 1826 dramatically revived the flagging catholic agitation. The catholic rent was reinstituted, liberal clubs were established in a number of counties, there was a general return of confidence and enthusiasm. Where the government was concerned, however, the elections had less impact than might at first be expected. The debate on the catholic question at Westminster is often seen as a mere adjunct to the ultimately triumphant progress of the catholic agitation in Ireland. In fact it had its own chronology, quite separate from that of extra-parliamentary events. There the real turning-point had been the introduction of Burdett's bill in March 1825. Although Liverpool and Peel had foreseen that the bill would be lost in the lords, they had expected that the margin of defeat would be so narrow that they would feel obliged to resign and make way for an emancipationist ministry. In fact the majority against had been an unexpectedly large one, removing the immediate pressure to resign. Nevertheless, for Peel and Wellington, the men who were eventually to be responsible for the granting of catholic emancipation, the events of March 1825 were decisive. Peel now came to believe that emancipation could

---

[1] Martin Cahill, 'The 1826 general election in County Monaghan' in *Clogher Rec.*, v (1964), pp 177–8.

[2] Malcomson, *Foster*, pp 311, 327–8.

not be resisted indefinitely. Since his own past stand on the matter precluded him from taking an active part in its introduction, this meant that he would at some point have to leave office while the matter was resolved. Meanwhile Wellington, taking a more pragmatic view, sought to prevent the break-up of the ministry by suggesting that the government should negotiate a concordat with the pope, whereby catholic emancipation would be granted, and the catholic church in Ireland supported out of public funds, in exchange for a measure of government control over ecclesiastical appointments. Yet, despite these conversions, there was no immediate change in government policy. After the loss of Burdett's bill Canning stated formally his view that the cabinet should no longer remain neutral on the emancipation issue. However, he was not prepared to bring about the dissolution of the ministry by pressing the matter. The outcome in Ireland of the general election may have strengthened still further the arguments of the emancipationists. In the United Kingdom as a whole, on the other hand, the result of the election was a modest but significant gain in the voting strength of the protestant party. When the question was again discussed, in March 1827, a resolution in favour of catholic claims was lost by four votes, the first such defeat in the commons since 1819. What finally broke the long stalemate between supporters and opponents of emancipation was not the pressure of events in Ireland, but rather an individual misfortune. On 17 February 1827 Liverpool, the one man who had held together a divided and fractious cabinet, suffered an incapacitating stroke; by the time of the debate it was clear that he would never be fit to resume his duties. The following month the king asked George Canning, the leading emancipationist in the cabinet, to form a new ministry.

The announcement of the new ministry on 10 April 1827 seemed at first sight to promise a major shift in policy on the catholic question. Peel, Wellington, and other prominent anti-emancipationists declined to serve under Canning, with the result that in the new cabinet supporters of emancipation out-numbered its opponents by nine to three. The former were further strengthened when a group of whigs under Lord Lansdowne joined the government. The emancipationist William Lamb (later second Viscount Melbourne) succeeded Goulburn as chief secretary, while Lansdowne later became home secretary. Yet these appearances were to some extent deceptive. Emancipation, despite the changed balance of opinion within the cabinet, remained an open question, and when Lansdowne's whigs had joined Canning's government they had done so on the understanding that he might not be in a position to take any immediate action on the matter. Whether Canning would eventually have been able and willing to coax or bully the king into giving his consent to an emancipation bill remains open to debate. As it was, he died on 7 August 1827, after only four months in office. The coalition of moderate whigs and liberal tories continued under Lord Goderich, but it was a government weakened from the start by internal dissensions. When it finally collapsed, at the beginning of 1828, the king turned to the duke of Wellington.

Wellington's cabinet, which took office on 22 January, was not firmly anti-emancipationist, any more than Canning's had been pro-emancipationist. Lansdowne, and the other whigs who had served with Canning and Goderich, returned to opposition, but Wellington also excluded the spokesmen for intransigent anti-catholicism, who had come to be known as the 'ultras'. The new cabinet in fact contained seven emancipationists and only six anti-emancipationists. The marquis of Anglesey, once considered a 'protestant' but now increasingly sympathetic to catholic claims, was appointed lord lieutenant as had been arranged under the previous ministry, with Lamb as his chief secretary. Meanwhile parliamentary pressure for a settlement of the catholic question was resumed. In May 1828 a motion in support of catholic claims passed through the commons with a majority of six votes. Peel, who had joined the cabinet as home secretary, told Wellington that in his view a settlement could no longer be deferred, and began to plan his own withdrawal from office. Wellington himself, it has been argued, by now had plans to introduce a relief measure, and some of his apparent gestures at this time towards the 'ultras' were in fact an attempt to build up a position of strength from which he could do so.[1] If this was the case, however, his actions were not so interpreted in Ireland. The Catholic Association, relatively restrained while Canning was in power, had already begun to show signs of impatience under Goderich's administration. On 13 January 1828 it organised 'simultaneous meetings' in no less than 1,600 of the 2,500 parishes in Ireland—a stunning demonstration of both organisational efficiency and popular support. Hostility to Wellington's ministry increased when the former followers of Canning withdrew in May, restoring the predominance of anti-emancipationists within the cabinet. In the reshuffle that followed, William Vesey Fitzgerald, M.P. for County Clare, was appointed president of the board of trade, and was consequently required to seek reelection. Fitzgerald was a popular landlord and a known supporter of emancipation: his appointment was in fact a gesture of conciliation. Nevertheless, the Catholic Association resolved that, as a member of Wellington's administration, he must be opposed.

The dramatic outcome of the County Clare by-election of 1828, like that of the general election two years earlier, was not the result of far-sighted planning, but rather of last-minute improvisation. At first the catholic leaders assumed that a liberal protestant would oppose Fitzgerald. They approached Major W. N. MacNamara and also, in what would have been almost as bold a stroke as that eventually fixed on, Lord William Paget, son of the lord lieutenant. However, both refused. It was only at this stage that it was suggested that Fitzgerald's rival should be O'Connell. The suggestion—originating, according to one account, in the half-joking comment of a protestant

---

[1] G. I. T. Machin, *The catholic question in English politics, 1820 to 1830* (Oxford, 1964), p. 117.

observer—was only reluctantly accepted. O'Connell's candidature was perfectly legal: catholics were excluded from parliament, not by any prohibition on their presenting themselves for election, but by the nature of the oaths required before those elected could take their seats. At the same time, such a move would be without precedent, both in the challenge it presented to the government and in what it demanded of the catholic freeholders. Once the campaign got under way, however, all doubts quickly vanished. The Clare election of July 1828 was the last and most dramatic demonstration of the control the Catholic Association exercised over its mass following. Almost as frightening, from the point of view of establishment observers, as the willingness of the freeholders to defy their landlords and vote for O'Connell was their discipline. Reports spoke of an estimated forty to fifty thousand people, many times the number entitled to vote, crowding into the town of Ennis, marshalled by officers of the Catholic Association and by their priests, refraining not only from riot and disturbance but even from liquor. In the words of Peel, 'We were watching the movement of tens of thousands of disciplined fanatics, abstaining from every excess and every indulgence, and concentrating every passion and feeling on one single object.'[1] When polling ended, O'Connell had received 2,057 votes to Fitzgerald's 982. Fitzgerald himself was unsure how he had polled even that many, since he had received the votes of scarcely any freeholders.

O'Connell's election represented the culminating triumph of the new style of popular politics that the Catholic Association had developed during the preceding five years. A broadside ballad circulated in Kilkenny combined a triumphant celebration of sectarian solidarity with an aggressive rejection of deference and subordination:

> We have good news today, says the Shan Van Vught
> And the parsons feel dismayed, says the Shan Van Vught,
> Now the Bible saints won't pray, but curse both night and day
> Since O'Connell gained the day, says the Shan Van Vught.
>
> O'Connell has an ass, says the Shan Van Vught,
> And Fitzgerald may kiss his arse, says the Shan Van Vught
> O'Connell has an ass, and he will let no one pass
> Only such as goes to mass, says the Shan Van Vught.[2]

For the government, meanwhile, O'Connell's election meant that the granting of catholic emancipation could be postponed no longer. The Catholic Association had shown that it had the ability and the will to undermine the Irish representative system. Even if the repeated election to parliament of individuals debarred from taking their seats were not unacceptable in itelf, the excitement generated by such contests would be certain sooner or later to spill

[1] Reynolds, *Catholic emancipation crisis*, p. 158, n. 111.
[2] G.-D. Zimmermann, *Songs of Irish rebellion: political street ballads and rebel songs, 1780–1900* (Dublin, 1967), p. 134.

over into open rebellion. On 1 August 1828 Wellington presented a memorandum to the king asking permission to discuss the whole question with Peel and with the lord chancellor, Lord Lyndhurst. Permission was granted and the three men quickly agreed that a catholic relief bill was now unavoidable. However, these discussions remained strictly secret. The next step was to obtain the king's consent that the question be formally discussed in the cabinet, and here Wellington was unable to make any progress. In December he faced a potentially serious embarrassment, when a private letter to the catholic archbishop of Armagh, in which he expressed his wish to see the catholic question resolved, was published in a Dublin newspaper. This was followed by a letter from Anglesey to the archbishop, also published, expressing surprise and pleasure at Wellington's change of heart. The cabinet, increasingly dissatisfied at what it saw as Anglesey's failure to deal firmly enough with the Catholic Association, had already decided that he should be replaced, and the publication of his letter led to his immediate recall. He was replaced in February 1829 by the duke of Northumberland, who had formerly opposed catholic emancipation, but now declared himself satisfied to see a final settlement of the question by parliament.

Meanwhile the state of Ireland had grown steadily more alarming. Two developments in particular had suggested that an explosion could not be held off much longer. The first was a revival of militant protestantism. Up to this point Irish Orangeism had put up a surprisingly weak resistance to the growing power of the Catholic Association. When the association was launched, Orange leaders were on the defensive, demoralised by their increasing rejection in official circles and by the knowledge that in the recent 'bottle' incident they had put themselves fatally in the wrong. In 1825 the order glumly accepted its dissolution under the unlawful societies act, and over the next three years its members remained in the background. By 1828, however, protestants both in Ulster and elsewhere had begun to build up a new organisation, the Brunswick clubs, dedicated to resisting the catholic challenge. In September open sectarian conflict was only narrowly avoided when the Catholic Association sent John Lawless on a propaganda tour of Ulster. Lawless's progress came to an abrupt halt when he and his party were confronted by a large force of protestants near Ballybay, County Monaghan, and only the intervention of magistrates and troops averted a pitched battle. Even more alarming than the revival of protestant militancy was the evidence that the Catholic Association might be starting to lose control of its own followers. During the summer of 1828 the association had organised a series of large popular assemblies, mainly for the purpose of putting an end to the feuds of local factions. These gatherings were carried on into the autumn, this time without the supervision of the association. Large bodies came together, accompanied by bands and in some cases wearing green insignia. Most of the gatherings were peaceful enough, but there were several violent clashes with troops and local protestants. Eventually the catholic leaders managed to have the processions discontinued, but government observers believed that they were no longer confident of maintaining their authority. Meanwhile more radical members of the association began to call for the adoption of bolder tactics: a commercial boycott of all who were known to oppose catholic emancipation, and an orchestrated run on the banks. To all of this, the government could respond with nothing more than preparations for an ultimate military emergency. By late 1828 25,000 of the total of 30,000 infantry in the United Kingdom were either in Ireland or at stations along the west coast of Great Britain from which they could be quickly dispatched across the Irish Sea.

The government's long and dangerous silence as to its ultimate intentions continued into 1829. The turning-point came in mid-January, when Peel agreed that he would not after all resign from office, but would remain to give the proposed emancipation bill his active support. This cleared the way for a display of cabinet solidarity sufficient to extract from George IV permission for the issue to be formally discussed in cabinet. When parliament assembled in February, the king's speech recommended that it consider the question of catholic disabilities. There was a last-minute crisis on 4 March when the king withdrew his consent to the proposed relief bill and accepted his cabinet's resignation. However, all concerned knew that there was no realistic alternative to the existing ministry, and within a few hours the consent had been renewed. Next day Peel introduced a motion for a committee of the whole house to consider the laws affecting catholics. The motion was carried by 188 votes to 160—a small house and an unexpectedly narrow margin. Thereafter, however, the combined votes of government supporters and whigs were sufficient to see the measure safely through, despite the bitter resistance of the 'ultras'. The catholic relief bill passed its third reading with a majority of 178, and had an unexpectedly easy passage through the lords. A last desperate attempt by the 'ultras' to persuade the king to withhold his consent ended in anticlimax when the planned mass demonstration attracted only derisory support, and the bill became law on 13 April 1829.[1]

The catholic relief act of 1829, compared at least with its many unsuccessful predecessors, was a relatively simple measure. Wellington's belief that it should include some guarantee of the future good behaviour of catholics, including at one point the suggestion that the laws excluding catholics from parliament should not be repealed but only annually suspended, was successfully resisted by his colleagues. The act did, it was true, contain clauses forbidding the holding of catholic religious services anywhere except in churches and private houses, and prohibiting the entry into the kingdom of members of catholic religious orders. Otherwise, however, the government was content to substitute for the former declarations against transubstantiation and other catholic doctrines a new oath in which catholics bound themselves to

[1] 10 Geo. IV, c. 7 (13 Apr. 1829).

accept the protestant succession, the existing church establishment, and 'the settlement of property within this realm, as established by the laws', as well as denying the pope's temporal jurisdiction and power to depose temporal rulers. On this basis, catholics were permitted to sit in parliament and to hold any civil or military office, other than those of regent, lord chancellor of either Great Britain or Ireland, and lord lieutenant of Ireland. The real attempt to limit the practical implications of the admission of catholics to full civil rights came in a separate bill, passed at the same time, which raised the county freehold franchise from 40s. to £10.[1]

The passage of the catholic relief act ended a controversy that had dominated British and Irish politics for over twenty years and had finally brought Ireland to the brink of renewed rebellion and civil war. But the manner in which the issue was resolved created its own problems. Supporters of catholic emancipation had long argued that the repeal of penal restrictions would remove a major cause of political discontent. To those who expressed fears for the safety of the protestant minority in Ireland, they replied that the abolition of religious distinctions would mean that the population was no longer divided along sectarian lines. Whether the granting of full catholic emancipation before 1824 would in fact have had these beneficial consequences, no one can say. As it was, emancipation was not granted: it was taken. Where reasoned argument had failed, the threat of force was allowed to succeed. In the process a large section of the catholic population received its first experience of serious political involvement in what inevitably presented itself as a religious conflict. Protestants, for their part, saw in the spectacle of an explicitly catholic mass agitation, spurred on by a rhetoric that seemed to promise much more than emancipation itself could ever bring about, a confirmation of all their worst fears concerning the ultimate nature of catholic ambitions.

Even in the short term the granting of 'catholic emancipation' did not bring political peace. Hostility between catholics and protestants, built up to new levels during the long wait for the government to declare its intentions, remained dangerously high. On 12 July 1829 Orange demonstrations in different areas were followed by serious violence. Meanwhile O'Connell and other catholic leaders had made it clear almost at once that they intended to proceed directly from emancipation to a campaign for repeal of the act of union. In addition, agrarian crime began to increase from the middle of 1829, and by the spring of 1830 a large part of the countryside was once again seriously disturbed. The resurgence of rural protest could be attributed partly to the removal of the discipline that the Catholic Association had been able to maintain during the emancipation campaign, and partly, perhaps, to disillusionment as it became clear that the aspirations to wider social change that had helped to give that campaign a popular following were not to be fulfilled. The

[1] 10 Geo. IV, c. 8 (13 Apr. 1829).

main reason, however, lay in economic conditions. Agricultural prices had once again fallen sharply, bringing hardship to all sections of the rural population and disaster to the poorest, while there had also been partial failures of the potato crop in 1829 and 1830. Once again the government was forced to make funds available for emergency relief measures. Meanwhile Peel, in consultation with Northumberland, began to plan a new package of Irish legislation. Its main elements were a police act, extending the constabulary and the professional magistracy, an education act, and the establishment of some permanent system of poor relief. Such a programme, combining provision for the more effective maintenance of order with measures of practical reform, had clear links with the approach to Irish government that Peel had sponsored as chief secretary between 1812 and 1818. To an even greater extent it looked forward to the policies that were to be adopted by later governments, including Peel's own, in the 1830s and 1840s. It was still at the planning stage, however, when Wellington's ministry fell from power in November 1830.

CHAPTER V

Poverty, population, and agriculture, 1801–45

CORMAC Ó GRÁDA

ACCOUNTS of this period are almost always coloured by its culmination in the great famine. This is easily explained: historians seek the origins of the calamity in features of the economy in preceding years. A useful economic history of the period, it seems, must be based on a model that 'predicted' the famine, or made it an increasingly 'likely' outcome. The problem with such models, however, is the assumption that what may appear inevitable after the event was also predictable before. That something like the famine was quite unimaginable to contemporaries may seem implausible to later generations, conditioned by Malthusian inference and nationalist rhetoric. But what if, on the basis of all the evidence and experience available to them, those who lived in Ireland before 1845 had predicted a disastrous famine—and acted accordingly? Perhaps then a different approach would be called for.

The famine will rightly continue to be seen as one of the main events in the history of the nineteenth-century economy. But even though the years 1801–45 were in many respects years of economic hardship and gloom, and probably of marked impoverishment for many—if not a majority—of the population, it is none the less misleading to depict them solely in terms of their disastrous finale. Such 'history written backwards' exaggerates both the difficulties facing the pre-famine economy and the extent of the failure to adjust in the face of challenge.

The early 1800s began gloomily enough, with severe food shortages in 1800–01. The succeeding war years may have been prosperous for farmers and landlords, but high food prices and the government's ravenous appetite for revenue probably increased hardship for almost everybody else. Population growth was at an all-time high, increasing labour supply and more than making up for the losses caused by enlistment. The depression in agricultural prices after the battle of Waterloo, which was exacerbated by poor potato crops and fever in 1816–18 and by the return of tens of thousands of discharged soldiers, culminated in the commercial crisis of 1820.[1]

---

[1] Above, p. 71.

'Like the salamander in fire',[1] the landed interest tended to thrive in war. After 1815 its Irish representatives seem to have regarded the two decades before 1815 as a golden age. Yet agricultural prices continued to rise relative to other prices in the long run, helping the typical farmer and landlord and prompting them to specialise in food production. Between 1815 and 1845 agricultural exports rose markedly, benefiting from an expanding and cheaper transport network and promoting the growth of ancillary industries. Flour millers, bacon curers, and butter merchants prospered, and on the eve of the famine coopers tellingly outnumbered most other skilled tradesmen. However, there is some evidence that agricultural expansion may have been tapering off before the famine.

The details of trends in the size and distribution of agricultural output are unknown, even at national level. Improvement in real terms in the lot of landlords and most farmers, with little change or deterioration for the rest, seems the most likely outcome of more knowledge of such trends. Outside agriculture, progress was made in banking, postal, and transport communications, and commercial organisation in general. The period is generally regarded as one of industrial decline, yet the timing, extent, and reasons for decline remain controversial. On closer inspection, industry's record was a mixed one; certain sectors (notably cotton and woollens) failed to keep pace with British competition, others held out or were successfully transformed from domestic to factory base. But the balance was certainly negative, and large parts of the country were 'deindustrialising' before 1845. Cotton is the best known example; others were woollens and tanning. Industrial decline and rising food exports had a common origin: the dramatic industrial expansion taking place in Britain. The abolition of separate British and Irish customs duties[2] and the assimilation of the two currencies[3] could only accentuate trends that were evident earlier.

Contemporary opinion was almost unanimous about the depth of Irish poverty. Most of the numerous travellers' accounts drew unfavourable comparisons between poverty in Ireland and in their home countries, with squalid houses and ragged clothes attracting most attention. The following excerpt from a report by Mr Twogood, a representative of the Fishmongers' Company, on conditions in the Sperrin foothills in 1820, is typical enough, though poverty was greater elsewhere.

In the course of the day we entered . . . many very wretched hovels, called cabins. The following picture will apply with variations to most of them. On entering the cabin by a door thro' which smoke is perhaps issuing at the time, you observed a bog-peat fire, around which is a group of boys and girls, as ragged as possible, and all without shoes

[1] *First report from the select committee on the state of Ireland, 1825*, p. 28, H.C. 1825 (129), viii (quoted in André J. Fitzpatrick, 'The economic effects of the French revolutionary wars in Ireland' (Ph.D. thesis, Manchester, 1973), p. 1).

[2] 5 Geo. IV, c. 22 (12 Apr. 1824).

[3] 6 Geo. IV, c. 79 (27 June 1825).

and stockings, sometimes a large pig crosses the cabin without ceremony, or a small one is lying by the fire, with its nose close to the toes of the children. Perhaps an old man is seen or woman, the grandfather or grandmother of the family with a baby in her lap; two or three stout girls spinning flax, the spinning wheels making a whirring noise, like the humming of bees, a dog lying at his length in the chimney corner; perhaps a goose hatching her eggs under the dresser; and all this in a small cabin, full of smoke, an earth floor, a heap of potatoes in one corner, and a heap of turf in another, sometimes a cow, sometimes a horse occupies a corner. In an inner room there are two or three wretched beds.[1]

Cobbett's report to his Surrey farm servant of what he found near Midleton, County Cork, in 1834 is similar, if bleaker in tone.

I went into several [hovels]. . . . They all consisted of mud walls, with a covering of rafters and straw. None of them so good as the place where you keep your little horse. I took a particular account of the first place that I went into. It was twenty-one feet long and nine feet wide. The floor, the bare ground. No fireplace, no chimney, the fire (made of potato-haulm) made on one side against the wall, and the smoke going out of a hole in the roof. No table, no chair; I sat to write upon a block of wood. Some stones for seats. No goods but a pot, and a shallow tub, for the pig and the family both to eat out of. There was one window, nine inches by five, and the glass broken half out.[2]

Remarks about housing are supported by the census of 1841, which showed that over two-fifths of all families lived in one-roomed cabins or tenements, where furniture was sparse, many lacking even bedsteads. Well documented cases of individual and family hardship abound, to shock even modern sensibilities dulled by ratios and averages. Crude contemporary attempts at drawing a rock-bottom poverty line placed two million or more (out of a total population of about seven million in 1821, or over eight and a half million in 1845) below the line, and one of the main arguments against introducing even the most niggardly of public relief schemes was that its cost would bankrupt those who had to pay for it.[3] Furthermore, by accepted criteria early nineteenth-century Ireland was very backward: it was relatively little urbanised or industrialised; it was overpopulated, in the sense that the continuing increase in population was associated with a more monotonous diet and the extension of cultivation to ever-poorer land; it was vulnerable to the ravages of diseases such as smallpox, cholera, and puerperal fever. Only a minority—37 per cent of males and 18 per cent of females—could read and write in 1841. Productivity in agriculture was low, and internal communications, though improving, were often primitive.

Yet there are grounds for believing that the situation was more complex and

[1] 'Mr Twogood's Irish journal', 1 Apr. 1820 (P.R.O.N.I., Fishmongers' Company records, Mic 9b/17).
[2] *Political Register*, 25 Oct. 1834, reprinted in Denis Knight (ed.), *Cobbett in Ireland: a warning to England* (London, 1984), p. 124.
[3] J. Stanley, *Ireland and her evils. Poor laws fully considered: their introduction into Ireland destructive of all landed interests* (Dublin, 1836).

somewhat less bleak than the bald facts would suggest. Visitors had a tendency to impose their own standards: tidy and organised themselves, they associated the prevalent lack of cleanliness with idleness and misery. In pointing to the bad clothing and housing, they often failed to note that the poor were relatively well heated and fed, since turf and potatoes were adequate substitutes—up to a point—for warm clothes, well insulated houses, and a more varied diet. The food, at least in dietary terms, was quite adequate most of the time, because in the potato the poor had chosen 'the only single cheap food that can support human life when fed as a *sole* article of diet'.[1] Moreover, although life expectancy was lower than in England, it was not significantly so: by 1840 it was forty in England and about thirty-eight in Ireland. The difference was probably more than accounted for by the higher Irish infant and child mortality. The Scandinavians and Dutch may have lived longer than the pre-famine Irish, but the French or the Germans apparently did not, and life expectancy in southern and eastern Europe was also probably lower. This point is important because economic welfare depends not just on how many potatoes or pairs of shoes one consumes annually, but on how many years are spent on such consumption.[2]

In order to overcome certain problems associated with the usual view of poverty, an alternative definition of poverty, emphasising the likelihood of disaster, has been proposed.[3] Its appeal is obvious: since Ireland was allegedly prone to subsistence crises long before 1845, it was by definition backward and poor. On the basis of such a definition, however, would one have predicted with confidence a massive crisis in the 1840s? Is there enough in the history of the years before 1845 to designate the probability of disaster in the 1840s as 'high'? The most readily available source on pre-famine subsistence crises— Sir William Wilde's report in the census of 1851[4]—was deeply influenced by the famine and created the false impression of almost annual subsistence crises before 1845. But the 1851 report must be compared with Wilde's 1841 report,[5] in which starvation and famine-related mortality are hardly mentioned. Indeed, Wilde's quantitative evidence for the ten years ending 6 June 1841 suggests that more people died from drowning (7,072), intemperance (1,239), suicide (792), or even from the hangman's rope (197) and accidental poisoning (139), than from starvation (117). This evidence almost certainly underestimates the numbers perishing from starvation; starvation moreover was rarely the immediate cause

[1] Stanley Davidson and Reginald Passmore, *Human nutrition and dietetics* (2nd ed., Baltimore, 1963), p. 285, quoted in Joel Mokyr, 'Irish history with the potato' in *Ir. Econ. & Soc. Hist.*, viii (1981), p. 10.

[2] E. A. Wrigley and R. S. Schofield, *The population history of England: a reconstruction* (London, 1982), pp 235, 529; Jacques Dupâquier, 'Population' in *New Camb. mod. hist.*, xiii, 105–8; P. P. Boyle and Cormac Ó Gráda, 'Fertility trends, excess mortality, and the great Irish famine' in *Demography*, xxiii (1986), pp 543–62; Dan Usher, *The measurement of economic growth* (Oxford, 1980), pp 223–58.

[3] Joel Mokyr, 'Industrialisation and poverty in Ireland and the Netherlands' in *Journal of Interdisciplinary History*, x (1980), pp 429–58.

[4] *Census Ire., 1851*, pt v, vol. i [2084-I], H.C. 1856, xxix, 261; vol. ii [2084-II], H.C. 1856, xxx, 1.

[5] *Census Ire., 1841*, pp i–lxxxiv [504], H.C. 1843, xxiv, 599–688.

of death in famines: during the great famine ten times as many deaths were attributed to 'fever' as to starvation. Wilde's 1841 report does not touch on famine mortality, even broadly defined. Admittedly, reliable figures on the subsistence crises of 1800–45 are lacking. Those of 1800–01, 1816–18, 1822, and 1831 are best known, and an excess mortality of 65,000 for what was probably the most serious of them, that of 1816–18, has been suggested. Even if this figure is somewhat short of the mark, excess mortality must have been far less than the normal natural increase and, more significantly, proportionately far less than the excess deaths recorded in several parts of Europe in the same years. The toll of 1816–18 was also probably *less* than that of several mid- and late eighteenth-century crises in Ireland.[1]

Other pieces of information point in the same direction. First, the results of a special poor inquiry questionnaire of 1835–6 on famine deaths are strongly negative, for only a handful of the many hundreds of answers mention cases of starvation during the previous decade or more.[2] Secondly, literary evidence for high mortality before 1845 is lacking. The sharp contrast between, for example, William Carleton's earlier writings and his *Black prophet*, written during the famine but recalling the year 1817 in his native Tyrone, is striking. The same is true of Trollope's Irish work. In sum, evidence that life was becoming progressively more precarious in the pre-famine decades is scarce, no matter how persuasive the retrospective case for it.

Yet this alternative definition of poverty takes into account one feature of Irish agriculture in this period that might be said to have invited disaster in the long run—the heavy dependence on potatoes.[3] At first the potato had added variety to the food of all classes and reduced the risk of subsistence crises, but by 1800 it had become both the staple food of the poor and the linch-pin of the whole system of tillage, without which corn-growing on a large scale would not have been possible. For the bottom third or so of the population, adult male consumption reached 12 lb daily, and access to alternatives had greatly diminished or disappeared. Pigs, hens, cows, and horses competed with humans for potatoes, and according to P. M. A. Burke, one-half of the crop was destined for fodder in the early 1840s.[4] Given the non-storability and high transport cost of the potato, the ultimate vulnerability of the system is striking in retrospect.

---

[1] Cormac Ó Gráda, 'Malthus and the pre-famine economy' in Antoin Murphy (ed.), *Economists and the Irish economy from the eighteenth century to the present day* (Dublin, 1984), pp 81–5; John D. Post, *The last great subsistence crisis in the western world* (Baltimore, 1977), pp 108–22; T. P. O'Neill, 'Fever and public health in pre-famine Ireland' in *R.S.A.I. Jn.*, ciii (1973), p. 10. Wilde's account of earlier famines was reproduced verbatim by O'Brien, *Econ. hist. Ire., union to famine*, pp 224–31. Some of the points made in this and the following three paragraphs are set out more fully in my 'Bochtaineacht, beatha, agus bás in Éirinn roimh an ngorta', to appear in *Studia Hib.*

[2] *Poor inquiry*, app. A, supp.

[3] Above, iv, 163, 164–6.

[4] P. M. A. Bourke, 'The use of the potato crop in pre-famine Ireland' in *Stat. Soc. Ire. Jn.*, xxi, pt 6 (1968), pp 72–96; P. M. A. Bourke, 'The potato, blight, weather, and the Irish famine' (Ph.D. thesis, N.U.I. (U.C.C.), 1965).

Yet although evidence on pre-famine yields is elusive, the potato's defenders, such as Mountifort Longfield and Maria Edgeworth, stressed its general reliability. Its yields, they claimed, varied no more than those of oats; and pigs were simply stored-up potatoes.[1]

In sum, then, nothing that happened to the potato before 1845 presaged the three annual failures of the late 1840s. The blight spelt disaster; but if the poor of any other European nation had lost their staple crop for several years in succession, disaster would have followed. The decline in starvation before 1845 may well reflect the increasing effectiveness of charity and bureaucracy in coping with ordinary bad harvests. But the potato failure of 1845–8 was much more drastic (output was only one-tenth of its normal level between 1846 and 1848) than the 50 per cent shortfall in a single year that was the traditional measure of subsistence crises in early modern Europe. In the circumstances non-storability was almost irrelevant, because no food producers would have anticipated such a massive and sustained failure. The undoubted problems facing the economy of Ireland in the early nineteenth century provided no inkling of what was to occur in the late 1840s.

At the height of the famine over three million people were seeking relief in the workhouses and soup kitchens. This was close enough to the number relying mainly for their subsistence on the potato, or living in 'fourth-class' accommodation (one room per family). These were the 'poor', landless labourers and their families for the most part, earning in cash and kind a family income of perhaps £15–20 a year. How much better off were the remaining better-off five million? Assuming a mean household size of five, the total income of the three million 'poor' amounted to between £9 million and £12 million. A tentative estimate of national income around 1840—say £80 million—highlights the extent of inequality, showing that the poorest 40 per cent of the population got 10–15 per cent of national income. Nevertheless, the distribution of income in pre-famine Ireland was no more unequal than that found in modern under-developed countries.[2] The £12 million in rents paid annually to about 10,000 landlords was the most visible feature of this inequality. The status and wealth of those in between—farmers, skilled and white-collar workers, the professional and mercantile classes—have been little studied. That a leading Dublin surgeon might earn £5,000 a year (certainly at least £200,000 in today's money), or that even ordinary merchants and small businessmen gave their daughters dowries of several hundred pounds, suggests a prosperous middle class. Among labourers it was widely noted that skill differentials were greater in

---

[1] Elizabeth Hoffman and Joel Mokyr, 'Peasants, poverty, and potatoes' in Gary Saxonhouse and Gavin Wright (ed.), *Research in economic history: supplement 3. Technique, spirit, and form in the making of the modern economics* (Greenwich, Conn., 1983), pp 115–45; Joel Mokyr, 'Uncertainty and pre-famine Irish agriculture' in T. M. Devine and David Dickson (ed.), *Ireland and Scotland, 1600–1850: parallels and contrasts in economic and social development* (Edinburgh, 1983), pp 92–4.
[2] T. P. O'Neill, 'Poverty in Ireland, 1815–45' in *Folklife*, xi (1974), pp 22–33; T. P. O'Neill, 'Clare and Irish poverty' in *Studia Hib.*, xiv (1974), pp 7–27; Mokyr, *Why Ire. starved*, pp 10–11.

Ireland than in Britain. Differences in the size of holdings and unequal access to land for tenants were also important features of life. Some 150,000 'strong' farmers controlled almost one-half of the land and an even higher proportion of the better land. Those same farmers owned in addition over one-half of the country's entire livestock capital. Yet while a situation like that in the midland barony of Ballybritt, King's County, in 1821, where seventy-four farmers held as much land as the remaining 1,008, might 'seem almost conducive to revolution', property relations were not radically questioned.[1]

Between 1800 and 1845 male employment on the land rose from slightly less than 1,000,000 to 1,700,000. The 1841 census prompts the following rough socio-economic breakdown.

Size of farms and share of land

class		size of farm (acres)	numbers	total land held (millions of acres)	percentage of total land held
I	landlords		10,000	3.5	17.5
	farmers:				
II	rich	80	50,000	4.0	20
III	comfortable	50	100,000	5.0	25
IV	'family'	20	250,000	5.0	25
V	poor peasants	5	300,000	1.5	7.5
VI	labourers, etc.	1	1,000,000	1.0	5

Those in the first three classes farmed most of the land; they were also substantial employers of labour from the poor peasants and labourers. Farmers with fifty acres or more enjoyed living standards far removed from the cottiers'; they ate well, and the famine passed them by largely unscathed. At the very top of the farming community in the 1840s stood some 7,000 farms of over £100 valuation, identified by Thomas Jones-Hughes.[2] Nearly half were located in Ireland's 'home counties' (Dublin, Kildare, Louth, Meath, and Westmeath). Thinner concentrations were found in the rest of Leinster, east Munster, and east Connacht. Not surprisingly, there were very few in Kerry or Mayo, and none in Connemara; more interesting was their scarcity in Ulster.

In terms of income, poor peasants and labourers overlapped considerably. Farmers who neither hired labour nor were hired out ('family' farmers, or those

[1] Lee Soltow, 'Age and economic achievement in an Irish barony in 1821' in *Explorations in Economic History*, xviii (1981), p. 393.
[2] Thomas Jones-Hughes, 'The large farm in nineteenth-century Ireland' in Alan Gailey and Daithi Ó hÓgáin (ed.), *Gold in the furze: studies in folk tradition* (Dublin, 1982), pp 93–100.

with 20 acres) were relatively few in pre-famine Ireland. The 1,300,000 who depended at least in part on hiring out were also involved in seasonal migration to Britain, in fishing, and in textile production; their stake in the land and in livestock capital was small. Conacre, a form of annual subletting of small, sometimes well fertilised plots of land, adapted the prevailing system of tillage to their poverty, but was a constant source of friction too. It made the labourer 'a commercial speculator in potatoes', mortgaging his labour against manure and seed, and paying the debt to the farmer by working for a certain number of days at an agreed rate. The conacre system grew up with tillage, and many graziers were drawn to it by high prices in the war years. Two examples of the system at work in Louth in 1808 and 1842 are reproduced below.

County Louth farmer's accounts with two cottiers, 1808/9 and 1842/3 [1]

A 1 May 1808–30 Apr. 1809

allowed to cottier	£. s. d.	value of labour	£. s. d.
balance br. forward	0.16. 9½	262 days at 7d.	7.12.10
6 barrels of coal	0.14. 2		
house, cow, and garden	3.10. 0		
one rood for flax	2. 0. 0		
9 perches potato land	0. 9. 0		
cash	0. 2. 0		
balance due	0. 0.10½		
	7.12.10		7.12.10

B 1 May 1842–30 Apr. 1843

allowed to cottier	£. s. d.	value of labour	£. s. d.
potato seed	3.15. 0	balance br. forward	2. 1. 3½
cash	2. 5. 6	277 days at 10d.	11.10.10
meal	1. 1. 3	balance cr. forward	3. 6. 9½
coal	0.15. 4		
furze	1.18. 0		
pig	0.13. 0		
cart and horse (1½ days)	0. 3. 0		
potato land	4. 1. 6		
house & garden	2. 0. 0		
misc.	0. 6. 4		
	16.18.11		16.18.11

[1] Based on P.R.O.N.I., D2738/1.

The plight of labourers' households has already been mentioned. Though their diet shielded them as a rule against ailments such as scurvy and ophthalmia (common enough among the poor elsewhere), they nevertheless had to withstand food shortages. To argue that the incidence of famine has been exaggerated is not to deny the occasional existence of partial failures and seasonal fluctuations in the availability of food, which, it is sometimes urged, were powerful enough to reduce workers' productivity in the early summer months.[1] The poor were the focus of much comment and of private charity, but public charity was far from generous. Though the government might ensure that few died of famine-induced starvation, the attitude to everyday destitution was tightfisted and dogmatic.[2] Ratepayers' greed and a strict application of the principle of 'less eligibility' combined to ensure that few of the new workhouses constructed after 1838 filled up before the great famine.[3] One long list of those relieved in the winter of 1844 suggests that only cases of extreme hardship or imminent death were admitted, or sought admission to the workhouse. A few examples help make the point.

Abbeyleix union: John Sinnott, aged 54; R.C.; stuff-weaver; married; ejected from farm; admitted (with wife and four children) 11 January, by board of guardians; himself bodily infirm, cripple, and bent together with pains in his limbs, the rest healthy; bad clothes; in want of food; emaciated looking; present condition, all healthy, but husband in bad health (will not recover).

Antrim union: Jane Barron, aged 32; presb.; married; deserted by husband; admitted by warden, 18 January; bodily infirm; out of health; ill clothed; conveyed seven miles to the workhouse (since dead).

Athy union: Mary Fitzpatrick, aged 55; R.C.; servant; widow; admitted by board of guardians 16 January; bodily infirm; cripple; in rags and filthy; present condition, in bad health; in idiot ward.

Bailieborough union: Edward Reilly, aged 70; R.C.; labourer; widower; admitted 11 March by board of guardians; hungry, dirty, and nearly naked; present condition, in good health.

Ballina union: Betty Deignan, aged 70; R.C.; married; no children alive; admitted by board of guardians, 22 January; bodily infirm; a cripple, came in a barrow; sickly and weak; in want of care; good clothes; present condition, in bad health; in infirm ward; her husband turned her out; she lived in a cabin, and got 1*s.* per week from her step-daughter; her husband is in the Marshalsea.[4]

For the rural poor, during spring and harvest full employment was fairly regular. Though underemployment at other times must have been exacerbated

---

[1] J. S. Donnelly, jr (ed.), 'The journals of Sir John Benn-Walsh relating to the management of his Irish estates, 1823–64' in *Cork Hist. Soc. Jn.*, lxxix (1974), p. 101.

[2] Above, pp 61–2.

[3] Below, pp 225–8.

[4] *Appendices A to C to the tenth annual report of the poor law commissioners*, pp 236–8 [589], H.C. 1844, xix, 254–6.

by the decline of domestic industry, the outsider's image of the poor, with 'indolent pertinacity', 'squatting leisurely among the potatoes' is no longer credible. The mainly seasonal character of unemployment is borne out by wage rates: the diary of Amhlaoibh Ó Súileabháin, for example, shows great fluctuations from month to month in the wages of casual labourers around Callan. Thus, though some of Callan's poor in late July 1830 were 'ag briseadh cloch ar tri pingine san ló .i. tri pingine ar carnan, ualach tri ccapall, do bhriseadh' (breaking stones at 3d. a day, that is at 3d. for breaking a heap of stones containing three horse-loads) by mid-August it was 'da tuistiun sa lo ag spailpinighe bochta' (poor migratory labourers have 8d. a day) and by late August 'cuig pingine deag sa lo do lucht corain' (15d. a day to sickle men).[1] Such evidence lends little support to underconsumptionist or 'glut' analyses of unemployment. That the scarcity of capital and land depressed the average and marginal product of labour, producing population pressure, is a different point.

The regional distribution of poverty was also important, being reflected in sharp educational and occupational contrasts. In 1841 Wicklow and Wexford, for example, had proportionately about twice as many boot- and shoemakers and three times as many carpenters as Mayo or Kerry, as well as literacy rates that were twice as high. Armagh had the highest population density, and agricultural holdings there were small (as throughout much of Ulster), yet its prosperity around 1801 could be seen 'even in the countenances of the dogs and cats'.[2] In the absence of regional cost-of-living figures, wage statistics are difficult to interpret with precision but seem to point in the same direction. The regional poverty pattern implied by sources such as the 1841 census is a good predictor of the distribution of excess mortality in 1846–9.

The degree of inequality seems to have grown between 1801 and 1845. As argued later, the real income of landlords and of farmers paying less than a full economic rent rose, but the condition of the poor almost certainly worsened. Mokyr's attempt to measure changes from contemporary subjective evaluations indicates a decline in the welfare of the poor in all counties except Wexford and Wicklow after 1815.[3] Taxation, which increased dramatically between 1801 and 1815 owing to war, and thereafter rose in line with population, may have increased inequality, but the main burden probably fell on the middle classes. By borrowing and increasing the national debt, Ireland avoided income tax—'the tax that beat Napoleon'—until 1853. The food, clothes, and housing of the poorest were kept free of tax, but the amalgamation of the exchequers in 1817 meant even higher rates on commodities such as tea, sugar, tobacco, and malt. The vocal middle-class opposition to tithes and poor rates

---

[1] *Cinnlae Amhlaoibh Uí Shúileabháin*, ed. Michael McGrath (4 vols, London, 1936–7), ii, 312–15, 328–9, 334–5.
[2] Letter from Thomas Mills, M.S., to Michael Mills, Loughbrickland, Co. Down, Aug. 1805 (Royal College of Physicians of Ireland, Dublin; Kirkpatrick MS 94).
[3] Mokyr, *Why Ire. starved*, p. 12.

in the 1830s and 1840s is a fair guide to the incidence of those contentious burdens.[1]

POPULATION reached a peak, probably at over 8,500,000, in 1845. It had risen by four-fifths in the previous half-century and had quadrupled since the catastrophe of 1740–41.[2] Nowhere else in Europe, with the possible exception of Finland, had growth been more rapid in those years. In both England and Scotland, for instance, the increase in the century before 1850 fell short of 200 per cent; in France it was only 50 per cent. The Irish population increase of the century before 1845 can rarely have been matched anywhere else in Europe. Between 1801 and 1845, however, if recent revisions of tax-related and censal estimates are reliable, the rate of increase was slackening.[3] The figures suggest a fall in the annual growth rate from 1.6 per cent between 1791 and 1821 to 0.9 per cent between 1821 and 1831 and 0.5 per cent in 1831–45. Growth was fastest in Munster and Connacht, indeed twice as fast as in a large diamond-shaped area to the east, bounded by Dublin, Derry, Athlone, and Waterford.

Why did population increase? Some of the best Irish economic historiography has been concerned with population, and explanations for this dramatic demographic performance are not lacking.[4] To the extent that population change was characterised by substantial regional variations, broad explanations are perhaps inappropriate. The eclectic model, however, emerging from long debate on the subject, deserves to be explained briefly. This model emphasises the role of food supply both in preventing and moderating subsistence crises and in facilitating earlier marriages and high marital fertility. It seems that early marriage had long been a feature of Irish society; the point here is that an elastic food supply kept the age at marriage from rising during the eighteenth century in the face of increasing population. During the years of rapid growth before 1801 the average age at which women married may well have been below the range allowed for by John Hajnal's 'European marriage pattern'.[5]

While age at marriage in Ireland was low, marriage fertility was apparently high. Unfortunately the figures needed to track the trend over time are unavail-

[1] A. J. Fitzpatrick, 'The economic effects of the French revolutionary wars in Ireland' (Ph.D. thesis, Manchester, 1973); Trevor McCavery, 'Finance and politics in Ireland, 1801–17' (Ph.D. thesis, Queen's University, Belfast, 1981), pp 215–23; David Dickson, 'Taxation and disaffection in late eighteenth-century Ireland' in Clark & Donnelly, *Ir. peasants*, pp 47–9.

[2] Above, iv, 146–7.

[3] See Stuart Daultrey, David Dickson, and Cormac Ó Gráda, 'Eighteenth-century Irish population: new perspectives from old sources' in *Jn. Econ. Hist.*, xli (1981), pp 601–28, and J. J. Lee, 'On the accuracy of pre-famine Irish censuses' in J. M. Goldstrom and L. A. Clarkson (ed.), *Irish population, economy, and society* (Oxford, 1981), pp 52–6.

[4] Above, iv, 159–63.

[5] John Hajnal, 'European marriage patterns in perspective' in D. V. Glass and David E. C. Eversley (ed.), *Population in history* (London, 1965), pp 101–43. For a recent survey of pre-famine population history see Joel Mokyr and Cormac Ó Gráda, 'New developments in Irish population history, 1300–1850' in *Econ. Hist. Rev.*, 2nd ser., xxxvii (1984), pp 473–88.

able. The high fertility has been variously explained. Economic explanations concentrate on the 'trivial expense' of extra children or on their investment value as future workers. The solvency of rural families, Newenham remarked in 1805, was 'always justly measured by the number of working hands ... four stout labourers being esteemed, in Ireland, equivalent to a considerable capital'.[1] Social historians refer to the prevailing taboo against contraception; even the fecundity-enhancing power of the potato has been suggested as a factor.[2]

The post-union decline in the rate of increase was probably achieved without a decline in life expectancy. Even if pressure on the food supply tended to increase mortality, the reduction in child mortality during these years should have offset this. Most of the decline in the growth rate was attributable to emigration, which increased dramatically after 1815.[3] But there is also evidence that the 'preventive check' was at work. In Dublin, for instance, the mean marriage age of working-class women rose by about 1.5 years between 1811 and 1841—quite an impressive change. A study of pre-famine Killashandra reports a similar rise.[4] An indirect approach, using the demographic technique of backward projection on available census and emigration figures for 1821 and 1841, gives the same results for the whole country, suggesting a fall in the birth rate of almost 10 per cent, from about 42 to 38 per thousand, between 1821 and 1841. As a consequence of demographic adjustment, the Irish were not by 1841 the early marriers of popular belief. The mean marriage age for women ranged from about 23 years in rural Connacht to perhaps 24.5 years in Leinster. Moreover, the proportion of the population that never married—over one in ten—was about as high as in England, Scotland, or France.

Elsewhere in western Europe population growth after 1800 was usually accompanied by massive urbanisation. In Ireland this was not so: according to both the 1821 and 1841 censuses, only about one-eighth of the population lived in towns or cities of 1,500 or more. Even if one allows for Dublin, still a big city by the standards of the day, Ireland remained one of the least urbanised countries in western Europe. Dublin itself was relatively small as a premier city, containing less than 3 per cent of the population in both 1801 and 1841. There were no other cities of even 100,000, though both Belfast and Cork had exceeded 80,000 by 1845. The slow pace of urbanisation, given low agricultural productivity, might be seen as a symptom—though hardly a cause—of economic backwardness. True, Irish towns, like towns elsewhere, attracted migrants from rural areas, some of whom lodged in the most wretched quarters

[1] Thomas Newenham, *A statistical and historical inquiry into the progress and magnitude of the population of Ireland* (London, 1805), pp 18–22.
[2] Michael Drake, 'Marriage and population growth in Ireland, 1750–1845' in *Econ. Hist. Rev.*, 2nd ser., xvi (1963), pp 311–13.
[3] Below, pp 120–22.
[4] Kevin O'Neill, *Family and farm in pre-famine Ireland: the parish of Killashandra* (Madison, 1984), pp 177–86.

in the vain hope of getting a day's work. But the real *bidonvilles* of the pre-famine Irish were Manchester and Glasgow rather than Dublin or Cork.

The course of Irish population growth before 1845 has often been seen as confirmation of the Malthusian 'principle of population', and the famine itself as the 'positive check' that inevitably follows when the population outstrips the food supply. Surprisingly, perhaps, Malthus paid little attention to the case-study on his own doorstep; yet in 1827 he effectively ruled out the prospect of population adjustment of the type here described before the select committee on emigration: 'Prolificness, and the causes that prompt to marriage, are likely to be the same, but, in all probability, the mortality is greater.'[1] He erred in this assertion: on the eve of the famine the Irish were already practising or at least moving towards the kind of moral restraint that he would have heartily approved but never gave them credit for.

SUSTAINED mass emigration, largely financed by the families of those who left, was a form of preventive check not envisaged by Malthus. That emigration was already substantial in the years between Waterloo and the famine is nowadays universally conceded. Yet the reluctance or inability of the Irish to leave in still greater numbers for distant lands before 1845 remains an important historiographical theme, and the image of peasant multitudes clinging to home, 'like sailors to the mast or hull of a wreck', is given point by the numbers that died during the famine. Nevertheless, by contemporary standards the pre-famine exodus was unparalleled, and it was probably unprecedented. Indeed, between 1815 and 1845 alone Ireland may have provided over one-tenth of all those who had voluntarily crossed the Atlantic since Columbus. Many accounts of the period stress, it is true, the inability of the poor to afford the crossing. But the 'full price' of the crossing, in which the fare counted for less than income forgone by emigrants in transit or seeking employment on the other side, equally deterred millions in other parts of Europe.

In all, well over one and a half millions left Ireland permanently between 1801 and 1845. The United States and Canada together took about 900,000, and Britain most of the remainder. Little movement occurred during the French wars, when official hostility and cumbersome regulation acted as deterrents, but the rate of emigration rose after 1815 and in the early 1840s was greater than ever before. By then emigration was removing one-half or more of the natural increase.[2] In addition, the disproportionate share of young adult males in the emigrant ranks promised to reduce marriage and birth rates further. This

[1] *Third report from the select committee on emigration from the United Kingdom, 1827*, p. 311, H.C. 1826–7 (550), v, 533.
[2] Maldwyn A. Jones, 'Ulster emigration, 1783–1815' in E. R. R. Green (ed.), *Essays in Scotch–Irish history* (London, 1969), pp 46–68; William Forbes Adams, *Ireland and Irish emigration to the New World* (New Haven, 1932); Cormac O Gráda, 'Across the briny ocean: some thoughts on pre-famine emigration to America' in T. M. Devine and David Dickson (ed.), *Ireland and Scotland, 1600–1850: parallels and contrasts in economic and social development* (Edinburgh, 1983), pp 118–30.

feature of the exodus runs directly against the Malthusian presumption that emigration leaves a 'vacuum' that the remaining population soon fills.

Through the study of such sources as passenger lists and emigrants' letters, the emigrants' profile is gradually becoming clearer. Before the famine emigrants were more likely to have been children, men, or members of a family group; they were also more likely to be drawn from the east and north of Ireland. The passenger lists also show that the female and 'unaccompanied' components, and the share from the poorer counties, were rising. The occupational structure of that portion of the American emigration can also be traced: the passenger lists suggest a largely proletarian outflow, the proportion of skilled workers being scarcely larger than in the population as a whole. Over two-thirds of those who went to New York and Boston in the 1820s and 1830s were labourers or displaced textile workers, and only one-sixth were artisans.

Government policy before 1845 did little directly to assist emigration. While Wilmot Horton, an ardent advocate of emigration, was under-secretary of state at the colonial office (1821–8) subsidised experiments were carried out, involving in all about 3,000 Irish emigrants. The first of these was something of an embarrassment, for the speculator engaged by the government to bring a shipload of indentured workers and their families to the Cape Colony in 1823 was a profiteer. Horton's other experiments were more successful. They were carried out in an area of north-west Cork that had experienced large-scale agrarian unrest in 1821–3.[1] With the aid of landlords, Horton's agent, Peter Robinson, selected and moved hundreds of young landless families, including potential and suspected troublemakers, to sparsely settled parts of Upper Canada (Ontario). Highly publicised at the time, the schemes were not continued. The 1828 passenger act,[2] prepared by William Huskisson and Horton, proved an enduring contribution. This piece of deregulation contained some consumer safeguards and helped to keep fares as low as the transport technology of the day permitted. Though Archbishop Whately's poor inquiry report of 1835–6[3] urged additional subsidised emigration, and though the Irish poor law of 1838 made provision for local spending, emigration continued to be financed primarily by the emigrants and their families.[4]

The advantages and disadvantages of emigration sparked off a vigorous debate that has proved lasting. Supporters invoked the law of diminishing returns and the authority of orthodox political economy. For them the size and persistence of voluntary emigration were ample proof that both those who went and those who remained benefited. Opponents drew attention to the allegedly high quality of the emigrants. The outflow of human capital—brains, skills, or

[1] Above, pp 71–2.
[2] 9 Geo. IV, c. 21 (23 May 1828).
[3] Below, pp 226–7.
[4] Wendy Cameron, 'Selecting Peter Robinson's emigrants' in *Social History/Histoire Sociale*, ix (1976), pp 29–46; H. J. M. Johnson, *British emigration policy, 1815–30: shovelling out paupers* (Oxford, 1977); MacDonagh, *Pattern of govt growth*; below, pp 599–602.

simply bone and sinew—could have hurt those who stayed. But this effect must be considered in conjunction with the likely surrender by emigrants of customary claims to land and other fixed property. The passenger lists, admittedly a poor guide, tell little about the quality of pre-famine emigration, suggesting that those leaving were no more numerous or skilled than the population at large. But the lists cannot identify those with 'drive' or 'risk preference', qualities allegedly in short supply in the post-famine period at least. A further consideration, stemming from the self-selective character of the emigration, is its age structure. Since those who emigrated tended to be in the prime of life, 'ready-made adults' for their country of destination, the cost of their upbringing may have fallen on the shoulders of those who stayed at home—unless remittances made up the deficit. Recent research into this possible source of loss from emigration in the pre-famine period suggests an annual cost of 1 or 2 per cent of national income. For a faltering economy such a loss was significant, but was probably outweighed by other benefits of emigration.[1]

ANY survey of the economy on the eve of the famine must start with agri- culture. To the outside expert of the day, inured to controversy about liquid manure, clay pipe drainage, and steam ploughing, the quality of Irish farming was far from impressive. Unfortunately this period is almost a statistical dark age as far as agriculture is concerned: Ireland's agricultural statistics did not begin until 1847. Nevertheless, with the help of the 1841 census and other sources, a reasonably detailed estimate of output may be pieced together here. These figures form the main basis for an appraisal of pre-famine agriculture. The major contribution made by the potato—about one-fifth of total output—comes as no great surprise. More striking, perhaps, is the massive role of tillage crops generally: claims of a pre-famine shift to pasture notwithstanding, tillage commodities still accounted for almost two-thirds of output in the early 1840s. Potato and grain used as fodder also generated a substantial share of the value of livestock. A corollary of this was a landscape radically different from today's. 'The view presented by the country in the months of July and August', one observer remarked in the 1830s, 'is an interwoven patchwork of potatoes, wheat, barley, and oats, with so little intervention of meadow and pasture, that one is surprised how the in- habitants contrive to maintain their cows, horses, and sheep.'[2] The table also confirms the generally high level of commercialisation in farming: since potatoes and oats were the only major subsistence items, and since two-fifths

[1] Black, *Econ. thought & Ir. question*, pp 203–38; Joel Mokyr and Cormac Ó Gráda, 'Emigration and poverty in pre-famine Ireland' in *Explorations in Economic History*, xix (1982), pp 360–84.
[2] Horatio Townsend, 'On the improvement of Irish agriculture' in *Quarterly Journal of Agricul- ture*, i, no. 3 (1829), p. 314.

Irish agricultural output (gross value added) at current prices, c.1845 [a]

commodities	£m
wheat	4.9
oats	8.1
barley	1.8
flax	1.3
potatoes	8.8
hay	0.6
other	1.4
total crops	26.8
cattle	4.7
butter and milk	4.8
pigs	3.4
sheep	0.8
wool	0.5
eggs	0.9
other	0.8
total livestock	15.9
total output	42.7

[a] For the calculations on which this table is based, and the reservations attached to them, see Cormac Ó Gráda, *Ireland before and after the famine: explorations in economic history 1800-1925* (Manchester, 1988), pp 47–50, 70.

of even the latter were marketed, as much as two-thirds of total output was sold for cash. Still, the degree of commercialisation had a regional and social aspect, being lowest in the west, where farms were smallest and dependence on the potato greatest.

How 'backward' was agriculture? To contemporaries, for whom British farming served as a standard, the pre-famine backwardness of Ireland was often defined in terms of Britain's chronological lead over Ireland. Such a definition, however, is unsatisfactory for the economic historian. If backwardness is defined instead in terms of productivity, how much is there to explain? Readily available acreage and employment figures prompt the following calculations. These figures suggest that the Whately commission did not grossly exaggerate in asserting that in the 1830s 'the agricultural produce of Great Britain [was] more than four times that of Ireland'. If due allowance is made for the lower prices obtained by Irish farmers, British superiority in terms of

Agricultural output and productivity in Ireland and
Great Britain, c. 1845

	Ireland	Great Britain
output (£m)	43	120–130
acreage (m)	15	30
employment (m)	1.7	2.0
output per acre (£)	2.9	4.0–4.3
output per employee (£)	25	60–65

output per worker was of the order of 2 to 1. Since British agriculture led the world in the 1830s and 1840s, the productivity gap is hardly astounding. Indeed, whether a gap of this size can accommodate all the explanations offered for Irish agricultural backwardness is doubtful. A recent estimate of the gap between Britain and France in the 1830s puts the British advantage at 1.8:1.[1] It would be rash to assume, therefore, that the productivity of Irish farmworkers before the famine was below the European average.

Tillage yields in Ireland on the eve of the famine were almost as high as in Britain, and very high indeed by contemporary European standards. This was due in part to the potato as a soil-cleansing crop, and to labour-intensive spade cultivation. In addition, nitrogen requirements were met by grasses and animal manure, as in Britain, and by large dressings of seasand and seaweed.[2] Irish productivity ratios in animal husbandry were also probably not far short of the British. But the gap in labour productivity is a better guide to relative backwardness.

The most obvious and important explanation for this gap was the difference in the land–labour ratio. Irish farmers and labourers had on average only about half as many acres on which to work as their British counterparts. Under less than heroic assumptions about the output elasticity of land, this factor alone may explain one-third to one-half of the initial gap in output per man. Not only was the land–labour ratio lower in Ireland, but soil quality there, acre for acre, may well have been lower also. Contemporary opinion was divided on this, but the evidence from modern soil maps is informative. Since inherent fertility is what is in question, the balance shown below is unlikely to have changed much

---

[1] Patrick K. O'Brien and Caglar Keyder, *Economic growth in Britain and France, 1780–1914: two paths to the twentieth century* (London, 1978), pp 90–91; see also Peter Solar, 'Agricultural productivity and economic development in Ireland and Scotland in the early nineteenth century' in T. M. Devine and David Dickson (ed.), *Ireland and Scotland, 1600–1850: parallels and contrasts in economic and social development* (Edinburgh, 1983), pp 70–88.

[2] P. M. A. Bourke, 'The average yield of food crops on the eve of the famine' in *Éire, Department of Agriculture, Journal*, lxvi (1969), pp 3–16, and G. P. H. Chorley, 'The agricultural revolution in northern Europe, 1850–1880: nitrogen, legumes, and crop productivity' in *Econ. Hist. Rev.*, xxxiv (1981), pp 71–93.

since the 1840s.[1] If we suppose that Ireland's disadvantage were made good and that 46.8 per cent instead of 30.1 per cent of Irish land were of the first quality, how would output have been affected? The contribution of soil quality to output can only be guessed; but if it is assumed that the output gain was measured by the rental increment on the better land (about 10s. per acre), then such an improvement would have been worth only about £1,250,000, or another 14s. per worker, which was trifling compared with the difference created by the limited supply of land.

Soil quality in Ireland and Great Britain
(percentage of total area)

class	Ireland	Great Britain
1	30.1	46.8
2	9.9	9.9
3	32.9	19.8
4	10.9	15.9
5	16.6	6.8
6	0.4	0.2

Several other factors are relevant, but it is impossible to measure their importance. The greater regional specification that quickly followed the introduction of railways in Ireland—more radical than anything occurring in Britain—suggests that poor internal communications were a real constraint for some kinds of farming, particularly cattle production.[2] Ireland's disadvantages in physical endowment, human skill, and education need not be emphasised. Indeed, lower levels of skill and education may have reduced the application of complementary physical capital inputs. A further constraint, easily documented from literary sources but impossible to quantify, was the influence on the productivity of the labour force of an inadequate diet during the summer months.

Like poor smallholders everywhere, the pre-famine Irish were censured by unsympathetic and uninformed outsiders. Harriet Martineau, for example, believed tales about peasants who wept when an agricultural instructor began

[1] O'Brien & Keyder, op. cit., pp 109–13; An Foras Taluntais, *General soil map of Ireland* (Dublin, 1969); M. J. Gardiner and P. Ryan, 'A new generalised soil map of Ireland and its land-use interpretation' in *Irish Journal of Agricultural Research*, viii (1969), pp 95–109. A qualification has been suggested by Mokyr: since soil quality is the product of nature and human effort jointly, a relative decline in the agricultural labour force would have reduced Irish soil quality relative to British somewhat since 1845.

[2] Liam Kennedy, 'Regional specialization, railway development, and Irish agriculture in the nineteenth century' in J. M. Goldstrom and L.E. Clarkson (ed.), *Irish population, economy and society: essays in honour of the late K. H. Connell* (Oxford, 1981), pp 173–93.

to thin their turnips, 'and said he was trying to rob them'. Others, she claimed, who 'had scribbled or shovelled four inches deep' in the fields, were delighted 'at being shown that a rich loamy soil lay six inches deeper'.[1] The dogmatic assistant secretary of the treasury, Charles Trevelyan, thought that the term 'lazybed' reflected the ease of the Irish way of growing potatoes, a reflection of both bias and deep-seated ignorance.[2] However, it is likely that the resource constraints explain much more of Irish backwardness than the traditional emphasis on slovenly farming. The figures in the tables on pp 123–4 above support a reinterpretation of farmers' and cottiers' performance that seeks to make better sense of behaviour formerly seen as the result of indolence and incompetence. Cases in point include lazybeds and the use of the spade, which seemed anachronistic to outsiders but suited Ireland because draught animals and heavy ploughs were luxuries not suited to small farms, small fields, and soils that were often wet or rocky. The marked regional variation in cultivation techniques and tillage implements is another example of methods that at first sight seem to reflect isolation and conservatism, but may simply show a determination to get the most out of what little capital there was. Even rundale, the much maligned Irish version of the open-field system, has been reinterpreted in this light, as an adaptation to difficult soil and cropping conditions.[3] The reluctance of the Irish to grow turnips was often criticised by 'improvers', but this complaint neglects the cleansing and fodder functions of the potato. 'In regard to the introduction of turnips,' admitted William Blacker, an energetic Ulster land agent, 'the opinion of even experienced farmers is very much divided.' Many preferred the potato. Accordingly Blacker did not insist on turnips but left it to the farmers 'to follow their own inclinations after making trial of each'.[4] In the circumstances the unprecedented extent of potato cultivation begins to make sense, and pleas such as the following, though perhaps in retrospect sounding disastrous, may have been good advice.

I will conclude ... by saying that the farmer who always grows plenty of potatoes will never be broke. They are good for sheep, pigs, poultry, horses, and horned cattle, and when steamed are best; they are the greatest improvers of ground, so much so that they are the best preparatory crop for wheat; and if grown for sale, I need not say how many wants the price of them will stop; but the farmer who is buying potatoes and has to pay rent for his land will soon be a beggar.[5]

---

[1] Harriet Martineau, *Letters from Ireland* (London, 1854), p. 10.

[2] Charles Trevelyan, *The Irish crisis* (London, 1848), p. 4.

[3] Eric L. Almquist, 'Mayo and beyond: land, domestic industry, and rural transformation in the Irish west, 1750–1900' (Ph.D. thesis, Boston, 1977), ch. 3; A. T. Lucas, 'Paring and burning in Ireland' in Alan Gailey and Alexander Fenton (ed.), *The spade in northern and Atlantic Europe* (Belfast, 1970), pp 99–147; John Donaldson, *A historical and statistical account of the barony of Upper Fews ... 1838* (Dundalk, 1923), pp 38–9.

[4] Blacker to W. C. Kyle, 18 Jan. 1836 (Letter-book, 1832–46, P.R.O.N.I., D1606/5/1).

[5] Daniel Ryan, *The Irish practical farmer and gardener* (Dublin, 1838), p. 80. See also Mountifort Longfield, *Lectures on political economy* (Dublin, 1834), pp 249–56.

Agricultural output increased substantially between 1801 and 1845. Besides feeding a population that grew from five to eight and a half million, it allowed agricultural exports to rise to about a quarter of output in 1845. Though the value of per capita food intake may have fallen somewhat, a rise of 80 per cent or more is still suggested. Admittedly, the rise was partly caused by a shift in the occupational composition of the labour force, since the decline of domestic industry led to greater specialisation in farming, particularly in the west and north. Against this, however, must be set the temporary loss each year from seasonal migration and sea fishing. The outflow of harvest migrants rose from a few thousand in 1801 to perhaps 80,000 in 1845; the increase in the number of mostly part-time fishermen was equally dramatic.[1] Agriculture can hardly have been unaffected by such leakages. Growth in output may therefore have matched that of labour input. To have countered the law of diminishing returns was no mean achievement. Malthus, after all, would have predicted a massive decline in productivity in the face of such an increase in numbers.

The reasons for this outcome can be identified but not quantified. The period was clearly one of significant diffusion of innovations. By 1845 iron ploughs and harrows had almost completely replaced wooden ones on larger farms and in lowland areas, and light carts with metal-shod wheels had replaced slide-carts and heavy carts with wooden wheels. The quality of livestock had improved as well.[2] English and Scottish strains of cattle, sheep, and pigs, which had already made an appearance by Arthur Young's time, seem to have taken over almost entirely by 1845. It was during these years that the cattle breeds most commonly seen on Irish farms until recently established themselves. As for sheep, Hely Dutton reported in 1824:

When I first came to Ballinasloe, having always heard so much of Connacht sheep, I was not a little surprised at seeing such multitudes with thick legs, booted with coarse wool down to their heels, and such a bushy wig of coarse wool on their heads, that you could scarcely perceive their eyes; at present they have nearly all disappeared, and given place to a fine breed, not to be equalled by the general stock of long-woolled sheep in England; this must be imputed to the introduction of Leicester rams.[3]

The result was heavier animals that matured far more quickly, thereby increasing productivity. Even in backward areas farmers paid great attention to breeding and crossing. Another livestock innovation was the donkey. So few in the late eighteenth century 'that a horse would shy on seeing one', donkeys numbered about 100,000 on the eve of the famine.[4] Land reclamation also added

---

[1] Barbara M. Kerr, 'Irish seasonal migration to Great Britain, 1800–38' in *I.H.S.*, iii, no. 12 (Sept. 1943), pp 425–80; Sarah Barber, 'Irish migrant agricultural labourers in nineteenth-century Lincolnshire' in *Saothar*, viii (1982), pp 10–23; John de Courcy Ireland, *Ireland's sea fisheries: a history* (Dublin, 1981), p. 48.

[2] Below, p. 221.

[3] Hely Dutton, *A statistical and agricultural survey of the county of Galway* (Dublin, 1824), pp 115–16.

[4] O'Donovan, pp 169–201; *Cinnlae Amhlaoibh Uí Shúileabháin*, ed. Michael McGrath (4 vols, London, 1936–7), i, 33; Lewis, *Topog. dict. Ire.*, county entries.

to output. Landlords showed little enthusiasm for the organised reclamation urged on them by improvers, but middlemen and larger farmers promoted thousands of small-scale schemes or allowed tenants to proceed themselves on a piecemeal basis. Most of the reclamation occurred in upland areas, though it is impossible to measure its extent. The 7 per cent added to Donegal's cultivated area between 1830 and 1849 may be less than what was added in the country as a whole between 1801 and 1845.[1]

Landlords conformed more to the traditional stereotype than their successors in the post-famine era. As a group, they were more improvident, they evicted more often, and they took a less active interest in their properties. On the eve of the famine one acre in ten lay hopelessly encumbered, and one in four remained in the hands of absentees, a group who typically had the attitudes of rentiers rather than entrepreneurs. The Devon commission, both in the evidence it heard and in its conclusions, lent considerable support to this image of a mercenary landlord class, largely removed from the day-to-day business of running their estates.[2] Historians have detected a growing concern for efficient estate management over the period, however, as more landlords replaced middlemen with agents, valuers, surveyors, and direct letting to occupying tenants, and consolidated farms in order to extract more rent. The ambitious and detailed estate surveys of the period, notably Abraham Collis's survey of the estate of Trinity College, Dublin, and Greig's of the Gosford estate, stand out as sources on the state of agriculture; the great vogue for farming societies (over a hundred by 1845) and market houses (over seventy built in Ulster alone between 1801 and 1845) also reflected a greater involvement by landlords. The emphasis in recent scholarship is to give fresh insights into the landlords' preoccupations and the constraints they faced.[3]

The traditional picture of Irish landlordism, criticised over the past two decades, has much in common with the recent American 'neo-abolitionist' literature on plantation slavery. To show how morality and economics pointed in the same direction was the aim of both. Debate on the relative efficiency of slavery continues, but in Ireland historians seem to believe that landlordism was a peripheral factor in agricultural retardation. Sometimes the argument is carried further: Raymond Crotty has suggested, for example, that rackrenting

---

[1] K. H. Connell, 'The colonisation of waste land in Ireland, 1780–1845' in *Econ. Hist. Rev.*, 2nd ser., iii (1950–51), pp 44–71.

[2] Mokyr, *Why Ire. starved*, pp 197–215. The implications of encumbrances for economic activity have been insufficiently researched, but for two notorious cases see William A. Maguire, 'The 1822 settlement of the Donegall estates' in *Ir. Econ. & Soc. Hist.*, iii (1976), pp 17–32; Ian d'Alton, *Protestant society and politics in Cork, 1812–1844* (Cork, 1980), pp 21, 26.

[3] Donnelly, *Land & people of Cork*, pp 52–72; William Greig, *General report on the Gosford estates in County Armagh, 1821*, with introduction by F. M. L. Thompson and D. Tierney (Belfast, 1976); General report of the Midleton estate surveyor, 1846 (P.R.O.I., 978/2/4/1); descriptive survey and valuation (T.C.D., MUNI/V/series 78/46–61); Lord Clements's instructions, 1839 (N.L.I., MS 3829); *Thom's Directory, 1845*, pp 292–5; C. E. B. Brett, *Court houses and market houses in the province of Ulster* (Belfast, 1973).

landlords, by forcing tenants to compete, guaranteed optimal use of the land. Short leases and tenancies-at-will did not threaten the competent farmer, but gave the landlord greater flexibility. Where long leases were required to secure investment, the argument continues, they were not wanting; strong farmers and industrialists usually found landlords accommodating.[1] Even the long-lived criticisms of absenteeism are no longer given much weight. The main charge against it, resting on the leakage abroad of massive rents, probably reaching £2 million or £3 million by 1845, is matched by the durable McCulloch–Martineau refutation.[2] In the words of Tracey, the absentee of Harriet Martineau's *Ireland: a tale*, 'my revenue must first be spent [in Ireland] before my agent can get it for me to spend anywhere else.' A more recent restatement of the same charge in Keynesian terms[3] presupposes the existence in pre-famine Ireland of a type of unemployment that could hardly have persisted in the long run.

A more plausible criticism of absenteeism contrasted the negligent absentee and the improving, paternalist, resident landlord.[4] The role of such 'good' landlords has been highlighted by James S. Donnelly and W. A. Maguire. Unlike the Waterford absentee who, 'supposing the tastes and wants of its people to resemble those of New Zealand or California . . . visited his estates with pockets full of beads, little mirrors, brooches, and other gew-gaws',[5] the 'good' landlord was resident and conspicuously active, patronising farming societies, attending agricultural shows, and promoting new techniques. But the importance of all this is questionable. Farm accounts and the farming press suggest that big farmers could be trusted to innovate in any case. As for the dozens of agricultural society jamborees of the pre-famine period, the reaction of a Cork farmer who attended one in 1844 hoping for 'some valuable information that he could communicate on return to show farmers' is sobering: 'he heard nothing but compliments passing from my lord *this* to my lord *that*, on his kindness to his tenantry', and he and his fellow Cork visitors were made to feel 'no more . . . than . . . bunk sweeps'.[6] The old orthodoxy was crude and sometimes silly, yet it sought to make the point that the landlords did precious little to justify their annual income. Perhaps there was little they could do; in any case, had *phytophthora infestans* destroyed landlords instead of potatoes in 1845, agricultural output would have been only marginally affected. In this Marxian sense the tenantry as a group were indeed being exploited.

[1] Raymond D. Crotty, *Irish agricultural production* (Cork, 1966), pp 51–65, 88–102; L. M. Cullen, *The emergence of modern Ireland* (London, 1982), pp 44–50; W. A. Maguire, *The Downshire estates in Ireland, 1801–1845: the management of Irish landed estates in the early nineteenth century* (Oxford, 1972).
[2] Black, *Econ. thought & Ir. question*, pp 72–85. [3] Ibid.
[4] A. P. W. Malcomson, 'Absenteeism in eighteenth-century Ireland' in *Ir. Econ. & Soc. Hist.*, i (1974), pp 15–35; Harriet Martineau, *Ireland: a tale* (London, 1834), pp 95–104; Black, *Econ. thought & Ir. question*, pp 72–85.
[5] Henry D. Inglis, *Ireland in 1834: a journey throughout Ireland during the spring, summer and autumn of 1834* (2 vols, London, 1834), i, 63–4.
[6] *The World*, 9 Nov. 1851.

Landlord earnings from their estates rose by 100 to 150 per cent between 1790 and 1815. Between 1815 and 1845 the movement is less clear. Those like Sir John Benn-Walsh who still had leases expiring after 1815 did well: Benn-Walsh achieved a 54 per cent rise on his Cork and Kerry properties between 1829 and 1847 as a result of taking over middlemen's land. However, an analysis of some individual estates shows that the 5 per cent rise in Lord Downshire's income between 1815 and 1845—not bad at all during a period of falling prices—was more typical.[1] The continued increase in landlord earnings is interesting in another sense: it shows that despite hardship and occasional famine, there was no sign yet of the doomsday predicted by Robert Torrens, when 'the whole rental of the country would be inadequate for the maintenance of those for whose labour there would be no demand'.[2]

The composition of farm output in 1845, taken in conjunction with trade statistics and farm accounts, rules out the possibility of any sharp shift to pasture before the famine. Even in north Leinster, where large farms were most numerous and population growth least, the undoubted increase that occurred in livestock numbers seems not to have occurred at the expense of the acreage under the spade and the plough.[3] The continued emphasis on tillage is to be explained by the fact that grain prices did not fall relative to livestock prices in the pre-famine decades.[4] In addition, labour was cheap and plentiful.

Before the famine it was commonplace to include crime and lawlessness as an explanation for Ireland's poor economic performance, not least in agriculture. Claims like Nassau William Senior's—that 'not merely is the introduction of capital prevented, but the capital formerly existing and employed in Ireland has been driven away'[5]—were typical. No doubt crime in strife-torn areas in bad years was frightening enough. The number of illegal and violent acts (3,280) reported in Clare during 1831, including 28 homicides, 420 attacks on houses, 293 robberies of arms, and 658 illegal meetings, was more than double that connected with the Swing riots of 1830–32 in all of England.[6]

[1] J. S. Donnelly, jr (ed.), 'The journals of Sir John Benn-Walsh relating to the management of his Irish estates, 1823–64', in *Cork Hist. Soc. Jn.*, lxxix (1974), p. 89; W. A. Maguire, *The Downshire estates in Ireland, 1801–1845* (Oxford, 1972), p. 39; Eric L. Almquist, 'Mayo and beyond: land, domestic industry, and rural transformation in the Irish west, 1750–1900' (Ph.D. thesis, Boston, 1977), pp 126–38; N.L.I., MSS 6077–81 (Fitzwilliam estate), 6915, 6923, 6969 (Lismore papers), 1740 (O'Callaghan, Shanbally), 1756 (Trant, Co. Tipperary), 12792–12805 (Mohill, Co. Leitrim); P.R.O.N.I., D16706/7A/34, 48 (Gosford estate, Co. Armagh), D623/C/4/1, 10 (Abercorn estate, Strabane part), D3531/12/2 (Shirley estate, Co. Monaghan); Kevin O'Neill, *Family and farm in pre-famine Ireland: the parish of Killashandra* (Madison, 1984), pp 51–7 (Hodson and Garvagh estates, Co. Cavan).
[2] Quoted in Black, *Econ. thought & Ir. question*, p. 93.
[3] The assistance of Dr Michael Kenny in making available his unpublished paper, 'Employment and wages of farm labourers in pre-famine Westmeath' is acknowledged with thanks.
[4] Below, pp 218–22.
[5] Nassau William Senior, *Letters, conversations and journals relating to Ireland* (2 vols, London, 1868), i, 31, 38, 41.
[6] *A return of the number and nature of offences reported to the government as having taken place in the county of Clare, in the years 1831 and 1832*, H.C. 1833 (79), xxix, 405; Eric Hobsbawm and George Rudé, *Captain Swing* (London, 1969), pp 304–5.

That ill-defined or hard-to-enforce property rights are bad for economic activity is axiomatic: if landlords were repaid in lead rather than in gold for trying to raise their rents through innovation or consolidation, not much could be expected of them. It is easy to understand why William Blacker's 'satisfaction' at being able to improve agriculture in Armagh was 'completely put an end to', on 'finding that [his] agriculturalist had twice narrowly escaped assassination'.[1] Landlords and their servants were rarely at risk, however. Both the perpetrators and those on the receiving end of agrarian 'outrage' were usually near the bottom of the socio-economic pyramid. Overall, rural crime was sporadic and uneven regionally. The replies to a poor inquiry questionnaire on unrest supported this generalisation. Of over 1,400 answers received to the query 'Has your parish been disturbed or peaceable [since 1815]?', only 2 per cent reported considerable or endemic unrest; well over half (four-fifths in Ulster) reported little or none. For the rest, one-third admitted occasional tension over tithes, and the remainder referred to secret societies and factional squabbles.[2]

Crime statistics present their own problems of interpretation, for definitions and coverage changed, and the proportion of crime that was reported probably increased. Yet when carefully used, the crime statistics that became available in the 1840s offer an antidote to the more sensational impressionistic claims.

Annual average committals in Ireland (1844-6) and England and Wales (1841-5)

category of crime	committals		committals per 100,000 population	
	Ireland	England & Wales	Ireland	England & Wales
murders (Ireland), homicides (England & Wales)	107	281	1	2
other crimes against the person	5,140	2,194	61	13
against property with violence	1,156	1,962	14	12
against property without violence	6,289	23,849	74	146
malicious offences against property	206	214	2	1
forgery and offences against the currency	103	545	1	3
miscellaneous	5,397	1,338	64	8

[1] Blacker to W. C. Kyle, 30 Mar. 1846 (P.R.O.N.I., D1606/5/1).
[2] Richard Whately, *A few words of remonstrance* (Dublin, 1848), p. 10; P.R.O.N.I., D1606/5/1, 30 Mar. 1846; *Poor inquiry, app. E, suppl.*, pp 1–393.

Broadly speaking, though they indicate that violent crimes and crimes against property and the person—which are at issue here—were more common than in England, the difference was not immense. If contemporary accounts sometimes give the impression that the whole country was controlled by 'banditti' in the early years of the century, a comparative perspective suggests a more peaceful picture in the early 1840s.

Before the famine the proportionate number of convictions was roughly equal in both countries, and the number of capital offences proportionately less in Ireland. Besides, the crime rate was falling and the conviction rate rising, trends probably explained by increasingly effective police.[1]

THE trend in output on the eve of the famine remains a puzzle. A long-term increase is not in doubt, but the trade statistics and other evidence point to a levelling out in the late or even mid-1830s—an indication perhaps that population had reached the dreaded point where the marginal product of labour was zero? This was not so, since the number of mouths to be fed at home continued to grow. Output growth may still have been slowing down; but before invoking sharply diminishing returns, another possibility—that farmers and exporters were simply responding in classic fashion to the low prices and bad harvests of those years—must not be overlooked. There is a good deal of evidence for this view. Many landlords granted rent abatements during these years because of bad harvests, economic slump, and cattle distemper. The 1845 trade figures began to reflect the emergence of producers from the 'straitened economic conditions in which four or five seasons of agricultural scarcity and deranged commerce . . . involved them'.[2]

The lack of a continuous output series makes the short-term fluctuations in agricultural conditions between 1801 and 1845 difficult to trace. Price and trade figures do not quite fill the gap, though they do capture some of the features and trends described in this chapter. In Figure 1,[3] showing grain exports to Britain, both a long-term rise and a deceleration after about 1830 can be detected; seasons of poor yields, such as 1810–11, 1825, and 1839–40, are also revealed. Figure 2,[4] a graph of Dublin bread prices over the period 1750–1849, suggests three broad phases—a gradual rise until the French wars, then a period of very high prices, and finally a gradual fall beteen 1815 and the famine.

[1] V. A. C. Gatrell, 'The decline of theft and violence in Victorian and Edwardian England' in V. A. C. Gatrell, Bruce Lenman, and Geoffrey Parker (ed.), *Crime and the law: the social history of crime in western Europe since 1620* (London, 1980), pp 238–370; Galen Broeker, *Rural disorder and police reform in Ireland, 1812–36* (London, 1970), pp 228–9; Édouard Ducpétiaux, *Statistique comparée de la criminalité en France, en Belgique, en Angleterre, et en Allemagne* (Brussels, 1835).

[2] *Belfast Mercantile Register*, 26 Nov. 1844, quoted in Philip Ollerenshaw, 'The Belfast banks 1820–1900: aspects of banking in nineteenth-century Ireland' (Ph.D. thesis, Sheffield, 1982), p. 106; *Irish Farmers' Gazette*, 27 May, 10 June, 8 July, 15 July, 16 Dec. 1843; *Bankers' Magazine*, ii (1844), pp 163–6; iii (1845), pp 234–5.

[3] Below, p. 136.

[4] Below, p. 136.

Other price series would presumably show a similar secular pattern, but would be less subject to short-term fluctuation. However, the creation and analysis of comprehensive price series is only in its infancy in pre-famine historiography.

To take a long view, Britain's buoyant market for foodstuffs made pre-famine Ireland a 'granary', and the progress of agriculture was in large part traceable to that market. The Anglo-Irish corn trade was relieved of restrictions in 1806. Britain's terms of trade were damaged by restricted markets for her exports and the isolation of some of her traditional food sources: between 1790 and 1815 it has been estimated that the relative price of corn in Britain rose by over one-quarter. In Ireland both grain farmers and provision merchants prospered.[1] After the wartime boom came a collapse in prices, but the corn law of 1815 sheltered Irish suppliers and gave them a considerably higher return than would otherwise have been available. The benefits were spread unevenly in Ireland, however. An appeal to Ronald Jones's three-factor trade model, well known to economic historians, is helpful and suggests that farmers who sublet and landlords benefited, while labourers and smallholders, who paid the rents and were relatively heavy consumers of food, were the losers. Perhaps it was a simple version of this model that prompted Daniel O'Connell to complain melodramatically about 'landlords' venison . . . sweetened with widows' tears' as an outcome of the corn laws. Yet petitions from Ireland against their repeal were frequent, and those strong farmers who formed much of O'Connellite voting support must have been unenthusiastic about his views. Peel's beliefs—that 'if there be any part of the United Kingdom which is to suffer by the withdrawal of protection . . . it was Ireland'—applies to such farmers at least.[2] This finding has a corollary: by improving Ireland's terms of trade the corn laws helped—if only in a modest way—both to deindustrialise and, in a sense, to enrich Ireland. Farmers could entice workers away from non-agricultural occupations without having to pay them more, and imported manufactures were substituted for native. The total effect was higher output.

[1] William Greig, *General report on the Gosford estates in County Armagh, 1821*, with introduction by F. M. L. Thompson and D. Tierney (Belfast, 1976), pp 106–11; Glenn Hueckel, 'War and the British economy, 1793–1815: a general equilibrium analysis' in *Explorations in Economic History*, x (1973), p. 389. See also Horatio Townsend, *A view of the agricultural state of Ireland in 1815; with observations on the causes of its depression, and the means of relief* (Cork, 1816), pp 13–17.

[2] Boyd Hilton, *Corn, cash, commerce: the economic policies of the tory governments, 1815–30* (Oxford, 1977); W. J. Fitzpatrick (ed.), *Correspondence of Daniel O'Connell, the Liberator* (2 vols, London, 1888), ii, 223–4.

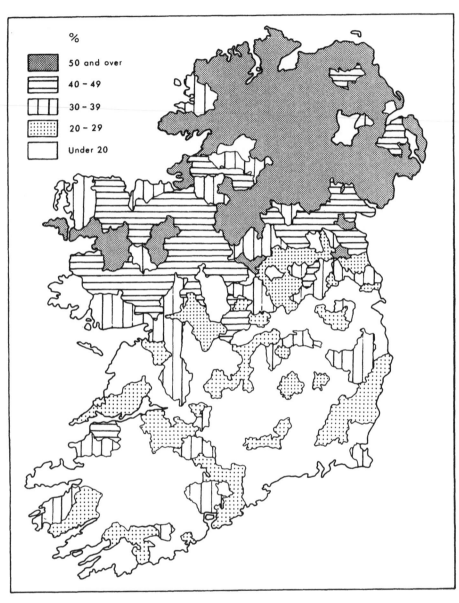

Map 1 PERSONS 'CHIEFLY ENGAGED IN MANUFACTURING,
TRADE, ETC.', AS A PERCENTAGE OF THE TOTAL OCCUPIED
POPULATION, 1821, BY BARONIES, by Cormac Ó Gráda

Census Ire., 1821, H.C. 1824 (577), xxii, 411.

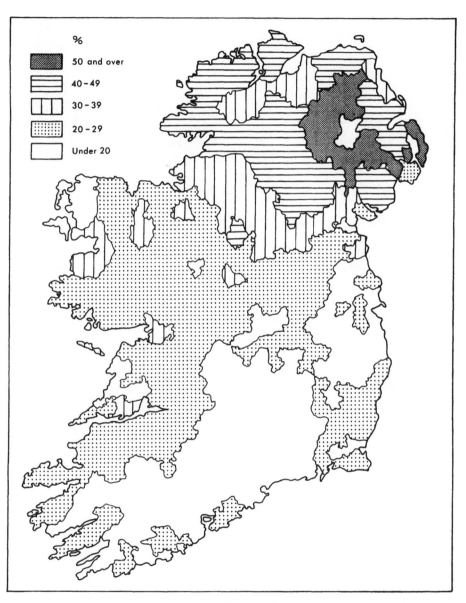

Map 2 PERSONS 'MINISTERING TO CLOTHING, LODGING, ETC.', AS A PERCENTAGE OF THE TOTAL OCCUPIED POPULATION, 1841, BY BARONIES, by Cormac Ó Gráda

Census Ire., 1841, p. 433 [459], H.C. 1843, xxiv, 541.

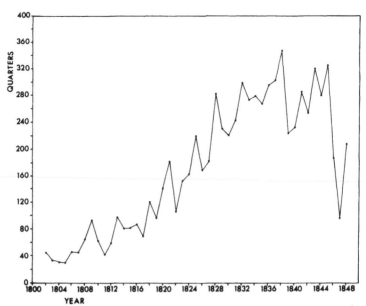

Figure 1 GRAIN EXPORTS TO BRITAIN, 1802–48, by Cormac Ó Gráda

Thom's Irish almanac and official directory . . . for the year 1850 (Dublin, 1850), p. 159, based on returns in parliamentary papers.

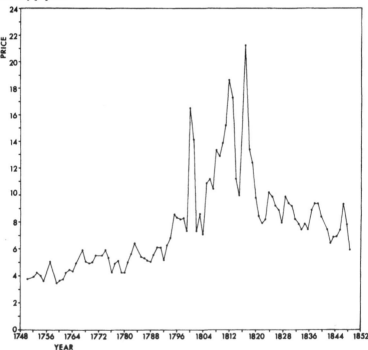

Figure 2 DUBLIN BREAD PRICES, 1750–1849, by Cormac Ó Gráda

John Swift, *History of the Dublin bakers and others* (Dublin, [?1948]), pp 370–71.

CHAPTER VI

Industry and communications, 1801–45

CORMAC Ó GRÁDA

EVEN economies that grow through increased specialisation in food production experience a fall in agriculture's share of the labour force. This generalisation holds true no less for modern Ireland than for New Zealand or Denmark.
Pre-famine Ireland was an exception to this well known process: the period
under review was marked by the decline of traditional cottage industries, obliging many 'to turn their attention to farming pursuits'.[1] Since about 1960 the
body of scholarly literature on those engaged in non-agricultural activities has
grown considerably.[2] A key point is that in traditional, largely rural economies,
such as that of pre-famine Ireland, occupations were less firmly defined—
hence the use of tentative categories such as '*chiefly* employed in agriculture'
and '*chiefly* employed in trades, manufactures, or handicraft' in the census of
1821. In south Londonderry in that year, according to a local schoolmaster's
account, for example, 'the division of labour is so little practised that a single
family can hardly be named, which subsists wholly by agriculture; nor again
any manufacturer, who does not consider himself a farmer'.[3] Such 'manufacturers' worked primarily in the home, but produced for local and foreign
markets rather than for subsistence. Their number grew significantly in the
eighteenth century, reaching perhaps one-quarter of the total occupied population in the years 1801–21. Based mostly in the countryside, they were engaged
primarily in textile production, but others who derived their livelihood mainly
from activities later to be mechanised should not be ignored. 'Protoindustrial'
workers might be independent commodity producers, as were most handloom

[1] John Donaldson, *A historical and statistical account of the barony of Upper Fews . . . 1838* (Dundalk, 1923), p. 62.
[2] Franklin F. Mendels, 'Protoindustrialisation: the first phase of the industrialisation process' in *Journal of Economic History*, xxxii (1972), pp 241–61; Rudolf Braun, *Industrialisierung und Volks-leben* (Zurich, 1966); Stephen Hymer and Stephen Resnick, 'A model of an agrarian economy with nonagricultural activities' in *American Economic Review*, lix (1969), pp 439–506; Joel Mokyr, 'Growing-up and the industrial revolution in Europe' in *Explorations in Economic History*, xiii (1976), pp 371–96.
[3] John McCloskey, *Statistical reports of six Derry parishes, 1821*, ed. David O'Kane (Draperstown, 1983), p. 16.

weavers in 1801, but early industrialisation generally brought about their pro-
letarianisation under the 'putting-out' system.

The Derry-centred shirtmaking industry began as such an 'outworking'
business in the 1840s. Between 1845 and 1851 its founder William Scott paid
about £500 weekly to seamstresses and ancillary workers who made shirts from
the cotton and linen that he supplied. Other masters operated over wider areas:
Derry weavers and Down needleworkers took out work from Glasgow capitalists. Some employers, like Coulsons of Lisburn, preferred to conduct a hybrid
system, combining urban workshops with the hiring of outworkers in the rural
hinterland. In south Londonderry in the 1840s poverty sometimes forced
another arrangement on weavers: 'the weaver is fed and attended during the
time he is weaving a web for his employer. As soon as he has finished it, he
purchases yarn and receives food and attendance while he is weaving one for
himself, and so on alternately'.[1] The 1841 census recorded 123,000 weavers of
various kinds, the great majority of whom were outworkers. But cottage
industry had reached its peak of prosperity some decades earlier.

The links between such industrialisation and the factory system—between
'manufacture' and 'modern industry' in Marxian terminology—are complex.
Both in the paradigmatic Belgian case and in Britain the former led to the latter
because many successful putting-out merchants had the funds and the markets
to switch to the factory system when the opportunity arose. Between 1800 and
1850 British textile factory employment and output increased over tenfold, and
textile exports rose by about 1,500 per cent. In much of Ireland, however,
cottage industry proved rather a dead end. The failure to convert a large protoindustrial base to modern industry, while the 'workshop of the world' was
being built next door, is of abiding interest to economic historians. Most comprehensive accounts run the risk of explaining too much; they lose sight of the
successful transformation in eastern Ulster in particular. Even outside Ulster
the record was mixed, for some industries that declined later in the century still
had much life left in them in 1845. Nevertheless, the new industrialisation was
first and foremost based on textiles, and textile mills employed only about
15,000 hands in Ireland in 1841, contrasting with 60,000 in Scotland and over
250,000 in England. Why did modern industry have such limited success in
Ireland? Generalisations based on developments elsewhere in Europe provide
an explanation:

Where good agrarian alternatives existed which would become relatively more profitable on the basis of comparative advantages arising from stronger industrialisation else-

---

[1] Hall, *Ire.*, iii, 20; see also Londonderry Teachers' Centre, *The shirt industry of the northwest of
Ireland* (Derry, 1980), pp 7–15; John Hume, 'Social and economic aspects of the growth of Derry,
1825–1850' (M.A. thesis, N.U.I. (Maynooth), 1964), pp 141–7; Diarmuid Ó Doibhlin (ed.), *Ordnance
survey memoir: parish of Ardtrea, 1833–1836* (South Derry Historical Society, 1983), p. 13. The assistance of Leslie Clarkson and Brenda Collins, in giving access to their unpublished paper, 'Proto-
industrialisation in an Irish town: Lisburn, 1820–21', is acknowledged with thanks.

where, a reversal to agriculture, or deindustrialisation of a positive kind, was likely. This tendency was reinforced if the initial rural industry had been relatively weak and dispersed and without a strong export market.[1]

Compared with those of Britain, most of Ireland's protoindustries in 1780 or 1800 were geared to local rather than distant markets and produced articles of low quality. Not surprisingly, as the terms of trade moved in favour of agriculture, Irish capital and labour also moved in that direction. Accordingly the large mills found in most towns on the eve of the famine, many of them recently built, produced flour rather than cloth. Ireland's contrasting position may be measured from the occupational profile of her main towns in 1841 (only Belfast and Derry recorded over two-fifths of the population employed in textile occupations) and from the rising share of farmers and farm labourers in the total labour force.

No comparable data are available for 1801, but the decline in non-agricultural employment between 1821 and 1841 may be measured from the occupation–distribution maps on pp 134–5. Rural industry was not replaced by jobs in towns; it is significant that towns with over 1,500 inhabitants in Munster or Connacht did not increase in size.[2] If the 1821 and 1841 census returns are to be credited, in the worst-hit districts of north Connacht and west Ulster the occupational shift from industry accounted for as much of the expansion in the agricultural labour force as did population growth. It was in areas of such industrial decline that the living conditions of the poor deteriorated most before 1845.

COTTON 'manufactories' began to appear in Ireland soon after their viability had been tested in Britain. Though Belfast may claim the status of pioneer (jennies were installed by the Charitable Society in 1779), the most spectacular early developments were in the south. A cursory listing of the better known suggests the characteristics of 'giantism' and hothouse growth: Robert Brooke's factory at Prosperous in the Bog of Allen (with a capital of over £40,000 and 2,500 employees, mainly outsiders), John Orr's at Stratford-on-Slaney (with £30,000 and 500 imported employees), the Sadleir brothers' factories at places near Cork (with £40,000 and 4,000 employees). Yet despite some sensational failures, including those of Brooke (1785) and the Sadleirs (1801), the industry in the south—shielded by a hefty tariff—proved resilient enough until the 1820s, when output was double its 1790 level. This modest success was largely founded on coarse cottons and on printing. In east Ulster over the same period output grew almost eightfold, to a considerable extent at the expense of linen. Production was regionally much more concentrated there, and notable for its emphasis on finer cloths and bleaching.

[1] Sidney Pollard, *Peaceful conquest: the industrialisation of Europe, 1760–1970* (Oxford, 1981), pp 76–7.
[2] Above, pp 119–24, for the effect of this failure on agriculture.

The industry was never important by United Kingdom standards, Irish cotton cloth output being about 5 to 7 per cent of British in 1801 and less than 3 per cent twenty years later. Yet as late as 1810 the industry was twice the size of that in Flanders.[1] Decline in Ireland was uninterrupted after 1825, gradual in the north (accompanying the mechanisation of linen spinning) and headlong in the south. Weavers' earnings tumbled: in Carrickfergus, for example, calico output that earned £1. 6s. in 1796 earned only 6s. thirty years later. Worst hit of all, perhaps, was Bandon, which boasted many mills and over 1,000 weavers at its peak, but where in 1837 'the mills were in ruin and not more than 100 weavers ... employed'.[2] The short-lived prosperity of cotton owed much to parliamentary grants and bounties, as well as to tariff protection. Had policy concentrated more on availing of external economies in one or two towns, instead of encouraging expensive locations, the industry might have fared better; though, given the phenomenal growth of Lancashire cotton, perhaps the main mystery is its survival until the 1820s. In parts of the south the decline of cotton brought considerable hardship and emigration. In the north-east it meant a switch to a closely related sector that enjoyed comparative advantage.

The manufacture of woollen cloth—carpets, broadcloths, friezes, blankets—also fell during the pre-famine period, shrinking to virtually nothing in such traditional strongholds as Kilkenny and Carrick-on-Suir. Changing fashions, arising from the availability of cheaper cotton substitutes, were part of the story, though it was reported in 1837 that 'three-fourths of the frieze generally worn by the peasantry throughout Ireland is now an article of import'.[3] Factory employment declined from 1,231 in 1839 to 553 in 1850. Isolated worsted factories sprang up too, but they were of little account.

THE 'success' industry of the day was linen. In the 1840s Mr and Mrs S. C. Hall, whose calculations were thought to be 'not more exaggerated than is usual with such general estimates',[4] put the value of linen output at £4 million, of which £1.2 million was in wages. While that means linen's share of national output was 3-4 per cent at the time, the growth of the industry was unspectacular by the standards of Lancashire cotton. Between 1801 and 1836 exports grew less than threefold and total output is unlikely to have grown any faster.

Coarse linen had been produced in Ireland since time immemorial, but development in the seventeenth and eighteenth centuries had owed much to immigration and mercantilist legislation. In 1801 linen was produced on a large scale in the northern half of the country and in isolated parts of Cork and

---

[1] David Dickson, 'Aspects of the Irish cotton industry' in L. M. Cullen and T. C. Smout (ed.), *Comparative aspects of Scottish and Irish economic and social history, 1600–1900* (Edinburgh, 1978), pp 105, 108; and Joel Mokyr, *Industrialisation in the Low Countries, 1795–1850* (New Haven, 1976), pp 28–36.

[2] Samuel McSkimmin, *The history and antiquities of the county of the town of Carrickfergus* (Belfast, 1909), pp 358–9; Lewis, *Topog. dict. Ire.*, i, 179.

[3] O'Brien, *Econ. hist. Ire., union to famine*, pp 297–308.

[4] Hall, *Ire.*, iii, 83.

Kerry. Competition from cotton and technical improvements in bleaching and spinning increasingly undermined the old system of independent household production after 1801. The impact of the expanding cotton industry on linen was twofold. First, as a good substitute for linen, it placed linen weavers' incomes under increasing pressure. Secondly, in Britain cotton machinery was quickly adapted to coarse-linen spinning. Despite prompting from the linen board, which as early as 1796 ordered 'several copies of exemplification of patents for spinning flax by machinery', mechanisation in this sector occurred only to a minor extent in Ireland, but the threat depressed hand-spinners' wages too. The hand-spinning sector largely succumbed in the late 1820s and the 1830s, when the wet-spinning process mechanised fine-yarn production. William Murland in Castlewellan and Andrew Mulholland in Belfast were the factory pioneers. Another twenty linen mills were established in 1835, nearly all of them in or around Belfast. Almost invariably they were set up by linen bleachers or cotton manufacturers. Employment in the mills grew from 3,400 in 1835 to over 17,000 by 1845, but mechanisation did not mean vast increases in yarn output. Factory yarn was sold in bulk to people who hired outworking weavers on a piecework basis. Throughout most of the linen country this development spelled doom for the independent weaver, who could buy yarn only in small amounts, selling the finished product himself.

Before 1820 the linen industry was not marked by much 'localisation', at least within Ulster. Its rural base and water requirements made for dispersion, and as late as 1820 the linen markets of Ballymena, Cootehill, Derry, Drogheda, and Omagh—outside the Lurgan–Belfast–Dungannon 'linen triangle'—were still important. Drogheda was unusual in having within its boundaries most of the weavers who supplied its market. Between 1780 and 1820 production there, mostly of unbleached 'market linen', grew impressively. Its lack of bleaching facilities and relative isolation brought crisis and decline in the 1820s, but other promising areas suffered too.[1] The centripetal forces that eventually concentrated nearly all British cotton production into one-third of Lancashire, and the American industry into eastern Massachussets and Rhode Island, were also at work later in Ulster.[2]

But why did such heavy concentration occur around Belfast? The old claim that the limited size of their markets and capital shortages prevented many Irish firms from reaping internal economies of scale, readily available elsewhere, may seem a good starting-point. Economic theory lends it only equivocal support, however. It may explain the absence of typesetters in Ballydehob or of bakers west of Dingle, but for industry in general a confined market should have produced *fewer*, not smaller, firms in equilibrium. The

[1] John Fitzgerald, 'The organisation of the Drogheda economy, 1780–1820' (M.A. thesis, N.U.I. (U.C.D.), 1972).
[2] D. A. Farnie, *The English cotton industry and the world market, 1815–1896* (Oxford, 1979), pp 45–77; J. S. Hekman, 'The product cycle and New England textiles' in *Quarterly Journal of Economics*, xciv (1980), pp 697–717. See occupational distribution maps, above, pp 134–5.

typical firm of the industrial revolution in Britain was, after all, quite small. Reassuringly for theory, Frank Geary's recent analysis of the cotton industry has effectively challenged the empirical basis for the argument in this important instance. He found that mills in the Belfast region in the 1830s probably had more capital than those elsewhere in the United Kingdom.[1]

External economies, however, are a different matter. Such economies, resulting from the presence of associated or ancillary firms and industries in the same area, might appear under many guises: they facilitated bulk transactions and reduced transport costs; they ensured reliable and continuous supply of spare parts, raw materials, and labour; they encouraged legal, consultancy, and trading services. The presence of external economies helps to explain the strong localisation or uneven development mentioned above; it also suggests that localisation tends to focus on a sizeable town or city.[2] For pre-famine Ireland this 'critical mass' argument remains in the status of a plausible hypothesis, difficult either to substantiate or refute. It seems to fit Belfast, which had been the principal textile port since the 1780s, and where the manufacture of looms and shuttles and, later, of steam-powered machinery quickly developed. Besides the usual printing, bleaching, and dyeing works, there were 'various manufactories for machinery, iron-forges, and other chymical products ... together employing about 1,000 persons';[3] the local foundries, moreover, soon began to invent and produce machinery specifically geared to local conditions.

After farming and textiles, the next biggest employers of labour were shoe-making (50,000), carpentry (40,000), and tailoring (35,000), all still small-scale and catering to local markets in the 1840s. Brewing and distilling were not yet heavy exporters, but their business was expanding.

POPULAR explanations of Irish industrial retardation concentrate on national resources and institutions. If such explanations carry less conviction nowadays, they still raise important issues. How important was energy supply, for example? Ireland's coal deposits were meagre. The mines at work between 1801 and 1845 met only a very small fraction of the country's demands—probably between 5 and 10 per cent.[4] Manufacturers using imported coal paid at least twice as much as their competitors in the north of England and lowland Scotland. This disadvantage is sometimes considered a factor in Ireland's industrial

[1] Mokyr, *Why Ire. starved*, pp 179–80; Frank Geary, 'The rise and fall of the Belfast cotton industry: some problems' in *Ir. Econ. & Soc. Hist.*, viii (1981), pp 30–49.

[2] Cf. Eoin O'Malley, 'The decline of Irish industry in the nineteenth century' in *Economic and Social Review*, xiv (1981), pp 21–42; E. M. Hoover, *Location theory and the shoe and leather industries* (Cambridge, Mass., 1937); Raymond Vernon, 'Production and distribution in the large metropolis' in *Annals of the American Academy of Political and Social Sciences*, cccxiv (1957), pp 15–29.

[3] Lewis, *Topog. dict. Ire.*, i, 194–5.

[4] Based on output and import estimates given in *Second report of the commissioners appointed to consider and recommend a general system of railways for Ireland, appendix B*, pp 69–90 [145], H.C. 1837–8, xxxv, 813–34.

decline, but the point must not be pressed too hard, for three reasons. First, energy was usually only a small component of total costs. In the cotton industry in Lancashire, for instance, coal accounted for about only 1 per cent of total costs. Secondly, other inputs—chiefly unskilled labour and land—were cheaper in Ireland and could presumably have been substituted to some extent for coal. Lowly paid workers might conserve fuel by keeping machinery in trim and by using every piece of coal available. Thirdly, as urged by Sir Robert Kane in 1844 and by Joel Mokyr recently, turf and water may have been viable substitutes for coal in certain circumstances.[1]

The mere presence of turf or water, however, would not have been enough. For Edward Wakefield the failure of factories to develop near the bogs was 'decisive proof that the expense of this kind of fuel has been too great to admit of any such improvement'. Against this, Kane pointed out that even though the calorific content of turf was only half that of coal, if it could be bought for a correspondingly lower price, it could have been—indeed should have been— used instead.[2] Turf had other drawbacks, however, notably its bulk and its susceptibility to wet weather. Industry in Dublin, Cork, and Belfast found coal cheaper. On the other hand, it probably would not have been profitable for entrepreneurs to operate near the bogs, where turf was a cheaper source of energy, even if it were free, for reasons quite unrelated to fuel.

More plausible are the claims for water power. G. N. von Tunzelmann has recently shown that steam was only marginally cheaper than water as late as 1850 in England.[3] Ireland's hillier topography and wetter climate may have tipped the scales towards water in many areas, thus helping to explain the relatively slow diffusion of steam. The eighteenth and early nineteenth centuries witnessed the greatly increased use of water power in Ireland. In 1839, 2,147 water horsepower were harnessed, compared with 1,503 steam horsepower.[4] Most mills were small affairs, but the largest rivalled those of Lancashire. The main wheel of Alexander's Fairbairn-built mill near Carlow produced 120 horsepower.

In the two establishments producing flour and oatmeal, there are twenty-two pairs of millstones at constant work; thirteen of which, with all the attendant machinery, are driven by the one wheel. The concern is able to manufacture annually 60,000 sacks of flour—'without', as one of the workmen expressed it, 'lighting a candle'. . . . Estimating flour at 60s. per sack, and the oatmeal at 30s., we have the aggregate concern yielding no less than £195,000 each year.[5]

Many other towns contained giant mills, and there was scope for more. If one compares water power harnessed in 1845 with what was available in theory

[1] Mokyr, *Why Ire. starved*, pp 157–8.
[2] Wakefield, *Account of Ire.*, i, 609; Kane, *Industrial resources*, pp 37–70.
[3] G. N. von Tunzelmann, *Steam power and British industrialisation to 1860* (Oxford, 1976), pp 116–60.
[4] Kane, *Industrial resources*, pp 71–117; H. D. Gribbon, *History of water power in Ulster* (Newton Abbot, 1969), pp 42–4, 86–96.
[5] Hall, *Ire.*, i, 404–7; Maurice Semple, *By the Corribside* (Galway, 1981), pp 44–50.

(3.5 million horsepower, according to Kane, 0.5 million horsepower, according to a subsequent and more sober estimate)[1] it becomes clear that great resources were not used. The comparison is somewhat misleading, however, because water power was already being fully used in and around cities and towns, where the prospect of factories being set up and succeeding was best. In Galway, for example, there were twenty-eight watermills, fed by an intricate system of artificial watercourses; the Boyne, Liffey, Dodder, and Slaney rivers were also intensively used. The problem resembled that with turf: the cost advantage of water power in Kerry, Mayo, or Donegal would attract few. That is why in Erris 'the available water power . . . though sufficient to work the machinery of 250 mills, even in the driest season, flows uselessly to the ocean'.[2]

The main theme of George O'Brien's *Economic history of Ireland from the union to the famine*, that 'the union had proved disastrous' to Irish industry, was a common contemporary refrain. Economic considerations, it is true, took a back seat in the union debates; if anything, Pitt and his advisers went out of their way not to hurt Ireland through economic, particularly fiscal, integration. Yet, later, great emphasis was placed by Irish, particularly Dublin industrialists on the dangers of removing the union duties of 10 per cent; and when industry continued to decline or languish in the 1820s and 1830s, nationalist writers were quick to see the removal as a primary factor.[3] To the modern historian the argument seems a bit strained, since, given the massive secular drop in the prices of Britain's industrial staples, an advantage of 10 per cent in favour of Irish products would have mattered little. More substantial tariffs might have reduced unemployment and given Irish industry a respite—as they did a century later—but at a cost in redistribution of wealth, if not in efficiency, that was politically inconceivable.[4] Because the amalgamation of the currencies came at a time of considerable economic crisis, this other element in the union settlement was also criticised. The ensuing appreciation of Irish money allegedly deflated the economy. In reality it made no difference, for most trade was denominated in sterling anyway, and prices and rents in Ireland quickly adapted to reflect what was in effect a revaluation of the Irish currency.[5]

The industrial decline blamed on free trade by George O'Brien was to persist after 1845. By 1885 Sir Robert Kane, so reassuring about prospects in his famous Royal Dublin Society lectures of 1844, had to admit that he could 'scarcely name a branch of industry that has not either become extinct or much more limited in its sphere, since the publication of my book, that is to say since

[1] Kane, *Industrial resources*, pp 71-3; Board of Trade, *Report of the water power resources of Ireland sub-committee* (Dublin, 1921), p. 5.

[2] Thomas Campbell Foster, *Letters on the condition of the people of Ireland* (London, 1846), p. 218.

[3] O'Brien, *Econ. hist. Ire., union to famine*, pp 419-27; Trevor McCavery, 'Finance and politics in Ireland; 1801-17' (Ph.D. thesis, Belfast, 1981), ch. I.

[4] For an early argument along these lines see Isaac Butt, *Protection to home industry: some cases of its advantages considered* (Dublin, 1846).

[5] George O'Brien, 'The last years of the Irish currency' in *Economic history* (supplement to *Economic Journal*), ii (1927), pp 249-58.

the year 1845'.[1] Not until the 1930s did an Irish administration give a fair trial to tariffs. While the new policy could be defended for its short-term anti-inflationary impact, the implied hopes of protectionist writers were not realised. Not even an average tariff level of over 40 per cent could produce more than a once-off, inward-directed spurt in manufacturing output.

WHAT of urban crime as a deterrent against investment?[2] In the cities craft unions had a reputation for ruthlessness. Disputes occasionally resulted in the death of recalcitrant fellow workers or foremen, and some industrial concerns cited union violence as a pretext for going out of business. But in general, craft violence—like Luddism—was confined to doomed sectors of the economy, and the buyers' market for labour guaranteed that union power could be neither pervasive nor entrenched. The true story of urban combinations after 1801 is less that of well publicised outrages—such as the gory Hanlon murder, for which four men were hanged—than of defeats in the struggle against determined masters.

To argue that contemporary accounts tended to exaggerate the effect of crime on business activity is still admittedly contentious. In support, one more piece of indirect evidence, from the records of the Sun Life Fire Insurance Company, may be added. This successful giant, which greatly increased the volume of its Irish business in the first half of the century, did so without having to charge a higher premium on policies in Ireland than in the rest of the United Kingdom.[3]

If the pre-famine industrialist faced handicaps in Ireland regarding the costs of energy and raw materials, contemporary observers are unanimous about a potential advantage: the lower wages commanded by ordinary workers. In rural areas adult male workers could be got for 5s. weekly or less—half the cost in England—and even along the more prosperous east coast labour cost one-third less than in Lancashire. This point was stressed both by contemporary advocates of Irish development and by historians. The implication that capital, Irish and foreign, was refusing 'bargains' does not follow, however, since low wages need not mean cheap labour. In Ireland an unskilled worker was less likely to be educated or accustomed to industrial discipline than in Britain. At certain times during the year he was also less likely to be well fed, and therefore less capable of hard physical work. It is tempting to conclude that lower Irish wages reflected lower efficiency. That would explain the alleged coexistence of large-scale unemployment and low wages, with farmers and others refusing to employ even at rock-bottom rates. It would also show that the pre-famine economy was caught in a 'poverty trap', low wages being both cause and effect

[1] *Report from the select committee on industries (Ireland); together with the proceedings of the committee, minutes of evidence, appendix, and index*, p. 136, H.C. 1884–5 (288), ix, 154.
[2] For agrarian crime, see above, pp 130–32.
[3] Sun Fire Insurance Company Records, MSS 11936, 11937 (Guildhall Library, London).

of low productivity. However, as Mokyr points out, conclusive empirical support for this view is lacking so far.[1]

SOME sectors of the economy registered steady progress between 1801 and 1845, and these must not be forgotten. Foremost among them were the processing industries linked to agriculture, such as flour milling and brewing. The massive increase in Irish wheat and oat exports in 1801–45 was matched by a proportionately greater rise in flour and meal exports, evidence of considerable capital formation, through mill-building and modernisation. Even in the 1840s new mills were being erected or enlarged in places as far apart as Cahirciveen, Cavan, Ennis, Enniscorthy, Gorey, and Navan.[2] The growth of butter and bacon exports also promoted ancillary industries; the livelihoods of the 10,000 coopers enumerated in 1841 were largely dependent on them. Though vulnerable to discomforts such as increases in excise duty or Fr Matthew's temperance campaign, both brewing and distilling expanded. Early in the century small-scale poteen-makers probably produced more—and better—whiskey than the legal distilleries. A new method of charging duty and efficient policing gradually shifted the balance; and between 1823 and the famine both the number of legal distillers and their output more than doubled. Production of beer, porter, and stout also increased: Arthur Guinness's sales rose from 10,000 barrels in 1800 to 67,000 in 1815, and 100,000 in 1846, by which date more than half were exports.[3]

There was considerable improvement in communications too, including the completion both of the Grand and Royal Canals and of the first railway lines. But it was in passenger traffic by road and in shipping that the biggest strides were made. A tolerably good road system already existed over much of the country, but in 1801 inland passenger transport was still usually slow and expensive. It was also occasionally subject to raids by highwaymen, forcing coaches occasionally to change routes and to carry armed escorts. Edward Wakefield reported in 1812 that extensive areas lacked any public transport whatsoever, while elsewhere travellers relied on posting and mail coaches. In the south there was little travelling 'by the mile'; one bargained as best one could with innkeepers over 'charges beyond all bound'. Yet even Wakefield conceded that communications were improving, reflecting and promoting the growth of business.[4]

By 1845, when Ireland's car and coaching system was at its most extensive, it covered a greater network of routes than the railway would ever do—travel

---

[1] Mokyr, *Why Ire. starved*, pp 222–5; J. S. Donnelly, jr (ed.), 'The journals of Sir John Benn-Walsh relating to the management of his Irish estates, 1823–64' in *Cork Hist. Soc. Jn.*, lxxix (1974), p. 101.

[2] Lewis, *Topog. dict. Ire.*, entries for Navan, etc.; Kevin O'Neill, *Family and farm in pre-famine Ireland: the parish of Killashandra* (Madison, 1984), p. 84.

[3] For an example of the fame of Guinness products in Britain, see Plate [3(b)].

[4] Wakefield, *Account of Ire.*, i, 665–74.

times had been cut substantially, and a regular service established between all towns of any size for about 1s. 5d. a mile. The huge concerns of Peter Purcell and Charles Bianconi were only the largest of many: in 1836 users of the system travelled a total of over thirty million miles.[1] To the commercial and professional people who were their mainstay, the coaches were a real boon. Between 1801 and the late 1830s journey times on the main routes were cut by one-third and fares by one-half or more. The economic savings to travellers were substantial. Reasonable assumptions about reductions in fares and the value of time saved produce estimates of the ensuing consumer gain ranging from 0.1 to 0.3 per cent of national income.[2]

Consumer surplus generated by passenger coach transport c. 1836, as percentage of national income

assumed price elasticity	4d. to 2d.	6d. to 2d.
0	0.18	0.27
−1	0.14	0.18
−2	0.09	0.12

Surplus as a percentage of national income at assumed price falls per passenger-mile.

The coaching concerns were not lacking in business acumen. Bianconi ably coped with competition from canals and railroads by rerouting his services, while Peter Purcell became the first chairman of the Great Southern & Western Railway Company.[3]

The success of coaching rested on an improving road network. Between 1801 and 1845 grand juries spent £300,000 to £400,000 annually on road repair and construction. More important for some areas were the schemes promoted by the board of works, notably under Richard Griffith and Alexander Nimmo.[4] Griffith's work in the south-west brought daily coach services to the main roads from Cork to Tralee and Killarney, and reduced the time of a journey on

[1] Calculated from 'Map of Ireland to accompany the report of the railway commissioners, showing the relative number of passengers in different directions by regular public conveyances. Constructed, under the direction of the commissioners, by Henry D. Harness, Lt. Royal Engineers, 1837', bound with the second report of the railway commission (see above, p. 142, n. 4).
[2] Cf. Jan de Vries, 'Barges and capitalism in the Dutch economy, 1636–1839' in *A.A.G. Bijdragen*, xxi (1978), pp 217–50.
[3] M. A. O'Connell, *Charles Bianconi: a biography, 1786–1875* (London, 1878), pp 72–98.
[4] P. J. O'Keefe, 'Richard Griffith: planner and builder of roads' in G. L. Herries Davies and R. C. Mollan (ed.), *Richard Griffith, 1784–1878: papers presented at the centenary symposium organised by the Royal Dublin Society, 21 and 22 September 1978* (Dublin, 1980), pp 57–75.

the latter from over a day to seven or eight hours. The new roads stimulated freight traffic too: a count kept on the Tralee road near Dromagh mill during 1838 revealed the passing to and from Cork, Killarney, and Tralee of 80,000 loaded carts carrying agricultural produce, lime, culm, iron, groceries, drink, and shop goods.[1] Better surfacing enabled such carts to carry freight of a ton or more. In this way the new roads prompted the growth of retailing and regional specialisation in production.

Before the creation of steamship routes the only regular crossings of the Irish Sea were by mail packet. Boats sailed 'when wind served', and communication was rather erratic. The famous *Rob Roy*, which began to ply the Belfast–Greenock route on 13 June 1818, was the first regular seagoing steamship in the world. The early routes, including the important Howth–Holyhead and the Belfast–Glasgow, catered mainly for passengers; the freight trade started with Charles Wye Williams's City of Dublin Steam Packet Company in 1824. Williams was the leading innovator, in terms of both service and technique, but he never established a monopoly. By the eve of the famine there were over one hundred sailings a week for man and beast, intense competition, and considerably lower fares. The proliferation of routes was a great boon to the trade in live animals, fresh butter, and even eggs and slaughtered meat. It made the large-scale export of fat cattle viable for the first time, and more and more of the butchers' meat of industrial Britain was Irish after 1820. Steam also encouraged more passenger movement; not least, it provided passages to thousands of seasonal migrants.[2]

Much has been claimed for canal transport during industrialisation in Britain. A recent evaluation of its contribution gives it a status equal to that of the railways.[3] Ireland underwent no radical canal revolution by comparison: in 1845 it had less than 600 miles of navigation. Whether the country was inadequately served in this respect is a moot point, however. In Ireland, unlike Britain, the canals were built with considerable government supervision and support. Entrepreneurs were given grants by the directors general of navigation, subject to observing conditions about construction and toll charges. Between 1801 and 1845 over £1,000,000 of public money was spent on inland navigation improvements, along with an equivalent amount in private funds. In theory canal charges were restricted by the directors general, but in practice that constraint was rarely binding, a far more serious threat being the competition from other modes for both passenger and goods traffic. In the circumstances the failure of the waterways to make profits despite such public aid

---

[1] Sean Ó Lúing, 'Richard Griffith and the roads of Kerry' in *Kerry Arch. Soc. Jn.*, viii (1975), pp 89–113; ix (1976), pp 92–124; N.L.I., MS 194.

[2] 'The cattle trade' in *Gore's General Advertiser*, 8 Jan. 1829. I owe this reference to Peter M. Solar.

[3] G. R. Hawke and J. P. P. Higgins, 'Transport and social overhead capital' in Roderick Floud and D. N. McCloskey (ed.), *The economic history of Britain since 1700* (2 vols, Cambridge, 1981), i, 248–9.

suggests a misallocation of resources on a large scale. The history of the canal companies thus seems to bear out the well known criticisms of Young and Wakefield.

The 1830s and 1840s were to prove the most prosperous in the life of the main Irish artificial water artery, the eighty-mile Grand Canal. Yet even at its pre-famine peak in the 1840s the canal was carrying only 250,000 tons a year, most of it heavy and bulky items such as building materials and turf. For other merchandise country dealers, even in the midlands, as a rule preferred to use the drays that plied all the main roads 'with great regularity ... on terms extremely moderate'.[1] Horse-carts charged 4d. to 6d. per ton-mile, or they could be hired for as little as 2s. 6d. a day. In the pre-famine decades these carts, rather than waterways or coastal shipping, handled the great bulk of inland carriage. The Grand Canal's famous but weaker rival, the Royal Canal Company, went bankrupt in 1812. A new company, with government aid, extended the Royal Canal to the Shannon but met with little success. The ninety-two-mile Royal never carried more than 100,000 tons a year; in 1845, to the great relief of directors, it was taken over by the Midland Great Western Railway Company. Traffic was light on most other lines too. When the Boyne Navigation Company petitioned for more public money in 1805 to extend its course to Trim and Navan, it was reminded that its most important potential customers, the Slane millers, were still sending their flour to Dublin by road, even though the toll between Slane and the sea was only 1d. per ton-mile. Again, the large sums spent on the middle Shannon in the 1750s and in the years 1802–6 generated little traffic, and the works were soon utterly dilapidated in places. By 1837 Lough Ree 'was but little used in a commercial way, not a trading vessel of any description crosses its surface'. Even in the more prosperous north only the Lagan and Newry canals proved successful. Traffic on the Coalisland was disappointingly light, and the Ulster Canal, linking Lough Neagh and Lough Erne, was a financial disaster.

Despite a great deal of discussion of proposed routes and investment flurries in 1825 and 1835–6, the period witnessed no railway revolution either. Daniel O'Connell was one of a group of speculators who dreamed of 'a general railway communication with various parts of this kingdom'[2] in early 1825; and in the next year the Limerick & Waterford was the first Irish line to obtain parliamentary sanction.[3] None of this came to anything, and Ireland's 'railway age' proper began during the famine. Fearing that private capital would not be forthcoming without some inducement, the Drummond commission recommended state support for a limited trunk system of some five hundred miles. Yet by 1845 only the Dublin–Kingstown, Dublin–Drogheda,

[1] 'Gleanings in the west of Ireland' (N.L.I., MS 10736), p. 6.
[2] D. L. Roose to Lord Oriel, 18 Jan. 1825 (P.R.O.N.I. D207/27/39, quoted in Thomas G. Ferris, 'The Ulster Railway, 1835–48' (M.A. thesis, Queen's University, Belfast, 1979), p. 24).
[3] 7 Geo. III, c. cxxxix (31 May 1826).

and Belfast–Portadown lines—less than seventy miles in all—were in operation. The government had helped to get the Dublin–Kingstown started in 1834 and later provided funds for others.

By 1845 Ireland had a cheap and extensive transport network. The roads and waterways could have carried several times more passengers and goods without pressure or a rise in costs. In this sense Ireland was 'an underdeveloped economy with a highly developed transport system'[1] even before the railway age, but the 'opening' of the country was also happening in a broader sense. Not only the rapidly rising number of travellers' accounts and statistical surveys (including the useful Dublin Society county surveys),[2] but parliamentary inquiries, the ordnance survey, and the censuses were making aspects of the real Ireland better known at home and abroad. In 1836 the engineer Charles Vignoles might lament, while sorting out potential railway gradients around 'Macromp' (Macroom) or 'Glengarram' (Glengarriff), that his maps were all 'miserably inaccurate' or 'execrably bad'; but the whole country was to be expertly mapped by Colby and his team a few years later. The railway commissioners (who employed Vignoles), the Whately poor inquiry, and the Devon commission produced much new information about people and places previously part of a 'hidden' Ireland, and the 1841 census was rightly regarded by its creators as a 'social survey'.[3] Much of the evidence produced was depressing; problems such as eviction, crime, poverty, and mortality were given a statistical dimension for the first time. While the figures may have had little short-term administrative impact, their very production in such bulk was unprecedented, and it may be surmised that, in the absence of the famine, they would have had more practical influence in time.

ANOTHER public service that changed out of all recognition was banking. In 1801 the Bank of Ireland was only seventeen years old, and private country banking was still finding its feet.[4] The older Dublin banks, such as La Touche's or Alexander's, limited their activities to exchange dealings, remitting money, and keeping accounts. There was no bank 'possess[ing] the means of regulating the circulation of the metropolitan district . . . and the rest of Ireland'.[5] By 1845 the Bank of Ireland had become a quasi-central bank, and the country had a solid network of joint-stock banks. These changes and their economic implications are worth examining briefly.

Economic development invariably means an increasingly sophisticated set

---

[1] J. J. Lee, 'The railways in the Irish economy' in L. M. Cullen (ed.), *The formation of the Irish economy* (Cork, 1969), p. 87.

[2] Above, iv, 673.

[3] Board of works, letter-book of Charles Vignoles, 1836 (P.R.O.I., I/10/3)); J. H. Andrews, *A paper landscape: the ordnance survey in nineteenth-century Ireland* (Oxford, 1975), pp 90–143.

[4] Above, iv, 150–59.

[5] [Mountifort Longfield], 'Banking and currency, part II' in *Dublin University Magazine*, xv (1840), p. 223.

of financial institutions. Are the latter a precondition for the former, or do they merely reflect economic growth? For financial historians this is an unresolved—perhaps insoluble—problem. According to one school of thought, development automatically generates the incentives necessary for the appropriate financial framework to emerge. The relative sophistication of the banking system is therefore just another index of economic development—unless an irresponsible government should create institutions ahead of demand. Another school argues that institutions do not develop everywhere in the short run with equal facility; laws, custom, education, and history play a part. Research in this tradition focuses, for example, on the number of banks in relation to national income as an independent explanation of subsequent economic performance.[1]

Before the suspension of cash payments in February 1797 specie had been the chief circulating medium in Ireland. The great variety of coin in use meant that, in effect, Ireland was on a bullion standard. This continued to be the case in Ulster, but elsewhere Bank of Ireland and other notes largely replaced gold and silver. The ensuing inflation and currency depreciation (the London exchange premium for Irish bills rose from 8.3 to 20 per cent) has been blamed 'almost entirely, if not solely, on an excess of paper'.[2] Note circulation seems to have trebled between 1797 and 1804. Some pointed the finger at the private country banks, which increased greatly in number after 1797 and aggressively expanded circulation, but the main culprits were surely the Bank of Ireland and the government, which increased the money supply from 1797. In expanding, reluctantly at first, its circulation four times faster than the Bank of England, the Bank of Ireland had betrayed the trust of those leading citizens who had announced publicly in 1797 their willingness to accept inconvertible notes in settlement of debts.[3] Such criticism of the Bank of Ireland in 1803–4 anticipated the later, more famous 'bullionist' criticism of the Bank of England in 1808–10.

Life was short for many of the new private banks. Only in Belfast was there stability: three new banks set up in the years 1808–9 all survived and developed through the province a system of agencies that anticipated the branch system of the joint-stock banks. The rest of the country, excluding Dublin, still had fourteen private banks in 1820, but the financial crisis in May and June of that year wiped out half of them. At a time of agricultural distress the deflation required by the partial restoration of cash payments at pre-1797 par proved too much for the others, and during the summer of 1820 most of Munster and south Leinster were left virtually without a medium of exchange.

[1] Lars Sandberg, 'Banking and economic growth in Sweden before World War I' in *Journal of Economic History*, xxxviii (1978), pp 650–80; Charles Kindleberger, 'Sweden as an "impoverished sophisticate": a comment' in *Journal of Economic History*, xlii (1982), pp 918–20.
[2] Report of the 1804 select committee on Irish currency, quoted in Frank W. Fetter, *The Irish pound* (London, 1955), p. 45.
[3] F. G. Hall, *The Bank of Ireland, 1783–1946* (Dublin and Oxford, 1949), p. 81; Trevor McCavery, 'Finance and politics in Ireland, 1801–17' (Ph.D. thesis, Belfast, 1981), pp 314–19.

The crisis was quickly followed by legislative reorganisation of the banking system. The existing law guaranteed that the Bank of Ireland's only competition would be small-scale banks. Now, however, business lobbyists vigorously demanded a more solid financial environment. Reform was opposed at every step by the Bank of Ireland, but the outcome was a joint-stock branch banking system along Scottish lines.[1] The new era was ushered in by the Northern (1824), quickly followed by the Hibernian and Thomas Joplin's Provincial (1825), and the Belfast (1827). Other banks—the National, Ulster, Agricultural & Commercial, and Royal (1834–6)—were the product of a frantic second wave of expansion. The only pre-1845 casualty was the well intentioned but badly managed Agricultural & Commercial.[2]

The banks in Ulster were formed with local capital, but all the others primarily with English and Scottish capital. Each bank developed its own style and specialisation: the Hibernian, for instance, nurtured a largely catholic business clientele, while the Provincial catered for landlords and gentry. The Belfast banks confined their business to Ulster, the others largely to the southern province. In the new competitive climate the Bank of Ireland was forced to adapt; it began to grant overdrafts and was nudged into branch banking, opening six agencies in 1825, and another eighteen before the famine. By 1845 the banks between them had 173 branches, well distributed over the country. Few towns with over 5,000 population were without a branch, and more than half of those with a population of 2,000 or more had at least one. Outside Dublin the era of private banking was past.

Pre-famine banking catered exclusively for the middle and upper-middle classes, and branch clienteles were small. Surviving records show, for example, that the average opening balance at the Provincial's Parsonstown branch during its first year was £250 (worth at least £10,000 today), while the humblest clients of its Youghal branch were small traders and merchants. Over three-quarters of the Hibernian's account holders were in commerce and the professions; the rest came from manufacturing, farming, or the wealthy leisured class.[3]

The Bank of Ireland continued until the act of 1845[4] to enjoy substantial 'special privileges', which brought it consistently high profits. The product of a more mercantilist age, it was accused of religious bigotry and undue caution in its business dealings. The small number of its branches may attest to the latter: the only towns of over 10,000 population without a branch bank in the act of

[1] Below, pp 231–2.

[2] Charles Munn, 'The coming of joint stock banking to Scotland and Ireland, c.1820–1845' in T. M. Devine and David Dickson (ed.), *Ireland and Scotland, 1600–1850: parallels and contrasts in economic and social development* (Edinburgh, 1983), pp 204–18.

[3] Allied Irish Banks archives, Foster Place, Dublin, signature book of the Hibernian Bank, 1825–46 (Bank of Ireland archives, College Green, Dublin).

[4] 8 & 9 Vict., c. 37 (21 July 1845).

1845 were in the bank's exclusive fifty-mile zone, and the bank had only three in towns of less than 10,000 population. On the other hand, it lent increasing stability to the financial system. Having been roundly criticised in 1804, it became more scrupulous about the value of its paper, and between 1804 and 1815 the Irish pound kept its value. It was to fall sharply again in the years 1815–16 and 1818–19, years of considerable economic distress, but regained its old value on both occasions in a matter of months.[1] Bank of Ireland notes became fully convertible in June 1821 at the old rate. In practice this meant the beginnings of a gold and sterling exchange standard that was to last until 1979.

Gradually the bank learned to behave more like a central bank. Less than two decades after its foundation it agreed to discount up to £80,000 of the bills of Beresford & Company, a private Dublin bank 'anxious to provide [them]selves against the possibility of an accident'. In 1814, and again during the great financial crisis of 1820, several banks appealed to it for urgent help, and none were turned away. In 1836 the bank once more took positive action, facilitating all joint-stock concerns except the ill-fated Agricultural & Commercial, and even their enemies conceded the useful role of the 'bashaws' of College Green.[2]

By 1845 the Bank of Ireland, as the main bank of issue, was 'fulfilling its duty in the most perfect manner', and the joint-stock network was healthy and expanding. Yet even though the banking system in 1845 had far more in common with that of 1900 than that of 1800, its relative sophistication is open to question. Comparison with neighbouring countries, using Cameron's index (number of bank branches per 10,000 population), is useful.[3] Between 1801 and 1845 Ireland moved from 'very low' to 'low' on this admittedly rather arbitrary scale. Like financial institutions everywhere, the Irish banks were accused of undue caution in their lending policies. Their accounts belie this charge to the extent that advances consistently exceeded deposits until the 1870s. The banks seem to have concentrated their lending on the provision of working capital through overdrafts, cash credits, and short-term loans, however, and shied away from long-term investment loans. Philip Ollerenshaw has recently lamented that 'no published history of an Irish bank contains significant analysis of lending policies, and no history of an Irish business contains systematic discussion of its sources of capital and credit.'[4] Yet even if further investigation only confirms that financial institutions were reluctant to provide venture capital, too much should not be made of the point, because even in

---

[1] Above, pp 61–3.
[2] Transactions of the court of directors, 10 Dec. 1799, 31 May–16 June 1820 (Bank of Ireland archives, College Green, Dublin); Charles Munn, 'The emergence of central banking in Ireland: the Bank of Ireland, 1814–1845' in *Ir. Econ. & Soc. Hist.*, x (1983), pp 19–32.
[3] Rondo Cameron and others, *Banking in the early stages of industrialisation* (Oxford, 1967), pp 12–13.
[4] Philip Ollerenshaw, *Banking in nineteenth-century Ireland: the Belfast banks, 1825–1914* (Manchester 1987), p. 192. 1.

Bank branches per 1,000 population c. 1800 and c. 1845:
Ireland and some other European countries

country	branches per 1,000 population
Ireland (1805)	0.08
Scotland (1800)	0.58
England (1800)	0.48
France (1800)	0.02
Ireland (1845)	0.21
Ulster	0.28
Munster	0.21
Leinster	0.19
Connacht	0.13
Scotland (1845)	1.4
England (*c.*1840)	0.7
Sweden (1840)	0.05
Prussia (1849)	0.27
France (1840)	0.1
Belgium (*c.*1835)	0.22

Britain financial institutions were slow to provide medium- and long-term loans to manufacturers.

Irish industry, however, did not languish for the want of long-term venture capital. In enterprises that must have seemed unattractive compared with British ones—banks, railways, mines—British capital came in support of Irish funds. True, these were joint-stock concerns, but the signs of a shortage of long-term venture capital—high realised rates of return where the capital has been found, company failures elsewhere, owing to undercapitalisation—were lacking. Moreover, since it is clear from insurance records that the capital outlay in brewing, food processing, and flour milling—areas in which Irish business thrived—often exceeded that required in factory industry, it may be surmised that had the latter been a better prospect in Ireland it would have been more to the fore. It may be supposed too—though further research is required here—that an informal market for term loans was supplied by the wealthy among the professional and commercial classes, often provided through lawyers.[1]

---

[1] Sun Fire Insurance Company Records (Guildhall Library, London, MSS 11936, 11937); Ollerenshaw, op. cit., pp 1–8; M. A. O'Connell, *Charles Bianconi: a biography, 1786–1875* (London, 1878), pp 18–19.

The banks, like the improving transport network, helped to reduce trans-action costs, thereby opening up local markets and helping to integrate the British and Irish economies. Other developments, such as a better postal service and increasing newspaper circulation (doubling between 1827 and 1844), worked in the same direction. Even where there were no roads to carry the mail coach, letters got through; those received by Maria Edgeworth while visiting the Martins at Ballinahinch, County Galway, in 1834 were carried three times a week from Oughterard by 'gossoons, or more properly bog-trotters . . . [their] bare, white legs thrown up among the brown heath'.[1] Such improve-ments prompted the movement of goods and the factors of production towards higher rewards.

TRADE statistics, though defective, reflect these changes. Irish trade statistics were a casualty of the act of union, disappearing with the last duties in 1826. Even for the years 1801–26 the figures are problematic. Incomplete and distorted by 'official' values, they have led to widely different corrected totals.[2] For the period after 1826 historians must presently make do with the imperfect estimates of the Drummond commission and isolated port statistics. Even so, the figures usefully illustrate several features of the changing economy. The following table reproduces the current value estimates of Anglo-Irish trade in the years 1804–6, 1814–16, and 1824–6 prepared by the late Ralph Davis, along with the Drummond commission's estimates for 1835. Some implications of the table are plausible. First and most obvious is the massive specialisation in food exports; nearly all the manufactured exports in 1835 were accounted for by linen. On the import side, tea, sugar, coffee, and drink made up the bulk of the food items; a massive increase in the volume of cottons is also indicated. Secondly, the trade figures underline the increasing openness of the economy. The share of exports in national income more than doubled between 1801 and 1845, reaching perhaps one-fifth by 1845. By both criteria Ireland was estab-lishing a pattern followed since by dozens of underdeveloped countries. The trade model produced by Stephen Hymer and Stephen Resnick in the 1960s[3] to explain aspects of economic change in such nations today also fits pre-famine Ireland well. Its doleful implications for those of the landless poor no longer able to make a living from handicraft production seem particularly apt. Thirdly, except in the period 1804–6, the figures indicate a sizeable positive balance of trade. Since massive invisible transfers in either direction are unlikely to have taken place, the surplus is to be expected and provides a rough guide to absentees' remittances. Yet because the figures are of poor quality, a

[1] Maria Edgeworth to M. Pakenham Edgeworth, 12 Mar. 1834 (*The life and letters of Maria Edge-worth*, ed. Augustus J. C. Hare (2 vols, London, 1894), ii, 232).
[2] Cf. Joseph Lee, 'The dual economy in Ireland, 1800–50' in *Hist. Studies*, viii (1971), p. 201; André J. Fitzpatrick, 'The economic effects of the French revolutionary wars in Ireland' (Ph.D. thesis, Manchester, 1973); Ralph Davis, *The industrial revolution and British overseas trade* (Leicester, 1979), pp 18–125.   [3] Above, p. 137, n. 2.

Irish foreign trade 1804–6, 1814–16, 1824–6, 1835

exports (£000s)

	1804–6	1814–16	1824–6	1835
manufactures				
linen	2,034	1,998	2,535	3,731
other	33	33	462	348
foodstuffs				
corn	678	1,779	2,914	3,401
meat	922	1,318	1,677	1,257
butter	696	1,038	1,008	1,400
spirits	109	43	16	76
other	104	218	192	207
raw materials				
fabric materials	186	341	363	421
hides and skins	72	83	16	46
other	105	184	231	660
total	4,939	7,035	9,414	11,547

imports (£000s)

	1804–6	1814–16	1824–6	1835
manufactures				
woollens, yarn	628	856	1,145	701
cottons, etc.	136	152	286	1,419
cotton yarn	332	101	210	40
linens, yarn	12	33	25	1,236
other apparel	347	209	385	488
iron and metal wares	539	333	533	288
other	562	451	561	752
foodstuffs				
sugar	340	531	234	775
other	949	875	1,152	2,471
raw materials				
metals	149	133	187	232
coal	246	330	318	803
other	983	1,182	1,091	1,713
total	5,223	5,186	6,127	10,918

The 1804–6, 1814–16, and 1824–6 figures refer to trade with Great Britain only, including re-exports from British ports.

reliable estimate of the Irish balance of payments during this period will probably never be established.

OWING to lack of figures, the performance of the pre-famine economy cannot
be assessed by reference to modern concepts such as national income and
productivity growth. Trends in inflation or unemployment cannot be precisely
measured either, though the cyclical peaks and troughs so easily identified with
such figures can be deduced from contemporary price and trade statistics.
However, none of these figures, even if available, would be good indicators of
how the welfare of the masses changed through time. National accounts tend to
tell a story about the minority with most of the wealth, often hiding important
shifts in the condition of the poor. Proper pre-famine national accounts, when
available, will surely support the account given here of an improving agriculture and considerable progress in other sectors as well. But they will fail to
show the growing inequality in income distribution, suspected on a number of
counts—the industrial revolution itself, population growth, lack of government
intervention—which weakened resistance to the potato blight when it arrived,
like a thief in the night, in the summer of 1845.

CHAPTER VII

The age of O'Connell, 1830–45

OLIVER MACDONAGH

THE years 1830–45 formed, to a remarkable extent, a little era in their own right. It was a petty age of reform and ruin alike. It goes without saying that its features were partially predetermined and anticipated; so it always is in history. To some extent the constitutional and political meaning of the union had already been clarified. It was not certain in 1801 that a separate Irish executive would survive. By 1830 its retention had been well and long confirmed. It was not certain in 1801 that Irish protestants would, in general, support the union. By 1830 there could be no doubt that the great majority of them, even the presbyterians of the north-east, saw it as their best, if not their only ultimate, security. It was not certain in 1801 that the catholic church and educated laity would, in general, reject the British connection. By 1830 the need to struggle for, and the length and nature of the struggle to secure, the emancipation act of the previous year, and the continued reliance of Great Britain on an exclusive protestant ascendancy for the internal management of Ireland, had left most catholics more or less 'disaffected'. None the less, it was 1830–45 rather than 1801–30 that set the pattern for Anglo-Irish relations in the later nineteenth and early twentieth centuries.

From the British standpoint, there were four notable developments in 1830–45. First, new attempts were made to broaden the basis of loyalism. One effect of the union had been to contract loyalism essentially to the protestant population; and no longer could piecemeal concessions to catholics serve to reconcile them to the constitution as a whole. Since 1808 the catholics' claims had been presented, and more and more peremptorily as the years went by, in terms of civil equality rather than supplication.[1] The interesting innovation of the 1830s and 1840s was the British effort (however partial and intermittent) to engender catholic loyalism by moves towards religious parity. Secondly, hand in hand with this dilution of protestant ascendancy went a more equal administration of justice and distribution of favours, and the opening, to a much greater degree, of offices of state and local government and membership of representative bodies to catholics and presbyterians.[2] The first steps towards power-sharing

---

[1] Above, pp 24–47, 74–107.
[2] For Peel's anticipation of these policies see above, pp 65–6.

and a neutral, supra-factional state in Ireland were being taken. Thirdly, Irish political dissidence was now meeting some positive response from, and an accommodation within, the British parliamentary system. The first of the 'liberal alliances' developed. These were party or group compacts whereby Irish nationalist members more or less regularly supported the whig-radical complex. In return they received a certain degree of influence over the Irish executive and Irish measures, and perhaps also some specific Irish reforms, if the whig-radicals were in office, or the promise of these things, if they were not. Finally, the tories in 1841–5 broke with the traditional policies of total reliance on protestant ascendancy for the control of Ireland, and indiscriminate resistance to change and pressure from below. *Fin-de-siècle* unionism was foreshadowed in the 1840s in the attempts to undercut nationalism, first by beginning to equalise Irish and British institutions and practice, and secondly by seeking 'safe' areas for reform, such as education, public works, some aspects of religion, or even the outworks of the landed system. Together these four developments represented a very substantial change in approach to the government of Ireland.

From an Irish standpoint, the vital development was the political articulation and organisation, and the extension of the range, of anti-unionism. Something of this had, of course, been foreshadowed in the campaign for catholic emancipation. The Catholic Association formed a model for all O'Connell's later bodies, and the basic techniques of fund-raising, popular agitation, and clerical management were all worked out in 1823–8. Moreover, from 1808 onwards, embattled with both Rome and Westminster on the veto issue, the movement was clearly coloured by nationalism. None the less, 1830 represented a new beginning, essentially. For the emancipation campaign, like most of the great constitutional agitations of the century 1750–1850, was directed at a single, well marked legislative object; and it was the assumption of the day that such movements instantly dissolved once the goal was reached. Twenty years later the Manchester radicals were to find themselves at a standstill precisely because they had identified free trade with the repeal of specific legislation; that done, and with 'Othello's occupation gone', they painfully discovered that few of the same men could be induced to fight a new campaign. For this reason—all else apart—O'Connell could not expect to transfer in any simple way the clerical–political machine, fashioned for the achievement of emancipation, to another, an unbounded and an amorphous conflict, or assume that mass agitation could be renewed at will and for general and continuing, instead of particular and circumscribed, ends.

Yet such a transfer and such renewals were precisely the achievements of the 1830s and 1840s. O'Connell did succeed in creating something like a national front and in keeping it in being even in collaborationist or relatively inactive phases; and he did succeed in drawing the catholic clergy, almost *en bloc*, back into political management and organisation, despite the hierarchy's resolutions of 1830 and 1834 forbidding such activity by the clergy, and despite Rome's stern endorsement of these injunctions in 1839 and 1844. Moreover, O'Connell pioneered not only effective popular participation and manipulation on a huge scale, but also the various tactics of deploying the forces he had conjured up against governments. The main forms of pressure he used were the independent political party at Westminster, his influence in rendering Ireland more or less governable, his capacity to mobilise and direct countless numbers, and the threat of mass disorders should he stand or be pushed aside or meet with a blank rejection. The device of alternative government—even if he stopped well short of any direct legal challenge—was also sketched out in the projected Council of Three Hundred, in Conciliation Hall, and in the assumption of quasi-police and quasi-judicial functions by the local repeal organisation. In fact almost every political technique subsequently employed in the Anglo-Irish conflict, other than those resting on violence and conspiracy, was explored and embodied during these years.

Correspondingly, almost the whole gamut of possible attitudes towards, and relationships with, British parties and movements was run in 1830–45. First came a period (1830–32) of independent support for the ministry in the house for a common legislative end, the reform bill, coupled with quasi-agitation in Ireland for further Irish ends—a tacit alliance abroad and pseudo-conflict at home. This was succeeded by a session of independent opposition at Westminster from 1832 to 1834, as much forced on as decided by O'Connell, which soon came to appear as a political cul-de-sac. Next, an awkward but gradually blooming courtship between the whig-radical and Irish parties developed in late 1834 and early 1835. This represented an oblique bargaining for office and for a share in the fruits of office, and for the right to control, to veto, or to influence legislation. A full-blown, if not frankly confessed, alliance, the forerunner of those of 1868–73, of 1886–90, and of 1910–14, followed. In its closing stages the alliance tended to become more and more contingent as O'Connell again threatened an independent agitation at home to counteract the growing sluggishness of the government and the house of lords' cavalier use of its blocking powers. Yet again, there were to be several later counterparts of all of these manoeuvres.

So far the pattern being woven concerned the whigs and liberals only, and the speed and thoroughness of its working out derived from the fact that the whigs were almost continuously in office during 1830–41. The opposite situation, particularly before the whig appetite for power began to return strongly in 1845, was equally prophetic. Minatory extramural massing and total opposition replaced parliamentary pressures and conditional cooperation. The state and the popular movement became mutually inimical; and the government worked to divide the national front instead of using it as a satellite organisation. Systematic obstruction was employed in the house of commons to resist coercion measures; Irish reforms were now seen in Ireland as sops and snares, as anathema to Irish nationalists where before they had been trophies. Yet again, the basic political actions and reactions of the next three-quarters of a century were being limned for the first time. All told, with the great exception of the 'Ulster' complication, there may be seen in 1830–45 models for almost every subsequent permutation and sequence manifested in Anglo-Irish 'constitutional' politics until 1914. In this sense, in setting the range, establishing the limits, and specifying the moves of the game, the period 1830–45 was a classical epoch.

In other respects, however, the dominant characteristics of this little era of Irish politics were being challenged even before it closed. In particular, three significant new notes were being sounded, albeit faintly and inferentially, by 1845. First, the Irish national movement had taken shape on the basis of a personal leadership and command. The hero at the centre, O'Connell, acted as the focus, marshal, and arbiter of aspirations, as champion, father-figure, and vicarious achiever all in one. But in 1844–5 counter-concepts, those of collective or committee leadership, and of accountability and answerability, were beginning to emerge from the nebulae of commonplace dissatisfaction. They may have been born out of Failure by Ambition rather than derived from any coherent democratic or representative theory. None the less, their gradual expression marked the opening of a conflict of principle over some of the fundamentals of political action in Ireland, which was to flare up spasmodically, and sleep uneasily in between, in the succeeding years.

Secondly, the rationalist and utilitarian basis of Irish nationalism from its French revolutionary origins onwards was beginning to be challenged in the mid-1840s by a new strain, derived ultimately (and perhaps also immediately) from Teutonic romanticism. *Gesellschaft*-type nationalism, built upon the theoretically free, isolated, and self-determined individual, was encountering for the first time in Irish history the *Gemeinschaft* type, built upon the supremacy of the organic community.[1] In this second strain cultural distinctiveness and group identity and coherence replaced universal assertions about the rights of man as the ground of the demand for independence and self-rule. The challenge was still somewhat incoherent in 1845, but with hindsight we can discern it, unmistakably, in formation. It was to be another, and probably the most fundamental, of the great dichotomies of later Irish politics.

Thirdly, sectarianism—or at least what was so regarded by the opposing faction—in Irish nationalism was under challenge towards the end of our

---

[1] 'The dichotomy of *Gemeinschaft* and *Gesellschaft* is associated, in modern times, with the sociological classic published under that title by Ferdinand Toennies in 1887. . . . *Gemeinschaft* tends to be used of an association that is internal, organic, private, spontaneous: its paradigm is the *Gemeinschaft* of marriage, the *communio totius vitae*. *Gesellschaft*—comparatively new as a word and as a phenomenon—is, on the other hand, usually something external, public, mechanical, formal, or legalistic. It is not an organic merger or fusion but a rational coming together for ends that remain individual.' (Eugene Kamenka, '*Gemeinschaft* and *Gesellschaft*' in *Political Science*, xvii (1965), p. 3.)

period. It was ironic that O'Connell, a lifelong asserter of civil rights and state indifference in religious matters, should ultimately have been assailed as a sectarian. The explanation lies partly in the swift march of concepts and events in this field in the second quarter of the century. The nationalist movement of 1830–45 was essentially catholic in both its mass support and its high degree of clerical leadership and control at local level. In the same period the catholic church was year by year growing more confident, more tridentine in doctrinal emphasis, and more reluctant to abate its full claims. All this limited O'Connell's freedom of manoeuvre. But he himself, as a *dévot* by now, would have inclined in any event towards some, though by no means all, of the newer attitudes. To label these simply as sectarian is to beg the question. On such an issue as education, the most intransigent catholic nationalist saw himself as claiming only that liberty of conscience was most truly served by each confession's developing, or being assisted by the state to develop, its own system. For him, secularism or centralism in such an area was but sectarianism in another guise. His opponents, contrariwise, condemned him as an agent of social divisiveness and asserted instead the primacy of supraconfessional citizenship as an educational goal for Irish children. Both parties were finally led on to conflicting notions of what was the right relationship between 'the church of the majority' and, on the one hand, the state and, on the other, the nation—or rather its vicars, the idea of nationality, and the organised national movement. O'Connell had not abandoned his original view of religious toleration, or of the composition of the Irish nation; nor did the catholic church ever conceive of itself as asking (what matter if in a more confident voice?) for more than the liberty to cultivate its own garden. But the very rapid advances in social aspirations, state activity, catholic power, and radical ideology in the period so altered the situation that what had once seemed simple matters amenable to consensus had become complex matters making for conflict by 1845. Yet another dualism was emerging here, casting its shadows already on the future.

As certain of the foregoing considerations suggest, Ireland was not only generating idiosyncratic ideas and institutions, but also participating in great contemporary movements and moods sweeping across the western world in the years between the 1830 and the 1848 revolutions. Let us point, in illustration, to three leading instances of this participation. In several respects the slowly maturing conflict between O'Connellism and Young Ireland was the counterpart of the confused struggle between liberalism and nationalism in many parts of continental Europe. It was not merely a matter of the antagonism between the *Gesellschaft* and the *Gemeinschaft* world-views, though this was of towering importance. Superimposed on this hostility was an international debate over priorities. Was it possible to achieve or secure either personal liberties or radical reform without political self-determination? Should one subordinate all else to unification, if one were German; or to repeal, if one were Irish? Again, the malaise of almost all Irish towns and cities in these years resembles that of many continental towns and cities, pushed into decline by the political and economic upheavals of the early nineteenth century. A vast war lasting more than twenty years had produced much political and economic consolidation. European states were markedly fewer and larger in 1815 than in 1789—and it might not be unprofitable to consider the union of 1801 in the context of scores of similar mergers and amalgamations on the Continent. Steam power was tending to change the location of production, wealth, and population according to the presence or absence of coal and iron. Free trade, or freer trade, was sending the economically weak faster to the wall. To pursue the German comparison (others might also be employed), a number of the state capitals in the German confederation were in essentially the same situation as Dublin in the 1830s, reduced to provincialism, saddled with redundant glories, luxury trades, and artisans, and sinking rapidly in wealth relative to the rising centres of political and industrial activity. Hundreds of German towns, dependent on markets and crafts, were in much the same slow decline as the lesser Irish towns, gradually retreating before the forces of mass production and cheaper communications, but still spared the massive disturbance of the railway. Yet again, the struggle of O'Connell and his class to break the closed ring of power, place, and honour, and their use of the masses and exploitation of the electoral system to this end, were closely matched by the Jacksonian democracy developing at much the same time—the 1820s and 1830s—in the United States. There is no question of imitation in either case. What we have, simultaneously, are two broadly similar responses to broadly similar challenges and frustrations.

IN each of these examples, Ireland reflected and expressed themes more or less general to the European and North American continents in 1830–45: the long-term effects of the French revolutionary experiences and wars, the immediate effects of early industrialisation, and the first stirrings of mass politics. But in Great Britain the 1830s and 1840s are specifically categorised as 'the age of reform', for the British emphasis was on concrete political and institutional changes. Whether or not it is useful to transfer the tag, unqualified, to Ireland, she was certainly affected by the British upheaval. Four aspects of the impact deserve special notice.

First, the alterations in the British political system in the early 1830s rendered Irish popular political pressures much more effective than before. Something approximating to a two-party system emerged in Britain from the struggle for parliamentary reform. It gradually became apparent, moreover, that the disparity in strength between the two great groupings at Westminster would be neither so large nor so fixed as to ensure prolonged periods in office for either, and that small independent elements in the electorate or a small independent faction in parliament might sway the balance. These changes produced much more favourable conditions for Irish disaffection.

Secondly, the British reforms inevitably raised the questions of whether or not they should extend to Ireland, and, if not, of the reality of the union. In the narrowly political field, in terms of the parliamentary and local government franchises and representation, for example, the disparity of treatment was greatly accentuated. In 1829 the Irish proportion of the enfranchised within the United Kingdom, already relatively small, fell drastically; and even after 1832 the British had roughly three times as many seats in the commons, *pro rata*, as the Irish. Had the redistribution of seats in 1832 gone in accordance with population, Ireland would have received nearly one hundred additions: instead she received five. The Irish municipal franchise qualification of 1840 was twice as high as the English of 1835, and the Irish 'reform' abolished most of the corporations and emasculated the survivors. Such unequal treatment presented ready-made new grievances to O'Connell. It also created *de novo* plain anomalies, the true reasons for which could not be explained without embarrassment and shuffling. It exposed for all to see the element of colonialism in Britain's attitude towards Ireland, and to that extent the hollowness of the pretended union.

On the other hand, in a different field Irish reforms strode ahead of the British. Some of these represented a greater measure of surrender or seizure of privileges than would have been conceivable in contemporary Britain. The inroads on the rights of the established church in Ireland, whether in terms of self-government, tithe, or education, are a prime example, representing a reluctant admission that the very bases of British and Irish society were likely to remain too different for a policy of uniformity to be sustainable. With religion as with the land system during 1830–45, two contrasting threads may be followed. Side by side with some efforts, and more hopes, to force Irish circumstances into conformity with English, to protestantise the population, and to introduce a three-tiered structure of capitalistic farming, went reforms or preparations for reforms that confessed that the two could not be brought into alignment. Elsewhere, in public works or public health, for instance, the relatively 'advanced' character of the Irish reforms sprang from other causes: Irish needs, Irish poverty, the weakness and self-seeking of both local government and the private sector in Ireland, and the extent and very effective expression of Irish discontent. Looking back on them, both types of reform, those 'positively' and 'negatively' motivated, seem pioneering work. Each was preparing the ground for the secular and collectivist state. But most contemporary Englishmen would have viewed the divergences in quite a different light. They would have taken them as unhappy indications that Britain was joined to a much more primitive society. Again, political union in the sense of political merger appeared to be receding, not advancing; and the alternative to political union was, for many Englishmen, frank acceptance of one's superior station in the chain of progress, and an Olympian arrangement and management of the inferior form.

Finally, there were areas in which the British reforms were applied, simply and unqualified, to Ireland. This was the case with new fields of state regulation such as factories, mines, and steam transport. Here a wholly centralised and uniform system, controlled from London, was developing. But more important still in this respect were the transferred reforms in the recruitment, conduct, self-image, and organisation of the public service.[1] These were gradually multiplying during the period. The Northcote–Trevelyan report of 1853 marked neither the beginning nor the end of this process of administrative transformation, but one event in a lengthy series. It was the 1830s that laid down the pattern of the changes. These moved, overall, towards the creation of the neutral state, distinct from politics; towards a meritocratic service; towards treasury control; and towards an ethos of passivity and candle-end saving in public finance. So far as might be, the Irish administration was subjected to the same remodelling. On the one hand, the instruments of Olympianism were being forged; on the other, the forms and conventions of any future Irish state were being assembled.

It would be misleading to emphasise only the innovatory character or the extraneous influences of the period. It was as much an age of ruin as of reform. It is as revealing to regard it as the ultimate, or penultimate, phase of various dying elements as to see it as the cradle or nursery of new. Perhaps the most telling single factor in the history of the preceding eighty years in Ireland had been population increase. No aspect of society, of the economy, or even of politics had been untouched by the massive augmentation. In the 1830s signs were already apparent that the end of this phenomenon was at hand. The rate of population increase declined sharply—in fact from 14.19 per cent in the 1820s it fell to 5.25 in the 1830s. Overseas emigration reached successive new peaks in 1831–2 and in 1841–2; and there was scarcely a year in the 1830s when some partial failure of the potato crop was not reported.[2] It was clear that the limit of the old expansion had been reached, and likely that the whole train of numerical growth would soon be put into reverse. Correspondingly, the economy inherited from the eighteenth century, in accelerating decline after 1815, was patently on the point of expiring. Cereal and potato acreages remained high, but only to provide the swollen population with subsistence. The localised economy survived beyond the eastern seaboard, but only because the canals provided a comparatively small and expensive commercial penetration of the interior, while the railways were as yet unbuilt. By 1830, however, the writing was already on the wall. Improved communications and full free trade within the United Kingdom would shortly produce the complete 'integration' of the Irish economy with the British. This meant the gearing of Irish agriculture to the growing British market for meat and dairy products, and (apart from a few industries that, because of various accidents, or skills, or

[1] Below, pp 538–61.   [2] Cf. above, pp 112–13.

their agricultural basis, developed on a significant scale) the furnishing of the Irish market with British products.

Partly for these and partly for other reasons, Gaelic Ireland was disintegrating before the famine. The proportion of Irish-speakers in the population, though declining, remained comparatively high, perhaps even as high as 40 per cent down to 1845. But almost all of Leinster, most of Ulster, north-east Munster, and even eastern Connacht had become predominantly English-speaking; and, what really counted in the long run, the proportion of monoglot Irish-speakers was falling much more rapidly than the proportion of those who could speak Irish.[1] For social and economic advancement depended on English. Not only the traditional language, but also the traditional life-patterns and culture in its general sense, were being pressed back into the poorest and least accessible regions and the most impoverished classes. It was a voluntary surrender to what were conceived of as the forces of the future, rather than a battle lost but bitterly contested. True, the first voices calling for the preservation of the remnants of Gaelic civilisation and peasant values were raised in the 1840s; and there were chairs of Irish not only at Maynooth but also at Trinity College and St Columba's. But, as has been wryly observed elsewhere, the glorification of 'the noble savage' usually seems to get under way at the point of his extinction.

At the other end of the Irish social, economic, and religious scale, the protestant Ireland of the enlightenment was also in its death-throes in 1830-45. It had been in decline since the 1790s when the movement towards equality for catholics became dangerously swift. More particularly, it failed after the 1798 rebellion had rendered security for protestant lives, interests, and property the overriding object. The disintegration continued in 1801-30. The rising tide of catholic assertion, and the growing realisation that the union was not threatening but shoring up protestant (even presbyterian) privilege, eroded the old confidence and pride. The *coup de grâce*, however, was delivered by the popular politics developed by O'Connell in the 1830s and early 1840s. These showed that the campaign for catholic emancipation was not to prove singular or inimitable, a nine days wonder, but that there were deep and permanent cleavages in Ireland that would in future be, to no small extent, expressed in terms of a religious power struggle. The bulk of Irish protestants reacted in fear by moving to the right politically, abandoning former liberal, democratic, and anti-British positions where these had been held, and sinking into confessional solidarity. Even northern presbyterian radicalism was modified, certainly on the issue of the union. The policies of Grattan and Tone alike were practically extinct among protestants by 1845, despite the handful of protestant leaders and opinion-shapers in the repeal movement and elsewhere who reexpressed these standpoints in a more modern idiom. The serene Anglo-Irish order and world-view were fading as quickly as their Gaelic counterparts.

[1] Above, iv, 383-7, 422-3.

Over and above 1830–45 being an era of reform or an era of ruin, it was, much more than most, the age of a single man. It is rare in the history of any country, particularly if it is a more or less open society, for an individual to leave so deep an impress on its organisations and opinion as did O'Connell on the Ireland of his day. There were several reasons why this should have been so. He was the pioneer, the first cartographer of an unexplored continent, that of the masses in constitutional politics; he was a many-sided political inventor and gadgeteer; he was responsive to an extraordinary range of the ideas and feelings of his day, not only in Ireland but also in Great Britain and the western world at large. He was perhaps fortunate in being cast, by the accidents of his situation, into the roles best suited for his political qualities—those of agitator, apologist, organiser, and broker. He could not have played a Bismarck or a Lenin. But neither could they have acted his particular part (although Bismarck, when young, admired O'Connell).

Although he was fifty-five in 1830, the future held much for him, and the next fifteen years saw the confirmation, exercise, and decline of his mastery in Ireland. His part in the later campaigns for catholic emancipation had both promoted him to a sort of a national leadership and cleared away what was, in many ways, a great cross-issue obstructing the path of reform. His entry into parliament in 1830 transformed his situation and both enabled and induced him to develop an entirely new grammar of pressure politics. For a decade he experimented with the uses of this form of power. Well before he shifted his focus from Westminster again, he had established his domination in catholic Ireland by persuading or compelling his political rivals, the trade unions, the priests, the catholic bourgeoisie, and the rural masses to support him, by and large, throughout his parliamentary manoeuvres. In short, he had turned catholic Ireland into something like a gigantic political party, which, of course, the leader had to tend and listen to, but which in the last resort he could count on to back him, even blindly. By the later 1830s he spoke and acted with commensurate authority.

The type of leadership that O'Connell exercised in the early 1840s was, in many respects, more dominating than that of ten or twelve years before. His organisational structures were more pyramidical, his associates more decidedly lieutenants, the nationalist newspapers more his instruments. It might also be argued that he had lost his 'best conscience' and his most useful critic when his wife died in 1836. But such an access of power had in the long run its political dangers, even for himself. It narrowed responsibility; it led to an excessive stress on palpable success and immediate achievement; and it rendered it more difficult for him to anticipate, and thus accommodate, contrary trends within the movement. By the autumn of 1845 there were several significant indications that, in its final form at least, his political system was in decay.

None the less, his influence in these fifteen years was immense and widely ramified. Most of the developments indicated above were crucially affected, and some quite clearly determined, by O'Connell's conduct and conceptions. The changes in British government and party attitudes towards Ireland, the growth of an Irish political ideology and battle tactics, and the progress of reform, not merely in Ireland but even Britain itself, were all, to some degree or other, of his moulding. Moreover, what he did not touch or tap was quite as noteworthy as what he did. In Britain, especially in its more 'advanced' industrial regions, the 1830s and early 1840s were years in which the old social controls—the magistracy, the corporations, the militia, the yeomanry, the army—and traditional family, work, and religious disciplines were breaking down. Locally and occasionally at least, this represented a fundamental crisis of order. To some extent the same phenomenon was discernible in Ireland. The virtual abandonment after 1833, under pressure from below, of the state's efforts to collect tithes, was a case in point. But O'Connell made no attempt to exploit this crisis, such as it was, in Ireland, or the more serious crises in Britain. In Ireland his influence was ever on the side of existing social structures *qua* structures. Even to secure the social changes that he desired, mainly equality 'within' established ranks and orders, he would not countenance popular repudiation of authority or the spread or enforcement of popular 'law'. He would not use issues or forces such as the land system, urban unemployment, the cultural collision, the Whiteboys, or catholic triumphalism to fuel his agitations. In Britain he worked happily and even eagerly with, for instance, the reformers of the Hampden Clubs or the Anti-Corn Law League, who were striving for a social rearrangement, but one which would reestablish social controls and order on a more 'moderate' and 'rational' basis than before. But chartism, threatening as it did in several of its manifestations to exploit the partial breakdown in government and legal enforcement, he eschewed.

All these various acts of self-restraint were, to some considerable degree or other, significant in their historical effect. It does not, therefore, seem too much to say that, in terms of omission no less than commission, O'Connell was—inevitable word—the colossus of his day. Negatively as well as positively, the period 1830–45 was peculiarly his age in Ireland; and much more than any other man of his time he was the constructor of the matrix from which later Irish history sprang.

CHAPTER VIII

Politics, 1830–45

OLIVER MACDONAGH

In general practical terms this period divides readily enough into three nearly equal parts. The first, 1830-34, was a phase of responses to a variety of new circumstances. The long struggle for formal catholic emancipation had just concluded; the next stage was obviously to translate the victory into actual and individual advancements. A second struggle, for social, professional, and economic parity, but within an unchanged class structure, was beginning. Another novelty was that O'Connell and other Irish popular representatives were now working within, instead of without, the house of commons. This raised new questions about the function and desirability of extra-parliamentary agitation; about the formation, durability, and character of an 'Irish parliamentary party'; and about the attitude that such a party should adopt towards the government. Thirdly, the whigs, after almost half a century of practically unrelieved opposition, had returned to power. What would be their Irish policy? What their reaction to nationalist and catholic demands and pretensions? How would protestant ascendancy fare in the new order? Finally, with the 'age of reform' dawning in Great Britain, the issue of parliamentary reform would at once overshadow, while it was in doubt, all Irish questions, and would furnish yet another Irish grievance when it was settled. The radical pressure for municipal reform, poor law reform, and full civil equality for dissenters would strengthen the Irish case for corresponding measures. The fact that legislation was rapidly coming to engross the time of parliament and that the cabinet was rapidly coming to engross the introduction and management of legislation would reinforce the arguments for reaching an accommodation with the ministry. The burgeoning professionalism and 'neutrality' of the British civil service, would, in the Irish context, tend towards the diminution both of local self-government by any particular group and of protestant ascendancy in general.

During 1835–41 a temporary resolution of most of these new problems and questions was achieved. An Irish parliamentary party had been formed by 1832. But with its organisation and discipline loosening in 1835, it now acted as a corps in a whig–liberal–radical army rather than independently. Meanwhile extra-parliamentary agitation was for all practical purposes abandoned. This reassertion of the two-party system at Westminster was an important, and in many ways unexpected, development; many had assumed that after reform the house of commons would be fragmented into numerous small and shifting groups. The development was important in Irish political history both for the precedent it afforded of the Irish participating in such a system, and because it laid down the constitutional pattern within which all Irish parliamentarianism had to operate over the next ninety years. Next, by 1835 the whigs had finally settled their Irish policy—largely in terms of the lowest price that must be paid for the support of O'Connell and his followers at Westminster and in Ireland. The price was to be paid, in part, by legislation, but mostly by changes in the administration of justice, the expenditure of public money, and the allocation of offices and honours. The years 1835–41 witnessed a belated effort to substitute a more detached, responsive, rational, centralised, and extra-territorial form of administration for the former indirect rule, based on protestant supremacy, which by and large had prevailed since 1801. This was accompanied by a train of British officials of a new kind, authoritarian, efficient, and dispassionate (in the sense of having only British and no peculiarly Irish prejudices)—men such as Thomas Drummond as under-secretary (1835–40), George Nicholls as poor law commissioner, James Shaw Kennedy and Duncan McGregor as inspectors-general of the constabulary, William Brereton as chief inspector of the revenue police, and, a little earlier, John Fox Burgoyne as chairman of the board of works. Most had been soldiers, as befitted their underlying concept of their role as that of pacifying a region of tribal disorder.

If 1835–41 saw the emergence of a new pattern of collaboration in Anglo-Irish relations, the next four years saw the emergence of new forms of antagonism. One innovation was 'Peelism', using the word to describe both Peel's own mature approach to the problem of political change and a novel British attitude to the Irish question. The Tamworth manifesto of 1835 was the first clear formulation of Peel's concept of judicious concession, the surrender under pressure of the most irrational, palpably inequitable, and anomalous elements in existing institutions in order to preserve their essentials and maintain political continuity. But direct challenges to authority were unacceptable and must be destroyed or dissipated by force. In Ireland this meant the modification of Peel's earlier blanket defence of protestant supremacy on the 'garrison' theory.[1] After 1835 he was not only willing but also anxious to compromise on such issues as tithe or municipal reform, to get them settled in (to his mind) the least unfavourable circumstances—with his opponents bearing the responsibility, the Irish muzzled by the needs of the liberal alliance, and the lords to be relied on to pare down to the bone what was yielded. But the opposing view was still powerful among the tories. In 1836 Lyndhurst, the leader of the ultras in the lords, restated the doctrine of ascendancy in its old Fitzgibbonite form:

[1] Above, p. 66; but see also p. 65.

One-fourth of her [Ireland's] inhabitants were English by descent, English in their habits, English in their usages, protestant in their religion, and unalterably attached to the English connection.... They had to contend with a population alien to Englishmen, speaking, many of them, a different language, professing a different religion, regarding the English as invaders, and ready to expel them at the first opportunity.[1]

As late as 1840 Wellington almost revolted on the final attenuated municipal reform bill because the concession of any degree of power to catholics endangered the protestant interest. For this reason even the temporary triumph of Peelism in the party's Irish policy in 1843–5 marked a watershed.

Superficially there was no insuperable barrier to O'Connell's doing political business with a tory government prepared to concede even minimal reform, and to extend its patronage even to a few catholics. But for thirty years Peel and O'Connell had been bitter personal as well as political enemies; O'Connell was a partisan and had long been a party man in British politics, and since 1833 he had taken it for granted that any tory ministry would work unceasingly for Orange domination in Ireland. It was not until 1844 that the ingratiating face of Irish Peelism showed itself at all, and by then the repeal conflict had deepened immeasurably their mutual hostility.

When, however, conciliatory conservatism did appear, it exposed anachronisms in O'Connell's political strategy and the relative fragility of the national combination he had built up. Peel drove wedges between the 'right' and 'left' wings of Irish catholicism and nationalism alike, the first by offering concessions that had to be publicly accepted or publicly rejected, the second by forcing a decision on the use of violence, or what might lead on to violence, on the repeal agitators.[2] After this it was clear that, quite apart from the rushing effects of age and infirmity on O'Connell, he would never regain the national authority, the parliamentary support, or the menacing visage needed to recreate the old liberal alliance. Two general patterns, then, often to be discerned over the next eighty years, made their first appearance in 1841–5. These were the tendency towards political disintegration in Ireland that followed immediately on phases of accommodation and assimilation at Westminster, and the tendency of hard-pressed unionist administration to attempt to undercut nationalism by economic, equalising, or confessional reforms, on the (for them) necessary assumption that the demand for self-rule was merely the distortion of some other cry of pain.

THE first political phase, from November 1830, when Wellington's government fell, until the dismissal of Melbourne's ministry four years later, was dominated by the campaign for, and the aftermath of, parliamentary reform and, in terms of Irish agitation, by the tithe issue. But personally it was dominated by Edward Stanley, the new chief secretary (1830–33), who was

---

[1] *Hansard 3*, xxxiii, 734–5 (9 May 1836).   [2] Kerr, *Peel, priests & politics*.

young, energetic, and domineering—but, as Greville noted in his diary, already
'half a tory'.[1] Stanley's Irish policy, which to a large extent he forced on Grey's
government, anticipated Peel's in 1841–5 and Balfour's nearly half a century
later. It would be too much to describe it as killing repeal by kindness: repeal was
scarcely a serious issue in 1830–34. But it was underlain by the assumption or
hope that administrative efficiency and economy and social aid of various kinds
would expose the hollowness of the nationalistic appeal. It was characteristic of
Stanley that he should have set up the boards of education and public works in
1831, the one to tackle the problem of mass ignorance, and the other the problem
of mass poverty, for men of his kind conceived of Irish disaffection as rooted in
Irish deprivation. Characteristic also were his efforts at administrative and
financial reforms in the Irish government, and at sweeping away archaic commercial restraints in Irish towns. All this was in the later Peelite mould, and had
indeed already shown itself in Peel's projected Irish programme of 1829–30.[2] But
Stanley's reforming zeal stopped short at the protestant ascendancy and the
Church of Ireland. He was prepared for a degree of modernisation even here—
the reorganisation of the grand jury system, for example, or the reordering of the
Church of Ireland's benefices and the substitution of a landed endowment for
the tithe. But he would resist any attempt to diminish that ascendancy or to
weaken the Church of Ireland as an establishment. He regarded both as indispensable for whatever degree of civilised order Ireland enjoyed.

No other whig minister, not even Grey himself, was as conservative as
Stanley on the basic issues of governing Ireland through the protestant faction
and by arrogant repression. Some, like Holland and Russell, fitfully attempted
to devise a wholesale alternative, and Stanley had to yield a little ground. He
was unable, for example, to secure a coercion act in 1831 or 1832, or to stave off
the church temporalities act of 1833, which suppressed ten bishoprics and
archbishoprics, set up an ecclesiastical commission with very wide powers to
reorganise and amalgamate livings, and taxed the richer clergy for the general
benefit of the church.[3] But these were minor setbacks. Overall, Stanley had his
way as chief secretary. The whigs' Irish legal officers were also 'half tories' at
least, and other 'full tories' at Dublin Castle were continued in 1830. The lord
lieutenant, Anglesey, may have had liberal and even radical impulses, but his
own folly and ineptitude, and the ministry's preoccupation with other matters,
left him virtually powerless *vis-à-vis* his chief secretary, who had moreover the
advantage of cabinet membership. Thus O'Connell's initial demands, as the
price of parliamentary cooperation, that 'the snappish, impertinent, overbear-
ing, high-church Mr Stanley'[4] be removed and that liberals and catholics be
given a large share of the Irish appointments, were disregarded.

---

[1] C. C. F. Greville, *The Greville memoirs*, ed. Henry Reeve (3 vols, London, 1874), ii, 382. As fourteenth earl of Derby, Stanley led tory governments in 1852, 1858–9, and 1866–8.
[2] Above, p. 107.
[3] 3 & 4 Will. IV, c. 37 (14 Aug. 1833).
[4] O'Connell to Duncannon, 4 Dec. 1831 (*O'Connell corr.*, iv, 371).

None the less, parliamentary cooperation was to come about; and in a pattern of alternating bouts of attraction and repulsion, it gradually grew warmer. The explanation was simple: up to a point cooperation was in the interests of both parties. The ministry needed O'Connell's votes and, at times, his voice. O'Connell wanted the fruits of patronage, more even-handed Irish government, and remedial legislation, which only a party in power could supply. It is important to remember, however, that in the early 1830s O'Connell and his 'tail' were quite a new phenomenon at Westminster. They lacked parliamentary experience, while the house of commons had never known a 'popular' party, appealing and responding, to some extent, to extramural and even extra-electoral forces. Moreover, the social prejudice against the O'Connellites reached absurd and very vulgar heights. Even Denis Le Marchant, an advanced liberal and well informed political observer, had this to note in his diary on their disreputability:

Daunt and O'Dwyer have more of the ruffian about them. Lalor shows that he has never been in gentlemen's society before. I believe it was only last year that Sir Henry Parnell brought him up to town to give evidence before a committee of the house, and presented [him] with a coat, being the first he had ever been the owner of, to appear in. Some of the others are not a whit better. They are understood to subsist on O'Connell. His large house in Albemarle Street is their hotel. They live there free of expense, much, as I hear, in the savage style of their own country.[1]

On either side, then, there had to be experiment and adjustment at first. The whigs had to learn to live with, flatter, and concede to 'blackguardism'. Some never would. But by mid-1834 the most obdurate of all, Stanley, Grey, and Graham, had virtually broken with or retired from the party. The radicals had to learn that although O'Connell was a leading British radical, his radicalism was already old-fashioned at some points and liable to collide with his Irish or catholic views at others. Radicals, who never felt the birch of the great school-master Office, were slow learners, politically. None the less, they gradually accommodated themselves to O'Connell's spasmodic leadership and occasional deviance. As to O'Connell's own politics in this phase, it is all too easy to be deceived by appearances, for they were, so to say, 'manic-depressive' in type, with rapid swings from enthusiasm to revulsion. This tended to obscure their steady trend. Beneath the incessant public gyrations we can discern a persistent endeavour to reach an understanding with the whigs. It was, in O'Connell's eyes, the strategy that promised most advantage at least cost. He had no desire to campaign squarely for repeal or to launch another mass agitation if he could make significant political progress otherwise. Each was useful, even necessary, as a threat. But both seemed, at this juncture, distasteful, unpromising, and dangerous as actualities.

Immediately the whigs took office in 1830 O'Connell attempted to come to

<hr>

[1] Arthur Aspinall (ed.), *Three early nineteenth century diaries* (London, 1952), p. 314.

terms with them, while they looked to him for forbearance. But before a month was out he was repelled, more by their determination to keep the Irish executive on its old course (as evidenced by their appointments, promotions, and retentions) than by any issue of political principle. He thereupon fell back on the tactic he had employed since early in the year, that of instituting associations (ostensibly to form launching-pads for a great repeal movement), which .the Irish executive swiftly suppressed seriatim. The government, anxious to establish itself as more royal than the king in the matter of public order, responded in January 1831 by arresting O'Connell for promoting unlawful organisations. Thus, within three months of their assuming office, the whigs were at open war with O'Connell.

It was characteristic of the relations between the two, however, that no sooner were they built up as antagonists than peace feelers began to be thrown out on either side. In this instance peace became urgent once the reform bill was introduced in March 1831. Although both the government and O'Connell denied that there was an understanding, prosecution of the latter was allowed to fail on technical grounds, while O'Connell became in effect a government supporter for the parliamentary session. The reform bill, which he warmly approved, did polarise all members of the house, and there was in contemporary eyes, no inconsistency in his subordinating the Irish question to its achievement. In November 1831, when reform seemed in great danger, he took the further step of instituting the National Political Union, to bring together all Irish reformers, whig, radical, liberal, and nationalist. This was the first of his attempts to establish an Irish 'popular front'. It was short-lived. When in January 1832 he and his sympathisers formed an embryonic party structure of their own, the 'National Council', and produced an Irish reform programme of reenfranchising the forty-shilling freeholders and increasing the number of Irish seats by twenty-five, they were rejected out of hand by the whig ministers, probably through Stanley's influence. There was no reenfranchisement, and Ireland received only five extra seats.

Thus the ground was prepared for a new breach with the whigs even before the reform bill was enacted. O'Connell determined that repeal should be the issue in the general election of 1832. His wholehearted adoption of repeal as his main platform reflected in part a reaction to disappointment with Westminster, with the corollary that only through self-government would Ireland win the reforms she needed, and in part a wild but temporarily strong hope that Irish nationalists and protestants would unite in an anti-whig and 'home rule' confederation. 'A conservative', he wrote to P. V. Fitzpatrick on 29 August 1832,

has but one fault, which is indeed a *thumper*: he wants ascendancy—a thing impossible to be revived. But he is, after that, Irish, often very very Irish, and whilst in opposition he may be made more Irish than the Irish themselves. An *Angleseyite*, on the contrary, is a suffocating scoundrel who would crush every Irish effort lest it should disturb the repose of our English masters.

I wish I could get Boyton and Shaw, the recorder, to join me for the repeal.[1]

As his last remark indicates, O'Connell strove hard to enlist the Irish tories, particularly in Dublin. Although it was a hopeless venture, it did not seem as absurd to contemporaries as it must to posterity. It was far from clear in 1832 that the patterns had already set. Irish protestants were undergoing a new experience, with so many of their bastions on the point of falling, and a British government that showed signs of regarding them as an obstacle rather than a bulwark. Might they not react as many of their forefathers had done half a century before? Might they not adjudge, as a considerable proportion had in 1800, that the union would undermine both their power and status? Might they not respond, as some of their descendants were to respond to similar deprivation and shock in 1869–70, by plumping for home government? From the start of his political career, moreover, O'Connell was prepared to pay a very high price in terms of 'securities' and all else for protestant collaboration. None the less, whatever our speculation, the Irish tories in 1832, with only a handful of exceptions, rebuffed O'Connell and preferred whiggery—if such it had to be—to 'ruffianism'.

O'Connell's insistence on a repeal pledge from popular candidates was partially successful. So numerous and various were the attempts to avoid a simple and absolute commitment that it is impossible to measure the success precisely. But certainly some forty of the new M.P.s of 1832 were clear 'repealers',[2] and several leading Irish liberals who had refused the repeal pledge had had to withdraw their candidatures or were defeated. O'Connell had his failures in the boroughs, but these he blamed on the careless or corrupt operations of the registration system. Now that he had an opposition party, defined by the issue of repeal and roughly equal in size to both the Irish liberals and the Irish tories, it might have been expected that his course for 1833 was clear. Far otherwise: he was reluctant either to oppose Grey's government generally or to press for repeal in parliament. Essentially nothing had changed since 1830–31—an understanding or tacit alliance with the whigs still offered most hope of gain and least cost or danger—except that a tory alternative had been shown to be illusory, and that O'Connell now found himself with a larger and more radical 'tail' and an obligation to take some positive action on repeal.

Thus 1833 proved to be a year of contrasts. On the one hand, O'Connell and the whigs drew together once again. The departure of Stanley from Ireland to the colonial office in March removed the greatest single source of bad

[1] *O'Connell corr.*, iv, 442. Rev. Charles Boyton, fellow of T.C.D., earlier described by O'Connell as 'that beastly caricature of a clergyman' (ibid., p. 387), and Frederick Shaw, tory M.P. for Dublin city (1830–31, 1832) and University (1832–48) and recorder of Dublin city (1828–76), were prominent Dublin tories.

[2] Forty-two 'repealers' were elected; after petitions and consequent by-elections the total was thirty-nine (below, ix, 638).

relations. With Edward Littleton, who became chief secretary in May, O'Connell was soon bargaining. In return for the abandonment or muting of parliamentary opposition, especially on Irish issues, O'Connell pressed, with some success, for the withdrawal of prosecutions of newspaper editors, the dismissal of Orange officials, and the amendment of the ministry's Irish bills dealing with the church and tithe arrears. On the other hand, not only did O'Connell face the 1833 session with a commitment to propose repeal, but he was also confronted with a whig coercion bill and with the need to establish or maintain his authority within his 'party'. Some ten or twelve of the repeal M.P.s were opposed to postponing the introduction of a repeal motion, and one of them at least, Feargus O'Connor, favoured a much more radical Irish programme than O'Connell, and was soon challenging his leadership. By contrast the right wing of the 'party' was not prepared to follow O'Connell's proposal that the coercion bill should be countered by systematic obstruction in the commons. There was moreover the problem of the allegiance of the fringe Irish liberal M.P.s who had neither rejected nor tied themselves to repeal. In these circumstances O'Connell probably felt not only that a repeal motion was virtually unavoidable, but also that it would have the incidental advantages of confirming his leadership and defining his followers. Certainly there seemed little else to be said for this course in 1833: without prospect, at that stage, of arousing a major popular agitation or of involving the catholic clergy in the campaign, O'Connell had no significant extra-parliamentary force at his back; and without it, a humiliating defeat in the house of commons was inevitable.

When at last, towards the end of April 1834, O'Connell, after more than a year of equivocation and hesitation on the brink, proposed his motion in favour of repeal of the act of union, it was defeated by the crushing margin of 523 votes to 38. Only one English member supported him, and the majority of the Irish did not. But there was political gain as well as loss in the affair. O'Connell's ascendancy over the Irish group was more firmly established, and his election pledge fulfilled. No longer did an obligation to press for repeal, in any immediate sense, hang about him like an albatross, and this particular barrier to collaboration with the whigs had been, for the near future at least, dismantled. Were it Parnell who was involved, historians might—almost automatically—set it all down to serpentine skill. O'Connell's garrulousness and childlike facility for throwing himself into the emotion or stance of the moment should not blind us to the fact that he was a superb politician, instinctively adept at manipulating others or extricating himself. At any rate, even if it meant some loss of face and diminution of threatening power, he had now extricated himself from his constitutional strait-jacket and was free to negotiate once again and more seriously with the whigs.

A third obstacle to a renewed alliance—Stanley and Anglesey, who had left their Irish offices in 1833, being the first, and the public commitment to repeal the second—was the coercion act of 1833.[1] O'Connell had fought its passage bitterly over many weeks, and although he had failed to prevent it reaching the statute book, his struggle had helped to hammer his group into something like an independent opposition party and also to drive a wedge between the right and left wings of the ministry and its regular supporters. Hard on the heels of the failure of the repeal motion, the coercion issue reappeared, with the question of its renewal after a year in operation. In June 1834 the liberal section of the cabinet came to a secret agreement that the new bill should be modified significantly; Grey and the conservative section repudiated them; and the upshot was Grey's resignation and the reconstitution of the ministry under Melbourne. As O'Connell summed up the change, 'we are on the way from a half whig, half tory government to one half radical, half whig'.[2] One minor but yet important by-product of the reconstitution was the appointment as home secretary of an Irishman, John William Ponsonby, who was raised to the peerage as Lord Duncannon on the same day. He was the minister most sympathetic and personally friendly to O'Connell, and the strongest advocate— from the whig standpoint—of the Irish alliance.

In fact the potential alliance failed to become actualised in the five months of Melbourne's first ministry (July–November 1834). The more conservative whig elements, most of all Melbourne himself (who had been chief secretary in 1827-8), were reluctant to go further, and William IV was decidedly hostile to either Irish church reform or his government's cooperation with O'Connell. For his part, O'Connell spent more time menacing than cajoling. The crisis was resolved, first, by the king's dismissal of Melbourne in November 1834, and secondly by the severe losses suffered by the whigs in the subsequent general election of January 1835. The first brought home to the whigs the disastrous political consequences of shelving *sine die* the question of a compact with O'Connell. To O'Connell it brought home the danger of admitting to power, through hostility towards the whigs, a tory government hell-bent, as it seemed to him it would be, on restoring protestant ascendancy and coercion in Ireland and stopping Irish reforms. His immediate reaction was to set up an anti-tory association to bring together once again, as in 1831, all Irish whigs, liberals, and repealers to face a common peril. The second, the whig electoral losses, profoundly changed the entire political balance. Although precision is impossible, the general election left, in round figures, the tories with a strength of some 270 votes in the house of commons, the whigs with about 200, the radicals with up to 100, and the 'Irish' with 60 or more, all of them more or less subject to O'Connell's influence and at least half of them, in the fullest sense, his party.[3] Clearly the whigs had now to choose between some form of an Irish

---

[1] 3 Will. IV, c. 4 (2 Apr. 1833); see below, pp 222–5.
[2] O'Connell to Richard Barrett, 11 July 1834 (*O'Connell corr.*, v, 151).
[3] Cf. below, ix, 638, 663, where the totals are given as 273 conservatives (including 37 Irish), 317 British liberals, 34 Irish liberals, and 34 repealers.

alliance and the loss of office. This was not merely a matter of the hour but quite possibly a permanent or at least protracted condition, as it seemed likely that toryism would maintain its recovered strength. O'Connell had to make the same choice in reverse. But he had also to choose between coalition or virtual amalgamation with the whigs; for the radicals proposed that the opposition 'parties' should work as separate bodies for agreed ends rather than merge. In the end O'Connell chose not only to collaborate with the whigs, but to form one party with them and, for the time at least, accept whig leadership. It was a fateful decision in terms of British as well as Irish political history.

Angus MacIntyre argues that O'Connell's rejection of the radicals' proposal destroyed for good their chance of forming a numerically significant and well knit party at Westminster.[1] Certainly it represented a triumph for the whigs: they were able to resume the leadership of one of the two major parties, after a momentary threat that they might be reduced to a body of less than two hundred members, which might moreover be expected to decline in time and to lose its distinctive marks, other than those of caste and anachronistic stances. At first sight, then, O'Connell erred badly in choosing to work within a whig–radical–Irish complex dominated by the traditional patrician leadership. Given his objects of 1835, however, the Lichfield House compact (as the formalisation of this choice has come to be known) was not unprofitable. The only specific commitment by the whig leadership was to appropriate some of the Irish tithes for secular purposes, and O'Connell was neither offered office himself nor permitted to nominate to it. But in practice he gained much more. Not only were the whigs effectively committed to Irish municipal and local government reform—in O'Connell's eyes equally vital matters—but they also, in 1835–7 at least, granted O'Connell a sort of informal veto on Irish bills and appointments. More important still, with Mulgrave as lord lieutenant (1835–9) and Thomas Drummond as under-secretary (1835–40), they provided the first Irish executive for a century and a half that worked against protestant ascendancy. It should not be forgotten that O'Connell's primary objective in the 1830s was the expansion of the 1829 bridgehead to a state of full religious and 'racial' parity in Ireland. Again it must be emphasised that all of these depended on controlling the levers of government, that is, cooperating with the party in power.

None the less, the question remains whether O'Connell might not have advanced his causes further in the long run by keeping his 'tail' autonomous and doing what he could to place the British radicals in an equivalent position. This applies particularly to legislation. Whig measures tended to be meagre in conception, stunted by cabinet compromise, easily abandoned in the face of opposition in the commons, and not earnestly fought for in the lords. Had the

---

[1] MacIntyre, *Liberator*, pp 144–6. On the Lichfield House compact generally and its impact on British radicalism see A. H. Graham, 'The Lichfield House compact, 1835' in *I.H.S.*, xii, no. 47 (Mar. 1961), pp 209–25.

government of 1835 been a coalition rather than a virtual merger, it is possible that, for example, Irish municipal reform might have come well before 1840 or that a ballot act might have been enacted some thirty-five years before 1872. Moreover, the 'collaborationist' strain in Irish parliamentary politics, with its attendant pains and bitterness, might never have developed. On the other hand, a coalition government might well have broken early and ushered in a long period of tory domination; and had this happened, O'Connell's prime objective at this stage, the weakening of the local power of an exclusive ascendancy, might have failed totally.

At any rate, with the Lichfield House compact the whig alliance was at last consummated. It was to govern Irish politics for six years, although from being an alliance *sans phrase* in 1835-8, it became a conditional alliance in 1838-41. As we shall see, however, this distinction represented a mere tactical variation on O'Connell's part; practically, his relationship with the government did not change. The alliance did not mean that O'Connell and the repealers invariably supported the ministry. On a number of humanitarian or 'advanced' issues, such as the abolition of flogging in the army or voting by ballot, they sided with the radicals against the main body of liberals—and, of course, the tories. On other questions, one of them the Irish poor law, they opposed the official measures bitterly. But none of these votes endangered the ministry's existence. When any did, O'Connell either found reasons for supporting the ministry or arranged a discreet absence from the house. The radicals accused him of desertion, but by the end of the 1830s he could reply 'tu quoque'; and in any event it was his constant, if frequently concealed, conviction that the *entente* paid better dividends than any alternative course of action. Even in terms of legislation, although O'Connell may have often failed to get what he wanted from a ministry palsied by cabinet dissension and badly outnumbered in the lords, he was normally assured that what he did not want would not be proposed: here the poor law of 1838[1] was the great exception. On one occasion, in 1839, when the chancellor of the exchequer introduced a bill renewing the Bank of Ireland's powers for much longer than O'Connell wanted, O'Connell fell back on systematic obstruction to such effect that the offending clause was eventually amended to his satisfaction.

The major gains were, however, where O'Connell expected them to be, in the field of Irish patronage and administration. Almost all judges, stipendiary magistrates, assistant barristers, and other law officers and police inspectors appointed during 1835-41 were either liberal protestants or catholics (who were almost by virtue of their religion liberal). Interestingly, the numbers in each category appear to have been more or less equal. To a lesser degree this also applied to the appointments to the ordinary magistracy and to the magistrates taking office under the constabulary act of 1836.[2] Here, and still more in the grander county offices of honour, the whigs were limited by their

[1] 1 & 2 Vict., c. 56 (31 July 1838).   [2] 6 & 7 Will. IV, c. 13 (20 May 1836).

concepts of appropriate station and property, particularly landed property. In general, wealth, titles, and massed acres tended to be tory. None the less, at every level there was some measure of liberal and catholic dilution.

But the changes transcended individual appointments, significant though these were cumulatively. Some structural alterations of the first order were either accomplished or attempted. On taking office as under-secretary in 1835 Drummond at once turned towards police reform.[1] He regarded the existing disparate county forces and the peace preservation force as necessarily partisan because they were recruited and rewarded by an almost exclusively protestant and 'ascendant' magistracy, and naturally took their cue from their masters.[2] In the constabulary bill, which he drafted in 1835 and which was let through without substantial amendment by the lords in the following year, the Irish police were centralised and rendered uniform and as politically neutral as might be practicable in the circumstances.

Coupled with this change went a considerable enlargement of the corps of stipendiary magistrates. Again it was expected—not without justification initially—that a more equal administration of the law would follow.[3] It is true that in the field of local government the whigs failed to carry through equivalent corrections. The grand jury system was 'reformed' by an act of 1837;[4] but in so far as this had any clear object it was to diminish corruption, not to produce a redistribution of power. The grand juries were to remain for more than half a century bastions of protestant and landed ascendancy—probably, once more, because of whig presuppositions about the social order. The ministry was not so culpable in the case of municipal reform. Six bills were lost, generally through the diehard resistance of the house of lords, before a measure finally passed in 1840.[5] The 1840 act was a compromise. Only by reducing the number of corporations to a handful, and curtailing the powers of these few survivors severely, were tory fears of demagoguery, peculation, and urban revenge on the protestants, who had misgoverned locally to their own advantage for so long, sufficiently allayed for any bill to be enacted. But municipal reform, however truncated, did tend towards the equalisation of the Irish parties; another outwork of exclusiveness had fallen.

The measure of most significance, however, in this field—was the Irish poor law of 1838. The boards of guardians set up under this act could and did reflect, to a considerable degree, middle-class catholic–liberal opinion in many districts. This counted increasingly in time because almost all the new powers heaped on local government after 1840 went to the boards of guardians. The former recipients of fresh functions, the grand juries and the magistracy, made no further advances after 1837. Within a generation a mass of legislation affecting the day-to-day life of hundreds of thousands had fallen, to some degree or

---

[1] See also above, pp 58–60, 71; below, pp 212–15, 551–2.   [2] Below, p. 213.
[3] Cf. below, p. 552.   [4] 7 Will. IV, c. 2 (24 Feb. 1837).
[5] 3 & 4 Vict., c. 108 (10 Aug. 1840); below, pp 215–17.

other, to the guardians to administer. This included sanitary, public health, district dispensary, pollution, veterinary, vagrancy, orphan, superannuation, and workshop acts.

Thus a marked, if not extensive, shift in power took place in Ireland under the first whig alliance; and this was O'Connell's major object. Up to a point it is to be explained in terms of a change of fortune, so far as the personnel of the Irish executive was concerned. O'Connell was as lucky in having the executive in the hands of Drummond, Morpeth, and Mulgrave in the later 1830s as he had been unfortunate in the tory Sir William Gosset (under-secretary 1831–5) and Stanley and Anglesey a few years earlier. But although personality might count for much—as Stanley's and Drummond's, for example, clearly did—it was the alliance itself, with a deep sense of mutual dependence as its underlying strength, that really drove the process forwards. Only a government could turn the tap on and off, and only O'Connell could ensure the necessary degree of nationalist forbearance and compromise. Though each party began to tire of the affair in time, the sense of mutual dependence lingered on till 1841; and in all these years the old ascendancy was being lopped and cropped, here and there, about the edges. As yet the losses may have been modest, but they were both irreversible and precedents for further spoliation.

TORY policy between 1841 and 1845 falls, broadly speaking, into two parts, with the line of demarcation somewhere in late 1843. The first two years were marked by a sort of dualism, or ambivalence. In part the government was pursuing a traditional 'protestant policy', in part it was taking over the whig policy of parity. This schizophrenia was personalised by the lord lieutenant, Earl de Grey, a right-wing tory with Irish protestant connections, and the chief secretary, Lord Eliot, a well meaning liberal tory. De Grey had the advantage of support in Dublin Castle from Irish tories such as Sir Edward Sugden, the new lord chancellor (1841–6), and Francis Blackburne, the new attorney general (1841–2); but Eliot could count on Peel or Graham reining in the ultra party when it threatened to bolt too far back along the road of learning nothing and forgetting nothing. De Grey, acting on his own initiative, promoted only opponents of the national education system to the higher offices of the Church of Ireland, and only protestants in the police force; restored some of the Orange magistrates dismissed by the previous regime; and was eager for prosecutions of the press for libels on the administration. Eliot, on the other hand, defended the national board of education, and in the end beat off the Irish tory campaign for state support for the Church of Ireland's schools. He upheld the whig poor law of 1838 and the 'democratic' franchise of 1832. But he also struggled for more positive ends, in particular for some catholic legal appointments and a modest programme of legislative reform. Two of his proposals for the 1842 session, an increase in the Maynooth grant and an extension of the franchise, were rejected by the cabinet. But he did introduce bills on medical charities, drainage, and law and grand jury reform, all of which were, in a mild way, inimical to the interests of the ascendancy. Irish tory opposition secured the defeat of the first and last of these, which promised some slight diminution in the powers of the local gentry. In 1843 he presented a poor law reform bill that epitomised the divided Irish policy. The proposal to increase the number of *ex officio*, at the expense of the elected, poor law guardians pleased the 'ultras', just as the proposal to exempt the poorest tenants from the poor rate pleased the liberal tories. Significantly, perhaps, the ministry, under pressure, dropped the first of these clauses in the house of commons, while the second was retained and enacted.

The strange dualism of 1841–3 is ultimately explicable only in terms of the cabinet's absorption in other matters: economic distress and social disaffection in Britain, the anti-corn-law campaign, Indian difficulties, and dangerously deteriorating relations with the United States and France. Yet almost half of Peel's cabinet consisted of former lords lieutenant and chief secretaries, and they might have been expected to keep the Irish question in the forefront. Moreover, Peel himself and Stanley had developed during their secretaryships particularly clear and elaborate views on the proper government of Ireland, and Peel's in particular should have opened the way to ambitious 'remedial' measures. He wrote to Sir James Graham in October 1843 that

mere force, however necessary the application of it, will do nothing as a permanent remedy for the social evils of Ireland. We must look beyond the present, bear in mind that the day may come—and come suddenly and unexpectedly—when this country may be involved in serious disputes or actual war with another power, and that it may be of the first importance that the foundations of a better state of things should have been laid.[1]

Perhaps Peel and his cabinet would have taken up Ireland in a large way, their foreign and domestic preoccupations notwithstanding, had they considered the Irish pressures of 1841–3 to be serious. But on the parliamentary front not only had the tories a very comfortable overall majority in the house of commons, but they also encountered only feeble Irish opposition there. In fact it is arguable that the Irish tories presented more trouble to the government than either the Irish whigs–liberals or repealers. So far as Irish agitation went, the repeal movement tended to be dismissed by the cabinet as a gigantic sham down to May 1843—a 'failing concern' was for long Peel's judgement—and there was no increase in Irish violence or disorder during 1841 or 1842. Thus Peel did not feel himself to be under sufficient pressure to work out any coherent Irish policy beyond alternate checks to the exuberance of de Grey and Eliot.

It would be wrong to speak of O'Connell as politically bankrupt at any stage of his career: he was much too sanguine and fertile a politician for that. But, his

---

[1] Parker, *Peel*, iii, 65.

dark last year apart, his resources were never lower than in 1841–2. It was clear from the general election of 1841 that his old tactics were exhausted. Only eighteen repealers were returned, but it was of still greater significance that not many more had put themselves forward for election. O'Connell was no longer placing much emphasis on a parliamentary party, or even attempting to work in tandem, electorally, with the whigs. The alliance had run its course, and for O'Connell the 'parliamentary method' had, over the years, narrowed itself to the alliance. On the other hand, the extra-parliamentary agitation of the repeal movement remained in a minor key until the last quarter of 1842, and O'Connell's self-imposed political neutrality as lord mayor of Dublin in 1841–2 was a further inhibition. His mayoralty was a ritualistic celebration of the triumphs of the 1830s, as well as a first fruit of the municipal reform act of 1840. In terms of the politics of the early 1840s, it was a cul-de-sac.

In these circumstances 1841 and 1842 were largely years of marking time. The post-election parliamentary session of 1841 was short and unproductive of legislation. But in the long and legislatively fruitful session of 1842 O'Connell was equally ineffectual and directionless. In so far as he developed a new strategy for Irish nationalism, it was a fresh form of alliance, now with an essentially extra-parliamentary British movement. He had been wary of chartism, although its formal programme was identical with his own in the field of elections and representation; but he was eager to cooperate with the Anti-Corn-Law League. Not only, once again, was the radical objective one that he himself shared, but he also linked the league's struggle with his own in Ireland. The anti-corn-law campaign, he observed in 1842, 'will compel the aristocracy to yield in England and to leave us Ireland to ourselves'.[1] The expectation that the government's will to coerce Ireland would be weakened by a dual assault on the landed interest was, however, a chimera. Peel was gradually to separate the government from the landed interest; and Cobden, though accepting O'Connell's valuable aid in persuading the Irish in England and particularly in Lancashire to support the league, gave no reciprocal assistance to the repealers. He felt, he wrote later, 'a complete antagonism and repulsion' against O'Connell and his party by the 1840s.[2] None the less, there was one special sense in which the anti-corn-law movement helped, although there appears to be no evidence that O'Connell included this in his calculations. The league was founded on the model of O'Connell's associations of the 1820s and 1830s, the same model that served again for the latest repeal association. If the latter were to be suppressed in 1841 or 1842, while the former was left untouched, there would have been a self-evident anomaly, all the more so as the league's spokesmen went much closer to 'sedition' and incitement to violence in 1842 than any of the repealers. On the other hand, if both were suppressed together, the government would face 'war' on two fronts, and

[1] O'Connell to P. V. Fitzpatrick, 11 Feb. 1842 (*O'Connell corr.*, vii, 134).
[2] John Morley, *The life of Richard Cobden* (London, 1903), p. 491.

Stanley, for one, believed that this might 'precipitate disastrous events in both countries at the same moment'.[1] Thus for two years the league at least provided a shield behind which the organisation and expansion of the repeal movement could be carried on.

The agitation in Ireland had begun to gather momentum in the winter of 1842-3, but it was not until the late spring or early summer of 1843, when the sudden tenfold leap in the membership and the repeal rent was reported, that the government took alarm. It had reason to do so. O'Connell's strategy, as revealed at successive meetings of the repeal association in April, was very shrewd. After Easter the great tour of Ireland, marked each Sunday by a 'monster meeting', would begin. The tour would demonstrate at once the peaceful character, the gravity, and the numerical strength of the demand. Concurrently a campaign of enrolment would proceed, with the object of recruiting three million members by the end of July. Next, each of the 'districts' into which the association had divided the country would select individuals to meet 'spontaneously' in Dublin (as the Council of Three Hundred) to plan a bill for repeal. This programme had the advantages of protracting the pressure, while yet increasing it steadily stage by stage over a period of five months, and of culminating in a full-blooded challenge to British authority, which would be very difficult either to avoid taking up or to meet by legal counter-measures. Perhaps the final outlines of the strategy were sketchy. But to an old professional like O'Connell five months would have seemed an aeon in politics. Meanwhile by May Peel and his cabinet were at last ready to take up the Irish question seriously and positively: the crises in Britain and abroad were over, for the time. This was the background to the development of their counter-policy of combined coercion and concession—the 'quick alternation of kicks and kindnesses',[2] in Locker Lampson's phrase—with which later generations of Irishmen were to become familiar. Peel was the true initiator of iron-handed conciliation, although necessity—the need to impose 'order' and win goodwill at once—was doubtless the mother of this particular invention.

But the kicks came first. The parliamentary session of 1843 was dominated, so far as Irish measures went, not by reform but by a repressive arms bill, giving the police virtually arbitrary powers of search and imposing the penalty of seven years transportation for being in possession of an unlicensed firearm. The bill appears to have been something of a panic measure, presupposing preparations for an armed uprising or at least large-scale armed disturbances, although there is no evidence that any such preparations were afoot. The manner of its passage through the house of commons was interesting politically. First, O'Connell, his sons (except Morgan), and other leading

[1] Graham to Peel, 7 May 1843 (B.L., Add. MS 40448, pp 297-8, quoted in MacIntyre, *Liberator*, p. 270).

[2] G. T. L. Locker Lampson, *A consideration of the state of Ireland in the nineteenth century* (London, 1907), p. 434.

repeal lieutenants were absent from all the debates, being engrossed in the popular campaign in Ireland: such was the measure of the decline in 'the parliamentary method' in 1843. Secondly, it was left to the more moderate Irish liberals to fight the bill in the commons. This they did with remarkable success. It took ten weeks to force it through the commons in the teeth of the concerted obstruction offered by Richard Lalor Sheil, William Smith O'Brien, Thomas Wyse, and their supporters. Sittings were spun out to 3 a.m. on occasion; the government majorities dropped sharply; and the measure was emasculated in the end.[1] More curious still was the marked (if temporary) radicalisation of many of the Irish liberals. At the end of the session they drew up a remonstrance against British policy in Ireland, adding that 'we recognise in you no superior title to political rights', and implying that they themselves might be driven, in exasperation and despair, into the repeal camp if the course of repression were continued.[2] Herein perhaps lay the seeds of the coming federalist movement, which represented an attempt to steer a course between union and repeal. The parliamentary struggle also precipitated the conversion of Smith O'Brien and others to the repeal cause.

For the six months May–October 1843 repression was in the ascendant in government ranks. Not merely was the arms bill its principal Irish business in parliament, but also twenty-four magistrates were dismissed for presiding over repeal meetings, thousands of additional soldiers were brought into the country, the decision was taken to proclaim the Council of Three Hundred, should it attempt to meet, and the search for a case against O'Connell himself was begun. The climax of this phase was the banning on 7 October of the last of the repeal meetings of 1843 and the arrest of O'Connell and eight of the subordinate leaders a week later on charges of conspiracy to subvert and intimidate the lawful government. Yet even before the proclamation of the Clontarf meeting or his own arrest O'Connell was already beginning to hedge his bets and toy once more with 'the parliamentary method'. He tried to ensure that the Council of Three Hundred could not turn in a revolutionary direction by proposing its conversion into an Irish parliament by the use of the royal prerogative, while at the same time he sounded out a former whig minister, Lord Campbell (lord chancellor of Ireland, June–September 1841), on the prospects of reviving the whig alliance.

In form, the conflict between the government and Irish nationalism, personalised as a political duel between Peel and O'Connell, began to alter in the last quarter of 1843. O'Connell had shot his bolt as a popular agitator, and the repeal campaign, as a mass movement, could not but recede after Clontarf. His natural inclination, and perhaps his only resource, was to attempt a return to the politics of the 1830s. 'O'Connell will run no more risks', Thomas Davis observed shrewdly during the course of O'Connell's imprisonment; '... from

[1] 6 & 7 Vict., c. 74 (22 Aug. 1843).
[2] MacIntyre, *Liberator*, pp 274–5.

the day of his release, the cause will be going back and down.'[1] Apart from the accuracy of this prediction of the effects of disappointment, defeat, confinement, and debility on an old man, the remark indicated that the long-restrained criticisms of the more 'advanced' nationalists would soon be openly expressed, and that eventually formal antitheses would be set up and the repeal movement divided. O'Connell's imprisonment in Richmond penitentiary was a climacteric in both respects.

Meanwhile Peel, Graham, Stanley, and Eliot began to explore the practicability of conciliation. They did not appreciate the opportunities of splitting Irish nationalism that O'Connell's arrest and imprisonment offered them. Here they had sown the seeds of division inadvertently. Instead they aimed at dividing the Irish catholic clergy and laity—O'Connell's two main bodies of support—and, in Peel's words, detaching from the repeal agitation 'a considerable proportion of the respectable and influential Roman Catholic population'.[2] Five major proposals, three of them directly religious, emerged from the cabinet papers and deliberations of the autumn and winter. First, it was decided to treble the annual grant to Maynooth (from £8,928 to £26,360) and to make it a permanent charge on the revenue, while providing a capital grant of £30,000 (the equivalent, roughly speaking, of £1,200,000 in terms of today's costs) for the renovation and extension of the college buildings. Here the government would bat on a strong wicket. The bishops had privately requested assistance in 1841 and 1842, and could not but welcome the new offer, all the more so as Peel would have to brave a protestant furore in Britain and confess to past illiberality in making it. Whether the government's further hopes that a better endowed college would produce more urbane and anglophilic parish clergymen were well grounded was, of course, another matter.

Secondly, the university question was raised, initially, in terms of clerical education. In the proposed provincial colleges at Cork, Belfast, and Galway 'young men destined for the priesthood might receive a liberal ecclesiastical education, in connection with a general education they would share with others'.[3] As the university bill was taking shape this aspect dropped largely out of sight, but the issue remained essentially religious—it was now the provision of third-level education for catholics and presbyterians. The government did succeed in its political objective here, although not quite in the form that it had intended. Concurrent endowment of denominational colleges, providing catholics and presbyterians with equivalents of the Church of Ireland Trinity College, was ruled out. It would probably have met fatal opposition in parliament from combined protestant and secularist forces and would in any event

---

[1] Randall Clarke, 'The relations between O'Connell and the Young Irelanders' in *I.H.S.*, iii, no. 9 (Mar. 1942), p. 22.

[2] Cabinet memorandum by Peel, 17 Feb. 1844 (Parker, *Peel*, iii, 106); Kerr, *Peel, priests, & politics*, pp 110–17.

[3] Stanley to Peel, 20 Mar. 1844 (B.L., Add. MS 40468, quoted in McDowell, *Public opinion & govt policy*, pp 212–13).

have tended to undo the anti-denominational work that the national schools were supposed to be carrying out, and on which many British hopes for the ultimate pacification of Ireland rested. Thus the government chose the non-denominational University of London as its model, and in so doing created a threefold division in the catholic–nationalist ranks. While the colleges bill, in its final form, failed to satisfy any body of Irishmen completely, almost half the Irish catholic bishops, almost all the Irish liberal and 'moderate' repeal M.P.s, and the bulk of the Young Ireland faction in the repeal movement were ready to accept it, at least as a *pis aller*, and to work within the new system.[1] The bare majority of the bishops, shepherded by John MacHale of Tuam, and the main body of repealers, following O'Connell, would probably have settled for nothing less than separate sectarian endowments. At any rate, they rejected the proposed colleges for their 'godlessness'. The cleavage within the church (which the ministry had doubtless hoped for, if they failed to carry the entire episcopate with them) was of only secondary importance and comparatively short-lived: by 1852 the bishops were at one in forbidding the colleges to catholics, except for purely professional qualifications.[2] The failure of O'Connell to carry such M.P.s as Thomas Wyse, Richard Lalor Sheil, and Richard More O'Ferrall probably mattered little at this stage when the prospects of re-creating an Irish parliamentary party in the near future were very small. But the bifurcation in Irish nationalism (which the ministry had never contemplated) was of critical significance in the long run, as it engendered 'clerical' and 'anticlerical' factions in most of the manifestations of national resistance in the second half of the nineteenth century.[3]

The third Peelite measure, the charitable donations and bequests bill, was the one that most damaged O'Connell's relations with the church. This bill,[4] representing an attempt to remove one of the catholic grievances, set up a new bequests board of thirteen, including five catholics, three of whom were to be catholic prelates. Property might be vested in the board in trust for the maintenance of catholic clergy or churches. It was immediately denounced by MacHale and O'Connell as discriminatory against the religious orders, insulting in annulling bequests made less than three months before the testator's death, and dangerous in facilitating outside intervention in the domestic concerns of the catholic church. It is difficult to believe that the nationalist leaders were not being disingenuous, for the bill certainly improved the position of catholics. The true reason for their opposition was, doubtless, apprehension that the issue would divide the church and render part of it sympathetic to the tory ministry. MacHale railed against the bill as associating 'catholics with the old and inveterate enemies of our faith . . . detached from

[1] J. R. Hill, 'Nationalism and the catholic church in the 1840s' in *I.H.S.*, xix, no. 76 (Sept. 1975), pp 371–95.
[2] Below, pp 396–8.
[3] See, on all matters in the above paragraph, Moody & Beckett, *Queen's, Belfast*, i, 1–80.
[4] Enacted as 7 & 8 Vict., c. 97 (9 Aug. 1844); below, pp 472–6.

their brethren and acting against the interests of their religion, dependent on the crown, fearful of its displeasure, and fawning on its caresses'.[1] It was quickly apparent that there was no prospect of defeating the bill in parliament: only seven Irish M.P.s voted against the second reading. But unless three 'fawning' prelates could be found to join the board, the act would be a dead letter, and the government proportionately humiliated and rejected. Thus the matter became another trial of strength between Peel and O'Connell, with the repealers, the repeal press, and the repeal bishops exerting the utmost pressure against any prelates who might be invited to take seats on the board. They failed. After some wavering and at least one defection, the archbishops of Armagh and Dublin, and Bishop Denvir of Down and Connor, were gazetted as members. Unquestionably the nationalists had suffered a moral and (with a breach now open between some leading churchmen and the repeal association) also a political defeat. Dublin Castle exulted: 'The Roman Catholic party, as such, has ceased to exist. O'Connell can no longer rely upon the support of the church,' wrote Eliot. 'We have erected a barrier—a line of churchmen—', Heytesbury, the new lord lieutenant, added, 'behind which the well thinking part of the Roman Catholic laity will conscientiously rally, and aid us in carrying out . . . measures of conciliation.'[2] While this exaggerated both the government's success and its significance, there could be no doubt that O'Connellism had been severely wounded.

The last two major measures of 'conciliation' devised in late 1843 and early 1844 were secular. First, at Graham's suggestion a royal commission to inquire into Irish land tenure (the Devon commission) was set up in November 1843. The approach to this great subject was timid: Graham's declared object was merely to give the government 'a distinct view of the causes of discontent in Ireland' and an opportunity to evince 'sympathy with the sufferings of an entire people'. 'I fear', he also wrote, 'the remedies are beyond the reach of legislative power.'[3] So it proved, as far as Peel's government was concerned. After the commission reported in February 1845, a modest bill, whose principal feature was compensation for improvements, met 'uncomfortable' opposition on its introduction in the lords and was postponed—*sine die*, as things turned out. None the less, the Devon commission represented a turning-point in Britain's Irish policy. For the first time the landed system as a whole was placed in the arena of potential reform; and the testimony of 1,100 witnesses and numerous written submissions exposed and delineated its evils authoritatively and for all time.

The last projected reform was interesting because it was designed as a step towards rendering the union more an association of equals and less an expression of British supremacy and superiority. The Irish county franchise was

[1] *The letters of the Most Rev. John MacHale* (Dublin, 1847), p. 583.
[2] Parker, *Peel*, iii, 132–3.
[3] Ibid., ii, 65–6.

much more restricted than the English, and had been narrowed further in 1837 by judicial decision on the meaning of the £10 freehold. Peel and Graham decided on a £5 freehold franchise for Ireland, even though it would probably cost the tories some Irish county seats. The registration bill embodying this proposal never proceeded beyond the second reading. But it did prepare the way for a similar measure in 1850;[1] and meanwhile its conception and introduction were emblematic of a new departure on the part of the tories. It was accompanied in 1845 by more catholic appointments to senior positions in Dublin Castle, and by the dismissal of an Orange deputy lieutenant and an Orange magistrate for their parts in Orange meetings protesting against the government's surrender to popery. Although the party processions act of 1832 was allowed to expire in 1845, a stronger act was passed in 1850.[2] Such moves represented the executive counterpart of the legislative conciliation, an assertion of the state's impartiality among Irish sects.

MEANWHILE, apart from one attendance in the commons in 1844 during the course of his appeal against his conviction in the state trials, O'Connell was absent from the house for about two and a half years during 1843–5. At first his absence was consequential on his popular campaigning; then it was enforced by incarceration; and finally it was a tactical retreat from a field in which nothing but a trouncing awaited him. The pitiful parliamentary performance of the repealers during the passage of the charitable donations and bequests bill in the spring of 1844 revealed the catastrophic decline that had taken place in the party's power in the commons. It had been reduced to a handful, some of them rogues or buffoons, working without steady support from any other corner of the house. In these circumstances O'Connell stood only to lose in repute and influence by appearing in the house. This was borne in on him with a vengeance when at last he returned there in mid-1845. He had been reluctant to take this step, and may have done so primarily to impress on Smith O'Brien and the repeal bishops and clergy that he was still in earnest. The colleges bill seemed to offer an opportunity for a new demonstration of militancy, and possibly some political success. But in the event he only suffered a drubbing. Under Peel's ministry, with a firm tory majority and the whigs listless and divided, 'the parliamentary method' as practised by the O'Connellites brought nothing but reverses and humiliation.

It seems fair to say that at any time after Clontarf O'Connell would gladly have renewed the liberal alliance on relatively modest terms. In a piece of private kite-flying at the beginning of 1844 he indicated what these might be: further instalments of the religious and political reforms of the 1830s (more measures promoting ecclesiastical equality, the enlargement of the parliamentary and municipal suffrages, and the secret ballot), together with the

[1] Below, p. 400.
[2] 2 & 3 Will. IV, c. 118 (16 Aug. 1832); 13 Vict., c. 2 (12 Mar. 1850).

repeal of the more onerous land legislation of recent years and the 'consideration' of fixity of tenure. It is true that he did not give up repeal in so many words. But in adding that such a programme would greatly diminish the pressure for repeal, he was undoubtedly playing the 'justice for Ireland' card again. But the whigs were unresponsive. This was, in part, because even O'Connell's limited 'terms' seemed too high for them: at that particular stage, while they would swallow further moves, legislative and executive alike, towards equality, they rejected both political and land reform. Mostly, however, they held him off because they were convinced that when they attained or were near to office they could easily make a better bargain with an O'Connell eager to have government on his side again. O'Connell's precipitate promise of support for Lord John Russell in a common anti-corn-law front, when the whigs looked like returning to power at the end of 1845, seems to establish the correctness of their calculation. He would have been all too happy to reenter and repeat the courses of the preceding decade.

Meanwhile, with the avenues of parliamentary pressure, mass demonstrations, and inter-party confederacy closed, it was natural for O'Connell, in the second half of 1844, to explore the possibility of widening his national front at home. With the sharp polarisation of repeal and unionism in 1843, a body of 'moderates' seeking a way between the two 'extremes' gradually came together around the apparent compromise of federation. The federalists were never a coherent or organised body, nor was there ever an agreed definition (or even perhaps any clear concept) of political federation in the British Isles: in fact such notions as emerged suggested mild devolution for Ireland rather than a federation of states or peoples. The federalists were of mixed political origin: some of them catholics, most protestants, some of them whig–liberals, most liberal–radicals or liberals plain. The landed, commercial, and professional interests provided almost all the members, and the movement had two 'capitals', Dublin and Belfast. Federalism had a special appeal for those Belfastmen who, although habituated to regarding themselves as radicals in politics, found separation repellent or frightening. Some years earlier, the *Northern Whig* had explained or rationalised the attitude of this group in economic terms: 'We are not devoid of national feeling as Irishmen, but as an industrious and enterprising people we are a thousand times more closely bound up with Liverpool and Glasgow, with Lanarkshire and Lancashire, than with all Munster put together.'[1]

Clearly, then, there were difficulties in O'Connell's coming to terms with a heterogeneous body that lacked both a formal organisation and a mouthpiece among the newspapers. But he determined, apparently quite suddenly, in the autumn of 1844 to fish openly for an understanding with them. He announced, in a manifesto from his home at Derrynane (12 October 1844), a preference for a form of federalism as against simple repeal. This move did not perhaps

[1] *Northern Whig*, 17 Oct. 1839.

represent so extensive a retreat as it has ever since been regarded. The federal system that O'Connell described in outline consisted of a single imperial parliament with two subordinate legislatures for Great Britain and Ireland. This was essentially the definition that O'Connell had given of the 'repeal demand' when under pressure to be specific during his British campaign of 1832. It reflected his own constitutional dualism, which embraced both the notion of national independence and that of participation in a world-wide imperial structure. It was in certain respects, in particular in placing Great Britain and Ireland on a level, a more advanced demand than that of home rule in a later generation. Moreover, Davis himself was negotiating with the northern federalists at much the same time as O'Connell appealed to them from Derrynane, and for much the same reason—that repeal, temporarily at least, had come to a dead end, and that an infusion of new men and tactics might revive the movement. None the less, O'Connell's ploy was presented to posterity as a surrender, and for this he has, if not himself directly, at any rate his original strategy to blame. One of the major political uses of the repeal slogan was its deceptive simplicity and negativity. It was paraded as a single lopping action, achievable by a ten-line act of parliament. But the obverse of this agitatory merit was that any variation of the plain and specific demand seemed, to the general mind, a retreat.

Perhaps O'Connell's pronouncement had to be *urbi et orbi* in the absence of any formal federalist party. But it was carelessly made, with no preparatory private correspondence with either his lieutenants or the federalist leaders or influential critics in the repeal movement. It was immediately repudiated by the *Nation* group on the grounds that the repeal association could not work against its own *raison d'être*, and that federation would perpetuate Ireland's cultural subordination to Great Britain. The Ulster federalists simply failed to respond at all, despite a meeting held in Belfast at the end of October 1844, presumably to consider O'Connell's overture. From Dublin there came only (and even at that from an unspecified group) a timid devolutionary scheme that went no further than proposing that local taxation, the poor law, and industrial development should belong to an indigenous Irish assembly. There was nothing in this on which to build a new departure, and O'Connell hastily retreated. A second declaration from Derrynane, issued on 8 November 1844, a month after the first, chided the federalists for their silence and the *Nation* group for its precipitate utterance, and wound up the whole business with a characteristic piece of compass-boxing—a gloss to the effect that O'Connell had never meant to accept for Ireland 'less' than she had enjoyed before 1801.

This exhausted O'Connell's resources. There was nothing left but thundering in Conciliation Hall, struggles to keep the repeal organisation in good repair, and his blessedly unfailing Micawberism. In June 1845 he was reduced to asking Smith O'Brien to decide for him whether his secession from parliament should continue. 'Decide for me as well as for yourself. . . . It will be no small sacrifice to give up my visit to my loved mountains but if you *continue* to think that sacrifice necessary I will readily make it.'[1] The sacrifice was made; but quite in vain. What was there now to do at Westminster but to watch the skies yet again for signs of another liberal dawning?

[1] O'Connell to Smith O'Brien, 9 June 1845 (*O'Connell corr.*, vii, 319).

CHAPTER IX

Ideas and institutions, 1830–45

OLIVER MACDONAGH

IRISH intellectual and cultural history has generally been entangled with politics; and rarely was this more the case than in the period 1830–45. Paradoxically, the pervasion of the political in the static arts, academic inquiry, and letters was in part the product of political deprivation. It is true that, in the ultimate sense, Ireland was a political dependency in the last quarter of the eighteenth century. But it was not felt to be so. Not only are there degrees in political dependency, but it should also be calibrated for feelings as well as constitutional and legal powers. By 1830, however, Ireland not only was, but was seen and felt by all to be, constitutionally inert; and over the next decade many of the surviving elements of self-rule contained in protestant ascendancy (creaturely though they might be) disappeared. Advancing colonialism may not always nip artistic flowering, but it generally does; and the meagre art of this condition is generally political. The corollary, that colonialism in retreat, or for that matter settled provincial government, commonly breed more or less apolitical 'renaissances', seems also valid; but this does not concern us here.

Perhaps the most obvious manifestation of political deprivation with cultural consequences was the steady withdrawal of Irish peers and the richest gentry from Dublin after the union. What Sir Walter Scott called in 1825 'the retreat of the most noble and opulent inhabitants'[1] was a gradual process; but by the end of the 1830s it had practically run its course. A quarter of a century later Engels was to comment: 'Dublin . . . bears the same relation to London as Düsseldorf does to Berlin, and has quite the character of a small one-time capital.'[2] The other side of this coin was the rise in social significance of the professional classes, especially lawyers and physicians, in the capital. Both L. M. Cullen and Gearóid Ó Tuathaigh have pointed out that this slow change in emphasis was symbolised in Dublin building.[3] The last of the great 'eighteenth-century' undertakings, Fitzwilliam Square, was completed in 1825. Meanwhile the

---

[1] Scott to Maria Edgeworth, 18 July 1825 (*The letters of Sir Walter Scott . . . centenary edition*, ed. H. J. C. Grierson and others (12 vols, London, 1932–7), ix, 190–91).
[2] *Marx and Engels on Britain* (Moscow, 1953), p. 489.
[3] Cullen, *Life in Ire.*, p. 135; Ó Tuathaigh, *Ire. before the famine*, p. 156.

growth of the 'comfortable' new suburbs just south of the Grand Canal was already under way. As Ó Tuathaigh puts it,

As the upper middle classes came to dominate the life of the capital, the new buildings began to reflect their preoccupations. The G.P.O., the King's Inns, and the College of Surgeons—clerks, lawyers, and medical men—are landmarks of the changing ethos.

The same metamorphosis was reflected in taste, design, and whatever manifested grander expenditure of money and time. Similarly, the medical sciences and geology, provinces of the 'new men', were among the few areas where scholarship in Ireland made a mark in the period, although a handful of the provincial gentry did maintain something of the gentleman-amateur tradition in the study of local antiquities and natural history.

The years 1830–45 were undistinguished in the arts generally in Ireland; and such as the artistic achievement amounted to, it served only too often as a vehicle for political didacticism. Propaganda was, of course, erected into a literary creed by the Young Ireland writers. Apart perhaps from the Hiberno-Carlyleanism of Mitchel, Davis was probably the most talented of this school. Such a poem as 'My grave' (though how suggestive the subject-matter!) establishes that he was more than a jingler:

> . . . on an Irish green hillside,
> On an opening lawn—but not too wide;
> For I love the drip of the wetted trees—
> I love not the gales, but a gentle breeze,
> To freshen the turf—put no tombstone there . . .

But Davis's gifts were harnessed to strident nationalism. Characteristically, the very forms he chose, the marching song and the martial ballad, marked the subordination of his minor art to a cause. But even the best Irish literary work of the period (and the very best might stand in most European company of the day)—the poetry of Mangan and the novels of Carleton—though far from simply propagandist, had strong political colouring. It seemed almost unavoidable; the very air men breathed seemed political. 'It is impossible', Maria Edgeworth wrote in 1834, 'to draw Ireland as she now is in a book of fiction. . . . We are in too perilous a case to laugh, humour would be out of season, worse than bad taste.'[1] The year 1834 was but early in this storm; and those writers who, unlike Edgeworth, had still their way to make over the next dozen years, had no alternative, short of sheer escapism, but to reflect, in some degree or other, contemporary political conflict in their looking-glasses.

Possibly the most original Irish work in 1830–45 was done in the field of economics. But this too was either overlain or debauched by politics. William Thompson's theories of communistic organisation, and his west Cork and the similar Ralahine experiments in cooperative enterprise, were largely unknown

[1] Frances Anne Edgeworth, *A memoir of Maria Edgeworth* (3 vols, London, 1867), iii, 85.

or unregarded in contemporary Ireland. They remain historical curiosities. Their significance and interest are still treated as altogether intrinsic or anti-quarian. Of more immediate importance and direct relevance to the Irish political battles of the day were the writings of a handful of Irish landowners, agents, and farmers, which collectively, challenged and ultimately helped to undermine classical economics. Within the period 1830–45, the British political economists did not modify their basic theory when confronted by its patent inapplicability to Ireland. Instead they demanded the modification of Irish conditions so that their basic theory might apply. Among other effects, this would have meant the removal of three-fifths of the rural population from the soil, a consolidation of holdings, and the institution of a three-tiered agricultural structure in the English fashion. Yet by 1845 all the main elements present in the property revolution of 1870–1903 in Ireland had reached the surface. These derived not from the theoretical economists but from men like William Conner, William Sharman Crawford, William Blacker, and James Fintan Lalor. In 1830 Conner argued for fixing rents by arbitration instead of competition, and for the absolute security of tenure subject to the payment of such a fixed rent. This was 'dual ownership' in embryo. From 1831 Blacker set out the justification on economic grounds of the small holding, and looked to 'durable and certain interest' to provide the other Irish desiderata, social security and conditions favourable to capital accumulation and investment. From 1835 on Crawford pressed for compensation for improvements. Lalor was later to combine social, economic, and political revolution. It was these advocates, then, who anticipated in all essentials the turnabout of the political economists in the late 1860s and the revolutionary land legislation of the following generation. But their triumph was posthumous. During 1830–45 the political deprivation described above left them without a domestic intellectual base from which to propagate their theories, and, enforced provincials, they were powerless to force an entry into the closed circle of British political economy. Political subordination left them powerless even to colour contemporary statutes.

Thus, in considering the ideas and institutions of the period, and particularly the new developments, it is the political and the governmental that appear to dominate the scene. In particular, the period was fertile in political ideology, political techniques, and organisational methods. It was almost as inventive in the field of central government and regulation. Here at least the parameters of Irish life for the next century were, to a remarkable degree, being set.

THE novel political ideas of the 1830s and 1840s were not products of the study or developed in either abstract or systematic form. Essentially they emerged from actual political engagement, and centred on the great practitioner, O'Connell. A necessary preliminary to their disentanglement is to understand the peculiar limitations that O'Connell's background, experience, and professional training placed on his liberty of speculation, for this power-fully affected the whole Irish ideological ferment almost to 1845. Here the salient fact was, of course, O'Connell's legal formation and thirty years practice at the bar. 'The law' was accepted by him unquestioningly as the legitimate circumscriber of political thought and action; and behind this acceptance of the 'lawful' lay an acceptance, again as a datum, of all the institutions of state, and even many of their private equivalents. Despite, and perhaps even more because of, this acceptance, O'Connell was an indefatigable and fecund legal and institutional reformer. Similarly, he conceived of desirable political change as piecemeal, a series of disparate modifications of or amputations from the existing body politic. It was not that he lacked generalised assumptions about the nature of social authority. Far from it. But his respect for the received order as a whole rendered him incapable of root-and-branch condemnation.

O'Connell's abhorrence of what he himself called 'physical force' doctrines may also have flowed from his legalism. Granted, his various experiences (uncomfortably close to first-hand) of revolutionary violence in the 1790s may have worked in the same direction.[1] None the less, his habitual obeisance to the lawful blocked for him any avenue of thought that led even to the contemplation of a *forcible* disturbance of the received order. Conversely, the lawyer-agitator was tempted constantly to consider (and often to test in practice) the legal brinks and borderlands. If he accepted such limits axiomatically, he was also inclined, advocate-like, to work to what he regarded as the edges of these limits and to assume that he knew their outermost bournes.

Given these peculiar mental inclinations, O'Connell's political philosophy, which was being stamped ineradicably on the emerging national consciousness, may perhaps be best approached through his specific demands, or apparent demands. The leading instance is probably repeal. Literally interpreted, the repeal of the act of union was politically nonsensical. 'Grattan's parliament' had rested on the bases of British political control, which depended increasingly in the 1790s on patronage, and of protestant (largely Church of Ireland) engrossment of local power and office in Ireland. By 1830 both, in their pre-1801 forms, lay in the dustbin of history. It would have been quite impracticable to reconstitute the Irish parliament in the 1830s without admitting a possible nationalist majority in the lower house and a sizeable catholic party in the upper. Exterior control in the old fashion—'indirect rule'—was no longer feasible. Moreover, any group dominated by O'Connell was bound to press for the full radical programme of parliamentary reform, including universal male suffrage and equal electoral districts. (He himself described the six points of the 'people's charter' as 'ancillary to . . . the great cause of repeal'.) It was therefore with some justice that Isaac Butt contended in the Mansion House debate of 1843 that 'repeal was revolution. . . . The proposition was not to return to any state of things which had previously existed in Ireland—not to adopt the consti-

[1] Cf. above, pp 93–4.

tution of any European state—but to enter on an untried and wild system of democracy.'[1]

As all this suggests, O'Connell did not intend, by launching his last movement for repeal, to make a specific proposition or demand. It was rather, in lawyer's language, an invitation to treat, an attempt to elicit a proposition from the government. Repeal was only apparently a demand; more truly it represented the sloganising of pressure designed to force out a counter-offer, as is apparent in this extraordinary passage towards the close of the Mansion House debate:

A parliament inferior to the English parliament I would accept as an instalment if I found the people ready to go with me, and if it were offered to me by competent authority. It must first be offered to me—mark that—I never will seek it. . . . I never will ask for or look for any other, save an independent legislature, but if others offer me a subordinate parliament, I will close with any such authorised offer and accept that offer.[2]

Like Parnell, O'Connell was a separatist whose measure of separation was relative, to be determined ultimately by Britain and expressed in essentially meaningless but apparently precise and precedented abstractions.

All this deepened and developed one great channel in Irish political thought. According to this canon, the boundaries to the march of the nation were constitutionality, law, and the parliamentary processes, and goals were to be reached by an adversarial system, a species of stylised conflict or trials of strength. As O'Connell himself expressed it shortly after the Mallow 'defiance', 'I will observe the spirit of the law—the letter of the law. I will, to be sure, shear it to its closest limits, but I will obey.'[3] However, empiricism, negotiation, and moral force were not O'Connell's only contributions to the stock of Irish political habits and ideas. He was also in the mainstream of late eighteenth- and early nineteenth-century British radicalism—one of the great branches of the historic liberal tradition of the enlightenment and the *philosophes*—and he transmitted many of its values and assumptions to his awakening countrymen. This was all the easier because other ideological progenitors such as Grattan and Tone had also been enlightenment men—of different schools, it is true, but none the less in the same master tradition. The centrepiece of this tradition was the individual person, his liberty, his equal rights, and his essential sameness, no matter what his creed, colour, race, or location. Its concept of liberty was negative—a series of 'freedoms from'. Its concept of equality was formal—that no man should be *legally* privileged by reason of his social station, beliefs, interests, or personal characteristics. Its concept of reform was universalist, placing little or no value on cultural distinctions, and regarding political

[1] *F.J.*, 1, 3 Mar. 1843.
[2] *A full and revised report of the three days' discussion in the corporation of Dublin on the repeal of the union*, ed. John Levy (Dublin, 1843), pp 191–2 (R.I.A., Haliday pamphlets, mdccclxxiii).
[3] *F.J.*, 20 May 1843.

conflict everywhere as essentially one. It was no coincidence that O'Connell should have greeted the news of Waterloo with: 'The scoundrels of society have now every triumph. The defeats and disasters are reserved for the friends of liberty.'[1] From such a frame of mind, diversely extended though it might be by men as different as Tone and O'Connell, two vital Irish nationalist assumptions derived: the one, that the end of British domination would produce an automatic resolution of domestic political problems; the other, that Irish nationality was synonymous with Irish domicile, and that, once Ireland was 'released', common domicile would dwarf and render insignificant religious, occupational, local, and all other differences among Irishmen.

Here we reach the great ideological bifurcation, developing towards the mid-1840s, between the universal, rational, private, and atomistic strain of the enlightenment, whose major contemporary carrier was O'Connell, and the strain that emphasised the race rather than the person, the group rather than the individual, instinct and emotion rather than reason. It is an oversimplification perhaps, but basically correct, to see the conflict between O'Connell and the more ardent element in Young Ireland as a conflict between these two forms of radicalism—a local engagement, in fact, in a titanic struggle that involved all Europe in the nineteenth century.

This second ideological influence probably derived in an unusually direct fashion from German romanticism, in particular from Davis's visit to Germany in 1839–40. As J. S. Kelly has suggested, Davis appears to have undergone an evangelical-like conversion when confronted by the works of Lessing, Fichte, and the Schlegels and by the example of Prussia, which he saw as having awakened, as it were from a trance, as soon as she had halted the advance of the French, militarily and culturally.[2] His conventional radicalism was replaced by the German romantics' assumption that national culture, national history, and national language were not merely ornamental but integral to national identity. But two deviations from the strict German model were forced on Davis by his circumstances. First, the culture to be rejected and resisted was, in Ireland's case, not French but English: hence Davis's denunciations of utilitarianism, industrialism, and urbanisation, much in the same strain as Cobbett or the tractarians. This also explains why, where O'Connell opposed the retention of the Irish language as a barrier to economic development, modernisation, and education, Davis was anxious to revive it precisely because it was a barrier—to anglicisation. Secondly, Davis could not follow the German model in stressing either religion or racial purity in the genetic sense: all else besides, this would have left him stranded, a creature apart from the mass of his fellow Irishmen. These two deviations help to explain how Davis could be, and is still, placed, however misleadingly, in a line of ideological succession from Tone onwards.

[1] O'Connell to Mary O'Connell, 12 July 1815 (*O'Connell corr.*, ii, 53).
[2] J. S. Kelly, 'The political, intellectual and social background to the Irish literary revival to 1901' (Ph.D. thesis, Cambridge, 1972).

There were apparent similarities in the cries in different generations to break the connection with England and to regard catholic, protestant, and dissenter as forming a single flock. But these appearances should not blind us to the reality, to the revolution that romanticism had wrought. The new emphasis was on *cultural* division and *cultural* hostility; on emotion rather than rationality; on group, rather than individual, rights; on a subjective and creative rather than a formal and negative concept of independence; and, of course, in the very long run, on race and language.

Thus, within the 1830s and 1840s, the ideological infrastructure of modern Irish nationalism was being finally formed and articulated. It was, in some senses, dualistic. To confine the dualism to the conflict between constitutional agitation and 'physical force' would be misleading. Of course, this conflict was, and was to remain, significant. But it was in part the end product of different world-views, and in part a false antithesis: the borderline between moral and martial pressure is not really easy to discern. Another, and perhaps more profound, aspect of the dualism was the clash between two major European theories of society and of the relationships and licit forms of conflict between societies, expressed in peculiarly Irish terms. In Ireland the clash was not to be concluded by victory for either. It was not to be concluded at all, but was to form a continuing tension, and alternation of emphases, a cohabitation of opposite tendencies, in the minds of millions of Irishmen in the future.

In other respects the ideological crop of 1830–45 was surprisingly thin. It might have been expected that Irish toryism, experiencing the loss of many of its redoubts, and depressing changes in British governments' concept of the loyalists' role in Ireland, would have reappraised their situation—all the more so as they possessed an intellectual centre in Dublin University, and men of outstanding mental calibre and imagination such as Charles Boyton and Isaac Butt. However, the tories continued to see themselves as mere defenders of their hereditary positions, and the representatives of, as the *Dublin University Magazine* once put it, 'the English interest, the protestant interest, the conservative interest' in Ireland.[1] It was left to British tories in the early and mid-1840s to consider anew how the act of union might be maintained and what it should imply in a period of growing popular power, political nationality, catholic self-assurance, and economic peril. The Irish liberals, on the other hand, did not leave all the running to their British counterparts. They were, of course, more acutely aware of the realities of Irish life, and under more constant pressure from the Irish 'left', the repealers. On issues such as public works, local government, and religious privilege, they (or some of them) frequently formed an *avant-garde* among the parliamentary whigs and liberals. But all this was a matter of occasional differences of degree. It was far from being an ideological difference of kind. Moreover, in three critical areas, the land system, the union, and the maintenance of 'order', they were, if anything,

[1] Below, pp 503–4.

less flexible than the mass of their British fellows. The dominance of whig peers and gentry in the upper ranks of the Irish liberal party was probably responsible for its extraordinary inflexibility on the land question. As for unionism, this was the very principle of distinction between them and the nationalists, as well as the apparent guarantor of their own security. It also necessarily implied phases of repression. Hence the Irish liberals were clamped by their own circumstances and interests into a basically conservative and uncreative mode of thought on the greatest questions.

Feeblest of all perhaps in the years 1830–45 was the once vigorous and steely radicalism of the north. It could continue or pursue such strains as free trade, popular education, peasant proprietorship, or dissenters' rights. But on the larger matters, Anglo–Irish or protestant–catholic relations, it was silent or confused or regressive. As with the Irish liberals, the Belfast radicals drew back quickly from the speculations that they had initiated on federalism. For them 1830–45 was a period of drifting, a phase in which their 'radicalism' ceased to be innovatory and became instead reactive to events and the ideas of others. Just as Irish toryism waited for Peel to redefine its ideology in nineteenth-century terms, and Irish liberals were to wait for Gladstone, the Ulster non-conformists were not to have a 'modern' spokesman until Chamberlain broke with his leader. It is perhaps symptomatic of the rigidity that the act of union induced in almost all the elements of Irish protestant society, as well as in the highest level of catholic society, that the reappraisals came in each case from across St George's channel.

THE field of institutional development to which Ireland contributed most in 1830–45 was probably that of political organisation. The forms and techniques pioneered there in these years were to influence later politics throughout the English-speaking world, partly, but only partly, because they were broadcast by the Irish diaspora. Much must be allowed for earlier organisational work in Ireland, for contemporary innovation in Britain, and for the general European cross-pollenisation in an age of Metternichian polarising and busy, peripatetic social analysts. None the less, O'Connell's Ireland was at once a species of laboratory and a kind of forcing-house for the new forms of mass politics.

At the core of all his systems stood the national bodies or associations centred in Dublin. Nearly a score of these were set up successively between the opening of the parliamentary intelligence office early in 1830 and the launching of the Loyal National Repeal Association on 15 April 1840 (though that particular variant of its name came only in the following July). Several were substitutions, part of O'Connell's mouse-and-cat game with repressive governments. Others, however, marked a change in political direction—the National Political Union (1831) and the Precursor Society (1838) are instances. Yet others, such as the Anti-Tory Association (1834), were especially designed to fight general elections. But all were structurally similar. The elected membership, with a subscription of at least £1 a year, was almost entirely middle-class; the business was transacted through a standing committee managed either by O'Connell directly or by his lieutenants, in particular his Admirable Crichton, P. V. Fitzpatrick; and protracted, eloquent, and widely reported public meetings were held weekly in the Corn Exchange. In general outline the organisations were modelled on the Catholic Association, and they also bore some resemblances to contemporary British developments, such as the politicisation of Brooks's Club or the Birmingham Political Union. But they were much more highly developed than their earlier or current counterparts. They constituted at once party headquarters and electoral clearing-houses; they were professionally managed; their existence was continuous; they formed so many ladders for administrative and political talent as well as outlets for the sense of individual participation; and they served as proto-parliaments, which sustained public interest and national pride and disseminated the party line on the issues of the hour. The repealers were not alone in this activity. The Irish Protestant Conservative Society (1831) was run on exactly the same lines. But this was, in R. B. McDowell's phrase, 'a tory imitation and at times parody of O'Connell's associations',[1] and its proceedings appear to have been generally desultory and defensive.

A second layer of political organisation was formed by the constituency associations. Here again the repealers led the way and easily dominated numerically; but in a few of the marginal constituencies the tories had produced equally formidable organisations by the late 1830s. On the repeal side, it is noteworthy that the local organisations were largely independent of the central body of the day. Occasionally there were national directives on voter registration and national endorsement of candidates. But essentially the constituency parties were autonomous. The necessary links were provided by O'Connell or some *alter ego*, commonly P. V. Fitzpatrick. O'Connell himself performed herculean labours in this field (in what organisational field did he not?), and it was for him the soundest of political investments. Unlike most of his British counterparts he grasped immediately the significance of the registration clauses in the reform act and showed extraordinary skill in manipulating the new system, for it was essentially a lawyer's problem. He also maintained direct personal correspondence with several of the local political managers, such as Rev. John Sheehan in Waterford and James Roe in Cashel. Thus his power over the nationalist movement as a whole was probably increased rather than diminished by the weak control exercised by the national over the constituency associations. Some of the smaller boroughs were, for all practical purposes, in his (though not necessarily in his party's) pocket; and even in the counties his personal (though not necessarily Dublin's) influence was often predominant. Paradoxically enough, his grasp of the levers of powers may have been least firm in the capital itself, and this largely because he himself stood for election

---

[1] McDowell, *Public opinion & govt policy*, p. 116.

there in 1832, 1835, and 1837. In these years the Dublin city contests were turned into national tournaments; and the great size of the Dublin electorate, the powerful Trades Political Union there, and the strength of the tory interest in the city all forced him to rely heavily on quasi-independent auxiliaries and the national executive.

The third level of organisation, relatively unused in the 1830s but in the fore-front in the next decade, was the local branch. This had, of course, its electoral uses; the parish, the village, and the small town were all units in the county constituency machine. But local organisation was far more important in agita-tion than in parliamentary contests, and consequently to the Loyal National Repeal Association than, say, to the Anti-Tory Association. It was the very basis of the mass movement, which depended for its effectiveness upon propaganda, political 'education', universal enrolment, the management of great numbers, the inculcation of a feeling of personal involvement, gigantic demonstrations, recurrent enthusiasm, and steady fund-raising. Shopkeepers, professional men, and, most of all, the priests throughout the countryside provided the local leadership, while reading-rooms and the network of repeal wardens and 'constables' formed institutional aids to the work of education and the maintenance of discipline. The force so organised was funnelled upwards through county and provincial councils. O'Connell himself was the final focus.

Even mechanically, mass mobilisation on such a scale represented an unprecedented and stupendous achievement, and it opened the way (though only a few tentative steps along it were taken in the 1840s) to the establishment of 'alternative government' in Ireland. But although, in its full flowering of 1843, national agitation was an essentially new phenomenon, it owed a great deal to other elements in the Irish experience, in particular to the experimental work in the same field of the Catholic Association, to the earlier harnessing of the catholic parochial structure, common worship, and priestly direction to political campaigns, and to two or three generations of Whiteboyism and Ribbonism throughout rural Ireland. It is true that Whiteboyism and Ribbon-ism were not only rivals but also enemies of constitutional agitation, and that O'Connell used all his influence to keep them within bounds—they were very far from being either superseded or inactive—during 1830–45. None the less, for more than half a century the secret agrarian societies had habituated people in the countryside to communal action, to political direction, to moral sanctions as well as physical, and to the use of their very numbers to intimidate authority. But the reworking, amalgamation, and drawing forward of these three elements by O'Connell and his marshals represented an original achieve-ment of the first magnitude.

Strangely enough, while these various forms were emerging, the most highly developed of existing Irish political organisations was in temporary decline. By 1835 the Orange Order possessed some 1,500 lodges and was extending far throughout the English-speaking world. It was, of course, more than a political organisation, and even its political aspect was unusual: it was neither parliamentary nor agitatory in emphasis. In one light, the Order represented a gargantuan, though exclusive, social security system; in another, it was an expression of mutuality; and in yet a third, it acted as an emollient, both in reducing class friction among protestants and in satisfying men's appetites for display, mystery, and conviviality. Politically Orangeism was essentially defensive; but since a jealous hold on power in all its forms was conceived of as its paramount function, it was a major force in contemporary politics, despite its other faces and the fact that it operated largely in surreptitious and clandestine ways.

In the early 1830s it came under radical and liberal attack in Britain for its alleged jobbery, intolerance, tampering with justice, and infiltration of the police and army. The tories found it awkward to champion what elsewhere they were foremost in denouncing—conspiracy, demagoguery, and disorder; and accordingly when in 1836, after a condemnatory report had been issued by Joseph Hume's select committee, the house of commons resolved that the crown should discourage the Order, the British tories acquiesced, and the Grand Orange Lodge of Ireland voted for its own dissolution. As with the Society of Jesus some sixty years earlier, the Order did not die with 'suppression'. But for the remainder of the period its activities were decidedly muted. Even the repeal campaign of the early 1840s produced no significant reaction in popular protestantism in the north. Presumably they evaluated the threat with their legendary shrewdness.

Finally, while the independent newspaper was of comparatively small importance to Irish unionism, it was of critical importance to O'Connellism in all its forms. The press was the principal disseminator of information and instruction in the country, for it underpinned all, but in particular national political organisation. The 1820s had broken the near-monopoly of this medium on the part of government, partly because Wellesley, as lord lieutenant, had withdrawn state subsidies and partly because various successes in the emancipation campaign had emboldened a few editors.[1] But the battle to establish and maintain independent newspapers was not quite over by 1830. Between 1831 and 1834 Dublin Castle instituted thirteen prosecutions of nationalist newspapers, manipulated newspaper stamps against them, and subsidised two new (but unsuccessful) newspapers from secret-service monies to propagandise for the whigs. But this final assault through the ancient modes failed; and the nationalist movement was effectively sustained and interlinked by three metropolitan newspapers, the *Morning Register*, the *Freeman's Journal*, and the *Pilot* (O'Connell's creature); and, equally important, by half a dozen major provincial organs, with support at most times from the liberal *Dublin Evening Post*. None of these could now be bribed, ruined, or muzzled. Together they provided the basic communications system of constitutional politics.

[1] For the position in 1813–14, see above, pp 49–50.

Their circulations were by modern standards minute, scarcely 1,500 copies on average. But their effective eventual dissemination rate per copy, with group purchases and readings, would have been many times greater than that of any modern newspaper.

The emergent independence of the Irish press in the 1830s meant independence of government, not of external influence. O'Connell expected a subservient press. His attitude towards the repeal newspapers was quasi-feudal. He was ready to go to extraordinary lengths—though not quite as far as the embattled editors themselves sometimes demanded or required—to shield them from official oppression or vengeance and to keep them solvent. In return they were basically (though, except for the *Pilot*, not slavishly) loyal to the movement. It was a rough and ready system of mutual obligations and benefits. The *Nation*, however, both constituted a new form of newspaper and expressed another conception of press freedom. Its sales, exceeding those of all the other metropolitan newspapers combined, were large even by international standards: a circulation of 10,000 copies would have been a very respectable achievement even in Britain, France, or the United States in the early 1840s. It was also a national newspaper in every sense, to a degree well beyond that of any of its Irish contemporaries. Its format was unusual, it was large in terms of pages, and its intellectual and technical qualities were at least correspondingly superior. All of these factors rendered it an important additional instrument in the later repeal agitation, even if the popular claim that it was primarily responsible for the extent, force, and relative success of that campaign must be regarded as a considerable exaggeration. On the other hand, its support of O'Connell's or any other movement was conditional. It had its own clearly—indeed rigidly—developed philosophy and programme. Broadly speaking, the repeal association and the *Nation* worked towards the same ends to 1844. Differences in tone, emphasis, and detail were occasionally discernible, but comfortably within the normal tolerances of such an alliance. But in 1844 and 1845 the fissures became more frequent, deep, and open. Down to the autumn of 1845 the discordance, though increasingly ominous, had not yet reached the point of rupture. It was, however, already apparent that the opposition within the national movement had an independent base, a factor of prime importance in the coming years, and that press independence had adopted a fresh meaning in Ireland. Institutional politics, in a sense beyond the manifold organisational ramifications of O'Connell's essentially personal system, were beginning to thrust themselves above the surface.

ALL the political ideas and machines were concerned to change or defend, capture or retain the government of Ireland. Although many aspects of the new relationship between Great Britain and Ireland were exhaustively discussed before the act of union, actual government was not. As we have seen, it was not clear for some years whether a separate Irish executive would be maintained at all, and the system that did survive and develop was cumbersome and anomalous in many ways, most of all perhaps in the retention of the lord lieutenancy and its appurtenances.[1] However, by 1830 it was clear that vice-regalism would remain, from the force of inertia if nothing else. Such leading whigs as Althorp and Russell favoured its abolition, but never took steps towards this end. Formally, then, the pre-union structure continued, although the chief-secretaryship, now that Ireland was represented at Westminster and her problems were growing in scale, number, and advertisement, was a much more important office than in the eighteenth century. Being a sort of irresponsible prime minister of Ireland, the chief secretary was generally more important politically than the lord lieutenant. But his actual power in any particular case depended to some extent on the relative weight of his own and his colleagues' personalities. Neither de Grey (lord lieutenant 1841–4) nor Eliot (chief secretary 1841–5), for example, was ever altogether master, although they collided repeatedly. Moreover, leading subordinate officers had on occasions superior claims to being the real governors of the country. Both Sir William Gosset and Thomas Drummond as under-secretaries had fair claims, successively, to such a title in the years 1833–40; and Lord Plunket and Sir Edward Sugden, as lord chancellors, had phases of extraordinary influence. Variation in the true location of ultimate power is, of course, a commonplace in politics. But the peculiar circumstances of the Irish executive, in particular its essential irresponsibility, greatly exaggerated this tendency from the outset.

In some ways the union had advanced administratively by 1830. For example, the armed forces, the revenue departments, and the postal services (1831) of the two countries were effectively amalgamated.[2] The amalgamation of the exchequers in 1817 was probably the most significant of all the junctions. Apart from an overall power of determining all questions of public finance, this gave the British treasury direct rule over certain Irish departments, such as the reconstituted board of works. Moreover, 'treasury control' from Whitehall extended to all branches of the Irish government, and it was applied quite rigorously even as early as the 1830s. This, imbued as it was with the current British orthodoxy on the proper limits of state action and state spending, held back appropriate social and economic reform in Ireland, particularly after 1840. Thenceforward the emphasis was on eliminating corruption and 'waste' in state expenditure, and if possible reducing it absolutely, not on stimulating economic growth or creating new employment. From his later experiences in the Irish famine, Charles Trevelyan, who became critically important in this field when he was appointed assistant secretary to the treasury in January 1840, was to learn something of Irish needs. But before 1845 Trevelyan and his acolytes at the treasury saw Ireland in terms of the British norms. Although

[1] Above, pp 1, 4.
[2] For the military reorganisation see below, pp 539–41. The revenue departments were consolidated by 4 Geo. IV, c. 23 (2 May 1823) and the post offices by 1 Will. IV, c. 8 (11 Mar. 1831).

they did not win every battle with recalcitrant Irish circumstances, they won most.

Again, in the 1820s and 1830s a new sort of state was being born in Britain. Central regulation of certain aspects of economic and social organisation through inspectorates quite suddenly got under way. In most cases this new activity was based, from the start, on the United Kingdom as a single administrative unit. Ireland might have its own inspector or inspectors, but only in the same way as Yorkshire or East Anglia. Thus the inspectors of mines and factories and the emigration officers, for example, were responsible directly to the home and colonial offices respectively. Even so vast and localised an undertaking as the Irish poor law of 1838 was ultimately managed by a parent body in London, with a member of the English board acting as the resident Irish commissioner, and with four of the first eight Irish poor law inspectors appointed from the English service. Again, this represented an advance (albeit in the particular instance a short-lived one) for the administrative union, and a further inroad on Ireland's administrative autonomy.

But it would be misleading to suggest that all the forces at work in the 1830s and 1840s were working for governmental uniformity within the United Kingdom under Whitehall overlordship. On the contrary, it is doubtful whether, for all their advances, they predominated over the forces of administrative idiosyncrasy in Ireland. In the fields of education, economic development, police, prisons, and public health—to take but leading examples—the state intervened to a degree and in a fashion scarcely conceivable in contemporary Britain. As Nassau William Senior told Alexis de Tocqueville, 'Experiments are made in that country [Ireland] on so large a scale, and pushed to their extreme consequences with such a disregard to the sufferings which they inflict, that they give us results as precious as those of Majendie [François Magendie, the physiologist].'[1] One reason was that the Irish ruling class was too few in number and too scattered in location to govern individually or in small groups as in Britain, and that Ireland was too poor for so small a unit as the parish to be administratively self-sufficient. As late as 1845 the English J.P.s and parishes had lost comparatively few functions to the central government; possibly, on balance, they had gained. In Ireland it was otherwise. By 1845 the local authorities had been shorn of many of their powers and replaced by national and centralised organisations. Whereas the first stage in administrative reform in English local government represented an attempt to broaden electorates and break the monopolies of church and squire, the equivalent phase in Ireland was marked by the passing of some of the old and almost all of the new functions of government from local to central control.

A second reason is that some measure of democracy was imminent in the 1830s in the Irish system of local government, even if it was likely to be still

[1] M. C. M. Simpson (ed.), *Correspondence and conversations of Alexis de Tocqueville with Nassau William Senior* (2 vols, London, 1872), i, 52.

more limited than that to be received by England and Wales. Any step in this direction meant, over most of Ireland, the admission of catholics and nationalists to some share in power. Faced with this possibility, Irish protestants, on the whole, acquiesced in centralisation. It often seemed to them to offer better security for their material interests, in much the same fashion as they had come to prefer the union to the dangers of active catholic participation in a domestic political system. The British governments of the 1830s and 1840s had corresponding reasons for working in the same direction. They saw any step towards democratisation in Irish local government as also enlarging the arena for agitation and factional and sectarian conflict. The first they feared; the second they were already beginning to approach in the spirit of a district commissioner faced with tribal conflict. On both counts it seemed desirable to minimise self-government.

To these considerations should, of course, be added the general poverty and disorder in Irish life, and the consequent traditions of both state intervention and central regulation, and of the government's almost automatic assumption of tutelary and authoritarian roles. The experience of the 1830s and 1840s did nothing to weaken these tendencies among those in power. The strains are well illustrated by much of the social and economic reform initiated or extended in the period. It is perhaps more illuminating to regard these reforms as contributions to the Irish polity and institutional framework rather than to Irish social and economic development, as such. In the long run, of course, the latter was deeply influenced by the changes. But in 1830–45 the ills of Irish society and the economy alike were so deep and widespread that ameliorative measures undertaken scarcely counted one way or another.

A PRIME illustration of these last generalisations is the new board of works set up in 1831.[1] This was both innovatory in degree rather than kind, and far more significant institutionally than materially. It superseded a number of late eighteenth-century and early nineteenth-century bodies, including the original board. But its administrative lineage should really be traced to the establishment in 1817 of a central loan fund for Irish public works, as a charge on the imperial revenue.[2] The advances from this fund were not confined to public buildings, roads, and bridges. Fisheries, mines, and even communal resettlement projects were also beneficiaries. The new Irish foundation presented an interesting contrast to the contemporaneous establishment of an English commission of public works. Though its grant was much larger, the English commission was charged only with organising *ad hoc* relief projects to cope with current economic distress. The Irish board, however, was intended to be permanent, and its works to be reproductive and part of a national plan. The Irish commissioners had also much more comprehensive powers; as Stanley put it, 'Their function was both deliberative and executive where the role of

[1] 1 & 2 Will. IV, c. 33 (15 Oct. 1831).   [2] Above, p. 62.

their English counterparts was deliberative only.'[1] This neatly captures the differences in the respective concepts of state activity and national need.

The new Irish board, with a national inspectorate of engineers, presents a remarkable instance of formal government growth in the 1830s and 1840s. At first its major work was in roads, ports, and harbours; and here the inspectors were often directly involved in construction, with all the concomitant practical 'interventions' that this implied. But in the later 1830s its activities quickly extended to railways, inland navigation, coastal fisheries, and land reclamation and drainage. The board supplied the majority of the members, and largely determined the conclusions, of the commissioners and committees that inquired into these various subjects of possible state interference. In the theoretical sense at least, its most striking 'success' was the second and final report of the Irish railway commission in 1838, which resulted in 1839 in Morpeth's bill to provide over £2,500,000 from imperial funds for the construction by the board of the trunk lines for a national railway system. Although the bill actually passed the house of commons, it was then dropped by the government: their own retention of power was uncertain, and the lords were hostile. To have come even as close as this, however, to establishing a pattern of state-built and state-managed railways in Ireland in the 1830s was a stupendous attainment.

Concrete, though more modest, achievement was marked by the Shannon navigation act of 1839 and by the Irish fisheries and drainage acts of 1842.[2] The first ended the much- and long-divided responsibility for the Shannon and its tributaries, and placed all under the autocratic control of a new commission, which was in fact a creature of the board of works—one might almost say, the board wearing another hat. The whigs fell from office before the report of the fisheries commission could be translated into a statute, and Peel approached state action in Ireland with the sourness and scepticism born of his earlier Irish experiences. 'Everybody in Ireland,' he once wrote, 'instead of setting about improvement as people elsewhere do, pester government about boards and public aid. Why cannot people in Ireland fish without a board if fishing be, as Lord Glengall declares it to be, so profitable?'[3] None the less, the tories did carry through the earlier fisheries recommendations, which gave the board of works considerable powers and responsibility in the development and organisation of both the river and the sea fishing industries. The drainage act of 1842 was significant constitutionally as well as practically; for not only did it charge the board with, in some senses, the regulation of land use, but it also empowered it to levy compulsory charges on the 'beneficiaries' of drainage schemes, even if they had opposed them, provided that two-thirds of the landowners affected were in agreement with the board.

[1] *Hansard 3*, v, 387 (26 July 1831).
[2] 2 & 3 Vict., c. 61 (19 Aug. 1839); 5 & 6 Vict., cc 89, 106 (5, 10 Aug. 1842).
[3] McDowell, *Public opinion & govt policy*, p. 211.

Apart from road construction, where its impact was immediate and powerful, the board prepared for the future rather than altered the present during the 1830s and 1840s. It had spent just over a million pounds in grants as well as loans by 1845. But this was trivial in terms of Irish need. None the less, not merely was the board being geared, unwittingly, for the impending crisis of the great famine, but it was also adumbrating a new form and philosophy of government—indeed, a revolutionary view of society. The inspectorate, as was not uncommonly the case with that new type of executive corps, tended to produce uniformity and coherence in administration and to initiate an unanticipated cycle of government expansion. Centralisation and the needs of supervision meant some degree of planning, if only to establish priorities in expenditure. In time the inspectors developed their own expertise, and the largeness of their task led them into distant fields; for example, they had virtually to determine the wage rates in areas—and there were many of these— where there was little cash employment outside the public works. This in turn forced them into the realm of wage policy and economic theorising. The railway commission was as much concerned with providing employment as with providing transport. The debate on drainage largely centred upon the increase in land resources. The ideas that the building of an economic infrastructure was the state's responsibility, that the economy should be continually primed and steered, and that the critical decisions should come from experts and from above, were all unfolding here. A new sort of policy was being prefigured.

A SECOND example of the same phenomenon, of the very early development of collectivist structures in society, lay in public health and its associated fields. In public health Ireland may have been *formally* one of the most advanced of European countries during the years 1830–45. As early as 1805 provision had been made for public dispensaries, half the cost of which was to be met by the local authorities.[1] In theory the dispensaries furnished free medicine and free medical attention to the sick poor. They spread rapidly; by the mid-1840s over 650 had been established. Their quality and effectiveness may have been very bad; and since each foundation depended on local initiative, their distribution was haphazard, sometimes originating in a physician's desire to supplement his income or secure his residence. But at least an organisation and a principle, which Britain was to lack for several decades, had been established; and both the network of dispensaries and the experience of conducting this sort of medical outdoor relief were necessary forerunners of the wholly public system set up in 1851.[2]

Moreover, every county, and every county of a city or town, inherited from the eighteenth century at least one infirmary and one fever hospital maintained largely by public funds; and by 1830 all appointments to these seventy-four institutions were being made by public authorities. Even the so-called private

[1] 45 Geo. III, c. 111 (10 July 1805). [2] 14 & 15 Vict., c. 68 (7 Aug. 1851).

hospitals were semi-state establishments in Dublin, being supported by initial or recurrent grants from the central government. In the 1830s and 1840s, apart from the 'poor law' hospitals, another seven—the Lock, Cowpox, Incurables', Rotunda, Meath, Steevens's, and Cork Street—continued to receive annual grants, despite many efforts at Westminster to bring the payments to an end on the ground that no other hospitals in the entire British empire were state supported. Again, Ireland possessed at this time not only elaborate emergency organisations like the Central Board of Health for Ireland, set up in the cholera epidemic of 1832, but also a permanent board of health, which had been constituted in 1820.[1] This body provided the government with information and advice on public health, in particular upon epidemics and the institution of local boards, while it provided the local boards and local authorities with instructions and financial supervision. There was no equivalent coordinating, centralised authority in public health in Britain for many years to come.

The Irish treatment of insanity was marked by two very interesting administrative developments, one of which culminated and one of which burgeoned in this period. The first was the grouping together of adjacent counties for the establishment of large regional mental hospitals. This process, completed by 1835, represented a startling break with the conventional divisions of local government, and it marked the entry of quantitative 'rationalisation' on the administrative scene. The second innovation was a centralised national system of control and inspection to ensure uniformity in the treatment of mental illness. The preparations for this development lay in the institution of a general board for the supervision of district asylums in 1817,[2] and in the duty laid on the inspectors of prisons in 1826 of inspecting all mental hospitals. In 1843 the board of works took over the supervisory tasks of the general board, so far as buildings and similar matters were concerned; a year earlier a licensing system for private asylums was set up, to be administered by the prison inspectors.[3] In 1845 a special Irish lunacy inspectorate was established, while the state took care of criminal lunatics entirely into its own hands.[4] In all of this, the contrast with British heterogeneity, localism, and *laissez-faire* is once more arresting.[5]

If one takes policy and structure as the criteria, therefore, Ireland had one of the most advanced health services in Europe in the first half of the nineteenth century. It was to a large degree state-supported, uniform, and centralised. It aimed at providing the poor—that is, the huge bulk of the population—with some security against both minor and major illness, and at rationalising and specialising the hospital services. For example, twenty-one of the thirty Dublin

[1] McDowell, *Ir. administration*, pp 168–9.　　　[2] 57 Geo. III, c. 106 (11 July 1817).
[3] 5 & 6 Vict., c. 123 (12 Aug. 1842).　　　[4] 8 & 9 Vict., c. 107 (8 Aug. 1845).
[5] It should perhaps be stressed once more that formal progress did not necessarily mean material. In fact, in this particular field, A. P. Williamson has argued that the introduction of uniform rules for all Irish district asylums in 1843, and with it the virtual abandonment of 'moral management' in favour of medical hegemony, was a retrograde step (A. P. Williamson, 'The origins of the Irish mental hospital service' (M.Litt. thesis, Dublin, 1970), pp 179–80).

hospitals in 1840 specialised in one branch of medicine or another. One cannot, of course, gauge the efficiency of this system, especially at so early a stage of modern medical science; and, however efficacious, it cannot possibly have sufficed to meet the needs of poverty in what was mainly a subsistence economy. None the less, the very mechanics of the system and the ideas that, consciously or unconsciously, it embodied were remarkably advanced. It cannot have been altogether a coincidence that the years 1830–50 constituted a golden age of Irish medicine and of medical discovery and research.

At first sight it might seem sinister that so much of the lunacy administration came within the orbit of the prison inspectorate; but such an impression would be misleading. The government of Irish prisons and Irish mental hospitals alike was, by contemporary standards, remarkably positive and humane—at any rate in declared intention and apparent endeavour. In addition, the history of Irish prisons exhibits the familiar pattern of early centralisation and nationalisation. A national inspector general had been appointed as early as 1786,[1] and he strove not only to improve the standards of decency and health in the forty-one county and borough prisons throughout the country, but also to establish uniform regulations and procedures. The system was reorganised in the 1820s, with two inspectors general now charged with promoting the segregation of prisoners according to their sex and the reasons for their imprisonment, the latter being divided into five classes.[2] (Since one of the inspectors general was himself imprisoned for debt in the 1830s, during his term of office, doubtless this last duty was seriously regarded.) The inspectors were also directed to ensure that all prisoners were provided with a specified diet, furniture, and bedding, and to report the misconduct of prison officers.

Thus by 1830 a characteristically hybrid and closely regulated system had developed. The bulk of the costs of prisons and much of their day-to-day administration were local authority matters. But state intervention and control were steadily increasing. The general policy of the inspectorate was to render the system as reformatory (as opposed to punitive) as practicable: hence their emphasis on penitentiaries and the segregation of criminals. 'Prisoners', they wrote in one annual report, 'have not forfeited their claims in society. On returning to the world they will be worse or better men, according to the use made of their imprisonment.'[3] In 1830, however, they complained that magistrates and local authorities generally were still deaf to such a penal philosophy. This was in part, presumably, because the philosophy made high demands on the local resources: penitentiaries and segregation demanded new and more expensive buildings and staffing. Still, prison reform progressed. Throughout 1830–45 more and more county prisons were either rebuilt or 'improved' to meet the new desiderata. Moreover, there were areas of prison

---

[1] 26 Geo. III, c. 27 (8 May 1786). See above, iv, 710–12.
[2] 3 Geo. IV, c. 64 (22 July 1822); 7 Geo. IV, c. 74 (31 May 1826). See also below, p. 545.
[3] *Seventeenth report of the inspectors general of prisons, Ireland*, p. 33, H.C. 1839 (91), xx, 435.

administration where the inspectors could innovate independently of the local authorities. In 1830, for example, the important step of withdrawing military guards from jails was taken; until his death in 1837 the medical inspector of convicts, Edward Trevor, worked with considerable success to improve their health and abate the inhumanity of their treatment; in 1837 a national penitentiary for female convicts was opened in Grangegorman;[1] and in 1845 an act was passed enabling the lord lieutenant to establish a central criminal lunatic asylum.[2] Thus here too state power and responsibility steadily advanced, stages ahead of Britain, and of the majority of European countries.

As the ultimate linkages of public health and prison reform indicate, it is not really easy to draw the apparently sharp distinction between ostensibly ameliorative and ostensibly coercive state machinery. Certainly police reform was complex in both its administrative and political implications. By 1830 Ireland had travelled, mainly in recent years, half the way towards the establishment of modern centralised police forces. The government already nominated the chief Dublin police magistrate and two-thirds of his fellows, and to that extent indirectly controlled the metropolitan force of some 700. The county police forces (over 7,000 strong) were still recruited and maintained locally. But they were equipped from government stores and the lord lieutenant appointed the inspectors general, who were to work towards common standards of discipline and conduct; and the lord lieutenant was also empowered to move constables out of their own counties. The revenue police, who dealt with smuggling and illicit distillation, were 'hired' by the various senior revenue officers and commanded by army lieutenants commissioned as excisemen for the purpose. This curious administrative arrangement defies exact categorisation: 'quasi-official' and 'semi-central' are perhaps the least misleading terms (the functions of the revenue police were transferred to the Irish constabulary in 1857).[3] Finally, there was one essentially national body, the peace preservation corps, which had been established by Peel in 1814.[4] This was a mobile paramilitary force, nearly 1,000 in number, detachments of which might be sent to any district proclaimed by the lord lieutenant. The peace preservation force possessed a hierarchical, military-like structure and was governed by police magistrates with the powers of J.P.s. Apart from this last, the Irish police forces were poorly organised, badly paid, untrained, and ill-educated. The revenue police were said to have been 'without discipline and without instruction of any sort or kind',[5] the majority of the Dublin police to

---

[1] The former Richmond general penitentiary, which had been converted by the prison commissioners under 6 & 7 Will. IV, c. 51 (13 Aug. 1836).

[2] Above, p. 210, n. 4.

[3] 20 & 21 Vict., c. 40 (17 Aug. 1857).

[4] Above, pp 59–60.

[5] *Report from the select committee . . . appointed to consider the consequences of extending the functions of the constabulary in Ireland*, p. 6, H.C. 1854 (53), x, 12.

have been 'decrepit, worn-out old men',[1] and the local forces to have been mere partisans, pandering to their selectors and masters, the local magistrates. 'They speak', wrote Drummond in 1835, 'of loyal inhabitants meaning thereby the protestant inhabitants.'[2]

The police and related reforms of 1835–6 contributed more perhaps than any other single venture to the diminution of protestant ascendancy. As Lecky wrote,

In 1833—four years after catholic emancipation—there was not in Ireland a single catholic judge or stipendiary magistrate. All the high sheriffs with one exception, the overwhelming majority of the unpaid magistrates and of the grand jurors, the five inspectors general, and the thirty-two sub-inspectors of police, were protestant.[3]

The centrepiece of the profound change that took place in the later 1830s was the constabulary legislation of 1836. Yet, strangely enough, constabulary reform had not ranked high on the repealers' programme, nor was it to prove another victim of the lords' powers of legislative veto. Rather did this reform spring from the new British strains of administrative rationalisation and suprafactional government, although immediately and in detail it was Drummond's work. The general political implications of the 1836 acts do not appear to have been appreciated by any party of the day. The tory acquiescence (for although the bills were delayed in the lords, they were neither strenuously resisted nor materially amended) is perhaps explicable in terms of police reform implying for many tories merely more potent and efficient instruments of authority. The repealers' lack of interest might be explained in much the same fashion. Habit and experience may have led them loosely to associate Irish constabularies of all kinds with political repression. Moreover, where radical or liberal viewpoints coexisted with nationalistic, the usual prejudices against 'French' or 'Austrian' modes of social control would have aggravated this sort of feeling. As for men like Morpeth and Drummond, they would doubtless have assumed that the elimination or balancing of partisanship in any element of the state machine was itself a non-partisan activity. At any rate, for one reason or another, the profound immediate political consequences of the police reforms were largely unforeseen.

The major measure of 1836 amalgamated the county and peace preservation forces into a single centralised police responsible for order over the entire country, except in Dublin, Belfast, and Derry. A second measure produced the equivalent reforms in a new Dublin constabulary, and provision was made for the reorganisation of the revenue police on the same principles.[4] The new forces

[1] Minutes of evidence taken before the select committee of the house of lords appointed to inquire into the state of Ireland, since the year 1835 . . ., pt III, p. 1002, H.C. 1839 (486-III), xii, 138.

[2] McDowell, Public opinion & govt policy, p. 185.

[3] W. E. H. Lecky, The leaders of public opinion in Ireland (revised ed., 2 vols, London, 1912), ii, 99–100.

[4] 6 & 7 Will. IV, c. 13 (20 May 1836); 6 & 7 Will. IV, c. 29 (4 July 1836).

together amounted to some 10,000 men, with the Constabulary of Ireland (to be designated the Royal Irish Constabulary from 12 September 1867) accounting for nearly 80 per cent of the whole. The essential novelties of the new police were their complete centralisation and coordination, their professionalism and mobility, and their quasi-military organisation and discipline. To some extent these structures and features had been foreshadowed in the peace preservation force; and the increasing involvement of the Irish executive in the recruitment and management of the county forces had represented a stage in the same development. However, the 1836 acts brought all Irish police under an ultimately united command, with an autonomous national inspectorate to enforce, as the original recommendation put it, 'one uniform system of rules and regulations for the entire Irish police establishment', and with a single, large training depot in Dublin to serve the whole body. Thus Ireland came to possess a coherent, stratified, paramilitary police at a time when the lonely, untrained village constable was still the instrument of law enforcement over most of rural England.

In the 1830s at least, police reform worked against the traditional ascendancies. The new forces were carefully selected, well paid, and drilled to perfection, and acted with quite unprecedented impartiality and efficiency. They were supported, in this drive towards state neutrality, by a further extension, under the constabulary act of 1836, of the Irish stipendiary magistracy, which had always been relatively more numerous and influential than their English counterparts. The permanent professional magistrates were at this juncture markedly less partisan and more legally literate than the ordinary J.P.s. The extension of their numbers and operations was a corollary of the new form of police action. The whig government further redressed the imbalance between the conflicting sections of Irish society by wholesale revisions of the ordinary magistracy (particularly in 1838), whereby more than one-third of the existing J.P.s were removed. Most of those dismissed were Church of Ireland clergymen, squireens, absentees, or land agents.

The police reform of 1836 could, however, turn into a repressive as well as a conciliatory direction. They provided the Irish executive with an instrument of rare efficiency, in terms of the Europe of its day, for the enforcement of law and policy. It happened that, initially, it was state policy to treat the nationalists and popular movements with unwonted mildness, and their opposites with unwonted severity. But a full-scale liberal alliance was not, to say the least of it, a permanent condition in Anglo-Irish relations; and in different circumstances the power and omnipresence of the Irish constabulary assumed a very different mien in the eyes of the populace. Moreover, its mode of officer recruitment, on a caste basis like that of the armed services, was bound to lead, over time, to a considerable measure of identification between the bias of the constabulary and the interests of the gentry. None the less, it would be quite wrong to regard the Irish constabulary as the oppressive engine of a police state of the Metternichian sort, or to suppose that it ever degenerated into either the gross partisanship or the disarray that had characterised the police of the early nineteenth century. Moreover, its work and significance were by no means exclusively political; it is arguable that they were not even primarily so. Possibly the most important consequence of the police reforms was the provision of a modern underpinning for nineteenth-century Irish society. Agricultural statistics were collected, as well as political information; national censuses were handled, as well as the registration of firearms. It was not only political violence that was repressed: faction fighting and a host of other contemporary manifestations of brutality were slowly worn down. A vast range of day-to-day duties, such as enforcing the current regulations on slaughterhouses or weights and measures or poison schedules, imperceptibly established a new and more evolved and responsible form of social organisation. Not least remarkable, as with so many of the administrative improvisations of the period, was the speed and thoroughness with which a highly articulated and nationally extensive system was set up. Here, as in several of the other areas, much must be attributed to the extraordinary number of military and naval officers whose administrative abilities had emerged in the forcing-house of the Napoleonic campaigns, but who, in the 1820s and 1830s, could be called on to use their organisational skills in creating a novel form of civilised order.

INSTITUTIONAL change faltered and even fell back, however, whenever self-government was involved; and Irish municipal reform was perhaps the most striking failure of the liberal–O'Connellite alliance of the 1830s. The civic government of Ireland in 1830 was both scandalous and damaging to whig, liberal, and catholic interests alike. The sixty-odd corporations that had survived in Ireland were almost exclusively and aggressively protestant and tory, as well as inefficient and corrupt in the comparatively rare cases where they possessed enough resources to make corruption worthwhile. They gave the tories a dozen seats in parliament before 1832, and they bloated tory influence in the other parliamentary boroughs. Most were small self-perpetuating oligarchies, 'in many instances, of no service to the community; in others, injurious; in all, insufficient',[1] to quote the hostile report of the commissioners of inquiry of 1835. Yet in addition to their influence over parliamentary representation, the Irish corporations also dispensed patronage, mercantile and other privileges, and local justice on a large scale and on a sectarian basis. They represented an area in which catholic emancipation and the substitution of a whig for a tory government had proved totally ineffectual in producing change in the early 1830s. They seemed an obvious and easy target for assault by the whig alliance.

Things turned out differently. In the years 1830–35 O'Connell was generally

[1] *First report of the commissioners appointed to inquire into the municipal corporations in Ireland*, pp 39–40 [23], H.C. 1835, xxvii, 45–6.

concerned to achieve power-sharing in the corporations rather than to change them structurally or to modernise them as instruments of local government: at one stage, indeed, he tried to bargain with the Irish tories on dividing the spoils. The whig government, on the other hand, was concerned with rendering the corporations more representative and more 'efficient' (often in the 1830s a euphemism for cheaper). But they were driven to such an approach by radical prodding rather than natural inclination, and they saw little advantage, at this juncture, in substituting an O'Connellite for a tory monopoly—for this they saw as the net effect, in the majority of Irish cities and towns, of democratising the municipal franchise.

With these cross-purposes and much double-shuffling, the matter never really came to an issue before 1835. In that year, however, the situation changed in two important respects. First, the English municipal reform act[1] was passed, and there was now a model for the Irish to aspire to. Secondly, it was a tacit part of O'Connell's new compact with the whigs that they should introduce an Irish municipal reform bill along the lines of the English measure. The English model appealed particularly to O'Connell. With a £5 household franchise, it was essentially political in objective, aimed at destroying anglican and tory power-bases, which is precisely what he himself wished to do. Moreover, it was now possible for him to argue the Irish case for reform on the favourable ground of parity within the United Kingdom. With his usual optimism, he looked forward at once, when an Irish bill substantially along the English lines was introduced in July 1835, to nationalist majorities and catholic and liberal officeholding in most municipalities, and to each Irish corporation serving as 'a normal school for teaching the science of peaceful political agitation'.[2]

But the tories countered the bill, not only by the now normal practice of voting down the whigs' Irish measure in the house of lords, but also by producing the alternative 'reform' of simply abolishing all Irish corporations and substituting for them the much more limited and humble boards of commissioners available under an act of 1828 to provide for urban 'lighting, cleansing and watching'.[3] The tory counter-proposal was defeated on several occasions in the later 1830s in the commons, but it lent respectability to the lords' resistance and provided the tories with something to bargain with over and above their phalanx of diehard lords. In 1836 it looked for a time as if the government might, on the issue of the municipal reform bill, resort to the creation of peers to carry the Irish measures that were being systematically rejected by the lords. But in the end they shrank, as ever, from this course, feeling that British opinion would not support them when it was Irish reform that was in question. Four sessions were to pass before a bill was finally enacted, after successive mutilations. Overall, the Irish municipal reform act of 1840[4] represented a victory for the house of lords. Only ten Irish corporations survived, and even

[1] 5 & 6 Will. IV, c. 76 (9 Sept. 1835). [2] *Hansard 3*, xxxi, 98 (4 Feb. 1836).
[3] 9 Geo. IV, c. 82 (25 July 1828). [4] 3 & 4 Vict. c. 108 (10 Aug. 1840).

these had their judicial, financial, and administrative functions much reduced. A £10 householder franchise and high property qualifications for election were meant to ensure an upper- and middle-class domination.[1]

This struggle and the result showed several interesting features of contemporary Anglo-Irish politics. It showed more clearly even than the tithe issue the limitations of the whig alliance. After 1835 the case pressed was the strongest possible, and one on which liberals, radicals, and Irish were at one. Yet so long as the house of lords itself was not assailed, and so long as O'Connell would go on backing ministry concessions lest the ministry collapse, the reformers had to accept in the end comparatively small concessions. Next, it demonstrated that Irish protestants, faced with admitting catholics to power, with their own share probably diminishing in time, and with factional struggles likely to develop in the representative institutions, acquiesced in centralisation and the loss of self-government. On the other hand, the episode also showed that O'Connellism could not be altogether held back. The gains here were very disappointing, but in terms of O'Connell's objects gains there were. Most of the surviving corporations were nationalist, and much of the corporations' activity was political even in a narrow party sense. But the negative gains seemed almost, or perhaps quite, as important: an 'Orange' monopoly had been broken, and even if much of the old 'Orange' power went not to catholics but to central government, it none the less diminished the redoubts of the ascendancy. Perhaps after all, it was sharing rather than power that was being sought throughout the decade.

The most striking single feature of the municipal reform debate was perhaps the general silence on the substance of civic government. Sanitation, arterial drainage, housing, roads, gas lighting, and similar matters, critical to the comfort and even tolerability of urban life, were practically ignored. Yet these were the subjects of rapid change in both theory and practice throughout Europe in the 1830s and 1840s. Here certainly politicisation was the enemy not only of reform but even of reality. People dwell, wash, walk, play, live noisomely or not, live in light or dark, die young or old, as well as struggle for vicarious power or snatch at tokens. The daily banalities did not enter much into the ideology of the period. Fortunately—though to no one's credit in particular—they found some lodgement in various of the institutional innovations.

[1] Below, pp 247, 553.

CHAPTER X

The economy and society, 1830–45

OLIVER MACDONAGH

As J. S. Donnelly, to whom the present author is much indebted for an understanding of pre-famine agriculture, has pointed out, the years 1830–45 mark the culmination of an extraordinary phase of Irish husbandry.[1] The phase ran from the late eighteenth century to the mid-nineteenth century. Both before and after it the Irish agrarian economy was dominated by the raising of animals and the production and processing of animal products. But from the 1780s to the 1840s the emphasis was increasingly on tillage and labour-intensive forms of cultivation. A process, begun apparently by protectionist legislation, and sustained and quickened by the enfranchisement of the catholic forty-shilling freeholders, and still more by the high corn prices during the revolutionary and Napoleonic wars, was self-perpetuating by 1815. The initial rapid growth in population itself ensured, under existing conditions, a further and faster enlargement, the fatal implications of which were fully apparent by 1830. By then the farming class consisted of some 700,000 families, more than thrice as many as today. Fully three-quarters of the farms, at twenty acres or less, were non-viable in every modern sense except that their wretched occupiers continued somehow or other to survive. Over one-half of them in fact were ten acres or under in extent. But a still more striking and significant contrast with modern Ireland was that in 1830–45 these farmers were quite outnumbered by a vast army of labourers.[2] Just as the Irish farmer of these years was a very different sort of being from his English counterpart, so too—and for the same reason—was the Irish labourer. Paradoxically, a large proportion of this last class might be termed 'landed'.

The pressure of population on resources after 1815 had led to a great and rapid expansion of the cottiers, a species of penniless entrepreneurs who in effect rented the means of subsistence, a cabin, a potato patch, and a cow or cows or pasture, from the farmers, and paid for them by labour. In some arrangements mere labour completed the transaction; in others the cottier

[1] See generally Donnelly, *Land & people of Cork*, pp 9–72.
[2] Above, p. 114.

earned cash over and above the rent; in yet others he paid cash as well as labour, generally through his main, and perhaps his only, 'cash crop', pigs.[1] The element of speculation in the cottier's situation was his gamble that the yield from what he 'rented' would provide his family with the means of life for twelve months. In these desperate gambles the odds against the cottier, already long in 1830, were lengthening, more or less steadily, throughout the period. This was partly because the terms on which he took his patch were worsening with rising competition, and partly because the quality of his mainstay, the potato, was declining, while reliance on it for survival was gradually increasing. But still more miserable than the cottier was the casual or unbound labourer, whether he took conacre, or attempted to live by purchase from his earnings, or intermingled both expedients. This was the class that grew fastest in the early 1830s, and whose multiplication was a sure indication that national disaster was possible. Not only was the weight of population pressing more people below the conventional economic structure, but the decline of weaving, handicrafts, and small-scale manufacture was throwing large numbers of new landless labourers on the market from the mid-1820s onwards.

But as one form of economy rushed to a common doom, the faint outlines of its eventual successor became discernible. The key to the new agriculture was the political and economic domination of Ireland by an industrialising Britain, resymbolised and reinforced by the act of union and the onset of free trade. Until 1845 the process of urbanisation and the growth and steadiness of manufacture in the other island had not yet gone far enough to revolutionise Irish agriculture—even if it had been free to be revolutionised. But many of the signs of radical change were already apparent, and some had worked to Ireland's disadvantage even before 1830. The development of free trade in the 1820s had, for example, ruined the important provisions trade to British North America and the West Indies, although the corn laws, much the most important element in the protective system of the United Kingdom so far as Irish agriculture was concerned, remained intact until 1846. But the other major implication of free trade, the creation of a vast market for imported agricultural produce in Great Britain, had also begun to manifest itself in the remarkable increase in Irish exports just before—and still more just after—1830. From an annual average of 125,000 tons at the close of the Napoleonic wars, Irish cereal exports, mainly oats, advanced to an annual average of some 450,000 tons during the 1830s, and actually reached their second highest level of the century, at 513,000 tons, in 1845 itself. Between the mid-1820s and the mid-1830s, the export of pigs grew by more than one-third, that of cattle by almost 50 per cent, and that of sheep by 150 per cent.[2] The exports of dairy produce and of stout and other beers also increased steadily, though not so markedly. There was probably an overall and more or less continuous increase in Irish production in all these items between 1830 and 1845; and this was accompanied by growing sales in both the home

[1] Above, p. 115.   [2] Cf. above, pp 123, 156.

and the British markets. Doubtless domestic *per capita* consumption was falling—the acreage under and yield from the great alternative food, potatoes, mounted fast to 1845[1]—but this fall was more than counterbalanced by the rise in population at all social levels. Thus the general increase in Irish cultivation, agricultural production, and exports in the second quarter of the century, and in particular in the years 1830–45, testified at once to the two opposite master trends: first, the apotheosis of the old economy in the race (by now quite hopeless) to keep resources abreast of population by more tillage and labour-intensive activity; and secondly, the coming of capitalistic, market- and export-directed, and essentially pastoral farming.[2]

For the ultimate implication of the union for Irish agriculture was to gear it to the British market and to increase the attractions of capitalistic farming. Before 1845 there were strict limits to the degree to which this could be realised. Generally speaking, the Irish landlords lacked the money, knowledge, and freedom of action to pursue such a course. Much of their land was in the hands of middlemen, often holding leases for ninety-nine years or three lives, in the pre-war or early wartime years; and almost without exception, the middlemen (whatever the covenants of their leases may have enjoined) refused to invest any money whatsoever in their temporary holdings, and instead did their utmost to bleed them white.[3] In practice the middleman system resembled tax farming in the *ancien régime*, most certainly in its vicious consequences for both the grantor and the victim of the concession. Even where the landowner retained control of his own land, he had to move towards clearance or consolidation slowly and stealthily if he hoped to avoid peasant counteraction. Even where he could move in these directions, he rarely had the economic wisdom, and still more rarely possessed the ready capital, to invest to a significant extent in permanent involvements. Wartime prosperity had encouraged in the landed class a level of expenditure, and a readiness to mortgage the future with abandon, that led to later indebtedness or insolvency. Bishop Doyle noted in 1830 the inability of the gentry to reduce their establishments to fit shrunken incomes: 'We all know how painful it is for a man to descend from a certain rank to another below it.'[4] Worse still, their expectations were rising. By 1830 the integration of standards and habits of the British and Irish gentry had gone far, and the British gentleman lived in a much more complex and expensive fashion than he had done in the eighteenth century.

None the less, the deeper assimilation of the Irish economy and gentry to the British was destined in the long run to revolutionise Irish agriculture, and the future pattern was increasingly evident as 1845 drew closer. As we have seen, the area of land cultivated, the amount of cereals grown, the number of animals raised, and the quantity of animal products processed were all apparently on

---

[1] Above, p. 123.   [2] Above, pp 126–7.   [3] Above, pp 128–30.
[4] *Second report of evidence from the select committee on the state of the poor in Ireland* . . ., p. 398, H.C. 1830 (654), vii, 572.

the increase in the years 1830–45, as indeed had been more or less the case since the conclusion of the Napoleonic wars. As we have also seen, this was probably not so much a sign of change as a final manifestation of the older form of agrarian activity and organisation. As the population pressed more heavily on resources, more and more waste land was drawn into production. When prices fell or rents rose, or both happened simultaneously, it was necessary to produce, by all possible means, more marketable goods to meet inescapable cash needs. Initially the gap might be covered by a reduction in the standard of living, but there was a final limit (very close in hundreds of thousands of cases) to the degree to which reduced standards of life could meet the shortfall. As large numbers of men, or their children, were pressed down to a lower level on the social scale, it was only to be expected that, for example, the raising of pigs should have become more intensive, and that the volume of pork products should rise. But this is only half, or at most three-quarters, of the story. The other part of the explanation of the leap in production is the arrival in Ireland of the 'agricultural revolution' of the early nineteenth century.

By the 1820s the new farming was drifting patchily south and west from its centres in the Scottish lowlands and East Anglia to Ireland. In 1830–45 all the usual marks of this enlightenment appeared more frequently and impressed themselves more deeply on the Irish countryside. Increasingly the iron plough replaced the wooden, and the scythe the sickle; green crops and modern crop rotation and diversification became more common; livestock strains were being steadily improved in cattle, still more in pigs, and most of all in sheep. Part of the improvement consisted in the better quality and increased weight of the animals, but more (at least in the case of pigs and sheep) in a marked shortening of the period of maturation. The main formal mechanisms for disseminating knowledge and reforming practice were the local agricultural societies, which multiplied after 1830. Of course, the societies and the new farming generally did not touch the vast lower agrarian groups, except perhaps, over time, in livestock strains. They touched only a minority even of the gentry and substantial farmers, and were much less developed and systematic than their British counterparts.[1] Still, they spread, and were by 1845 sufficiently extensive and coherent to constitute an unmistakable harbinger of the future order.

For the present, however, it was the rush towards the Niagara of the old order rather than the early intimations of the future that contemporaries rightly emphasised, although they might also have noted the desperate ingenuity with which Irish society had reorganised itself to stave off mass starvation for as long as possible. For the cottiers, the farm workers, and, most of all, the swelling horde of casual labourers were now pressing very close to the margin of utter ruin. The decline in living standards after 1830 was both dangerous and rapid. Housing, firing, furniture, implements, and clothing had long been so mean and scarce for labourers that little room remained in them for further

[1] Above, p. 129.

degeneration. But food was a different and, of course, a critical affair. By 1830 milk had practically disappeared from the diet of the poorest two million of the population. More and more of this 25 per cent may have owned pigs. But pigs were reared for money, and their growing numbers in 1830–45 were an index, paradoxically, of increasing desperation, not of hope. The extraordinary growth in potato cultivation, to almost one-quarter of the total area under tillage by 1845, was also an index of declining standards. It represented at once the facilitator and the consequences of rising population. But what really implied catastrophe was, first, the increasing proportion of the cottiers' and labourers' incomes—it already exceeded 50 per cent in 1830—that had to be devoted to renting potato land;[1] and, secondly, the decline in the quality of the potato and the stretching of the summer hunger gap. The 'lumper' potato, which had come to predominate by the 1830s, did not store well. Year after year more and more people were closer and closer to starvation in the months between June and October, and especially in August. The social weight hanging from the single thread of one root crop was growing ever heavier. The slowing of the rate of population growth and the general increase in emigration levels in the early 1840s were both too small and too late to affect the issue, except marginally.

In these very dreadful circumstances an extroardinarily high level of agrarian counteraction might have been expected. But while even approximate quantification in such a field is difficult, the evidence generally suggests that in 1830–45 Whiteboyism and its equivalents, powerful though they continued to be in their effects, were yet on a lower level than in either the immediately preceding or the immediately succeeding decades. If this is true, what weight are we to attribute to the opposition, the alternative, and the brake provided by pacific political agitation? Contrariwise, what is to be ascribed to the inverse of de Tocqueville's law that revolutions spring from rising living standards? These are nice points. Certainly the interaction of the two factors produces the first successful large-scale conflation of constitutional methods and quasi-revolutionary action in Ireland, thereby setting a pattern for the agrarian movements of the later nineteenth century. The issue, tithes, was ideal for such a development. It divided the landed classes, naturally inflamed the catholic clergy, touched the self-interest of the farmers, lent itself to the application of passive disobedience, and was readily comprehensible by and congenial to British liberals and radicals. It deserves close attention as an index of the particular character of the period.

For almost seventy years opposition to tithes had been a staple of Irish agrarian resistance, although the opposition was usually to their level or incidence rather than to tithes as such. But the 'war' that opened in November 1830, at Graiguenamanagh, County Carlow, was much more intense, wide-

[1] Above, p. 115.

spread, and bitter than anything that Ireland had known before. This was due partly to the 1823 composition act,[1] which had tied tithes in many instances to cereal prices that no longer obtained, partly to the agitatory vacuum left after the conclusion of the emancipation struggle, and partly to the dimension of catholic–protestant conflict that the particular issue involved. In the first phase of the 'war', to mid-1833, the catholic clergy, the urban and middle-class repealers, and O'Connell and many landlords of his kind assumed leadership of the campaign. It is true that, in quite considerable numbers, protestant farmers and even landlords (by no means all presbyterians) withheld tithes in these years, for basically the issue was economic. None the less, the agitation was heavily impregnated initially by nationalist and sectarian feeling.

By mid-1832 less than half the tithes were collected, while the number of dead and wounded among both resisting peasants and the constabulary and yeomanry mounted spasmodically. Meanwhile the government, while freely using the machinery of the state to try to enforce the claims of incumbents and lay tithe-owners, was too preoccupied with the reform bill and other troubles to devise any new policy or extraordinary measures of coercion. Then on 1 June 1832, by 2 & 3 Will. IV, c. 41 (commonly known as the 'attorney general's act', because the relevant powers were placed in his hands), the government was authorised to pay some of the arrears and to collect those for 1831 by force if necessary. Later in 1832 Stanley's composition act[2] tried to solve the problem by making the assessment an official proceeding instead of a private arrangement; by slightly reducing the actual level of tithes payable; by exempting the poorest—the yearly tenants and tenants-at-will—from direct liability for tithes; and by allowing landlords or superior tenants who chose to take responsibility for the payment a rebate of 15 per cent. At the same time the principle that surplus revenues might be appropriated for catholic or secular purposes was in effect rejected. Although the act foreshadowed much of the final settlement of 1838, immediately the problem grew instead of being solved. In 1833–5 less than one-third of the tithe due was collected. Meanwhile the government expeditions to collect the arrears of 1831 brought only a miserable harvest, one worth less than half of what it cost to garner, and violence continued in late 1832 and early 1833.

The second phase, from June 1833 until early 1835, was marked by the barely concealed retreat of both sides. By the 'church million act' of 1833[3] (so named because of the sum advanced), the government assumed responsiblity for the payment of all the arrears of 1831–3, inclusive, subject to some scaling-down of the actual amounts that would be paid. At the same time it became clear that the state would make no further effort to collect the arrears, and that it would be far less zealous in giving its aid to pursue future defaulters. On the other

[1] 4 Geo. IV, c. 99 (19 July 1823).
[2] 2 Will. IV, c. 119 (16 Aug. 1832).
[3] 3 & 4 Will. IV, c. 100 (14 Aug. 1833).

hand, the catholic clergy and most Irish nationalists had been alarmed by the course of events in the early 1830s. The clergy, and O'Connell with them, were appalled by the bloodshed that had accompanied the agitation, and feared that the violence would spread not only all over the country, but to issues other than tithes. O'Connell and most of his supporters feared that rents might soon follow tithes and that the whole social fabric might come, step by step, under assault, if the campaign continued unabated and indefinitely. Hence by mid-1833 the catholic church was dissociating itself from the agitation, and the Irish liberals and repealers were, in general, ready for a compromise on the issue. This became apparent in July 1834, when O'Connell accepted the government's bill for commuting tithes once it was agreed in committee to accept his amendment substituting 60 for 80 per cent of the existing composition as the basis of a settlement. The house of lords rejected the amended bill; but meanwhile it was clear that O'Connell and the bulk of the Irish members, as well as of educated Irish opinion, had abandoned full-scale and absolute opposition to the tithe.

By the third stage of the affair, beginning with the Lichfield House compact of March 1835,[1] the violence had died away, and the focus had shifted from tithes *per se* to the principle of appropriation of the supposed surplus for extra-ecclesiastical objects. Appropriation had formed the ideological basis for the junction of whigs, radicals, and Irish in 1835 in much the same way as disestablishment was to form the basis for a similar junction between the roughly corresponding groups in 1868.[2] Ironically, however, the bulk of the members involved were not in their hearts committed to appropriation. Only Russell and a handful of the whigs, some of the radicals, and a few of the Irish led by William Sharman Crawford in what was possibly a challenge to O'Connell's leadership, genuinely cared about the principle—which was tangential, if not actually irrelevant, to the tithe issue. Yet for three sessions all the whig tithe-reform bills failed because they incorporated appropriation in some form or other, as an obeisance to what had made possible the compact of 1835. In the end the act of 1838[3] omitted any appropriation clause and followed much the same lines as the 1834 bill had done, except that the terms were rather less favourable to the tithe-payers. The composition was fixed at 75 per cent and became a rent charge payable by landlords, who received a bonus of up to 25 per cent for assuming the responsibility. Thus the 'war' ended in a further minor reduction in the level of tithes, in a confirmation of the exemption of yearly tenants and tenants-at-will, in the treasury paying the bulk of the arrears accumulated over eight years, and in the landlords replacing the clergy in the firing line if hostilities should ever be renewed. The relatively tame conclusion to the affair is explicable partly in terms of the most inflammatory section of the peasantry being freed (apparently) from the burden as early as 1832; partly in terms of the apprehensions of both the catholic clergy and O'Connell and his

---

[1] Above, p. 178.   [2] Below, pp 441–4.   [3] 1 & 2 Vict., c. 109 (15 Aug. 1838).

colleagues; partly in terms of the government's growing reluctance to coerce and of its growing willingness to pick up the unpaid bills; and partly in terms of the improved cereal prices of the later 1830s, which effectively augmented the value of the reductions of 1832 and 1838. The Church of Ireland was removed as a major target for nearly thirty years; the landlords had made themselves still more vulnerable; and much of the history of the land war and land reforms of the 1880s had been foreshadowed. 'During all these troublous times', recalled W. R. Le Fanu, son of the dean of Emly in County Limerick in 1831–4, 'the landlords looked on with indifference, and showed little sympathy with the clergy in their difficulties. My brother used to say: "Never mind, their time will come; rents will be attacked, as tithes are now, with the same machinery, and with like success."'[1]

TITHES, however, represented only an outwork of the land system. Strangely, the system as such was never subject to a serious political assault in 1830–45. In so far as its modification or even the mitigation of some of its deleterious consequences were concerned, it was—equally strangely—a poor law that offered the only real prospect of achievement. Yet—once more oddly—the poor law of 1838 was the one major Irish measure of the whig government that owed more to British than to Irish pressure. Poor law reform was second only to parliamentary reform in arousing fears, speculation, and interest in Britain in the early 1830s. On the one hand it seemed that the English agricultural labour force was, under the current poor law system, being rapidly transformed into an army of paupers, idle and expensive. On the other hand, mass starvation and even peasant revolution seemed possible if relief were suddenly withdrawn and 'the forces of the market' liberated. It was because it was supposed to steer a way between these two dangers that Chadwick's 'less-eligible' workhouse scheme was generally acceptable, and in the end partially enshrined in the English poor law amendment act of 1834.[2] Given this absorption in the question in Britain and the fact that Irish poverty was palpably more intensive and extensive, it was not surprising that British M.P.s were almost unanimous in pressing for an Irish poor law, or that the whig government proffered it as a reform in 1833, with the usual preliminary of a royal commission to inquire and report. British opinion had its reasons for supporting this with almost malevolent enthusiasm. As Archbishop Whately put it,

The feeling of the English was a mixture of revenge, compassion, and self-love. They pitied the suffering poor of Ireland; they had a fierce resentment against Irish landlords, whom they hastily judged to be the sole authors of those sufferings; and they dreaded calls upon their own purse.[3]

[1] W. R. Le Fanu, *Seventy years of Irish life* (London, 1893), pp 66–7.
[2] 4 & 5 Will. IV, c. 76 (14 Aug. 1834).
[3] E. J. Whately, *Life and correspondence of Richard Whately, D.D., late archbishop of Dublin* (2 vols, London, 1866), i, 401–2; D. H. Akenson, *A protestant in purgatory: Richard Whately, archbishop of Dublin* (Hamden, Conn., 1981).

This last referred particularly to the rising tide of Irish immigration, now facilitated by very cheap, quick, and frequent cross-channel steamer passages, which ended so often, it was thought, in Irish paupers living off British rates. Racialism and religious prejudice, added to motives of local economy, swelled the chorus of 'Irish, go home!'

There were Irish pressures too, some from orthodox liberals for an orthodox poor law, but more from priests and resident landowners, face to face with destitution, and thinking on very different lines. For them the poor law was but an element in some larger and more positive undertaking than merely ensuring that the very poorest Irish should not die of hunger. Bishop Doyle, for example, was widely known as an advocate of an Irish poor law; but his main object was to secure an injection of capital and skills into an underdeveloped economy. Again, Sharman Crawford, another celebrated advocate of a poor law, saw it as subordinate to, though important in, the creation of a peasant proprietary. But the mass of Irish opinion was indifferent or hostile to the entire proposal. The leading opponent was O'Connell, who in fact made this the occasion (it may even have been a cause as well) of his breaches with Doyle and Crawford. O'Connell's opposition was partly theoretical, a doctrinaire aversion to meddling with the market forces; but mostly he was generalising from his own experience of landowning in Counties Cork and Kerry. He feared that a poor rate would ruin landlords, and that poor law institutions would destroy the network of mutuality and deference that rendered Irish poverty more endurable by creating a measure of personal kindliness and humanity in the countryside. This last was a tribal view of Irish rural society, as seen from the chieftain's eminence. O'Connell's apprehension was self-interested, but also shrewd, and probably more in accord with contemporary Irish sentiment than the notions of his opponents.

The 1833 commission, presided over by Whately, did not report for three years, for it took a large view of its allotted task. Basically, like Doyle, it saw the problem in terms of a backward economy, brought to such a pitch that it was incapable of generating significant improvements from its own resources and by its own unaided efforts. Conventional asylums were recommended for the very young, very old, and unfit poor. But otherwise the report was exclusively concerned with increasing production and setting off processes of economic growth. It proposed massive expenditure on bringing waste land into cultivation, and on drainage and other improvements for existing farms; agricultural instruction to raise the standard of farming; state loans to construct or extend the economic infrastructure generally; and large-scale assisted emigration to reduce the weight of population on resources. All this cut across British assumptions and interests. It would be vastly expensive—the assisted emigration project alone might have cost £20 million for a merely temporary relief. It would call for elaborate and practically unbounded state intervention. There were no models to work from. Not least important, it would feed rather than assuage the 'English feeling' to which Whately had referred.

In these circumstances Lord John Russell in 1836 had no hesitation in throwing over the report and so arranging matters that the English poor law of 1834 (curiously, the Scottish system does not appear to have been considered) should be simply transferred to Ireland with the minimum number of amendments. It was a practicable—in fact a very easy—course because the British parties had long been agreed on this 'solution'. With some independent Irish support, they were sure of huge majorities; and O'Connell's opposition in the commons was correspondingly muted. O'Connell also refrained from making much stir in Ireland. The case was hopeless; to press it hard might divide his following and tarnish his prestige. Ironically, the only serious, though futile, resistance came from the peers with interests in Irish land, normally O'Connell's *bête noire*. The report on 15 November 1836 of George Nicholls, the English poor-law commissioner, dispatched by Russell to Ireland to arrive at a preordained conclusion within weeks—'to get one bottle of water out of the Liffey and one out of the Shannon, and then persuade the English people that he can give them a better poor law than we who have been three years considering it', as Whately sourly observed[1]—deviated in only one major particular from the British system. For obvious reasons of economy, or even solvency, poor relief in Ireland was to be a matter of selection, not of right. The workhouses were planned to hold only 80,000 persons—a small fraction of the destitute.

The 1834 poor law was inappropriate even for England and Wales. The impotent poor were as surely condemned to a 'less-eligible' existence as the able-bodied, and a measure designed for redundant agricultural labourers was applied equally to the urban unemployed. But whatever its relevance to England, the principle of 'forcing labour on to the open market' was meaningless in Ireland, where virtually no demand was matched by a practically limitless supply. Moreover, Nicholls specifically stated that his poor law was designed to facilitate the development of capitalist farming in Ireland, and that it was not meant to cover large-scale catastrophe such as famine. But if the able-bodied Irish poor threw up their land, most of them would also throw up all hope of reentering their own economy; and if they clung to it, the problem of poverty would remain untouched until masses of them broke under some sudden strain and overwhelmed the meagre workhouse system. In short, the English poor law could neither ward off the impending disaster in Ireland nor cope with its effects when it arrived.

Thus the Irish poor law of 1838[2] failed to deal seriously with the effects, not to add the causes, of poverty or to provide a relief system nearly adequate for the famine that struck within two years of its completion. None the less, it was

[1] Morpeth to Russell, 5 Oct. 1836 (P.R.O. 30/22/2C, quoted in MacIntyre, *Liberator*, p. 215).
[2] 1 & 2 Vict., c. 56 (31 July 1838).

of first importance in three respects. First, as has been pointed out above, the extensive new powers conferred on local government from 1840 on went, almost without exception, to the boards of guardians, who were relatively popular and democratic bodies. Secondly, it diverted attention for a dozen years—which could be very ill-afforded—from the questions of land tenure and the formation of wealth in Ireland. It is significant that almost all the Irish reformers who supported a poor law thought of it as subordinate to land reform and economic development. It was possible to narrow one's purpose to the provision of 80,000 workhouse places only if one knew nothing of Ireland at first hand. But, as things fell out, the government's purpose was so narrowed from 1830 to 1843 at least; and the famine apart, the consequences of the following of this false trail, so far as Irish society was concerned, were tragic. Finally, as Angus MacIntyre points out, 'in isolation . . . the whole tendency of the poor law was towards breaking up the fabric of rural society'.[1] It aimed at subtracting 'worthless' members from that society; and what was 'worth' in pre-famine Ireland? Although its scale was small initially, it was soon to develop into a massive instrument of effective depopulation.

By 1830 certain of the lineaments of the Irish industrial and commercial, no less than the Irish agrarian, economy for the remainder of the century were already discernible. The 1820s had seen several critical developments. Of overriding importance was the total abolition in 1824 of the surviving duties that still protected several Irish industries from British competition.[2] The textile industries were the main victims. Silk, woollen, and cotton manufactures were reduced to less than half their output and employment-provision within a decade; leather goods, glass, furniture, and other products of the kind suffered similarly. In only one instance was there a successful substitution—or rather revival. In the north-east linen stepped more or less into the shoes of the expiring cotton manufacture. James Kay's invention of the wet-spinning process in 1825 made possible the spinning of fine linen by machine. Much of the capital, labour, and plant employed in the Belfast cotton industry was soon transferred to linen. By 1838 there were fifteen flax-spinning mills, as against three or four surviving cotton mills, in the town. By 1845 a large-scale and largely mechanised linen industry was concentrated in the Belfast–Lisburn district, with the application of steam power and the factory system to weaving as well as spinning soon to come. Steam was a vital factor in the general decline in Irish manufacture. It was introduced in 1830–45 into the very largest units of a few of the traditional Irish industries, such as brewing, distilling, and milling. But, generally speaking, it was the enemy of Irish industry in this phase. For it was the rapidly increasing use of steam in British manufacture in the second and third decades of the century that, combined with the removal of the last of

[1] MacIntyre, *Liberator*, p. 225.
[2] 5 Geo. IV, c. 22 (12 Apr. 1824).

the protective duties by 1825, gave the British products their overwhelming price advantage.

A second innovation of the 1820s that had profound effects over the next fifteen years was the development of cheap and frequent steamship communication between all the major Irish and British ports, and especially between those on the Irish eastern and the British western coasts. This greatly facilitated and strengthened the British export drive in large and important parts of the Irish market. It also facilitated the British use of Irish labour, both seasonally and permanently. Deck fares were reduced to very small amounts, and passages rendered comparatively short, certain, and safe. Further economic consequences were the temporary differentiation, to some degree, of the economy of the eastern seaboard from the remainder of the Irish economy, and the decline of the Irish provisions trade. The carriage of livestock across the Irish Sea, which the steamships rendered economic, advanced the store cattle as it diminished the dead-meat trade—particularly when this was combined with the rapid development of a British railway system in the 1830s. Live-cattle exports trebled between 1830 and 1845. To a lesser degree, the same trend was discernible in live-sheep and live-pig exports. This had obvious repercussions on the Irish meat-processing plants and, for cattle, on the changeover to pasturage in the vicinity of the greater export centres.

Conversely, two other aspects of Irish economic life during 1830–45 are largely explicable in terms of the steam age's not having yet arrived. One was commerce and travel in the interior. Even by 1845 there were less than seventy miles of railway in the country, confined to the immediate vicinity of Dublin and Belfast.[1] It is true that road and canal traffic expanded considerably in the period. The parliamentary grants available for road-building since 1822 were freely called on, especially after the board of works entered directly the business of road construction in 1832.[2] The most notable development was the opening of west Connacht and the north-western and south-western regions, which had been virtually inaccessible before; but everywhere the network of road communications was improved and extended. The change was often immediate and dramatic. Sir Robert Kane noted in 1843:

When this [road construction] is done, it is remarkable how instantly the very poorest of the people hasten to avail themselves of its benefits. When Mr Nimmo was engaged in the construction of the Connemara roads, his workmen were actually inconvenienced by the country cars conveying produce and objects of traffic, even up to the spot which the engineers were at the moment commencing to render passable.[3]

All this meant a quickening and a concentration of trade. But both the scale and the character of the development were comparatively insignificant. Broadly speaking, the larger the inland town, the more it gained. This did not necessarily mean an increase in commerce or productive population. More

---

[1] Above, pp 149–50. [2] Above, pp 207–9. [3] Kane, *Industrial resources*, p. 388.

often perhaps, the change merely helped to offset the growing ease of British penetration of the Irish markets, and to sustain for a little longer local small-scale manufacture, handicrafts, and skilled services.

The new roads and the canals were, then, of only marginal importance.[1] This becomes very clear when we consider the transformation that railways would have brought—and were shortly to bring. Even at the level of the cheapest fares (second-class canal and Bianconi long car) it would have cost a labourer his entire week's wages to travel fifty miles in 1840; and freight was correspondingly expensive. Most public transport did not exceed a speed of five miles per hour. Even in their heyday of the early and mid-1840s, the canals carried only some 150,000 people annually and provided access to comparatively narrow strips of the country. It was therefore of the highest economic and social significance to the period that Ireland did not then, as she could conceivably have done, enter the railway age, with passenger and goods rates and journey time halved and practicable loads multiplied many times. This meant that the *ancien régime* (economically and socially speaking) of interior Ireland was only mildly modified, instead of being materially reordered, before 1845.

The second area in which the impending steam revolution had not yet got under way by 1845 was that of deep-sea shipping. During the 1820s steam power had established itself for most of the Irish estuary and cross-channel work. But it was not until 1850 that it made significant advances on the Atlantic or other oceans. As a consequence, the Irish shipping industry and Irish ports were able to maintain, during 1830–45, more or less the level of activity that they had reached by the early nineteenth century. The Irish industry was small in scale (only 50,000 tons in all), and much divided in ownership and port of origin; and the vessels themselves were minuscule, 200 tons at most. But at least it provided some degree of employment and diversification in a dozen or so Irish ports. It also kept alive hopes that a major shipbuilding industry, or a major Atlantic port, or both might be established. As early as 1815 a paddle steamer was built at Passage West, County Cork, and in 1845–6 iron-hulled vessels and screw-propelled steamers were launched at Cork. In 1843 Sir Robert Kane argued (with Valentia, Berehaven, or Tarbert in mind) that the coming of steam on the Atlantic would not neutralise Ireland's westerly advantage. 'The freight of goods on steam vessels on long voyages is far too high to allow of their being generally used ... and passengers also would naturally prefer to start from the extremest point of land.'[2] Thus it was of some importance, psychologically as well as materially, that this little sector was still spared what was to prove (despite Sir Robert) the fatal challenge of steam. For soon after 1845 steam power was to render all the Irish ports mere vestibules of Liverpool, Glasgow, Bristol, and London, and to sweep almost all Irish shipping from the North Atlantic and the continental trades.

Thus much of the old commercial order still hung on, and the surest

[1] Cf. above, pp 146–9.   [2] Kane, *Industrial resources*, p. 346.

measure of its survival was in the very small scale and the slow growth of urbanisation. In 1841 even Dublin was well under one-quarter of a million in population, and Belfast only 75,000. The eight largest Irish cities between them housed less than 500,000 people. Apart from the Lagan valley and a few new towns at the junctions or termini of the road and canal systems, the urban population was growing more slowly than the rural: even Dublin, for example, grew by only 16 per cent between 1801 and 1841. One consequence of this was a very densely populated countryside in 1830–45. With five to six times as many rural dwellers as in Ireland today, country life must have been very different from the stereotypes of rural living that have come down from the later nineteenth century. The agrarian social web before the famine was probably closer to equatorial delta settlement than to any western agricultural community of the present day.

As with farming, however, the urban economy of the period was marked by intimations of the future: again, the overlying traditional pattern was being pierced by modernity. One example of fundamental change, which was like the decline in manufacturing and the improvement in cross-channel communications rooted in the 1820s, was the growth of a commercial banking system. After the Bank of Ireland's monopoly had been partially sundered in 1821,[1] the Provincial, Ulster, and National Banks, set up in the decade 1825–36, and indeed the Bank of Ireland itself as well, quickly spread branches throughout the provincial towns. This represented a major step in the general process of modernisation in Ireland. Its immediate utility to the Irish economy is doubtful. It institutionalised and channelled much Irish saving; but the flow was—like that of the English provincial banks—largely directed to the London money markets. The banks did not conceive investment in Ireland as one of their leading functions. Doubtless their establishment facilitated the provision of credit; but they were cautious in management and outlook, and would in general have preferred London interest rates to the return from native entrepreneurs and improvers, even had the latter constituted a numerous and clamorous category of would-be borrowers. Financially Ireland's condition was no less—indeed probably more—'colonial' after the development of branch banking on a national scale than before; for the business was at bottom London-dominated. A similar case was the insurance business. Of the seventeen major insurance companies operating in Ireland in 1844, fifteen were London-based. One of the other two, the National, included in its objects 'being closely identified with the commercial interests of this country, and aiming to retain a portion of the vast sums which are annually remitted to England in insurance premiums'.[2] But this company was small, ephemeral, and possibly (to judge from the composition of its directorate) no more than a consortium of Dublin businessmen providing easy finance for themselves. Banking and

[1] 1 & 2 Geo. IV, c. 72 (2 July 1821); above, pp 150–52.
[2] *Post-office directory and calendar* (Dublin, 1844), p. 493.

insurance have been noted as particular instances of what were, notwithstanding Bombay-like poverty and decaying streets and markets, two important general tendencies of the period—the greater integration of the Irish into the British commercial order, and the development of sophisticated financial and business systems in the midst of dearth.

I T was, as we have already noted in the case of the political economists,[1] characteristic of 'reformers' in the second quarter of the nineteenth century to attempt to alter circumstances where they did not fit the orthodoxies of the day. This helps to explain the stress laid on education by contemporaries. At many points the poor (broadly speaking, the lower four-fifths of the population) were aggrieved by the patterns and institutions of society; in certain fields and regions and at certain times their rage and misery seemed to endanger the established order. To some extent that order was modified in response to these frightening pressures, although the modifications of the 1830s and 1840s were often not what the downtrodden confusedly demanded, but what the enlightened proclaimed to be either inevitable or useful. But the residual (or sometimes consequential) problems could be dealt with only by force or persuasion. There was force in plenty in Ireland, but it was not by itself enough. So persuasion had also to be enlisted, and persuasion meant education. This is not meant to suggest a cynical, predetermined project of indoctrination. Rather did the enlightened think in terms of a sober undertaking to bring the masses to a realisation of the folly of flouting the social and economic laws, and the necessity to work within their ambit. Ignorance bred crime, vice, and disaffection; knowledge and self-discipline were to be the deliverers.[2]

By 1830 the state's first major effort to promote elementary education was in ruins. The Kildare Place Society, despite an annual parliamentary grant of £30,000 and the apparently innocuous object of 'undenominational' religious teaching, had long been rejected by the catholics. Five years earlier it had been condemned by a royal commission as resting on a 'compromise . . . which, even if realised, no person is of opinion would have been completely satisfactory'.[3] In fact it rested on two compromises, one governmental, the other religious, for it sought state ends without direct state involvement or responsibility, and aimed at 'contracting out' education to a body that, although professedly neutral in religion, was in fact dominated by members of the Church of Ireland. Both compromises failed, with the catholics at least, and in a sense the education of the catholics was the *raison d'être* of state support. The current Irish alternatives were repellent to the government. The hedge (or 'pay', or 'popular') schools were too few, too various in quality, and too haphazard in conduct

---

[1] Above, p. 195.
[2] For the development of the national school system see also below, pp 523–37.
[3] *First report of the commissioners on education in Ireland*, p. 58, H.C. 1825 (400), xii, 63; see above, pp 74, 79.

to be considered as a 'private system'. A later generation romanticised them and wildly exaggerated both their classicism and their numbers. Despite occasional excellence, they were but stop-gaps. Next, an independent catholic system might conceivably develop in the course of time. But the new or newly deployed teaching orders were only scratching the surface of the problem as yet. Even if they did expand sufficiently to enrol the next generation of the urban poor—and this would have called for very rapid and extensive growth— the urban religious schools would be deficient in capital and revenue alike, to say nothing of being likely to instil both 'sedition' and 'superstition'. Meanwhile the countryside would remain virtually untouched.

In 1828 a commons' select committee had recommended the establishment of a board to supervise Irish elementary education and distribute an annual parliamentary grant among societies and individuals organising or maintaining primary schools, and the whigs saw an extension of this course as their way out of the dilemma. Stanley's establishment of a board of national education in 1831 was bolder in scope and action than the committee had been in words. In effect, under the new scheme, two-thirds of the costs of buildings, equipment, salaries, and other running expenses were to be provided out of public funds. This state aid carried with it state control over much of the syllabus and teaching, and a state veto on appointments. The inspectorate established by the board to report on the schools and to set and maintain standards ensured that central regulation and a high degree of uniformity were realities almost from the outset. Moreover, 'model schools' were soon set up, and eventually only teachers trained there might teach in the state system. By 1840 several training colleges were in operation and the entire country had been divided into inspectoral districts—roughly one in each county. The next stage was the gradation and promotion of teachers, and the fixing of their salaries, by the board. By 1845 there was, in form, truly a state system of education, with some 4,000 schools (a number of them formerly independent) and over 400,000 pupils in its empire.

The Irish 'national' system was a model pressed later by liberals in many parts of the English-speaking world. But how close was it to the celebrated liberal slogan, 'free, compulsory, and secular'? Even though the state met the lion's share of the costs, private and local funds were also called on. School attendance was voluntary, and the worst feature of the want of compulsion may have been not the number who never attended but the irregularity of the attendance of the rest. The 'secularism' of the 1831 system consisted in common classes for everything but religious instruction, and the commissioners' duty and endeavours to eliminate 'sectarian' matter from the syllabus. However, even this programme was objectionable to sections of all the three major denominations, and the system gradually turned into one that was (in R. B. McDowell's phrase) 'denominational in practice with a conscience clause'.[1] Such a result was

[1] McDowell, *Ir. administration*, p. 244.

intrinsically likely in a country of both high religious feeling and a high degree of confessional concentration among the population. Thus the Irish system fitted the later liberal slogan rather ill. But it was none the less, within the context of the United Kingdom in the 1830s, a revolutionary experiment in state planning, management, and secularity.

It was also, in certain important respects, a successful one. As fast as population and poverty were growing between 1830 and 1845, popular education grew still faster; and one important effect was the dramatic fall in the national illiteracy rate. By 1841 it had dropped to 53 per cent of those aged five and over, and by 1851 to 47 per cent,[1] impressive figures by contemporary European standards, especially in the light of the composition and destitution of the Irish population.

The system had other profound consequences for Irish society. By 1845 a considerable majority of the Irish children attended, albeit many irregularly, the national schools. There were pockets of overtly denominational education, sustained by organisations such as the Church Education Society (maintaining over one thousand Church of Ireland schools), by prelates such as MacHale, and by teaching orders such as the Irish Christian Brothers, but the numbers involved were comparatively small and the instruction was generally similar to that in the state system. This sudden and very extensive growth of primary education affected Irish society in three main ways. First, it hastened the breakup of the traditional rural pattern of life by teaching quite different sets of values, by failing (despite a few gallant and imaginative endeavours) to provide a significant measure of vocational training, and by weakening the rising generation's ties to the soil. Secondly, it facilitated (one is tempted to say, rendered practicable) the massive emigration from countryside to town in Ireland, or to Britain or North America, which became established in the 1840s. Almost without exception, the overseas emigrants appear to have been capable of speaking English. Most seem, too, to have had considerable preparation for a British-type milieu. Thirdly, the new schools accelerated 'anglicisation'. In this context 'anglicisation' does not mean the crude and total displacement of one culture by another, but rather the steady modification and attenuation of what was distinctively Gaelic, with language perhaps the leading sufferer. Half a century later these processes of depopulation and deracination, hastened (though by no means started) by the national schools, were coming to be deplored. But they were not deplored in 1830-45, except by an occasional 'advanced' churchman like MacHale and by the urban pioneers of cultural separatism. Even the few 'native' articulators of what survived of the Gaelic world seem to have been resigned to its imminent extinction and to have looked to religion rather than race or language as the rallying-point. In fact it is altogether characteristic of these years that the conflicts over the educational

[1] *Census Ire., 1841*, pp 438-9 [504], H.C. 1843, xxiv, 546-7; *Census Ire., 1851*, pt IV, pp 184-5 [2053], H.C. 1856, xxix, 256-7.

system were not cultural at all, but almost exclusively confessional, with the Church of Ireland generally hostile, the catholics initially favourable but increasingly disenchanted, and the presbyterians the most successful in wringing concessions from the national board. Otherwise, the schools were popularly regarded as so many ladders by which it might be possible to climb carefully from the pit. But if the whigs hoped that the national schools would produce either political or religious latitudinarianism, or acquiescence in the current economic or social structures, they were to be altogether disappointed. In the long run literacy made discontent more clearly articulated, more precisely directed, and more politically effective.

Secondary education was, on the other hand, virtually ignored by the state in the 1830s and 1840s, although this was as true of England and Wales as of Ireland. The catholic sector continued to grow slowly from the first ventures of the religious orders and diocesan authorities during the revolutionary and Napoleonic wars; but it was still minute in 1845, for the church lacked the resources to extend it fast. The other religious communities were comparatively well served, mostly with schools long established under charities or by statute. In many instances it would be wrong to regard these as narrowly denominational, although their tone and teaching may have been generally 'protestant'. Over much of Ireland they had a more or less considerable catholic enrolment at this stage—a fact that may help to explain certain of the differences in nuance between the nationalism and radicalism of, say, the third and the fourth quarters of the nineteenth century. Meanwhile the neglect of secondary schooling by governments in 1830–45 remains, in the light of their expectations from education, somewhat curious. Here the N.C.O.s at least in forming opinion and leading agitation in the future would be trained.

Superficially, this makes it all the stranger that Peel should have taken up tertiary education in 1844. But perhaps the colleges bill was not so much an educational reform as a strand in his policy of killing repeal, if not by kindness, at least by *douceurs* that might win over a section of the catholics and divide the church politically.[1] There had been some pressure for provincial colleges in the late 1830s. But this was not especially clerical—or especially catholic.[2] On the other hand, it was obviously only a matter of time before the rising assurance and ambitions of the catholic hierarchy would lead them to express more positively their dissatisfaction with the University of Dublin. We should also, however, allow for the possibility that Peel's adoption of the university issue was accidental. The better endowment and the physical reconstruction of Maynooth were an essential part of his plan to court the more susceptible of the hierarchy and perhaps also to soften the Irish parish clergy of future years; and the 'new Maynooth' was first proposed as a system of combined clerical and lay tertiary education. The bishops having frowned on this combination, the element of lay catholic university training was adrift. Herein lies the immediate

[1] Above, pp 186–7.   [2] Above, p. 76.

origin of the colleges bill of 1845, even though it was later extended, as that was, to cover the other major dissidents, the presbyterians. Maynooth may have also influenced the matter in another sense. It had been possible for Peel to negotiate quite successfully with the bishops on Maynooth by intermediary 'soundings'. He repeated this *modus operandi* on the colleges issue; but the second matter being new and complex, the method here proved disastrous. The institution of the queen's colleges and their development lie outside the period. But the immediate political effects do not. In this respect Peel's venture recoiled upon the government. True, it played an unanticipated part in dividing Irish nationalism when Old and Young Ireland split on the question of denominationalism in university education. But it failed to divide the catholic church, despite its initial promise to do so. On the contrary, the episcopate eventually united in condemnation of the colleges at the synod of Thurles in 1850.[1] They had been presented with a standing grievance rather than a sop; and to a lesser extent this was true of the catholic laity as well. In fact, as with the national schools, it was probably the presbyterians who gained most from, and were best reconciled by, the undertaking.

EVEN education, the sphere perhaps in which the most far-reaching social changes of the period occurred, was, therefore, largely determined by religious considerations. It was indicative of the ultimate supremacy of religion in Irish life in this period, as in so many others. For these were the years in which the powerful and passionate revival of Irish protestantism was met by a catholic counterpart. The divisions within Irish protestantism in the early nineteenth century were numerous and bitter, in particular among presbyterians and methodists.[2] But on balance these were outweighed by common purposes, plights, and characteristics. The liberal and rational tone of eighteenth-century protestantism in Ireland, its tranquil ease of effortless superiority, its readiness to await the withering, in the natural course of things, of popish superstition and priestcraft, were widely and swiftly replaced by evangelicalism in the post-union era. Not until 1842 did an avowed evangelical actually become a bishop of the Church of Ireland. But well before that date evangelicalism had its centres in scores of parishes and even coloured the spirituality of many thousands of members of the Church of Ireland who might not have recognised themselves as members of any particular church party. In northern presbyterianism, the fundamentalists and strait observants had been in the ascendant since 1800, and by 1828 the 'new light' faction had finally captured the general synod of Ulster.[3] In the following year the small and dwindling band of liberal presbyterians seceded to form the remonstrant synod, which met in 1830; and a decade later in 1840 the general synod of Ulster united with the ultra-orthodox secession synod (itself the fruit of earlier struggles against liberalism)[4] to

[1] Below, pp 396–9. [2] Above, pp 76–8.
[3] Above, pp 76–7. [4] Above, iv, 104.

constitute the General Assembly of the Presbyterian Church in Ireland, a decidedly unbending and evangelistic body. Meanwhile methodism, both within and without the established church, was marked by the usual Wesleyan enthusiasm, zeal for souls, and stress on personal illumination and witness.

One expression of this great and general 'revival' was a spate of church- and chapel-building and parochial and circuit reorganisation and reform. This was at its fullest flood in the second and third decades of the century; but the after-flow continued in the 1830s and 1840s. A more aggressive manifestation was the formation of national missionary societies, replete with schools, tracts, travelling preachers, Gaelic bibles, and scripture readers, aimed at the conversion of Irish catholics. Between 1806 and 1820 no less than seven national societies were set up, four of them within the Church of Ireland and one interdenominational. While it would be absurd to try to pin this vast movement and wave of feeling unerringly on a chronological chart, the evidence does suggest that a climax was reached shortly before 1830. This would march well with the relative confidence of Irish protestants in the first quarter of the century that they could maintain indefinitely their various degrees of political and social ascendancy.[1] The belief that theirs was the 'forward', advancing religion and that numerous conversions among the people were at hand would hearten them in their defence of privilege and appear to offer some insurance against the onset of democracy. Conversely, the upsurge of catholic power in 1826–9 constituted a scandal and served as a new spur to evangelicals. Still more, however, did it seem a fresh menace, if not a deadly blow.

For catholicism too had been undergoing a revival (though in a more ordinary and less theological sense) in the post-union era; the emancipation campaign was but one of its products. The years 1830–45 marked the culmination of the first phase of this catholic resurgence. Since the 1790s the reconstitution of the parochial system, alike in terms of churches, other ecclesiastical buildings, and priests, had been gathering pace. By 1845 it was virtually complete. Ireland had then almost the same number of fully worked parishes and of parish priests as in 1901.[2] The only later development of note was in the number of curates, and even these increased by no more than 50 per cent between 1845 and 1901. The post-famine period is often spoken of as an era of church-building, and so it was. But it must not be forgotten that most of this building was the replacement of earlier, humbler structures. The later work may have been an expression of group wealth, stability, and pride. But it was not the provision of a network. This was the accomplishment of the pre-famine years.

On the other hand, several striking features of late nineteenth-century Irish catholicism were still comparatively undeveloped in 1830–45. Primary and secondary education by religious was, as we have seen, still on a small scale, though fast increasing. The same was true—indeed to a higher degree—of

[1] Cf. above, pp 77–9.   [2] Kerr, *Peel, priests, & politics*, pp 33, 353.

hospital and other social work by religious. Irish missionary activity overseas was in its infancy. Apart from a small and unsuccessful foray in India, there had been none as yet except to countries where Irish immigrants were comparatively numerous. Even there the supply of a chaplaincy for the diaspora was still at a rudimentary stage in 1845. This task was to be an outstanding venture of Irish catholicism in the second half of the nineteenth century, in much the same way as Asian and African missionary work was to be an outstanding venture in the first half of the twentieth. Overall, then, what the 1830s and 1840s witnessed was the completion of the initial stage of the reconstruction of the catholic church in Ireland—the provision and effective deployment of a secular clergy and of the basic ecclesiastical materials they required. But although the emancipation campaign rested on the quiet assemblage of an infrastructure in earlier years, that campaign in turn transformed the public bearing and private self-esteem of catholics, and in particular of the clergy. The old passivity and timidity in the face of British power was generally replaced by confidence and even, in many cases, truculence. To some extent the degree of change was a matter of generation; for instance, almost every bishop who later joined the repeal association had been appointed after 1825, and most of those who did not were pre-1825 appointments. None the less, all were more or less influenced by the 'famous victory' of 1829 and the experience of open involvement in the agitation that preceded it. The new catholic confidence and belligerency may also have owed something to the earlier confidence and belligerency of the protestant churches. Nothing was more likely to develop religious pugnacity and 'manliness' than theological and ecclesiastical conflict of the sixteenth-century type—especially if one felt that one was winning.

Politics was, in Irish circumstances, the area predestined for the most public exhibition of these traits and trends. In 1846 *The Times* observed: 'The people follow their pastors; their pastors are guided by their prelates; the hierarchy are devoted to O'Connell. . . . The grand secret of O'Connell's success must be found in the religious accompaniments of his agitation.'[1] The remark exaggerated the subservience both of laity to clergy and of priests to bishops, but basically it was correct. The countenance of hierarchy probably was, as O'Connell had told Bishop Doyle as early as 1827, essential to the success of any national agitation.

At first the post-emancipation church seemed determined to eschew further political engagement. In a joint statement of 1830 the bishops counselled all clergy to keep aloof from political activity of every kind in future; and at a meeting in the synod of January 1834 they passed unanimously two resolutions, one repeating in stronger terms the injunction of 1830, and the other forbidding the use of ecclesiastical buildings for any political or secular purpose. In fact, however, most bishops—and a still higher proportion of the priests—interpreted politics, charity, and religion with a convenient catholicity. The

[1] *The Times*, 13 Apr. 1846.

defeated candidate for County Kerry in the general election of 1831 attributed his rout to 'the priesthood ... marshalled under a Jesuit bishop'.[1] In October 1834 Bishop Michael Blake of Dromore actually presided over an 'O'Connell tribute' meeting in the grounds of his cathedral, arguing that no breach of the episcopal resolutions of January was involved because the meeting was held outside and not inside a church and because rewarding O'Connell was a charitable and not a political affair. Again, Edward Nolan, one of the many bishops who intervened openly in the general election of 1835, observed publicly that although, like every other bishop, he wished his clergy to eschew political activity, 'we are bound to give them [the laity] our assistance by instruction, advice, exhortation, and it is necessary to explain to the electors the real nature of the question they are now called on to determine by their votes'.[2] These various reactions, hot on the heels of synodal decrees, show clearly that the bishops' resolutions constituted no real obstacle or even discouragement to clerical participation in politics.

Had O'Connell pressed the repeal campaign of the early 1830s wholeheartedly, the bishops might have proved difficult. But as things went, they were generally amenable, even enthusiastic, and unreserved in support of his leadership. This was particularly the case during the years 1835–9, when O'Connell was the leading advocate of and actor in the whig alliance, which the hierarchy favoured. The main benefits that the alliance promised—tithe reform, civil equality, a diminution of the protestant ascendancy, and the opening to catholics of new doors to local place and power—seemed sufficiently religious in character to need no baptism.

In 1839, however, Cardinal Fransoni, prefect of Propaganda, complained to Archbishop William Crolly of Armagh that MacHale and other bishops were presiding over political banquets, denouncing the government, and exciting popular passions. Crolly was instructed to dissuade them not only from all political action but even from all semblance of political involvement.[3] But Rome's intervention had little apparent effect. As soon as the repeal association was set up in 1840, MacHale and half a dozen bishops became open adherents and actively engaged in the struggle as O'Connell's allies. In all these dioceses the mass of the clergy worked for repeal; to a lesser extent the same was true even in 1840 in dioceses where the bishops were 'neutral' or covertly hostile. Over the next three years many other bishops joined the association until it included two-thirds of the hierarchy in its ranks. Even when, in October 1844, a letter from Fransoni (procured by the British government) sternly reminded prelates that it was their sacred duty to avoid politics, to inculcate subjection to the temporal power in civil matters, and to dissipate popular excitements, there

---

[1] Maurice Fitzgerald to Croker, 23 Feb. 1831 (Croker papers, Duke University Library, N.C.).
[2] Letter to clergy of Kildare and Leighlin, 7 Jan. 1835 (*Pilot*, 12 Jan. 1835).
[3] J. F. Broderick, *The holy see and the Irish movement for repeal of the union with England* (Rome, 1951), pp 110–11.

was no abatement. No priest or bishop resigned from the association or even reduced the ardour of his banquet orations. Generally the letter of 1844 was dismissed as sound doctrine doubtless, but not applicable to Irish circumstances—the very line to be taken later by Archbishop Croke in setting aside the rescript of 1888 condemning the 'plan of campaign'.

Yet at another level the Fransoni letter can be seen as a turning-point in 'the church in politics' in Ireland. One-third of the bishops and some proportion, though much lower, of the lower clergy remained aloof from the repeal campaign. None opposed it openly; even oblique moves by Daniel Murray to enforce the Roman policy in his archdiocese of Dublin created such an outcry that they were quickly abandoned. None the less, there was now a discernible fissure in clerical ranks and in the nationalist–catholic front. It was this that Peel sought to enlarge, with some success, in 1844–5. Peel's move represented the first major use of the counter-checks of the Roman stick and the concessional carrot since the full development of nationalist–clerical political organisation. For the next three-quarters of a century they were to continue to weave in and out of the story of Anglo-Irish relations.

Still, the remarkable feature of the years 1830–45 as a whole was the intertwining of denominationalism and politics; and its most striking advertisement was the renewal and extension of clerical participation in the nationalist movements. Synods and Propaganda might anathematise, O'Connell strive for a supra-sectarian party, and liberals, members of the Church of Ireland, and presbyterians might struggle to stem the retreat to the politics of religion in their own ranks, but clerical management and mobilisation were the organisational cement of the new party structure and agitations all over Ireland, and especially in the smaller towns and in the countryside. It was impossible to call in the priests without catholicising and anti-catholicising popular politics. Not that the catholic clergy could fairly be described as either free or creative politically. Propelled from beneath and steered from above, the priests and bishops lacked genuine initiative or controls—indeed, probably lacked any positive desire for them. None the less, they checked and limited both popular pressure and the lay leadership.

O'Connell himself was constrained by the alliance with the church. For example, his professions of loyalty to the throne and his ostentatious repudiation of violence were trump-cards of the repeal bishops in their game with Rome; and although other interests and inclinations might have pressed O'Connell in the same direction, his dependence on the bishops undoubtedly limited his options in these respects. Again, on such an issue as the colleges bill, O'Connell, whatever his views, would have been forced to follow the lead of the clerical repeal faction. Moreover, his decline after 1844 changed the nature of his political system. His party and organisation became partisan rather than national and began gradually to disintegrate. In the process the repeal priests and bishops identified themselves with a faction rather than a popular front, and then retained their habits of political command despite the loosening and finally the disappearance of the structure in which they had had an allotted place.

The 'church in politics' did not revert to anything like its O'Connellite form until the 1880s. Meanwhile, however, with the clergy easily assuming that they were surrogates for all catholics, it expressed the confident, not to say arrogant, tone of the generation that had grown up after emancipation. Contrariwise, the protestant churches and congregations, outside the north-east at least, fell into defensive and exclusive attitudes, tacitly accepting the roles of garrisons and chaplaincies. The contractions of privilege forced on them in the 1830s, the mobilisation and massing of catholic numbers in the early 1830s, and above all the refusal of a tory government in 1841–6 to attempt a return to the politics of ascendancy and spoils, had the same effect on them secularly as had the meagre gains of the 'Second Reformation' religiously. In tune with this, the spiritual mark of Irish protestantism might be said to have been, by 1845, fundamentalism without evangelicalism (as might have been expected, tractarianism made little headway in Ireland, unless indeed the *Nation* school be regarded as a transferred and secularised form of the same phenomenon). As to the catholics, ultramontanism without papalism—an equally unusual disjunction—was increasingly the note in the immediate pre-famine years.

In one light, this conclusion seems to mark a return to the past. In another, however, it throws the modern elements, the novelties, into relief. Herein religion was of a piece with much of the rest of the story. The years 1830–45 were, to an unusually high historical degree, a sort of February. Everywhere the last season, ravaged and rotting, still covered the land. But almost everywhere, too, the shoots of a new year might be perceived if one looked closely.

CHAPTER XI

Land and people, *c.*1841

T. W. FREEMAN

IF printer's ink could have solved the problems of Ireland it would have become an earthly paradise long ago. Not only Irishmen but residents and visitors of widely varied origin were impelled to write about it, to travel widely, to note down what they saw, and even to moralise on the ways of life that would lead to improvements. Men of science looked forward hopefully to a time when peat bogs would be made to blossom as the rose, or at least to give bountiful crops, when new roads would carry commerce, education, and civilisation to the remotest mountains and the most deserted western shores, when nationally owned railways would be so profitable that tax could be abolished, when vast mineral resources would be opened up to profitable exploitation. A succession of royal commissions drew attention to the stark realities of the time, such as the apparently endemic poverty, the near-famines that occurred in various areas when unexplained disease hit the potato crop, the undercurrent of unrest that occasionally flared out into violent action, the pathetic eagerness with which every bit of land was not only sought but defended against all competitors, and even the fierce struggle to gain the lease of an acre or two of highly rented conacre land to grow the potatoes that could at least keep body and soul together. Some of the travellers spoke of the great patience shown by the Irish in adversity, and many found them an endearing people who were worthy of every possible encouragement and help. The times were certainly out of joint, but nobody seemed to know how to put things right.

On every hand the picture was dark. Many industries had failed, especially the woollen trade; the land was crowded with tenants wresting some sort of a living from a few—very few—acres; a large proportion of the houses in the countryside were one-roomed hovels; the towns had squatters' settlements on their fringes, known as cabin suburbs, and their streets swarmed with beggars. Any public works such as road- or rail-building attracted an abundance of labourers, and the cry of the time was 'For God's sake, give us work.' Emigration was a possible outlet for the enterprising, but it was always regarded as a social evil as it led to the break-up of families, to the departure from friends, and to moral as well as physical risk to those who went away. The economic compulsion to emigrate has always, and quite explicably, been resented. Only in the north-east were there signs of the industrialisation that could provide an adequate living for the people. Travellers from England such as Mr and Mrs Samuel Carter Hall felt quite at home in Belfast, for it had the same pulsating energy and growth that they knew in British cities such as Manchester and Birmingham. Factories were being built, new and neat cottages were lining straight little streets between one main road and the next, and on the pleasant higher ground around the Lagan lowland, handsome terraces of houses for the professional and merchant community were built, with mansions for the really successful. Domestic industry still survived in the north-east, though it had virtually disappeared everywhere else. That it was to disappear quite soon was hardly appreciated.

Disparities of wealth between rich and poor were regarded as a natural feature of social life by many observers. The possession of wealth gave a social responsibility that included providing work for others, not only as servants and labourers but even as workers in factories capitalised by the rich. But the poverty of Ireland was plain to see. The Devon commissioners, for example, commented:

We cannot forbear expressing our strong sense of the patient endurance which the labouring classes have generally exhibited under sufferings greater, we believe, than the people of any other country in Europe have to sustain.[1]

Their idea was that more employment must be provided by various means, some of which are discussed, and they looked to the landlords and other people of substance for help in creating work. The census commissioners of 1841 were obviously concerned to assist the people and stated categorically that 'a census ought to be a social survey, not a bare enumeration';[2] and so indeed it was, for it covered such details as housing, education, farmers' resources, emigration, and the value of agricultural produce. Also included was a long and detailed analysis of deaths by Surgeon (later Sir) William Wilde (1815–76). Contemporary writers in their various ways helped to diagnose the problem, and the knowledge of Ireland was strengthened by the work of the Griffith valuation and the publication of the six-inch maps for the whole country between 1833 (Londonderry) and 1846 (Kerry). The Griffith valuation gave, for its time, a sound scientific assessment of the agricultural possibilities of a country in which land must inevitably remain a basic resource, and the mapping gave a basis for further survey of population distribution, of railway development, of new routes for roads, and of other public works. To the historical geographer of a later time it gave, with the census of 1841, various commission reports, comprehensive gazetteers such as the maligned but useful Samuel Lewis's *Topographical dictionary of Ireland* (1837), and even the accounts of travellers or journalists, a source that can make the landscape come to life.[3] But to what extent?

[1] *Devon comm. digest*, p. 1116.　　　　[2] *Census Ire., 1841*, p. vi [504], H.C. 1843, xxiv, 6.
[3] Lewis's book was favourably received by the *Dublin University Magazine*, xii (1838), pp 226–32: see T. W. Freeman, *Pre-famine Ireland* (Manchester, 1957), p. 315.

It is a fascinating exercise to wander through an Irish town or village, or even through the countryside, and see what really survives from the period immediately before the famine. In Cork, Dublin, Limerick, and many other towns there are houses, even whole streets, that were built long before 1845, of which some are still carefully preserved. Similarly in some parts of the countryside there are old demesnes with their stately mansions, which have changed very little, for even if they have been taken over by institutions the grounds may be kept much as they always were, and in a few cases even the gentry survive. Nevertheless, scores of mansions have crumbled into dust, and many demesnes only retain the old high walls that are so marked a feature along many roads, especially in the vicinity of Dublin. Many of the smaller country houses, however, remain, and not a few still have wonderful sheltered walled gardens. Equally, some of the older farmhouses of the more substantial type still exist. But of the smaller houses that dotted the countryside so plentifully in the early 1840s there is little trace. Some villages and even towns have rows of ruined cottages long since abandoned; and in many of the clustered settlements of former times, especially but not exclusively in the west, it is possible to discern the layout of the houses, many of which are now used as outbuildings. There are also relics of old mills and factories in a number of towns. That survivals from this period are worthy of further investigation has been shown by E. R. R. Green[1] and by various writers on canals, which, with railways, appeared to offer hope to Ireland. Sir Robert Kane and others wrote optimistically about the future in the ten years or so before the famine, for two main reasons. First, all the resources of science were available at a time when economic activity was expanding and the world was being opened up by new and swifter means of communication; secondly, the position was so bad that it could hardly deteriorate, and any change must be an improvement. Only the wildest pessimist could have foreseen the tragedy that was to come so soon.[2]

In this chapter the story ceases at the beginning of the last act of the drama that culminated in the famine years. It deals with an Ireland that was never to be the same again, when the population was still increasing from the 8,175,124 of 1841 to an unknown total, perhaps about 8,500,000, by 1845. Dependence on the land was marked, even extreme, for only one-fifth of the population lived in the towns and villages so carefully recorded in the 1841 census. Not surprisingly, the six-inch mapping of the country was a cadastral survey showing the division of land into fields, parks, demesnes, and other visible features as well as boundaries, roads, settlements, and other normal expressions of the mapmaker's craft; unfortunately it did not show contours, as some observers noted when roads were planned to traverse impossibly steep hillsides through using the maps rather than the actual countrysides as

---

[1] E. R. R. Green, *The industrial archaeology of County Down* (H.M.S.O., Belfast), 1963.
[2] Above, pp 108–13.

a basis.[1] The organisers of the survey penetrated every remote corner of the land, undeterred by weather or any other difficulties: the work was organised by Thomas Frederick Colby (1784–1853) and three junior officers of the Royal Engineers, Thomas Drummond (1797–1840), Thomas Aiskew Larcom (1801–79), and Joseph Ellison Portlock (1794–1864), of whom the last lived under canvas at 2,000 feet in County Donegal in the depths of winter while working on the local triangulation. Colby worked in Ireland from 1824 to 1828, but Drummond stayed to his death and was a main contributor to the valuation survey under Sir Richard John Griffith (1784–1878). He was also, as under-secretary (1835–40), the main author of the report of 1837–8 on the possible routes of Irish railways.[2] Larcom produced the only ordnance survey memoir[3] that was published (the Templemore memoir), but it was so elaborate and expensive that the scheme was dropped. He remained a much respected figure in Ireland and was one of the commissioners for the 1841 census and under-secretary from 1853 to 1868. The 1841 census was more successful than its two predecessors of 1821 and 1831, partly because at least the enumerators (the constabulary) had maps before them on which the administrative boundaries were defined. These will now be considered, following which attention will be given to the landscape, communications, population, and economic activity.

IN theory administrative divisions could easily be recognised, as there was a fivefold system of provinces, counties, baronies, parishes, and townlands. In 1841 the ordnance survey was complete except in the south-western counties of Cork, Kerry, and Limerick, where the mapping was finished in 1842. The basis of the entire system was the townland, still extant in Ireland and invariably known to the local residents. Not invariably, however, were the exact townland boundaries known, and in some cases the lines drawn on the maps were a compromise, perhaps even an invention made by the workers in the Griffith valuation, who dug a low earthen ridge as a boundary. Others were drawn when the electoral divisions were formed as part of the poor law unions. But once a townland was on a map it had identity and some degree of permanence.

Parishes were traditional units for ecclesiastical and social purposes in Ireland as elsewhere, but the census commissioners found that the civil and ecclesiastical parishes differed from one another. The civil parishes were grouped into baronies, of which there were several in each county. Neither the parishes nor the baronies, however, appeared to provide the government with a satisfactory basis for administering Ireland. As in Britain, the relief of poverty became a national concern, and therefore Ireland was divided into 130 poor law

[1] See J. H. Andrews, *A paper landscape: the ordnance survey in nineteenth-century Ireland* (Oxford, 1975).
[2] *Second report of the commissioners appointed to consider and recommend a general system of railways for Ireland* [145], H.C. 1837–8, xxxv, 469–863.
[3] *Ordnance survey of the county of Londonderry*, i, *parish of Templemore* (Dublin, 1837).

unions, each of which was to have a workhouse under the act of 1838.[1] Five years earlier a commission had been appointed 'to inquire into the condition of the poorer classes in Ireland and into the various institutions at present established by law for their relief': in one of their many publications, dated 1836, it was reported that there were thirty-six infirmaries, about five hundred dispensaries (though only one in County Mayo), and only five workhouses.[2] Definition of the poor law unions began from 1838, and 127 out of 130 were in existence by the end of 1841. Their definition eroded the earlier traditional parish and barony definitions of the counties, though it used the townland as its base. The legislation was clear:

The commissioners may . . . unite as many townlands as they think fit to be a union for the relief of the destitute poor. . . . Whenever a union is declared, a board of guardians is to be elected, for which purpose the commissioners may divide the union into electoral divisions, and from time to time alter the same; but in making or altering such electoral divisions, no townland is to be divided.

In the following year, 1839, it was noted that 'the boundaries of many townlands [are] not accurately drawn' and arranged that 'the commissioners may . . . declare any place not known as a townland to be a townland'.[3]

By 1845 there were 123 workhouses with 42,068 inmates, compared with 5,468 in four workhouses in 1841. The poor law rate was collected in all the unions except four: Cahirciveen, County Kerry; Clifden, County Galway; and Glenties and Milford in County Donegal. There was some resistance to such payments, for which more than a million persons were liable, but a report of 1844 noted that in ninety-eight unions 92 per cent of the amount due had been paid.[4] Nevertheless, there were incidents, such as the arrival at Kilmallock workhouse, County Limerick, of all the ratepayers from a certain electoral district, demanding the release of their poor, who were then escorted home with rejoicing. Some electoral divisions coincided with large estates, as the landlord would naturally pay most of the rates and therefore contribute most to the needs of his people.[5] Today many of the old workhouses seem austerely handsome buildings externally, and it was fortunate that the original idea of using old barracks was discarded. The original directive said that 'the style of building adopted' was to be 'of the cheapest compatible with durability: and effect was to be obtained through harmony of proportion and simplicity of arrangement, all mere decoration being studiously excluded'.[6]

Counties were established at various times in Ireland[7] and numbered thirty-

[1] 1 & 2 Vict., c. 56 (31 July 1838).

[2] Nicholls, *Ir. poor law*, p. 125.

[3] Summary, 2 Vict., c. 1 (15 Mar. 1839), to amend 1 & 2 Vict., c. 56 (cited in Nicholls, *Ir. poor law*, p. 125).

[4] Nicholls, *Ir. poor law*, p. 323.

[5] William L. Feingold, *The revolt of the tenantry: the transformation of local government in Ireland, 1842–1886* (Boston, 1984), pp 15–17.

[6] Nicholls, *Ir. poor law*, pp 243–4. See also below, p. 558.   [7] Above, ix, maps 43–5.

nine in 1841, for as well as the familiar thirty-two there were four counties of cities (Cork, Dublin, Limerick, and Waterford) and three counties of towns (Carrickfergus, Galway, and Drogheda). In addition, Tipperary was divided into north and south ridings for the assizes, and Cork into east and west ridings for general sessions of the peace. Between 1839 and 1849 numerous minor adjustments of territory between counties were made by government proclamation, generally to assimilate exclaves to the counties surrounding them. Each county had its officials, its jail, and its assizes. Presentments for public works were made before the grand jury, which received plans for building new roads, bridges, and other works, with estimates of their cost. These schemes were scrutinised and, if approved, implemented with assistance from the county cess.[1] Town definition offered many problems to the 1841 census commissioners, and they compromised by using the word 'civic' for places with more than 2,000 inhabitants. They saw that this was an artificial limit, though they noted that

in Ireland, although a town of 2,000 inhabitants seldom possesses any manufacture or trade of sufficient consequence, or any division of occupations sufficiently distinct, to give it the principal characteristic of a town; yet we found that when that number was accumulated the evils of crowded habitations, which constitute another characteristic of a town, began to be felt, especially in a sanatory point of view.[2]

Concern about health measures as a possible, indeed an inevitable, responsibility of town commissioners was characteristic of the time.[3] In scores of towns corporations had ceased to exist, and therefore an act of 1828[4] provided that town commissioners should be elected by all householders occupying property valued at more than £5 per annum; the commissioners themselves were to be holders of houses valued at £20 or more, which meant that the choice was restricted to a few wealthy citizens. Sixty-five towns adopted this scheme. By 1840 only ten towns were boroughs: Dublin, Belfast, Cork, Limerick, Waterford, Derry, Sligo, Kilkenny, Drogheda, and Clonmel. Under the 1828 act it was ruled that any town of 3,000 people could become a borough if a petition, signed by a majority of the people paying poor law rates, was presented, but only Wexford applied. The county towns normally had a jail and a courthouse. At Carrick-on-Shannon, for example, the intimidating courthouse was linked by a dark underground corridor to the jail. Samuel Lewis refers[5] to several of the jails as built 'on the new radiating principle', with separation of male and female prisoners and possessing a treadmill; but all this was the fashion of the

---

[1] Wakefield, *Account of Ire.*, i, 657–62; ii, 348–51.
[2] *Census Ire., 1841*, p. viii [504], H.C. 1843, xxiv, 8.
[3] J. J. Webb, *Municipal government in Ireland* (Dublin, 1918), pp 238, 251; above, pp 209–11, 217; below, pp 552–3, 560.
[4] 9 Geo. IV, c. 82 (25 July 1828).
[5] Lewis, *Topog. dict. Ire.*, i, 276, Carrick; 370, Clonmel; 419–20, Cork; 600, Ennis; 606, Enniskillen; 648, Galway; ii, 260, Lifford; 273, Limerick.

age. The towns were varied in commercial strength and industrial activity, but the weekly markets were universal, and fairs were normally held a few times a year rather than monthly, for in 1841 the rural produce included crops, butter, bacon, eggs, poultry, vegetables, and even homespun textiles as well as cattle, sheep, and pigs. Most of the larger country towns had banks by the 1840s, which were either branches of the Bank of Ireland or of other joint-stock enterprises, of which the first foundations were the Northern Bank and the Hibernian Banking Company, both of which opened for business in 1825.[1] In Ireland, as elsewhere, the administration of justice and the provision of some care, however grimly given, for the sick and destitute, became localised in the towns along with a fluctuating commercial life.

Four provinces cover Ireland, but they have never had any separate government in modern times. The 1841 census commissioners spoke of them as divisions 'so little used in the country, that its chief object in these tables is to afford limits for contrasting one part of the country with another'.[2] To the census commissioners of 1841 these contrasts were clear and dramatic, as this passage shows.

The remarkable difference in the duration of life in favour of Leinster and Ulster over Connacht and Munster is too striking to be overlooked. The latter are the most exclusively agricultural, and from the analogy of Great Britain should . . . present the longest, rather than the shortest, average duration of existence. We fear, however, that the very low state, as to food and accommodation, of the rural population of these provinces, would be found, by a more searching inquiry and comparison, to place them in a sanatory point of view, more nearly equal with the crowded inhabitants of the western parts of England and Scotland, rather than the healthy rustics of the English and Scotch agricultural counties.[3]

Maps 3 and 4 show that the poorer western areas had the highest incidence of illiteracy and the worst housing, and map 5 shows that there was little trade from western ports, except at Limerick and to a minor extent at Galway and Sligo.[4] In short there were two human regions, one of poverty west of a line roughly from Derry to Cork and one in happier, if hardly fortunate, circumstances east of this line.

EVEN now one thinks of Ireland as a rural land of farms, of peat bogs and mountains, of gently flowing rivers and lakes surrounded by luxuriant if at

---

[1] Anthony Marmion, *The ancient and modern history of the maritime ports of Ireland* (London, 1856), pp 104–16 (an interesting contemporary account of banking). See also G. L. Smyth, *Ireland, historical and statistical* (London, 1849), pp 3, 350. Marmion says that the Hibernian Banking Company was the earliest, as it was open for business in June 1825 and the Northern Bank on 1 Aug. 1825; but Smyth gives primacy to the Northern Bank, as its deed of settlement was dated 1 Aug. 1824 compared with 11 Apr. 1825 for the Hibernian. See Smyth for a general review of banking; see also above, pp 150–55.

[2] *Census Ire., 1841*, p. vi [504], H.C. 1843, xxiv, 6. The constabulary system of 1822–36 placed an inspector-general in charge of the police of each province.

[3] Ibid., pp l–li.   [4] Below, pp 265–7.

times over-watered pastures. At intervals of ten to twenty miles there are towns, but most of them are small and only on the coast are there larger towns, associated in the past, and in some cases still, with the country's overseas trade. Some Irish towns have grown considerably since the 1840s, notably in Ulster, but the scene is still predominantly rural as it has been for centuries. In 1841 the census showed that only 20.2 per cent of the population lived in towns, villages or hamlets having twenty houses or more (in Connacht the figure was 10.3). Many of the hamlets and smaller villages were groups of farms though a large proportion of the villages had trading links with the countryside. Just over one-eighth of the people lived in towns of 2,000 or more, to use the figure chosen by the census commissioners as appropriate for a town.

During the seventy years, or possibly the fifty years, before 1841 Ireland's population had doubled, but the increasing labour force found little work in towns, so pressure on the land mounted steadily. Ironically, the poorest parts of the country had the highest density per square mile of 'arable' (or improved) land, with more than 400 to the square mile in Donegal, Kerry, and Mayo, and in the four Ulster counties of Cavan, Down, Monaghan, and Tyrone. In County Armagh, however, the density was 511 to the square mile, but this was due to the widespread combination of farming with domestic spinning and weaving. Hardly less densely peopled than the western and Ulster counties were five others, three of them in Connacht—Leitrim, Roscommon, and Sligo—with two others, Clare and Longford.[1]

Well intentioned people discussed all kinds of methods of alleviating population pressure, such as the intensification of production by improved farming methods, the spread of farming on hillsides and cleared peat bogs, the rearrangement of fields into compact and remunerative holdings, the stimulus to thrift and hard work given by the good example of model farms and agricultural schools. Rural problems must be solved within the rural areas themselves, for permanent migration, either to the towns or overseas, could never be more than a useful contribution to an eventual solution, rather than a solution in itself. The outward movement, year by year, of scores of thousands of harvesters to Britain (57,651 in 1841) and the movements of smallholders to richer farms for seasonal work were accepted features of rural life that gave useful financial returns. With a view to raising revenue, the Griffith valuation covered Ireland from 1830 onwards. It also gave a useful assessment of the actual, and even the potential, resources of the land, on which, it was predicted, between five and six million people must continue to depend for a livelihood.

Like the ordnance survey mapping, the Griffith valuation began in the north, in County Antrim and County Londonderry. It was described[2] as an effort to

[1] Below, p. 268.
[2] *Devon comm. digest*, pp 724–37; for Griffith's instructions to valuators appointed under 7 Geo. IV, c. 62 (26 May 1826), 1 & 2 Will. IV, c. 51 (20 Oct. 1831), and 2 & 3 Will. IV, c. 73 (1 Aug. 1832) see *Report from the select committee appointed to inquire into the duties, salaries and fees of the officers paid by*

assess the natural capabilities and qualities of the soil. The valuator was to act as if he were employed by a liberal landlord to assess the land for letting to a solvent tenant, on a twenty-one year lease. Standards were set for a norm, fixed as land in an ordinary situation, ten to fifteen miles distant from an export market, with due allowance for local climate and soils. There was a thorough study of soils with a sharp appreciation of their physical properties (as clays, loams, sands, and gravels), their depth, water content, and drainage. The permanent pastures were assessed according to the number of cattle and sheep that were normally grazed through all or part of the year, the quality of herbage, and the usual price charged locally for grazing. Water meadows such as the 'callows' beside the Shannon proved difficult to assess, as in dry years they gave bountiful crops of hay but in wet years they were flooded. It was known that the callows were let at very high prices, and it was agreed that the rateable value should be half or five-eighths of the letting value, with an allowance for the average damage from flooding.

Favourable circumstances raised the valuation, including nearness to cities and towns, to good roads to markets and to limestone quarries, seashores with seaweed and sand for manuring, convenient access to peat bogs for fuel, and a locally favourable climate, especially 'moderately elevated situations' with shelter from injurious winds. Conversely, reductions were made for distance from the market, bad roads, difficulties of access, distance from supplies of lime, seaweed, and peat, or unfavourable climatic circumstances. Land near Dublin, Cork, Belfast, or Limerick, the four largest towns, was valued at double similar land in other situations if not more than three-quarters of a mile from the built-up area and at a decreasing amount thereafter up to five miles. In the case of the larger market towns there was an increased valuation for lands within two miles, but for the smaller towns and villages, with populations of 700–1300, only the first three-quarters of a mile had an inflation of value, and even that was slight. Fields immediately beside houses in still smaller places were given a slightly higher rating. Two examples given in the report of the Devon commission are of interest.[1] In both, the land—of medium quality—is valued at 16s. or 15s. 6d. an acre. In the first case, it is ten miles from the nearest town (Derry), and therefore a reduction of 2s. is made, giving 14s.; in the second case, the land is at 600 feet in the upland country of west County Tyrone, and therefore a reduction of 3s. 6d. is made for distance and 2s. 6d. for elevation and climatic difficulties, lowering the amount to 9s. 6d. The survey was thorough: each townland was divided into lots of not more than thirty acres, to coincide with a single farm or a group of farms; soil samples were dug, and their potential fertility was assessed by two valuers working independently; a third valuer adjudicated in cases of disagreement.

counties in Ireland, etc., and into the presentments compulsory on grand juries therein . . . appendix, pp [10]–[33], H.C. 1836 (527), xii, 170–93.

[1] *Devon comm. digest*, p. 728.

Vast disparities of inherent wealth were revealed by the valuation survey, due in part to differences of climate and soil and also to the lack of efficient cultivation. But not everywhere: an account of 1834 for six parishes between Carrick and Clonmel, north of the river Suir, show conditions of some prosperity.[1] The whole district had nearly 8,000 inhabitants in 1841, and over four-fifths of its area, forty square miles, was improved land. This was divided into a number of large farms, and even some of more than 160 acres (100 Irish acres), used mainly for pasture. But in the whole district over half the improved land was tilled, and the proportion given to crops was potatoes 23 per cent, wheat 20 per cent, oats 11 per cent, barley 1 per cent, and fallow 1 per cent. Near the towns the higher valuations of the Griffith survey were apparently justified by the enhanced rents, for it was easy to sell milk, butter, grain crops, and vegetables.

In the 1841 census livestock were counted on all the farms of the country, with subtotals for counties and for farms of various sizes. Farms of 5–15 acres generally had two cattle, and the figure rose to an average of thirteen on those over 30 acres; two sheep were kept generally on the small farms, but many more on larger ones, especially in County Galway, where both the lowland east and the mountainous west had considerable flocks. Pigs were kept on most farms.[2] Contrary to general belief, poultry did not predominate on the small farms. Far more were kept on larger holdings, with an average of six on farms of 1–5 acres, nine on 5–15 acres, fifteen on 15–30 acres, and twenty-three on farms of more than 30 acres. Asses were kept on few farms, and it was thought that the number of horses was needlessly high. Barony figures were also compiled, but these were not published. They were, however, used to make a map[3] showing the relative wealth per 100 acres of total area, not—be it noted—the area of improved land. As improved land covered one-tenth, or even less, of the whole area in many baronies of western Ireland, the map means little there. But it shows the significance of stock farming in some of the richer grazing areas such as the belt of land from County Meath southwards into the counties of Kildare, Dublin, and Wicklow, in County Down, around Wexford and Cork, and also in County Limerick. The statistical basis could be questioned, for obviously there is no such thing as a standard cow. The estimated value of stock was horses and mules £8 each, asses £1, cattle £6. 10s., sheep £1. 2s., pigs £1. 5s., and poultry 6d.

Stock provided only part of farmers' incomes before the famine,[4] and weekly markets were held in all the towns and a number of smaller places that would now be regarded as villages. Many of these are mentioned in Lewis's *Topographical dictionary*, and a thorough investigation made in 1853[5] showed that

[1] R. C. Simington, 'Tithe applotment books of 1834' in *Éire, Department of Agriculture, Journal*, xxxviii, no. 2 (1941), pp 239–42, 246–7.
[2] *Census Ire., 1841*, pp 452–7 [504], H.C. 1843, xxiv, 560–65.
[3] Ibid., plate 1 (MS p. 55).   [4] Above, p. 123.
[5] *Report of the commissioners appointed to inquire into the state of the fairs and markets in Ireland* [1674], H.C. 1852–3, xli, 79.

there were 349 markets. Probably there were at least as many before the famine. There were also 1,297 fairs, held not only in towns and villages but in many rural areas as well. Some patents authorising markets and farms dated from the fourteenth century: in County Louth, for example, both markets and fairs were authorised in Dundalk in 1338, and in Carlingford in 1358. Wexford had a market patent dating from 1317, with several others later. In County Kildare Kilcullen (1403), Athy (1515), and Kildare (1515) had patents for markets, and Maynooth (1340) had a fair. Most of the surviving patents had been granted in the seventeenth and eighteenth centuries, but a number were lost. In 1853 it was noted that no patent could be found for 125 markets and 485 fairs and that 103 markets and 324 fairs were held on different days from those originally set forth. Many were said to have existed from time immemorial.

Both the markets and the fairs were essential to the farming community, but both had acute disadvantages. Some towns had market houses, many of which had been built by landlords, but most were small and of little use. Town commissioners were permitted under the 1828 act to levy tolls, but east of a line from Derry to Youghal they rarely succeeded in doing so. Fair greens were provided in some places, but it proved difficult to persuade people to use them, and consequently 'the high road . . . is injured: the thoroughfare is rendered impassable for the day: life and property are in danger: horses, cattle, sheep, and pigs are mingled together, to the great inconvenience of buyers and sellers, and the annoyance of the inhabitants'.[1]

Markets declined after the famine as grain and other crops became a less significant source of income, but the fairs survived in strength, though their number declined. Some fairs were renowned such as that at Ballinasloe, County Galway, held for five days beginning on the first Tuesday of October. This fair was invariably held on a large open space between the town and the entrance to the demesne of the earl of Clancarty, who was regarded as a good landlord. Records of sales from 1790 onwards[2] show remarkable consistency from year to year. In 1841, for example, 77,189 sheep were offered, of which only 7,061 were unsold, and 14,164 cattle, of which 2,210 were unsold. The fair gathered surplus stock from the west for sale to farmers and dealers from the east; Ballinasloe had four other fairs, at which sales included pigs for the bacon factories in Limerick and Dublin. Some fairs had a special character: for example, at Aughrim, five miles from Ballinasloe, there was an October turkey fair at which 20,000 birds were sold. In 1841, as before and after that date, many towns and villages were galvanised into a brief spell of active life on the market and fair-days.

Farm sizes for 1841 are given in the 1841 census. There were 685,309 holdings, which supported 952,631 families, and a further 135,134 holdings of less

---

[1] *Report of the commissioners appointed to inquire into the state of the fairs and markets in Ireland*, pp 4, 6–7, 38 [1674], H.C. 1852–3, xli, 86, 88–9, 120.

[2] G. L. Smyth, *Ireland, historical and statistical* (London, 1849), pp 3, 52–4.

than one acre. Of the farms of one acre upwards, 45 per cent were of 1–5 acres, 36 per cent of 5–15 acres, 12 per cent of 15–30 acres, and only 7 per cent of more than 30 acres.[1] Whether these figures are for statute acres, or for the larger Irish or Cunningham acres (the latter used in parts of Ulster) has been questioned; it is probable that the 1841 statistics included only the 'improved' areas of arable and pasture. Even if all the returns were given in Irish acres (1.6 statute acres), the majority of the farms would still be very small (only 5 acres and less) especially in Connacht and in County Donegal: for County Mayo the proportion was 73 per cent, Sligo 61 per cent, Leitrim 51 per cent, Roscommon 64 per cent, Galway 62 per cent, and Donegal 46 per cent. Although no county had less than one quarter of its farms under 5 acres, the lowest were Wicklow, 28 per cent, and Wexford, 29 per cent. The more substantial farms (over 30 acres, but if Irish acres were given in whole or in part, nearer 50 statute acres) were most prominent in Kildare (23 per cent), Dublin (22), Waterford (21), Wicklow (21), Meath (19), Westmeath (13), Wexford (13), Cork (12), and Kilkenny (12), but towards the Shannon the proportion fell to 10 per cent in the King's and Queen's Counties, 9 per cent in Tipperary, and only 4 per cent in Longford; in Ulster only 4 per cent, and in Connacht only 3 per cent were over 30 acres.

Housing in the countryside was poor for the greater part of the population. The 1841 census commissioners divided the houses into four classes, of which the lowest generally consisted of mud cabins with only one room, and the third class cottages 'still built of mud but varying from two to four rooms and windows'.[2] These two classes included three-quarters of all the houses in Ireland, with 40 per cent in the fourth class and 37 per cent in the third. The second class consisted of houses having five to nine rooms, and the first class those of a higher standard. Only in and around Dublin was the first class represented by even one-tenth of all the houses, but the second class included 20–40 per cent of all houses in an area bounded by a line from Dublin to Cork and in parts of Ulster, notably the counties of Armagh and Down and in the Bann valley. In general these were good farm houses or houses in town streets. Map 3[3] shows that west of a line from Derry to Cork the proportion of houses in the fourth class was at least 40 per cent almost everywhere (and in some places over 80 per cent) and that over four-fifths of all houses were in the third and fourth classes. The census returns show that the standard of housing was higher in the towns than in rural areas, but in fact many large houses in towns were shared: in Dublin, for example, 10,171 first-class houses were shared by 27,176 families. This may not indicate overcrowding, as in many cases the caretaker or married servants had their own quarters. In the rural areas sharing of

---

[1] *Census Ire., 1841*, pp 454–5 [504], H.C. 1843, xxiv, 562–3; P. M. A. Bourke, 'The extent of the potato crop at the time of the famine' in *Stat. Soc. Ire. Jn.*, xx, pt 3 (1959–60), pp 1–26. A statute acre has 4,840 square yards, an Irish acre 7,840 square yards, and a Cunningham acre 6,250 square yards.

[2] *Census Ire., 1841*, p. xiv [504], H.C. 1843, xxiv, 14.   [3] Below, p. 265.

large houses was not common. The census commissioners assessed the actual quality of accommodation, according to a specified scale of values.

Enormous numbers of houses in the fourth class have disappeared, either without trace (as investigation on the ground with original ordnance survey maps clearly shows) or into a pile of stones with the mud washed away. But of the more substantial houses in the upper classes many survive, associated with the larger farms. In many areas demesnes were prominent. Clearly marked on the six-inch maps of the period, they ranged in size from what would now be regarded as large farms of perhaps 200 acres or less to parklands covering several square miles. In County Tipperary as a whole substantial areas were covered by demesnes, but in Kerry and west Cork the only large demesnes were the famous ones in the vicinity of Killarney and Glengarriff, large areas of which were in woodland. Many areas of scenic attraction had numerous demesnes, for example around Cork harbour, in the Lee valley and the Blackwater valley, or in the valleys of the Wicklow mountains. In many western areas the land within the demesnes available for agricultural settlement, the 'untenanted areas', proved, under legislation some sixty years later, to be far less spacious than was expected.

That a vast number of the farms were too small to provide a living nobody doubted. The Devon commission dealt with the problem by asking what area was needed to support a family having no supplementary income, how many occupiers had less, and how the problem could be solved. Assuming that $10\frac{1}{2}$ acres were needed 'to support a family of five individuals such as the present ignorant occupiers', 8 acres for a 'better instructed' occupier, and $6\frac{1}{4}$ acres if the farm had 'all the requisite permanent improvements' such as good drainage, access, storage space, and barns, there were 326,000 occupiers below this level.[1] The land they occupied could be reallocated in consolidated holdings, but new holdings would be needed for 192,000 families. Griffith's valuation had shown that 6,290,000 acres, approximately one-third of Ireland, were waste land, but of this it was estimated that only 2,535,000 acres were 'unimprovable' and that of the remaining 3,755,000 acres, 1,425,000 acres could be used for tillage and the rest for pasture. It would, therefore, be possible to provide land for the 192,000 families who needed it, giving them 8 acres each if only the first-quality land was used, and as much as 20 acres if second-quality land were also used.[2] The provision of adequate holdings would reduce the number of labourers perhaps by as many as 500,000, for many who had a tiny holding or even no land at all would become farmers with land adequate to support themselves and their families. The hope was that many cleared boglands could be made into remunerative farmland by thorough draining and the use of lime, and that in uplands vast areas would be available: for example, County Donegal had 769,000 acres of unimproved land, but of this 150,000 acres could be used for

[1] *Devon comm. digest*, pp 398–9.   [2] Ibid., pp 563–6.

cultivation and another 250,000 acres for rearing young cattle.[1] The remainder, 369,000 acres, consisted of land over 800 feet in altitude, which could only be profitably used in a few sheltered places, or bogs resting on 'crystalline rock, not decomposed', which is now called blanket bog and when removed leaves only the solid impregnable rock exposed. There were encouraging reports from areas where roads had been constructed: Clifden, County Galway, established in 1815, had grown to a town of 1,509 people with markets twice a week and fairs four times a year, and a strong trade in corn and butter, some of which was sent by boat to Liverpool.[2] Belmullet, County Mayo, founded in 1822 around a new coastguard station, had 637 people with a considerable trade in oats and barley, some of which was collected by steamers, and there was comparable growth at Binghamstown (population 437) on the Mullet peninsula. At its pier corn and potatoes were collected for shipment to Westport.[3] The benefits given by new roads were undoubted and help to explain the optimistic forecasts about possible land reclamation.

Unfortunately the hopes of reclaiming large areas of mountain pasture and cleared peat bog proved vain. Nobody suggested that the thousands of acres used as parklands around the homes of the gentry could be divided among needy farmers, who continued the struggle to obtain possession of enough land to feed their households, to grow some crops for sale, and to feed their stock. Over their lives the uncertainty of tenure remained an abiding worry. For those who had a lease, there might still be the fear of poverty. Tenant right, most frequent in Ulster, might cost as much as forty times the annual rent, so security was bought at a high price, probably paid only by permanent debt to a moneylender. If the tenure was yearly, they had no incentive to make any improvements that would permanently improve the land or the buildings; if they were on a long lease, subdivision might result from the need to provide land for sons or other dependants: if they hired land on conacre, that is, the right to use it for the growing season each year, the price charged in a competitive market could be cripplingly high. The mass of the rural population, therefore, lived in a state of poverty from which only the relatively few holders of the larger farms were exempt. The landlords saw with dismay the continuing subdivision of the land when they gave long leases; some of them tried to encourage emigration, as they saw only too clearly that too many people were living on inadequate holdings. Naturally the landlords were an easy target for political agitators. Some were good and some were bad; some cared and some did not; some knew their people and others did not. At their best, they were frustrated by a human problem for which there was no easy solution.

COMPARED with many countries at the time, Ireland was well provided with roads, as from 1760 many 'presentment' roads had been constructed with funds

---

[1] Ibid., p. 579.   [2] Lewis, *Topog. dict. Ire.*, i, 339–40.
[3] *Devon comm. digest*, p. 153; Lewis, *Topog. dict. Ire.*, i, 202, 208.

provided by the county cess. The main coach roads had a metalling of broken stones, 18–21 feet wide, 8 inches deep in the centre, and 5 inches at the side with gravel borders. The local roads from one market town to another had a metalling of stones or screened gravel 15–18 feet wide, and minor roads of 12–15 feet.[1] The various coach services, with the 'cars' of Charles Bianconi (1786–1875) from 1815, when he ran his first service from Clonmel to Cahir, gave a useful form of public transport. By 1841 only a few areas in the extreme west were more than ten miles from coach, Bianconi cars ('bians'), or canal passenger services.[2]

Of the passenger services on canals and rivers, the best known are those on the Grand Canal from Portobello bridge in Dublin to Shannon Harbour, where connections were available with the steamships on the Shannon to Athlone, Portumna, and Killaloe, where horse-drawn boats conveyed passengers to Limerick.[3] The Grand Canal passenger boats were 52 feet long and nearly 10 feet wide, with accommodation for forty-five first-class and thirty-five second-class travellers. Hotels were built at Dublin, Sallins, Robertstown, Tullamore, and Shannon Harbour. From Dublin it was possible to take the day boat to Tullamore or Shannon Harbour, stay the night at the canal hotel, and proceed to Limerick on the following day. From Limerick there were steamship services to Tarbert and Kilrush, on which nearly 24,000 people travelled in 1836. The canal passenger services began to suffer from the competition of mail and stage coaches by the 1830s but riposted by providing 'fly-boats' drawn by three horses at a speed of ten miles an hour by day and six miles an hour by night. Passenger services were available also on the Royal Canal.[4]

The river navigations and canals were used for goods services: in Ulster, for example, on the Newry canal, opened in 1742, coal from Coalisland was conveyed from quays on Lough Neagh until 1787, when the Tyrone navigation gave a water route from Coalisland. The Lagan navigation was opened in 1794 and gave a continuous inland waterway from Belfast to Newry. Between 1830 and 1850 the Newry canal became a ship canal, but Newry was losing significance as a port by the 1840s, and Belfast was rising to the dominant position it was to enjoy later.[5] Expectations of a large export of coal from Coalisland proved false. The Ulster canal from Lough Neagh to Lough Erne, opened in 1841, was never successful,[6] but the short canal, just over four miles long, from the tidal river Foyle to Strabane, constructed by the marquis of Abercorn in 1791–6, brought considerable prosperity to the town of Strabane, where the

---

[1] These details are given in *Summer assizes, 1840: city and county of Londonderry, a copy of the presentments* (Derry, [1840]), no pagination (R.I.A., Haliday pamphlets, mdccxc).

[2] Below, pp 269–70.

[3] V. T. H. and D. R. Delany, *The canals of the south of Ireland* (Newton Abbot, 1966), pp 58–68, 186–95, 240–41.

[4] Ibid., pp 77–88, 244–5.

[5] W. A. McCutcheon, *The canals of the north of Ireland* (Dawlish and London, 1965), pp 17–35.

[6] Ibid., pp 98–108.

exports included grain, flax, provisions, and beer, and the main imports were timber, iron, groceries, and coal.[1]

Further south the Grand Canal attracted a reasonable volume of goods traffic in the 1840s and for a long time afterwards, but the Royal Canal was far less successful, for it suffered from the competition of the Grand Canal, with its links to the Barrow river navigation and so to Waterford. In 1845 the canal was sold to the newly formed Midland Great Western Railway Company, whose line ran for scores of miles beside the canal.[2] Two canals across the Irish central lowland were not needed; in fact it was difficult to support even one. The Barrow navigation, constructed between 1759 and 1790, was well used, and a number of grain mills were built beside it, some of which were later adapted as malt-houses.[3] The Nore was used by boats to the tidal limit at Inistioge, but the navigation from Kilkenny to Inistioge was never completed.[4] On the Suir boats travelled from Waterford to Carrick, the normal tidal limit, and beyond it to Clonmel, described by Wakefield in 1812 as 'having more internal trade than any other town in Ireland' and by Lewis in 1837 as having 120 lighters engaged in its trade, though navigation was difficult owing to shallow water.[5] The ruins of former mills, factories, and warehouses on Suir Island, and the old quay, now transformed into a riverside promenade, are indicative of the river's significance in the 1840s. On the Blackwater the duke of Devonshire built a canal one mile long to Lismore by 1814,[6] but generally the river is more famed for salmon than for navigation. The Slaney was used for lighters in the 1830s from quays at Enniscorthy, apparently built by local traders who had also financed some river dredging, but when the railway was built this trade diminished sharply.[7] The Boyne was navigable for nineteen miles from Drogheda to Navan, of which the first thirteen miles to Slane were improved between 1759 and 1789 and the remaining six miles by 1800. Very little traffic used the navigation, however, though boats served various mills and carried grain, flour, and meal to Drogheda for local sale and export.[8]

Of all the forms of transport in the 1840s, the system established by Charles Bianconi was the most interesting. There were other services, such as those of the Purcell and Gosson firms in Dublin, but Bianconi perceived the problem of travelling between provincial towns and by 1840 had extended his system over much of Ireland to the south and west of a line from Sligo to Wexford.[9] Together the various firms covered the country so effectively that only a few western areas of County Donegal (with the extreme north of Inishowen), of

[1] Ibid., pp 86–9.   [2] Delany, op. cit., pp 88–9.
[3] Ibid., p. 136. See also above, iv, 258.   [4] Delany, op. cit., pp 142–4.
[5] Ibid., pp 144–6; Lewis, Topog. dict. Ire., i, 369–71; Wakefield, Account of Ire., ii, 22.
[6] Delany, op. cit., pp 153–5.
[7] Ibid., pp 148–9.   [8] Ibid., pp 149–51.
[9] I. J. Herring, 'The bians' in U.J.A., 3rd ser., ii (1939), pp 130–37; iii (1940), pp 115–22; iv (1941), pp 1–11. Lists of the actual services are given in M. A. O'Connell, Charles Bianconi: a biography, 1786–1875 (London, 1878), pp 95–8. See also map 7 below, p. 269.

County Mayo and of County Cork, were more than ten miles from some form of public transport. Bianconi showed great flexibility in organising his business. The true 'bian' was an outside car on which the passengers sat over the wheels and facing the roadsides. Developed from the jaunting car, in time it was enlarged to become the 'long car' with accommodation for twenty passengers. The smallest type, the two-wheeled car, was used on the less frequented routes, but four-wheeled cars were generally used, and there were coaches on a few major routes, such as Clonmel to Waterford, Waterford to Dungarvan, Limerick to Tralee, and Longford to Castlerea. Bianconi's business was centralised at Clonmel, which had car manufacturing workshops with wheelwrights, painters, and smiths, as well as harness rooms, a hospital for sick horses, provision lofts, and quarters for grooms and drivers. Bianconi read a paper at the Cork meeting of the British Association in 1843, in which he commented on the want of a cheap and easy means of locomotion in the countryside, and the hardship inflicted on a farmer 'living twenty or thirty miles from his market town' who 'spent the day in riding to it, a second day doing his business, and a third day returning'.[1]

The task of the Drummond commission of 1836 was to find the most suitable routes for railway lines, and on the evidence available they recommended two main trunk lines: the first from Dublin to Cork and Limerick, and the second from Dublin to Belfast, each with numerous branches. The Dublin–Cork line was to have branch lines to Kilkenny round both sides of the Castlecomer plateau, a branch to Limerick from Thurles, and a connecting line from Waterford to Limerick crossing the main line between Cashel and Cahir. On the basis of inquiries about the use of canal and coach services, and assuming that four times as many people travelled in public as in private conveyances, they estimated that 342 persons and 87 tons of merchandise would traverse every single mile of the railway each day. For the Belfast line, similar calculations gave an average of 456 passengers and 67 tons of merchandise. The commissioners, however, recommended an inland route for the Dublin–Belfast line through Navan and Armagh, with a branch to Enniskillen from Navan. After prolonged argument before parliamentary committees, the coastal route was chosen and the Dublin–Drogheda railway was constructed, and was formally opened on 24 May 1844.[2] Meanwhile the Ulster railway from Belfast had reached Lisburn in 1839, Lurgan in 1841, and Portadown in 1842.[3] The Dublin and Belfast junction railway was opened from Drogheda to Dundalk and Castleblayney in 1849, but it was only in 1855, when the Boyne viaduct at Drogheda was opened, that trains ran uninterruptedly from Belfast to Dublin.[4]

Suburban traffic was restricted to the first seven miles of the Ulster railway

[1] *Report of the thirteenth meeting of the British Association for the Advancement of Science; held at Cork in August 1843* (London, 1844), notices and abstracts, p. 92.

[2] E. M. Paterson, *The Great Northern Railway of Ireland* (Lingfield, 1962), pp 17–19.

[3] Ibid., pp 6–8.

[4] Ibid., pp 25–7; and below, p. 374.

to Lisburn, which had 1,200–1,300 passengers a day, and the line from Dublin to Kingstown, opened in 1834, which had 4,000 passengers a day. Already the villages on the south side of Dublin Bay were becoming suburbs, and the trains were well filled during rush hours and at holiday periods. If Thackeray is to be believed, travelling on this railway was a fashionable pastime, for the Dublin dandies appeared to spend a large part of the day promenading around the stations or travelling from one place to another.[1] The Sunday excursions on the Ulster railway were condemned by preachers of decided views, who said that the company was 'sending souls to the devil at the rate of 6d. apiece' and that 'every sound of the railway whistle is answered by a shout in hell'.[2]

In the 1840s it was thought that railways could only be successful in the more populated and industrialised areas of Ireland, and that for the remaining areas coach and canal services could handle the traffic. Sir Robert Kane suggested that numerous canals could be built,[3] as indeed several were after the 1840s, and there were also proposals that river navigation could be improved. Goods traffic was mainly to and from the ports. The analysis of trade through the ports given to the Drummond commission shows that most of Ireland was an exporter of agricultural produce and an importer of coal and manufactured goods with a limited quantity of raw materials for industry. Only in the northeast was there any real sign of industrial growth, chiefly in the linen trade. Hopes that further investigation might show that Ireland's coal and other minerals were of considerable value were widespread: Kane, for example, said that the Munster coalfield was 'the most extensive in the British empire' and that the coal, though slaty, could be useful in lime-burning.[4] A characteristic port of rural Ireland, Wexford, had exports valued at £312,000 and imports at £627,000. Of the exports the largest item was grain, meal, and flour (£175,000), followed by butter (£54,000), wool (£3,000), cows (£36,000), sheep (£15,000), and pigs (£12,000). Of the imports, woollen manufactures (£120,000) were the largest item, but no other category reached even £30,000, with coal at £26,000, iron £28,000, wines and spirits £22,000, and a wide range of manufactured goods: small imports of oak bark (£2,300), hides (£1,600), and tallow (£1,600) were industrial raw materials. Clearly grain and meal were major exports, with live animals in a secondary but significant position. Some ports had a large sale of provisions, especially the larger ones such as Cork (£2,020,000), Derry (£273,600), Sligo (£181,800), and Waterford (£712,600). The provisions trade included eggs, poultry, salt beef, and bacon. Cork had a well established connection with Newfoundland and the West Indies for the sale of pork, beef, and butter, but Dublin was the main centre for overseas trade, with Belfast rising to a position of rivalry. Other significant ports on the east coast were

[1] M. A. Titmarsh [W. M. Thackeray], *The Irish sketch-book* (2 vols, London, 1843), ii, 128–9.
[2] Paterson, op. cit., p. 7.
[3] Kane, *Industrial resources*, pp 351–63.
[4] Ibid., pp 11–12.

Newry, Dundalk, Drogheda, and Wexford, and there was also an export of copper ore valued at £63,100 from Wicklow, though its other trade was small. On the south coast, Cork and Waterford were dominant, but from all the western ports trade was small, with Limerick as the largest port. Derry's trade was growing at this time, but its main industrial and commercial development came after the famine. Many smaller places had some export and import trade and no doubt received coastal vessels at intervals.

While too much reliance cannot be placed on the figures in detail, the relative trading strength of the various ports was assessed by the Drummond commissioners and illustrated by a map by Lieutenant H. D. Harness (1804–83) of the Royal Engineers with a line shading of fine craftsmanship on which map 5[1] is based. No record was kept of coasting trade, from one port to another in Ireland with periodic journeys to other countries, and the records of imports and exports are in effect estimates. Nevertheless, the main features of the trade were clear and excellently summarised in the report written by Harness. Of Ireland as a whole he says

Her inland traffic is almost exclusively confined to the conveyance of articles to and from the ports. She has no great manufacturing inland towns receiving a variety of materials from different parts, and returning their commodities in complicated streams for exportation, or consumption; with the exception of the trade occasioned by four collieries, as yet of small importance, the linen, and some cotton manufactures in the northern counties, there does not appear to be any transit worthy of notice, of other than agricultural produce. The inland towns are only important in proportion as they offer good markets for such produce; and it is, in almost every case, to the facilities afforded by a navigation, that those of note owe their superiority.[2]

Nothing could be clearer. Underlying this terse summary of the situation there was the hope that the coalfields might develop as industrial areas; but it was not to be. Government servants and independent travellers saw clearly that there was one main problem in Ireland—population pressure.

No exact figures are available for birth and death rates before the famine, though the 1841 census commissioners estimated that the birth rate was 30 per 1,000 and the death rate 21 per 1,000. Only a small proportion of the population remained unmarried, calculated to be 8 per cent for men and 12 per cent for women over fifty-five in rural areas, and 10 per cent for men and 15 per cent for women over fifty-five in the towns. But the census commissioners noticed, and cautiously mentioned, a tendency to delay marriage.[3] Then as now, women lived longer than men, though the higher proportion of women in the senior age groups could be due partly to the greater emigration of men. Efforts were

[1] Below, p. 267.
[2] *Second report of the commissioners appointed to recommend on general system of railways for Ireland . . . appendix*, p. 42 [145], H.C. 1837–8, xxxv, 640.
[3] *Census Ire., 1841*, p. xlii [504], H.C. 1843, xxiv, 42.

made to calculate the overseas migration in the ten years preceding the census. Between 1831 and 1841, of 214,000 people who went from Irish ports, 121,000 were men. Another 153,000 Irish-born people went from Liverpool, and allowing 10 per cent for imperfect returns the total movement overseas was 403,463. This did not include emigration to Britain, where the 1841 census showed that 419,256 people were of Irish birth, of whom perhaps one-quarter had come since 1831, nor did it include the seasonal harvesters, who were counted as 57,651 between 13 May and 31 August 1841, almost certainly an underestimate as some travelled on cargo boats not included in the returns.[1] How many of these settled down eventually as permanent residents in Britain nobody can say, but it is a reasonable assumption that many did so, especially if navvying jobs or industrial employment was available. Long before the 1840s emigration had entered deeply into the fabric of Irish life. Within the country there was seasonal movement to the richer areas for the harvest, and on a lesser scale for the spring ploughing and sowing of crops. In 1835 it was noted at Naul, County Dublin, that 'the harvest of this parish and of the surrounding country could not be made up without the assistance of the spalpeens or Connacht men'. At Ratoath, County Meath, it was stated that 'in harvest and seed time we have an overflow of Connacht men to get on the work, the population being very thin'.[2] There were similar reports from the richer parts of Counties Dublin, Kildare, Meath, and Wicklow, and also from areas of tillage in Counties Kilkenny (notably around Fiddown and Thomastown) and Tipperary. Some of the harvest labourers were recruited from poorer areas in the vicinity, but many came from the west, including Connacht, Kerry, and west Cork. In County Donegal there was a well established movement from west to east; in the barony of Raphoe North one witness in 1835 noted that

labour is so much in request here, that during the harvest we have numbers of strangers, who come from a distance of about forty miles to cut down our crops. The labouring population, though quite enough for usual purposes, are not so for that particular season.[3]

It would be easy to exaggerate such resources as the employment lasted only for a short time and labourers abounded. Nor was there much hope for the needy in the towns, even in the richer parts of the country. County Meath was in part covered with lush pastures, in part with cropped land, and presented an impression of wealth that, the Halls noted, was 'so refreshing to the eye, and so cheering to the mind when associated with ideas of comfort and prosperity'.[4] Yet in the towns there was obvious squalor, even in County Meath. To quote the Halls,

The towns ... into which the poor have been driven, are thronged with squalid countenances; starvation stalks at noonday through the streets; and perhaps in no part

[1] Below, pp 565–6, 567–71. [2] *Poor inquiry, app. A, supp.*, pp 56, 169.
[3] Ibid., p. 327. [4] Hall, *Ire.*, ii, 373.

of the world could be found so much wretchedness 'huddled' together in an equal space as in the town of Navan. All around the suburbs, the cabins are filthy to the last degree; a very large proportion of them have no other outlets for smoke but the broken windows; the roofs of many have fallen in. . . .¹

Similar accounts of Irish towns are numerous, and the 'cabin suburbs' were notorious. This was notably so in Drogheda, yet the Halls found the centre of the town (population 17,300) alive with trade, with shipping in the river, and a linen market that gave 'token of an approach towards the manufacturing north'.² Dundalk, though smaller (population 10,782), was a port, market, and industrial centure. Newry (population 11,972) was the chief market centre for the area south of Lough Neagh, with a considerable goods trade on its canal, and with iron foundries, distilleries, and several flour mills, many of its inhabitants going to work at the linen mill in Bessbrook, two miles away. Nevertheless, even in Newry there was poverty: '. . . hundreds in this town have no beds but the cold damp earthen floor, without even straw in some cases . . . and frequently cannot procure as much potatoes as would support nature'.³ Although Drogheda and Dundalk, with smaller places such as Collon (population 936), County Louth, with its flax mill and bleach green, heralded the textile-dominated area of 'the north', it began effectively in the south of County Armagh. Here the domestic industry survived, for the Halls found 'the cheerful hum of the loom in the home' with 'almost every dwelling . . . a linen factory . . . the whole of the inmates, from the very aged to the very young . . . made in some degree, useful'.⁴ This was the true north, an area of dense rural population, of flax retting in the rivers, of flax scutching in small mills beside them, of spinning and weaving culminating in sales in the markets and linen halls of the towns. But the return for home labour was pitifully small, for some spinners earned only 2*d.* or even 1*d.* a day. A high proportion of the total population in 'the north' depended on home industry.

Belfast aroused enthusiasm among travellers. H. D. Inglis found it comparable to 'the most flourishing among the manufacturing and commercial cities of the empire' and—a Scotsman himself—ascribed it to the sterling qualities of the Scottish element in the population. 'It is impossible', he comments, 'that Cork, Limerick, or Waterford, should ever become altogether like Belfast; because the character of the Scotch and the Irish is essentially different.'⁵ The Halls were equally enthusiastic, for Belfast, 'is a new town, and has a new look. It is the healthiest manufacturing town in the kingdom', densely populated but having 'far less wretchedness in its lanes and alleys, and around its suburbs than elsewhere in Ireland'. Societies of an improving character abounded, and

¹ Hall, *Ire.*, ii, 373.
² Ibid., p. 424.   ³ *Poor inquiry, app. A, supp.*, p. 363.
⁴ Hall, *Ire.*, ii, 453.
⁵ Henry D. Inglis, *Ireland in 1834: a jouurney throughout Ireland, in the spring, summer and autumn of 1834* (2 vols, London, 1834), ii, 251.

included one founded in 1836 for the 'encouragement and reward of good conduct in female servants'.[1] Bleach greens lined the valleys, cotton had been almost supplanted by linen, and a variety of industries had been attracted to the town, which in 1841 had 75,308 inhabitants. The Lagan was canalised, though far more trade came to the town by road and the building of the railway had begun. The outlook was bright, and the travellers were right in sensing that economic progress was certain, with Belfast as Ulster's major city and regional capital.

HAD one lived in Ireland in 1841, it is unlikely that one would have foreseen the disaster that was to come in a very few years.[2] True, one might have heard of the near-famines that had struck certain areas at intervals, but that famine would come to the whole countryside (with the only possible exceptions being some northern districts where oatmeal was the basic diet) would have seemed improbable. The big question is 'was Ireland overpopulated?', and the answer is an emphatic 'yes', given that overpopulation is assessed in relation to the development of resources at one chosen time, say 6 June 1841 when the census was taken. By this time the problems were known. Commission after commission had collected evidence on poverty, on rural life, on the possible use of peat bogs, on railway and other transport, on ports and harbours, and on much else besides. The census added more, including medical information. The country was effectively mapped and its administrative divisions exactly defined. Travellers, writers, and politicians all had their say at considerable length, and voluntary bodies such as the Royal Dublin Society had conducted county surveys. Information about Ireland's problems abounded, but the means of solving them was hard to find.

Administratively the county was a recognised unit, provided with an income from local taxes by which roads could be built under the presentment system. Central government money had financed canals and river navigations, and a beginning had been made with railway-building using private capital. Communications were relatively good, and by various means ports had been developed for the overseas trade. Unhappily this consisted mainly of the export of agricultural produce and the import of manufactured goods. Except in the north-east, travellers from town to town spoke of empty woollen mills, of abandoned factories, of widespread unemployment, of desperate people settled in one-roomed cottages in squalid suburbs or yards behind main streets. In many of these towns the poor law commission built workhouses that, however maligned, gave shelter to famine victims later.

Having little if any hope of employment in towns, the rural population depended on their land almost exclusively, with occasional labouring, public works, or seasonal emigration as possible additional resources. There were four or five times as many people on the land then as now. Marriage was almost

[1] Hall, *Ire.*, iii, 53.   [2] Above, p. 108.

universal, and there was a high natural increase of population, not exactly known but perhaps as much as 9 per cent in each decade.[1] Emigration provided a way out, but all friends of Ireland regretted its necessity and even tried to find ways of removing its compulsive power. Projects for reclaiming vast areas for new farms were seriously studied, but the country's area of improved land, at 65 per cent, was much the same as now. Scientists such as Sir Robert Kane wished to see an industrialisation similar to that of Britain, with work for the surplus rural population in towns and villages, new mines opened, and industrial wealth growing apace. The evils of excessive rents and insecurity of tenure on the land were well known. It was all too easy to blame the people for intemperance—in fact Fr Mathew's great total abstinence campaign was in progress—or for a feckless attitude to life. Most of the land had to be used for growing food for the family and fodder for the stock, but grain was normally too valuable to consume at home, and so too was the butter, bacon, poultry, and eggs that could have given a varied diet. Some of the lassitude came from ill-health, and some of the resultant poverty and squalor was due to illiteracy, bad housing, fear of the future, sorrows of the past.

Most of all, the differences between the west and the east were marked. In this chapter attention has been drawn to the line from Derry to Cork as a divide. It is a useful generalisation, but it is nothing more. For example, to the west of Derry one enters the Laggan, a fertile area, but one is soon in the more typical Donegal of small farms, extensive bogs, and rough pastures and mountains. West of the Shannon in the central lowland there is a difference of standard, with farmland no longer continuous as to the east, but interspersed with heaths and peat bogs. Farther south the Limerick lowland is, and was in the 1840s, a countryside of some prosperity, already beginning to show some of the specialisation in grazing dairy cattle that was to become so marked later, but here, as further south, there was a clear decline in farming resources as one moved westward. The conclusion is inescapable and simple: there were too many people on the land, and the problems of Ireland in the early 1840s were much like those of India and Pakistan today. And even in the north, domestic industry was giving pitiably small returns when faced by factory competition. Ireland of the 1840s was a vastly different land from that of today, for in areas now having perhaps a dozen farms and fifty or sixty people to the square mile there might be sixty or more farms and 300 (or even more) to the square mile. The changes have been greater than anyone living in the 1840s could possibly have foreseen.

[1] Cf. above, p. 118.

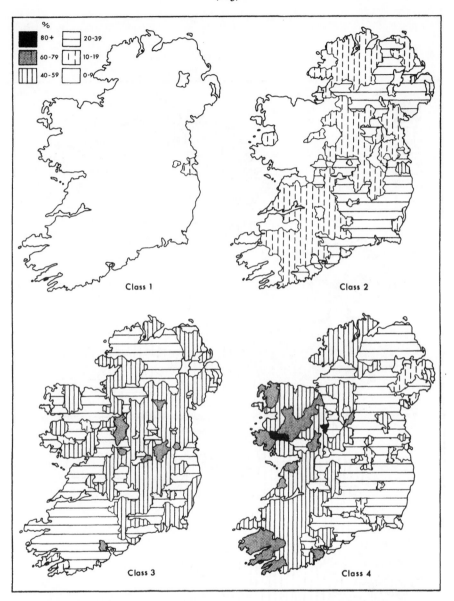

Map 3 HOUSE TYPES, 1841, BY BARONIES, by T. W. Freeman

Redrawn from T. W. Freeman, *Pre-Famine Ireland* (Manchester, 1957), p. 150. The fourth class included 'all mud cabins having only one room'; the third, 'a better description of cottage, still built of mud, but varying from two to four rooms and windows'; the second, 'a good farm house, or in towns, a house in a small street, having from five to nine rooms and windows'; and the first, 'all houses of a better description than the preceding classes' (*Census Ire., 1841*, p. xiv [459], H.C. 1843, xxiv, 14).

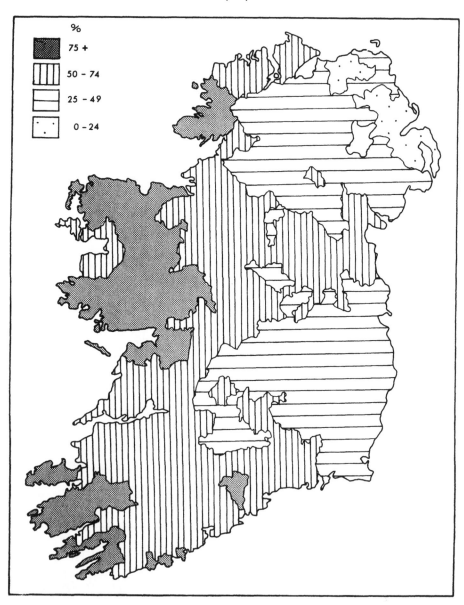

Map 4 ILLITERACY, 1841, BY BARONIES, by T. W. Freeman
Redrawn from T. W. Freeman, *Pre-famine Ireland* (Manchester, 1957), p. 134.

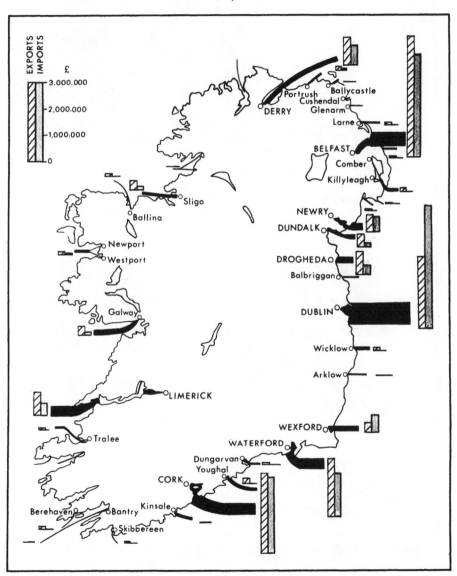

Map 5 OVERSEAS TRADE, 1836, by T. W. Freeman

Redrawn from T. W. Freeman, *Pre-famine Ireland* (Manchester, 1957), p. 80.

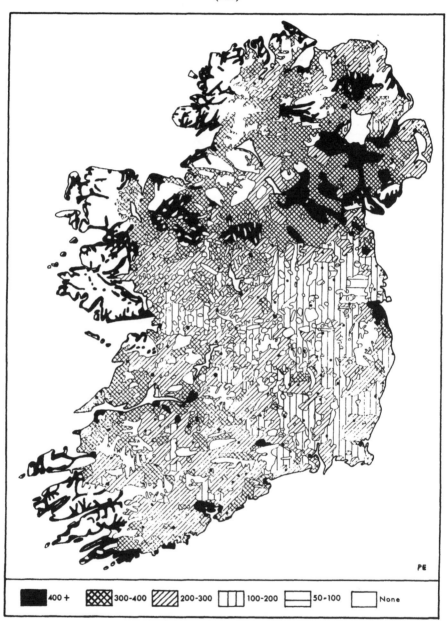

PE

| 400 + | 300-400 | 200-300 | 100-200 | 50-100 | None |

Map 6 POPULATION DENSITY, 1841, by T. W. Freeman
Reproduced, with key added, from T. W. Freeman, *Pre-famine Ireland* (Manchester, 1957), p. 18.

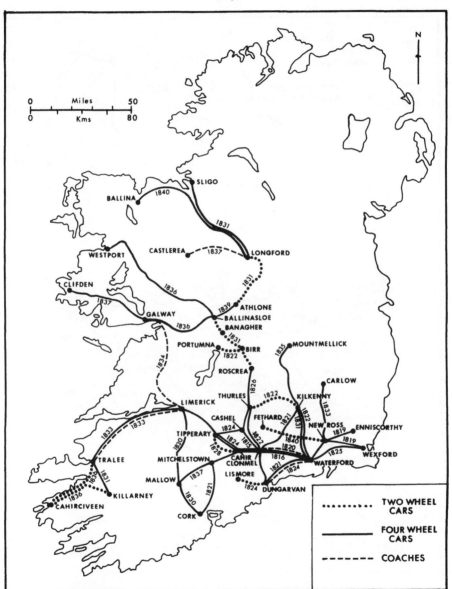

Map 7 BIANCONI SERVICES, 1815–40, by T. W. Freeman
Redrawn from T. W. Freeman, *Pre-famine Ireland* (Manchester, 1957), p. 115.

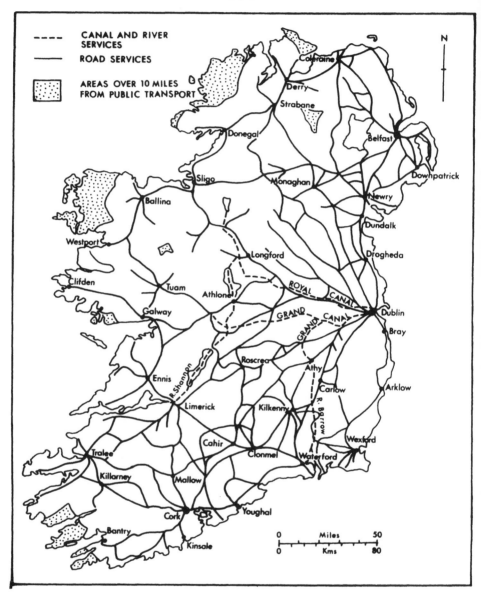

Map 8 CANAL AND ROAD SERVICES, *c.* 1841, by T. W. Freeman

Redrawn from T. W. Freeman, *Pre-famine Ireland* (Manchester, 1957), p. 112.

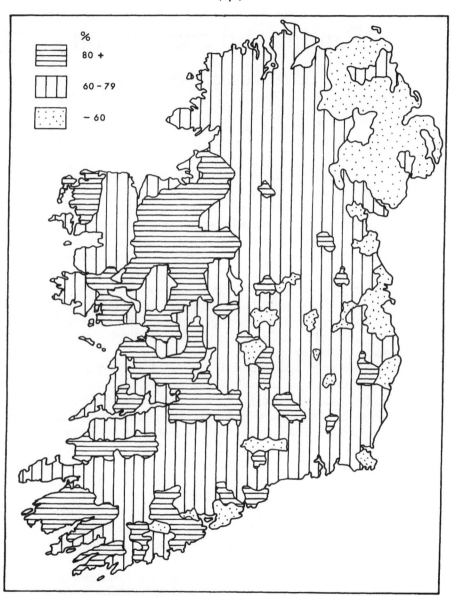

Map 9 PERCENTAGE OF FAMILIES OCCUPIED IN
AGRICULTURE, 1841, BY BARONIES, by T. W. Freeman
Redrawn from T. W. Freeman, *Pre-famine Ireland* (Manchester, 1957), p. 57.

CHAPTER XII

Famine and government response, 1845–6

JAMES S. DONNELLY, JR

THE great accident of nature that struck Ireland beginning in 1845 was a raging epidemic of the fungal disease *phytophthora infestans*, commonly known as potato blight or potato murrain. Before the sudden advent of blight early in September of that year, there had of course been potato shortages, some of which were serious enough to be classed by contemporaries as failures. These shortages or failures were attributable either to bad weather or to plant diseases much less destructive than *phytophthora infestans*. In exceptionally wet years potatoes became waterlogged and rotted in the ground; in seasons of drought the lack of moisture stunted their growth. Before blight appeared in Ireland or elsewhere in Europe, there were only two major plant diseases that attacked the potato periodically: one was a virus popularly known as 'curl', while the other was a fungus that non-scientists called 'dry rot' or 'taint'.

Exactly when and how the new disease—a minute fungus of the genus *Botrytis*—entered Europe are matters not surprisingly shrouded in some obscurity. Into these dark corners P. M. A. Bourke has shed some valuable light.[1] Almost certainly, potato blight was not present anywhere in Europe before 1842, and it probably did not gain entry until 1844. The source (or at least one source) of the infection may have been the northern Andes region of South America, particularly Peru, from which potatoes were carried to Europe on ships laden with guano, the seafowl excrement so much in demand as a fertiliser on British and continental European farms during the 1840s. An even likelier source of the deadly infection was the eastern United States, where blight largely destroyed the potato crops of 1843 and 1844. Vessels from Baltimore, Philadelphia, or New York could easily have brought diseased potatoes to European ports.

Once blight had been introduced from the new world into the old, its diffusion among the potatoes was extremely rapid, indeed even faster than the spread of the dreaded cholera among humans. This was essentially a function

[1] P. M. A. Bourke, 'Emergence of potato blight, 1843–46' in *Nature*, cciii (1964), pp 805–8; see also his 'The potato, blight, weather, and the Irish famine' (Ph.D. thesis, N.U.I. (U.C.C.), 1965).

of the nature of the disease. The mould fungus that grew on the undersurface of blighted potato leaves consisted of multitudes of extremely fine, branching filaments, at the tips of which were spores. When mature, these spores broke away and, wafted by the wind, settled on other plants, restarting the process of destruction. Rain was, like the wind, a vector of the disease, since water-borne spores from the leaves and haulms penetrated to the tubers below ground. The blight's conquest of European potato fields was apparently the work of a single season or perhaps a little more. By the late summer and early autumn of 1845 it had spread throughout the greater part of northern and central Europe. The area of infection stretched from Switzerland to Scandinavia and southern Scotland, and from Poland to the west coast of Ireland. The ravages of the disease, however, were not the same everywhere. In regions stricken by blight early in the summer of 1845, crop losses were severe, whereas in areas not affected before mid-September, the damage was generally much less extensive, unless the harvest season was unusually wet. Thus Belgium, Holland, northern France, and southern England, all stricken by mid-August, were heavy sufferers, while Bavaria and Prussia among the German states, touched later and enjoying a dry harvest, escaped with only slight damage. Ireland occupied an intermediate position in this spectrum of loss. On the one hand, blight did not make its first reported appearance until early in September, more than two months after the disease had originally been spotted near Courtrai in Belgium. On the other hand, much of the harvest season in Ireland was exceptionally wet, and the rains materially aided the progress of the disease.

F o r several reasons the early public reaction in Ireland to reports of blight was restrained. Everyone agreed that the oat crop had been unusually abundant—'the best crop, in quality and quantity, we have had for ten years past', declared one northern observer at the end of September.[1] It was also apparent that a larger acreage had been sown with potatoes in 1845 than in the previous year, and this increase was initially rated as considerable. Lastly, no reliable calculations of the deficiency could even begin to be made until after general digging of the 'late' crop began in the second and third weeks of October.

But the absence of alarm at the outset rapidly gave way to deepening gloom and even panic in the last ten weeks of the year. Day after day, letters testifying to the ravages of the blight poured in from anxious, frightened gentlemen and clergymen, and general estimates of the destruction naturally swelled. The Mansion House committee in Dublin (established on 31 October 1845), to which hundreds of such letters were directed from all over Ireland, claimed on 19 November to 'have ascertained beyond the shadow of doubt that considerably more than one-third of the entire of the potato crop . . . has been already destroyed'.[2] At the beginning of December the *Freeman's Journal* asserted in an editorial that as much as 'one-half of the potato crop has been already lost as

[1] *F.J.*, 1 Oct. 1845 (quoting *Northern Whig*).   [2] Ibid., 20 Nov. 1845.

human food'.[1] What was so discouraging, and what lent credibility to even the most despondent reports, was that potatoes that appeared sound and free of disease when dug became blighted soon after they had been pitted or housed. To many, it seemed that there was no stopping the rot. Typical of this despair was a Dublin market report at the end of October: 'the general impression now is that with the greatest care the crop will be all out by the end of January, be prices what they may, as the tendency to decay, even in the best, is evident'.[2]

There was no shortage of putative remedies for staying the progress of the disease. As E. C. Large has remarked sardonically, 'the potatoes were to be dried in lime, or spread with salt; they were to be cut up in slices and dessicated in ovens; and cottagers were even to provide themselves with oil of vitriol, manganese oxide, and salt, and treat their potatoes with chlorine gas, which could be obtained by mixing these materials together'.[3] The most prominent and widely publicised remedies were those offered by a scientific commission that Peel's government appointed in October.[4] Two of its three members were Dr Lyon Playfair, an undistinguished Scots chemist with good political connections, and Dr John Lindley, an accomplished English botanist with both commercial experience and high academic standing (as professor of botany in University College, London), who was also the editor of the *Gardener's Chronicle and Agricultural Gazette*. To these two was added Professor Robert Kane of Queen's College, Cork, whose recent book on Irish industrial resources had attracted wide attention, and who already headed a subcommittee of the Royal Agricultural Improvement Society of Ireland that was investigating the blight.

The commissioners had the triple task of recommending what should be done to preserve seemingly healthy potatoes from infection, to convert diseased potatoes to at least some useful purposes, and to procure seed for the 1846 crop. In addressing the seed question, the commissioners could not ignore the fundamental issue of what had caused the blight in the first place. Here they went badly astray. Without pretending to certainty in the matter, they strongly inclined to the view that since the minute *Botrytis* fungus must have existed as long as the potato itself, the fundamental cause of the *epidemic* of blight was not the fungus but rather the cold, cloudy, and above all, wet weather that had so visibly accompanied its progress. Without endorsing it, the commissioners did acknowledge the conflicting opinion of Rev. M. J. Berkeley, 'a gentleman eminent above all other naturalists of the United Kingdom in his knowledge of the habits of fungi', who believed that this particular fungus was itself the basic cause of the epidemic.[5] Berkeley's 'fungal hypothesis', though generally rejected when he elaborated it in 1846, was eventually proved correct.

[1] *F.J.*, 1 Dec. 1845.	[2] Ibid., 29 Oct. 1845.
[3] E. C. Large, *The advance of the fungi* (London, 1940), p. 27.
[4] T. P. O'Neill, 'The scientific investigation of the failure of the potato crop in Ireland, 1845–6' in *I.H.S.*, v, no. 18 (Sept. 1946), pp 123–38.
[5] *F.J.*, 10 Nov. 1845.

Yet even Berkeley admitted that wet weather greatly promoted the growth of fungi.

The commissioners therefore felt it safe to recommend that healthy potatoes from the blight-affected 1845 crop could be used for seed, since even if the germs of the disease were still present, they would be activated and spread only if the country had the great misfortune to be visited in 1846 by the same combination of bad weather that had prevailed in the current year. Any deficiency in home-grown sets of sound potato seed could be met, said the commissioners, by importing supplies from southern Europe (generally disease-free) on private commercial account. No active role as a direct purchaser was contemplated for the government. In this aspect of their work the commissioners greatly underestimated both the shortage of seed that would exist in 1846 and the difficulty of ensuring that no slightly diseased potatoes from the 1845 crop would be planted through accident or ignorance in the following year.

In an earlier report the commissioners had grappled with the other two main parts of their charge. What could usefully be done with blighted potatoes depended on the extent of the decay. Potatoes only slightly diseased—with up to a quarter-inch of discoloration—could be eaten by humans without risk, said the commissioners, provided that the diseased parts were cut away before the potatoes were boiled. No time should be lost in consuming such potatoes, they urged, because the advance of the rot would soon render them useless as food. But if the discoloration went deeper and the potatoes gave off a tell-tale stench, there was nothing to be done but to break them up into starch. Though not food by itself, the starch could be used to make a wholesome bread after being mixed with meal or flour.[1] (Since the commissioners were concerned to maximise the amount of food that would be available for humans, they abstained from pointing out that diseased potatoes could also be fed to livestock, and farmers did this on a considerable scale.[2])

What everyone wanted to know, however, was not so much what to do with rotting potatoes, but how to keep good potatoes sound. Besides insisting that the bad potatoes should be segregated from the good, the commissioners' basic message was that the crop must above all be kept dry. In place of the traditional method of pitting the potatoes, which would bring 'certain destruction to them', the commissioners strongly advocated the adoption of a system of ventilation. Their plan called for shallow trenches in which the potatoes were to be placed in layered rows; the potatoes were to be separated from each other by a mixture of lime and dry clay, or of earth and the ashes of turf or sawdust; the rows were to be divided by sods of turf, which would provide the ventilation. The heap was to be crowned with a little roof of thatch.[3] These recommendations, which were actually based on a plethora of pit ventilation schemes already being discussed, were given extremely wide publicity. Of the 70,000 copies of the instructions printed by the government, each parish priest in the

---

[1] Ibid., 5 Nov. 1845.   [2] Ibid., 19 Dec. 1845.   [3] Ibid., 5 Nov. 1845.

country received thirty, and the Royal Agricultural Improvement Society distributed 10,000 copies to local agricultural societies.[1]

Little attention was paid to this avalanche of paper, and rightly so. The rot advanced in spite of ventilation, where that was tried. The commissioners further undermined their already shaken credibility when they publicly suggested that the steeping of diseased potatoes in bogwater might arrest the progress of decay—this less than a week after a report in which they insisted that the greatest desideratum was to keep the tubers absolutely dry! Understandably, the *Freeman's Journal* dismissed the whole exercise: 'the present commissioners have satisfactorily proved that they know nothing whatever about the causes of or remedies for the disease'.[2]

Privately, the commissioners seemed to have as gloomy a view of the impending food crisis as their worst Irish critics. In their report of 15 November to Sir James Graham, the home secretary, Lindley and Playfair concluded that 'one-half of the actual potato crop of Ireland is either destroyed or remains in a state unfit for the food of man'. As if this assessment were not sombre enough, they also remarked that theirs was 'a low estimate', that the most recent rains had 'in all probability' extended the destruction, and that not all of what now remained sound could be accounted safe because Irish circumstances would prevent their proposals for preservation from being fully implemented. Lastly, they pointed out that since at least one-eighth of the 1845 crop would be required in 1846 for seed (on the assumption of a constant acreage), only three-eighths of the 1845 crop could 'at this moment' be considered available as food.[3] Whatever else might be said about the commissioners and their work, they certainly did not underestimate the extent of the potato deficiency in 1845; indeed, unknowingly, they exaggerated it. This readiness to paint a pessimistic scenario, P. M. A. Bourke has argued, helped to elicit government relief on a larger scale than if greater optimism had prevailed.[4]

Historians have generally credited Peel's government with reacting promptly to the partial potato failure of 1845.[5] A strong case can be marshalled in favour of this view. Most of the important policy decisions were taken in London before 1845 was over, but these did not pay dividends immediately. In the closing months of the year it seemed to many people in Ireland, and not to nationalists alone, that Dublin Castle, headed by Lord Heytesbury, the lord lieutenant, was so dilatory as to be guilty of criminal neglect.[6] Castle officials

---

[1] T. P. O'Neill, 'The scientific investigation of the failure of the potato crop in Ireland, 1845–6' in *I.H.S.*, v, no. 18 (Sept. 1946), p. 128.

[2] *F.J.*, 10 Nov. 1845.

[3] *Copy of report of Dr Playfair and Mr Lindley on the present state of the Irish potato crop and on the prospect of approaching scarcity (dated 15th November 1845)*, p. 1, H.C. 1846 (28), xxxvii, 33.

[4] P. M. A. Bourke, 'Emergence of potato blight, 1843–46' in *Nature*, cciii (1964), p. 807.

[5] Cf. above, pp 61–2, for government action in 1816–17.

[6] *F.J.*, 14, 17 Nov. 1845.

appeared to believe that alarmists were exaggerating the ravages of the blight, and that even if the shortage of potatoes turned out to be serious, the food gap would be at least partly filled by the abundant harvest of oats. The Irish constabulary had been instructed to estimate the extent of the loss in every county, and its returns for December were somewhat reassuring: they showed that the damage was less extensive than many had claimed, for the proportion of the 1845 crop deemed 'lost' in the country as a whole was somewhere between one-quarter and one-third. Deficiencies of more than one-third of the crop were reported in only six counties: Kilkenny, Limerick, Louth, Queen's, Roscommon, and Wexford. The counties along the west coast from Kerry to Donegal generally suffered less than the national average, and the lowest proportional losses occurred in Ulster, especially in Fermanagh, Londonderry, and Tyrone, where less than one-seventh of the crop had been destroyed. Furthermore, the constabulary returns indicated that the total potato acreage was about 6 per cent greater in 1845 than in 1844.[1]

If Dublin Castle was inclined to cautious optimism, deep pessimism was characteristic of a broad spectrum of Irish public opinion. It struck many as scandalous that while the potato crop was melting away, the abundant oat crop, widely touted as a partial substitute, was rapidly being depleted through export, which the government refused to stop. For those with no choice but to buy their food, prices had risen steeply. By early December retail potato prices had more than doubled, and grain prices had reached a level at least a third higher than the averages for 1843 and 1844.[2] Within just a few more months at most, there would be, if not actual famine, then acute and widespread distress. Action now to meet the developing crisis was insistently demanded of the government. At public meetings held in Dublin at the end of October, Peel's ministry was urged to allow the duty-free importation of foreign grain (i.e., to repeal or suspend the corn laws); to forbid the export of oats from Ireland; to raise a loan of £1 million for the relief of distress; to establish public granaries; and to provide employment for the destitute.[3] This was a great deal to ask of Peel's ministry, though many of those doing the asking professed not to think so. With some elaboration and addition, these proposals were forcefully recommended to Peel on 7 November by Lord Cloncurry as chairman of the Dublin Mansion House committee. Cloncurry urged that the loan (at least £1.5 million was now specified) be applied 'in the first instance' to raising the quantity and lowering the price of food in Ireland. It was also essential to set 'the people to work without any delay', and Cloncurry suggested that to accomplish this, the government should promote and assist railway construction, drainage schemes, and 'other works of general or local utility'.[4]

The final Irish verdict on Peel's relief programme was to be highly positive,

---

[1] *Correspondence explanatory of the measures adopted by her majesty's government for the relief of distress arising from the failure of the potato crop in Ireland*, p. 5 [735], H.C. 1846, xxxvii, 57.
[2] *F.J.*, 3 Dec. 1845. [3] Ibid., 3 Nov. 1845. [4] Ibid., 13 Nov. 1845.

but since the government's approach to the crisis involved large elements of secrecy and delay, applause remained a scarce commodity for quite some time. Among the earliest measures was the secret purchase of £100,000 worth of Indian corn and meal in the United States through the agency of Baring Bros & Co., one of the great London trading houses. This clandestine purchase Peel himself initiated early in November 1845, and the public remained perfectly ignorant of the transaction for about three months. The arrival of these supplies from America was a protracted affair, extending from February to June 1846. Additional quantities of Indian corn (maize) and some oatmeal were bought in Britain at a cost of £46,000 and also shipped to Ireland. Altogether, the treasury calculated that it had spent £185,000 by August 1846 on the purchase of Indian corn, a sum that covered not only the food itself, but also the costs of water freight, kiln-drying, and grinding. (The full outlay must have been considerably higher because this account excluded the expense of conveyance within Ireland and the wages of officials involved in the enterprise.) This expenditure made possible the official importation of an estimated 44 million lb (almost 20,000 tons) of Indian corn and oatmeal, a quantity said to be sufficient, at a rate of 1 lb a day per head, to feed 490,000 persons for three months.[1]

The efficient distribution of this food was the joint responsibility of a central relief commission (set up by Peel's government in November 1845) and of the hundreds of local relief committees that came into existence during the spring and summer of 1846. (Almost 650 local committees were at work by 10 August 1846.) The most important member of the central commission was undoubtedly Sir Randolph Routh, the head of the commissariat branch of the army in Ireland. Beginning in February 1846, the commissariat established a network of food depots. The west was to be served by depots at Galway, Kilrush, Limerick, Sligo, and Westport; the south and east, by depots at Clonmel, Cork, Dublin, Dundalk, and Waterford; and the midlands, by depots at Athy, Banagher, Longford, and Tullamore.[2]

It was not the government's intention, except under extraordinary circumstances, to become engaged in the distribution of free food from its depots or to sell food directly to those in want. Rather, the main burden of providing for the destitute was to be borne by the local committees, with the government selling food to them at cost price. The committees were to secure the means to purchase by raising subscriptions, chiefly among local landowners, and were in turn to sell at cost to the poor. Provision was made, however, for the lord lieutenant to supplement monies raised locally if, despite vigorous efforts, these proved inadequate. Eventually, government donations totalling nearly £68,000 (up to 7 August 1846) were made to local committees in aid of

---

[1] *A statement 'of the total expenditure for purposes of relief in Ireland since November 1845 . . .'*, p. 1, H.C. 1846 (615), xxxvii, 477.
[2] T. P. O'Neill, 'The organisation and administration of relief, 1845–52' in Edwards & Williams, *Great famine*, pp 215–16.

subscriptions collected for the purchase of food.¹ It was also recognised that there would be districts where local relief committees could not be established or where their resources would be woefully inadequate, and in such areas the central relief commission promised to set up depots for the sale of food at cost price. (Gratuitous distribution was contemplated only when the ability to pay was 'absolutely wanting'.) In the event, the need for such stores—designated subdepots—was much greater than officials had anticipated: the coastguard opened as many as seventy-six subdepots along the south and west coasts, and the constabulary operated twenty-nine more, mostly in the interior parts of Connacht and Munster.²

Relief officials engaged in a concerted effort to delay the opening of the depots as long as possible while at the same time meeting truly urgent cases of extreme distress. By exercising this policy of severe restraint, they sought to conserve their own limited supplies for the three-month period of greatest pressure between mid-May, when spring planting operations ceased, and mid-August, when the 'early' potatoes normally became available. By the same strategy they hoped to force Irish landlords, regarded in official circles as a slothful, negligent crowd, to be more zealous in furnishing relief; lastly, they wanted to check 'over-speculation', that is, the withholding of food supplies from the springtime market by private dealers greedily waiting for prices to rise still further in the summer. Routh told Charles Trevelyan, the assistant secretary of the treasury, on 4 April 1846, when pressures for the general release of government stocks were already mounting, 'I ... preach economy and reserve to all the [commissariat] department, so that nothing may be premature, or done without reflection. If I were to throw open our depots now, there is not an effort nor a landlord that we could enlist through any other channel.'³ A few depots began sales in restricted quantities before the end of March, but most kept their doors shut until sometime in April or May. By the beginning of June nearly all were open for business.⁴

Officials and relief committees promoting the use of Indian meal at first encountered considerable opposition to what was contemptuously decried as 'Peel's brimstone' (because of its bright yellow colour it was likened to sulphur). A large part of this popular resistance could be traced to the physical discomfort associated with the switch from a habitual diet of potatoes (over 10 lb daily for adult males) to one of meal (a daily ration of about 1 lb). As Routh put it, the Irish 'are accustomed to potatoes, which satisfy by repletion, and a more nourishing substance, which does not fill the stomach, leaves a craving sensation, a want of support and strength, as if they had not eaten enough'.⁵

¹ Statement 'of total expenditure', p. 1.
² O'Neill, op. cit., p. 216.
³ Correspondence explanatory of measures adopted ..., p. 90 [735], H.C. 1846, xxxvii, 142.
⁴ Correspondence from July 1846 to January 1847 relating to the measures adopted for the relief of distress in Ireland and Scotland (commissariat series), p. 2 [761], H.C. 1847, li, 24.
⁵ Routh to Trevelyan, 6 Mar. 1846 (Correspondence explanatory of measures adopted ..., pp 56–7).

Another important reason for popular opposition, and a far more serious problem, was that much of the Indian corn that entered Ireland early in 1846, having been imported unmilled, was not sufficiently ground by private millers. When it was sold in a coarse, lumpy condition and eaten without being boiled long enough, it was liable to cause severe bowel complaints. Some of the Indian corn also arrived in an unmerchantable condition, and unlike official imports found to be in this state, was treacherously foisted on a hungry populace. Circumstances such as these help to explain why, for example, the paupers in the Limerick workhouse refused to eat Indian meal; and why, at Waterford workhouse, reports circulated that people who had eaten it became ill and died.[1]

But the resistance was short-lived: Indian meal was 'much too good a thing to be long rejected by starving people'.[2] The government assisted in eroding opposition by publishing a cheap halfpenny pamphlet containing simple cooking instructions. The little tract was extremely popular; demand for it was 'beyond credibility' by early April.[3] Also, millers were instructed in the special grinding requirements for Indian corn. It was officially urged that oatmeal be added to Indian meal in a ratio of one part to three, and this mixture was widely found to be more palatable and hence more acceptable.[4] Very quickly, resistance vanished, to be replaced by an almost insatiable demand. Routh declared in mid-April that he 'could not have believed that the Indian corn meal would have become so popular',[5] and two months later, after virtually all the depots had been opened, Deputy Commissary-general Hewetson observed, 'the people everywhere have eagerly taken to its use, but they all want *ours*, with the queen's mark, it being so very superior to that imported and manufactured by the trade'.[6]

The original choice of Indian corn as a substitute food had largely been dictated by its cheapness. For a government reluctant to interfere with private commerce, Indian corn possessed the added advantage that it had not previously been a substantial item in Irish trade. Admittedly, it was not an entirely novel component of Irish lower-class diets in 1846, but only limited quantities had been imported in earlier years.[7] The government could therefore argue that since there was no large established trade in this commodity, its interference with private commerce was minimal. What increasingly weakened

[1] Woodham-Smith, *Great hunger*, pp 64–5, 73, 134–5.

[2] Edward Pine Coffin to Trevelyan, 30 Mar. 1846 (*Correspondence explanatory of measures adopted . . .*, p. 84).

[3] Routh to Trevelyan, 2 Apr. 1846 (ibid., p. 88).

[4] T. P. O'Neill, 'The organisation and administration of relief, 1845–52' in Edwards & Williams, *Great famine*, p. 216.

[5] Routh to Trevelyan, 15 Apr. 1846 (*Correspondence explanatory of measures adopted . . .*, p. 105).

[6] Hewetson to Trevelyan, 7 June 1846 (ibid., p. 158).

[7] E. M. Crawford, 'Indian meal and pellagra in nineteenth-century Ireland' in J. M. Goldstrom and L. A. Clarkson (ed.), *Irish population, economy, and society: essays in honour of the late K. H. Connell* (Oxford, 1981), pp 113–15.

this argument was that unofficial imports of Indian corn swelled enormously in the first three quarters of 1846, and that the government's agents ostentatiously employed official imports to curtail private profiteering and to lower the price of alternative food. Relief officials were in no doubt that their efforts had been quite successful, and historians have generally believed that official imports were on a scale sufficient to give the government the leverage over food prices that it desired. 'The entry of the government into the market', commented T. P. O'Neill, 'was a spectacular example' of Peel's willingness to defy current economic orthodoxy, and 'it gave him an effective means of price control so as to defeat monopolists'.[1] Yet Bourke has recently propounded a much less heroic view: 'the extent of "government interference" with the grain trade was trifling in comparison with the overall figures [of imports]; Routh was not exaggerating when he described the official imports as "almost only a mouthful"'.[2]

Can these two apparently conflicting interpretations be reconciled? In the first eleven months of 1846, total Irish imports of Indian corn and meal amounted to almost 122,000 tons, whereas official imports of food to the end of August 1846 did not exceed 20,000 tons.[3] If these official imports had been released into the market gradually during the course of the year, their effect on prices would have been quite limited. But as already indicated, the government threw the bulk of its supplies on to the market in a concentrated period of three months (15 May–15 August 1846), with June and July accounting for most of its sales. In this period government issues of meal constituted a sizeable fraction of the total amount of food available for consumption. As a result, they did have the effect of restricting profiteering and significantly dampening prices. It should also be stressed that the impact of the government's food relief operations was greatest in the west and the south-west, where private wholesaling and retailing facilities were weakest. Lastly, and not least important, the government's 'interference' with the grain trade, together with its famous decision to repeal the corn laws, helped to transform what had been a minor trade in Indian corn before 1846 into a major international commercial enterprise. It is no doubt true that the forced retention in Ireland of the entire grain harvest of 1845, or even the prohibition of the export of oats and oatmeal alone, would have been sufficient to offset the partial loss of the potato, but only if the government had been prepared to subsidise the purchase of higher-priced native produce. Thus oatmeal, costing around £15 a ton in the spring and summer of 1846, was about 50 per cent more expensive than Indian meal. But strong arguments could be and were made against such a policy, and in retrospect relief officials could only praise the decisions reached by the government.

[1] O'Neill, op. cit., p. 222.
[2] P. M. A. Bourke, 'The Irish grain trade, 1839–48' in *I.H.S.*, xx, no. 78 (Sept. 1976), p. 163.
[3] Ibid., p. 167; *Statement 'of total expenditure'*, p. 1.

Deputy Commissary-general Hewetson informed Trevelyan early in June 1846:

I am assured, from the best authority, that in all the localities where our meal is in use, the general health of the people has wonderfully improved, and that where at this season, gastric complaints were numerous, there are scarcely any; such is the wholesome and nutritious quality of the meal, so superior in every point of view to the potato. The mass of the peasantry are really grateful to the government for their timely interposition. . . . I know not what horrors and misery would have ensued had not these precautionary measures been taken when they were; and I often think of the vile abuse heaped upon the ministers, at the very time they were deeply considering all these arrangements, for their callous neglect, as they were pleased to call it.[1]

R ELIEF officials may have enthused about the results of their food distribution programme. But they were much less happy with the public works undertaken to provide employment and thus to furnish the money that the destitute needed to buy food. In part, the dissatisfaction stemmed from the character of the public works. Peel's government had clearly hoped that many of the works would be of a reproductive nature, permanently strengthening the Irish economy while furnishing temporary relief. Thus one of the four bills[2] that the prime minister presented to parliament in January 1846 was aimed at promoting the development of piers and harbours; the second sought to give increased encouragement to thorough drainage and other permanent improvements on landed estates. But under neither of these was much money spent or much employment furnished: pier and harbour projects consumed slightly less than £10,000, and the new land improvement legislation was practically a dead letter, mainly because it offered no increased financial incentives. Instead of reproductive works, road improvements became the chief source of employment. These were carried out under the direction of either the grand juries or the board of works. When grand juries sponsored the schemes, the entire cost was to be borne ultimately by the county, although in the first instance the treasury advanced the full amount as a loan. Nearly £134,000 was thus advanced. On the other hand, when the board of works undertook the schemes, only half of the cost was liable to be repaid to the treasury, while the other half was treated as a grant chargeable to the consolidated fund. Inevitably, these more generous terms meant that the expenditures of the board of works (£453,000, with half recoverable) far exceeded those of the grand juries.[3]

Government officials soon came to regard 'the half-grant system' as a major legislative blunder. Trevelyan bitterly complained in mid-April that it offered 'such advantages to the landlords as to have led to a general demand for it,

---

[1] Hewetson to Trevelyan, 7 June 1846 (*Correspondence explanatory of measures adopted.* . . . , p. 158).

[2] Enacted as 9 Vict., cc 1–4 (5 Mar. 1846).

[3] *Statement 'of total expenditure'*, p. 1; T. P. O'Neill, 'The organisation and administration of relief, 1845–52' in Edwards & Williams, *Great famine*, pp 219–21.

whether relief *for the people* was required or not; so that instead of a *test of real distress*, we have a *bounty on interested exaggeration*'. Rather than dig into their pockets, landlords, it was said, spoke openly and unashamedly of getting 'their share' of the public grants. The treasury did what it could to 'resist the torrent' of allegedly premature and ill-considered applications by demanding proof of distress and asking for contributions from proprietors. But these efforts were in the end largely ineffectual. As Trevelyan painfully realised, delays in granting requests placed the government 'in the awkward and invidious position of hesitating to apply a remedy which it has itself devised, and withholding the relief which it had itself previously been supposed to offer'.[1] Even when works were initiated under grand jury presentments, with the whole expense falling on the county, officials were convinced that the landlords who were grand jurors often approved schemes more from fear of courting intense unpopularity than from an honest belief that such works were essential for relieving acute distress.

These complaints by no means exhausted official dissatisfaction with the operation of public works. Payment of wages by the day rather than by the task led, it was claimed, to widespread indolence, and the rates of pay (usually 9d. or 10d., but sometimes as much as 1s.) were high enough to entice labourers away from farmers and other private employers. The harshest criticism, however, was reserved for the manner in which individuals were chosen for employment on the board of works schemes. The selection was made by the local relief committees, which were supposed to issue tickets only to destitute persons and only in accordance with prescribed rules. But many tickets were dispersed by individual committee members 'in the most irregular manner'; some were 'sold and distributed by persons unconnected with committees'; and often tickets were issued in much larger numbers than the works could possibly accommodate efficiently.[2] Above all, the relief committees generally neglected to scrutinise the applicants' means and allowed many who were not destitute to secure a place.

Lacking direct control over the recruitment of labourers for its schemes, the board of works could do little to restrain the dramatic extension of its responsibilities in the summer of 1846. From a daily average of about 21,000 persons during the month of June, the number employed soared to 71,000 by mid-July and reached a peak of almost 98,000 in the first week of August. It has been estimated that another 30,000 persons obtained work on schemes supervised by the grand juries or on pier and harbour projects, and that perhaps 10,000 more received employment on schemes undertaken directly by local relief committees.[3] If these estimates are correct, then approximately 140,000

[1] Trevelyan's memorandum, 15 Apr. 1846 (*Correspondence explanatory of measures adopted.* . . . , p. 304).
[2] Commissioners of public works to lords of the treasury, 8 Aug. 1846 (ibid., p. 352).
[3] Ibid., pp 332, 351; O'Neill, op. cit., pp 220–21.

people were given work at one time or another by the various agencies that Peel's government had set in motion. To assign four dependents to each of these 140,000 labourers would raise the total number of beneficiaries to 700,000.

Clearly, officials believed that the public purse had been opened much too widely, a view epitomised in the lament that 'every labouring man in the country was directed to look to the board of works for employment'.[1] As the number of workers on its schemes was nearing 100,000 early in August, the board flatly asserted that the figures were 'not an index to the state of distress or of the amount of employment necessary to be given to afford relief'.[2] Statistics showing the distribution of employment by county lend much support to this conclusion. Five-sixths of all those who worked under the board's supervision on roads in July were concentrated in only seven counties. Ranked in descending order, these were Clare, Limerick, Galway, Tipperary, Kerry, Mayo, and Roscommon. What is even more remarkable is that slightly over 40 per cent of such employment was confined to only two counties, with Clare accounting for 26 per cent and Limerick for 15 per cent.[3] In most of these counties the deficiency in the 1845 potato crop did not exceed the national average, and in three (Clare, Kerry, and Mayo) the deficiency was actually below the average. Obviously, to measure the level of distress from the extent of the potato deficiency alone would be short-sighted, but it is clear from these statistics on public employment, and especially from the dramatic case of Clare, that the board of works was right to complain that the numbers employed on its relief schemes in different counties were no fair guide to the geographical distribution of distress. Even if one rejects the official view that the government seriously overspent in relation to the country-wide level of distress, it is difficult to resist the conclusion that there was a substantial waste of public resources.

But what appeared to be unnecessary extravagance from the perspective of officials had an entirely different aspect for its beneficiaries. The employment provided, and especially the food distributed, by the government prompted an extraordinary outpouring of popular gratitude. Commissariat officers took delight in quoting the effusive comments of the poor in reference to relief measures. Said one labourer: 'This is the sort of repeal for Ireland, and may the Almighty bless our queen'. Another remarked: 'After all, Peel is a true man to old Ireland, and the right sort.'[4] The country people, observed Assistant Commissary-general Edward Pine Coffin, readily declared that they had 'been rescued from a state of frightful misery, or, to use their own strong but common expression, that "only for the government meal, thousands would have been now dying by the roadside"'.[5] These golden opinions were not confined to the

[1] Commissioners of public works to lords of the treasury, 8 Aug. 1846 (*Correspondence explanatory of measures adopted*..., p. 352).

[2] Ibid., p. 351. [3] Ibid., p. 349.

[4] Major Simmonds to Trevelyan, 4 July 1846 (ibid., pp 191–2).

[5] Coffin to Trevelyan, 24 June 1846 (ibid., p. 175).

peasantry. As Routh gleefully told Trevelyan in mid-June 1846, 'even the radical papers have ceased to speak of us in any other way than praise'.[1]

But if governments can cover themselves with glory when their actions are perceived as having overcome a major crisis, they can also cover themselves with infamy when their inaction is perceived as having turned a crisis into a catastrophe. The record of Peel's government in responding effectively to the partial potato failure of 1845 embedded the expectation that in the face of some far worse crisis in the future, relief fully equal to the vast needs of the people would be delivered, and delivered promptly. The total failure of the potato crop in 1846 meant that infinitely more was expected of Peel's whig successors, and the infamy they earned in Ireland had a great deal to do with the perception of how far short they fell of the high standards established by their distinguished predecessor.

[1] Routh to Trevelyan, 17 June 1846 (ibid., p. 167).

CHAPTER XIII

Production, prices, and exports, 1846–51

JAMES S. DONNELLY, JR

In 1846 blight attacked the potato much earlier and far more destructively than in the previous season. Reports of the havoc made by the disease now began to appear in mid-July. 'God help the poor people who paid in advance for their gardens', exclaimed one observer in the Fermoy district of Cork.[1] Under blackened stalks and leaves the tubers lay completely rotten or were as small as marbles; fields affected by the blight gave off an intolerable stench. With these sights and smells in the summer of 1846, the great famine began. The speed with which the devastation occurred etched itself deeply into the national consciousness. Writing on 7 August, Fr Theobald Mathew, the celebrated 'apostle of temperance', conveyed to Charles Trevelyan a vivid picture of what a vast difference a week had made:

On the 27th of last month I passed from Cork to Dublin, and this doomed plant bloomed in all the luxuriance of an abundant harvest. Returning on the 3rd instant, I beheld with sorrow one wide waste of putrifying vegetation. In many places the wretched people were seated on the fences of their decaying gardens, wringing their hands and wailing bitterly [at] the destruction that had left them foodless.[2]

Even before the 'late' crop could be lifted, government officials believed that the loss would amount to three-fourths of that crop.[3] When the constabulary tabulated the results of its county-by-county survey in late October, it was painfully obvious that the earlier estimates had not been nearly gloomy enough. According to the constabulary figures, the average yield per acre in recent years had been almost eight tons, whereas in 1846 it was barely more than one-third of a ton. Though there was wide geographical variation in yields, in no county did the average exceed one ton per acre.[4] Almost certainly, potato yields in the

---

[1] *Cork Examiner*, 15 July 1846.
[2] *Correspondence from July 1846 to January 1847 relating to the measures adopted for the relief of distress in Ireland and Scotland (commissariat series)*, p. 4 [761], H.C. 1847, li, 26.
[3] Ibid., p. 7.
[4] Ibid., p. 57.

early 1840s were lower than the constabulary figures indicated (say, six tons in a normal year), and the actual yield in 1846 may have been higher than the constabulary estimates. P. M. A. Bourke has suggested a 'highly speculative' yield of 1.5 tons per acre.[1] But quite obviously, to use the adjectives 'total' and 'universal' in reference to the failure of 1846 is hardly exaggeration. As if it were possible to darken a picture already pitch black, the disruption of the conacre system and the shortage of seed after the partial failure of 1845 led to an estimated decline of 21 per cent in the acreage planted in 1846.[2] To say, as Fr Mathew did to Trevelyan, that 'the food of a whole nation has perished' was excessive, but under the circumstances his assertion was understandable and excusable.[3]

In several crucial respects the virtually total failure of the potato in 1846 paved the way for an equally great catastrophe in 1847. First, the traditional relationship between farmers and their bound labourers was thoroughly disrupted. Under the customary system such labourers had been willing to give work in exchange for a patch of potato ground, a cabin, and a few so-called privileges. But as soon as blight blasted their potato gardens, money wages (at higher rates than usual) became absolutely essential if they were to avoid starvation. The widespread refusal of farmers to make cash payments compelled the labourers to surrender their plots and to flee to the public works or, as a last resort, to the workhouses. Secondly, the failure of 1846 deranged the conacre system. Conacre lettings were even less extensive in 1847 than they had been a year earlier. Massive default by unbound labourers in the payment of conacre rents in the autumn of 1846 had taught farmers to insist that these rents must be paid in advance, but this demand was never more difficult to meet than in the spring of 1847, after the labourers' cash reserves had been totally exhausted.

To these two causes of the neglect of potato cultivation in 1847 must be added a third, which was indeed the most important—the enormous deficiency of seed, one that dwarfed the shortages of 1846. Though urged to buy and distribute seed, the government refused to do so for a variety of reasons, the most myopic of which was that people would thereby be discouraged from preserving their own. In fact, with Indian meal selling at famine prices in the winter of 1846–7 and the subsequent spring, labourers and smallholders had no choice but to consume their seed potatoes if they wanted to stay alive. When they should have planted, they could not. 'I have asked them [i.e., the parishioners of Templecrone, County Donegal] why, instead of being idle, they do not dig their land,' reported a commissariat officer in February 1847, 'and get but one answer—they have neither food to eat while working [for themselves], nor seed to put in, which is the case, for they have no person to

---

[1] P. M. A. Bourke, 'The extent of the potato crop in Ireland at the time of the famine' in *Stat. Soc. Ire. Jn.*, xx, pt 3 (1959), p. 11.

[2] Ibid.   [3] Above, p. 286, n. 2.

help them.'[1] The combined effect of these adverse circumstances was an enormous decline in the potato acreage, which amounted in 1847 to a mere one-seventh of what it had been a year earlier, and to only one-ninth of the estimated acreage in 1845. The cruel irony of this situation was that the warm, dry weather of the spring and summer of 1847 kept the destructive blight at bay, and the national average yield of 7.2 tons per acre (this was the first year of official agricultural statistics) was excellent. But because of minimal planting, the total crop was no larger and perhaps even smaller than in the catastrophic season of 1846.[2]

The general absence of blight in 1847 led to an extraordinary effort early in 1848 to bring the potato back from near-oblivion. This valiant attempt was made in the face of great obstacles, the chief of which was the continuing scarcity of seed. Reporting from the Rosscarbery district in Cork in April, a quaker remarked: 'I know of a great many instances of the poor people fasting for eight and forty hours, trying to save the little remnant of their potatoes for seed.'[3] Such sacrifices helped to boost the acreage planted to a level three times higher than that of 1847 (810,000 acres compared with only 284,000). But in contrast to the previous season, the summer of 1848 was exceptionally wet, and blight again raged all over the country, sharply cutting the average yield to only about half of the 1847 figure. The net result was that total output in 1848 remained a small fraction of production in pre-famine years.[4]

The drastic fall in potato production was the worst, but not the only, problem that beset Irish agriculture in the late 1840s and early 1850s. Some of these additional problems stemmed from the famine crisis itself, while others arose independently. To the former category belong the enormous decline in the number of pigs and the substantial, though less serious, contraction in the number of sheep. From a total of 2.1 million in 1841, sheep fell to 1.8 million in 1849, though by 1851 they had regained the level of a decade earlier and stood on the verge of a remarkable advance. Pig numbers were cut by more than half between 1841 and 1847, declining from 1,400,000 to 622,000 over that period, and they still had not fully recovered by 1851, when the total fell short of 1.1 million.[5] As the export figures strongly suggest, the reaction of labourers and smallholders to the succession of potato failures was to dispose of their pigs and sheep without being able to restock. The shipment of pigs from Ireland to Britain plunged from 481,000 in 1846 to only 68,000 in 1849, while the export of sheep dropped from 324,000 in 1847 to less than 152,000 in 1851.[6] For

---

[1] Captain Giffard to Trevelyan, 27 Feb. 1847 (*Correspondence from January to March, 1847, relating to the measures adopted for the relief of the distress in Ireland (commissariat series)*, pt ii, p. 178 [796], H.C. 1847, lii, 524).

[2] P. M. A. Bourke, 'The extent of the potato crop in Ireland at the time of the famine' in *Stat. Soc. Ire. Jn.*, xx, pt 3 (1959), p. 11.

[3] Ibid., p. 12.   [4] Ibid., p. 11.

[5] *Returns of agricultural produce in Ireland in the year 1853*, p. xix [1865], H.C. 1854–5, xlvii, 19.

[6] *Thom's Irish almanac and official directory* (Dublin, 1855), p. 402.

the sharp contraction in sheep numbers there were other causes in addition to forced export without replacement. Farmers thinned their flocks because they could not protect them from nocturnal plunder and slaughter by famished labourers and cottiers. Flocks were also reduced by a widespread epidemic of liver-fluke disease spawned by heavy rains in the spring and summer of 1848.

The bad weather of 1848 also led to what was the worst grain harvest of the late 1840s. Wheat was hit especially hard, the average yield per acre declining to 4.5 barrels in contrast to 6.6 barrels in 1847. Despite the substantial fall in output there was no compensating rise in price. On the contrary, wheat prices began to slump badly in 1848, and by 1851 they were as much as one-third lower than they had been as recently as 1847. This contracting demand, combined with another poor wheat harvest in 1850, prompted a large-scale abandonment of wheat farming throughout the country. Between 1847 and 1852 the area planted with wheat plummeted from 744,000 to less than 354,000 acres, or by 52 per cent.[1]

The other grain crops fared much better than wheat in the late 1840s and early 1850s. The yields of oats and barley were steadier, and their acreage underwent no serious decline. The production of oats did fall modestly in 1848 and 1849, but by 1852 it had risen slightly above the 1847 level. Oats were of course by far the most important grain crop, with an acreage in 1847 over twice as large, and in 1852 almost four times as large, as that of wheat and barley combined.[2] Thus the maintenance of oat production and prices at reasonably good levels over these years provided a significant element of stability in the otherwise dislocated tillage sector of the economy.

Yet even though the output of oats and barley did not falter seriously, tillage farmers were unable to convert these crops into income-earning exports at the usual rate of former years. The din of contemporary protest over the continuing flow of food out of the famine-stricken country has often been allowed to conceal the large-scale diversion of Irish grain from export to home consumption. The following table, showing Irish exports of corn, meal, and flour to Britain from 1843 to 1849, highlights the extent of this diversion.[3] One major reason for this diversion was the need of Irish livestock producers to secure a substitute for the fodder that plentiful potatoes had once furnished. On the eve of the famine, as much as 5 million tons of potatoes, or about one-third of the total annual production, were fed to livestock. Almost 56 per cent of this was allotted to pigs, and another 40 per cent was consigned to cattle over the winter and early spring.[4] Largely because of the enormous deficiencies in

[1] Returns of agricultural produce in Ireland in the year 1847, pt i: Crops, p. vi [923], H.C. 1847–8, lvii, 6; Returns of agricultural produce ... 1853, pp vii, xii; Thomas Barrington, 'A review of Irish agricultural prices' in Stat. Soc. Ire. Jn., xv, pt 101 (Oct. 1927), p. 251.   [2] Ibid.
[3] 'Corn exported from Ireland to Great Britain' in Ledgers of imports, England, 1843–9 (special abstract on last pages of each ledger), nos 32–5, 37, 39, 41 (P.R.O., Customs 5).
[4] P. M. A. Bourke, 'The use of the potato crop in pre-famine Ireland' in Stat. Soc. Ire. Jn., xxi, pt 6 (1968), pp 83–7.

Exports of corn, meal, and flour from Ireland to Great Britain, 1843–9 (thousands of tons)

year	oats	oatmeal	wheat	wheatmeal & flour	barley	total
1843	218	152	40	48	20	478
1844	211	103	42	52	16	424
1845	235	95	78	89	17	514
1846	134	50	39	45	17	285
1847	69	30	26	13	9	147
1848	133	84	30	32	14	293
1849	93	64	21	29	8	215

the potato crop after 1845, the breeding of pigs went into eclipse until the early 1850s. But the raising of cattle increased substantially, and this expansion, together with the potato losses, made it necessary for farmers to feed a much higher proportion of their oat crop to their cattle.

What lowered grain exports even more, of course, were the appallingly large needs of humans. Insofar as grain retained in Ireland was marketed there to feed the starving, farmers' incomes benefited. Indeed, before 1848 the strength of domestic demand was such that fat profits (in 1846, obscene profits) accrued to that minority of farmers with large surpluses of grain to dispose of. But for the majority of tillage farmers, greatly increased subsistence needs cut deeply into the grain supplies that they could offer for sale. In County Cork even 'respectable farmers' holding thirty acres or more were said early in 1847 to be suffering acutely on this account: 'they are obliged to consume in their families and in their stables the corn which in former years procured clothes and other comforts for them'.[1] If this was true of the bigger farmers, smaller landholders must have had even less corn to place on the market. Thus, although the diversion of grain away from export was partly a matter of off-farm sales within Ireland, the scale of on-farm consumption rose so sharply in the late 1840s that this factor must be ranked among the leading causes of the serious erosion in tillage farmers' incomes.

Amid this general picture of crisis and malaise, however, there were some bright spots. Among the sectors of Irish agriculture that advanced in the late 1840s was dairying, a pursuit concentrated in the south-east and south-west. In the absence of separate figures before 1854 on the number of milch cattle, we must turn to the available figures of butter exports for indirect information about the course of dairy output. These statistics are not national in scope, but since they pertain to the Cork butter exchange, which was the largest single market in the country and drew its supplies from a wide area of Munster, they

---

[1] *Cork Constitution*, 21 Jan. 1847.

can be said with assurance to reflect accurately the general Irish trend. The rise in receipts of butter at Cork, shown in the following table, strongly suggests that production increased moderately in the late 1840s.[1]

Receipts of butter at Cork exchange, 1841–51
(thousands of cwt)

year	cwt	year	cwt
1841/2	134	1846/7	148
1842/3	155	1847/8	162
1843/4	168	1848/9	192
1844/5	149	1849/50	201
1845/6	159	1850/51	180
average, 1841–6	153	average, 1846–51	177

There is some reason to believe that a portion of the enlarged receipts in the years 1846–51 (about 15 per cent higher than in the previous five seasons) resulted from a decline in on-farm consumption, as the pressure of both rents and poor rates drove dairy producers to maximise their marketed output. But the effect of this on the level of receipts seems to have been relatively small.

If most of the increase in supplies sent to Cork market was the result of a rise in production of similar magnitude, the reason for growing output was not a greater demand for Irish butter in Britain. The price of first quality Cork butter in the years 1846–50 was virtually the same, on average, as in the previous quinquennium.[2] What made dairying attractive in the late 1840s was the high price of store cattle, of which dairy farmers were the chief suppliers. In 1847 and 1848 young stores (less than two years old) were about 50 per cent higher in price than in 1845, and older stores had risen even more in value, indeed, by as much as 80 or 90 per cent.[3] In the aftermath of the repeal of the corn laws, the long-term prospects of tillage in Ireland appeared bleak, whereas the future of pastoral farming seemed bright, given the country's natural advantages of soil and climate as well as the potential expansion of British demand for meat and butter. Even after the prices of butter and young stock declined sharply beginning in 1849, landlords considered it an unmistakable sign of lasting improvement when tenants enlarged their dairying operations. As Sir John

[1] Account of the total annual quantity of butter in casks, firkins, and kegs passed through the weigh-house, 1770–1869 (Cork Public Museum, Cork Butter Market MSS, C. 38). Because of a computational error the figures given in Donnelly, *Land & people of Cork*, p. 77, are incorrect.

[2] T. J. Clanchy and Co., *Half-a-century's butter prices...* (Cork, 1892).

[3] Thomas Barrington, 'A review of Irish agricultural prices' in *Stat. Soc. Ire. Jn.*, xv, pt 101 (Oct. 1927), p. 251.

Benn-Walsh recorded in his journal in August 1851 while visiting his estate in north Kerry,

the great criterion in these times is to watch whether the farmers are increasing their cow and dairy stock. If they are reducing their cattle and ploughing up their lands, depend upon it, they are going to the bad, but if they are adding a collop or two to their stock, the productiveness of their farm and the security for their rent are both increasing.[1]

Indeed, the Irish cattle enterprise as a whole was growing in the late 1840s and early 1850s, which represented a continuation of the rising trend of the early 1840s. The official statistics, however, need to be treated with caution. As P. M. A. Bourke has pointed out, the number of cattle reported in the 1841 census—a total of 1,863,000—did not include 'calves of the current year', with the result that the enumeration was deficient by some 16 to 20 per cent. A comparison of the higher corrected total for 1841 (2,233,000 cattle) with the figure for 1847 (2,591,000) reveals an increase of at least 16 per cent during the interval.[2] But if the effect of this correction is to reduce the extent of the growth in cattle numbers between 1841 and 1847, a countervailing consideration must be kept in mind. The impact of the partial potato failure of 1845 and the nearly total loss of 1846 forced cottiers and small farmers to dispose of their cattle in large numbers before agricultural statistics were collected in 1847. Had this crisis not occurred, the rise since 1841 would have been appreciably greater. In the four years following 1847, the national cattle herd increased by another 15 per cent, to a total of 2,967,000 in 1851. This latter rise, however, was anything but evenly distributed among the farms of different sizes. On holdings of fifteen acres or less, the number of cattle actually decreased, and it was stationary on farms of fifteen to thirty acres; the whole of the increase was thus confined to large farms exceeding thirty acres.[3] This is a striking illustration of a general phenomenon of the late 1840s—a drastic widening of the gap between rich and poor in Irish rural society.

Even well-to-do farmers, however, were hammered by the general depression in agricultural prices that started in 1849. The price declines were smaller for grain crops, which (apart from the exceptional year of 1846, when corn soared in value) had already shown a tendency to fall even before 1849; the decreases were much larger for store cattle, which had risen in price to great heights between 1845 and 1848. Graziers, together with dairy farmers who reared young stock, were hit especially hard. The great October fair at Ballinasloe in 1849 was sorely disappointing to the sellers of both cattle and sheep.

[1] J. S. Donnelly, jr (ed.), 'The journals of Sir John Benn-Walsh relating to the management of his Irish estates, 1823–64' in *Cork Hist. Soc. Jn.*, lxxix (1974), p. 115.

[2] P. M. A. Bourke, 'The agricultural statistics of the 1841 census of Ireland: a critical review' in *Econ. Hist. Rev.*, 2nd ser., xviii, no. 2 (Aug. 1965), pp 381–2.

[3] *Returns of agricultural produce in Ireland in the year 1847*, pt ii: *Stock*, p. iv [1000], H.C. 1847–8, lvii, 112; *Returns of agricultural produce . . . 1853*, p. xix.

'I have been attending the fair of Ballinasloe for the last twelve or thirteen years', remarked the special correspondent of the *Freeman's Journal*, 'and never witnessed such indifferent prospects nor heard such general complaints on the part of breeders of stock.'[1] The cattle fair in particular was 'characterised by a dulness [*sic*] hitherto unknown'; indeed, it was 'admitted by all to have been the worst cattle fair ever experienced in Ballinasloe'.[2] By 1850 younger stores had declined in value by 43 per cent since the peak attained in 1847, and over the same period the price of older stores fell by 32 per cent. In addition, the value of both butter and beef tumbled, the first by 30 per cent between 1846 and 1850, and the second by 26 per cent between 1848 and 1850.[3] Although the worst was nearly over by the end of 1851, there was no real recovery in prices until the outbreak of the Crimean war.

[1] *F.J.*, 5 Oct. 1849.
[2] Ibid., 9 Oct. 1849.
[3] Thomas Barrington, 'A review of Irish agricultural prices' in *Stat. Soc. Ire. Jn.*, xv, pt 101 (Oct. 1927), p. 251.

CHAPTER XIV

The administration of relief, 1846–7

JAMES S. DONNELLY, JR

'"WE know your honour will help us again" is the consoling remark with which [the poor] wind up their tale of disappointment and prospective want, and this seems to them, after their late experience [of government intervention in the grain trade], a sufficient security against the risk of famine.' So Charles Trevelyan was told on 18 August 1846 by Sir Edward Pine Coffin, the assistant commissary general in charge of the Limerick depot. Coffin knew that the relief operations of 1846–7 would be conducted very differently from those of 1845–6, and as if to justify the change, he said of the attitude of the poor: 'It is a characteristic feeling, but one replete with mischief to themselves and to the community.'[1] Before the new relief system could be installed, the old one needed to be terminated, and this could safely be done, it was felt, because the harvest season was about to start. Employment on the public works was gradually reduced from the second week of August. By the end of that month the number of persons employed by the board of works had fallen to a daily average of 38,000, and it continued to fall for several weeks thereafter.[2] (The corresponding figure for the week ending on 26 September was slightly less than 15,000.) The food depots also reduced their sales, with a view to a complete cessation of operations at the close of August.

The relief policies of the new whig administration had been disclosed to parliament by Lord John Russell, the prime minister, in mid-August 1846, when all the available evidence already pointed to a calamitous failure of the potato crop. Russell announced that the cabinet was opposed to any general interference by the government with the grain trade. The primary emphasis in any new crisis would be placed less on the sale of food and more on the provision of employment through a revised system of public works. In adopting these policies, the cabinet was basically accepting the proposals made by

[1] *Correspondence from July 1846 to January 1847 relating to the measures adopted for the relief of distress in Ireland and Scotland (commissariat series)*, p. 15 [761], H.C. 1847, li, 37.

[2] *Correspondence from July 1846 to January 1847 relating to the measures adopted for the relief of the distress in Ireland, with maps, plans, and appendices (board of works series)*, pt i, p. 76 [764], H.C. 1847, l, 96.

Charles Trevelyan. In an important memorandum submitted to the cabinet on 1 August, Trevelyan insisted that 'the supply of the home market may safely be left to the foresight of private merchants', and that if it became necessary for the government to interfere at all, its purchases should be restricted to the home market in order to encourage the private importation of food. As anxious as Trevelyan was to allow full scope to private enterprise, he recognised (though not sufficiently) that in parts of Ireland grain importers and retail traders either did not exist or were too few in number to provide adequate supplies in a period of extreme scarcity. Even so, he proposed minimal intervention: government food depots should be set up only on the west coast, but not even there should they issue food while supplies could be purchased from dealers or obtained from other private sources. In essence, then, the government committed itself to acting as a supplier of last resort west of the Shannon. Everywhere else (around the north, east, and south coasts from Derry to Dublin and Cork, as well as east of the Shannon generally), ministers and relief officials considered themselves bound to a policy of non-intervention, and pledges to that effect were actually given to merchants.[1]

The partial potato failure of 1845 had allowed the government a period of six or seven months to prepare its relief machinery before having to set it in motion. But the new crisis was utterly different. The almost total failure of 1846 permitted virtually no breathing space before the destitute masses sought to throw themselves on government resources. With respect to food, those resources were shockingly inadequate, even for the west alone. By the end of August all but a few of the depots had closed, and the stocks remaining had dwindled to less than 2,100 tons of Indian meal and about 240 tons of oatmeal.[2] When the prospect of a total potato failure became all but certain in August, Trevelyan scrambled to increase official stocks by employing as corn factor the London merchant Eric Erichsen. His initial purchases were quite small, and on 19 September Routh protested to Trevelyan: 'it would require a thousand tons to make an impression, and that only a temporary one. Our salvation of the depot system is in the importation of a large supply. These small shipments are only drops in the ocean.'[3] The problem, as Trevelyan explained a few days later, was that 'the London and Liverpool markets are at present so completely bare of this article [Indian corn] that we have been obliged to have recourse to the plan of purchasing supplies of Indian corn which had been already exported from London to neighbouring continental ports'.[4] Partly through such expedients Erichsen was able during August and September to buy about 7,300 tons of Indian corn, 200 tons of barley, and 100 tons of Indian meal.[5]

---

[1] T. P. O'Neill, 'The organisation and administration of relief, 1845–52' in Edwards & Williams, Great famine, pp 223–4.
[2] Correspondence from July 1846 to January 1847 . . . (commissariat series), p. 31.
[3] Ibid., p. 80.
[4] Trevelyan to Routh, 22 Sept. 1846 (ibid., p. 83).
[5] Ibid., p. 103.

These imports, however, did little to raise commissariat reserves because the depots could not be kept shut altogether. The largest issues were made from the depot at Sligo, which served the north-west, where acute distress became evident as early as mid-August. Over 650 tons of Indian meal and oatmeal were distributed from here alone between 10 August and 19 September. Heavy pressure persisted for many weeks thereafter, and it was not until early November, after the first local arrival of private imports, that relief officials were able to close the Sligo depot.[1] The combination of small government imports and unavoidable issues from some of the depots caused the total stocks in government depots to remain for a long time well below the minimum level of 8,000 tons that Routh considered necessary before there could be any general opening of the western depots. Official stocks did not surpass 4,000 tons until the end of November, and a month later they barely exceeded 6,000.[2] Even so, at the end of December the treasury finally consented to throwing open the western depots 'for the sale of food as far as may be prudent and necessary'.[3]

Could the government, by prompt action, have secured enough food from Britain or foreign countries to open its depots in the west of Ireland much sooner? It has been suggested that if Trevelyan had been willing to move decisively into the grain market as soon as he received the first reports of the reappearance of blight in mid-July, adequate supplies could have been accumulated. T. P. O'Neill has pointed out that Trevelyan was urged by Hewetson in late July to purchase 4,500 tons of Indian meal immediately. 'This warning had been ignored', O'Neill observes, 'and purchases began too late in the season to ensure the arrival of sufficient quantities before Christmas.'[4] But the matter is more complicated. Hewetson clearly did not anticipate issuing the meal until the spring of 1847.[5] On the other hand, it is true that Erichsen's purchases for the government did not begin until 26 August, and that of the 22,600 tons of Indian corn bought through his agency up to mid-January 1847, only about 6,800 tons had actually arrived by that time in Ireland or Britain.[6] The government, in fact, had to contend with two serious obstacles. The first was the unavoidable delay of one to three months between the date of purchase and the date of delivery, and the second was that after such heavy imports in the first six or seven months of 1846, Indian corn was in short supply in the London and Liverpool markets as well as on the Continent. Trevelyan had ruled out direct government orders to the United States, but even if he had not done so, American maize was not quickly accessible. As Routh noted of the requests

---

[1] *Correspondence from July 1846 to January 1847 . . . (commissariat series)*, pp 93–6, 265.
[2] Ibid., pp 318, 428.
[3] Trevelyan to Routh, 28 Dec. 1846 (ibid., p. 425).
[4] T. P. O'Neill, 'The organisation and administration of relief, 1845–52' in Edwards & Williams, *Great famine*, p. 225.
[5] *Correspondence explanatory of the measures adopted by her majesty's government for the relief of distress arising from the failure of the potato crop in Ireland*, p. 215 [735], H.C. 1846, xxxvii, 267.
[6] *Correspondence from July 1846 to January 1847 . . . (commissariat series)*, pp 22, 506–7.

forwarded by Irish merchants to America in September, 'these orders cannot be executed so as to arrive in the United Kingdom before the end of November, and then only the old corn of last year [1845], for the new corn of this year will not be ready for shipment before January'.[1] This much is clear: if Erichsen had been authorised to begin his purchases in late July instead of late August, there would have been considerably more food in the western depots before the end of 1846; perhaps the depots would have opened a month or so earlier than they did. But this would not have been enough to avert the onset of famine and epidemic disease.

Since relief officials did not expect the first large supplies of foreign corn to reach Irish ports before December, they were especially anxious to see the domestic harvest brought to market as rapidly as possible. One excuse offered for keeping the western depots closed most of the time and for not establishing depots outside the west was that this policy would accelerate the process of converting the grain harvest of 1846 into food. It soon became apparent, however, that in spite of steeply rising grain prices at home, exports on a large scale, though smaller than in 1845, were again taking place. Routh was alarmed and more than once hinted at the desirability of stopping them. 'The exports of oats have amounted since the harvest to 300,000 quarters', he told Trevelyan at the end of September. 'I know there is a great and serious objection to any interference with these exports, yet it is a most serious evil.' As he remarked in another letter, 'the people, deprived of this resource, call out on the government for Indian corn, which requires time for its importation'.[2] But Trevelyan promptly and brusquely turned Routh's suggestion aside. 'We beg of you', he said, 'not to countenance in any way the idea of prohibiting exportation. The discouragement and feeling of insecurity to the [grain] trade from such a proceeding would prevent its doing even any *immediate* good; and there cannot be a doubt that it would inflict a permanent injury on the country.'[3] Trevelyan's decision, never questioned by his political masters, seems to have been based more on his rigid adherence to *laissez-faire* economic doctrines than on a careful assessment of its practical short-term consequences. To have forbidden exports from the 1846 grain harvest might well have led to some reduction in food imports late in 1846 or early in 1847, but it would hardly have paralysed the trade, and it would have helped materially to fill the fateful gap in domestic food supplies until the Indian corn ordered from America began to reach Irish shores in December.[4] Most scholars would agree that this refusal to prohibit exports, even for a limited period, was one of Trevelyan's worst mistakes, although the blame was of course not his alone. More than any other single decision, it provided at least some substance to the later nationalist charge that

[1] Routh to Trevelyan, 22 Sept. 1846 (ibid., p. 84).
[2] Routh to Trevelyan, 29, 30 Sept. 1846 (ibid., pp 97, 104).
[3] Trevelyan to Routh, 1 Oct. 1846 (ibid., p. 106).
[4] P. M. A. Bourke, 'The Irish grain trade, 1839–48' in *I.H.S.*, xx, no. 78 (Sept. 1976), p. 165.

the British government had been prepared to see a large proportion of the Irish people starve.

Allowing unhindered exportation certainly contributed significantly to the remorseless rise of Irish food prices between September and the end of the year. As long as the wholesale price of Indian meal remained at £10 or less per ton, as it did through August, there was little risk of famine, but as each succeeding month brought higher prices, malnourishment increased, eventually to the point of starvation, and along with it, susceptibility to nutrition deficiency diseases, the greatest scourge of all. At Cork the price of Indian meal rose from £11 a ton at the beginning of September to £16 in the first week of October, and before the end of that month it stood as high as £17 to £18; only slight reductions (to £16 or £17) were recorded in November and December.[1] When food was sold from the depots, as happened periodically before late December, the prices were purposely regulated by those prevailing in the nearest market town or by the current trade prices. This was justified on the grounds that private traders had to be allowed to make reasonable profits, and that if they were undersold, there would be such a rush to the depots that the limited supplies would quickly be exhausted.

The latter argument contained some truth, but the former displayed, to say the least, undue tenderness for grain importers and dealers, whose profits swelled. Even commissariat officers conceded the point. As Hewetson told Trevelyan in late October, 'the corn dealers and millers are everywhere making large profits, but I trust Christmas will see prices much lower'.[2] Among the biggest beneficiaries were G. W. & J. N. Russell, 'the great corn factors and millers of Limerick', who at this time were grinding over 500 tons a week.[3] Their prices tended to regulate the cost of food not only in Limerick but also in north Kerry, Clare, and Tipperary. In mid-November, Hewetson pressed the Russells to reduce their prices and extracted a promise that the charges for Indian meal and oatmeal would at once be lowered to £16 and £20 a ton respectively. Yet 'even this is too high a figure for any length of time', and though the firm deserved what Hewetson called encouragement, he feared that if the matter were 'left altogether to the few houses in this city (theirs giving the tone), reductions will be very gradual in operation'.[4] And so they were, without effective government intervention and with ever more doleful consequences. Indeed, the depots actually made substantial profits on their sales: in mid-January 1847 the commissariat was charging £19 a ton (as high as £22 or even £24 'in some situations') for Indian meal that it had purchased a few months earlier for about £13.[5] This situation reflected Trevelyan's inflexible view that

[1] *Correspondence from July 1846 to January 1847 . . . (commissariat series)*, pp 48, 128, 199, 304, 313, 326, 335, 366.
[2] Hewetson to Trevelyan, 23 Oct. 1846 (ibid., p. 185).
[3] Hewetson to Trevelyan, 20 Oct. 1846 (ibid., p. 181).
[4] Hewetson to Trevelyan, 18 Nov. 1846 (ibid., p. 278).
[5] Ibid., pp 479–82, 506.

unless prices were allowed to attain the full market rate, Ireland would be even worse placed to attract foreign supplies and to retain home-produced food. Or as he said in a little lecture to Routh late in September 1846, 'imports could not take place into a country where prices are artificially depressed, but, on the contrary, the food already in the country would be exported to quarters where a fair market price could be obtained'.[1] This, needless to say, was to make a religion of the market and to herald its cruel dictates as blessings in disguise.

Against this pattern of non-intervention and general passivity with respect to the food supply in late 1846 must be set the burst of activity in public works. It will be recalled that there had been intense dissatisfaction among relief officials with many aspects of the system of public works during the previous season of distress.[2] The new system, devised mainly by Trevelyan in August 1846, was intended to avoid the inefficiency, waste, and extravagance that in the official view had characterised earlier operations. Instead of allowing the grand juries to initiate and direct a significant proportion of the employment projects, it was decided that the board of works should assume complete responsibility for all public schemes.[3] Rather than continue the practice under which the treasury paid half the cost of projects controlled by the board of works, it was decided that in future all charges should ultimately be met out of local taxation. Though the treasury would advance the money for public works in the first instance, the county cess was to be used to repay these loans in full. Irish property must support Irish poverty: much was to be heard of this maxim, a favourite of British politicians and civil servants, during the famine years. In sum, then, the government created a system that combined local financial responsibility with thoroughgoing centralised control of employment projects. By design the schemes were not to be 'reproductive', since Trevelyan wanted to restrict applications from landlords. This policy was soon modified under pressure from landlords, but the practical results of the alteration were meagre, and in the new season of distress, as in the old, the building or repair of roads and bridges was the most common activity. Cutting hills and filling hollows were the main tasks.[4]

With the assumption of complete control by the board of works came the imposition of time-consuming bureaucratic procedures. (The board itself was on the verge of becoming a mammoth bureaucracy, with 12,000 subordinate officials.) Only the lord lieutenant himself could authorise the holding of an extraordinary presentment sessions, and the relief schemes proposed at the sessions had first to be scrutinised by the board's officials, who then might request the treasury to sanction them. Adherence to these procedures caused agonising delays in starting public works, not only when the new system was

[1] Trevelyan to Routh, 30 Sept. 1846 (ibid., p. 101).
[2] Above, pp 282–4.
[3] 9 & 10 Vict., c. 107 (28 Aug. 1846).
[4] This and the next two paragraphs draw heavily on T. P. O'Neill, 'The organisation and administration of relief, 1845–52' in Edwards & Williams, *Great famine*, pp 227–34.

inaugurated but also, to some degree, throughout its whole duration, since at any given time, while some works were being closed, others were being opened. Delays, however, were particularly numerous at the outset. The lord lieutenant had ordered public works to be restarted early in September, but it was not until October that the new schemes began.

Even though the problem of delay was never eliminated, the sheer pace and scale of operations soon became quite extraordinary. Indeed, the extension of the bureaucratic apparatus could hardly keep pace with the headlong expansion of employment. Between the first and the last week of October the average daily number of persons employed by the board of works soared from 26,000 to 114,000; throughout November the figure climbed steadily, reaching 286,000 in the fourth week. Though the rate of increase slowed somewhat during December, 441,000 persons were employed daily by the end of the year. The peak was reached in March 1847, when during one week as many as 714,390 persons were employed daily. Naturally, the expenditure was great. By the time that the system of public works was terminated in the spring of 1847 and replaced by the distribution of free food (in a terribly belated confession of failure), the accumulated costs of these relief schemes amounted to the staggering sum of almost £4,850,000. It could now be said that Irish property was paying, or rather was beginning to pay, for Irish poverty.[1]

As enormous as expenditures were, they had not been nearly sufficient to bring enough food within the financial reach of the rapidly increasing masses of destitute people. The fundamental problem was the inadequacy of the wages paid on the public works. Beginning in September 1846, the board of works tried to substitute a system of task labour for the daily wages that had prevailed previously. The main reason for this drastic change in policy was to eliminate or at least to reduce the general indolence that had allegedly prevailed among labourers during the past season of relief operations. The board instructed its officials that 'the sum to be paid for each portion of [task] work should be sufficient to enable an ordinary labourer to earn from 10*d.* to 1*s.* per day, and a good labourer who exerted himself, from 1*s.* 4*d.* to 1*s.* 6*d.* per day'.[2] As a punitive incentive designed to win acceptance for task work, those labourers who were unwilling (or unable) to do it were to be paid no more than 8*d.* per day.[3] This was from one-fifth to one-third less than previous daily rates for customary unmeasured work, even though food prices were already rising when the reduction was ordered.

The introduction of task labour was fiercely resisted by the workers, often to the point of violence, and many projects had to be stopped, at least temporarily, before popular opposition could be overcome. Officials tended to attribute the

---

[1] *Correspondence from July 1846 to January 1847 relating to the measures adopted for the relief of the distress in Ireland, with maps, plans, and appendices (board of works series)*, pt i, pp 195, 344, 486 [764], H.C. 1847, l, 215, 372, 574; O'Neill, op. cit., pp 232, 234.

[2] *Correspondence from July 1846 to January 1847 . . . (board of works series)*, pt i, p. 140.

[3] Ibid., pp 68, 150–51.

resistance they encountered to the labourers' unfamiliarity with task work or to their unreasonable fears of unfair treatment if they consented to do it. But there were serious practical problems, only too evident to the labourers, which the senior officials of the board were inclined to minimise or overlook. Any delay in the setting out of task work, and delays were unavoidable in view of the rapidly growing scale of operations, meant (or was supposed to mean) that wages had to be paid at the low daily rate of 8d. On the other hand, when task work was set out but not measured immediately, as was usually the case, the labourers were paid on account, the rule being that they were to receive three-fourths of the agreed value of the assigned work, for example, 9d. on account for a task worth 1s. Delays in making measurements, occasioned by the shortage of qualified staff and by other factors, often caused severe hardship, and there were complaints that payments on account fell short of the stipulated three-fourths.[1]

Another reason for popular opposition to task work was that the scarcity of implements seriously reduced wages, for many labourers in the closing months of 1846 were unable to earn even half the 'ordinary' rate of 10d. to 1s. because they lacked the proper tools: among one gang of seventy-five men near Cong, County Mayo, there were only two wheelbarrows, two crowbars, and a wooden lever. The few possessing implements received up to 10d. a day while the rest earned as little as $3\frac{1}{2}d.$ to 4d. Labourers whose task work formerly entitled them to 1s. a day but whose health declined were later unable to claim more than 6d. while toiling at the same job.[2] Indeed, the system of task labour operated to the general detriment not only of the sick or infirm but also of the old, women, and adolescents, for some labour gangs excluded them from their ranks because their presence would have lowered the rates of wages that physically strong and healthy adult males could earn.

To judge from the reports of the board's inspecting officers, however, a majority of workers in many districts eventually accepted and even approved of task labour. To many, it offered or seemed to offer the possibility of increasing their wages to keep pace with the rapid advance of food prices; it was particularly attractive to younger adult males in sound health, who could make the most of it or at least avoid being engulfed in the rising sea of misery around them. Another reason was that workers were often able to subvert the system to their advantage. Local overseers were subjected to great pressure by the labourers to exact less work for a given rate than the application of strict standards would have required. Harsh overseers risked being beaten, and the fear of assault (along with humanitarian feeling, in many cases) inclined others to leniency in enforcing standards. Senior officials of the board of works complained that there was widespread collusion to raise wages between their subordinates and workers engaged in task labour. Early in December the

[1] Ibid., pp 152, 230, 346.
[2] T. P. O'Neill, 'The organisation and administration of relief, 1845–52' in Edwards & Williams, Great famine, p. 228.

chairman of the board of works, Lieutenant-colonel Harry David Jones, told Trevelyan: 'I am quite convinced from reading our last week's reports, and from other sources, that our task system is not working as it ought to do; the men are receiving much larger sums than they ought to do. . . . I believe everybody considers the government fair game to pluck as much as they can.'[1]

Yet the sad truth was not that too many earned too much, but that too many earned too little to enable them to ward off starvation and disease. A signal defect of the task-work regime was the growing physical debility of many labourers suffering from malnutrition, a condition that made it impossible for them to earn the sums of which 'ordinary' workers were considered capable. In west Clare, for example, debilitated labourers were seen to stagger on the public works at the beginning of 1847, and 'the stewards state that hundreds of them are never seen to taste food from the time they come upon the works in the morning until they depart at nightfall'.[2] Barely more than a month after telling Trevelyan that task-work wages were too high, Lieutenant-colonel Jones had to admit that the opposite was often true: 'In some districts the men who come to the works are so reduced in their physical powers as to be unable to earn above 4*d.* or 5*d.* per diem'.[3]

In many parts of the country where public works had been opened, task labour had not been introduced at all, or had been only partially adopted, or had been abandoned after a period of trial. In numerous instances the nature of the work to be performed or the character of the terrain was considered unsuitable for the adoption of task labour. In other cases the subordinate officials of the board of works were incapable of shouldering the additional technical and supervisory burdens associated with task labour. 'It is extremely difficult to carry out the board's wish respecting task work,' remarked the inspecting officer for north Kilkenny in late December 1846, 'the nature of the soil being so different in various places that nothing like a fixed list of prices can be established, and the overseers are not capable, in most instances, of measuring and valuing excavations, &c., were the staff of the engineers sufficient to overlook the works properly.'[4] The board itself pointed out in mid-January 1847 'the impossibility of finding overseers qualified to estimate and measure tasks for 10,000 separate working parties'.[5] In the many localities where day labour remained the dominant or exclusive form of public employment, wages were even more likely to be inadequate to sustain health than in areas where task work prevailed. It is true that the rule limiting payment by the day to 8*d.* was not always scrupulously observed, but the wage for this type of work rarely

[1] Jones to Trevelyan, 10 Dec. 1846 (*Correspondence from July 1846 to January 1847 . . . (board of works series)*, pt i, p. 334).

[2] *Clare Journal*, 7 Jan. 1847 (quoted in *Correspondence from January to March 1847 relative to the measures adopted for the relief of the distress in Ireland (board of works series)*, pt ii, p. 3 [797], H.C. 1847, lii, 13).

[3] Jones to Trevelyan, 18 Jan. 1847 (ibid., p. 17).

[4] *Correspondence from July 1846 to January 1847 . . . (board of works series)*, pt i, p. 442.

[5] *Correspondence from January to March 1847 . . . (board of works series)*, pt ii, p. 14.

exceeded 10*d.*, and such sums condemned the recipients and their families to malnutrition and disease.

This became a common complaint in the weekly reports of the inspecting officers beginning in December 1846, though other commentators had called attention to the general insufficiency of earnings much earlier. From one inspecting officer in County Leitrim came the report that 'the miserable condition of the half-famished people is greatly increased by the exorbitant . . . price of meal and provisions, insomuch that the wages gained by them on the works are quite inadequate to purchase a sufficiency to feed many large families'.[1] Another inspector in County Limerick declared: 'I greatly fear that unless some fall shortly takes place in the rate of provisions, a great proportion of the families now receiving relief on the public works will require additional support, and that without it they will not long exist.'[2] Because the retail price of meal in County Limerick was as high as 2*s.* 8*d.* per stone, one labourer from a family of six or more could no longer furnish himself and them with enough food, obliging the inspecting officer to allow a second member of such families to be placed on the public works. (From other counties there were reports at this time of even higher retail prices for Indian meal: 2*s.* 10*d.* per stone in Galway, 3*s.* in Meath, and up to 3*s.* 4*d.* in Roscommon.)[3] A month earlier (at the end of November), the inspector of north Tipperary, where Indian meal was much cheaper (2*s.* 2*d.* a stone), remarked: 'The country people are generally in the greatest distress. Tenpence a day will, I believe, only give *one* meal a day to a family of six persons.'[4] A west Cork observer made a similar calculation early in January 1847: 'Indian and wheaten meal are both selling at 2*s.* 6*d.* per 14 lb; at this rate a family consisting of five persons cannot, out of the wages of one person, say 6*s.* per week, have even two meals per diem for more than four days in the week.'[5] Almost everywhere 8*d.* a day was literally a starvation wage for the typical labouring family, and so too, in most places, was 10*d.* Yet a high proportion of the labourers on the public works throughout the country earned no more than these sums, and many earned less. No wonder, then, that work gangs so often engaged in strikes, demanding at least 1*s.* a day, that overseers and check clerks were so frequently threatened or assaulted, and that in the winter of 1846–7 labourers on the works commonly collapsed from exhaustion.

Two other serious deficiencies exacerbated the general inadequacy of wage rates. One was frequent delay in the payment of wages. To this chronic problem several factors contributed: dishonesty or lack of zeal on the part of the pay clerks, who numbered 548 at the beginning of March 1847 (some of them were also robbed); shortages of silver; breakdowns in the elaborate system of paperwork; and the failure or inability of the overseers to measure

---

[1] *Correspondence from July 1846 to January 1847 . . . (board of works series)*, pt i, p. 445.

[2] Ibid., p. 448.

[3] Ibid., pp 441, 444, 446.

[4] Ibid., p. 285.

[5] *Correspondence from January to March 1847 . . . (board of works series)*, pt ii, p. 5.

task work promptly. Delays of one to two weeks were not unusual, and in some districts interruptions lasting as long as five weeks occurred occasionally. When in late October 1846 a labourer named Denis McKennedy dropped dead by the roadside in the Skibbereen district of Cork, with his wages two weeks in arrears, a coroner's jury declared that he had 'died of starvation due to the gross negligence of the board of works'.[1] This was the first in a string of similar verdicts, though not all of them involved alleged interruptions in the payment of wages. Persistent efforts were made to overcome this problem, and delays were reduced in duration, but they could not be eliminated altogether.

The other serious defect was the government's unwillingness to pay normal wages whenever work had to be curtailed because of bad weather during the winter of 1846–7. When the issue was first discussed in September 1846, the lord lieutenant directed that if labourers were prevented from working by wet weather, they should be 'sent home and paid [for] half-a-day's work'.[2] After frost arrived in early December, Trevelyan observed to Lieutenant-colonel Jones: 'Now that the hard weather is come, you will, I presume, act upon the rule long ago settled by you with the lord lieutenant, that on days when the weather will not permit the people to work, they will receive a proportion of what they would otherwise earn; this is clearly the right way of meeting the exigency.'[3] To pay only half of what was already in many cases a starvation wage was scarcely right, but at least it was straightforward. Yet the board of works apparently never gave a clear instruction in this matter to its local officials. Some of them adopted a half-pay standard, but others—indeed, the vast majority—simply allowed the works to proceed. For obvious reasons, labourers in general did not wish to stop working if that would mean the interruption of their pay. But in bad weather they were rarely able to earn much. When heavy snow fell in County Donegal in mid-December, 'the people continued work during the whole time, but could do nothing but break stones' for low wages.[4] At the same stage in King's County an inspecting officer declared that 'earnings this week, after measurement, are much reduced owing to the frost'.[5] Extremely bad weather in the second week of February 1847 brought about the first reduction in public works employment since the previous October. Because of a heavy snowfall, the number at work fell from a daily average of 615,000 to slightly less than 608,000. But in the third and fourth weeks of that month alone, another 100,000 persons crowded on to the works in spite of the cold and the inadequate wages.[6]

---

[1] T. P. O'Neill, 'The organisation and administration of relief, 1845–52' in Edwards & Williams, *Great famine*, p. 229.

[2] Jones to Trevelyan, 12 Sept. 1846 (*Correspondence from July 1846 to January 1847 . . . (board of works series)*, pt i, p. 89).

[3] Trevelyan to Jones, 5 Dec. 1846 (ibid., p. 299).

[4] Ibid., p. 414.

[5] Ibid., p. 413.

[6] *Correspondence from January to March 1847 . . . (board of works series)*, pt ii, p. 189.

Already, however, those responsible for relief policy had reluctantly concluded that the mammoth system of public works must soon cease to be the centrepiece of the battered strategy for warding off starvation and disease. By January 1847 mass death had begun in some localities, and inspecting officers of the board of works anticipated heavy mortality 'within a very short period' in the counties of Clare, Cork, Galway, Kerry, Leitrim, Mayo, Roscommon, Tipperary, and Wicklow.[1] In mid-January the board confessed itself to be near the end of its powers and resources. Its officers, having already fought a losing battle to keep small farmers with holdings valued at £6 or more off the works, could now do almost nothing to limit the constantly swelling mass of claimants for employment. For their inability they castigated the local relief committees, whose only object, declared Lieutenant-colonel Jones, echoing innumerable complaints by his subordinates, 'is to get as many persons employed as possible, instead of anxiously endeavouring to keep the numbers as low as the existing calamity will permit'. In rejecting 'undeserving' applicants designated as destitute by the committees, the inspecting officers drew 'down upon themselves and the board all the odium and vindictive feelings of the poorer classes'.[2] It was not unknown for inspectors to be denounced to their faces as the authors of starvation.

Even if those deemed undeserving could have been thrown back on their own resources, supposing they had some, the undeniably destitute would more than have filled their places. 'The number employed is nearly 500,000,' Jones and his colleagues told the lord lieutenant on 17 January 1847, 'and 300,000 or 400,000 in addition will shortly require it.'[3] As many as one-third of those listed as destitute by the local relief committees were not yet on the public labour rolls. Even for those currently employed, work to do on the roads was almost exhausted. Indeed, the main roads had been made much worse, not better. Landlords, who had 'voted thousands and thousands of pounds' for such schemes, 'cry out that the great communications of the country are destroyed,' Jones acidly remarked, 'and I have no doubt that for this season they are all more or less severely injured and many nearly impassable, but whose fault is that? Not ours.' His board, he insisted to Trevelyan, could not possibly accommodate the additional multitudes likely to be driven to the public schemes in the coming months by want of food; 'we have neither staff nor work upon which we can employ them'. Even if there were scope for a wide extension of the road projects, the system of task labour could not be retained. 'The fact is', Jones finally admitted, 'that the system ... is no longer beneficial employment to many; their bodily strength being gone, and spirits depressed, they have not power to exert themselves sufficiently to earn the ordinary day's wages.'[4] Task labour had lost its original purpose, he and his colleagues declared, because

[1] Jones to Trevelyan, 13 Jan. 1847 (ibid., p. 8).
[2] Ibid., p. 7. [3] Ibid., pp 14–15.
[4] Jones to Trevelyan, 13, 16, 19 Jan. 1847 (ibid., pp 7–8, 13, 18).

'the idleness of the idle' could no longer 'be distinguished from the feebleness of the weak and infirm'.[1] Taking all these circumstances into account, Jones was led to what for him was the distasteful conclusion that 'it would be better in many cases to give food than to be paying money away, as we are now obliged to do'. Like many others, he had been deeply impressed by the results of the distribution of soup to the starving by private groups such as the quakers. 'You will perceive the great benefits derived from the soup establishments', he told Trevelyan, 'and how very cheap is the preparation.'[2] Economy in public expenditure being one of the gods that Trevelyan worshipped, the assistant secretary of the treasury had not missed the significance of soup. Indeed, he was even ready to displace temporarily another of his idols—the general sanctity of the private food market—to exploit its enormous potential. The distribution of free food by agencies of government in virtually all parts of the country was soon to begin. Needless to say, it was too long, and for thousands too late, in coming.

[1] Commissioners to lord lieutenant, 17 Jan. 1847 (ibid., p. 14).
[2] Jones to Trevelyan, 19 Jan. 1847 (ibid., p. 18).

CHAPTER XV

The soup kitchens

JAMES S. DONNELLY, JR

ONCE the government recognised at the very end of 1846 that its schemes of public works were failing disastrously to hold starvation and disease in check, a new system of relief designed to deliver cheap food directly and gratuitously to the destitute masses was gradually put into place. The government always intended that its new initiative would be temporary, lasting only until the harvest season of 1847, when a revised poor law system would begin to function. In the short term, soup was supposed to bring salvation. Even before the necessary legislation—popularly known as the soup kitchen act[1]—was hurried through parliament in late January and February 1847, relief officials in Ireland were busily promoting the installation of boilers for the making of soup. Their efforts had been anticipated by numerous individuals and groups during the closing months of 1846. The soup kitchens operated by the Religious Society of Friends in Cork city (from November 1846) and elsewhere had won deserved acclaim, and these were matched by the generally unheralded enterprises of many other private philanthropists. Their collective success (in limited geographical areas and within the severe restraints imposed by their restricted resources) was largely responsible for the enthusiasm with which government agents belatedly embraced the new policy.

To decide to adopt a new policy was one thing, but to implement it rapidly, as the deteriorating situation required, was another matter. The first necessity was to erect new administrative machinery. Supervisory responsibility for implementing the scheme was entrusted to a relief commission. Among its six members were representatives of the board of works (Lt-col. Jones), the commissariat (Sir Randolph Routh), the constabulary (Duncan McGregor), and the poor law commission (Edward Twistleton). The chairman was Sir John Fox Burgoyne, previously the inspector-general of fortifications in Ireland, and joining these five was Thomas Redington, the under-secretary at Dublin castle. The central staff of the relief commission was drawn from the commissariat department, and the inspecting officers, who served as agents of the commission in the localities, were selected from either the board of works or the commissariat, thus assuring an experienced contingent of central officials.

[1] 10 & 11 Vict., c. 7 (26 Feb. 1847).

To regulate expenditures and the distribution of food at the local level, two types of committee were established: a small finance committee of two to four persons in each poor law union (there were then 130 unions), and district relief committees, with a much larger membership, whose area of responsibility generally coincided with the boundaries of the electoral divisions of the poor law administration (there were 2,049 electoral divisions in the country).

Because the relief commission was firmly determined to impose administrative order and strict financial accountability on this extended bureaucracy, the machinery was not activated as quickly as the alarming circumstances demanded. The mere preparation, printing, and distribution of the forms and documents considered necessary—over 10,000 account books, 80,000 sheets, and 3,000,000 ration tickets—constituted a vast undertaking in itself, consuming valuable time.[1] It was not until 4 March 1847 that the lord lieutenant's order specifying the membership of the district relief committees was promulgated. This was followed within a matter of days by the issue of detailed regulations for the inspecting officers, finance committees, and district relief committees. The actual distribution of food rations was authorised to begin on 15 March in those districts where the relief committees were willing and able to comply with the regulations.[2]

But weeks elapsed in many areas before the new regime was instituted. As late as 15 May only about 1,250 electoral divisions had come under the operation of the soup kitchen act (almost 2,000 would eventually do so). And in their report of the same date the relief commissioners themselves expressed 'considerable disappointment that this progress should have been so slow, seeing no good reason why the measure might not, by this time, have been in full activity all over the country'.[3] The fault, insisted the commissioners, rested with the local relief committees. Some of them merely wanted to exhaust their own financial resources before adhering to the new scheme, but many others wished to see the public works system of relief extended for as long as possible. In spite of all their defects, the public works were a known quantity; they required labour in return for assistance and thus were not 'demoralising' like gratuitous aid; and they were less vexatious to the local committees than soup kitchens.

The relief commissioners were unwilling to tolerate this foot-dragging. The cost of the public works was fearsome, and so were starvation and disease—in spite of them. In conjunction with the board of works, the commissioners had already directed that from 20 March the number of labourers on the public works was to be cut by at least 20 per cent, beginning with landholders occupying ten acres or more; even those with less land had to be discharged until the

---

[1] *Treasury minute, dated 10th March 1847, and first report of the relief commissioners . . .*, p. 8 [799], H.C. 1847, xvii, 26.

[2] Ibid., pp 12–15, 22–4.

[3] *Second report of the relief commissioners . . .*, p. 3 [819], H.C. 1847, xvii, 77.

quota was reached. Further reductions were to take place in stages as the new system of relief was brought into operation.[1] Only by such pressure, the commissioners believed, could the recalcitrant local committees be compelled to inaugurate the soup kitchen scheme. A second cut of 10 per cent was ordered to be implemented as of 24 April, and in a dangerous move (it appeared reckless even to Trevelyan), all engineers in the service of the board of works were commanded to close the works in their districts entirely on 1 May unless they received specific instructions to the contrary before then.[2] Yet the destitution was so overwhelming, and the prescribed alternative to the public works was still so often absent, that this deadline simply could not be met. Although 209,000 labourers had been dismissed by the end of April (a reduction of 29 per cent from the peak of 714,000 in March), only another 106,000 (15 per cent) were dismissed during the whole month of May. The respite for most of the remainder, however, was indecently brief. By the last week of June 1847 all but 28,000 (4 per cent) had been discharged.[3]

Even though the pace of dismissals from the public works was less rapid than the relief commissioners had originally wanted, it was still too fast to be fully accommodated by the slow extension of the new scheme of assistance. As the table below indicates, at the beginning of May the number of rations issued daily in the 1,063 electoral divisions then covered by the soup kitchen act had reached 826,000, and because children received less than a full ration, the total number of persons relieved was about 994,000. But this scale of distribution was almost certainly insufficient to reach all of the 209,000 labourers who had by

Scale of daily relief under the soup kitchen act, May–September 1847

date	electoral divisions	rations	persons relieved
8 May	1,063	826,325	944,372
5 June	1,989	2,388,475	2,729,684
3 July	1,989	2,643,128	3,020,712
31 July	1,990	2,205,329	2,520,376
28 Aug.	1,098	967,575	1,105,800
11 Sept.	623	442,739	505,984

Second report of relief commissioners, p. 26; *Third report* . . ., p. 29 [836], H.C. 1847, xvii, 131; *Fourth report* . . ., p. 5 [859], H.C. 1847, xvii, 147; *Fifth report* . . ., p. 6 [876], H.C. 1847–8, xxix, 34; *Sixth report* . . ., p. 7 [876], H.C. 1847–8, xxix, 59; *Seventh report* . . ., p. 7 [876], H.C. 1847–8, xxix, 79.

[1] *Treasury minute dated 10th March 1847*, pp 4–5.
[2] *Second report of relief commissioners*, p. 7.
[3] Woodham-Smith, *Great hunger*, p. 288.

that time been discharged and who, together with their dependants, probably numbered 1,045,000 (if we calculate the average family size at five persons). And this problem persisted. By the first week of June the daily ration count had soared to 2,388,000, and the total number of persons relieved with soup or other food was then estimated at 2,730,000. The continuing inadequacy of this vastly increased distribution can partly be judged from the fact that up to the end of the first week of June the number of discharged labourers amounted to 633,000. The addition of their dependants raises the total to 3,165,000 persons (again on the assumption that the average family contained five members). This means that even in the most sanguine view almost 15 per cent of the population directly affected by the dismissals were still excluded from the relief furnished under the soup kitchen act. To these should be added the destitute who had been unable to obtain employment on the public works before the discharges started in late March. Even at the point of its widest extension during the first week of July, when rations were distributed to as many as 3,021,000 people a day, there is good reason to believe that the provision remained insufficient. For by the end of June the population directly affected by the closure of public works had grown to perhaps 3,530,000, and this figure again leaves out of account the destitute who had never found employment on such schemes.

In assessing the defects and benefits of the system after its termination early in September, however, the relief commissioners did not find fault with themselves, or, in general, the local committees for failing to throw open the gates more widely. If anything, they were convinced that the scale of assistance had been excessive, though not wildly so. That some abuses did exist can hardly be denied. In a small proportion of electoral divisions the number of persons appearing on the relief lists actually exceeded the total population recorded in the 1841 census; and in some others, popular intimidation, deceit, illegitimate influence, or simply the liberality of committee members secured places on the lists for persons who were not utterly destitute or (in a few cases) not even poor. The most serious problem of this kind concerned able-bodied labourers who were in receipt of wages. In contrast to the three categories of the poor who were now entitled to gratuitous relief (the infirm, destitute unemployed labourers, and destitute landholders), working labourers were barred from obtaining free food. If their wages were insufficient to enable them to feed their families, they were allowed only to *purchase* food, paying at least the cost price. The relief commissioners were adamant that there must be no gratuitous assistance that would supplement wages, however inadequate. The inevitable result of this policy was that unemployed labourers often obtained more food without having to pay for it than employed workers who were charged for it. In such cases there was obviously a disincentive for those in work to remain so, and many of them abandoned their employers in order to qualify for gratuitous relief. Farmers also entered into collusive arrangements under which they formally discharged their regular labourers, thus entitling them and their dependants to free food, but still employed them 'at odd times'. Relief committees not infrequently tolerated this practice. In particular, they did not strictly enforce the rule requiring the attendance of all able-bodied members of a family at the soup kitchen before rations could be issued to any of them.[1]

But if the system was open to abuse, it was increasingly operated in such a way as to exclude or discourage many more people who would have benefited from a less stringent and demeaning regime. The controversy over whether food should be distributed in an uncooked or a cooked form highlights this problem. The relief commissioners were generally opposed to the issue of uncooked rations, and the central board of health strongly supported their position.[2] The medical arguments against the distribution of uncooked food by local committees were quite sound. Either through popular ignorance or more often because adequate cooking facilities were lacking, the practice led to the consumption especially of Indian meal in a raw or badly cooked state, thus aggravating the diarrhoea and dysentery that were already so widespread. In addition to the medical case against it, the distribution of uncooked meal or flour also led to fraud, as when it was subsequently sold in order to raise money for tea, tobacco, or whiskey. Nevertheless, many local committees long persisted in dispensing uncooked food. This was less troublesome than erecting, staffing, and supervising soup kitchens; it was somewhat cheaper in terms of unit costs; and it was the method that most of the poor, at least at the beginning, strongly preferred.[3]

But the relief commissioners and their inspecting officers were convinced that besides the other evils that attended it, the issue of uncooked food attracted many people who were undeserving of assistance. As one inspecting officer insisted in May 1847, 'the issue of raw meal or flour must lead to great imposition; I have heard hundreds say they would go for meal, when they would reject the cooked food'.[4] Thus, although cooking the rations raised unit costs, this increase was more than offset by the decline in the number of claimants for relief. 'The introduction of cooked food', declared an inspecting officer, 'has reduced the numbers of applicants wonderfully, and it is generally liked by the really destitute, and immeasurably better for them than the uncooked Indian meal.'[5] Another inspecting officer also observed that cooked food served as a fitting test of destitution: 'In consequence of cooked food being issued, not more than two-thirds of the usual numbers attended for rations, and many of those who did [attend] indignantly refused the cooked

[1] *Third report of relief commissioners*, pp 23–4; *Supplementary appendix to the seventh and last report of the relief commissioners*..., pp 5–6 [956], H.C. 1847–8, xxix, 125–6.
[2] *Treasury minute, dated 10th March 1847*, pp 22–3; *Second report of relief commissioners*, p. 4.
[3] *Second report of relief commissioners*, pp 6, 17; *Supplementary appendix to seventh and last report of relief commissioners*, p. 6.
[4] *Third report of relief commissioners*, p. 24.
[5] Ibid.

food, which was really of better quality and as well cooked as that which I daily breakfast upon.'[1]

The main reason for the popular resistance was plain enough, though it was not sufficiently appreciated by the relief authorities. The demeaning business of requiring the whole family to troop every day to the soup kitchen, each member carrying a bowl, pot, or can, and waiting in a long line until their number was called, painfully violated the popular sense of dignity. Among many similar incidents, one crowd at Templetouhy, County Tipperary, collected around the kitchen, yelled that they would not accept soup, and 'ill-treated a female who had been engaged to attend to the soup kitchen'; another crowd at Milltown Malbay, County Clare, burst into the kitchen and destroyed the boiler.[2] Under the unrelenting pressure of the central relief authorities, the great majority of local committees eventually fell into line with the policy of restricting rations to cooked food alone, though only after the inspecting officers in some districts had been subjected to 'threats of personal violence and conflict with members of committees in urging its adoption'.[3]

For many local committees the most telling argument in favour of the soup kitchen regime was its economy. With individual rations costing $2\frac{1}{2}d.$, and eventually only $2d.$, on the average, it was much less expensive than the public works had been. Indeed, many committees claimed that 'in their respective districts it only cost one-third of the expense' of the discarded system.[4] The substitution of cooked for uncooked food was also a considerable economising factor through its effect in reducing the relief lists. The overall impact of this effect is impossible to measure precisely, but there is no doubt that it was substantial. The relief commissioners adduced the example of two electoral divisions that were reputedly alike in all respects except that in one division uncooked food was issued while in the other cooked food was distributed. In the former the proportion of the population receiving relief was as high as 58.5 per cent, whereas in the latter the figure was only 36 per cent.[5]

The ever present desire to restrain costs had also been evident in the early administrative decision about the size of the daily ration. This could hardly be described as generous. The relief commissioners stipulated in their original instructions to local committees that the soup or other food was to include either 1 lb of meal or flour (of any grain), or 1 lb of biscuit, or $1\frac{1}{2}$ lb of bread for all persons over nine years of age, with those under nine receiving a half-ration.[6] Sharply criticised for the inadequacy of this scale, the commissioners replied that the ration 'must be reduced to what is strictly necessary', and they endlessly invoked the authority of the central board of health for its reasonableness.[7] In practice, the raw ration usually consisted of two-thirds Indian meal

[1] *Third report of relief commissioners*, p. 24.   [2] Woodham-Smith, *Great hunger*, p. 295.
[3] *Supplementary appendix to seventh and last report of relief commissioners*, p. 6.
[4] Ibid., p. 7.   [5] Ibid., p. 6.
[6] *Treasury minute dated 10th March 1847*, p. 23.
[7] *Second report of relief commissioners*, p. 4.

and one-third rice (when obtainable). This mixture, when cooked with water as 'stirabout' or porridge, swelled into a ration weighing 3 to 5 lb. Some local committees, however, took it on themselves to reduce the raw ration below the 1 lb stipulated by the commissioners, and others 'issued only two pounds weight of cooked food, instead of the full weight produced by the pound of meal'.[1] Especially at the beginning of the scheme much of the soup was very thin; instead of soup for the poor, it was a case, as has been said, of poor soup. The commissioners conceded as much: 'The soup originally issued, before the "stirabout" was brought into use, is reported to have been highly obnoxious to the people; and in Clare [and not only there] it was found necessary to discontinue it.'[2] Even when the approved ration was not diminished by local parsimony even greater than that of the central authorities, there were other problems to which the board of health drew attention. One was the lack of solidity (too much liquid) in the ration, which intensified the normal relaxation of the bowels coincident with the coming of warm weather, and another—far more serious—was the absence of variability in the food portion of the soup, which gave rise to scurvy.[3]

The varied efforts to practice and enforce economy produced financial results that the relief commissioners deemed to be more than satisfactory. Like the public works system, the soup kitchen scheme had been designed to place the heaviest burden on local ratepayers, with supplementation of the rates through private subscriptions from local landlords and others. The government's fiscal responsibility was limited to advancing loans to the finance committees (to be repaid out of the poor rates) and to making grants or donations, normally to be in an amount equal to the combined proceeds of rates and private subscriptions, although larger donations could be given in extremely urgent cases. In practice, however, the government had to shoulder by far the greater part of the burden. Private subscriptions or voluntary assessments did not exceed £46,000, and the government gave an equivalent sum, without reference to the rates collected locally. Much more important, the loans advanced by the treasury on the security of the rates were almost never repaid. Even so, the cost of the soup kitchen scheme to the government was not considered excessively heavy by the relief commissioners, who brought the scheme to a close in September 1847 without spending £530,000 that had been voted for loans and grants under the act. Total government outlays amounted to £1,725,000, consisting of £953,000 in loans, £717,000 in grants and donations (including £118,000 for fever hospitals), and £55,000 in staff salaries and expenses.[4] Substantial savings were effected by both the treasury and the local relief committees when the arrival of massive quantities of foreign grain and

[1] *Supplementary appendix to seventh and last report of relief commissioners*, p. 7.
[2] Ibid., p. 6. See also Woodham-Smith, *Great hunger*, p. 178.
[3] *Second report of relief commissioners*, p. 7; *Fourth report*, pp 17–19.
[4] *Supplementary appendix to seventh and last report of relief commissioners*, pp 16–17.

meal led to a drastic fall in prices. The cost of Indian corn fell from as much as £19 a ton in mid-February 1847 to £13 at the end of March and to only £7. 10s. by the end of August.[1]

By contrast, total expenditures for the relief works carried out from October 1846 to June 1847 had amounted to £4,848,000. Although this entire sum was supposed to be repaid to the government out of the poor rates and county cess, prospects for the recovery of the money from this source were dismal. In the nine months during which the public works were in operation, slightly less than £450,000 of rates could be collected, and the gap between what was owed and actual receipts was widening in 1847 with almost every passing month.[2] In the likelihood that only a small portion of public works outlays would be recouped by the treasury, the alternative system of soup kitchens was considerably less expensive.

For all its shortcomings the soup kitchen scheme must be judged more than a qualified success. As one relief committee remarked, 'however easy it may be to find fault, it is not so easy to feed more than three millions of souls'.[3] Though many additional thousands should have been fed, and though all should have been fed more generously, the scheme was by far the most effective of all the methods adopted by the government to deal with starvation and disease between late 1846 and 1851. Indeed, the most profound regrets that might be voiced are that the system was not introduced much earlier, and that it was not continued after September 1847. While it lasted, and for those whom it reached, starvation was generally averted and disease (with the major exception of typhus) considerably lessened. The distribution of cooked food in particular greatly reduced the incidence of diarrhoea and dysentery, and where proper care was taken to vary the rations and to include vegetables in the mixture, scurvy was reduced as well. Even the awful scourge of typhus, which had already taken hold in many districts before the scheme was instituted, and which was undoubtedly spread by the gathering of crowds around the kitchens, was reportedly less often fatal among food recipients. The members of one relief committee in the Macroom district of Cork expressed the general view when they declared at the end of the scheme that 'had they not witnessed it themselves, they could scarcely have conceived it possible that such a change for the better could have been brought about in the health and appearance of the poor, in so short a time, and at comparatively so small an expense'.[4] The relief commissioners understandably took pride in having accomplished so much under the soup kitchen act, but with an ineradicable dogmatism they insisted that because of 'its many dangers and evils', the measure 'could only be justified by such an extreme

[1] Nicholls, *Ir. poor law*, p. 326.
[2] *Papers relating to proceedings for the relief of the distress and state of the unions and workhouses in Ireland; fourth series, 1847*, p. 258 [896], H.C. 1847–8, liv, 294.
[3] *Supplementary appendix to seventh and last report of relief commissioners*, p. 12.
[4] Ibid., p. 7.

occasion, including a combination of circumstances that can hardly be expected to occur again'.[1] Yet history did repeat itself, and more than once, and now the official responses to extreme occasions were murderous in their consequences, though not in their intentions.

[1] *Seventh report of relief commissioners*, p. 3.

CHAPTER XVI

The administration of relief, 1847–51

JAMES S. DONNELLY, JR

WHEN the soup kitchen scheme was ended early in September 1847, the government resorted to the poor law system as the principal means of affording relief to the destitute. The adoption of this approach was one measure of the rising impatience of the governing elite in Britain with the intractability of the famine crisis in Ireland. It was also a measure of the government's unwillingness to allow what it considered the enormous dead weight of Irish poverty to burden—endlessly, it seemed—the financial resources of the British treasury. The legislation that defined the general conditions of public relief for the rest of the famine years was enacted in June and July 1847,[1] that is, before anyone could know if the vast potato deficiencies of 1846 would be perpetuated or if typhus and dysentery would continue their appalling ravages of the recent past. Admittedly, with foreign grain and meal pouring into the country, food prices had fallen drastically by the late summer and autumn of 1847. But the private labour market had sharply contracted and was incapable by itself of providing employment and wages on a scale sufficient to ensure a general absence of mass death.

Ministers recognised the nature of this problem. As the prime minister, Lord John Russell, told the chancellor of the exchequer, Sir Charles Wood, in March 1847, 'it is more than ever necessary that between this time and the harvest of 1848 as much employment as possible should be given. Otherwise we shall see our poor law utterly fail from not getting a wind to take it out of harbour.'[2] But to raise that wind the government was mainly relying on its loans to Irish landlords for agricultural improvements. The stimulation given to private employment by means of these loans was not insignificant. But the near-insolvency or utter bankruptcy of a substantial section of the landlords was so apparent by 1848 that the government had devised a measure—the encumbered estates bill—that it hoped would rid Ireland of its impoverished

[1] 10 & 11 Vict., c. 31 (8 June 1847); 10 & 11 Vict., c. 90 (22 July 1847).
[2] G. P. Gooch (ed.), *The later correspondence of Lord John Russell, 1840–1878* (2 vols, London, 1925), i, 172.

gentry. Sir Charles Wood expressed the unanimous view of the British cabinet when he told Russell in May 1848: 'There is no real prospect of regeneration . . . for Ireland till substantial proprietors possessed of capital and will to improve their estates are introduced into that country.'[1] In short, the strong wind on which Lord John Russell had counted for the salvation of the revised Irish poor law system had largely failed to materialise.

When Irish landlords did not fill the employment gap, the deficiencies of the poor law system were glaringly exposed. Its defects were so serious that they gave plausibility to charges (then and later) that there was a genocidal intent at work. Before these charges can be fairly assessed, the policies that governed the revised system and the local practices that prevailed under it must first be considered. The main poor law act of June 1847 provided that the destitute who were not able-bodied (the aged, the infirm, the sick, orphans, and widows with two or more legitimate dependent children—often called the 'impotent' poor) were to be relieved either in or out of the workhouse, with the local boards of guardians having the right to choose either mode of assistance. In addition, the able-bodied, if without employment and destitute, were also declared entitled to relief. But this had to be administered in the workhouse (as a test of destitution) unless there was no room or unless the prevalence of infectious disease had rendered the workhouse unfit for their reception. Where accommodation was exhausted or disease rife, the poor law commissioners could authorise the local guardians to furnish outdoor relief to the able-bodied for a maximum of two months, but only in the form of food and only to those willing to engage in the hard labour of stone-breaking (another test of destitution). Lastly, no one occupying more than a quarter of an acre of land could be relieved out of the poor rates.[2] This provision, the infamous quarter-acre clause, was appended to the law at the urging of Sir William Gregory, a Galway landowner and M.P. for Dublin city. Its purpose was to arm landlords with a weapon that would enable them to clear their estates of pauperised small-holders who were paying little or no rent. Only by surrendering their holdings to the landlord could these tenants qualify themselves and their families for public assistance.

Conditions within the workhouses greatly contributed to making the poor law system work so badly. The 130 union workhouses of Ireland in 1847 had been planned and built for relieving the distress of a poor country in normal times, not to contend with the mass starvation and disease of a catastrophic famine. In March 1847 less than 115,000 inmates could be accommodated at one time, and the facilities available for separating the diseased from the healthy were initially not merely inadequate but often disastrously so. At the beginning of March, for example, the Fermoy workhouse in County Cork, with proper accommodation for only 800 persons, was inundated by more than 1,800

[1] Ibid., p. 228; below, pp 346–9.
[2] 10 & 11 Vict., c. 31 (8 June 1847), sect. 10.

paupers. In the absence of a fever hospital at Fermoy the sick and the still healthy were all mixed up together, and the consequent mortality was appalling: out of 2,294 persons admitted since 1 January 1847 and not discharged, as many as 543, or nearly 24 per cent, had died.[1]

Many other workhouses in the south and west were in a state like Fermoy's. The average *weekly* rate of mortality per thousand inmates rose from four at the end of October 1846 to thirteen at the end of January 1847 and then almost doubled to twenty-five in the middle of April—the highest rate of workhouse mortality recorded during the famine years.[2] Already there was a marked tendency for the seriously or fatally ill to delay their entry into the workhouse until they were so debilitated by disease that medical attention was virtually useless. Resigned to death, many entered merely to assure themselves of a coffin and burial at public expense. This pattern was to persist throughout the famine years and was largely responsible for making the workhouses places of notoriously high mortality and refuges of the very last resort—a mutually reinforcing process.

The workhouse horrors of the early months of 1847 compelled the relief authorities to institute a series of changes: the construction of separate fever hospitals and additional dispensaries, the expansion of workhouse accommodation (both permanent and temporary), and the granting of outdoor relief even to the able-bodied poor. The building of the fever hospitals, making possible medical differentiation among paupers, was an unmixed blessing. It kept workhouse mortality from again reaching the fearsome peaks of early 1847. Even so, the sanitary condition of the workhouses at the beginning of 1848 was anything but reassuring to potential applicants for admission, to say nothing of actual inmates. The average *weekly* mortality rate stood as high as eleven or twelve per thousand inmates during the months of January and February. Much lower rates generally prevailed thereafter, mainly because of the institution of outdoor relief on a greatly extended scale. The outbreak of cholera in March 1849, however, again pushed workhouse death rates up to the high levels prevailing at the start of 1848. The average *weekly* mortality rate per thousand inmates increased from 7.7 in mid-January 1849 to 9.4 at the beginning of March and 12.4 by early May, before falling to 6.3 at the end of June.[3]

Together with this relative improvement in sanitary conditions in 1848 and 1849, there occurred a gradual expansion of workhouse accommodation. Between September 1847 and September 1848, the original accommodation was increased by about one-third, thus creating space for a maximum of over 150,000 inmates at any one time. This enlargement of facilities continued over the next twelve months, so that by September 1849 the total number of places available in the workhouses, auxiliary buildings, and fever hospitals had

---

[1] Minute book, Fermoy board of guardians, 1847-8, 10 Mar. 1847, pp 26-9 (Cork Archives Council).

[2] Nicholls, *Ir. poor law*, p. 318.   [3] Ibid., pp 351, 404.

reached about 250,000. Even with this steady expansion, however, some work-houses in the south and west continued to suffer from severe overcrowding at the periods of maximum seasonal pressure in the winter and spring. An extreme example was the Skibbereen workhouse, which was originally designed to accommodate only 800 inmates, but contained nearly 2,800 early in December 1848, even though the local guardians had provided only three small timber sheds as additional room.[1]

The persistence of overcrowding was usually attributable to the determined efforts of local boards of guardians to avoid giving outdoor relief to the able-bodied poor or to restrict such assistance as narrowly as possible. In those districts of Munster and Connacht where labourers and cottiers dominated the social structure, the guardians dreaded that the abandonment of the workhouse test of destitution would bring incalculable hordes of poverty-stricken people on to the outdoor relief lists. This common view was forcefully expressed to the commissioners at the end of March 1848 by Captain Arthur Kennedy, the poor law inspector in Kilrush union in west Clare, where appointed vice-guardians had recently replaced an incompetent and probably corrupt group of elected guardians:

A formal closing of the house under any circumstances would swamp the union and the vice-guardians together. The great danger of giving outdoor relief in this union to any but the impotent classes arises from the wretched wages given. Any number of men can be procured for 5d. per day without their food; so that [the outdoor relief] ration on the lowest scale would be in nine cases out of ten worth more than their wages. Six days' wages at 5d. would be but 2s. 6d., not an equivalent to two and a half stones of meal, which a small family on outdoor relief would be entitled to.[2]

In order to have workhouse places available to test the destitution of able-bodied applicants for assistance, the guardians of Kilrush and other unions repeatedly shunted the qualified impotent poor who were not seriously ill to the outdoor relief rolls. In addition, the poor law commissioners authorised the granting of outdoor relief to certain classes of persons who technically were not entitled to such assistance: widows with only one dependent child, childless widows over sixty years of age, women deserted by their husbands before June 1847, and orphans whose relatives or friends were prepared to shelter them.[3] But above all, it was essential in the eyes of relief officials to increase work-house accommodation so as to restrain the otherwise irresistible pressure for outdoor relief. It was notorious among relief officials that the poor loathed the harsh discipline of the workhouse and dreaded contracting fatal disease there. As Captain Kennedy informed the poor law commissioners in February 1848, 'the repugnance to enter the workhouse is beyond credence, and I am satisfied

[1] Ibid., pp 342–3, 351–2; *Cork Examiner*, 8 Dec. 1848.
[2] *Papers relating to proceedings for the relief of the distress and state of the unions and workhouses in Ireland; sixth series, 1848*, p. 811 [955], H.C. 1847–8, lvi, 849.
[3] Ibid., p. 810; above, p. 317.

the outdoor relief list might be reduced one-third by testing them'. He rejected the idea of actually doing this as 'neither politic nor humane', given the undoubted destitution of those on the list and 'an utter absence of any employment or mode of earning'.[1] Yet like relief officials generally, he was extremely anxious to acquire additional workhouse accommodation as a defence against a great and very costly increase in outdoor assistance. Reasons of economy and not of humanity basically controlled the near-tripling of workhouse places from slightly more than 114,000 in March 1847 to almost 309,000 by March 1851.

Once the workhouses of the south and the west were filled to capacity in February and March 1848, however, the poor law commissioners were compelled to sanction outdoor relief for the destitute able-bodied poor as well as for certain categories of women and children technically not eligible for such assistance. The extension of outdoor relief under the second section of 10 & 11 Vict., c. 31, to others besides the impotent poor had begun in the last few months of 1847, and already by the first week of February 1848 over 445,000 persons were receiving outdoor relief. Of this number, almost one-quarter consisted of the able-bodied and others qualified under the second section of the act. By the end of June the outdoor relief rolls had swelled to nearly 834,000, and now the proportion qualified under the second section had increased to slightly more than two-fifths of the total. The pressure of destitution was so great in 1848 that in as many as 71 out of the 131 unions the poor law commissioners authorised outdoor relief in the form of food under the second section of the act. Only in 23 of these 71 unions, however, was such assistance sanctioned 'without distinction of class'. In 35 other unions outdoor relief was restricted to the impotent poor under the first section of the act, and in the remaining 25 unions no assistance was granted outside of the workhouse, apart from occasional urgent cases. The same pattern was repeated in the following year. The outdoor relief rolls expanded from 423,000 persons at the beginning of January 1849 to 784,000 in the first week of July, and the portion represented by the able-bodied and others qualified under the second section rose over the same period from 18 to 37 per cent.[2]

In 1850, on the other hand, assistance outside the workhouse was confined almost exclusively to the impotent poor, whose numbers fluctuated between 100,000 and 150,000 at any one time between January and June. The great increase in workhouse accommodation over the previous three years allowed the local guardians to apply the workhouse test rigidly to the able-bodied, and the total number of inmates rose to 264,000 in the third week of June—the highest level so far attained. In 1851 even the impotent poor were invariably required to submit to workhouse discipline, since in that year outdoor relief was virtually eliminated altogether. The workhouses themselves, however, were still

---

[1] *Papers relating to proceedings for relief of distress; sixth series, 1848*, p. 796.
[2] Nicholls, *Ir. poor law*, pp 343, 404.

nearly full in the first half of 1851, at least in Munster and Connacht, with over 263,000 inmates early in June of that year.[1]

Throughout the famine years cost was a primary consideration in nearly all administrative decisions about the character and quantity of relief. On a per capita basis outdoor relief was actually far cheaper than the expense of main-tenance in the workhouse. Thus in the week ending on 1 July 1848 the total cost of providing outdoor relief to almost 834,000 persons amounted to £21,800, or slightly more than 6d. per head. By contrast, the average weekly expense of maintaining a pauper in the workhouse was as much as 2s. 4d. throughout 1847, 1s. 9d. in 1848, and 1s. 7d. in 1849.[2] The relative cheapness of outdoor relief on a per capita basis was not the result of the handsomeness of the workhouse diet but rather of lower overhead costs in outdoor assistance and the avoidance of expense for such things as clothing, bedding, firing, and medicine.

But for the economy-minded authorities, the much lower per capita cost of outdoor relief was completely cancelled by the almost universal preference of the poor for this form of assistance and their eagerness to avail of it wherever it was offered. Unless this eagerness could be restrained, the resources of local ratepayers would be overwhelmed. The enormous difficulty that the guardians experienced in collecting the rates throughout most of Munster and Connacht was a constant reminder of the financial fragility of the poor law system. Another motive for fiscal restraint was the common assumption of officials that the Irish poor were thoroughly unscrupulous in claiming public assistance, capable of almost limitless imposition and duplicity. (It rarely occurred to the authorities that the niggardliness of the poor law system itself greatly encouraged cheating and lying.) Erecting defences against the profligate abuse of outdoor relief by those who craved it therefore became an unending official preoccupation.

One such defence was the insistence of the poor law commissioners that only cooked food be issued by the local guardians to those qualified for outdoor relief, and that these paupers come each day to receive it. When food rations were distributed once a week instead of every day (Sundays excepted), observed the commissioners, the thriftless paupers too often consumed their weekly supply in three or four days.[3] This problem might have suggested to the commissioners as well as the local guardians that the cause of the premature exhaustion of a weekly supply was less the paupers' improvidence and more the inadequacy of the rations. These usually contained 1 lb of Indian meal a day for an adult and ½ lb for a child under twelve years. A dietary scale very similar to this had been sanctioned by the central board of health early in 1847 as suffi-cient to prevent malnutrition. In some unions, however, the guardians distri-buted less than the recommended quantity or its equivalent in soup. And yet

[1] Ibid., p. 404.
[2] Ibid., pp 397, 404.
[3] *Papers relating to proceedings for relief of distress; sixth series, 1848*, pp 297–8.

even the approved scale was eventually recognised to be seriously inadequate. Early in May 1848, after having again sought the opinion of the board of health but this time with a different result, the commissioners informed boards of guardians that 'the daily allowance to an able-bodied man [who is] required to work for eight to ten hours each day should be not less than $1\frac{3}{4}$ lb of raw meal or $2\frac{1}{2}$ lb of baked bread—a scale which ... may be considered applicable to the daily ration of oatmeal, Indian cornmeal, or wheaten meal'.[1] The numerous reports of deaths among paupers in supposedly regular receipt of outdoor relief probably prompted this belated reassessment by the central authorities, but it does not appear that local boards of guardians generally increased the rations.[2]

This is hardly surprising. The insistence of the commissioners on the daily issue of cooked rations was prompted at least as much by their desire to cut costs as by their concern to ensure adequate nutrition. As they told the vice-guardians of Clifden union in west Galway in March 1848, 'the great point to be borne in mind is the due relief of destitution in the manner which is at the same time the most effectual and the most economical'.[3] It was obvious (or it should have been) that such factors as sickness, infirmity, inclement weather, and the necessity for long walks to the depots all served to reduce the number of claimants when rations had to be collected as often as once a day. (Some boards of guardians, however, did grant weekly allowances in food or money to the impotent poor relieved outside the workhouse.) It was also commonly observed by relief officials, as pointed out earlier, that the substitution of cooked food for raw meal also had the effect of lessening the number of claimants for assistance, and largely for this reason the commissioners strongly urged local boards of guardians early in 1848 to set up again the soup boilers that had been used so effectively and so economically in 1847.

But it proved extremely difficult to resurrect the elaborate local administrative machinery that had sustained the soup kitchens. Boards of guardians found it much easier to delegate the task of food distribution to meal contractors or shopkeepers. As a result, many fewer soup kitchens were set up or reestablished, thus often leaving the destitute with longer journeys to make for their cooked rations. By placing their boilers four miles apart, the Clifden vice-guardians hoped in March 1848 to limit the travels of the poor in that union to a maximum of two miles coming for soup and two miles returning home. But in numerous unions this level of density was not achieved. Unless the length of the journey could be kept within reasonable bounds, the cooked food carried by able-bodied labourers to their dependants was apt to spoil by the time they arrived home, and, in addition, the impotent poor were liable to suffer extreme hardship. In the great majority of unions the guardians were therefore unable

---

[1] *Papers relating to proceedings for the relief of the distress and state of unions and workhouses in Ireland; seventh series, 1848*, p. 13 [999], H.C. 1847–8, liv, 333.

[2] T. P. O'Neill, 'The organisation and administration of relief, 1845–52' in Edwards & Williams, *Great famine*, p. 252.

[3] *Papers relating to proceedings for relief of distress; sixth series, 1848*, p. 298.

to comply with the commissioners' instructions. In May 1849 all food rations were distributed raw in as many as twenty-three of the thirty-one unions that then employed labourers outside of the workhouse. In six other unions some of the food was issued cooked and some in a raw state; only in the remaining two unions was cooked food alone distributed.[1]

The labour test of destitution was a great deal more effective as a defence against what the authorities considered the inveterate propensity of the poor to abuse outdoor relief. The work usually assigned—stone-breaking—was itself hated. The popular attitude towards such work was epitomised by some applicants for outdoor assistance in Newcastle union (County Limerick), who declared in February 1848 that 'they would rather die than break stones'.[2] Many ratepayers objected to this type of unproductive labour as well, believing that their precious money might have been put to better use. But the poor law commissioners patiently explained that such barren work was the best calculated to hold down the rates, or rather to keep them from rising even higher. Just as the nature of the labour itself discouraged applicants, so too did the long hours of toil. At first, as many as ten hours were prescribed by the commissioners, although later eight hours of stone-breaking were required in most unions. The overseers initially employed to enforce this harsh regime often showed too much laxity and were replaced by tougher ones. The overseers were generally obliged to call the roll of all the labourers in each working party two or three times a day, and those not in attendance (a substantial portion frequently were not) could be and often were removed from the outdoor relief lists.

The last major test of destitution—the Gregory clause barring from public relief anyone holding more than a quarter-acre of land—was by far the worst in its consequences. Before this draconian provision was inserted in the poor law in June 1847, the central relief authorities had regularly urged local boards of guardians to extend assistance to smallholders and their families on the sensible grounds that a refusal to do so would only increase the likelihood that their current destitution would become a permanent condition. Once the law was altered drastically in this respect (and it is only fair to stress that the law was changed not at the behest of the whig government but rather at the insistence of Irish landlords), the poor law commissioners believed that they had no choice but to enforce the new provision. At first, the general inclination of the commissioners and inspectors was to regard the change as beneficial. They saw the Gregory clause as another effective instrument for a more economical administration of public relief, another valuable bulwark against the deceptions and impositions practiced by the poor.

But it soon became all too apparent that the drawbacks of the clause were

[1] O'Neill, op. cit., p. 252.

[2] Captain Maxwell to commissioners, 12 Feb. 1848 (*Papers relating to proceedings for relief of distress; sixth series, 1848*, p. 584).

quite serious even from the administrative viewpoint and that they were no less than murderous from a humanitarian perspective. On the one hand, the poor law commissioners received a stream of reports in 1848 and 1849 that landlords in the south and west were using—and abusing—the quarter-acre clause to turn bankrupt smallholders out of possession *en masse*. This was a matter of deep concern at least partly because the mass evictions reduced the effectiveness of the various tests of destitution, raised the costs of relief substantially, and further weakened the already precarious financial structure of the poor law system. In response to early reports of clearances the commissioners lamely asked their local officers to furnish written statements, given under oath, about the evictions. This time-wasting bureaucratic punctilio eventually gave way to a more sensible insistence that local relieving officers be given sufficient prior notice of impending evictions—itself a recognition that in the face of the law or even abuses of the law, there was little or nothing that the commissioners or their local agents could do to stem the rage for clearances.[1]

On the other hand, it also became obvious that the quarter-acre clause was indirectly a death-dealing instrument. A second stream of reports from Munster and Connacht conveyed to the commissioners the news that destitute smallholders were starving themselves and their families to death by refusing to surrender all but a quarter-acre of their holdings, thus disqualifying them from assistance out of the poor rates. Hardened relief officials could of course say, as they often did, that they were powerless to help those who would not help themselves by doing what the law required. But when specific cases of 'voluntary' starvation were investigated closely, it was repeatedly found that the victims had substantial reasons for their refusals, particularly the entirely justifiable fear of the demolition of their houses or the loss of an opportunity for landlord-assisted emigration.[2] As the vice-guardians of Scariff union in west Clare explained to the commissioners in February 1848,

There is the greatest reluctance to surrender to the landlord, even in cases where many years' arrears of rent are due; in most cases the land would be given up if the cabin could be retained, but the consequence of surrendering the cabin with the land is that the cabin is immediately demolished, and the recent tenant becomes a permanent pauper, without a home.[3]

Cottiers who retained only their cabins and then secured assistance in the workhouse often found that landlords took advantage of their absence to unroof their houses. Other tenants were cajoled into giving up possession of their land with false assurances that they would be granted outdoor relief. Still others engaged in bogus surrenders, but these were usually detected by their landlords or the guardians (often the same people). Under these circumstances

[1] Below, pp 332–49.
[2] Below, pp 337–44.
[3] *Papers relating to proceedings for relief of distress; sixth series, 1848*, p. 506.

a great number of smallholders simply clung to their land against the odds of survival. The case of Michael Bradley, who 'died from want' early in 1848, was typical of thousands of others. Bradley 'held two or three acres of land [near Louisburgh in County Mayo], and, therefore, never applied to the relieving officer for assistance; but left his home for the purpose of begging, and died on the side of the road, within two miles of the town of Westport'. Bradley's neighbours were also 'now actually starving; but still are unwilling to abandon their little farms'. In concluding his report on the Bradley case to the poor law commissioners, the inspector of Westport union remarked: 'I may add that such cases are not peculiar to Louisburgh, but are to be found in almost every district in the union.'[1] Indeed, his observation was applicable all over the south and west of Ireland.

Although the poor law commissioners steadfastly adhered to the strict letter of the law against relieving the actual occupiers of more than a quarter-acre, the Gregory clause was eventually relaxed for their wives and children. For almost a year after its enactment in June 1847, the commissioners had opposed giving assistance to such dependants, even when assured that they were starving. But in late May 1848, after taking legal advice on this question, the commissioners sent a circular letter to all boards of guardians informing them that the destitute dependants of 'obstinate' smallholders were now eligible to be relieved in the workhouse or even out of doors if the workhouse was full.[2] The guardians were needlessly cautioned, however, against granting assistance 'systematically and indiscriminately to the wives and children of persons occupying more than a quarter of an acre of land when the legislature has expressly declared that such occupiers are not to be deemed destitute'. Rather ludicrously, the guardians were also instructed that they could prosecute such occupiers under the vagrancy laws if through wilful neglect they allowed their wives or children to become destitute and chargeable to the rates. (That wilful neglect would be hard to prove in the midst of famine seems to have been grudgingly admitted.) The commissioners concluded by congratulating themselves for giving to the local guardians the legal means 'for the better securing [of] an object which must be regarded as the principal aim of every poor law, viz, the preservation of human life'.[3] How hollow this expression of sentiment rings in the modern ear!

Once again, however, the perceived problem of imposition and deception resurrected itself. Already, the local guardians were contending with innumerable applications for relief from women who asserted that they had been deserted by their husbands, and from children whose parents had allegedly died or abandoned them. Most such applications were bona fide, but a substantial number were bogus in the sense that the husbands or fathers (and sometimes

---

[1] *Papers relating to proceedings for relief of distress; seventh series, 1848*, p. 9.
[2] Ibid., pp 10–11.
[3] Ibid., p. 12.

mothers) were unwilling to submit themselves to workhouse discipline or to stone-breaking out of doors. After the dependants of destitute smallholders were declared eligible for assistance in May 1848, the difficulties of identifying bogus claimants were compounded. Almost all boards of guardians felt duty-bound to make the effort, but many experienced frustration and anger as they went about the task. The guardians of Mallow union in County Cork complained to the poor law commissioners in June 1849 that 'thirty individuals having twenty-three children have this day applied for admission to the work-house, stating that they had been deserted by their wives or husbands respect-ively, an increasing evil for the prevention of which the legal remedies are not found efficacious'.[1] In some unions the guardians adopted a restrictive inter-pretation of the policy on dependants enunciated by the commissioners. Thus in Bandon union the guardians instructed the master of the workhouse in September 1848 to discharge all paupers whose husbands, fathers, or mothers were outside the house, although he was cautioned to 'use a discretion in [the] case of children who were too young and not strong enough to be sent away'.[2]

What made the rigid enforcement of the quarter-acre clause as well as the workhouse and labour tests of destitution seem so essential to central and local relief officials was the inability of the financial structure of the poor law system to sustain a greatly increased burden. On this vital point British policy was terribly misguided. The dictum that Irish property should carry the full weight of relieving Irish poverty may have been a reasonable proposition for ordinary times and circumstances, but in the face of a catastrophic famine, it was a prescription for both horribly inadequate resources and the ruin of much Irish property. Though the famine years witnessed intense conflict between land-lords and tenants, they were both agreed on at least one point: the British government and parliament had scandalously abdicated their responsibility for meeting a major share of the costs of famine relief after September 1847. Irish landlords were not happy to pay rates. Indeed, the active or passive opposition of ordinary ratepayers to the collection of taxes was often attributed to the instigation or bad example of their disgruntled betters among the landed elite. Landlord hostility to the poor law system during the famine was thoroughly understandable. First of all, they were responsible for discharging the entire rates of every holding valued at £4 or less and for paying half the poor rates of all holdings valued at more than £4. The former liability served as a major inducement to the mass eviction of bankrupt smallholders so that the landlords would not have to endure simultaneously both heavy rates and unpaid rents. Second, each poor law union was supposed to be self-financing, and landlords whose estates were located in the impoverished unions of the south and west

---

[1] Minute book, Mallow board of guardians, 1849–50, 15 June 1849, p. 100 (Cork Archives Council).
[2] Minute book, Bandon board of guardians, 1848–9, 23 Sept. 1848, p. 288 (Cork Archives Council).

felt deeply aggrieved that the burden of providing for an extraordinary calamity like the famine should fall so disproportionately on their shoulders. They saw no reason why they should be held financially accountable for the peculiar geographical incidence of an event for which the responsibility should have been national and ultimately imperial.

Above all, it was the overwhelming burden of the rates in unions where mass destitution prevailed that condemned the poor law system in the eyes of its ratepaying critics. In the province of Munster, with thirty-six unions, there were as many as eleven where rates of between 5s. and 10s. in the pound would have been necessary to meet the expenses incurred under the poor law during the year ending 29 September 1848. In two additional Munster unions—Kenmare in Kerry and Scariff in Clare—average poor rates of 10s. 3d. and 12s. 6d. respectively would have been required. The position in Connacht was even worse. In more than half of the unions there (ten out of eighteen), a sum equal to at least 25 per cent of the valuation (5s. in the pound) would have been necessary in rates to satisfy poor law expenditures in the year 1847–8. In four Connacht unions—Ballina, Ballinrobe, Clifden, and Westport—rates exceeding 50 per cent of the valuation would have been required. In Clifden union, the worst placed in this respect in the country, not even a sum equivalent to the whole valuation would have sufficed, for an average rate of 24s. 4d. in the pound would have been necessary to discharge expenditures.[1] As if this were not bad enough, 1848–9 brought even heavier financial pressures.

Not surprisingly, where the poor rates actually levied surpassed 25 per cent of the valuation, resistance to their collection was widespread. Indeed, opposition was common even in some unions where they did not reach that level. Little of the resistance involved violence. Ratepayers hid their livestock from the collectors and engaged in generally non-violent rescues when cattle, sheep, or pigs were seized. But the guardians and their collectors were relentless in pursuing defaulters, and the massive arrears of 1847 were greatly reduced in 1848 and 1849. Apart perhaps from scrutinising applications for relief, the business of supervising the collection of the rates occupied more of the time of the guardians and inspecting officers than any other issue.

In the most distressed unions of the south and the west, however, the guardians were unable to collect enough money to meet their liabilities, and they often hesitated to strike additional rates in the knowledge that to do so would be largely futile or even counterproductive for the collection of rates that had been struck earlier. As arrears accumulated in these unions and bills fell due, the government had to issue loans from its own coffers or to call on the funds of the philanthropic British Association. The need was actually greater in the financial year 1848–9, when expenditures under the poor law reached nearly £2.2 million, compared with £1.7 million in the previous year.[2]

[1] *Papers relating to proceedings for the relief of the distress and state of unions and workhouses in Ireland; eighth series, 1849; appendix*, p. xl [1042], H.C. 1849, xlviii, 480.   [2] Nicholls, *Ir. poor law*, p. 395.

By mid-1849 twenty-two unions in the west and the south-west, with a combined population of almost one and a half million, were more or less bankrupt; some of them in fact had been in that condition for many months. Characteristically, the government was unwilling to continue subsidising them with loans. It therefore instituted in June 1849 what was called a rate-in-aid. This device entailed the levying of a special rate of 6*d.* in the pound, 2.5 per cent of the valuation of all electoral divisions throughout the country, and was designed to raise nearly £323,000. A second rate-in-aid of 2*d.* in the pound was imposed in December 1850 and netted about £99,000.[1] Outside of the unions that benefited from them, the rates-in-aid were highly unpopular. There were loud complaints that if the act of union meant anything tangible, these special rates should have been levied not on Irish unions alone but on those of England, Scotland, and Wales as well. Harried ratepayers in Connacht and Munster could now say that the government had in effect conceded their point about the unfairness of the fiscal structure of the Irish poor law, but the step had been taken so belatedly and its effects were so restricted that even in the west and the south the government reaped little credit from its decision.

It will be convenient here to summarise the contributions of the British government towards the costs of famine relief in Ireland. The treasury calculated in 1850 that its total outlay since 1845 amounted to £8.1 million. Of this sum, less than half consisted of grants from imperial resources. The most important grant came in 1848 when the government remitted half of the total cost (£4.8 million had been spent altogether) of the public works carried out between October 1846 and June 1847. This remission, together with the grants extended under the relief schemes of 1845–6 and the soup kitchen act of 1847, amounted to less than £3.6 million. The rest of treasury outlays—a sum of slightly more than £4.5 million—consisted of loans that were supposed to be repaid out of Irish taxes. But only a small portion of these (less than £600,000) had been discharged by 1850, when most of the outstanding debts (about £3.7 million) were consolidated and refinanced, with repayment to come in annuities extending over forty years and bearing interest at an annual rate of 3.5 per cent. The burden of liquidating these debts fell most heavily on the western and south-western unions, which continued to be distressed after 1850 and therefore had great difficulty in paying their annuities. Finally, Lord Aberdeen's coalition government decided in 1853 to cancel all remaining debts completely, although it destroyed any possibility of Irish gratitude for this concession by increasing duties on Irish spirits and by extending the income tax to Ireland at the same time.[2] Thus in the end, taking into account treasury grants since 1845 and the annuities remitted in 1853, British governments—

---

[1] Nicholls, *Ir. poor law*, pp 359, 375–6.

[2] 16 & 17 Vict., c. 34 (28 June 1853); T. P. O'Neill, 'The organisation and administration of relief, 1845–52' in Edwards & Williams, *Great famine*, pp 255–6; below, p. 411.

Peel's, Russell's, and Aberdeen's—contributed about £7 million to the costs of famine relief.

While it has frequently been said that this was not nearly enough, it has less often been pointed out that the British government contribution was considerably less than what was raised in Ireland itself. By far the most important Irish contribution to the costs of famine relief came through the collection of poor rates. Altogether, expenditures under the poor laws from 30 September 1846 to 29 September 1851 amounted to almost £7.3 million. To this figure should be added about £300,000 incurred for poor law expenses in the first nine months of 1846 (the sum of £435,000 was spent during that year as a whole).[1] Although a small portion of poor law outlays was covered by advances (unrepaid) from the treasury, the great bulk of the money was actually extracted from Irish ratepayers. The other main Irish source of famine relief was the exceptional employment furnished by landlords. In part, this was financed out of private income, and we can only guess at its magnitude. But most of the money was borrowed from the government under the land improvement acts, and nearly all of these loans were eventually repaid. Between mid-1847 and the end of 1851 landlords borrowed a total of £1.2 million for land improvement projects, the great majority of which were designed to alleviate distress associated with the famine.[2] Even if private subscriptions for relieving destitution that were raised within the country are left out of account (perhaps they amounted to £1 or £2 million in addition), it is clear that Ireland itself contributed more to the costs of famine relief than did the well endowed but miserly treasury.

But the treasury, or rather the political elite that controlled its disbursements, was not always miserly, and that is just the point. In assessing the woeful inadequacy of government outlays for famine relief, Joel Mokyr has drawn attention to the fact that Britain spent no less than £69.3 million on 'an utterly futile adventure in the Crimea' in 1854–6, and as Mokyr plausibly maintains, 'half that sum spent in Ireland in the critical years 1846–9 would have saved hundreds of thousands of lives'.[3] Another way of putting British government expenditure on famine relief into perspective is to note that British outlays for national defence since 1815 had averaged over £16 million a year, and that the annual average tax revenue of the United Kingdom in the late 1840s was about £53 million.[4] Had the political will existed to do more for the starving masses in Ireland, what happened there could have been far less tragic.

After this extended consideration of the application of British relief policies in Ireland during the famine, it is appropriate to ask if there is any justification for the charge of genocide levelled by (among others) the revolutionary Irish

---

[1] Nicholls, *Ir. poor law*, pp 323, 395.

[2] *Fiftieth annual report from the commissioners of public works in Ireland, with appendices, 1881–82*, p. 16 [C 3261], H.C. 1882, xx, 302.

[3] Mokyr, *Why Ire. starved*, p. 292. Cf. above, pp 297–9.

[4] G. R. Porter, *The progress of the nation . . .* (London, 1851), p. 506; J. H. Clapham, *An economic history of modern Britain: free trade and steel, 1850–1886* (Cambridge, 1932), p. 397.

nationalist John Mitchel (1815–75) and the respected British historian A. J. P. Taylor. In his extraordinary book *The last conquest of Ireland (perhaps)*, first published in 1861, Mitchel passionately maintained that Britain possessed the power and wealth needed to save Ireland from the famine disaster and that the withholding of the means of salvation could only be ascribed to malignant motives. In spite of his evident distortions of fact and his suppression of evidence that did not fit his thesis, Mitchel's scathing book has great rhetorical force, a power that it gains from its savage irony. As Thomas Flanagan has well said, 'surely, the reader of Mitchel's account finds himself thinking against his will, surely this intricate machinery of ineffective relief, these proliferating committees and commissions which produce nothing save lists of the dead and the starving, could not have issued from a wholehearted desire to keep the Irish people alive, however great the expense to British trade and the British treasury?'[1]

Without attributing malevolent intentions to the responsible British ministers and officials, A. J. P. Taylor has also characterised their policies as genocidal. In reviewing Cecil Woodham-Smith's *The great hunger: Ireland, 1845–9* (London, 1962) in the *New Statesman* shortly after its publication, Taylor compared famine-stricken Ireland to Bergen-Belsen ('all Ireland was a Belsen'—a gross exaggeration) and declared: 'The English governing class ran true to form. They had killed two million Irish people.'[2] But unlike Mitchel, Taylor does not argue that the English rulers of Ireland deliberately chose to pursue a campaign of extermination. As he points out, 'Russell, Wood, and Trevelyan were highly conscientious men, and their consciences never reproached them'. Instead, they were led hopelessly astray by their economic convictions: 'they were gripped by the most horrible, and perhaps the most universal, of human maladies: the belief that principles and doctrines are more important than lives. They imagined that rules, invented by economists, were as "natural" as the potato blight.'[3]

If the charge of genocide could be sustained simply by showing that blind adherence to the doctrines of *laissez-faire* led to countless thousands of deaths (though certainly not two million) in Ireland during the late 1840s, then it may be taken as proved. But if, as most scholars would hold, there must also be a demonstration that British statesmen and their agents in Ireland were knowing and willing collaborators in a deliberate campaign of extermination, then the allegation of genocide is not only unproven but not even worth making. Still, that the charge has been levelled at all is one measure of how radically mistaken were the actions and inactions of the politicians and administrators responsible for relief measures during the great famine. It is true that at times, especially

[1] Thomas Flanagan, introduction to John Mitchel, *Jail journal* (University Press of Ireland ed., 1982), p. xxxi; see also below, pp 507–8.
[2] A. J. P. Taylor, *Essays in English history* (Harmondsworth, 1976), pp 73, 78.
[3] Ibid., p. 74.

during the operation of the soup kitchen scheme, accepted economic principles were reluctantly abandoned. Yet what made by far the greater impression was not how many people were kept alive by soup in the late spring and summer of 1847, but rather how many people were allowed to die at other times because they were not fed when they could have been. Many aspects of British relief policy deserve censure, but the severest condemnation should be aimed at the paltry level of financial aid rendered by the British government after September 1847. In this sense A. J. P. Taylor is essentially correct in saying of Peel's successors that 'when crisis arose, they ran away from it'.[1]

[1] Ibid.

CHAPTER XVII

Landlords and tenants

JAMES S. DONNELLY, JR

I T was possible for Irish landlords who looked back on the great famine from the vantage point of the mid-1850s to regard that cataclysmic event as advantageous, on balance, to their interests. A Kerry landlord who dined with the visiting Sir John Benn-Walsh in October 1852 crudely went 'the whole length of saying that the destruction of the potato is a blessing to Ireland'.[1] But it was much more difficult for landlords to adopt such a view during the famine itself. Over much of the country the difficulties created by the famine seemed decidedly to outweigh the opportunities that it opened up. The two most serious problems facing landlords, especially in the west and the south, were those of collecting rent and finding the means, out of their diminished incomes, to discharge heavy poor rates and to provide additional employment. Though no landlord is known to have starved during the famine, a substantial number wound up in the encumbered estates court established for insolvent Irish landlords in 1849.[2]

Because there were enormous variations, even within the same region, it is dangerous to generalise about the degree to which the rental incomes of landowners were reduced during the famine years. It is essential, however, to distinguish between the fortunes of the larger landlords and the losses of small landlords, especially those who held only or mostly intermediate interests and were not owners in fee. Two highly important determinants of the rate of collection or default were of course the location of the estate in the varied geography of destitution and the size of holdings on the estate. Whereas many owners of the overcrowded estates in the west and south-west were threatened with ruin because of unpaid rents, their counterparts in the north-east, the east midlands, and the south-east often escaped with modest or light losses. In addition, a great deal depended on whether the landlord generally let his land directly to the occupiers or to intermediate landlords, commonly called middlemen, who sublet their holdings to smaller tenants and cottiers. For a variety of reasons but especially because it entailed a loss of income and of

---

[1] J. S. Donnelly, jr (ed.), 'The journals of Sir John Benn-Walsh relating to the management of his Irish estates, 1823–64' in *Cork Hist. Soc. Jn.*, lxxix (1974), p. 119.
[2] 12 & 13 Vict., c. 77 (28 July 1849).

control over tenant access to land, the middleman system had been under attack from landlords and their agents since the late eighteenth century. But its eradication was a highly protracted process, lasting much longer on some estates than on others, and not completed in many districts until the famine or even later. A survey of the estates of Trinity College, Dublin, carried out in 1843 showed that there were 12,529 tenants on the 195,000 acres owned by the college in sixteen different counties, mostly in Kerry and Donegal. But less than 1 per cent of these 12,500-odd tenants 'held directly from the college, while 45 per cent held from a college lessee, and 52 per cent held from still another middleman who was a tenant to a college lessee'.[1]

For perhaps a majority of the middlemen who had escaped eradication earlier, the famine and the agricultural depression of 1849–52 spelt the extinction of their position as intermediate landlords. They were ground into dust between the upper and nether millstones. Head landlords, having long wanted to oust them and to appropriate their profit rents, generally refused to grant them abatements. 'I have never made an allowance to middlemen or tenants having beneficial interest [i.e., the benefit of a long lease]', declared the agent of the Cork estates of Viscount Midleton in February 1852,[2] and few agents or their employers departed from this rule: it was either pay up or leave. But to pay up was a tall order. In the typical case the minor gentleman or large farmer who assumed the role of middleman had as his tenants a horde of small farmers, cottiers, and sometimes labourers—the very classes that were reduced to destitution or worse by the famine. When his tenants defaulted in their payments, sometimes in spite of large abatements, the middleman's profit rent sharply contracted or disappeared altogether, and he himself often fell into serious arrears in discharging the head rent owed to the proprietor. Some intermediate landlords whose profit rents were greatly reduced still managed to meet their obligations to the head landlord, but when they did not, the head landlord was usually quick to oust them.

The liquidation of middlemen had been the consistent policy of Sir John Benn-Walsh ever since he succeeded to extensive estates of over 10,000 acres in Cork and Kerry in 1825, and the impact of the famine allowed him to bring the process almost to completion. At Grange near Cork city, as he noted in August 1850, the main middleman 'got greatly into arrear and I brought an ejectment for £800', a sum that represented more than twice the annual head rent.[3] On Benn-Walsh's much larger Kerry property three townlands near Listowel were in the hands of a middleman named Leake, whose doubtful legal title and financial embarrassment made him a tempting target for attack. By 1850 Leake 'was getting into arrear, and in consequence of the distressed state of the

[1] Samuel Clark, *Social origins of the Irish land war* (Princeton, 1979), p. 35.
[2] Thomas Foley to Joseph Tatham, 12 Feb. 1852 (Midleton papers, Guildford Muniment Room, Surrey).
[3] Donnelly, op. cit., p. 111.

country we understood that he had little or no profit out of the farm', observed Benn-Walsh. 'We accordingly brought an ejectment, to which Mr Leake took no defence, and entered into possession last July [1851].'[1] Among the other middlemen remaining on his Kerry estate at the start of the famine, one was evicted in 1846, the lease of a second expired in 1849 and was not renewed, and a third, noted Benn-Walsh in 1850, 'has fallen a victim to the times'.[2]

But while the impact of the famine enabled Benn-Walsh to oust nearly all of the surviving middlemen on his estates, it also greatly reduced the income that he derived from his Irish properties. Because he had been methodically removing middlemen long before the famine, when that crisis arrived, he had to contend directly with a mass of defaulting smallholders. This problem was especially acute on his Kerry estate, which was entirely concentrated in the poor law union of Listowel. Destitution in Listowel union was not nearly so bad as in Kenmare or several of the Connacht unions, but it was still severe. As Benn-Walsh recorded with alarm and dismay in mid-August 1849, 'since last year the debts [under the poor law] have increased eightfold and the union owes about £40,000. There are now 22,000 paupers on outdoor relief out of a population by the last census of 78,000, now probably 10,000 less.'[3] Even though destitution on Benn-Walsh's own property was probably substantially less than in the rest of Listowel union, he could hardly expect well paid rents. The combined annual rental of his Cork and Kerry estates in 1847 was £5,317, but as Benn-Walsh later pointed out, during the famine years his rents were 'merely nominal'.[4] The surviving documents do not permit any precise estimate of his losses, but to judge from a telling remark made in October 1852, they must have been enormous. The collection of the half-year's rent then payable had netted only £1,200, and yet Benn-Walsh observed with some glee, 'this is the best haul I have had since the famine'.[5] Allowances to his tenants for agricultural improvements certainly contributed to his losses, and so too did the heavy burden of poor rates, both directly and indirectly. 'The vice-guardians', he fumed in mid-August 1849, 'have already collected all the produce of the butter in rates, and they are prepared to strike another in September to secure the produce of the harvest. The fact is that the landed proprietors are now the mere nominal possessors of the soil. All the surplus produce is levied by the poor law commissioners.'[6] The bitter experience of Sir John Benn-Walsh, whose rental income may have fallen by more than half between 1846–7 and 1852, can probably be taken as representative of the fortunes of landowners with a multitude of small direct tenants in regions of acute destitution.

A strikingly more favourable situation existed for another and greater Kerry proprietor, the earl of Kenmare. His huge property was concentrated in the poor law union of Killarney, where the degree of destitution was almost as

[1] Donnelly, op. cit., p. 113.   [2] Ibid., pp 102, 105, 108.
[3] Ibid., p. 106.   [4] Ibid., pp 89, 119.
[5] Ibid., p. 120.   [6] Ibid., p. 106.

severe as that in Listowel, and yet Lord Kenmare managed to collect as much as £69,500 out of £81,100, or 86 per cent of the rents due between 1846 and 1850. In his case the explanation is simple: of the twenty-three townlands on his estate in Killarney union, no less than nineteen were still in the hands of middlemen as late as 1850, and these middlemen neither defaulted heavily (a rare happening in this region during the famine) nor received any abatement from Lord Kenmare. On all of his property in Kerry in 1850, the earl had only 300 direct tenants—a tiny fraction of the total number of occupiers—and they paid an average rent of almost £56.[1]

Other proprietors did almost as well as Lord Kenmare and occasionally better, even when they were not so heavily shielded by rent-paying middlemen. On the duke of Devonshire's great estates in the counties of Cork and Waterford, his agents were able to collect 84 per cent of the total of £359,200 due from the tenants between 1846 and 1853. But his properties, besides having been carefully managed for decades, were favourably situated—around Lismore in Waterford and around Bandon in Cork—with respect to the geography of destitution. Even at their worst in 1850 his payments for poor rates and other taxes represented only about 9 per cent of his annual rental.[2] A much smaller landowner, Sir Charles Denham Jephson-Norreys, whose estate was centred in and around the town of Mallow in Cork, received as much as 90 per cent of the rents owed by his tenants between 1846 and 1853. Well might his agent tell him in August 1850: 'Taking everything into account, you have come off well with your tenants. Indeed, you are the only man I know who gets anything like his income.'[3] Partly, the reason was that a relatively high proportion of the receipts came from town tenants and that the holdings of the rural ones were apparently much larger than average in size. Moreover, the estate was again favourably situated. As measured by poor law expenditures in the year 1847–8 in relation to its valuation, Mallow had less pauperism than any other union in the county.

But even landlords in districts with comparatively low levels of destitution could not expect to be as fortunate as Jephson-Norreys if their tenants were not large farmers. The experience of Robert Cole Bowen is instructive. From his tenants in the counties of Cork and Tipperary, Bowen managed to collect 81 per cent of the rents actually due from 1848 to 1853. But his income was not preserved even as well as this figure might suggest. Over the same period his yearly rental declined by about 14 per cent as tenants failed or were evicted

---

[1] Rental of the earl of Kenmare's estates, 1830–50 (Kenmare papers, in the possession of Mrs Beatrice Grosvenor, Killarney, Co. Kerry); *Cork Examiner*, 31 Dec. 1849.

[2] Rent receipts and disbursements of the duke of Devonshire's estates, 1818–90 (N.L.I., Lismore papers, MS 6929).

[3] Rental of the Jephson-Norreys estate, 1846–55; J. W. Braddell to Sir Charles Denham Jephson-Norreys, 9 Aug. 1850, in folder marked 'Mallow workhouse and poor law commissioners, 1847–50' (Jephson-Norreys papers, formerly in the possession of Commander M. C. M. Jephson, Mallow Castle, Mallow, Co. Cork).

without the prompt reletting of their farms. That numerous tenants disappeared from the rent roll is not at all surprising. On neither his Tipperary nor his Cork estate were the holdings large. On the Tipperary property the average yearly rent payable by the 144 tenants of 1848 was £19, and by the 111 tenants of 1853 it was £23. On the Cork estate the corresponding figure for the 37 tenants of 1848 was £27, and for the 28 tenants of 1853 it was £23.[1] To have numerous small or middling tenants spelt substantial losses for proprietors even when, as in this case, their estates lay outside zones of heavy pauperism.

If many landlords in relatively advantaged regions lost between 15 and 25 per cent of their rents during the late 1840s and early 1850s, it is easy to appreciate how badly the proprietors of Mayo, west Galway, and much of Clare must have fared. There the appalling degree of destitution and the extremely small size of holdings combined in a doubly destructive assault on landlord incomes. This combination was at its worst in County Mayo. According to a parliamentary return of 1846, no less than 75 per cent of the agricultural holdings in that county were valued at £4 or less for poor law taxation.[2] This meant, on the one hand, that the vast majority of tenants there quickly became unable to pay rent, and it also meant, on the other hand, that proprietors and other landlords were responsible for bearing nearly the whole burden of the poor rates. The marquis of Sligo, whose property was concentrated in Westport union, informed Lord Monteagle in October 1848 that for three years he had received no rent from his tenants. Though Lord Sligo undoubtedly obtained at least some money, it must have been only a small fraction of his nominal rental of about £7,200 a year, for in Westport union as many as 85 per cent of the occupiers had holdings valued at £4 or less. As early as March 1848 Lord Sligo owed almost £1,650 to the Westport board of guardians, a body that he served as chairman. This debt he was able to discharge only by borrowing £1,500, thus adding to his already heavy encumbrances, which reportedly cost him £6,000 annually. As he told Lord Monteagle, his dire financial condition placed him 'under the necessity of ejecting or being ejected'.[3]

Evict their debtors or be dispossessed by their creditors—this perceived choice provided a general rationalisation among landlords for the great clearances of defaulting or insolvent tenants that were carried out during the famine and its immediate aftermath. 'The landlords are *prevented* from aiding or tolerating poor tenants', declared the large Galway proprietor Lord Clanricarde at the end of 1848. 'They are compelled to hunt out all such, to save their property from the £4 clause.'[4] Time diminished only slightly the force and currency of this exculpation. In 1866 the owner of Mallow, Jephson-Norreys,

[1] Rental of Robert Cole Bowen's estates in the counties of Cork and Tipperary, 1847–53 (Tipperary County Library, Thurles, Bowen papers).

[2] *A return from the poor law commissioners . . .*, pp 34–5, H.C. 1846 (262), xxxvi, 502–3.

[3] Woodham-Smith, *Great hunger*, p. 364. See also D. E. Jordan, jr, 'Land and politics in the west of Ireland: County Mayo, 1846–82' (Ph.D. thesis, University of California–Davis, 1982), p. 85.

[4] Woodham-Smith, *Great hunger*, p. 364.

was still insisting that the £4 rating clause had 'almost forced the landlords to get rid of their poorer tenantry'.[1] From his experience as a poor law inspector in Kilrush union, Captain Arthur Kennedy (later Sir Arthur) carried away a different perspective. Many years later, he bitterly recalled: 'I can tell you . . . that there were days in that western county when I came back from some scene of eviction so maddened by the sights of hunger and misery I had seen in the day's work that I felt disposed to take the gun from behind my door and shoot the first landlord I met.'[2]

There was remarkably little resistance and still less shooting. Some large clearances occurred in 1846, but the great campaigns of what were soon branded as 'extermination' got under way in 1847 as the quarter-acre clause, starvation, and disease loosened the grip of smallholders on their land, and as the mounting tide of poor rates and arrears of rent propelled landlords into frenzied destruction of cabins. The number of evictions for the years 1846–8 can only be estimated roughly from the records of ejectments, but beginning in 1849 the constabulary office kept count of the evictions that came to the knowledge of the local police. In the earliest years of this effort, when estates were being cleared wholesale as well as piecemeal, it is likely that the police figures considerably understated the real total of dispossessions. From the two sets of statistics it is clear that evictions soared in 1847 and increased every year until 1850, when they reached a peak; they remained high in 1851 and 1852 before trailing off to a much lower level by 1854. Altogether, as the following table shows, the police recorded the eviction of 65,412 families from 1849 to 1854, but of this number, 16,672 families were readmitted to their holdings either as legal tenants (after paying rent) or as caretakers (without payment). Thus a minimum of 48,740 families were permanently dispossessed between 1849 and 1854. The average evicted family included about five members, and the total number of persons dispossessed amounted to almost a quarter of a million.[3]

This figure, however, leaves out of account the 'voluntary' surrenders of possession by tenants headed for the workhouse or the emigrant ship, or simply reduced to begging along the roads and especially in the towns. Although such surrenders usually were not reckoned officially as evictions, they often amounted to virtually the same thing, and they were legion. The Kerry and Cork estates of Sir John Benn-Walsh, for example, were 'very much weeded both of paupers and bad tenants during the famine'. This had been decorously managed by his agent, noted Benn-Walsh in September 1851,

---

[1] *Cork Constitution*, 2 June 1866.

[2] Sir W. F. Butler, *Sir William Butler: an autobiography* (2nd ed., London, 1913), p. 12. It was Butler who recorded what Kennedy said to Lord Carnarvon. Some transference of guilt was involved, since Kennedy had worked to keep a substantial number of the destitute from obtaining poor law relief.

[3] *Return . . . of cases of evictions . . . from 1849 to 1880 inclusive*, p. 3, H.C. 1881 (185), lxxvii, 727. See also *Returns . . . of the number of ejectments* [1846–9], H.C. 1849 (315), xlix, 235.

Evictions recorded by the constabulary, 1849–54

	evicted		readmitted		not readmitted	
	families	persons	families	persons	families	persons
1849	16,686	90,440	3,302	18,375	13,384	72,065
1850	19,949	104,163	5,403	30,292	14,546	73,871
1851	13,197	68,023	4,382	24,574	8,815	43,449
1852	8,591	43,494	2,041	11,334	6,550	32,160
1853	4,833	24,589	1,213	6,721	3,620	17,868
1854	2,156	10,794	331	1,805	1,825	8,989
total	65,412	341,503	16,672	93,101	48,740	248,402

without evictions, bringing in the sheriff, or any harsh measures. In fact, the paupers and little cottiers cannot keep their holdings without the potato, and for small sums of £1, £2, and £3 have given me peaceable possession in a great many cases, when the cabin is immediately levelled.[1]

Some of the clearances were associated with landlord-assisted emigration.[2] One of the largest such schemes was carried out by Francis Spaight, a famine-enriched partner in the 'great firm of merchants and corn dealers at Limerick', after he bought the Derry Castle estate around Killaloe in 1844. Spaight told an obviously impressed Sir John Benn-Walsh in 1849 that he 'had emigrated 1,400 persons, that this estate was now to be formed ... into an electoral division to itself, and that he then anticipated that the poor rates would be within his control and that the property would be a valuable and improving one'.[3] Spaight reported elsewhere that he had spent £3. 10s. per emigrant,[4] so that the whole operation, which extended over several years, probably cost just under £5,000. An even more far-reaching scheme was undertaken for the marquis of Lansdowne by William Steuart Trench after Trench became the agent for Lansdowne's congested estate in bankrupt Kenmare union in south Kerry during the winter of 1849–50. As Trench analysed the daunting situation, some 3,000 of the 10,000 paupers then receiving poor law relief in that union were chargeable to Lansdowne's property. For the landlord to give employment to so many people, Trench rejected as thoroughly impractical after a short and partial experiment. To maintain them in the workhouse would, he claimed, cost a minimum of £5 per head a year, thus leaving Lansdowne with an annual

[1] J. S. Donnelly, jr (ed.), 'The journals of Sir John Benn-Walsh relating to the management of his Irish estates, 1823–64' in *Cork Hist. Soc. Jn.*, lxxix (1974), p. 117.

[2] Below, pp 591–7.

[3] Donnelly, op. cit., p. 107.

[4] Oliver MacDonagh, 'Irish overseas emigration during the famine' in Edwards & Williams, *Great famine*, p. 474, n. 9.

bill for poor rates of £15,000 when the entire valuation of his property there barely reached £10,000 a year. He explained to Lansdowne that 'it would be cheaper to him, and *better for them* [i.e., his pauper tenants], to pay for their emigration at once than to continue to support them at home'.[1] Lansdowne concurred, and over the course of three or four years in the early 1850s, slightly more than 4,600 persons were shipped off to the United States or Canada. The total expense exceeded £17,000, and the average cost per emigrant (£3. 14s.) was a few shillings more than that incurred by Francis Spaight.[2]

Most proprietors who undertook such schemes did so, like Spaight, in 1846–8, when landlord-assisted emigration was at its height. In contrast to Lansdowne, very few landowners engaged in the practice extensively after 1850. The schemes of both men, however, were highly atypical in their scale. Oliver MacDonagh has concluded that landlord-assisted emigration from all of Ireland in the years 1846–52 'can scarcely have exceeded 50,000 in extent'.[3] Since all of Spaight's 1,400 tenants as well as about 3,500 of Lansdowne's had departed before 1853, this would mean that these two proprietors alone were responsible for nearly 10 per cent of the estimated total. But like the usually much smaller emigration enterprises of other landlords, those of Spaight and Lansdowne were portrayed as entirely voluntary. Spaight insisted that his tenants left willingly and without rancour,[4] and according to Trench, Lansdowne's paupers greeted the offer of free passage to any North American port as almost 'too good news to be true' and rushed to seize the unexpected opportunity.[5] Everyone who accepted, Trench asserted, did so 'without any ejectments having been brought against them to enforce it, or the slightest pressure put upon them to go'.[6] Yet by no means all of those whom landowners assisted to leave were given a choice between staying and going. For a great many, the choice, sometimes implicit and at other times made quite explicit, lay between emigrating with modest assistance and being evicted. Moreover, as MacDonagh has argued, it was a pretence to say that a pauperised tenant without the ability to pay rent or to keep his family nourished had a 'free' choice in the matter.

Yet even if the choice was highly constrained, it was far less inhumane than the total absence of an alternative, which is what the vast majority of estate-clearing landlords offered. West Clare in particular presented throughout the years 1848–50 the appalling spectacle of landlords cruelly turning thousands of tenants on to the roadside. This heartless practice first became intense in the winter of 1847–8 and the following spring, as one landlord after another joined the campaign. Furnishing a list of the many cabins unroofed or tumbled on six different properties in just two of the electoral divisions of Kilrush union, Captain Arthur Kennedy informed the poor law commissioners early in April

[1] W. Steuart Trench, *Realities of Irish life* (London, 1868), pp 122–4.   [2] Ibid., pp 132–3.
[3] MacDonagh, op. cit., p. 335.   [4] Ibid., p. 474, n. 9.
[5] Trench, op. cit., p. 124.   [6] Ibid., p. 125.

1848 that 'I calculate that 1,000 houses have been levelled since November and expect 500 more before July.' Those dispossessed, he declared, 'are all absolute and hopeless paupers; on the average six to each house! Enough to swamp any union or poor law machinery when simultaneously thrown upon it.'[1] Deceit and small sums of money were used to bring about acquiescence: 'the wretched and half-witted occupiers are too often deluded by the specious promises of under-agents and bailiffs, and induced to throw down their own cabins for a few shillings and an assurance of outdoor relief'.[2] Many of the evicted

betake themselves to the ditches or the shelter of some bank, and there exist like animals till starvation or the inclemency of the weather drives them to the workhouse. There were three cartloads of these creatures, who could not walk, brought for admission yesterday, some in fever, some suffering from dysentery, and all from want of food.

Other dispossessed families crowded into cabins left standing in neighbouring townlands 'till disease is generated, and they are then thrown out, without consideration or mercy'. The larger farmers in the vicinity of these clearances took advantage of them by getting 'their labour done in exchange for food alone to the member of the family [whom the farmer] employs, till absolute starvation brings the mother and helpless children to the workhouse; this is the history of hundreds'.[3] It is little wonder that Kennedy wanted to take his gun and shoot the first landlord he met.

This was in fact the history not alone of hundreds in Kilrush union in 1848 but of thousands throughout Clare during the famine years. A greater number of permanent evictions occurred in Clare in the period 1849–54, relative to the size of its population in 1851, than in any other county in Ireland. For that period as a whole its eviction rate was 97.1 persons per thousand. Altogether, nearly 21,000 people were permanently dispossessed in Clare from 1849 to 1854, according to the constabulary returns. Thus a county that comprised only 3.2 per cent of the population of Ireland in 1851 experienced 8.3 per cent of the total number of officially recorded evictions between 1849 and 1854. The eviction rate for Clare was even much higher than that for nearly all the other western counties. The corresponding rates for Kerry and Galway were 58.4 and 65.3 per thousand respectively, although for west Galway alone the rate of dispossession was much closer to that for Clare.[4]

Only in Mayo were evictions, relative to population, almost as numerous as those in Clare. From 1849 to 1854 over 26,000 Mayo tenants were permanently dispossessed, a figure that represented a rate of 94.8 persons per thousand of the 1851 population. With only 4.2 per cent of the inhabitants of the country,

[1] *Papers relating to proceedings for the relief of distress and state of the unions and workhouses in Ireland; sixth series, 1848*, p. 821 [955], H.C. 1847–8, lvi, 859.
[2] Kennedy to commissioners, 13 Apr. 1848 (ibid., p. 823).
[3] Kennedy to commissioners, 16 Mar., 13 Apr., 6 Apr. 1848 (ibid., pp 803–4, 823, 817).
[4] *Return . . . of cases of evictions from . . . 1849 to 1880 inclusive*, pp 8–10, H.C. 1881 (185), lxxvii, 732–4.

Mayo was the scene of no less than 10.5 per cent of all evictions in Ireland during the years 1849–54. But the temporal pattern of the clearances in Mayo was strikingly different from that in Clare, the rest of Connacht, or indeed the rest of Ireland. Whereas the total number of evictions in Ireland declined sharply after 1850, the toll in Mayo remained remarkably high during the early 1850s. Permanent dispossessions were more numerous there throughout the years 1851–3 than in 1849 and dropped below the level of 1849 only in 1854.[1] Part of the reason for this difference between Mayo and the rest of Ireland, it has been argued, is that Mayo landlords had less cause to engage in clearances before 1850 because a much higher proportion of the tenants there, 75 per cent of whom occupied holdings valued at £4 or less, surrendered their tiny plots to the landlords in order to qualify themselves for poor law assistance.[2] In addition, Mayo provided a much higher than average share of insolvent proprietors to the encumbered estates court, and there is an abundance of evidence that the new purchasers of these properties actively engaged in extensive evictions during the early 1850s.[3]

But even by long-established proprietors, and before 1850, there were some enormous clearances in Mayo, with entire villages of smallholders being erased from the map. Among the greatest of these depopulating landlords was the earl of Lucan, who owned over 60,000 acres. Having once said that he 'would not breed paupers to pay priests', Lord Lucan was as good as his word. In the parish of Ballinrobe, most of which was highly suitable for grazing sheep and cattle, he demolished over 300 cabins and evicted some 2,000 people between 1846 and 1849. Some of those dispossessed here may have been included among the almost 430 families (perhaps 2,200 persons) who, as Lucan's surviving but incomplete rent ledgers show, were 'removed' between 1848 and 1851. In this campaign whole townlands were cleared of their occupiers. The depopulated holdings, after being consolidated, were sometimes retained and stocked by Lord Lucan himself as grazing farms and in other cases were leased as ranches to wealthy graziers.[4]

Also belonging to the 'old stock' of Mayo proprietors who cleared away many tenants was the marquis of Sligo. His policy, he claimed in 1852, was rigorously selective. Though 'large evictions were carried out', only 'the really idle and dishonest' were dispossessed, while 'honest' tenants were 'freed from all [arrears] and given at a new fairly valued rent'. Once he had finished implementing this policy, he thought, perhaps one-quarter of his tenants would be forced to leave. Despite his earlier assertion that his was a case of 'eject or be ejected', Lord Sligo had a troubled conscience about his evictions.

[1] Ibid.
[2] D. E. Jordan, jr, 'Land and politics in the west of Ireland: County Mayo, 1846–82' (Ph.D. thesis, University of California–Davis, 1982), pp 90–91.
[3] P. G. Lane, 'The general impact of the encumbered estates act of 1849 on Counties Galway and Mayo' in *Galway Arch. Soc. Jn.*, xxxiii (1972–3), pp 45–51.
[4] Jordan, op. cit., pp 92–3.

He despised more indulgent landowners, such as Sir Samuel O'Malley and his own cousin G. H. Moore. He professed to be convinced that by refusing to evict for non-payment of rent, they were pursuing a course that would ultimately make necessary clearances far greater in scope than his own. To prove his point, he cited the fact that the indulgent O'Malley was eventually forced to evict on a large scale: for on O'Malley's property in the parish of Kilmeena near Westport 'the houses are being levelled till at least half [the tenants] are evicted and legally removed'. He severely upbraided Moore, saying that he would become 'a second Sir Samuel'. In concluding his shrill, self-exculpatory letter to Moore, Lord Sligo declared: 'In my heart's belief you and Sir Samuel do more [to] ruin and injure and persecute and exterminate your tenants than any [other] man in Mayo.'[1]

But while the old stock of Mayo proprietors did a fair share of the 'extermination' for which landlords were assailed in the national and local press, they received a strong helping hand in the early 1850s from the numerous new purchasers under the encumbered estates act. Quite a few of the new owners had in fact invested their money in the west of Ireland on the explicit understanding that the property that they were buying had already been or was in the process of being cleared of superfluous tenants. As the prospectus for the sale of the Martin estate in the Ballinahinch district of Galway delicately put the matter,

the number of tenants on each townland and the amount of their rents have been taken from a survey and ascertained rental in the year 1847; but it is believed many changes advantageous to a purchaser have since taken place, and that the same tenants by name and in number will not be found on the land.[2]

When new owners discovered that the contrary was true, they secured special court injunctions for the removal of such tenants, or they simply proceeded to oust the unwanted occupiers themselves, sometimes avoiding formal evictions by persuading the tenants to accept small sums as inducements to depart. Among the numerous new Mayo purchasers who behaved in one or another of these ways were Edward Baxter at Knockalassa near Cong, Captain Harvey de Montmorency at Cloongowla near Ballinrobe, Joseph Blake on the Abbey Knockmoy estate, and Lord Erne at Barna near Ballinrobe. Similar scenes— the succession of new landlords followed by the eviction of the old tenants and the consolidation of their holdings into much larger units—were occurring during the early 1850s in west Galway and parts of adjacent counties, where among the clearance-minded new owners were John Gerrard at Kilcoosh near Mount Bellew, Francis Twinings at Cleggan near Clifden, and James Thorngate on the Castlefrench estate.[3] 'In the revolution of property changes',

[1] Joseph Hone, *The Moores of Moore Hall* (London, 1939), pp 158–60.
[2] Lane, op. cit., p. 48.
[3] Ibid., pp 48–9.

observed the *Roscommon Journal* in July 1854, 'the new purchaser accelerates the departure of the aborigines of the country, by which he seems to imagine he has not only rid himself of their burden but enhanced the value of his property.'[1]

These clearances in Mayo and west Galway set the stage for a considerable expansion of the grazing or ranch system there during the 1850s. Both the old proprietors who escaped the encumbered estates court as well as the new owners avidly promoted the grazing system. Many of them retained at least part of the depopulated holdings in their own hands and, like Lord Lucan, stocked the land with cattle and sheep. But they also leased recently cleared tracts to new settlers, a substantial number of whom were of Scottish or English origin and set themselves up as graziers on a large scale. The land agent Thomas Miller estimated in 1858 that as many as 800 English and Scottish farmers had secured leases of large holdings in Mayo and Galway, which were almost exclusively devoted to the raising of livestock. Miller indicated that there were particularly heavy concentrations of new settlers in the districts of Hollymount, Newport, and Westport in Mayo as well as around Ballinasloe and Tuam in Galway.[2] In a few cases the new settlers were the victims of agrarian violence, but the vast majority escaped any immediate retribution, as did the proprietors who facilitated their entry into the western countryside. Yet the local resentment against these intruders from England and Scotland remained strong for decades and would eventually erupt into violence during the various phases of the land war in the late nineteenth and early twentieth centuries. Like the clearances themselves, their beneficiaries were remembered with a poisonous, ineradicable hatred.

By means of the great clearances of the late 1840s and early 1850s, as well as because of mass emigration and mass death, Irish landowners were able to achieve their long-desired objective of the consolidation of holdings on a large scale. The painstaking work of P. M. A. Bourke has convincingly demonstrated that the statistics on farm size appearing in the 1841 census cannot be used to gauge the degree of consolidation that took place between 1841 and 1851. The two most serious flaws of those statistics for comparative purposes are that in 1841 farm size was overwhelmingly expressed in terms of the larger Irish acre (1.62 statute acres), and that in the computation of farm size, waste land was excluded in 1841. 'Together,' declares Bourke, 'the two factors led to *a reduction of about one-half* in the apparent farm size' in contrast to the real picture that would have emerged if, as in 1847 and later, the statute acre had been taken as the invariable unit of measurement and waste land had been included along with pasture and arable.[3] Though it is possible to reconstruct the 1841 figures by applying some rough corrections to those data, Bourke has found it

---

[1] Ibid., p. 50.

[2] Thomas Miller, *The agricultural and social state of Ireland in 1858* (Dublin, 1858), pp 7, 12.

[3] P. M. A. Bourke, 'The agricultural statistics of the 1841 census of Ireland: a critical review' in *Econ. Hist. Rev.*, 2nd ser., xviii, no. 2 (Aug. 1965), pp 378–9.

Landlords and tenants

preferable to use in a modified form the returns on farm size compiled in 1844 or 1845 by the poor law commissioners. These returns are not fully comparable in all respects with the figures that appear in the annual series of agricultural statistics beginning in 1847, but the discrepancies are relatively minor. The results of Bourke's reworking of the poor law returns, together with the official statistics for 1847 and 1851, are presented in the following table.[1]

Changes in the distribution of holdings by size in Ireland, 1845–51

year	1 acre or less		1–5 acres		5–15 acres		over 15 acres	
	no.	%	no.	%	no.	%	no.	%
1845	135,314	14.9	181,950	20.1	311,133	34.4	276,618	30.6
1847	73,016	9.1	139,041	17.3	269,534	33.6	321,434	40.0
1851	37,728	6.2	88,083	14.5	191,854	31.5	290,404	47.8
% change, 1845–51		−72.1		−51.6		−38.3		+5.0

The discarding of the 1841 census data on farm size results in making the change effected by the events of the famine 'less sensational' but nevertheless quite striking. The number of holdings in the two smallest categories of size declined between 1845 and 1851 by almost three-fourths and by slightly over one-half respectively, and even holdings of five to fifteen acres fell in number by nearly two-fifths. Farms above fifteen acres increased modestly in number between 1845 and 1851, and rather dramatically in proportional terms—from less than a third of all holdings in 1845 to almost a half by 1851. There was never again so sudden and drastic a change in the structure of landholding in Ireland as that which occurred during and immediately after the famine. Though consolidation continued in the post-famine generations, it was usually a very gradual and piecemeal process. Furthermore, for that half of Irish tenants whose holdings did not exceed fifteen acres, there were severe limits to the gains that could be conferred even by a long period of agricultural prosperity like that of 1853–76, and such tenants of course remained highly vulnerable to the effects of economic downturns on their precarious condition.

In undertaking clearances of pauper tenants, landlords proved to be pitiless creditors, but they too had creditors who became equally remorseless in pressing their claims during the famine. A lavish style of living assumed before 1815 and not easily supportable under the conditions of depressed markets and lagging rents in peacetime, together with defective laws that permitted the accumulation of debts far beyond the value of estates, meant that already before

[1] Bourke, *Agricultural statistics*, p. 380.

the famine a substantial number of landlords were in a precarious financial condition. In fact, a significant number of heavily indebted landlords were past rescue. In 1844 receivers appointed by the court of chancery were administering 874 Irish estates with a combined annual rental of almost £750,000.[1] The owners of some of these properties were simply minors or lunatics, but most were bankrupts. Under different circumstances these insolvent proprietors might have satisfied their creditors by selling all or part of their estates. But because of defects in the law, especially the great difficulty and cost of tracing the encumbrances in separate registers in different courts and in the registry office of deeds, prospective purchasers were extremely wary of buying Irish land. Many estates of bankrupts continued under chancery administration for years (some for decades), and thus the backlog of insolvent landlords was very slow to be cleared. From such landlords tenants obviously received little or no assistance during the famine.

The great famine had the short-term effect of exacerbating the extreme sluggishness of the land market. On the one hand, it added substantially to the number of bankrupt and acutely embarrassed proprietors. Lost rents, heavy poor rates, and (in some cases) significant expenditures for employment erased what was for many a narrow margin of safety between income and out-goings even before 1845. Foreclosure notices and execution warrants soon began to rain down upon the heads of landlords unable to discharge the claims of mortgagees, bond holders, annuitants, and other creditors. As early as December 1846 one newspaper reported that 'within the last two months twelve hundred notices have been lodged in the Four Courts to foreclose mortgages on Irish estates'.[2] Certain landlords known to be embarrassed were hounded from pillar to post. Against Earl Mountcashell 'execution upon execution was issued ... until in December 1849 there were in the sheriff's hands executions to the amount of £15,000', and others in 1850 soon brought the total to about £20,000.[3] The earl derived some temporary relief from the fact that his son Lord Kilworth was then the high sheriff of County Cork, and his agent was the sub-sheriff, but other landowners in similar straits were not even that lucky.

On the other hand, the famine and the agricultural depression of 1849–52 had the result of greatly lowering the value of Irish land. According to one reliable report, the average rate of sale had fallen from twenty-five years' purchase of the annual rental before 1845 to only fifteen years' purchase by the spring of 1849.[4] Even though financially embarrassed proprietors needed to sell at least some property to stay afloat, they were generally unwilling to let it go at so great a sacrifice, and therefore they themselves were not about to initiate such ruinous transactions. Even creditors might not wish to force sales in cases where there was reason to fear that the proceeds would not be sufficient to

[1] *Return from the registrar's office of the court of chancery in Ireland...*, H.C. 1847–8 (226), lvii, 213.
[2] *Cork Examiner*, 14 Dec. 1846.   [3] *Cork Constitution*, 24 Nov. 1857.
[4] *Cork Examiner*, 13 May 1849.

discharge their claims in full because of a low sale price. Yet unless prices were low, and unless secure titles could be obtained, it was difficult to imagine that purchasers would be forthcoming, since the immediate prospects for reasonable returns on their investments were anything but attractive.

After an abortive effort to resolve the problem in 1848 by using the cumbersome machinery of the court of chancery,[1] the government finally broke the deadlock in July 1849 by passing the encumbered estates act, which established a new tribunal with drastic powers.[2] The three commissioners or judges of the court received authority to order sales on the application of a single encumbrancer as long as the annual charges and interest payments exceeded half the net yearly income of the land or leasehold. The creditors' interests were taken into account in the provision that allowed all encumbrancers to bid for the property or lease offered for sale, with the single exception of the encumbrancer on whose application the sale had been ordered, and even he could become the purchaser with the consent of the commissioners. The judges were also authorised to arrange exchanges and divisions, even of lands not subject to be sold under the act, if such steps would facilitate the sale of the encumbered property. They were also empowered to sell lands included in different applications in the same sale. Finally, the court received the authority to grant to purchasers of property sold under its aegis an indefeasible parliamentary title, secure against the claims of all previous creditors. The passage of the act signalled that the long-standing log jam in the land market was about to be broken, and throwing so much property into the market at once could only drive land values still lower. Even landlords who had no reason to expect forced sales themselves were disheartened. 'I am deeply affected by this most heavy stroke,' moaned Sir John Benn-Walsh in August 1849, 'by which my Irish property is rendered as valueless as a Jamaica estate.'[3]

The early operations of the court confirmed the worst fears of heavily indebted proprietors. In one of the largest sales some 62,000 acres in Cork and Antrim belonging to Lord Mountcashell, with a combined yearly rental of £18,500, were bought for £240,000, or thirteen years' purchase. During the proceedings a distraught Mountcashell 'was heard to exclaim that it was bad enough to have his estates confiscated, but to be sold up by a dwarf in a garret was more than he could endure!'—a reference to Commissioner Charles Hargreave, a very short man whose office was located in the bedroom storey of a house on Henrietta Street in Dublin.[4] An even greater loser was Viscount Gort, whose case aroused widespread popular sympathy because he had opposed clearances and had reputedly evicted no one from his property around Lough Cutra in south Galway. Moreover, though his unsettled estates were charged

[1] 11 & 12 Vict., c. 48 (14 Aug. 1848).
[2] 12 & 13 Vict., c. 77 (28 July 1849).
[3] J. S. Donnelly, jr (ed.), 'The journals of Sir John Benn-Walsh relating to the management of his Irish estates, 1823–64' in *Cork Hist. Soc. Jn.*, lxxix (1974), p. 106.
[4] A. M. Sullivan, *New Ireland* (2 vols, London, 1877), i, 197.

with debts of about £60,000, they had been valued at £150,000 as recently as 1842. When a mortgagee who had not received his interest during the famine forced their sale in the court, the various purchasers acquired great bargains. Thirteen years' purchase was apparently 'the highest [price] given at this sale' and 'many lots were sold at five'.[1] Lord Gort was even forced to part with his mansion, Lough Cutra Castle, which was also sold for much less than its value.

The many victims of this drastic process of course protested bitterly, but the commissioners stoutly defended the prevailing prices. In May 1851 they asserted that to calculate the rates of purchase from the printed rentals was a 'fallacious' exercise for several reasons: first, because the rents specified were often excessive even before 1846; secondly, because arrears amounting to several years' rent were usually owed to the previous owners; and thirdly, because the generally dilapidated condition of the property 'would necessarily require a heavy outlay by the incoming purchaser'.[2] Their case, however, is not very persuasive, nor was it then. The cheapness of most of the property sold before 1854 was repeatedly demonstrated by the far higher prices given for the same lands when they were resold through the court only a few years later. In fact, there was considerable speculation in the underpriced estates of bankrupt landowners during the early 1850s. The London *Morning Herald* reported in November 1853 that two English land companies were pooling small capitals to buy Irish property with the intention of selling it again at a substantial profit.[3] Solvent Irish proprietors were hardly above playing the same game of speculation, and the rewards could be handsome. The west Cork landowner John Becher was said to have bought a portion of the Holybrook estate in 1853 for £1,950 and to have resold it six years later for £4,050.[4] The Castle Hyde estate, purchased in December 1851 for £14,425 by Vincent Scully (M.P. for County Cork, 1852–7, 1859–65), was sold again in court in 1860 for nearly £45,000.[5] The superior of the Sisters of Mercy had paid £17,000 for Lord Gort's castle on Lough Cutra, intending to convert it into a noviciate for her order, but this plan was dropped and the castle was soon resold at a tidy profit of £7,000 above the original purchase price.[6]

Prices were at their lowest (generally from ten to fifteen years' purchase) during the early 1850s, when in fact the bulk of the most heavily encumbered estates were sold. Of the almost 4,300 petitions for sale presented to the court between January 1850 and March 1858, over three-quarters were lodged before 1855.[7] By the late 1850s Irish land had not only recovered but had now probably surpassed the levels of the late 1830s and early 1840s. By that time a large

---

[1] Ibid., p. 292. See also ibid., pp 291, 293–4.

[2] Report of commissioners to lord lieutenant, 3 May 1851, quoted in *Dublin Evening Post*, 13 May 1851.   [3] *Cork Examiner*, 28 Nov. 1853 (quoting *Morning Herald*).

[4] *Bessborough comm. evidence*, pt ii, p. 916 [C 2779–II], H.C. 1881, xix, 166.

[5] *Cork Examiner*, 11 Dec. 1860.

[6] Sullivan, op. cit., i, 292.

[7] *Hansard 3*, cl, 27.

portion of the petitions for sale were actually being lodged by necessitous land-owners themselves rather than by their creditors. Only six of the first 100 petitions to the court in 1849 had come from the owners, but as many as fifty-three out of the last 100 before September 1857 emanated from them.[1] There was little reason to hang back now that the land market was so buoyant. When the earl of Thomond sold almost all of his property in Clare and Cork in 1857, the 48,000 acres involved, with a total yearly rental of about £13,500, realised nearly £360,000, representing over twenty-six years' purchase. His 39,000-acre Clare estate alone, situated in the Ennis district, brought in more than thirty-two years' purchase. The buyers of his property were almost exclusively Irish; in the case of his Clare estate they were all said to be 'connected with that county and resident in it'.[2]

This was not what the whig ministers who framed the encumbered estates act had anticipated. They had fervently hoped that large numbers of wealthy British capitalists would invest their money in Irish property and begin to manage their new possessions on the most advanced lines. To some educated Britons, it seemed that no part of Ireland stood in greater need of British investment or was more likely to receive it than the impoverished west. 'In a few years more', *The Times* had declared hopefully at the start of this experiment, 'a Celtic Irishman will be as rare in Connemara as is the Red Indian on the shores of Manhattan.'[3] In fact, however, although most of Connemara did fall into the hands of the English Law Life Assurance Society, British capitalists formed only a small proportion of the purchasers throughout Ireland. Out of a total of 7,489 buyers up to the end of August 1857, just 309, or 4 per cent, were of English, Scottish, or foreign background; all the rest were Irish. Admittedly, the non-Irish purchasers often bought large estates, but of the gross proceeds of all sales conducted between October 1849 and August 1857 (about £20.5 million was realised), they provided only £2.8 million, or less than 14 per cent.[4]

A. M. Sullivan (editor of the *Nation* 1858–76) is mainly responsible for the legend that the overwhelmingly Irish purchasers were drawn predominantly from a commercial background. In his popular work, *New Ireland*, first published in 1877, Sullivan claimed that the new owners were 'chiefly mercantile men who have saved money in trade and invest it for a safe per-centage. They import what the country people depreciatingly call "the ledger and day-book principle" into the management of their purchases, which contrasts unfavourably in their minds with the more elastic system of the old owners.'[5] The appearance of a significant number of individuals, though not even close to a majority, from outside the ranks of the traditional landowning class naturally attracted contemporary attention, and the fact that some of them

---

[1] Sullivan, op. cit., i, 295.   [2] *Cork Constitution*, 29 Dec. 1857.
[3] Quoted in Sullivan, op. cit., i, 286.
[4] Ibid., p. 296.   [5] Ibid., p. 298.

aroused intense popular hostility by raising rents, pressing for arrears, or carrying out evictions gave rise to a prevalent view that the new owners in general were a breed different from and worse than the old masters of the soil whom they replaced. But a systematic analysis of the social backgrounds of the purchasers under the encumbered estates act in County Cork indicates that most of the new owners there came from the established landed and professional elites, with the sons of the gentry and nobility as well as landed gentlemen and aristocrats themselves constituting the most numerous group of buyers.[1]

Moreover, for every indulgent Lord Gort or Lord Kingston who crashed in the encumbered estates court, there was a Lord Lucan or a Lord Sligo who was anything but lax or elastic. The new owners in Mayo and Galway may have intensified the clearances there during the early 1850s, but whether the eviction rate in those counties would have been substantially lower without their coming is doubtful. Given what the old landlords were doing in Clare before 1850, tenants in that county would presumably have applauded a thoroughgoing change. There is, in short, no need to invent an invasion of the ranks of landowners by commercial men after 1850 to account for the tighter administration of Irish estates. What Sullivan termed 'the ledger and day-book principle' (this was not a country expression) was as evident among the continuing owners as among the new purchasers. The transformation of estate management and of landholding among tenants was the product of historical forces larger than mere changes of personnel.

[1] Donnelly, *Land & people of Cork*, p. 131.

CHAPTER XVIII

Excess mortality and emigration

JAMES S. DONNELLY, JR

L. M. CULLEN has argued that the great famine 'was less a national disaster than a social and regional one'.[1] This provocative statement has the merit of drawing attention to the wide social and regional variations in the incidence of famine-related destitution, mortality, and emigration. But to hold that the famine had the character of a national calamity is a defensible position, especially if one considers the combined effects of both excess deaths and emigration on the population levels of individual counties. Only six of the thirty-two counties lost less than 15 per cent of their population between 1841 and 1851. In another six counties the population in 1851 was from 15 to 20 per cent lower than it had been a decade earlier. Of the remaining twenty counties, nine lost from 20 to 25 per cent of their population, while eleven lost over 25 per cent between 1841 and 1851.[2]

Since the intensity of excess mortality and that of emigration often differed in individual counties, it will be best to consider these two matters separately. With respect to mortality, both the overall magnitude and the regional variations are now known with some statistical precision. The geographer S. H. Cousens did the pioneering work on this subject. Cousens based his calculations mainly on the deaths that were either recorded on census forms in 1851 or reported by institutions, though he had of course to estimate 'normal' death rates before and during the famine. His calculations for each of the thirty-two counties yielded a countrywide total of excess mortality amounting to 800,645 persons for the years 1846–50. Cousens also suggested that the inclusion of the excess deaths that occurred in the first quarter of 1851 (census night was 31 March) would raise the total to approximately 860,000.[3] For more than two decades historians were content to regard Cousens's estimates as generally reliable.

Recently, however, Cousens's dependence on the 1851 census data has been sharply and effectively criticised by the economic historian Joel Mokyr. His

---

[1] L. M. Cullen, *An economic history of Ireland since 1660* (London, 1972), p. 132.
[2] Vaughan & Fitzpatrick, *Ir. hist. statistics*, pp 5–15.
[3] S. H. Cousens, 'Regional death rates in Ireland during the great famine, from 1846 to 1851' in *Population Studies*, xiv, no. 1 (July 1960), pp 55–74.

chief objection is to the serious undercounting of deaths in the census, a deficiency arising from the fact that when whole families were obliterated by mortality or emigration, there was no one to report the deaths in such families to the census takers. Cousens was in fact aware of this problem, but his attempt to offset it must now be regarded as insufficient. Adopting a different approach, Mokyr calculates excess death rates as a residual for each county (and for the country as a whole) by comparing the estimated population of 1846 with the officially reported population of 1851 after first accounting for births, emigration, and internal migration. As he frankly admits, the results of these elaborate calculations are not free from ambiguities and possible sources of error. The chief uncertainty is how steeply the birth rate fell during the famine years and whether or not to count averted births as a part of the excess mortality. This problem is sensibly resolved by the presentation of lower-bound and upper-bound estimates of excess deaths between 1846 and 1851. (Actually, Mokyr offers two slightly different versions of these sets of estimates and the discussion here relates to the second version in which the national totals are insignificantly higher.) According to these figures, overall excess mortality in 1846–51 amounted to 1,082,000 persons if averted births are not counted, and to 1,498,000 if they are. To count averted births among the casualties of the great famine is a thoroughly defensible procedure, though some might not wish to go so far.[1]

How were the excess deaths distributed geographically? Excluding averted births, the provincial breakdown is as follows: Connacht accounted for 40.4 per cent of the total, Munster for 30.3 per cent, Ulster for 20.7 per cent, and Leinster for 8.6 per cent. With even relatively prosperous Leinster and Ulster recording 93,000 and 224,000 excess deaths respectively, it could be argued that although its geographical incidence was heavily skewed towards Connacht and Munster, the famine still had the dimensions of a national disaster. It is useful and instructive to disaggregate the provincial statistics since these mask significant intraprovincial variations. Mokyr's lower-bound estimates of excess mortality by county[2] are set forth in the following table.

Even within Connacht the difference between Mayo and Leitrim was substantial, though the most noteworthy fact is that all five counties in that province registered higher rates of excess deaths than any county elsewhere. In a second group of counties covering most of Munster and the southern portion of Ulster, excess mortality was also fearfully high. On the other hand, the rate of excess deaths was comparatively moderate in mid-Ulster (Tyrone and Armagh) and in west Leinster, while a low rate was characteristic of east Leinster and the northern portion of Ulster. Given what is known of their social structures, it is somewhat surprising that Limerick in the south-west and Donegal in the north-west escaped the brutal rates of excess mortality suffered by the rest of the west of Ireland.

[1] Mokyr, *Why Ire. starved*, pp 263–8.   [2] Ibid., p. 267.

Average annual rates of excess mortality by county, 1846—51
(per thousand)

county	rate	county	rate
Mayo	58.4	King's	18.0
Sligo	52.1	Meath	15.8
Roscommon	49.5	Armagh	15.3
Galway	46.1	Tyrone	15.2
Leitrim	42.9	Antrim	15.0
Cavan	42.7	Kilkenny	12.5
Cork	32.0	Wicklow	10.8
Clare	31.5	Donegal	10.7
Fermanagh	29.2	Limerick	10.0
Monaghan	28.6	Louth	8.2
Tipperary	23.8	Kildare	7.3
Kerry	22.4	Down	6.7
Queen's	21.6	Londonderry	5.7
Waterford	20.8	Carlow	2.7
Longford	20.2	Wexford	1.7
Westmeath	20.0	Dublin	−2.1

In seeking to explain these wide geographical variations, Mokyr used regression analysis to test the potency of an assortment of independent variables. The results of the regressions indicate that neither the pre-famine acreage of potatoes nor rent per capita was related to the differing geographical incidence of the famine. The factors that correlate most strongly with excess mortality are income per capita and the literacy rate. The counties with the lowest incomes per capita and the highest rates of illiteracy were also the counties with the greatest excess mortality, and vice versa. In addition, the proportion of farms above and below twenty acres correlates positively with excess death rates. As the proportion below twenty acres increases, the excess mortality becomes progressively worse, and as the proportion above twenty acres rises, the excess deaths progressively fall. The grim reality was that poverty, whether measured by dependence on wage labour or by reliance on inadequate landholdings, greatly increased vulnerability to the mortality of the famine. This was true even in regions of the country usually regarded as relatively prosperous. Sheer location offered little protection to labourers and smallholders cursed with inadequate personal resources. Ultimately, the successive failures of the potato claimed as many victims as they did in Ireland because so high a proportion of the population had come to live in a degree of poverty that exposed them fully to a horrendous accident of nature from which it was difficult to escape.[1]

[1] Mokyr, *Why Ire. starved*, pp 268–75.

Emigration, of course, did offer the chance of escape, and that chance was seized by no fewer than 2.1 million Irish adults and children between 1845 and 1855. Of this horde, 'almost 1.5 million sailed to the United States; another 340,000 embarked for British North America; 200,000–300,000 settled permanently in Great Britain; and several thousand more went to Australia and elsewhere'. As Kerby Miller has observed in his recent monumental study, 'more people left Ireland in just eleven years than during the preceding two and one-half centuries'.[1] A significant portion of those who departed in these eleven years would undoubtedly have left even if there had been no famine, for the emigrant stream had been swelling in the decade immediately before 1845. As many as 351,000 had sailed from Ireland to North America alone between 1838 and 1844—an average of slightly more than 50,000 a year, as compared with an annual average of about 40,000 from 1828 to 1837. If the rate of increase recorded between these two periods had simply been maintained in the years 1845–51, then 437,500 people would probably have journeyed to North America anyway. But the actual number of Irish emigrants who went overseas in those years amounted to more than a million. Departures during the immediate aftermath of the famine were almost as enormous as during the famine years themselves. Of the total of 2.1 million who left between 1845 and 1855, 1.2 million fled before 1851 but as many as 900,000 departed over the next five years.[2]

From what social groups were the emigrants of 1845–55 drawn? We are better informed about the emigrants of the early 1850s than about those of the late 1840s. It would appear that in the years 1851–5 between 80 and 90 per cent of all Irish emigrants consisted of common or farm labourers and servants. Skilled workers never constituted more than 11 per cent of the total in the early 1850s (the unweighted average was about 9 per cent), and farmers never accounted for more than 8 per cent (the unweighted average in their case was less than 5 per cent). In the late 1840s the lower-class composition of emigrants was less pronounced but not markedly so. According to manifests of vessels sailing to New York city in 1846, three-quarters of the Irish passengers were either labourers or servants; artisans made up 12 per cent and farmers only 9.5 per cent of the remainder.[3] Admittedly, it was notorious that Irish emigrants disembarking at United States ports were much superior in condition to those arriving in British North America. But the exodus to Canada, though favoured by the poorest because of the lower fares, was also much smaller in scale and could not have changed the picture greatly. The conclusion is inescapable that in both the late 1840s and the early 1850s the overwhelming majority of

[1] Kerby A. Miller, *Emigrants and exiles: Ireland and the Irish exodus to North America* (New York and Oxford, 1985), p. 291.
[2] Ibid., pp 199, 569.
[3] Ibid., pp 295, 582. The low percentages of farmers among the emigrants of both the late 1840s and the early 1850s are undoubtedly a reflection of the youthfulness of a large proportion of those who went overseas. Many of those recorded as farm labourers and servants were the sons and daughters of farmers.

emigrants were drawn from the lowest classes of Irish society. Compared with pre-famine emigrants, they were less likely to be skilled or to have been farmers. And as Kerby Miller has emphasised, they were more likely to be catholic, Irish-speaking, and illiterate.[1]

From which parts of Ireland was the exodus heaviest? Three areas stand out as having experienced high or very high rates of emigration: south Ulster, north Connacht, and much of the Leinster midlands. The same areas had been notable for a heavy stream of departures in the years 1815–45, and thus the famine period saw the continuation of the pre-famine trends in this respect. As Cousens has shown, the prominence of these regions in the pre-famine exodus was mostly the result of the contraction and virtual collapse of domestic textile industry, especially the home spinning and weaving of linens, under the withering impact of the industrial revolution in Britain and the north-eastern corner of Ireland. Although the decline of cottage industry was already far advanced by the late 1830s, with hand spinning having become altogether obsolete, the ruin of the handloom weavers was delayed until the 1840s, when many of them joined the famine exodus.[2]

But high rates of emigration during the famine years were usually the result of a combination of factors. According to Cousens, the extensive movement from Leitrim and Roscommon as well as from Longford and Queen's County was mainly owing to the coincidence of a heavy preponderance of small holdings with high rates of eviction. In addition, the pressure of heavy poor rates was a factor of considerable importance in promoting emigration from Cavan, Monaghan, Leitrim, and Longford, where not only were the rates high but a relatively large proportion of the ratepayers also occupied holdings valued at £4 to £5, or just above the threshold of liability to rates.

On the other hand, relatively low emigration was characteristic of most of Ulster, the south-west, and the south-east. Flight was reduced in most of the northern counties by the moderate level of destitution, the correspondingly low poor rates, the scarcity of evictions, landlord paternalism, and the availability of internal migration and factory employment as alternatives to emigration. By contrast, the high levels of destitution that prevailed throughout most of the south and in the far west operated to restrict departures among smallholders, agricultural labourers, and farm servants. Even though labourers and farm servants constituted the most numerous category of emigrants during the famine, they were also the groups who least possessed the resources needed to depart. This difficulty seems to have been most acute in the Munster counties, four of which (Clare, Cork, Kerry, and Tipperary) actually experienced an increase in the ratio of farm workers to farmers between 1841 and 1851. In

[1] Miller, op cit., pp 293–8.
[2] S. H. Cousens, 'The regional variation in emigration from Ireland between 1821 and 1841' in *Transactions and papers of the Institute of British Geographers*, no. 37 (Dec. 1965), pp 15–30; Miller, op. cit., p. 293.

Waterford there was a substantial decline, but the ratio there was still higher in 1851 than in any other Irish county (Dublin excepted), and not surprisingly, Waterford's rate of emigration was one of the lowest in the country.[1]

Destitution, however, did not always act as a sharp brake on emigration. In fact, four of the five counties with the highest rates of excess mortality during the famine years (Leitrim, Mayo, Roscommon, and Sligo) also ranked among the counties with the heaviest rates of emigration. Perhaps the likeliest explanation for this apparent anomaly is that north Connacht, as noted earlier, had been a centre of emigration before 1845, and that remittances from previous emigrants relieved their relatives and friends who now followed them from having to depend exclusively or largely on their own resources. In south Ulster as well, emigration was not checked by destitution. The exodus from Cavan, Monaghan, and Fermanagh was extraordinarily heavy, even though in all three counties the rate of excess mortality was considerably above the average. This region too had been remarkable as a centre of emigration in the pre-famine years, and presumably remittances again allowed many of its poor to escape abroad.

Apart from south Ulster and north Connacht, however, the relationship between emigration and excess mortality was usually inverse, as Kerby Miller has observed. This pattern was perhaps clearest in the mid-west and the southwest. In Galway, Clare, and west Cork, where excess deaths were high, emigration was relatively low. Conversely, in Donegal and Limerick, where excess mortality was quite low, emigration was either very heavy (Donegal) or moderately high (Limerick). An inverse relationship similar to that prevailing in Limerick and Donegal was also strikingly evident among certain of the Leinster counties. Carlow, for example, ranked very low in the scale of excess deaths but very high in the scale of emigration, and the same was true of Kildare, Kilkenny, and especially Louth. To be sure, the inverse relationship was often less pronounced, but it was rare for a low level of excess mortality to be associated with anything less than a moderate level of emigration. Even Wexford and Dublin, which ranked lowest in the excess mortality scale, experienced moderate rates of emigration.[2]

Even though emigration was already a normal occurrence in certain regions of the country before 1845, its acceptability increased enormously throughout most of Ireland in the late 1840s and early 1850s. The exodus of the late 1840s was characterised by an often panic-driven desperation to escape that swept aside the prudential considerations and customary restraints of former years. Neither reports of adverse conditions abroad, nor lack of adequate sea stores

---

[1] David Fitzpatrick, 'The disappearance of the Irish agricultural labourer, 1841–1912' in *Ir. Econ. & Soc. Hist.*, vii (1980), p. 88.

[2] My discussion of variations in the rate of emigration at the county level is based on an elaborate set of statistical calculations made by Joel Mokyr and not published in *Why Ire. starved*. I am deeply grateful to him for placing these data at my disposal.

and landing money, nor the absence of safe vessels could check the lemming-like march to the ports. Most of those who left embraced emigration as their best—or their only—means of survival, even if it entailed, as it did for thousands, the perilous crossing of the North Atlantic in the middle of winter.[1] Inevitably, departures under such conditions produced disasters at sea or on landing. By far the worst year in this respect was 1847, and the worst conditions were to be found among passengers to Canada. With lax regulations and with cheap fares that attracted the poorest emigrants, the voyage to Quebec was often lethal. Even apart from the 'coffin ships', with their horrific toll of deaths on board, the situation was dreadful. The mortality rate among emigrants to British North America in 1847 (including deaths at sea, in quarantine on the notorious Grosse Isle, or in hospital) was as much as 17 per cent. Fortunately, the vast majority of emigrants escaped such depths of suffering. In 1848 the death rate among passengers to British North America fell to barely more than 1 per cent, and voyages to the United States were throughout the famine years much less dangerous to the health and safety of Irish emigrants, largely because of stricter regulation of passenger ships.[2]

At first, the mass exodus aroused little hostile comment in Ireland. Land-lords who encouraged departures were not initially condemned, provided that they gave some modest assistance towards the emigration of their tenants; instead, such landlords were frequently praised for their generosity. For a time after 1845, catholic priests generally accepted and often even promoted emigra-tion, and nationalist newspapers and politicians usually acquiesced in it. But by late 1847 and early 1848 the whole tone of public discussion on the subject had changed drastically. Priests, editors of popular newspapers, and nationalist politicians of all factions were joining in a loud chorus of denunciation, stig-matising emigration as forced exile. This radical shift in opinion coincided with, and was largely prompted by, the bitter realisation that the British government had laid aside any conception of the famine as an imperial respon-sibility and had terminated all major schemes of direct relief funded by the treasury. The hypercriticism of emigration evident among clerics and national-ists by 1848 did nothing to stem departures. But along with other factors, it helped to undermine earlier popular conceptions of the famine as divine punishment for sin or as the will of an inscrutable providence.[3] Increasingly after 1847, blame for emigration and indeed for the famine itself was laid at Britain's door, and political events, to be discussed below, had much to do with this fundamental and long-lasting development.

[1] Miller, op. cit., pp 298–300.

[2] Mokyr, *Why Ire. starved*, pp 267–8. According to Oliver MacDonagh, however, 'at least 20,000 immigrants [into Canada], some 30 per cent of the entire Irish emigration, had perished by the close of 1847' (Oliver MacDonagh, 'Irish overseas emigration during the famine' in Edwards & Williams, *Great famine*, p. 371); below, p. 582.

[3] Miller, op. cit., pp 301–7.

CHAPTER XIX

A famine in Irish politics

JAMES S. DONNELLY, JR

IN Irish politics the famine years coincided with the splintering and decline of
the once powerful popular movement for the repeal of the act of union.[1]
Already before the famine the unity of the repeal movement had been badly
shaken by the consequences of the failure of its basic strategy. The great
'monster meetings' of 1843 were intended to intimidate the British government
into granting legislative independence to Ireland, just as an enormous popular
agitation under Daniel O'Connell's masterful leadership in the 1820s had
coerced the Wellington–Peel administration into conceding Catholic emancipation in 1829. But in the early 1840s the use of essentially the same strategy
and tactics as in the 1820s failed to produce a similar political breakthrough.
This was not because the implied threat of possible revolution appeared less
credible in British eyes than it had earlier, but rather because British politicians feared the consequences of catholic emancipation far less than they did
those of repeal. However much O'Connell might stress Irish catholic loyalty to
the crown and to Queen Victoria personally, the British political elite persisted
in regarding the repeal agitation as a crypto-revolutionary movement whose
goal, if achieved, would lead ultimately to the disintegration of the British
empire. Given this dominant attitude towards repeal in British political circles,
and given O'Connell's deeply rooted aversion to violence, the result of the so-
called showdown at Clontarf in October 1843 was entirely predictable. When
the tory government of Sir Robert Peel banned this planned monster meeting
and dispatched troops to prevent it from taking place, O'Connell called it off
rather than risk serious bloodshed.

This decision was not repudiated by the Young Ireland allies of O'Connell
who had done so much to boost his movement and to trumpet in the weekly
Nation their own special cause of Irish cultural nationalism. But privately the
Young Irelanders harboured misgivings, and these were intensified when
O'Connell showed in the aftermath of Clontarf that he was willing to negotiate

---

[1] Thorough treatment of the politics of this period will be found in Nowlan, *Politics of repeal*;
Robert Kee, *The green flag: a history of Irish nationalism* (London, 1972); and Malcolm Brown, *The
politics of Irish literature from Thomas Davis to W. B. Yeats* (Seattle and London, 1972). In this chapter I
have relied most heavily on Nowlan's excellent work.

with both the whigs and the federalists. O'Connell did not embrace federalism, and there was as yet no question of a formal alliance with the whigs. But the mere readiness of O'Connell to enter into discussions with these groups was profoundly disturbing to the Young Irelanders, who were especially haunted by the not unreasonable fear of a repetition of the O'Connellite–whig alliance of 1835–41. That earlier episode had in effect required O'Connell to shelve his demand for repeal in return for distinctly inferior concessions that were not widely applauded or appreciated in Ireland. For most of the Young Irelanders, repeal was a non-negotiable minimum demand, and its eventual achievement was inseparably linked in their eyes with maintaining the political independence of the O'Connellite party at Westminster.

The fissures that opened up in 1844 between the idealistic Young Irelanders and the opportunistic O'Connellites were considerably widened in 1845 by their sharp clash of views over the colleges bill.[1] This was one of three measures devised by Peel's government with the general aim of undercutting catholic support for repeal by detaching moderates, especially catholic churchmen, from the O'Connellite political machine. During the debates over the bill in the repeal association in Dublin, it became evident that despite the strictures of most catholic bishops against the proposed colleges, many of the leading Young Irelanders took a favourable view of the measure. Strongly associated as they were with a non-sectarian cultural nationalism, and including numerous middle-class protestants within their ranks, the Young Irelanders were not bothered by the refusal of Peel's government to entrust control of the colleges to the catholic hierarchy or to provide public money for the teaching of catholic theology. On the contrary, these omissions actually enhanced the attractiveness of the colleges from their point of view. The projected establishment of non-denominational institutions of higher education in Belfast, Cork, and Galway was fully consistent with the non-sectarian cultural nationalism that Thomas Davis, John Blake Dillon, and Charles Gavan Duffy had been propagating in the *Nation*. According to Young Ireland ideology, even the protestant landed gentry might be won over to repeal through the power of the nationalist ideal to blunt sectarian and class divisions. So deep was this faith that the impact of the famine itself was slow to dislodge it.

O'Connell, however, cast himself as the political guardian of the interests of the catholic church on this issue, and in a lamentable display of rhetorical excess he branded the proposed colleges as 'godless' or 'infidel'. In May 1845 there was an ugly row over the issue in the repeal association, with O'Connell in one of his most insensitive and belligerent moods. The fundamental differences of opinion were at once papered over by mutual expressions of personal regard, and the opportunity for further acrimony was reduced by another round of monster meetings as well as by the common grief over the premature

[1] Kerr, *Peel, priests, & politics*, pp 290–351; see also above, pp 186–7.

death of the young Thomas Davis in September 1845. But the uniform nation-alist reaction to this latter event could not conceal that the breach between the two groups was growing steadily wider and might soon produce an open rupture.

When it came, the rupture was linked in a roundabout way with the famine, and the famine helped to make it permanent, except for a brief interlude in 1848. At the end of 1845 and in the early months of 1846 the energies of Peel's government were directed to repealing the corn laws, largely as a means of alleviating the food crisis created in Ireland by the partial failure of the 1845 potato crop. The measure was regarded as base treachery by a large group of dissident tories, whose anxiety to maintain agricultural protection in Britain led them at this stage to minimise Irish suffering. The votes of Peelite, whig, and O'Connellite M.P.s were more than sufficient to assure the repeal of the corn laws in June 1846.[1] But the protectionist tories were so enraged by their defeat that, oblivious to their own past political behaviour, they joined with the whigs and the O'Connellites in voting against an Irish coercion bill sponsored by Peel's government. Thus the dissident tories and the O'Connellites provided the ladder by which the whigs climbed back into office early in July under the leadership of Lord John Russell.

O'Connell's desire to oust Peel and to give general political support to the whigs, provided that the whigs reciprocated with what he called 'sweeping measures' for Ireland,[2] was a primary consideration in the decision to force a showdown with the fractious Young Irelanders in the repeal association. Six months earlier, in December 1845, when it seemed that the whigs might be able to form a government because of a split in Peel's cabinet over the corn laws, O'Connell soothingly told the future Young Ireland leader William Smith O'Brien exactly what he wanted to hear: 'we ought to observe a strict neutrality between the two great English factions, supporting good measures as they may be proposed by either, and creating for ourselves an Irish national party entirely independent of both'. O'Connell assured Smith O'Brien that he could never be a party to 'placing the Irish nation under the feet of the English whigs'.[3]

By late June 1846, O'Connell had conveniently forgotten these fine words. No longer was he stressing either parliamentary independence or the urgency of repealing the act of union. Instead, he was insisting that 'something must be done by the [whig] government for the benefit of the Irish people during the present session' of parliament.[4] Accordingly, O'Connell asked the repeal association to endorse a list of eleven measures that he hoped to persuade the whigs to adopt. The list contained few items that were new. Included were proposed reforms of the franchise, municipal government, the grand jury

---

[1] 9 & 10 Vict., c. 22 (26 June 1846).
[2] *O'Connell corr.*, viii, 61.
[3] Ibid., vii, 349–51.   [4] Ibid., viii, 66–7.

system, and landlord–tenant relations, coupled with a tax on the rents of absentee proprietors and the provision of denominational university education.[1] Except for the last item, which resurrected the contentious issue of the 'godless colleges', the Young Irelanders were not hostile to these measures in themselves. But the whole package implied much greater O'Connellite fraternisation with the whigs than the Young Irelanders could stomach. Moreover, O'Connell apparently considered it essential to demonstrate to the whigs that he was in complete control of the repeal movement, and that it was free of even the slightest taint of unconstitutionality or illegality. Such a demonstration would presumably make it easier for the whigs to adopt, and for parliament to accept, the O'Connellite package of reforms.

The device chosen by O'Connell to dramatise his control came to be known as the 'peace resolutions'. At this juncture only a tiny minority of the Young Irelanders could even be suspected of harbouring thoughts of armed revolution. Nevertheless, O'Connell demanded that every member of the repeal association agree to an all-embracing renunciation of the use of physical force to achieve repeal or any other political objective, whether in Ireland or elsewhere. As the key resolution put it, 'we emphatically announce our conviction that all political amelioration . . . ought to be sought for . . . only by peaceful, legal, and constitutional means, to the utter exclusion of any other. . . .' Despite serious objections to such a sweeping repudiation of physical force under virtually all circumstances (only defence against unjust aggression was to be allowed), the Young Irelanders at first sought to avoid a break. With only one dissentient (Thomas Francis Meagher), the statement of which this resolution formed part was adopted by acclamation by the repeal association on 13 July 1846. But further debate about its meaning and interpretation led to the secession of the principal Young Irelanders before the end of that month.[2]

The showdown that O'Connell had deliberately provoked had ended much as he had expected. Immediately, his own leadership position was strengthened. The seceders were relatively few in number, and as individuals, they had no considerable following in the country. But otherwise, O'Connell's political calculations missed their mark. Once again, and this time disastrously, he had overestimated the willingness and capacity of the whigs to 'do something' for Ireland, and his successful assertion of control failed to pay political dividends in the parliamentary arena.

Though the social and economic condition of Ireland had almost nothing to do directly with the split of July 1846 within the repeal association, it had a great deal to do with the course of Irish politics after the total failure of the potato crop in the autumn of 1846. The beginning of mass death in the winter of

[1] *Nation*, 4, 11 July 1846.
[2] See O'Connell to Smith O'Brien, 18 July 1846, and editorial note 2 in *O'Connell corr.*, viii, 70–71. For a different interpretation of this episode, see Maurice R. O'Connell, 'O'Connell reconsidered' in *Studies*, lxiv, no. 254 (summer 1975), pp 112–14.

1846-7 and the tragic shortcomings of the whigs' relief measures emphasised for most nationalists the folly of disunity between O'Connellites and Young Irelanders. If the whigs were to be persuaded to alter their policies, it seemed highly desirable to achieve a reunion among nationalists and, if possible, to broaden the basis of political cooperation even more by including non-repealers. O'Connell's denunciation of whig relief measures in December 1846 narrowed the gap separating him from the Young Irelanders, and the growing disenchantment of Irish landlords with whig policies appeared to create an opportunity for repealers and non-repealers to join hands in an effort to push the whigs into adopting a different course.

To heal nationalist divisions, however, proved an impossible task. The conference on reunion held in December 1846 ended in failure when neither side displayed sufficient readiness to compromise. O'Connell refused to jettison the notorious peace resolutions; at most, he was willing to limit their application to Anglo-Irish relations alone. He also declined to discuss certain other issues, such as cooperation with the whigs and the acceptance of government jobs by repealers, until the Young Irelanders rejoined the repeal association. There was too little in these proposals to tempt the Young Irelanders to terminate their secession.[1]

Instead, they decided to launch in January 1847 their own organisation, which they christened the Irish Confederation. The confederation was eventually to acquire a solid base of support among the artisans of the towns, but it began its life with, and long retained, completely unrealistic hopes about the power of nationality to resolve sectarian and class divisions within Irish society. There was a naive belief among confederate leaders such as Gavan Duffy and Smith O'Brien, a protestant landlord, that if they eschewed 'the ultra-democratic and ultra-catholic tendencies' that they ascribed to the repeal association, they would be able to attract substantial support from protestants and landlords as well as from moderate catholics and tenant farmers.[2] Special emphasis was placed on the landed gentry, whose conversion to repeal in significant numbers was thought possible. They were by now intensely dissatisfied with whig relief measures, which neglected reproductive works and laid heavy fiscal burdens on landlord shoulders. Though he was soon to repent his faith in the landlords, at this point even John Mitchel firmly believed that they had an important role to perform in the nationalist movement.

Overtures to the landed gentry were hardly confined to the Young Irelanders of the Irish Confederation. For several months O'Connell had been sounding the same note just as insistently, and in December 1846 he called publicly for a great national conference that would include the landlords and address the calamity facing the country. Though not really a national conference, the meeting held in Dublin on 14 January 1847 could reasonably claim to speak for the

---

[1] Nowlan, *Politics of repeal*, pp 113-15.
[2] Gavan Duffy to Smith O'Brien, 26 Dec. 1846 (ibid., p. 128).

Irish upper and middle classes, protestant and catholic alike. In attendance were several peers, twenty-six Irish M.P.s, and many landowners and professional men. Broad agreement was reached on four points: private enterprise alone could not be expected to satisfy the food needs of a starving population; the imperial exchequer should bear all the costs of emergency employment schemes because the famine was an 'imperial calamity'; in so far as possible, relief monies ought to be spent on reproductive works, such as thorough drainage, waste land reclamation, and harbour construction; and legislation should be passed that would provide evicted or departing tenants with reasonable compensation for their agricultural improvements. This gathering was the prelude to a new political departure. In its immediate aftermath as many as eighty-three Irish peers and M.P.s, including the O'Connellites, agreed to act in unison as an Irish parliamentary party, with the object of pressing on the government the proposals adopted at the Dublin meeting. This was the high-water mark of Irish political unity during the famine years, but it was an unnatural alliance fated to endure for only a few months.[1]

Divisions within the party began to appear as early as February 1847 over the proposal of the tory protectionist leader Lord George Bentinck to have the British treasury advance as much as £16 million for Irish railway projects. Once the minimisers of Irish suffering, the tory protectionists now came forward as the saviours of the famishing population. Here was a grand scheme of reproductive works bound to appeal to almost all political factions in Ireland. But the measure actually split the Irish M.P.s after Russell threatened to resign if Bentinck's bill were given a second reading. Thus weakened, the Irish parliamentary party collapsed altogether when faced with its next big test. What caused the collapse was the varied reaction of Irish M.P.s to the whigs' Irish poor relief bill. Irish tory M.P.s strongly opposed the bill for two main reasons. First, it made the relief of the destitute in effect a wholly local responsibility, with no prospect that other relief schemes such as public works or soup kitchens would ease the enormous pressure on the poor law system. Secondly, under certain circumstances the bill authorised outdoor relief not only for the impotent poor but also for the able-bodied, a provision whose anticipated costs frightened the landlords even more.[2]

If the repeal M.P.s had been faithful to the terms by which the Irish parliamentary party came into existence, they would have voted against this bill because it was at the opposite pole from making relief of the famine an imperial responsibility. But the O'Connellites fixed their attention on the limited authorisation of outdoor relief. Though dissatisfied with other provisions of the bill, they found in the issue of outdoor relief sufficient reason to support the measure, albeit reluctantly. O'Connell's last parliamentary speech came on 8 February during the debates over this bill, and he pathetically told the commons that he was willing to accept anything likely to help the poor. Had

---

[1] Nowlan, *Politics of repeal*, pp 125–9.   [2] Above, p. 317.

O'Connell known how the bill would be administered after it became law, he would perhaps have been less ready to see his cooperation with the non-repeal Irish M.P.s terminated, as it soon was, over this measure.[1] It is a sad comment on the last phase of O'Connell's career that he gave even grudging approval to the measure that, above all others, signalled the disengagement of British ministers from bearing fiscal responsibility for the famine.

By the time that the poor law amendment act reached the statute book in June 1847,[2] Daniel O'Connell was in his grave. Partly on the advice of his doctor that a warmer climate might improve his health, which had been deteriorating sharply for several months, and partly because O'Connell himself recognised that his end was near, he decided to make a pilgrimage to Rome. On his way there in May, at Genoa, he died. In accordance with his last wishes, his heart was taken to Rome, while his body was returned to Ireland for burial. No other leader of the modern era dominated Irish politics for as long as O'Connell, with the exception of de Valera, and no other leader, again excepting de Valera, was held in greater popular esteem by his catholic contemporaries.

But whereas de Valera made a career of setting British governments at defiance, O'Connell in two notable phases of his public life shaped his policies in such a way as to persuade whig ministers to 'do something' for Ireland. Each time the results were disappointing, and during the famine profoundly so. Admittedly, O'Connell had to work within a political system that made the task of a constitutional nationalist leader exceedingly difficult. The Irish parliamentary franchise was still so restricted, and the limited electorate was so variable in its socio-economic composition, that O'Connell's following at Westminster bore little relation to the real strength of his grassroots support in Ireland.[3] As a result, he was unable to acquire the kind of tactical leverage that Parnell exploited later in the century.

But a comparison with Parnell also suggests that O'Connell's overwhelming aversion to violence and his strong faith in the rights of private property severely restricted his willingness to use agrarian unrest for worthwhile political ends. Parnell also knew how to harness the energies of fenians in the cause of Irish nationalism, whereas O'Connell forced the Young Irelanders out of the repeal association almost against their will. Parnell could justify his alliance with the Gladstonian liberals in the years 1886–90 on the grounds that the liberal party was firmly committed to Irish home rule and strongly anti-landlord in temper, but O'Connell could make no similar defence of the whigs. His last years as the preeminent Irish political leader were surely not his best, and his final year was almost unrelieved agony. He saw the abyss into which the

[1] Nowlan, *Politics of repeal*, pp 132–7.
[2] 10 & 11 Vict., c. 31 (8 June 1847).
[3] For the complexities of the Irish parliamentary franchise and the variability in the social composition of the electorate during the period 1832–50, see K. T. Hoppen, *Elections, politics, and society in Ireland, 1832–1885* (Oxford, 1984), pp 1–73.

country was falling and called for heroic measures to avert catastrophe. When these were not forthcoming, he denounced whig policies as hopelessly inadequate. But he could not bring himself or the movement he led to the point of resolute, thoroughgoing opposition because he regarded the tories as a far worse alternative. Whether the tories, Peelite or protectionist, would have performed much better during the famine than the whigs can be debated, but what is certain is that the whigs never came close to proving the worth that O'Connell saw in them.

Although O'Connell's death was not an event of great political significance, his passing made it even less likely that repealers of either faction would be able to breathe new life into the Irish body politic. On the Liberator's death the mantle of leadership within the repeal association fell to his son, John O'Connell, who lacked his father's charisma and the capacity that his father had once shown for political decisiveness. Besides having these defects, John O'Connell possessed neither the policies nor the funds needed to revive his largely moribund organisation. The Young Irelanders were in no better shape. As the general election of mid-1847 demonstrated, they were widely held responsible for having hastened the death of the revered Liberator. Moreover, their chief leaders Gavan Duffy and Smith O'Brien still clung tenaciously to the forlorn hope of converting the landed gentry to repeal and ensured that the Irish Confederation adhered strictly to a constitutionalist and conservative nationalism in which agrarian agitation, much less social revolution, had no place. The overall result was that neither group was capable of accomplishing anything.

Various attempts were made in 1847 both to achieve a nationalist reunion and to resuscitate the spirit that had propped up the Irish parliamentary party. With the whig alliance so thoroughly discredited, the ground separating John O'Connell from the Young Ireland leaders was much narrower than it once had been. And in negotiations with the confederate chieftains John O'Connell was more conciliatory than his father on such points as the interpretation to be placed on the peace resolutions and the barring of place-hunting by repealers. But he rejected the Young Irelanders' insistence that an entirely new repeal organisation should take the place of both the confederation and the repeal association.[1] And just as these efforts at reunion failed, so too did the attempts of both groups to win any significant number of landlord recruits to a strategy of broad-based opposition to government policy. That many landlords were deeply discontented with the whig ministry was obvious, but nationalist leaders were extremely reluctant to admit that the unionism of the landed gentry was much stronger than their current alienation from the whig government. Many landlords also had reason to doubt the soundness of repealers on the land question.

The land question, and more specifically tenant right, became the focus of

[1] Nowlan, *Politics of repeal*, p. 140.

much political discussion as the clearances gathered momentum in late 1847 and as the destitute multitudes faced another winter of starvation and pestilence.[1] Among Irish politicians who advocated tenant right as a solution to the problem of insecurity of tenure, there was no agreement as to its precise meaning or as to how it might be given legislative embodiment. For William Sharman Crawford, the best known Irish advocate of tenant right and its foremost parliamentary champion, the phrase had no radical implications. A claim to tenant right, he held, arose only in those cases where the tenant had made substantial permanent improvements to his holding; in such instances the tenant deserved reasonable compensation if his landlord evicted him or if he wished to surrender his farm. Under this interpretation the achievement of tenant right would have been of limited practical significance during the famine years. Only a small proportion of the tenants then facing eviction or planning to emigrate could legitimately have claimed to be responsible for really substantial improvements. In contrast to Sharman Crawford, John O'Connell apparently took a more advanced position and viewed the tenant 'as having, in effect, a property right in the land itself, once he had paid his rent'.[2] But as much as O'Connell was interested in somehow linking the demand for tenant right to the cause of repeal, he showed no disposition to subordinate the latter to the former (not even temporarily) or to lead a popular agitation with tenant right as one of its primary goals.

Such views, however, were forcefully advocated by James Fintan Lalor in the pages of the *Nation*, and they were eventually taken up and pressed by John Mitchel and other radicals in the Irish Confederation.[3] Lalor was the crippled son of a prosperous farmer in the Abbeyleix district of Queen's County; his father, Patrick Lalor, had played a prominent part in the great anti-tithe agitation of the early 1830s and had briefly sat in parliament as an O'Connellite M.P. for Queen's County (1832–5). But Fintan Lalor had no time for the O'Connells or their policies. While regarding himself as a nationalist, he rejected repeal as 'an impracticable absurdity', not attainable by constitutional methods and much too abstract to have any real attractiveness in the famine-stricken Irish countryside. Although he accepted private property as the basis of the social system, Lalor repudiated the notion of absolute ownership in land. He held instead that the land belonged ultimately to the whole community, and he insisted that the current occupiers of the soil possessed rights amounting to coownership with the proprietors. From this premise it followed that the tenants were entitled at least to fair rents and security of tenure. Perhaps more important than Lalor's radical philosophy was his advocacy of what he called

[1] Ibid., pp 145–58.
[2] Ibid., p. 148.
[3] For Lalor's political career, ideas, and influence, see L. M. Fogarty, *James Fintan Lalor, patriot and political essayist (1807–1849)* (Dublin, 1918); Tomás Ó Néill, *Fiontán Ó Leathlobhair* (Dublin, 1962); Nowlan, *Politics of repeal*, pp 148–51, 153–6; Robert Kee, *The green flag: a history of Irish nationalism* (London, 1972), pp 259–61.

'moral insurrection', which meant in practice a national strike against the payment of rent until the British government and Irish landlords conceded a new agrarian order that would recognise the justice of the tenants' claims to economic security.[1] Lalor was convinced that the traditional agrarian regime was collapsing under the destructive impact of the famine, so that replacing it should not be all that difficult. With the help of local activists he tried to start a militant tenant right movement in south Leinster and north Munster.

Lalor's strategy, however, failed to win acceptance either at the grassroots or within the confederation. Strong farmers would not begin to show deep interest in a tenant right movement until 1849 or 1850, after an agricultural depression took hold. And even tenant right seemed remote from the elemental concerns of smallholders and agricultural labourers in the years 1847–8. There was truth in Gavan Duffy's biting criticism that Lalor's 'angry peasants, chafing like chained tigers, were creatures of the imagination—not the living people through whom we had to act'.[2]

Lalor was no more successful within the confederation. By the end of 1847 John Mitchel had at last abandoned his earlier hopes that the landlords would concede tenant right without open warfare. Though he did not endorse all Lalor's views, Mitchel now agreed that the confederation ought to give enthusiastic support to the kind of agrarian campaign that Lalor advocated. A few others in that body had also come to the same conclusion. But the moderate majority still accepted the judgement of Gavan Duffy and Smith O'Brien, who decried class conflict and insisted upon adhering to constitutional agitation alone. In disgust Mitchel and his friends began to sever their ties with the confederation. They concurred with the *Nation* writer who declared: 'It is indeed full time that we cease to whine and begin to act. . . . Good heavens, to think that we should go down without a struggle.'[3] There was no whining in Mitchel's new newspaper, the *United Irishman*, which began publication early in February 1848. It preached revolution more or less openly, but few were listening to its message. Futility and division seemed to have an iron grip on Irish politics as the year 1848 opened.

Everything appeared to change, however, when beginning in February the fever of revolution swept across Europe. Especially invigorating was the spectacle of the overthrow of Louis Philippe in France by an almost bloodless revolution in Paris. It encouraged Irish nationalists to believe that repeal could now be won without spilling much blood—without having to make a real revolution. To instil fear would be enough. If British ministers should lose their nerve, as others had, the goal could be attained. Fearful of attack by revolutionary France, fearful of social revolution by domestic chartists, and fearful of nationalist revolution in Ireland, Britain would soon concede repeal.

[1] *Nation*, 17 July 1847.
[2] Sir Charles Gavan Duffy, *Four years of Irish history, 1845–1849: a sequel to 'Young Ireland'* (Dublin, 1883), pp 476–7.   [3] Quoted in Kee, op. cit., p. 261.

It was quickly made plain, however, that the new revolutionary government in France, valuing good relations with Britain, would not commit itself to open support of Irish nationalism. An Irish nationalist delegation to Paris, headed by Smith O'Brien, came away empty-handed early in April. The chartists were much more accommodating. In the north of England numerous combined chartist and confederate meetings were held in the spring of 1848, and Irish confederates were much in evidence at the great chartist demonstration on Kennington Common in London on 10 April, when Feargus O'Connor extolled the justice of Ireland's cry for repeal. But the main lesson to be drawn from the Kennington Common episode was that social revolution by chartists was simply not in the offing. Consequently, it was hardly necessary for whig ministers to concede repeal to Irish nationalists so as to be able to concentrate on the chartist menace at home. Thus nationalists in Ireland were gradually thrown back on their own resources, which were still divided and mostly rhetorical.[1]

Then the government unintentionally rescued the nationalists from their divisions, though not from their rhetoric. In March 1848 the authorities decided to prosecute three of the leading Young Irelanders on charges of sedition: Mitchel for articles appearing in the *United Irishman*, and Smith O'Brien and Thomas Francis Meagher for inflammatory speeches. The lord lieutenant feared that unless the agitators were muzzled, they would raise a storm throughout the country, and because the government had no new measures of relief to offer, their opportunities for making mischief or worse would be much enhanced. Those officials who advised against the prosecutions for fear of making martyrs were overborne, but they had the cold comfort of seeing their predictions confirmed when the trials occurred in May. The prosecutions of both Smith O'Brien and Meagher failed and the prisoners were discharged amidst nationalist jubilation when the juries could not reach a verdict. After this stinging defeat the authorities went to great lengths to pack the jury in the case of Mitchel, who was tried ten days later under the recently passed treason-felony act,[2] the earlier charges of sedition having been dropped. Mitchel was duly convicted and sentenced to fourteen years' transportation. The severity of the sentence, together with the flagrant packing of the jury, at once aroused a wave of sympathy for Mitchel among all nationalist factions. Not for the first or last time, it was difficult for Irish political moderates to gainsay the spell cast by a martyr, however unpalatable his extreme views.[3]

The character and outcome of Mitchel's trial increased the pressures for a nationalist reunion, especially within the repeal association, which was financially crippled and faltering badly under John O'Connell's less than masterful

---

[1] Nowlan, *Politics of repeal*, pp 182–93.
[2] 11 Vict., c. 12 (22 Apr. 1848).
[3] Nowlan, *Politics of repeal*, pp 194–6, 202–5.

leadership. And on this occasion, though O'Connell fought a rearguard action against merger, the negotiations finally led in early June 1848 to the establishment of the short-lived Irish League, which replaced both the repeal association and the confederation. The terms of the merger were more favourable to the Young Irelanders than to O'Connell and his followers, since the confederate clubs scattered around the country were not only allowed to remain in being but were also permitted, as the nucleus of a national guard, to arm themselves. Thus, even though the league was officially a constitutionalist organisation, its members were left free as individuals to champion the use of physical force.[1]

In practice, nationalist reunion signified little. Attention was focused not on building up the league but rather on extending the network of local confederate clubs. In the dispiriting circumstances of the time this work was bound to proceed slowly. Even at their widest extent the clubs never numbered more than about seventy, each with a membership reportedly ranging from 200 to 500. If the average membership is generously assumed to have been about 300, the total may have slightly exceeded 20,000. Had club members been properly armed and well trained, they might have constituted a potentially troublesome, if not really formidable, force. But arms were in short supply and drilling was sporadic. Moreover, the clubs were very unevenly distributed geographically. Almost all of them were concentrated in the towns, with nearly half located in Dublin alone; organisation in the countryside, not surprisingly, was virtually non-existent.[2] Under such conditions the prospects for the success of a possible rebellion were scarcely encouraging, as the Young Irelanders themselves recognised in their sober-minded moments.

In the end, the principal Young Irelanders or confederates became the prisoners of all their bold talk of action. By calling on the people to arm themselves so that they might be ready if the day for action ever came, the confederate leaders instilled the belief that they meant business, sooner rather than later. They felt wounded when some of their fanatical adherents in effect accused them of being fine talkers rather than courageous men of action. As a result, they themselves drifted aimlessly towards action. They were helped along this path by the widespread notion that the preservation of self-respect, their own and that of a famishing people, required action. This attitude was strengthened in July, when the government suspended habeas corpus, instituted a series of arrests, and declared illegal the holding of arms in Dublin and certain other counties. It was only by a small majority that the council of the Irish League voted against an immediate rising in response to the government proclamation. Instead, the majority, still awaiting a better opportunity to strike, opted for a policy of defensive resistance against efforts to disarm the clubs. As the main proponent of immediate action bitterly declared, they were forever

---

[1] Nowlan, *Politics of repeal*, pp 206–10.
[2] Kee, op. cit., p. 268.

waiting—till aid came from France or America, 'till rifles are forged in heaven and angels draw the trigger'.[1]

It is unnecessary to rehearse here the confused events of late July, which finally brought the Young Ireland leaders to their brief and inglorious encounter with the police in the Widow McCormack's cabbage garden near Ballingarry, County Tipperary. As Robert Kee has well said, the so-called rising of 1848 'was not in any practical sense a rising at all, nor until the very last minute was it ever intended to be one'.[2] Its reluctant, halfhearted leaders had made hardly any preparations. They had nothing that could be dignified with the name of a strategy. They discovered again what they already knew—that the peasantry in the south-east were incapable of being roused or were too intelligent to take the risk. And even in the towns where clubs existed, they found that most members were without firearms. It was a pure mercy that such a ridiculous escapade collapsed almost as soon as it started. Mitchel's acid comment when he received the news two months later was apposite: 'What is this I hear? A poor extemporised abortion of a rising in Tipperary, headed by Smith O'Brien.' Coming from the arch-revolutionary, this might be considered strange criticism, but Mitchel professed to know his business: 'In the present condition of the island, no rising must *begin* in the country. Dublin streets for that.' The revolt, he added, 'has been too long deferred', implying that if only the rebels had taken up arms earlier and in Dublin, they would have given a much better account of themselves, though even Mitchel accepted that the ultimate military outcome would have been the same.[3] He seems to have wanted what would later be called a blood sacrifice, one that would redeem military defeat by the political success of its after-effects, and his disappointment over the pathetic farce of a revolution was acute.

But Mitchel's immediate reaction to the rising was unduly pessimistic, just as Sir Robert Peel was too optimistic when he wrote to Graham in late August 1848 that 'Smith O'Brien has rendered more service than I thought he was capable of rendering, by making rebellion ridiculous.'[4] In spite of the pathetic character of the rising, its political effects were profound and literally far-reaching. Some of these were slow to mature, while others manifested themselves more quickly. Many Young Ireland rebels evaded arrest and took ship to North America, where they later helped to give focus and a sharp edge to the anti-English hostility of the famine emigrants and their children. A few others escaped to Paris, where they continued to nurture their fierce resentment against British misrule. This small band included James Stephens and John O'Mahony, the co-founders in the late 1850s of the fenian movement in Ireland and America. Indeed, in its leadership before 1865 and in its ideology, fenianism was essentially the product of 1848.

[1] Ibid., p. 275.   [2] Ibid., p. 270.
[3] John Mitchel, *Jail journal* (Dublin, 1913; reprint, with introduction by Thomas Flanagan, 1982), pp 72–3.   [4] Nowlan, *Politics of repeal*, p. 215.

Other Young Irelanders, however, paid the price for their involvement in the events of 1848 either by imprisonment in Ireland or by transportation to Van Diemen's Land. The judicial repression that followed the rising was by no means severe. Presented with the gift of a ridiculous rebellion, the government was not disposed to throw it away through an excess of repressive zeal. Not a single one of the captured rebels was executed. Four of them (Smith O'Brien, Meagher, Terence Bellew McManus, and Patrick O'Donoghue) were convicted of high treason and sentenced to death, but the authorities were strongly against letting the law take its course. And when the four state prisoners embarrassingly refused to ask for the pardons that would have allowed their death sentences to be commuted to transportation, the government resolved the difficulty by quickly carrying into law a measure that made transportation permissible in treason cases without pardon.[1] But for all its calculated restraint the government could not prevent the martyr's crown from descending on those convicted in its courts. By refusing to crave pardons, the four state prisoners elevated and ennobled their farcical rising. Their steady courage during and after their trials, together with their eventual dispatch to Van Diemen's Land, captured the Irish popular imagination at home and abroad. A hero's welcome greeted McManus, Meagher, and Mitchel when they arrived in California in 1853 after escaping from Van Diemen's Land.[2]

Though less idolised, the Young Irelanders imprisoned at home also benefited politically from their rebel past and penal confinement. The fact that they were soon released did not prevent them from claiming some share in the martyrology of Irish nationalism, even when, chastened by their recent experience, they again embraced constitutionalism and non-violence.[3] Most of them soon resumed their political careers, and quite a few drew important lessons from their political isolation in 1848. Gavan Duffy, among others, recanted one of the cardinal tenets of the moderate Young Irelanders before the rising, namely, their belief in the necessity of avoiding class conflict between landlord and tenant. Soon after emerging from jail, he revived the *Nation* on 1 September 1849 and at once announced that in the short run the quest for independence must give way to efforts 'to bring back Ireland to health and strength by stopping the system of extermination'.[4] A week later, he declared it to be 'the first duty of a national association to assault' the current land system.[5] Though not in the same words, many others—churchmen and politicians, catholics and presbyterians—were now saying much the same thing. Capitalising on this increasing public sentiment in favour of agrarian

---

[1] 12 & 13 Vict., c. 27 (26 June 1849). See Kee, op. cit., pp 286–9; Nowlan, *Politics of repeal*, pp 216–17.

[2] Mitchel, op. cit., pp 349–50.

[3] Kerby A. Miller, *Emigrants and exiles: Ireland and the Irish exodus to North America* (New York and Oxford, 1985), p. 310.

[4] *Nation*, 1 Sept. 1849.

[5] Ibid., 8 Sept. 1849.

reform in the south as well as in Ulster, Duffy was instrumental in organising a national conference in November 1849 that helped to lay the basis for the great tenant right agitation of the early 1850s.[1]

Collectively, what the Young Ireland rebels did was to politicise the events of the famine, especially its appalling mortality and its mammoth emigration.[2] The interpretation of famine deaths as a grotesque act of genocide, perpetrated by the British government, owed much to the Young Irelanders. Long before John Mitchel in 1861 gave systematic expression to this view in his book *The last conquest of Ireland (perhaps)*, even the moderate Gavan Duffy was calling the famine 'a fearful murder committed on the mass of the people'—in the *Nation* at the end of April 1848.[3] Similarly, the interpretation of famine emigration as forced exile or banishment found some of its most vociferous exponents among Young Irelanders who were themselves compelled to flee their native land. Not only did they dramatise in their own persons that emigration was forced exile, but they also propagated the same view relentlessly in their venomously anti-English writings and speeches in those countries to which they had been 'banished'. Of course, these interpretations of mortality and emigration were not the exclusive property of the politically sophisticated, middle-class Young Irelanders. Often, they arose spontaneously at the popular level out of bitter common experience. But the Young Irelanders certainly gave them a currency and respectability that they would not otherwise have had.

However acquired, such views gained wide popular acceptance in Ireland and among the famine Irish abroad largely because they served a deep psychological need to displace personal guilt. Apart altogether from 'extermination' by landlords and the deadly callousness of officials, the records of the great famine are replete with anti-social behaviour and acts of gross inhumanity— committed by wealthy farmers and shopkeepers against the poor, by the poor against others of their own class, by parents against their children, and by sons and daughters against their parents. By their very nature prolonged famine and epidemics of fatal disease lead to the large-scale erosion or collapse of traditional moral restraints and communal sanctions. For many of the survivors of the great famine of the late 1840s, the recollection of their anti-social conduct against neighbours and even close relatives was a heavy psychological burden crying out for release and displacement. What made the displacement of this guilt on to Albion's shoulders so compelling was not only that England represented the ancient oppressor but also that its whig government during the famine had such a damning record in Ireland. Who today should be surprised that many of 'Erin's boys' wanted 'revenge for Skibbereen'?

[1] Nowlan, *Politics of repeal*, pp 230–31. For the origins of the Tenant League, see below, pp 399–401, and Whyte, *Indep. Ir. party*, pp 1–13.
[2] In this paragraph and the next I am heavily indebted to the analysis of Miller, op. cit., pp 310–12.
[3] *Nation*, 29 Apr. 1848; above, pp 329–31.

CHAPTER XX

Ireland 1850–70: post-famine and mid-Victorian

R. V. COMERFORD

IN the obvious sense the 1850s and 1860s are the post-famine decades, but something more than chronology is conveyed by the term 'post-famine Ireland'. It is loaded with connotations of the gloom and depression with which the period has been so frequently characterised in the past. There was indeed much to be gloomy about, but there was much else besides, and the general drift of recent scholarship has been towards a more positive depiction of the era.[1] Even more important than this corrective colouring is a willingness to admit the distinctiveness of the period. From this point of view 1870 is not a terminal date, for the years between the great famine and the land war constitute an integral era in the social, economic, political, and cultural history of the country. Like much else in Irish history, this era has had its distinctiveness largely ignored or distorted by the preoccupation of popular historiography with the mythic march of the nation. From that perspective the quarter-century after the famine is fundamentally of little interest apart from the emergence of fenianism: the 'nation' hangs helplessly on the ropes for a few years, then gradually recovers sufficient spirit to put up a splendid fight, under Mr Parnell's coaching, in the next important bout of Irish history. But there are continuities, more meaningful than that of inevitable nationalist progress, into which aspects of the age can be inserted. Equally helpful are the transverse lines of reference, those linking with the wider contemporary context. Post-famine Ireland is also mid-Victorian Ireland.

Historians have convincingly portrayed the years between the depression of the late 1840s and the depression of the middle and late 1870s as the golden age of capitalism, a period of previously unparalleled economic expansion and growth in communications, during which vast numbers of people around the

---

[1] Works that have helped to transform appreciation of the post-famine decades include the following: L. M. Cullen, *An economic history of Ireland since 1660* (London, 1972); J. J. Lee, *The modernisation of Irish society, 1848–1918* (Dublin, 1973); Samuel Clark, *Social origins of the Irish land war* (Princeton, 1979); Mary Daly, *Social and economic history of Ireland since 1800* (Dublin, 1981); Donnelly, *Land & people of Cork*; W. E. Vaughan, *Landlords and tenants in Ireland, 1848–1904* (Dublin, 1984).

globe were incorporated into, or subordinated to, one great economic system. It is partly because Ireland participated—in its own way—in the developments of this British-dominated era that the term 'mid-Victorian Ireland' has more than merely chronological validity. Besides, fenianism notwithstanding, Ireland between the famine and the land war was settling as never before, or after, into an accommodation with English power within the United Kingdom. And English culture with its attendant values was being absorbed in Ireland on a wider scale than ever before and with less reservation than ever after. On both sides of the Irish Sea new levels of decorum were taking hold in public and private life. As older forms of communal entertainment were being modified or suppressed in England the same happened in Ireland. The notorious Donnybrook fair, which for generations had made the name of the County Dublin village synonymous with disorder, drunkenness, casual violence, and debauchery, was held for the last time in August 1854. The suppression was the work of a committee that raised a sufficient sum of money to buy the fair's 650-year-old charter from its private owner. Zeal for propriety was matched by respect for property.

'Mid-Victorian Ireland' has a depth of meaning that 'early Victorian Ireland' or 'late Victorian Ireland' do not have. This distinctive quality of the period does not depend on the sudden appearance of new trends or structures, but rather on changes in the relative strength and importance of features carried over from earlier periods. Thus, the industrialisation of the north-east, the consolidation of agricultural holdings, the devotional revolution, the decline of the Irish language, and even regular emigration were in evidence before 1850, and most of them long before it. Now, along with other established aspects of Irish life, they were cast in new combinations and a new order of precedence, partly in reaction to the famine crisis and, even more, in response to conditions in the world outside.

The structure of the administration is a good example of something that contributed to the new order, though itself unchanged in any major respect from immediate pre-famine times. The work of Dublin Castle attained new levels of efficiency and coherence during the period owing to the continuity of Thomas Aiskew Larcom's tenure of almost sixteen years as under-secretary (1853–68). The hallmark of Larcom's administration was efficient perform-ance, rather than any daring innovation. Well organised archives probably constitute a fitting monument to it. The public record act of 1867,[1] a counter-part of contemporaneous English developments, made enlightened arrange-ments for the public record office and the state paper office. Larcom took his own papers with him on leaving office, as was then still the general custom. They now rest in the National Library of Ireland and the library of Trinity Col-lege, Dublin, in hundreds of uniformly bound volumes, each a valuable collec-tion of material on some aspect of the public life of that age. The

[1] 30 & 31 Vict., c. 70 (12 Aug. 1867).

most impressive treasure bequeathed by this epoch of confident administration is the *General valuation of Ireland*[1], which sets out the findings of a cadastral survey of the entire country conducted under the direction of Richard Griffith in the 1850s and early 1860s. Griffith's valuation and its regular updating by the valuation office provided an acceptable basis for local taxation for over a century and a frame of reference for numerous other purposes over shorter periods. With its comprehensive listings by townland of occupiers and lessors and of the sizes, descriptions, and valuations of holdings, it will always remain the single most important source of information on modern Ireland.

Local government continued to be an amalgamation of *ancien régime* institutions (notably the grand jury) and rational innovations of the 1830s, most importantly the poor law system. New tasks related to their original areas of responsibility were assigned to the boards of poor law guardians as needs became apparent. Thus in 1851 they were put in charge of a revamped medical dispensary system[2] and in 1866 were made the sewer authorities in rural areas.[3] In the sphere of municipal government the towns improvement act of 1854[4] provided for the erection of town commissioners in towns with a population of over 1,500. By 1871 almost eighty towns had a local administration provided under this act, bringing the total number of municipal authorities in the country to over one hundred and ten. The Public Libraries (Ireland) Act, 1855[5] facilitated the provision by these bodies of a service, the growing demand for which was a feature of the age. Another instance of the refinement of Irish local government was the setting up of the Dublin port and docks board by an act of 1867.[6] All in all this was an age of real, but moderate rather than major, change in the structures of Irish administration.

Ireland participated spectacularly in the mid-Victorian transport and communications boom. The compulsory standardisation of the Irish main-line gauge in 1846[7]—as railway mania reached its apogee in Britain—presaged a dramatic countrywide expansion of the railways, previously confined to the Dublin and Belfast areas. The year 1850 opened with over four hundred miles of line in commission, linking Belfast with Carrickfergus, Ballymena, Armagh, Castleblayney, and Drogheda, and linking Dublin with Mullingar, Carlow, Bagenalstown, Limerick (by way of Kildare, Maryborough, and Thurles), and Kilbarry, which served as a temporary station for Cork while the last few miles to the city were being tunnelled. A few more years of rapid expansion ensued and then decades of inevitably slower but nevertheless noteworthy growth. The opening of the Boyne viaduct at Drogheda in 1853 closed the last gap on the line between Dublin and Belfast. By 1855 the railway had reached Derry, Omagh, Enniskillen, Longford, Navan, Galway, Killarney, Clonmel, Kilkenny,

---

[1] *General valuation of rateable property in Ireland* (202 vols, Dublin, 1852–64).
[2] 14 & 15 Vict., c. 68 (7 Aug. 1851).   [3] 29 & 30 Vict., c. 90 (7 Aug. 1866), sects 56–69.
[4] 17 & 18 Vict., c. 103 (10 Aug. 1854).   [5] 18 & 19 Vict., c. 40 (26 June 1855).
[6] 30 Vict., c. lxxxi (17 June 1867).   [7] 9 & 10 Vict., c. 57 (18 Aug. 1846).

Waterford, and Wicklow. Cookstown joined the network in 1856; Birr, Dungannon, Monaghan, and Clones in 1858; Tralee and Ennis in 1859; Carrickmacross, Cootehill, Fermoy, and Youghal in 1860; Sligo, Carrick-on-Shannon, Claremorris, and Castlebar in 1862; Nenagh and Enniscorthy in 1863; and Dunmanway and Westport in 1866. By 1870 the length of lines open was almost two thousand miles. In twenty years the number of passengers carried annually had more than doubled to reach over fourteen millions. With fares at about a penny per mile (varying with the class of seating accommodation and the railway company) long-distance travel was still comparatively expensive, but it was incomparably cheaper, and more efficient, than it had ever been before. Even more impressive than the growth in passenger numbers was the expansion in goods traffic, receipts from which grew more than fivefold between 1850 and 1870.

The railways multiplied traffic not only in persons and goods but also in what are often referred to rather grandly as 'ideas'—the bulk of it communication of a most pedestrian type and not at all calculated to turn the world upside down. The postal service could operate at a new level of efficiency. Letters were collected and delivered from one end of the country to another with a speed, regularity, and frequency quite beyond the capacity of earlier ages and—for different reasons—of our own. In 1839, the year before the introduction of the penny stamp, just over nine and a quarter million letters were delivered by the Irish postal system. This was the equivalent of just over one letter per head of the population per annum. The average number of letters delivered each year from 1851 to 1855 was over thirty-nine million, the equivalent of six letters per head of the 1851 population. In 1870 the total number was over sixty-five million, the equivalent of almost twelve letters per head of the population. Admiration for this progress must be tempered by a comparison with the rest of the United Kingdom. In Scotland in 1870 letters delivered amounted to more than twenty-five per head of the population and in England and Wales the comparable figure was thirty-one.

The railways also facilitated the expansion of a novel and even faster means of sending messages, the electric telegraph; railway lines provided secure and virtually unimpeded routes for telegraph poles and wires. In June 1852 the completion of a submarine cable from Howth to Holyhead incorporated the Irish telegraph into a much larger system, which was in the process of transforming communications around the globe. Ireland's geographical position gave it a strategic place in the network, astride the line from North America to Britain and Europe. On 20 August 1858 the station at Valentia Island received the first message on the newly laid North Atlantic cable. A serious break subsequently developed, but from July 1866 an improved cable provided an uninterrupted link. Within the country the system was extending impressively and by the early 1870s well over four hundred towns and villages had telegraph offices. The speedier communication to distant parts of information about births and deaths, which was now possible, amounted at least to a minor boon for humanity. Of considerably greater importance was the impact on business communications and especially on the dissemination of public news. In at least one sense the telegraph invented news. Together with other factors it transformed the newspaper business.

In the early 1850s newspapers were on the brink of important changes. In 1853 the tax on advertisements was repealed. Two years later the compulsory stamp on newspapers was abolished; this had stood at 1*d.* per copy since 1836. In 1860 the tax on paper disappeared. All of this, together with technical changes in printing, led to a dramatic reduction in costs, to lower newspaper prices, and so to the possibility of greatly increased circulation. The old *Nation* of Duffy and Davis in the 1840s had cost 6*d.* In late 1861 the same journal was selling at 3½*d.* and by 1868 it was down to 2*d.* The *Irish Times* when founded in March 1859 appeared three times a week and cost 1*d.* A few weeks later Dublin got the country's first penny daily, the *Morning Post*. In response to this challenge the *Freeman's Journal* dropped its price from 2½*d.* to 1*d.*

The number of newspapers increased. In 1852 something short of one hundred newspapers were publishing in Ireland once a week or more frequently, about seventeen of them in Dublin. By 1871 the national total was well over one hundred and forty, of which Dublin had twenty-two. Unfortunately no reliable statistics are available for circulation figures after 1855, when the stamp was abolished. Subsequent statements by the papers themselves about their circulation are probably as useful as their partisan editorial comments on politics, which is to say never absolutely trustworthy as to exactness but cumulatively likely on interpretation over a period to yield some truth, however incidentally. The strong impression comes across—supported by independent sources—that total sales of newspapers had increased very substantially, probably much more than the approximately 50 per cent increase in the number of publications. The significance of the latter figure is greatly enhanced by the fact that newspapers appeared more frequently over the two decades. In the early 1850s the country's three daily newspapers were all Dublin publications. Twenty years later Dublin had eight dailies, Belfast four, Cork four, and Waterford one. Not all of the extra fourteen dailies were new publications. For instance, they included the *Cork Examiner*, founded in 1841, which had come out three times a week in the late 1850s. Whatever it is that newspapers spread—ranging perhaps from the occasional idea to notions of self-importance on the part of the readers—penetrated new zones of Irish life, both geographical and social, early in the second half of the nineteenth century. By later standards it was still superficial penetration, but it did bring the country along in line with the advances in the wider world.

The invention of photography in 1839 brought a new dimension to communications, and to human experience. Dublin and Belfast had commercial photographic studios from the early 1840s. In the 1850s and 1860s more flexible and less expensive processes led to a dramatic expansion of photography both as a business serving an eager public and as a hobby. Surviving photographs of outdoor scenes, rare for the 1840s, are sufficiently plentiful for subsequent decades to be a historical source in their own right. The most frequently represented places include the lakes of Killarney and the Giant's Causeway. Such material helped to fuel the new, cheaper, and easier type of tourism made possible by the railways.

The new British-oriented world system into which Ireland was incorporated in these decades produced an increase in the volume of traffic of all kinds, but this increased traffic tended to run along fewer lines—though of course in much greater concentration—than the more diffuse commerce of earlier times. Thus it was that Irish shipping, while undoubtedly carrying greater amounts of goods than ever before, became less and less diversified in its patterns. This was simply the culmination of a trend that had been in evidence long before 1850. In 1825 87 per cent of Ireland's recorded export and import trade had been with Britain. Complete figures for Anglo-Irish trade do not exist for subsequent years because with the phasing-out of duties on trade between Ireland and Britain the keeping of relevant records was discontinued. Of Ireland's non-British trade in 1825, estimated at a value of £2 million, exports amounted to about 33 per cent. Thereafter exports to non-British destinations (even including reexport of British goods) plummeted in both absolute and percentage terms. In twenty years the absolute figure halved. From 1848 to 1870 it was virtually static, at considerably less than half the 1825 figure in twenty-two of these twenty-three years. Of every thousand pounds' worth of goods exported from the United Kingdom in 1870, only just over one pound's worth went directly from Irish ports. This, for a period when the volume of commerce in general was multiplying, strikingly illustrates the British orientation of Irish trade.[1]

Irish direct imports from sources other than Britain had remained virtually static (at a value of around £1½ million) between 1825 and 1845. Thereafter they rose dramatically. The figure for 1850 was just over £6 million. Twenty years later it was almost £8¾ million. The increase from 1845 onwards was made up preponderantly by the extra wheat and Indian corn that came initially in response to the great famine and the repeal of the corn laws and then continued to find a place because of the fall in Irish tillage production and changing dietary habits.[2] The corn imports came mainly from North America and up to 90 per cent was landed at six ports—Dublin, Belfast, Cork, Waterford, Limerick, and Derry. Thanks to the railway, the remotest parts of the country could have the benefit of ready supplies of Indian meal and flour from these

[1] The annual *Thom's Irish Almanac and Official Directory of the United Kingdom* is a good source for the regrettably incomplete Irish trade statistics of the period.
[2] E. Margaret Crawford, 'Indian meal and pellagra in nineteenth-century Ireland' in J. M. Goldstrom and L. A. Clarkson (ed.), *Irish population, economy and society: essays in honour of the late K. H. Connell* (Oxford, 1981), pp 114–17.

centres. The benefits of handling and processing the imported corn to produce the meal and flour were enjoyed preponderantly by the principal ports and reasonably adjacent centres (such as Clonmel, which was accessible by barge and rail from Waterford). The increased non-British import business of the larger ports was evidence not of any independent development but of the country's fuller incorporation into the British-centred system. The ports of second rank along the west coast—Sligo, Ballina, Westport, Galway, and Tralee—suffered a dramatic decline in their non-British trading contacts, both incoming and outgoing, in the 1850s and 1860s. So, absorption into the new economy of the steam age took place at the expense of an older, more diversified order. Beginning in the early 1850s an effort was made to win a place for the port of Galway in the new order by establishing it as the terminus for a transatlantic steamship service. The dream was realised briefly between 1857 and 1861, but to withstand any longer than that the pull of the New York to Liverpool route proved impossible. Queenstown (as Cobh had been renamed in 1849 to mark Queen Victoria's first Irish visit) was better placed for coming to terms with ineluctable reality, and from 1859 ships of the Inman line called there regularly for passengers and mail. But most American-bound Irish traffic still had to go east before going west.

The new economic system not only rendered older patterns of commerce obsolete but extended the scope of commercial activity at the expense of subsistence living. People who formerly would have lived almost entirely on the produce of their own holdings began to buy flour or Indian meal for at least part of the year and so for the first time, or at least to a greater extent than before, became part of a wider money economy. Maize in one form or another had for generations been the mainstay of the economically marginal over much of southern Europe while similarly circumstanced people in Ireland were coming to rely on the potato. In the form of Indian (or 'yellow') meal, maize now came to supplement the no longer dependable potato in Irish diets. However cooked or baked it was coarse and unpalatable food but it was cheap and it was available all the year round. Indian meal brought the very poorest into the commercial economy. From the spectacular rise in the Irish consumption of tea and tobacco after the famine it is clear that many more people than before were spending money on these commodities. And if home-produced food could be replaced by a market product, so too could home-produced clothing. One of the prime functions of the railway was to distribute throughout the land products of the industrial age, whether these were replacements for old basic necessities, or new-fangled products generating needs and meeting them at the same time. All this meant a big extension of retailing in mid-Victorian Ireland, especially in the western areas, which had been least commercialised. In some western localities, retailing arrived abruptly during the famine, and so as part of a painful disruption and without any of the safeguards provided by experience and custom. Shopkeeping was inseparable from credit, especially in an agricultural society. The money-lending shopkeeper of the west—the gombeen-man—became a figure of controversy, not to say hate, in the absence on both sides of an adequate cultural context for the easy conduct of such relationships. Even where commerce was long established the developments of the age produced tensions. In the towns and cities the artisan-tradesman who sold what he had made in his workshop came under increasing pressure from the retailer of mass-produced goods. Tradesman and shopkeeper alike were threatened in the cities by the emergence of department stores ('monster houses') with their economies of scale, smartly attired assistants, and low-priced consumer durables, frequently imported. The impact of cheaper factory-produced goods on employment in the crafts was in evidence both before and after 1850. The foundation of the United Trades Association in Dublin in 1863 suggested that the artisans felt their interests to be under threat, but it proved equally that there was plenty of life left in them as an interest group, as did the elaborate turn-out of numerous and varied trades for a number of political demonstrations in the 1860s.

Free trade and economic union between Britain and Ireland became a legal fact in 1825,[1] but acquired a new reality with the communications revolution of the railway age. It is a commonplace that by the end of the century the north-east had made use of free trade to construct an intensively industrialised economy, while the remainder of the country was virtually denuded of significant industry with the exception of a few successful giants in brewing, distilling, and biscuit-making. However, teleology can be as misleading in economic as in political history, and the economy of the mid-Victorian period deserves to be considered in its own right and not simply as part of some ineluctable process. Dismissing an industrial or economic activity in history as worthless because hindsight shows it to have been 'doomed' is not very sensible in an age such as ours when twenty years is regarded as a satisfactory life-span for even the most expensive industrial projects. Similarly, the later preeminence of Belfast shipbuilding cannot be projected backwards to the 1850s when Harland & Wolff was established as a medium-sized venture.

Already by 1850 the linen industry of the north-east was self-evidently Ireland's best example of successful adaptation to the new industrial age. The spinning process had been fully mechanised and was carried on in over seventy factories using a total of about half a million spindles. Mechanisation of the weaving stage was beginning and a handful of factories were engaged in this. Continued expansion in the 1850s gave way in the early and mid-1860s to a boom as the American civil war starved the cotton industry of its basic raw material. By 1870 over 900,000 spindles and nearly 15,000 power looms were in production in a total of 154 factories, employing 55,000 people, two-thirds of them females. That was about 35,000 more than the industry's factories had employed twenty years earlier. The impressive 175 per cent increase has to be

[1] Above, p. 109.

set against the concomitant loss of employment among domestic hand weavers. Other textile industries, too, though admittedly starting from a much lower base, displayed remarkable vigour in the 1850s and 1860s. Woollen factories, numbering eleven in 1850, came to a total of sixty-one in 1870. These, however, were different in many respects from the linen factories, being scattered widely throughout Munster, Leinster, and Ulster, generally utilising water power rather than steam, and employing on average about twenty-five workers each. These were the factories of an earlier age reopened in response to moderately encouraging market conditions. The cotton factories presented a much different picture. These too had numbered just eleven in 1850 but in 1870 they had increased to a mere fourteen. However, on average these fourteen factories employed 300 workers each, and they were powered predominantly by steam. The largest of them, at Portlaw, County Waterford, was three times as large as the average linen factory in the north.

Milling prospered in these decades—a decline in employment in the 1860s notwithstanding—and provided a good instance of a native industry adapting well to the fullness of free trade. Expanding home demand was supplied from the vast direct imports of wheat and Indian corn already mentioned, supplemented by smaller volumes of foreign grain coming by way of Britain. Surplus flour production was exported to Britain (as was a small amount of wheat). Surplus native production of oats permitted the millers to keep up a very substantial export of oatmeal to Britain.

The most celebrated example of an individual Irish business taking advantage of new conditions at this time is provided by Guinness's brewery. From its Dublin base it had already established a sound market in Britain before providing the classic Irish instance of an enterprise exploiting modernised transport and communications to create a national market and expand at the expense of less capitalised competitors. Between 1855 and 1870 the volume of sales of Guinness's stout and porter almost trebled in Dublin city and almost quintupled in the rest of the country. That reflected a considerable rise in beer consumption generally, but far more significant was the expansion of Guinness's at the expense of other firms. If small, locally orientated breweries were closing down in large numbers, the position was even more critical in distilling. Consumption of spirits was hit badly by excise increases in the 1850s and 1860s and many small distilleries went out of business. The total of fifty-one in 1851 dropped to twenty-two in 1868. Annual production of whiskey fell by one and a half million gallons in the same period, but at just short of six million gallons in 1868 (one-fifth of which regularly went in exports to England) it was still a very important industry.

The main trends in Irish agriculture were inseparable from the general economic patterns of the period. There was a decline in the production of grain, which could be supplied from outside, and a major swing towards pastoral farming, whose products were in growing demand on the increasingly accessible British market. From 1851 to 1871 the acreage under corn decreased by 30 per cent, while the area devoted to hay and pasture was rising by almost 20 per cent. The total number of cattle went from almost three million to almost four million. The potato acreage increased by approximately 10 per cent: total dependence on potatoes might be a thing of the past, but they were still central to the diet of the majority of Irish people; besides, they were used also as fodder.

The trend from arable to livestock farming had important implications for the structure of rural society. Pastoral farming was in general less intensive, so that larger farms now enjoyed a relatively greater advantage than before. The failure of the potato as a subsistence crop in the late 1840s had almost wiped out the smallest pre-famine holdings. The decline of tillage had somewhat similar consequences for large numbers of farms below fifteen acres that had survived the famine. Many were absorbed or amalgamated into larger holdings. True, even more remained, but not as truly self-supporting units. Their occupiers survived on emigrants' remittances or by their own earnings through temporary work elsewhere. Tens of thousands of these from Connacht travelled annually to Britain for seasonal work, and they were able to do so with new-found ease owing to the railways. Meanwhile large numbers of landless labourers were making one-way railway trips to the emigrant ship. Well before 1850 there were insufficient hired hands available, even for the reduced harvest, in parts of the country. This encouraged the introduction of the scythe (in place of the sickle[1]) and of the horse-drawn reaping machine, which in turn sent more labourers to America. The switch to livestock was important above all because it was profitable for those with the resources and good luck necessary to take advantage of it. Between 1850 and 1870 the prices of store cattle, mutton, pork, and butter rose by proportions varying from 33 per cent to 50 per cent, while grain prices advanced but a little. This was a direct consequence of the prosperity of mid-Victorian England, and it produced a prosperity in Ireland that had profound and long-lasting effects on the country. Many farmers, and those who shared their wealth—especially shopkeepers and priests—experienced an unprecedented flush of good fortune. There had long been a comfortable farming class, but its members now found circumstances better than for more than a generation; and they were now joined by a multitude of emulators of their lifestyle. Manifestations of new-found prosperity could take a myriad shapes depending on circumstances, especially the starting point of the individual: meat for dinner a few days a week; a trap for going in style to church; a piano in the parlour; a parlour where there had not been one before; a son entered for a profession; a small garden behind the house; an entrance gate with piers; a new deal table. The most widespread signs of success were three: money in the bank; increased numbers of increasingly valuable livestock; and extra land acquired from less successful neighbours.

---

[1] Above, p. 221.

Progress was interrupted in the early 1860s by a series of difficult seasons but by 1865 another decade of sustained advance had begun.[1]

The extent of this agrarian prosperity is perhaps less important than the manner in which its achievement and sustainment affected many of those concerned. Extra wealth may have accrued easily to the graziers,[2] but at the lower levels the agricultural boom brought not easy or immediate prosperity but the opportunity to achieve it by effort. Farmers holding from fifteen to, say, fifty acres had to work for their success as hard and as singlemindedly as any baron of the industrial revolution. Not surprisingly, therefore, theirs was the most productive segment, acre by acre, of Irish agriculture. The last traces of communal farming at this level disappeared, and a wide band of peasantry was transformed into modern economic beings competing with one another in the market place. Wife and children had to toil with the farmer, and whether the man or the woman dominated on any given farm depended on the force of personal character. With family life firmly subordinated to the economic welfare of the farm, it made sense to ensure that marriage was similarly subordinated. Dowries and matches arranged with an eye to economic benefit had always been common, in Ireland as elsewhere, among people with family wealth or territory to worry about. The newly prospering farmers now followed the example of those who had preceded them to wealth, but, having no scope for mistakes, they adopted the practice with unexampled ruthlessness and inflexibility, so that their matchmaking became a byword for mercenary bargaining, and their marrying the epitome of calculation. Their late, calculated marriages soon made a noticeable impression on Irish demography.

The Representation of the People (Ireland) Act, 1850,[3] greatly expanded the parliamentary franchise in Irish counties by giving the vote to tenants of holdings valued at £12 or more, even when they had no beneficial interest in the property. This was a major departure from previous principles and was the first instance in the United Kingdom of a county franchise based on valuation without reference to ownership. Here was practical recognition of a major new reality in Irish life—the rising social importance of the middling and large tenant farmers as a class. (Very roughly, a holding valued at £12 would amount to about twelve statute acres of good land.) This recognition had come even before the advent of the era of high prices and prosperity. The landlords had proved to be a disappointment during the famine; or, rather, the famine had demonstrated what observation could have shown at any time, that Irish landlordism was but imperfectly analogous to English or Scottish landlordism. With a view to resolving the gigantic financial problems that afflicted so many Irish landowners, the encumbered estates court had been set up in 1849. Large

---

[1] See J. S. Donnelly, jr, 'The Irish agricultural depression of 1859–64' in *Ir. Econ. & Soc. Hist.*, iii (1976), pp 33–54.

[2] See W. E. Vaughan, 'Farmer, grazier, and gentleman: Edward Delany of Woodtown, 1851–99' in *Ir. Econ. & Soc. Hist.*, ix (1982), pp 60–61.

[3] 13 & 14 Vict., c. 69 (14 Aug. 1850).

amounts of land changed hands by auction in the court in the following years. This served to restore the solvency of landlordism but also tended to dispel any aura of sacrosanctity attaching to the functions of landed proprietor. Even before the famine tenants had been seeking legal changes to enlarge their rights in the relationship with the landlord. From 1850 their vocal representatives gave evidence of a widespread belief that such legislation was desirable and possible. Tenant farmers in the 1850s and 1860s did not reject landlordism, but they challenged it. The best evidence of their success in this was the failure of landlords to put up rents in line with the increasing income of the farmers. Landlords were comparatively prosperous in these years because most farmers could afford to pay their rents promptly, but proportionately the farmers were getting more of the extra wealth. This of course is to talk in global terms. Some landlords did increase rents in line with agricultural prices, and no tenant without a lease (the case of the great majority), no matter how reasonable his rent, could be confident that his landlord, or a successor, would not demand a substantial increase. Similarly, although after the early 1850s only a tiny proportion of tenants were evicted in any year, some notoriously unfair evictions did occur from time to time and the threat was always there.[1] The fact is that the successful working of a commercial landlord–tenant relationship requires the existence of a complex of understandings and usages. It is a socio-cultural accomplishment that cannot be conjured into existence by even the most sophisticated legislation. Given time and stability it can develop, but throughout most of Ireland the length of time between the famine and the land war was not sufficient. The celebrated 'Ulster custom', so liable to turn to dust at the touch of the legislator's hand (and of the historian's), was a cultural phenomenon. This made possible the sale, by an outgoing tenant to an incoming tenant, of his interest in the holding, even a yearly one, and even where no valuable improvements had been made, although such an interest had no legal existence whatsoever. Such sophistication did not by any means imply absence of tension between landlord and tenant; it did give evidence of practised capacity for channelling tension.

Despite the prosperity that this period brought for many, industry and agriculture were unable, severally or jointly, to support a sufficient number of people to maintain the existing density of population. In 1851 the country had just over 6.5 million people; by 1871 the number had dropped to 5.4 million. Rising expectations and the spread of economic individualism meant that an even higher proportion of the population experienced the need for remunerative work. Indirectly, by furthering this mentality, successful industry and agriculture worsened the problem. They also added direct aggravation. The move to livestock farming seriously reduced the employment prospects of

---

[1] For a survey of the problem and a detailed analysis of one celebrated case see W. E. Vaughan, *Sin, sheep and Scotsmen: John George Adair and the Derryveagh evictions, 1861* (Belfast, 1983).

tillage-oriented labourers (because increases in dairying and the acreage under hay, the only highly labour-intensive branches of livestock farming, did not equal the decline in tillage). Worship of the farm unit demanded undivided inheritance, and so surplus children were turned adrift on reaching early adulthood. Mechanisation of the linen industry left numerous domestic workers seriously underemployed. Add to this the fact that in the less prosperous parts the disastrous failure of the potato economy put ineluctable pressure on the survivors of the famine. Thirty of the thirty-two counties lost population between 1851 and 1871. The exceptions were Dublin, where the figures remained virtually static, and Antrim, which showed a considerable increase. However, the Antrim increase is explained by the dramatic growth of Belfast. Excluding Belfast, Antrim too showed a notable decline. An average of 6,609 natives of that county emigrated yearly between 1851 and 1871. By 1870 there were about three million Irish-born people residing abroad, mainly in North America and Great Britain.[1]

While population declined dramatically in the countryside, it held its own in the towns. The actual number living in towns with an average population of more than 2,000 increased slightly from 1851 to 1871, giving a significant increase of urban population as a proportion of total population from 17 to 22 per cent. This reflects the intensification of commercial activity: wholesaling and retailing were thriving sufficiently to offset substantially the decline of crafts and small industry. At this time numerous towns assumed the character of market centres primarily serving the needs of the agricultural community. Such a role was comparatively more beneficial to small towns than it could be to larger ones. Cork, Galway, Limerick, Sligo, and Waterford had sluggish growth or none at all. Even Dublin, with the lion's share of the shipping trade, performed unspectacularly. Impressive urban population growth, which was so much a feature of the age elsewhere, was confined in Ireland to Belfast and Derry. Derry's share was attributable to the shirtmaking industry located there from the 1850s. With or without large-scale population growth the bigger cities developed elegant residential areas of enduring attractiveness, tangible evidence that more than a few people were enjoying wealth and comfort. The Malone Road and university area of Belfast, in which successful businessmen settled down at a distance from the grime of the city, has its equivalent in the Dublin suburbs of Rathmines, Pembroke, Kingstown, and Blackrock. If Victorian culture was an invader in the Irish countryside, here it was as much at home as in any London suburb.

WEIGHING the gains and losses of any phase of economic and social development is a futile game. Since happiness and success, depression and failure, are ultimately measured by the subjective standards of individuals, there is no point in trying to decide whether the economic and demographic upheaval of

[1] Below, pp 562–607.

the decades under review was good or bad for 'Ireland' or the 'Irish nation' or the 'Irish race'. Nevertheless, categories of winners and losers can be discerned. The winners have to include, along with those left in comfortable circumstances in Ireland, the vast numbers who found a satisfying existence for themselves abroad, not excluding those of them who attained sufficient leisure to be able to nurture and put on record an undying dissatisfaction with exile. It has to be remembered that even the ease with which it was possible to emigrate was a boon of the new age. Losers included, in addition to those failing to make their way as immigrants in Britain, Canada, or the U.S.A., those in Ireland who had to fall back on the poor law for succour. In 1851 the workhouses were still crowded with famine casualties. By the middle of the decade a 'normal' level had been established and until 1870 an average of a little short of 1 per cent of the population appears to have been in receipt of indoor relief in any one week. Meanwhile just over 10 per cent of registered deaths occurred in workhouses; obviously many of the poor were taken to the workhouse hospital in their final illness. While nobody is ever likely to compose a convincing idyll of life in the Irish workhouse, it must not be forgotten that it provided minimal comforts for those who would otherwise have been utterly destitute. The more humane ethos evident from the mid-1850s was codified in the Poor Relief (Ireland) Act, 1862.[1]

Rapid change of the type undergone by Ireland by the middle of the nineteenth century has typically been the occasion of widespread adoption of a mass identity by people who previously felt no need for the like. The question of identity may have been posed in Ireland particularly early and with particular intensity. In any event a large proportion of the population had answered by 1850 and there was serious divergence in the answers. For reasons that are to be sought in the previous thirty to sixty years (rather than the preceding three hundred or six hundred), the divergence was on strict confessional lines. The catholic majority—catholics accounted for 78 per cent of the population in 1861—saw themselves as a political community. For observers, and especially for many later historians, matters were often confused by ideologues making believe that the community in question was not defined by its catholic allegiance. The catholics had a mighty arsenal of historical grievances at their disposal, that served to add weight to the actual grievance that afflicted them, namely, that they did not enjoy the measure of dignity, power, and influence in the land to which they felt entitled. These they might hope for in a self-governing Ireland, which was what O'Connell appeared to be working for in the mid-1840s. The famine experience induced doubt about the country's capacity for self-government, but that had no effect whatsoever on the underlying drives of politicised catholics seeking a larger place in the sun. There was no essential reason why Irish catholics, like Scottish presbyterians, could not have their demands satisfied within the United Kingdom. The problem lay not with

[1] 25 & 26 Vict., c. 83 (7 Aug. 1862).

the union but inside Ireland itself, for, if catholics were to have more, protestants would have less. Those protestants who might have been amenable to arguments based on the appeal to justice and equality had, with a small number of exceptions, been brushed aside in the polarisation of the O'Connell era. So, protestants adopted a defensive posture, convinced that they had to hold on to their privileges or face losing them all in a catholic-dominated country. There were, needless to say, divergent interests within the larger unity on each side of the great divide. Contemporary usage restricted the term 'protestant' to the Church of Ireland and its members—almost 12 per cent of the population in 1861. The presbyterians (9 per cent of the population) were as distinct from the established church in socio-political as in ecclesiastical terms. Well before 1850 it had become clear that in the event of a straightforward confrontation with militant catholicism the presbyterians would always take a firm stand; but on other issues a section at least of the presbyterian community was quite ready to challenge the establishment in church and state.

Sectarian tension had been heightened at every level of church life by competition for adherents. From early in the century, when many catholics had quite poor contact with their clergy, waves of evangelical protestant missionaries had set out to rescue Irish souls from catholicism.[1] The catholic church (itself just entering that era of heightened self-assertiveness conveyed by the term 'ultramontanism') responded to the protestant initiative by means of structural reorganisation and batteries of apologetic writing and preaching. By the early 1850s there remained a handful of protestant communities—mostly spread along the western seaboard, but in other isolated places too—that were the fruits of the evangelical crusades. A catholic missionary counter-campaign in the 1850s overran these pockets almost completely. Thereafter active competition for the adherence of individuals was concentrated on those whose allegiance might be affected by public institutions. Although the days of government subsidisation of protestant missionary agents were past, the established church still enjoyed some inherent advantages in workhouses, reformatories, prisons, and the armed services. One of the leading political themes of the period is the campaign for the elimination of the legal advantages of the Church of Ireland until, by 1871, it had been disestablished and all Irish churches were on an equal footing before the law.

The successful campaign was spearheaded by Paul Cullen, archbishop of Armagh from 1850 and of Dublin from 1852. His name has come to symbolise the attainment of a certain quasi-classical form by the Irish catholic church. He introduced nothing substantial that had not been there before him. Most of what he accomplished would probably have been achieved without him. Yet Cullen is an outstandingly important figure. He had the vision, energy, and patience to bring important trends to thorough and country-wide completion

[1] Above, pp 78–9.

in a generation. He homogenised the Irish catholic church, admittedly in an age that was conducive to the process. Just as the Irish economy came to be orientated with an unprecedented exclusiveness on England, the religion of Irish catholics was concentrated with new intensity on Rome. Direct links with the church in Spain, France, and Belgium atrophied perceptibly with the triumph of ultramontane attitudes.

During Cullen's episcopacy economic and social developments permitted the culmination of previously evident trends towards the intensification of catholic religious identity and practice in Ireland. Following the virtual elimination of the pauperised subsistence sector, the inhabitants of remaining pockets of primitive indifference were brought into line. The newly progress-ing—if not universally prosperous—multitudes of rural society were ready for a lifestyle more obviously 'respectable' than that of their parents. This they found in the observance of ecclesiastical precepts and elaborate religious practices with a decorum and thoroughness that was achievable by only a minority a generation or two earlier. The widespread abandonment of old religious customs such as pattern days at holy wells in favour of approved devo-tions in church illustrates well the coincidence of the search for social decorum with the triumph of the 'devotional revolution'. Increasing clericalisation of Irish catholic society was both product and cause of change. In 1850 there was one priest for approximately every 2,100 catholics in Ireland. By the mid-1870s there was one for approximately 1,300. In the same period the number of nuns had increased threefold and by 1870 there was one nun for every 1,100 catholics.[1]

The pervasive confessional animus of mid-nineteenth century Ireland was not amenable to any easy solutions. British rulers have often been accused of encouraging Irish sectarianism, acting on the principle of *divide et impera*. This charge may be thoroughly justified with reference to periods of crisis, but in general the Westminster politicians and Dublin Castle officials can be far more justly criticised for not having paid sufficient attention to the sectarian question in Ireland. The British political system and its Irish extension, despite its considerable democratic element, still accorded a major role to property and especially to the landed interest. In Ireland this meant in practice a continuing imbalance in favour of protestants in the administration of justice, in govern-ment, and in public employment, at both national and local levels. At local level the balance was partly restored—but only partly—by the stipendary magistrates and by the assistant barristers (or 'county chairmen') who presided at the quarter sessions. Mainly because of the influence of these state-appointed functionaries, who were evidently more detached than the ordinary

[1] Emmet Larkin, 'The devotional revolution in Ireland, 1850–75' in *A. H. R.*, lxxvii, no. 3 (June 1972), pp 625–52 (reprinted in Emmet Larkin, *The historical dimensions of Irish catholicism* (New York, 1976; Washington, D.C., 1984), pp 57–89), remains a *locus classicus*, though its thesis has undergone considerable modification elsewhere.

justices of the peace, the courts of summary jurisdiction were largely accepted by catholics as impartial. The stipendiary magistrates included a far higher proportion of catholics than the corps of lay justices of the peace. Catholics had also gained admission on a considerable scale to the ranks of the higher judiciary from which the judges of assize were chosen for the twice-yearly circuits of the counties to try serious cases. It seems clear that by and large the judges were accepted as fair and impartial arbiters, with a few notable exceptions, the most notorious being, ironically, a catholic, William Keogh, who moved from parliament to the bench in 1856.

The principal catholic grievance with the judicial system concerned the composition of the petty juries, which brought in the verdicts at assizes. While large numbers of catholics were on the county lists of jurors by virtue of property or other qualifications, the effective list—or panel—for any assize was chosen by the sheriffs acting totally on their own discretion, and on occasion sheriffs used their power effectively to exclude catholics. Historically the attempted manipulation of jury selection by the authorities has been a feature of the system almost everywhere it has existed. In nineteenth-century Ireland this all too easily became a matter of real or apparent religious discrimination. When catholics were excluded from the Kerry jury at the Phoenix Society trials in 1859 the prisoners' sympathisers raised a cry against jury packing.[1] Even more indignant was the catholic bishop of Ardfert, David Moriarty; his complaint was that catholics had been insulted by the insinuation that they could not be called on to do their oath-bound duty.[2] There is little likelihood that those directly involved in such instances greatly regretted their exclusion. Despite such problems it can be said that seldom before or since has the jury system worked more fairly and more effectively throughout the country than it did in the mid-Victorian period.

The accession of Keogh (judge of the court of common pleas, 1856–78), Rickard Deasy (baron of the court of exchequer, 1861–78; lord justice of appeal, 1878–83), Thomas O'Hagan (lord chancellor, 1868–74, 1880–81), Christopher Palles (chief baron of the court of exchequer, 1874–1916), and other catholics to the highest reaches of the judicial system was paralleled only imperfectly in other branches of the public service. In general, protestants (many of them Englishmen or Scots) very significantly outnumbered catholics at the higher levels, even though the number of catholic appointees was increasing steadily in the 1850s and 1860s. At the lower levels, where selection by competitive examination was becoming the norm from the 1850s, catholics had less cause for complaint. In any case, just as the pessimist's glass is half empty when the optimist's glass is half full, statistics for the employment of catholics can be viewed from either end, as an index of opportunity denied, or, on the other hand, as evidence of advancement achieved. Taking the latter perspective a Dublin priest writing for a Roman audience in 1859 made an impassioned plea

[1] Below, pp 418–19.   [2] *Nation*, 23 Apr. 1859.

for the elevation of Archbishop Cullen to the college of cardinals on the grounds that such a compliment was due to Irish catholics, 'a population growing every day in wealth and social importance', which could boast of having five out of twelve judgeships in the supreme courts, 'almost one half of the administrative power' in the banks, the control of three great railway lines, and landed property in the hands both of old gentry and of 'numberless others who in the late transfer of landed property have acquired by purchase large territorial possessions'.[1] If protestants enjoyed privilege in access to higher positions it must not be forgotten that another species of privilege, access to secondary education, determined who would pick up the catholic share. In the 1850s and 1860s there was a burgeoning of secondary education in which catholics were well to the fore. Older schools expanded and new ones were founded, among them Newbridge College in 1852 and the French College (Blackrock) and Terenure College, both in 1860.

If opportunities in Irish government service were limited, the young men coming from these institutions could enter the professions, or aspire to careers in the army or in the imperial or foreign service. From this time very significant numbers of Irish catholics of gentry, commercial, and strong farming stock began to enter the service of the British empire. Irish protestants and catholics of the officer class were outnumbered by the Irish of the rank and file in the army, though these declined somewhat with the fall of the Irish population. If Irishmen had a common empire to provide them with places in the sun, they had a diversity of churches that could be used for the same purpose. The Irish famine emigrants were followed with little delay by swelling contingents of priests: after 1850 Maynooth and the other seminaries produced a large surplus, even with the creation of many new posts in Ireland itself. (At the first Vatican council in 1869–70 no less than 10 per cent of the participating bishops were Irish-born.) Similarly Trinity College produced a great surplus of clergymen who found livings in England and elsewhere in the English-speaking world. Mid-Victorian Ireland was dependent, for its economic progress and for the defusing of employment-related sectarian tensions, on the existence of many opportunities abroad.

The economic exploitation of Ireland was something that nineteenth-century British politicians scarcely thought about. That was occurring spontaneously, and given the enormous pulling power of British industry and commerce it is not at all certain that any conceivable political change, such as Irish self-government, could have altered the situation very much. From time to time worry about the possible invasion of Ireland by another power weighed on the minds of ministers more than we can now readily imagine. They had consolation in the strength of the navy and in the presence in Ireland of a sizeable military force, usually of between 20,000 and 30,000 men. The latter could

[1] Emmet Larkin, *The making of the Roman Catholic church in Ireland, 1850–60* (Chapel Hill, N.C., 1980), p. 447.

also be called on as a last resort in dealing with internal problems, whether of disaffection or of social or confessional strife. Because of such problems limitations were occasionally (and very reluctantly) imposed in Ireland on the exercise of certain civil rights that by mid-century were considered inviolable in Britain, such as habeas corpus and the right to carry arms. The party processions act[1] interfered with the rights of public assembly in Ireland: it was intended to suppress the Orange parades, which were the occasion of much sectarian provocation and violence.

A major divergence between British and Irish law enforcement arrangements was the existence in Ireland of an armed, centrally-controlled constabulary, given definitive shape in 1836.[2] It proved reasonably effective at keeping Orangemen and militant nationalists in check. There was another dimension to its work, one that came fully to fruition in the mid-Victorian period, namely, the enforcement throughout the land of order based on the rule of laws and publicly administered in the courts. This is probably the least appreciated achievement of the era. Before the famine a large proportion of the population was subjected to other types of social control operated by anonymous and irresponsible persons through secret societies or less formal combinations (frequently denominated as 'Ribbonmen' because police inspectors and other people behind desks like to have names for things). These have been naively idealised as enforcers of some 'popular' or 'native' code of justice, enshrining the rights of an oppressed people. In fact Irish secret societies were simply a local manifestation of a baleful primitive system that modern governments have had to tackle in many areas in Europe. The Mafia is the result of the failure of the Italian government in Sicily after 1860 in this task. 'Ribbonism', like the Mafia, meant the infliction of arbitrary and cruel punishment without due process. Secret societies had not completely disappeared from Ireland in the 1850s, but their extent and scope were very remarkably reduced. In north Connacht and south Ulster the habits of primitive collective violence endured, and over a much wider area disputes about land could provoke similar manifestations. But as regards law and order most of the country had undergone something of a transformation. It was not simply that secret conspiracy had been tamed: serious crime in general was drastically reduced. By 1850 Ireland had a total of nearly fourteen thousand police under direct government control (counting the Dublin Metropolitan Police along with the constabulary, but not counting the revenue police or the local forces of Belfast and Derry). This figure was virtually unchanged in 1870, giving one policeman for approximately every 425 of the population. This means that Ireland was in proportion to its population twice as heavily policed as England and Wales and two and a half times as heavily policed as Scotland.

With so many factors working in its favour it is scarcely surprising to find

---

[1] 13 Vict., c. 2 (12 Mar. 1850), strengthened by 23 & 24 Vict., c. 141 (28 Aug. 1860).
[2] Above, pp 212–15; below, pp 551–2.

that the literacy rate grew steadily in the 1850s and 1860s. The proportion of the population over five years of age reported unable either to read or write declined between the 1851 and 1871 censuses from 47 per cent to 33 per cent. The improvement was spread fairly evenly throughout the country but was most noticeable in Connacht, where the figure had just dipped below 50 per cent by 1871. The principal agent that inculcated literacy was the national school.[1] The number of children studying the three Rs under the auspices of the national board increased steadily. Like school systems everywhere the national system was as effective as the society it served wished it to be. The anxiety of so many clergymen and nationalist ideologues that the national school could be used to seduce the youth of the country from the world-view fashioned by church and family seems in retrospect quite unnecessary. On the other hand the system imparted very effectively what parents wanted from it, the boon of literacy in English, and numeracy. If the national schools contributed to the continuing decline of Irish, they were able to do so because of popular attitudes to the language. In the mid-nineteenth century, as both before and after, ordinary people deliberately cut off their children from several features of the inherited way of life—including the Irish language and much oral tradition and social customs—in order, as they assumed, to prepare them the better for life in the new age. That life might be spent at home or abroad.

Literary historians have an understandable preoccupation with the small minority of works that are of outstanding merit, and with their authors. This approach can seriously distort the social and contextual history of literature and lessens appreciation of the major uses of literacy that are of concern to cultural history. The impression has sometimes been given that literary life in Ireland in the two decades after the famine was limited to a diminished William Carleton, scribbling unworthy addenda to a previously complete corpus until his death in 1869. These years in fact witnessed varied and vibrant literary activity. The question of how many deathless masterpieces resulted is an interesting one, but not the most important for present purposes. A great volume of work first saw the light in monthly or weekly magazines. Periodical literature in the 1850s and early 1860s was dominated by the Monaghan-born Dublin publisher, James Duffy. Collectively, and even individually, his overlapping series of magazines presented a *mélange* of fiction ('tales'), history, topography, verse, and piety, most of it in easy popular shape.[2] Literary taste, like so much else in Ireland had become denominational, and Duffy's religion was insistently, even if not always aggressively, catholic. The mixture in his periodicals was repeated even more successfully in his book catalogues. He published scores of works, some of Young Ireland and pre-famine vintage, but most with

[1] Below, pp 523–37.
[2] *Duffy's Irish Catholic Magazine*, no. 1 (Feb. 1847), etc.

a catholic or nationalist appeal. He built up an empire in meeting the needs of the newly emergent mass literacy of Irish catholicism. 'Empire' is no exaggeration, for his market extended to North America, Australia, New Zealand, India, and virtually every town in Britain. His achievement was a commercial symbol of the world-wide success of Irish catholicism. From the *Spirit of the Nation* to Dean Richard O'Brien's novels, from Moore's *Melodies* to *Simon Kerrigan, or the confessions of an apostate*, and from Mitchel's *Jail journal* and Cobbett's *History of the reformation* to *The cross and the shamrock, or how to defend the faith, an Irish-American catholic tale of real life, etc.*, Duffy's books responded to and further strengthened the sense of identity of a new, predominantly literate politico-religious community. His enterprise was Dublin-based, giving direct employment to over one hundred people (not including printers) in a city where, when he started his business in the 1830s, book publishing was in a parlous state. Neither as a cultural nor as a commercial phenomenon has his achievement received due recognition. Like Guinness's, and the linen manufacturers of Belfast, he exploited the conditions of the age to sell an Irish product to a wider market. That is not to say he had a monopoly—or anything like it—even of the ethno-religious market for which he principally catered. The most impressive new work of fiction addressed to this audience before 1870, Charles Kickham's *Sally Cavanagh, or the untenanted graves*, was not first published by Duffy but by W. E. Kelly of Dublin jointly with Simpkin, Marshall & Co. of London (1869). Another Dublin firm strongly represented in the same market was that of McGlashan & Gill, whose many new publications at this time included Patrick Kennedy's *The banks of the Boro* (1867) and *Evenings in the Duffrey* (1869).

If Duffy did not have a monopoly, neither was his list exclusive. In 1863 he was selling the first edition of *The house by the churchyard* by Joseph Sheridan Le Fanu, who was the proprietor and editor of the protestant and tory *Dublin University Magazine*. Whereas the generality of Duffy's authors were addressing themselves to a newly viable and well defined audience, Le Fanu and his protestant contemporaries such as Charles Lever and William Allingham (whose *Laurence Bloomfield in Ireland* appeared in 1864) were writing for a mainstream English-language readership, even when their subjects were Irish. Some new militantly protestant Irish books continued to appear—glorifying the adventurous labours of missionaries in Connacht or Munster, for instance—but the market was not expanding and was adequately met by a series of mostly short-lived periodicals. By contrast the long-lasting *Dublin University Magazine* (founded 1833) was one of the handful of leading British periodicals. The same was true of the London-published *Dublin Review* (founded 1836), a vehicle favoured by Irish catholic ecclesiastics. In 1864 the catholic clergy acquired a new periodical, the *Irish Ecclesiastical Record*, destined to be one of the longest-lived (1864–1968) of many specialist periodicals launched in this period. It quickly became the professional journal of possibly the most influential elite in the country. Founded at the behest of Paul Cullen, it epitomised the character of the age, providing for the rapid dissemination of centrally approved ideas and directives to an ever more uniform army of consciously or unconsciously standardising agents. An early item was the text of Pope Pius IX's 'syllabus of errors' (1864). Along with papal and episcopal pronouncements of various kinds, the *I.E.R.* carried expert elucidations of great and small points in moral theology, canon law, and liturgical practice. Related but wider interests were catered for by book reviews and learned articles, most of them on historical subjects.

While engaged on the ordnance survey in the 1830s Larcom had assembled a team of outstanding pioneers in the study of Irish antiquities, language, and literature—George Petrie, John O'Donovan, and Eugene O'Curry, all of whom lived and worked into the 1860s. Societies had been formed to promote and publish work such as theirs, and two of these merged in 1853 to form the Irish Archaeological and Celtic Society. All this, combined with the wider contemporary enthusiasm for the editing and publication of historical records and the writing of history closely based on them, created an impressive list of publications: John O'Donovan's edition of the *Annals of the four masters* (1848–51), John T. Gilbert's *History of Dublin* (1854–9), George Petrie's *The ancient music of Ireland* (1855), Eugene O'Curry's *Lectures on the manuscript materials of ancient Irish history* (1861), the first volume of the *Ancient laws of Ireland* (1865), J. P. Prendergast's *Cromwellian settlement* (1865), William Barnes's edition of Poole's *Glossary* [1] (1867), and the first series of P. W. Joyce's *The origin and history of Irish names and places* (1869). In a different category was W. E. H. Lecky's *Leaders of public opinion in Ireland* (1861). The Royal Irish Academy embarked on publication of some of its more significant manuscripts under the direction of J. H. Todd, its president from 1856 to 1861. The *Transactions of the Kilkenny Archaeological Society* made its first appearance in 1850, to be followed by the *Ulster Journal of Archaeology* in 1853.

The *Dublin Builder* (launched in 1859 and renamed the *Irish Builder* in 1867) was a very different kind of publication but one equally redolent of the age. This fortnightly provided news and commentary about building and engineering projects throughout the country. It exuded enthusiasm for improvement of every kind, not least in the provision of public services such as piped water and sewerage. New buildings and plans for new buildings—banks, churches, private houses, and public institutions—were described and assessed from a viewpoint that combined the aesthetic with the practical. Style, quality, and achievement were lauded, lapses from good taste gently but unequivocally reprimanded. Irish distinctiveness was respected without any breach of neutrality in political matters. The *Irish Builder* is an example of the flourishing in Ireland of some of the better features of the Victorian outlook—progressive,

---

[1] Jacob Poole, *A glossary . . . of the old dialect of the English colony in the baronies of Forth and Bargy*, ed. William Barnes (London, 1867; new ed. by T. P. Dolan and Diarmaid Ó Muirithe, Wexford, 1979).

didactive, public-spirited, and prepared to assume that the prose of a trade journal should be as well-turned as that of a literary review.

Attitudes of a similar kind lay behind the exhibition movement of the age, in which Ireland took at least a modest part. The Royal Dublin Society, with its headquarters at this time in Leinster House, staged exhibitions of Irish 'arts and industries' in the 1830s and 1840s that contributed to the genesis of the great Crystal Palace exhibition of 1851 in London. That in turn set the standard for ambitious efforts in many countries, including Ireland. Cork had a celebrated national exhibition in 1852 and Dublin followed with international exhibitions in 1853 and 1865.[1] The first two were housed in temporary, specially designed halls, the latter in what was intended to be a permanent exhibition, entertainment, and cultural centre where the expected educative and socially ameliorative effects of the exhibitions would be constantly at work, to the destruction of the spirit of Donnybrook fair.

Queen Victoria and Prince Albert visited the 1853 exhibition and the prince and princess of Wales that of 1865. Landed aristocrats gave fulsome approval. However, all three major exhibitions were made possible by the patronage of wealthy Irish businessmen, notably Benjamin Lee Guinness and William Dargan. The latter, a native of County Carlow, was one of the most notable Irish achievers of the century. A brilliant engineer and entrepreneur, he had pioneered railway construction in Ireland. In 1853 he was lord mayor of Dublin and was honoured by the queen with a visit to his private residence.

Another Irishman exuding the spirit of improvement was Sir Robert Kane, a graduate of Trinity College, Dublin, and first president of Queen's College, Cork. He was a passionate believer in the possibilities of Irish progress through a combination of education, science, technology, and industry. He was the founder in the 1840s of the Museum of Irish Industry, which in 1867 became the Royal College of Science under the tutelage of the department of art and science in South Kensington (founded in 1853 to perpetuate the scientific education mission of the great exhibition of 1851).

The hope that exhibitions would effect a revitalisation of Irish industry proved to be illusory. But the movement did do much for the higher cultural life of Dublin, especially in making painting, sculpture, and antiquities (including many of the treasures of early Christian Ireland) available for public viewing. The many works of art from outside the country exhibited in 1865 included loans from Pope Pius IX and Queen Victoria. The 1853 exhibition inspired the assembling by public subscription of a permanent collection of painting and sculpture that, with government assistance, became the National Gallery of Painting and Sculpture, officially opened in 1864. The Royal Dublin

[1] John Turpin, 'Exhibitions of arts and industries in Victorian Ireland' in *Dublin Hist. Rec.*, xxv (1981–2), pp 2–13, 42–51; A. C. Davies, 'Ireland's Crystal Palace, 1853' in J. M. Goldstrom and L. A. Clarkson (ed.), *Irish population, economy, and society: essays in honour of the late K. H. Connell* (Oxford, 1981), pp 249–70.

Society had used the large exhibitions to put samples of its rich and varied treasures on public view. An act of 1877[1] provided for the society's collections to be hived off to form a national library and (together with the Irish antiquities of the Royal Irish Academy) a national museum where they would be regularly on view to the public. Ireland's national repositories are largely the gift of the mid-Victorian improvers. It is also noteworthy that twentieth-century Ireland has provided itself with a national concert hall by converting a surviving section of the Dublin Exhibition Palace and Winter Garden that housed the international exhibition of 1865.

[1] 40 & 41 Vict., c. ccxxxiv (14 Aug. 1877).

CHAPTER XXI

Churchmen, tenants, and independent opposition, 1850–56

R. V. COMERFORD

THE inauguration of a new era after the great famine was symbolised in timely fashion by the holding of a national synod of the Irish catholic church, the first for centuries, under the direction of the newly appointed archbishop of Armagh, Paul Cullen, at Thurles, from 22 August to 10 September 1850. The new primate came from a long apprenticeship in Rome, armed with ultramontane crusading zeal and the greatest possible measure of authority from the pope—the warrant of apostolic delegate. His coming and the plenary synod that he quickly set about summoning have to be seen as fitting into the same phase of Roman initiative as the almost contemporary restorations of catholic hierarchy in England and the Netherlands. Cullen exuded a confidence that arose from his awareness of riding on the tide of history. The obstacles to be overcome in the Irish part of the grand design were to be found both outside and inside the church. At Thurles measures were adopted to deal with these internal and external problems; the series of statutes adopted there—and subsequently approved by Rome—crowned the work of earlier provincial synods and became the basis of subsequent Irish catholic ecclesiastical law. In so far as seemed at all practicable, church discipline and devotional practice were decreed to be brought into line with the general law, thus abolishing exceptions and idiosyncrasies that had evolved over centuries. Measures to counteract protestant missionary efforts were adopted. And government education schemes, especially the queen's colleges, were opposed. On the university issue there was serious opposition to Cullen, whose views prevailed only after very strenuous efforts. The details of the university question need not concern us here, but the issues involved are of fundamental political import.[1]

The ultramontane offensive, especially in the lands of protestant ascendancy—such as England, the Netherlands, and Ireland—was made possible by

---

[1] A chapter by Dr Susan M. Parkes on higher education, 1793–1908, appears in vol. vi, below.

the partial triumph of liberalism. This may seem paradoxical, since ultra-montanists denounced liberalism incessantly and much of what they stood for was undeniably reactionary. In fact the papacy was taking advantage of an emerging *laissez faire* in religion of which it could not approve in principle. The governments concerned were equally confused and uncertain about what was happening. By mid-century the old tension between church and state had taken on a new complexity, and in many countries much of the remainder of the century and beyond was to be spent in working out the new relationship, especially in the area of education. A state-approved system of education that was not subservient directly to the state or to the state church would have been unthinkable in earlier times. The Irish national school system[1] was a half-way house on the road to a form of 'pluralism'. So was Sir Robert Peel's answer to the problem of Irish university education, the queen's colleges scheme of 1845. The state would fund a system open to members of all denominations but connected with none. Straightaway one section of the Irish catholic church led by Archbishop MacHale of Tuam—it had already practised its postures on the national schools issue—demanded more, namely, state support for a catholic-controlled university like Louvain. In 1847 the relevant Roman con-gregation, Propaganda, declared the government scheme unacceptable to catholics. Denunciation of the queen's colleges was urged by the then rector of the Irish college in Rome, Paul Cullen. When, at the Thurles synod, he proposed a policy of total non-cooperation by catholics with the new colleges he was supported by MacHale and, as it turned out, a majority of those present. Equally, he was opposed by a very substantial minority led by Archbishop Daniel Murray of Dublin who, while prepared to join in ritual condemnation of the colleges, favoured practical cooperation. Whichever policy prevailed, there would be church–state tensions on higher educational issues in sub-sequent decades. By pitching its claim as high as it did the catholic hierarchy made its own contribution to the impasse that delayed accommodation until 1908. The minority of twelve or thirteen, mostly older men of a more cautious frame of mind, may have had a more practical attitude than the confident ultramontanes.

The history of the catholic university suggests as much. Its establishment was a logical corollary of the rejection of the queen's colleges, and it was resolved on at Thurles. Some years of preparatory work led up to the formal launching on 18 May 1854. Despite some good national collections and finan-cial support from abroad, the new university could never build up the resources that it would have needed to succeed. Notwithstanding the impres-sive investment being made by Irish catholics in their churches and religious houses, there was a limit to what they could, or would, do on a voluntarist basis.

The question of Cullen's political programme, or of whether he had one at

[1] Below, pp 523–37.

all or not, has been given some attention in more recent times as historians have begun to appreciate his significance. He has been depicted both as an unqualified unionist and as a determined nationalist, and both views can be supported by evidence, which suggests that the question needs to be approached from another angle. From his earliest years, as the son of a family that had suffered in the suppression of the 1798 rising, to the end of his life Cullen seethed with everything that went to make up the mentality of an Irish catholic nationalist. He was an ardent supporter of O'Connell's repeal campaign. What he envisaged for a post-repeal Ireland need not concern us here, for when he came to Armagh in 1850 repeal was a dead letter. In the mind of Cullen the archbishop there was no distinction between the achievement of his ultramontane dream for Ireland and the vindication of Irish catholic nationality. Henceforth the question about civil government that mattered to Cullen was not whether it was native or foreign, but the extent to which it could be used to advance his national religious ideal. Gradually, and no doubt unconsciously, he came to see that the union suited his catholic and national purposes. A Dublin parliament would have strong—perhaps dominant—protestant representation; and Irish protestants were likely to resist concessions to the catholic church with more determination than Westminster governments. Besides, Dublin government would foster on the catholic side new political cadres that might complicate matters for bishops and priests. The union had one very positive advantage in that it gave Ireland access to the empire and opened up for the Irish catholic church a prospect of overseas expansion. Cullen was not concerned to achieve national self-government, because he was preoccupied with transforming national life in a much more far-reaching respect.

After their combined efforts at Thurles against the queen's colleges, Cullen and MacHale drifted apart. The island was probably too small to hold them both in comfort. Apart from a clash of personality and style it is not easy to pinpoint the fundamental difference between them, but it can best be understood in terms of divergent visions of how the assertive catholic nationalism that they had in common was to be realised. MacHale, who had a magnetic effect on crowds, had set his heart on demonstrative politics of the kind that he had revelled in during O'Connell's campaigns. He also delighted in public controversy. Cullen, who had no platform charisma in any case and intensely disliked publicity, concentrated his efforts on the duller business of institutional structures and treated politics as a means, not an end. MacHale never fully appreciated the importance of the things that preoccupied Cullen, especially the revitalisation of ecclesiastical structures, including the new flexibility (and the possibility of multi-faceted contact with the faithful) provided by confraternities, religious orders, parochial missions, and the like. It was significant that MacHale made very heavy weather of opposing protestant missionaries in his diocese while elsewhere in the country Vincentians and

Redemptorists prompted by Cullen were achieving an unprecedented measure of popular devotional expression.[1]

SELF-GOVERNMENT for Ireland may or may not have been a feasible proposition at the height of O'Connell's campaign for repeal, but millions assumed it was. By 1850 that assumption was no longer tenable. Not only was repeal obviously unattainable but the famine had raised unresolvable doubts about the capacity of Ireland to fend for itself. These realisations were quickly reflected on the political scene. The efforts of John O'Connell in late 1849 and early 1850 to resume the indoor public meetings that had been such a typical feature of the repeal movement failed for want of support. The three dozen or so M.P.s elected as repealers for Irish constituencies in 1847 sat in parliament during the 1850 session as so many liberals, bringing the total number of Irish members of that tendency to over sixty. There were nearly forty Irish tories, not counting four Peelites. Among the latter was the up-and-coming young lawyer William Keogh, member for Athlone, who had displayed considerable enterprise in having himself, though a catholic, returned as a tory.

The abandonment of campaigning for self-government did not mean the end of campaigning. When Charles Gavan Duffy reestablished the *Nation* in September 1849 he was impelled, by his own crusading public spirit and by the need to foster circulation, to find a replacement for the moribund repeal agitation that had been his stock in trade in earlier years. The land question was the answer. It had always been one of Duffy's minor themes and an important subsidiary element in the repeal movement. There were in reality many land questions, but the one with political potential was the cause of the tenant farmers against their landlords. The general upheaval of the famine years, and especially the collapse of prices after the repeal of the corn laws,[2] had brought inherent landlord–tenant tensions to the point of open collective conflict. As 1850 began, presbyterian tenants in Ulster were well advanced into a campaign to obtain legislative endorsement of the Ulster custom. The custom was under pressure from landlords because of the difficult times; and as a consequence of the Devon commission report there was the threat of land legislation that would effectively outlaw the custom by ignoring it. The Ulster custom was based on (among other features of socio-cultural life in the north-east) the susceptibility of landlords to collective tenant opinion on matters concerning levels of rent, and evictions. The Callan tenant protection society, founded in October 1849 on the initiative of the local catholic curates, Tom O'Shea and Matthew O'Keeffe, was a successful attempt to introduce a constraint of the same kind on landlords in a southern district on behalf of substantial tenants (as distinct from the violent pressures formerly exerted by lower-placed

[1] See James H. Murphy, 'The role of Vincentian parish missions in the "Irish counter-reformation" of the mid-nineteenth century' in *I.H.S.*, xxiv, no. 94 (Nov. 1984), pp 152–71.
[2] Above, pp 292–3.

elements within the peasantry). By early 1850 the Callan model was being followed in dozens of other districts in Leinster and Munster: a committee of farmers, priests, and shopkeepers, highlighting the plight of hard-pressed tenants, and prepared to direct the full force of non-violent public opinion against anyone who might consider taking a farm from which the previous tenant was deemed to have been unfairly evicted.

The charge of 'socialism' and 'communism' was frequently levelled against tenant right advocates at this time when the fear of subversion of property rights, set off by the revolutions of 1848, was still strong in many quarters. But the tenant righters could in turn deflect this fear from themselves on to those below them in the socio-economic order. The Callan tenant protection society had as one of its professed objects the provision of industrial employment for 'the labouring classes'. There was undoubtedly humanitarian concern in this, but there was also an anxiety to keep down poor rates and to ward off the menace of the landless. The Irish Democratic Association, a vehicle for militant artisans who refused to accept that the cause of revolution in Ireland had been lost in 1848, flourished until the middle of 1850. Its stated aims included 'the return of the exiles', a proposal fraught with threatening implications for those tenant farmers in possession of the post-famine land.

By August 1850 the tenant right activists, north and south, were joined in one organisation, the Irish Tenant League. The league was concerned primarily with seeking parliamentary support for change in land law and left the local organisations to look after disputes with individual landlords. The parliamentary campaign was an excellent venture from the journalistic viewpoint. Newspaper proprietors provided not just support in their papers but actual leadership and direction. In addition to Duffy of the *Nation* there was John Gray of the *Freeman's Journal* and Frederick Lucas, founder of the *Tablet*, which he had brought across from his native England in search of a cause to serve with his convert's zeal. Equally enthusiastic were James MacKnight of the *Banner of Ulster* (Belfast) and John Francis Maguire of the *Cork Examiner*.

The extension of the franchise in 1850 to include thousands of additional farmers in every county opened up hitherto inconceivable prospects for a parliamentary tenant right campaign.[1] Duffy persuaded the others of the feasibility of building up a parliamentary party pledged to the advancement of tenant right, and not simply relying on M.P.s with previous party commitments. That would mean contesting elections, and a campaign of public meetings and petitions would also be essential. Campaigning got under way in the autumn of 1850 with a series of outdoor demonstrations held mostly in Munster and Leinster. However, support was but a pale shadow of that for repeal five years earlier. Local leadership was dominated by clergymen—both catholic and presbyterian—but their dedication could not overcome the fact

---

[1] The county electorate rose by 125 per cent, from 60,597 in 1832 to 135,245 in 1851–2, while the borough and university electorates fell slightly; see below, ix, 635.

that they were a minority of their respective orders. Very few sitting M.P.s came forward to endorse the league's programme. True, almost all of them were tied directly or indirectly to the landlord interest, but they could have been expected to show signs of eagerness if the tenant movement looked like sweeping the board on the new franchise. In the event the matter was never put to a straight test at the polls; an issue of far wider interest intervened before general elections were held.

The English catholic hierarchy was restored in 1850 in a manner that caused an amount of unnecessary concern to those wary of Romanism. Government and parliament responded with a measure that combined minimal effectiveness with a massive amount of offence to catholics—the ecclesiastical titles act of 1851.[1] Irish catholics were in the forefront of the protests against the act. It proposed to infringe the liberty of their church, which was bad enough; worse still, it threatened their self-respect by its implications of second-class citizenship. Up and down the country priests and bishops addressed protest meetings inside and outside chapels. Most of the Irish liberal members voted against the first reading of the bill in February 1851, although this meant opposing a liberal government's measure. Their determined resistance at subsequent stages delayed the passage of the act until August. The most vociferous parliamentary opponents of the legislation were dubbed 'the Irish Brigade' by the admiring *Tablet* (and 'the pope's brass band' by a less favourably disposed later commentator). About twenty of them went so far as to threaten opposition to the government on every issue until the offending act should be repealed. Their support for the tory opposition in an important vote on 19 February 1851 actually caused the resignation of the prime minister, Lord John Russell, but he quickly resumed office as there was nobody willing and able to take his place at that stage.

The Brigadiers sat together in the commons. They promoted the formation of the Catholic Defence Association of Great Britain and Ireland, which was launched at a meeting in Dublin on 19 August 1851 with Archbishop Cullen in the chair. Three members of the Brigade stood out from the others: William Keogh, George Henry Moore, and John Sadleir. Moore and Sadleir were both catholic landlords, but of very different stamps. Moore, elected as a liberal for County Mayo in 1847, lived the life of a squire on the proceeds of ancestral acquisitions supplemented by timely victories on the racecourse, and had never had need to learn the art of cautious speech. Sadleir, returned for Carlow Town as a repealer, had started from small beginnings on the building of an ambitious personal empire in land, railway shares, and banking. (He was the original of Mr Merdle in Charles Dickens's *Little Dorrit*.) With leaders like this the Catholic Defence Association could not have been expected to care very much about tenant right. Yet in a very short time the Irish Tenant League had come to an understanding with the association. The reasons for this are not

[1] 14 & 15 Vict., c. 60 (1 Aug. 1851).

difficult to understand. Each group had the purpose of maintaining a parliamentary party dedicated to its aims. The aims were different, but over most of the country the two groups depended on the same body of voters and the same local leadership—that of the priests. Failure to cooperate would split their available support and ruin the prospects of both. So they agreed to cooperate, despite the misgivings of Gavan Duffy, the presbyterians, and the priests active in the league. The agreement, arrived at in August 1851, was virtually forced on the league by one of its indispensable friends, William Sharman Crawford, owner of almost 6,000 acres in County Down, radical M.P. for Rochdale, and long-standing advocate of tenant right in the house of commons. The Brigade consented to support tenant demands in parliament but only in a watered-down version as contained in a draft bill agreed with Crawford and providing for fair rent and free sale but excluding fixity of tenure. There was no meeting of hearts. Brigadiers and tenant leaguers showed an intense distrust of one another, which was increased when it became known that Sadleir was planning to launch a new newspaper in competition with the *Nation*, the *Tablet*, the *Freeman's Journal*, and the others. It appeared in January 1852 as the *Telegraph*.[1]

The government fell in February 1852 and was succeeded by a minority tory administration. There was an understanding that an election would follow later in the year. In the interval the new government proceeded to stoke the fires of religious animosity by prohibiting catholic processions in England. Catholic opinion in Ireland accused the government of fomenting the serious sectarian rioting at Stockport, Cheshire, in June 1852 in which catholics came off second best. Religious tension put steam into the Irish elections of 1852. Throughout the three southern provinces, assenting to the sentiments of tenant right and religious equality and promising not to support any government failing under these headings proved to be a sure means of securing support from the key catholic middle-class and clerical figures who in so many constituencies controlled the liberal nomination. Many outgoing liberals sought to secure their return by assenting to such sentiments; and a number of newcomers to parliamentary politics found openings by dint of their enthusiasm for the religious–agrarian campaign. The Irish tories entered the contest with an enhanced sense of collective awareness fired by the opposing combination of catholic assertiveness and tenant menace. Despite the obvious appeal of an anti-papist front, and despite the unashamed identification of the questions of land and religion in the south, the northern tenant right leaders pressed forward with their own slate of candidates, who received the support of a good proportion of presbyterians in Counties Armagh, Down, Londonderry, and Monaghan. In this election the presbyterians faced the dilemma characteristic of their situation for much of the nineteenth century: whether to assert their

---

[1] Throughout 1852 the *Telegraph* appeared thrice-weekly. There was also a *Weekly Telegraph*; the latter was discontinued from the year's end, while the former continued until 1856 when it was renamed the *Catholic Telegraph*.

anti-ascendancy interests and tendencies, or to support the ascendancy in the face of a threatening catholic nationalism. In July 1852 the latter course was taken by a number sufficiently large to thwart the hopes of Ulster tenant right candidates. The only success of the northern tenant righters was in the borough of Newry, where they helped to elect William Kirk, who, however, quickly disowned their cause. Sharman Crawford failed in his native County Down, even though he had abandoned his English constituency, Rochdale, to raise the flag of tenant right at home.

Pan-protestant solidarity was not the only reason why a significant proportion of presbyterians voted tory in 1852. For the tory landlords and their agents made a determined effort to dictate the voting of their newly enfranchised tenantry. Far from being a boundless source of support for popular causes, the new franchise produced a species of voter who was especially vulnerable to pressure from landlords as well as from public opinion. This opinion was directed in much of the three southern provinces by the priests, and many thousands of enfranchised tenants had to face the distasteful choice of disappointing the priest or disappointing the landlord. The landlord's wishes prevailed frequently enough for the tories to increase their number of seats, with losses in Newry, County Carlow, County Clare, Cork city and Counties Galway and Sligo being more than offset by gains in Armagh city, Belfast, County Down, County Monaghan, Dublin city, County Wexford, County Wicklow, Youghal, and County Leitrim.[1] But the main, if unintended, effect of the vigorous and well financed tory campaign was to further galvanise the clerical and tenant right cadres and ensure their influence over the outcome in a large number of constituencies. Of the M.P.s returned close on fifty had identified themselves with the catholic–popular–tenant movement and its demand that M.P.s should remain independent of any government not giving the required guarantee of legislation on tenant right and religious equality. The exact figure was uncertain because many were essentially loyal liberals who had committed themselves to the independent policy only out of necessity and with as much ambiguity as the circumstances of their individual constituencies permitted. In any case, what was intended by a policy of independence?

Clarification of a sort came in September 1852 at a conference in Dublin organised by the tenant right newspaper proprietors, three of whom had themselves been elected to parliament—Lucas (for County Meath), Gavan Duffy (for New Ross), and John Francis Maguire (for Dungarvan). Their objective was to achieve united action in parliament that would embrace even the lukewarm. Of the forty-eight M.P.s invited to the conference, forty-one attended. They were joined, and outnumbered, by a few hundred of the country's leading tenant right activists. Some of the parliamentarians put on record their philosophical reservations about appearing to accept dictation from the conference. The chair was taken by Sharman Crawford, whose compromise bill of August

[1] Below, ix, 638; see also Whyte, *Indep. Ir. party*, p. 91.

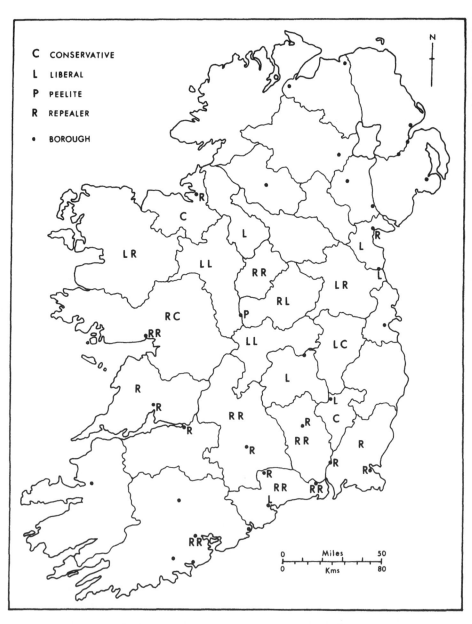

Map 10 POLITICAL COMPLEXION IN 1847 OF SEATS WON BY
'INDEPENDENTS' IN 1852, by W. E. Vaughan

Brian M. Walker (ed.), *Parliamentary election results in Ireland, 1801–1922* (Dublin, 1978), pp 75–86.

1851 had been adopted as the minimum acceptable measure of tenant right. The conference reaffirmed the commitment of all present to the principles of this bill. But how were these principles to be forwarded in parliament? Forty of the M.P.s present, including all the leaders of the Irish Brigade, assented to the 'opinion' of the meeting that it was

essential to the proper management of this cause that the members of parliament who had been returned on tenant right principles should hold themselves perfectly independent of, and in opposition to, all governments which do not make it a part of their policy and a cabinet question to give to the tenantry of Ireland a measure fully embodying the principles of Mr Sharman Crawford's bill.[1]

An equivalent formula was adopted at a similar but smaller conference on the religious question, held on 28 October. The demands of this meeting included not merely repeal of the ecclesiastical titles act but the removal of all remaining disabilities including special tests and exclusion from certain public offices. Twenty-six M.P.s assented to the 'independent opposition' pledge on this occasion, twenty-four of whom had already done so at the tenant league conference.

Accordingly, the independent Irish party entered the new parliament on 4 November 1852 with a pledged membership of forty-two, more than half of them pledged twice over, and five or six less thoroughly committed supporters. The party was in the apparently enviable position of holding the balance of power in the commons. Since the mid-1840s the party system at Westminster had been in some flux, which was one reason why the notion of an Irish party, unworkable in O'Connell's time, seemed feasible in the late 1840s and early 1850s. Just how feasible it was remained to be seen. The new parliament was a cauldron of intrigue as the tory government, short of a majority, endeavoured to hold on to office while liberals and Peelites conspired not simply to remove them but to do so in such a way as to influence the formation of a new government and forward their individual careers. The contrived unity of the Irish independent group was quite unequal to the challenge. A government feint of considering Sharman Crawford's bill—now handled by Serjeant Shee (member for County Kilkenny) as Sharman Crawford had now no seat in parliament—and other concessions induced about twenty of the 'independents' to decide in favour of supporting the government in the first vote of confidence. Defending his right flank in the upper house, however, the prime minister, Lord Derby, disclaimed any intention of accepting the principles of Shee's bill. As a consequence, the independent Irish party members all voted against him, thereby bringing about the resignation of his government on 17 December 1852. In fact about half of the 'independent' members never

[1] Whyte, *Indep. Ir. party*, p. 88; any subsequent account of Irish politics in the 1850s is of necessity indebted to this standard monograph and also to Professor Whyte's 'Political problems, 1850–60' in Corish, *Ir. catholicism*, v, fasc. 2.

moved from their basic affinity with the liberals. The new liberal–Peelite government formed under Lord Aberdeen on 19 December was secure because it could depend on the support of at least twenty of them. The inclusion of the Peelites served to neutralise the aura of anti-Roman prejudice that had recently rendered the liberals unacceptable to catholic opinion. The new prime minister was a Peelite who had opposed the ecclesiastical titles act. His accession to office was a guarantee that the act would be a dead letter, and so was a form of victory for the Brigadiers and the Catholic Defence Association. In making his Irish appointments Aberdeen took considerable care not to offend catholic sensibilities. No other government likely to be produced under the circumstances would be as sensitive to the catholic viewpoint. Yet all this fell very far short of the important changes demanded at the Dublin conference of 28 October. On the tenant right front nothing tangible had been gained (although the government did allow consideration of Shee's bill and related measures to proceed in both houses during 1853).

On a strict interpretation of the pledges there was little justification for supporting the new government, but in practical political terms this was a very reasonable and defensible course of action. Less defensible was the acceptance of office by two of the pledged members, William Keogh, who became solicitor general for Ireland, and John Sadleir, who became a junior lord of the treasury. Their alleged treachery subsequently became a *cause célèbre* in Irish political debate, and in the process came to be seen out of all reasonable perspective. It is a mistake to cast the question in the form: did they ever believe in the cause, and, if so, when did they abandon it in their hearts? Like most politicians they served self and cause together without being clearly conscious of the distinction. The cause in whose defence they had achieved such widespread public attention—the rights of catholics—was essential to the achievement of their own ambitions. And they did continue to stand up for it even at apparent risk to their careers. On 2 June 1853 both tendered their resignations in protest against a slur cast by Lord John Russell, then foreign secretary, on the loyalty of Irish catholics; in the event the prime minister publicly rebuked Russell, and Sadleir and Keogh remained in office. Being in office had obvious advantages for Sadleir in his intended progress to wealth and fame. For Keogh, as for any ambitious lawyer, government or judicial office was the *sine qua non* of success in life, and he appears to have conducted himself so adroitly that he received offers from both major parties, having been approached by Lord Naas on behalf of the tories when they were forming their administration in February 1852. (He was, after all, or had been, a member of the Carlton Club.) His rejection of that offer may have been owing to principle or strategy, but most likely to an inextricable combination of the two. A number of others who had taken the independent opposition pledge in 1852 accepted official positions at later stages in the life of the same parliament.

The newspaper controversy that followed the 'defection' of Sadleir and

Keogh signified and intensified the split within the independent Irish party. One section was returning to the loosely knit fellowship of the liberal party, which it never really abandoned: the number was to go on increasing throughout the decade. The other group, including G. H. Moore, Gavan Duffy, and Lucas, proclaimed its own continuing allegiance to the independent policy, turned Sadleir and Keogh into bogeymen, and continued to demand land legislation. This still substantial remnant sat as a group on the opposition benches, began to be called the independent opposition party during 1853, and continued to campaign for tenant right, even though much of the steam had gone out of the issue in the Irish countryside with the advent of the new agricultural prosperity. The division partly reflected divergent socio-economic interests: catholic whigs-in-the-making opposed the largely self-appointed representatives of farmers and shopkeepers. But essentially it was a factional split only partially explicable in terms of any rational or policy considerations. For example, the landlord, and anti-repeal liberal of 1847, G. H. Moore, was now among the tenant right activists (though it is by no means certain that the tenants on the Moore Hall estate noticed any change). The split at Westminster was reflected in the Irish constituencies, where the older and more staid clerical and commercial interests tended to support the pro-government line while independent opposition was forwarded by a smaller but much more active group, mainly Tenant League priests and enthusiasts of Young Ireland inspiration. To some extent the cleavage coincided with that which had divided O'Connellites from Young Irelanders. But Archbishop MacHale, who had been among the most outspoken critics of O'Connell's opponents in the mid-1840s, was now the most eminent supporter in the country of Gavan Duffy's faction.

A number of other bishops had denounced Sadleir and Keogh when they first accepted office, but in the course of time it became evident that the preponderant weight of episcopal support was with the catholic–liberal group rather than the independent oppositionists. In particular the oppositionists began to experience the antipathy of the archbishop of Dublin. Cullen had various reasons for taking the side he did. For one thing, the cadre of independent opposition priests was given to a style of political activity that ran counter to the decorum and restraint he was determined to impose on the Irish clergy. A few priests on the independent opposition side became over-enthusiastic from time to time, but enthusiastic priests were of the essence of that party. Action by a united priesthood when catholic interests appeared to be at stake—as in the 1852 general election—was one thing; unceasing public activity in aid of a cause that was not specifically catholic, and set priest against priest, was quite another matter.

Considerations weightier than decorum were influencing Cullen. As J. H. Whyte has so pertinently pointed out, a policy of independent opposition meant the abandonment of hopes of influencing government. Week in, week out, public offices were being filled in Ireland by ministerial patronage. For Cullen it was a matter of the most intense concern that as many as possible of these should be filled by catholics. That could only be brought about through members of parliament cooperating with a favourably disposed government. Cullen was not willing to waste the opportunities provided by the Aberdeen ministry. His plentiful correspondence with Irish M.P.s supporting the government, including Sadleir, reveals that from the start he was soliciting appointments for suitable catholics.[1] More serious than appointments was the question of legislation. Even a rigidly disciplined independent opposition party holding the balance of power could not prevent the passage of government-sponsored measures inimical to catholic interests, if any should be proposed, because such measures would gain the support of the tory opposition. This was what had happened in the case of the ecclesiastical titles act. The one way to prevent unwelcome legislation was to exert influence on the government. It was not a matter of groundless concern. In 1853 and again in 1854 leave was granted in the commons for the tabling of bills that would have placed constraint on the existence and functioning of convents. The government rejected both after Cullen had put pressure on Irish liberal M.P.s. A government bill of 1854 to provide for Irish reformatories was deemed unsatisfactory by Cullen. Following representations by Irish members it was dropped.

Cullen's taking of sides against the independent oppositionists is sometimes assumed to have been inspired by an antipathy to Gavan Duffy as a Young Irelander and supposed fellow-traveller of the Mazzinians whom Cullen had seen chase the pope from Rome in 1848. He certainly referred to Duffy in these terms and allowed himself to feel accordingly. However, as we shall see later, he cooperated freely in the mid-1860s with John Blake Dillon (whose 1848 record was far more lurid than Duffy's). Dillon was then pursuing a political policy that suited the archbishop. Cullen used his influence to have David Moriarty, a priest well known to have had Young Ireland leanings, promoted coadjutor bishop of Ardfert in 1854. The archbishop's antipathy in the early 1850s to the quite orthodox Duffy was prompted basically by the latter's stubborn advocacy of independent opposition rather than by his political philosophy. This is not to deny that there were ideological differences between the two. They had in common the atavistic sense of repression on which Irish catholic nationalism was based, but while Cullen's formula for salvation was the assertion of catholic rights in Ireland, Duffy had adopted the ideal of his friend, Thomas Davis, who envisaged a 'pluralist' Irish nation state. The Davis–Duffy vision obviously seems the more attractive today, but Cullen's approach had at least the virtue of being more in tune with the sectarian reality of Irish life then and later. Much more evident than any insurmountable antipathy to Young Irelanders was Cullen's deep-seated antipathy to the tories, whom he identified with the Irish protestant ascendancy. A preference for the

[1] J. H. Whyte, 'Political problems, 1850–60' in Corish, *Ir. catholicism*, v, fasc. 2, pp 21–2.

whigs rather than the tories was a political tendency of long standing for Irish catholics. A basic point about the independent opposition strategy was the assumption of an attitude of indifference as between the two parties. Cullen never identified with the whigs, but he instinctively looked to them as allies.

Relations between the archbishop of Dublin and the independent oppositionists deteriorated in 1854. The latter began to see evidence of an apparent episcopal conspiracy, guided by Cullen, to undermine their cause. Provincial synods had introduced restrictions on priestly involvement in politics, and the national synod of 1854 followed suit; a number of tenant right priests had been disciplined by their bishops; and the last straw was the banning from all political activity of O'Keeffe of Callan on no more weighty a pretext than that a private (and critical) letter of his to an M.P. had appeared in the press— through no doing of his own. Frederick Lucas, M.P. for County Meath, was devoted to both tenant right and the interests of the catholic church as he understood them, and he had a blind faith in the correctness of independent opposition as the righteous way of forwarding both causes. In October 1854 he announced that he and others were to appeal to Rome against the Irish episcopal opponents of the policy. Lucas arrived in Rome in December 1854 and during a stay of five months was treated very courteously, even being received in audience by the pope. But with his plain-spoken quaker formation he may not have comprehended some of the more subtle Roman ways of replying in the negative. Even taken on its merits his case would have had little to recommend it to Rome, demanding as it did papal support for anti-government politics in Ireland. But whatever his case he had no hope of success in Rome with Archbishop Cullen against him. At most Lucas achieved a minor modification in the new Irish ecclesiastical statutes governing priestly participation in politics. Two very definite consequences of his initiative were the embitterment of the conflict in Ireland and the withdrawal of some significant support from the oppositionists, including that of a number of bishops and Dr John Gray, the editor of the *Freeman's Journal*. (Gray did not break completely until 1857.) Against this background Gavan Duffy announced in August 1855 that he was giving up the struggle. He resigned his seat, disposed of the *Nation*, and left Ireland in November for Australia, where his talents quickly received due recognition. Lucas had died the previous month, aged forty-three. In 1854 the party had lost the services of Serjeant Shee after he had disobeyed instructions from the Tenant League on parliamentary tactics. The league continued to be one of the main pillars of independent opposition in the country. The league in its turn seems to have depended more and more on its central organisers and its nucleus of priests, as farmer enthusiasm for agitation diminished with the upsurge in agricultural prosperity.

If support for the Tenant League was at a low pitch it was apparently spread as widely as ever over most of the country. The exception was Ulster. Most of the northerners had broken their direct links with the league by the end of 1853, though there were a few exceptions, one of whom, Thomas Neilson Underwood, we shall meet again in another context.[1] Sharman Crawford, James MacKnight, and the generality of presbyterian tenant righters looked very favourably on the Aberdeen government and approved of Sadleir and Keogh taking office. That alienated them from Duffy, Lucas, and company. As late as 1856 the Tenant League collected a quarter of a million signatures in support of its proposed legislation. Land law reform was seen as desirable by large numbers of people who were not prepared to do much about it beyond signing petitions. The league saw to it that tenant right bills were introduced in each session of parliament, but to no avail.

If the leadership of the independent opposition was undergoing upheaval, their erstwhile companions Sadleir and Keogh were also in the news. Sadleir's tenure of public office was short-lived; he was forced to resign early in 1854 when some illegal behaviour on his part during the 1852 election came to light. Subsequently his financial affairs went out of control; he had overstretched himself and then tried to retrieve the situation through forgery. When collapse could no longer be averted he took his life in February 1856 on Hampstead Heath. Relations and associates shared his disgrace if not his fate. His brother James, manager of one of Sadleir's major enterprises, the Tipperary joint-stock bank, was expelled from parliament. Small depositors with the bank—who lost all their money—became damning propaganda fodder for independent oppositionists who had been maintaining for three years that the pledge-breakers were also dishonest self-seekers. Meanwhile Keogh had become attorney general for Ireland in 1855 after Lord Palmerston's appointment as prime minister. In early April 1856 he was promoted to the promised land of the Irish bench.

Before his departure for Australia Gavan Duffy, in a valedictory leading article in the *Nation*, declared that there seemed to be—in a subsequently celebrated phrase—'no more hope for the Irish cause than for the corpse on the dissecting table'.[2] It is hardly unfair to interpret this as meaning that there was no hope of making a living out of independent opposition politics. His colleague, Lucas, had already said as much to MacHale: 'Duffy's real reason is want of means; he sold his paper; but he wants to go off in poetry rather than in prose.'[3] A. M. Sullivan, Duffy's successor at the *Nation*, looking back twenty years later at the Ireland of 1856, wrote a moving evocation of the political torpor of that year.[4] This is surely further evidence of hard financial times at the *Nation*. Sluggish circulation of political journals went hand-in-hand with the lack of any widespread political excitement that characterised most of the decade. Although the cause of independent opposition and tenant right retained much support in the country, including a widespread cadre of

---

[1] Below, p. 424.   [2] *Nation*, 18 Aug. 1855.
[3] Lucas to MacHale, 30 July 1855 (Whyte, *Indep. Ir. party*, p. 120).
[4] A. M. Sullivan, *New Ireland* (2 vols, London, 1877), ii, 1–4.

activists, it was incapable of generating an intense political movement, and not only because the farmers were enjoying prosperity. Under the premiership of Aberdeen (December 1852 to February 1855) and, even more so, that of Palmerston (February 1855 to February 1858 and June 1859 to October 1865) government and parliament were airily dismissive of agitations for popular causes, English, Welsh, Scottish, or Irish. With no prospect of success such agitations simply did not flourish. Under the circumstances advocates of unrequited causes resorted logically enough to a demand for electoral reform, and especially the secret ballot. Experience of the 1852 election in Ireland had proved that extension of the franchise was of little benefit while open voting lasted; the independent oppositionists were among the advocates of the ballot from 1853 onwards.

If the independent oppositionists were having no influence on the legislature, this is not to say that there was no important legislation for Ireland in these years. In a series of three budgets beginning with that of 1853 the chancellor of the exchequer, W. E. Gladstone, wrought a profound change in the Irish taxation regime, which was now for the first time assimilated to that of Britain. It is a remarkable measure of the selectivity of politics and political history that so little has been heard of or written about this part of Gladstone's Irish involvement, although over a period of more than half a century it may have impinged more frequently on the daily lives of more Irish people than any of his more celebrated initiatives. The changes in question were perhaps too complex and too diverse in their impact to become political matters. The 1853 budget introduced the income tax to Ireland but this affected too small a proportion of the population to become a 'national wrong'. In any case it was presented as a quid pro quo for the extinction by the government of the huge debts accumulated by the Irish poor law unions during the famine, whose repayment was imposing a crippling burden on ratepayers, including all except the smallest farmers. A threefold increase in the already substantial tax on spirits hurt some very badly but their annoyance was counteracted by the satisfaction of the temperance lobby and the relief of the brewing interests, who were getting off lightly. Duties on whiskey, tobacco, and tea shifted the tax burden in relative terms towards lower income groups. The newspapers had no reason to complain. For Gladstone conferred an inestimable boon on the press by removing the stamp duty and the tax on advertisements in 1853 and 1855.[1] His subsequent career was helped by the goodwill he thereby earned from newspapermen on both sides of the Irish Sea.

The demoralisation of the independent opposition provided a resounding line of propaganda for the ideologues who proclaimed the doctrine of revolutionary Irish nationalism. They were few in number, a small splinter of Young Ireland, which had been itself a minority tendency. Gavan Duffy, virtually alone among the Young Ireland leaders, had not left the country in 1848 or 1849.

[1] Above, p. 376.

John Mitchel, John Martin, William Smith O'Brien, Thomas Francis Meagher, Terence Bellew McManus, Kevin Izod O'Doherty, and Patrick O'Donoghue were transported to Van. Diemen's Land. John Blake Dillon, Patrick James Smyth, Thomas D'Arcy McGee, Richard O'Gorman, and Michael Doheny fled to America (as did scores of lesser figures, the local leaders of the confederate movement). The U.S.A. became home for Mitchel, Meagher, and McManus when they escaped from Van Diemen's Land after breaking parole.

The year of revolutions, 1848, was marked by a highly important arousal of Irish-American interest in Irish politics. As revolution swept through Europe and seemed imminent in Ireland, tens of thousands of Irish in New York, Philadelphia, and elsewhere were mobilised in sympathy with the eagerly anticipated Irish republic. The mobilisation was done largely at the behest of local vote-garnering politicians—1848 was presidental election year—but it was possible because so many Irish-Americans desperately needed Irish nationalism for the sake of their own self-respect. The 1848 excitement came to nothing as far as Ireland was concerned, but henceforth Irish-American support would be available for Irish revolutionary projects, and militant Irish nationalism would be inseparable from Irish-American nationalism. John Mitchel resumed in his own New York newspaper, the *Citizen*, the advocacy of Irish intransigence, but proved himself incapable of practical cooperation with anyone. Meagher, McManus, and O'Gorman became symbols of Irish resistance but, not surprisingly, began to devote more and more of their time to earning a living and finding a place in society. McGee publicly rid himself of the trammels of revolutionary sentiment and went to live as a constructive British subject in Montreal. Dillon and Smyth returned quietly to Ireland, in 1855 and 1856 respectively, to resume their careers. Smith O'Brien, Martin, and O'Doherty were set free in 1854, initially on condition that they did not return to Ireland; that restriction was lifted in 1856. O'Doherty set about completing his medical studies and then emigrated to Australia. Martin settled quietly on his County Down property. Smith O'Brien returned to Cahirmoyle House, County Limerick. At every opportunity he defended the action he had taken in the peculiar circumstances of 1848 but he made it clear that his public career was over and he consistently eschewed the popular admiration that his name evoked.

By 1856 most of the leaders of the Young Irelanders had become pillars of respectability and not many of them represented even a verbal threat to the constitutional position of Ireland. It is to a small group of their followers— much younger men—that one must look to find the potential cadres of a revolutionary movement. They were well read young men of that rare but often influential variety that has to live for a cause rather than the more mundane rewards of existence. Through the writings of Davis, Mitchel, and Lalor they had all found that cause in romantic nationalism. They were an intelligentsia *manqué*; a number of them had been destined by their families for university or the professions, but partly because of their political preoccupations few of them graduated. All had highly developed scribal tendencies, towards journalism especially. John O'Mahony and James Stephens fled to Paris in 1848 after conspicuous involvement in the attempted rising of that year. Charles Kickham, who had been less seriously implicated in the same event, remained on quietly in Mullinahone. A number who participated in the revolutionary efforts of 1849 were similarly able to stay in Ireland. They included John O'Leary, Thomas Clarke Luby, Philip Grey, Joseph Brennan, and Denis Holland. A. M. Sullivan belongs with them all, though he had not seen any action, having been intercepted by members of his family on the way from his Skibbereen home to join Smith O'Brien's rising in July 1848. All were devoted to the apparently discredited and unfashionable notion of separate Irish nationhood.

Joseph Brennan was editor of the *Irishman* newspaper (Dublin, 1849–50) for at least part of its short career, but otherwise opportunities of congenial employment were scarce in the early 1850s. Holland was employed on the even shorter-lived *Ulsterman* (Belfast, 1852), which was an attempt to revive radical nationalist journalism, defunct since the demise of the *Irishman*. The *Tribune* (Dublin, 1855–6) provided Luby with some brief editorial experience. Kickham and Sullivan were deeply involved with a contemporary provincial newspaper of advanced views, the *Tipperary Leader* (Thurles, 1855–6). Even before the *Leader* collapsed, Sullivan had moved on to become a member of the partnership that bought the *Nation* from Gavan Duffy when he was about to depart for the antipodes.

The *Tribune* and the *Tipperary Leader* were both founded by people who hoped that the Crimean war (1854–6), by drawing the army away from the United Kingdom and possibly causing a crisis in British affairs, would promote disaffection in Ireland. Both the hope and the expectation of this were confined to a small section of opinion in Ireland. Extreme views about the country's future flourished much more freely across the Atlantic. From the beginning of the Crimean war John Mitchel proclaimed this to be the irresistible opportunity for Irish revolution (as he had previously claimed for the great famine). Mitchel even approached the Russian ambassador at Washington, to solicit a supply of arms, but his efforts came to nothing. One of the small societies into which Irish-American extremists were fragmented, the Emmet Monument Association, decided rather ambitiously to launch an invasion of Ireland in September 1855. The leading figures in the Emmet Monument Association were Michael Doheny and John O'Mahony, the latter having moved from Paris to New York in 1853. They engaged a Kilkenny-born tailor, Joseph Denieffe, returning on private business from New York to Ireland in the summer of 1855, to prepare the way for their invasion. Denieffe sought out a number of artisans and tradesmen in his native Kilkenny, in Callan, and in Dublin city, whom he knew to have been implicated in the 1849 movement. This small group constituted the only rank-and-file forces available for an Irish rebellion. At least in Dublin they appear to have preserved some form of organisation since 1849 under the leadership of the lath-maker Peter Langan, but they seem to have numbered only a few score in all. Denieffe informed them of the projected invasion and sought their cooperation, which they appear to have agreed to give without question.

By early 1856 the promised invasion had come to nothing and James Stephens was back in Ireland from Paris for the first time in over seven years. No doubt the excitement created by the war was at least part of his reason for returning. However, he was determined to discourage the idea that the time was ripe for rebellion. He had travelled by way of England, testing radical artisan opinion on the way, and he told his Irish friends that the country had no business contemplating rebellion until England too was in the throes of a democratic revolution. He himself was preoccupied with the composition of a book. He supported himself by giving French lessons in upper-class households and amused himself by means of lengthy tours through the country, visiting places of historical, literary, and scenic interest.

CHAPTER XXII

Conspiring brotherhoods and contending elites, 1857–63

R. V. COMERFORD

In Ireland the general election of spring 1857 was conducted without that nationwide polarisation that had distinguished the 1852 election. Instead the ambition of local notables manipulated the various electoral interests and influences in each separate constituency. Under these circumstances questions of political policy were outweighed by considerations such as connection, family, patronage, and ability to provide the vast sums of money—sometimes thousands of pounds—required to meet election expenses, both formal and informal. Party affiliation usually mattered in all of this, but more as a badge of connection than as an earnest of attachment to any set of principles. The tories gained some new seats in 1857 to bring their total for Ireland to the mid-forties.[1] The great majority of those 1852 independents who had reverted to straight-forward liberal affiliation were either reelected themselves or succeeded by other liberals. Similarly most of the dozen or so surviving independent opposition M.P.s were returned. The tories displaced two of them—Tristram Kennedy in Louth and Richard Swift in County Sligo—but these losses were offset by the return of two new members for County Clare and Athlone. In a few constituencies there was cooperation between independent opposition and tory interests, something that was already in evidence at by-elections in 1856. The extent and depth of the antipathy between catholic whigs and independent oppositionists was not fully represented at the polls, partly because the oppositionists had few people who could afford to stand as parliamentary candidates. Enough of these were forthcoming, however, to provide for stiff contests with whigs in half a dozen constituencies, especially in Counties Kilkenny and Mayo. Elsewhere the conflict was resolved by the making of independent opposition noises on the part of liberal candidates who found it advisable to fudge distinctions in order to maximise support.

The over-enthusiastic efforts of clerical partisans of independent opposition in the Mayo election led to the unseating, on petition, of their candidate,

[1] All students of Irish elections under the union are enormously indebted to the tables in B. M. Walker, *Parliamentary election results in Ireland, 1801–1922* (Dublin, 1978).

George Henry Moore, who had defeated his whig opponent at the polls. The removal of Moore left a void in the leadership of the movement, which in any case had never been the subject of a formal arrangement. In the next session of parliament John Francis Maguire more than adequately made up for the absence of Moore in the commons. Outside parliament the movement's leading light over the next half-decade was a young protégé of Moore, Daniel O'Donoghue, otherwise the O'Donoghue of the Glens. This 'young chieftain' had some natural qualities of leadership that were enhanced for many by his stylish title and by the fact that he was a grand-nephew of the Liberator. As early as 1853 he had identified with the independent oppositionists and so had gone against his O'Connell cousins. He was in his twenty-fifth year when elected to parliament for the first time in a County Tipperary by-election a few weeks before the general election of 1857. That particular battle against a catholic liberal had been so ferocious that the opposing factions could not face a renewal of the conflict at short notice, and both contestants were returned unopposed in the general election.

Palmerstonian rule continued after the general election of 1857 but gave way in February 1858 to a minority conservative government under Derby. As between liberals and tories the hard core of the independent opposition faction had developed a preference for the tories, and they eagerly supported the new administration. The government in its turn was eager for any outside support that could be won. Throughout 1858 and early 1859 there was a steady stream of measures and gestures calculated to appeal to Irish catholic and national opinion: concessions to catholic chaplains in the army; support for the provision of a national gallery in Dublin; government business for the Galway transatlantic packet; and an act[1] providing for government financing of denominationally controlled reformatories, such as Archbishop Cullen had sought in vain from the whigs. There was the additional consideration that tory foreign policy appeared to be less inimical than that of Palmerston to the temporal power of the papacy, now being threatened by Italian nationalists. However, the independent oppositionists would keep up their support, in the long term, only in return for concessions to tenant right. On 19 June 1858 a delegation of independent opposition M.P.s received from the chancellor of the exchequer, Benjamin Disraeli, an offer of a new land law giving Irish agricultural tenants compensation for improvements, but only for those made subsequent to the legislation's coming into effect. This was far short of the minimum demands of the tenant league, and accepting it would not be at all easy for the independent oppositionists. In fact the government had done nothing to introduce formally even these limited measures before the debate and vote on the reform bill that brought it down in March 1859. In the crucial vote the independent opposition group was split down the middle and the movement was never the same again. That is not to say it was destroyed. The

[1] 21 & 22 Vict., c. 103 (2 Aug. 1858).

tenant league, which was the movement's formal extra-parliamentary institutional expression, did not meet again after 1858, but the independent opposition faction formed in the 1850s continued to be a fact of political life in the Irish constituencies until sometime in the 1870s.

The vote that split the independent oppositionists on 31 March 1859 brought down the minority tory government and precipitated the general election of May 1859. Known or declared independent oppositionists had quite satisfactory results and the number returned, though impossible to calculate precisely, certainly was not reduced. Quite a few of them were assisted at the hustings one way or another by the tories. This election marked the high point of electoral cooperation between independents and tories. The tories benefited even more than the independents from the friendly feelings that had been fostered by the concessions of the outgoing government and by its less offensive policy on the Italian question. Campaigning under the general direction of the chief secretary, Lord Naas, they angled for catholic support, which at other times they could not expect to receive, and succeeded in winning enough extra seats to give them altogether fifty-five of the country's one hundred and five M.P.s.[1] In Britain, by contrast, the elections had favoured the liberals and on 12 June 1859 Lord Palmerston resumed office as prime minister with a comfortable majority.

The Italian question, which helped the tories in the 1859 election in Ireland, was but one of a series of crises or threatened crises that affected political life in the late 1850s. In the second half of 1857 and early 1858 the Indian mutiny appeared to pose a grave threat to British power and prestige. This was superimposed on an apparently even graver threat of Anglo-French hostility, which had been growing since the end of the Crimean war in 1856. News that Napoleon III was building ironclad warships possibly capable of carrying armies across the Channel through Britain's long-impregnable naval defence started an invasion scare in England that resulted in more than one hundred thousand civilians buying themselves arms and uniforms and joining in newly instituted volunteer corps. Thoughts of 'England's difficulty' and of Frenchmen 'on the *say*' brought no pleasure to that majority of Irish people, of every religion, who had no desire for political upheavals. But for a significant minority the crisis brought back to public affairs a sense of occasion that had been lacking for some time. And for a small number of these the dream of independent nationhood was given a new lease of life.

It was a more plausible dream in New York and Philadelphia than in Dublin or Cork (not to mention Belfast). As in 1855, so in the autumn of 1857, the Emmet Monument Association, responding now to news of the Indian mutiny, resolved that 'Ireland's opportunity' should be seized by a liberating army of Irish-Americans. This time it was decided to place responsibility for

[1] K. T. Hoppen, 'Tories, catholics and the general election of 1859' in *Hist. Jn.*, xii, no. 1 (1970), pp 48–67; Hoppen, *Elections, politics, and society in Ireland, 1832–85* (Oxford, 1984).

preparations in Ireland on the shoulders of James Stephens. Partly because of the choice of Stephens, but even more because of the enhanced sense of threat to British power, the 1857 initiative had more enduring consequences than that of 1855. On 17 March 1858 Stephens founded in Dublin the secret, oath-bound, and originally anonymous society that has become known to history as 'the fenians' or the I.R.B. The initial following consisted of Joseph Denieffe's organisation, recruited with his full cooperation. The first expansion was achieved among people of the same kind—artisans who had been radicalised in 1848 and younger associates who had grown up in the meantime. Stephens was seeking an immediate national response to the promise of early action with Irish-American support, but his success was confined within fairly clearly defined social lines. Fenianism was launched in response to an external, international stimulus; it flourished in the 1860s because it answered some of the social needs of a stratum of the youth in the towns of Ireland, large and small, where an increasingly disciplined, prosperous, and 'respectable' society produced young men of good education but no property, and limited their opportunities for self-expression and social mobility. Even in 1858, when fenianism was still a preparation for imminent national crisis and opportunity, its appeal was largely confined to these people. For more than a year before the founding of the I.R.B. the young artisans and shopboys of Skibbereen, County Cork, had been devoting their leisure time to the Phoenix Literary and Debating Society. In the summer of 1858 this society came into contact with Stephens and was incorporated into his movement. The Skibbereen men spread fenianism to the other towns of south-west Cork and south Kerry, scattering Stephens's message more effectively than he had been able to do himself, and apparently reaching significant numbers of rural people. By the autumn the south-west was seething with an almost millenarian expectation of French invasion, of national uprising, and of material reward for those who enrolled in good time with the conspirators. There was talk that every man would get 1s. 6d. a day and free land. Magistrates, policemen, bishops, and priests were appalled by what they sensed to be happening among a large section of the local population. Priestly influence had already exerted some dampening effects before the police moved in the second week of December to arrest a few dozen key conspirators in Skibbereen, Bantry, Kenmare, and Killarney. The new year opened with these in custody and the promise of invasion unfulfilled. In the early days of 1859 half a dozen young men were arrested in Callan, County Kilkenny, on charges of illegal oath-taking and conspiracy. They, too, were members of Stephens's organisation. Before the end of 1859 all were free, having made a number of court appearances in the meantime.

The leading light in the original Phoenix Society was Jeremiah O'Donovan Rossa, an undeniable, if not fully typical, example of the kind of neo-Young Irelander referred to earlier, a pen-wielding, book-reading, socially unsettled young man, a natural leader of artisans and shopboys but essentially not one of them, disposed to find a panacea in the rhetoric and emotions of nationalism. It was an important part of Stephens's achievement that he rallied many—though by no means all—such men around him for a few years. Before Rossa he had already engaged the support of Thomas Clarke Luby, who was to be his most faithful and effective lieutenant from 1858 to 1865. Towards the end of 1858 John O'Leary agreed to lend his support. By contrast, Stephens's approaches to the original Young Irelanders were totally unproductive. In Ireland Smith O'Brien rejected his overtures during 1858. Before the year's end Stephens went to America with the objective of securing his support there, and in particular of ensuring a steady flow of money to finance his operations at home. A determined effort to obtain the backing of Mitchel, Thomas Francis Meagher, and Richard O'Gorman failed after some early promise of success. Stephens was left with his original New York collaborators in the Emmet Monument Association including two old acquaintances, John O'Mahony and Michael Doheny. All three were involved in the foundation early in 1859 of an organisation that superseded the Emmet Monument Association and was named the Fenian Brotherhood at O'Mahony's suggestion. It was intended to be the American counterpart of Stephens's home-based organisation (to which it later unintentionally gave the 'fenian' designation). O'Mahony and Stephens were the leaders of their respective organisations but there was never a satisfactory understanding about how they stood vis-à-vis one another.

Owing to the refusal of the Young Irelanders to cooperate, Stephens's greater ambitions for the American visit had not been realised, but he did come away with a good sum of money, and leaving his Irish-American collaborators in newly organised condition and apparently all set to provide a steady supply of money. But the organisation in Ireland scarcely justified such intimations of foreign aid. At its best it had been limited in numbers and confined to a few areas in Leinster and Munster. The arrests had seriously demoralised it, and it stagnated during 1859, although the international situation was still favourable to its basic illusions for war between France and Austria had broken out in April. At the trials of the Phoenix prisoners there had been many references by prosecution witnesses to Stephens himself (though not under his own name) so that he was wary of returning to Ireland, thinking that he would be arrested on landing. To give vent to his own frustrations and to exonerate himself from blame in the eyes of his associates at home and abroad, Stephens seized on a scapegoat, in the person of A. M. Sullivan of the Nation. Sullivan had indeed discouraged support for fenianism both privately and in the leader page of his newspaper. He had done this in a discreet manner and only after obtaining a letter of approval from Smith O'Brien, who was proof against any charge of dishonourable or anti-patriotic activity. After the arrests Sullivan was indefatigable in his work for the welfare and final release of the prisoners. Nevertheless Stephens chose to declare unlimited war on the proprietor of the Nation, alleging that the arrests had been brought about by his disclosures in his paper, and branding him as a 'felon-setter'. Stephens did that kind of thing most effectively; but if it showed his capacity for influencing the minds of his associates, it also cast doubt on his capacity for leading any broadly based movement.

Stephens left America in March 1859, bound not for Ireland but for France. He settled in Paris, from where he directed his Irish organisation through intermediaries, especially Luby, who flattered him with the sobriquet of 'captain'. He devised grandiose schemes to provide military training for his men. O'Mahony was prevailed on to send home some Irish-Americans with army experience to drill the fenians of their native localities. But financial arrangements broke down and the drill-masters struggled back to the U.S.A. in disarray. Similarly a plan to bring key men in the Irish organisation to Paris for military instruction did not work out as envisaged and the attempt came to nothing.

In August 1859 the Irish catholic bishops launched a new initiative on the education question, calling for popular and political pressure for the provision of a separate state-financed primary education system for catholics. Writing to Rome a few months later, Archbishop Cullen mentioned that the time was right for seeking concessions because, among other reasons, the English feared war and were in a mind to conciliate catholics.[1] The fact that both Stephens and Cullen agreed about the opportunities created by international crises in the late 1850s should impress any historian who has difficulty appreciating the impact of crises that have simmered threateningly without boiling over, of the Sarajevos that have not led to world war.

Many Irish people other than Stephens and his followers were keenly interested in France in 1859. The triumphantly successful excursion of the French army into northern Italy in early summer was certain to heighten that interest. Here surely was evidence that the emperor Napoleon III was his uncle's nephew. For those who were so inclined, dreams of Bonapartist intervention in the British Isles were given new encouragement. And to add colour to the stuff of these dreams, the French commander who covered himself in glory at the victorious battles of Magenta and Solferino was a MacMahon. In quick time Irish newspapers were illustrating Pierre Edmé Patrice de MacMahon's 'wild geese' ancestry by means of lovingly detailed pedigrees which went back beyond Aughrim, and the Boyne, and Brian Boru's father, in the direction of Adam. The *Irishman*, a recently founded weekly, carried the excitement to the point of reporting a reader's comment that Ireland might soon be in need of a king as Belgium had been in 1830 and that MacMahon would be an obvious candidate.[2] The *Irishman* and the *Nation* cooperated to promote the collection of subscriptions to make a presentation to MacMahon from 'the people of Ireland'. The object decided on was a sword of honour, and soon a self-

[1] Emmet Larkin, *The making of the Irish catholic church, 1850–60* (Chapel Hill, N.C., 1980), p. 479.
[2] *Irishman*, 2 July 1859.

appointed MacMahon Sword Committee was in being in Dublin. The amount of money required—not very much, in fact—was quickly collected, but making the sword took nearly a year. It was presented to MacMahon at Châlons on 9 September 1860 by a delegation that included the O'Donoghue, M.P. Ironically, MacMahon's Italian exploits had by then become a source of embarrassment to Irish catholics, for they had set in train a chain of events that left Piedmont-Sardinia at the head of an emerging kingdom of Italy and poised to destroy the temporal power of the papacy.

A sense of alarm about the papal states had been growing among Irish catholics since the autumn of 1859. During the winter the priests organised numerous public meetings at parish and diocesan levels to register support for Pius IX. In early 1860 a collection was launched, which eventually raised nearly £80,000. In the early summer of 1860 a military agent of the papacy arrived in Dublin in search of recruits; it had been decided, rather late in the day, to raise volunteers from catholic Europe to resist the threatening Piedmontese aggression. There was no difficulty whatsoever in finding Irish volunteers. Indeed the main task facing the organisers—most of them parish priests—was to select the most suitable of the many young men offering their services, and to arrange for their discreet departure—in small groups and as ordinary travellers—for the papal states.[1] About one thousand were sent altogether. On arrival they were embodied as the battalion of St Patrick. Before they had time to settle into military ways they were overwhelmed by the invading Piedmontese at Spoleto and Castelfidardo in September 1860. The Irish suffered a few score casualties. The survivors surrendered and were moved under detention to Genoa. In defeat they provided a rallying point for Irish catholic-nationalist sentiment. This was encouraged unintentionally by slighting comments in the English press, which provoked Irish papers to produce paeans of inflated praise for the heroism of 'the Irish brigade', now a most serviceable army which could inspire everyone from John Mitchel to Archbishop Cullen. Before its defeat it was a potential source of embarrassment to the latter because he disliked armies, and to the former because it was fighting against the triumph of nationality. The volunteers returned home before the year's end to an enthusiastic and prolonged welcome.

The Italian crisis had given vogue to the plebiscite as a method of determining nationality. Through this device the annexation by Piedmont-Sardinia of Tuscany, Parma, Emilia, Modena, and the Romagna had been legitimised in the spring of 1860, with the loud approval of liberal politicians in many countries, including Britain. The *Nation* of 14 April demanded that Britain allow Ireland's future constitutional status to be decided in the same way. Soon a petition to this effect was being promoted by a Dublin-based

[1] In May 1860 the government issued a notice drawing attention to 59 Geo. III, c. 69 (3 July 1819), which prohibited foreign enlistment. In 1870 this act was repealed and replaced by 33 & 34 Vict., c. 90 (9 Aug. 1870).

committee. Signatures were collected in various parts of the country during the summer months, but the campaign reached a new level of intensity in the autumn and winter, at the same time as the public excitement about the papal battalion. Collection of signatures continued until April 1861, after which the great mass of accumulated paper was taken to Westminster and formally presented by the O'Donoghue, M.P. The organisers claimed to have collected more than 423,000 signatures. The total was impressive; and although the petition merely asked for a plebiscite it could be plausibly argued that every signature was a vote for repeal of the union. Self-government for Ireland had become a subject of public debate once more, thanks to the impact of international events over the period 1857–61. Closer examination of the 'national petition' suggests that though repeal may have become mentionable once again the solid majority, even of Irish catholics, were not interested. The instructions issued from Dublin to local organisers had specified that signature should be sought from males over the age of fifteen. The total number collected came to less than a quarter of all males over fifteen recorded in the census of 1861 and did not amount to more than 30 per cent even of catholic males over fifteen. Besides, the signatories counted included unspecified numbers of Irishmen residing in Britain. Of course there must be very large reservations about treating this exercise as an adequate consultation of public opinion. A loosely organised *ad hoc* group could scarcely have achieved thorough coverage of the target population. On the other hand there was immense scope for exaggerating: it would have been easy to persuade many to sign without making fully clear what was at stake; people regularly sign petitions solely in order to please importunate canvassers; and a great many signatures could have been forged without risk of detection. It would be surprising if at least a few of the organisers were not carried away by their enthusiasm to the point of fabricating signatures.

The national petition campaign had been largely directed from the offices of the *Nation* and the *Irishman*. (It was well suited to increasing newspaper circulation.) Priests and middle-class catholics generally seem to have steered clear of the campaign at local level, though names seem to have been collected at many chapel doors without the objections that certainly would have been raised against something of which the clergy strongly disapproved. On the other hand, a petition actively proposed by the majority of the catholic clergy would in the conditions of the time have been signed by at least twice as many. This is not to say that the priests were dictating the political policy of the catholic community; rather, they were reflecting the views of what they saw as the *major et sanior pars* (to which they themselves as a body belonged). In much of the country the petition brought into public view as political activists educated young men of no property of the kind already referred to in connection with fenianism. Some were ideological nationalists; most were ripe for political activity because of their social needs. As a group they were to find a place for themselves for a few years in the fenian movement. This came to pass not because they had any particular sympathy for the ideology of Stephens—or Wolfe Tone—but because Stephens played his hand more successfully than others in a complicated political struggle that began in 1861.

By late 1860 the original fenian organisation was in a sorry condition and Stephens was still in Paris. It was a visit to Ireland at this juncture by an exasperated O'Mahony that forced Stephens to return to his post: he could not be seen to fear arrest while O'Mahony braved it. And besides there was the danger that O'Mahony might interfere in the Irish organisation to the detriment of Stephens's influence. At a meeting in Dublin early in 1861 they hammered out a new misunderstanding. Their organisations had been founded to prepare for an apparently imminent crisis; by 1861 that had passed and a new *raison d'être* had to be found. They agreed that preparations would go ahead with a view to fomenting a rising irrespective of international circumstances, and on the amount of American aid in men and arms that would make such a rising feasible. It is doubtful if either Stephens or O'Mahony in his heart of hearts seriously contemplated a rising except as part of a wider international conflagration. Certainly Stephens did not, but he was to make use of the pretence for six years.

From early 1861 fenianism entered a new phase of expansion, with Stephens and Luby embarking on organising tours throughout the country. The most important development was the establishing of contact with the cadres of the national petition campaign, especially in Dublin, where they were to be found especially among the educated young countrymen employed in large numbers by the new 'monster' stores. Before the middle of 1861 large numbers of these appear to have taken the fenian oath. That did not mean they had become discreet disciplined members of a secret army awaiting every word of command from the fenian leadership. On the contrary, fenianism and its pastime activities were inextricably intermixed; and the young men in question were available to join any other political movement offering congenial opportunities to answer their social needs. Such was the National Brotherhood of St Patrick, founded in March 1861. It emerged out of a complex of endeavours and intrigues (involving a large number of people) to set up—and of course to control—a national movement; the fenians were about to be drawn into this maze.

Since 1858 the possibilities of a national organisation (aiming at some form of self-government and ready to take advantage of an international crisis) had been tossed around with more or less enthusiasm among a group consisting of G. H. Moore, the O'Donoghue, Young Ireland leaders (such as P. J. Smyth, John C. Pigot, John Martin, and Smith O'Brien), and newspaper proprietors (especially A. M. Sullivan, and Denis Holland of the *Irishman*). The most active individuals were the O'Donoghue and A. M. Sullivan, but despite a flurry of effort including the MacMahon sword movement and the national petition, nothing solid had been achieved in the way of organisation by the end of 1860. In March 1861 the *Nation* announced that the certain rejection of the national petition would be followed by a summons to all Irish nationalists to join in a new organisation. But already another initiative was under way, which would have to be either crushed or adopted. The initiator was Thomas Neilson Underwood of Strabane, a well known advocate of tenant right who had arrived in Dublin in late 1860, fresh from the Inner Temple in London and burning to make his mark as a leader of opinion. In January 1861 he used the *Irishman* to . launch the idea of having formal St Patrick's day banquets in Dublin, Cork, Belfast, and centres of Irish population in Britain. The response was so encouraging that the *Irishman* took up the project. The young Dublin-based activists of the petition campaign, many of them already fenians, joined in with enthusiasm. As the weeks passed and more details of the preparations were revealed it became clear that Underwood, and the inevitable committee now forwarding the business, intended to use the banquets for the initiating of a permanent organisation, to be known as the National Brotherhood of St Patrick, which would not only arrange banquets in future years but have much wider responsibilities as well. A. M. Sullivan gave as little encouragement as he dared. The O'Donoghue accepted an invitation to the Dublin banquet and used his influence to have Sullivan included in the list of speakers. Underwood launched the new organisation in the opening speech of the Dublin banquet, held in the Round Room of the Rotunda on Monday 18 March. Later speakers, including not only Sullivan and the O'Donoghue but also G. H. Moore and John Martin, made no reference to the new movement just launched before their very eyes. Notwithstanding this pointed discouragement the National Brotherhood established itself rapidly. Within two months it had twenty-three fully accredited branches. Each branch was required to provide a reading-room and other facilities for social contact between members. But before it had an opportunity to become immersed in such mundane matters the brotherhood was faced with handling the spectacular funeral of Terence Bellew McManus.

McManus died in San Francisco on 15 January 1861 and was duly buried there. A few months later it was decided to disinter his remains and send them to Ireland for final rest. The motives behind this are uncertain and may have been concerned originally with the internal politics of the San Francisco Irish with little or no thought for events in Ireland itself. In any case there were at least three McManus funerals, in San Francisco, in New York, and in Ireland. First word of the affair reached Ireland after the middle of May 1861. The Dublin branch of the National Brotherhood arranged a public meeting for 3 June at which a McManus funeral committee was formed. The membership consisted predominantly of young men who had been active in the national petition campaign a few months earlier. Impressive funeral cortèges for revered personalities were a well established feature of Irish life at local and national level. The McManus funeral came at a time when (by contrast with much of the previous decade) the public mood was right for supporting large-scale demonstrations. The committee members undoubtedly had a sense of this from their work on the petition. McManus's comrades from Young Ireland days were perhaps surprised, but certainly pleased, at the prospect of one of their own having his memory honoured. Smith O'Brien, John Blake Dillon, Fr John Kenyon, and John Martin expressed their approval, assuming implicitly that they would be determining the tone of the affair, and occupying leading positions. The O'Donoghue and A. M. Sullivan made similar assumptions about their roles. Stephens determined to deprive them of their expected triumph, because he saw, as they did, that it could provide a basis for a permanent political movement dominated by some or all of them. It was Stephens's first opportunity to display his outstanding skills at a particular kind of political in-fighting. Ably assisted by Luby, he provided the young men on the committee with the courage, determination, and tactics necessary to resist the Young Irelanders, the *Nation*, and the O'Donoghue. Thus he effectively took charge of an affair with which he had no connection until quite late in the day. It was undoubtedly under Stephens's influence that the committee came into dispute with Archbishop Cullen about the ecclesiastical part of the obsequies, and then definitely let it be known that they would do without any formal religious rites, resisting the strenuous efforts made by A. M. Sullivan to find a formula satisfactory to both sides. The dispute with Cullen served Stephens's interests admirably as it stirred up bitterness that would tend to discourage any future cooperation by Cullen with Young Irelanders. The remains arrived in Dublin on 4 November 1861 (by train from Queenstown and Cork) and were put to lie in state at the Mechanics' Institute. The great procession to the final resting place in Glasnevin cemetery took place on 10 November. Smith O'Brien, Dillon, Martin, and the O'Donoghue were there in carriages. Seven or eight thousand marchers, marshalled by men on horseback, came behind, including many of the Dublin trades in full regalia and other groups marching with military precision. Most impressive, however, was the vast number of people who lined the streets of Dublin to see the procession. This was subsequently represented as evidence of mass support for McManus's ideals. It meant nothing as precise as that.

Much the same crowds, perhaps even greater in numbers, turned out less than nine months later—on 20 July 1862—for a demonstration called by Cullen in favour of the catholic university. It took the form of a march from the city to Drumcondra, where the foundation stone was laid for what was intended to be a new building to house the university. The trades marched as they had for McManus, and every other aspect of the funeral was matched, if not excelled. But the fact that more than 100,000 people had turned out to support Cullen's demonstration did not mean that there was any widespread support for his 'idea of a university' (which as we have seen was doomed to failure for want of public interest).[1] Similarly, the great display of public interest in the earlier demonstration was no evidence of popular attachment to the ideas associated with the late Terence Bellew McManus.

The McManus funeral was a victory for Stephens in his contest with other nationalist leaders. It deprived Young Irelanders of an expected public triumph and it won influence for Stephens with the young activists over and above that of any of his rivals. However, his organisation was still anonymous, and those outsiders becoming aware of his growing influence identified it with the National Brotherhood of St Patrick. The brotherhood bore the full brunt of catholic episcopal assault in 1862 and 1863, with membership becoming a reserved sin, at least in Dublin. A meeting of the bishops in August 1863 condemned the brotherhood by name on the ground that it administered an oath of support for an Irish republic. Because of the considerable overlap of membership this confusion was very understandable, but the truth was that Stephens tolerated the overlapping only until such time as he felt strong enough to destroy the rival organisation. The National Brotherhood was a loose collection of people with nothing in common except the vaguest attachment to the principles of nationality. It attracted radicals of one kind or another—as well as many who were in no sense radicals—and for that reason appeared all the more suspect to Cullen and others. These had been given a particularly large stick with which to beat the brotherhood in March 1862 when there became publicly available the text of an anti-clerical address from the San Francisco branch to the Dublin branch. Attempts to explain away the address's embarrassing sentiments were futile.

For the first few years of its existence the National Brotherhood spread widely through Ireland, with branches reaching some level of development in dozens of towns. Among the Irish in Britain it was even more successful. Early in 1862 Underwood claimed that one hundred and sixty branches had already been formed. The brotherhood's celebration of St Patrick's Day took place in 1862, 1863, and 1864. By 1864 it was going into decline, and that decline was greatly accelerated by pressure from Stephens, who appears to have prevailed on fenians in the National Brotherhood to withdraw as and when he felt strong enough to do so. Plotting the progress of fenianism in this period is made all the more difficult by the overlapping of its membership with that of the National Brotherhood. It does seem certain, however, that expansion occurred mainly in Dublin and Cork and in the towns and villages of Leinster and Munster. And even within those limits there were gaps: there appears to have been little success in Limerick city or County Clare before the summer of 1863. Ulster and Connacht proved unresponsive to Stephens, and fenianism was effectively introduced to these provinces by John Nolan and Edward Duffy in 1861 and 1862 respectively.

The setting up of the National Brotherhood of St Patrick and Stephens's

[1] Above, pp 396–7.

manipulation of the McManus funeral both set back the O'Donoghue's hopes of having a broadly based organisation to his own liking. They came in a year in which he had conducted a wide range of negotiations and was clearly considering some very interesting lines of action. In a public speech in December 1860 he had declared his conviction that an Irishman had 'no business in the house of commons'.[1] One of the group with whom he was most in contact, P. J. Smyth, was at this time advocating a clearly enunciated policy of constitutional abstentionism.[2] John Mitchel had left America to live in France in 1859, because like so many others he expected serious Anglo-French complications that might affect Ireland's relations with Britain. In May 1861 the O'Donoghue crossed to meet him at Boulogne. The M.P. unveiled the outline of a plan of action based on withdrawal from Westminster. Mitchel was very impressed by his attitudes and ideas, and in effect promised his goodwill for the initiative that the O'Donoghue hoped to launch. He wrote to John O'Mahony recommending the fenians to throw their weight behind the O'Donoghue, whose new movement was to be within the law but would 'cooperate with all other nationalist movements'.[3] The policy planks that won Mitchel's approval probably proved unacceptable to other groups that the O'Donoghue wished to please. In any case, Mitchel let it be known in the autumn that negotiations about a new national organisation either had failed or had been postponed.

The O'Donoghue and A. M. Sullivan attempted a fresh start a few weeks after the McManus funeral. The American civil war had been in progress since the preceding April. In the third week of November 1861 news broke of a serious incident on the high seas in which the federal navy, in search of confederate agents, had boarded a British ship, the *Trent*. An exchange of angry diplomatic notes followed, and Anglo-American war seemed likely. This prospect renewed the hopes concerning 'Ireland's opportunity' that had subsided since 1860. The *Nation* of 30 November announced a public meeting at the Rotunda on 5 December 'to take into consideration the position of Irish national affairs at the present momentous crisis'. It was planned to get a mandate from the meeting for the formation of a committee charged with preparing plans for a 'national' organisation; and the intention was that the committee would consist of individuals chosen by Sullivan, the O'Donoghue, and their friends. With a scintillating display of tactical prowess, Stephens manœuvred the meeting into placing on the new committee a large number of young unknowns who happened to be close associates of his own. They outnumbered the 'respectable' members, including the O'Donoghue, G. H. Moore, and P. J. Smyth, and thus were able to sabotage the intentions of the organisers. Stephens was proving to be a formidable opponent. Significantly,

[1] *Irishman*, 8 Dec. 1860.
[2] *Irishman*, 15 Dec. 1860, 13 Apr. 1861.
[3] Mitchel to O'Mahony, 8 May 1861 (quoted in Joseph Denieffe, *A personal narrative of the Irish Revolutionary Brotherhood, giving a faithful report of the principal events from 1855 to 1867, written at the request of friends* (New York, 1906), pp 164–5.

the next major attempt to launch a public nationalist movement was moved away from Dublin and from easy reach of Stephens: a banquet was arranged in honour of the O'Donoghue at Thurles, in his own constituency, for May 1862. This was merely a pretext for bringing together a large number of prominent nationalists and giving them a platform. Smith O'Brien devoted considerable effort to devising lines of action that the meeting could adopt in order to move towards the desired permanent organisation. The banquet was cancelled at short notice, almost certainly because it threatened to be a failure. Throughout the remainder of 1862 and all of 1863 the nationalist newspapers continued to call for the formation of a public organisation, but to no avail. We cannot be certain that the O'Donoghue would have succeeded in his efforts to create a broadly based consensus even if there had been no Stephens. But the fenian leader very effectively and deliberately destroyed whatever chances he had.

The O'Donoghue also failed with the other wing (perhaps one should say the main body) of Irish nationalism, represented by Dr John Gray, the catholic bishops, and most of the clergy. Both the O'Donoghue and A. M. Sullivan had the old repeal association before their minds and realised that a new national movement without episcopal support would be incomplete, to say the least. But a movement evincing even a hint of the rhetoric of self-government held no attractions for Cullen, nor, more importantly, for the catholic middle classes generally. The catholic university procession of 20 July 1862 was enormously reassuring to Cullen and those close to him politically. The very next evening a group of them set up a committee 'to proclaim Ireland's grievances'. That was further evidence of that disillusionment with the whigs already evinced by Cullen in 1859,[1] and of agreement with the O'Donoghue and his associates on one point: that there was need for an organised campaign to put pressure on the government. The new committee found an ideal outlet in September 1862 when it latched on to a campaign to honour O'Connell with a monument in Dublin's main thoroughfare. This was a further flexing of political muscles by the moderate catholic interest, and can be seen as part of a rejoinder to the McManus funeral. People such as Sullivan, Smyth, Archbishop MacHale, and the O'Donoghue had no choice but to approve of the idea of a monument to the Liberator. When they went on from that to criticise the organisers for stressing O'Connell the winner of religious equality and playing down O'Connell the repealer, they were tacitly acknowledging that their opponents had made a very clever move. The O'Connell monument committee was living evidence that the dominant elements in Irish catholic society were interested in concessions to Irish catholics but not in the hazardous business of constitutional change.

The impetus for renewed political activity in Ireland provided by the international crisis of the late 1850s faded briefly and then was revived, in 1861, by the American civil war. Resentment on the part of the federal government against any evidence of British partiality to the confederates raised the

[1] Above, p. 420.

possibility of an Anglo-American war sooner or later. The preponderance of Irish catholic (and nationalist) opinion, represented in various ways by liberal M.P.s, the *Freeman's Journal*, and Cullen, did not wish even to envisage this outcome, much less to see it. The O'Donoghue's best hopes lay with other individuals, elites, and cliques who for one reason or another were prepared to strike an overtly nationalist pose and implicitly or explicitly to be seen ready to grasp any opportunities that might arise for the assertion of Irish nationalist claims. Stephens thwarted the O'Donoghue's ambitions because he was not himself prepared to accept subordination to anyone. But the only elite prepared to follow Stephens was a section of the 'neo-Young Ireland' group to which he himself belonged; people of higher social standing such as the original Young Irelanders would have nothing to do with him. There were divisions on numerous questions of policy, tactics, and personality, as there usually are in such circumstances unless an able leadership emerges, but what ultimately defined the fenians was not any question of principle—such as republicanism, physical force, or oath-taking—but willingness to be led by Stephens. His limited share of the available officer corps was further reflected in the narrowness of the social groups from which he drew his rank and file. He won and retained their allegiance by means of exaggeration about the American aid at his disposal, and by means of his own tactical skills and the hard work of loyal lieutenants, especially Luby. To retain his following the continuous exercise of skill and effort was required. His struggles with the O'Donoghue and the Young Irelanders have already been touched upon. There were also numerous local challenges to his authority, as when Peter E. Gill of the *Tipperary Advocate* (Nenagh) published plans for a series of public meetings throughout County Tipperary in the summer of 1863. Only by the astute use of a prominent local 'neo-Young Ireland' supporter, Charles J. Kickham, was Stephens able to suppress a scheme that would have had his Tipperary followers travelling around the countryside Sunday after Sunday at the directions of a rival.

Dependence on Stephens alone was a condition into which the chief manipulated his followers. On many occasions numbers of them displayed an inclination towards some kind of committee system of government within the organisation. At the suggestion of some fenians in the south John O'Mahony forced Stephens at their Dublin meeting early in 1861 to agree to the formation of county committees. It was an arrangement that Stephens had no intention of implementing. In the summer of 1863 the activists in Dublin argued vociferously for a directory to head the organisation. Again, Stephens astutely quelled this challenge to his dictatorial authority.

Mention of Gill serves as a reminder that the press was intimately involved in the popular politics of these years. Renewed political excitement ended the apathy that had Sullivan feeling so miserable in 1856. At the same time the effects of the dramatic drop in the costs of newspaper production were coming to be felt in Ireland.[1] In the closing years of the 1850s the tone of much of the provincial press was changed by the accession to editorial chairs of younger men of Young Ireland inspirations such as Gill, John F. O'Donnell, A. W. Hartnett, William Kennedy, and Martin A. O'Brennan. Sullivan entered the newly flourishing market of the dailies in 1859 and was in keen competition with the *Freeman's Journal* until 1864 with his *Morning News* and *Evening News*. The older paper emerged from the contest stronger than ever and firmly entrenched as the organ of moderate catholic opinion. The more explicit nationalism of Sullivan and his like found the weeklies more congenial. From July 1858 the *Nation* was being challenged for readership and influence by the *Irishman*, owned and edited by Denis Holland. The challenge intensified in April 1859 when Holland removed his paper from Belfast to Dublin. The *Irishman* took a marginally more intransigent editorial line than the *Nation*, but the two papers represented competing business enterprises, cliques, and personalities rather than competing opinions. Holland had an informal working relationship with the National Brotherhood of St Patrick, which nevertheless considered from early on the launching of a journal of its own. Efforts in this direction were renewed in 1863 after Holland, under financial pressure, disposed of his paper to P. J. Smyth. In the event the brotherhood came to an understanding with the proprietor of the *Galway American*, which from 25 July 1863 was published as the *Galway American and United Irishman*. Stephens also had found the *Irishman* cooperative. The replacement of Holland and the advent of a weekly controlled by the National Brotherhood posed problems for the fenian leader. His response was to start a paper of his own, the *Irish People*, which after months of preparatory work made its first appearance on 18 November 1863.[2]

[1] Above, pp 376, 411.
[2] R. V. Comerford, *The fenians in context: Irish politics and society, 1848–82* (Dublin, 1985), pp 96–8.

CHAPTER XXIII

Gladstone's first Irish enterprise, 1864–70

R. V. COMERFORD

IN January 1864 at a meeting in Dublin John Martin crowned his years of participation in the debate about a new national organisation by instituting the Irish National League. This did not mean that the debate had come to a successful conclusion, but that one rather disingenuous participant had arrived at his own answer. As Martin was a man without enemies, who declared the sole aim and object of his league to be 'the restoration of a separate and independent Irish legislature', his initiative was greeted with expressions of goodwill by his fellow Young Irelanders and the nationalist press; even James Stephens was not moved to try nipping it in the bud. Regarding the National League's prospects of actually achieving anything in the way of mobilising the population, even the most favourably disposed commentators were not optimistic. If the league had had any hope of making a mark, somebody more politically nimble than John Martin would have been at the head of it. The National League provided a monthly occasion for speech-making and also published some propagandist pamphlets.

The O'Donoghue identified himself prominently with Martin's league, but in fact it was an unintentional and implicit embarrassment to him and A. M. Sullivan in their search for something greater. The following month they found another excuse to spread their wings. Dublin corporation voted on 15 February 1864 to allocate a site on College Green for a memorial to the royal consort, Prince Albert. Sullivan, who was by now a member of the corporation, immediately launched a campaign to have the site designated instead for a statue of Henry Grattan. Among the contending elites Grattan was being made into a symbol of self-government, to be set off against O'Connell, who had been appropriated by the Cullenites. For the populace Grattan was another totem on a pole. As a large and enthusiastic crowd gathered for a public demonstration in the Rotunda on 22 February, Sullivan seemed to have found a certain winner. Scattered strategically through the crowd, however, were knots of well tutored fenians; Stephens was determined to deny Sullivan an ovation. When the O'Donoghue, in the course of his address to the gathering, made a complimentary reference to the proprietor of the *Nation*, the fenians took their cue. Abuse and accusations of felon-setting were hurled from the floor; then violent-looking I.R.B. men, who perhaps were carrying things further than Stephens intended, climbed on to the platform and sent its occupants scurrying through the back door to safety. Sullivan and the O'Donoghue responded by calling a meeting on the same topic for the same location one week later. By distributing tickets beforehand and placing a strong guard on the doors, they procured a peaceful meeting. But it had been shown once again that Stephens had the capacity to sabotage any open political agitation by which he felt threatened. The O'Donoghue signalled the abandonment of his aspirations to national leadership in January 1865 by transferring from County Tipperary to the borough of Tralee when a convenient by-election occurred in that constituency. He could not afford to contest a large county in the forthcoming election from his own resources; and he had failed to generate a political movement that might have paid his expenses.

Meanwhile the new O'Connellites were making their move. The foundation stone of the monument was laid on 8 August 1864 at the culmination of a procession that put all demonstrations within living memory—even O'Connell's funeral—in the shade. It was a triumph for Sir John Gray[1] and Archbishop Cullen. At a subsequent banquet Archbishop Leahy of Cashel hinted strongly that the catholic bishops were prepared once again, as in O'Connell's time, to be associated with a movement of political agitation. Palmerstonian intransigence had alienated the majority of them since 1859 at least. Since the summer of 1863 Leahy had been in indirect contact with the Liberation Society of England, a body that was devoted to ending state support for churches. The prospect of political cooperation with British radicals dawned for many politically minded Irish catholics in May 1864 with the publication of Gladstone's famous speech on the extension of democratic principles. Even the *Nation* and the *Irishman* grew excited, the former confidently declaring that Gladstone was a prime minister in the making.[2] It was against this background that Leahy spoke on 8 August 1864 and went ahead in subsequent months with a series of negotiations aimed at agreement on a new organisation. This was inaugurated on 29 December 1864 at a public meeting in the Rotunda addressed by Cullen. Precautions had been taken against any possible fenian disruption. A message from John Bright brought out explicitly the tactical understanding with the British radicals. The new body was named the National Association of Ireland, and its stated objectives were disendowment of the established church, state support for denominational education, and reform of the law on landlord and tenant.

The establishment of the National Association was an admission by all concerned that redress of grievances on any considerable scale could not be achieved through cooperation with the existing government. Rule 3 of the asso-

---

[1] He was knighted in June 1863.   [2] *Nation*, 14 May 1864.

ciation laid down that candidates for parliament should be required to give a pledge not to support any party that had an unsatisfactory policy on the land and church questions. This was independent opposition all over again, and it was significant that almost all liberal M.P.s, protestant and catholic, kept clear of the association. For a different set of reasons the stalwarts of the independent opposition clique, with the exception of John Francis Maguire, M.P. for Dungarvan, remained aloof, refusing all invitations to join. MacHale and G. H. Moore, in particular, refused to cooperate with Cullen unless he admitted having made a mistake (or worse) in repudiating independent opposition in the 1850s. Cullen showed no inclination to confess his errors and so no reconciliation was achieved. Cullen's heart was never fully in the association, partly no doubt because it was too close to the policy of independent opposition for his liking.[1] He was still prepared to do business with the Palmerston government without setting conditions, if it seemed inclined to concede something.

The association made very little impact in the general election of July 1865. Admittedly, three important figures in the association were returned for the first time—Sir John Gray, Edward Synan, and John Blake Dillon, the Young Irelander. However, the latter two campaigned under the banner of 'independent opposition', and that slogan had proved as attractive as in the two previous elections and helped to reelect more than a dozen M.P.s who had nothing to do with the National Association. Though it continued in existence until the 1870s, the association was never much more than a talking shop. Its importance was that it had been a harbinger of important developments, and it was the occasion of Dillon's entry to parliamentary politics.

Dillon sensed the opportunity being created by the new stirrings among the British liberals. He saw that independent opposition in a constructive form now offered hope of success for the first time since 1852. Palmerston continued in office after the election, until his death in October. Although Lord John Russell succeeded, there was a widespread assumption that Gladstone's day was coming ever closer. Using the National Association as a flag of convenience, Dillon summoned a meeting of M.P.s for early December 1865 in Dublin; independent oppositionists and liberals with a leaning to popular causes were invited. At least twelve of the twenty-one who attended had been elected as independent oppositionists. Dillon's purpose was clearly to create a coherent parliamentary group prepared to bargain with the liberals. He may also have hoped for agreement that the liberals were already showing sufficient promise to justify support. If so, he had to wait some months longer. The new year brought the great debate about Russell's reform bill. A section of the government party seemed set to oppose it, so that the votes of the Irish independents could be of crucial importance. Under Dillon's informal leadership all except three of the independent oppositionists supported the government in the vote of 27 April 1866 on the second reading of the bill, which

[1] Above, pp 407-9.

was carried with a majority of five. The bill was lost at the committee stage on 18 June 1866 (as a consequence of which the government fell), but the negative majority included only two independent oppositionists. Dillon died suddenly on 15 September 1866, aged fifty, having made a remarkable impression at Westminster during a parliamentary career of just one year. His achievement had been to persuade the independent opposition party to reconstitute itself as a parliamentary force and then to transcend its earlier tactical limitations in order to act effectively in unprecedented circumstances. He showed the independent oppositionists that in 1866 they could best advance their political aims by supporting the new reforming tendency within the liberal party. Within a few years of his death this strategy proved spectacularly successful.

Meanwhile the main topic of public interest in Ireland was not these important political developments, but fenianism. The year 1864 opened with the movement reaching an unprecedented level of recognisability. Police, priests, and people were coming to recognise that intimations of secret organisation in preceding years were largely traceable to one society distinct from the National Brotherhood, and that it had close links with a formidable-sounding American organisation, the Fenian Brotherhood. Hence they began to talk of 'the fenians'; the category 'fenianism' was introduced to the index of the registered papers at the chief secretary's office, Dublin castle, early in 1864.[1] The unintentional acquisition of a name was an advantage, all the more so as it was a name without any obvious meaning. The recently launched *Irish People* contributed significantly to the awareness of fenianism and to the way in which it was perceived. Opponents now had a clearer target. Archbishop Cullen sought from Rome a denunciation of the fenian society by name, and proceeded to attack it and the *Irish People* in pastoral letters. Bishop Moriarty of Ardfert was similarly outspoken in his dealings with the fenians. Other bishops who were equally opposed to the movement—such as Leahy of Cashel—combated it in a more circumspect fashion; and Rome followed until 1870 Leahy's advice against explicit denunciation. Bishops and priests, with very few exceptions, regarded the fenian formula—military aid from abroad and revolution—as a prescription for disaster; so did the preponderance of Irish catholics who had any opinion on the matter at all. But the clergy opposed fenianism before they knew what it stood for politically, because at ground level it amounted to a revival of secret conspiracy and social insubordination. Reminders from Cullen about the spiritual and canonical implications no doubt provided the texts of many sermons, but it is a mistake to envisage many young men agonising about the theological implications of joining, or remaining in, the condemned society. Those who did agonise are more likely to have been torn between the fear of clerical authority on the one hand, and, on the other, the attractions of conspiratorial association with their peers.

[1] See Breandán Mac Giolla Choille, 'Fenian documents in the State Paper Office' in *I.H.S.*, xvi, no. 63 (Mar. 1969), pp 258–84.

The exact extent to which the *Irish People* acted as an indispensable aid to the expansion of fenianism is difficult to compute. The paper never explicitly identified itself with the secret society, and its leading articles were addressed to the Irish public at large. In any case its inception coincided with the beginning of a further phase of spectacular fenian expansion. Fenianism seems to have been introduced on a large scale to the Irish in Britain only with the advent of the *Irish People*, whereupon it flourished. The conceit that fenianism was essentially a secret military organisation was abandoned in Britain far more openly than in Ireland. In England and Scotland fenianism replaced the National Brotherhood of St Patrick as a social movement. When Luby went to Britain on a tour of organisation in 1865 he found himself expected to address large groups in public halls as if he were a peripatetic preacher. All of this is not to deny that the fenian oath was being taken, or to deny that arms were being purchased—perhaps much more extensively than in Ireland. At home 1864 and 1865 witnessed considerable expansion in the north and the west, with Rossa, Luby, and Stephens himself embarking on extensive recruiting tours. Nevertheless, the movement in Ireland continued to have its strength located preponderantly in the east and south.

How strong numerically was Stephens's organisation at its high point in 1865? He himself put the figure at well over 100,000 on several occasions. No written records were kept and in any case this was not the kind of organisation that had a very clear dividing line between members and non-members. No doubt many a young man took the fenian oath in a public house at night, only to repent next morning (or sometime later), and never return to the same company again. Working from the findings of American fenian agents in Ireland, it can be confidently stated that 50,000 (as a round figure) was the maximum number of men ready and willing to participate in a fenian rising in 1865.[1] The actual figure may have been very much below that, but there were certainly tens of thousands of them. There is a similar lack of exactness about the numbers of one rather special section of fenians—those recruited from among regiments of the British army in Ireland. Canvassing of soldiers began in a systematic way in late 1863 or early 1864 on the initiative of an eccentric Irish-American, Patrick ('Pagan') O'Leary, and only after Stephens's initial objections had been overcome. O'Leary and his two successors in this hazardous work, W. F. Roantree and John Devoy, were arrested one after the other in the space of just two years. Devoy claimed many years later that during his period in charge of the work there were 8,000 fenians among the regular army in Ireland; recent research suggests that the actual figure may have been much lower.[2]

Whatever about their numbers, how well were the fenians prepared and

[1] R. V. Comerford, *The fenians in context* (Dublin, 1985), pp 123–5.
[2] John Devoy, *Recollections of an Irish rebel* (New York, 1929), pp 128–84; A. J. Semple, 'The fenian infiltration of the British army in Ireland, 1864–7' (M.Litt. thesis, Dublin, 1971), pp 161–6.

equipped for insurrection? They seem to have had a great amount of practice at marching and drill, acquired at night or in isolated places that could be visited on Sunday walks. The drill masters appear to have been drawn mainly from the ranks of the militia. Training in the use of arms was much less widespread, reflecting their scarcity. Only as late as 1864 did Stephens make serious arrangements for the acquisition of arms on a regular basis; and even then one of the two main types in supply was the pike head, which was being manufactured in Dublin on Stephens's authority. More realistically, rifles were being purchased in Britain and brought across discreetly to Ireland. Both pikes and rifles were allocated by Stephens, who made a point of being seen as the dispenser of arms. Supplies to fenians outside Dublin had to be collected by agents who were required to wait on 'the captain'. The ending of the American civil war in April 1865 was followed by a slump in the price of rifles on the British market, which must have made their acquisition by fenians considerably easier. The largest number of firearms that the fenians can have possessed by the summer of 1865 was 6,000. That may be a considerable exaggeration of the true number, and may include old weapons of varying character and quality acquired locally in various ways. Moreover, there was little ammunition available. In short, fenianism was not very formidable as a military machine, and Stephens's main preoccupation was not with making it formidable but with keeping it under his control. Without straining things too far we could say that fenianism was a voluntary social movement posing as a military organisation. This is not to deny that in certain eventualities it could have made a very definite strategic mark. One shrewd observer put the point like this: 'If England were emptied of troops by some foreign war such as that in the Crimea, the Stephens gang would have a much better chance of making head in this country.'[1]

Fenianism as a social phenomenon is explicable by reference to contemporary Irish conditions; in political, military and strategic terms it made sense only by reference to considerations external both to Ireland and to the United Kingdom. Nobody in Ireland in the 1860s imagined an Irish insurrection to be possible without an international crisis, or Irish-American aid, or both. The establishment of an Irish republic was the subject of far more intense and widespread yearning in the U.S.A. than in Ireland. Even very enthusiastic Irish-Americans, however, were slow to subscribe their dollars unless they could see something convincing in progress in Ireland. Yet Stephens could not provide anything spectacular in Ireland without American money. This, however, came irregularly and amounted to much less than promised, and the situation became even less satisfactory when American fenians in their tens of thousands went to join the rival armies in the American civil war. O'Mahony's policy was one of waiting for the war to end and then starting up again where things had left off. As the war dragged on, this policy became less and less satis-

[1] Entry for 7 July 1866 in journal of William J. O'Neill Daunt (N.L.I., MS 3041).

factory to Stephens, and to some of O'Mahony's immediate subordinates. In response to the restiveness of the latter, the first convention of the Fenian Brotherhood was held in November 1863 at Chicago. In the aftermath of the convention a group implicitly dissatisfied with O'Mahony's leadership set about organising a fair, again in Chicago, to raise funds and generally to provide the Brotherhood with a sense of something doing. Stephens attended the Chicago fair himself and then embarked on an extensive tour taking in many camps of the union army. It was possibly the most brilliant episode of his entire career, and it put American fenianism on a new level of appeal; when the second convention of the Fenian Brotherhood was held, at Cincinnati, in January 1865, 273 circles were represented, an increase of more than 200 over the Chicago convention of a mere fourteen months earlier. That expansion was largely attributable to Stephens's impact. But his success had been achieved by means of a very hazardous stratagem: he had painted a glowing picture of the battle-readiness of the fenians at home, and he had solemnly declared that, irrespective of the situation in the U.S.A. or internationally, they would rise before the end of 1865.

The ending of the American civil war in April 1865 raised the hopes of fenians on both sides of the Atlantic that an Anglo-American war was imminent, and greatly exaggerated prospects of this were held out for many months. Hoping, no doubt, that the international situation would prevent his bluff being called, Stephens brought the organisation to a high state of expectancy, reiterating throughout the summer of 1865 that this would be the year of action. It was indeed, as one of his associates remarked ruefully later on, but the action was taken by the government. On 15 September the police raided the office of the *Irish People* and arrested most of the principal persons associated with the paper including Luby, O'Leary, and O'Donovan Rossa. Stephens evaded the net until captured in hiding at Sandymount on 11 November. Within two weeks of his arrest Stephens escaped from jail, thus adding enormously to hopes and fears that he was well-nigh invincible. He lay low for some time, evading a most intensive police search, and made his way by France to America, reaching New York on 10 May 1866. He found the Fenian Brotherhood distressed and divided. An influential faction opposed to O'Mahony—the 'senate wing'—had taken up the idea of striking at Britain by invading Canada. O'Mahony, who never wavered from the view that the purpose of fenianism was to foment an Irish rebellion, had nevertheless felt obliged to keep his wing of the brotherhood in the eye of Irish-America by some quick gimmick. So an attempt had been made in April 1866 to occupy, on behalf of the United States, the disputed island of Campo Bello in the Gulf of St Lawrence. The outcome was failure and a serious loss of face. Stephens took over the discredited O'Mahony wing and went about setting up another convincing scenario for an early Irish rebellion. The year 1866, he decided, would now be the year of action. This man who had slipped almost at will from the clutches of Dublin Castle spoke with such conviction that he raised $60,000 during the summer and early autumn of 1866. At a rally in New York on 28 October he was consistent with the 'line' he had been selling in the previous months, and declared that his next public appearance would be in Ireland at the head of a rising. He had finally manœuvred himself into a cul-de-sac. Habeas corpus had been suspended in Ireland in February 1866, permitting the detention without trial of suspected fenians. The hundreds of arrests made over the following months had struck a far more severe blow at the movement than had the *Irish People* arrests of 1865. Stephens knew that even if he returned to Ireland to take charge personally he could not hope to start a serious insurrection. The international crisis that would have made all the difference had failed to materialise. So a less flamboyant Stephens reappeared among the New York fenians in mid-December 1866, advocating another postponement. He was at once deposed from all authority by a group under the leadership of Thomas J. Kelly, a former captain in the federal army but with the rank of colonel in the American fenian roster. He was now styled chief executive of the Irish Republic (C.E.I.R.), an adaptation of a title previously bestowed by the Fenian Brotherhood on Stephens—chief organiser of the Irish Republic (C.O.I.R.).

In January 1867 Kelly and a number of his associates went to England, where they made contact with an emerging committee leadership—there was more than one committee—of fenianism in Ireland and Britain, which was pushing ahead with plans for a rising in February. Kelly obtained agreement to a postponement until early March, but owing to deficiencies in command or communications, or both, there was a premature outbreak in the Iveragh peninsula, County Kerry, on 12 February and an attempt to raid the arms depot at Chester castle on 11 February. The arms seized in Chester were to have been hurried by train and boat to Ireland for an immediate uprising. By this time fenianism was leaking information like a sieve, and the authorities, warned just in time of what was planned, placed such a secure guard on Chester castle that the thousand or so fenians who descended on the town by various forms of transport soon saw that they had lost the advantage of surprise on which their plan depended. Similarly in the case of the March rising in Ireland the authorities knew in advance almost all that they needed to know in order to anticipate events. Over the previous fifteen months the army in Ireland had been increased and its dispositions modified so as to have it ready to intervene at any point at short notice. On the evening of 5 March 1867 many hundreds of fenians, variously armed, left Dublin city in a southerly direction, the main body moving towards Tallaght. By the following morning they had been scattered and many of them taken prisoner. Simultaneously hundreds and perhaps thousands of fenians moved from Cork city in the direction of Limerick Junction, sixty miles away. Minor setbacks and a general sense of unreality brought on early demoralisation, and by the morning of 6 March they too were being scattered. In the following days there were minor incidents in Counties Limerick, Tipperary, Clare, Louth, and Queen's County. Mopping-up operations continued for several weeks, but the military challenge of the rising had been very weak. Of course the fenians had taken the field under very adverse circumstances, but even making allowances for that their demeanour—with some notable exceptions—bears out the belief that they were essentially part of a social movement rather than members of a military conspiracy. Very few people had seriously believed that a successful rising was likely, but the 'fenian fever' of 1865–7 had nevertheless made a major impact on the public mind in Ireland (and in Britain and the U.S. too). It had exercised a mesmeric effect on much of the population and temporarily inhibited popular participation in the reform movement then gathering momentum elsewhere in the United Kingdom.

OUT of office from June 1866, the liberal party was rapidly transformed into the first thoroughly popular parliamentary party in British history; or to be more exact Gladstone became the first popular parliamentary leader in Britain, and as such took control of his party. He rose to this prominence at the head of an impressive public movement orchestrated by John Bright and involving the reform league and various nonconformist and minority interests. It had been clear as early as 1864 that Gladstone and Bright intended to hitch Irish catholicism to their wagon. In November 1866 Bright made a short visit to Ireland (originally suggested by John Blake Dillon, who died in September) that demonstrated that he—and of course Gladstone—had a most impressive following among Irish catholic and popular interests. He was hailed by the *Nation*, the *Irishman*, and the *Freeman's Journal*, the latter proclaiming that he was the first Englishman to make himself thoroughly popular in Ireland. A banquet in his honour in the Rotunda was addressed by the O'Donoghue and Dean Richard O'Brien of Limerick. Next day he was received by Cardinal Cullen (raised to the purple the previous June). He addressed an enthusiastic gathering of Dublin tradesmen; and he met a delegation from the Cork Farmers' Club. Nobody had commanded this range of support in Ireland since O'Connell's day, and the cause of Gladstone and Bright would certainly have been hailed at this time by great public demonstrations but for the way in which the fenian threat had paralysed the body politic.

Once the fenians had been shown to pose no serious threat of revolution they became objects of sympathy and a pretext for public demonstrations. On 16 March 1867 the *Irishman* began a campaign to highlight the prison sufferings of fenians arrested in 1865 and sentenced to serve terms of penal servitude in English jails. It had for a text a letter smuggled from prison by O'Donovan Rossa. More startling charges of ill-treatment of fenian convicts were published by the same paper on 13 April. The first major politician in Ireland and Britain to identify with this incipient sympathy for the no longer dangerous fenians was John Bright. On 3 May he presented to the commons a petition, signed by several British radicals, concerning the treatment of Rossa and his companions. At least five Irish members, including Gray and Maguire, declared themselves as sharing Bright's concern. Bright had not so much made the fate of fenian prisoners into one of the minority causes on board the Gladstonian bandwagon; rather had he sensed intuitively, ahead of others, that it would become such. Meanwhile scores of new convictions were on the way as those arrested in connection with the attempted rising went on trial. In Dublin Thomas F. Bourke (one of the Irish-American officers assigned to provide the military leadership) was condemned to death; the execution was to take place on 29 May 1867. Requests for clemency poured in and the government commuted the sentence. This, and the cases of others sentenced to death later (and also reprieved), brought the prisoners to the centre of public notice. The commutation of the death sentence was approved by virtually all politically minded Irish catholics. By the summer of 1867 most of Ireland was apparently returning to normal political life, having acquired a new 'grievance'—the continued incarceration of what were now seen as well intentioned if misguided young rebels—but with the certainty that all grievances would in due course be dealt with by Gladstone. And even with the existing tory government there was a sense of understanding. It too was setting about the remedying of Irish grievances, although less convincingly than the liberals. With the return of normality, public meetings and processions became feasible once again. A leading fenian in Belfast jail had died in March 1866 and had been buried without any public demonstration; after another prisoner, William Harbinson, had died in the same prison in September 1867 tens of thousands participated in his funeral. A recently released prisoner, William Kelly, died in Limerick in October 1867, allegedly from the effects of his imprisonment; his burial was accompanied by a massive demonstration.

It is against this background that one must see the reaction in Ireland to the execution in Salford on 23 November 1867 of William Philip Allen, Michael Larkin, and Michael O'Brien for the murder of a police sergeant in the course of the rescue of Col. Thomas J. Kelly and another fenian from custody in Manchester. British opinion saw the affair in a very serious light: the use of firearms against the police was the violation of an almost sacred convention. In the view of a great many Irish people the death of Sergeant Brett had been an accident. The executions were seen in Ireland as the violation of the recently achieved understanding between 'Irish opinion' and 'English opinion', one not easily expressed in words but symbolised by the fact that the leaders of the rising were not executed. Many priests recited requiem masses for the deceased. Protest demonstrations soon began to take the form of mock funerals. Tens of thousands marched in such a demonstration in Cork city on 1 December and on the same day similar demonstrations took place in many other towns. A week later up to thirty thousand marched in a Dublin 'funeral' procession organised by a committee under the chairmanship of John Martin;[1] the ceremonies concluded at McManus's graveside in Glasnevin cemetery. The *Nation* had been in the forefront of the protests from the start; on 7 December it carried the words of a song by T. D. Sullivan with the defiant invocation of Allen, Larkin, and O'Brien in the dock as refrain: 'God save Ireland'. It was to become a kind of Irish national anthem; its combination of vagueness of intent with a popular American civil war air was not totally inappropriate. Irish indignation at the Manchester executions was deflected by news of multiple deaths and injuries among residents of Clerkenwell, London, on 13 December 1867 in an explosion intended to facilitate the escape of a prominent American fenian from the nearby jail.

About May 1867 Ireland had entered a phase of excitement and flux in its political affairs that was to endure for three years or so; the country was joining in the ferment that marked the rise of Gladstone to popular eminence in Britain. Some of his convoluted public utterances and his general demeanour had been interpreted as a pledge that in future Ireland would be governed 'in accordance with Irish ideas'. The campaign of protest that followed the execution of the 'Manchester martyrs' was not an expression of support for the physical-force separatism of the fenians, or evidence that the priests, the Sullivans, and Martin had belatedly come to adopt the ideas of Stephens, but an assertion of the Irish catholic demand for recognition that the fenians had come to symbolise and Gladstone was expected to satisfy. One Irish idea given a new airing at this time was that of self-government. In January 1868 Dean Richard O'Brien and some of his fellow priests from Limerick diocese issued a declaration, signed on 23 December, in favour of repeal of the union, to which a few hundred more clergymen subsequently subscribed. Obviously the subject was no longer unmentionable even in clerical circles. But it evoked only slight interest and was very far from being practical politics. With Gladstone apparently undertaking to remedy all wrongs there was minimal popular interest in national self-government. For a few years Gladstone offered the same illusion of possessing a panacea that any popular nationalist leader offers, and the same opportunity for mass emotional satisfaction. The waves of concern for fenian prisoners that surged through these years were an expression of a sense of national identity that was perfectly compatible with maintenance of the union. It should be clear that it was not the fenians who put Ireland on Gladstone's agenda, even if once or twice it suited his purposes to imply that they had. If the I.R.B. had never existed there would still have been in the later 1860s an Irish catholic community eager and willing, just like the nonconformist majority in Wales, to give their support to Gladstone in return for the promise of enhanced collective status and recognition that he summed up as 'justice'. Gladstone had a well publicised and sincere conscience about such matters but his conscience never ran ahead of his pragmatic political practice. The fundamental source of

[1] Above, p. 431.

Gladstone's interest in Ireland at this time was neither moral conviction, nor fenianism, but votes.

Nothing was better calculated to secure Irish catholic support than an undertaking to disestablish the Church of Ireland. With a stroke of political genius Gladstone made Irish disestablishment an issue in Britain also. It rallied the grand coalition of anti-establishment interests throughout Britain that was propelling Gladstone to power; but it implicitly left the English establishment untouched, so that antagonism from that quarter would not be provoked. The Clerkenwell outrage of 13 December 1867 added a further dimension. There was fear that it might presage a campaign of mass murder in British cities; special constables were sworn in by the tens of thousands as in 1848 when the chartists had appeared to threaten. Gladstone managed to create the scarcely spoken assumption that disestablishment would defuse fenian bombs. He was thus seen to be offering Britain an insurance policy on which Irish protestants would pay the premium. So it was that Gladstone secured his following in both Britain and Ireland when on 23 March 1868 he moved resolutions in the commons in favour of the disestablishment of the Irish church. These were carried by majorities of fifty and more against government opposition on 3 April 1868. Despite this defeat the government was able to remain in office because neither side was ready for a general election. In the summer the Representation of the People (Ireland) Act, 1868, was passed.[1] The only major change was the reduction of the rated occupier franchise in the boroughs from £8 to 'over £4'.

The general election came in November 1868. For the first time since 1852 the Irish election was a crusade. The catholic bishops and clergy were exceptionally active on behalf of supporters of Gladstone, and catholic electors were left in no doubt about their duty. As in 1852 presbyterian opinion was divided, but this time sufficient of it went against the establishment to give the liberals a handful of Ulster seats—in Belfast, Derry, Newry, and County Cavan. This presbyterian support, together with that of the catholics and the whig interest, gave Gladstone an impressive sixty-six Irish seats. Ireland thus provided Gladstone with over half of the handsome majority in the commons that made him prime minister on 3 December 1868. His pledge on Irish disestablishment received prompt attention. By early March 1869 Gladstone, having hammered out a formula that would provide for the changes to which he was committed, was able to introduce his Irish church bill. Many conservative-minded people who nevertheless accepted the need for change in Irish ecclesiastical arrangements favoured some form of 'levelling up' whereby, side by side with the established church, the church of the majority would acquire a share of the country's ecclesiastical endowments. 'Concurrent endowment' was anathema to the radical proponents of voluntaryism on whose support Gladstone was very dependent in Britain and whose principles demanded an end of all state support of churches. Meeting

[1] 31 & 32 Vict., c. 49 (13 July 1868).

in October 1867 the Irish catholic bishops had declared themselves unwilling to accept endowments for their church; they did this because of sensitivity to the political weight of the British voluntaryists and because they had themselves strong inclinations towards voluntaryism. The alternative was 'levelling down', disendowment of all churches, which would leave them all on an equal footing, and free of legal links with the state. That was provided for by Gladstone's bill. It passed through the commons with very clear majorities, but was sent back from the tory-dominated house of lords with major amendments. The commons restored the bill to its original shape and returned it to the lords, where after some tense deliberations it was passed on 22 July 1869. Under the Irish Church Act[1] the property of the established church was taken into the possession of a church temporalities commission. About half of it, approximately £8 million, was returned to the church to make provision for the incomes of existing occupants of livings and for other purposes. Another £1 million, approximately, went to compensate the presbyterian church for the loss of its long-established state subsidy, the *regium donum*, and to compensate Maynooth college for the loss of its parliamentary grant. The remaining £7 million was set aside for eventual expenditure on charitable purposes. While the Church of Ireland retained places of worship actually in use, those that were abandoned or ruined passed to the care of the board of public works. In this way many ancient ecclesiastical sites, such as the Rock of Cashel, became in due course public monuments.

The disestablishment of the church was an event of the highest significance in the history of nineteenth-century Ireland. It was the acceptance by Westminster of the principle that Irish majority opinion should decide a major Irish constitutional issue. In some interpretations of history this is seen as a step on the way to self-government and the breaking of the union. It can with equal justice be seen as a new beginning for the union. Was Scotland any less part of the United Kingdom for having distinctive ecclesiastical and legal systems? Again, it is almost universally recognised that ending the monopoly enjoyed by the Church of Ireland was a prerequisite for the maintenance of a democratic consensus based on justice. However, the rhetoric about absolute equality should not be allowed to obscure the possibility that, whatever its theoretical attractions, this total abandonment of the confessions to their own devices may have been a further cause of mistrust between them. It is just possible that a well managed system of concurrent endowment would have left the churches with less perceived reason for mutual fear.

The trouble about 'Irish ideas' as a yardstick of government was that on any particular topic there was likely to be in Ireland more than one indigenous 'idea' passionately entertained. Whether it might have been otherwise or not, the progress of 'justice for Ireland' occurred in a manner that awakened the deepest resentments in many protestants and promoted a militant sense of

[1] 32 & 33 Vict., c. 42 (22 July 1869); below, pp 727–33.

communal identity, mirroring that of the catholics. Since 1850 the style of Orange parading had been hampered by the party processions act, amended,— and strengthened—in 1860.[1] This legislation also inhibited catholic and nationalist demonstrations. But the McManus funeral escaped precisely because it was a funeral and so a religious occasion. The catholic university procession of July 1862 had a similar pretext: it was all part of the ceremony of blessing a foundation stone at Drumcondra. Casuistry of this kind was extremely trying to protestants, but when the O'Connell monument demonstration of August 1864 was passed off as not being a 'party' procession their patience was exhausted. The Dublin Orangemen had threatened in advance that they would wreak havoc if the affair went ahead. In the event the backlash came not in Dublin but in Belfast. On 8 August O'Connell was burned in effigy on Sandy Row. This signalled the beginning of eighteen days of sectarian rioting in which twelve people were killed and one hundred injured. A subsequent investigation recommended the disbandment of the local police force and the admission of the Irish constabulary to the town. This was speedily done.[2] Protestants, like catholics, took to public demonstrations with renewed fervour after the fenian rising. On 12 July 1867 a particularly large Orange march from Newtownards to Bangor very deliberately defied the processions act. At the head of the demonstration was a minor County Down landlord, William Johnston of Ballykilbeg. He was subsequently charged with a breach of the act—something for which he was not unprepared—and on 29 February 1868 he was given one month in prison. The punishment was all the more galling because it was upheld and carried out without respite by a tory lord lieutenant, the duke of Abercorn. In November Johnston was a candidate for Belfast in the general election. His platform was one of opposition to the party processions act and the tories and of assertion of protestant rights. He headed the poll by well over a thousand votes, with the liberal candidate following and two 'official' tories bringing up the rear. Johnston has been described as the first 'popular' representative of Irish political protestantism to sit in parliament. The more conventional tory candidates in predominantly protestant constituencies were equally firm in their opposition to concessions to catholics that were felt to constitute a threat to the heritage of Irish protestants. Although the financial settlement made by the act was generous to their church, many Irish protestants saw the manner in which it came to pass as something of a humiliation.

AFTER the attempted rising of March 1867 Col. Thomas J. Kelly brought about the dissolution of the committee (or 'provisional government') that had called it, and set about reorganising the movement under his own control. During the summer of 1867 he toured the remnants of fenianism in Ireland announcing himself as C.E.I.R.[3] and Stephens's successor. Meanwhile the

---

[1] 13 Vict., c. 2 (12 Mar. 1850); 23 & 24 Vict., c. 141 (28 Aug. 1860).
[2] 28 & 29 Vict., c. 70 (29 June 1865).   [3] Above, p. 438.

'senate wing' of the Fenian Brotherhood was endeavouring to win influence with the fenians of Ireland and Britain. Its leader, William R. Roberts, sent agents to Ireland within weeks of the rising. They gleefully pointed out how the O'Mahony wing had proved to be a broken reed. By a date in early June 1867 a more or less representative sample of leading fenian activists was assembled in Paris for a meeting with Roberts himself. He persuaded them to acknowledge his organisation as the one true fenian society in America, and to give him authority over the Irish organisation. In return he promised regular and adequate supplies of money and arms. It was agreed that fenianism in Ireland and Britain would henceforth be under the control of an elected body, the supreme council. Roberts's secretary, Daniel O'Sullivan, was commissioned to travel through Britain and Ireland and arrange conventions for the election of the seven members. This he proceeded to do, helped by the fact that he had an adequate supply of money for incidental expenses. All of this was a serious threat to the position of Col. Kelly, whose authority was based on the claims of the O'Mahony wing. In an effort to secure his control he held a convention of fenians in Manchester on 17 August 1867. The meeting readily recognised him as C.E.I.R. and successor to Stephens, but then took back much of what it had given by adopting a resolution that proposed cooperation with 'honest men' on both wings of the Fenian Brotherhood. This can only mean that a large body of opinion, even at this conference assembled by Kelly himself, was favourably disposed to the Roberts initiative. What was most appealing about that was the introduction of elected committee government, something that Kelly had repudiated. But on other scores there was a noticeable preference for the O'Mahony wing, as against Roberts's faction, and widespread suspicion of the level of control over the Irish organisation being sought by Roberts. When the supreme council met for the first time in mid-February 1868 in Dublin, Daniel O'Sullivan was excluded, much to his chagrin. The first published statement of the supreme council of which we have knowledge appeared in April 1868 and contained a warning to Irish-Americans not to interfere in the running of the I.R.B., as the organisation in Ireland and Britain was now officially named.

Gladstone's new government set free almost fifty fenian convicts in the early days of March 1869. Only one of the leading elite of the pre-1865 movement was included, Charles J. Kickham. The others had been men of lesser significance but some had the capacity and will to make a larger impact in the future. These, and others who had escaped imprisonment, quickly came to form a new type of fenian elite that included such people as J. F. X. O'Brien, James O'Connor and his brother John, James J. O'Kelly, John Daly, Charles G. Doran, John O'Connor Power, and John Nolan. They were closely associated with Richard Pigott, who was extremely useful as proprietor of the *Irishman*. A dislike of Stephens's style was one of their strongest common attitudes, and they threw their weight behind the concept of the supreme council. They also had the strength to recast the council according to their own ideas, getting strong representation on it themselves in the process. The supreme council, thus newly reinforced, convened on 18 August 1869 and adopted the first known I.R.B. constitution. The style and functions of the 'new' fenianism were so different from those of Stephens's organisation that it is probably misleading to represent one as the continuation of the other. All major decisions were now taken in accordance with prescribed procedures. The supreme council had a president, but his capacity for acting alone was severely circumscribed. Ordinary members were expected to be more businesslike than formerly, and this included the acquisition of arms by each individual at his own expense. The importation of arms was put on a regular footing; by January 1870 Dublin Castle was being informed from a number of sources that the fenians were better armed than ever before. Nevertheless, fenianism was less important in relative terms than it had been in the mid-1860s; then there had been something like a vacuum in political life; by 1869 the country was on a heavy diet of politics.

Unlike Stephens, the supreme council had no desire to disrupt the efforts of politicians. Some leading I.R.B. men were in close contact with G. H. Moore, who had been returned to parliament in the election of 1868 and had hopes of involving the fenians in open politics under his guidance. The contradiction of maintaining a policy of non-participation in the midst of an open political society would test the cohesion of the new fenian elite and eventually fragment it. In 1869 they all subscribed to the ideal of an Irish republic; and among their rank and file was probably a much larger number of individuals with fixed convictions on this than had ever followed Stephens. But even at that, their rigid formula appealed to a very small proportion of the population, and they faced in the years that followed a ineluctable choice between compromise on principle and irrelevance.

In the run up to the general election of November 1868 there was a popular assumption in Ireland that Gladstone, once in office, would as a matter of course free the fenian prisoners. From early 1868 the term 'amnesty' was in widespread currency. It was called for by a number of town and city councils, and some liberal candidates in the general election agreed to commit themselves to it as a matter of urgent policy.[1] The amnesty committee that emerged in Dublin in the autumn of 1868 was taken over after the election by Gladstone's Irish supporters. They were prepared to be much more explicit and enthusiastic about the subject now that the danger of alienating electoral support for Gladstone in Britain was no longer relevant. The measure of amnesty granted in early March 1869 was a disappointment. The most prominent fenian convicts were still in prison, some in England and the rest in Western Australia. By June 1869 the amnesty committee had been superseded by the Amnesty Association, which was dominated by a group of fenians

[1] Maurice Johnson, 'The fenian amnesty movement, 1868–79' (M.A. thesis, Maynooth, 1981).

headed by John Nolan. They were not acting in accordance with any official I.R.B. strategy, or scarcely even with the approval of the supreme council; they had simply succumbed to the temptation to become involved in public affairs. They were encouraged, and perhaps manipulated, by the enigmatic Isaac Butt. A brilliant barrister of strongly protestant and tory background who had acted as defence counsel for the Young Irelanders in 1848, and more recently for the fenian prisoners, he was setting out at the age of fifty-five to create an accommodation, along hitherto untried lines, between warring Irish interests. He hoped to win support from disgruntled protestants and to wean popular catholic support away from Gladstone. The Amnesty Association arranged a campaign of over fifty public meetings in the autumn of 1869. This culminated in a mass meeting at Cabra, near Dublin, on 10 October, attended by well over 100,000 people. On 18 October 1869 Gladstone formally rejected the call for an extension of the amnesty, pointing out that some of the meetings seemed to be demanding as a right what could only be granted as an act of clemency. As Butt well realised—and perhaps John 'Amnesty' Nolan did also—the tone of the association's campaign, far from helping the prisoners, made it impossible for Gladstone to obtain the cabinet's agreement to any further releases. The campaign had not been well calculated to obtain the release of the prisoners. Nolan obviously enjoyed organising public meetings, and he did it very well indeed; Butt was availing himself of an opportunity to appear in Irish catholic eyes as a popular leader. Thanks to Butt's propaganda a seriously mistaken notion about the importance of the amnesty campaign of 1869 has found its way into historical accounts. The campaign resembled the McManus funeral of 1861 in this, as also in the non-clerical, unpropertied cadres that organised it. But the amnesty demonstrations were but one manifestation of the political excitement of these closing years of the 1860s in Ireland, and the question of the prisoners never loomed as large as that of tenant right.[1]

Butt knew that his most important contest would be that for the confidence of the tenant farmers. He had ingratiated himself with the few farmers' clubs in existence in the mid-1860s, and had made himself more widely known through the newspapers as a friend of the tenants, by means of propaganda on the land question. Meanwhile Gladstone had come to see that any attempt to win widespread favour in Ireland would have to provide for concessions to the farmers. Bright had gladly raised the flag of anti-landlordism on his Dublin visit in 1866, and Gladstone himself was soon musing aloud, in more careful terms, on the desirability of a reform of Irish land law. No other 'Irish idea' carried remotely as much power as the demand for a change in the balance of land legislation in favour of the tenant. The power derived directly from the actual social and economic strength of the farming class in mid-Victorian Ireland, though the demand was justified by historicist rhetoric about racial dispossession. The Irish tenants and their friends expected land legislation

[1] R. V. Comerford, *The fenians in context: Irish politics and society, 1848–82* (Dublin, 1985), pp 171–9.

from Gladstone as firmly as they expected disestablishment. Many of them did not wait for the legislation, or even the general election, but began to display impatience with the various restrictions and burdens associated with landlordism. The result was a wave of agrarian unrest. The most notorious incident in this spate of disturbances occurred at Ballycohey, County Tipperary, on 14 August 1868, when tenants successfully resisted by force of arms the serving of grossly unjust ejectment proceedings taken by their landlord, William Scully, whose bailiff, together with a sub-constable of the R.I.C., was killed in the consequent affray. When suitably dressed up in the Irish and British press, the agrarian unrest—and especially the Ballycohey affair—served as an argument in favour of the land legislation, expectation of which had exacerbated the trouble in the first place.

By the end of July 1869, with the ecclesiastical legislation safely on the statute book, the land question was next in line for serious attention. The time was opportune for a public campaign to press for maximum concessions; many liberals believed that nothing was called for beyond compensation for improvements. At this very juncture Butt gave his approval to (and possibly inspired) the series of public demonstrations in favour of amnesty, which, as we have seen, were certain not to advance amnesty. The suspicion has to be that he did not wish to see a campaign on the land question precisely because that could produce results. Butt had a twofold motivation for being wary of a tenant right campaign: if very successful it might secure worthwhile concessions that would win the farmers permanently to Gladstone; and, successful or not, it would antagonise the landlord class, which he intended to woo into a grand coalition. Of course he did not repudiate tenant right. The farmers' clubs looked to him as to their leader, and he was careful not to alienate their confidence. He went along with them as they set about the formation of a nation-wide organisation, and he was the central figure in the meeting at which it was formed in Tipperary town on 28 September 1869. It was named the Irish Tenant League, and its striking failure under favourable conditions was almost certainly owing to Butt's lack of enthusiasm for it.

The most effective attempt at organised agitation on the land question in these crucial months was made by Sir John Gray, M.P., of the *Freeman's Journal*. He arranged a large series of public meetings, which, all things considered, were at least as impressive as the amnesty gatherings. In fact tenant right speeches were delivered at many amnesty meetings, and there was a number of meetings described as joint amnesty and tenant right demonstrations. The great majority of those attending any of the meetings would have been prepared to cheer for either cause, or both. In the mid-1860s the farmers had seen fenianism as a threat. There had been an apprehension that a successful revolution would lead not just to expropriation of the interests of landlords but to a redistribution of farms to benefit the landless. Now that the spectre of revolution had vanished, the imprisoned fenians had become symbols of all popular demands, not excluding tenant right, and farmers felt few qualms, if any, about supporting the call for amnesty. However, some fenian activists had no great interest in tenant right and resented the existence of any movement competing with the amnesty campaigns for the attention of the populace. Acting without the authority of the supreme council, local I.R.B. men in a number of places attempted to disrupt tenant right meetings, succeeding spectacularly on one notorious occasion in Limerick on 1 November 1869. An outbreak of serious friction between the two movements was averted largely through the efforts of Isaac Butt.

A by-election in County Tipperary in November 1869 provided an obvious opportunity for a spectacular demonstration in favour of tenant right by the county's enfranchised farmers. They found an ideal candidate in Denis Caulfield Heron, but he was to be denied his expected triumph. At about this time opponents of Napoleon III were putting foward political prisoners in French parliamentary elections to embarrass the regime. Inspired by this a group of fenian activists had O'Donovan Rossa, the most celebrated of the fenian prisoners, nominated for Tipperary. The motivation was the same as that for the disruption of tenant right meetings. Faced with two causes of which most of them approved, the majority of the electors were rather mesmerised. On by-election day, 17 November, 70 per cent of the Tipperary voters remained at home. Under the circumstances the election of O'Donovan Rossa by a majority of 103 out of 2,171 votes cast, although it returned a very remarkable member to parliament, did not signify the upsurge of fenian revolutionism that British politicians and leader-writers discerned at the time. Rossa was declared ineligible to take his seat, as an unpardoned felon, and another by-election was called. This time Heron was opposed by the pardoned fenian, Charles J. Kickham, nominated against his own wishes, who took no part in the campaign. In a somewhat larger poll on 28 February 1870, Heron was victorious by a margin of four votes.

Although Butt had not encouraged Rossa's candidature, the episode helped to advance his objectives by hardening British opinion against far-reaching concessions on the land issue. Gladstone in these months was pushing a draft bill through the cabinet in the face of much scepticism on the part of his fellow ministers. Now opponents of a far-reaching measure, both within and without the cabinet, could declare that the election of Rossa at the expense of a liberal within months of the church act showed how little Ireland appreciated concessions. Gray's campaign to influence the forthcoming legislation reached its climax with a land conference in Dublin on 2 and 3 February 1870. Resolutions were adopted in favour of the most extensive measures of tenant right. On 15 February Gladstone introduced his Irish land bill. Its measures were far short of what its author would have wished and of what the leaders of Irish tenant opinion were demanding. No major changes were made in the bill in its passage through parliament, except for the addition of clauses advocated by

Bright making provision for state loans to help tenants to buy out their land-lords. This was to produce very little result, as it placed no compulsion on owners to sell.[1] By contrast the main provisions of the bill did constitute an invasion of the strict proprietorial rights of landlords. The Ulster custom was given the force of law wherever it existed, and for the rest of the country an attempt was made to call equivalent practices into existence by law. Within specified limits tenants were to receive compensation for disturbance in the event of eviction for causes other than non-payment of rent; and complex arrangements were made governing compensation for improvements made by the tenant on surrendered holdings. The Irish land act of 1870[2] did mark the interference of parliament with previously sacrosanct property rights. It was an interference not in the interests of collectivism but of the class of small capital-ists who in Ireland were not only more numerous but on balance more power-ful than landlords or factory owners. The land act had given them less than they had hoped for, but they interpreted it, taken together with disestablish-ment and Gladstone's obeisance to 'Irish ideas', as meaning that henceforth majority opinion—their opinion—would determine Irish institutions. But to assert that the union was thereby doomed is to interpret history backwards.

---

[1] Below, pp 466–7.
[2] Below, pp 464–7, 746–58.

CHAPTER XXIV

Legal developments, 1801–79

J. C. BRADY

THE eighteenth century had seen relatively little statutory law reform. During that period the courts, and more particularly the chancery courts, had sought to adapt legal principles to changing conditions. Judicial activism in the area of law reform was a feature of eighteenth-century jurisprudence, and the dividing line between policy, which has been regarded traditionally as a matter exclusively for the legislature, and legal principle, which is properly within the purview of the courts, was sometimes crossed by eighteenth-century judges. The nineteenth century was to see a reversal of roles, with the judges for the most part carefully eschewing law reform, the burden of which was increasingly assumed by parliament. The intellectual precursors of the growth of statutory law reform were the utilitarians, the most prominent and influential of whom, Jeremy Bentham, argued that progress was dependent on a rational planned programme of legislative action.

The short period of Irish parliamentary independence saw the Irish parliament conform to the legislative pattern in Britain and relatively few additions were made to the statute book. The act of union, however, ensured that Ireland shared, directly or consequentially, in the new climate of law reform that was to obtain at Westminster, and the legislative triumphs of Benthamite utilitarianism were to be substantially paralleled in Ireland. Irish M.P.s did not initially add much to the weight of radical opinion at Westminster, since they represented the protestant landowning, and thus conservative, interest, while the protagonists of catholic rights were preoccupied with catholic emancipation and, following that, the resolution of the tithe problem and the repeal of the act of union. Be that as it may, Ireland's constitutional status following the act of union was to make her the sometimes unwilling beneficiary of progressive legislation.

The first half of the nineteenth century was to see important and fundamental changes in such disparate areas of the law as those relating to succession, charities, the limitation of actions, prescription, and the land law. Problems associated with the nature of ownership and leasing of land were to dominate political life for much of the nineteenth century, and the resolution of the land problem was ultimately to depend on fundamental changes in the nature of the landlord and tenant relationship, but in the early decades of the century reforms in the land law were principally of a technical nature aimed at modernising practices and principles, many of which reflected the needs and preoccupations of an obsolete feudal society. Legislation was also needed in a developing society to permit public bodies to acquire land for the provision of essential amenities such as roads, railways, bridges, and canals. Examples of the latter, such as the Bridges (Ireland) Acts of 1813 and 1834 and the Canals (Ireland) Act, 1816,[1] which enabled public bodies to acquire land, compulsorily if need be, were consistent with the utilitarian principle that the public good took precedence over the rights of individuals; but the prevailing political and philosophical commitment to the essential inviolability of private property required that such legislation contain detailed provisions for the payment of compensation to those from whom lands were appropriated.

Reforms in the land law were also enacted to remove anachronisms that made conveyancing practice unnecessarily complicated, dilatory, and expensive. An example of such reform was the Fines and Recoveries (Ireland) Act, 1834,[2] which, duplicating an English measure of the previous year, abolished the collusive actions by means of which the courts had kept alive the principle of the alienability of land following the statute *De donis conditionalibus* of 1285 that had sought to prevent the barring of entails.[3] The fictional actions of fine and recovery, which allowed the life tenant in family settlements to bar his successors, had become purely formal rituals, but remained complex and expensive. The act of 1834 remedied this by providing that the tenant-in-tail could bar the entail simply by the execution of a 'disentailing assurance', which meant, in effect, the execution of a conveyance using words that a fee-simple owner would have to use in order to pass the fee simple. Conveyancing practice was futher simplified by the Real Property Act, 1845,[4] which gave to a simple deed of grant the same efficacy in relation to the transfer of all corporeal hereditaments and tenements as the ingenious but convoluted form of conveyance that combined the bargain and sale concept with that of lease and release. The act of 1845 thus established the ordinary deed of grant as the standard form of conveyance.

Other land law reforms peculiar to Ireland were statutes allowing the conversion of certain leases into fee-farm grants, enabling tenants to acquire the fee simple of their holdings subject to the payment of a perpetual rent. Such conversion fee-farm grants uniquely combined the grant of a freehold estate with leasehold tenure. The earliest example was the Church Temporalities (Ireland) Act, 1833,[5] which gave to tenants holding under bishops' leases the right to purchase the fee simple subject to a fee-farm rent that was calculated

---

[1] 53 Geo. III, c. 77 (2 July 1813); 4 & 5 Will. IV, c. 61 (13 Aug. 1834); 56 Geo. III, c. 55 (20 June 1816).

[2] 4 & 5 Will. IV, c. 92 (15 Aug. 1834).

[3] 13 Edw. I (Westminster), c. 1.   [4] 8 & 9 Vict., c. 119 (8 Aug. 1845).

[5] 3 & 4 Will. IV, c. 37 (14 Aug. 1833), sect. 128.

by reference to the rent and the average annual value of renewal fines of the former leasehold. Fee-farm rents were recoverable in the same manner as leasehold rents. All further such conversion grants ceased following the Irish Church Act, 1869,[1] which instructed the church temporalities commissioners to sell by January 1874 the unencumbered fee simple of lands still subject to unconverted leases. Thus ended the earliest application of the principle of leasehold enfranchisement, which was ultimately to provide the solution to the land problem.

Another form of conversion fee-farm grant derived from the renewable leasehold conversion acts. It was quite a common practice in Ireland during the eighteenth and first half of the nineteenth centuries for landowners to grant leases for lives, usually three lives, renewable forever. Such a lease would contain a covenant for renewal, subject to the payment of a fine, by granting a new lease for another life when one of those whose lives measured the lease died. The Devon commission, which estimated that one-seventh of tenanted land was held under leases for lives, was told that they originated in the practice following the seventeenth-century confiscations and settlements of lands, whereby grantees who were often absentees employed them as a way of asserting their proprietorship from time to time while enjoying rents and additional periodic payments by way of fines. The popularity of such leases is also attributable to the fact that they combined the best of both worlds, giving to the landowner the extensive remedies available to a landlord while giving to the tenant an estate that approximated in status to a fee simple. The Renewable Leasehold Conversion Act, 1849,[2] gave statutory weight to that status by providing that such lessees had the right to acquire fee-farm grants from the lessor subject to a rent that was to be the old leasehold rent plus an estimated sum based on the average annual value of renewal fines.

Technical reforms in the land law were not confined to the simplification of conveyancing practice and the removal of anachronisms, for the quickening pace of statutory law reform in the 1830s saw the enactment of measures that provided, and in some instances still provide, the basis of the modern law in relation to the application of the principle of limitation to actions for the recovery of land and the application of the analogous, but distinct, principle of prescription to the acquisition of easements and profits. The latter principle, which exemplified the complex and fictional character of much contemporary land law, provided that if a claimant could show long enjoyment of an easement, such as a right of way, the court would presume that there had been an actual grant of such easement from the owner of the so-called servient land, even though there was no extant evidence of such a grant. The theoretical requirement that easements lay in grant led the courts to develop a complex body of law that involved the absurd presumption that the easement was enjoyed from time immemorial, fixed at 1189, and the concomitant fiction of a

---

[1] 32 & 33 Vict., c. 42 (26 July 1869), sect. 34.   [2] 12 & 13 Vict., c. 105 (1 Aug. 1849).

lost modern grant. The Prescription Act, 1832, which was extended to Ireland by the Prescription (Ireland) Act, 1858,[1] introduced less complicated procedures for the acquisition of easements and profits.

While the law governing prescription in Ireland was on all fours with that in England after 1858, the Irish courts differed from the English in one important respect: they were prepared to hold, as the English were not, that the doctrine of prescription applied to leasehold as well as to freehold property. J. C. W. Wylie has argued that the different approach of the Irish courts is explained by the fact that so much Irish land, unlike that in Britain, was subject to tenancies for the greater part of the nineteenth century.[2]

In 1833 fundamental changes were enacted in the law governing the principle of limitation as it applied to actions for the recovery of land. Limitation, which is a creature of statute in our legal system, provides for the extinction of stale claims and obsolete titles to land, by requiring a dispossessed owner to initiate an action for recovery within a given time, or lose his right to recover the land.[3] Before the Real Property Limitation Act, 1833,[4] which applied to Ireland, the courts had construed the words 'adverse possession' in the earlier statutes of limitation in such a way that time did not run in favour of an adverse possessor merely by reason of his occupation of the disputed land: there had to be something in the nature of an ouster of the true owner. The words 'adverse possession' were accordingly omitted from the act of 1833 in order to exclude the technical connotation that those words had acquired in the courts; but whether or not possession by a squatter would cause time to run against the owner remained a matter to be determined by the courts with reference to the particular circumstances of each case. The act of 1833 also effected a radical change by providing that both the right of action and the *title* of the dispossessed owner were extinguished at the end of the limitation period. The earlier statutes of limitation had barred only the former and not the latter.

The Wills Act, 1837,[5] which applied to Ireland, laid down a uniform code for the execution of wills of both real and personal property. It still obtains in Northern Ireland, and many of its provisions are reproduced in the Republic of Ireland's Succession Act, 1965.[6] The statute of wills, 1634, which was the Irish equivalent of a sixteenth-century English statute, had required wills of real property to be in writing, but there was no need for the testator's signature or for witnesses.[7] The Irish statute of frauds, 1695,[8] added the requirement that such wills be not only written but also signed by the testator and attested in his presence by at least three witnesses. The act of 1837, which applied to all wills,

---

[1] 2 & 3 Will. IV, c. 71 (1 Aug. 1832); 21 & 22 Vict., c. 42 (23 July 1858).
[2] Wylie, *Ir. land law*, p. 325.
[3] See generally J. C. Brady and Tony Kerr, *The limitation of actions in the Republic of Ireland* (Dublin, 1984).
[4] 3 & 4 Will. IV, c. 27 (24 July 1833).
[5] 7 Will. IV & 1 Vict., c. 26 (3 July 1837).
[6] 1965/27 [R.I.] (22 Dec. 1965).
[7] 10 Chas. I, sess. 2, c. 2 (15 Dec. 1634).
[8] 7 Will. III, c. 12 (22 Oct. 1695).

whether of realty or personalty, required a will to be in writing and signed at the foot or end thereof by the testator (or some person in his presence and by his direction) in the presence of at least two witnesses. The courts' strict interpretation of the requirement that a will be signed by the testator at the foot or end led to the enactment of the Wills Act Amendment Act, 1852,[1] which provided that a signature would otherwise be valid if it should be apparent on the face of the will that the testator intended to give effect by such signature to the writing signed as his will.

The updating of the statutory rules governing the execution of wills and other technical reforms of the land law were essentially uncontentious and apolitical measures, which no doubt accounts for their enactment by a parliament that, though increasingly reformist, was still controlled by the traditional governing class, the landowners, who dominated both main political groupings. Changes in the system of land tenure that obtained in Ireland, and more particularly changes in the law governing the relation of landlord and tenant, which were to provide the eventual solution to the land question, were to raise fundamental questions about the nature of ownership of property that were not to be so easily resolved.

A formidable obstacle for those who espoused the land tenure explanation of Ireland's many social and economic woes was the fact that a similar system obtained in England without similar malign consequences; indeed the legal basis of the landlord–tenant relation was the same in both countries until the Landlord and Tenant Law Amendment (Ireland) Act, 1860.[2] In both countries, for example, when a tenancy ended the principle *quicquid plantatur solo, solo cedit* applied, and the landlord was legally entitled to resume possession not only of the land but also of any appurtenances that became attached to it during the tenancy. In England, however, improvements such as buildings and fencing were customarily made by the landlord, but in Ireland by the tenants, so the plight of an outgoing tenant in Ireland was exacerbated by the law. This clear disincentive to a tenant to invest in his holding provides the basis of the argument that the Irish system of land tenure militated against economic development. This argument derived further support from the relatively prosperous and quiescent state of the north where the evolution of the tenant right, or Ulster custom, gave to tenants who had invested in their holdings the right to compensation when the tenancy ended.

Those who sought fundamental changes in the law governing the relation of landlord and tenant, and particularly the provision of compensation for improvements by the tenant, argued that tenant right should be given statutory effect for the entire country. In 1835 the chief protagonist of this view, William Sharman Crawford, then M.P. for Dundalk, moved for leave to bring in a bill to amend the law. It contained a modest provision to compensate evicted tenants

---

[1] 15 & 16 Vict., c. 24 (17 June 1852).
[2] 23 & 24 Vict., c. 154 (28 Aug. 1860); below, pp 458–63.

for improvements they had made. Crawford's proposals were not enacted, but his persistent and indefatigable advocacy of tenant right led to the setting up in 1843 by Sir Robert Peel of the Devon commission to inquire into the occupation of land in Ireland.

Since the commission consisted of Irish landlords presided over by the earl of Devon, an English landlord with an estate in County Limerick, it was not likely to propose radical changes in the system of land tenure obtaining in Ireland. The report of the commission did, however, confirm the argument of Sharman Crawford with regard to the beneficial effects of tenant right, for it admitted that, although the custom was anomalous when 'considered with reference to all ordinary notions of property', 'the district in which it prevails has thriven and improved, in comparison with other parts of the country'. The commission did not draw the obvious inference from this conclusion; and, rather than considering whether statutory weight should be given to tenant right, considered whether the law should be used to limit its exercise, but concluded:

Although we foresee some danger to the just rights of property from the unlimited allowance of this 'tenant right', yet we are sure that evils more immediate, and of a still greater magnitude, would result from any hasty or general disallowance of it, and still less can we recommend any interference with it by law.[1]

On a more positive note the commission recommended the introduction of a bill to give tenants a fair return on improvements, since it believed that 'no single measure can be better calculated to allay discontent and to promote substantial improvement throughout the country'.[2] Lord Stanley introduced a bill in June 1845 that provided for the payment of compensation for tenant improvements, but it failed to survive the opposition of those who represented the Irish landlord interest in parliament, whose hostility was directed mainly at the proposal to establish a new office of commissioner of improvements. In the event the famine opened the way for the application to the land problem of the current panacea for economic ills, which was the principle of free trade. Free trade in land in Ireland, however, required the removal of legal barriers to the movement of capital, since only 'by cutting this Gordian knot of legal entanglement, it was argued, might economic prosperity be revived in Ireland'.[3] The latter policy was embodied in two measures, in 1848 and 1849,[4] which facilitated the sale of encumbered estates in Ireland. The second of these provided for the appointment of commissioners who were to constitute a court for the express purpose of selling out insolvent landlords. The act of 1849 accordingly provided that where any land, or lease of such, was subject to encumbrances the value of which exceeded half the net rent, it would be lawful for any encumbrancer on such land or lease to apply to the commissioners for the sale of such

---

[1] *Devon comm. rep.*, p. 15.   [2] Ibid., p. 17.
[3] J. E. Pomfret, *The struggle for land in Ireland, 1800–1923* (Princeton, 1930), p. 44.
[4] 11 & 12 Vict., c. 48 (14 Aug. 1848); 12 & 13 Vict., c. 77 (28 July 1849).

land or lease for the purpose of discharging the encumbrances thereon. All encumbrancers, except the person on whose application the sale had been ordered, and even the latter if he obtained the leave of the commissioners, could bid for the encumbered property, and the successful bidder was vested with an indefeasible title by the commissioners.

The act of 1849, despite the proposals on compensation contained in the report of the Devon commission, did not provide that any part of the purchase money should go to tenants who had carried out permanent improvements. As far as tenants were concerned the act merely allowed for the replacement of one species of landlord by another, and the latter was often a speculator in land who was determined to get full value for his investment. The Bessborough commission was later to point out that it was customary to insert in advertisements of sales under the encumbered estates court a note to the effect that the rent was capable of considerable increase on the falling-in of leases.[1]

The legal climate was made more favourable for such new entrepreneurial landlords by an extension of the remedy of ejectment for non-payment of rent. Originally such an action could be brought only in the case of lettings under a written agreement that contained a clause allowing the landlord to reenter and avoid the lease on the failure of the tenant to pay the rent. Although the right to bring such an action when one whole year's rent was in arrear had been extended to all cases of lettings under a written agreement, whether or not the latter contained a reentry clause,[2] it did not apply to the numerous cases of implied tenancies that arose, not under a written agreement, but from the fact of payment of rent. The Civil Bills Courts (Ireland) Act of 1851[3] accordingly extended the remedy of ejectment, as far as those courts were concerned, to tenancies where no written agreement existed, provided that the annual rent of the holding was under £50 and there was a year's rent in arrear.

Tenants were afforded a measure of compensation for improvements by 'Cardwell's act' which provided that a tenant of agricultural land could, on certain conditions, one of which was the landlord's consent, carry out improvements for which he might be compensated by way of an annuity, provided that the improvements were not such as he was compelled to make by contract or custom.[4] The conditions contained in the act, however, severely limited the circumstances in which a tenant might receive compensation for past improvements. This modest measure in favour of tenants was followed immediately on the statute book by a statute that was to alter fundamentally the law governing the relation of landlord and tenant in Ireland.

---

[1] *Bessborough comm. rep.*, p. 6.
[2] 25 Geo. II, c. 13 (7 May 1752).
[3] 14 & 15 Vict., c. 57 (1 Aug. 1851).
[4] Landed Property (Ireland) Improvement Act, 1860 (23 & 25 Vict., c. 153 (28 Aug. 1860)).

THE Landlord and Tenant Law Amendment (Ireland) Act, 1860,[1] otherwise called 'Deasy's act' after Rickard Deasy (attorney general for Ireland 1860–61), was based on one of four bills that had been introduced in 1852 by Joseph Napier (attorney general for Ireland 1852–3). Deasy's act sought to simplify, consolidate, and amend the law regulating the relation of landlord and tenant in Ireland, but it also effected a radical change in the theoretical nature of that relation, which has been attributed to the prevailing policy of free trade in land. The fundamental changes in the law governing the relation of landlord and tenant wrought by Deasy's act can best be illustrated by a brief review of the law before 1860.

Leasehold interests had developed outside the feudal system of estates, which recognised only the three estates of freehold: the fee simple, the fee tail, and the life estate. Originally leases, or terms of years, were regarded not as property interests but as personal contracts binding only on the parties, and it was not until the end of the fifteenth century that the leaseholder was protected against other persons. Gradually, however, leases came to be regarded as estates in land, and by a process of analogy the concept of tenure, by which all land was held in return for services, was applied to them, the tenant holding in return for a service, which was the payment of rent. The payment of rent and the fulfilment of other covenants in a lease, however, were not treated as conditions precedent on which the tenant was entitled to retain possession. This right was referable not to the contract of hiring but to the fact that the tenant was considered to have acquired an *estate* in the land demised for the term specified. The tenant's interest, accordingly, was not forfeited by non-payment of the rent or non-fulfilment of other covenants in the lease but by the determination of the lease. An important consequence of this development of the lease by way of analogy with the freehold estate was that a landlord would not be entitled to avail of the usual remedies against a tenant unless he was entitled to a reversion, which meant in effect that he would be entitled to possession of the land when the lease expired. Alexander Richey gives the following example: if A, entitled to the land for twenty years from 1 January 1840, let these lands to B for ten years from 1 January 1850 the relation of landlord and tenant did not arise, but it would have arisen if A had let them for ten years from 31 December 1849.[2]

It was thus essential for a prospective landlord to grant a lease for a period less than his own interest, and in *Pluck* v. *Digges* (1832), 5 Bligh (N.S.) 31, a case involving a lease for lives in which the tenant had purported to grant a sublease for the same lives as those named in the lease under which he himself held, the house of lords reversed the opinion of the courts of common pleas and exchequer in Ireland and affirmed the need for a reversion in the landlord. This latter requirement created particular problems in Ireland, where it was not uncommon for middlemen to grant their entire interests to tenants. The

---

[1] 23 & 24 Vict., c. 154 (28 Aug. 1860).   [2] Richey, *Ir. land laws*, p. 43.

person entitled to the reversion might be a mortgagee or trustee or someone who had no connection with the lease, and the person who ordinarily received the rent and otherwise acted as the owner of the land demised might not legally be entitled to take proceedings against the tenant.

The requirement of a reversion in the landlord and the technicalities that circumscribed the remedies available to the landlord, which were attributable to an obsolete system of real property, were anathema to the protagonists of free trade in land, who argued for the establishment of the relation of landlord and tenant on a modern commercial basis. Richey put it thus:

The landlords' estates being purchased in the encumbered estates' court as simply and expeditiously as furniture at a sheriff's sale, the mercantile principles had to be applied to the properties purchased by the new capitalist landlords. If capitalists were to invest their money in the purchase of estates, they were entitled to the same freedom of dealing with their lands as was applicable to the case of any other commodity.[1]

The necessary fundamental change in the legal basis of the relation of landlord and tenant was contained in section 3 of Deasy's act, which provides that

the relation of landlord and tenant shall be deemed to be founded on the express or implied contract of the parties, and not upon tenure or service, and a reversion shall not be necessary to such relation, which shall be deemed to subsist in all cases in which there shall be an agreement by one party to hold land from or under another in consideration of any rent.

The placing of the relation on a contractual basis would, arguably, have removed the need for a reversion, but since the latter was the cornerstone of the old system its specific exclusion in section 3 underlined the fundamental change in the legal basis of the relation that was being enacted.

Despite the clear and unambiguous language of section 3, controversy has raged in judicial and academic circles over whether it was intended to alter the legal basis of the relation of landlord and tenant or whether it simply provides that such relation can now obtain where previously it could not for want of a reversion. The latter view was taken by Fitzgerald, who said in *Gordon* v. *Phelan* (1881)[2] that 'the intention of the act of 1860 seems to have been to maintain the known relation of landlord and tenant with its incidents, even though there were neither tenure nor service to support it, provided there was a contract to create the relation'. The same view was taken by O'Hagan, who said in *Chute* v. *Busteed* (1865)[3] that Deasy's act could not be said 'to constitute within itself a complete code, so as to dispense with the consideration of the principles of law which were in force at the time of its enactment, and are still in force, notwithstanding its operation'. In the same case, however, a contrary view was expressed by Christian, who believed that the relation of landlord and

[1] Ibid., p. 48.
[2] 15 I.L.T.R. 69, 71. Special abbreviations used in this chapter are listed below, p. 481.
[3] 16 I.C.L.R. 222, 235.

tenant after Deasy's act had been discharged of the element of tenure and reversion and rested exclusively on contract.[1] Fitzgerald took much the same view in *Russell* v. *Moore* (1882),[2] when he said that the relation rested 'not as in England, on tenure at common law, but on contract alone'.

J. C. W. Wylie has this to say of section 3:

We can see now after over a hundred years that, while it no doubt had great importance, especially in establishing or confirming concepts and practices which became common in Ireland during the eighteenth and nineteenth centuries, it did not have the striking or revolutionary effect on the development of the law that might appear from a first reading of it. Indeed, to some extent there is still uncertainty as to all its consequences, and this tends to give credence to the view that much of the controversy has been of academic significance only.[3]

Perhaps it is not altogether surprising that Irish lawyers, faced with the revolutionary statement of principle in section 3, should cling to the familiar law of landlord and tenant, and this conservatism was manifested in relation to other, less radical, sections of the act. Sections 12 and 13 had swept away a vast array of legal erudition deriving from *Spencer's case* (1583),[4] which dealt with what covenants would or would not 'run with the land'. These sections expressly provided that covenants entered into by tenants and landlords would be enforceable by and against their respective assignees. Despite these express provisions the Irish courts often insisted on referring to the older principles, a phenomenon that prompted Gibson to say in *Lyle* v. *Smith*: 'The express language of sections 12 and 13 cannot be restricted or altered by forcing on it *Spencer's case* applicable to the law of covenants at common law, which was so precious in the eyes of legal schoolmen that they could hardly conceive a statute disregarding it.'[5] Gibson, for his part, had no doubt that Deasy's act 'was intended to put the law of landlord and tenant on a modern, simple, and intelligible basis, getting rid of feudal technical rules. . . . It introduced a wholly new and revolutionary principle, substituting contract for ancient real property law.'[6]

Despite the controversy that ensued over the precise effect of section 3 and the curious neglect of sections 12 and 13, other sections of Deasy's act did have an immediate and important effect on the relation of landlord and tenant. Thus section 40, which was borrowed from the civil law, provides that the destruction of the substantial subject matter of the letting, otherwise than by default of the tenant, and in the absence of any covenant on the tenant's part to repair, gives to the tenant the right to determine the letting by surrender. This section repealed a rule of English common law that bound the tenant to pay the rent

---

[1] 16 I.C.L.R. 222, 247   [2] 8 L.R.I.R. 318, 330.
[3] Wylie, *Ir. land law*, p. 730.   [4] 5 Co. Rep. 16a.
[5] (1909) 2 I.R. 58, 76.
[6] See J. A. Dowling, 'The Landlord and Tenant Law Amendment Act (Ireland) 1860' (Ph.D. thesis, Belfast, 1985), para. 6.40ff.

covenanted during the term, notwithstanding the destruction of the subject matter of the letting. The common-law rule that fixtures attached to the demised premises by the tenant had to be surrendered by him on the termination of his interest was altered by section 17. The courts had already relaxed this rule by providing that a tenant could retain trade, ornamental, and domestic fixtures if they could be removed without doing substantial damage to the premises, and the Landlord and Tenant Act, 1851,[1] had allowed tenants to remove agricultural and trade fixtures and buildings if the land was left in as good a condition as before. These provisions were superseded by section 17 of Deasy's act, which enacted that all personal chattels, engines, machinery, and buildings accessorial thereto, affixed to the freehold by the tenant at his sole expense, for any purpose of trade, manufacture, or agriculture, for ornament, or for his domestic convenience, could be removed by the tenant if the removal could be effected without substantial injury to the freeholder or the fixture, and if the fixture had not been erected in pursuance of any obligation or in violation of any agreement.

The new contractual regime had other important consequences for the tenant, since compensation for improvements would now depend on express or implied contract and, not least, because it was made easier for a landlord to avail of his remedies against the tenant. With regard to an action for non-payment of rent, section 52 provided that whenever a year's rent was in arrear in respect of lands held under any fee-farm grant, lease, or other contract of tenancy, or from year to year, and whether by writing or otherwise, it was lawful for the landlord immediately thereon, and before the expiration of the time, if any, limited for reentry in any lease or agreement, to proceed by ejectment for the recovery of the possession of the land in any of the superior courts or, where the rent did not exceed £100 a year, in the court of the chairman of the county (county court).

The ejectment statutes had been held to be inapplicable to tenancies from year to year, where created by parol, and to contracts of tenancy, for whatever term, or however created, where the landlord had no reversion. The first class of cases had been partially remedied, as far as the civil bill courts were concerned, in 1851,[2] and was now wholly remedied by section 52. The problem posed by the second class was cured with the abolition of the need for a reversion by section 3 of Deasy's act.[3] Despite the wide language of section 52, which refers to a 'lease or other contract of tenancy', the availability of the remedy of ejectment under the section has been confined to tenancies from year to year or for a longer term. Madden in *O'Sullivan* v. *Ambrose*,[4] a case involving a monthly tenancy, refused to accept the proposition that all distinction between different classes of tenancies, so far as regards procedure by

---

[1] 14 & 15 Vict., c. 25 (24 July 1851), sect. 3.
[2] Above, p. 457.   [3] Above, p. 459.
[4] (1893) 32 L.R.Ir. 102.

ejectment, must be taken to have been abolished by Deasy's act. That proposition appeared to him 'to be supported neither by reason nor authority'.[1]

It might well have been expected that an up-to-date law of landlord and tenant, based on contract, would have no place for the ancient remedy of distress, with its aura of self-help, which involved the landlord seizing goods on the demised premises, selling them, and retaining arrears of rent out of the proceeds.[2] Indeed, before Deasy's act distress had fallen into disfavour, and it was said that it

required the performance of so many technical forms, introduced for the benefit of the tenant, and the failure to comply with these legal technicalities, by rendering the whole proceedings void *ab initio*, exposed the landlord to such heavy damages, that a proceedings by distress for the recovery of rent was always most reluctantly adopted.[3]

Nevertheless, distress survived Deasy's act, section 51 of which provided that a landlord could not recover by distress more than the rent of the preceding year.

The contractual regime after Deasy's act permitted the creation of the landlord–tenant relation in respect of interests at both ends of the property spectrum. Thus, since the definition of 'lands' in section 1 includes both corporeal and incorporeal hereditaments, the relation can be created by the grant of minor interests such as shooting or fishing rights.[4] At the other end of the spectrum is the fee-farm grant, involving the conveyance of a fee simple, which approximates in our legal system to absolute ownership, subject to the payment of a perpetual rent by the grantee and his successors to the grantor and his successors. The wording of section 3, and more particularly the exclusion of the need for a reversion, permitted the making of a fee-farm grant that creates the relation of landlord and tenant between the grantor and grantee. There were some initial doubts about the application of section 3 to the grant of a fee simple, deriving from the fact that the statute *Quia emptores*, which prohibited subinfeudation, had not been repealed by Deasy's act.[5] Wylie points out that these doubts arose from confusion between the feudal relation of lord and tenant and the modern relation of landlord and tenant to which *Quia emptores* did not apply. The language of section 3 was otherwise wide enough to embrace fee-farm grants, and in *Chute* v. *Busteed* (1865) Christian dismissed the argument that *Quia emptores* would prevent section 3 applying to fee-farm grants. Having stated that he would not be much appalled if the non-repeal of *Quia emptores* by Deasy's act meant that section 3 would not apply to fee-farm grants, Christian went on:

But it does not, I think, necessarily follow. For I think it might fairly be argued that an instrument, executed after this statute has been passed, ought to be construed with

---

[1] (1893) 32 L.R.Ir. 107.
[2] Richey, *Ir. land laws*, p. 53.   [3] Ibid., p. 40.
[4] *Bayley* v. *Conyngham*, [1863] 15 I.C.L.R. 406, and Wylie, *Ir. land law*, p. 731.
[5] *Quia emptores* (18 Edw. I, c. 1).

reference to the new law founded by the statute; and that worded as this deed is, like an ordinary lease, it should be held to embody an agreement that the new statutable relation of landlord and tenant should exist—a relation discharged of the element of tenure and reversion, and resting exclusively on contract.[1]

The radical change in the legal basis of the relation of landlord and tenant had other more significant consequences for the great mass of Irish tenants than that fee-farm grants might come within the ambit of section 3. In so far as Deasy's act placed the relation of landlord and tenant on a contractual basis, it could be said to have proceeded on the same assumption as the civil law systems, particularly the French, that the relation was merely a species of hiring. While some of those urging reform in the 1850s were indeed impressed by the simplicity and equity of the French law on the subject, there is no direct evidence to suggest that Deasy's act was a conscious attempt to introduce civilian principles into Irish law, although provisions with specific and limited effect, such as section 40, were undoubtedly borrowed from the civil law.[2] Moreover, there are important differences between the relation of landlord and tenant as contained in Deasy's act and its French counterpart, and Richey points out that 'while it [Deasy's act] treated the relation of landlord and tenant as an ordinary contract, it treated this relation as against both parties, as one *strictissimi juris*, and not to be tempered by the equities so much favoured by the Roman lawyers'.[3]

Deasy's act contains no obvious bias, since reforms in the landlord's favour are reciprocated by reforms in the tenant's favour. Thus under section 41, unless it is otherwise expressly provided in the lease, two covenants are implied on the part of the landlord: first, that the landlord has a good title to make the lease; and secondly, that the tenant will have quiet and peaceable enjoyment without interruption by the landlord or any other person during the term of the lease. Section 42 implies on the part of a tenant covenants to pay the rent and to give up quiet possession of the premises in good and substantial repair and condition on the termination of the lease. Despite this equality of treatment for landlord and tenant, the placing of the relation on a contractual basis was more likely to favour the landlord, given the prevailing view of contract that was expressed in the celebrated dictum of Sir George Jessel, master of the rolls in England, to the effect that 'if there is one thing more than another which public policy requires, it is that men of full age and competent understanding shall have the utmost liberty of contracting, and that their contracts, when entered into freely and voluntarily, shall be held sacred and shall be enforced by courts of justice'.[4] That view rested on two interrelated concepts of mutual agreement and free choice that were scarcely the common currency of rural life in mid-nineteenth-century Ireland.

[1] 16 I.C.L.R. 222, 247.
[2] Above, p. 460.
[3] Richey, *Ir. land laws*, p. 55.
[4] *Printing and Numerical Registering Co.* v. *Sampson*, [1875] L.R. 19 Eq. 462, 465.

SIMPLIFICATION of the law governing the relation of landlord and tenant was not calculated to improve the lot of tenants, since, as Richey put it, 'every improvement in the real property law has been injurious to the tenants; to a man in possession, a defendant in ejection, no system of law is so advantageous as one hopelessly entangled and incomprehensible'.[1] Richey went on to point out that the statutory declaration of the principle of free trade in land had failed to improve the condition of Ireland, and

it became necessary either not to enforce the new theory of law until the population was so improved as to be capable of appreciating an advanced code (an event certainly not likely soon to occur), or to introduce legislation of an admittedly retrograde character, for the purpose of palliating patent evils and allaying not ill-founded discontent.[2]

With respect to Richey, who was writing in 1880, it was not altogether the relatively backward state of Ireland that made the full-blooded application of mercantile principles of contract law to the relation of landlord and tenant inappropriate in the second half of the nineteenth century. Wylie has made the point that perhaps 'the most striking feature of landlord and tenant law in Ireland, as in other countries, has been the extent to which legislation has sought to control the agreements made between landlords and tenants'.[3] It is certainly true that virtually every piece of legislation dealing with the relation of landlord and tenant since Deasy's act has attempted to redress the contractual imbalance, which favoured landlords, and the relation is now largely governed not by contractual terms made by the parties but by statute.

Within ten years of Deasy's act such legislation was introduced by Gladstone.[4] Its purpose, according to Gladstone, was to adapt the law to the customs of the country, and to that end statutory effect was given to Ulster tenant right and analogous customs throughout the country. Thus within ten years one of the underlying premises of Deasy's act, that the relation of landlord and tenant should be governed by mercantile principles of contract, was abandoned.

The act of 1870 also contained important new provisions by which a tenant who did not enjoy the benefit of Ulster tenant right or analogous customs could be awarded compensation for disturbance and for improvements. Gladstone apparently subscribed to the traditional wisdom that the question of compensation for tenant improvements lay at the heart of the Irish land question, and he had not been impressed by the counter-argument that tenants of holdings that were too small to be economically viable would not be helped by compensation for improvements that they would have been unable to make in the first instance.

Compensation for disturbance, which was dealt with in section 3, was

---

[1] Richey, *Ir. land laws*, p. 44.   [2] Ibid., p. 61.
[3] Wylie, *Ir. land law*, p. 728.
[4] 33 & 34 Vict., c. 46 (1 Aug. 1870); below, pp 751–4.

confined to such loss 'which the court shall find to be sustained by [the tenant] by reason of quitting his holding' and was available to tenants of holdings with an annual rateable valuation of not more than £100, held by them under yearly tenancies, existing on or created after 1 August 1870, if disturbed by the act of their immediate landlords. Deductions might be made from such compensation, both for arrears of rent and for damages in respect of any deterioration of the holding arising from non-observance on the part of the tenant of any express or implied covenant. Further, any tenant who sublet or subdivided his holding without the written consent of the landlord, or who, despite a written prohibition by the landlord or his agent, let any part of the holding in conacre, was disentitled to compensation. The scale of compensation adopted by the act was not based on the value of the tenant's interest but on the rent paid by him, and Richey pointed out the absurdity of compensating a tenant in the direct, and not in the inverse ratio of his rent.[1] Compensation could in no case exceed £250 and this sum was rarely achieved by a dispossessed tenant. Fitzgerald observed in *Ward* v. *Walker*: 'The maximum compensation should only be given where capricious eviction takes place, or where some act of misconduct has been committed by the landlord, as for instance, where an improving tenant, paying the best rent to be obtained for the land, is capriciously ejected.'[2]

The right to compensation for improvements to be awarded to a tenant in quitting his holding, which was contained in section 4, was also circumscribed by exceptions that reduced its beneficial effect for many tenants. Deductions might be made from the amount awarded for outstanding taxes payable by the tenant in respect of his holding, and any loss occasioned by the non-observance by the tenant of express or implied covenants. The court was also required in awarding compensation for improvements to 'take into consideration the time during which such tenants may have enjoyed the advantage of such improvements, also the rent at which such holding has been held, and any benefits which such tenant may have received from his landlord in consideration, expressedly or impliedly, of the improvements so made'.

Statutory effect for Ulster tenant right and analogous customs, together with the new provisions regarding compensation for disturbance and improvements, represented a significant advance; but they fell short of what the tenants most wanted, which was security of tenure. Gladstone had to proceed circumspectly in this regard, since any explicit guarantee of fixity of tenure would have left him open to the charge of unjustifiable encroachment on the property rights of landlords. In the event Gladstone sought to provide security of tenure for the tenants by making the cost of eviction prohibitively high in terms of the compensation payable by the landlord. He explained in a letter to Cardinal Manning that his intention was 'to prevent the landlord from using the terrible

[1] Richey, *Ir. land laws*, p. 68.
[2] Wicklow summer assizes, 1872 (Robert Donnell, *Reports of one hundred and ninety cases in the Irish land courts: with preliminary tenant-right chapters* (Dublin, 1876), p. 391).

weapon of undue and unjust eviction, by so framing the handle that it shall cut his hand with the sharp edge of pecuniary damages'.[1] The great mass of Irish tenants wanted not compensation for the loss of their farms but to be allowed to continue in occupation at fair rents. Indeed the compensation provisions in the land act presented a tenant with something like a Hobson's choice, in that

> in order to raise a question before the court, he is forced to begin by a surrender of the only thing for which he cares. The plaintiff in a land claim, if he fails to prove his case, is turned out without the compensation that he claimed; but if he proves it, he is turned out all the same.... In a word, once the tenant comes into court, all the law can give him is compensation in money.[2]

Given the realities of Irish rural life, it was not uncommon for the compensation payable to be made by the incoming tenant.

The tenants' quest for security of tenure was not helped by the failure of the land act to establish a regular jurisdiction in relation to questions of rent. The absence of some mechanism by which fair rents might be settled was to have harmful consequences, particularly since an ejectment for non-payment of rent was not deemed a disturbance within the act unless the rent was less than £15 a year and 'the court shall certify that the non-payment of rent causing the eviction has risen from the rent being an exorbitant rent'.[3] The Bessborough commission pointed out that the use of the word 'exorbitant' rendered the latter provision virtually inoperative.[4] The employment of local valuators to determine the value of a holding for the purpose of fixing a fair rent had been a feature of Ulster tenant right, but the land act did not define the incidents of tenant right, and the latter practice was one of the casualties of that omission. Indeed, the onus lay on a tenant to prove the existence of tenant right, and the absence of a statutory definition presented the courts with considerable difficulties.[5]

The legislators also hoped, in the land act, to provide greater security for tenants within the parameters of existing property law by stimulating the grant of long leases, and provided that a tenant had no right to compensation for disturbance if he held for a term exceeding thirty-one years. The Bessborough commission found that this provision failed, largely because of the indifference of yearly tenants, who regarded the long lease as 'not a lengthening of the legal yearly tenancy, but a shortening of the continuous traditional tenancy'.[6] Of much more importance to the long-term solution of the Irish land question was the inclusion in the land act of the principle of state-aided land purchase.

The latter principle was contained in the 'Bright clauses', which were

[1] J. E. Pomfret, *The struggle for land in Ireland, 1800–1923* (Princeton, 1930), p. 93.
[2] *Bessborough comm. rep.*, p. 7.
[3] Sect. 9.
[4] *Bessborough comm. rep.*, p. 21.
[5] E.g. *Stevenson* v. *earl of Leitrim*, I.R.R. & L. 121, and *Friel* v. *earl of Leitrim*, I.R.R. & L. 101.
[6] *Bessborough comm. rep.*, p. 6.

incorporated in the act at the insistence of John Bright, the president of the board of trade and the most influential advocate in the cabinet of a policy of tenant proprietorship.[1] A purchase scheme devised by Bright had been incorporated in the Irish church act of 1869, and the clauses in the land act were on similar lines. They provided that the landlord and tenant of any holding in Ireland might agree on the sale of the holding to the tenant at such price as might be fixed between them, and on such agreement being made they might jointly, or either of them might separately with the assent of the other, apply to the landed estates court for the sale to the tenant of his holding. The board of works, if satisfied with the security, could advance to a tenant a sum not exceeding two-thirds of the price, and the holding was to be charged with an annuity of £5 for every £100 of such advance, which was to be repayable in the term of thirty-five years.

Unlike the land purchase provisions in the church act, which proved remarkably successful, the purchase provisions in the land act were not availed of to any significant degree by the tenantry, many of whom were probably unaware of the new land purchase scheme. Those tenants who were aware may well have simply found the costs prohibitive, and a measure of the modest success of the scheme was the fact that a total of only 469 loans, for a total of £347,480 in respect of an area of 39,924 acres, were made by the commissioners of public works under the provisions of the act.

ENGLISH equity, from which Irish equity derived, evolved as an ameliorating jurisdiction that permitted the adaptation of general and abstract legal rules to the particular circumstances of the individual case. That concept of equity is not unique to the legal system that Ireland shared with England, and similar concepts are to be found in most developed legal systems. What was peculiar to English equity was its development in a separate court structure, the chancery courts, a development that had no rational basis but was largely an accident of historical circumstances. The growth of a separate chancery jurisdiction in England was closely followed by the growth of a similar jurisdiction in Ireland, and this trend was continued, and indeed accentuated, following the act of union.

By the beginning of the nineteenth century equity jurisdiction in England was ceasing to be characterised by the discretionary interference with general rules in order to do justice in the particular case, and was acquiring characteristics that were to make it a system competing with, rather than ameliorating, the rigidity of the common law. The reduction of equity to a system of rules and principles that were as predictable and certain as those of the common law is popularly attributed to Lord Eldon, who during two periods as lord chancellor of Great Britain (1801–6, 1807–27) set about ridding equity of all traces of unbridled discretion and arbitrariness. The closeness of Irish and English equity, which was underpinned by the translation of

[1] Above, pp 449–50.

English judges to the Irish bench in the early nineteenth century, ensured that the systematisation of equity in England was to be followed in Ireland.

Occasionally English appointees to the Irish bench were lawyers of the first rank, but often they were men whose attainments were slight and whose appointment owed more to family influence or political expediency than distinction in the law. In the former category was Lord Redesdale (lord chancellor 1802–6), whose reputation as an equity lawyer had been established by his treatise on chancery pleadings and whose reputation prompted a series of nominate reports that covered the period of his chancellorship, and in the publication of which he sometimes cooperated by revising the notes of the reporters. Redesdale, who was not indifferent to money, had succumbed to the inducement of an annual salary of £10,000 sterling and the assurance that it was cheaper for an Englishman to live in Dublin than in London. Apparently he did not find this to be the case. Lord Manners, who was a cadet of the Rutland family, fell into the category of appointees who owed their appointment to political favour and family influence, and during twenty years on the Irish woolsack (1807–27) he added little to the body of Irish equity jurisprudence. Perhaps his most significant decision was one in 1823, in which he declined to hold a bequest for memorial masses void as being for a superstitious use, and held the bequest valid and charitable.[1]

Manners was succeeded by Sir Anthony Hart (1827–30), who was offered the chancellorship at the age of seventy-three over the head of William Conyngham Plunket (created Baron Plunket 1 May 1827), the outstanding Irish equity lawyer of his generation, apparently because George IV refused to countenance the appointment of Plunket, who had championed the cause of catholic emancipation. Sir Anthony, a native of St Kitts in the West Indies, clearly had reservations about coming to Ireland and was persuaded to do so only on the understanding that 'of papists and Orangemen he was to know nothing'.[2] Shortly after taking up office Hart's unfamiliarity with Irish procedure involved him in a bitter wrangle with the master of the rolls, Sir William MacMahon, over whether petitions in the rolls court could be heard without first being signed by the lord chancellor's secretary. Judicial functions had been restored to the master of the rolls in Ireland by an act of 1801,[3] and the dispute was in large measure attributable to the assertion by MacMahon of a status equal to that enjoyed by the master of the rolls in England. That dispute continued during the chancellorship of Lord Plunket, who succeeded Hart in 1830, and during the early part of whose chancellorship MacMahon was still master of the rolls.[4]

Lord Plunket, whose earlier promotion had been frustrated by the king, was

---

[1] Below, p. 472. [2] Ball, *Judges*, ii, 268.
[3] 41 Geo. III, c. 25 (18 Apr. 1801).
[4] MacMahon was master of the rolls 1814–37. He was succeeded by Michael O'Loghlen, the first catholic to hold the office.

the second distinguished legal author to sit on the Irish woolsack in the nineteenth century. Although his appointment was no more than his standing as the leading Irish equity lawyer of his generation merited, he was apparently not successful in gaining the confidence and goodwill of the profession, and appeals 'were taken from his decisions and allegations of nepotism were made against him in parliament'.[1] Many of Plunket's decisions, however, are consistent with his high reputation as an equity lawyer, and none more so than those in which his view of the law was in conflict with that of Sir Edward Sugden, in which cases the house of lords tended to confirm Plunket's view. One such case was *Shaw* v. *Lawless*,[2] in which Plunket had decreed in 1833 that precatory words did not establish a trust. Sugden, the outstanding English equity lawyer of the day, who had succeeded Plunket while the tories were in office from January to April 1835, took a different view, but the house of lords affirmed the earlier decree of Plunket and reversed Sugden's.[3] Before *Shaw* v. *Lawless* the courts had tended to construe precatory language (words expressing hope, confidence, or desire) as creating a trust, and Plunkett's decree in that case prefaced an important shift in judicial policy towards precatory trusts.

Sugden, the third distinguished legal author to sit on the Irish woolsack, served again in 1841–6 in succession to Lord Campbell; he was to be the last, and also the most gifted, of the expatriate Englishmen to become lord chancellor of Ireland. When he was first appointed his reputation as a legal author was unrivalled, and his brief tenure of office confirmed his mastery of equity. His second period as chancellor spawned no less than five sets of nominate reports that bear eloquent testimony to his great erudition and legal knowledge, and it was said of him that 'he was one of the greatest lawyers that ever lived'.[4] Sugden, who was succeeded by Maziere Brady, became lord chancellor of Great Britain in 1852, being raised to the peerage as Lord St Leonards.

The translation of English judges to the Irish bench ensured the parallel development of Irish and English equity, but the derivative nature of much Irish equity also owed much to the dominance of the English reports in the early part of the nineteenth century before the regular reporting of Irish cases began. This dominance is reflected in an anecdote of a case in which Plunket appeared as a counsel before Lord Manners, then lord chancellor, who asked him if he was sure that what he stated was the law. 'It unquestionably was the law half an hour ago', replied Plunket, looking at his watch, 'but as the packet is now due, I'll not be positive.'[5]

Nineteenth-century chancery practice in both England and Ireland was characterised by inordinate delays and excessive expenses, abuses that were savagely caricatured by Charles Dickens in the notorious suit of *Jarndyce* v.

[1] Ball, *Judges*, ii, 279.
[2] 1 Dr. & Wal. 512.
[3] J. R. O'Flanagan, *Lives of the lord chancellors . . . of Ireland* (2 vols, London, 1870), ii, 585–6.
[4] *The Times*, 26 Nov. 1875, quoted in Ball, *Judges*, ii, 288.
[5] O'Flanagan, op. cit., ii, 482–3.

Jarndyce in *Bleak House*. An extra expense for Irish litigants was the cost of taking an appeal to the British house of lords, a practice that had ceased in 1783 but was renewed following the act of union. Defects in chancery proceedings can be attributed to two principal causes. First, the aim of equity to achieve justice *inter partes* required that the closest attention be given to the facts of the particular case and this led inevitably to delays in the adjudication process. Secondly, the composition of the chancery courts involved too few judges determining too many cases. Until reforms in the early nineteenth century in England, the lord chancellor sat as sole judge in chancery. When judicial functions were given to the master of the rolls the position was little improved, since appeals could be taken from the rolls court to the lord chancellor. A single vice-chancellor was appointed in England in 1813 to help discharge judicial business; but since an appeal could be taken from him to the lord chancellor, arrears continued to accumulate. Two more vice-chancellors were appointed in 1841 but it was not until 1867 that a vice-chancellor was first appointed in Ireland.[1]

The need for chancery reform was constantly brought to the attention of parliament and certain jurisdictional changes that were enacted in England were subsequently extended to Ireland. Thus in 1831 bankruptcy jurisdiction in England was transferred from the chancery to a chief judge in bankruptcy, and a similar transfer was enacted for Ireland in 1857.[2] The equity jurisdiction of the court of exchequer, which was transferred to the court of chancery in England in 1842, was similarly transferred in Ireland in 1850.[3] A court of appeal in chancery was established in England in 1851 for the purpose of hearing appeals from the master of the rolls, the vice-chancellors, and the chief judge in bankruptcy; within five years a court of appeal in chancery was established in Ireland.[4] The office of taxing master, which had been introduced to the court of chancery in England in 1842, was established in the court of chancery in Ireland in 1867.[5]

Reforms in the composition and jurisdiction of the chancery courts, however desirable, were calculated to emphasise rather than to diminish the anomalous position of equity as a separate and sometimes competing jurisdiction. Some cases fell on the borderline between equity and common law, and in one such case, *Marquis of Waterford* v. *Knight* (1844),[6] litigation went on for fourteen years before it was discovered that the action should have been initiated in the other jurisdiction. A series of royal commissions that examined the respective constitutions of the court of chancery and the common-law courts recommended changes that were intended to reduce, if not altogether to eliminate, the harm-

---

[1] Chancery (Ireland) Act, 1867 (30 & 31 Vict. c. 44 (15 July 1867)).
[2] Irish Bankrupt and Insolvent Act, 1857 (20 & 21 Vict., c. 60 (25 Aug. 1857)).
[3] Exchequer Equitable Jurisdiction (Ireland) Act, 1850 (13 & 14 Vict., c. 51 (29 July 1850)).
[4] Chancery Appeal Court (Ireland) Act, 1856 (19 & 20 Vict., c. 92 (29 July 1856)).
[5] Chancery (Ireland) Act, 1867 (30 & 31 Vict., c. 44 (15 July 1867)).
[6] 11 Cl. & Fin. 653.

ful and wasteful consequences of two disparate and competing jurisdictions. As a result a series of measures were enacted in the 1850s that provided for the exercise by the common-law courts of powers that had been peculiar to the court of chancery, and for the exercise by the latter of powers that had been peculiarly within the competence of the common-law courts. Thus by the Common Law Procedure Act, 1854, which was extended to Ireland in 1856,[1] the common-law courts were enabled to compel discovery of documents in all cases in which a court of equity could do so, and were given a limited power to grant injunctions and permit equitable defences to be pleaded. The Chancery Amendment Act, 1858,[2] otherwise 'Lord Cairns's act', which applied to Ireland, gave to the court of chancery discretionary power to award damages either in addition to or in substitution for specific performance. Before that act damages could be awarded only in the common-law courts; Lord Cairns' act gave the court of chancery the power to award damages but only in cases where it might otherwise have granted the equitable remedy of specific performance.

Despite this partial fusion of common law and equity, the essential problem created by the existence of two separate court systems remained, and a royal commission was appointed in 1867 to recommend changes and improvements that might be made to provide for the more speedy, economical, and satisfactory dispatch of judicial business. The whole matter had apparently acquired a fresh urgency with the growth of limited-liability companies, whose directors were regarded as both agents and trustees; as the former they could be sued in the common-law courts, and as the latter they could be pursued simultaneously in the court of chancery. The commissioners, in the first of two reports, referred to the fact that the evils of this double system of judicature, and the conflict and confusion of jurisdiction deriving from it, had long been known and acknowledged. They accordingly recommended the consolidation of all the superior courts of law and equity, together with the courts of probate, divorce, and admiralty, into one supreme court, which consolidation they felt would 'at once put an end to all conflicts of jurisdiction'.[3] These recommendations were given effect in the Supreme Court of Judicature Act, 1873, as amended by the Supreme Court of Judicature Act, 1875. The Irish judicature act of 1877, which was closely modelled on the English act of 1873, consolidated the existing courts of queen's bench, common pleas, exchequer, admiralty, probate and divorce, and chancery into one supreme court of judicature, which was divided into a high court of original jurisdiction and a court of appeal.[4]

Initially there were five divisions of the new high court, each of which could exercise both legal and equitable jurisdiction. Since a court could find itself in

[1] 17 & 18 Vict., c. 125 (12 Aug. 1854); Common Law Procedure Amendment (Ireland) Act, 1856 (19 & 20 Vict., c. 102 (29 July 1856)).

[2] 21 & 22 Vict., c. 27 (28 June 1858).

[3] *Judicature commission: first report of the commissioners*, p. 9 [4130], H.C. 1868–9, xxv, 9.

[4] 36 & 37 Vict., c. 66 (5 Aug. 1873); 38 & 39 Vict., c. 77 (11 Aug. 1875); 40 & 41 Vict., c. 57 (14 Aug. 1877).

difficulty when a rule of equity was in conflict with a rule of law, the first ten subsections of section 28 of the act of 1877 provided for the resolution of such conflict in specific areas, while the eleventh subsection provided that 'in all matters, not hereinbefore mentioned, in which there is any conflict or variance between the rules of equity and the rules of common law, with reference to the same matter, the rules of equity shall prevail'. Despite the invitingly wide language of section 28 (11) it was judicially accepted that the union of judicature had effected merely a procedural and not a substantive fusion of law and equity. Chief Baron Palles said of the act of 1877: 'that act changed forms of procedure, but did not alter rights or remedies'.[1] The effect of the union of judicature was later summed up in Ashburner's celebrated phrase to the effect that the two streams of jurisdiction, law and equity, 'though they run in the same channel, run side by side and do not mingle their waters'.[2]

THE first half of the nineteenth century was to see important developments in the substantive law of charity and in the law regulating the administration of charities, which had important consequences for the catholic church, for it relied largely for the maintenance of its clergy and buildings on private benefactions. When the penal laws were relaxed, there seemed to be no reason in principle why bequests for catholic services such as the mass should not be held as charitable under the rubric of the advancement of religion,[3] which is one of the four heads of charity. In a case in 1823 involving the validity of a bequest for masses for the repose of the testatrix's soul Lord Manners, the lord chancellor, otherwise a virulent anti-catholic, confirmed the report of the master of the rolls that the bequest was a valid charitable one and not void as being for a superstitious use. That case, *Commissioners of charitable donations* v. *Walsh*, was not reported other than in the newspapers, and some twenty years later the question whether a bequest for masses was void was again raised in *Read* v. *Hodgens* (1844).[4] Two reasons may be suggested for this renewed challenge to the status of mass bequests. First, in England in 1835, Sir Charles Pepys, master of the rolls, declined to hold charitable bequests to catholic priests for prayers and masses, on the ground that such bequests were void as being for superstitious uses, a decision that caused some ripples in Ireland. Second, although he was not considering the question of superstitious uses, Sir Edward Sugden (later Lord St Leonards), the last and arguably the most distinguished Englishman to sit on the Irish woolsack, held in *The Incorporated Society* v. *Richards* (1841)[5] that the law of charity in Ireland was coterminous

[1] *Barber* v. *Houston*, [1884] 14 L.R.Ir. 273,276. See Wylie, *Ir. land law*, p. 87.
[2] Walter Ashburner, *Principles of equity* (London, 1902), p. 23; cf. Lord Diplock in *United Scientific Holdings Ltd* v. *Burnley Borough Council*, [1978] A.C. 904, 925.
[3] See generally O. D. Tudor, *Law of charities* (6th ed., London, 1967); G. W. Keeton and L. A. Sheridan, *The modern law of charities* (2nd ed., Belfast, 1971).
[4] 7 Ir. Eq. Rep. 17.
[5] 4 Ir. Eq. Rep. 177.

with that in England. Before Francis Blackburne, as master of the rolls, addressed the question of 'superstitious uses' in *Read* v. *Hodgens* he was apprised of the earlier decision of Lord Manners, which he was bound to follow, and so ended the brief history of 'superstitious uses' in Ireland. Bequests for masses were thereafter regarded as legally charitable until that status was successfully challenged by the crown on a ground other than superstition in *Attorney general* v. *Delaney*[1] in 1875.

Catholics had less reason to be satisfied with legislation dealing with the administration of charities in Ireland. In the last year of the Irish parliament the first charitable bequests board was set up, consisting of the archbishops and bishops of the Church of Ireland, together with other named ecclesiastics, the twelve judges of the superior courts, and the judge of the prerogative court. The legislature's primary purpose in setting up this board was to prevent the misapplication and concealment of funds given for charitable purposes, and it achieved some success.[2] The board was also given power to apply funds cy-près, which meant that in cases where the application of funds in the manner laid down by the donor would be inexpedient, unlawful, or impractical, such funds could be applied to purposes that the commissioners considered to be the nearest and most conformable to the intentions of the donor. Since the board's business was conducted almost entirely by the clerical commissioners, who were exclusively protestant, their power to apply funds cy-près made catholics reluctant to make charitable bequests, and this was a source of grievance to the catholic church, which was thereby deprived of funds. O'Connell accordingly had sought reform of the board in 1830; but that, and later efforts at reform in 1834 and 1838, were of no avail. In February 1840 the catholic bishops addressed a memorial to the chief secretary praying that the board should be rendered more useful and popular by the addition to it of catholic members. In 1844, however, some fifteen years after the emancipation act, only one of the board's fifty members was catholic.[3]

One of the major grievances of the catholic clergy had been that they could not take grants and conveyances in perpetuity without the intervention of trustees, the appointment of whom was troublesome and expensive. O'Connell had introduced a bill in March 1844 that sought to meet this difficulty by constituting every catholic bishop a body politic and corporate with perpetual succession. This solution would have given catholic bishops the same legal status as bishops of the Church of Ireland, but while the government did not formally oppose its introduction, it proceeded no further, a fact in part at least attributable to O'Connell's imprisonment within weeks of the bill's introduction.

Peel had assured O'Connell in March 1844 that it was the government's

---

[1] I.R. 10 C.L. 104.
[2] V. T. H. Delany, *Law relating to charities in Ireland* (Dublin, 1962), p. 181.
[3] Kerr, *Peel, priests, & politics*, p. 122.

intention to introduce a bill that would provide for the supervision and protection of charitable funds in Ireland, and this bill was introduced in the house of lords in June 1844. Catholic criticism of the board established by the earlier legislation was to be met by the setting up of a new board consisting of ten nominated members, of whom five were to be catholic, and three *ex officio* members. Peel's decision that three of the members of the new board should be catholic ecclesiastics was to prove crucial in defusing catholic opposition to the measure. When the appointment of three catholic bishops was officially announced in the *Gazette*, they were given their full ecclesiastical titles, though without reference to territory, and accorded precedence over the members of the peerage on the board. 'This is the first time, since the enactment of the penal laws', remarked the *Morning Chronicle*, 'that the Roman Catholic prelates have been recognised, by their titles, in an official document emanating from the queen in council.'[1] Section 15 dealt with the problem of perpetuity in relation to grants for catholic purposes by providing that donors could vest such property in the new commissioners to be held in trust for such purposes. It was also provided that when questions concerning the catholic church arose they would be dealt with exclusively by catholic commissioners, who would then give a certificate of facts to be acted on by the board. The commissioners' power under the earlier legislation to apply funds cy-près, which had been a cause of disquiet to catholics, was omitted from the bill.

Despite these safeguards the bill was perceived by many catholics not as an enabling measure but as an attempt to legislate for the catholic clergy and bring them under state control. A particular source of disquiet was the proviso in section 15 that nothing contained therein should be construed as rendering lawful any donation in favour of a religious order proscribed by the Roman Catholic Relief Act, 1829. Opponents of the bill argued that this proviso would involve catholic commissioners in helping to put the penal clauses of the emancipation act into effect.[2] A still more serious cause of catholic disquiet was section 16, the 'mortmain' section, which provided that no disposition of real property for pious or charitable uses would be valid unless the deed, will, or other instrument creating the same should be duly executed at least three months before the death of the person executing it. The equivalent English legislation, the Georgian mortmain statute of more than a century earlier,[3] had been more severe in its requirement that such disposition be made twelve months at least before the death of a donor. Sir Edward Sugden, as lord chancellor, had observed in *The Incorporated Society* v. *Richards* in 1841 that he would be glad if the law on charities in Ireland and England was further assimilated by the extension to Ireland of the Georgian mortmain statute.[4]

---

[1] Kerr, *Peel, priests, & politics*, p. 190.
[2] Ibid., p. 141.
[3] 9 Geo. II, c. 36 (20 May 1736).
[4] J. C. Brady, *Religion and the law of charities in Ireland* (Belfast, 1976), p. 129.

The argument in favour of some statutory restriction on death-bed dispositions in favour of charity, which were often made at the expense of the donor's family and others dependent on him, was made more pressing by the removal of penal restrictions on catholic benefactions, since catholics were more likely to make this sort of disposition. This latter point was underlined, somewhat ironically, by Archbishop MacHale's criticism of section 16 that it 'would consign the deathbed penitent to all the horrors of despair'.[1] Indeed, the mortmain provision was originally included in section 15 of the bill and confined to catholic bequests, but catholic criticism led to its being put in a separate section and made applicable to all denominations. Catholic hostility to the section was also muted somewhat by O'Connell's opinion that it could easily be circumvented by making not a grant of land but a sum of money chargeable on the land for the charitable purpose.[2] Later the 'O'Hagan clause' was routinely inserted in wills of realty to neutralise section 16 by providing that if a device for charitable purposes should fail for any reason, a gift over (a gift of money exceeding the value of the land) would take effect to a named clergyman for his own benefit absolutely.[3]

The history of the Charitable Donations and Bequests (Ireland) Act,[4] from 1844 until its repeal in both parts of Ireland in the 1960s, shows that catholic fears were largely groundless. Particularly groundless was O'Connell's claim that the 'monstrous extent of powers' given to the commissioners authorised them to decide many questions of catholic doctrine and to determine questions touching the succession of prelates and priests in various dioceses and parishes in Ireland.[5] The board established by the act of 1844 proved to be scrupulously neutral between the denominations and played an important role in a country where charitable benefaction, particularly that mediated through the churches, has been, and remains, an important aspect of life.

An interesting development that affected the fiscal privileges accorded to a purpose deemed charitable in law followed the enactment of legislation in the 1850s dealing with the rating and valuation of premises in Ireland. Section 2 of the Valuation (Ireland) Amendment Act, 1854, provided that in making out the lists or tables of valuation the commissioner of valuation should distinguish, in order to exempt from rating, all hereditaments and tenements, or portions of the same, of a public nature, or used for charitable purposes, or for the purposes of science, literature, and the fine arts.[6] The Irish courts were later to hold that the act of 1854 was so dependent on and interwoven with the Poor

[1] MacHale to Peel, 2 July 1844 (Kerr, *Peel, priests, & politics*, p. 131).

[2] Kerr, *Peel, priests, & politics*, p. 133.

[3] Brady, op. cit., pp 136–9.

[4] 7 & 8 Vict., c. 77 (9 Aug. 1844).

[5] O'Connell made this claim in a professional opinion dated 24 Aug. 1844. See V. T. H. Delany, *Law relating to charities in Ireland* (Dublin, 1962), p. 188.

[6] Section 2 of the act of 1854 (17 & 18 Vict., c. 8 (12 May 1854)) replaced section 15 of the Valuation (Ireland) Act, 1852 (15 & 16 Vict., c. 63 (30 June 1852)).

Relief (Ireland) Act, 1838,[1] that the 'charitable purposes' referred to in section 2 must be treated as being coterminous with the exempt purposes set out in the proviso to section 63 of the act of 1838, which ran as follows.

Provided also, that no church, chapel, or other building exclusively dedicated to religious worship, or exclusively used for the education of the poor, nor any burial ground or cemetery, nor any infirmary, hospital, charity school, or other building used exclusively for charitable purposes, . . . or . . . for public purposes, shall be rateable, except where any private profit or use shall be directly derived therefrom. . . .

The effect of this singular interpretation by the Irish courts of section 2 of the act of 1854 meant that to merit exemption from rates the occupying charity had to be invested with the same character as the exempt purposes set out in the proviso to section 63 of the act of 1838. Thus schools that were otherwise charitable as being for the advancement of education, and religious institutions, such as retreat houses, that were otherwise charitable as being for the advancement of religion, were all subject to rates unless of an eleemosynary character. The house of lords was later to reject this interpretation of section 2 in a case that came before them in an appeal from Northern Ireland.[2] The narrower interpretation, however, still obtains in the Republic of Ireland.[3]

AT the beginning of the nineteenth century the benchers of the Honourable Society of King's Inns exercised wide powers of control over both branches of the legal profession: barristers, who constituted the 'senior' branch of the profession, and attorneys and solicitors, who constituted the 'junior' branch. The benchers, who were appointed from the judges, were thus in a singular position to lay down conditions for those who wished to appear before the courts. In December 1793, for example, the judges passed a number of resolutions affirming their control over the attorneys' profession. All attorneys wishing to take apprentices were obliged to become members of the King's Inns and on admission to membership pay a 'deposit for chambers', the proceeds of which were to be used for the erection of residential quarters. The money thus paid was never used for the stated purpose and was later the subject of a claim by the Law Society against the benchers, which was finally resolved only in 1874, when the benchers granted to the Law Society a 999-year lease of premises at the rear of the Four Courts at a nominal rent.

Membership of the King's Inns and payment of yearly dues did not mean that attorneys and solicitors, who were more numerous than barristers, shared in the government of the Inns. Indeed the reverse was true, since the benchers were selected exclusively from the barristers, and this undemocratic state of

---

[1] 1 & 2 Vict., c. 56 (31 July 1838).

[2] *Campbell College* v. *Commissioner of valuation for Northern Ireland*, [1964], N.I. 107; see R. L. E. Lowry, 'Some reflections on rating' in *N.I. Legal Quart.*, xvii (1966), pp 256–75.

[3] *Governors of Wesley College* v. *Commissioner of valuation*, unreported supreme court judgment, delivered 9 Dec. 1982.

affairs led the attorneys and solicitors to assert their professional independence and ultimately to secede from the Inns. The earliest professional association for attorneys and solicitors was the Law Club of Ireland, set up in 1791, which was followed by the Law Society of Ireland, founded in 1830 by Josias Dunne to promote and protect the rights and privileges of attorneys and to adopt 'such measures as may best be calculated to ensure respectability to the profession and advantage to the public'. From its inception the Law Society concerned itself with the professional education of its aspirant members. The only statutory provision for such legal training was contained in an Irish statute of George II that obliged an applicant for admission as an attorney to prove by affidavit that he had served an apprenticeship for five years, and in a statute of George III that provided for moral examiners to be appointed by the courts; but such examinations were perfunctory and were no real test of the candidates' legal knowledge.[1] A solicitor commentator was later to observe acidly that the strongest qualification for the legal profession 'was the expression of an extreme willingness to send the pope and his followers to warm quarters'.[2]

The absence of any effective statutory provision for legal education was compounded by the benchers' abject failure to provide teaching facilities for either branch of the profession, a failure that led in 1839 to the setting up of the Dublin Law Institute for the purpose of giving a systematic legal education to both branches of the profession. The institute, which was largely the brainchild of a Dublin barrister, Tristram Kennedy, was governed by a council composed of distinguished members of the Irish bar, with Kennedy as its principal. Kennedy did not seek a charter of incorporation for the institute, but the benchers of the King's Inns were invited to become members of the council and a grant of £400 was secured from King's Inns funds. Further grants of £100 each were provided by two of the English inns, Gray's and Lincoln's. The rapport between the institute and the King's Inns was short-lived, however, and in the following year the benchers refused to renew their grant, apparently because of agitation on the part of students at the institute to have the requirement of keeping terms in London ended. This requirement was not ended until 1885.[3] Lack of funds soon led to the closure of the institute and the end of a most interesting and innovative experiment in legal education. Instruction at the institute was through formal lectures and classwork, but the students also attended the courts and apparently it was not unusual for professors in certain departments to make available to their students pleadings in pending cases. Professorships in equity, property, medical jurisprudence, and common law had been established, and the last chair was held by Joseph Napier, later to become lord chancellor (1858–9). Kennedy had been in correspondence with Joseph Story and Simon Greenleaf, whose appointments at Harvard in 1829

[1] 7 Geo. II, c. 5 (29 Apr. 1734); 13 & 14 Geo. III, c. 23 (2 June 1774).
[2] W. F. Littledale, *The Society of King's Inns, Dublin* (Dublin, 1859), p. 18.
[3] Barristers Admission (Ireland) Act, 1885 (48 & 49 Vict., c. 20 (21 May 1885)).

and 1833 respectively had given a new vitality and direction to the teaching of law in the universities. Story warned Kennedy of the opposition he was likely to encounter from the disposition, so common in the legal profession, 'to resist innovation, even when it is an improvement'.[1]

The activities of Story and others at Harvard, which caused some ripples in educational circles on this side of the Atlantic, and the widespread interest generated by the lectures of Andrew Amos and John Austin at the University of London drew attention to the need for reforms in legal education, and in 1846 a parliamentary select committee on legal education was appointed under the chairmanship of Thomas Wyse. That committee, which considered evidence from Great Britain, Ireland, continental Europe, and the United States, was extremely critical of the state of legal education in Ireland, although it paid a well earned tribute to Kennedy's institute. The committee was particularly critical of the role of Dublin University, which it said provided little education for the professional or unprofessional classes and 'what it does provide is rendered nugatory by the circumstances with which it is connected'.[2] One such afflicting circumstance could well have been the fact that professors were very much part-time teachers, since double, triple, and even quadruple jobbing were not perceived as social evils in the eighteenth and early nineteenth centuries. Patrick Duigenan, regius professor of feudal and English law in Dublin University, was at the time of his death in 1816 vicar general of the diocese of Armagh, a judge of the court of prerogatives and faculties, a member of parliament, and a privy councillor. The detrimental effect of this dilettantish approach to legal education in the university is perhaps best summed up by the admission of John Anster, regius professor of civil and canon law, to a royal commission in 1853 that he could not instance one case of a student being refused the degree of bachelor of laws on account of the way in which he performed his exercises; and, while an examination by the professor of a candidate for the degree was contemplated, in point of fact no such examination existed.[3] That university law teachers were not only dilettantish, but also timidly conservative and resistant to change and innovation, is well exemplified by the evidence on the desirability of teaching criminal law given by Mountifort Longfield, regius professor of feudal and English law in Dublin University, to the select committee in 1846: he had never lectured in criminal law, 'not considering it worth calling the attention of students to. There are no fixed principles in it, except that men must not commit certain crimes, and if they do, there are certain punishments'.[4] This extraordinarily dismissive approach was in stark contrast to that which prevailed in Tristram Kennedy's

[1] V. T. H. Delany, 'The history of legal education in Ireland' in *Journal of Legal Education*, xii (1960), p. 403.

[2] *Report from the select committee on legal education*, p. vii, H.C. 1846 (686), x, 7.

[3] Delany, loc. cit., p. 400.

[4] Ibid., p. 403.

short-lived institute, where criminal law, and the new discipline of medical jurisprudence, had prominent places in the curriculum.

The select committee recommended the improvement and extension of university law teaching and the institution of examinations. The committee reported in the year following the setting up of the queen's colleges, and drew attention to the opportunity that their establishment offered of 'introducing a popular course of elementary law or jurisprudence for all classes, and attendance in which, being required for the attainment of a degree, would ensure its extension to all those to whom such elementary knowledge would be applicable'.[1] Each of the new colleges was endowed with a professorship in law, and in time was enabled to conduct courses leading to degrees in law under the aegis of the federal Queen's University in Ireland, but it is a curious fact that the first full-time professor of law was not appointed until 1934, when J. L. Montrose was appointed in Belfast.

Despite the strong language used by the select committee, little was done immediately to remedy the situation; but the benchers, following further criticism from a member of the profession, embarked in 1850 on a joint venture with the professors of Dublin University. Attendance at classes in the Inns and Trinity was made compulsory for aspiring barristers, but no provision was made for compulsory examinations, and the system governing admission to the bar was little improved. A more positive response by the benchers to criticism was the establishment of two professorships in 1850. Further insistent calls for improvements in legal education came from the Law Society, which had been reconstituted in 1841 as the Society of Attorneys and Solicitors of Ireland. The society obtained in 1852 a charter of incorporation, which recited, *inter alia*, that the attorneys and solicitors of Ireland had associated themselves for the purpose of founding an institution for facilitating the acquisition of legal knowledge and the better discharge of other professional duties. The society, in pursuit of the object of its charter, presented several petitions to the benchers between 1855 and 1860, drawing attention to the absence of any provision for legal education for apprentices. In a memorial submitted to the benchers in 1855 the society sought the implementation of the recommendations of the select committee of 1846, including the proposal that applicants for admission as apprentices should be required to pass a preliminary or entrance examination, and that before admission as attorneys they should be required to pass examinations in law and practice. The memorial also requested that lectures be provided for apprentices and that the library of the King's Inns be open to them.

The benchers referred the memorial to their 'legal education committee', which responded to the request for lectures for apprentices with the bald statement that funds were not available for the establishment of such lectures. As to

---

[1] *Report on legal education*, p. xlvi. For a contemporary view of the contribution of the new colleges to law teaching, see W. F. Littledale, *The Society of King's Inns, Dublin* (Dublin, 1859), pp 41–2.

the request for admission of apprentices to the library, the committee saw no sufficient grounds for concluding that apprentices, if admitted to the library, would 'devote their limited leisure to legal study in preference to lighter and more agreeable reading. We are informed that actual experience of the class of books most read in the King's Inns Library would lead to the opposite inference.'[1] Admission of apprentices to the library was thus refused on precisely the same ground as that on which, for many years, undergraduates were refused admission to the library of Trinity College.

It was not until 1860 that the benchers agreed to institute a system of lectures and to hold examinations to ascertain the fitness of persons aspiring to be apprentices and of apprentices aspiring to be attorneys, but by then it was too late to arrest the movement towards secession that came with the enactment of the Attorneys and Solicitors (Ireland) Act, 1866.[2] This act, in providing that attorneys and solicitors should not, in future, be obliged to be members of the King's Inns, marked the passing of control of legal education of apprentices from the benchers to the Society of Attorneys and Solicitors; but the judges continued to exercise a disciplinary jurisdiction over the profession until 1898.

[1] Littledale, op. cit, p. 40.
[2] 29 & 30 Vict., c. 84 (6 Aug. 1866).

EDITOR'S NOTE

Since this chapter was written, the development of professional training in law has been covered in Dáire Hogan, *The legal profession in Ireland, 1789–1922* ([Dublin], 1986).

SPECIAL ABBREVIATIONS

THE following abbreviations are current among writers on law, and have therefore been used in this chapter. They are listed separately here, being formed on different models from the abbreviations used elsewhere in *A new history of Ireland*. As examples of their application, 'I.R. 10 C.L. 104' denotes p. 104 of volume x of I.R.C.L., and '16 I.C.L.R. 222' denotes p. 222 of volume xvi of I.C.L.R.

A.C. [appeal cases]	*The law reports . . . house of lords and judicial committee of the privy council and peerage cases* (London, 1927–)
5 Bligh (N.S.) 31	*The English reports, volume V: house of lords. Containing Bligh, N.S., volumes 4 to 9* (Edinburgh and London, 1901), pp 219–20
11 Cl. & Fin. 653	*The English reports, volume VIII: house of lords. Containing Clark & Finnelly, volumes 8 to 12* (Edinburgh and London, 1901), p. 1250
Co. Rep.	*The English reports, volume LXXVI: king's bench division V, containing Coke, parts 1, 2, 3, and 4* (Edinburgh and London, 1907)
Dr. & Wal.	W. B. Drury and F. W. Walsh, *Reports of cases argued and determined in the high court of chancery during the time of Lord Chancellor Plunket* (2 vols, Dublin, 1839–42)
I.C.L.R.	*Irish common law reports: reports of cases argued and determined in the courts of queen's bench, common pleas, exchequer, exchequer chamber, and court of criminal appeal* (17 vols, Dublin, 1852–67)
I.L.T.R.	*Irish Law Times Reports* (monthly supplement to *Irish Law Times*, 1867–)
I.R.	*The Irish reports . . .* (Dublin, 1894–)
I.R.C.L.	*The Irish reports, . . . containing reports of cases argued and determined in the superior courts in Ireland . . . common law series* (11 vols, Dublin, 1868–78)
I.R.R. & L.	*Irish reports. Registry appeals in the court of exchequer chamber and appeals in the court for land cases reserved, 1868–76* (Dublin, 1886)
Ir. Eq. Rep.	*Irish equity reports, particularly of points of practice argued and determined in the high court of chancery, the rolls court, and the equity exchequer* (13 vols, Dublin, 1839–52)
L.R. Ir.	*The law reports (Ireland) . . . containing reports of cases argued and determined in the court of appeal, the high court of justice, and the court of bankruptcy in Ireland* (32 vols, Dublin, 1879–93)
L.R. Eq.	*The law reports: equity cases before the master of the rolls and the vice-chancellors* (20 vols, London, 1866–75)
N.I.	*The Northern Ireland law reports: containing reports of cases argued and determined in the high court of justice and on appeal therefrom to the court of appeal in Northern Ireland* (Belfast, 1925–)

CHAPTER XXV

Literature in English, 1801–91

THOMAS FLANAGAN

IF the political history of nineteenth-century Ireland is measured from the act of union to the death of Parnell, its literary history stretches from Maria Edgeworth's *Castle Rackrent* (1800) to the early poetry of Yeats. In both this opening and this close there is a strong and suggestive connection between the political and the literary event. *Castle Rackrent*, which was published in the shadow of the impending union, is Maria Edgeworth's sardonic elegy on the morally and socially bankrupt 'nation' of the eighteenth century; Yeats, writing shortly before Parnell's death, predicted 'an intellectual movement at the first lull in politics'.[1] In neither case is the connection one of simple coincidence, for the strands of art and politics have been intricately intertwined in the cultural history of modern Ireland. This chapter will attempt to define this intricate relationship by exploring the ways in which developing notions of cultural identity found expression in the assumptions and attitudes of Irish writers.

The century opens and closes on statements that address themselves explicitly to the question of cultural identity. 'Nations as well as individuals gradually lose attachment to their identity', the preface to *Castle Rackrent* hopefully remarks, looking forward to the time when 'Ireland loses her identity by an union with Great Britain'.[2] But Douglas Hyde, in the lecture on 'The necessity for de-anglicising Ireland', which he delivered before the Irish National Literary Society in 1892, was to argue that Ireland, after a century of union, had half lost her old identity without gaining a new one, and was 'at present in a most anomalous position, imitating England and yet apparently hating it'.[3] Hyde's contention that the botched and fateful work of a century must be undone, that 'we must strive to cultivate everything that is most racial, most smacking of the soil, most Gaelic, most Irish',[4] takes issue with Maria Edgeworth on ground that lies deeper than that of historical prediction and hindsight. What separates Hyde from Edgeworth is the history of the nine-

[1] W. B. Yeats, *Autobiographies* (2nd ed., London, 1955), p. 199.
[2] Maria Edgeworth, *Castle Rackrent* (London, 1800; reprint, with introduction by R. L. Wolff, New York and London, 1978), p. xi.
[3] Douglas Hyde, 'The necessity for de-anglicising Ireland' in C. G. Duffy, George Sigerson, and Douglas Hyde, *The revival of Irish literature* (London, 1894), p. 121.
[4] Ibid., p. 159.

teenth century, which includes the changing modes in which men perceived, judged, and cherished cultural existence. Their implicit quarrel arises from different notions of the nature of culture itself, and requires an historical explanation. The intellectual and literary history of modern Ireland is in some measure the history of such notions. Irish history is the history of ideas about Ireland.

Castle Rackrent is usually called the first Irish novel. Certainly it is the first in which a writer sought, by the ordering and clarifying techniques of fiction, to present a coherent vision of Irish life. The history of the Irish novel therefore begins ironically with a denial of the power of national identity, and yet the life of *Castle Rackrent* itself argues warmly against its prefatory assumption. The successive generations of the Rackrent family, Old Patrick, Murtagh, Kit, and Condy, suggest rather, in their emblematic fashion, that such identity derives from sources deep within the life of the society, and this argument is sustained, even more powerfully, by the voice and personality of Thady Quirk, the servant who narrates the history and fate of the family. Maria Edgeworth's Irish novels—*Castle Rackrent*, *The absentee*, *Ennui*, and *Ormond*—argue that Ireland did indeed possess an identity, but one that had been shaped almost entirely by abnormal and baneful circumstances. But the venal, profligate, and ramshackle society she hoped to see submerged within the larger British culture was also one she cherished with an ill-concealed affection, and the consequence was a duality of attitude that was to appear in the work of later ascendancy writers.

Maria Edgeworth, like her father Richard Lovell, viewed with a rationalist's scorn the sentimental nationalism of the late eighteenth century, but in this she differed only in degree from a colonial patriot like Grattan or a separatist like Tone. The preservation of a specifically Irish culture was not merely absent from the political thought of Grattan and Tone; it was entirely alien to their tastes and habits of thought. In the end, Grattan was to move with ease if not with pleasure to the British parliament, and Tone was to discover in revolutionary France a country of the imagination that was as truly his as ever Ireland had been. Tone, who loved French plays and Italian operas, summed up the matter in his impatient comment on the traditional musicians who marred his second visit to Belfast: 'strum strum and be hanged'.[1] That Belfast harp festival of 1792,[2] organised by enthusiasts who included both loyalists and republicans, may now be seen as a preface to the history of Irish cultural nationalism as it moved by tortuous indirections from antiquarianism to rebellion. But the belief that Ireland possessed a culture, which like every culture has both roots and being in language, habits, traditions, the words of poets, the aspects of landscape, was developed only by a later generation.

A national literature is one that is informed by a specific culture, and it possesses the coherence of a tradition when that culture is recognised and accepted by its writers. Nineteenth-century Ireland did indeed possess a rich,

[1] Tone, *Life*, i, 157.   [2] Above, iv, 603.

contradictory, and thick-textured culture woven from many strands, Gaelic and English, native and planter, catholic and protestant. But it was only during the course of the century that writers sought consciously to explore and to define this culture. This is not surprising, nor does it mark a condition peculiar to Ireland. The nations of Europe are centuries old, but nationality in the modern meaning of the term was a nineteenth-century discovery. To that century we owe the discovery that nations possess unique existences from which are shaped the sounds of their music and the cadences of their verses. It was in particular the Romantic poets and historians who sought to trace back the links of history that bind present and past, and to celebrate those refractory habits and loyalties that the eighteenth century had hoped to flatten to a benign uniformity. The Romantic historian, a Michelet or a Carlyle, sought to find the shape of a society in the actions and spirit of its people, rather than in the sequence of its dynasties. The Romantic critic, a Renan or an Arnold, in discussing the poetry of 'the Celtic races', sought to define the particular attributes of a literature by relating it to the presiding life and imaginative genius of its society. The instances here chosen, it will be seen, have both a general and a specific bearing on the development of nineteenth-century Irish literature.

If the history of that larger literature is to be read properly, it must be placed within the larger contexts both of British and of European thought and art. Yeats rightly regarded Standish James O'Grady as a writer thwarted and shackled by his provincialism, but O'Grady, besides sharing the passion for Carlyle that was common among the writers of Victorian Ireland, was an acute reader of Shelley and Whitman, and these unlikely enthusiasms helped to shape his attitude toward the Irish sagas. It must equally be borne in mind, of course, that the literature of nineteenth-century Ireland was the expression of specific, and in some instances unique, social pressures. It was a deeply divided land, and the ancient barriers that separated catholic from protestant, peasant from landlord, had been hewn from native stone. Throughout much of the century Irish writers were not addressing their fellow countrymen (who rarely bothered to listen) but rather a neighbouring stranger. The audience for Irish books was in part at least a British one, and writers were therefore concerned to 'interpret' Ireland, to exploit as local colour or as provincial genre-painting whatever seemed unique, particular, or 'romantic' in Irish life. One of the deepest divisions within Irish life was that of language itself. Gaelic, in which was vested virtually all of the traditional culture of the island, was losing ground steadily, decade by decade, through the operation of a process that the century chose to regard as inexorable. The literature of the Irish nineteenth century was predominantly a literature in English, which instinctively made use of English modes and conventions. As regards language, the centuries-old conflict between native and planter cultures had seemingly come to a decisive close.

The central theme of much of Ireland's literature in English, in part because of the paradox that that phrase implies, has been the exploration of Irish identity. 'I think, look you, under your correction', says Fluellen to Shakespeare's only Irishman, 'there is not many of your nation ...', and Macmorris bursts out in anger, 'Of my nation? What ish my nation? Ish a villain, and a bastard, and a knave, and a rascal. What ish my nation? Who talks of my nation?' 'What is your nation, if I may ask', says Joyce's Citizen, three centuries later, and Bloom replies, with cogent but misleading simplicity, 'Ireland. I was born here. Ireland.'[1] Even, perhaps especially, in works clearly addressed to an English audience, the Irish writer has been concerned, like Macmorris and Bloom, to know what was his nation, and to explore the puzzles and paradoxes of his identity.

In the novel, especially, writers found a form that enabled them to consider their society and their relationship to it. The examination began with *Castle Rackrent*. Written at the deathbed of the eighteenth-century 'nation', it is a demonstration more persuasive than any political treatise of why that nation failed, and why it deserved to. Four generations of Rackrents move from improvident wealth to impotent ruin—the drunken Patrick, the grasping Murtagh, Kit the gambler and duellist, and the weak, generous Condy. Their history is given both structure and meaning by the deceptive voice of Thady, the old servant who narrates it. His chief concern is apparently for the honour of the family, to which he yokes a sublime inability to perceive the actual nature of his masters. Gambling was 'the only fault he had, God bless him', Thady says of Kit, after having revealed that he kept his wife locked in her room for seven years while courting the daughters of the neighbouring gentry.[2] But 'honest Thady', as he is called by successive generations of Rackrents, is not at all the simpleton he makes himself out to be. His attention to his own interests is shrewd and unflagging, and he knows that these are best served by uncritical flattery of all Rackrents. It is Thady who ruins young Condy by teaching him a fanciful version of the family history, and it is Thady's gombeen son Jason who probably will come into possession of the Rackrent lands. *Castle Rackrent* is an extraordinarily poised and subtle work of art; its disingenuous narrative voice and its remarkable use of compression as a way of giving characters the weight and significance of cultural symbols are devices we encounter again only in fiction of a much later period. But it is equally impressive as social history. Why follow the fortunes of them that have none left, a peasant girl asks as she turns away contemptuously from Condy's deathbed,[3] and by her question she passes judgement on his family and his class.

Maria Edgeworth's later novels of Irish life are further explorations of the

[1] William Shakespeare, *Henry V*, III, ii; James Joyce, *Ulysses. The corrected text*, ed. H. W. Gabler (London and Harmondsworth, 1986), p. 272.
[2] Maria Edgeworth, *Castle Rackrent* (New York and London, 1978), p. 53.
[3] Ibid., p. 173.

same theme, the relationship of the Anglo-Irish to their land. The subject is most fully developed in *Ormond*, a rich and elaborate book in which the hero confronts three cultures—the Anglo-Irish world of his witty and corrupt uncle Ulick, the dense, tribal world of his Irish uncle Corny, and the proper, responsible world of the English Annaly family. The choices are presented to the hero in convincing detail, and with a scrupulous regard for the values and weaknesses of conflicting cultural traditions. Like *Castle Rackrent*, it looks beyond itself toward certain directions that the Irish novel was to take. From Charles Lever's *The Martins of Cro' Martin* to *The big house of Inver* by Somerville and Ross, Irish novels, and especially those by writers of the ascendancy, have sought to trace social destiny in the history of a family or an estate. But the destruction by fire of the big house of Inver is prefigured in the fall of Castle Rackrent. Maria Edgeworth's novels, like Lever's final works, suggest how deep and prophetic a sense of the actualities of Irish experience could be embodied in the traditional forms of the English novel.

A wide gulf would seem to separate her novels from the *Irish melodies* of her near-contemporary, Thomas Moore, for she was supremely a rationalist, while Moore's songs are the perfect, minor expression of certain Romantic impulses and themes. The antiquarian and dilettante Celticism that she mocked in her *Essay on Irish bulls* (1802) supplies both the background and the substance of the *Irish melodies* (1808). These take on as a theme the vast distance between a past imagined as splendid and chivalric, and a present, urbane but diminished, in which the vanished splendours may be recalled in comfort. Kinkora and Mononia, the ruined wall of palace and abbey dreaming in the moonlight, the minstrel boy fallen in ancient battle, the triumphs of Brian and Malachi were bright barbaric images which Moore subdued and set afloat across Merrion and Mountjoy Squares. Behind the *Melodies* lay pseudo-history, the musings of General Vallancey and of the absurd Joseph Cooper Walker,[1] who in an excess of rationalism had supposed that the banshee's wail was produced by the wind moving through harps hung on branches of trees. Eugene O'Curry has recorded how Moore, encountering some ancient manuscripts at the Royal Irish Academy, exclaimed in wonder that the men who composed such works, which to him were unintelligible, could not have been fools. But this did not dissuade him from the many-volumed *History of Ireland* which he was doggedly preparing. That history, with its judicious speculations as to whether the round towers had been constructed by fire-worshipping Babylonians,[2] is a monument to the belief that a nation's history can be set forth in utter ignorance of its language. But the *History* has the value of many mistaken monuments, for it summarises with elegance a century of amateur and genteel scholarship, and it established a notion of the Irish past that persisted far into the nineteenth century.

[1] Above, iv, 416–17, 468–9.
[2] Thomas Moore, *The history of Ireland* (4 vols, London, 1835–45), i, 29–34.

Moore's attitude to that past must be taken in conjunction with his attitude to the Ireland of his own day. The footnotes to the *Irish melodies* are rich in references to Edward Ledwich, Ferdinando Warner, and Sylvester O'Halloran,[1] to Edward Bunting's collections of traditional airs, to manuscript translations from the Irish that were collected 'under the direction of that enlightened friend of Ireland, the late countess of Moira'. But other notes, and some of the most celebrated of the *Melodies*, suggest a more immediate political perspective. The references to liberty, patriotism, courage, and national loss evoke the complex of feelings produced by the speeches of Grattan and by faded engravings of the Volunteers, and the 'nation' that was swept away by the act of union. The immediate past is thus joined to the vanished, antique world of Brian and Malachi. The delicate achievement of the *Melodies* is to form from ancient and recent past a coherent world of feeling, sentiment, tone, and atmosphere in which the legendary countryside of ruins exists beside Malton's Dublin streets.

Moore's prose works, in particular the *Memoirs of Captain Rock*, and the *Life and death of Lord Edward Fitzgerald*, define his own political position, whiggish and sentimentally patriotic. It is natural that although he supported catholic emancipation and, less enthusiastically, repeal of the union, he should have detested O'Connell. For although O'Connell was lavish in his praise of 'Ireland's national poet', he seemed to Moore a florid and leather-lunged demagogue who had transposed to a vulgar key his own national sentiments. Yet O'Connell's oratory and Moore's poetry worked together to create the characteristic nationalism of the first half-century, a nationalism that retained firm links with eighteenth-century assumptions and stances.

The conjunction of whiggish liberality and antiquarian patriotism that characterises Moore's work appears also in the novels of Lady Morgan.[2] *The wild Irish girl: a national tale* is the daydream of a governess, the absurd account of an Irish 'prince' and his erudite daughter, living in a ruined castle at the edge of the Atlantic. As such fantasies often do, however, it captured with utter fidelity the very essence of a specific Romantic attitude toward the Irish past. Later novels, *O'Donnel* and *Florence Macarthy*, are slightly more sophisticated and to that degree lack its naive intensity. For all her posturing and theatricality, she was capable of one first-rate book, *The O'Briens and the O'Flahertys*, an oddly shaped, quirky, and intelligent story, which draws on a genuine sense of history. The story is rooted deep in eighteenth-century Galway, and although it depends heavily for its facts on Hardiman's *History of Galway*, the meanings with which it is invested are drawn from her memories and fantasies of the past of her own family. Its subject is the conflict between competing notions of Ireland, and it takes culture itself as theme, in a manner that was to characterise other writers.

[1] Above, iv, pp lxi–lxii; see, e.g., *Irish melodies* (London, 1846), p. 257.
[2] Sydney Owenson married Sir Thomas Morgan in 1812. *The wild Irish girl*, *Patriotic sketches*, and other early work appeared under her maiden name. See also above, iv, 429, 597.

In an early volume of *Patriotic sketches* Lady Morgan offers us her melancholy and sunset-hued meditations as she stands before the O'Connor tomb in Sligo abbey.[1] The reverie, at once theatrical and true in feeling, is made to serve both a sentimental and a political purpose, for in a manner suggestive of Moore she manages to imply that although Irish nationality lies safely buried in the historied past, it justifies and demands present patriotic indignation. Although she called her novels 'national tales' and used them for the ostentatious display of a perfervid patriotism, she was not seriously dismayed that the actual restoration of Irish nationality was a most remote possibility. Like Moore, she trafficked in the politics of nostalgia, and like Moore she despised and feared O'Connell, whose politics inclined towards the actual. As an ally of the whigs, he was barely tolerable, but as a tribal chieftain of the catholic masses he seemed to her a gross and scheming menace. In 1837 she departed for London (abandoning the Kildare Street *salon* where she had presided in 'a red Celtic cloak, formed exactly on the plan of Grannuaille's'),[2] noting waspishly in her journal, 'creatures of temperament and temper, true Celts, as Caesar found your race in Gaul, and as I leave you, after a lapse of two thousand years'.[3] She was not to be the last Irish writer driven to exile by the harsh intrusion of an actual on an imaginary Ireland.

History, the actual and the imaginative commingled, was to dominate much of the literature of the first half of the century, as the landscape of prairie and mountain was to dominate American romantic prose, as though the two cultures were seeking definition, the one in time and the other in space. Sir Walter Scott, in his famous tribute to Maria Edgeworth, praises the example that she had set him of the ways in which the novel can be used for the exploration of a culture.[4] But Scott, in his turn, was to pass on to Irish writers the design of the historical novel, in which the patterns of social and political identity may be traced in the lineaments of remote conflicts. The most impressive and substantial of these novels is *The Boyne Water* (1826), by John and Michael Banim, a book that lifts itself above its rivals by its clear and impartial historical judgements. The Banims were catholics and moderate nationalists, but they renounced partisan polemics in their explorations of the social and religious tensions of the late seventeenth century. Yet their novel drifts toward a contrived irresolution, and for a significant reason. Scott's Waverley novels, which celebrate a culture that had resolved its conflicts, are an emblematic assertion of the resolution. They are profoundly conservative for reasons that lie far beneath Scott's tory preferences, for they assert that Scottish culture has received its final form. But although the battle of Culloden marked, at least in

---

[1] Sydney Owenson, *Patriotic sketches of Ireland, written in Connaught* (2 vols, London, 1807), i, 18–30.

[2] Lionel Stevenson, *The wild Irish girl* (New York, 1936), p. 295; cf. plate 13b.

[3] *Memoirs, autobiography, diaries and correspondence of Lady Morgan*, ed. William Hepworth Dixon (2 vols, London, 1862), ii, 427.

[4] Sir Walter Scott, *On novelists and fiction*, ed. Ioan Williams (London, 1968), p. 413.

the political sense, the end of Scotland's national history, the Boyne was but one crucial chapter in the history of Ireland, with long shadows falling into the present. Maria Edgeworth's novels, Scott writes, 'may be truly said to have done more toward completing the union, than perhaps all the legislative enactments by which it has been followed up'.[1] This may be read either as a graceful tribute to the powers of art or, more mordantly, as a comment on the efficacy of the legislative enactments. It may have occasioned a satirical if respectful smile at Edgeworthstown, which Scott visited in 1825, setting down in his journal a remark more in accordance with the state of things, 'their factions have been so long envenomed, and they have such narrow ground to do their battle in, that they are like people fighting with daggers in a hogshead'.[2]

Although Maria Edgeworth lived until 1849, her pen had been silent on Irish affairs for some three decades. But her letters make clear her attitude towards the agitations of the 1820s and 1830s, which she saw only as 'a restless desire to overthrow what is, and a hope—more than a hope—an expectation of gaining liberty or wealth, or both, in the struggle; and if they do gain either, they will lose both again and be worse off than ever'.[3] The Banims, however, capture the mood of the period in their Tales by the O'Hara family (1825–6), which are among the first Irish stories written to portray the life of a particular region—in this case, the Kilkenny countryside. 'Peep o' day' and 'Crohoore of the billhook' are startlingly brutal stories of the '98 rebellion, lit by fitful and lurid flames, but their actual subject is a later Ireland of Ribbon and Rockite conspiracies, as though the untended fires of agrarian insurrection remained smouldering on hillsides and in glens. The great strength of the Banims lay in provincial genre-painting, and their weaknesses, perhaps a corresponding one, in their constant effort to 'explain' Ireland to their British audience.

The effort itself is understandable. In the 1820s and 1830s, events were compelling Britain to pay reluctant attention to her unruly sister island. It seemed to British eyes a dark and savage land, picturesque in appearance, but fitfully revealing its true nature in flashes of violent murder. When the Banims, like other Irish writers, sought to demonstrate the causes of this violence and to urge its remedies, they were having recourse to the novel as an instrument of social instruction and change, precisely as Dickens was in England. But the Irish writers found themselves in the position of barristers, arguing the cause of one country before the bench of another, and they slipped easily into the arts of the special pleader, cajoling, extenuating, preaching. The Banims' genuine literary gifts, not great but considerable, are often hidden beneath a blanket of moral purpose, although at times they shone through, as in a novel like 'The Nowlans' (1826), which Yeats admired. Perhaps the art and the pleading must

---

[1] Ibid., p. 413.
[2] J. G. Lockhart, Life of Sir Walter Scott (10 vols, Edinburgh, 1839), viii, 25.
[3] The life and letters of Maria Edgeworth, ed. A. J. C. Hare (2 vols, New York, 1895), ii, 511.

be taken together as composing an authentic statement of the situation in which nineteenth-century Irish writers found themselves.

That much of the literature of the century was written with a British as well as an Irish audience in mind is a fact that does not require extensive documentation. Its consequences, however, were complex and at times contradictory. A novelist like Gerald Griffin, a teller of tales like William Carleton, a folklorist like Thomas Crofton Croker, inevitably saw himself as an interpreter of his society, and this in turn demanded from him some clear and coherent idea of the nature of that society. As writer, he stood at one remove from his people, judging the shape and manner of their lives and sketching what a literary cliché of the period termed 'the lights and shadows of Ireland'. And indeed the cumulative effect on English readers must have been precisely that of chiaroscuro drawing. Ireland appealed to the early Victorian taste for untamed and picturesque landscape, a close-at-hand Sicily. Its people, however, were shrouded in the mysteries of unfathomable paradox: loyal, cheerful-hearted, and unjustly oppressed, according to the accounts of some writers; sullen, vindictive, and murderous, according to others. A people, in short, who defied and perhaps did not deserve explanation save that offered by Scott's terse simile of men fighting with daggers in a barrel. For the Irish writer, however, a serious issue was at stake: in defining his society, he was defining himself. The complexities of the issue are apparent in the novels of Gerald Griffin, a writer of remarkable gifts and intelligence.

Griffin, like the Banims, began by writing stories shaped for a British market, but even his early *Tales of the Munster festivals* (1827) have an intensity and an imaginative energy that the O'Hara stories lack. He was fiercely introspective, but this quality was surprisingly yoked to shrewd social judgement and to a warm delight in the world of social experience. *The collegians* (1829), his masterpiece, is a profound and moving study of passion and ambition, of murder and conscience. Most Irish readers were familiar with it, for it became a popular classic, in its own right and in the deplorably sentimentalised versions of Boucicault's play and Benedict's opera.[1] Hardress Cregan, a Limerick squireen, contracts a misalliance with a rope-maker's daughter, regrets what he has done, and with the help of his creature, Danny the Lord, murders her. But this plot, while it gives the novel its centre, does not fully embody its theme. The true subject is the society of provincial Ireland— Cregan's world of 'half-sirs' and squireens with loaded whips, the middle-class catholic world of his friend Daly, the farmers of the countryside, the peasants in the hills, the servants of the big houses, the schoolmasters and cattle-dealers. Cregan, the Byronic, passionate, and childish hero is joined so fully to his society that his crime is made to seem the inevitable consequence of its

---

[1] Dion Boucicault's 'The colleen bawn' (first public performance 1860) and Julius Benedict's 'The lily of Killarney' (first public performance 1862). The theme of all three derives from the murder of Ellen Hanly in July 1819.

tensions. Griffin's vision of Irish life is subtle and complex, and his instinct for place and manner is unerring. *The collegians* is a chapter in the history of the Irish conscience.

Daniel Corkery, in *Synge and Anglo-Irish literature*, was to write of *The collegians*:

> In this we have an Englishman to whom the quaintness of the folk is exhibited with the accompanying stream of comment, exactly in the colonial manner. This normal Englishman is really the symbol of the public for whom the book was written; and the writer of it, Gerald Griffin, may be taken as the type of the non-ascendancy writer who under the stress of the literary moulds of his time wrote colonial literature.[1]

But it is Corkery rather than Griffin who writes out of the deforming insecurities of a colonial situation. Griffin accepts the fragmentary, incoherent nature of his society, and seeks by imagination to puzzle out its pattern. Indeed, the conflict between native and colonial values is one of his explicit subjects. But Corkery, in his gnarled and censorious manner, poses a genuine question: how may the literary forms or 'moulds' of one culture express the cultural life of another? The question may be perplexing in the abstract, yet not in particular instances. Griffin was responsive to the culture he lived in and saw about him— the broken Gaelic world he perceived through songs and customs, and the ascendancy world that both attracted and repelled him. It is rather Corkery's own notion of the hidden Ireland[2] that might properly be described as an imperfect work of fiction, the will doing the work of the imagination. Griffin possessed the Virgilian piety of place, and it served him well.

The problem reappears, however, with William Carleton, the one writer with whom every student of nineteenth-century literature must come to difficult terms. Carleton, a prodigally gifted Tyrone peasant, sought to capture and express the life of the Irish countryside in a score of books, but most vividly and successfully in his *Traits and stories of the Irish peasantry* (1830) and in his unfinished autobiography.[3] Farm boy, aspirant to the priesthood, schoolmaster, Carleton wandered to literature and to the streets of Dublin from that other Ireland of hedge poets, wakes, and faction fights. The autobiography, written with a freshness and freedom from artifice not always present in his novels, captures this world in its brightest and its darkest colours—the girls behind the hedges, the fiddlers and prophecy-men, the cottagers and labourers, Ribbonmen and thieves. It is one of the great literary documents of the Irish nineteenth century. By temperament, Carleton had much in common with the hedge poets, lazy, cunning, adventurous, relishing language and character. He set off from Tyrone to Dublin with a copy of *Gil Blas* in his pocket, and he makes of this a journey as long and as eventful as any in Le Sage;

---

[1] Daniel Corkery, *Synge and Anglo-Irish literature: a study* (Dublin and Cork, 1931), pp 8–9.
[2] Above, iv, 129–30.
[3] Below, p. 493, n. 1.

the few counties he travels through seem as wide and as thickly peopled as the plains of Spain.

Had Carleton been a less remarkable writer, he would still be an important repository of knowledge concerning peasant life in pre-famine Ireland. His defects as a writer are many and large—an imperfect hedge-school education he sought to conceal beneath coatings of 'literary' English, a stiff and awkward sense of construction, a clumsy indifference to the resources of the novel. But these faults, although they maim, do not destroy his subjects. The best of the novels—*Fardorougha the miser* (1839), *The black prophet* (1847), and *Valentine M'Clutchy* (1845)—are concerned with the constants of peasant experience: famine, avarice, and land; and their power of vision is concentrated and terrible. He knew that he was expressing for the first time in English a civilisation that lay hidden behind the hedges, and his knowledge that an entire world lay within his imaginative possession lent power, at times bravado, to his pen.

It is significant that his best fiction is to be found not in the novels but in *Traits and stories of the Irish peasantry*. Their looseness and openness of form is exactly suited to his genius, which is that of the story-teller, not the novelist. 'The Lough Derg pilgrim', 'Denis O'Shaughnessy going to Maynooth', 'Tubber Derg', 'The hedge school', live in their accumulated wealth of affectionate detail, and in the warm sardonic colours of his memory and his imagination. 'Wild Goose Lodge', the fictionalised account of a Ribbon outrage, savagely executed and as savagely punished, reads less like literature than like a hypnotic evocation of a dreadful folk memory. Had Corkery chosen Carleton rather than Griffin to develop his theory of 'colonial literature' he would have been on firmer ground, for Carleton's novels are marked by the painful conflict between his creative energies and the literary 'moulds' in which he felt compelled to form them. The problem extends beyond literary form to general ideas. Carleton has always been an embarrassment to the conventional literary nationalist; a chronicler of the catholic peasantry, himself risen from its ranks, he was a tory in politics and a zealous convert to protestantism. The toryism has its simple explanation in the peasant's shrewd, cautious conservatism, sceptical of enlightened liberal panaceas. The religious issue, as it struggles towards articulation in the stories, is more complex, but part of the explanation lies in his deeply ambivalent attitude towards the society he chronicles. Yet neither the politics nor the religion, although abundantly present in the novels, serves to illuminate the culture he strives to depict. His ideas lie athwart his tales, which tend to assume life and meaning of their own.

Traits and stories of the Irish peasantry is a suggestive title. Like Thomas Crofton Croker's *Fairy legends and traditions of the south of Ireland* (1825–8) and Anna Maria Hall's *Sketches of Irish character* (1829–31), it makes an assumption that is as much sociological as literary. Some of the most powerful of the stories have as their formal purpose an attempt to define by illustration some 'trait' of the peasantry. The effect of such distancing often is not to bring the peasant closer to hand, but rather to place him yet further in the distance, the dweller in some alien world to which the writer has special access. Carleton, who in his later years acquired the unfortunate habit of referring to himself as 'the great peasant', was not above exploiting the authority of his experience. The effect on English readers is incalculable, but may well have contributed to the notion that the peasantry of Ireland were remote, mysterious, and therefore tragically un-English. Certainly in the course of the century an English image of the Irish peasant developed that was at least in part a literary invention. Like that equally celebrated stereotype, 'the stage Irishman', it became part of that shorthand by which nations misunderstand each other. But for Irish readers Carleton has been a troublesome writer—harsh, often graceless, powerful, and sardonic, and deeply divided in his aims. He is a universal writer, says Patrick Kavanagh, who much resembled him, 'as good, say, as Cervantes, but with no opening into the world'.[1] The phrase captures perfectly his plight, islanded between two cultures of ebbing and advancing tides.

It is common to invoke the name of Charles Lever when speaking of the stage Irishman, and he remains part of literary history by virtue of his early tales, *Charles O'Malley* (1841) and *Harry Lorrequer* (1839), picaresque romances of rakehell heroes moving through a dowdy, amiable, and inefficient society of fox-hunts, garrison towns, and ruined big houses. There may be some truth to the dour suspicions of nationalists that such ebullient cartoons served not merely to flatter English self-esteem but also to argue that Ireland, whether or not it stood in need of help, was ill-prepared to put it to good use. But 'the world of Charles Lever' has its authenticity as well as its charms, and the scenes by which it is created are brilliantly evoked—priests and magistrates taking their ease over hot whiskies in a Galway parlour, dragoons courting the daughters of bankrupt landlords, hunts spilling along long hills and over broken walls. Lever's point of view is substantially but not entirely that of the hero of 'Jack Hinton' (1843), a young English guardsman posted to the south of Ireland, who becomes willingly involved in the racketting, hard-drinking lives of the Munster squireens. This point of view is shrewdly manipulated, however, for Lever had his own tart, tory view of Irish affairs.

It is unfortunate, however, that these early novels have obscured his later work, for he developed into a serious and urbane commentator on the Irish scene, the one genuine novelist of Victorian Ireland. In the series of novels that extends from *The Martins of Cro' Martin* (1847) to *Lord Kilgobbin* (1872), most of them written when he was serving as a British consul in Italy, he developed an intricate and strangely neutral picture of the country he had left. They are marked by slow and leisurely plot, a carefully composed background, a sharp and impartially satirical eye and ear. Lever was a tory by both instinct and principle—he had been an editor of the *Dublin University Magazine* and

[1] William Carleton, *The autobiography of William Carleton*, with preface by Patrick Kavanagh (London, 1968), p. 9.

continued contributing to *Blackwood's*—but his peppery prejudices, although they enliven the pages of his 'Cornelius O'Dowd' papers (1864-5), are largely absent from the late novels. *The Martins of Cro'Martin*, based closely on the history of a well known Connacht family, is a thickly woven chronicle of social experience, involving much political intrigue, but it serves no polemical purpose. On the contrary, its tonic effect derives from its buoyant and even-handed satire. These are the least provincial of nineteenth-century Irish novels, as though Lever, in the safety of his Italian sinecure, had discovered fresh perspectives on Ireland.

Lever's inquiries into the nature of Irish identity take strange forms in his late novels, which were never popular and now are almost forgotten, as in that entirely grim and enigmatic book *Luttrell of Arran* (1865), with its embittered hero, half gentleman and half rebel, self-exiled on a western island; or his last and finest book *Lord Kilgobbin*, in which magistrate, landlord, priest, and fenian are treated with equal sympathy. They are elegaic books, and not merely because they were written towards the close of his life. By the 1860s, his high-tory sentiments had mellowed. Like his friend Isaac Butt, he had grown less certain of the fate of the social class to which he was allied, and his final novels are tentative and probing, suffused with a sense of impending loss. The novels themselves also represent a loss, for the Ireland of that period was badly in need of writers who possessed his gifts of social perception and comic energy.

When Carleton was dying, he spoke of himself and his surviving contemporaries as the end of a brief tradition, and predicted that half a century would pass before literature flourished again in Ireland. A tradition of the novel had not established itself in the first half of the century, although, as we have seen, a number of variously gifted writers had turned to the novel as a literary form eminently suited to the exploration of social experience and to the imaginative resolution of cultural issues. Such explorations of identity at times took unexpected and subterranean channels, as in the novels and tales of Joseph Sheridan Le Fanu. Elizabeth Bowen has suggested that the English setting of Le Fanu's masterpiece, *Uncle Silas* (1864), is deceptive, and that the story makes fullest emotional sense when it has been transposed back to the Irish country-side.[1] The observation holds true for others of his books. His early novels, *Cock and anchor* (1845), for example, and *The house by the churchyard* (1863), are set firmly in eighteenth-century Dublin, but it was later practice to place his stories, in their final version, in an English setting. The process by which 'A passage in the secret history of an Irish countess' was transformed into *Uncle Silas* is typical, but his motives are far from clear. A big house set against a remote and lonely landscape is essential to *Uncle Silas*, but surely Westmeath would have served him as well as Derbyshire, if not better. It is tempting to discover in this

[1] J. S. Le Fanu, *Uncle Silas* (London, 1864; reprint, with introduction by Elizabeth Bowen, 1947), pp 8-9.

evidence of Le Fanu's fastidious withdrawal from the contemporary Irish scene. He is remembered today for his tales of the eerie and the irrational, but in his youth he was deeply involved in Irish life, and his knowledge of the eighteenth-century ascendancy was exhaustive. There is a remarkable line among certain writers of the ascendancy, running from Charles Robert Maturin at the beginning of the century to Bram Stoker at its close: compounders of fantasies and tales of the grotesque, set everywhere save in Ireland. But it might be well to remember that the best-known of such novels, Maturin's *Melmoth the wanderer* (1820), opens in the ruined corridors of an Irish big house. Perhaps also to remember that when Oscar Wilde went into European exile he assumed the name 'Melmoth', from the tale written by his distant kinsman. Such imaginative exiles, the spirit alone taking ship or turning inward on its own resources, form a small but significant chapter in the history of English-speaking Ireland. The books of such writers are like small houses enclosed by alien and threatening hills.

IN a dedicatory poem for a book of stories selected from the Irish novelists, Yeats was to write:

> We and our bitterness have left no traces
> On Munster grass and Connemara skies.[1]

It is an exact evocation. We have been discussing the writers of pre-famine Ireland, and when reading them we sense an Ireland in some ways discontinuous with our own. We can sense this almost in the atmosphere they create of a multitudinous and thickly peopled island. The impression is one we share with those who survived the disaster. Patrick Murray, writing in 1852, was to claim as one of Carleton's chief merits that he had recorded the vanishing peasant civilisation.

It is in his pages, and in his alone, that future generations must look for the truest and fullest—though still far from complete—picture of those, who will ere long have passed away from that troubled land, from the records of history, and from the memory of man for ever.[2]

He could have been writing of Carleton's own Clogher valley, which the novelist visited in 1847, to discover that that rich, Chaucerian hive of countryfolk, the source for his *Traits and stories*, had been swept bare. George Petrie, introducing in 1855 his collection of Irish music, writes movingly of 'the calamities which, in the year 1846–7, had struck down and wellnigh annihilated the Irish remnant of the great Celtic family'.[3] An awful, unwonted silence had fallen upon the land, he writes, and this silence, stretching across valleys that once

[1] W. B. Yeats, *The poems*, ed. Richard J. Finneran (London, 1984), p. 45.
[2] [Patrick Murray], 'Traits of the Irish peasantry' in *Edinburgh Review*, no. cxcvi (Oct. 1852), p. 389.
[3] George Petrie (ed.), *The ancient music of Ireland: the Petrie collection* (Dublin, 1855), p. xii.

had echoed with song, struck fearfully on the imagination. Petrie was persuaded that he was collecting the song and the music of a shattered race.

Of the old, who had still preserved as household gods the language, the songs, and traditions of their race and their localities, but few survived. Of the middle-aged and energetic whom death had yet spared, and who might for a time, to some extent, have preserved such relics, but few remained that had the power to flee from the plague- and panic-stricken land.[1]

And those chains of traditions and peculiarities of feeling that had bound the young within a community of feeling had been snapped. Petrie was a remarkable man, gifted beyond most others of his day in his perception of the close intermingling of art and society, but the view he expresses here was far from uncommon. The peasant civilisation of Ireland had been shattered by the famine, although less entirely and less permanently than it must have seemed at the time.

The famine was to leave its heavy and sombre mark not only on Irish society but on its literary consciousness. From that time until almost the close of the century writers were to write in the knowledge that they dealt with a stricken land, ill with a sickness that lay far beneath political formulation. The memory of the famine, however, was to be joined to that of a second, exactly contemporary, and seemingly unrelated event—the rise and fall of Young Ireland. 'Against the dark and tragic background of the great famine', F. S. L. Lyons has written, 'the posturings of most of the individual actors seem unimportant and almost ludicrously irrelevant.'[2] And so they must inevitably seem. Thomas Francis Meagher, declaiming on the beauties and potencies of the sword in paragraphs of dropsical eloquence as the land sank into starvation and disease, is not today an impressive, nor even an attractive picture, however much it may have impressed his young colleagues.[3] But for the cultural historian the emergence of Young Ireland has its importance and its inevitability. When Thomas Davis, John Blake Dillon, and Charles Gavan Duffy took their famous walk through the Phoenix Park and laid down their plans for the *Nation*, they introduced into Ireland, in its specific terms, the modern notion of nationality. By a paradox, and not one they fully intended, they brought Ireland into Europe, for the doctrine of an integral nationalism, 'racy of the soil' and binding together all classes, all creeds, all particular interests, was a powerful element in the political consciousness of nineteenth-century Europe. The task assumed by Davis and his colleagues was that of translating the doctrine into Irish terms, and in the few years available to them before the débâcle of 1848 they performed the task with zealous attention to detail.

[1] Petrie, op. cit., p. xii.
[2] F. S. L. Lyons, *Ireland since the famine* (London, 1971), p. 93.
[3] Speech at Conciliation Hall, 26 July 1846, in *Meagher of the sword: speeches of Thomas Francis Meagher in Ireland 1846–1848*, ed. Arthur Griffith (Dublin, 1917), pp 35–7.

Davis's brief essays in the *Nation*, on literature, history, politics, manners, music, and a host of other subjects, are the work of a talented journalist, written in haste and often bearing its mark. The *Nation* came into being as a journalistic ally of O'Connell's repeal movement, and for a time the alliance was mutually rewarding. As a skilful propagandist, Davis offered the repeal party an organ of opinion of which it was sorely in need, but he was also attractive to O'Connell on other grounds. He was a recruit from the ranks of the protestant gentry and professional class, with numerous friends in the social and cultural life of Dublin, and with a following of earnest and articulate young men. Davis, for his part, recognised that O'Connell's programme coincided in rough outline with his own, and was therefore prepared to support him without reservation. But the specific differences that shortly before Davis's death were to separate the two men were implicit from the first, and not entirely unrecognised by either. They issued from Davis's conception of nationality and the values that he attached to the word 'nation'.

Like the ideologists of nationalism in other countries, Davis was partly an historian, partly a cultural enthusiast, partly a politician. He regarded Ireland as a distinctive culture, deeply rooted in history, or rather in the histories of the several races that had gone into its making, and believed that his primary task, both as writer and as politician, was that of creating and fostering a sense of this distinctiveness. The historic Irish nation was for Davis a reality, unrecognised by most of his contemporaries, which transcended immediate political issues. It is significant, however, that his first extended work, *An address read before the Historical Society, Dublin* (1840), is devoted to an elaboration of the simple assertion that 'Ireland *is* a nation', and that the address is pointed specifically towards his own class. (The title 'The young Irishman of the middle classes' was applied to this work in later reprints.) History was for Davis the full accretion of the past, and he was prepared to cherish all those institutions and legends in which he could discern the germ of nationality—the 'patriot' parliament of James II, the apprentice boys of Derry, the confederation of Kilkenny, the rebels of 1798. Although he was to lift the United Irishmen into romantic legend (for a generation they had been regarded either as ogres or as misguided idealists), his notion of Irish nationality was one that Tone would have regarded with indifference, for its centre of gravity was not political but cultural.

The man who would write the history of Ireland, he wrote,

must fathom the social condition of the peasantry, the townsmen, the middle classes, the nobles, and the clergy (Christian or pagan) in each period—how they fed, dressed, armed, and housed themselves. He must exhibit the nature of the government, the manners, the administration of law, the state of useful and fine arts, of commerce, of foreign relations. He must let us see the decay and rise of great principles and conditions—till we look on a tottering sovereignty, a rising creed, an incipient war, as distinctly as, by turning to the highway, we can see the old man, the vigorous youth, or the infant child.[1]

It is not surprising that the models he holds out are Jules Michelet's *Histoire de France* (1833) and Augustin Thierry's *Histoire de la conquête d'Angleterre* (1825), for he had adopted wholeheartedly the romantic conception of national history. The nation of Ireland had been shaped by its people, by their experiences, and by their institutions, and in its turn it claimed from them an allegiance that did not transcend but might at times compete with the claims of creed or class. It was to be Davis's misfortune, as it was also his vindication, that he held these views somewhat in advance of his times. O'Connell, who has passed into orthodox legend as his great adversary, knew far more of Ireland and of Irish history than Davis did, but the romantic doctrine of nationalism was almost as alien to him as it would have been to Tone. The quarrel between the two men over the colleges bill[2] can well be viewed as a quarrel over the nature of nationality. Legend has made Davis the moral victor in that quarrel, but the legend exists because Davis and those who followed him in the Young Ireland movement did their work so thoroughly. Young Ireland's perception of its country as a culture struggling against an alien bondage was neither novel nor revolutionary; its achievement was that of placing the conflict within the context of nineteenth-century political feeling.

The specifically romantic content of Young Ireland's nationalism is most fully exhibited in Davis's attitude to English culture. As he was well aware, he was himself a product of that culture in one of its provincial variants, his mind moulded by English literature and thought. Indeed, many of Davis's topographical and antiquarian essays read like the reports of an impressionable historical society for one of the more picturesque English counties, and his poems, which were to become the marching songs of insurrection, are modelled on Macaulay's *Lays of ancient Rome* (1842). His knowledge of Gaelic civilisation, although extensive, was superficial and inexact, and he knew no Irish, although retrospective piety has credited him with a wish to remedy this defect. He deeply disliked the growing materialism and commercialism of modern life, and he identified these with England, but this was common romantic doctrine and many British writers would have agreed with him— among them Carlyle, who was his literary master, as he was the master of almost all the writers of the Young Ireland movement. Davis's wish to see Ireland emerge as a modern nation, equipped with steamships, standing armies, factories, and the other attributes of sovereignty, existed comfortably beside his belief that Irish civilisation was superior to English precisely because it had avoided—or rather, had been denied—industrialisation. The paradox was one he left for later generations of nationalists to resolve.

[1] Thomas Davis, 'Irish history' in *Essays literary and historical by Thomas Davis*, ed. D. J. O'Donoghue (Dundalk, 1914), p. 305.

[2] Above, pp 358–60.

By identifying England and materialism, and by invoking the idea of Ireland as a counter-principle against them, Davis wove an essential thread into the fabric of Irish nationalism. John Eglinton, in an acute and malicious essay on 'The de-Davisisation of Irish literature', was to write:

It was Davis . . . who gave a sort of religious or idealistic status to modern Irish patriotism which it has retained; for since Davis the true religion of the Irish nationalist has been patriotism; and it remains to be decided whether this confusion of two essentially different things, idealism and patriotism, has bestowed upon Irish national literature the germs of new developments or is not rather that which must be got rid of before even the meaning of the term 'national literature' is understood.[1]

Eglinton was writing a half-century after Davis's death, at a time when the forms and conventions of pietistic nationalism had produced a literature notably lacking in creative energy, but his judgement, however ill tempered, is essentially sound. Davis invested the political struggle for self-government with the passions and emotions of a conflict between opposing cultures. Throughout much of the nineteenth century, however, he was a prophet more often honoured than read, and was honoured as the founder of 'Young Ireland', an amorphous body of patriotic belief and feeling. Davis himself possessed a strong and clear intelligence, and a prose style capable of impressive eloquence:

This country of ours is no sandbank, thrown up by some recent caprice of earth. It is an ancient land, honoured in the archives of civilisation, traceable into antiquity by its piety, its valour, and its sufferings. Every great European race has sent its stream to the river of Irish mind: if we live influenced by wind and sun and tree, and not by the passions and deeds of the past, we are a thriftless and hopeless people.[2]

This passage, generous in sentiment and in expression, comes close to suggesting the force Davis exerted on his contemporaries, a force Yeats rightly calls that of personality. It is by an historical irony, however, that Davis is today remembered as the formulator of a programme of cultural nationalism that was in fact the work of other men. The 1830s and 1840s are notable for the scholarly and literary activity centred on the work of the ordnance survey, then directed by Thomas Colby and Thomas Larcom, of the Royal Engineers.[3] Larcom wisely chose as his assistant George Petrie, one of the ablest and most variously gifted scholars of his generation, and Petrie, in turn, gathered a staff of writers and artists that included the great Celtic scholars John O'Donovan and Eugene O'Curry. Larcom's ambitious scheme failed for lack of government support, but his introduction to the one completed volume, the 1835 survey of a Londonderry parish, suggests the scale upon which his group proposed to work.

---

[1] John Eglinton, *Bards and saints* (Dublin, 1906), p. 38.
[2] Thomas Davis, '"The Library of Ireland"' in *Essays literary and historical by Thomas Davis*, ed. D. J. O'Donoghue (Dundalk, 1914), p. 355.
[3] Above, pp 244–5.

A perfect map, with a perfect memoir, should constitute the statistics of a country: such a combination has been attempted in the survey of Ireland, and though it is not to be assumed that perfection has been attained, no pains have been spared to fulfil the enlightened intentions of the legislature. Geography is a noble and practical science only when associated with the history, the commerce, and a knowledge of the productions of a country; and the topographical delineation of a county would be comparatively useless without the information which may lead to and suggest the proper development of its resources.[1]

Larcom's statement contrasts interestingly with Davis's as illustrating complementary aspects of the nineteenth-century mind. Larcom possessed the insatiable Victorian passion for copious and accurate information, coupled with the equally Victorian belief that such information was essential to the march of progress. But he was fortunate to have encountered in Ireland a group of imaginative and enthusiastic scholars. George Petrie had already established himself as an antiquarian, but it is possible that O'Donovan and O'Curry, poor and self-taught countrymen, would not have pressed forward their researches had it not been for the assistance and encouragement given them by the ordnance survey. Petrie and his staff worked for some eight years in the back parlour of his house, 21 Great Charles Street, and if only a part of their work survived in published form, the enterprise itself left its mark on the public and literary life of Ireland.

The work of this band of mid-century scholars was prodigious both in its ambitions and in its accomplishments. O'Donovan's massively annotated translation of the *Annals of the Four Masters* (1851), O'Curry's two sprawling volumes on the history and literature of ancient Ireland, Petrie's study of an ancient ecclesiastical architecture and his collections of songs, and the linguistic and historical researches of university scholars who were associated with them suggest an unprecedented burst of scholarly energy. Petrie, in the *Dublin Penny Journal*, which he edited, gave to Ireland an instrument of popular education that far surpassed the *Nation*. The talented men who formed this group were not merely scholars. They possessed a sense of nationality that was clear, articulate, and subtle. Samuel Ferguson, their finest writer, expressed their aim in an 1840 essay on the *Dublin Penny Journal*.

What we have to do with, and that to which these observations properly point, is the recovery of the mislaid, but not lost, records of the acts, and opinions, and condition of our ancestors—the . . . bringing back to the light of intellectual day the already recorded *facts*, by which the people of Ireland will be able to *live back*, in the land they live *in*, with as ample and as interesting a field of retrospective enjoyment as any of the nations around us.[2]

---

[1] Quoted in M. C. Ferguson, *Sir Samuel Ferguson in the Ireland of his day* (2 vols, Edinburgh and London, 1896), i, 63–4.

[2] Ibid., i, 109.

What Ferguson is arguing, as Frank O'Connor says, 'is that the aim of any civilised nation must be cultural identity, and cultural identity can be achieved only by total acceptance of a common past'.[1] Ferguson's series of essays (1834), which have as their ostensible occasion the publication of James Hardiman's *Irish minstrelsy: bardic remains of Ireland* (1831), displays an acute understanding of the ways in which literary, musical, and social culture are related. To measure his article on O'Donovan's *Annals of the Four Masters* against Davis's essays on Irish history is to see how large an area of agreement the two men shared, and how much deeper and more complex was Ferguson's thought. Ferguson, far more than Davis, possessed a sense of the ways in which culture is embodied in language. Yet Ferguson had fallen into obscurity by the end of the century, while Davis remained a bright legend. The explanation is in part political. Ferguson, like Petrie and the other members of his group, was a unionist in politics, and the nationalism he espoused was almost entirely cultural in character. In his old age, he was to describe himself as one who had sympathised with, but had not supported, the Young Ireland party. The sympathy ran deep, as we know from the deeply felt article he wrote on the occasion of Davis's death, and from his fine memorial poem. It stopped short of support, however, in part because of Ferguson's innate conservatism and in part because of his distrust of popular movements.

Thomas Davis and the young Samuel Ferguson, standing at the mid-century mark, exemplify what was to become a vital division between Irish writers and intellectuals. It would reappear in the quarrels between Yeats and the orthodox literary patriots at the end of the century and in Douglas Hyde's reluctance to involve the Gaelic League in nationalist politics. Broadly speaking, it is the quarrel between cultural and political nationalism, but these terms are too general properly to define the issue. Ferguson was a learned and indefatigable student of the literature and the antiquities of Ireland, and a poet whose verses and songs display a deep and almost instinctive sympathy towards the several cultures of Ireland. The poetry of Young Ireland, enshrined by several generations of patriots, seems ephemeral and journalistic beside Ferguson's 'Lark in the clear air' or his 'Welshmen of Tirawley'. His affection for the people of Connacht and the Aran Islands was based not on literary preference but on familiarity, and his descriptions of his visits among them are bathed in the warmth of a genuine liking and admiration. His essays of the 1840s and 1850s, written chiefly for the *Dublin University Magazine* or for *Blackwood's*, are extraordinary in their ability to seize on and to celebrate the elements of national culture, and extraordinary in the passion with which Ferguson argues the case for national identity.

The literature of the Young Ireland movement, on the other hand, fails to survive the most superficial inspection. Its poets, of whom the ablest were probably Denis Florence McCarthy and Thomas D'Arcy McGee, were at best

[1] Frank O'Connor, *The backward look: a survey of Irish literature* (London, 1967), p. 151.

limp versifiers, much preoccupied with Celtic virtue and Saxon guilt. Their newspaper, the *Nation*, although ably edited by Davis and Gavan Duffy, fell far below the level set by Petrie's *Dublin Penny Journal*. It set itself the task of instructing and educating an unsophisticated audience towards an understanding of political and social issues, and it performed the task with zealous efficiency. A once familiar woodcut suggests the sense of mission that animated Young Ireland: the weekly number of the *Nation* has arrived in a village, and the villagers are gathered around an elder who is reading aloud from it. The point of this sentimental pastoral was at once educational and political: by quickening the national pride of the people, the writers of the *Nation* hoped to organise them politically. They coined the vocabulary and the iconography of an easily available patriotism, and the coinage survived the movement itself. Yeats, writing of his own first efforts at nationalist propaganda, says:

> The greater number of those who joined my society had come under the seal of Young Ireland at that age when we are all mere wax; the more ambitious had gone daily to some public library to read the bound volumes of Thomas Davis's old newspaper, and tried to see the world as Davis saw it.[1]

Yeats had reason to know the power of that vision, for his own mentor, the old fenian John O'Leary, had been converted to nationalism by an encounter with Davis's poetry. By the end of the nineteenth century, Young Ireland had come to seem both a body of nationalist doctrine and an unachieved national renaissance; young writers recognised their role as that of completing its works.

Yet this assumption involved a misreading of history, not serious, perhaps, but significant. The 'renaissance' of the mid-century was in good measure the work of Ferguson and Petrie, of scholars like Whitley Stokes and James Henthorn Todd, of translators like O'Donovan and O'Curry. Their journal, if they may be said to have had one, was the *Dublin University Magazine*, which in political matters maintained a belligerently tory line. The friendship between Davis and Ferguson was based not on personal affection alone, but on a recognition of shared aspirations and attitudes. Gavan Duffy, in his biography of Davis and in his history of Young Ireland, would have us believe that the patriotic fires of Young Ireland burned so fiercely that they kindled the spirits even of the Trinity tories. The facts are quite different. The early 1840s witnessed a remarkable interest in Irish history and culture among educated Irishmen of all factions—Butt, Sheridan Le Fanu, and Lever all published novels that were termed 'national'. Davis parted from these, his natural allies, on a crucial point: he cast his lot with O'Connell and the overwhelmingly catholic repeal movement, and he was to discover before his death that Irish divisions of class and sect ran far deeper than patriotic formulations.

Much of the credit for sustaining, if not indeed for magnifying, the legend of Young Ireland must be given to Gavan Duffy. In the years of his retirement, he

[1] W. B. Yeats, *Autobiographies* (2nd ed., London, 1955), p. 205.

produced four copious and engaging books[1] that may be read as a long, unrolling canvas on which are painted in bold and vivid colours the chief characters of what is in substance a morality play. The men of Young Ireland are the heroes of the play, with Davis as their almost faultless champion, appearing in two volumes as the chief actor, and in the others as a kind of tutelary angel, by whom other men are judged, nearly always to their disadvantage. The outlines of the drama need not be rehearsed, for as a version of history it is still widely known. In this version, Davis, his patriotism quickened by the Genius of Nations, moves beyond the grey, indifferent walls of Trinity to rouse his countrymen to cultural and political energy, succeeds splendidly, and then is checked by O'Connell, a tribal chieftain in whom greatness and meanness are compounded on so lavish a scale as to render all definition impossible. The account is misleading not merely as a representation of the political history of the period, but in what it suggests as to the literary life of the mid-century period. From Duffy's histories, one gains the impression that the 1840s witnessed a remarkable burst of creative energy, centring on the offices of the *Nation*. In fact Duffy, although he himself possessed a supple and trenchant prose style, was an entirely conventional judge of literature, and as an editor allowed political virtue to atone for a myriad of literary defects. The genuine intellectual life of the period was sustained by the *Dublin University Magazine*, which was truculently described by Butt, its second editor, as 'the monthly advocate of the protestantism, the intelligence, and the respectability of Ireland'.[2]

Under Butt (1834–8), and under Lever, who also served as its editor (1841–5), the *Dublin University Magazine* made clear its belief that the three terms of this trinity were interchangeable: it regarded itself as the intellectual organ of the protestant ascendancy, and maintained a running war against O'Connell and repeal. Its attitude to Davis was more complicated, however, and it dealt with the men of Young Ireland in terms of mocking yet friendly banter. The *Dublin University Magazine* writers regarded themselves as 'national' in their own way, and were at times described, half jokingly, as 'Orange Young Ireland'. 'It was noticeable', Owen Dudley Edwards remarks, 'that "Orange Young Ireland" seemed to have a greater degree of humour, to take itself less seriously, to possess a greater knowledge (however condescending) of the Irish lower classes, and to employ a greater mastery of economics than was the case with its nationalist counterpart.'[3] This is not surprising, for it was the very crux of their political case that Ireland was a province, kept in perpetual turmoil by internal demagogues, and mismanaged from a distance by ignorant British ministers.

[1] Charles Gavan Duffy, *Young Ireland: a fragment of Irish history* (London, 1880); *Four years of Irish history* (London, 1883); *The league of the north and south* (London, 1886); *Thomas Davis: the memoirs of an Irish patriot* (London, 1890).

[2] Terence de Vere White, *The road of excess* (Dublin, [1946]), p. 10.

[3] Owen Dudley Edwards, 'Ireland', in Owen Dudley Edwards, Gwynfor Evans and Ioan Rhys, and Hugh MacDiarmid, *Celtic nationalism* (London, 1968), pp 119–20.

The colonial position can easily encourage a zestful appetite for the oddities of native life, about which patriotic literature is apt to be evasive or apologetic. Butt's bellicose essays on politics and Ferguson's humane and sensitive studies of Gaelic culture exist together somewhat incongruously within the pages of the *Dublin University Magazine*, but without actual contradiction. The ascendancy position of the 1840s held, and held the more fiercely in the face of O'Connell's agitation, that the union was unalterable. Ireland's status as a province was a necessary corollary of that belief. But one may be loyal to a province, as to a nation, and Butt and Ferguson regarded themselves as patriotic Irishmen, eager to explore and to foster Irish culture. The union was a political and social necessity, but it was neither inviolable nor sacred: in 1848 Ferguson served as secretary to the short-lived Protestant Repeal Association, and Butt was of course to become leader of the movement for home rule. By 1885, however, under the pressure of a far fiercer and more violent campaign than O'Connell had waged, Ferguson was writing:

I sympathised with the Young Ireland poets and patriots while their aims were directed to a restoration of Grattan's parliament in which all the estates of the realm should have their old places. But I have quite ceased to sympathise with their successors who have converted their high aspirations to a sordid social war of classes carried on by the vilest methods. I was comrade in that sense of Davis, and possibly, but with far less sympathy, of some of his companions. But it was in sympathy only. I never wrote in the *Nation*. To say that I have upborne their banner, therefore, is more than I would like to vouch.[1]

The legend of Young Ireland, which was put to the service of a programmatic nationalism, distorts the complexities of the cultural life of mid-century Ireland, with its confusions and discontinuities. Some of these are reflected, if almost by accident, in the battered and incoherent career of James Clarence Mangan, its most remarkable poet. Mangan, unlike Ferguson, published both in the *Dublin University Magazine* and in the *Nation*, but then he published in every Dublin periodical of the time, from the *Comet* to the *Irishman*. The facts of his melancholy life, if we set aside his passionate and unreliable autobiography, are probably unrecoverable. In 1897 D. J. O'Donoghue assembled, after a fashion, the bare bones of the biography[2] but did little to dispel the shadows in which the life had been lived. The son of a bankrupt tradesman, Mangan grew up in bitter poverty, served for a time as copyist for Petrie at the ordnance survey, and thereafter lived on such meagre sums as his verse and journalism brought him. A drunkard and a laudanum addict, he scraped through a miserable existence on the edges of literary Dublin, solitary and eccentric, and endlessly prolific.

The problem posed by Mangan to his critics is that he possessed poetic gifts

[1] Quoted in Ferguson, op. cit., i, 254.
[2] D. J. O'Donoghue, *The life and writings of James Clarence Mangan* (Edinburgh and Dublin, 1897). Mangan's autobiography (R.I.A., MS 12.P.18) has been published in an edition by James Kilroy ([Dublin], 1968).

of a very high order, which only rarely manifested themselves amid a welter of jokes, sentimentalities, and dead timber. Nationalist critics, beginning with Duffy and John Mitchel, have sought, either directly or by implication, to relate the broken quality of his work with the disturbed condition of the Ireland in which he lived, but the defects of his art, its facileness and lack of discipline, issued directly from his temperament. There is, however, a point of juncture between Mangan and his culture: he lacked any sense of identity, and indeed exploited this bewildering absence of definition. He worked most easily through the masks of actual or pretended translations, and most of his poems are presented as 'versions' recast from a variety of languages. The numerous versions from the German, although not remarkable for their accuracy, may properly be called translations, for he had acquired a working knowledge of that language and possessed a genuine sympathy for the minor German romantics. His versions from Italian, Arabic, Kurdish, Persian, and other, more exotic tongues are transparent hoaxes, but hoaxes he found necessary to expression. His verses 'more or less from the Irish', his 'oriental versions and perversions', his 'oversettings from the German', suggest both the unease he felt at directly confronting his experience and his uncertainty as to his own poetic tradition. Unlike Moore, who understood all too thoroughly the forms he employed, Mangan was adrift amid conventions and genres.

Mangan's 'translations' of Irish poetry, on which his celebrity chiefly rests, wander far indeed from their originals, although often they are based on translations made available to him by O'Curry, Ferguson, and, later, John O'Daly. John O'Donovan dismissed them as 'concoctions' that were less than 'the shadow of a shade',[1] and yet 'Dark Rosaleen' and 'O'Hussey's ode to the Maguire' are extraordinary poems. The latter, that 'torrent of nineteenth-century romantic eloquence', as Frank O'Connor calls it,[2] is notable both for its hallucinatory power ('Rolls real thunder? Or was that red, livid light only a meteor?') and for its deliberately harsh eccentricities of diction:

> Where is my chief, my master, this bleak night, mavrone!
> O, cold, cold, miserably cold is this bleak night for Hugh,
> Its showery, arrowy, speary sleet pierceth one through and through,
> Pierceth one to the very bone![3]

Yet these versions are based on no settled notion as to the nature of Irish poetry, and the sense of the Irish past they convey is fitful and distorted. Mangan did not turn to Gaelic material as to a lost but insistent historical memory. Rather, it offered him yet another opportunity to experiment with language, metre, and mood, another mask behind which he could disappear. The tone of his 'O'Hussey's ode' is continuous with that of his finely wrought

[1] O'Donoghue, op. cit., p. 121. The word 'concocted' is used by O'Donoghue.
[2] Frank O'Connor, *The backward look: a survey of Irish literature* (London, 1967), p. 101.
[3] *Poems of James Clarence Mangan*, ed. D. J. O'Donoghue (Dublin and London, 1903), p. 8.

'Siberia', a personal utterance brought to its appropriate form. Even his auto-biography is an exercise in disguise, his life cast in the form of romantic confession. Like the bulk of his prose, like 'The man in the cloak' and 'An extraordinary adventure in the shades', it derives a curious emotional complexity from its arrangement of aspects and versions of the self. Mangan's figure, cloaked and topped by a 'broad-leafed and steeple-shaped hat', haunted Dublin decades after his death, and perhaps haunts it still, an image of fantastic and eloquent incoherence.

Mangan's verbal wit, an uncontrollable energy that quickened his prose and ruined his verse, places him within an odd and almost inexplicable tradition. In 1849, his last, terrible year of life, he published a sketch of William Maginn that is written with understandable fellow-feeling: 'Maginn wrote alike without labour and without limit. He had, properly speaking, no style, or rather he was master of all styles, though he cared for none.'[1] Maginn had died five years before in circumstances that resembled his own—a penniless drunkard forcing out penny-a-line journalism that mingled erudition with buffoonery. They differed in origins and training: Maginn, the precocious son of a Cork school-master, protestant and high tory, had brought with him to Grub Street a mind disciplined and honed on the classics. But they resemble each other in one particular. Maginn, like Mangan, was a master of mimicry, a writer who delighted in tricks of language, puns, mock-solemn and fake translations, elaborate verbal jokes. One of his achievements in this line, a translation of 'Chevy Chase', into and out of demotic Latin, to the accompaniment of wicked burlesques of Wordsworth and Southey, earned Mangan's special praise. In a similar fashion, Maginn's friend Francis Mahony, who wrote as 'Father Prout', composed his essay on 'The rogueries of Tom Moore', in which the poet's most idiosyncratic verses are turned into Latin and French 'originals' so that he may be accused of plagiarism. That these three mid-century writers, a Dubliner and two exiled Corkmen, should have shared an obsessive skill at linguistic manipulation may be no more than coincidence, but the same skill, greatly magnified, was to appear in later writers, among them Joyce, Beckett, and Flann O'Brien. The Irish delight in verbal wit is as elusive of explanation as any other cultural trait. The argument most often advanced, that it issued from the tensions of a culture caught between two languages, is specious. It is unlikely that Maginn, whose background was entirely urban, had even the most fleeting contact with Irish speakers; his essay on 'Irish songs' is a mass of inaccuracies and misconceptions. The fact of a fascinated and endlessly resourceful attention to language remains. 'It was his language before it was mine', Stephen Dedalus thinks as he stands before the English-born dean of studies.[2]

[1] Quoted in D. J. O'Donoghue, *The life and writings of James Clarence Mangan* (Edinburgh and Dublin, 1897), p. 115.

[2] James Joyce, *Portrait of the artist as a young man*, ed. Richard Ellman (London, 1968), p. 194.

One figure stands out among the Young Ireland group, both as writer, and as a political and cultural portent. John Mitchel, Yeats was to say, was the only writer of that generation to possess a genuine style, one with the qualities of 'music and personality, though rancorous and devil-possessed'.[1] Yeats correctly derives this style from Carlyle: Mitchel learned Carlyle's lessons, literary and philosophical, and turned them inside out, putting them at the service of rebellion. But he achieved an authentic voice, one of the most extraordinary of the nineteenth century, which is present in everything he wrote, from his elaborate *History of Ireland* (1869) to the most casual of his personal letters. 'May 27, 1848. On this day, about four o'clock in the afternoon, I, John Mitchel, was kidnapped, and carried off from Dublin, in chains, as a convicted "felon".' The voice finds itself in the opening sentence of the *Jail journal*, a fierce, corrosive irony joined to a sullen consciousness of personal integrity.[2] 'Mitchel's influence', Yeats writes, 'comes mainly, though not altogether, from style, that also a form of power, an energy of life', and he speaks of Mitchel's 'long, martyred life, supported by style'.[3] Its sources may be found in the Bible and the classics, in Swift and Cobbett and Carlyle, but he made all his masters subordinate to his own vision. Harsh, yet musical, his style is the direct expression of his personality, by which it is endowed with tense, nervous strength. That personality was indeed devil-possessed, haunted by hatreds and obsessions that run through his sentences like stiff, inflexible wires. The *Jail journal*, which is at once the most complex and the most personal of his books, is carefully composed to reveal him as he would have himself be seen—a rebel with a savage wit, the constant and deadly enemy of 'English' rule, but the enemy also of all cant, sentimentality, and false humanitarianism. In his later books, as in the manner of his later exile, he shaped this image of himself into a moral and passional stance, as though with him the conscience and intellect of Ireland itself had passed into exile.

This style is not a matter for merely literary consideration, for Mitchel's greatest achievement was the creation of his own exemplary role. His austere, unyielding nationalism, expressed with the sardonic eloquence of a settled fanaticism, supplied the century with a lasting and satisfactory image of political intransigence. The *Jail journal*, which provided extreme Irish nationalism with an entire arsenal of attitudes and ideas, has rightly been called the Bible of republicanism, and like other scriptural revelations it derives its authority from its bleak and unyielding singlemindedness. Like Mitchel's own life, it is shaped on the single principle of rebellion against British rule, and it is with Mitchel that hatred of England, a passion raised to a principle, makes its appearance in the thought of modern Ireland. Tone had written in his Paris

---

[1] W. B. Yeats, *Autobiographies* (2nd ed., London, 1955), pp 204, 225.
[2] John Mitchel, *Jail journal* (Dublin, 1913; reprint, with introduction by Thomas Flanagan, 1982), p. 1. The work was first published in New York (1854).
[3] Yeats, op. cit., p. 516.

journal: 'I was led by a hatred of England, so deeply rooted in my nature, that it was rather an instinct than a principle.'[1] But the sentence stands alone in Tone's journals, and seems an afterthought, one of his several attempts to impose a coherent meaning on the tangle of motives that had carried him to Paris. Davis discerned in England not merely a political power that he opposed, but a culture he distrusted; hatred on a Miltonic scale, however, was alien to his nature. The roots of Mitchel's hatred were mysterious even to himself, although he was understandably awed by the depth of his own passions.

Now, in looking back, and trying to analyse my own feelings, or principles, or whatever it was that made me write and act as I did in Ireland, I have found that there was perhaps less of love in it than of hate—less of filial affection to my country than of scornful impatience at the thought that I had the misfortune, I and my children, to be born in a country which suffered itself to be oppressed and humilitated by another; less devotion to truth and justice than raging wrath against cant and insolence. And hatred being the thing I chiefly cherished and cultivated, the thing which I specially hated was the *British* system —everywhere, at home and abroad, as it works in England itself, in India, on the continent of Europe, and in Ireland. Living in Ireland, and wishing to feel proud, not ashamed of Ireland, it was there, first and most, that I had to fight with that great enemy.[2]

Mitchel burned into the Irish popular imagination the notion that the famine was a devastation deliberately contrived by England for the annihilation of the Irish peasantry, but for Mitchel himself this was merely further monstrous evidence against an enemy he already hated with a consuming rage. His was a personality that defined itself through opposition, and his ultimate enemy was the modern world, of which England was the most powerful and most proximate incarnation. He shaped nationalism into a messianic cult that demanded unwavering loyalty, an unending war against an omnipotent foe, in which victory lay not with political or military success, but with the unwavering affirmation of a limitless spirit of rebellion. He earned precisely the reward on which he had calculated: he became, in the long failure of his life, the very model of the Irish rebel, incorruptible and uncompromising. The chemicals of Mitchel's wrath, compounded in deep recesses of his character, were to work powerfully on the Irish imagination.

The central importance of the *Jail journal* to the tradition of Irish separatism has been underestimated: it affected powerfully men as different from each other as John O'Leary, Arthur Griffith, and Padraic Pearse. Without it, fenianism would have been a movement without a literature. Griffith, in the preface to his edition of the book, argues manfully that Mitchel's 'hatred of England was the legitimate child of the love of Ireland that flowed in the heart of the man who spent his leisure scaling her hills, tramping her ways, and commun-

[1] Tone, *Life*, i, 55.
[2] William Dillon, *Life of John Mitchel* (2 vols, London, 1888), ii, 104–5.

ing with her kindly peasantry.'[1] But there is no evidence that he ever communed with the peasantry; had he done so, they might have warned him against relying on their support in 1848. Mitchel's power derives, rather, from his fierce indictment of English civilisation and his steely insistence that Ireland must defy it upon behalf of principles that he prudently leaves half-formulated. His defiance, although theatrical, is heroic, and it was passed as a legacy to later generations. The body of received opinion among separatists of the fenian generation was the history of Ireland as it had been interpreted and codified by the essayists and poets of Young Ireland. John O'Leary tells us that he was converted to fenianism by a reading of Davis's poetry, but fenianism was made of sterner stuff than Davis's metres, and to the degree that it possessed an ideology, it was one shaped from Mitchel's Manichean vision. Mitchel's voice possessed the clarity that is the only recompense for exile: his 'campaign' against England, lifting itself above the complexities of actual social issues, possessed the power and simplicity of myth.

ON levels less exalted than the mythological, however, the decades that stretch between the collapse of the Young Ireland movement and the literary revival of the 1890s fail to present a coherent cultural pattern. Davis and his disciples in Young Ireland had sought to create a nationalism that could flourish without seriously disturbing the existing class structure. In fact, however, the class structure, like the religious divisions with which it was intertwined, was far stronger than any nationalist doctrine. Not one but many 'Irelands' existed, if by this term is meant neither a geographical expression nor a society, but rather a perception of cultural identity. Ireland of the 1850s, with the famine as its terrible and unforgotten background, was paradoxically situated. The O'Connellite agitation for repeal had made clear the fact that political nationalism was a cause that claimed a predominantly catholic following, but the church in the 1850s, under the spiritual leadership of Archbishop Cullen, was intensely suspicious of political nationalism.[2] The relationship between nationalism and religion in Ireland, never less than complicated, now began to assume a particularly tortuous shape. For different, although not entirely unrelated, reasons the catholic hierarchy and the protestant ascendancy were disinclined to nurture nationalist sentiment, and nationalism was therefore deprived of that intellectual, or at least educated, leadership that Davis and his followers had regarded as essential.

Accordingly, there was no climate of opinion favourable to the creation of a new literary movement, while those impulses that had stimulated the literary activities of the early decades were now exhausted. Few novelists appeared in the post-famine years to 'explain' Ireland to English readers, and England, for its part, displayed no eagerness to receive such explanations. The famine itself, a monstrous, inexplicable visitation, had destroyed, at least for several decades,

---

[1] Mitchel, *Jail journal* (1982), pp 370–71.   [2] Above, pp 397–8.

the notion of Ireland as a picturesque hinterland. Matthew Arnold tells us that in his youth his father had never wearied of explaining to him the impassable barrier that separated the English from the Irish: 'He insisted much oftener on the separation between us and them than on the separation between us and any other race in the world; in the same way Lord Lyndhurst, in words long famous, called the Irish "aliens in speech, in religion, in blood".'[1] These barriers were never higher than in the decades following the famine, as though England had resolutely locked the door against an ugly, insoluble mystery. Ireland itself was locked in with the mystery, a land of incoherences, half-formed ideals, and warring images.

The representative, and also the most popular, Irish novel of the later nineteenth century is Charles Kickham's *Knocknagow* (1873). Kickham was a fenian of impeccable credentials, his principles being shielded by his deafness, but although it has its social and political points to make, the dominant mood of *Knocknagow* is that of affectionate genre-painting. A gentle and almost interminable book, sentimental, garrulous, and clumsily written, it lives through its rambling, meticulous accumulation of detail. It is one of the very few novels of the century that attempted to represent, on a broad canvas, the lives of Irish country people. That it did so in pious and conventional terms scarcely weakened its appeal to middle-class readers, but it may be supposed that the book owed its popularity to the fullness with which it served one of the primary purposes of fiction: it offered its readers a recognisable if idealised image of their own country. *Knocknagow* is set in the recent past, and at its close the village of Knocknagow itself has vanished, victim of a distant enemy. England, 'the stranger', exists in the novel as an invisible, malignant presence, hostile to the settled way of life that the book cherishes and celebrates. Kickham combined his fenian beliefs with an intense social conservatism and a deep religious piety; the combination allowed him to work out the terms of a nineteenth-century Irish pastoral, quiet in manner, bucolic, and sweet-tempered. *Knocknagow* abounds with life, but its ending is sombre. 'It is an omen', says Hugh Kearney, pointing beyond the desolate farms to a family in a cornfield. 'The Irish people will *never* be rooted out of Ireland. Cromwell could not do it; the butchers of Elizabeth could not do it.' The doctor answers him: 'But there is a more deadly system at work now. The country is silently bleeding to death.'[2]

To discover in literature the emotional and social contours of late nineteenth-century Ireland, one must turn to writers whose point of view was determined, at least in part, by their political stance and by their position within Irish society. By the time the land war had worked its course, and partly in consequence of that war, a significant development had taken place. It is best

---

[1] Matthew Arnold, 'On the study of Celtic literature' in *The complete prose works of Matthew Arnold*, vol. iii: *Lectures and essays in criticism*, ed. R. H. Super (Ann Arbor, 1962), p. 300; cf. above, p. 171.

[2] Charles Kickham, *Knocknagow; or, the homes of Tipperary* (Dublin, 1879; reprint, with introduction by R. L. Wolff, New York and London, 1979), p. 625.

defined in terms of the religious divisions, and best illustrated by two writers who fall outside our chronological boundaries—Emily Lawless and Canon Sheehan. Put briefly, it was the identification of the Irish 'nation', defined in emotional rather than political terms, with the catholic population. This was far indeed from the conscious intentions of nationalist politicians, who held to the non-sectarian ideals of their tradition, but it was in some ways close to the social and political actualities. The land war, being a 'war' against the propertied classes, was almost by definition a 'war' against the protestant ascendancy; moreover, it carried emotional overtones that extended well beyond its stated programme. Even by the close of the century, the Irish propertied and educated classes remained strongly protestant, and while this may have been a cause of satisfaction to protestant squires, it deprived a protestant writer like Lawless of that easy and confident sense of identification with the people on which a catholic writer like Sheehan could draw.

The consequent bitterness is evident in the novels of Lawless, and especially in *Hurrish* (1886), the book by which she is best known. Her affection for her countrymen was genuine and deep, but it sustained itself against the pressures of political actualities by nurturing the belief that an organic community that once had embraced landlord and tenant had been shattered by unprincipled and socially ambitious demagogues.

Like every Irishman of the reigning generation, Maurice Brady cherished dreams of ambition,—dreams too, by no means destitute, as it seemed to him, of solid foundations. If every recruit of the Grand Army carried a marshal's baton in his knapsack, surely every nationalist recruit, that can read, write, and spell, carries an appointment in the coming Irish republic somewhere or other about his personal possessions.[1]

In Lawless's Ireland, some young Maurice Brady or Egan Shaughnessy is forever aspiring to use nationalist politics as a way of rising above haberdashery or provincial newspaper, and usually at the expense of the 'Hurrish' O'Briens, simple, broad-shouldered men, content to live in the immemorial fashion of their forebears. It is not an ungrounded assumption: nationalist politics was class warfare on the petty as much as on the grand scale. She elevates this perception, however, into social myth, a fable based on fact that she uses to explain her sense of a broken community. Her chosen setting is rural Ireland, a land without effective law, which has fallen victim equally to an uncomprehending government and the base ambitions of agitators. The same myth, although elaborated with a far greater sophistication and with colours far less lurid, is present in Somerville and Ross's novel *Mount Music* (1919). Lawless's use of it is striking precisely because her conflicts of feeling are expressed in an open and unguarded manner. *Hurrish* closes with her wish for a 'new departure' in Irish life, founded on elements that 'have nothing, fortunately, to

---

[1] Emily Lawless, *Hurrish: a study* (2 vols, Edinburgh and London, 1886; reprint, with introduction by R. L. Wolff, New York and London, 1979), i, 92–3.

say to politics—of any complexion'.[1] It was an improbable, even a desperate wish, and yet one on which her own sense of Ireland depended. She was living through years in which her class had been defined as 'anti-national' and as 'un-Irish'; politics, 'of any complexion', strengthened the terms of that definition.

The sense of being caught within a broken community, which is so painfully evident in Emily Lawless's books, and which Somerville and Ross draw on for their splendid autumnal comedy, is entirely absent from the novels of Canon Sheehan. A complex and emotionally charged drama is being worked out in these novels, but it is based on the simple and unwavering premise that Ireland is a catholic culture. Stephen Gwynn was right to call them 'the best documents about the catholic church in Ireland',[2] but he understated the case: Sheehan defines Ireland almost entirely in terms of its catholicism. He sees Ireland from the windows of what had become the snuggest and strongest bastions in the land—the seminary and the presbytery. The implications of his premise pass unnoticed in such light-hearted books as *My new curate*, in which the presbytery is the centre about which life revolves, much like the big house in ascendancy novels.

It is quite natural that Sheehan should centre his world on the clerical life, which he knew best; in practice, he identifies the priesthood as both the repository and the guardian of Irish cultural values. Father Dan, the narrator of *My new curate*, traces in detail the generations of Irish priests of the nineteenth century, beginning with the 'polished, studious, timid priest',[3] educated at continental seminaries, slightly tinged with Gallican ideas and inclined to fraternise with landlords. The successive generations are increasingly national, and of the present one it can be said that 'their passionate devotion to their faith is only rivalled by their passionate devotion to the motherland'.[4] The motherland, in its turn, is noteworthy among the nations for its fathomless receptivity to the spiritual and ethical values of catholicism. The very faults that Sheehan perceives in his people are but virtues disguised, for if they are inclined to inertia, it is because they dwell in a region of the mind 'where time was never counted', and though their lives are narrow they possess a noble 'contempt of physical comfort'.[5]

Sheehan possessed intellectual and literary resources of a high order, including a fair knowledge of continental literature and an alert, though scarcely a dispassionate, understanding of social and cultural issues. If he was capable of the mawkish and avuncular sentimentalities of *My new curate*, he was capable also of a novel like *Luke Delmege*, a novel of clerical life that commands the reader's interest and admiration. One of the chief points of interest in this

[1] Lawless, op. cit., ii, 302.
[2] Stephen Gwynn, *Ireland* (London, 1924), p. 164.
[3] P. A. Sheehan, *My new curate* (Boston, 1899), p. 228. The work first appeared serially in the *American Ecclesiastical Review* from May 1898.
[4] Ibid., p. 231.
[5] P. A. Sheehan, *Luke Delmege* (London, 1905), p. 458.

novel, however, rests on the elaboration of an attitude to Ireland that illumin-
ates with blinding clarity a group of issues, attitudes, and feelings that had
slowly been gathering together. Luke Delmege's adventures as a pastor of
souls, harassed by his pride and his spiritual perplexities, is joined to a second
theme, an inquiry into the nature of Irish society and the mission of Irish civilisation. Sheehan regards these as related themes, and the power with which he
persuades us of the relationship is one of the novel's chief successes. Delmege's
task is twofold: to discover the true vocation of his ministry, and to discover the
true form of that culture to whose people he ministers. He moves towards these
dicoveries along different roads, but in the novel's resolution they are joined.
Sheehan assumes the existence in Ireland of a civilisation that is catholic, rural,
and culturally autonomous, but has not yet found its form, in good measure
because it has been subjected to an alien and corrupt society. Like Thomas
Davis, he perceives England as a cultural threat, but for reasons that would
have disturbed Davis, for Sheehan regards only the culture of catholic Ireland
as authentic and valuable. Virtuous, even exemplary, protestants exist in his
novels, but only on sufferance. The identification of nationality with religion is
impressive in its comprehensiveness. Catholic Ireland, moreover, has been
summoned to a 'mission' that is nothing less than warfare against modernity. A
passage from the sermon with which *Luke Delmege* closes suggests the terms of
the issue:

And, as the two illusions disappeared—that of Ireland, built from its ruins on purely
material and selfish principles; and that of an Ireland, built without the foundation of
security and independence, the young priest woke up suddenly to the vision of his
country, developing under new and stable conditions her traditional ideas; and becoming, in the face of a spurious and unstable civilisation rocked to its foundation by revolution, a new commonwealth of Christ. The possibility of such an event had been vaguely
hinted at by priests, who evidently were struggling to evolve coherent ideas from a mass
of sensations and instincts, righteous and just, but yet unformed. It was foreshadowed
by the manner in which the people, untrained and illiterate, groped after and grasped
the highest principles of Christian civilisation; it was foretold by the energy with which
men contemned the mere acquisition of wealth, and felt ashamed of possessing it; it was
outlined in the simple, human lives, with all their Spartan severity toward themselves,
and all their divine beneficence toward others.[1]

Ireland is thus given by Sheehan not merely form and body, but a purpose
and a direction. The struggle for political and economic independence, the
claims of traditional pieties, and the opposing principles of English and Irish
cultures are stages on the road to the 'new commonwealth of Christ'. The
notion of an Irish identity conceived in terms that are exclusively catholic is
here given literary expression, not for the first time, and not, most certainly, for
the last. The essential point is that it is a dynamic notion: Ireland is seen not

[1] Ibid., p. 563.

merely as a catholic nation, but as a nation charged with the task of accomplishing a specific spiritual and social mission. History in Sheehan's novels, whether of agrarian conspiracy as in *Glenanaar* or of fenian rebellion as in *The graves of Kilmorna*, is a process moving towards the reassertion of certain cultural values, certain 'traditional ideas' that are Irish and catholic. How widely this view was held cannot be known, but it seems likely that he was giving specific expression—perhaps uncomfortably specific—to ideas and feelings that were powerfully at work. The messianic overtones may have been peculiar to Sheehan, but not the conjunction of religious and national emotions.

South of Canon Sheehan's parish of Doneraile in County Cork stood, on the steep coast, Drishane House, where Edith Œnone Somerville and Violet Martin ('Martin Ross') lived and wrote. Its imaginative climate is pleasantly free from such portentous issues, in part because the world of their *Irish R.M.* is delicately suspended in time, a provincial world of immense lazy charm and good humour, in which everything is falling quietly and courteously into ruin. The utter authority of these stories issues from their authors' vast, shrewd knowledge of the society with which they deal, but they embody an argument that has political implications: that nothing in Ireland is going to change, save slowly and probably for the worse. Most Irish readers, with the exception of the more rabid political purists, have always had a sneaking and entirely justified affection for the 'Irish R.M.' stories, which are held, bathed in their russet and autumnal light, in the long late afternoon of the ascendancy. The affection is a response not merely to Somerville and Ross's sense of social comedy, which was superb, but to their sense of community. The world of Mohona, 'our champion village, that boasts fifteen public houses out of twenty buildings of sorts and a railway station',[1] is a fully realised community, from the terrifying old Mrs Knox of Aussolas through Larry the auctioneer to Slipper, the carman and poacher. Everyone is certain of his place in this community, even the half-hero, Flurry Knox, who is 'a stableboy among gentlemen and a gentleman among stableboys'[2]—a confusion of roles that comes more easily to gentlemen than to stableboys. It is a community expressed through a wealth of precisely observed detail, an unerring accuracy of gesture and speech, and judgements that manage to be at once benevolent and faintly mordant.

But we know from their other novels, especially from *Mount Music* and *The big house of Inver* (1925), that Somerville and Ross were intensely conscious of changes in the structure of Irish society, and on the whole hostile to them. Dick Talbot-Lowry, the master of Mount Music, which he had loved with an affection described as 'the solitary strand of romance in his nature, the feudal feeling that Mount Music tenants were his, as they had been his ancestors'',[3] is forced at last to leave it with his wife, 'too agitated by their coming journey to

---

[1] E. Œ. Somerville and Martin Ross, *The Irish R.M. complete* (London, 1928; reprint, 1973), p. 70.
[2] Ibid., p. 11.
[3] E. Œ. Somerville and Martin Ross, *Mount Music* (London, 1919), p. 160.

have a spare thought for sentiment; too much beset by the fear of what they might lose, their keys, their sandwiches, their dressing-boxes, to shed a tear for what they were losing, and had lost'.[1] The big house of Inver is burned by the last of the Prendevilles, and the only gainers are the Weldons, an aspiring local family of land agents and solicitors. In each case, the defeat has been dual, an inner weakness exploited by the agents of a class rising to power—the middle-class, nationalist catholics of the towns. Indeed, *The big house of Inver* elaborates a biological law of social power and decay, by which governance passes to those who are most fit to exploit it. The novels of Somerville and Ross, unlike their 'Irish R.M.' stories, take as theme the decline of ascendancy power, and although they were themselves embattled members of that class, they were far too clear-headed to sentimentalise the theme.

The decline of the ascendancy, as it was viewed by a romantic and fiercely proud member of that class, is also the theme of Standish James O'Grady's gallant and faintly absurd address to 'the landlords of Ireland'. O'Grady's political position is not easily sorted out, and does not entirely justify the effort: in essence, it was born of the impact of Carlyle on a lightly ballasted intellect. His noble scorn of the ascendancy—and it is expressed in language that does indeed possess a genuine nobility—sprang from his belief that the landlord class had abdicated both its powers and its responsiblities. 'I believe there never will be', he writes with a ferocity that Michael Davitt must have envied, 'as I know there never has been within the cycle of recorded things, an aristo-cracy so rotten in its seeming strength, so recreant, resourceless, and stupid in the day of trial, so degenerate, outworn, and effete.'[2] O'Grady's vituperations against his class were of course intended to serve purposes quite contrary to Davitt's: he hoped to rouse the landlords, in their final hour, to a chivalric acceptance of their duties and their roles. His methods were hopelessly quixotic: men who, as he alleges, had not studied Carlyle could not be expected to heed a Standish O'Grady, and functional illiteracy ranked high among their defects: 'Christ save us all! You read nothing, know nothing.'[3] But in point of fact, O'Grady's social analysis is as romantic and as irrelevant as his prescrip-tions. Social classes fall from power not because they have failed to read the classics of English prose but because the bases of their power have been eroded.

The descriptions of O'Grady as a 'fenian unionist' are not far from the mark. He roved back through the cycles of Irish history, seeking out those periods in which a ruling class, whether native or colonist, had governed wisely and well—no easy task, when it is considered that Ireland was the victim of almost continuous misgovernment. His political prescriptions, it need scarcely be

---

[1] Ibid., p. 284.
[2] Standish [James] O'Grady, 'Ireland and the hour' in O'Grady, *Selected essays and passages*, with introduction by E. A. Boyd (Dublin, [1918]), p. 200.
[3] Ibid., p. 223.

said, went unheeded, but his eloquent denunciations of the ascendancy were greatly appreciated by nationalists. They regarded him, with fair accuracy, as an eccentric Jeremiah, urging the reform of a class that had proved itself incapable of wisdom or simple prudence. O'Grady himself, however, was in deadly earnest, a provincial Ruskin or Carlyle, arguing the claims of aristocratic sacrifice and austerity. As with Ruskin, however, his political writings have the charm of a forlorn gallantry, and they are given resonance by his other books—the series of semi-historical adaptations of ancient bardic materials by which he made available to a generation the legends of heroic Ireland.

O'Grady's 'histories', to which Yeats and other writers of the literary revival have paid generous tribute, are odd and prodigious achievements. He has given us an often quoted account of their inception.[1] One rainy day he found himself in the library of a country house in the west of Ireland and began reading Sylvester O'Halloran's *A general history of Ireland from the earliest accounts to the close of the twelfth century* (1778)[2]—one of the books that Maria Edgeworth, in her *Essay on Irish bulls*, had singled out for derision. It persuaded him that his country, of which he had known virtually nothing, possessed a rich and astonishing history, ample and heroic in its proportions, illuminated by the broken lights of a great, forgotten poetry, and compounded of history, legend, and imaginative truth. He took on himself, as a kind of sacred mission, the task of bringing this past to life. The language of religion is not inappropriate to his task as he perceived it, for O'Grady was a clergyman's son, raised on strict principles in a remote west Cork rectory, and he brought an evangelical fervour to his work. The obstacles that confronted him would have daunted lesser men. The history of ancient Ireland, as he understood the term, was of course recorded in Irish, a language of which he was utterly ignorant, and lay scattered and broken in scores of manuscripts. Some of his sources had been translated and published by O'Curry and earlier scholars; others existed as manuscript translations in the library of the Royal Irish Academy. He recognised, moreover, that this 'history' was a twisted skein of fact and poetry, told and retold over a period of centuries. On the whole, his ignorance of Irish was an advantage, for it shielded him from the knowledge that his ambition was both grandiose and misconceived.

The method, or rather the several methods, that he employed were touched with an odd, grave beauty. An ancient heroic civilisation had flourished in Ireland, he believed, with its deeds recorded in an epic poetry rivalled only by the Homeric. His task therefore was twofold: to reconstruct the actual history, using the bardic poetry as his source of evidence, but also to communicate, in all its grandeur, a sense of the poetry itself. It was a mad enterprise, doomed from the start, and the succession of books in which he tells and retells his story, changes and defends his methods, testifies to his troubled recognition of

---

[1] O'Grady, op. cit., pp 3–5.
[2] Above, iv, pp lxi, 468.

the problems that beset him. The centre of his work is a two-volume *History of Ireland*, of which the first, *The heroic period*, was published in 1878, and the second, *Cuculain and his contemporaries*. Between the two, however, he published a study of *Early bardic literature* (1879), a vindication both of the literature and of his method, which was incorporated in the second volume. Then, in 1881, he published the first volume of a *History of Ireland: critical and philosophical*, in which he seeks to tell his story by more conventional means, and in which he apologises for the errrors of his earlier method. The second volume never appeared, but in 1882 he published *Cuculain: an epic*, composed of materials drawn from the earlier volumes, and asserting, by its very title, an aesthetic claim. Finally, and much later, he retold the entire story of Cuculain in a trilogy of novels—*The coming of Cuculain*, *In the gates of the north*, and *The triumph and passing of Cuculain*—of which the first appeared in 1894 and the third not until 1920. By the time the third had appeared, O'Grady had himself become a legendary figure, the revered 'father of the Irish literary revival'.

The muddle in which O'Grady found his materials is compounded by his own muddled methods. As a historian, he attempted 'the reconstruction by imaginative processes of the life led by our ancestors in this country',[1] but

> the blaze of bardic light which illuminates those centuries at first so dazzled the eye and disturbed the judgement, that I saw only the literature, only the epic and dramatic interest, and did not see as I should the distinctly historical character of the age around which that literature revolves.[2]

O'Grady remained dazzled by that blazing light to the end. His efforts to climb to the firm ground of historical fact were unceasing, but served only to thrust him more deeply into the bog of bardic fancy. The most eloquent pages in the *Bardic history*, as the two-volume work came to be called, are those that testify to the confusions of mind into which he was plunged by his material.

> But all around, in surging, tumultuous motion, come and go the gorgeous, unearthly beings that long ago emanated from bardic minds, a most weird and mocking world. Faces rush out of the darkness, and as swiftly retreat again. Heroes expand into giants, and dwindle into goblins, or fling aside the heroic form and gambol as buffoons; gorgeous palaces are blown asunder like a smoke-wreath; kings, with wand of silver and ard-rōth of gold, move with all their state from century to century; puissant heroes, whose fame reverberates through and sheds a glory over epochs, approach and coalesce; battles are shifted from place to place . . . buried monarchs reappear. . . . The explorer visits an enchanted land where he is mocked and deluded. Everything seems blown loose from its fastenings. All that should be most stable is whirled round and borne away like foam or dead leaves in a storm.[3]

This passage suggests the qualities of his own imagination, eccentric and excitable, constantly and cheerfully risking foolishness and error. The *Bardic*

[1] Standish [James] O'Grady, *History of Ireland* (2 vols, London, 1878–80), i: *The heroic period*, p. v.
[2] Ibid., ii: *Cuculain and his contemporaries*, p. 32.   [3] Ibid., i, 28.

history is a triumph of this imagination, its energy deriving from the fierce imposition of coherence on materials that seek to shift and change beneath his pen. O'Grady believed himself to be the lonely possessor of a great secret, which he struggled ceaselessly to articulate; he had chanced on the fragments of a great literature, and the memorials of a timeless past. His description of himself as an explorer exactly states his situation. His histories, published at his own expense and almost unnoticed at the time of their publication, are flawed but extraordinary works of art, products of a mind obsessed by a singular vision. It is possible to trace the constituent parts of this vision; thus, his insistence on the imaginative truth of history, and on imagination as an instrument of historical reconstruction, bears the marks of his wide, eclectic readings in romantic literature. His celebration of Cuculain as the towering figure of ancient saga, attaining in his final struggle a superhuman grandeur and nobility, is clearly influenced by nineteenth-century conceptions of the saga hero. His style suggests, inevitably, Carlyle, and, more surprisingly, Whitman, of whose work he was an early and perceptive admirer. But the full effect of the *Bardic history* is that of an original talent of a very high order, solitary, gnarled, and powerful.

O'Grady sought to reconstruct 'the life led by our ancestors in this country'; in this lies one source of his intensity. The heroes and events of which he treats were important to him not as an *Arabian nights* spectacle, but as what he believed to be the early history of his own country and his own people. His own attitude toward that country was complicated. He was descended from an ancient Gaelic family, but one that had centuries before embraced protestantism; if he denounced the landlords of Ireland, it was because he wished to strengthen and purify their claims to social leadership; he was a vigorous opponent of the British parliament, but a loyal defender of the British crown. The complexities into which he was led are everywhere evident, even in the footnotes to his edition of the *Pacata Hibernia* (1896) and his romances of Elizabethan Ireland. If problems of cultural identity were common in the nineteenth century, O'Grady nevertheless remains a special case. He compounded the disparate elements of his background and his assortment of loyalties and passions, and made of them an eccentric but gallant unity.

Ernest Boyd devotes a chapter of *Ireland's literary renaissance* to O'Grady, whom he describes, in a term which had become commonplace, as 'the father of the revival'. His terms of praise are vague and are pitched to a high level of intensity.

Here at last was heard the authentic voice of pagan and heroic Ireland; in the story of Cuculain, modern Irish literature had at length found its epic. How pale is Ferguson's *Congal* beside this glowing prose, where poetry springs from the very power and beauty of the imagination as it conceives the life and struggles of the divine being. With his proud affirmations of belief in the ancient deities, and his wonderful evocations of the past, Standish O'Grady revealed to his countrymen the splendour of their own idealism, and restored to them their truly national tradition. All eyes were now turned towards the shining land of heroic story and legend, the footsteps of all were directed upon the path which led back to the sources of Irish nationality.[1]

The implications of this passage are extraordinary. It assumes that a single writer, labouring under difficulties and limitations that he readily acknowledges, not merely restored to a people its national tradition but persuaded them that this tradition was idealistic in nature. Behind the passage rests Boyd's assumption that the writers of the revival—Yeats and George Russell ('AE') in particular—discovered in O'Grady's work an heroic literature that wedded spiritual mysteries to the landscapes of Ireland. There is a certain validity to this assumption. One of the passages from O'Grady that both writers admired, the description of Slieve Gullion in *The flight of the eagle*, points forward both to Yeats and to AE, and suggests the fascination that O'Grady held for certain writers of the revival.

O melancholy lake, shaped like the moon! lake uplifted high in the arms of Slieve Gullion; boggy, desolate, thick-strewn with grey boulders on thy eastern shore and, on thy western, regarded askance by thy step-child the rosy heather, ruddy as with blood— aloof, observant of thy never-ending sorrow; unfathomable, druid lake; home of the white steed immortal; bath of the Caillia-Bullia, the people's dread; thy turbid waves aye breaking in pale foam upon thy grey shore strewn with boulders and the wrecks of the work of men's hands; horror-haunted, enchanted lake; seat of dim ethnic mysteries, lost all or scattered to the winds; with thy made wells and walls and painted temples, and shining cairns, and subterrene corridors obscure—walked once by druids gold-helmeted and girded with the sun;—scene of religious pomps, and thronging congregations hymning loud their forgotten gods obscene or fair; what mighty tales, what thoughts far-journeying, Protean, sprang once in light from thy wine-dark, mystic floor, Lough Liath! Sky-neighbouring lake vexed by all the winds! mournful, sibilant, teeming fount of thy vast phantasmal mythus, O Ultonia![2]

The prose is a jumble of fustian and eloquence, faintly ridiculous, but dignified by its strength of feeling. For those who admired it, its power rested not in its one clear image, the moon-shaped lake, but in the 'dim ethnic mysteries' at which it hinted. O'Grady's talent, someone in George Moore's *Hail and farewell* suggests, resembles 'the shaft of a beautiful column rising from amid rubble-heaps'.[3] The outlines of the column are elusive although the heaps of rubble are visible and jagged. In this, his work bears a striking resemblance to what he took to be his ancient sources. Both the landscape and the old literature of Ireland were for O'Grady haunted by the troubling presences of a shattered mythology, living and powerful, but reduced now to incoherence. Its present life is suggested throughout his work, and is intimated

[1] E. A. Boyd, *Ireland's literary renaissance* (Dublin, 1916), pp 52–3.
[2] Standish [James] O'Grady, *The flight of the eagle* (London, 1897), pp 256–7.
[3] George Moore, *Hail and farewell* (London, 1914; reprint, ed. Richard Cave, Gerrards Cross (Bucks.), 1976), pp 132–3.

even in his account, in *The story of Ireland* (1894), of Parnell's funeral. But his sense of Ireland's past was linked directly to his political position and social attitudes.

Yeats, whose understanding of O'Grady was both shrewd and sympathetic, writes that

he had given all his heart to the smaller Irish landowners, to whom he belonged, and with whom his childhood had been spent, and for them he wrote his books, and would soon rage over their failings in certain famous passages that many men would repeat to themselves like poets' rhymes. All round us people talked or wrote for victory's sake, and were hated for their victories—but here was a man whose rage was a swansong over all that he had held most dear, and to whom for that very reason every Irish imaginative writer owed a portion of his soul.[1]

Although it is a Yeatsian exaggeration to suppose that O'Grady composed his elaborate historical reconstructions for the edification of so restricted and unbookish an audience as 'the smaller Irish landowners', it is true that O'Grady himself came to perceive a relationship between the ancient Ireland of which he wrote and the increasingly embattled class that claimed his loyalty. In this instance at least, therefore, the literary revival was linked to an anti-democratic, if not a reactionary, political stance.

But in fact, of course, the politics of the Irish literary revival were complex and paradoxical. The early works of Yeats and Hyde, the activities of the several Irish literary societies in London and Dublin, all of the carefully charted landmarks of the revival, present at first glance a deceptive simplicity. The first history of the revival, which was published as early as 1894,[2] is very much an act of parochial piety, a faithful and insipid chronicle of all Irish writers, however trivial, who had turned to Irish themes and materials. In this respect it is probably faithful to the spirit of the times, for the revival, in its first period, was an innocent and intellectually unsophisticated enterprise, an effort to revive 'the spirit of the nation', by which was meant simply an effort to complete the work of Thomas Davis. That the complex and extraordinary work of the 'renaissance' should have flowered forth from such humble origins has always been one of the mysteries of Irish literary history. Perhaps there is no explanation: it is one of the chief virtues and powers of art that its operations are mysterious. But it is equally true that literary culture has deep roots in the society to which it responds.

BY the turn of the century, conceptions of Irish identity and of the nature of Irish experience were coming forward that would have seemed incomprehensible equally to Maria Edgeworth and to Tone, although Thomas Davis

---

[1] W. B. Yeats, *Autobiographies* (2nd ed., London, 1955), p. 220.
[2] Above, p. 482, n. 3.

might have given them his puzzled assent. The bland and conventional formulations of Young Ireland were being challenged by the powerful and wayward art of richly gifted imaginative writers—among them, Yeats, AE, Douglas Hyde, Lady Gregory, and Synge. These writers owed debts to their nineteenth-century predecessors that they readily acknowledged, at times graciously and at times with condescension. There are close links, for example, between Hyde's work and Samuel Ferguson's, between Lady Gregory's work and Standish O'Grady's. But on the whole, their work has seemed a break with the immediate past, an assertion of the power and autonomy of art against the opposing pieties of conventional nationalism. Yeats argued this case on a number of occasions, but nowhere more explicitly than in his essay on 'J. M. Synge and the Ireland of his time', in which the literature of the nineteenth century is dismissed as at best a superior journalism, imprisoned within the ideas and images of a virtuous but sterile patriotism.[1] Synge's work, and by implication that of Yeats himself, is quite properly seen within the terms of this argument as that of a fierce and reckless imagination, moving toward a lonely and authentic voice and vision.

This argument, however, requires modification. The literature of the renaissance, even that of the supposedly detached and indifferent Synge, was created not in a vacuum, but within the context of specific social and cultural circumstances. The title of Yeats's essay suggests such a relationship, although it is not explored in the essay itself. It might indeed be argued that the remarkable creative vitality of the first decade of the twentieth century was nurtured by changes and challenges within Irish society. The belligerent and strident nationalism that Yeats and Synge confronted was not that of Thomas Davis, although it invoked his name and made use of his slogans. Neither did the Ireland of their day, after land wars and land acts, after Parnell and Davitt, after Balfour and Wyndham, greatly resemble the Ireland of Thomas Davis. But it is equally misleading to assume, as Yeats does for the purposes of his argument, that the literature of nineteenth-century Ireland can be defined in simple terms.

Ireland of the nineteenth century was a land of incoherences and broken aspirations, a fragmented and richly diverse society. Its best writers were conscious of this, and the knowledge informs the best of their art. The novels of a Gerald Griffin or a Charles Lever, although separated by far distances in their social assumptions and allegiances, share equally a sense of social complexity. Their work moved, almost inevitably, from the recognition of complexity to the assertion of simplicity; that is, they sought to impose on their fragmented world the clarifying order of a political or social thesis. Not one but many Irelands find expression in the fiction and in the poetry of the century, a multitude of voices striving towards the definition of a society that resisted

[1] W. B. Yeats, *Essays and introductions* (London, 1961), pp 311–42.

articulation. In few other literatures has the definition of self been bound so inextricably to the definition of that culture by which the self is surrounded and shaped. If the pressures placed on the literature are suggested by this circumstance, so also does it suggest the source of the century's creative energy.

CHAPTER XXVI

Pre-university education, 1782–1870

D. H. AKENSON

In 1831 an event occurred about which the period covered by this chapter pivots: E. G. Stanley (chief secretary 1830–33) founded the 'Irish national system of education'. This was a system whereby the government underwrote most of the expenses of erecting schools and paid the salaries of the teachers. A central board controlled the textbooks and lesson materials; local managers were responsible for the day-to-day management and maintenance of the schools, and controlled the appointment of the masters. This state system of education antedates by almost a full four decades the establishment of a similar system in England, a nation well advanced along the path of industrial and urban change. Why, then, did the Irish system of state primary education appear at such a relatively early date?

To answer this question let us first step back and note that, despite the British stereotypes of the troglodytic Irishman, the Irish peasant of the late eighteenth and early nineteenth centuries evinced a striking avidity for education. Various acts of the late seventeenth and early eighteenth centuries[1] in theory prohibited catholics from having schoolmasters and in practice made it extremely difficult. Significantly, the peasantry did not allow itself to be ground into illiteracy, but responded by supporting its own clandestine 'hedge schools' with a tenacity born of desperation. One of the necessary pre-conditions for the eventual creation of the national system of education was a readiness of the catholic peasants to accept and support local schools, and this readiness stemmed in part from the reflexes imprinted on the peasant mind by the penal code.

But there was more to the catholic peasant's affirmation of the value of schooling than a mere Newtonian response to social oppression. The peasant culture was to a remarkable extent a word culture, one in which the acquisition of verbal and mathematical formulae was highly regarded. The Irish language had throughout the middle ages been a highly cultivated oral and written

[1] 7 Will. III, c. 4 (7 Sept. 1695); 2 Anne, c. 6 (4 Mar. 1704); 8 Anne, c. 3 (30 Aug. 1709); 1 Geo. II, c. 20 (6 May 1728); 13 Geo. II, c. 6 (31 Mar. 1740).

medium; and until it declined in the late eighteenth and early nineteenth centuries, its modes of expression retained their semi-classic flavour. A normal indoor pastime on a winter evening was the hearing of ancient literary tales, which in their telling over several centuries had been moulded into a distinct literary form. Hence, with the repeal in 1782, 1792, and 1793 of the most pernicious of the penal measures relating to education (minor impediments on catholic endowments remained), the hedge schools flourished.

Because the hedge schools serve as the chief evidence of the remarkable indigenous drive for schooling on the part of the peasantry, they deserve our attention.[1] While the penal laws were enforced, the catholic hedge schoolmasters taught as members of a quiet but widespread conspiracy. Their fellow conspirators were the students who formed their classes and the parents who sheltered them and paid their fees. In many localities a hedge school was literally that: a collection of students and a teacher holding class in a ditch or hedgerow, with one of the pupils serving as look-out for law officers. As the penal laws were relaxed the master was able to make himself and his pupils a bit more comfortable, settling in the comparative luxury of a sod hut or an unused barn for his classroom. The best available estimates indicate that in the mid-1820s three to four hundred thousand catholic children were being educated at parental expense, a very useful index of the peasantry's enthusiasm for schooling.[2]

We should avoid romanticising the hedge schools. Some of them were taught by men of high scholarly attainments (it is reported that one later hedge schoolmaster was offered an honorary degree by Dublin University), but such men were rare. Most hedge schoolmasters, it appears, knew something more than the 'three Rs', but because of the impediments to catholic education few had been to universities or even to secondary schools. Much showy, useless pedantry was usually part of the hedge schoolmaster's intellectual gear, and this was sufficient to awe the parents who paid the fees. Bishop Doyle, however, noted that the masters 'in many instances are extremely ignorant'.[3] Thus, the 'three Rs' were the typical fare of most hedge schools, although some masters did not teach all three, and others, in contrast, taught higher subjects such as modern and ancient languages and various technical skills. Most children, it appears, attended for three to five years and therefore had time to learn little more than the fundamentals. By the beginning of the nineteenth century English was rapidly replacing Irish as the medium of instruction in the hedge schools, and elementary literacy was usually an attainment of the English rather than of the Irish language.

[1] The standard work on the hedge schools is Patrick J. Dowling, *The hedge schools of Ireland* (Dublin and Belfast, 1935; 2nd ed., Cork, 1968). Also useful on the early period are Martin Brenan, *Schools of Kildare and Leighlin, A.D. 1775–1835* (Dublin, 1935), and Philip O'Connell, *The schools and scholars of Breiffne* (Dublin, 1942). See also above, iv, pp li–lii, 55, 98, 380–81, 692.

[2] Akenson, *Ir. education experiment*, p. 57.

[3] Doyle to Sir Henry Parnell, 22 Apr. 1821 (W. J. Fitzpatrick, *The life, times, and correspondence of the Right Rev. Dr Doyle, bishop of Kildare and Leighlin* (2 vols, Dublin, 1861), i, 168).

While the common people were willing to support popular educational institutions, the Irish government had a tradition of intervening in educational matters stretching back to the sixteenth century. This contrasted sharply with the reluctance of the British government to involve itself in educational affairs at home and partially explains why the Irish system of state education ante-dated the English. 'National education in Ireland began in 1537', Michael Sadler claimed somewhat extravagantly, 'when the Irish parliament estab-lished parochial schools . . .'.[1] The act Sadler referred to required all beneficed clergyman to keep or cause to be kept within their vicarage or rectory an English-language school.[2] Originally the statute (which considerably precedes the better known Scottish parish schools act of 1696) was effective only within the Pale and its marches. But with the extension of English control during the seventeenth century the law was extended to all Ireland. The basic act was modified in the eighteenth century.[3] Whereas the Tudor statute had focused on the teaching of the English language and customs, the renewing acts emphasised the advancement of the protestant religion. It is clear that in reality the network of parish schools was embarrassingly thin: at its most prosperous, in 1823, there were only 782, enrolling 36,498 children.

Much the same is true of the attempt, beginning in the reign of Elizabeth I, to establish a system of protestant diocesan schools. Like the parish schools act of Henry VIII, the diocesan schools statute[4] was essentially defensive in origin, being intended to shore up the drifting allegiance of the middle classes. It enacted that 'there shall be from henceforth a free school within every diocese of this realm of Ireland, and that the schoolmaster shall be an Englishman, or of the English birth of this realm'. Despite this decree, diocesan schools were founded only in a few places, and the 'system' (if so it was) had to be buttressed by acts of 1662, 1725, and 1755. Those few diocesan schools that were created taught both elementary literacy and, in contrast to the parish schools, higher subjects. An investigation in 1791 revealed that only eighteen of the thirty-four protestant dioceses possessed schools, enrolling a total of 324 pupils. Another inquiry, in 1808–9, found seventeen diocesan schools operating, but only eleven of these had their own separate schoolhouse and of these one was in a 'ruinous state', another had been 'begun twelve years ago but never finished', and a third was a thatched cabin 'in tolerable repair'. A return of 1831 showed only twelve diocesan schools extant, enrolling 419 pupils.

The early Stuarts followed Tudor precedent and were active in educational affairs, but with greater success in the long run. As part of the Ulster plantation, a free grammar school was to be founded in each of the planted counties (Armagh, Cavan, Donegal, Fermanagh, Londonderry, and Tyrone), with land

[1] Michael E. Sadler, 'The history of the Irish system of elementary education' in Michael E. Sadler (ed.), *Special reports on educational subjects, 1896–97* (London, 1897), p. 211.
[2] 28 Hen. VIII, c. 15 (13 Oct. × 20 Dec. 1537).
[3] 8 Geo. I, c. 12 (18 Jan. 1722); 5 Geo. II, c. 4 (10 Mar. 1732).
[4] 12 Eliz. I, c. 1 (26 June 1570).

reserved in each county to pay for their maintenance. In 1612 James I directed the lord deputy to see that the lands intended for schools were conveyed immediately to the respective protestant bishops, but nothing was done. Only after several subsequent orders were four 'royal schools' operating in 1621 and five in 1625. Charles I attempted to build on James I's wobbly foundation, making regrants of the land given for educational endowments and adding land for royal schools in King's County and in County Wicklow. In contrast to the diocesan and parish schools, most of the royal schools seem to have been reasonably well maintained. In 1831, 343 students were enrolled in the royal schools, seventy being free scholars. Five of the six still exist, at Armagh, Cavan, Dungannon, Enniskillen, and Raphoe.

A further element in the long tradition of state intervention in educational affairs is the case of the protestant charter schools. The Irish charity school movement began early in the eighteenth century under voluntary auspices. In most cases the charity schools enrolled both protestant and catholic children, but permitted instruction only in the protestant faith. In 1717 the Society in Dublin for Promoting Christian Knowledge was formed, under the leadership of Dr Henry Maule, later protestant bishop of Meath (1744–58), and by 1725 the society was operating 163 schools containing 3,000 pupils. With Maule as the link, a similar society was able to obtain a royal charter in 1733, its full title being 'The Incorporated Society in Dublin for Promoting English Protestant Schools in Ireland', but it was usually known as the 'charter school society'. The charter greatly aided the society in its fund-raising, and from 1738 to 1794 it also received £1,000 annually from successive kings. In 1747 the Irish parliament granted the society the proceeds from the licensing duty on hawkers and peddlers, and it was only a small step from this for parliament to make an outright grant to the society. The parliamentary grants began in 1751 and continued until 1831. Altogether it is estimated that during that period a total of more than £1,250,000 sterling was voted to the society from public funds. But its record was far from creditable. It operated chiefly as a proselytising agency (indeed, from 1775 to 1803 only catholic children were admitted to the charter schools). John Howard, the prison reformer, inspected the schools in 1784 and in 1787. 'The children, in general,' he averred, 'were sickly, pale, and such miserable objects, that they were a disgrace to all society; and their reading had been neglected for the purpose of making them work for the masters.'[1] Subsequent nineteenth-century investigations confirmed Howard's charges in detail. In the mid-1820s roughly 2,100 children were enrolled in some thirty-four schools, institutions that now were regularly denounced by the Roman Catholic clergy and viewed with increasing embarrassment by the Irish government.

Obviously none of the institutions described above—the parish, diocesan, royal, or charter schools—could be considered as serious attempts to educate

[1] *First report of the commissioners of Irish education inquiry*, p. 7, H.C. 1825 (400), xii, 11.

the mass of the people. But the actions of the Irish and, later, of the United Kingdom parliaments in allocating resources to certain schools established a tradition of state action that was a necessary pre-condition for the formation of a full system of state schools in the nineteenth century.

Two more components must be added to the explanation of the foundation of the national system of education. These are the evolution in the years 1783–1830 of an agreed body of 'conventional wisdom' within the Irish government about the nature of mass education, and the willingness of the Roman Catholic clergy to accept the emergent official consensus.

The initial link in the train of official reasoning that led eventually to the establishment of the national system was the announcement to the Irish parliament by John Hely Hutchinson in October 1783 of a rather modest scheme for the creation of two major public schools on the English model in Ireland. Hely Hutchinson presented an elaboration of this scheme of two 'great schools' to Thomas Orde, the chief secretary, in late 1785, expressing the belief that two such schools would serve as models on which other schools throughout the country would pattern themselves. The most important result of Hely Hutchinson's plan was that Orde became convinced of the need for new educational legislation and sufficiently concerned to raise the matter in the commons. He developed a plan presented to parliament in 1787, involving the reinvigoration of the parish schools, the creation of four technical academies, the improvement of the diocesan schools, and the establishment of two superior schools as preparatory schools for the university—all this in addition to a proposal for a second university for Ireland, to be located somewhere in the north.[1]

Orde left office before his plan could be implemented, but his successor, Alleyne Fitzherbert (1787–9), capitalised on the momentum of Orde's administration and induced parliament to sponsor an investigation into the condition and conduct of all endowed schools in Ireland, both public and private. This commission's report was completed in 1791, and for eighteenth-century Ireland it was a remarkable document. It suggested that the control of the local parish schools should be taken from the protestant clergy and placed in the hands of a local body composed chiefly of laymen, and that Roman Catholics be admitted to this body; it implicitly frowned on proselytising in the parish schools and suggested that clergy of each denomination be allowed into the parish schools to teach the religious doctrines of their respective faiths; it proposed that the lord lieutenant and the privy council should appoint a schoolmaster in each county and thus make the diocesan school system a full reality; to ensure that the diocesan schools functioned properly, the report suggested that all building expenses and one-half of the teachers' salaries should be borne by the central government; and most remarkable of all, the

[1] Above, iv, 283.

report recommended the creation of a national board of control to supervise all endowed schools in educational as well as in financial matters.

The immediate fate of the 1791 report was as undistinguished as its contents were remarkable. It was not published (probably because it was so critical of the existing protestant schools), and was never debated in parliament. Yet its compilation was not a fool's errand, for an act of the British parliament in 1806[1] explicitly revived the act of the Irish parliament that had initiated the education inquiry. This new commission took the unpublished 1791 report as its starting point for an investigation that lasted nearly seven years and yielded fourteen reports. For our purpose the fourteenth, or summary, report is the crucial one, for it greatly influenced Irish educational practice. It postulated that to bring order out of the chaos of 'ill-taught and ill-regulated schools' a permanent body of education commissioners should be established to administer parliamentary grants to schools for the poorer classes. Significantly the report stated that no plan could be successful 'unless it be explicitly avowed, and clearly understood, as its leading principle, that no attempt shall be made to influence or disturb the peculiar religious tenets of any sect or description of Christians'.[2] The new education commissioners should, the report stated, have control over all texts used in the schools, and it was recommended that ordinary classroom instruction in literary and moral matters be kept strictly separate from the study of dogmatic religion. The former was to be provided and controlled largely by the state, the latter entirely by the local clergymen.

At first the work of the 1806–12 commission had little immediate effect (save for the establishment of a commission to oversee endowed schools), largely because the Irish government was deeply committed to aiding financially a cohort of protestant educational societies, the most important of which was the Association for Discountenancing Vice and Promoting the Knowledge and Practice of the Christian Religion. These were repugnant to the catholic clergy, however, and as the catholic population became increasingly powerful the government cast about for an educational agency that would be acceptable both to the ascendancy and to the catholics. This they found in the Society for Promoting the Education of the Poor in Ireland, usually known as the Kildare Place Society. Established in 1811, following the success of a virtually non-denominational school founded in 1786, the Kildare Place Society operated schools for the poor, schools that were religiously neutral, or almost so. The Bible was read daily in the society's schools, but doctrinal matters were not raised. The society's style of operation seemed to the government to be in harmony with the recommendations of the 1806–12 commission for the establishment of an undenominational system of education for the poor. Hence, in 1816, when the Kildare Place Society applied for a parliamentary grant, its

---

[1] 46 Geo. III, c. 122 (21 July 1806).

[2] *Fourteenth report of the commissioners of the board of education, in Ireland*, p. 2, H.C. 1821 (744), xi, 144.

petition was successful. An annual grant of £6,000 was given in 1816, reaching a peak of £30,000 just before it ceased in 1831. The magnitude of these grants becomes clear when they are compared with the first parliamentary grant for education in England, in 1833, which was only £20,000.

To be national in any true sense a school system in Ireland needed to have the approval of the catholic clergy and leading laymen; and for a considerable time the Kildare Place system had that approval. O'Connell was on the society's board of governors, catholic gentry became patrons of individual schools, and the clergy gave their cautious sanction to the society's activities. Educationally, the society was a considerable success, publishing the first major series of sequential textbooks in the British Isles, establishing efficient model schools for the training of teachers, and pioneering the creation of an efficient system of school inspection. By 1820 the society was operating 381 schools, enrolling 26,474 pupils.

But then things began to go awry.[1] Up to 1819 the catholics had expressed only two objections to the society's operations: they did not approve of the large protestant majority on the managing board and they were uneasy about the reading of the scriptures without note or comment. In 1820, however, the Kildare Place Society abandoned its neutral stance and began to allocate part of its own income to the schools of various protestant proselytising societies, such as the London Hibernian Society, the Baptist Society, and the Association for Discountenancing Vice. Simultaneously, protestant clergy and lay patrons violated with increasing boldness the society's rules prohibiting the denominational exposition of the scripture readings. At the society's annual meeting of 1819 O'Connell raised some of the catholic grievances, and in 1820, not having obtained satisfaction, he resigned. Thereupon he led an agitation against the society, and gained the adherence of such leading prelates as John MacHale and James Doyle.

The catholic complaints, especially as articulated in a petition signed by the leading catholic bishops, led to the establishment in 1824 of yet another official inquiry into Irish popular education. This inquiry put forward a plan for a central board to superintend 'schools of general instruction' wherein catholic and protestant children were to be given literary and moral instruction together and denominational instruction separately, an arrangement that was approved by the catholic bishops. These basic principles were subsequently confirmed by a select committee, appointed in 1828, to which the reports of the 1824–7 commission were referred.

The reasons why the national system of education was created so comparatively early may be summarised: Irish people evinced a remarkable appetite for schooling for their children; successive Irish governments were willing to use legislative and prerogative mechanisms to facilitate the provision of educational institutions; the Roman Catholic clergy and laity became strong enough

[1] Cf. above, p. 79.

to resist the imposition of proselytising societies, while being willing to accept a non-denominational system of education; and there emerged an official consensus on the need for a national system of popular education, a system that would be neutral between religious denominations and would be super-intended by a state board.[1]

WHEN in the autumn of 1831 the chief secretary, Stanley, issued his 'instruc-tions' for the establishment of a national school system, he was setting an educational pattern that survives in modified form to the present day. Stanley's plan was a mixture of central control and local initiative. At the centre, he created the 'commissioners of national education in Ireland' to oversee the new system. The commissioners, unpaid, were men of distinction in various fields—barristers, professors, and bishops. At first the board was dominated by protestants, but in time the proportion of catholics was regularly increased, until by the end of the century they had achieved numerical parity. The super-intendence of the new system by a board of distinguished citizens gave it a prestige no group of civil servants would have been likely to match, and the unpaid board was able to be more independent in thought and action than professional civil servants. Of course the daily administrative chores were performed by full-time professionals, but the commissioners kept full control of policy.

In practice, the commissioners' activities were fourfold. First, they made grants towards the construction of primary schools (almost always referred to in the nineteenth century as 'national schools'), which covered most of the building costs. Secondly, they paid almost the whole salary of each school-teacher. Thirdly, they issued a list of approved texts for use in the schools and made associated regulations for the conduct of the schools; inspectors were appointed to see that the approved practices were followed. Fourthly, they published an excellent set of school texts, a series that was used not only in Ireland but throughout Great Britain and its empire.

Each school was under the control of a local manager. In catholic schools the manager was almost always the parish priest, and in protestant schools the rector, minister, or landlord. The manager's powers were quite extensive, since he was entrusted with the daily oversight of the school: he had the right to appoint teachers (subject in theory but not in reality to the commissioners' veto); in practice he could dismiss teachers whenever he pleased; he chose which of the several approved sets of textbooks the school would use, and, within broad limits, arranged the school's timetable. Thus, the national system of education was at once highly centralised and strongly localised. Tensions

---

[1] A well argued monograph, which indicates the carry-over of practices from the Kildare Place system to the national school system, is Eustas Ó hEideáin, *National school inspection in Ireland: the beginnings* (Dublin, 1967). A summary of catholic attitudes is given by Ignatius Murphy, 'Primary education' in Corish, *Ir. catholicism*, v, fasc. 6, pp 1–52.

were inherent in the relationship between the commissioners and the local school managers, but overt conflicts were surprisingly rare. Teachers were appointed and dismissed at the manager's whim; until late in the nineteenth century they had no appeal against arbitrary dismissals. They were not civil servants and had none of the protections or prerogatives of civil servants. Indeed, they were treated as if they were day labourers and not as educated men. The parents had as few rights as the teachers. There was no reasonable way for a parent to influence the conduct of the local national school. The school manager was not an elected official or a representative of a local government body. The commissioners themselves were an appointed, not an elected, group, so the entire educational mechanism was insulated from local civic influence.

If enrolments are any indication, the national system of education was a great success.

Number of schools and children enrolled, 1833–70

year	schools	children	parliamentary grant £
1831/3[1]	789	107,042	30,000
1840	1,978	232,560	50,000
1850	4,547	511,239	125,000
1860	5,632	804,000	294,000
1870	6,806	998,999	394,200

[1] The figures of schools and attendance are for 1833; the parliamentary grant is that of 1831.

When we turn from discussing structure to describing the curriculum of the national schools we are really turning to the national school textbooks published by the commissioners, for although their use was not compulsory they were almost universally adopted. This was in part because they were cheap and in part because the texts were among the best available at any price. The most important were the six reading books, which formed a logical, integrated sequence of instruction, taking the child from elementary literacy to fairly sophisticated lessons in geography, science, and literature. Although most pupils stayed on only through the first two books, the fourth and fifth books contained material of secondary-school level. Thus a pupil could receive the basis of a secondary education in the local national school, given the good fortune of a competent teacher and of parents who allowed him to remain in school.

Three points about the books bear emphasis. First, the school books, while containing instruction in science and mathematics, contained little material relevant to everyday Irish life, and were rigidly academic. The closest the commissioners came to providing practical instruction was an agricultural class book, which attempted to teach how best to manage a small farm and a kitchen garden. The book was an admirable popularisation of contemporary agricultural theory, but without practical work in a school garden it remained a statement of theory. Secondly, the school books were not noticeably Irish; they contained a few references to Ireland as a geographical entity but little else. History as a subject was only an incidental for the advanced classes, and even then it was British history of the distant past. Thirdly, and most important, it is crucial to realise that the textbooks, while neutral among Christian denominations, were not secular in the modern sense of the word but were full of moralising and religiosity. James Carlile, the presbyterian author of most of the original series of reading books, modelled them on those of the Catholic Book Society. The first lesson book, far the least religious of the series, told the children that God is love and that He sent his son for man's salvation. The second included a great deal of biblical history and basic theology, including a paraphrase of the creation story and other Old Testament material. In the fourth book, the birth and work of Christ were covered and the doctrine of salvation presented. The books were sufficiently religious to be adaptable to denominational purposes while being sufficiently neutral dogmatically to give little or no offence.

Whatever their flaws (and they were many) the school books can fairly be claimed to have been at mid-century the most popular series of school texts in the British empire. The commissioners supplied them to more than a dozen countries in the empire, the most important being Upper Canada (Ontario), where, for a time, they were used to the almost entire exclusion of all others. From 1836 the commissioners employed a London agent to sell books directly to English schools, and in the late 1840s they began supplying large quantities to the committee of the privy council on education in England. In 1851 about 100,000 Irish school books were sold in England, and by 1859 the number was approximately 300,000. According to a conservative estimate, in 1859 there were nearly one million Irish school books being used in England. The royal commission on popular education in England, which disapproved of the Irish school texts, was forced to admit that in 1861 they were the most popular and widely used school books in England.[1]

THE effect of the national school system on Irish people is extremely difficult to determine, but one thing is certain: the basic premise on which E. G. Stanley founded the system, that it would facilitate the social integration of protestants

[1] I am indebted to the late Tarlach Ó Raifeartaigh, who provided me with manuscript material on the influence of the Irish system abroad and on the teaching of history in the national schools.

and catholics, was unsound. By mid-century the system, which Stanley intended to be non-denominational, was effectively denominational.

Stanley intended that three practices would guarantee the non-denominational character of the national system. The first was that local control of the schools should be what we would today call 'ecumenical'. In his original instruction he stated that the commissioners of national education would look with 'peculiar favour' on applications for recognition made jointly by protestant and catholic clergy, by protestant and catholic laymen, and by clergy of one denomination and laymen of the other. When an application proceeded exclusively from one denomination the commissioners were to make special inquiry and, it was implied, look sceptically at the request for funds. His second intention was that catholic and protestant children would be educated together; for the instructions urged that not only should the schools be open to children of all faiths but that a positive effort should be made to mix the children as a remedy for the denominational estrangement and strife that so marred Irish social and political life. Thirdly, in order to make the mixing of the faiths possible in a religiously sensitive society, he stated that a clear and inviolable line should be drawn between literary and moral education on the one hand and religious education on the other. Religious education was to be conducted by the different clergy on a special day set aside for it, or before or after the secular school day. The rules were scrupulously fair: clergy of every denomination having children in the school had the right to enter the school-room at the time set apart for religious instruction or, if they preferred, to take the children to a place of their own choosing.

Unfortunately for Stanley's objectives, none of the three original conditions was maintained. To begin with, the commissioners undercut Stanley's plan by failing to encourage interdenominational applications for school manager-ships. Being anxious to spread their system as quickly as possible, they from the start granted aid to anyone of good character and sound social standing. As a result, in 1852 only 175 schools, or less than 4 per cent, were under joint managerships. Moreover, the local control of the national schools became not only denominational but clerical as well. There being no real tradition in Ireland of local government at the parish level, religious leaders, especially among the Roman Catholics, stepped forward to assume command. The great majority of the catholic schools were soon under clerical control, as were roughly two-thirds of the presbyterian schools. Only among the members of the Church of Ireland did lay leadership develop, for approximately two-thirds of their schools were managed by laymen. But overall, of the 4,547 schools in operation in 1850, 3,418 (75 per cent) were under the exclusive control of clergymen of a single denomination.

Naturally, the system of denominational managerships meant that teachers were recruited by denomination. In 1867 only 10.7 per cent of the national schools had managers who appointed teachers of other than their own faith, and in most of these it was a manager of one protestant denomination appointing a teacher of another. In only 6.8 per cent of the schools did a protestant manager appoint a catholic teacher or a catholic manager a protestant teacher.

Despite honest efforts the commissioners of national education were unable to keep religious and secular instruction apart. Partly this was their own fault, for, as mentioned earlier, their textbooks for combined instruction were full of material that, although technically neutral as between denominations, was bound to raise religious questions. By the late 1830s, moreover, the commissioners were allowing school managers to designate any time during the day as the period of religious training, provided that this period was specified in advance. Then, in the mid-1860s, the commissioners began permitting religious instruction to take place in a schoolroom adjoining the main room at the same time as the non-denominational literary instruction was being given in the main schoolroom. In practice, therefore, the line between secular and religious instruction became very blurred.

Of the Irish denominations, the presbyterians were at first the most hostile to the national school system. In the commissioners' original rules, clergymen of all faiths had the right to enter any school to give religious instruction to children of their own faith. To the presbyterians this meant that catholic priests would be allowed to teach in schools built in part with presbyterian funds. This view, when combined with the misinformed belief that the commissioners were 'mutilating' the Bible, produced a vitriolic presbyterian agitation. During the 1830s presbyterian extremists intimidated national schoolmasters, destroyed some schoolhouses, and defaced others with slogans identifying the schools with the pope and the devil. The more responsible presbyterian leaders engaged in a long negotiation with the commissioners, who in 1840 capitulated to their demands and permitted the redefinition of a category called the 'non-vested schools', built solely from local funds and receiving financial aid only for teachers' salaries and books. In return for accepting less money, the managers of such schools acquired the right to prevent clergymen of denominations other than their own from giving religious instruction. The national system's conscience clause continued to operate, however; catholic and Church of Ireland children could not be forced to attend presbyterian religious instruction if their parents objected. Once the new category of schools was established, the presbyterians joined the system with enthusiasm. But they were not the only denomination to choose the non-vested status: in 1850 68 per cent of all national schools were non-vested, and in 1870 74 per cent.

It is thus not surprising that Stanley's goal of integrating children of different faiths was unrealistic. Even in an encouraging social climate it would have been difficult to mix religiously schoolchildren in large areas of Ireland, for in many parts of the south and west there were very few protestant children. County Clare, the most extreme case, was 97.8 per cent catholic in 1861. Moreover, from its foundation many Church of Ireland clergymen were strongly opposed to the national system. Their grounds ranged from the belief that the established church had the right to control all popular education, to opposition to the separation of religious and secular instruction, and to general distaste for any creation of the whig government. Whatever their reasons, the majority of Church of Ireland clergy refused to cooperate with the commissioners of national education, and in 1839 founded an educational network of their own, the Church Education Society. At its peak, in 1848, the Church Education Society enrolled more than 120,000 children, roughly half of whom were Church of Ireland.[1] Thereafter the society declined, encountering severe financial difficulties in the late 1850s and early 1860s. In the first three decades of the national school system's existence, strong forces inhibited the enrolling of many Church of Ireland children, and this inhibition in turn greatly reduced the possibility of the national schools becoming non-sectarian.

Unlike the members of the Church of Ireland and presbyterians, the Roman Catholic clergy for the most part were positively disposed towards the national system, although a minority, led by Archbishop MacHale of Tuam, strongly opposed any connection. In the 1830s and 1840s the catholic church's attitude towards non-denominational education was not as clearly defined as it was later to become. In any case, in the years before the famine the church was financially pinched and was willing to accept government grants without quibbling about the terms. Thus, the commissioners' annual report for 1835 was able to note that 941 catholic clergymen had applied for grants. This adhesion to the national system was the one action that would most reinforce the effects of the Church of Ireland's abstention: at the very time that the latter were holding aloof, the national schools were being filled with Roman Catholic pupils, the result being that in the south and west of Ireland most national schools were attended only by catholic children, as shown in the following table.

Percentage of national schools attended by protestant and catholic children, 1870

Ulster	82.6
Munster	40.5
Leinster	46.7
Connacht	48.6
total	58.8

These percentages (which were to decrease with each passing year) overstated the degree of religious integration taking place, because a school was counted as mixed even if there was a solitary protestant in a catholic school, or vice

[1] Cf. above, p. 531, for the number enrolled in national schools in 1850.

versa. The figures below for the year 1870 indicate that in only a few of the religiously integrated schools can there have been any semblance of a balance between the religious groups.

Children in mixed schools

	catholics	protestants
children in mixed schools staffed exclusively by catholic teachers	364,154 [37]	25,076 [3]
children in mixed schools staffed exclusively by protestant teachers	29,540 [3]	125,260 [13]
children in mixed schools staffed both by catholic and protestant teachers	12,887 [1]	14,226 [1]

The figures in square brackets give the attendances as percentages of the total children at national schools in 1870 (998,999). 42 per cent of children attended religiously-homogeneous schools.

It is fair to conclude that by 1870 the national system of education had become denominational in fact, even if still non-denominational in theory. Only three major rules distinguished the national system from a formally denominational system: the time of religious instruction had to be stipulated in advance; no child could be forced to remain in attendance during religious instruction of a faith other than his own; and except in non-vested schools, clergy of all denominations had the right of access during the hours of religious instruction.

Whereas Stanley's original intention had been that the Irish national system of education should unite the Irish denominations, it seems likely that it actually reinforced the walls between them. The plan of integration was replaced with the practice of segregation. The school system that had been intended as an antidote for Ireland's sectarian problem had become not the solution but a part of the problem.

ALTHOUGH the national system of education failed to heal Ireland's sectarian wounds, it deserves credit for making Ireland a country of literates. The percentage of persons aged five years and above who were neither able to read nor write was 53 in 1841; 47 in 1851; 39 in 1861; and 33 in 1871. This achievement was of great consequence for Ireland's later political history. Though the system was unfavourable to nationalist sentiment in its formal curricula, it aided nationalistic propaganda by creating a populace that could be reached by newspaper and pamphlet; when revolution came, it was not revolution conducted by or for illiterate men.

Undeniably, in making Ireland a country of literates the national school system made them literate in English, but it is a mistake to conclude that the system was a British machine for destroying the Irish language. The first reliable statistics on Irish speakers were compiled in 1851, when 23.3 per cent of the population was recorded as able to speak Irish; the percentage in 1861 was 19.1, and in 1871 it was 15.1. If one projects the trend-line determined by these figures backwards, it appears highly probable that Irish had ceased to be the majority language of Ireland before the national school system was created.[1]

Clearly, however, the system had something to do with the decline of Irish, for the schools served as a convenient place for children to acquire the much-valued English. In this situation, it must be emphasised, the schools served as a mechanism for furthering a pre-existing cultural trend, not as a primary cause of that trend. Most Irish peasants wanted their children to speak and read English, and the schools were therefore in support of, not in opposition to, the national will.

As for the commissioners, did they plot to destroy the Irish language? Hardly. They were not hostile so much as unaware. Until the late nineteenth century the rules of the national system concerning the use of Irish were noteworthy for their virtual non-existence. There was no rule against its use, but hardly anyone seems to have even considered that it might be a useful medium of education. On only three occasions between 1831 and 1870 did the commissioners deal with the Irish language, twice in relation to individual schools. Only during the mid-1850s, when a strong case was made for its use in Irish-speaking areas by one of the head inspectors, was the issue discussed on a policy level. Nothing was done, however, and even the inspector later became convinced that a knowledge of Irish was not necessary for teachers in Irish-speaking districts. In doing nothing about the language the commissioners were not making a strenuous assault on Irish but were following the educational line of least resistance. It was the easiest to follow because it was the course of action most acceptable to the Irish people.

[1] Cf. above, iv, 383–7, 420–23.

CHAPTER XXVII

Administration and the public services, 1800–70

R. B. McDOWELL

THE union, it was believed, would prove the harbinger of change in Ireland, but during the debates on the measure in the British and Irish parliaments and in the correspondence of experienced officials over the terms of union, little or nothing was said about administrative reorganisation. 'Those who contrived the union', Clare's successor as lord chancellor indignantly wrote, 'seem to have thought only of carrying that measure, without considering how the machine was to work afterwards.'[1] But some remodelling of the administrative structure was almost bound to follow the union. Obviously the existence in a united kingdom of separate departments performing similar functions was likely to arouse critical comment. Moreover, the union was carried at a time when the administrative reform movement in Britain was well under way. During the American war of independence rising taxation and the belief that the influence of the crown had increased and should be reduced had given a powerful impetus to the economical reform movement. As Burke, with a grasp of administrative practicalities and sparkling humour, demonstrated, economical reform meant rationalisation and promoted efficiency. As the influence of the executive in parliament was being weakened, public opinion was becoming more powerful, better informed, and more sensitive than ever to the cost of government (tending to display in fact what Castlereagh, a confirmed administrator, once termed 'an ignorant impatience to be relieved from the pressure of taxation').[2] Moreover, the business habits and the urge towards technological improvement bred by the new industrialism influenced administrative standards. Ireland during the latter years of the eighteenth century was not unaffected by the administrative reform movement, but vested interests were strong and the Irish administration, which was expected by the British government to control the Irish parliament, was naturally reluctant to take any steps that would weaken its influence.

A few months after the union a new administration took office in Ireland. The new lord lieutenant was the earl of Hardwicke, a public-spirited nobleman

[1] *Fortescue MSS*, viii, 25.   [2] *Hansard 1*, xxxii, 45 (13 Feb. 1816).

who was very conscious that he possessed administrative standards above those current in Ireland. His chief secretary was Charles Abbot, an administrative reformer who had introduced the first census act, taken steps to improve the publication of the statutes, and acted as chairman of a committee of inquiry into the finances. According to his step-brother, Jeremy Bentham, Abbot had

more talent than all the tories put together. His finance reports are the first of their kind; their order and method are admirable; yet it is well he is not in office, he would do nothing but mischief, he has no relish for physical science, for nothing but grimgibber.[1]

Abbot was certainly not a thoroughgoing utilitarian but during the six months he spent in Dublin he attempted to survey systematically all the aspects of the administration. He paid great attention to the revenue departments, recommending the adoption of British methods, and he claimed that

the frauds long extensively practised upon the quays of Dublin were greatly checked, and a stricter discipline established throughout this department, where, by the confession of all the principal commissioners, taken down by myself in writing, it had been shamefully and corruptly relaxed.[2]

While the viceroy and chief secretary were busily engaged in planning, studying, and improving the administration, they became involved in a somewhat acrimonious controversy with the home secretary. Portland, who was home secretary at the time of union, seems to have suggested that the lord lieutenancy might be abolished—a suggestion that Hardwicke, who had recently arrived in Ireland, dismissed as impossible and impolitic.[3]

Shortly afterwards Portland's successor Pelham (home secretary 1801–3) put forward a plan for reorganising the administration of Ireland. He suggested that all the military and financial departments should be placed under British supervision, the lord lieutenant being left with the responsibility for the maintenance of law and order. The office of chief secretary would become superfluous, the home secretary supervising Irish affairs and taking charge of Irish business in parliament. The reaction of the lord lieutenant and chief secretary to this scheme was, as might be expected, unfavourable. Attacking it they employed an argument that would soon be considered outmoded and improper. They pointed out that generally speaking the lord lieutenant ought to control Irish patronage. He had the necessary local knowledge, and 'a lord lieutenant with contracted and enfeebled powers' could scarcely 'soothe or allay the bitter tempers, party animosities, and divisions of the inhabitants'.[4] Pelham, who was not a very forceful politician, did not press his plan, and nothing came of another suggestion for reorganising the Irish administration on its highest level, put forward by Redesdale, the lord chancellor. He thought

---

[1] Jeremy Bentham, *Works*, ed. John Bowring (11 vols, London, 1838–43), x, 121.
[2] *Colchester corr.*, i, 281. [3] Above, pp 1–2.
[4] *Colchester corr.*, i, 309.

the chief secretary should be in charge of the financial administration of Ireland, and that there ought to be a second secretary, 'an Englishman, who would come to Ireland before the meeting of parliament, receive all the chief secretary's plans and orders for conducting the government during his absence, wait his return . . . and then return to England to carry to ministers the chief secretary's plans and views, and to execute his orders in England. . . . This country will not be well governed until governed by English minds'.[1]

Abbot, though very keen on administrative reorganisation, was chief secretary for only nine months, and his eight immediate successors, who held the chief-secretaryship on an average for sixteen months each, seem to have been concerned themselves with routine problems rather than with projects for large-scale reorganisation. But other forces were working to modify the administrative structure. Even before the union the king had tried to ensure that units on the Irish military establishment should conform in their training and discipline to the British military pattern. In 1798 his son, the duke of York, was appointed commander-in-chief. The duke had not been a conspicuously successful commander in the field but as a military administrator he was conscientious, competent, and eager to encourage professional efficiency by concentrating military patronage in the hands of the commander-in-chief. Naturally then, with the union the lord lieutenant's share in military patronage, so far as the regular army was concerned, vanished, the duke of York merely making the easy promise that he would try to meet the lord lieutenant's wishes.[2] Immediately after the union Irish and British military finances were consolidated; the Irish ordnance was 'consolidated with the British into one system', under the British master-general.[3] The judge advocate-general of Great Britain was given a new commission authorising him to take cognizance of court martial proceedings in Ireland, and when in 1820 the pre-union Irish judge advocate-general at last retired, the British judge advocate-general appointed a deputy for Ireland.

On their arrival in Ireland, Hardwicke and Abbot inquired into the working of the Irish barrack board, with painful results.[4] Its accounts were in arrears and it was rumoured that Lord Tyrawley, the chief commissioner, who, 'from a very moderate beginning',[5] had become a large landowner, had prospered at the public expense. Tyrawley was persuaded to resign, and the Irish barrack board was placed under the supervision of the British barrack master general. This step annoyed the lord lieutenant, who thought that his deputy, Quin John Freeman, would not be able to supervise properly the Irish department and argued with some vehemence that 'the transferring the whole of the patronage of the department to the barrack master in England will deprive the Irish government of the means of obliging many Irish interests, as well as many

[1] *Fortescue MSS*, viii, 26.   [2] Above, p. 2.
[3] *Colchester corr.*, i, 292.   [4] Above, iv, 200, 698.
[5] *Colchester corr.*, i, 289.

meritorious officers'.[1] Hardwicke's pessimism was justified. Freeman was unable to supervise efficiently a large department, working under wartime strain. Barrack masters' accounts were carelessly kept; some neglected their duties and some had corrupt relations with contractors for repairs and supplies. As a remedy for this state of affairs the Irish barrack department was placed under the control of the ordnance department in 1822, and immediately afterwards its establishment was reorganised. In the previous year the Irish commissariat was fused with the British, and with all the other Irish military departments integrated into the British administration, naturally enough the department for auditing Irish military accounts was abolished in 1822, it being enacted that military accounts in Ireland should be audited by the secretary at war.

By the early 1820s the process of consolidating the British and Irish financial departments was also well under way, partly as a result of parliamentary pressure. During the war public opinion was not only aware of the burden of taxation but very sensitive to the cost of collection, and in the house of commons politicians belonging to opposing groups vied with one another in their anxiety to reform the Irish financial administration. Sir John Newport, a whig, referred to 'the want of arrangement which prevailed in the collection of its [Ireland's] revenues' and declared that it was necessary 'to adopt ... the same excellent mode and plan' that existed in England. John Foster, a more conservative politician, for many years chancellor of the Irish exchequer, was unsparing in drawing attention to the defects in the system—he pointed out that in one day twenty to thirty tons of wine had been taken from the quay in Dublin without paying duty and that there was 'scarcely a distiller in Dublin who has not openly and honestly avowed to me that he has defrauded the revenue'.[2] In 1804 a statutory commission was created to inquire into the emoluments in certain government departments in Ireland. This commission, which concentrated on the revenue departments, carried out a most systematic inquiry. Returns were demanded, a number of officials had to answer questionnaires, and in addition many had to give verbal evidence on which they were often cross-examined. The commissioners seemed to have had a grim satisfaction in displaying in detail in their reports how the departments functioned, with full emphasis on the administrative anomalies and human frailties that they discovered. By the time the commission finished its work in 1830, one of the principal reasons for maintaining separate financial departments in Ireland was disappearing. At the time of the union it could be argued that to require Ireland, which had a national debt in proportion to its resources considerably smaller than the British, to merge its finances with those of Great Britain would be unfair, and the continuance of different systems of taxation seemed a good reason for maintaining separate financial departments. But by

[1] Hardwicke to Addington, 22 July 1803 (B.L., Add. MS 35772).
[2] *Hansard 1*, iv, 9 (13 Mar. 1805); vii, 35, 43 (7 May 1806).

1811 the national debts stood in the same ratio to each other that had been anticipated in the act of union, and in 1816–17 their finances were consolidated.[1] This had the immediate result that the treasuries of the two countries were fused, one treasury board becoming responsible for the finances of the United Kingdom. This meant in practice that the British treasury was placed in control of the Irish financial departments. The Irish treasury, as has been pointed out was an inert department. The British treasury was already developing a tradition and technique that would enable it to exercise considerable control over the working of other departments, and it had become a persistent agent of administrative reform. Efficiency and economy were its ideals, and in any official sphere in which it was empowered to act, it tried to enforce the simple rules that a departmental establishment should be fixed in accordance with its responsibilities, that official duties should be defined, and that official remuneration should be fixed in relation to the work to be done. Sinecures, the employment of deputies, fees, and reversions were, of course, to be swept away.

The Irish financial departments, to some extent insulated from the new reforming currents by distance from London, were suddenly exposed to the full force of metropolitan administrative idealism. Soon after the new treasury board was constituted a group of customs and excise officials were sent to Ireland to investigate the working of the Irish departments. They quickly came to the conclusion that too many officials were employed and that administrative standards were slack (for instance, landing officers at Dublin habitually came on duty scandalously late). At this stage the Irish revenue commissioners, rather pathetically, produced a series of suggestions for reorganisation, which in fact underlined the need for reform. In 1821 a second statutory commission of inquiry into the Irish revenue departments was constituted. It sat for eight years and produced twenty-two reports. In its second report it recommended that the Irish customs and excise departments should be fused with the British, and this was implemented in 1823.[2] Once the major financial departments were consolidated, the remaining sections of the Irish financial system were soon absorbed by their British equivalents. Two Irish departments were doomed by the reports of the commission of 1821, the post office and the stamp office. The Irish post office had been in some respects an enterprising department. Between 1797 and 1822 the number of post towns had increased by 60 per cent; the department had endeavoured from about 1790 to substitute mail coaches for carts, and after 1815 it had used 'bians' on the more difficult roads of the south and west. But the two postmasters general, who were at the head of the office, were both official absentees, issuing instructions (which could be contradictory) to the secretary from their country seats. Officials were allowed to remain in office when past their work, there was carelessness over mail coach contracts, the financial checks were defective, and franking was permitted on

[1] Above, pp 62–3.　　[2] 4 Geo. IV, c. 23 (2 May 1823).

a scandalously lavish scale. The commission recommended fusion with the British post office, and in 1831 it was enacted that there should be one post-master general for the United Kingdom.[1] Immediately afterwards an expert in detecting official irregularities was placed in charge of the office and a period of brisk reorganisation began. Deplorable administrative behaviour was discovered to be prevalent in the stamp office. The chief commissioner, having got into pecuniary difficulties and persuaded his subordinates to back his bills, was living on the Continent to avoid his creditors. The secretary was frequently absent from his office; the head of the Dublin warehouse and his deputy were most irregular in their attendance and frequently absent from the office; the accounts of the Dublin distributor of stamps were in hopeless confusion, and it was clear he owed the office a very large sum of money. The treasury acted promptly on receiving the commission's report. Some officials were at once dismissed and the stamp commissioners themselves removed from office, the administration of the department being taken over by a group of civil servants until in 1827 the stamp commissioners for Great Britain were constituted stamp commissioners for the United Kingdom.[2] In the same year the land revenues of the crown in Ireland were placed under the management of the commissioners of woods and forests, who, incidentally, took control of that historic Irish office, the quit-rent office.

The effort to achieve administrative economy and efficiency, which was growing in strength during the first three decades of the nineteenth century, led, as has been shown, to the elimination of a number of Irish government departments. Even when their duties continued to be performed by United Kingdom departments there was a reduction in the number of officials employed in Ireland. It must be added that during these decades *laissez-faire*, a powerful, coherent, and compelling system of economic doctrine, was beginning to dominate British thinking not only on economic issues, but on a wide range of social problems. *Laissez-faire*, with its continuous emphasis on making the most effective use of resources, automatically encouraged administrative reform. To an adherent of *laissez-faire*, administrative reform not only cut the cost of government but also lessened the danger of state intervention in the community's life. Paradoxically, however, it was during the very era when, theoretically, state intervention was being restrained within the narrowest limits and private enterprise emphatically admired and trusted, that the state began to expand its activities. Economic expansion and change were creating problems that it was believed could be dealt with only by government action. This was especially so in Ireland; Irish conditions, it was widely held both in Ireland and Great Britain, demanded an unusual degree of state interference, even in the economic sphere.

However, the form in which the nineteenth-century state first enlarged the range of its activities in Ireland could not be criticised even by the upholders of

---

[1] 1 Will. IV, c. 8 (11 Mar. 1831).   [2] 7 & 8 Geo. IV, c. 55 (2 July 1827).

laissez-faire. It was universally agreed that the state was responsible for the preservation of law and order, and at the beginning of the nineteenth century a combination of sedition, agrarian discontent, faction fighting, and general lawlessness was producing grave disorders in wide areas of rural Ireland.[1] The police, appointed and managed by the counties, were ineffective. The constables were comparatively few in number, scattered, and often of poor calibre. As for the local magistrates they were amateurs who 'could not be expected to devote the whole of their time to the public service'.[2] The government in the past had tried to deal with serious disorder by legislation that increased penalties and enlarged the powers of the magistracy. But Peel, who became chief secretary in 1812, soon came to the conclusion that what was essential was an effective police force.[3] He began by sending to disturbed areas paid officials who were technically justices of the peace but were expected to be continuously engaged in stamping out crime. 'Their minds', he pointed out, 'being wholly turned to one employment, they became, of course, more skilled in the mode of detecting and apprehending offenders' than the unpaid justices of the peace, and in addition they had 'no local allurements or interests to sway their judgement'.[4] The success of this experiment encouraged Peel to make legislative provision for the employment of police magistrates paid and appointed by the government. The peace preservation act of 1814[5] empowered the lord lieutenant to proclaim a district as being in a state of disturbance. In such an area the lord lieutenant could appoint 'a chief magistrate of police' with the powers of a justice of the peace, with a clerk, a chief constable, and a force of sub-constables. Peel indignantly repudiated the suggestion that the government's aim was 'to multiply the means of patronage', explaining that he constables were to be selected from a list of discharged N.C.Os. who could produce 'the strongest certificates of personal ability, good conduct, and character', and he argued that the cost of the force, which fell on the proclaimed area, might induce 'the inhabitants of the neighbouring districts to unite, and to act with energy, for the preservation of the peace, in order that they might escape the tax'.[6] The detachments serving under the police magistrates formed the peace preservation force, and it soon proved its worth in disturbed areas. Some years after its foundation an attempt was made to reform the baronial police by giving the government a measure of control over them. In 1822 the lord lieutenant was empowered to appoint a chief constable for each barony, to direct the justices of the peace to nominate a sufficient number of constables, and, if they failed to do so, to make the nominations himself. The force so raised was to be equipped by the government at the expense of the county.[7] The lord lieutenant was also empowered to appoint four inspectors general of constabulary and (in 1828) to move constables out

---

[1] Above, pp 56–8.   [2] *Hansard 1*, xxviii, 170 (23 June 1814).   [3] Above, pp 59–60.
[4] *Hansard 1*, xxviii, 171 (23 June 1814).   [5] 54 Geo. III, c. 131 (25 July 1814).
[6] *Hansard 1*, xxix, 336–7 (18 Nov. 1814).   [7] 3 Geo. IV, c. 103 (1 Aug. 1822).

of their own county.[1] The appointment of stipendary magistrates and police reform were accompanied by an effort to improve the quality of the unpaid magistracy—the justices of the peace. When Ponsonby was lord chancellor during the short-lived whig administration of 1806-7 he had begun a revision of the magistracy, requesting peers and privy counsellors to give him confidential reports on persons they thought unsuitable to be on the commission of the peace, and in 1822 Wellesley embarked on a systematic revision of the names of those holding the commission. About the same time a check was imposed on individual failings and eccentricities by the development, under government encouragement, of the practice of holding petty sessions. This meant that cases would be decided by at least two justices of the peace sitting together, and the petty sessions act of 1827[2] provided that the sessions should be held at fixed times, and that there should be a clerk and fixed fees.

In another area connected with the preservation of law and order, prisons, the technique of employing government agents to assist and stimulate local authorities was employed.[3] There was at the beginning of the century considerable interest in penal reform, and R. B. Sheridan, influenced by the reports of 1805, and of the Irish inspector general for prisons in 1808, raised the question in the house of commons and secured the appointment of a committee of inquiry. As a result of its work a prisons act was passed in 1810,[4] the first of a series of measures consolidated in the great Irish prisons act of 1826,[5] a measure of 142 clauses, which *inter alia* embodied a detailed code of regulations. The object of this measure was to ensure uniform and efficient standards of prison administration. Prison officials were absolutely forbidden to receive fees and could be summarily dismissed by the court of king's bench if found guilty of any offence. There was to be a rigorous division in all jails between male and female prisoners, and in county prisons and houses of correction there was to be a more complete system of segregation—between debtors, vagrants, persons convicted of misdemeanour or felony, and persons awaiting trial—and there were elaborate provisions for preserving the prisoners' health and cleanliness.[6] The grand jury remained responsible for prison administration within its county but was to act through a board of superintendents, of which half were to be justices of the peace. Plans of prisons had to be approved by the lord lieutenant; there were to be government depots or hulks for convicts awaiting transportation. The lord lieutenant was to appoint two inspectors general of prisons who were required to visit all Irish jails regularly and report on their condition, and were empowered to report prison officials guilty of misconduct to the king's bench and to direct, if necessary, that prisoners should be supplied with certain requisites at the expense of the county. The inspectors general were active and alert, and the annual reports they published,

[1] 9 Geo. IV, c. 63 (15 July 1828). [2] 7 & 8 Geo. IV, c. 67 (2 July 1827).
[3] Above, iv, 710-12. [4] 50 Geo. III, c. 103 (20 June 1810).
[5] 7 Geo. IV, c. 74 (31 May 1826). [6] Above, p. 211.

detailed and readable, were sure to influence local authorities. They were strongly opposed to 'tyranny or over-indulgence'. They wanted prison governors to be gentlemen, and turnkeys to be put into uniform and given clearly demarcated duties. Prisoners were to be detained in healthy surroundings and compelled to observe an industrious and strictly disciplined routine.

Writing a quarter of a century after their office was instituted, the inspectors general drew a grim picture of the condition of nearly all Irish prisons about 1820. 'They were for the most part scenes of filth, fraud, and vice, with scarcely one good resident officer, without accommodation, clothing, classification, employment, inspection, school instruction, order, or cleanliness.'[1] Spirits were being openly sold in jail, the expenditure on food in some prisons was so high that the prisoners' families were being fed on the surplus of food issued to the prisoners, and prisoners were even allowed what was called 'street liberty', being able to go to work daily from the jail. By 1845 the inspectors general considered that the administrative evils had been to a great extent corrected and they were eager to raise the standards of prison administration. One sign of this was the amount of prison building that marked the first half of the nineteenth century. New prisons were built and old ones enlarged and improved, with the result that the jail was often one of the most impressive architectural features of an Irish town. Prison planning was of course influenced by penology. By the 1830s penal reformers were vigorously debating which was the better system, 'entire separation' or silence. The former was officially approved for Ireland in 1840 but could not be put into operation in many jails because of insufficient cells. Each system was later to be strongly criticised, but at least the adoption of either encouraged the provision of a separate cell for each prisoner, which was probably all to the good.

Law and order was a sphere in which state intervention was taken for granted even by those who wished a large share of the responsibility for preservation of the peace to be left to the local authorities. Economic life on the other hand was a sphere in which the state was to refrain from meddling, and it is interesting to notice that in the 1820s a government agency, the linen board, established by the Irish parliament to encourage and control an important Irish industry, was abolished. In spite of a few administrative scandals, largely due to the fact that the board was composed of unpaid trustees whose attendance at meetings was erratic, it functioned satisfactorily enough, and in 1822 a parliamentary commission drew attention to the fact that the board had 'given scope to experiments beyond what individuals in the trade, without their encouragement, would have risked'.[2] But it was argued in the commons that the linen board was both shackling private initiative and spending public money on a successful industry that might well be left to stand on its own feet. In 1827 the

---

[1] *Prisons of Ireland: twenty-fourth report of the inspectors general*, p. 8 [697], H.C. 1846, xx, 264.

[2] *Report from the select committee on the laws which regulate the linen trade of Ireland*, p. 5, H.C. 1822 (560), vii, 453.

board's grant was sharply cut and in 1828 the board was abolished.[1] The other agency for encouraging economic advance set up by the Irish parliament, the directors of inland navigation, surprisingly enough, managed to survive to the beginning of the 1830s. In 1813 they were entrusted with the completion of the Grand Canal, the Grand Canal Company being hopelessly insolvent, and having extended the canal to the Shannon they handed it over to the old company's debenture holders. They also managed a few short waterways, and in 1829 a parliamentary committee, having commented on the amount they had spent and on what a high proportion of their annual grant was being expended on their own salaries and their Dublin office, recommended they should be abolished.

The state was in other directions intervening in the economy. In 1809 Sir Arthur Wellesley, the chief secretary, was concerned over the probable want of flax seed in Ireland at a time when linen and hemp were essential war materials. He suggested a commission should be appointed to inquire into the possibility of large-scale drainage operations, and in the summer of 1809 such a commission was constituted by statute.[2] The lord lieutenant was empowered to appoint five unpaid commissioners who were to conduct an inquiry into the extent of the Irish bogs and the feasibility of draining them. The commissioners immediately after their appointment set up their headquarters in the Dublin Society's house in Hawkins Street, arranged for the society's assistant secretary to act as their secretary, and built up a staff of nine engineers (of whom two, Richard Griffith and Alexander Nimmo, were later to have distinguished careers in state employment), forty surveyors, and a number of staff-men, chainmen, and labourers. The commissioners worked for four-and-a-half years and produced very full reports relating to over a million acres, which it was said showed that there was in Ireland an immense amount of land 'easily reclaimable, convertible to the production of grain almost without limit'. But the commission, having provided a useful survey of the bogs, did not suggest further state intervention. In fact it firmly recommended that the improvement of the bogs should be left to private enterprise, hoping that at the end of the war Ireland would become a field for British investment. The only step the commission recommended the state to take was to set up 'a commission of perambulation' to determine the boundaries of estates, since the fear of litigation might discourage proprietors from starting drainage schemes.

The post-war slump affected Ireland adversely: there was widespread distress, advertised by agrarian disturbance, and state intervention seemed to be imperative. Two bodies, composed of unpaid commissioners nominated by the lord lieutenant, were set up: the commissioners for advancing money from the consolidated fund—who had £250,000 at their disposal—appointed in 1817,[3] and a commission to advance loans to merchants and manufacturers who were

---

[1] 9 Geo. IV, c. 62 (15 July 1828).   [2] 49 Geo. III, c. 102 (15 June 1809).
[3] 57 Geo. III, c. 34 (16 June 1817).

temporarily distressed, appointed in 1820.[1] The commissioners for advancing money from the consolidated fund employed a small staff, a solicitor, a secretary, and inspecting engineers, and they seem to have closely scrutinised the projects put up to them by individuals or local bodies. However, they advanced a considerable amount of money for a variety of objects. They were especially ready to assist schemes for improving communications by building roads and bridges. These schemes not only provided employment in poor areas but it was hoped they would promote economic development by opening up the country. The state made another specialised effort to help the poor areas by encouraging the fishing industry. In 1819 a fishery board, composed of unpaid commissioners appointed by the lord lieutenant, was set up and given an annual grant.[2] It had a small staff, including local inspectors and four inspectors general, and it paid bounties on boat-building and catches, made loans for boats, built small piers, and employed engineers to make a survey of the coast. The board considered that helping a struggling industry with great potentialities was of the greatest value, and in 1829 pointed out that the number of Irish fishermen had almost doubled since it had begun operations. Its critics thought that the bounty system, already going out of fashion, was attracting excessive labour to the industry, and in 1830 the board was abolished.

The ambiguous attitude of public and parliamentary opinion towards state intervention in Irish economic life was well summed up in the report of a parliamentary committee published in 1819. The committee explained that they found themselves 'in a great measure controlled by the unquestionable principle that legislative interference in the operations of human industry is as much as possible to be avoided'. But they went on to explain 'there are nevertheless considerable exceptions to such a rule, either when injurious artificial impediments are to be removed or where any branch of national industry which cannot in its commencement be without great difficulty carried on by individual exertion and solely by private funds may be encouraged and facilitated by parliamentary regulation'.[3]

Education was another sphere in which the desirability of state intervention was taken for granted even by supporters of *laissez-faire*, the education of the poor being regarded as a social service, which would benefit the community in general and which it was felt the state ought to promote. The Irish parliament had made grants to institutions that provided primary education, and after the union the practice was continued by the imperial parliament. This meant that large sums of public money were being spent by private societies that were not subject to inspection. In 1811 a commission of inquiry into Irish education recommended that a permanent commission

---

[1] 1 Geo. IV, c. 39 (8 July 1820).

[2] 59 Geo. III, c. 109 (12 July 1819).

[3] *Second report from the select committee on the state of . . . the labouring poor in Ireland*, p. 95, H.C. 1819 (409), viii, 459.

should be constituted, empowered to set up and supervise a sufficient number of primary schools 'to gratify the desire of information which manifests itself among the lower classes of the people'.[1] In 1825 another commission on education emphatically reiterated this recommendation, and a similar scheme was suggested by a select committee of the house of commons in 1829. But by the beginning of the 1830s little had been done. In 1831 a board composed of *ex officio* and nominated members, usually known as the commissioners of education, was constituted, with a very restricted sphere of responsibility, being given very limited supervisory powers over some of the endowed schools that provided education at a secondary level. At the end of the 1820s the grants for primary education began to be rapidly reduced, as catholic opinion, which was becoming more self-assured and vocal, resented the payment of public money to societies that were under protestant control.

By 1830, with the civil service largely reformed, with administrative techniques improved and improving, and with a vast amount of factual information accumulated by inquiries into different aspects of the community's life, the state stood poised and ready for increased activity. That the first three decades of the century had been by no means a static era is illustrated even in the limited sphere of Irish administrative history. But reform tended to be piecemeal and empirical. From 1830, however, the momentum of change accelerated. Reformers had settled their principles and worked out their programmes. Public opinion expected political action to produce solutions for a whole range of acute problems. With a demand for new measures there came a dramatic change of government. In November 1830 almost a quarter of a century of tory political predominance ended, a whig cabinet under Lord Grey took office, and for the following ten years, with a brief interval, the whigs were in power. The whigs were, of course, very far from being radical, doctrinaire reformers. Temperamentally the true whig had a distaste for extremes and prided himself on his moderation and common sense. The whigs were, however, fair-minded, liberal, tolerant, and receptive. Their commitment to catholic emancipation, which had provided a party suffering badly from dissensions with a unifying principle, had kept them out of power for years. It had also increased their interest in Ireland. Some of the leading members of the party—George Ponsonby, Lord Fitzwilliam, William Conyngham Plunket, Sir John Newport, Thomas Spring-Rice, Lord Duncannon—were closely connected with Ireland. The *Edinburgh Review*, the great organ of intellectual whiggery, had during the 1820s steadily stressed the importance of the 'condition of Ireland' question. In grappling with Irish problems they put their trust in a blend of common sense and fair play. Catholic emancipation, the discouragement of subdivision of farms, and efficient and impartial administration would, they believed, make Ireland a contented part of the United Kingdom. In retrospect they can be

[1] *Fourteenth report of the commissioners of the board of education, in Ireland*, p. 5, H.C. 821 (744), xi, 147.

criticised for over-optimism or for basing their policy on an oversimplification of the whole situation. But what cannot be denied is the energy with which they went to work. Since they were confident that vigorous and rational, if limited, state intervention in carefully selected areas of Irish life would produce most beneficial results, their policy led to a considerable extension of the Irish administrative machine.

During its first year in office, Lord Grey's administration, in a bold drive to improve Ireland, created two new departments, entrusted with heavy responsibilities in very different spheres, the board of works and the commissioners of national education. In 1831 a new Irish board of works, composed of three commissioners, was set up.[1] It took over from the existing board of works responsibility for constructing and maintaining government buildings and was empowered to make loans to public bodies and individuals for public works or private improvements. As time went on its functions multiplied: it was given important duties under the drainage acts; it was made responsible for works on the Shannon to improve navigation and prevent flooding; between 1842 and 1869 it was responsible for enforcing the regulations on river and deep-sea fishing under the fishery acts. The department between 1831 and 1914 advanced £49,000,000, a remarkably large sum, by nineteenth-century standards, for the state to invest in economic development, and it seems to have made a substantial contribution to the improvement of the country. But its work—except during the famine—was not spectacular, and it did not evolve a long-term strategy for the provision of state assistance to Irish economic development. Probably the commissioners were overburdened by their multifarious duties, and the fact that the department was under the treasury meant close and continuous control over its activities.[2]

In the same month as the board of works was constituted, steps were taken to set up another board whose work was to have far-reaching effects, the commissioners of national education. An unpaid board, carefully balanced denominationally, it was empowered to administer an annual grant for primary education in Ireland. If an individual or committee was prepared to meet at least part of the cost of building a school and contribute towards its upkeep, the board might assist in its building and maintenance, provide cheap textbooks, and make a grant towards the teacher's salary. It was hoped to solve the religious problem, which had loomed so large in the discussions on primary education in the 1820s, by laying down that in the schools supported by the board there should be united secular and separate religious instruction. The application of this neat formula was to lead to acrimonious disputes over whether the two forms of instruction should be separated, and if it was possible, where the boundary between them lay. But as the century progressed nearly all primary schools in Ireland became connected with the board; the fact that in practice

---

[1] 1 & 2 Will. IV, c. 33 (15 Oct. 1831).
[2] Above, pp 207–9.

all, or nearly all, the pupils in a vast majority of the schools belonged to the same denomination made the system widely acceptable.[1]

The board went to work with a sense of mission and soon built up a great department with a central staff and inspectorate (by 1914 over seventy strong) that spread its influence throughout the country. An unpaid board of busy men would have found it very difficult to manage such a large department in contact with so many units (by 1914 the national schools numbered 8,200). Though the board supervised the general working of the system, routine administration was directed by the resident commissioner. The national education commissioners had a somewhat anomalous relationship with the government. The board's revenue was voted by parliament, the staff of the office and the inspectors were civil servants, and it was accepted from the outset (and legalised in 1855) that the board should not change any fundamental regulations without the sanction of the lord lieutenant. On the other hand, since the members of the board were unpaid and in practice irremovable, they possessed a considerable degree of independence when it came to dealing with the Irish government. In its regulations the board emphasised the simple virtues of diligence, precision, tidiness, and obedience. The system, with its emphasis on the elements of a relatively simple, carefully graded curriculum being firmly instilled into the mind of the pupils by teachers who were expected to be dedicated and were kept up to the mark by inspection, laid the foundation for much intellectual effort and played a great part in equipping Irishmen for the battle of life.

There was still another way in which the whigs attempted to influence for the better the whole tone of Irish society. It was by the strengthening of the agencies of law and order. For the whigs the maintenance of law and order in Ireland had a twofold significance. It was an essential element in building up conditions that would encourage economic development; and impartiality in the administration of the law would create throughout society confidence in the established order. What was obviously needed was an impartial magistracy in the counties and a police force uninfluenced by local pressures or political partisanship, and quickly responsive to government direction. In 1836 two police forces were created, the Dublin Metropolitan Police, responsible for Dublin and the surrounding countryside, and the Irish constabulary, stationed throughout the rest of Ireland. The Dublin Metropolitan Police was commanded by two commissioners—usually retired army officers—appointed by the government, all its other officers being promoted from the ranks. The D.M.P., with its men recruited on very high physical standards, was an impressive body of men, closely resembling an English civic police force. The constabulary, a much larger force, was under the command of an inspector general, almost always an army officer (the first two inspectors general were in fact distinguished Peninsular war veterans) who was expected to keep in close

[1] Above, pp 532–6.

touch with the Irish executive. The men, carefully recruited, were generally of good farming stock, drilled on military lines, clothed in a uniform resembling that of the rifle brigade, and well disciplined—the first inspector general produced a detailed manual covering the work of the force, which, much amended, remained in use throughout its history. Though a high proportion of the constabulary was stationed in small barracks scattered throughout Ireland, a punctilious performance of its duties was insisted on. From the force's formation most of its officers were directly commissioned, entering and being trained as cadets. In time this policy was modified to the extent that half the vacancies in the rank of district inspector (the title before late 1883 was 'sub-inspector') were filled by promotion from the ranks, but the high proportion of directly commissioned officers, together with the military element in its training, had an undoubted effect on the force, giving the men a fine bearing and endowing them with a remarkable readiness to act with cohesion and courage in daunting circumstances. Besides performing routine police work, the constabulary from the beginning coped with sectarian rioting and agrarian disturbances. Twice during the nineteenth century it was faced with armed rebellion, in 1848 and 1867, its services during the fenian rising earning it the title 'Royal'. As time went on the constabulary, a body of well trained, disciplined men stationed throughout the country, were used by other government departments, an early and striking example being their employment with great success as emumerators for the census of 1841. The practice also soon developed of the constabulary making regular reports from all over Ireland to Dublin Castle, providing the government with a valuable means of feeling the pulse of the country.

In 1836 the whigs took another step by which they hoped to strengthen respect for law and order by ensuring its efficient and impartial administration. The constabulary act of that year[1] empowered the lord lieutenant to appoint magistrates to reside in such districts as he thought fit. These 'resident magistrates' had the powers of a justice of the peace and were full-time paid officials. Soon sixty had been appointed and were distributed all over the country. Their principal duty was attending petty sessions and setting standards for the unpaid magistracy, sometimes by their professional training as barristers, soldiers, or police officers, and always by growing experience and common sense.

The other whig measures that were to lay the foundations for the development of local government and the social services in Ireland, the municipal reform bill and the Irish poor law bill, were both based on recent British legislation that reflected the influence of utilitarianism in politics.[2]

In 1833 a group of young whig barristers was appointed to investigate the Irish boroughs. Their reports, objective, systematically arranged, and packed

[1] 6 Will. IV, c. 13 (20 May 1836).   [2] Above, pp 215–17.

with damning detail, provided the government with a justification for the Irish municipal reform bill it introduced in 1835, which was placed on the statute book, after strenuous struggles, in 1840.[1] Based on the English municipal reform act of 1835,[2] it was a thoroughgoing and rational measure. The old borough corporations were all swept away but ten boroughs continued to be corporate towns with severely functional constitutions, their governing bodies, which were given wide powers, being elected by the ratepayers. Any town with a population of over 3,000 could apply for a charter but only Wexford availed itself of this provision and joined the original ten corporate towns. Other boroughs could adopt the provisions of the act of 1828 that empowered them to elect a body of commissioners with limited powers in municipal matters. About twenty-five towns formed governing bodies under this act, and a further twenty went on later to bring into force the provisions of a 'revised edition' of the act, which was enacted in 1854 and widely adopted throughout Ireland.[3]

County government was also reformed by the whigs, though less dramatically than borough administration. In the period of post-war economy that followed Waterloo the steady growth of county cess aroused intense criticism and in 1817 it was provided that the justices of the peace should report on presentments before they were placed before the grand jury.[4] This method of controlling county expenditure was elaborated by the act of 1836[5] that set up baronial committees composed of justices of the peace and ratepayers to examine and sanction the plans and estimates—which were to be prepared on clearly defined lines—for public works, before they were voted on by the grand jury. It was also provided that county surveyors were to be appointed by what in practice was a competitive examination, conducted by engineers of some standing. As a result of this legislation corruption and mismanagement were to a great extent eliminated from county administration, being replaced by a cautious respect for the ratepayer's pocket.

Poor law reform was a major subject of political debate in Britain during the first half of the nineteenth century. It was a subject that involved economic, administrative, and ethical problems; and it was widely held that a wrong decision on poor law policy might well inflict a damaging blow on the whole economy. In the discussion on the poor law Ireland was bound to figure. During the eighteenth century there had been a certain amount of both seasonable and permanent migration from Ireland to Britain, and after the union, with the Irish population steadily increasing, Irish emigration stepped up and Irish working-class colonies were formed in the great British cities. An Irish labourer might acquire by residence a 'settlement' in an English parish, and even if he had not a settlement, the alternative to receiving him (and possibly

[1] 3 & 4 Vict., c. 108 (10 Aug. 1840).
[2] 5 & 6 Will. IV, c. 76 (9 Sept. 1835).
[3] 9 Geo. IV, c. 82 (25 July 1828); 17 & 18 Vict., c. 103 (10 Aug. 1854).
[4] 57 Geo. III, c. 107 (11 July 1817).
[5] 6 & 7 Will. IV, c. 116 (20 Aug. 1836).

his family) was to ship him back to Ireland as a vagrant—at the expense of the parish. In 1826 that great and gloomy economic expert Thomas Malthus prophesied before a house of commons committee that the Irish population would continue to grow, that emigration to England would increase, and that the living standards of the English labourer would be forced down to the Irish level; a view dramatically summed up in the formula that the question seemed to be 'whether the wheat-fed population of Great Britain shall or shall not be supplanted by the potato-fed population of Ireland'.[1] When the reform of the English poor law was being discussed in the early 1830s the presence of Irish paupers and beggars (noted for their pertinancy and ingenuity) attracted attention. (A beggar, in *The Pickwick papers*, is one of the few Irish characters in the works of Dickens.)

Another matter also attracted attention: the absence of an Irish poor law. The Irish parliament had, as has been said, refrained from large-scale legislation on poor relief, restricting itself to sanctioning local schemes—a few workhouses and houses of industry. But by the 1830s it was being urged that systematic steps must be taken to cope with the mass of wretchedness in Ireland. Moreover, it was pointed out that the attempt to improve the condition of the English poor through the working of the new poor law of 1834[2] would fail if there was an influx of Irish labour, attracted by the prospect of relief and facilitated by the cheap transport. It was also urged that the introduction of a poor law into Ireland would stimulate Irish economic development, for taxing Irish landowners would provide a disincentive to economic inertia. The existence of a system of poor relief would both minimise the suffering inevitably accompanying the consolidation of agricultural holdings, which agrarian reformers regarded as highly desirable, and by promoting social peace encourage capitalists to invest in Ireland. There was, however, an argument that received considerable support from Irish landowners against the introduction of a poor law. Ireland, it was said, could not afford it. Any attempt to grapple with the problem of Irish poverty by a compulsory rating system would cost far too much. (Malthus, with typical pessimism, said it would absorb all the rental of the country; O'Connell, more cautiously, asserted it would swallow one-third.) Charity, it was said, should be the immediate resort of the destitute; and for long-term solutions reliance should be placed on emigration—state-aided—and economic growth stimulated by the consolidation of holdings, a reduction of county taxation, and a programme of public works. But the argument that a poor law would prove impossibly expensive was weakened by the administrative framework set up by the English poor law act of 1834. The local area for poor law purposes was to be the union, a group of parishes, which meant that the local poor law authority, the guardians, though

[1] *Third report from the select committee on emigration from the United Kingdom*, p. 7, H.C. 1826–7 (550), v, 229.

[2] 4 & 5 Will. IV, c. 76 (14 Aug. 1834).

elected, would be less subject to local pressures than a vestry and would probably usually be fairly large ratepayers. More important was the brake applied by the government-nominated board, the poor law commissioners, with power to supervise and to some extent control the boards of guardians. Centralised supervision, combined with the general acceptance of the principle of 'lesser eligibility', enforced by the workhouse test, would, it was thought, make it possible to combine essential assistance with economical administration.

Even before the reform of the English poor law, M.P.s, English and Irish, were pressing for the introduction of some form of poor relief in Ireland. In May 1833 John Richards, M.P. for Knaresborough, seconded by James Grattan, M.P. for County Wicklow, asked the house to agree to the extension of the Elizabethan poor law to Ireland. Lord Althorp, the leader of the house, probably not ungrateful for an excuse for postponing action, met the motion by agreeing to a suggestion by Sir Robert Peel that before any step was taken an inquiry should be held, and a strong commission, headed by Archbishop Whately, was appointed to inquire into the condition of the Irish poor. It carried out its task with enthusiasm and skill. A number of sub-commissioners were appointed, who toured the country and collected a vast amount of information relating to the management of local charities, the cost of living, and earnings. Much of the evidence given at gatherings of local people to the sub-commissioners was printed verbatim and provided an almost photographic picture of conditions in some areas. While the commission was conducting this great social survey the government was growing impatient, and at the beginning of 1836 Lord John Russell, the home secretary, said he would wind up the commission if it did not soon produce a report. A few months later the commission presented its report, a bold, diffuse, and comprehensive piece of work, recommending the creation of a board to plan and supervise large schemes of national improvement, including the drainage of waste land, road-building, and fencing, and it was to be empowered to permit tenants for life to grant long leases if they included improvement clauses. The board's schemes were to be financed by loans from the board of works and a local rate. Local boards were to be responsible for the care of the infirm, sick, aged, and lunatic poor and would be empowered to compel vagrants to emigrate. These boards were to be supervised by an Irish poor law commission. Emigration from Ireland was to be managed by this commission and the colonial office, and to be financed partly by a national rate and partly by the landlords of the locality from which emigrants went. The report of the commissioners also suggested that the financial powers of the grand juries should be transferred to elected county boards and that a tithe composition scheme should be adopted that, while respecting the financial interests of the tithe owners, would yield a surplus that could be used for charitable purposes.

The commission, in addition to amassing information, had laid down definite lines of action. But it was unfortunate in two respects. Any government might well have hesitated to adopt proposals that demanded complex and controversial legislation and, at the beginning at least, would require considerable advances from the treasury. Lord Melbourne's government, after 1835, was not in a strong parliamentary position; Russell, the home secretary, noted for his fixity of opinion, was convinced they should attempt to perform only a very limited range of functions; and the Irish executive, with other problems on its hands, does not appear to have given much attention to the question. Furthermore, while the commission had been engaged on its great social survey, the new English poor law had been enacted and the system had got under way. The government, therefore, had an alternative to the commission's proposals at hand. The government's inclinations were indicated by the fact that Russell referred the commission's report to English economists, Nassau William Senior and George Cornewall Lewis. Lewis, a strong supporter of the new poor law, pulverised it in a powerful memorandum. What was even more significant, Russell asked George Nicholls, one of the English poor law commissioners, to visit Ireland and inquire into its needs. Nicholls, a pioneer in poor law reform, had a crusading faith in the principles of the new act. Before leaving for Ireland he expressed the view that the act should be extended to Ireland; during the six brisk weeks he spent there he found most people he talked to agreed with him, and on his return he reaffirmed the view he had expressed before leaving for Ireland. Nicolls's report was lucid, assured, and highly practical. He considered a well administered poor law, based on the workhouse test, was the best available remedy. He admitted that it was difficult to make 'the lodgings, the clothing, and the diet of the inmates of an Irish workhouse inferior to those of the Irish peasantry', but he was confident that the rules and discipline imposed would render the house unattractive enough. He thought the commission of inquiry had grossly overestimated the number it had stated of those who required relief. In his opinion the number demanding relief in normal conditions would be about 60,000. Also, he protected the system against strain by recommending that a legal right to relief should not be granted and that relief should be given *only* within the workhouse. He did not expect the introduction of the poor law to work an economic miracle in Ireland. But he thought it would help the country through the transition from an agrarian system characterised by minute holdings to one where farms were large and labourers paid in money wages. He was careful to point out that famine was a contingency 'altogether above the power of a poor law to provide for' but he hoped that, as time went on and standards rose, the Irish peasantry would develop habits of prudence and provide for emergencies.[1]

Even after they had received Nicholls's definite and well defined recommendations, the government as a whole was hesitant. But Russell accepted

[1] George Nicholls, *Three reports . . . to her majesty's principal secretary of state for the home department* (London, 1838), pp 24, 64, 96, 15–16, 37–8.

Nicholls's basic principles and detailed advice wholeheartedly, and in 1837 introduced a bill extending the English poor law to Ireland, which was passed in the following session.[1] The debates on the bill did not follow party lines. As might be expected there were those who were reluctant to grant relief to the able-bodied and those who favoured a degree of outdoor relief. Two important matters of principle were raised. It was suggested that a law of settlement should be introduced into Ireland. This proposal was rejected on the grounds that it would tie the labourer down. It also, of course, might have led to the admission of a right to relief, which the bill, following Nicholls's recommendations, did not grant. The other important question raised was a burning one in England: how extensive were the powers which should be granted to the poor-law commissioners? Lyndhurst in the lords made a vigorous attack on what an eminent lawyer in the twentieth century was to term 'the new despotism'. He complained that the bill was full of blanks to be filled up at the discretion of the commissioners. But as the tory leader in the lords, Wellington, supported the bill, characteristically remarking that it might make Irish landlords manage their properties properly, Lyndhurst's attack was futile. Some years later Daniel O'Connell (who thought 'Ireland was too poor for a poor law') declared that the poor law commissioners were unpopular partly because 'they would not yield to local feelings and circumstances but maintain their own "cast iron" system', and partly because of the 'flippancy and impertinence' they displayed when dealing with boards of guardians.[2]

Once the bill was on the statute book Nicholls was sent over to Ireland to start the system functioning. He was in Ireland for four years, but administrative uniformity was maintained by his being required to submit all regulations requiring the commission's seal to his colleagues in London. (After he left Ireland the Irish poor law was controlled by two of the assistant commissioners, who of course reported to London; in 1845, when the membership of the board was raised from three to four, the additional commissioner was stationed in Ireland.) Nicholls brought with him four assistant commissioners, whom he soon reinforced by the same number of newly recruited Irishmen, and he and his staff went to work with the sustained drive, efficient grasp of detail, and crusading zeal that distinguished so many of the early Victorian administrators. They were working in an administrative vacuum but they were not confronted by the vested interests and habits (Nicholls would certainly say bad habits) bred in England by centuries of poor law administration. Very quickly Ireland was mapped out for poor law purposes, the parishes being grouped in one hundred and thirty unions and provision made for building workhouses in each union and for setting up boards of guardians composed of ratepayers' elected representatives, and of justices of the peace who were to make up one-quarter of the boards' membership. The building of workhouses

[1] 1 & 2 Vict., c. 56 (31 July 1838).
[2] *Hansard 3*, xl, 780 (5 Feb. 1838); lxv, 510 (22 July 1842).

involved the poor law commissioners in humiliating disputes with boards of guardians in which the local authorities triumphed. Logically the workhouses should have been built by the board of works, but it was understandably reluctant to be burdened by an additional duty. So Nicholls engaged an architect and staff to plan and supervise the operation. The architect produced standardised plans for workhouses of different sizes, in Tudor Gothic, a style that it was thought gave a pleasing appearance without being expensive to build.[1] The work went forward briskly but there was carelessness over contracts and some unions complained that they had been saddled with expenses that should not have been incurred. After two independent inquiries had been held, the treasury relieved the unions of some of their liabilities. However, in so far as the poor law commission had blundered it was from excessive eagerness to get the system under way and they made every effort to ensure that the workhouses were used effectively.

The new poor law had scarcely become fully operative before the potato crop failed in 1845, and the results of the famine were so far-reaching that the new poor law, though it provided a useful enough 'ambulance wagon', lost the opportunity of proving itself to be an important factor in Irish economic development. But another department created by the whigs in the 1830s, the ecclesiastical commission, was by a strange chance the administrative ancestor of the land commission, a department that played a decisive part in reshaping the Irish agrarian system. In 1833, in an attempt to deprive the critics of the established church of an easy target, the government set up a board of ecclesiastical commissioners to reorganise and redistribute part of the church's revenues.[2] The commission was composed of the archbishops of Armagh and Dublin, the lord chancellor, four bishops nominated by the crown, and three paid commissioners, of whom one was appointed by the two archbishops and two by the crown. It administered the temporalities of ten dioceses (each of which had been united to a neighbouring diocese) and certain suspended dignities, and it could levy tax on benefices worth more than £300 per annum. It used its revenue to build and repair churches, to augment poorer benefices, and for other ecclesiastical expenses. The commission does not seem to have considered itself a government department, but as the government-nominated commissioners supervised its working and its establishment, it at least considerably resembled one. What perhaps is most interesting about its activities is that it was managing land scattered throughout Ireland and thus training a small nucleus of officials for work in a sphere into which the state would advance towards the close of the century.

In the mid-1840s, the Irish administration, largely the creation of the age of reorganisation and reform that may be said to have begun at the close of the

---

[1] Hundreds of plans were discovered in 1985 in the cellars of the Custom House, Dublin, where they had lain for decades.

[2] 3 & 4 Will. IV, c. 37 (14 Aug. 1833).

eighteenth century, had to face an exceptionally severe test, the great famine. Responsibility for coping with the results of this catastrophe devolved on four departments, the poor law commissioners, the board of works, the commissariat, and the treasury. The poor law commission had been entrusted a few years earlier with the task of dealing with distress and it had just finished building up its machinery when the crisis began. From the beginning the commissioners adhered strictly to a fundamental principle of their system, that relief should be given only in the workhouse, though they encouraged guardians to enlarge their workhouses and erect fever hospitals. Soon the sheer mass of poverty to be relieved over wide areas threw an unendurable strain on parts of the system. Boards of guardians in the west lost heart, ceased to perform their duties, and were replaced by vice-guardians, nominated officials who doggedly carried on. With the workhouses crammed and acute poverty prevalent, the rules in the end were relaxed, and in 1847 the guardians were empowered to grant outdoor relief to the aged, infirm, and sick poor and, with the permission of the board, for limited periods to able-bodied paupers.[1] The board of works also played a large part in relieving destitution. From early in the crisis local bodies were encouraged to suggest public works—usually in practice drainage projects or roads—on which the poor might be employed, and it was the duty of the board of works to plan and supervise these. As the position grew more desperate an increasing number of schemes was initiated. By the beginning of 1847 the board, with a staff expanded to 14,000, was trying to supervise relief schemes all over the country on which hundreds of thousands of labourers were employed. The commissariat was also at work from early in the famine, opening and managing a number of depots from which food was supplied at cost price to local relief committees. It also provided inspecting officers to visit the relief committees and encourage them to keep proper accounts and to act on sound administrative principles.

All this manifold activity was supervised by the treasury. The commissariat was a treasury department, the board of works was under direct treasury control, and the poor law commissioners relied on the treasury for advice on making advances to boards of guardians. In addition the treasury made arrangements for the purchasing, milling, transportation, storage, and distribution of the supplies of corn provided by the government. The position of the treasury throughout the crisis was of enormous significance. Not only did it play an essential coordinating role, but inevitably it exercised a considerable influence over policy. This commanding and strong-willed department exemplified most forcibly the virtues and limitations of the new administrative outlook. The new school of civil servants prided themselves on their diligence, disinterestedness, and devotion to duty. They were profoundly impressed with the importance of seeing that the best use was made of available resources. This meant of course that requests involving expenditure should be carefully

[1] Above, pp 317–18.

scrutinised and that people should not be helped to do what they could accomplish by their own unaided efforts: the state should only intervene when local and individual effort was exhausted. Precipitancy would both interfere detrimentally with the beneficial working of the laws of supply and demand and weaken individual initiative. Charles Trevelyan, who as assistant secretary to the treasury directed much of the government's activity in Ireland, and had considerable influence on policy, was a firm adherent of the *laissez-faire* school. He believed that if the catastrophic situation in Ireland was handled on the right lines society would be reconstructed on a sound basis, and he reflected at the end of the crisis that, as often before, 'Supreme Wisdom has educed permanent good out of transient evil.'[1] He worked incredibly hard, showed remarkable administrative skill in coping with novel problems, inspired his subordinates with his own devotion to duty, and was impervious to local or parliamentary pressures and arguments that conflicted with his own principles. Some may regard the treasury's attitude as narrow and stultifying. But it was based on considered principles and applied consistently. What cannot be denied is how hard the civil servants concerned both in London and Ireland worked to mitigate the disaster—and how often they displayed initiative and courage.

Two important changes in the administrative structure followed on the famine. In 1847 a separate poor law commission for Ireland was created and in 1851 it was made the department responsible for public health.[2] The question of medical relief for the Irish poor had been under discussion for years, but little had been achieved. The famine showed starkly that it was urgently necessary to provide a nation-wide health service, and the dispensaries act of 1851 directed that poor law unions should be divided into dispensary districts and that in each district—there were in all 700—there should be a committee composed of justices of the peace, poor law guardians, and the larger ratepayers. Each committee was to appoint a medical officer and maintain a dispensary, the expense being met from the rates, and a pauper who obtained a ticket from a member of the committee was to be entitled to medical assistance. The working of the system was closely supervised by the poor law commissioners, who from the middle 1860s devoted a considerable amount of attention to public health matters.

The 1850s and 1860s were a period of consolidation in British life, and during these decades no striking modifications occurred in the Irish administrative structure although change was quietly taking place. The reorganisation of the offices attached to the superior courts (begun in 1844) was completed; the public record office was founded (1867); the vestry was abolished as a local government unit (1864), and a series of improvements were made in prison administration that culminated in the prisons act

[1] Charles Trevelyan, *The Irish crisis* (London, 1848), p. 1.
[2] 10 & 11 Vict., c. 90 (22 July 1847); 14 & 15 Vict., c. 68 (7 Aug. 1851).

of 1877, which empowered the goverment to administer directly all Irish gaols.[1]

It was during this comparatively placid period that momentous decisions were made on the recruitment of the civil service. In the early decades of the century an immense amount had been done to rationalise the establishments of government departments, but entry to the civil service was still by nomination and many of those admitted were very poorly qualified for the duties they were expected to perform. In 1853 the government appointed two commissioners, Sir Stafford Northcote and Sir Charles Trevelyan (K.C.B., April 1848), to consider the staffing of government offices. They reported in favour of admission by competitive examination. Official opinion was not prepared for a complete revolution in recruitment procedure but in 1855 the civil service commission was constituted and empowered to conduct qualifying tests to which persons nominated for civil service posts had to submit themselves. Competitive examinations for the civil service were strongly advocated by several well known Irishmen. Vincent Scully, M.P. for County Cork, tried unsuccessfully in 1855 to persuade the government to substitute competitive for qualifying examinations. Charles Graves, a fellow of Trinity and a distinguished mathematician, argued in a powerful memorandum that admission by competitive examination would deprive 'democrats and socialists . . . of a staple grievance' and would go far to abate national and religious jealousies and encourage industry and resolution, virtues in which 'the native character' was deficient. 'Having three sons and little interest to push them forward in the world', Graves, as soon as he heard the government were considering introducing entry by competitive examination 'resolved . . . to direct their education in such a way as they might be fitted for the proposed competition'. The prospect, he wrote 'diminishes my anxieties about providing for my family as much as if I had received an access of fortune'. Larcom, the under-secretary, one of the great civil servants of his time, declared that if a system of open competition was adopted it would encourage throughout Ireland 'industry and self-reliance'. Larcom in 1854 pointed with pride to the fact that for twenty years county surveyors in Ireland had been appointed by competitive examination. Immediately after the civil service commission was set up, the Irish departments under the control of the chief secretary's office began to recruit by open competitive examination.[2]

[1] 40 & 41 Vict., c. 49 (14 Aug. 1877).
[2] *Papers on the reorganisation of the civil service*, pp 21–32, H.C. 1854–5 (1870), xx, 69–70.

CHAPTER XXVIII

Emigration, 1801–70

DAVID FITZPATRICK

Few Irish people of the nineteenth century would have agreed with Falstaff
that they 'were better to be eaten to death with rust than to be scoured to
nothing with perpetual motion'. Only a small minority were both able and
willing to spend their lives in the house or farm of their upbringing: indeed, for
many generations in many regions of Ireland, the likelihood was that their
working lives would be conducted in another country. The migratory experience was seldom that of direct translation from home in Ireland to settlement
abroad. Migration usually involved reiterated if not 'perpetual' motion,
impelled by the ubiquitous scarcity of secure employment, the enduring
illusion that the next town or country would after all be paved with gold, and
also the cumulative restlessness and rootlessness of those habituated from
childhood to migration. Three personal chronicles must serve to exemplify the
tortuous paths that were often followed from one place of settlement to
another, paths that only occasionally crossed the borders patrolled by official
enumerators and therefore left no clear imprint on the statistics of migration.

Daniel O'Sullivan was born at Castletown, County Cork, in about 1825, but
three years later migrated with his parents to Listowel, County Kerry, where at
the age of ten he found employment as a stable-boy. Shortly before his parents'
death during the early famine years, Daniel left his employer and roamed
through Munster and 'most of Ireland' to Belfast, where he spent four months.
In March 1849 he crossed to Glasgow and

stopped there but two nights, after that I went through small Towns to Berwick-on-
Tweed, to Newcastle in England, to Leeds and Liverpool stopping in each place but
two or three nights, came over to Dublin the 5th or 6th of May last [1849], where I only
stopped one night, and have been travelling since through the country. I never done
work all the time and supported myself by Singing in Irish—I cannot speak English, but
can understand what is said to me.

In Cavan he was apprehended as a suspected vagrant, his case being deemed
an 'outrage' worthy of special report as prejudicial to the peace; but his subsequent movements are unrecorded, since Dublin Castle ordered that having

given no grounds for suspicion he should be released. He probably escaped enumeration as either a departing or returning migrant: in another age, he might have been classed as a tourist visiting Britain.[1]

Owen Mangan was born at Billy Hill, County Cavan, just before the 'big wind' of 1839. His father had been constantly on the move, being a drover, occupant of two farms, market vendor, and even ('having too much spare time on his hands, particularly in the winter') illicit distiller. He died just after his release from prison on the last account, leaving five sons of whom Owen, aged two, was the youngest. His widow promptly remarried a spoiled priest turned choleric schoolmaster, an event that 'scattered our family so that we never after met under the same roof'. The eldest son was hired by a farmer ('a quaker in religion, but by all accounts a good man') before emigrating to New Orleans; the second went to sea, was shipwrecked, reemerged briefly, and disappeared; the third settled and married in Durham, then fled ahead of his family to Philadelphia to escape arrest as a suspected fenian; the fourth, after working for a Drogheda druggist and a dry-goods merchant in Newry, served with the pope's army, returned to Newry, married, emigrated alone to the United States, and eventually brought over his family.

Owen himself was briefly fostered by a neighbour but spent much of his childhood pursuing his elusive stepfather and mother to Monaghan, Cootehill, Bailieborough, Cootehill once again, and Drogheda. There, after an uneasy reunion with his stepfamily, Owen finally broke away after a quarrel over a penalty of three shillings when he 'missed a cut of each loom' at the cotton mill where he had been put to work. With three 'chums' he made for Preston via Liverpool in 1853, soon abandoning cotton for more remunerative factory work. Owen, too, married in England but soon got itchy feet, taking up evening classes, serving as a policeman at St Helens for six months, returning to his old job supplemented by work as a bell-ringer at three pounds a year, and using his savings to set up a grocery store. The store lost custom in 1867 after an Irish neighbour had been implicated in the killing of Sergeant Brett at Manchester, and Owen emigrated alone to Philadelphia where he began training as a cooper under his brother. In order to save the cost of his family's emigration he soon resumed occupational and residential mobility. He signed on at a local woollen mill, spent a fortnight in Monnyut before returning to Philadelphia to try 'all my relations' for loans (without avail), sought hotel work, 'landed in among my old chums' from Preston and Drogheda at Fall River (Massachusetts), tired of his Irish connections, and took up loom-fixing in Rhode Island, where he finally landed his family in 1870. The resumption of family life did not quell Owen's restlessness, and for much of his remaining half-century he drifted between factory work, storekeeping, shoemaking, and peddling insurance policies. If the Mangans were ever enumerated they would probably have been listed by the Irish constabulary as 'temporary emigrants' to Britain and by

[1] S.P.O., outrage papers 4/162 (21 July 1849).

British emigration officers as unaccompanied passengers to America. The complexity of their migratory strategies, and the family cleavages and unities that determined them, would have had no statistical manifestation.[1]

Wilson Benson, a weaver's son born at Belfast in 1821, was also launched into migration on rejection by the second family of a widowed parent. After his mother's death the infant was taken to Portadown, County Armagh, where his father married a widow, whose family subsequently ejected both father and son. Wilson entered the workforce, aged twelve, as an apprentice reedmaker, but soon moved with his married sister to Scotland in search of employment as a weaver and cotton-piecer. They tramped towards Edinburgh, then back to Glasgow and Belfast, before Wilson settled in Bottlehill, County Armagh, for nearly four years as an apprentice linen-weaver. There he married, but emigrated in 1841 armed with 'letters from friends in Ireland to friends in Canada'. His wife (masquerading as a sister) became successively a servant, dressmaker, and storekeeper, but Wilson found employment less accessible. Yet, sometimes alone and sometimes in partnership with relatives, he tried his hand at farm labouring, factory work, cooking, peddling a cure for ague that had appeared to him in a dream, storekeeping, and farming. Between 1841 and 1874 he had at least eight places of residence and twelve occupations, some reiterated. Wilson has been designated as 'a representative Canadian first and foremost because he was a transient', fluctuating rather than progressing in his residence and occupational status.[2] Yet he was also a representative Irish migrant, a protestant Ulster Canadian whose life story closely matched those of catholics and southerners choosing other destinations. For people like Benson, Mangan, and O'Sullivan, migration was not an isolated episode but a habit of life.

These illustrations suggest that any official return of the volume of Irish migration would be fragmentary, being based upon mere snapshots of a continuing movement. Several conflicting statistical sources are available, differing in criteria as well as reliability. Gross outward movement by sea was enumerated at several points, with strikingly disparate results. The Irish constabulary attempted from 1851 to enumerate all those leaving Irish ports with the intention of residing elsewhere for at least a year; customs or emigration officers abstracted the manifests of most passenger vessels leaving the British Isles for non-European destinations after 1825, recording birthplace from 1853; and immigration agents in the United States from 1819, and also elsewhere, collected the manifests of arriving ships and in many cases noted the nationality of passengers.[3] No such returns were compiled for movement of passengers into Britain or Ireland; while for the first quarter of the century even

---

[1] Owen Peter Mangan's autobiography; typescript, 1912 (N.L.I., MS 22462).
[2] Michael B. Katz, *The people of Hamilton, Canada West* (Cambridge, Mass., 1975), pp 94–111.
[3] N. H. Carrier and J. R. Jeffery, *External migration: a study of the available statistics, 1815–1950* (London, 1953); Cormac Ó Gráda, 'A note on nineteenth-century Irish emigration statistics' in *Population Studies*, xxix, no. 1 (1975), pp 143–9.

outward movement must be reconstructed from surviving manifests or newspaper reports of emigrant sailings. Migration may also be measured indirectly by analysing census returns giving birthplace and age-group. The recorded birthplaces of the populations of Ireland, Britain, and foreign countries enable us to estimate the geographical distribution of Irish natives and net intercensal displacement; while comparison of Irish populations aged 5 to 24 at one census with those aged 15 to 34 a decade later provides us with a useful proxy for net outward migration of the age-group most susceptible to migration ('cohort depletion').[1] The most detailed returns of Irish migration tend also to be the least complete, so that details derived from one set of returns must often be grafted on to other skeletons in order to construct a credible profile of the movement. In order to elucidate the causes of migration and its functions in Irish society between 1801 and 1870, we must first examine its magnitude, flow, and composition. How many people, with what attributes, left different parts of Ireland to arrive at different destinations?

Long before the famine, the intensity of Irish emigration had become remarkable in the context of contemporary Europe. The pre-revolutionary movement to America, which had been dominated by Ulster presbyterians and indentured servants, had already given place to a broader emigration between the treaty of Versailles in 1783 and the renewal of Anglo-American hostilities in 1812. Despite interference from war, prohibition of artisan emigration, and the severe passenger legislation of 1803, 100,000 people are thought to have left Ireland for North America during those three decades. Most of them were paying passengers rather than servants imported under contract, while many were southerners and catholics. Even more probably made for Britain, where recognisable Irish enclaves developed in cities such as London, Manchester, and Glasgow.[2] After the resumption of peace in 1815, emigration resumed and intensified. A million Irish emigrants are estimated to have crossed the Atlantic between 1815 and 1845, with half that number taking the cheaper British alternative and some 30,000 obtaining state assistance to undertake the much longer journey to Australia.[3] Before the famine this huge egress curtailed, but did not reverse, Irish population growth: the century-long decline began in the late 1840s, when emigration was an even more important agent of depopulation than famine-related mortality. Movement out of Ireland probably exceeded a million between 1846 and 1850, yet did not peak until 1851 when the worst

[1] Cohorts are of course depleted by mortality as well as out-migration; but for the age-group specified, decadal mortality would seldom have exceeded 6 per cent (possibly 10 per cent over the 1840s). In order to estimate net intercensal displacement from birthplace statistics, one must posit assumptions concerning the probable age-distribution and mortality of those living outside their birthplace.

[2] Maldwyn A. Jones, 'Ulster emigration, 1783–1815' in E. R. R. Green (ed.), *Essays in Scotch-Irish history* (London, 1969), pp 46–68; David Noel Doyle, *Ireland, Irishmen and revolutionary America, 1760–1820* (Dublin and Cork, 1981), pp 209–12.

[3] Adams, *Ir. emigration to New World*, pp 69, 410–28. Australian statistics exclude the 40,000 involuntary emigrants who were tried in Ireland and transported between 1787 and 1868.

ravages of dearth and disease had passed in most regions.[1] Between 1851 and 1870 the recorded level of gross outward movement oscillated about a slowly declining axis; yet, as figure 3 suggests, even years of Irish prosperity such as 1857 or 1866 generated more emigration than any but the most desperate pre-famine years. Net outward movement remained remarkably intensive, and during both the 1850s and 1860s the probability that a young person would 'disappear' over a decade was close to a third.[2] The volume of emigration over this period may variously be estimated at 2,100,000 (using the constabulary returns of gross emigration), 2,400,000 (using an index of net emigration based upon cohort depletion), or 2,600,000 (combining estimated net movement to Britain with the recorded outflow of Irish passengers from the British Isles).[3] All told, at least five million people left Ireland during the first seven decades of the century.

Though vast in magnitude and tortuous in path, Irish emigration was usually conducted over long distances and seldom reversed. The unexpected similarity between our estimates of gross and net movement out of post-famine Ireland suggests that few of those leaving Ireland returned to live in their native country. It is true that much circular and seasonal migration to Britain took place from certain regions; while by the 1870s there was also considerable traffic from America to the British Isles of Irish passengers on business or vacation.[4] Yet the shortages of land and employment that encouraged emigration also discouraged permanent return, especially since those left behind were often reluctant to readmit well-heeled expatriates to the restrictive markets of rural Ireland. Whereas the predominantly male 'new' immigrants from southern or eastern Europe often preferred to spend a few years in the United States, saving for their eventual marriage and resettlement at home, the Irish of both sexes usually intended from the outset to marry and settle abroad. Though some left with the dream of retirement and 'death in Erin', their determination tended to soften into ineffectual nostalgia after experience of relative liberty and prosperity elsewhere. Those who did return faced an uneasy blend of resentment arising from their assets or accents, and contempt for their evident inability to 'make it' overseas: 'Oh, that is a man who has come home; he has failed through his own fault.'[5]

The 'Yank' nevertheless became a familiar figure in rural folklore, a symbol

---

[1] For various estimates of the scale and changing intensity of Irish emigration, see Jacques Verrière, *La population de l'Irlande* (Paris, 1979), pp 79, 328–44, 507; and above, pp 120–22.

[2] Below, p. 617.

[3] My estimates of net emigration are derived from 'cohort depletion' over a decade of the group initially aged 5–24, assuming that decadal mortality was 6 per cent and that the cohort's share of total net emigration was equivalent to that of corresponding age-groups in the gross emigration from Irish ports as enumerated by the constabulary. More direct estimates of net emigration are unfeasible in the absence before 1864 of registration of births and deaths.

[4] For seasonal migration, see above, pp 127, 261.

[5] Evidence of William Keane, bp of Cloyne (1857–74) (*Report from the select committee on Tenure and Improvement of Land (Ireland) Act . . .*, p. 194, H.C. 1865 (402), xi, 546).

of loneliness: the woman bringing home a fat fortune with which to find a husband and 'redeem' his farm; the man flourishing ready cash to secure land or pub; the lost offspring summoned home to take over from faltering parents. As early as 1835, a Sligo witness referred to 'many instances of persons having saved money in America, and having returned in their old days to their place of birth, where they have given excessive prices for small portions of land'.[1] Since no reliable statistics of reverse passenger movement were compiled, it is difficult to test either the extent of reverse migration or the accuracy of the familiar stereotypes. Census returns of Irish residents born abroad show that very few emigrants returned with foreign-born children.[2] More revealingly, analysis of passenger lists from America preserved in connection with the fenian scare (1858–67) suggests that the typical reverse migrant was very different from the stereotype distilled from folklore surveys by Schrier. Since two-thirds of those sampled were male, while half of the female minority were already married, it is clear that husband-hunters did not predominate. The median age of returning men was 29.8 years compared with 26.5 years for women, indicating a sojourn in the United States of only 7 and 4 years respectively. In occupational distribution they differed little from America's resident Irish population, though labourers and servants were far less conspicuous among returning than departing migrants. 'Yanks' seem to have been unusually inclined to settle in the north-west or in northern Leinster, where the land market was probably more open than in the south and west of the country.[3] No doubt returned migrants helped diffuse information about foreign lands and thus accelerated further emigration; yet the failure of most emigrants to return home is more significant than the contribution of those few who did so.

Internal as well as reverse migration was inhibited by paucity of employment and low wages throughout Ireland. Census statistics of birthplace and residence give no indication of local movement within counties, which must have been considerable as the result of marriage, changed employment, or displacement from one holding to another. Some hint of short-distance movement during the famine is provided by returns of poor relief, which distinguish the proportion of recipients who had not lived in the immediate locality for at least thirty of the preceding thirty-six months. The mean proportion of migratory paupers was usually about one-seventh, being slightly higher in the summer months of most acute shortage. It was relatively low in major centres such as Dublin, Belfast, and Galway, but extremely high in certain western unions of Munster and Ulster.[4] Yet even the convulsions of the famine decade

---

[1] Arnold Schrier, *Ireland and the American emigration, 1850–1900* (Minneapolis, 1958), pp 129–43; Marjolein 't Hart, 'Irish return migration in the nineteenth century' in *Tijdschrift voor 'Economische en Sociale Geografie*, lxxvi, no. 3 (1985), pp 223–31; *Poor inquiry, app. F*, p. 134.

[2] 't Hart, 'Irish return migration', pp 227–9. The number of persons aged under 20 and born in America was 2,426 in 1861 and 3,053 in 1871.   [3] Ibid., *passim*.

[4] Evidence of Thomas Larcom (*Fourth report from the select committee of the house of lords appointed to*

brought only a modest increase in the number displaced from their county of birth to some other Irish county. That number never exceeded 550,000 even in 1851, though as a proportion of Ireland's population it rose from 5 per cent in 1851 to 9 per cent by 1871. About two-thirds of these inter-county migrants had merely crossed county borders, while Dublin was the only major city to draw migrants from a broad catchment zone, to the extent that nearly one-third of its population in 1851 had been born in other counties. Displacement both inwards and outwards was most intensive in the east, being relatively rare along the Atlantic seaboard and in much of Ulster. The regional patterns of displacement changed very little between 1841 and 1871, reflecting the static distribution of employment opportunities and the continuing restriction of urban and industrial expansion.[1] The character of demand for labour in nineteenth-century Ireland was also evident in the sexes and occupations of inter-county migrants. Except in parts of the west, females slightly outnumbered males among those resident away from their counties of birth. Women often migrated as a consequence of marriage; but those with specified occupations were disproportionately likely to be teachers or domestics, predictably often spinners or dressmakers, and seldom weavers or farmers. Male migrants were heavily over-represented in the professional and clerical categories of the census between 1841 and 1861. Skilled tradesmen, grocers and dealers, domestics, and carmen were other favoured groups, whereas labourers as well as farmers were disinclined to migrate between counties.[2] Thus Irish inter-county migration was generally sluggish, but particularly scanty in poorer regions and among the unskilled rural population.

The regional distribution of the migratory population is summarised in table 2.[3] By 1871 more than three and a half million natives of Ireland were living outside their counties of birth, a number not far short of the non-migratory population. The chief regions of settlement were invariably the United States, followed by Britain, other Irish counties, Canada, and Australia; but the regional distribution altered significantly over time. The United States

---

inquire into the operation of the Irish poor law..., pp 819-21, H.C. 1849 (365), xvi, 843-5). Paupers were charged to the union at large unless resident in their district electoral division for the period stated.

[1] Birthplace data for thirty-one county units (Antrim, Down, and Belfast being combined) were used to compute (a) natives of a county resident elsewhere in Ireland and (b) persons from elsewhere in Ireland resident in a county, as a proportion of that county's population in 1841, 1851, 1861, and 1871. Taking the county distributions of outward displacement (a) in 1841 and 1871, we obtain r = +.96 (for n = 29, excluding the aberrant rates for the Dublin and Belfast regions). For inward displacement (b), r = +.88. The correlation between the distributions of (a) and (b) was r = +.73 (1841) and r = +.78 (1871). See also Ruth-Ann Mellish Harris, 'The nearest place that wasn't Ireland' (Ph.D. thesis, Tufts, 1980), pp 101-15, 129-47.

[2] After 1861 no census tabulation of migrant occupations was provided. As in all subsequent references to the 'over-representation', etc., of an occupation in a certain group, our index gives the ratio of (a) to (b), where (a) is the proportion of occupied members of that group following the stated occupation, whereas (b) is the proportion of persons occupied in Ireland following the same occupation.

[3] Below, p. 609.

became the majority destination only in the 1860s, and probably housed fewer Irish migrants than Britain until the late 1840s. After the famine Australia as well as the United States took an increasing share of the displaced Irish, whereas the number of first-generation residents in Britain and Canada declined, at first relatively and after 1861 absolutely. The distributions taken from census birthplace returns are marred by the fact that many Irish people enumerated in Britain and Canada in 1851 were temporary residents intending to proceed to the United States. This problem is still more acute in the case of the returns of passenger movement from the British Isles, which specify place of disembarkation rather than intended settlement, thus greatly inflating Irish emigration to Canada.[1] Nevertheless, the available evidence clearly indicates that heavy migration occurred from Ireland to several destinations apart from the United States. It cannot be assumed that common factors governed all of these movements.

The relative ease with which Irish settlers achieved either 'assimilation' or ethnic 'community' in each region should be gauged from intensive study of each immigrant experience rather than statistical surveys. Even so, useful hints may be derived from analysis of Irish patterns of settlement in each major receiving region, when the Irish diaspora was at its greatest about 1870. In terms of residence, Irish settlers were most huddled together in regions with relatively small and often embattled Irish minorities: the existence of Irish enclaves usually signified individual weakness rather than communal power. As table 2 reveals, the Irish component of foreign populations was only 3 per cent in Britain and 5 per cent in the United States, but 6 per cent in Canada and 13 per cent in Australia. The extent of residential clustering by Irish settlers was predictably minor within the Australian colonies; somewhat greater in New Zealand and New York State as well as in Ontario and New Brunswick; and very marked in the United States as a whole, Britain, Nova Scotia, and Quebec. In Britain and the United States, with their large and entrenched native-born majorities, Irish settlers tended to congregate in clearly marked regions such as the north-eastern United States, northern England, and south-western Scotland. These patterns of clustering were specific to Irish settlers, who generally showed no tendency to congregate with other immigrant groups. The Irish in the United States and Britain were massed in certain cities and towns, being abnormally disinclined to penetrate agricultural districts.[2] Within their favoured urban settlements, however, the Irish seldom formed or inhabited 'ghettos', except perhaps in the immediate aftermath of the famine exodus. They tended to reside in low-quality housing in central rather than peripheral zones, and to share rough working-class

[1] Constabulary returns showing intended destinations for 'permanent' residence (for a year or more) were not compiled until 1876.
[2] David Fitzpatrick, 'Irish emigration in the later nineteenth century' in *I.H.S.*, xxii, no. 86 (Sept. 1980), pp 126–43.

neighbourhoods with others of similar occupations. No ward in New York city in 1855 had less than a thousand Irish-born inhabitants, and the Irish components of each ward's foreign-born population varied only between 26 per cent and 72 per cent.[1] In general, the Irish were quite evenly dispersed within cities, states, and countries where their total weight as a component of population was great. In Ontario and Australia, for example, Irish settlers were scarcely over-represented in cities, often engaged in farming and less inclined to avoid districts dominated by the native-born.[2] Thus Irish 'clannishness', in so far as it is reflected in patterns of residence, was not an invariable attribute of Irish emigrant mentality but a response to specific host environments.

Smaller pockets of Irish settlement developed in all other anglophone countries, though only in New Zealand and South Africa would their number (if recorded) have significantly swollen that given in table 2. Cape Colony had been the site of one of the earliest state-subsidised emigrations from Ireland: a rather disreputable transaction whereby a Cork merchant imported a group of indentured servants and labourers from his native town at treasury expense.[3] The dream of founding a South African colony for 'all those of the Roman Catholic Irish who are anxious or are necessitated to leave Ireland' possessed James Edward Fitzgerald as late as in 1849; but Irish–African movement remained sluggish until the last decades of the century.[4] Despite the prominence of Irishmen such as Fitzgerald and John Robert Godley in the early development of New Zealand, immigrant intake up to the 1870s was largely British, apart from the overspill of Irish gold-miners following the rushes from Victoria to Otago or Westland.[5] Irish emigration to non-anglophone countries was oddly sparse by comparison with the German or Italian influx to South America. Even so, some 7,000 Irish emigrants seem to have reached Argentina between 1801 and 1870. A Westmeath observer reported in 1844 that 'a great many' had made for Buenos Aires on hearing that 'the natives are obliged to take up arms, and strangers get employment'. The climate agreed with them 'very well; and the only difficulty they find is, that they have not potatoes to eat. The bread and the meat, and the constant eating, is what disagrees with them'. Speculators promoted several schemes to bring Irish settlers to Latin America, such as MacCann's Argentinian proposal of 1848 and Edward Cullen's

---

[1] Data for the twenty-two wards of New York city in 1855 are given in Robert Ernst, *Immigrant life in New York city, 1825–1863* (New York, 1949), pp 193–6. The coefficient of variation for the Irish-born component of the foreign population was only .22, very close to those for the divisions of Sydney and Melbourne (Australia) in 1871: see Fitzpatrick, op. cit., p. 140.

[2] D. H. Akenson, *The Irish in Ontario* (Kingston and Montreal, 1984); A. Gordon Darroch and Michael D. Ornstein, 'Ethnicity and occupational structure in Canada in 1871' in *Canadian Historical Review*, lxi, no. 3 (1980), pp 305–33; Fitzpatrick, op. cit., pp 135–7.   [3] Above, p. 121.

[4] *Report from the select committee on emigration from the United Kingdom*, pp 283–5, H.C. 1826 (404), iv, 283–5; H. J. M. Johnston, *British emigration policy, 1815–1830* (Oxford, 1972), pp 73–5; G. B. Dickason, *Irish settlers to the Cape* (Cape Town, 1973), pp 21–6; Fitzgerald to Stephen de Vere, 26 July 1849 (T.C.D., MS 5053/11).

[5] Murray McCaskill, 'The goldrush population of Westland' in *New Zealand Geography*, xii (1956), pp 32–50; Richard P. Davis, *Irish issues in New Zealand politics* (Dunedin, 1974), ch. 2.

campaign for creation of an Irish 'New Granada' in Panama a decade later.[1] But the great bulk of prospective emigrants continued to limit their choices to Britain, Australia, and North America with their established and self-perpetuating networks of Irish residents.

The regional origins of Irish emigration have been widely misconstrued, mainly because of reliance on the defective returns collected by the Irish constabulary. *Pace* Cousens, the regional distribution of net outward migration (as indicated by 'cohort depletion') was largely determined during the 1840s and replicated throughout the remainder of the century.[2] It contrasted sharply with the pre-famine distribution.[3] Between 1821 and 1841, depletion had been greatest in a cluster of Ulster and Leinster counties, though even then virtually every country had been subject to considerable emigration. During the 1840s the epicentre of emigration moved westwards, and Connacht lost nearly half of its youthful population as a result of massive outward movement as well as mortality. Over the following decade emigration from Munster and the south-west probably increased slightly, whereas movement out of other provinces diminished, though the contrast with the 1840s is far less pronounced than Cousens and others have suggested (see table 1 and map 14c). By the 1860s (map 14d) the regional distribution of the famine period had been mainly restored, emigration from the less 'backward' eastern counties having been relatively minor at all periods.[4] The catastrophe of famine thus generated an immediate and lasting transformation in the regional patterns of outward migration. The counties most devastated by famine were also those in which the 'adjustment' of heavy emigration was most emphatic.

These overall patterns and continuities mask significant diversity in the regional origins of emigrants choosing different destinations. The maps showing 'cohort depletion' are largely governed by movement to Britain and the

[1] Evidence of Thomas Glennon (*Devon comm. evidence*, ii, 315); William B. Ready, 'The Irish and South America' in *Éire-Ireland*, i, no. 1 (1965–6), pp 59–60; Thomas Murray, *The story of the Irish in Argentina* (New York, 1919), p. 163; [Edward Cullen], *The republic of New Granada* (Dublin, 1858); L. M. Cullen, review in *Ir. Econ. &Soc. Hist.*, x (1983), pp 131–33, of J. C. Korol and H. Sabato, *Cómo fue la immigración irlandesa en Argentina* (Buenos Aires, 1981).

[2] Cormac Ó Gráda, 'Some aspects of nineteenth-century Irish emigration' in L. M. Cullen and T. C. Smout (ed.), *Comparative aspects of Scottish and Irish economic and social history* (Edinburgh, 1977), pp 65–73. The findings of S. H. Cousens (that emigration from the west was sluggish and sporadic until about 1880) appear in numerous articles, including 'The regional variations in population changes in Ireland, 1861–1881' in *Econ. Hist. Rev.*, 2nd ser., xvii, no. 2 (1964), pp 301–21.

[3] Maps 14a and 14b, below, p. 620.

[4] Below, pp 608, 620. For conflicting analyses of the pre-famine regional distribution of emigration, see Adams, *Ir. emigration to New World*, pp 158, 188–9; S. H. Cousens, 'The regional variations in emigration from Ireland between 1821 and 1841' in *Transactions and papers of the Institute of British Geographers*, xxxvii (1965), pp 15–30; J. H. Johnson, 'The two "Irelands" at the beginning of the nineteenth century' in Nicholas Stephens and Robin E. Glasscock (ed.), *Irish geographical Studies* (Belfast, 1970), pp 234–6. For subsequent patterns see Ó Gráda, op. cit.; Oliver Mac-Donagh, 'The Irish famine emigration to the United States' in *Perspectives in American History*, x (1976), pp 421–3. If the regional distribution of 'cohort depletion' between 1841 and 1851 (for thirty counties excluding Dublin and Antrim) is correlated with those for other decades, we obtain $r = +0.35$ (1821–41), $r = +0.32$ (1851–61), $r = +0.72$ (1861–71) and $r = +0.64$ (1871–81).

United States, while only scattered evidence survives concerning the origins of less important movements. The minor streams, often generated by favourable reports from a few pioneers giving rise to chain migration from isolated neighbourhoods, tended to be far more localised. Sir John Forbes remarked in 1852 that

it is curious to observe how the tide of emigration flows in different directions from different parts. Canada seems the favourite resort of the people of the Tralee district.... Accident, at first, generally determines the destination; and the news of success, which is almost sure to follow, whatever be the place of exile, confirms the selection.[1]

A similar axis was reported between pre-famine Corroneary, County Cavan, and Canada, where there was a presbyterian congregation 'almost exclusively formed of persons who emigrated from this neighbourhood'.[2] Analysis of catholic marriage registers at Halifax, Nova Scotia, shows that between 1801 and 1845 three Irish spouses in four were natives of five adjoining counties in the south-east, whereas few came from the northern region, which invariably supplied the bulk of Irish movement to British North America as a whole. The same five counties dominated Irish movement to nearby Newfoundland, long after that migration had ceased to be controlled by merchants contracting for fishermen at certain coastal towns.[3] Westmeath, Longford, and Wexford seem to have supplied most of the Argentinian Irish; and the departure of the 'twelve matchless youths' from Kilrane to Buenos Aires in April 1844 is still remembered in a ballad.

> On Wexford's Quay the thirteenth day there were many to bid farewell;
> They stayed conversing with their friends till the sound of the last bell.
> Then gave three cheers for Ireland that echoed with hurray,
> And with one for Dan O'Connell they boldly sailed away.[4]

'Localism' likewise coloured the much larger movement to the Australasian colonies. The regional origins of the 40,000 Irish convicts naturally reflected the incidence of crime, so that few of those transported to New South Wales or Van Diemen's Land between 1787 and 1852 were tried either in northern or western counties. Transportation was most intensive from the disturbed counties of eastern Munster and the Leinster midlands, together with the environs of Dublin and Belfast.[5] Convict settlers generated further chain

---

[1] John Forbes, *Memorandums made in Ireland* (2 vols, London, 1853), i, 160.

[2] Report by agent of Greville estate (1845), quoted in Philip O'Connell, *The schools and scholars of Breiffne* (Dublin, 1942), p. 367.

[3] Terence M. Punch, 'Some Irish immigrant weddings in Nova Scotia' in *Ir. Ancestor*, vi, no. 2 (1974), pp 101–12; vii, no. 1 (1975), pp 39–54; vii, no. 2 (1975), pp 104–20; viii, no. 1 (1976), pp 53–68; viii, no. 2 (1976), pp 124–39; ix, no. 2 (1977), pp 33–45. See also John J. Mannion (ed.), *The peopling of Newfoundland* (Newfoundland, 1977), p. 8. The five dominant counties were Kilkenny, Waterford, Tipperary, Cork, and Wexford.

[4] L. M. Cullen, review (see above, p. 571, n. 1), p. 132; Robert L. Wright, *Irish emigrant ballads and songs* (Bowling Green, Ohio, 1975), p. 166.

[5] L. L. Robson, *The convict settlers of Australia* (Melbourne, 1965), pp 178, 186.

migration from these districts, but from the early 1840s onwards the foci of assisted immigration were north Munster and mid-Ulster. During the 1850s, when immigration from Ireland was greatest, two-fifths of those assisted to New South Wales and Victoria came from Clare, Tipperary, and Kilkenny. To a considerable extent this pattern had been established by the private 'bounty' immigration of the early 1840s; and despite the reiterated efforts of immigration agents to attract more northern protestant settlers, the pattern remained remarkably stable for several decades.[1] The county imprint of Australia's Irish population was exported to parts of New Zealand through gold rushes, and the tombstones of the Westland Irish suggest origins strikingly similar to those applying to mid-century Victoria.[2] Thus the Australasian Irish tended to be helped out of fairly prosperous counties in rural Ireland, rather than being driven from the poorest counties of the west, which fed Britain and the United States.

EDWARD Gibbon Wakefield observed in 1849 that 'an equal emigration of the sexes is one essential condition of the best colonisation. . . . You may induce some men of the higher classes to emigrate without inducing the women; but if you succeed with the women you are sure not to fail with the men.'[3] By the mid-nineteenth century Ireland, alone among the countries supplying the cities of the New World, was generating 'an equal emigration of the sexes'. Previously men had predominated among Irish transatlantic emigrants also, but the male component had declined fairly steadily from two-thirds in 1803–5 and three-fifths in the 1820s to a bare majority just before the famine. At least among long-distance emigrants leaving Irish ports, this trend was temporarily reversed between 1846 and 1848, when panic emigration was prevalent.[4] After 1856, as table 3 confirms, males again slightly outnumbered females among those enumerated by the constabulary: thus 'preponderance of women' was not a general 'feature of post-famine migration' as Clarkson has suggested. Even so, women continued to contribute more heavily to Irish emigration than to most other international movements.[5] By about 1870 these fluctuations in the sex

---

[1] David Fitzpatrick, 'Irish emigration in the later nineteenth century' in *I.H.S.*, xxii, no. 86 (Sept. 1980), p. 134, n. 17. If the counties of origin of all Irish bounty emigrants (January 1841–June 1842) are compared with those for emigrants assisted to New South Wales between 1877 and 1887, the resultant correlation (32 counties) is r = +0.59.

[2] Murray McCaskill, 'The goldrush population of Westland' in *New Zealand Geography*, xii (1956), pp 43–4.

[3] Richard Charles Mills, *The colonization of Australia* (London, 1915), p. 119.

[4] Below, p. 610; Cormac Ó Gráda, 'Across the briny ocean' in T. M. Devine and David Dickson (ed.), *Ireland and Scotland, 1600–1850* (Edinburgh, 1983), pp 124, 126; *Colonial land and emigration commissioners: general reports*, 1843–54, in H.C., *passim*; *Census Ire.*, *1841*, pp 450–51 [504], H.C. 1843, xxiv, 558–9 (showing overseas emigration from Irish ports, by sex, for 1832–June 1841). Females predominated in 1845 and 1850–54, though the male proportion was larger for those leaving Liverpool.

[5] L. A. Clarkson, 'Marriage and fertility in nineteenth-century Ireland' in R. B. Outhwaite (ed.), *Marriage and society* (New York, 1982), p. 249; William Petersen, *Population* (3rd ed., New York and London, 1975), pp 289–92.

composition of emigration had virtually balanced out, leaving only a slight female majority in the home population. The sex of Irish residents in North America is not recorded, but in England and New South Wales parity had been attained. There were substantial male excesses in New Zealand and Queensland and small majorities in Scotland and Western Australia, compared with small surpluses of Irishwomen in Victoria and Tasmania and a marked surplus in South Australia. These variations reflected regional differences in demand for female servants as against male labourers; but throughout the Australasian colonies at least, the female component was greater for the Irish than for other immigrant populations. The sex of emigrants was also influenced by their regions of origin: as map 15a indicates,[1] the female proportion tended to be greatest in the vicinity of Connacht with its high overall emigration rates. Between 1851 and 1855 most counties outside the north and south-east sent out more females than males. Over the following decade that zone had shrunk to a band of counties in Connacht and the north midlands, while no county recorded a female majority between 1866 and 1875. Yet inter-county variation in sex composition remained quite minor, and women as well as men flowed out of every region of Ireland into almost every region of settlement.[2]

Irish responsiveness to the patterns of foreign demand for immigrant labour was manifest in the composition of the emigrant stream by age and family status as well as sex. Those with the best chances of finding immediate employment overseas tended to be women rather than men, unmarried rather than married, young adults rather than children or older people. In many European countries women were nevertheless restrained from emigrating alone, while 'push' factors often encouraged family rather than individual emigration, so swelling the host population with unwanted children and aged dependents. In Ireland, even in the first half of the century, these constraints upon maximising the immediate utility of the newcomers were relatively feeble. The fairly even balance of the sexes was achieved not by universal family movement but by heavy emigration of unattached girls as well as young men. Though the majority of transatlantic emigrants before the famine travelled with others of the same surname, this proportion is reported to have exceeded three-fifths only in 1803–05. The family component of Irish emigration to the United States was much smaller than in the British case (1831), declining to a nadir of 51 per cent in the later 1830s before recovering during the famine years. The importance of family-group emigration varied according to region of origin, being greatest in Ulster and smallest in Connacht in cases as far removed as movement to the United States (1803–05) and Victoria (1855–6).[3]

---

[1] Below, p. 621.

[2] The coefficient of variation (thirty-two counties) for the ratio of female to male emigrants (as enumerated by the constabulary and adjusted for non-specification of origin) was 0.08 (1851–5); 0.12 (1856–65); 0.14 (1866–75).

[3] Ó Gráda, op. cit., pp 124–5; Charlotte Erickson, 'Emigration from the British Isles to the

The extent of family movement after the famine was not explicitly recorded, but probably corresponded closely in its regional and temporal variation with the proportion of emigrants aged under 15. During the 1820s and 1830s just under one-fifth of transatlantic emigrants had been children, a proportion that rose slightly in 1847–8 in reflection of the heavy family emigration of the famine. Children were more prominent in long-distance emigration from Irish than from British ports during the early 1850s, though this was partly because unaccompanied Irish emigrants tended to choose the cheaper and rougher journey via Liverpool.[1] The constabulary returns abstracted in table 3 show that the proportion of emigrants aged under 15 dropped from almost one-quarter in the early 1850s to one-eighth by the late 1860s. As map 15b indicates,[2] the regions supplying numerous child emigrants included not only the south-east and north-east Ulster, but also Mayo and south-west Munster. These trends in child and family movement were reflected negatively in the proportion of young adult emigrants, which quickly surpassed its pre-famine level during the 1850s. By the 1860s over one-third of all emigrants were aged between 20 and 24, females being typically somewhat younger. In the case of Munster (1851–5), annual emigration for both sexes amounted to almost one-tenth of the initial population in that age-group. Though family movement subsequently declined, massive emigration of young adults continued.

Most emigrants, when asked to state their occupation on embarkation, claimed neither status nor skills. From about 1830 to the famine the majority of Irish emigrants to Boston and New York were returned as 'labourers' or 'servants'. The unskilled component grew fairly steadily from under one-third in the early 1820s to about three-fifths in the 1840s. Farmers, who had accounted for about one-third of emigrants sampled before 1825, remained a substantial but decreasing minority. Mokyr shows, however, that farmers and labourers together were no more predominant among male emigrants than in Ireland's pre-famine population (1841). Textile, clerical, and commercial personnel were under-represented; but industrial and construction workers, as well as artisans such as carpenters, were markedly prone to emigrate to New York.[3] After 1850, as table 4 demonstrates, labourers overwhelmed all other categories of male emigrants and outnumbered even farmers by at least ten to one. No other group (except clerks) was over-represented among men leaving Ireland between May 1851 and December 1855, when compared with the Irish population in 1851. Sailors, tailors, carpenters, shoemakers, and masons were however more disposed to emigrate than blacksmiths, domestic servants,

U.S.A. in 1831' in *Population Studies*, xxxv, no. 2 (1981), pp 184–5; *Reports from the immigration agent, 1855–56*, in Victorian Legislative Council, *Votes and proceedings*.

[1] For statistical sources see above, p. 573, n. 4; figures for emigration from Irish ports between 1843 and 1847, and in 1853–4, refer to children under 14.

[2] Below, p. 621.

[3] Cormac Ó Gráda, 'Across the briny ocean' in T. M. Devine and David Dickson (ed.), *Ireland and Scotland, 1600–1850* (Edinburgh, 1983), p. 125; Mokyr, *Why Ire. starved*, p. 250.

farmers, or weavers. Emigration of female textile workers was also markedly sluggish. The predominance of labourers was peculiar to emigrants, whereas over three-fifths of those returning from the United States, as well as inter-county migrants, could boast superior attainments.[1] The abnormality of the Irish emigrant's occupational profile is illustrated by table 5, which offers comparisons with England and Scotland.[2] At all periods the British emigrant component of labourers was far smaller than the Irish, though this was partly due to differences in occupational structure between Ireland and Britain. More significantly, fewer Irish emigrants were farmers, despite Ireland's far larger agricultural sector. These contrasts applied to all major destinations in 1857 and 1867, though by the latter year labourers were far more conspicuous among Irish passengers to the United States than to Canada or Australasia. In 1857 virtually all female emigrants of each nationality were either servants or without occupation; but a decade later this remained true only of the Irish.[3]

It is tempting to cite the predominance of menial workers as evidence that relatively little 'human capital' was lost as the result of post-famine if not pre-famine emigration.[4] Such a conclusion, however true, would be invalid. The description of a twenty-year-old as 'labourer' or 'servant' reveals little about the emigrant's class background or expectations of future status in Ireland. Most children of farmers and shopkeepers, as well as labourers, would have so described themselves, as would many young people hoping to succeed to a farm in later life. Moreover, Ireland's endemic underemployment ensured that most occupational descriptions were assertions of intention rather than fact; those about to enter the workforce through emigration tended to choose occupations accessible to them abroad rather than those of their parents. The occupational returns of emigration, therefore, embody a tangle of incongruous factors such as the 'life-cycle effect', future hopes, past experience, and also the visual perceptions of shipping clerks or policemen making out registers in a hurry. No firm inferences should be drawn from occupational comparisons between Irish emigrants and other groups, whether 'standard' populations or other emigrant samples. To test such inferences we must have recourse to alternative sources.

Since the unusual is more newsworthy than the commonplace, contemporaries may have exaggerated the frequency of emigration by the more comfortable classes. Press reports before, during, and after the famine might be cited as evidence of recent increases in emigration by, for example, 'respectable farmers and artisans, with their families' (Donegal, 1842); 'small farmers from the interior, or tradesmen, shopkeepers, and dealers' (Dublin, 1848); or simply

[1] Below, p. 611. [2] Below, p. 612.
[3] Comparison of statistics showing servants as a proportion of occupied females is hindered by variant terminology. For 1857 emigrants, however, these percentages were 94.6 (Irish), 93.2 (English), and 95.7 (Scottish); whereas in 1867, when cabin passengers were evidently included, they were 92.1 (Irish), 62.3 (English), and 66.9 (Scottish).
[4] Cf. above, pp 121–2.

'a better class' (Tipperary, 1867). Significant emigration of farmers with capital was reported at eight out of eighteen baronial examinations for the Whately commission in 1835; and there are scattered reports of surprising amounts of gold being secreted by emigrants who often displayed every other sign of destitution.[1] In about 1848 evidence abounded of farmers who had sold their tenant right and emigrated in expectation of further decline in the value of land; and it was asserted that 'the very poorest classes do not go in any way; parties, in fact, who are scarcely human, of whom there are great numbers, especially upon the sea-coast, whom everybody would be anxious to remove'.[2] It seems likely that most Irish emigrants from the famine onwards were surplus offspring of farmers and rural labourers, drawn from a broad band of social strata but largely excluding both strong farmers and destitute squatters or beggars. Emigration became an aspect of the rural life-cycle rather than that of any class within rural society. As maps 16a and 16b suggest, the counties marked by intensive emigration also tended to have large agricultural sectors, from which farm workers were 'disappearing' much faster than farmers during the period 1851–81. The correlation between heavy 'cohort depletion' and rapid disappearance of farm workers was most pronounced in the 1860s and 1870s.[3] Since, however, these 'farm workers' included assisting relatives from every stratum of rural society, their disappearance through emigration signified changes in household rather than class structure.

The paucity of middle-class emigration from Ireland is reflected in table 6, which shows the relative propensity of literate and illiterate young adults to 'disappear' between censuses.[4] Even in the 1860s the majority of these victims of 'cohort depletion' were unable to read and write, illiteracy being most widespread among females. Emigrants were less likely to have basic writing skills than their contemporaries at home, a contrast that held good for every county of Ireland in the 1860s. Yet this over-representation of illiterates among emigrants applied to men more than women, a contrast that was to become more marked later in the century as persistent overseas demand for literate female servants encouraged Irish girls to prepare for departure by attending to their elementary education. By the 1860s the 'cohort depletion' of Mayo females was no longer affected by their educational attainments, being 47 per cent for both literates and illiterates.[5] The national education system, which

[1] *Longford Journal*, 14 May 1842; *Sidney's Emigrant's Journal*, 12 Oct. 1848; Lord Dufferin, *Irish emigration and the tenure of land in Ireland* (London, 1867), p. 292; *Poor inquiry, app. F*, pp 130–41; *Third report from the select committee on emigration from the United Kingdom*, p. 113, H.C. 1826–7 (550), v, 335; Richard J. Purcell, 'The New York commissioners of emigration and Irish immigrants, 1847–1860' in *Studies*, xxxvii (1948), p. 39; Adams, *Ir. emigration to New World*, pp 104–11, 192–3, 238.

[2] Evidence of Edward Senior (*First report from the select committee of the house of lords appointed to inquire into the operation of the Irish poor law*, p. 166, H.C. 1849 (192), xvi, 170).

[3] Below, p. 621; David Fitzpatrick, 'The disappearance of the Irish agricultural labourer' in *Ir. Econ. & Soc. Hist.*, vii (1980), p. 75, n. 30. 　　　　　　　　　　　　[4] Below, p. 613.

[5] For fuller discussion see David Fitzpatrick, '"A share of the honeycomb": education, emigration and Irishwomen' in *Continuity and change*, i, no. 2 (Sept. 1986), pp 217–34.

developed after 1831, proved well suited to catering for prospective emigrants. Even though the national commissioners' textbooks deplored emigration, at least among 'those who can live at home, and those who could not live abroad', the practical consequences of teaching Irish children the geography of every country but their own, of providing basic instruction in domestic economy, and, above all, of diffusing literacy in English, were (in the words of a fenian journal) to educate 'the Irish to emigrate by millions'.[1] The same factors that encouraged emigrants to become literate in English also helped to destroy Irish as a vernacular language, a process likewise reinforced by the omission of Irish from the school programme as either a subject or a medium of instruction. As a Galway fenian recollected: '"What is the use of Irish for children going to America?" the old people used to say; and many of them actually got their children punished at school for speaking Irish at home.' Though many famine emigrants from the west of Ireland must have understood Irish, there are few references to its public use, for Irish was an incubus rather than an asset in the countries of Irish settlement.[2] Thus the concentration of prospective emigrants in regions marked by poverty, general illiteracy, and widespread Irish-speaking was counteracted by their determination to aid their escape from all these contexts through preliminary acculturation.

Though catholics dominated Irish emigration, protestant movement was never negligible. Early in the century there was intensive emigration from northern counties with large protestant populations, though from the 1840s onwards the continuing northern emigration was swamped by that from the catholic-dominated south and west. Evidence from Antrim and Londonderry in the 1830s indicates that presbyterians were more disposed to emigrate than either catholics or anglicans, while noteworthy non-catholic emigration was also reported from southern districts such as Bandon, County Cork.[3] Even in 1851 up to one-third of passengers leaving Derry were identified as protestants, and a year later an Armagh priest tesified that the emigration rate per capita from the Crossmaglen district did not vary according to denomination.[4] The

[1] Commissioners of National Education, *Agricultural class book* (Dublin, 1854), p. 51; J. M. Goldstrom, *The social content of education* (Shannon, 1972), p. 85; *Irish People*, 11 June 1864, quoted in Robert S. Fortner, 'The culture of hope and the culture of despair' in *Éire-Ireland*, xiii, no. 3 (1978), p. 47.

[2] Mark F. Ryan, *Fenian memories* (Dublin, 1945), p. 4. A rare report of Irish-speaking on shipboard is cited by Edwin C. Guillet, *The great migration* (Toronto, 1937), p. 71. See also Oliver MacDonagh, 'The Irish famine emigration to the United States' in *Perspectives in American History*, x (1976), p. 382. For the view that Irish-speaking was not uncommon in mid-nineteenth-century America, see Kerby A. Miller, *Emigrants and exiles: Ireland and the Irish exodus* (New York, 1985), pp 297–8.

[3] Adams, *Ir. emigration to New World*, p. 191; Cormac Ó Gráda, 'Across the briny ocean' in T. M. Devine and David Dickson (ed.), *Ireland and Scotland, 1600–1850* (Edinburgh, 1983), p. 127; *Poor inquiry, app. C*, pp 84–5.

[4] Evidence of E. A. Smith (*Report from the select committee on passengers' act*, p. 629, H.C. 1851 (632), xix, 671); evidence of Rev. Michael Lennon (*Report from the select committee on outrages (Ireland)*, p. 354, H.C. 1852 (438), xiv, 372).

pre-famine influx of Ulster protestants into Canada and Scotland left an enduring imprint: in both countries the Orange Order flourished and catholic settlers faced particular hostility from their protestant fellow countrymen, while in Ontario the catholic proportion of those claiming Irish stock remained static at about a third between 1842 and 1871.[1] Thus the general preponderance of catholic emigrants masked important variations according to regions of settlement as well as origin.

The composition of Irish emigration to eastern Australia was somewhat aberrant, since most emigrants received state assistance in accordance with official selection procedures. Table 7 provides an instructive indication of the limited ability of administrators to twist a voluntary emigration into a satisfactory immigration.[2] Colonial legislators would usually have preferred to have assisted fewer Irish immigrants, more women, more protestants, and fewer illiterates: but the cost of imposing severe quality controls was to risk failure of demand for passages. During the 1840s and 1850s the provision of more generous subsidies to young women did generate a marked female majority, though by the 1860s the usual sex parity had been attained among Irish arrivals in New South Wales. Under the bounty regulations of the mid-1840s a disappointingly large proportion of Irish immigrants were children, and this incubus was only temporarily relieved by the importation of mature 'female orphans' from 1848 to 1850. Subsequently the proportion of children declined in movement to Australia as elsewhere. The colonies were undoubtedly successful in attracting unskilled labourers and servants from Ireland as they failed to do from Britain, and the labourer component of male immigrants was consistently greater than the overall Irish figure.[3] It was in matters of religion and education that colonial preferences proved least efficacious. Until 1848 vigorous recruiting in the north and east of Ireland had secured a sizeable protestant minority; but thereafter that minority steadily dwindled to less than one-fifth by the late 1850s. Except in the late 1840s and 1860s most Irish immigrants were illiterate, though the proportion declined sharply in later periods. By comparison with the Irish counties from which they came, the immigrants of the 1850s and 1860s were only slightly less likely to be either catholics or unable to read.[4] Thus in the Australian case the effect of state control was to modify but not to transform the profile of the characteristic Irish emigrant.

THESE changes of composition signified a remarkable diffusion of the habit of emigration. Regional, occupational, and religious groupings, once disinclined

[1] D. H. Akenson, *The Irish in Ontario* (Kingston and Montreal, 1984), pp 26–7.

[2] Below, p. 614.

[3] The relatively low proportions of labourers among Irish emigrants choosing Australasia in 1857 and 1867 (see table 5, p. 612) are perhaps accountable to inclusion of non-assisted emigrants.

[4] David Fitzpatrick, 'Irish emigration in the later nineteenth century' in *I.H.S.*, xxii, no. 86 (Sept. 1980), p. 132, n. 12.

or unable to leave Ireland, rapidly discovered that heavy and unremitting emigration could improve the quality of life for those staying at home as well as those departing. By the 1850s the obstacles hindering emigration had clearly become feeble by comparison with the logic that encouraged it. Yet during the first half of the century the obstacles raised by the workings of the passenger trade were formidable: the historian can but wonder at the alertness and ingenuity with which so many Irish people circumvented them. The removal from Ireland of several million people naturally required massive provision of shipping, yet specialised passenger transportation was slow to develop. People long remained a rather unwelcome substitute for more profitable cargoes on both the cross-channel and transatlantic routes, filling empty holds in ships returning to pick up further merchandise. Since few passengers sought to travel eastwards across the Atlantic, it is not surprising that pre-famine passenger vessels typically carried fish and oil from Newfoundland, timber from Canada, flaxseed from New York and Philadelphia, or cotton from Baltimore and elsewhere. During the famine a three-way trade developed for ships plying between Liverpool, New York, and New Orleans, with coal or manufactures replacing people at New York and cotton being transported between New Orleans and Liverpool.[1] The extension of specialist passenger shipping was progressively encouraged from the 1840s onwards by the increasing predictability of demand as emigration from Europe became endemic rather than episodic; by increasingly rigorous passenger legislation that made it more difficult to convert cargo holds into human quarters; and finally by increasing reverse movement of passengers from America. The entrepreneurial risks associated with passenger shipping, whether in one or both directions, were invariably greater in the case of Irish rather than British ports. Since the 'ceiling' for pre-famine annual movement from Irish ports was only about 35,000, most Irish passengers bound for the United States from the late 1820s onwards were obliged to travel indirectly via Liverpool. In 1843 no less than 93 per cent of these passengers probably used Liverpool, which remained the majority port of embarkation until the late 1860s, when Queenstown (Cobh) began to meet the demand from Munster and Connacht.[2] Even during the famine exodus, shippers had been reluctant to invest in Irish ports, predicting an early end to massive emigration. As William Le Fanu observed in 1851, when a transatlantic packet station was being mooted for Galway, 'the emigration from Ireland, as it is now going on, cannot last; and it is not to be relied upon as

---

[1] Adams, *Ir. emigration to New World*, pp 71, 402–5; MacDonagh, *Pattern of govt growth*, pp 45–7; evidence of A. C. Buchanan (*Report from the select committee on emigration from the United Kingdom, minutes of evidence*, pp 174–5, H.C. 1826 (404), iv, 174–5).

[2] Oliver MacDonagh, 'Sea communications in the nineteenth century' in Kevin B. Nowlan (ed.), *Travel and transport in Ireland* (Dublin, 1973), p. 131. Between 1853 and 1872, the nativity of overseas emigrants from each port in the British Isles was given in the general reports of the colonial land and emigration commissioners. For earlier years we follow the official assumption that two out of three Liverpool emigrants were Irish, rising to 90 per cent from 1841.

supplying a permanent freightage for transatlantic steam packets'.[1] Despite such gloomy prognoses, Irish emigration became regular enough to permit extension to Ireland of a flourishing passenger shipping industry later in the century. Emigrants bound for Canada had always tended to use Irish ports, while by the late 1860s those making for the United States were also spared the inconvenience of crossing the Irish Sea.

The direct costs of emigration were influenced by legislation as well as market factors. Passenger legislation restricting the ratio of passengers to tonnage tended to increase the price as well as comfort and safety of emigration. The harsh British legislation of 1803 gradually gave place to virtual absence of control by 1828, and the appointment of the colonial land and emigration commissioners in 1840 did not lead to any rapid and effective regulation of passenger traffic. This was achieved only between 1847 and 1855, while the application of statutory controls to shipping within the British Isles was negligible until 1863. In 1819 supervision of shipping was initiated in the United States, whose more rigorous requirements ensured that fares generally exceeded those to British North America until the 1850s.[2] Irish bargain-hunters adeptly exploited the wild fluctuations in fares to America according to demand, season, shipping line, and ports of departure and arrival, though the average fare probably changed little between the 1830s and mid-century. In 1832 a steerage passage from Ireland to New York cost 90 shillings, a pound less than the fare from Bristol, but three times the fare from Irish ports to Quebec. During and just before the famine tickets might often be had for less than £3, and even in the mid-1850s the price was only a few shillings greater. This was nevertheless a substantial sum even for a small farmer, comparable with half the cost of a heifer, a summer's earnings, or the annual rent for a typical western holding. Since a similar outlay was normally required for 'outfit', inland transportation, landing money, and perhaps port taxes, emigrants without funding from their predecessors had to show much resourcefulness in order to escape from Ireland. Those bound for Australia, for which the full fare was between £10 and £15 in 1848, could seldom hope to travel without state assistance. But the majority making for the United States displayed a keen market sense, often travelling to distant ports in search of cheap or discounted tickets, frequently taking the cheaper routes via Canada despite the arduous onward journey to the United States that this might entail. For those headed for America, and even more so Britain, the costs of passage were seldom an impassable barrier to emigration.

The indirect costs and risks associated with emigration were also more

[1] *Mr Le Fanu's report... on the port of Cork as a packet station for communication with America* (Dublin, 1851), p. 11.
[2] Adams, *Ir. emigration to New World*, pp 160–63; MacDonagh, *Pattern of govt growth, passim*; Charlotte Erickson, 'Emigration from the British Isles to the U.S.A. in 1831' in *Population Studies*, xxxv, no. 2 (1981), p. 175; E. P. Hutchinson, 'Notes on immigration statistics of the United States' in *Journal of the American Statistical Association*, liii (1958), pp 1016–17.

apparent than prohibitive. Until 1850, when the introduction of iron-hulled screw steamers reduced the emigrant's passage to about a fortnight, the Atlantic crossing typically took more than a month. For emigrants forgoing employment at home the opportunity-cost was therefore considerable; but since most were either unemployed or underemployed in Ireland, the length of transit imposed little burden except for the cost of provisions beyond the statutory requirement,[1] and the risks of discomfort, seasickness, susceptibility to infection, and shipwreck. Only about fifty-nine passenger vessels plying between the British Isles and America were wrecked between 1847 and 1853; but those wrecks were widely publicised and fear of a watery death was doubtless exaggerated. The same applied to shipboard mortality, which was only a severe risk in the case of the 'coffin ships' making for Canada in 'Black '47'. The fetid holds provided a congenial breeding ground for lice-borne fever bacilli, and 'ship fever' ravaged the famine-weakened emigrants both during and after the voyage. Of nearly 100,000 emigrants who embarked for Quebec in 1847 over one-sixth died on board ship, in the hospital on Grosse Isle, or elsewhere in Canada East or West while still under official scrutiny. Those leaving Cork and Liverpool were particularly at risk. A medical officer at Grosse Isle observed 'a stream of foul air issuing from the hatches as dense and as palpable as seen on a foggy day from a dung heap'; while the philanthropist Stephen de Vere noted 'water covered with beds cooking vessels etc. of the dead. Ghastly appearance of boats full of sick going ashore never to return. Several died between ship and shore. Wives separated from husbands, children from parents etc.'[2] Despite this appalling carnage the risk of death in other seasons and other routes than the Canadian was seldom greater than 2 per cent. Between 1842 and 1846 recorded shipboard mortality among all overseas emigrants from the British Isles was one in 160, while by 1858 it had fallen back to one in 500.[3] The lingering nightmare of the coffin ships did not impede emigration, serving merely to divert it elsewhere and to instil a lasting distaste for Canada as a destination. And if the urgent desire to leave Ireland could overcome that horror, it is scarcely surprising that emigrants brushed aside the more humdrum inconveniences of seasickness, infestation, cramped and insanitary accommodation, appalling food, despotic ships' officers, and hostile fellow passengers; not to speak of the predatory crooks, touts, runners, or sharpers who preyed upon them before, during, and after the voyage. Neither death nor discomfort could staunch the flow out of Ireland.

[1] Above, p. 576.
[2] J. D. Gould, 'European intercontinental migration, 1815–1914' in *Journal of European Economic History*, viii, no. 3 (1979), pp 593–679; ix, no. 1 (1980), pp 41–112; ix, no. 2 (1980), pp 267–315 (see especially first article, p. 613); Terry Coleman, *Passage to America* (London, 1972), pp 120, 236–8; MacDonagh, *Pattern of govt growth*, pp 183, 187–8, 213, 304; *Papers relative to emigration to the British provinces in North America*, pp 13–18, H.C. 1847–8 (964), xlvii, 385–90; Woodham-Smith, *Great hunger*, p. 224; diary of Stephen de Vere, 16 June 1847 (T.C.D., MS 5061).
[3] MacDonagh, *Pattern of govt growth*, pp 187, 304.

Whereas the impediments to emigration were ineffectual, the agencies promoting it were sophisticated and operative from an unexpectedly early date. The 'diffusion' of the mental readiness to emigrate, which according to Gould was a process that took many decades to accomplish in most European countries, was completed in a matter of months in the Irish case. As already shown, emigration became a national rather than a local experience in the famine period, after which 'feedback' served to reinforce the existing regional patterns of emigration rather than to generate further 'diffusion'.[1] Clearly such an abrupt extension of the emigrant mentality could not have been accomplished without the prior existence of networks of information and marketing capable of penetrating even the most remote townlands. In fact the passenger-broking business, initiated in Dublin and Belfast by Francis Taggart, got under way immediately after the peace of 1815. By 1827 the Canada Company had agents in Dublin, Cork, Limerick, and Omagh as well as Liverpool and New York; while fifteen years later the Cork agent of a single 'bounty' contractor for Australia retained no less than thirty-eight sub-agencies in all four provinces.[2] Naturally the larger passenger trade to the United States gave rise to even denser networks of local agents, often merchants or shopkeepers in small towns, whose advertisements and advice on current bargain fares made emigration seem a routine as well as attractive option. Local newspapers, their readership being extended after the abolition of the stamp tax in 1855, carried notices of forthcoming sailings into humble rural households; while bills and posters began to decorate walls, shopfronts, and even schoolrooms. Indeed, as early as 1834 Henry Inglis 'noticed in one of the poorest cabins, in the neighbourhood of Youghal, where scarcely any furniture was to be seen, one of the printed bills, announcing the approaching departure of a ship for Canada, stuck upon the wall'.[3] Those whose interest had been aroused were inundated with guides and manuals offering practical advice, often with an unmistakable commercial motive but sometimes in the disinterested hope of redirecting emigrants from the urban slums of the New World to 'the interior of the country'. As Edward Hale observed in his letters of guidance published in 1851, 'the competition between different lines of packets and different shipping houses has been enough to scatter through the most barbarous parts of Ireland full information as to the means of passage to America'.[4]

The most important source of practical guidance was the correspondence of the emigrants themselves. The 'American letter' was already an institution in

[1] J. D. Gould, 'European intercontinental migration, 1815–1914' in *Journal of European Economic History*, ix, no. 2 (1980), pp 281, 292–3.

[2] Adams, *Ir. emigration to New World*, pp 76–81; *Third report from the select committee on emigration from the United Kingdom*, p. 463, H.C. 1826–7 (550), v, 685.

[3] Henry D. Inglis, *Ireland in 1834* (2 vols, London, 1834), i, 181.

[4] *Wiley and Putnam's emigrant guide* (London, 1845), p. 136; Edward E. Hale, *Letters on Irish emigration* (Boston, 1852), p. 6.

much of rural Ireland long before the famine, though the prevalence of illiteracy meant that many letters had to be dictated abroad and read aloud at home. Apart from enclosing money (the most eloquent argument for emigration), these letters served to convey information, nominate further emigrants, and reinforce the bonding of separated kinsfolk. In the 1830s transatlantic postage was still expensive and slow, often being entrusted to agents who negotiated with captains or passengers to act as couriers. Yet between 1833 and 1835 over 700,000 letters from New York passed through Liverpool post office, eleven times the reverse correspondence; the bulk of these were probably letters from Irish settlers.[1] Clergymen often provided a combined banking and posterestante service for their flocks. Bishop Doyle of Kildare stated in 1830 that he provided embarking emigrants with testimonials, made block bookings on their behalf through a friend in the shipping trade, read their invariably favourable letters from America, and passed on their remittances. Fr Theobald Mathew testified in 1847 that he had forwarded 'hundreds and hundreds' of emigrant letters: 'being so well known I am a kind of agent'. Three years earlier the parish priest of Schull, County Cork, had remarked that 'when they write home, the friends come to me to read them. The accounts are very flattering. The general observation they make in the letters to friends is, that there is no tyranny, no oppression from landlords, and no taxes.'[2]

Since few of the surviving emigrants' letters have been published or analysed for content, their typical themes and attitudes remain conjectural. Since a primary function of letter writing was to foster further emigration, their tone tended to be enthusiastic, as in this case of a Canadian settler writing home to Crossmolina, County Mayo, in 1831: 'I would recommend any sober, industrious person to come here, where in a few years there will be neither *landlord nor bailiffs to torment us*. I have good times here, I feel myself as good as landlords in Ireland, and much better. Spirits is cheap here, and provisions of every description.'[3] This letter was enthusiastic enough to merit publication in an emigration guide; and it is likely that those letters that were found worth preserving form a biased sample with more orotund phrases and fewer shopping lists than normal. One survey of 189 American letters shows that employment conditions in the United States were less often discussed than religious practices, the weather, or the heavenly host. Irish politics, British tyranny, and even American public affairs were also seldom referred to. Other collections, such as those used by Schrier and those directed to the Spring

[1] Arnold Schrier, *Ireland and the American emigration, 1850–1900* (Minneapolis, 1958), pp 18–42; Marcus Lee Hansen, *The Atlantic migration, 1607–1860* (Cambridge, Mass., 1940), p. 152; *Tables of the revenue, population, commerce, etc., of the United Kingdom and its dependencies, pt VI, 1836*, p. 166 [137], H.C. 1837–8, xlvii, 176.

[2] Evidence of Most Rev. James Doyle (*Poor inquiry, rep. 2*, pp 396–7, 400); evidence of Rev. Theobald Mathew (*Report of the select committee of the house of lords on colonization from Ireland*, p. 248, H.C. 1847 (737), vi, 264); evidence of Rev. James Barry (*Devon comm. evidence*, ii, 959).

[3] *The emigrants' guide* (Westport, 1832), p. 128.

Rices of Foynes, County Limerick, from Australia, concentrated on more mundane matters. These letters often provided statistics of wages, prices, rents, and transportation costs; so conveying to Irish readers and auditors not merely a favourable vision of life abroad, but also precise indications of where to go and what to do upon arrival. Though despair and discontent occasionally intruded, those who 'failed' as emigrants usually ceased to correspond with their connections at home except, on occasion, to solicit reverse remittances.[1]

WHILE emigration remained localised and fitful, many politicians, political economists, and proponents of colonisation advocated some form of state-funded movement out of Ireland. 'Voluntary' emigration was deemed to be removing the wrong people from the wrong regions, taking individuals rather than entire households from localities relatively unburdened by 'overpopulation'. While most commentators denied that emigration could 'cure' Ireland's economic maladies, many treated it not only as a necessary temporary palliative but also as a fact of life; the state's duty was to redirect the existing migratory impulse in order to maximise the benefit for both Ireland and the empire. In the later 1820s J. R. McCulloch, Robert Torrens, Sir Henry Brooke Parnell, and T. R. Malthus all argued that state-funded emigration was a necessary condition for averting famine and unrest in Ireland, though not in itself sufficient. Associated measures such as restriction of subdivision, consolidation of farms, and destruction of vacated cottages were also required in order (as Parnell expressed it) to 'make sure of preventing the vacancies occasioned by it from being filled up', and to render the rural economy attractive to investors. Irish emigration might serve at least two imperial functions. For McCulloch, Parnell, and also Lord Monteagle, the priority was to channel the flow of Irish labourers away from Britain towards the New World; whereas for Torrens the main function of emigration was to provide an industrious and well balanced population for existing or projected colonies. During the 1830s most of Edward Gibbon Wakefield's circle contemplated peopling the colonies with the British, rather than the Irish, surplus; but Torrens, though architect of the least Irish of all colonisations in South Australia, urged establishment of a state-funded 'New Erin' in Canada, New Zealand, or East Africa.[2]

The political clamour for state intervention was greatest at periods when subsistence crises gave practical urgency to theoretical debate, such as the

---

[1] John Hanley, 'A content analysis of nineteenth- and twentieth-century emigrant letters to Ireland' (typescript, 1982); Arnold Schrier, *Ireland and the American emigration, 1850–1900* (Mineapolis, 1958), pp 18–42; N.L.I., MS 13400; Patrick O'Farrell, *Letters from Irish Australia, 1825–1929* (Sydney and Belfast, 1984). See also Kerby A. Miller, *Emigrants and exiles* (New York, 1985), *passim*.

[2] Evidence of Sir Henry Parnell (*Second report from the select committee on emigration from the United Kingdom*, p. 167, H.C. 1826–7 (237), v, 167); Robert Torrens, *Self-supporting colonization: Ireland saved, without cost to the imperial treasury* (London, 1847); Black, *Econ. thought & Ir. question*, esp. pp 203–38.

early 1820s, mid-1830s, and later 1840s. Numerous parliamentary inquiries urged removal of Ireland's 'excess of population' in order to rectify the imbalance 'now existing between the number of the people and the amount of capital which can be profitably employed in creating a demand for labour'.[1] Almost all protagonists in the poor law controversy of 1835–7 proposed some form of state emigration in combination with relief at home. Whately's rejected report called for a temporary but massive investment to permit resettlement in the colonies of all poor people eager and fit for emigration. More modest assistance schemes were proposed in dissenting reports by J. E. Bicheno, Cornewall Lewis, and Nassau William Senior; while even George Nicholls, whose recommendations were substantially implemented, favoured assisted emigration from overpopulated localities as a means of relieving pressure on workhouse relief.[2] In 1837 O'Connell himself urged government aid to emigration, 'which he justly looked upon as the only remedy that was adequate to the disease'; though eight years later he was 'very strongly of opinion that emigration is not a remedy for the evil which at present exists'. His fellow repealer, the landlord William Smith O'Brien, was a more consistent advocate. In 1840 he criticised R. J. Wilmot Horton's scheme for the removal of tenants occupying land wanted for consolidation, on the grounds that this would exclude the class most in need of assistance for emigration, labourers. O'Brien deplored defiance of 'the mandate of heaven—"Be fruitful and multiply"—given to the early fathers of mankind', and urged instead the translation of surplus Irish and English families (at state rather than landlord expense) to 'the unpeopled territories which acknowledge the sway of Great Britain'.[3] Thus support for state funding transcended party divisions in both Ireland and Britain before the famine.

During the famine the familiar arguments were rehearsed with unprecedented vigour. In March 1847 John Robert Godley presented the prime minister with a memorial signed (if not always supported in detail) by eighty 'noblemen, gentlemen, and landed proprietors' including Whately and prominent nationalists such as Maurice O'Connell and Sir Colman O'Loghlen. The memorial urged the creation of Irish colonies in rural Canada under clerical direction, since the Irish had 'no natural leaders but their priesthood', who constituted 'their chief security against falling into a state of anarchy or barbarism'. The *Nation* denounced the 'gang of coward landlords and knavish whigs' who had thus proposed 'wholesale depopulation for the benefit of Canada';

[1] *Report of the select committee on the state of the poor in Ireland*, p. 49, H.C. 1830 (667), vii, 49; *Devon comm. evidence*, i, 28; see also above, pp 121–2.

[2] *Poor inquiry, rep.* 2; *Poor inquiry, rep. 3*, pp 9, 17, 27; *Poor inquiry, app. H, pt II*, p. 40; *Poor inquiry, Lewis remarks*, pp 13–25; *Poor inquiry, Senior letter*, pp 9–10; *Poor inquiry, Nicholls rep. 1*, pp 30–32; *Poor inquiry, Nicholls rep. 2*, pp 22–3.

[3] W. E. H. Lecky, *The leaders of public opinion in Ireland* (revised ed., London, 1871), p. 276; evidence of Daniel O'Connell (*Devon comm. evidence*, ii, 940); William Smith O'Brien, *Emigration* (London, 1840), p. 4.

while *The Times* warned against any 'dangerous experiment to settle a large Celtic sept under its natural and hereditary chiefs in a remote dependency of the crown'.[1] Even Lord Monteagle, for several decades the most persistent and influential whig advocate of state intervention, deemed the scheme too drastic. His own more flexible plan to extend current Australian-directed assistance at an annual charge of £180,000 rather than to colonise Canada at a total cost of £9,000,000, was in turn designated by Clarendon, then lord lieutenant of Ireland, as being 'somewhat too liberal': 'although as an Irish proprietor you would have no difficulty in advocating the project you might hesitate to propose it if you were still chancellor of the exchequer'. The lord lieutenant himself, the prime minister, and the colonial secretary all promoted emigration schemes during the famine years; but their efforts were confounded by mutual bickering, colonial opposition, and effective resistance from Charles Trevelyan, assistant secretary to the treasury, whose opposition was framed in terms of *laissez-faire* doctrine: 'Emigration is open to objection only when the natural checks and correctives have been neutralised by the interposition of the government, or other public bodies.'[2] Yet it was problems of funding rather than principle that thwarted those campaigning for state intervention, divided as they were between raising loans or making grants, paying fares or providing cheap land overseas, and charging expenditure against colonial, imperial, Irish, or local revenues. Any massive expenditure would almost certainly have been levied on Irish proprietors through taxes, rates, or rent charges; but neither landlords not politicians could agree on the area of application or the extent of that additional burden. Thus, even at the height of famine, heavy state commitment was precluded by conflicts of interest and strategy both within and beyond Ireland. Thereafter, the widespread bankruptcy of proprietors and the obvious ubiquity of 'voluntary' emigration meant that state intervention ceased to be regarded as a practical option. State organisation of the Irish exodus, always desirable, but seldom practicable, now seemed unnecessary.

State assistance, where it occurred, was usually either lavish but localised or pervasive but parsimonious. Its most effective intervention was negative and costless: as Beaumont observed in 1863, the state deserved neither praise nor blame for emigration, 'mais son vrai mérite est de l'avoir laissée libre'.[3]

---

[1] Evidence of J. R. Godley (*Report of the select committee of the house of lords on colonization from Ireland*, pp 167–8, H.C. 1847 (737), vi, 183–4); *appendix*, pp 202–16, H.C. 1847 (737-II), vi, 776–90; Oliver MacDonagh, 'Irish emigration during the great famine, 1845–1852' (M.A. thesis, N.U.I. (U.C.D.), 1946) pp 55, 68; [*The Times*], *Great Irish famine of 1845–1846* (London, 1880), p. 98. Smith O'Brien, though not a signatory, had made a similar proposal in January 1847 in his *Reproductive employment* (Dublin, 1847), pp 48–50. For the private doubts of several signatories see Monteagle papers, N.L.I., MS 13400.
[2] Monteagle to Clarendon, 21 Oct. 1848, and Clarendon's reply, 30 Oct. (N.L.I., MS 13400/2); Clarendon to Monteagle, 28 Jan. 1849 (N.L.I., MS 13399/6); MacDonagh, 'Ir. emigration 1845–52', pp 35–6; Lord Monteagle, *Emigration—Ireland* (London, 1847); Charles Trevelyan, *The Irish crisis* (London, 1848), p. 150.

[*See p. 588 for n. 3*]

Between 1788 and 1824 the emigration of skilled artisans had been rather ineffectually prohibited, but those embarking in later years faced no statutory impediments. Restriction of movement, apart from the removal of Irish paupers from Britain under the vagrancy acts and poor law, was thus left to overseas administrations. A capitation tax on passengers arriving in British North America was introduced in 1832 and sharply increased in 1847; while in Massachusetts and New York capitation charges were briefly applied during 1847–8 to supplement the paralysed bonding system. The effective legal exclusion of Irish indigents was accomplished only in the last quarter of the century, when it was no longer necessary.[1]

Early beneficiaries of positive assistance included convicts, the 'free settlers' who followed them, crown witnesses, and military pensioners. Other assisted groups included those sent by James Buchanan from Ulster via New York to Upper Canada (1817), by Richard Talbot from Cloughjordan, County Tipperary, to London in Upper Canada (1818), and by John Ingram from Cork to the Cape of Good Hope (1823).[2] The first major scheme was implemented in 1823 and 1825, when Peter Robinson took 2,592 emigrants from Munster to the Bathurst and Newcastle districts of Upper Canada. The emigrants of 1823 came from the Fermoy region; but those of 1825 were drawn from 50,000 applicants in over ninety parishes, largely belonging to eight estates in the disturbed Blackwater valley. They were mostly catholics, 'in a lower condition of life, who are not possessed of any capital whatever'. As with the Talbot emigration the state's function was to help landlords to clear away surplus households on their estates, and many emigrant families had recently been dispossessed of land despite Wilmot Horton's desire to remove 'paupers'. Yet immense pains were taken to settle them in well planned townships, local support was expressed by priests as well as landlords, and most reports deemed the experiment a success. Robinson and his sponsor Horton hoped to remove 90,000 others through similar schemes. But the very factors that made it successful precluded its repetition: the provision of a free passage supplemented by bread, meat, and whiskey, as well as oatmeal and potatoes, preparation of settlements, and payment for internal transportation in Canada, ensured that the expense per capita was over £20, four times the amount usually spent by later benefactors.[3] Countless petitions were presented on behalf of

[3] Gustave de Beaumont, *L'Irlande sociale, politique et religieuse* (7th ed., 2 vols, Paris, 1863), i, p. xxiv.

[1] See, e.g., W. A. Carrothers, *Emigration from the British Isles* (reprint, London, 1965), pp 154, 197–8; Marcus Lee Hansen, *The Atlantic migration, 1607–1860* (Cambridge, Mass., 1940), pp 257–60.

[2] See H. J. M. Johnston, *British emigration policy, 1815–1830* (Oxford, 1972), *passim*.

[3] Wendy Cameron, 'Selecting Peter Robinson's Irish emigrants' in *Histoire Sociale*, ix, no. 17 (1976), pp 29–46; Alan G. Brunger, 'Geographical propinquity among pre-famine catholic Irish settlers in Upper Canada' in *Journal of Historical Geography*, viii, no. 3 (1982), pp 265–82; evidence of Robert Owen (*Report from the select committee on the employment of the poor in Ireland*, p. 79, H.C. 1823 (561), vi); R. W. Horton, *Ireland and Canada* (London, 1839), p. 53; evidence of Peter Robinson (*Third report from the select committee on emigration from the United Kingdom*, pp 347–8, 416–31, H.C.

aspirant emigrants, but Horton's hopes were frustrated; as were those of the 'Canadians' of the Kerry coast who sold their possessions, went to Cork in expectation of passages, and eventually returned home in a body, 'pitching, like a flock of plover, upon a bog in the same place they left'.[1]

The state's second experiment in clearing a locality of surplus population was undertaken on various crown estates in Roscommon, Galway, Cork, Kerry, and King's County (1847–52) by the quit-rent office and the commissioners of woods and forests. Just over a thousand emigrants in 240 households were removed at the cost of about six guineas a head, still a lavish provision by comparison with that offered by private benefactors.[2] In Ballykilcline, County Roscommon, the state consciously emulated neighbouring landlords who had offered passages to tenants evicted from their holdings in a context of widespread agrarian unrest and refusal to pay rent. Despite initial protest, it was claimed that all emigrants 'went with their own consent, and seemed to be very happy and very grateful for being sent off'. Lord Monteagle remarked that 'the lands are now freed from the locusts. ... There is peace likewise where formerly there would have been insubordination, and they have transformed into consumers of British manufactures abroad men who would only have been White Boys and Molly Maguires without either principles or breeches at home.'[3] Yet no further local clearances were attempted with state involvement until the 1880s, when hardship reminiscent of that in 1847 would momentarily restore the issue to practical politics.

A more lasting function of state funding was to subsidise the emigration of individual paupers as an instrument of poor relief. Even before the poor law of 1838, several groups of 'female orphans' had been dispatched to Australia, at state expense, from institutions such as the Cork foundling hospital. Subsequent legislation enabled meetings of ratepayers (1838) or boards of guardians (1843) to raise rates for the emigration of paupers.[4] The guardians might also contribute a third of the cost of removing non-pauper smallholders if their landlords paid the residue (1847); borrow money on easier terms and send emigrants outside the empire (1849); and draw on a national rate-in-aid (1850–51).[5] Only about twenty-seven paupers benefited from these enactments before 1844, and 306, from nineteen (mainly northern) unions, departed in

1826–7 (550), v, 569–70, 638–53); Jebb papers, T.C.D., MS 6391 (letters from landlords involved). The mean size of emigrant family groups was 5.7 (1823) and 6.5 (1825).

[1] Abstracts from petitions are given in *Report from the select committee on emigration from the United Kingdom*, pp 357–63, H.C. 1826 (404), iv, 357–63; *Third report . . .*, pp 484–99, H.C. 1826–7 (550), v, 706–21. For Kerry's 'Canadians' see *Poor inquiry, app. F, supp.*, p. 211.

[2] Eilish Ellis, 'State-aided emigration schemes from crown estates in Ireland' in *Anal. Hib.*, no. 22 (1960), pp 329–94. Mean group size was 4.4.

[3] Evidence of William Ash and George Knox (*First report from the select committee of the house of lords on colonization from Ireland*, pp 87–90, 96–8, 197, H.C. 1847–8 (415), xvii, 91–4, 100–02, 201); Monteagle to Clarendon, 21 Oct. 1848 (N.L.I., MS 13400/2).

[4] 1 & 2 Vict., c. 56 (31 July 1838), sect. 51; 6 & 7 Vict., c. 92 (24 Aug. 1843), sect. 18.

[5] 10 & 11 Vict., c. 31 (8 June 1847), sect. 13; 12 & 13 Vict., c. 104 (1 Aug. 1849), sect. 26.

1844-6. Later amendments made the law less repugnant to ratepayers, so that 965 emigrants were assisted from twelve unions (principally in Wicklow or Clare) in 1848-9, and 871 from eighteen unions in the following year. Over the next two decades some 26,000 recipients were helped to British North America and other destinations from a wide range of unions.[1] In most cases the beneficiaries were women or children whose passages were paid by relatives or landlords, with the guardians merely providing outfit and transportation to the port of departure. By these means the South Dublin union in 1854 'got rid of a great many refractory girls', many of whom 'turned out very badly; they got a pound on being landed at Montreal, and many of them immediately got drunk'.[2] Between May 1848 and April 1850 the government implemented a separate and better organised scheme for removing female orphans from Irish workhouses to the colonies, whereby unions contributed five pounds per capita for outfit and conveyance to Plymouth, while free passages were provided out of colonial land revenue. All told, 4,175 'orphans' from 118 unions were dispatched in 22 shiploads (11 to Sydney, 6 to Port Phillip, 3 to Adelaide, and 2 to the Cape).[3] Many girls were eager to make the journey, believing 'that on landing husbands would be provided for them' (Birr, 1848); those selected were usually neatly boxed and dressed, and often surprisingly sturdy. A senior official told Nassau William Senior of a Clare orphan who 'weighed 15 stone. "How had she been fed?" I asked. "On potatoes", he answered, "and Indian meal porridge, slightly flavoured with onions. No animal food whatever."'[4] The orphans aroused hostility as well as excitement among the men of New South Wales, Victoria, and South Australia; mainly because of confusion with an earlier shipload of prostitutes recruited in England, they were at first denounced as immoral ('thoroughly bad girls', as the censorious but not irreproachable Sir Charles Dilke later declared). Yet their utility as servants, mistresses, or wives was quickly recognised, and even a group of foul-mouthed female pilferers from Ulster speedily found employment after being banished to the interior.[5]

The bulk of state assistance was funded from colonial land sales rather than

---

[1] Joseph A. Robins, 'Irish orphan emigration to Australia, 1848-1850' in *Studies*, lvii (1968), pp 372-4; Henry Herbert Phear, *Emigration: a summary of the acts* (London, 1886), pp 19-24; Oliver MacDonagh, 'Irish emigration during the great famine, 1845-1852' (M.A. thesis, N.U.I. (U.C.D.), 1946), pp 227-36; *Emigration (Ireland): summary of a ... return of the persons who have emigrated at the expense of the different poor law unions in Ireland, in the years 1844, 1845, and 1846*, H.C. 1847 (255), lvi, 199; Irish poor law commissioners, annual reports, in H.C., *passim*.

[2] Evidence of G. G. Place (*Report from the select committee on poor relief (Ireland)*, pp 214-15, H.C. 1861 (408), x, 236-7).

[3] *Third annual report of the commissioners for administering the laws for relief of the poor in Ireland*, table XVII, pp 133-4 [1243], H.C. 1850, xxvii, 593-4; Robins, op. cit., pp 372-87.

[4] MacDonagh, 'Ir. emigration 1845-52', p. 247; Nassau William Senior, *Journals, conversations and essays relating to Ireland* (2 vols, London, 1868), i, 284.

[5] Robins, op. cit.; Charles Wentworth Dilke, *Greater Britain* (New York, 1869), p. 358. Some unions continued to assist groups of orphan emigrants, where supplementary funding was available, after termination of the government scheme: see S. C. O'Mahony, 'Emigration from the Limerick workhouse, 1848-1860' in *Ir. Ancestor*, xiv, no. 2 (1982), pp 83-94.

Irish taxes or imperial revenue, though the provision of emigrant passages and crown lands was seldom coordinated. Most of the beneficiaries were selected and shipped by the emigration commissioners in London, yet the scale and composition of movement was largely determined by the colonial authorities. After the Robinson experiment the peopling of British North America was accomplished with virtually no state intervention before landing; when Earl Grey proposed free passages from imperial funds for those taking up uncleared lands with a view to future purchase, his scheme was derided as unworkable by colonial politicians and land companies alike.[1] Only in Australia was extensive colonisation attempted. Many forms of assistance to New South Wales were provided, including loans to prospective emigrants (1831); 'bounties' towards the cost of passage for emigrants in certain categories selected by colonists or shipping agents (1835): similar provision for persons selected by the emigration commissioners (1831); and 'nomination' schemes enabling relatives or friends to fund further emigration in conjunction with colonial governments (1848). Assistance was administered spasmodically to about 3,000 recipients between 1832 and 1838; 25,868 bounty and assisted passengers between 1839 and 1845; 13,328 orphans, assisted and nominated emigrants between 1846 and 1850; and another 100,945 in the same categories between 1851 and 1872. Thus the volume of Irish assisted movement to Australia was probably under 150,000, at a cost of well over a million pounds.[2] By comparison, other forms of state assistance benefited only about 3,444 Irish emigrants between 1818 and 1845; 2,826 between 1846 and 1850; and 26,554 between 1851 and 1870. By 1870 the state's lethargy had been elevated into a virtue, causing the under-secretary of state for the colonies to inquire if 'the poor Irish who went over to America and half-starved themselves . . . to pay for the emigration of their friends, would have contributed anything had they known that by dragging at the public coffers they would be able to procure the money?'[3] Ireland had depopulated herself without serious burden on the public purse.

SINCE 'improving' landlords had a clear interest in promoting systematic emigration to cushion the impact of 'clearances', it is not surprising that some of the major architects of state assistance were Irish landlords and their numerous representatives in both houses of parliament. Landlord collaboration with

[1] H. J. M. Johnston, *British emigration policy, 1815–1830* (Oxford, 1972), pp 110–12; MacDonagh, 'Ir. emigration 1845–52', pp 10–12.
[2] R. B. Madgwick, *Immigration into Eastern Australia, 1788–1851* (reprint, Sydney, 1969); Margaret Kiddle, *Caroline Chisholm* (Melbourne, 1950), pp 25–9, 87; Albert A. Hayden, 'New South Wales immigration policy, 1856–1900' in *Transactions of the American Philosophical Society*, n.s., lxvi, pt 5 (1971), pp 1–60; *Returns . . . of the number of emigrants sent out by the government emigration board, . . . 1840 to 1862*, H.C. 1863 (504), xxxviii, 29–36. The last return estimated that the cost of assisted emigration of Irish people to Australia (1840–62) had been £1,176,822, an additional £97,597 having been contributed on their behalf by private nominators.
[3] G. R. C. Keep, 'Official opinion on Irish emigration in the later nineteenth century' in *I.E.R.*, lxxxi (1954), p. 414.

the state was overt in the Talbot, Robinson, and crown estates ventures; implicit in the poor law assistance administered by guardians under landlord direction; informal in the selection of emigrants for Australia, where the Monteagles' personal interventions with T. F. Elliott enabled several hundred inhabitants of the Foynes estate to obtain subsidies. The inadequacy of state provision generated reiterated protest from landlords, of whom 600 attended a meeting at Dublin's Rotunda in January 1846 to demand intervention.[1] A year later Monteagle's nephew Stephen de Vere, who had himself endured a steerage journey to Quebec with a group of his labourers in order to publicise the horrific conditions of passage, stressed that 'a great effort must be made by the state, the counties, the landlords, and the people, in combination, to locate elsewhere the hands that cannot here be paid for their labour, and the mouths that cannot otherwise be fed'.[2] Persistent state recalcitrance left landlords with the options of bewailing official parsimony or providing private funding, or both; the fact that the strongest advocates of state assistance were themselves aiding emigration weakened their appeal *ad misericordiam* while securing their moral impregnability. Few landlords without extensive external income could offer much personal assistance where and when it was most needed. As that great benefactor Earl Fitzwilliam protested in March 1848, 'Shall great public interests be allowed to hang upon accidental private interests? . . . Some have the means, but not the will; some the will but not the means; while others, again, have neither the will nor the means.'[3] The third category probably constituted the majority.

Private benefaction was often crucial in forging local chains of emigration, which soon became self-sustaining, yet it probably affected even fewer emigrants than did state assistance. In Quebec the emigration agent attempted to enumerate passengers assisted from Ireland, being 'dependant entirely on personal inquiry of the individuals themselves, who very often return unsatisfactory replies'. Between 1846 and 1850 he recorded the arrival of 14,213 Irish emigrants with private assistance travelling on 216 ships: over one-twelfth of all Irish arrivals at Quebec and Montreal. Recorded assistance had virtually ceased by 1852.[4] A more impressionistic guide to the scale of private assistance is provided by the medley of memoirs, estate records, and parliamentary and newspaper reports on which map 17 is based.[5] References were found to about 175 cases of assistance by individuals (usually landlords) or groups, who probably aided at least 12,000 emigrants between 1826 and 1845; 22,000 between 1846 and 1850; and 14,000 between 1851 and 1870. Pre-famine assistance was

---

[1] Aubrey de Vere, *Recollections* (New York and London, 1897), pp 223–4.

[2] Ibid., pp 252–4; Stephen de Vere to (?) Lord Monteagle, 13 Mar. 1847 (T.C.D., MS 5053/4).

[3] Earl Fitzwilliam, *A letter to the Rev. John Sargeaunt* (London, 1848), p. 24.

[4] *Papers relative to emigration to the British provinces in North America*, H.C. *passim*, covering 1846–59 with less systematic reports for earlier years; the passage quoted is on p. 10 [777], H.C. 1847, xxxix, 28.

[5] Below, p. 622.

virtually limited to Leinster and Munster, and even after 1845 more aid was offered in Leinster than in Connacht and the afflicted western seaboard. Benefactors were clustered in the south-east, with secondary concentrations in the vicinity of the Shannon and of Sligo. Most of the recorded private assistance was administered by ten proprietors aiding between 1,000 and 7,000 emigrants each. In roughly descending order of their investment, these benefactors were as follows: the fifth Earl Fitzwilliam (Coolattin estate, County Wicklow); Charles Wandesforde (Castlecomer, County Kilkenny); the third marquis of Lansdowne (Kenmare, County Kerry); the fourth marquis of Bath (Farney, County Monaghan); the third Viscount Palmerston (Cliffony, County Sligo); Col. George Wyndham (Tulla, County Clare); Sir Robert Gore-Booth (Lissadell, Co. Sligo); Francis Spaight (Derry, County Tipperary); the third Viscount de Vesci (Abbeyleix, Queen's County); and Major Denis Mahon (Strokestown, County Roscommon). The records of these emigration schemes provide insight into the character and functions of landlord assistance.[1]

The reported subvention per capita seldom exceeded £5, as indicated by table 8.[2] Most major patrons saved expense by chartering entire vessels or negotiating bulk bookings, often in association with other landlords. They usually provided clothing and 'outfit', conveyance and provisions up to the port of embarkation, and a small gratuity or 'landing money' to enable emigrants to make their way 'up country'. Little attempt was made to superintend emigrants after arrival, though one of Wyndham's shiploads was shepherded inland, while an ancestor of W. B. Yeats went to Canada with a group of Gore-Booth's charges in a vain attempt to secure them employment.[3] Additional compensation to outgoing tenants was not consistently provided, depending on local customs of tenant right and the solvency of estates and of individual tenants. Fitzwilliam was probably unusual in offering occasional compensation for surrendered land, whereas most landlords timed their assistance to coincide with expiration of leases, to accompany evictions, or to follow repudiation of leasehold agreements. Spaight and Mahon allowed compensation for abandoned cattle or crops but not land; Bath merely forgave arrears of rent; but Wandesforde, Gore-Booth, and eventually Wyndham also valued household materials and improvements. Compensation was also given by Mahon to unfit members of emigrating households; and by Gore-Booth, Wyndham, and Fitzwilliam to solvent tenant households that declined to emigrate.[4] In many other

[1] The major sources relating to all but two of these proprietors are listed under table 8. MacDonagh, 'Irish emigration to the United States of America and the British colonies during the famine' in Edwards & Williams, *Great famine*, p. 335, offers an upper-bound estimate of 50,000 for landlord-assisted emigrants (1846–52).

[2] Below, p. 615.

[3] Evidence of Sir Robert Gore-Booth (*Third report from the select committee of the house of lords on colonization from Ireland*, pp 124–5, H.C. 1849 (86), xi, 614–15).

[4] Major Mahon's agent, in a report dated 23 July 1847, stressed the relative cheapness of emigration: the annual cost of a pauper at the Roscommon workhouse was £7. 3s. 0d., or £3. 0s. 8d.

cases, no doubt, landlords promoted emigration less directly by merely waiving rent and arrears, permitting sale of tenant right, or providing compensation, without also offering a free passage. Their aim, after all, was not to create colonies but to clear estates at minimum expense.

Control of the selection of emigrants and disposition of vacated property was essential if landlords were to recoup their investment. Spaight made it 'a rule never to take an individual or part of a family; I take the whole family or none, and the house is levelled'. Most benefactors concurred, though Mahon sent a few solitary emigrants and Wyndham assisted single as well as married tenants, while by the 1850s both Fitzwilliam and Wandesforde were relaxing their insistence on emigration in family groups (perhaps in order to reunite strays with those already departed).[1] Table 8 suggests that the mean size of emigrant groups as well as Irish rural households in general was about six.[2] The composition of emigrant groups also reflected prevailing household structure, at least in the case of groups approved for emigration by Fitzwilliam's agents between 1847 and 1856. In percentage terms, 63.9 were simple family households, whereas 1.5 were solitaries, 2.1 simple families with a parent, 5.6 groups of unmarried people such as siblings, 8.0 multiple and 18.9 otherwise extended family households.[3] Landlords usually confined assistance to direct tenants or sub-tenants on land falling out of lease, though Fitzwilliam's agents sometimes removed sub-tenants on condition that middlemen occupied vacated property themselves. Lansdowne's agent, however, evidently offered passages to all paupers chargeable to the estate, so causing alarm among the Kenmare guardians as swarms of emigrants presented themselves at the workhouse to pass his poverty test. Gore-Booth 'had applications to a very considerable amount above those that I sent out', despite restricting his offer to direct tenants. But his rule was flexible: preference was given to 'what might be termed the bad characters' such as poteen makers; stowaways were treated indulgently; and unexpected vacancies were allocated less restrictively to those standing by.[4]

By investing in emigration, landlords hoped to curtail subdivision and promote consolidation of holdings. Aided, of course, by later 'voluntary' emigration, they were usually successful; though one of Wyndham's neighbours in Clare claimed just before the famine that subdivision had not

for a person receiving outdoor relief (*First report from the select committee of the house of lords on colonization from Ireland*, pp 202–4, H.C. 1847–8 (415), xvii, 206–8).

[1] Quoted in Charlotte Erickson, *Emigration from Europe, 1815–1914* (London, 1976), p. 35.
[2] Below, p. 615.
[3] My analysis is drawn from the Coolattin emigration accounts, N.L.I., MSS 4974–5. 'Simple' families consist of a couple with or without children, or children with a parent; 'multiple' families include at least two simple family units. The proportion of simple family groups steadily increased between 1847 and 1856, while that of extended family groups decreased.
[4] Evidence of Sir Robert Gore-Booth (*Second report from the select committee of the house of lords on colonization from Ireland*, pp 261, 265–6, H.C. 1847–8 (593), xvii, 269, 273–4). He could prove that his first shipload had carried £1,500 with them.

been prevented. Most donors believed that clearances softened by assisted emigration benefited the recipients as well as themselves. As J. L. Foster put it in 1827,

you thus also apply your benevolence to the class, which of all others requires it the most; no language can adequately describe the sufferings of those unfortunate persons ejected, often in great numbers, with their wives and children, from their habitations, and without money or food, and scarcely with clothing, thrown upon society, everywhere unwilling to receive them; you thus also remove the class which is of all others most likely to disturb the peace of the country.[1]

But landlord benevolence had a sharp edge, exposed by a Galway proprietor in 1844: 'The people are very anxious to get rid of the population, which is a very bad stock, and to put the land into grass as much as possible. [What has become of the tenants?] Some of the agents have sent them away. . . . They all get rid of them, more or less.' As O'Connell exclaimed in January 1845, 'one of the great mischiefs in Ireland I think is, that it seems to be taken for granted that man is a nuisance'.[2] The assisting landlords endeavoured not only to remove nuisances but also to prevent their subsequent reappearance in the guise of relatives claiming their former holdings. Spaight required emigrants to level their own houses to prevent repossession, while Fitzwilliam further insisted that there be a house to be levelled. His agents' enquiries into applications for assistance offer a unique insight into the convoluted housing arrangements adopted by the Wicklow peasantry. Apart from scribbling notes such as 'No house to come down therefore will not be sent', they queried cases where houses were subdivided, where only part of the normal household was seeking emigration, or where some of the applicants were normally resident elsewhere. A son-in-law was rejected because 'he lives in the barn—a separate dwelling'; a father of five was queried for having let 'a *part* of his house to a man from Ballybegg about a year back who is still in possession'; whereas it was thought 'desirable to get rid of' a widow as her evicted brothers-in-law 'still frequent her house'. The virtual restriction of landlord assistance to households with something to surrender meant that those most in need of removal from Ireland (squatters, labourers, or paupers) were least likely to receive it.[3]

Despite the harsh and restrictive economic logic underlying landlord emigration schemes, most donors received more applications than they could satisfy. Up to the 1850s most tenants were prepared to accept free passages as an alternative preferable to eviction and ruin at home. Spaight 'never pressed

---

[1] *Third report from the select committee on emigration from the United Kingdom*, pp 310–11, H.C. 1826–7 (550), v, 532–3.

[2] Evidence of J. H. Burke (*Devon comm. evidence*, ii, 551–2); evidence of Daniel O'Connell (*Devon comm. evidence*, iii, 940). See also David Fitzpatrick, 'Irish emigration in the later nineteenth century' in *I.H.S.*, xxii, no. 86 (Sept. 1980), p. 133.

[3] N.L.I., MSS 4974–5. Wandesforde, however, assisted many labourers and colliers who held cabins with little or no land: in 1847, only about one-quarter of families assisted were currently holding land. See William Nolan, *Fassadinin* (Dublin, 1979), p. 207.

one individual to go'; Wandesforde's emigrants left 'all at their own earnest request'; Mahon noted 'the anxiety of the tenants to emigrate' even without the encouragement of ejectment decrees; and the parish priest at Drumcliffe, County Sligo, testified that Gore-Booth's scheme 'was perfectly voluntary, and ... that they were all well clothed, well fed, and were supplied with good bedding at your expense', so securing 'for you and your family a very large and enviable amount of sincere affection'. Reluctance was greater on the Bath estate, where 'a great many persons refused to take the benefit of the offer'; and the Wyndham estate, whence some surplus tenants 'would not go, and they are now squatting about ... in the most miserable condition'. Many accepted or sought assistance *faute de mieux*; thus a Sligo tenant seeking compensation for his land and crops from Charles O'Hara had

> Decided on going to Meraca. ... Ptr [Petitioner] never would go if he could over come the Calamity that Surrounds the Countery and the land of his birth, but to become a pauper in the Countery Ptr Shuders and Chills at the thoughts of it. Ptr has three Acres of oats and Barley on his ground cabages And all other things that dos become a Small farm.

But other beneficiaries of assistance rushed joyously to the quays, like Lansdowne's pauper emigrants who celebrated their arrival in Cork by dashing semi-naked through the streets, 'all in the most uproarious spirits'.[1]

There is little evidence of popular resistance to emigration schemes, though the estate 'improvements' that followed sometimes generated unrest or violence. 'Grabbers' who had taken land vacated by emigrants were occasionally attacked by kinsmen or neighbours, as in the case of a northern protestant named Brock who took a farm on the Lorton estate at Ballinamuck, County Longford, and was murdered in 1835. Lord Lorton thereupon announced that 'he would clear the town, and have every house thrown down' in reprisal, an action not calculated to enhance the benevolent reputation of assisting landlords.[2] Major Mahon of Strokestown was himself assassinated in 1847 after removing 217 families from an estate from which no rent could be collected. The plot was evidently conceived against his agent by tenants fearing eviction; but hostility against the landlord was reinforced when one vessel put back in distress and rumour had it that Mahon had hoped to drown his tenantry. Fifteen years later another 'very rich, and very liberal' landlord was the target of a murder conspiracy on account 'of his having emigrated some people, and drowned them on their passage'.[3] Landlords sending 'coffin ships' to Canada in

---

[1] Charlotte Erickson, *Emigration from Europe, 1815–1914* (London, 1976), p. 33; *Report from the select committee on outrages (Ireland)*, p. 254, H.C. 1852 (438), xiv, 272; evidence of Rev. Patrick Shea (*Devon comm. evidence*, ii, 647); Micheal Foard to Richard Beere, agent (N.L.I., MS 20376); W. Steuart Trench, *Realities of Irish life* (London, 1868), pp 125–6; sources from Wandesforde and Gore-Booth as for table 8.

[2] Evidence of Thomas Courtenay (*Devon comm. evidence*, iii, 803); Oliver MacDonagh, 'Irish emigration during the great famine, 1845–1852' (M.A. thesis, N.U.I. (U.C.D.), 1946), p. 196.

[3] Evidence of George Knox (*First report from the select committee of the house of lords on colonization*

1847 were often blamed for shipboard mortality and denounced for culpable negligence, though official investigations unsurprisingly exonerated such proprietors as Gore-Booth, Palmerston, Wandesforde, Fitzwilliam, and de Vesci. Canadian vituperation against the 'worthless and unprincipled hirelings' organising these emigrations should be balanced against the grandiloquent expressions of gratitude to landlords and captains that were published by 'committees of passengers' on several of the ships involved. Passengers on the *Aeolus* at St John's, New Brunswick, thanked 'our ever-to-be-remembered late landlord, Sir Robert Gore-Booth, Bart., Sligo: he was always kind to his tenants; it was not tyranny which forced us to emigrate—it was the loss of our crops for two years past'.[1] In the circumstances of famine it was those who were refused assistance who were more inclined to condemn it as 'tyranny'. After the early 1850s landlords rapidly lost enthusiasm for both estate reorganisation and investment in emigration as the land market subsided from volatility into stagnation.

The philanthropic urge, unless activated by the profit motive, proved predictably feeble in generating assistance. An exception was Vere Henry Lewis Foster, who later in the century was to squander his inheritance in promoting emigration, instead of promoting emigration in order to preserve his inheritance. Foster's aim was to assist single girls out of Ireland, rather than to uproot families. Between 1849 and 1857 he aided 1,250 girls from Louth and Clare as well as 40 labourers, providing up to £8 a head for passage, provisions, utensils, bedding, clothing, and landing money. He circulated a quarter of a million free copies of his unusually useful emigrant manual, made two steerage crossings of the Atlantic, and personally arranged ancillary services abroad. Such largesse naturally made Foster an object of general suspicion. His appeals for subscriptions raised only £109 from donors other than his eldest brother Frederick, while the tenantry of Louth was still more hostile than the gentry. When one party of his emigrants arrived at Drogheda

there was the greatest excitement on the quay. Many of the farmers were mad with me for reducing the supply of labourers and servant girls; and alternate entreaties, threats, and force were used to prevent many of my party from embarking, cries being got up that my intention was to make protestants of them; that they were to be bound for a term of years; to be sold to 'the blacks', to the Mormons, etc., etc.[2]

Other philanthropists whose venal motives could not be confirmed, such as Caroline Chisholm in New South Wales, were calumniated likewise for their

from Ireland, pp 199–206, H.C. 1847–8 (415), xvii, 203–10); MacDonagh, 'Ir. emigration 1845–52', pp 194–5; Nassau William Senior, *Journals, conversations and essays relating to Ireland* (2 vols, London, 1868), ii, 218 (relating a conversation with Lord Rosse in 1862 concerning a Clare man returning from Melbourne).

[1] *Papers relative to emigration to the British provinces in North America*, p. 36 [932], H.C. 1847–8, xlvii, 342, and *passim*; J. Elizabeth Cushing and others, *A chronicle of Irish emigration to Saint John, New Brunswick, 1847* (St John, 1979), p. 18.

[2] Mary McNeill, *Vere Foster, 1819–1900* (Newton Abbot, 1971), pp 89, 57, 83–6, 95, 100; Vere

attempts to ease the female emigrant's path to the New World. Such suspicions were indeed often justified in the case of the many 'Irish emigration societies', which sprang up in all the major cities of Irish settlement. These bodies helped administer immigrant reception centres such as Castlegarden in New York (opened in 1855); offered benefit schemes, lodgings, and advice on employment; and sometimes exploited newcomers under the cloak of benevolence.

The only other likely source of institutional assistance towards emigration was the catholic church, for which emigration carried the promise of spreading the gospel in the New World as well as the threat that the faith would perish in cities of sin. The Irish clergy did little to assist emigration beyond acting as brokers, agents, or postmasters, though a few priests contemplated accompanying their parishioners to more salubrious homes abroad and establishing 'catholic colonies'. Godley, Fitzgerald, Smith O'Brien, and even Earl Grey had favoured colonisation under clerical leadership, and ineffectual attempts were made to solicit support from Archbishop MacHale of Tuam.[1] Two parish priests did propose colonisation schemes in 1849: James Maher of Graigue, County Carlow, and Thomas Hore of Killaveny, County Wexford. Maher formed a Leinster Emigration Society in the hope of founding New Carlow on a tract of public land by the Mississippi; but he was opposed by other priests and did not accompany his parishioners. Hore induced 1,200 farmers to gather in Liverpool, where however he lost control of them before the intended removal to Arkansas could take place. It is worth noting that Hore had sought support from Fitzwilliam:

he says that several families would go with him if they got even small assistance from you, a few pounds, say £5 or £10, for each family. He is anxious that they should go with him but affects very strongly that the holdings in that parish must be put together and enable tenants to pay for them, and in many cases new tenants put into them.[2]

More serious attempts to establish Irish catholic colonies were initiated by clergy in America and Australia, who were alarmed at immigrant concentration in cities and hoped to reinforce their spiritual solidarity through segmentation. The most celebrated scheme was promoted by Bishop John Ireland at St Paul, Minnesota, in the 1870s; but half a century earlier Bishop John England had urged creation of catholic colonies in the West, while other bishops supported

Foster, *Work and wages* (5th ed., London, 1855); M. A. Busteed, 'A Liverpool shipping agent and Irish emigration in the 1850s' in *Transactions of the Historic Society of Lancashire and Cheshire*, cxxix (1979), p. 153.

[1] For MacHale's position, see J. E. Fitzgerald to Stephen de Vere, 26 Aug. 1849 (T.C.D., MS 5053/13); Lord Ashburton to Spring-Rice, 28 Mar. 1847: 'if John of Tuam is up to such a task such a scheme might be rendered practicable but I fear John's energies are all for mischief' (N.L.I., MS 13400/1).

[2] Oliver MacDonagh, 'Irish emigration during the great famine, 1845–1852' (M.A. thesis, N.U.I. (U.C.D.), 1946), pp 47–50; Robert Chaloner to Lord Milton, 14 May 1850 (Wentworth Woodhouse Muniments, Sheffield Central Library, G 35/238a).

colonies in Maine, Arkansas, Iowa, Minnesota, and Nebraska. The Young Irelander Thomas D'Arcy McGee summoned an Irish Emigrant Aid Convention at Buffalo, New York, in 1856, which raised many promises but few dollars towards establishing Irish rural communities, 'with church and school', in several western and Canadian locations. The failure of most of these schemes was due as much to their obvious financial unsoundness as to the desire among many American bishops to 'Americanise' rather than segregate immigrant catholics.[1] An unusually successful scheme was initiated by Bishop Quinn in Queensland, who imported 6,000 Irish settlers during the 1860s. With the help of his brother (a priest in Dublin) and a visiting Australian priest, Fr Patrick Dunne, Quinn was able to overcome both clerical opposition in Ireland and the baneful effects of a fire at sea that gutted the ship bearing the second contingent. Queensland officials reluctantly conceded that the bishop's emigration society, though 'essentially of a private character', had acted 'in accordance with the existing regulations'; and agreed to honour land orders, provide reception facilities, and leave selection and shipping of further emigrants to the society.[2] In general, however, the church's role both in Ireland and abroad was to exhort and minister to the streams of emigrants rather than to select, superintend, or settle them.

OF the five million emigrants who left Ireland between 1801 and 1870 only about one in twenty received state or private assistance, amounting to less than £2 million. Since that assistance was both localised and largely directed towards less impoverished regions and classes, most 'pioneer' emigrants had to rely on their own sparse resources of cash, derived from dowries, tenant right payments, sale of livestock, or wages. In November 1847 the emigration commissioners reported

that long beforehand, the people were engaged in their preparations to escape from the want and misery of their own country. All the money that could be spared was laid by, and the savings banks were laden, as is well known, with deposits, which the best informed persons did not doubt to be destined for this purpose. No emigration could have been more thoroughly spontaneous.[3]

Communal resources were sometimes redistributed in response to appeals from poor would-be emigrants. In Limerick (1847) they went about 'collecting half-crowns and shillings, and all persons, even the poor, are willing to give what they can to assist such an object'. In Down (1835) as in Galway (1852),

[1] See for example Maldwyn Allen Jones, *American immigration* (Chicago, 1960), pp 122–3; Carl Wittke, *The Irish in America* (Baton Rouge, 1956), pp 64–72; James P. Shannon, *Catholic colonization on the western frontier* (London, 1957).

[2] James Francis Hogan, *The Irish in Australia* (Melbourne and Sydney, 1888), pp 155–64; R. G. W. Herbert to Bishop James Quinn, 7 May 1862 (N.L.I., MS 22942).

[3] *Papers relative ● emigration to the British provinces in North America, and to the Australian colonies*, p. 32, H.C. 1847–8 (50), xlvii, 38.

watches or 'trifling articles' were raffled to raise passage money; while subscriptions were often raised in pubs and shebeens to enable the chosen perpetrators of outrage to escape abroad.[1]

Once enough pioneers had raised funds for their own passages, emigration would soon become self-sustaining in the locality. Those who assisted emigration often marvelled at the mechanism they had activated. Lansdowne's removal of paupers was soon followed by the voluntary emigration of many smallholders and 'vast numbers' of cottiers and sub-tenants; Wandesforde's emigrants brought out their siblings from home; Palmerston's 2,000 beneficiaries of 1847 paid the passages of twice that number within eighteen months; while ninety-two of Vere Foster's girls from Clare had remitted £1,058 and sent for ninety-seven further emigrants within four years of their own departure in 1852. More modest benefactions were equally reproductive, as in the Donegal case of a widow's son who borrowed his passage money from an uncle in 1845, sent home enough to maintain his family through 1846 and 1847, and with the help of another expatriate son and fifty shillings raised locally was able to bring out his four remaining brothers and mother in 1848.[2] Irish emigrants quickly acquired the reputation of being unusually generous towards their home connections and willing to sacrifice individual for family interests. 'Invitations' and 'entreaties' were already encouraging further movement from Cork in 1826; while by 1834 'the humbler class of protestants' in Ulster were emigrating in succession, using fares paid to captains in America by their relatives. The Whately commission showed that emigrant remittances (even apart from prepaid passages) were contributing to household income in almost three-fifths of the 106 parishes examined, the proportion exceeding three-quarters in both Leinster and Ulster.[3] Several investigations in the later 1830s confirmed the peculiar propensity of emigrants to send both remittances and prepaid passages, and remittances from the United States were thought to exceed a million dollars in 1846.[4] Reports of emigrant largesse abounded in 1847, when for example the New Brunswick emigration agent referred to this 'pleasing proof of the strength of their family ties, and of the sacrifices they cheerfully make in the discharge of their filial and parental duties'.[5] From 1848 onwards

---

[1] Evidence of Aubrey de Vere (*Report of the select committee of the house of lords on colonization from Ireland*, p. 537, H.C. 1847 (737), vi, 553); *Poor inquiry, app. F, supp.*, pp 322–4; G. R. C. Keep, 'The Irish migration to North America' (Ph.D. thesis, Dublin, 1951), p. 39.

[2] W. Steuart Trench, *Realities of Irish life* (London, 1868), p. 127; evidence of John Walsh (*Report of the select committee of the house of lords on colonization from Ireland*, p. 193, H.C. 1847 (737), vi, 209); MacDonagh, *Pattern of govt growth*, p. 30; McNeill, *Vere Foster*, p. 86; evidence of J. V. Stewart (*Second report from the select committee of the house of lords appointed to inquire into the operation of the Irish poor law*, pp 466–7, H.C. 1849 (228), xvi, 478–9).

[3] Evidence of Redmond O'Driscol (*Report from the select committee on emigration from the United Kingdom*, p. 196, H.C. 1826 (404), iv); Lewis, *Local disturbances*, p. 457; *Poor inquiry, rep. 1*; *Poor inquiry, app. A*.

[4] George W. Potter, *To the golden door* (Boston and Toronto, 1960), pp 119–20.

[5] *Papers relative to emigration to the British provinces in North America, and to the Australian colonies*, p. 67, H.C. 1847–8 (50), xlvii, 73.

official statistics of doubtful quality were collected from shippers and bankers dealing with the North American passenger trade. From half a million pounds in 1848, the stated volume of remittances rose to a million in 1850 and to a peak of a million and three-quarters in 1854. It declined fairly steadily over the following decade but recovered to three-quarters of a million in 1870. In 1868, as in 1848, about two-fifths of these payments were through prepaid passages, enough to bring out up to three-quarters of all emigrants from the British Isles to North America. The trend in remittance payments roughly corresponded to those in both emigration and the American business cycle, though year-by-year fluctuations cannot be explained in terms of recent variations in the intensity of emigration.[1] 'Emigration begets emigration', as the emigration commissioners observed in 1849; and within a few years the 'stream of gold' had penetrated even the most remote districts of Ireland.[2]

Particularly in the first half of the century, it was common practice for a young husband (or occasionally a wife) to emigrate alone in the hope of earning or borrowing enough to bring out their family after a year or so. Once abroad, pioneers like the Mangans of Cavan[3] would fret about their spouses and children and family cohesion. As a husband in Baltimore wrote to his Galway wife in 1848:

I send home this 10 pound; I hope that it will not be long untill I send for ye all. I would make aragement to send for some of ye, But I expect to bring ye all from Liverpool. I would rather ye would be all Together than to seperate ye from each other. . . . I hope that my fine children is all Together. . . . We are all very clean here; every one in this Country wash their faces and comes their hair three times a day.[4]

It was reported in Longford (1835) that sometimes 'a married man, driven to despair by his hopeless condition, takes the extreme step of deserting his family, and absconding to America, leaving his wife and children with very slender means of subsistence'; though always with the 'fixed intention' of sending for them when able.[5] During the famine husbands were particularly inclined to exploit the public relief system: able-bodied men would desert their families and 'proceed to America immediately, and probably they are not heard of for months, and a great many when they get out there marry again; they forget that they have wives and families at home, and their wives and families remain as permanent paupers in the workhouse'. Monteagle, however, felt that such forgetfulness was characteristic of those choosing England rather than

---

[1] Arnold Schrier, *Ireland and the American emigration, 1850–1900* (Minneapolis, 1958), pp 103–28. Correlation of year-by-year changes in the reported volume of remittances with emigration to North America four years earlier was insignificant.

[2] Report from Moher (Co. Clare), xxxix, 380 (department of Irish folklore, U.C.D.); evidence of T. W. C. Murdoch (*Fifth and sixth reports from the select committee of the house of lords appointed to inquire into the operation of the Irish poor law*, p. 972, H.C. 1849 (507), xvi, 1004).

[3] Above, pp 563–4.

[4] James H. Tuke, *Report of visit to Connaught* (2nd ed., London, 1848), p. 48.

[5] *Poor inquiry, app. A*, p. 403.

America; while in 1871 another Limerick witness stated that desertion by emigrating husbands was limited to towns, where 'the social ties have been broken in a way that they would not have been if they had been left in the country'.[1] In general, the fact that wives consistently outnumbered husbands on census night indicates the geographical extension rather than break-up of Irish families.

After about 1850, as rural society stabilised and the removal of entire households became less common, another model of chain emigration became predominant. In 1852 an Armagh linen merchant, who had handled numerous remittances and 'thousands of their letters', discerned 'almost an organised system' in his locality: 'a son or daughter goes first, acquires some money, and sends it home; ... the money which is sent takes out another member of the family, and at length the whole family go'. To render this system possible, the pioneers would adopt 'habits of very low living' for the first three or four years, but then tended to fall 'into the more expensive habits of the people of the States, and rarely remit much money home'.[2] This system enabled the surplus children of a rural household to emigrate successively, though on occasion remittances were forthcoming not merely from siblings but 'from uncles and aunts, and even from friends'. Irish emigrants were indeed notable for the broad range of kinship obligations that they honoured. In 1853, for example, a Melbourne grocer's assistant and his wife told the Monteagles that they would 'ever pray for the Lady and your Lordship, for sending us from a starved Country to where we can have good earnings and enough to Eat. My lord, I hope you will send out both my Brothers in laws for this order of Twelve pounds, 8£ for the two Michael and Richard Hartnett and 4£ for my cousins in law.'[3] The changing pattern of emigrant remittances is illustrated by table 9,[4] which compares drafts sent home from pre-famine Canada with nominations lodged in post-famine Victoria. The Canadian transactions represent a transfer of resources from men to women, who constituted three-fifths of recipients but only one-fifth of donors. Wives and mothers each constituted one-quarter of all beneficiaries; but since the median draft to a wife was twice that to a mother, it seems likely that the intention was to assist wives to Canada while paying pensions to mothers in Ireland. Siblings and children together accounted for only a quarter of those receiving payments, and tended to receive less money than wives.[5] The statistics of payments lodged in Victoria on behalf of

[1] Evidence of Col. W. A. Clarke (*Fourth report from the select committee of the house of lords appointed to inquire into the operation of the Irish poor law*, pp 754-5, H.C. 1849 (365), xvi, 778-9); Monteagle to Senior, 6 Sept. 1852, in Nassau William Senior, *Journals, conversations and essays relating to Ireland* (2 vols, London, 1868), i, 302; evidence of J. B. Hewson (*Report from the select committee on law of rating (Ireland)*, p. 204, H.C. 1871 (423), x, 216).

[2] Evidence of William Kirk (*Report from the select committee on outrages (Ireland)*, pp 451-2, H.C. 1852 (438), xiv, 469-70).

[3] Evidence of E. A. Smith (*Report from the select comittee on passengers' act*, p. 622, H.C. 1851 (632), xix, 664); Patrick Kelly to Lord Monteagle, 9 June 1853 (N.L.I., MS 13400/3).

[4] Below, p. 616.

[5] The most common relationships of recipient to sponsor (with median amount of remittance)

nominees in the British Isles, though relating only to passage money, reveal a different pattern. The majority of recipients were siblings, while very few were parents, children, or wives. By comparison with persons nominated in Victoria for emigration from Britain, the Irish nominees were far more likely to be 'cousins' or 'friends', less likely to be children, and less likely to be nominated as part of a family group.[1] The peculiar importance of the chain mechanism to Irish emigration is exemplified by Irish eagerness to exploit the nomination schemes available in New South Wales and South Australia as well as Victoria. By the later 1850s most Irish assisted emigrants to all colonies were being sponsored by colonial connections, compared with small minorities of English and Scottish emigrants. In 1861–2 virtually all Irish arrivals, but few from elsewhere, were so funded.[2] Irish emigration had become overwhelmingly a movement of individuals within a family chain that progressively bore away the surplus of each maturing generation.

Thus Irish emigration was essentially a family movement. Most emigrants left alone, but in response to family pressures at home and with assistance from family abroad. For this reason the emigration cannot be explained in terms of 'push' or 'pull' factors acting on individuals governed by self-interest. Even so, push factors often contributed to the critical decision to initiate emigration from a household. In the prelude to famine, emigrants were pushed out of a widening region by estate reorganisation, by declining domestic textiles production, by static demand for farm labour as against increasing supply, and above all by recurrent subsistence crises. The importance of the decline of textiles was reflected in the concentration of intensive emigration in northern counties (map 14A). The effect of short-term food shortages is illustrated by the violent fluctuations in overseas movement traced in figure 3, though the regions of worst shortage as yet had relatively light emigration. Peaks in outward movement occurred in 1831–2, 1834, 1836–7, and 1841–2; whereas partial but major failures in the potato crop were reported in 1829–30, 1832–4, 1836, 1839, and 1841–2. Thus food shortages were usually followed by a sharp

were mothers (56, £3. 15s. 0d.); wives (54, £7. 10s. 0d.); fathers (51, £6. 5s. 0d.); brothers (26, £6. 5s. 0d.); sisters (20, £5. 0s. 0d.); sons (7, £7. 0s. 0d.; and daughters (6, £3. 15s. 0d.). Cases involving multiple recipients are excluded from these statistics, though not from table 9. The median remittance from male donors was £6. 5s. 0d. compared with £5 from female donors; by coincidence, the same differential applies to recipients.

[1] The most common relationships of Irish recipients to Geelong sponsors were sisters (188), brothers (180), mothers (23), sons (18), daughters (10), fathers (7), and wives (7). Corresponding numbers of non-Irish recipients were 75, 38, 5, 67, 55, 4, and 30 respectively. 45 per cent of Irish recipients were nominated in groups of three or more, compared with 70 per cent of non-Irish recipients.

[2] *Returns ... of the number of emigrants sent out by the government emigration board, ... 1840 to 1862,* H.C. 1863 (504), xxxviii, 29–36. In 1861–2 the percentage ratio of *statute adults* sent out after nomination in the colonies, to all assisted *emigrants*, was 85 (Irish), 39 (English), and 24 (Scottish) for New South Wales; 62 (Irish), 17 (English), and 7 (Scottish) for Victoria; and 91 (Irish), 21 (English), and 10 (Scottish) for South Australia. Since some assisted emigrants were under 12 years, the true proportions of nominated emigrants were somewhat higher.

increase in emigration.[1] The convulsive 'push' of the famine years, when alternative strategies for coping with shortages became ineffectual, generated heavy emigration from all regions dependent on potato production: as J. B. Byles put it, 'the furies of want, misery, and despair scourge the emigrants from our shores'. In local if not national terms we may accept MacDonagh's suggestion 'that the potato blights of 1845–9 caused a volte-face in the general attitude to emigration'. Yet the famine's longer-term impact was not so much to relax 'the peasant's desperate hold upon his land and home' as to replace the conviction that a peasant holding could sustain an entire Irish family with the belief that it could sustain half a family. During and after the famine, though not before, the pseudo-Malthusian model of emigration as a 'prudential check' on overpopulation is starkly confirmed by the regional distribution of out-migration rates.[2]

In 1851 *The Times* asserted that 'emigrations commonly begin in repulsion, and go on with attraction'.[3] The fact of previous emigration certainly intensified the 'pull' from abroad, both by diffusing favourable reports and by generating practical mechanisms for translating longing into realisation. In Ulster the impact of American 'pull' factors was noted by A. C. Buchanan as early as 1827.

We can always tell in the season before, in the north of Ireland, whether we are likely to have a large emigration; it depends upon the success that the emigrants met with in the preceding year; they write home letters, and if the season has been favourable, if there has been any great demand for labour, like the Western Canal, that absorbs a great many of them, they send home flattering letters, and they send home money to assist in bringing out their friends.

Yet variations in the pull exercised by American demand for labour had little detectable impact on fluctuations in the overall movement out of Ireland until the 1850s. Indeed the two major periods of build-up in pre-famine emigration outside Europe (1828–31 and 1838–42) coincided with recessions in the United States (1825–30 and 1837–43). The famine years were marked by low but stable prices in the United States, whereas Britain was experiencing an unmistakable economic downturn; consequently the Irish were often 'pushed' out of Britain as well as Ireland.[4] The coincidence of Irish famine, British recession, and

[1] Below, p. 617. For a summary of potato failures, following Wilde, see Connell, *Population*, p. 145.

[2] John Barnard Byles, *Sophisms of free trade* (8th ed., London, 1851), p. 311; MacDonagh, 'Irish emigration to the United States of America and the British colonies during the famine' in Edwards & Williams, *Great famine*, p. 331.

[3] J. D. Gould, 'European intercontinental migration, 1815–1914' in *Journal of European Economic History*, viii, no. 3 (1979), p. 632.

[4] Evidence of A. C. Buchanan (*Third report from the select committee on emigration from the United Kingdom*, p. 110, H.C. 1826–7 (550), v, 332); B. R. Mitchell, *International historical statistics: the Americas and Australasia* (London, 1983), p. 835 (wholesale price index for the United States). There was no significant correlation between year-by-year fluctuations in that index and in Irish overseas emigration lagged by a year (1825–70).

American stability was probably a major factor in diverting the majority of Irish emigrants from Britain to America. Thereafter the chain mechanism sustained this imbalance for nearly a century.

From the later 1850s, short-term fluctuations in emigration were largely determined by 'pull' factors (interpreted as differences in attainable living standards between Ireland and the host societies). As Lasteyrie wrote in 1860: 'it is no longer the destitution of Ireland, but the wealth of Canada, of the United States, and of Australia, which now promotes Irish emigration'.[1] Figure 3 indicates that year-by-year fluctuation had become much milder than before the famine; while the fluctuation that occurred could no longer be attributed to Irish 'push' factors. Major declines in potato production occurred in 1855–7, 1858–61, and 1864–6; yet in each case less emigration occurred in the following year than hitherto.[2] The volume of emigration was now subject to longer-term cyclical movement rather than short-term deviation. European migration from the 1860s onwards followed a cycle closely akin to the trans-atlantic building cycles: that is, heavy emigration was associated with extensive building activity in America and inactivity in Britain. The fact that the British and American cycles now moved in opposite phase may itself have been a manifestation of the flow of migratory labour, which tended to 'overreact' to changes in relative living standards and so generate changes in the reverse sense. Thomas concludes that 'the timing of the mass immigration into the United States in the late forties and early fifties was determined by expulsive forces in the Old World. After the structural change of the late sixties it would seem that the "pull" element is as evident in the long cycles of migration as it is in the short cycles.' This analysis may plausibly be applied to the Irish case, with the caveat that the linkage of the three cycles was probably achieved by 1860. Irish emigration touched its lowest volume since the famine in 1861, only two years before British building activity peaked; whereas emigration tended to increase between 1867 and 1873, a period during which American building activity reached a summit. 'Pull' factors also helped determine fluctuations in Irish emigration from year to year, though differences in employment levels seem to have carried more weight than income differences.[3] Thus the ebbs and

---

[1] Jules de Lasteyrie, *A few observations upon Ireland* (Dublin, 1861). The sentence quoted closely follows an earlier essay published in 1853.

[2] Except in the 1870s, there was no significant negative correlation between year-by-year fluctuations in tonnage of potato production and in Irish emigration lagged by a year (1852–1914). Emigration was lower in 1858 than in 1855–7; lower in 1862 than in 1860–61; and declined steadily between 1863 and 1868. We therefore reject the hypothesis of inverse correlation presented in Stanley C. Johnson, *History of emigration from the United Kingdom to North America, 1763–1912* (London, 1913), pp 52–3.

[3] Brinley Thomas, *Migration and economic growth* (2nd ed., Cambridge, 1973), pp 103, 116, 158, 175–8, 411–13; Richard A. Easterlin, 'Influences in European overseas emigration before World War I' in *Economic Development and Cultural Change*, ix, no. 3 (1961), p. 347 (taking long swings in rate of growth in real product per capita rather than building activity); J. D. Gould, 'European intercontinental migration, 1815–1914' in *Journal of European Economic History*, viii, no. 3 (1979),

flows of movement now reflected economic calculation rather than the blind desire to escape destitution at home.

The persistence of intensive emigration from generation to generation cannot however be explained by reference to individual calculations of self-betterment. Economic fluctuations after the 1840s affected the timing of emigration (and, to some extent, its direction), but the intention to emigrate was not governed by the same factors that hastened or postponed its realisation. Movement out of Ireland was renewed with each generation not merely by the chain mechanism, but because it provided a continuing justification for rearing more children than could hope to find employment or marriage partners at home. Irish couples persisted in rearing an average of six children because, above all, they regarded children as potential assets, provided that most of them emigrated. Some at least of one's emigrant offspring could be expected to provide supplementary income for 'uneconomic' households, social insurance for ageing parents, and passages for yet more emigrants. Children, in short, were frequently 'reared for emigration'. In the words of a ballad set in Sligo,

> My father was a farming man, used to industry,
> He had two sons to manhood grown, and lovely daughters three,
> Our acres few that would not do, so some of us must roam,
> With sisters two I bade adieu to Erin's lovely home.[1]

Thus emigration became a phase of the rural life-cycle, to the extent that 'the structure of family and social life has become conditioned to a continued reorganisation as members move away'.[2] Since emigration normally occurred shortly before marriage became probable, and close to the moment when household control was transferred from one generation to another, the decision to emigrate may be treated as the outcome of a choice between marriage and succession, celibacy and dependency in Ireland, and departure. The choice of both emigrants and successors was made within a family rather than individual context, since the allocation of roles had vital consequences for all members of the household productive unit. The third alternative, unmarried dependency, was usually the unwanted outcome of missing both the match and the boat. It may plausibly be argued that heavy continuing emigration was a necessary condition for perpetuating a social system marked by high marital fertility, infrequent marriage, restricted subdivision of land, and an archaic rural structure propped up by 'American money'. Yet analysis of the workings of post-famine society is clearly not a topic properly treated under the heading of emigration, since the latter was only one component of a system, however far-reaching its

pp 646-52. Gould provides a useful epitome of the mass of econometric studies of temporal fluctuations in European emigration to the United States.

[1] 'The emigrant's tragedy (Answer to "Erin's lovely home")' in Robert L. Wright, *Irish emigrant ballads and songs* (Bowling Green, Ohio, 1975), p. 104.

[2] John Archer Jackson, *The Irish in Britain* (London, 1963), p. 30.

consequences. It would be enough to have shown that the practical expectation of future emigration was built into the mentality of the representative Irish child, so becoming a fact of life to be coped with rather than desired or rejected. In the words of Edward Senior, poor law commissioner, in 1855, 'everybody has one leg over the Atlantic'.[1]

NOTE ON MAPS 14-16

In these maps the counties of Ireland are shaded according to rank order, in eight groups, each including four counties ranked 1–4, 5–8, 9–12, 13–16, 17–20, 21–4, 25–8, 29–32. The following table shows for each map the highest value in each group and also the lowest value among the thirty-two counties. All figures are percentages.

	rank								
map	1	5	9	13	17	21	25	29	32
14a	51.62	42.06	40.60	40.06	37.24	34.41	29.99	26.29	9.79
14b	51.75	49.03	44.65	42.90	40.59	38.64	36.80	30.73	0.14
14c	48.40	40.99	40.24	38.98	37.70	35.81	32.77	28.42	8.52
14d	41.77	38.25	36.49	35.81	33.78	32.03	30.35	26.94	9.46
15a	51.90	49.34	48.52	48.28	48.01	46.73	44.86	43.70	38.69
15b	19.42	18.53	18.04	17.78	17.17	16.68	16.05	15.55	14.29
16a	83.51	81.69	79.46	74.66	71.42	69.22	64.48	55.23	14.06
16b	60.45	50.33	37.38	35.15	28.92	24.29	20.32	16.14	−2.72

[1] *Report from the select committee on poor removal*, p. 232, H.C. 1854–5 (308), xiii, 246. For a brief survey of the consequences of emigration, see David Fitzpatrick, *Irish emigration, 1801–1921* (Dublin, 1984), pp 31–42.

APPENDIX

1 RATES OF OUT-MIGRATION FROM IRELAND, 1821–71

	cohort depletion				emigration from Irish ports	
	1821–41	1841–51	1851–61	1861–71	1851–60	1861–70
Leinster	34.05	33.27	31.21	25.75	15.92	10.89
Munster	29.34	39.41	41.25	34.38	27.36	21.33
Ulster	38.85	37.68	30.26	28.30	18.17	14.24
Connacht	33.42	47.97	39.85	39.04	15.58	13.71
Ireland	33.99	38.99	35.25	31.01	19.70	15.16
coefficient of variation	18.1	14.3	15.0	12.7	25.7	29.1

Source: *Census Ire., 1821–71*; *Agricultural statistics, Ire., 1856–70*. For full bibliographical references see Vaughan & Fitzpatrick, *Ir. hist. statistics*, pp 355–61, 365–6.

Cohort depletion is the percentage depletion over an intercensal decade of the cohort initially aged 5–24 years (6–15 years in the case of depletion over the two decades 1821–41). Rates of emigration from Irish ports give the number of 'permanent' emigrants enumerated by the constabulary (adjusted for non-specification of origin, using data of origin for emigrants from each major port) per 100 of the mean census population for the decade. In order to allow for lack of returns for the first four months of 1851, statistics for 1851–60 are inflated by one-fourteenth of the emigration recorded between May 1851 and December 1855. The coefficient of variation gives the standard deviation of percentages for 30 counties (excluding Dublin and Antrim) multiplied by 100, and divided by the mean percentage for those counties.

2 DISTRIBUTION OF IRISH-BORN OUTSIDE THEIR NATIVE COUNTIES, 1851–71

year	Ireland	Britain	U.S.A.	Canada	Australia	total (5 cols)	native county
			thousands				
1851	549.6	727.3	961.7	227.0	70.2	2,535.8	5,952.1
1861	459.9	805.7	1,611.3	286.0	177.4	3,340.3	5,260.7
1871	489.2	774.3	1,855.8	223.3	213.8	3,556.3	4,817.6
			% OF MIGRATORY IRISH-BORN IN EACH REGION				
1851	21.7	28.7	37.9	9.0	2.8	100	
1861	13.8	24.1	48.2	8.6	5.3	100	
1871	13.8	21.8	52.2	6.3	6.0	100	
			% OF LOCAL POPULATION IN EACH REGION				
1851	8.4	3.5	4.1	9.2	17.4	4.7	
1861	7.9	3.5	5.1	8.7	15.4	5.2	
1871	9.0	3.0	4.8	6.0	12.9	4.7	

Statistics are derived from national census returns for dates close to the stated years (preceding year for U.S.A.). Precise criteria of enumeration varied between countries: the military are excluded from the Irish statistics (1851), the Channel Islands and the Isle of Man from the British, and outlying territories from the Canadian. Figures for Australia involve estimation. Irish settlers in other regions such as New Zealand, South Africa, and South America are ignored.

3 AGE-DISTRIBUTION OF EMIGRANTS FROM IRISH PORTS, 1851-70

age-groups	age-groups as % of total emigrants			
	1851–5	1856–60	1861–5	1866–70
MALES				
under 15 years	11.41	7.97	9.19	6.46
20–24 years	13.81	17.82	17.57	21.76
all males	49.87	53.28	52.67	58.48
FEMALES				
under 15 years	11.10	7.61	8.84	5.99
20–24 years	14.17	15.02	16.12	15.62
all females	50.13	46.72	47.33	41.52
TOTAL EMIGRANTS (000s)				
	748.0	415.4	467.3	382.5

Source: *Census Ire., 1851*, pt vi, p. lv [2134], H.C. 1856, xxxi, 55; *Agricultural statistics, Ire., 1856-70*.

Males and females, distinguishing those belonging to two age-groups, are given as percentages of all 'permanent' emigrants enumerated at Irish ports for whom ages were returned. The first quinquennium excludes the first four months of 1851.

4 OCCUPATIONS OF IRISH MALE MIGRANTS, 1820–67

destination	years	labourers	farmers
		as % of male emigrants	
Boston[1]	1822–39	62.7	10.4
New York[2]	1820–48	56.8	15.7
extra-European	1857[3]	81.1	8.1
extra-European	1867[4]	83.4	6.4
returned from U.S.A.[1]	1858–67	37.7	8.4
all	1851–5	86.0	4.5
		as % of males resident outside native county	
Ireland outside native county[5]	1841	37.2	7.0
	1851	37.4	7.5
	1861	32.5	9.5
		as % of total Irish males	
Ireland[5]	1841	54.4	19.4
	1851	50.3	20.2
	1861	45.7	23.1

Sources: for Boston, Cormac Ó Gráda, 'Across the briny ocean' in T. M. Devine and David Dickson (ed.), *Ireland and Scotland, 1600–1850* (Edinburgh, 1983), p. 125; for New York, Mokyr, *Why Ire. starved*, p. 250; for 'extra-European', *Return of the numbers of emigrants* [1848–67], H.C. 1868–9 (397), l, 487–92; for 'returned from U.S.A.', Marjolein 't Hart, 'The returned emigrants in nineteenth-century Ireland' (M.A. thesis, Groningen, 1981), p. 42; for the remainder, *Census Ire., 1841–61*. Statistics for Boston, New York, and 'returned from U.S.A.' are based on samples from passenger manifests.

The table shows the percentage of all males (with specified occupations) who were returned as labourers (including agricultural and general labourers, farm servants, and other skilled agricultural workers, but not domestic servants), and as farmers (including graziers and proprietors).

[1] Servants included with labourers.
[2] Excluding children under 15 years.
[3] Excluding cabin passengers.
[4] Including cabin passengers.
[5] Excluding soldiers.

5 OCCUPATIONS OF MALE MIGRANTS ACCORDING TO BIRTHPLACE, 1831-67

destination	years	% of male emigrants					
		labourers			farmers		
		Ireland	England	Scotland	Ireland	England	Scotland
U.S.A.[1]	1831	39.1	9.5	17.3	20.2	24.6	15.3
returned from U.S.A.[2]	1858-67	37.7	19.4	9.8	8.4	12.4	11.3
U.S.A.[3]	1857	81.4	36.4	24.2	6.4	17.6	20.7
British North America[3]	1857	84.1	54.3	35.9	10.9	16.4	14.4
Australasia[3]	1857	79.7	41.0	56.4	11.9	10.2	12.3
total extra-European[3]	1857	81.1	40.1	40.5	8.1	13.5	15.5
U.S.A.[4]	1867	85.4	48.0	40.3	5.6	7.2	6.4
British North America[4]	1867	66.2	29.0	17.4	13.9	16.6	22.8
Australasia[4]	1867	72.3	22.1	58.6	10.2	9.4	12.5
total extra-European[4]	1867	83.4	41.8	38.0	6.4	8.3	11.4

Sources: for U.S.A. in 1831, Charlotte Erickson, 'Emigration from the British Isles to the U.S.A. in 1831' in *Population Studies*, xxxv, no. 2 (1981), pp 175-98; returned from U.S.A., 1858-67, Marjolein 't Hart, 'The returned emigrants in nineteenth-century Ireland' (M.A. thesis, Groningen, 1981), p. 51; for the remainder, *Return of the number of emigrants* [1848-67], H.C. 1868-9 (397), l, 487-92. Statistics for the U.S.A. in 1831 and 'returned from U.S.A.' are based on samples from passenger manifests.

The table shows the percentage of all males (with specified occupations) who were returned as labourers (including agricultural and general labourers, farm servants, and other skilled agricultural workers, but not domestic servants), and as farmers (including graziers and proprietors).

[1] The criteria for inclusion are unclear, and labourers specified as agricultural may have been counted as farmers. Those under 20 years are excluded, and the figures are apparently based on place of departure rather than birthplace.

[2] Servants included with labourers.

[3] Excluding cabin passengers.

[4] Including cabin passengers.

6 COHORT DEPLETION AND LITERACY FOR IRELAND AND MAYO, 1841–71

cohorts	Ireland			Mayo		
	1841–51	1851–61	1861–71	1841–51	1851–61	1861–71
			DEPLETION AS % OF COHORTS			
literates						
males	43	39	39	50	34	42
females	41	40	35	44	47	47
illiterates						
males	56	56	54	64	52	53
females	52	52	46	59	51	47
			% OF TOTAL DEPLETION			
literates						
males	41	40	48	21	21	32
females	22	29	39	7	13	23

Source: *Census Ire., 1841–71*.

Cohort depletion is the percentage depletion over an intercensal decade of the cohort initially aged 15–24 years (16–25 years in the case of 1841–51 and 1851–61), calculated separately for each sex and for the literate and illiterate cohorts. The depletion statistics slightly overstate the out-migration of persons initially unable to read, since some people aged over 15 years presumably became literate thereafter. The category of 'illiterates' includes those returned as able to 'read only'.

7 IRISH EMIGRANTS ASSISTED TO EASTERN AUSTRALIA, 1844-69

categories	% of Irish assisted emigrants							
	N.S.W.	N.S.W. (Sydney)					Victoria (Port Phillip)	
	1844-5	1848-50	1853-5	1856-60	1861-5	1866-9	1848-50	1852-9
males	46.4	30.6	34.7	52.3	51.4	48.7	30.9	30.2
labourers as % of males	81.1	86.3	86.8	91.4	85.9	87.0	90.8	93.6
under 14 years	26.9	13.9	17.5	11.5	9.7	8.9	16.1	15.6
Roman Catholics	54.5	70.2[1]	78.0	80.5	81.4	83.4	65.3[1]	80.5
literates	52.1	41.6[1]	44.8	48.4	58.9	67.4	41.6[1]	45.3
number of emigrants	2,163	6,566	12,062	12,219	11,400	2,059	3,628	26,845

Sources: *Copy of the report of the committee of the legislative council of New South Wales on the subject of immigration*, H.C. 1846 (418), xxix, 225; *Papers relative to the emigration to the Australian colonies . . .* [1163], H.C. 1850, xl, 29; *Copies of extracts of any despatches relative to emigration to the Australian colonies . . .*, H.C. 1851 (347), xl, 9; *Papers relative to emigration to the Australian colonies* [1489], H.C. 1852, xxxiv, 417; *Reports of the immigration agent for N.S.W.* (1853-69) and Victoria (1852-9), in *Votes and proceedings* of the N.S.W. Legislative Assembly and the Victorian Legislative Council, *passim*. For other years data are missing.

New South Wales excludes the Port Phillip district (1848-50), which became Victoria in 1851, and excludes Queensland after its separation in 1859. Statistics of 'bounty' emigration (1 Jan. 1844 to 31 Aug. 1845) include Port Phillip. Child emigrants are those under 12 rather than 14 years in the case of N.S.W. (1859, 1861-9).

Occupational statistics give the proportion of male emigrants other than children returned as (agricultural) labourers, herdsmen, etc.; literacy statistics show the proportion of emigrants other than children who could read and write.

[1] 1848 only.

8 COST AND FAMILY GROUPING OF LANDLORD-ASSISTED EMIGRATION, c.1835-55

landlords	period of assisted emigration	cost (£)	number	cost per capita	family groups		
					number	families	mean size of family group
Fitzwilliam[1]	1842–6	–	–	–	560	124	4.5
Fitzwilliam[2]	1847–56	19,018	5,903	3.2	5,924	889	6.7
Wandesforde[3]	to 1847	14,525	4,854	3.0	–	–	–
Wandesforde[4]	1847–53	–	–	–	2,844	668	4.3
Lansdowne[5]	from 1851	17,059	4,616	3.7	–	–	–
Bath[5]	from 1851	7,988	2,459	3.2	–	–	–
Wyndham[6]	1839–47	7,634	1,582	4.8	1,582	238	6.6
Gore-Booth[7]	1835–42	784	262	3.0	262	42	6.2
Gore-Booth[7]	1847–8	5,936	1,122*	5.3*	–	–	–
Spaight[8]	from 1846	6,000	1,400	4.3	–	–	–
Mahon[9]	1847	3,571	883*	4.0*	883*	217	4.1*

Asterisked figures refer not to individuals but to 'statute adults' (children under 12 years counted as half units; infants omitted). In some cases the reported cost of emigration probably excludes ancillary expenses. 'Family groups' often include kinsmen or friends not immediately related to the head of the emigrating household. The Fitzwilliam emigration registers are inflated slightly by inclusion of persons approved for emigration who did not embark.

[1] N.L.I., MSS 18429.

[2] N.L.I., MSS 4974–5; Finlay Dun, *Landlords and tenants in Ireland* (London, 1881), p. 32ᴬ

[3] *Report of the select committee of the house of lords on colonization from Ireland; together with the minutes of evidence . . .*, p. 193, H.C. 1847 (737), vi, 209.

[4] N.L.I., MS 4178.

[5] *Report from the select committee of the house of lords on the Tenure (Ireland) Bill [H.L.], together with the proceedings of the committee, minutes of evidence, and index*, pp 18–19, H.C. 1867 (518), xiv, 458–9.

[6] As in note 3 (p. 140).

[7] *Second report from the select committee of the house of lords on colonization from Ireland; together with the further minutes of evidence . . .*, pp 258–9, 260–61, H.C. 1847–8 (593), xvii, 266–7, 268–9.

[8] *Report from the select committee on law of rating (Ireland); together with the proceedings of the committee, minutes of evidence, appendix, and index*, p. 436, H.C. 1871 (423), x, 448.

[9] N.L.I., MS 10138; *First report from the select committee of the house of lords on colonization from Ireland; together with the minutes of evidence*, p. 201, H.C. 1847–8 (415), xvii, 205.

9 RECIPIENTS OF REMITTANCES FROM CANADA AND VICTORIA, 1843–61

source of remittance	recipients	years	total	female	sibling	spouse	parent	child	cousin
					relationship to sponsor				
NUMBERS									
Canada Company	Irish	1843–5	269	157*	60	57	119	33	n.a.
Geelong	Irish	1856–8	744	410*	368	63	43	126	144
Geelong	other	1856–8	499	279*	113	85	13	239	49
Victoria	Irish	1861	2,526	1,535	1,299	203	81	363	580
Victoria	other	1861	3,984	2,407	940	1,019	100	1,549	376
PERCENTAGES									
Canada Company	Irish	1843–5	100	62.3*	22.3	21.2	44.2	12.3	n.a.
Geelong	Irish	1856–8	100	55.4*	49.5	8.5	5.8	16.9	19.4
Geelong	other	1856–8	100	56.7*	22.6	17.0	2.6	47.9	9.8
Victoria	Irish	1861	100	60.8	51.4	8.0	3.2	14.4	23.0
Victoria	other	1861	100	60.4	23.6	25.6	2.5	38.9	9.4

Sources: for Canada, Gerald Merrick, 'Canada Company remittances' in *Ir. Ancestor*, xii, nos 1–2 (1980), pp 84–7; xiii, no. 1 (1981), pp 4–9; xiv, no. 2 (1981), pp 99–104; for Geelong, 'Immigration remittance regulations of 1st August 1856' (Geelong Immigration Officer, 1 vol.), in Public Record Office of Victoria (Laverton), Trade and Customs: ser. 22, no. 15; for Victoria, *Reports of emigration and immigration for 1861* in *Votes and Proceedings* of the Victorian Legislative Council, 1861–2, iii, 1415.

The table shows the sex, and relationship to sponsor, of recipients of remittances sent through the Canada Company (Jan. 1843 to May 1845) and the Victorian government, from the Geelong district (Aug. 1856 to Apr. 1858) and from all Victorian districts (1861). The figures exclude a few cases where no precise relationship was specified (Canada Company). In asterisked cases the breakdown by sex excludes a few recipients whose sex was unclear. The categories of 'sibling', 'parent', and 'child' include some less immediate relatives of the same generational level; the 'cousin' category includes 'friends' and others who could not be classified by generational level. All 'heads of family', as returned in the Victorian statistics (1861), are counted as spouses; though some of the 82 Irish and 346 non-Irish male heads were presumably fathers of nominators rather than husbands, as only mothers were separately returned.

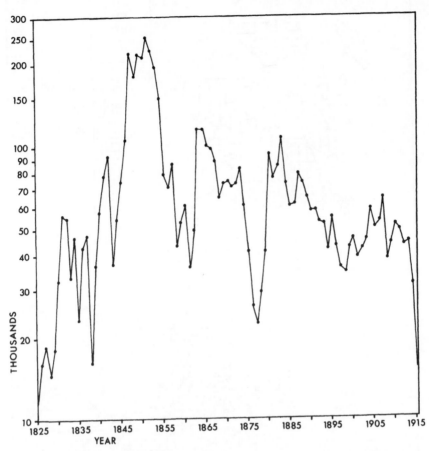

Figure 3 IRISH OVERSEAS EMIGRATION, 1825–1915: NUMBERS
LEAVING THE UNITED KINGDOM PER ANNUM,
by David Fitzpatrick

Commission on emigration and other population problems, 1948–1954: reports (Dublin, 1955), pp 314–16.
Erroneous returns up to 1842 have been corrected.

Statistics refer to Irish-born passengers leaving United Kingdom ports for destinations outside
Europe and the Mediterranean. Precise criteria were altered several times, and the graph is most
useful as a guide to short-term and cyclical fluctuations.

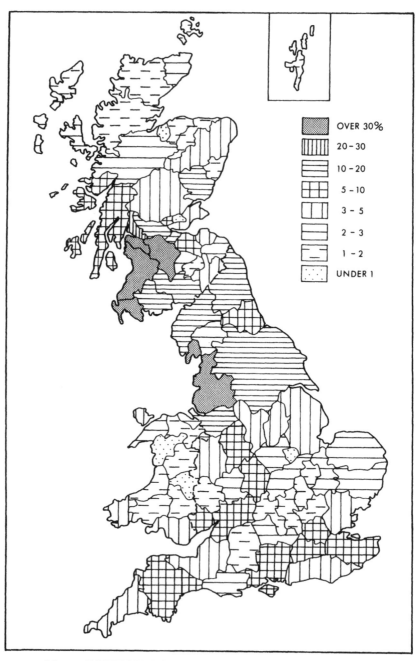

Map 11 BRITISH COUNTIES, 1841: IRISH-BORN AS
PROPORTION OF POPULATION BORN OUTSIDE COUNTY OF
RESIDENCE, by David Fitzpatrick

Census G.B., 1841 [496], H.C. 1843, xxii, 1.

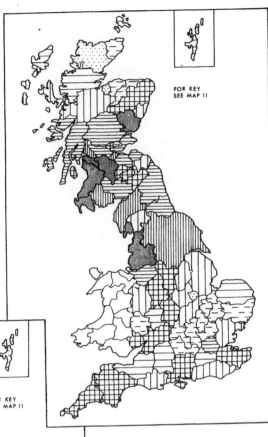

Map 12 BRITISH COUNTIES, 1851: IRISH-BORN AS PROPORTION OF POPULATION BORN OUTSIDE COUNTY OF RESIDENCE, by David Fitzpatrick

Census G.B., 1851, pt II, i [1691-I], H.C. 1852–3, lxxxviii, pt I, 1; ibid., vol. i [1691-II], H.C. 1852–3, lxxxviii, pt II, 1. Data for Welsh counties are not available.

FOR KEY SEE MAP 11

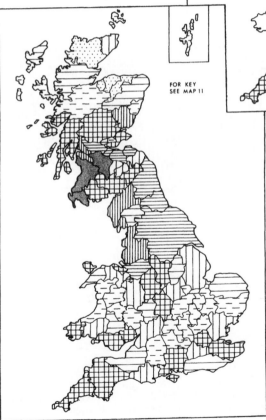

FOR KEY SEE MAP 11

Map 13 BRITISH COUNTIES, 1871: IRISH-BORN AS PROPORTION OF POPULATION BORN OUTSIDE COUNTY OF RESIDENCE, by David Fitzpatrick

Census Eng., 1871 [C 872], H.C. 1873, lxxi, pt I, 1; *Census Scot., 1871* [C 841], H.C. 1873, lxxiii, 1.

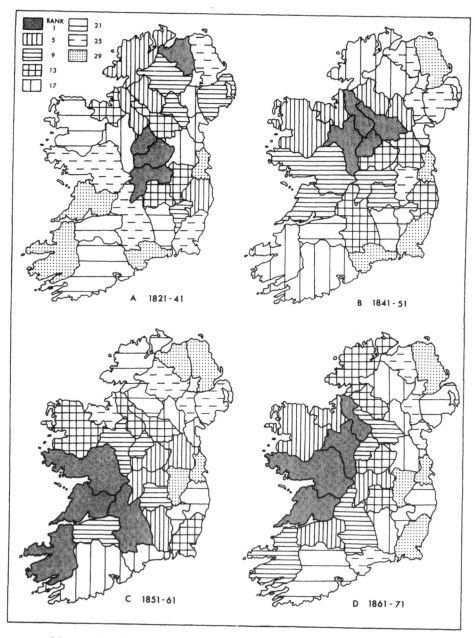

Map 14 COHORT DEPLETION, 1821–71, by David Fitzpatrick

Census Ire., 1821–71. See notes on tables 1 and 6 above, pp 608, 613. Each map shows the percentage depletion over an intercensal decade of the cohort initially aged 5–24 years (6–15 years in the case of depletion over the two decades 1821–41). The key is explained above, p. 607.

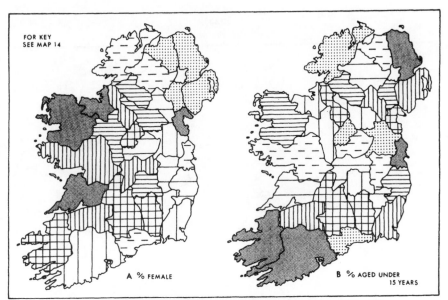

Map 15 EMIGRANTS FROM IRISH PORTS, 1851–75,
by David Fitzpatrick

Census Ire., 1851, pt VI, p. liv [2134], H.C. 1856, xxxi, 54; *Agricultural statistics, Ire., 1856–75*; see also Vaughan & Fitzpatrick, *Ir. hist. statistics*, pp 269–343.

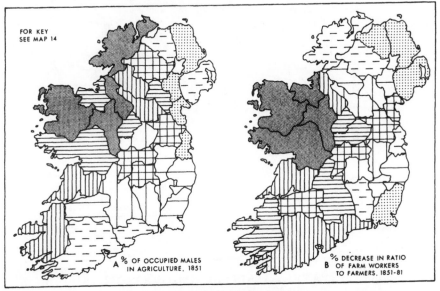

Map 16 OCCUPIED MALES IN AGRICULTURE, 1851; DECREASE
IN RATIO OF FARM WORKERS TO FARMERS, 1851–81,
by David Fitzpatrick

Census Ire., 1851 [2134], H.C. 1856, xxxi, 1; *Census Ire., 1881*, pt I, i [C 3042], H.C. 1881, xcvii, 1; ii [C 3148], H.C. 1882, lxxvii, 1; iii [C 3204], H.C. 1882, lxxviii, 1; iv [C 3268], H.C. 1882, lxxix, 1.

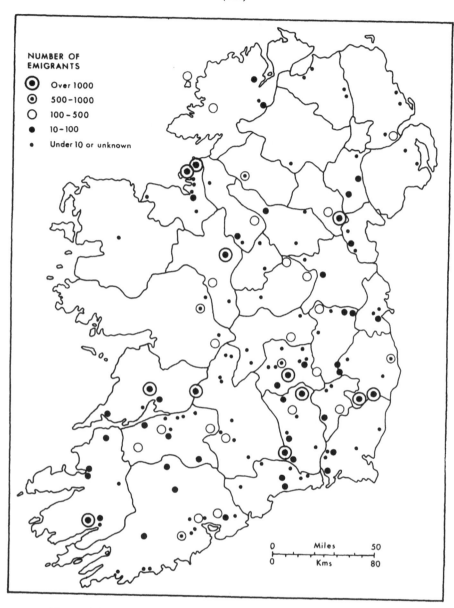

Map 17 PRIVATELY ASSISTED EMIGRATION, 1826–70,
by David Fitzpatrick

Data are drawn from a wide, but not exhaustive, range of parliamentary reports, estate records, and historical works; for examples, see table 8, above, p. 615. Approximate locations of recorded cases of assistance are shown; a few could not be located. Lower-bound estimates are given for the numbers of emigrants receiving any financial assistance from landlords or other non-official benefactors.

CHAPTER XXIX

'A peculiar tramping people': the Irish in Britain, 1801–70

DAVID FITZPATRICK

England is guilty towards Ireland; and reaps at last, in full measure, the fruit of fifteen generations of wrong-doing. . . . Crowds of miserable Irish darken our towns. . . . The uncivilised Irishman, not by his strength, but by the opposite of strength, drives out the Saxon native, takes possession in his room. There abides he, in his squalor and unreason, in his falsity and drunken violence, as the ready-made nucleus of degradation and disorder.[1]

DURING the first seventy years of the union, the Irish and British peoples came more and more into contact with one another. Personal interaction occurred as a result of migration in both directions across the Irish Sea, but by 1861 there were twelve times as many Irish in Britain as British in Ireland. Migration gave a personal twist to the Anglo–Irish relationship, and was crucial in the formulation of Irish attitudes towards the British as well as British attitudes towards the Irish. Thus study of the Irish in Britain provides a testing ground, not only for the development of 'Anglo-Saxon attitudes' concerning a subject people who could not be ignored, but also for the resilience of Irish *mores* when transplanted to an alien context. Irish movement to Britain engendered feelings of rage, fear, and resentment on both parts, so reflecting the broader political conflict. Yet personal experience and pursuit of self-interest often served to undermine the hostile rhetoric, and towards the end of the period host and guest were edging towards a *modus vivendi*, which was to have its political counterpart in the home rule movement. In its ambiguity as well as its disharmony, the interaction of Irish minority with British majority epitomised the Anglo–Irish connection.

There was no universal British stereotype of the Irish immigrant. As Gilley points out in his telling critique of Curtis's highly coloured model of apes against angels, the immigrants were not always despised as 'reckless of life, violent, intolerant, and superstitious, they were also extolled for their conviviality, generosity, industry, chastity, piety, and patience in suffering'.[2]

[1] Thomas Carlyle, *Chartism* (2nd ed., London, 1840), pp 27–8.
[2] Sheridan Gilley, 'English attitudes to the Irish in England, 1780–1900' in Colin Holmes (ed.), *Immigrants and minorities in British society* (London, 1978), p. 88.

Interpretation of Irish characteristics oscillated between vice and virtue according to the current state of politics, with simian features seldom adorning the cartoon Irishman except in years of rebellion such as 1848 or 1867. Yet the oscillation evident in British attitudes was skewed, ranging between grudging condescension and bullish vituperation. Carlyle's apocalyptic vision of the Irish influx was shared by many polemicists with very different ideologies. Engels, for example, protested that 'these people having grown up almost without civilisation, accustomed from youth to every sort of privation, rough, intemperate, and improvident, bring all their brutal habits with them'. Yet barbarity did 'not hinder the Irishman's competing with the Englishman, and gradually forcing the rate of wages, and with it the Englishman's level of civilisation, down to the Irishman's level'.[1] Immigrant barbarity was variously attributed to race, religion, nationality, poverty, and misgovernment in numerous combinations. But most observers, including Carlyle and Engels, believed that the reduction of Irish poverty, helped by state intervention, might lead to the gradual amelioration of national, religious, or racial character. Indeed the presence of 'crowds of miserable Irish' darkening their towns was a powerful factor in generating legislative reform to benefit the Irish at home. Many influential proponents of land reform, state-subsidised emigration, and a far-reaching Irish poor law were driven to action by fear rather than compassion.

The Irish influx to Britain was, self-evidently, far from homogeneous. Out of the jumble of prejudice, stereotype, and observation that expressed contemporary perceptions of the Irish immigrant, we may extract several characteristic responses to distinct strands of migration. Most menacing was the strand that threatened to create an Irish community of 'permanent' immigrants in the industrial heartland of Britain. Irish settlers were widely perceived as a cohesive and alien presence: clustering in Irish quarters to the exclusion of the natives, competing for employment and undercutting wages, posing a moral, religious, and political menace to the host society. 'Even without express combination', so The Times thundered in July 1852, the race, religion, and habits of the immigrants rendered them 'a virtual conspiracy'. Only slightly less abhorrent to the British mind was that more transient species of immigrant, the vagrant Irish pauper. As a poor law inspector remarked in 1848, 'this horrible evil not only presents the spectacle of an inferior civilisation and semi-barbarous mode of existence to the English labourer, but it sets him an example of living without labour'.[2] The wandering Irish cadger might present no enduring political or industrial threat, but was resented as the carrier of disease, criminality, and drunkenness, as a parasite on the parish.

[1] Friedrich Engels, 'The condition of the working-class in England' in Karl Marx and Friedrich Engels, On Britain (Moscow, 1953), pp 124, 111.

[2] E. D. Steele, 'The Irish presence in the north of England, 1850–1914' in Northern History, xii (1976), p. 225; Reports to the poor law board, on the laws of settlement and removal of the poor, p. 86 [1152], H.C. 1850, xxvii, 229.

British benevolence was largely reserved for a third class of Irish expatriate, the 'reaper' or seasonal labourer seeking to supplement his Irish subsistence with British cash. He was transient, mobile, industrious, and necessary: 'nearly', indeed, 'an unmixed good'. The equally mobile Irish railway navvy gained a less favourable reputation than his agricultural counterpart; yet even Carlyle, on inspecting the workforce of the Caledonian railway in 1846, was moved to declare privately that 'not without glad surprise I find the Irish are the best in point of behaviour'. While English workers prodigally guzzled beef and whisky, the Irish remained thrifty and supportive of their kinsmen at home.[1] Those Irish were most feared who 'herded together', most resented who 'forced down wages', most despised who could not find employment, and most praised who departed expeditiously. To what extent did British perceptions— so colourful, so confident, and so diverse—correspond to the realities of Irish migration to Britain as interpreted by social historians?

For the hordes of Irish deck passengers disembarking at Liverpool, Bristol, or the Clyde, Britain was seldom the desired or promised land. Even immigrants who hoped to find gold in the streets expected to spend it elsewhere. As the earl of Donoughmore remarked in 1854, 'I think that the whole aspirations of the people are turned towards America, and that they come to England as a temporary expedient.'[2] Between about 1835 and 1865 most Irish transatlantic emigrants embarked from Liverpool, while many chose Clydeside or other British ports. Each year tens of thousands of emigrants crossed the Atlantic after only a brief spell in Britain, either waiting (often for many weeks) for the boat to leave or earning the price of a passage. During the great famine about a quarter of a million passengers from Ireland reached Liverpool annually, but about two-thirds of these proceeded overseas, while many of the rest returned to Ireland after a period of labouring, harvesting, or cattle jobbing. Yet many migrants remained in Britain despite the impermanence of their intentions: as the Liverpool nationalist John Denvir remarked, 'many of them have set out from Ireland, intending to go to America, but, their little means failing them, have been obliged to remain in Liverpool'. Once caught in the British web the reluctant immigrant would restlessly explore its filaments, unwilling either to go home or to settle down in Britain. As a Stafford magistrate remarked of 'a certain class of Irish' in 1833, 'they travel in a circle, and ... the nearer they get to their own homes, the greater is their tendency to fly off'.[3] Unsettled, transient, centrifugal in their drift, those arriving in Britain

---

[1] *Fourth report from the select committee of the house of lords appointed to enquire into the operation of the Irish poor law, and the expediency of making any amendment to its enactments; and to report thereon to the house; together with the minutes of evidence*, p. 713, H.C. 1849 (365), xvi, 737; Terry Coleman, *The railway navvies: a history of the men who made the railways* (London, 1965), p. 25.

[2] *Report from the select committee on poor removal; together with the proceedings of the committee, minutes of evidence, appendix, and index*, p. 162, H.C. 1854 (396), xvii, 174.

[3] John Denvir, *The life story of an old rebel* (Dublin, 1910), p. 7; *Report from the select committee on Irish vagrants, with the minutes of evidence taken before them*, p. 39, H.C. 1833 (394), xvi, 361.

seldom betrayed the sense of joyous homecoming and social fulfilment that cushioned resettlement in the United States.

For the intending emigrant from Ireland, Britain's attraction was largely negative: the costs of getting there, and indeed of returning home, were relatively low. Emigrants to distant America or Australasia might dream of returning to the old sod, but few did so. Having broken out of the British Isles, usually with the financial help of relatives already overseas, the long-distance emigrants normally set about making a new life and a new home. By contrast, those staying in Britain left their options open. Fares between Ireland and Britain, though sometimes higher for the return journey, were usually low and often negligible. The first steam service, inaugurated in 1818 between Belfast and Glasgow, at first charged fourteen shillings for a steerage berth. This was equivalent to a couple of weeks' wages for a farm labourer, though it fell far short of the prevailing transatlantic fare of up to ten pounds. Subsequently, the cost of travel to Britain declined even more steeply than that to America. In 1824 and 1833 tickets could be found for five or six pence, while competition on the Cork–Bristol route generated offers of free passages from one company and free loaves of baker's bread from another. As late as 1850, coal boats returning from Cork were often stabilised with emigrants 'brought over as ballast, without any payment for their passage. The captains, it appears, find it cheaper to ship and unship this living ballast than one of lime and shingles.' During the famine years fares to Britain generally remained low, ranging between half a crown and half a sovereign according to the distance travelled. Even after the end of the 'price war' between steamship companies in April 1851, which had 'continued with unabated violence for upwards of seventeen months', a passage could usually be obtained for less than a week's wages, whereas a ticket to America cost as much as a heifer.[1] Indeed the cost of the ticket was often dwarfed by that of the preliminary inland journey, board and lodging on arrival, and the actuarial risk involved in braving the Irish Sea. Steamers, though more resilient than the sailing vessels, which they largely displaced from the 1830s onwards, were wrecked with alarming frequency. Casualties were often excessive because of reckless overcrowding and inattention to safety: when the P.S. *Queen Victoria* went down in 1853 with the loss of fifty-nine lives, still more would have died but for a seaman who showed 'presence of mind in putting his finger in the plughole of the [life] boat, and by unremitting exertions prevented her from sinking'. Regulation of passenger traffic within the British Isles remained rudimentary, despite the belated introduction of loading controls for vessels plying between Ireland and Liverpool, after the smothering between decks of seventy-two passengers on the P.S. *Londonderry*

[1] D. B. McNeill, *Irish passenger steamship services. Volume 1: north of Ireland* (Newton Abbot, 1969), p. 20; *Select committee on poor removal*, pp 475–6; City of Dublin Steam-packet Company, *Report* (Dublin, 1851), p. 3.

in 1848.[1] But the risk of shipwreck, not to speak of seasickness, was relatively small compared with that for transatlantic emigrants. Overall, Britain was the low-cost and low-return option for Irish emigrants.

Given the casual, impermanent, and unregulated character of migration within the British Isles, it is not surprising that no reliable statistics were compiled of net movement from Ireland to Britain. The best indicator is provided by the birthplace returns of the British census from 1841 onwards, though a considerable but unknown proportion of Britain's Irish population on census day consisted of visitors, lodgers, jobbers, or harvesters awaiting passage home or overseas. As table 1 shows,[2] the number of Irish-born counted in Britain rose from about 400,000 just before the famine to three-quarters of a million during the following decades. In 1851 there were almost as many Irish people in Britain as in the United States, and well over one-quarter of all Irish natives who had migrated out of their home counties were counted in Britain. By 1871 the proportion had fallen to one-fifth, yet far more natives of Ireland were counted in Britain than in Irish counties other than their counties of birth. These birthplace returns reveal not only the impact of famine, which almost doubled the Irish population in Britain, but also the magnitude of pre-famine movement across the Irish Sea. George Cornewall Lewis's painstaking survey of the Irish in extra-metropolitan Britain, conducted for the 'poor inquiry' in 1834, indicates that intensive Irish immigration dated only from the 1820s.[3] The drift towards Britain, though accelerated by famine, was set in motion by the rapid development of urban industry in Britain and rural poverty in Ireland after the Napoleonic wars. If Britain's attraction as an emigrant destination seemed negative when judged in rural Ireland, its expanding industries and relatively high wages often prevailed on newcomers to linger a while, and perhaps a lifetime.

The regional origins of Irish settlers in Britain were naturally affected by the topography of the British Isles. Northerners tended to travel from Derry to Glasgow and thence to southern Scotland; Munster people from Cork to Bristol and thence to London and southern England. In 1834, Bishop Scott of Glasgow remarked that 'almost all the Irish in this city and neighbourhood come here from the northern counties of Ireland', a fact confirmed by studies of Dundee, Paisley, and Greenock. Lees reports that two-thirds of the London Irish in 1861–71 were born in 'western Munster', though a well placed Liverpool witness claimed in 1834 that more Irish was spoken in London than Liverpool because immigrants from Connacht habitually passed on to London.[4] Less obvious but also explicable was the link between Connacht and

---

[1] *Report of Captain Walker, of the naval department of the board of trade, on an inquiry into the nature, circumstances, and causes attending the wreck of the 'Queen Victoria'; together with the minutes of evidence*, p. 5 [1606], H.C. 1852–3, xcviii, 361; Lowe, 'Irish in Lancashire', pp 142–8.

[2] Below, p. 658.

[3] *Poor inquiry*, app. G.

[4] Ibid., pp 105, 138, 21; Brenda Collins, 'Irish emigration to Dundee and Paisley' in J. M.

the north of England. For most Connacht emigrants Dublin was the most convenient port of embarkation, while Liverpool was the closest major British port to Dublin. Studies of census schedules for various Yorkshire towns between 1851 and 1871 indicate disproportionately high rates of emigration from counties such as Mayo and Sligo, which together accounted for only one-sixteenth of Ireland's population in 1851. In Leeds about one Irish settler in seven came from these counties, in Bradford over one in four, in York up to one in two. Connacht people also dominated Irish movement to Staffordshire towns such as Wolverhampton and Wednesbury, though data is regrettably lacking for Lancashire.

Significantly, Connacht emigrants usually outnumbered those from Leinster, which was still more convenient to Liverpool via Dublin. Though Dublin itself contributed heavily to the Irish populations of Leeds and York, while Queen's County sent an excess of emigrants to Leeds and Bradford, it was generally the poorest and most agricultural counties of the west of Ireland that peopled the Irish settlements of industrial England.[1] Since Irish settlers were notably concentrated in these regions,[2] it seems likely that aggregate movement to Britain broadly conformed to the general pattern of Irish emigration, which from the famine onwards occurred most intensively from the poorest counties. Indeed, since the poorest emigrants could not afford the transatlantic passage until enough 'pioneers' had reached America to set up a self-perpetuating 'chain migration', the correlation between poverty and emigration was both precocious and exaggerated in the British case. It was not, however, exaggerated to the extent suggested by the preacher Father Cahill at Liverpool in 1853: 'the very nature of their case sends them to this country naked, and hungry, and friendless, and exterminated, and broken-hearted. . . . This is the sickbed of Ireland, the hospital of Ireland, the churchyard of Ireland.'[3] Not long after the famine, many of those leaving southern and western counties for England were no longer the poorest products of their admittedly poor environments. On the Cork–Bristol route, the 'poor and destitute' of 1849–50 had already given place by 1854 to 'the strong working people . . . the labouring classes; servant boys and girls', though their intention was usually to save in England for a ticket to America.[4] In their county origins

Goldstrom and L. A. Clarkson (ed.), *Irish population, economy, and society* (Oxford, 1981), p. 202; Lynn Hollen Lees, *Exiles of Erin: Irish migrants in Victorian London* (Manchester, 1979), p. 51.

[1] Terence Dillon, 'The Irish in Leeds' in *Publications of the Thoresby Society*, cxix (1973), p. 6; C. Richardson, 'The Irish in Victorian Bradford' in *The Bradford Antiquary*, xlv (1971), p. 315; Frances Finnegan, *Poverty and prejudice: a study of Irish immigrants in York* (Cork, 1982), pp 69, 94–5; Roger Swift, 'Crime and ethnicity: the Irish in early Victorian Wolverhampton' in *West Midlands Studies*, xiii (1980), p. 1; M. A. G. Ó Tuathaigh, 'The Irish in nineteenth-century Britain' in *R. Hist. Soc. Trans.*, xxxi (1981), p. 165.

[2] Below, pp 633–4.

[3] D. W. Cahill, *Important letter . . . to the catholics of Liverpool* (Dublin, 1853), pp 5–6.

[4] *Report from the select committee on poor removal*, p. 99, H.C. 1854 (396), xvii, 111.

and their class background, the emigrants to Britain were not unlike those making for America a few years later.

This seems also to have been true of their demographic profile, though inference must be tentative from the patchy returns of birthplace. In general, Irish emigration was remarkable for its even balance of the sexes, with a slight male majority before the famine and a slight female majority immediately after it. This pattern was reflected in the British case, as table 1 illustrates.[1] Except in 1861, Irish-born males somewhat outnumbered females, the male excess being greater in Wales and Scotland than England. But in certain noteworthy cases, such as Lancashire, Cheshire, London, and Dundee, female settlers predominated even before the famine. Local variations in the balance of sexes among Irish immigrants were doubtless influenced by fluctuating demand for female employment, and the regions of male predominance changed markedly over time.[2] As with most migrations, movement was concentrated among young adults, the most easily mobilised and adaptable group in any population. This is confirmed by local studies of the age-distribution of Irish settlers at the end of the famine, which usually resembled a lozenge rather than the familiar pyramid. Yet there was also considerable family movement, at least during the famine years. Many Irish families probably moved to Britain in procession rather than ensemble, the father 'pioneering' while his wife and family waited at home or in the workhouse until he had earned enough to bring them across the water and offer them bed and board. But by 1851 over one-quarter of Britain's Irish population was younger than twenty, quite a high proportion given the exclusion from census statistics of the British-born children of Irish settlers. Twenty years later the proportion had dropped to one-eighth, a change that reflected not merely the reduction of family emigration after the famine panic, but also the ageing of an immigrant population which had mainly left Ireland several years earlier.

Historians of the Irish in Britain have rightly stressed the predominance of Roman Catholics among the immigrants, but wrongly neglected the locally significant minorities of protestants among Irish settlers. One is tantalised by Denvir's casual observation that the Scotland Road and Toxteth Park districts in Liverpool, later renowned as slightly up-market colonies of catholic Irish, had once been strongholds of Irish protestantism. Even in the late 1850s, up to one-fifth of Irish paupers admitted to the Liverpool workhouse were protestants, a fact that suggests a still higher protestant proportion for the Liverpool Irish outside the workhouse.[3] But in the absence of a reliable religious census,

[1] Below, p. 658.
[2] Analysis of the ratio of Irish-born males to females in the 32 Scottish and 37 English counties (excluding home counties) gives coefficients of variation (C.V.) for Scotland of .38 (1841) and .23 (1871), and for England of .32 (1841) and .22 (1871). The correlation coefficient (r) for the distributions of 1841 and 1871 is -.02 for Scotland and +.40 for England.
[3] John Denvir, *The Irish in Britain from the earliest times to the fall and death of Parnell* (2nd ed.,

Ireland's elusive protestant expatriates have been widely ignored, except in the guise of an 'Orange rabble' of mixed nativity intermittently menacing the security of the catholic and Irish 'community'. Rather more attention has been paid to the protestant Irish presence in Scotland, with its heavy influx from Ulster. In pre-famine Scotland a few attempts were made to estimate catholic as against Irish populations. It seems that for every hundred Irish natives there were only about 41 declared catholics in Paisley (1821), 66 in Glasgow (1819), 65 in Glasgow (1831), and perhaps 50 in Girvan (1834).[1] Yet even in the Scottish case, where the religious division of Irish immigrants was probably similar to that in Canada or New Zealand, we know all too little of the divergences and also parallels between the catholic and protestant experiences of migration. The religious history of Irish settlement in Britain ought to be more than a catalogue of catholic pietism, protestant anti-popery, and broken heads.

SEASONAL migration from Ireland to Britain requires separate treatment, since its determinants and functions were distinct from those of the predominant drift from rural Ireland to urban Britain. The relationship between seasonal, 'permanent', and indeterminate migration is of course tangled, since many Irish people who left for Britain intending to undertake a season's farm work went on to find casual labour in towns, or seek poor relief, and settle in the regions of Britain with which they became familiar. In terms of Irish mentality, seasonal migration had countervailing influences on the disposition to resettle abroad: by accustoming home communities to British *mores* and wages it strengthened the 'pull' across the water, yet by propping up the home economy through seasonal earnings it mitigated the 'push' out of Ireland. For the period before 1880, data on seasonal migration is still more uncertain than for Irish settlement in Britain. The Irish reaper was already a familiar figure in the summer landscape of eighteenth-century England, and by about 1834 it seems from the poor inquiry's parish survey that some forty thousand reapers were migrating annually to Britain. A defective count during the 1841 season recorded nearly sixty thousand departures of deck passengers to Britain, but these seem to have included visitors and jobbers as well as seasonal workers. Six-sevenths of these travellers were male and three-fifths were aged between sixteen and thirty-five.[2] Historians have disagreed about changes over time in

London, 1894), p. 110; Denvir, *The life story of an old rebel* (Dublin, 1910), p. 23; Lowe, 'Irish in Lancashire', p. 260.

[1] *Poor inquiry, app. G*, pp 129, 149; James Cleland, *The rise and progress of the city of Glasgow* (Glasgow, 1820), p. 288; Cleland, *Enumeration of the inhabitants of the city of Glasgow* (Glasgow, 1832), pp 209–11. For Glasgow, including its suburbs, the figure for 1831 is 54. It seems likely that Cleland's 'Irish' included Scottish-born children of immigrants, while his 'Roman Catholics' excluded many returned wrongly as 'episcopalians'. All these statistics should be treated with caution.

[2] *Census Ire., 1841*, pp 450–51 [504], H.C. 1843, xxiv, 558–9.

the pattern of seasonal migration, but O Gráda plausibly suggests that the volume continued to increase during and after the famine to a peak of about one hundred thousand in the mid-1860s.[1]

Seasonal workers came broadly from the same regions as the settlers recorded at the census, which from 1851 onwards occurred in spring before the seasonal influx had begun. In 1841 one-third of the migrants came from Ulster, of whom three-quarters were bound for Glasgow. Over two-fifths were from Connacht, and all but one-seventh of these proceeded to Liverpool. The surveys of 1834 and 1841 indicate that seasonal migration was already concentrated in the impoverished north-western counties well before this applied to 'permanent' emigration from Ireland, and it was always to remain a far more localised phenomenon. In 1843 Donegal, Leitrim, Mayo, Roscommon, and Sligo were all sending out at least sixteen migrants per thousand of population, whereas half the counties of Ireland sent less than five. Inter-county variation was more than three times as marked as that for post-famine permanent emigration.[2] Bishop Doyle, in 1830, attributed the paucity of seasonal movement from the east coast to the fact that 'it is more advanced in civilisation, and the habits of the people more domestic', though he noted that unemployed weavers from the north and from Queen's County also migrated, being 'a kind of roving and unsettled population, who have no resting place, and who think very little of going from one country to another'. In general, it was the poorest denizens of the poorest regions who were prepared to tramp long distances in search of summer employment. The poverty of the reapers appalled seasoned visitors such as Johann Kohl, who before his visit to Edgeworthstown in 1842 had 'seen migrations of harvesters somewhat similar, in many parts of Europe, but nowhere did they produce so melancholy an impression upon me as in Ireland'.[3] In Ireland the epithet 'spalpeen' came to be applied not merely to migratory labourers, but to any Irishman who was deemed dirty, degraded, and deprived.

Yet, wretched though they seemed, the migratory labourers were widely considered to be more serviceable to the British economy than other Irish workers. As early as 1758, they were characterised as being 'useful, faithful, good servants to the farmer, and as they are of real use to the kingdom, deserve protection and encouragement'. Their thrift was fabled, and the Victorian mind admired them for being 'willing to undergo every toil for good pay'. On the Liverpool packet they were well behaved, unlike their 'uniformly drunken'

---

[1] Cormac Ó Gráda, 'Seasonal migration and post-famine adjustment in the west of Ireland' in *Studia Hib.*, xiii (1973), pp 48–76.

[2] For 1841 passengers to Britain expressed as a proportion of each county's population, C.V. = .98 (32 counties). The corresponding figure for all 'permanent' emigrants leaving Irish ports between May 1851 and Dec. 1860 is C.V. = .28.

[3] *Second report of evidence from the select committee on the state of the poor in Ireland. Minutes of evidence: 18 May–5 June*, pp 418–19, H.C. 1830 (654), vii, 592–3; J. G. Kohl, *Ireland, Dublin, the Shannon, Limerick, Cork, and the Kilkenny races, the round towers, the lakes of Killarney* . . . (London, 1843), p. 15.

and 'very troublesome' social superiors on board, the cattle drovers.[1] Their
services were generally reckoned to complement rather than rival those of
native workers, and as one Lincolnshire witness stated in 1860, it would be
'impossible' to get in the harvest 'without them or some foreign labour'. They
also pleased farmers by consistently accepting lower wages than those that
continued to be paid to local labourers, a fact that gives the lie to the notion that
their presence forced down the prevailing agricultural wage.[2] As well as being
cheap and industrious, they were mobile and flexible: valuable attributes in an
industry whose demand for labour varied not only between seasons but also
from year to year, according to weather conditions, yields and the density of the
crop. In slack seasons regular Irish reapers sometimes found themselves in
collision with idle and resentful local workers, but in years of heavy demand
Irish labour was indispensable. The inelastic supply of native rural labour
encouraged employers to dip their buckets into the bottomless well of Irish
poverty whenever shortage occurred. Irish labour was usually plentifully available at the numerous 'hiring fairs' in the north of England, but might also be
got by contracting with a 'gaffer' or group leader to bring out the required
number of his relatives or neighbours. The half-acre 'family patrimony' of
Carleton's Phelim O'Toole had been won by his grandfather 'from the Sas-
senah at the point of his reaping-hook', when Grandfather O'Toole obtained
eight guineas and a new hat as his reward for leading a 'resolute little band' of
spalpeens to England. The gang system was to persist, at least in the case of
Scotland, throughout the nineteenth century.

Demand for seasonal labour fluctuated, but the Irish were adept at tapping
sources of relatively high wages and accessible employment. Many trudged
from farm to farm and county to county in obedience to the agricultural
calendar, following the progression from hay to corn to turnips to potatoes, or
moving north and west towards cooler weather and later harvests. The introduction of more efficient tools did not at first reduce demand for Irish labour.
The Irish were less resistant than native workers to innovation, proving quick
to increase their earnings by substituting reaping hooks for sickles, and later
scythes for reaping-hooks. The rapid growth in output attributable to these
modest technical advances ensured that aggregate demand for farm labour
scarcely diminished between 1835 and 1870, and only at the end of this period
did the belated diffusion of reaping-machines (itself encouraged by a temporary contraction in the supply of Irish labour) threaten to render the spalpeen

---

[1] *Report of George Coode, Esq., to the poor law board on the law of settlement and removal of the poor; being a
further report in addition to those printed in 1850*, p. 305, H.C. 1851 (675), xxvi, 495; W. Neilson
Hancock, *On the condition of the Irish labourer, being a paper read before the Dublin Statistical Society*
(Dublin, 1848), p. 8; *Poor inquiry, app. G*, p. xliv.

[2] *Report from the select committee on irremovable poor; together with the proceedings of the committee, minutes
of evidence, appendix and index*, p. 97, H.C. 1860 (520), xvii, 115; E. J. T. Collins, 'Migrant labour in
British agriculture in the nineteenth century' in *Econ. Hist. Rev.*, xxix (1976), pp 38–59; cf. below,
pp 642–3.

redundant in the grain harvest. Meanwhile, however, many Irish workers had drifted out of farming into more remunerative seasonal trades. Occupations such as railway construction, building, and brick-making required excess labour in the drier summer months, and even before the famine the Irish had become prominent in these trades. For the struggling peasant households of Mayo or Donegal, the few pounds saved over a long British season were often essential for paying the rent, shop-debt, or emigrant passage; and the temptation was strong to earn an extra pound by working off the land. When it came to deciding between sickles and scythes, or between harvesting and navvying, Irish beggars had to be canny choosers.

Except for the reapers, the Irish influx to nineteenth-century Britain was mainly directed towards major towns. As Cornewall Lewis reported in 1834, 'they settle exclusively in towns, and, for the most part, in very populous towns'. He maintained that 'the *general diffusion* of the Irish over Scotland and England is more remarkable than their *numbers*.... Their roaming and restless habits appear to have carried them to every place where there was any prospect of obtaining profitable employment.' This judgement, though based upon a thorough and imaginative social inquiry notably unwarped by conventional stereotyping, requires some qualification.[1] Though the census from 1841 onwards recorded the presence of Irish natives in every British county, their diffusion was markedly uneven. Taken as a proportion of all those resident outside their county of birth, the Irish were prominent in a virtually solid block of counties ranging in latitude roughly from the Mersey to the Clyde, most of all in the western counties adjoining Liverpool and Glasgow. Secondary clusters developed in the home counties and south Wales. The Irish generally settled in districts with heavy urban demand for labour and small farming sectors, being part of the massive drift from rural to urban areas that characterised the British Isles in the nineteenth century. Despite their preference for settlement near the western seaports, the Irish were far less restricted in their choices than were migrants from rural England, who showed a strong inclination to move to nearby towns rather than risk transplantation to faster growing but unfamiliar cities. The urban expatriate, like the reaper, was an opportunist, aware that many districts and occupations were closed to him, but tireless in his search for the most remunerative employment available.

Irish conspicuousness in Britain cannot be explained in terms of crude numbers. In 1841, when popular dread of Irish immigrant hordes was already acute, Irish natives comprised less than 2 per cent of the English population and 5 per cent of the Scottish. Even at their peak shortly after the famine, these proportions did not exceed 3 per cent for England and 7 per cent for Scotland (see table 1).[2] The Irish were excessively obvious partly because of their concentration in a handful of large towns. Nearly half of Britain's Irish population in 1841 was found in the four major cities (London, Manchester,

[1] *Poor inquiry, app. G*, pp xvii, vii.   [2] Below, p. 658.

Liverpool, and Glasgow), while only one-third lived outside the 'principal towns' of Britain. As table 2 shows,[1] these proportions had been reversed by 1871 as a result of the gradual diffusion of Irish settlers into smaller towns. But the Irish remained heavily over-represented in the great manufacturing centres and in some of the major ports, though not in the metropolis. In mid-century Liverpool, Glasgow, and Dundee about one-fifth of the population was Irish-born, with Irish components of at least one-tenth in Manchester and Salford, Stockport, St Helens, Newport, Paisley, and Kilmarnock. Since these proportions exclude the British-born children of Irish immigrants, they represent local Irish clusters that could not be ignored.

Irish visibility was further enhanced by the immigrants' patterns of settlement within British cities. Both contemporaries and many later historians have been prone to exaggerate Irish residential segregation, on the premise (stated by the *Morning Chronicle* in 1849) that 'the Irish invariably herd together'. The various 'Irish quarters' of British towns were taken as proof of segregation, and Victorian sociological lore was replete with colourful references to Liverpool's Irishtown (formerly Welshtown), Wolverhampton's Caribee Island, the Bedern in York, Rock Row in Stockport, the Rookery of St Giles in London, and, above all, Manchester's Little Ireland. As Engels wrote of Little Ireland in 1844: 'in a rather deep hole, in a curve of the Medlock and surrounded on all four sides by tall factories and high embankments, covered with buildings, stand two groups of about two hundred cottages, chiefly back to back, in which live about four thousand human beings, most of them Irish'.[2] Little Ireland and other Irish enclaves have sometimes been designated as 'ghettos', but the model of the Jewish ghetto (a sector restricted to Jews, to which Jews were restricted) does not fit Irish settlement in urban Britain.[2] Irish immigrants undoubtedly tended to cluster in particular streets and districts, often as lodgers in rooms sublet by Irish tenants. But they were not restricted to these quarters, and in most British towns there were few districts entirely bereft of Irish residents. In 1851 all thirty-six divisions of London contained sizeable Irish components, ranging from 15 per cent in St Olave (Southwark) to 1 per cent in Bethnal Green. Variation was only half as marked as that between the Irish components of English county populations. As Londoners drifted from the centre towards the periphery the Irish drifted with them, though they remained slightly over-represented in the central divisions. Irish householders in Liverpool were only slightly more 'segregated' in 1871 than other migrants from England, Wales, or Scotland, and their residential patterns were actually more like those of native Liverpudlians than was the case for either Scottish or Welsh settlers.[3]

[1] Below, p. 659.

[2] *Morning Chronicle*, quoted in Colin Holmes (ed.), *Immigrants & minorities in British society* (London, 1978), p. 45; Friedrich Engels, 'The condition of the working class in England' in Karl Marx and Friedrich Engels, *On Britain* (Moscow, 1953), p. 94.

[3] Variation in the proportions of Irish-born is given by C.V. — .60 for London (36 divisions,

Even the 'Irish quarters' were seldom exclusively Irish. A single parish contained over one-fifth of York's Irish population in 1841, yet the 'Irish' (including their spouses and children) made up less than one-seventh of the population of that parish. No ward in Leeds (1839) was more than one-sixth Irish, though in Liverpool (1851) three-fifths of the residents of the Waterloo Road dockside quarter were from Ireland. In a few towns such as York (1851), Cardiff (1851), Birkenhead (1855), and Newcastle upon Tyne, there is evidence that between one and five streets were virtually monopolised by Irish settlers. Elsewhere, social historians in search of a ghetto have discovered still more minuscule Irish concentrations, such as that at Cochrane's lodging house in Barrhead, near Paisley (1862), which was partitioned into separate sections for Irish and Scottish girls employed at a bleaching works.[1] Irish settlers in British towns showed a marked tendency to settle in working-class zones, but they were neither confined to these zones nor without near neighbours of different ethnic stock. This is confirmed by several studies of the likelihood that an Irish resident of a British town in 1851 would find another Irish resident next door, directly opposite or diagonally opposite. The probability was three-fifths in Preston, one-half in South Shields, two-fifths in Oldham, and zero in Northampton.[2] In the towns of Britain, as in North America and Australia, the Irish herding instinct was to some extent a figment of alien imagination.

The geographical patterns of Irish settlement in Britain were broadly established before the famine, and the mighty influx that followed tended to settle in cities or towns already notable for Irish clusters. Comparison of the Irish components of each county's immigrant population in 1841 and 1871 indicates that about three-quarters of inter-county variation in 1871 may be 'explained' by that recorded thirty years earlier. Variation remained marked throughout the period, and the distribution remained heavily skewed towards the few

1851), cf. C.V. − 1.26 for England (37 counties, 1851). Likewise, C.V. − .62 for Glasgow Royalty (9 parishes, 1819), C.V. − .53 for Glasgow and suburbs (17 divisions, 1831), cf. C.V. − 1.47 for Scotland (32 counties, 1841). Statistical data from census returns (James Cleland, *The rise and progress of the city of Glasgow* (Glasgow, 1820), p. 288; Cleland, *Enumeration of the inhabitants of the city of Glasgow* (Glasgow, 1832), pp 209–11). See also Lynn Hollen Lees, *Exiles of Erin: Irish migrants in Victorian London* (Manchester, 1979), pp 56–62; Colin G. Pooley, 'The residential segregation of migrant communities in mid-Victorian Liverpool' in *Transactions of the Institute of British Geographers*, ii, no. 3 (1977), pp 369–72.

[1] Frances Finnegan, *Poverty and prejudice: a study of Irish immigrants in York* (Cork, 1982), pp 6, 45–8; Terence Dillon, 'The Irish in Leeds' in *Publications of the Thoresby Society*, cxix (1973), pp 9–10; R. Lawton, 'The population of Liverpool' in *Transactions of the Historic Society of Lancashire and Cheshire*, cvii (1955), p. 104; C. Roy Lewis, 'The Irish in Cardiff in the mid-nineteenth century' in *Cambria*, vii, no. 1 (1980), p. 24; *Report from the select committee on poor removal; together with the proceedings of the committee, minutes of evidence, appendix and index*, p. 178, H.C. 1854–5 (308), xiii, 194; T. P. MacDermott, 'Irish workers on Tyneside in the nineteenth century' in Norman McCord (ed.), *Essays in Tyneside labour history* (Newcastle upon Tyne, 1977), p. 159; J. E. Handley, *The Irish in modern Scotland* (Cork, 1947), p. 133.

[2] Michael Anderson, *Family structure in nineteenth-century Lancashire* (Cambridge, 1971), p. 101; John Foster, *Class struggle and the industrial revolution: early industrial capitalism in three English towns* (London, 1974), p. 129.

counties of intensive Irish settlement.[1] Between 1841 and 1871, Irish settlers regularly comprised at least one-third of the immigrant populations of Ayr, Lanark, and Wigtown, one-fifth in Cumberland, Lancashire, Dumbarton, Forfar, and Renfrew, and one-tenth in Cheshire, Northumberland, Yorkshire, Linlithgow, and Stirling. Yet in other counties with substantial immigrant sectors, such as Berkshire, Gloucester, Worcester, Selkirk, and Peebles, the Irish continued to be represented only sparsely. These peculiarities of Irish settlement were reinforced by Irish adherence to the 'chain' mechanism of migration, whereby immigrants joined their relatives or former neighbours in foreign cities. The Irish ranged widely in their search for urban employment in Britain, but their range of choice was guided by the networks of 'friends' who might provide lodgings, introductions, or jobs for the newcomers.

The statistical stability of Irish settlement patterns masked extremely rapid geographical mobility for individuals. Nineteenth-century town dwellers were in general very mobile people, with few remaining at the same address from one census to the next.[2] But immigrants were more mobile than natives, and Irish immigrants were more mobile than most. The Irish in Britain moved restlessly from city to city, street to street, or house to house within well defined Irish circuits. As a Leeds poor law official complained in 1847: 'they are a peculiar tramping people; they never stay long in one place unless they are well to do in the world, as it were'.[3] Local studies of Leeds and also York point indeed to an Irish condition of perpetual transience. In the Irish precinct of Wellington Yard, Leeds, only one-third of householders had the same address in 1861 as in 1851, though one-tenth had moved house within the yard. In York's Brittania Yard, none of the 154 Irish residents of 1851 remained a decade later, and only five had moved to other York addresses.[4] These findings suggest that the Irish in Britain were inclined to persist in long-distance migration to other cities or countries, even if they were resident in towns far removed from the migratory 'clearing-houses' of Liverpool or Glasgow. The case of Isabella Charles, a lunatic pauper removed from Edinburgh to Ireland in 1849, illustrates the 'peculiar tramping' habits of the Irish migrant. Born in Kildare in about 1810, Isabella accompanied her Scottish mother to Castlehill, Edinburgh parish, in 1832. After three and a half years they moved to St Cuthbert's parish, and thence after a similar period to Old Assembly Close, city parish. After brief

---

[1] Analysis of the ratio of Irish-born inhabitants to those born outside the county of residence gives the following C.V. for Scotland: 1.33 (1841), 1.03 (1851), 1.09 (1871); and for England: 1.12 (1841), 1.16 (1851), 1.11 (1871). Correlation of the Scottish distributions for 1841 and 1871 gives r = +.92, the English figure being r = +.94. For units, see above, p. 629, n. 2.

[2] See Michael Anderson, *Family structure in nineteenth-century Lancashire* (Cambridge, 1971), pp 38–42; Richard J. Dennis, 'Intercensal mobility in a Victorian city' in *Transactions of the Institute of British Geographers*, ii, no. 3 (1977), pp 349–63.

[3] *Sixth report from the select committee on settlement, and poor removal: together with the minutes of evidence and appendix*, p. 37, H.C. 1847 (409), xi, 439.

[4] Terence Dillon, 'The Irish in Leeds' in *Publications of the Thoresby Society*, cxix (1973), pp 10–11; Frances Finnegan, *Poverty and prejudice: a study of Irish immigrants in York* (Cork, 1982), pp 39, 48.

spells in the Close, in Dublin, and in Glasgow, Isabella returned for another two years to the Close, only to depart for further terms in Dublin and Glasgow. Just before her entry to the Morningside asylum and consequent deportation, she spent a few weeks each in Edinburgh's Potter's Row and Crosscauseway.[1] The concept of 'settlement' had little relevance to the experience of much of Britain's Irish population, forever on the move in search of better jobs or cheaper lodgings.

Residential mobility was but one consequence of low social status and lack of security. Another consequence, which suffused British perceptions of the Irish immigrant, was conspicuous poverty—manifest above all in Irish dependence on British poor relief. Since paupers in Britain were sustained largely through 'outdoor relief' rather than incarceration in the workhouse as in Ireland, many British observers believed that the Irish poor preferred to migrate towards British mendicity offices rather than languish in penury or the poorhouse at home. During the famine and its immediate sequel Irish immigrants were undoubtedly over-represented among recipients of relief, despite the concurrence of famine in Ireland with recession and cholera in British cities. At the worst period of immigrant distress in 1847–8, the Irish proportion of all recipients of outdoor relief exceeded two-fifths in Liverpool and one-third in Manchester (double the Irish proportion of the population in those towns). Over 26,000 Irish natives received outdoor relief each week in Liverpool alone, not to speak of thousands of others in the workhouse or in fever hospitals. In Leeds, where only one-fourteenth of the population was Irish, there was actually an Irish majority of claimants at the mendicity office during most of the period 1847–53.[2]

Both before and after the famine, however, only a small proportion of Britain's Irish population was thrown on poor relief. Returns for Liverpool and Manchester in 1845–6 indicate that the Irish were not over-represented during a period of fairly low overall demand for relief. Miscellaneous returns for the Scottish towns of Glasgow, Edinburgh, Greenock, Paisley, and Kilmarnock at periods between 1832 and 1843 indicate a slight excess of Irish recipients of relief, but except in the case of Edinburgh the proportion of Irish paupers was less than double that of the Irish in the local population.[3] Irish pauperism again diminished in absolute terms after 1850, though Irish recipients remained unduly prominent in the major Lancashire towns and in Leeds. Irish immigrants, being at the base of the occupational ladder, were still particularly vulnerable to employment fluctuations. Thus during the great winter frost of

---

[1] Scottish Record Office, Edinburgh, AD.58.121.

[2] *Report from the select committee on poor removal*, pp 592, 442–5, H.C. 1854 (396), xvii, 604, 454–7; Lowe, 'Irish in Lancashire', pp 168 ff; Terence Dillon, 'The Irish in Leeds' in *Publications of the Thoresby Society*, cxix (1973), pp 21–2. The 'Irish' proportion of paupers is swollen by inclusion of their British-born families.

[3] Lowe, 'Irish in Lancashire', pp 168 ff; J. E. Handley, *The Irish in Scotland, 1798–1845* (2nd ed. Cork, 1945), pp 157–203.

1855, nearly all the recipients of additional 'casual' relief in Birmingham and in many London parishes were natives of Ireland.[1] But in normal seasons the Irish no longer imposed an outrageous charge on the rates. Many poor immigrants, even before the famine, obtained relief privately through kinsmen, through charities such as the London Mendicity Society, or through bodies such as the Liverpool District Provident Society, which between 1830 and 1853 dispensed relief to ten thousand families a year, of whom over half were Irish.[2]

Irish dependence on poor relief would doubtless have been greater but for the threat of 'removal' home to Ireland. English parishes were entitled, at the expense of ratepayers, to remove persons on the poor roll to Ireland if so ordered by two magistrates. Irish paupers were immune from removal only if they had a parochial 'settlement', or if they had been continuously resident in the parish for five years (1819), three years (1861), or one year (1865). In fact many parishes ignored these provisions, moved by either compassion or expediency. Numerous removals were ordered, however, in the major western seaports and in London. Certain migratory workers ruthlessly exploited the removal system in order to obtain free passages home, and in 1859 it was claimed by a vestry official that many came 'to Liverpool for the sole purpose of being passed' across the Irish Sea. Certainly most of those removed, particularly from Liverpool, had been locally resident for very short periods. Yet for most poor Irish settlers removal home constituted a threat rather than a promise. As the Loyal National Repeal Association claimed in March 1845, this threat caused many immigrants to 'submit to the greatest privations when thrown out of employment' rather than risk seeking relief.[3] A substantial minority of Irish immigrants were removed at British expense, though some returned to Britain by the next boat while others evaded their overseers. The number actually passed from Liverpool annually never exceeded nine thousand between 1823 and 1831 or between 1850 and 1853, peaking at about fifteen thousand in 1847. In addition some ten thousand Irish paupers were removed from Scottish ports in both 1847 and 1848, together with a few from other English ports.[4] Far more Irish paupers entered Britain than were removed from it, but the practice of removal served at once to discourage immigrant reliance upon the rates and to foster feelings of resentment against the reluctant host country.

The vast majority of the Irish in Britain were not reliant on either poor relief or charity for their subsistence, except perhaps in the cruellest seasons of the

---

[1] *Report from the select committee on poor removal*, pp 2-3, 117, H.C. 1854-5 (308), xiii, 18-19, 133.

[2] *Third report from the select committee on emigration from the United Kingdom*, p. 590, H.C. 1826-7 (550), v, 812; *Report from the select committee on poor removal*, p. 593, H.C. 1854 (396), xvii, 605.

[3] *Minutes of evidence taken before the select committee on irremovable poor; together with the proceedings of the committee, appendix, and index*, p. 155, H.C. 1859 (146, sess. 2), vii, 163; 'Second report of subcommittee on removal from England of poor persons born in Ireland' in *Reports of the parliamentary committee of the Loyal National Repeal Association of Ireland*, ii (Dublin, 1845), p. 172.

[4] Statistics collated from five parliamentary reports.

late 1840s. Yet many Irish settlers lived in poverty and squalor, often accentuated in the vision of British observers by Irish indifference to furnishings, cleanliness, and appearances. Working-class squalor was not, of course, uniquely Irish, and occasionally the Irish were compared favourably to other 'outcast' groups. Thus as early as 1843, the clerk of Holborn Union, which embraced the notorious Rookery of St Giles, reported that 'the Italians are much worse than the English, or the Irish; all manner of refuse' being found in their congested lodgings, from which they emerged by day 'with their organs, or selling images'.[1] But no group was more prone than the Irish to overcrowding, of which cases abound from almost every town of Irish settlement. Thus in 1849 Michael Harrington of Cardiff provided lodgings in a room measuring 15′10″ × 17′2″ × 8′6″, which contained two 'stump' beds, orange boxes, and piles of shavings. Fifty-four lodgers were found living, eating, and sleeping in this room, which emitted an 'overpowering' stench of mainly Irish origin, while additional casual lodgers were admitted by night for a few pence each. Letting out patches of floor was a lucrative occupation for Irish settlers 'with a little prudence': as early as 1765 Mrs Farrell, late of St Giles, left more than £6,000 accumulated from twopenny lodgers, 'chiefly her own countrymen, harvesters or labourers from Ireland'. As Lees has shown for London nearly a century later, wives with young children often took lodgers instead of working outside the home, so that nearly one-quarter of Irish households at this stage of their development cycle included lodgers in 1851.[2] In mid-century Lancashire towns almost two-fifths of all households with Irish heads contained lodgers, and despite gradual reduction of this proportion it remained consistently above that for non-Irish households. Nevertheless, by 1871 the housing standards of the Lancashire Irish had become 'virtually indistinguishable from [those of] the poorer members of the English working class'. Hitherto, Irish households had tended to be somewhat larger and more densely packed into houses, as well as being more crowded with lodgers, though the differences had been less marked than contemporary observers believed.[3] Irish living conditions were appalling, but little worse than those of other marginal groups in the grim towns of nineteenth-century Britain.

The key to Irish overcrowding, transience, and settlement patterns was the narrow range of occupations open to immigrant workers. Everywhere the Irish were over-represented among unskilled and semi-skilled workers, under-represented among skilled and professional people. Studies of London, Cardiff, and York in 1851 show that well over two-thirds of occupied Irish

[1] *First report of the commissioners for enquiring into the state of large towns and populous districts*, p. 257 [572], H.C. 1844, xvii, 279.

[2] John Hickey, *Urban catholics* (London, 1967), p. 75; Bernard Bogan, 'History of Irish immigration to England: the Irish in Southwark' in *Christus Rex*, xii, no. 1 (1958), p. 38; Lynn Lees, 'Mid-Victorian migration and the Irish family economy' in *Victorian Studies*, xx, no. 1 (1976), pp 33–5.

[3] Lowe, 'Irish in Lancashire', pp 81 ff; John Haslett and W. J. Lowe, 'Household structure and overcrowding among the Lancashire Irish' in *Histoire Sociale*, x (1977), pp 57–8.

workers were without significant skills, more than twice the proportion for the entire working populations of Cardiff and York. In Liverpool, Manchester, Salford, and especially in York, London, and Bradford, Irishmen were far more likely than other workers to be returned as general labourers at the census. Statistics for subsequent years in York, Greenock, and the three Lancashire towns indicate that virtually no improvement occurred in the relative status of Irish workers.[1] This static occupational distribution reflects a dual failure on the part of the Irish in Britain: earlier immigrants did not in general move up in the world, despite their increasing age, experience, and familiarity with British life; while later immigrants were no more successful in securing skilled employment than their famine-driven predecessors. Indeed pre-famine settlers in York were markedly more likely to occupy skilled positions than their successors in 1851, 1861, or 1871. Throughout the period the Irish remained at the fringe of the British economy, often indispensable in their restricted sphere of occupations but without much hope of breaking down the formidable social barriers with which Britain greeted its 'foreign' guests.

The particular occupations followed by the Irish in Britain, though generally humble, varied according to local industrial specialisation. In ports such as Liverpool, London, Cardiff, and Greenock many immigrants found harsh but profitable employment as dock labourers. In Greenock they were also over-represented in sugar-refining; in Bradford, among woolcombers and railway workers; in York, among chicory hands. Only to a small extent were Irish immigrants able to apply skills or experience gained in Ireland. Clearly an Irish upbringing was of little use to those seeking work in the chicory or sugar industries, or to the daughters of peasants in pre-famine Connacht who were imported at moments of labour shortage to wind silk in Manchester. Trades-men whose skills were overabundant in Ireland, such as shoemakers, tailors, masons, joiners, and carpenters, were prominent among the Irish in post-famine Greenock (as also among those migrating between counties within Ireland itself). In Dundee, where demand for handloom weavers remained strong until the 1870s, surplus linen-workers from mid-Ulster were able to reapply their expertise abroad when the home textile industry began to fail in the 1840s. Over one-half of Dundee's workforce of spinners were Irish girls in 1851, while two-thirds of the weavers were Irishmen.[2] In Aberdeen, though not in Paisley, there is further evidence that unemployed Irish weavers managed to change country without changing occupation. In the cotton towns of Lanca-

[1] Lynn Hollen Lees, *Exiles of Erin: Irish migrants in Victorian London* (Manchester, 1979), pp 256, 93, 119; C. Roy Lewis, 'The Irish in Cardiff in the mid-nineteenth century' in *Cambria*, vii, no. 1 (1980), p. 25; Lowe, 'Irish in Lancashire', pp 600–06; C. Richardson, 'Irish settlement in mid-nineteenth-century Bradford' in *Yorkshire Bulletin of Economic and Social Research*, xx, no. 1 (1968), p. 52; Frances Finnegan, *Poverty and prejudice: a study of Irish immigrants in York* (Cork, 1982), pp 108–09, 99, 103, 105; R. D. Lobban, 'The Irish community in Greenock in the nineteenth century' in *Ir. Geography*, vi, no. 3 (1971), pp 271–2.

[2] Brenda Collins, 'Proto-industrialisation and pre-famine emigration' in *Social History*, vii, no. 2 (1982), p. 145.

shire and Cheshire, such as Manchester, Salford, Stockport, and Stalybridge, large proportions of Irish immigrants found employment in the cotton mills. Here, however, any rudimentary skills acquired in rural Ireland were largely irrelevant to the sophisticated process of production. On the whole one must accept the harsh judgement of Sir James Tennent in 1860, that 'untaught any handicraft, and unskilled in any mechanical art, the Irish immigrant competes only for the coarsest, the least remunerative and generally the most repulsive descriptions of labour'.[1]

Two of the worst paid and 'most repulsive' occupations available to immigrants deserve separate treatment: military and domestic service. The census returns of birthplace often neglect those in the armed services, who comprised an important element in the Irish migratory population of the British Isles. Soldiering was often the occupation of last resort for Irish towns-men without regular employment, and was thus a result as well as an origin of migration. Many Irishmen joined British regiments in British towns. Even at the period of the peninsular war, one-quarter of those enlisted for Scottish regiments were Irish. Between 1830 and 1870 about 50,000 'other ranks' in the British army were usually Irish-born, though the Irish component in the army dropped steadily from two-fifths to one-quarter. This meant that the Irish were consistently over-represented in the army by about one-third, just as protestant Irishmen were over-represented in the officer class.[2] Returns of army medical inspections between 1860 and 1863 suggest that Irish over-representation was largely owing to heavy immigrant enlistment. Less than three-fifths of Irish-born recruits in those years were enlisted in Ireland, whereas one-third joined up in England and almost one-tenth in Scotland. Over one-quarter of all recruits in the Liverpool and Glasgow districts were returned as Irish-born, a proportion well in excess of the Irish share of the total population of Glasgow or Liverpool in 1861.[3]

Another menial occupation conventionally associated with Irish immigrants was domestic service. This was indeed a major occupation, particularly for single girls and widows, yet in some towns the Irish found employers reluctant to engage their services. As a Glasgow clergyman remarked in 1841, 'it may be a prejudice on the part of the Scotch but they generally prefer the Highland females in their families; . . . the Highlanders have many friends in Glasgow to

---

[1] Quoted in Catherine Jones, *Immigration and social policy in Britain* (London, 1977), p. 46.

[2] J. E. Handley, *The Irish in Scotland, 1798–1845* (2nd ed., Cork, 1945), pp 80–81; H. J. Hanham, 'Religion and nationality in the mid-Victorian army' in M. R. D. Foot (ed.), *War and society: historical essays in honour and memory of J. R. Western, 1928–71* (London, 1973), pp 176–81; census returns of birthplace for army 'effectives' at home and abroad, 1851–71. The last source indicates that Irish natives were consistently under-represented in the Royal Navy, Royal Marines, and merchant navy. Before 1861, members of the services were excluded from the general returns of birthplace; thereafter, only those serving in Great Britain were included.

[3] *Army medical department: statistical, sanitary, and medical reports for the year 1860* [–63], p. 153 [3051], H.C. 1862, xxxiii, 161; p. 148 [3233], H.C. 1863, xxxiv, 158; p. 169 [3464], H.C. 1864, xxxvi, 267; p. 185 [3566], H.C. 1865, xxxiii, 195.

whom they apply'. Irish girls were likewise crowded out by better connected Highland immigrants in Paisley and Greenock, exemplifying the fact that the Irish in Scotland were disadvantaged by comparison with other migratory groups as well as the native-born.[1] In English towns domestic service often accounted for more than one-third of occupied Irishwomen, yet there was only a slight excess of Irish servants in mid-century Manchester and Bradford, and a slight deficit in London and possibly Liverpool. No appreciable change has been documented for the two subsequent decades.[2] The Irish in Britain were probably told more often than those in America or Australia that 'no Irish need apply' for domestic 'situations', perhaps because in Britain alone was there an adequate supply of non-Irish immigrant women.

So long as their ambitions were confined to occupations unsought by other groups, Irish immigrants were tolerated by the labour force and welcomed by employers. But whenever the immigrants found themselves in competition with British workers, tolerance was easily displaced by hostility, resentment, and polemical economics. In 1827, Malthus prognosticated that continued population growth in Ireland would 'be most fatal to the happiness of the labouring classes in England, because there will be a constant and increasing emigration from Ireland to England, which will tend to lower the wages of labour in England, and to prevent the good effects arising from the superior prudence of the labouring classes in this country'. A less sober contemporary predicted that continued encroachment of 'Scotch and Irish labour upon English industry' would help to extinguish 'the English name, or, at least, English power, and English blood, in England'; while many modern historians have followed Carrothers in asserting that Irish immigration served 'to depress the standard of life of the labourers'.[3] The truth of the thesis that the wage level would be depressed by increasing the labour supply through immigration depends on several factors: whether home supply was adequate to meet growing industrial demand for labour; whether Irish and British workers competed for employment in the same sectors; and whether immigrant workers undermined 'combinations' seeking to safeguard working-class conditions of life.

In aggregate terms, Irish immigration did not demonstrably lower industrial any more than agricultural wage levels. In both sectors the immigrants tended

[1] Cited in T. M. Devine, 'Temporary migration and the Scottish highlands' in *Econ. Hist. Rev.*, 2nd ser., xxxii (1979), pp 352–3; Lobban, op. cit., p. 274.

[2] Lowe, 'Irish in Lancashire', pp 600–06; C. Richardson, 'Irish settlement in mid-nineteenth century Bradford' in *Yorkshire Bulletin of Economic and Social Research*, xx, no. 1 (1968), p. 52; Lynn Hollen Lees, *Exiles of Erin: Irish migrants in Victorian London* (Manchester, 1979), pp 93, 119; R. Lawton, 'Irish immigration to England and Wales in the mid-nineteenth century' in *Ir. Geography*, iv (1959), pp 51–3. Statistics given by Richardson and Lawton for Bradford and Liverpool respectively refer to servants of both sexes.

[3] *Third report from the select committee on emigration from the United Kingdom*, p. 312, H.C. 1826–7 (550), v, 534; E. A. Kendall, *Letters to a friend, on the state of Ireland, the Roman Catholic question, and the merits of constitutional religious distinctions* (3 vols, London, 1826), ii, 635; W. A. Carrothers, *Emigration from the British Isles* (London, 1965), p. 43.

to cluster in regions of persistently high wages. In 1834 a Manchester cotton manufacturer denied that immigration had reduced wages, protesting that 'it might with more show of reason be asserted, that where Irish labourers are most numerous, wages are the highest. The simple explanation is, that the profitable employment of capital having raised the rate of labour, labourers resort to those places, and the greatest numbers flow from those parts where labour is the lowest.'[1] Immigrants were readier than natives to uproot themselves in order to service developing industries, though a recent historian has ingeniously chastised the Irish for snapping up jobs while potential internal migrants were left napping, so accentuating regional wage disparities.[2] Occasionally Irish workers were able to exploit their initial indispensability by taking control of future labour recruitment. In Greenock, where one sugar manufacturer despaired of finding alternative sources of labour except by importation from Germany, Irish workers established the right to distribute jobs among their own relatives and friends. The secretary of the London Mendicity Society claimed in 1826 that the Irish had obtained a monopoly in 'some particular descriptions' of bricklaying labour; and eight years later a Manchester builder ascribed Irish domination of that sector to the effective combination and 'malicious tricks' of the Irish rather than to the alleged reluctance of Englishmen to 'carry the hod'. In general, however, Irish workers proved highly vulnerable whenever British labour became readily available. As another cotton manufacturer remarked in 1834, 'ten or twelve years ago we could not have done without the Irish. . . . Now there is an abundance of English hands, and we could dispense with the Irish.' He had decided to rid himself of nine-tenths of his Irish weavers, with their 'slovenly' habits and 'mutinous disposition'.[3]

Though the functions of British and Irish workers were more often complementary than competitive, enough localised clashes of interest occurred to foster enduring disharmony. As early as 1834, Irish operatives were driven out of a Pontypool ironworks by Welsh colleagues who accused them of undercutting the standard wage. The most frequent and bloodiest clashes occurred on the railways, where Irish navvies were prominent from the 1830s onwards. Resentment, sometimes sparking into ethnic confrontation, was fostered by primitive working conditions, violent fluctuations in demand for labour, and mutual suspicion that contractors preferred to employ other ethnic groups. Trivial incidents could provoke the burning of Irish huts, marches and counter-marches, assaults and reprisals. Thus the major riot at Penrith in 1846 was sparked off by an Irish navvy's refusal to exchange his shovel for a pick when ordered to do so by an English ganger. Some railway contractors

[1] *Poor inquiry, app. G*, pp 79–80.

[2] E. H. Hunt, *Regional wage variations in Britain* (Oxford, 1973), pp 286–305; E. H. Hunt, *British labour history 1850–1914* (London, 1981), pp 34, 171–6.

[3] Lobban, op. cit., p. 274; *Report from the select committee on emigration from the United Kingdom*, p. 215, H.C. 1826 (404), iv, 215; *Poor inquiry, app. G*, pp 140, 71, 64.

followed the example of a Lancashire alkali manufacturer by separating their Irish and British workforces into separate segments, but this merely transformed communal into trench warfare.[1] The intensity of ethnic hostility in northern Britain was manifested in Dunfermline in 1850, Irish labourers having become 'obnoxious to the colliers and weavers of the District, from interfering as it is alleged with the demand for labor'. Several thousand operatives 'assembled in a tumultuous manner' and tried to eject 'all Irish labourers' from their lodgings, in reprisal for which the Irish fatally injured a Scottish weaver. As the sheriff substitute reported, the Scots then 'tried to march them down to North Queensferry and to ship them off across the Irish [Sea], but I got there before them and balked them and marched the Irishmen back to Dunfermline in spite of their talk'. He believed that this was 'a preparatory move to a strike for the Irish not being in the unions they cannot carry a strike out'.[2]

On occasion the Irish became actual rather than potential 'knobsticks' or 'blacklegs', as a Liverpool clergyman delicately intimated in 1854. When English workers demanded extravagant wages, 'we are very frequently able to put on the screw of the Irish competition'; and 'very great assistance from the Irish' had been obtained in connection with 'some strikes which have taken place'. But strike-breaking was a risky enterprise for a scattered immigrant minority. When Irishmen were brought in during a colliery strike at Bute Merthyr, south Wales, in 1857, the strike was indeed broken. So, a few months later, was the peace, crockery, and some of the heads of the Irish population, which was driven out of the village by an armed mob of a hundred and fifty Welsh colliers. Three years earlier in Preston, many 'knobsticks' imported from the Belfast workhouse during a major mill dispute had turned tail at the first sight of pickets, whereas other more resilient Irish strike-breakers had been thrown out of work on settlement of the dispute.[3] Those foolhardy enough to break strikes were more often paupers summoned from Ireland for the purpose than Irish residents in Britain.

Despite the vulnerability of 'blacklegs' and the evident benefits of trade union membership, the organisational gap between Irish and British workers was only gradually closed. Many writers have attributed this to spirited propaganda against trade 'combinations' on the part of Daniel O'Connell and the catholic clergy, which promoted its own rival network of provident and benefit societies and on occasion withheld its sacraments from trades unionists. Nationalist and catholic opposition has also been held responsible for Irish reluctance to participate in the radical and chartist agitations of the 1830s

[1] John Hickey, *Urban catholics* (London, 1967), pp 53–4; Terry Coleman, *The railway navvies* (London, 1965), pp 85–7; letter of Peter McDonough in *Liverpool Mercury*, 8 Nov. 1839, cited in J. H. Treble, 'Irish navvies in the north of England, 1830–50' in *Transport History*, vi, no. 3 (1973), p. 238.

[2] Scottish Record Office (Edinburgh), AD.58.75.

[3] *Report from the select committee on poor removal*, p. 370, H.C. 1854 (396), xvii, 378; Hickey, op. cit., pp 54–5; Lowe, 'Irish in Lancashire', pp 176–8.

and 1840s. Such explanations of group affiliation are unconvincing, since neither the church nor any nationalist body exercised effective social control over the immigrant population. The disorganisation of the Irish labour force was a predictable consequence of immigrant concentration in unskilled occupations, whereas radical and trade union activity was concentrated among skilled workers and artisans. Individual Irishmen such as John Doherty in Manchester were prominent in attempts to establish national organisations for unskilled workers, such as the Grand General Union of Operative Cotton Spinners (1829), but these general unions soon became defunct. Even these ephemeral bodies often had little Irish support: John Doherty was one of the few adult Irish male cotton spinners in Lancashire. The dreaded alliance of chartism and Irish disaffection, seemingly achieved at Manchester's Free Trade Hall on St Patrick's day 1848, was in fact illusory. Neither the Irish confederate clubs nor the chartist bodies that united in 1848 had much popular following among the immigrants, and orthodox Young Irelanders as well as repealers remained fearful of conspiring with the 'physical force' chartists. In most English towns there was a sprinkling of Irishmen among the chartist leadership, usually favouring the militancy of Feargus O'Connor, but sometimes advocating moral force as in the case of Arthur O'Neill in Birmingham. 'Irish' radicals such as O'Connor (a protestant landlord) and 'Bronterre' O'Brien (a graduate of Trinity College, Dublin) had strong negative appeal for catholic immigrants. The Irish of mid-century Britain were variously castigated as strike-breakers and as class-conspirators, but seldom merited either insult. Unskilled, disorganised, too few to alter the prevailing wage level, the immigrants occupied a marginal and vulnerable position in a society which grossly overestimated their capacity for subversion.

This aggregation of relatively poor, ill-housed, impermanent, and often unwelcome immigrants has frequently been classified as a 'community'. Several witnesses to the poor inquiry 'described them as forming a distinct community in the midst of the English, and compared them in this respect with the Jews'. Irish distinctiveness in England, and to a smaller extent Scotland, was attributed to catholicism, the Irish language, and enforced segregation.[1] In effect, Lewis offered three propositions: that the immigrants were subjected to native exclusivism leading to segregation from all but 'the lowest class'; that they remained culturally alienated; and that in self-defence they formed a 'community'. Having explored the character of Irish residential and social segregation, it remains for us to test the extent of cultural alienation, and to establish whether the combination of segregation and alienation gave rise to a community or merely to a condition of enduring rootlessness.

Evidence of cultural alienation abounds both in rhetoric and in social archives. Interaction with immigrants engendered strong popular beliefs about Irish distinctiveness, expressed in the Welsh proverbs *dyna hen das Gwyddel*

[1] *Poor inquiry, app. G*, p. xiv.

(that is an old Irish trick) and *maen nhw yn byw fel Gwyddelod* (they live like Irish people).[1] Other observers noted that the Irish not only lived but died distinctively. The Irish custom of 'waking' the corpse with the help of porter, whiskey, and conviviality was reenacted in immigrant households as far apart as London, Liverpool, and Greenock. This provoked British ridicule, indignation, and sometimes alarm, since the survivors occasionally offered violent resistance when officials tried to remove infected bodies, as during the cholera epidemics of 1832 and 1849.[2] Cornewall Lewis reported that the immigrants often re-created their domestic environment of rural Ireland in the cellars of urban Britain, stocking their households with swine rather than furniture, and consuming potatoes, milk, and salt herring rather than meat. British contempt for an alien culture was confusingly mixed with fear of 'moral pollution' for British workers associating with the Irish, feebly counterbalanced by hope of moral uplifting for the degraded Irish. A Manchester cotton-spinner lamented in 1834 that

one of the chief evils of the Irish influence arises from the habits of the women; the English women are clean, orderly, and attentive to their families; the Irish women are negligent, inattentive, and slovenly, and fond of going to each others' houses for the sake of gossip; hence they often go into the houses of the English and hinder the English in their work, and teach them bad habits.

A few Scottish witnesses reversed this model of interaction by complaining of the baneful moral effects of immigration on the Irish themselves. Thus the owner of an Anderston spinning mill remarked that on arrival the immigrants were 'in general very decent and respectable in their appearance and manner', subsequently deteriorating from their former condition as a result of 'mixing with the lowest dregs of our working population'. A correspondent of Glasgow's catholic *Free Press* warned the Irish in 1864 that 'if we do not gather ourselves from among them, they will corrupt the hearts of even the wise and good amongst us'.[3] But despite mutual anxiety as to the consequences of cultural interaction between hosts and guests, the predominant theme of commentators up to 1870 was immigrant alienation.

The most notorious of all manifestations of Irish estrangement in Britain were drunkenness and criminality. Opinions differed as to whether these characteristics were imported from Ireland or acquired as a result of experiencing working-class misery in Britain. The solicitor to the Licensed Victuallers' Association claimed in 1853 that 'drunkenness and dissipation' were most

[1] Donald Attwater, *The catholic church in modern Wales: a record of the past century* (London, 1935), p. 223.
[2] Michael Durey, 'The survival of an Irish culture in Britain, 1800–1845' in *Historical Studies* (Melbourne), xx, no. 78 (1982), p. 32; Lynn Hollen Lees, *Exiles of Erin: Irish migrants in Victorian London* (Manchester, 1979), pp 186–7; *Poor inquiry, app. G*, p. 139.
[3] *Poor inquiry, app. G*, pp xi–xii, 63, 106–7; W. M. Walker, 'Irish immigrants in Scotland: their priests, politics and parochial life' in *Hist. Jn.*, xv (1972), p. 651.

often found in towns with 'an immense influx of Irish' such as Glasgow and Liverpool. Denying that this arose from the easy availability of liquor, he attributed it to 'the habits of the people coming there, who have been accustomed to these indulgences' and who tended to 'corrupt and destroy the population of Liverpool and Glasgow'. Cornewall Lewis also stressed the durability of Irish drinking habits among immigrants, who 'often drink with their wives and children, not only in their own houses, but even take their entire families to the tavern', so encouraging female inebriety. Nevertheless, immigrant drinking habits conformed more closely to those of the British working class than the Irish peasantry, for whom fairday rather than payday determined the rhythm of drinking. Irish as well as British workers were induced in mid-century to reduce their alcoholic consumption, by a combination of temperance campaigning, increasing excise duty, and 'the great cheapness of tea, coffee, and sugar'. Yet for both groups the temptations of 'wabble shops', 'dram shops', and 'bush houses' as well as public houses remained powerful in the absence of other diversions.[1] If drinking was evidence of alienation, it was characteristic of the British proletariat rather than the Irish immigrant population alone.

Immigrant criminality was the other major theme of anti-Irish rhetoric and, by extension, of the 'no-popery' agitation. Immigrant spokesmen such as John Denvir did not deny the prominence of the Irish among those arrested in Britain, but attributed this to the multitude of petty offences committed by hawkers and of crimes of violence attributable to drink. Lewis likewise reported 'that the Irish in the large towns of Lancashire and Scotland commit more crimes than an equal number of natives of the same places; but that their crimes are not in general of a very dangerous character, being for the most part brutal assaults committed in a state of drunkenness'. Premeditated violence against the person was far less common among the Irish in Britain than at home, while serious crimes against property were rarely perpetrated by a people 'not having been regularly trained for housebreaking'.[2] Contemporaries and historians have generally accepted Lewis's finding that Irish criminality in Britain was commonplace but casual and unskilled.

The immigrant's reputation for criminality is confirmed by birthplace statistics for those arrested in various English towns during the period 1832–71. At its peak (usually soon after the famine) the Irish proportion of offenders reached two-fifths in Liverpool, about one-third in Oldham and Manchester, one-quarter in Preston, York, Wolverhampton, and Bradford, and less than one-fifth in Salford and Widnes. Table 3 reveals that the Irish were about twice as prominent among offenders as among the general population in

---

[1] *Report from the select committee on public houses, etc.; together with the proceedings of the committee, minutes of evidence, appendix, and index*, pp 588, 229, 397–8, H.C. 1852–3 (855), xxxvii, 600, 241, 409–10; *Poor inquiry, app. G*, p. xiii.

[2] John Denvir, *The Irish in Britain* (2nd ed., London, 1894), p. 253; *Poor inquiry, app. G*, pp xx, xxii.

Liverpool, Manchester, Salford, Widnes, and York, but at least three times as prominent in Preston, Oldham, Bradford, and Wolverhampton. The immigrant's relative criminality changed remarkably little over the period, despite major changes in the scale and character of the Irish influx. Other records of committals to local prisons confirm Irish propensity for crime, though the Irish excess was quite modest in the case of the Glasgow bridewell in 1834 and of various London prisons inspected by Mayhew and Binny.[1] National statistics compiled from 1856 onwards show that England's prison population contained about five times as large a proportion of Irish natives as did the population outside. This was partly due to the concentration of Irish immigrants in crime-prone regions such as Lancashire, where the index of Irish criminality was somewhat below the national aggregate figure. The Irish nevertheless accounted for one-quarter of Lancashire's male prisoners and no less than two-fifths of the women committed in 1861. How should we interpret the unmistakeable prominence in crime of Britain's Irish population?

The likelihood that an Irish immigrant would be arrested in Britain is at best a highly ambiguous indicator of group alienation. Criminal as well as drinking patterns were probably determined by neighbourhood and class more than by ethnic affiliation, and the Irish were clustered in towns and classes with high crime rates. Furthermore, several writers have stressed the hostility shown to Irish settlers by urban policemen and magistrates, who may have provoked riots or assaults by their aggressive intrusion on parties of carousing Irish devoid of criminal impulse. In many towns policemen regarded Irish enclaves as danger zones, and seemed readier to draw their cutlasses against immigrants than against locals. Yet the excess of Irish arrests, evident in so many towns with different police authorities and different occupational structures, cannot plausibly be attributed to police discrimination or class factors alone. The peculiar contribution of the immigrant experience to British criminality may be elucidated by analysing the categories of crime that the Irish were most inclined to commit.

As so many contemporaries attested, the Irish showed a significant propensity for violence when drunk. This is manifested in the Irish contribution to various categories of crime in Manchester, Salford, Liverpool, Oldham, Bradford, York, and Glasgow at dates between 1834 and 1871.[2] In most cases, an excessive proportion of Irish offenders were charged with drunk and disorderly behaviour or assaulting the police. Though related offences such as

[1] *Poor inquiry, app. G*, p. 121; Henry Mayhew and John Binny, *The criminal prisons of London and scenes of prison life* (London, 1862), pp 199, 241, 284, 402–4, 632. For Glasgow the index of over-representation rose from 1.3 (1 Mar. 1834) to 1.8 (Glasgow prison, decade to 30 June 1860: see John Strang, 'Ten years' chronicle of the prison of Glasgow' in *Transactions of the National Association for the Promotion of Social Science*, 1860 (London, 1861), p. 466).

[2] Statistics were analysed for Manchester (1846, 1851, 1861, 1871); Salford (1849); Liverpool (1863, 1871); Oldham (1864, 1871); Bradford (1853–4); York (1850–51, 1860–61, 1870–71); and Glasgow (1 Mar. 1834). For sources, see table 3, below, p. 660.

common assault, malicious damage, rioting, or breach of the peace were not uniformly prominent in Irish crime, it does seem that immigrants were slightly more conspicuous in crimes of violence against the person than in other offences. Their penchant for drunk and disorderly behaviour was not however powerful enough to reverse the secular trend towards increasing sobriety during the famine years of peak immigration. Between 1842–6 and 1847–51, the rate of arrests on these charges fell sharply in towns such as Manchester, Birmingham, Bristol, and Edinburgh, while even in the traditionally drink-sodden towns of Liverpool and Dundee a slight reduction occurred. When disorderly behaviour again became prevalent towards 1870, Irish offenders kept pace with their British contemporaries.[1] The Irish record in other sectors of crime also suggests that the conventional image of the bleary-eyed, hot-blooded, but good-natured Hibernian lout requires qualification. Prostitution accounted for a greater proportion of Irish than British arrests, at least in Manchester, while the Irish were particularly well represented among forgers and currency offenders in Glasgow (1834), Manchester (1849), and Bradford (1853–4). Even theft, which occasioned a relatively small proportion of Irish arrests, was committed more frequently by the Irish than by the British. In both Liverpool and Oldham about one-third of those arrested for larceny offences in the early 1860s were Irish-born. Thus the Irish immigrant, though distinctively prone to offences against the person rather than property, was also more likely than his British neighbour to commit crimes of virtually every category. In crime as in the labour market, the immigrant betrayed an exaggerated state of class alienation as well as alienation from the rest of his class.

Irish alienation from other sections of the proletariat was evident in the frequent ethnic party fights, which tended to arise from the drunkenness and result in the criminality already discussed. As we have seen, these battles sometimes arose from economic grievances; but more often they gave the appearance of racial or religious confrontations. As one railway excavator in Cheshire protested in 1839, 'it was often hinted to me that I ought to consider myself a fortunate kind of Irish animal, because I was not driven from the place with sticks or stones, as many of my countrymen had been before my coming, for no other reason than being Irish'. The writer remembered cases of 'Irish men hunts' resulting not merely in the conventional stoning but also the more recherché penalty of rolling up coats in hot bricks.[2] Ethnic confrontations between railway navvies often took the form of ritualistic trials of strength, with Irish gangs armed with 'bludgeons, scythes, and bayonets on sticks, reaping hooks, iron rods etc.' responding to formal challenges from their Highlander or

[1] *Abstract of the return of persons taken into custody for drunkenness and disorderly conduct in each city and town in each year, from 1841 to 1851*, H.C. 1852–3 (531), lxxi, 295; Lowe, 'Irish in Lancashire', figs. 20, 21, pp 218 ff.

[2] ' H. Treble, 'Irish navvies in the north of England, 1830–50' in *Transport History*, vi, no. 3 (1973), p. 239.

other adversaries.[1] Ritual also governed the seasonal clashes between Orange and Green, which were modelled upon the party contests of Ulster but which involved religious and political factions recruited from the British as well as the immigrant working class. Though peak membership of the Orange order in Britain may not have exceeded 6,000, it had considerable support in Lancashire towns such as Liverpool, where the twelfth of July was known as 'Carpenters' day' in honour of protestant Irish domination of Liverpool's shipbuilding workforce. Orange processions, often resulting in riotous clashes with 'Ribbonmen' or other catholic factions, were curtailed by the suppression of the order in 1836 and the banning of processions in Liverpool in 1852. But ugly scenes occurred in Liverpool in 1846, 1850, and 1851, while provocative Orange processions were held in subsequent years outside borough limits. The grimmest confrontations occurred in Scotland, where catholic and protestant Irish miners in Paisley fought on the Twelfth as late as 1859. Two hundred Orangemen 'with some women' were met at Linwood Bridge by an equal force of catholics. Pistol shots were fired, 'stones were thrown by both parties and knives and sticks with spears were used by some as well as bludgeons and other legal weapons', a catholic was stabbed to death, and several Orangemen were injured. As usual, the battle was over before pensioners or soldiers could be drafted in.[2] Ethnic clashes also occurred intermittently under the guise of 'no-popery' riots, though these were somewhat less ferocious than London's Gordon riots of 1780. The anti-catholic movement that greeted the restoration of the English hierarchy in September 1850 was not simply anti-hibernicism under a new label, but it did involve the ransacking of catholic chapels and Irish enclaves, and it did generate organised resistance among the battered survivors of Irish famine. Set battles ensued, Irish gangs often trading or even initiating atrocities against their protestant adversaries. These battles were episodic rather than endemic, with a further outbreak in the late 1860s provoked by the rabble-rouser William Murphy, who had been baptised a catholic in Limerick but was later persuaded that 'every popish priest was a murderer, a cannibal, a liar, and a pickpocket'.[3] Ethnic violence of one form or another was a recurrent nightmare for Irish immigrants in many of Britain's industrial towns.

THE immigrant's sense of Irishness was to some extent a defensive posture, adopted in response to the hostility and prejudice of British neighbours and fellow proletarians. Irish drunkenness, violent behaviour, and party fighting owed more to the harshness of life in urban Britain than to the cultural inherit-

---

[1] Scottish Record Office, AD.58.66. This confrontation, which occurred near Linlithgow in June 1841, arose out of 'a quarrel about a subscription for a snuff box to be given to one of the sub-contractors'.

[2] Scottish Record Office, AD.56.309/3.

[3] Walter L. Arnstein, 'The Murphy riots: a Victorian dilemma' in *Victorian Studies*, xix, no. 1 (1975), p. 58.

ance of rural Ireland. Yet the British conviction that these traits were intrinsic to Irishness left its imprint on immigrant imagination, causing many settlers to revel in misconduct that might otherwise have been a matter of shame. Thus alienation originating in class experience was transformed into cultural alienation, reinforcing authentic Irish otherness in matters of diet, domestic organisation, and sociability. But the sense of estrangement from British *mores* and the persistence of home-formed habits by no means entailed the creation in Britain of a cohesive Irish 'community'. The reality of that community must be judged by analysing the strength and pervasiveness of those social institutions that brought immigrants together in common enterprises.

One such institution was marriage, which determined whether immigrants would construct their households within or beyond their ethnic group. The extent of ethnic exogamy is hard to determine, since little is known about the partners of immigrants marrying outside the catholic church. The majority of Irish immigrants married by catholic priests in Britain probably found other immigrants as partners. In Paisley (1834) it was reported that 'the Irish frequently intermarry with the natives here', but in contemporary Greenock two-thirds of catholic Irish marriages involved pairs of Irish partners. In 1855 this proportion had risen to four-fifths, a considerably higher rate of intragroup marriage than that experienced by protestant Irish or Highlander immigrants. Census schedules for London in 1851 and 1861 show that only one-fifth of 'Irish' couples included an English partner (often with an Irish surname), but in York (1841) the proportion exceeded two-thirds. York's Irish men were notably more successful than the women in finding English-born spouses. The scanty data so far assembled leave uncertain the extent to which intra-group marriage helped foster an Irish community, though one historian has neatly evaded the issue by ruling that anybody marrying an Irish immigrant thereby became 'Irish'.[1]

The most prominent institution serving to incorporate and provide guidance for immigrants was the catholic church. The church was itself profoundly altered by the Irish influx. Between 1800 and 1870 it was transfigured from being a small, proud, rich, and unpopular body to become a large, prudent, poorer, and unpopular body, with a vast majority of Irish adherents. However reluctantly, it was hibernicised to a greater extent than any of the presbyterian or protestant churches that catered more silently for the needs of immigrants from Ulster. As in Boston or Sydney, the clergy and especially the hierarchy were slow to respond to the Irish takeover of most urban congregations. Many British priests were loath to adapt their pastoral priorities to the urgent

---

[1] *Poor inquiry, app. G*, pp 134, 138; R. D. Lobban, 'The Irish community in Greenock in the nineteenth century' in *Ir. Geography*, vi, no. 3 (1971), pp 278–9; Lynn Hollen Lees, *Exiles of Erin: Irish migrants in Victorian London* (Manchester, 1979), pp 153–4; Frances Finnegan, *Poverty and prejudice: a study of Irish immigrants in York* (Cork, 1982), p. 6. In Girvan (1834) as in York (1841–71), those Irish immigrants who intermarried with the local population were usually men (see *Poor inquiry, app. G*, p. 149; Finnegan, op. cit., pp 6, 70–71).

demands of impecunious Irish worshippers rather than the daintier requirements of munificent, loyal, and often anti-Irish native laymen. Until the famine crisis the church was backward in providing charitable or social provision for the poor Irish, and despite the growing influence of prelates such as Walsh and Wiseman in Birmingham and London, old-fashioned patricians continued to preside over many dioceses with heavy Irish settlement. The priesthood long resisted Irish infiltration, and even Wiseman at Westminster was accused of anti-Irish discrimination in recruitment. One-third of London's secular clergy were Irishmen in 1842, and Irish natives dominated the post-famine priesthood in Liverpool. But in other Lancashire towns such as Preston, St Helens, and Widnes there were no Irish clergy in 1855, while the Scottish church, under the pugnacious leadership of Bishops Scott and Murdoch in Glasgow, remained unmistakeably Scottish. As late as 1864, a meeting of twenty-two Irish priests in Glasgow protested

that while more than nineteen-twentieths of the faithful and half of the priests of the vicariate are by birth or parentage Irish, Scotch clergymen are nevertheless for the most part trustees of all our ecclesiastical properties, lands, churches, chapels, houses, schools, colleges, convents, reformatories, cemeteries, etc.

The church put up a stout fight before partially succumbing to hibernicisation, and the faithful English proclaimed their detachment from the immigrants by addressing their clergy as 'Mr', while northern Irish catholics said 'Priest' and southerners 'Father'.[1]

Dissonance between the institution of the church and its laity doubtless contributed to the laxity of religious observance by the immigrant Irish long after the mid-century tightening of church discipline in Ireland. Catholic publicists might proclaim that the Irish in Britain were 'much more likely to forget their country than to forget their faith', but in private they were less triumphalist. A Marist priest in Spitalfields (London) reported in 1852 that 'the seven or eight thousand catholics who live here are devoid of all religious instruction, living and dying without the sacraments'; and a Vincentian who witnessed a Sheffield Sunday school a decade later likened the pupils to 'wild Indians; they seemed never to have seen a priest before; and their wild disregard of order or of authority almost disheartened me'.[2] Attendance at mass and performance of the Easter duty were discouraged by a combination of shortages of priests, consecrated space, and lay enthusiasm. In London, where the church had longer experience than elsewhere of poor Irish parishioners,

[1] Sheridan Gilley, 'The Roman Catholic mission to the Irish in London' in *Recusant History*, x, no. 3 (1969), p. 141; Lowe, 'Irish in Lancashire', p. 278; J. E. Handley, *The Irish in modern Scotland* (Cork, 1947), p. 78; John Denvir, *The Irish in Britain* (2nd ed., 1894), p. 113.

[2] William G. Todd, *The Irish in England. Reprinted with additions, from the Dublin Review* (London, 1857), p. 20; Lynn Hollen Lees, *Exiles of Erin: Irish migrants in Victorian London* (Manchester, 1979), p. 173; G. A. Beck (ed.), *The English catholics, 1850–1950: essays to commemorate the centenary of the restoration of the hierarchy of England and Wales* (London, 1950), p. 269.

chapel seating was available for less than one-fifth of the catholic population in 1851. Even this provision was often barred to immigrants, since two-fifths of places were appropriated to well-padded renters of pews. Not one catholic in three attended mass in London on census Sunday, and fifteen years later mass attendance was only slightly more common in the Liverpool diocese. Attention to the Easter duty was still less widespread, though certain groups such as young children and decrepit adults were exempted. The proportion of catholics taking the mandatory confession and communion ranged from about one-tenth in London (1839) and Cardiff (1841), through one-quarter in post-famine Cardiff, Liverpool (1866), and Wigan (1866), up to one-third in Liverpool (1834) and the minor towns of the Liverpool diocese in 1866. Only in Preston, with its abnormal majority of English catholics, did as many as two catholics in five observe the church's requirements in that year. The available statistics show no general improvement over time, and in both Liverpool and Cardiff religious observance seems to have become less common after the famine.[1] Though catholics were probably more punctilious than most other early Victorian flocks in manifesting their faith, they could not match the performance of their counterparts in post-famine Ireland.

Confronted by a largely indifferent laity, the church under Wiseman's direction worked energetically to provide guidance and social amenities for its members. Provision of catholic schooling remained inadequate, despite energetic exploitation of the system of state grants to denominational schools between 1847 and 1870. By about 1870 most catholic children in Salford and Oldham could find places in church schools, but this did not apply in Liverpool or Manchester. Despite notable improvement in class attendance, catholic pupils remained more inclined than others to drop out or play truant. The church vastly extended its social provision for other groups from mid-century onwards, building up an imposing network of guilds, sodalities, confraternities, friendly societies, and the like. In Spitalfields, where religious observance was so exiguous in 1852, the Marists claimed to have enrolled one-seventh of their parishioners in lay societies less than a decade later. The Catholic Young Men's Society, introduced to Lancashire in 1854 to encourage 'mutual improvement, and the extension of the spirit of religion and brotherly love', established several branches in Liverpool and Manchester and provided reading rooms, lending libraries, burial, sickness, and provident funds, and even building society services. Temperance campaigns, such as those organised by Fr Nugent in Liverpool, proved intermittently effective. But the church's attempts to educate and train its largely Irish laity in the ways of piety, sobriety, and respectability had only partial success. The creation of a catholic 'community' was uncompleted in 1870.

---

[1] Gilley, op. cit., pp 125, 132, 142; Lowe, 'Irish in Lancashire', pp 247–87; Lynn Hollen Lees, *Exiles of Erin: Irish migrants in Victorian London* (Manchester, 1979), pp 180–81; John Hickey, *Urban catholics* (London, 1967), pp 91–2; *Poor inquiry, app. G*, p. 22.

Neither was a political community any more firmly established. Not surprisingly, immigrants played little part in either local or national politics. Even in the few towns where the Irish formed a substantial part of the population, their transience and low social status tended to cause their exclusion from the electoral registers. It is true that London had a catholic lord mayor (Thomas Kelly) as early as 1836, but very few immigrants were elected to vestries even in parishes of intensive Irish settlement, and of those few most solicited non-catholic support. Liverpool had a catholic club of middle-class membership from 1844 onwards, but it was unable to break the tory monopoly of local government between 1841 and 1892. Excluded from local political participation, immigrant activists were restricted largely to aping the political movements of Ireland itself. Ribbon lodges were active in many British as well as Irish towns, their enthusiasm being fostered by heavy drinking on the premises of their publican leaders, and also by the truculence of their equally thirsty Orange opponents. The repeal association, like all nationalist bodies in Ireland, developed a network of wards in Britain, implausibly claiming eighty thousand associate members in London alone by 1844. St Patrick's day provided an opportunity for the various political and catholic societies to celebrate the woes of Ireland in concerts, dinners, or public processions, in addition to public houses. But the underlying tension between Irish nationalism and British catholicism was frequently evident on these occasions, with the church deploring not only drunken revelry but also ostentatious displays by militant political bodies such as the Ancient Order of Hibernians ('Ribbonmen') or the repeal association. Repealers and priests clashed over the processions of 1846 and 1847 in Liverpool, and after some ugly incidents in subsequent years the holding of public demonstrations ceased from 1852. Preachers such as Father Cahill sought to give the church credit for this 'sacrifice' intended to 'soothe political rancour' and increase 'social virtue and domestic happiness'; though in fact the banning of party processions in Liverpool was probably a more powerful agent of repression than church interference.[1]

The limited capacity of the church to direct the political life of its flock was manifest in the support given by many immigrants to organisations seeking the overthrow by force of British rule in Ireland. Though immigrant participation in these bodies has probably been exaggerated, it seems likely that the Irish in Britain spent a greater part of their smaller political involvement dreaming about revolution than was the case for the Irish at home. The confederate movement of 1848, though never winning mass allegiance in either Ireland or Britain, did establish clubs in many English towns and also clandestine arms shops in Liverpool and Manchester. The National Brotherhood of St Patrick, founded in 1861 'to secure the national independence of Ireland, whether by

---

[1] D. W. Cahill, *Important letter . . . to the catholics of Liverpool* (Dublin, 1853), p. 2; Lowe, 'Irish in Lancashire', pp 355–9.

parliamentary agitation or other means remains to be shown',[1] spread from Liverpool to other Lancashire towns and London despite clerical condemnation. Many of its branches were recruiting agencies for the Irish Republican Brotherhood, which seems to have won rather more support among the urbanised expatriates than among the rural population at home. Thomas Clarke Luby, who did his best to organise the I.R.B. in Britain in 1865, remarked on the enthusiasm, high spirits, and openness of the movement in Britain by comparison with that in Ireland. He recollected that he

must have addressed, in those countries [England and Scotland], a short time, mark, before we were arrested, at least twelve or fifteen hundred men. Of course this was in violation of the strict 'I.R.B.' regulations. But 'twas unavoidable, under the circumstances. I spoke, to them, fiery stuff about the coming time and the *diversion* and destruction they could make in England.[2]

There was undoubtedly a network of fenian circles in northern England, often centred on men of that 'dirty and repulsive-looking' breed known to the police as 'Irish Yankees'. Police information about fenianism in Britain only became plentiful and reliable after the aborted rising of 1867 and its English fringe performances at Chester castle, Clerkenwell, and Hyde Road, which moved the home office to take the movement seriously once it was no longer dangerous. But the scanty evidence of earlier police reports does not confirm Lowe's conclusion that fenianism had widespread support among the Lancashire Irish and 'was the expression of a social, cultural, and national community'. It is true that an Irish detective in Liverpool claimed five months before the rising that 'the great majority of the Irish labourers in this town, London, Manchester, Birmingham, Sheffield, Leeds, and Newcastle, as well as those residing in towns of less note through this country, if not actually enrolled members of the brotherhood, are strongly impressed with the spirit of fenianism.' But British administrators were rightly sceptical of alarmist reports from Irish detectives, eager to suggest that the heart of unrest lay in Britain rather than in Ireland. The home secretary dismissed the report quoted as being 'very loosely drawn as regards fact', and his officials placed more credence in a Scotland Yard investigation indicating that 'there has been (as we supposed) gross exaggeration as to the Liverpool dangers'. The Liverpool police consistently maintained 'that, although the fenian spirit exists in Liverpool, there is no extensive organisation, and that no drilling or meetings of fenians in numbers takes place'. Superintendent Ryan of the Dublin Metropolitan Police supported the Irish detectives, but imprudently revealed that their chilling interpretation of immigrant mentality was derived not from exhaustive enquiries throughout industrial Britain but from evening chats over pots of beer with their fellow

[1] Above, p. 424.
[2] Memoirs of T. C. Luby (N.L.I., MSS 331–3), p. 340.

lodgers in Liverpool.[1] The popular appeal of fenianism in Britain remains uncertain, though it seems clear that Ireland long remained the focus of immigrant politics, and that conspiracy rather than institutional pressure remained the preferred means of political agitation for an unknown number of zealots until the fiasco of 1867. The Irish in Britain practised the politics of alienation, but with insufficient enthusiasm to justify the notion that they constituted a political community.

If evidence of community is weak, that of a powerful and enduring bond between the expatriates and their Irish connections is strong. As in the better documented case of America, immigrants sent home substantial sums as 'remittances', so subsidising the domestic economy as well as funding further migration. Thus, by the mid-1820s, migrants from Lord Dillon's Connacht estates to the world of London bricklaying were sending home over one thousand pounds annually, usually in sums varying from ten shillings to a couple of pounds. Many observers noted the diligence with which Irish settlers, unlike their more individualist British counterparts, saved on behalf of their distant families and parents. During the famine countless poor immigrants despatched remittances to their only slightly poorer relatives in Ireland including 866 postal orders from Irish labourers in York alone during the first ten months of 1847. Others reversed the traffic in affection by trying to import their 'aged parents', an impulse which even the chairman of the Scottish poor law board could only applaud (despite the resultant expense to ratepayers when the newcomers were thrown on the parish) since it arose 'from a feeling so natural, so proper, so good in itself'.[2]

The Irish in Britain generally retained their national identity without forming strong communal bonds away from home. By comparison with Irish emigrants elsewhere they remained more transient, more likely to return home or pass on overseas, less content to carve a humble niche in an alien environment. Those who failed to escape from Britain before death were sometimes repatriated by their children, the bodies being sent 'at a considerable expense, to be buried in Ireland'.[3] In the incongruous context of some industrial town, the transient Irish kept up the familiar routines of eating potatoes, drinking with their families, waking their dead. Stealthily, though, there crept on this 'peculiar tramping people' a novel and more convenient identity. Alienation from British customs and celebration of Irishness gradually became immaterial to the lives of those long settled in Britain. Grudgingly, the survivors found themselves thinking of Britain rather than Ireland as home. In 1860 Captain

---

[1] P.R.O., HO 45/7799, ff 884, 976–7, 863–4, 580; Lowe, 'Irish in Lancashire', pp 598, 529 (citing the quoted report from Head Constable McHale to the inspector general, Irish Constabulary, 18 Oct. 1866).

[2] *Report from the select committee on the laws relating to Irish and Scotch vagrants*, pp 7–8, H.C. 1828 (513), iv, 209–10; Frances Finnegan, *Poverty and prejudice: a study of Irish immigrants in York* (Cork, 1982), p. 181; *Select committee on poor removal*, p. 216, H.C. 1854 (396), xvii, 228.

[3] *Poor inquiry, app. G*, p. 87.

McBride, deputy harbourmaster at Belfast, reported that the Irish paupers removed home from Scotland usually felt themselves to be 'strangers in Ireland ... they have been so long away'. McBride had offered one repatriate his dinner and train fare home to Monaghan, but the 'poor fellow' declined. 'He said "I will not go to Monaghan, I am able to work." I then gave him 2s. and said "Will that do for you?" He thanked me, and I met him at the boat [that] evening, and he said "I want to go back again; I have been 15 years away," and I sent him back; his whole tale is here; there is not a line in it, but there is a volume.'[1] If transience and alienation coloured the history of Irish settlement in Britain between 1801 and 1870, adaptation to British life was to dominate the immigrant experience over the following half-century.

---

[1] *Report from the select committee on irremovable poor*, pp 234, 235, H.C. 1860 (520), xvii, 252, 253.

APPENDIX

1 IRISH-BORN POPULATION OF GREAT BRITAIN, 1841–71

year	number	as % of population	% female	% under 20
		ENGLAND AND WALES		
1841	289,404	1.82	47.74	n.a.
1851	519,959	2.90	n.a.	25.65
1861	601,634	3.00	50.35	17.37
1871	566,540	2.49	50.01	11.97
		SCOTLAND		
1841	126,321	4.82	47.35	n.a.
1851	207,367	7.18	n.a.	29.14
1861	204,083	6.67	49.42	17.75
1871	207,770	6.18	47.79	14.43

2 IRISH-BORN POPULATION OF BRITISH TOWNS, 1841–71

year	London	Liverpool	Manchester	Glasgow	other towns	elsewhere	Britain
			AS % OF LOCAL POPULATION				
1841	3.90	17.33	11.58	16.17	2.92	1.08	2.24
1851	4.60	22.29	13.08	18.17	4.72	1.94	3.49
1861	3.81	18.91	11.31	15.70	4.20	2.26	3.48
1871	2.80	15.56	8.59	14.32	3.42	2.04	2.97
			AS % OF TOTAL IRISH-BORN POPULATION IN BRITAIN				
1841	17.59	11.94	8.25	10.67	16.63	34.92	100
1851	14.92	11.52	7.22	8.22	20.23	37.88	100
1861	13.27	10.42	6.46	7.71	19.22	42.92	100
1871	11.77	9.91	5.59	8.82	19.08	44.82	100
			INDEX OF OVER-REPRESENTATION				
1841	174	772	516	721	130	48	100
1851	132	638	374	520	135	56	100
1861	109	543	325	451	121	65	100
1871	94	524	289	482	115	69	100

Figures refer to the 72 districts designated in the 1861 census as 'principal towns', being 'a selection of towns most remarkable for population and importance in their several counties, or for some other distinguishing feature'. Enumeration limits varied from census to census. Manchester includes Salford. The index of over-representation is the quotient of the Irish-born percentage of each district's population and that of the British population:

$$\left(\frac{\% \text{ Irish-born in each locality}}{\% \text{ Irish-born in Britain}} \times 100 \right).$$

3 IRISH-BORN OFFENDERS IN BRITISH TOWNS, c.1841-71

	as % of all offenders				index of over-representation			
	1841	1851	1861	1871	1841	1851	1861	1871
ARRESTS								
Bradford¹		26 [1853-4]	19 [1860]	24 [1870]		2.9	3.3	4.2
Liverpool²	32 [1832-3]	40 [1849]	37 [1863]	34	1.9	1.8	2.0	2.2
Manchester²	23 [1846]	27	30	22	1.8	1.8	1.9	2.3
Oldham²		36 [1856]	31 [1859]	32		5.5	3.9	7.4
Preston²			26	28			3.1	5.2
Salford²		19 [1849]				1.7		
Widnes²		18 [1849-52]				2.3		
Wolverhampton³		23 [1854]	19 [1857]			3.3	3.3	
York⁴	3	26	21	16	1.3	3.7	2.6	2.1
COMMITTALS⁵								
London			16	12			4.2	4.2
Lancashire			31	28			3.5	4.0
England and Wales			15	14			4.9	5.7

Arrests refer to all Irish-born placed in custody, except for York, where figures refer to those of Irish ethnicity mentioned in newspaper court reports. Committals refer to all Irish-born committed to local prisons, excluding convict, military, and debtor prisoners, during the year stated. Years referred to are those of census, except where indicated by dates in square brackets. The index of over-representation is the quotient of the Irish percentage of offenders and the percentage of Irish-born in the local population. Many figures are approximations.

¹ Report from the select committee on poor removal; together with the proceedings of the committee, minutes of evidence, appendix, and index, p. 317, H.C. 1854-5 (308), xiii, 331 (1853-4); C. Richardson, 'The Irish in Victorian Bradford' in The Bradford Antiquary, xlv (1971), p. 311 (1860, 1870).

² Lowe, 'Irish in Lancashire', pp 222 ff (figures read off graphs); Poor inquiry, app. G, p. 19 (Liverpool, 1832-3); Report from the select committee appointed to inquire into the operation of the act 8 & 9 Vict., c. 117, relating to the removal from England of chargeable poor persons born in Scotland, Ireland, and the isles of Man, Scilly, Jersey, and Guernsey..., pp 358-60, H.C. 1854 (396), xvii, 370-72 (Liverpool, 1849).

³ Roger Swift, 'Crime and ethnicity: the Irish in early Victorian Wolverhampton' in West Midland Studies, xiii (1980), p. 1.

⁴ Francis Finnegan, Poverty and prejudice: a study of Irish immigrants in York (Cork, 1982), p. 153.

⁵ Judicial statistics, 1861. England and Wales..., pp 64-6 [3025], H.C. 1862, lvi, 600-02; Judicial statistics, 1871. England and Wales..., pp 64-6 [C 600], H.C. 1872, lxv, 114-16.

CHAPTER XXX

The Irish in Australia and New Zealand, 1791–1870

PATRICK J. O'FARRELL

THE first fleet of convict ships that began the settlement of Australia reached Sydney harbour in the colony of New South Wales in January 1788; the first convicts sent direct from Ireland—133 males and 22 females—arrived from Cork aboard the *Queen* on 26 September 1791. In the 1820s and 1830s Irish convicts were arriving at an average rate of about a thousand a year. By the time transportation to Australia's eastern colonies ended in 1853,[1] almost 40,000 convicts (29,466 males and 9,104 females) had been sent direct from Ireland. Of those convicts sent from Britain, estimates suggest that about 8,000 were Irish-born and perhaps a similar number of Irish descent. In all, the Irish-born element represented about a quarter of all convicts transported,[2] and this convict element accounted for about 90 per cent of the Irish-born quarter of the colony's population in the 1830s.

Irish-Australian historical tradition has depicted Irish convicts as honourable victims of gross injustice, social oppression, and national persecution, or as heroic rebels. Recent research suggests that this legend of injured innocence requires serious qualification.[3] In the strictly nationalist sense, political rebels

---

[1] Convicts were sent in relatively small numbers to Western Australia up to 1868: the last convict ship sent to Australia reached Fremantle on 10 Jan. 1868 carrying, among other prisoners, 63 fenians.

[2] These figures and conclusions are drawn from the standard general authority, A. G. L. Shaw, *Convicts and the colonies: a study of penal transportation from Great Britain and Ireland to Australia and other parts of the British empire* (London, 1966), and from the particular study of Irish catholic convicts in James Waldersee, *Catholic society in New South Wales, 1788–1860* (Sydney, 1974). In relation to Irish convicts these books supersede previous studies, the most notable of which are L. L. Robson, *The convict settlers of Australia* (Melbourne, 1965); Charles Bateson, *The convict ships, 1787–1868* (Glasgow, 1959); T. J. Kiernan, *Transportation from Ireland to Sydney, 1791–1816* (Canberra, 1954); and Eris M. O'Brien, *The foundation of Australia* (2nd ed., Sydney, 1950).

[3] Waldersee, *Catholic society*, pp 42–71. For a detailed study of the 'rebel' group, see George Rudé, 'Early Irish rebels in Australia' in *Historical Studies*, xvi, no. 62 (Apr. 1974), pp 17–35; George Rudé, *Protest and punishment: the story of the social and political protestors transported to Australia, 1788–1868* (Oxford, 1978). See also B. W. O'Dwyer, 'Michael Dwyer and the 1807 plan of insurrection' in *Journal of the Royal Australian Historical Society*, lxix (Sept. 1983), pp 73–82. For a contemporary critical account, see W. T. Southerwood, 'New light on the foundation of Australian catholicism' in *Australasian Catholic Record*, lxi, no. 2 (Apr. 1984), pp 164–75.

among the Irish convicts were relatively few: about 1½ per cent, less than 600 in the entire history of transportation, of whom nearly 500 arrived in the very early years of the colony, before 1806. Social rebels—those convicted of crimes of violent protest against poverty and landlordism—made up about a fifth. Almost four-fifths of Irish convicts, therefore, can be properly described as ordinary criminals, mostly thieves.

Here were men dishonest and cunning, often violent, no less so than their British counterparts. Thieves made up about three-quarters of all convicts, British and Irish. Of the Irish, about a third had previous convictions, and multiple convictions were quite common. Nor can the Irish be depicted as an older and more responsible element: less than one-fifth were over thirty. Even that minority of political and social rebels was not necessarily of a different stamp from the mere criminals. Joseph Holt described his followers in the 1798 rebellion as

a band of ruffians. . . . Many of the men were inclined to become robbers. . . . They were desperate and bloody minded. . . . Religion . . . was a pretext and excuse for their deceit. . . . The political feeling, or sense of injury, which brought them out in the first instance, was forgotten; and living so long at free quarters made them think robbery and murder lawful.[1]

Nor can their catholicism be necessarily presumed a civilising restraint. Holt recounts the occasion of his men crowding into a mountain chapel: when the priest protested at their bringing in weapons, one man threatened to kill him at the altar if he did not proceed with mass.[2] There was ample confirmation within the convict colony of the violent criminality of the Irish. If one discounts Sir Thomas Brisbane's report in 1824 that 'every murder or diabolical crime which has been committed in the colony since my arrival has been perpetrated by Roman Catholics',[3] there is still the letter of the free settler and future bank manager, John O'Sullivan, to Archbishop Murray of Dublin in May 1830.

Some of our unfortunate and wretched countrymen are foremost in perpetrating the shocking crimes that mark this colony. I did not think the Irish character capable of performing the villainous deeds that are daily blazoned forth. . . . The bloodthirsty and treacherous acts of the ruffians are enough to make the genuine Irishman hide his face in shame.[4]

No doubt the murderous and violent Irish in early New South Wales were a tiny minority, but it was a very spectacular one, which did much to set an adverse public image. The Irish of good life and respectable position found themselves saddled with an image generated by the worst elements of Irish society.

[1] T. Crofton Croker (ed.), *Memoirs of Joseph Holt* (2 vols, London, 1838), i, 236–7, 245–7.
[2] Ibid., pp 199–203.
[3] Sir Thomas Brisbane to Earl Bathurst, 28 Oct. 1824 (*The historical records of Australia* (35 vols, Sydney, 1914–25), 1st ser., xi, 382).
[4] P. F. Moran, *History of the catholic church in Australasia* (Sydney, [1896]), pp 128–9.

However, even in felony the Irish tended to be a distinctive group. Some, small in numbers but significant in their prominence, were men of integrity, guilty of political or social protest, but not common criminals. The Irish were nearly all catholics, whereas the British were protestants. Most were peasants (though about a third possessed manual skills of some kind), while most of the British came from towns. Though the literacy rate of Irish males was not markedly different from that of British males (about 60 per cent could read and between 40 and 50 per cent could also write), many of the Irish did not speak English among themselves, but Gaelic. Here, generally, was a distinctive minority in the Australian colonies. Probably in nothing were the Irish more distinctive than in their cultural background, world view, historical experience, and sense of values, all of which were distinct from those of the British majority; moreover, the hostile relationship between Irish and British in the old world was transported to the new.[1]

Nevertheless, the Irish were not a homogeneous group. There were important differences, and even wide social and moral gulfs among them. There were those (only about 500 by 1828) who had come to the colony as free settlers; and there were convicts, some of whom were violent and vicious while others were not. There were emancipated convicts who had utterly reformed, and those who returned to crime or its shady environs. There were those who achieved considerable prosperity, and the failures, and all the economic grades between. There were also catholics and protestants. Up to 10 per cent of Irish convicts were protestants, and during some periods of assisted free immigration they rose to 20 per cent of the total.[2] Perhaps there were differences also between the Irish who came direct from Ireland and the considerable number—up to 20 per cent of the total Irish-born—who had lived for some time in Britain.

Among the Irish convicts, the small group of political rebels has captured most historical attention, and their unusual characteristics have tended to appear in Irish-Australian mythology as typical of the whole. The most prominent rebels were often men of some previous substance, educated, high-principled, and quite often protestants. The colonial governors did not treat such men as ordinary convicts. Some, like James Meehan the surveyor, were recruited into the government service; others, like Joseph Holt, were employed as farm managers; some, such as Michael Dwyer, had not been convicted and were allowed to become settlers. All were pardoned or emancipated relatively quickly. Very much in the same superior category, but much less relevant to Australian history, were the famous leaders of the 1848 rebellion, transported to Tasmania—William Smith O'Brien, John Mitchel, Thomas Francis Meagher,

[1] This theme of the exporting to the first Australian colonies, New South Wales and Van Diemen's Land (Tasmania), of the cultural differences and historic antagonisms of the old world is dealt with evocatively by C. M. H. Clark, *A history of Australia*, vol. i: *From the earliest times to the age of Macquarie* (Melbourne, 1962), pp 102–10.

[2] Robert J. Schultz, 'The assisted immigrants, 1837–1850' (Ph.D. thesis, Australian National University, 1971), p. 304.

Patrick O'Donoghue, Terence Bellew MacManus, Kevin O'Doherty, and John Martin. Even more than the transportees of 1798, the 1848 rebels were men of standing in business, professions, or politics, educated, intellectual—and often protestant. Much more than the 1798 men did they regard themselves as temporary exiles,[1] bent on returning to the centres of Irish affairs—Ireland or America—as soon as they could. O'Doherty was the only one (apart from Charles Gavan Duffy, who was never convicted, and left Ireland in 1855) to have any substantial Australian career.

Of the 1798 rebels, some returned to Ireland—Joseph Holt and the catholic priests James Dixon, Peter O'Neil, and James Harold are examples.[2] Others— the great majority—remained to become the central figures in the early Irish community in New South Wales. In the early 1820s the most prominent and most prosperous Irishmen in Sydney—James Meehan, William Davis, James Dempsey, Edward Redmond, and Michael Hayes—were all '98 veterans. And '98 veterans, centring on a group of Wicklow rebels, formed such a landholding concentration to the south-west of Sydney as to attract to the district the initial name of Irishtown (now Bankstown).[3] From 1809 a considerable number of '98 men were given land grants close to each other, a concentration apparently contrived by James Meehan as government surveyor. This initial farming settlement from the Liverpool to the Illawarra districts acted as a continuing magnet to further concentration, as other settlers were attracted to the vicinity by the prosperity and society of their fellow countrymen, or were actually employed on their farms. The '98 men, when freed, promptly showed that obsession with the acquisition of land and livestock that was characteristic of early Irish emigrants to Australia. They pioneered a path many Irish were to follow—from convict status, through emancipation, to land acquisition or commercial activity, to modest prosperity and social respectability.

Analysis of the 1828 census of New South Wales, when the population was under 40,000, permits an appraisal of the Irish population at that time.[4] Catholics were about 10,000, of whom nearly 2,000 were colonial-born, leaving about 8,000 Irish-born. Of these, about a third were convicts; of the 5,000 who were then free, only one in ten had come to the colony free; the rest were emancipated convicts. What is remarkable about the bulk of the Irish emancipists is their relative prosperity. About 20 to 25 per cent of free Irishmen in the colony held land or livestock or both, and some were among the leading landholders or flockmasters in their districts. Others were well established in the

[1] O'Donohoe's Tasmanian newspaper was called *The Irish Exile and Freedom's Advocate* (1850–52), and the same point is made in the titles of the books that deal with the 1848 leaders: T. J. Kiernan, *The Irish exiles in Australia* (Melbourne, 1954), and J. H. Cullen, *Young Ireland in exile: the story of the men of '48 in Tasmania* (Dublin and Cork, 1928). See also Blanche M. Touhill, *William Smith O'Brien and his Irish revolutionary companions in penal exile* (Columbia and London, 1981).
[2] For the story of the priests, see Harold Perkins, *The convict priests* (Gardiner, Victoria, 1984).
[3] See Errol Lea-Scarlett, *The faith of Irishtown: a history of St Felix parish, Bankstown* (Sydney, 1982).
[4] See Waldersee, *Catholic society*, ch. III.

middling areas of commerce. The 1828 New South Wales census substantially modifies the traditional historical depiction of the early Irish as restricted to the bottom of the socio-economic scale. It shows that if very few were wealthy, many were reasonably prosperous, a conclusion also indicated by the middling but numerous donations to the building of St Mary's chapel. This highlights a feature of colonial society that was to be the basis of relatively easy Irish assimilation in Australia—that however hostile the Anglo-Saxon protestant majority might appear, it was still possible for the Irish to make their way up in the Australian world even from positions of the gravest disadvantage.[1]

However, circumstances in early New South Wales were peculiarly advantageous: the Irish were a sufficiently large proportion of the initial population, and with adequate leadership, to take advantage of a favourable economy. Their situation in the other early Australian colony, Tasmania, was markedly different.[2] Over a third of New South Wales convicts were Irish, but only one-fifth of Tasmania's convicts were Irish-born—and most of those came after 1840 when transportation ceased to New South Wales. Before 1840—that is, in the decisive period of early settlement—the Irish-born were probably significantly less than 10 per cent. By mid-century, in contrast to New South Wales, very few Tasmanian Irish had obtained land or succeeded in business. They tended to conform strongly to the traditional stereotype, congregating in the major towns, mostly unskilled labourers, and almost totally excluded from the social or economic establishment.

Irish success in New South Wales was achieved in the face of considerable suspicion and hostility from two main sources: attitudes and prejudices brought out from the British Isles, and the simple fact that New South Wales was a convict colony. So far as the governors and local administration were concerned, the major factor governing their attitudes towards the Irish seems to have been not so much anti-Irish or anti-catholic prejudice as fear of violence and sedition. As Governor Hunter wrote to the duke of Portland in January 1798, 'if so large a proportion of these lawless and turbulent people, the Irish convicts, are sent into this country, it will scarcely be possible to maintain the order so highly essential to our well-being'.[3] The fear that the garrison of the prison colony might be overwhelmed by an Irish uprising appears very early in the history of New South Wales, certainly before 1798. That rebellion, and those transported after it, greatly increased such fears, which were strengthened by the reputation that Irish convicts speedily acquired within the

[1] For some direct testimony from Irish convicts of their success in Australia, see O'Farrell, *Letters from Ir. Australia*, pp 9–18.

[2] See John Williams, 'Irish convicts and Van Diemen's Land' (M.A. thesis, University of Tasmania, 1970); Williams, 'Irish convicts and Van Diemen's Land' in *Tas. Hist. Assoc.*, xix (1972), pp 100–120; Williams, 'Irish female convicts and Tasmania' in *Labour History*, no. 44 (May 1983), pp 1–17.

[3] *Historical records of New South Wales* (7 vols, Sydney, 1893–1901), iii, 348.

settlement for being insolent, turbulent, ignorant, violent, and forever conspiring and attempting to escape. This highly unfavourable image was vindicated by the discovery of some United Irishmen plotting in 1800, and by the rebellion that occurred in March 1804 at Castle Hill, on the outskirts of Sydney, striking terror and panic into the tiny settlement. Led by Philip Cunningham, an Irishman transported for his part in the 1798 rebellion, over 300 men assembled to march on Sydney and take vengeance on their jailers. The rebellion was quickly and bloodily repressed.[1] Although it seems to have involved British as much as Irish, it was officially given an Irish identity, for the Irish convicts had acquired a virtual monopoly of the image of turbulent tendencies and rebellious intentions. Suspicion of Irish loyalty remained an enduring theme in Australian history.

When fear of Irish assemblages and of instigators of Irish rebellion was expressed in the prohibition or regulation of the celebration of the mass, or the exclusion or restriction of priests, official policy appeared as religious persecution. There was also hostility deriving from anti-catholicism, usually mixed with social and cultural antagonism. In 1807 Rev. Samuel Marsden, anglican chaplain in New South Wales, contended that 'if the catholic religion was ever allowed to be celebrated by authority . . . the colony would be lost to the British empire in less than one year'. Marsden reasoned thus:

The number of catholic convicts is very great in the settlement; and these in general composed of the lowest class of the Irish nation, who are the most wild, ignorant, and savage race . . ., men that have been familiar with robberies murders and every horrid crime from their infancy . . .; governed entirely by the impulse of passion and always alive to rebellion and mischief, they are very dangerous members of society. . . . They are extremely superstitious, artful, and treacherous. . . . They have no true concern whatever for any religion nor fear of the Supreme Being; but are fond of riot, drunkenness, and cabals; and was the catholic religion tolerated they would assemble together from every quarter not so much from a desire of celebrating mass, as to recite the miseries and injustice of their punishment, the hardships they suffer, and to inflame one another's minds with some wild scheme of revenge.[2]

Marsden's proposed remedy to the Irish threat was simple—prohibit catholicism and impose protestantism, so producing industry, prosperity, and peace. This remedy was not adopted; on the contrary, the arrival of official catholic chaplains from 1820 begins an increasing official tolerance of the religion of most of the Irish. But the judgements and attitudes expressed so candidly by Marsden were long to remain deeply ingrained in the Australian community.

[1] The most recent and extensive account is that of J. E. Gallagher, 'The convict rising at Castle Hill, 1804' (B.A. thesis, University of New England, N.S.W., 1970). The most extensive published account is R. W. Connell, 'The convict rebellion of 1804' in *Melbourne Historical Journal*, v (1965), pp 27–37.

[2] Samuel Marsden, 'A few observations on the toleration of the catholic religion in N. South Wales', quoted in Patrick and Deirdre O'Farrell, *Documents in Australian catholic history* (2 vols, London, 1969), i, 73.

Such prejudices contained elements of truth: it could hardly be expected that the Irish convicts should not be depraved and brutalised with the rest, and that their catholicism, without priests for thirty years and with very few for another twenty, should not be in many cases merely nominal. Those few Irish catholics who maintained devotions before 1820 were, again, the men of '98, probably less than a hundred. The apathy, indifference, and dereliction, characteristic of the great majority of the first Irish catholics, was to persist until the 1860s at least.[1]

It was the tiny pious fragment of an otherwise torpid whole, in conjunction with the first priest, the aggressive Irishman John Joseph Therry, who arrived in 1820, that determined the development of the initial character of Irish catholicism in Australia.[2] In the early 1820s the interreligious atmosphere was harmonious, reflecting the small size and quiet and discreet ways of the active Irish catholic group, as well as the general temper of catholicism before catholic emancipation in 1829. However, as Therry pursued his missionary work energetically, he moved into a state of constant abrasion with the authorities and the colonial establishment, so much so that by the late 1820s he was well known as a friend of the most prominent critics of the administration—the colony's democratic politicians—and was something of a symbol of opposition to authority. In the process he split the catholic community into pro- and anti-Therry factions, acquiring among the majority (the lower orders, not the respectable) an immense popular following and the reputation of a saint. He became the venerated leader of an Irish catholic clan, valued not less for his challenges to the administration than for his ministry. So Irish catholicism, as dominated by Therry, became identified with the challenge to the status quo of British social conservatism and anglican religion (a prevailing ethos inherently anti-Irish and anti-catholic), and its relations with the authorities declined accordingly. Therry's policy in coping with the non-catholic establishment was generally one of assertive confrontation, to stand up and fight, a policy pursued with truculence and intransigence. This catholic pushing set the stage for sectarian conflict, which was becoming evident by the late 1830s. At first, catholic agitation was for religious causes—freedom and equality in worship, and defence of catholic doctrines. But by the time of the laying of the foundation stone of Sydney's second church, St Patrick's, Church Hill, in August 1840, catholic assertiveness had taken on an Irish nationalist aspect.

[1] Patrick O'Farrell, *The catholic church and community: an Australian history* (Sydney, 1985), pp 8–11; Waldersee, *Catholic society*, ch. VII; Gregory Haines, 'The laity: a review of Father English's submission prior to the 1885 plenary council' in *Australian Catholic Record*, xlix, no. 4 (Oct. 1972), pp 292–313.

[2] The Irish element in Australian catholicism is surveyed in J. J. McGovern and Patrick J. O'Farrell, 'Australia' in Corish, *Ir. catholicism*, vi, fasc. 6, pp 1–75. For an older biography of Father Therry, whose conclusions have been challenged by recent research, see Eris M. O'Brien, *Life and Letters of Archpriest John Joseph Therry* (Sydney, 1922). For the first important influx of Irish priests see 'John O'Brien' [P. J. Hartigan], *The men of '38 and other pioneer priests*, ed. T. J. Linane and F. A. Mecham (Kilmore, 1975).

Festivities to mark St Patrick's day had begun very early in the colony's history, but its significance was convivial.[1] Joseph Holt, writing of his farming in 1803, explained: 'My usual time for commencing to sow was the first Monday after St Patrick's day, it requiring a few days to get my men sober.'[2] Protracted celebrations of a similar kind among the Irish catholics of Bathurst were reported to Fr Therry on 27 March 1833: 'they have been keeping St Patrick's day since the 12th inst., and not ended it yet'.[3] The day had little if any significance beyond an excuse for drinking, albeit in national groups. On St Patrick's day 1840, the *Australasian Chronicle*—Australia's first Irish catholic newspaper, founded the previous year—looked in vain 'for a proof that Irishmen have not forgot their country, save in the tavern and taproom'.[4] However, later in that year the beginnings of a change became evident. The colony's English Benedictine bishop, John Bede Polding, who had arrived in 1835, and his vicar general, Dr William Ullathorne, were strenuously opposed to the non-denominational education system proposed by the governor, Sir George Gipps. When he told them that he doubted if they had significant support, they decided on a public demonstration of strength, the laying of the foundation stone of St Patrick's church to be the occasion.

This brought to the surface the basic realities of the catholic situation in Australia. By the late 1830s a whig–catholic–Irish connection existed. Irish catholics, under English Benedictine leadership, were claiming and asserting religious equality against anglican dominance. At the same time, Irish catholics who were emancipists were joining the 'democratic' popular movement, which sought to break the monopoly of political, social, and economic power enjoyed by the old colonial establishment. At first these catholic pressures had no specifically Irish content. But catholic claims to equality were, of their nature—in that they were claims with civil implications that had to be urged and defended in the public arena—tantamount to political demands made in the face of powerful established interests and prejudiced resistance. However reasonably and moderately these claims might be urged by catholicism's articulate leadership, their ultimate backing was the catholic body, and that was predominantly Irish. Any action that called on the energies of that body would have to take the Irish with the catholic. Given the tendency of confronta-

---

[1] A brief history of St Patrick's day celebrations up to 1870 is given by K. S. Inglis, *The Australian colonists: an exploration of social history, 1788–1870* (Melbourne, 1974), pp 86–104. See also Patrick O'Farrell, 'In search of the hidden Ireland' in *Jn. Relig. Hist.*, xii, no. 3 (June 1983), pp 323–30. For later St Patrick's day celebrations, see Oliver MacDonagh, 'Irish culture and nationalism translated: St Patrick's day, 1888, in Australia' in Oliver MacDonagh, W. F. Mandle, and Pauric Travers (ed.), *Irish culture and nationalism, 1750–1950* (London and Canberra, 1983), pp 69–82; and Malcolm C. Campbell, 'St Patrick's day in Sydney in the 1890s: an exploration of the influences upon, and dimensions of, the celebration' (B.A. thesis in History, University of New South Wales, 1984).

[2] T. Crofton Croker (ed.), *Memoirs of Joseph Holt* (2 vols, London, 1838), ii, 178.

[3] James Waldersee, 'Old St Mary's: Sydney's debt to Father Therry' in *Journal of the Australian Catholic Historical Society*, ii, pt 3 (1968), p. 53.

[4] *Australasian Chronicle*, 17 Mar. 1840.

tions to reduce themselves to the basic simplicities of power, it would draw on the bitter resentment, the latent aggression, and the quasi-tribal unity of the Irish proletariat.

Before the projected St Patrick's church demonstration, as Ullathorne wrote, 'national distinctions had been instinctively avoided in the colony; all prided themselves as being Australians'.[1] Now 'a warm national feeling' appeared among the Irish catholics, who resolved to make the ceremony a national demonstration, with green banners and scarves and other Irish emblems. The government was alarmed, fearing an Orange counter-demonstration and violence. Ullathorne persuaded the organisers to abandon the Irish emblems, but the procession was the largest and by far the most impressive seen in Australia up to that time. The emblems may have been put aside, but the catholic Irish were on the march.

The St Patrick's day following, in 1841, saw the first formal celebration of that day, a procession that ended with high mass and then dinner in the evening for a hundred gentlemen. The purpose seems to have been to demonstrate the respectability, loyalty, and community spirit of affluent Irish emancipists, both protestant and catholic. The stimulus and control were clerical, centring on Fr Francis Murphy, then vicar general. Murphy proposed the first toast at the dinner—to the queen: 'As Irishmen we owe her a special debt of gratitude, which we can never repay, for the kindness and justice with which she has treated a long-suffering and persecuted people (cheers).'[2] Though Daniel O'Connell received mention, the occasion was innocent of any real Irish nationalism.[3] However, it set out clearly some major themes in the history of the Irish in Australia. The first was the constant effort of the Irish clergy to mobilise and control the Irish and Irish nationalism for their own religious purposes. On this occasion it was in relation to fund-raising to build St Patrick's church. The second theme is that of the assertion of pride in national identity, allied with the quest among the more affluent Irish for respectability and social acceptance. These Irish were affronted by the *Sydney Morning Herald*'s observation that those attending the 1841 St Patrick's day dinner were not 'gentlemen' but 'respectable citizen-artisans'. They, and their clergy, were anxious to rid the Irish of their reputation for drunkenness and violence. The third theme is that of division, between the wealthier and conservative elements, who wished to blend harmoniously with their Australian environment, and the working class, often truculent, radical, aggrieved with their lot, prone to see Irish national causes as symbolic and expressive of their own sense of local oppression. In 1843 there were two simultaneous St Patrick's day dinners, one for the top of the Irish-Australian social pyramid, the other for those less well placed.

[1] H. N. Birt, *Benedictine pioneers in Australia* (2 vols, London, 1911), i, 468.
[2] *Australasian Chronicle*, 18 Mar. 1841.
[3] For O'Connell's influence, see Patrick O'Farrell, 'The image of O'Connell in Australia' in Donal McCartney (ed.), *The world of Daniel O'Connell* (Dublin, 1980), pp 112–23.

This tension, sometimes amounting to a division, continued to exist among the Irish in Australia. It did not, however, become established structurally, for its components changed, both with immigration and the continued upward mobility of the lower elements. Transportation of convicts to New South Wales ended in 1840. Thereafter, until 1853, they were sent to Tasmania. But until 1840 almost all the convicts from Ireland had been sent to New South Wales, with the result noted in 1837 by a hostile observer, the presbyterian minister J. D. Lang, that no less than a third of the colony's population were Irish catholics, nearly all of whom were convicts or emancipists,[1] or, he might have added, their children. Indeed in 1840 W. A. Duncan, who edited the *Australasian Chronicle*, claimed that more than half the white inhabitants of the colony were Irish, either by birth or descent.[2] Then, in the 1840s came an acceleration of Irish free migration, which became a flood in the 1850s and 1860s. This virtually submerged the tiny group of established Irish who sought the community's regard as 'gentlemen'. It overwhelmed the conformist tone that had developed among the early Irish, and reemphasised aggressive confrontation. Both in terms of its magnitude and character it is not surprising that the development of free Irish immigration provoked the active expression of community hostility.

BEFORE the 1850s, free Irish migration was substantially government-assisted, that is, financed from the sale of colonial lands by individual Australian colonies that sought a labour force for development.[3] Relatively few at this stage (less than a thousand a year) paid their own passage out—an Australian voyage cost five times an American one. In the 1840s the colonies wanted British settlers, but English and Scots were not forthcoming, so the emigration commissioners were compelled to send Irish, mainly the poor and destitute, particularly from Cork and Tipperary. The result was a succession of colonial complaints that Australia was being flooded with ignorant, uncivilised, degraded, catholic paupers.[4] The loudest critic was Rev. J. D. Lang in Sydney, but such criticism was voiced Australia-wide, still being strident in Queens-

[1] J. D. Lang, *Transportation and colonisaton* (London, 1837), pp iv–v. Up to 1840, out of a total of 67,980 convicts sent to New South Wales, 20,480 were Irish.

[2] *Australasian Chronicle*, 17 Mar. 1840.

[3] See Robert J. Schultz, 'The assisted emigrants, 1837–1850' (Ph.D. thesis, Australian National University, 1971); Oliver MacDonagh, 'Irish emigration to the United States of America and the British colonies during the famine' in Edwards & Williams, *Great famine*, pp 317–88.

[4] The Irish immigrants who attracted the most concentrated adverse attention were workhouse orphans. See Joseph A. Robins, 'Irish orphan emigration to Australia, 1848–1850' in *Studies*, lvii (winter 1968), pp 372–87; also Robins, *The lost children: a study of charity children in Ireland, 1700–1900* (Dublin, 1980), pp 197–221. For a general study of prejudice against Irish immigration to Australia, see Pauline Hamilton, '"No Irish need apply": prejudice as a factor in the development of immigration policy in New South Wales and Victoria, 1840–1970' (Ph.D. thesis, University of New South Wales, 1979); Pauline Hamilton, '"Tipperarifying the moral atmosphere": Irish catholic immigration and the state, 1840–1860' in Sydney Labour History Group, *What rough beast: the state and social order in Australian history* (Sydney, 1982).

land when it was settled in the 1860s, and in New Zealand in the 1870s.[1] This reaction sprang from the feeling that these Irish menaced the future development of a civilised British society, because they threatened the dominance of English and Scots. Hostility was sharpened by observation of the incapacity of some Irish migrants when faced by colonial situations, and by resentment that public money should be spent on them.

What was the justification for this fear and antagonism? Statistically, none: between 1828 and 1861, the catholic proportion of the New South Wales population remained almost constant, while its Irish-born component was shrinking rapidly.[2] It seems that the hostility, sometimes verging on hysteria, that greeted Irish migrants was related not to proportion but to simple increase in their numbers, to their concentration of arrival in some years, and to their tendency to concentrate in the lower areas of employment, labouring and domestic service. The accusation that they were all shiftless, unstable paupers was baseless, for some were skilled and perhaps half were in family groups, many coming from the same county, even the same Irish town.[3] Nevertheless, the adverse image has its truth. Of the Irishmen who came to Victoria in the 1850s and 1860s, 89 per cent were unskilled.[4] The parliamentary select committee that investigated the condition of the Sydney working class in 1860 found there a large Irish component, an Irish immigrant unwillingness to move on from the city to the country, and a remarkably high proportion (around half) of persons of Irish descent among convicted juvenile prostitutes and vagrants.[5]

[1] For Queensland, see M. E. R. MacGinley, 'A study of Irish migration to and settlement in Queensland, 1860–1885' (M.A. qualifying thesis, University of Queensland, 1970); and M. E. R. MacGinley, 'A study of Irish migration to and settlement in Queensland, 1885–1912' (M.A. thesis, University of Queensland, 1972). For South Australia, see Christopher Nance, 'The Irish in South Australia during the colony's first four decades' in *Journal of the Historical Society of South Australia*, no. 5 (1978), pp 66–73. For New Zealand, see Richard P. Davis, *Irish issues in New Zealand politics, 1868–1922* (Dunedin, 1974), ch. 2.

[2] In New South Wales between 1828 and 1846 the catholic proportion increased from 28.4 per cent to 30.5 per cent, but fell to 28.3 per cent in 1861. In 1861 the Irish-born were 15.6 per cent; in 1871, 12.5 per cent; and in 1881, 9.2 per cent. The actual numbers remained fairly constant: 54,829 Irish-born in 1861, 69,192 in 1881.

Victoria exhibited a similar picture. The catholic percentage was 18.83 in 1857; 20.44 in 1861; 23.32 in 1871; 23.60 in 1881; 21.80 in 1891. The Irish-born percentage was 15.89 in 1857; 16.23 in 1861; 13.73 in 1871; 10.06 in 1881; 7.48 in 1891. The Victorian census that recorded the highest number of Irish-born was that of 1871, when there were 100,468.

For a demographic analysis of the Victorian Irish see Oliver MacDonagh, 'The Irish in Victoria, 1851–91: a demographic essay' in *Hist. Studies*, viii (1971), pp 67–92. All other colonies had markedly smaller Irish proportions.

[3] Waldersee, *Catholic society*, pp 160–85; Neil Coughlan, 'The coming of the Irish to Victoria' in *Historical Studies*, xii, no. 45 (Oct. 1965), pp 76–8. For further demographic detail see David Fitzpatrick, 'Irish emigration in the later nineteenth century' in *I.H.S.*, xxii, no. 86 (Sept. 1980), pp 126–43; Fitzpatrick, 'Irish immigrants in Australia: patterns of settlement and paths of mobility' in *Australia 1888*, bulletin no. 2 (Aug. 1979), pp 48–54.

[4] Coughlan, op. cit., p. 84. For a consideration of the reaction to Irish immigration and political involvement in Victoria, see Frances O'Kane, *A path is set: the catholic church in the Port Phillip district and Victoria, 1839–1862* (Melbourne, 1976); and Margaret Pawsey, *The popish plot: culture clashes in Victoria, 1860–1863* (Sydney, 1983).

[*See p. 672 for n. 5*]

The spectacular increase in Irish migration to Australia in the 1850s and 1860s was related to gold rushes, particularly in Victoria. But the gold rushes were essentially a passing phase in the more basic process of Irish settlement. This was marked by the desire and effort to acquire farming land, the tendency to concentrate closely in certain areas, and the practice of encouraging, by letter and remittances of money, friends and relations to come to Australia.[1] These characteristics, evident in New South Wales by the 1820s, developed and magnified. The heavy initial concentration of Irish settlers south-west of Sydney, and around the northern Maitland area, became bases for Irish movement into adjacent areas as pioneering expansion opened the squatting age in the 1840s and 1850s. Most marked was the movement south-west from Sydney into the Yass and Goulburn areas, the south coast, and eventually northern Victoria. In Victoria, similar concentrations of Irish developed in the mixed farming districts north of Melbourne around Kilmore, and Belfast and Warrnambool on the west coast.

These concentrations reflected the Irish gravitation towards rural areas and pursuits. In Victoria, for instance, the Irish-born and catholic population of the towns and cities were, to the end of the century, below the average for the colony.[2] An Irish settler told the Queensland parliament in 1877: 'Our clear aim is a peasant proprietary in the Irish tradition.'[3] In part, Irish migration to Australia was related to unfavorable factors in America, such as periodic depressions and the civil war. Indeed the American civil war formed the background to the successful establishment, in 1862, of the Queensland Immigration Society, Bishop James Quinn's project to settle Irishmen in Queensland.[4] But positive factors were more important—Australia's reputation during the gold-rush period as an El Dorado, the promise of ample land, and, above all, personal relationships. The main force that moved the stream of Irish who came to the little-known colonies of Australia and New Zealand was the fact that their friends and relations already there encouraged them to do so, and that the voyage was made possible either by remittances or by government assistance. At first sight, the fact that 85 per cent of the Irish who came to Victoria in the 1850s and 1860s were single conveys the suggestion of lonely exile, but it is certain that very many of these were related to each other—brothers, sisters, or cousins—or friends and acquaintances. On arrival in Australia, they settled close to established family or friends, often being

---

[5] *Report from the select committee on the condition of the working classes of the metropolis ... New South Wales legislative assembly, votes and proceedings, 1859–60*, pp 1366–1423.

[1] The most substantial primary documentation of this process is in the P.R.O.N.I. collection of emigrant letters from Australia, many of which are published in O'Farrell, *Letters from Ir. Australia*.

[2] MacDonagh, 'Irish in Victoria', p. 75.

[3] D. B. Waterson, *Squatter, selector and store-keeper: a history of the Darling Downs, 1859–93* (Sydney, 1968), p. 108. It should be noted, however, that initial settlement patterns did not always persist: the Irish in Queensland (and elsewhere in Australia) tended to drift from the land into country towns.

[4] See MacGinley, 'Study of Irish migration ... 1860–1885', pp 72–84.

employed by them, frequently marrying within the group. That great champion of Irish immigrants, Caroline Chisholm, fostered the concentration because she found it easiest to place Irish servant girls in the homes of the Irish settlers of south-western New South Wales, where they were much in demand as wives.[1]

This process of Irish aggregation has been detailed for the 1840s in the small town of Bungendore, New South Wales.

> Bungendore quickly became a very Irish place. ... John Dwyer's arrival began the steady flow of families related to his father, the Wicklow chieftain. ... Soon Sheehans and Byrnes, Doyles and Donoghoes—all part of the Dwyer connection—were in the district, revering almost as a patriarch John Dwyer. ... Rubbing shoulders with the Wicklow men were smaller groups of Tipperary folk associated with Thomas Shanahan who bought 'The Briars' at Molonglo, and not far away from them were other Irish workmen consciously collected on Carwoola by William and Thomas Rutledge.[2]

Such Irish often had very large families—commonly ten to fifteen children—which led to more intensive concentrations as large initial holdings were divided, or new adjacent land acquired. Other Irish provided services within these farming areas: in the south-west they virtually monopolised the coach service and inn-keeping. This was a society strongly influenced by the patriarchalism of a few dominant and often wealthy personalities, though few had domains so great as the emancipist Edward Ryan of Galong, who had nearly a quarter of a million acres by the 1840s.[3] Even in the cities there was Irish paternalism: the New South Wales solicitor general J. H. Plunkett frequently extended his patronage and help to Irish families who needed assistance.[4] But it was in the countryside that paternalism was strongest, and clannish communities handed down their customs and brogues to succeeding generations.

The melting-pot influences of the Australian city were to come later; in the 1850s and 1860s it was the goldfields that accelerated the process of Irish assimilation. Indeed it was gold that first attracted a considerable Irish immigration to New Zealand. In both countries the Irish contributed much to the colour of the gold-rush period and to the romantic legendry that surrounds it, not only through the flamboyance of many of the Irish personalities in the fields, but because a very high proportion of the diggers were Irish, as were many of the goldfields hotels: the centres of digger sociability blazoned forth

---

[1] Both biographies of Caroline Chisholm devote substantial attention to her work in settling Irish immigrants: Margaret Kiddle, *Caroline Chisholm* (Melbourne, 1950); Mary Hoban, *Fifty-one pieces of wedding cake: a biography of Caroline Chisholm* (Kilmore, 1973).

[2] Errol Lea-Scarlett, *Queanbeyan—district and people* (Queanbeyan, 1968), p. 230.

[3] The story of Edward Ryan and his property is told by Max Barrett, *King of Galong castle: the story of Ned Ryan, 1786–1871* (Lewisham, N.S.W., 1978).

[4] Plunkett, a quiet graduate of Trinity College, Dublin, represents a mild Irish catholic tradition, often in sharp contrast to the more aggressive one dominant in the colonies from the 1850s. See John N. Molony, *An architect of freedom: John Hubert Plunkett in New South Wales, 1832–1869* (Canberra, 1973).

their Irishness with names like Brian Boru, Harp of Erin, and Shamrock. Possibly over a quarter of the 1867 goldfields population of the west coast of New Zealand's South Island was of Irish birth, although the Irish comprised only 13 per cent of New Zealand's population.[1] Within the goldfields, the Irish were prominent in just those eruptions of turbulence that attracted most widespread attention, such as the so-called 'fenian riots' in Hokitika, New Zealand, in 1867,[2] and, most famously, in the Eureka stockade rebellion at Ballarat, Victoria, in 1854.[3] The Irish reputation for violence is also evident in the image of Irish prominence among bushrangers, an association elevated to the heights of Australian heroic myth in the person of Ned Kelly, for 'mad Ireland had fashioned Ned'.[4]

In the case of bushranging, and of violence generally, the statistics bear out the popular image. Many of the most notorious bushrangers—or rather, bestknown, for they often acquired reputations as gallant heroes—were Irish or of Irish descent. In 1861 15.6 per cent of the New South Wales population was Irish-born, but in 1859–61 more than a third of convictions at circuit courts for general crime, and more than a quarter of convictions at quarter sessions, were of Irishmen. In 1871, 118 prisoners in New South Wales gaols had been convicted of armed robbery. Of these 76 per cent were Irish—21 Irish-born and 69 catholics—a strong indicator of Irish descent.[5]

If the Irish were prominent among the criminals, they were also prominent in the counter-attack: in 1872 there were 803 men in the ranks of the New South Wales police, of whom 479 were Irish-born. The size of the Irish element in the British army in New Zealand became of colonial significance when soldiers discharged after the Maori wars in the 1860s were given land grants. The result was a notable Irish farming settlement in the Auckland province.

Australia's great population increase between the 1850s and the 1870s contained several distinctive strands of Irish immigration. The gold-rush element was largely ephemeral, dissipating quickly to other rushes, or to land settlement, or other employment. Within the major continuing Irish influx, the

[1] P. R. May, *The west coast gold rushes* (Christchurch, 1962), p. 284.

[2] Ibid., pp 307–9; P. R. May (ed.), *Miners and militants: politics in Westland, 1865–1918* (Christchurch, 1975), pp 31–2; Richard P. Davis, *Irish issues in New Zealand politics, 1868–1922* (Dunedin, 1974), pp 11–24.

[3] C. H. Currey, *The Irish at Eureka* (Sydney, 1954). A more balanced estimate of the role of the Irish at Eureka is given by James Murtagh, 'The significance of Eureka' in *Manna*, no. 6 (1963), pp 20–29.

[4] [Charles] Manning [Hope] Clark, 'Good day to you, Ned Kelly' in C. F. Cave (ed.), *Ned Kelly: man and myth* (Melbourne, 1968), pp 12–39. Kelly was Australian-born of Irish parents, and the extent of Irish influence on his behaviour is a matter of debate among historians. For an interpretation that stresses Irish elements, see John N. Molony, *I am Ned Kelly* (Melbourne, 1980). For a placing of these in a broader context of social banditry, see John McQuilton, *The Kelly outbreak, 1878–1880* (Melbourne, 1979).

[5] R. B. Walker, 'Bushranging in fact and legend' in *Historical Studies*, xi, no. 42 (Apr. 1964), p. 207. Victorian statistics are similar. See Neil Coughlan, 'The coming of the Irish to Victoria' in *Historical Studies*, xii, no. 45 (Oct. 1965), pp 84–5.

most massive tendency is obvious: the south-west of Ireland, Munster generally, was overwhelmingly the source of Irish immigration from the 1840s to the 1880s; that is, in the period of the greatest number of arrivals.[1] In the 1880s Leinster, especially County Dublin and King's County, became more prominent, taking the lead in the late years of the century, but this was not a consequence of the growth of the Leinster migration, but of the decline of Munster migration. By 1907 the provincial balance had changed again, this time in favour of Ulster. Before this, Ulster had been a major source of Irish migration to New Zealand, even to the extent of a small Ulster colony being established at Katikati in the Bay of Plenty in the 1870s.[2] Ulster migration, which remained predominant until 1915, made a considerable contribution to the flavour of New Zealand life, not only for its distinctive qualities and personalities—such as W. F. Massey, prime minister from 1912 to 1925[3]—but because of its substantial harmony with the large Scots presbyterian element there.

Nineteenth-century Irish-Australia, however, was colonised from Munster in the main, and in part reflects its character, that of a backward peasant community.[4] The image acquired by the Munster Irish continued and reinforced that of the convict Irish—barbarians, often Gaelic-speaking, often drunken, frequently fighting among themselves, mixing peasant superstition and primitive catholicism. Initially primitive and ignorant, the Munster immigrants produced few leaders of their own, which made them particularly open to the dominance and leadership of the catholic clergy, though this saved them from the political tribalism of the American Irish.

The common Munster Irish were separated by a great gulf in education, sophistication, social background, and usually religion from those of their fellow countrymen in Australia who were most prominent and influential in public and political life, and who tended to be Anglo-Irish gentry. This element, particularly concentrated in Victoria, and mainly graduates of Trinity College, Dublin,[5] gave much to colonial life and development, but in the general sense of adding their cultivated talents and professional abilities, mainly in law. Most were protestants. They came to Australia because of 'a

---

[1] See G. M. Tobin, 'The sea-divided Gael: a study of the Irish home rule movement in Victoria and New South Wales, 1880–1916' (M.A. thesis, Australian National University, 1969), pp 15–16; Coughlan, op. cit., pp 73–6.

[2] Arthur J. Gray, *An Ulster plantation* (Wellington, 1950); N. C. Mitchel, 'Katikati: an Ulster settlement in New Zealand' in *Ulster Folklife*, xv–xvi (1970), pp 203–15. Ulster migration to Australia is perhaps more heavily documented in the surviving personal correspondence than emigration from the other provinces. See O'Farrell, *Letters from Ir. Australia*, for this documentation, and for an explanation of it.

[3] W. F. Gardner, *William Massey* (Wellington, 1969).

[4] For an account of better placed Munster migrants, see S. M. Ingham, *Enterprising migrants: an Irish family in Australia* (Melbourne, 1975).

[5] See Geoffrey Serle, *The golden age* (Melbourne, 1963), p. 43; J. J. Auchmuty, 'The Anglo-Irish influence on the foundation of Australian institutions' in *Melbourne University Gazette* (May 1969), pp 2–8.

superfluity of ingenious and educated men' in the United Kingdom, particularly at the bar, and the group grew as the first arrivals wrote back to encourage their friends to come. They encountered no problem of assimilation. Their abilities, social graces, protestantism, and generally conservative politics assured them a welcome in the upper levels of Victorian life in the period of rapid colonial growth between 1850 and 1900. In fact this Anglo-Irish administrative and professional element had been a founding element in all Australian colonies and New Zealand, given that this was a major constituent of the 'imperial class' of soldiers, officials, and administrators who conducted the day-to-day work of the British empire. Such Anglo-Irish—educated, talented, often liberal and reforming—occupied a wide variety of positions in the colonial service and colonial life: Sir Richard Bourke, governor of New South Wales (1831–8), exemplifies this element at its best, as a dimension of British colonial officialdom. In Victoria, for the beginnings of settlement there, it was supplemented by another facet of the Anglo-Irish world, that of substantial landowning. Victoria's first elite was the 'Irish cousinage', a small group of interrelated Anglo-Irish landholders who had seen in the new colony opportunity for expansive living.[1] The Anglo-Irish professional classes of middling lawyers, doctors, journalists, educated men of enterprise, made up a later addition to an Irish-Australian colonial world of the upper orders, seeking, in various ways and degrees, wealth, openings for talent, and satisfaction of ambition. Charles Gavan Duffy, premier of Victoria in 1871, exemplifies this as a social process (though his catholicism and radicalism were quite untypical, allowing him to offer a popular leadership to the mass of the Irish). This group of Anglo-Irish and Irish 'gentlemen' reached its peak in numbers and influence between 1850 and 1880. Thereafter its power declined. It was not reinforced from Ireland, and the increasingly democratic and radical complexion of colonial life and politics rendered its somewhat patrician conservatism less relevant.

P. S. Cleary, in *Australia's debt to Irish nation-builders* (1933), devotes much attention to that Irish and Anglo-Irish element that is prominent in the public life and political development of Australia. But he immediately concedes that this kind of enumeration ('We have counted a hundred and thirty-seven in the lists of cabinet ministers'[2]), based on Irish surnames, is no guide whatever to the Irishness of these persons' contribution to Australian life. To put this vital point in Gavan Duffy's words: 'To strangers at a distance who read of Murphys, Barrys, MacMahons, and Fitzgeralds in high places, it seemed the paradise of the Celt—but they were Celts whose forefathers had broken with

---

[1] For the 'Irish cousinage' in Victoria, see Paul de Serville, *Port Phillip gentlemen and good society in Melbourne before the gold rushes* (Melbourne, 1980). For some comments on the links between the experience of the Anglo-Irish in Ireland and their colonial dispositions, see Julian Gormly, 'Some aspects of the history of the Anglo-Irish in Australia in the nineteenth century' (B.A. honours thesis, University of New South Wales, 1984).

[2] P. S. Cleary, *Australia's debt to Irish nation-builders* (Sydney, 1933), p. xiii.

the traditions and creed of the island.'[1] Overall, the Irish in high places in Australia exhibited little that was distinctively Irish in any nationalist sense, nor did they attempt leadership of the mass of the Irish.

A further strand of Irish migration to Australia and New Zealand was that from protestant Ulster.[2] Orange lodges were formed in both countries in the 1840s. The Orange movement was seriously checked by the gold rushes, but revived in spectacular fashion after the attempted assassination in Sydney of the duke of Edinburgh in March 1868 by an Irish catholic (and alleged fenian), Henry James O'Farrell.[3] It claimed 10,000 members in New South Wales in 1872.[4] In comparison with the Munster Irish, the Ulster protestant element was small, but its extremist elements gave some countenance to Gavan Duffy's contention that Ulstermen were trying to reconstruct in the colonies the same type of domination over the southerner that they enjoyed in Ireland.[5] Twelfth of July celebrations were frequently the occasion of riots, especially in the 1880s and 1890s. The protestantism of Ulstermen allowed them to merge more readily into colonial life; but when extreme elements asserted protestantism and ultra-loyalty against what they regarded as the threat of catholicism, they stood out clearly on the far right of colonial life and politics. Only at times of patriotic intensity, notably the first world war, did Orangeism exercise any considerable public influence. However, its existence, and the considerable number of Irish-born clergy within the protestant denominations, forms one element in the sectarian tension and bitterness that disfigured Australian and New Zealand life from the 1840s on. Many of the Ulster emigrants exhibited characteristics identical with those from Munster—a gravitation to the rural areas, a tendency to group together—but as a body they were more skilled, and some arrived with reasonable, even considerable, means. They tended towards the trades and more skilled employment generally, while some of them were sufficiently wealthy to establish themselves easily in new farming areas or in city commercial life. But the bulk of Ulster protestant immigrants, coming in Australia particularly in the 1880s, had little patience with divisive Irish politics or sectarian animus. Their considerable correspondence back to Ireland shows them to have been conscious of their distinctive brand of Irishness, of the

---

[1] Charles Gavan Duffy, *My life in two hemispheres* (2nd ed.; 2 vols, London, 1898), ii, 139; H. W. Coffey and M. J. Morgan, *Irish families in Australia and New Zealand, 1788–1978* (4 vols, Melbourne, 1978–80; revised vol. i, A–D, 1983), provides a detailed set of short biographies of the prominent Irish.

[2] For commentary on some few of those emigrants, see Grenfell Morton, 'Ulster emigrants to Australia, 1850–1890' in *Ulster Folklife*, xviii (1972), pp 111–20. For greater detail, see O'Farrell, *Letters from Ir. Australia*.

[3] K. S. Inglis, *The Australian colonists: an exploration of social history, 1788–1870* (Melbourne, 1974), pp 90–104. The most detailed study of the Orange lodge movement is in Mark Lyons, 'Aspects of sectarianism in New South Wales, c. 1880' (Ph.D. thesis, Australian National University, 1972).

[4] Richard McGuffin, *The rise and progress of Orangeism in N.S.W. vindicated* (Sydney, 1872), p. 4.

[5] *Civil and religious liberty: speech of C. Gavan Duffy, Esq., at Melbourne . . . August 20th 1856* (Melbourne, [1873]).

values of family, respectability, and hard work. They sought a quiet, decent life, integrating rapidly into all aspects of the Australian colonial scene.[1]

The most influential Irish group was the smallest, the catholic clergy and religious.[2] About 2,000 priests came to Australia in the nineteenth century. Nearly all were Irish; and increasingly from the 1860s, and virtually entirely from the 1880s to the 1930s, they exercised a dominating monopoly of the church in Australia. Their influence was supplemented, through the catholic schools system, by that of religious teaching orders from Ireland,[3] so that the entire formation of Australian catholics, from childhood to adulthood, came under intense Irish influence. This group had continuity and great power, having control of education and of the resources of the church, resources of authority, decision-making, and money, that also gave it control of the Irish-Australian press. Newspapers that were simply Irish in a nationalist sense were ephemeral, but those that enjoyed continuity—such as the Sydney *Freeman's Journal*, the Melbourne *Advocate*, and the Adelaide *Southern Cross*—were those with clerical approval, content, and involvement, and financial backing. This also reflected the fact that the clergy was the only intelligentsia possessed by the mass of the Irish, their leadership in public affairs.

The rapid growth of a catholic education system from the 1880s is testimony not only to religious loyalty and solidarity, but also to the aspirations of the Munster Irish to social betterment, to their determination that their children would, through education, rise higher than themselves. Nor would it be correct to see the remarkable growth of large and imposing catholic buildings—churchs, schools, hospitals—as entirely religiously motivated, for they also proclaimed the worldly ambitions of Irish catholics and, of course, their increasing prosperity. For the Munster Irish, the catholic church in Australia was not only the road to salvation, it was also their defiant profession of separ-

---

[1] Much of the content and commentary in O'Farrell, *Letters from Ir. Australia*, illustrates these latter observations: see particularly ch. 7, 'The fortunes of a family, 1883–1929'. The same is evident in the quaker letters of Joseph Beale: see Edgar Beale, *The earth between them: Joseph Beale's letters home to Ireland from Victoria, 1852–53* (Sydney, 1975).

[2] See Patrick O'Farrell, *The catholic church and community: an Australian history* (Sydney, 1985), and J. J. McGovern and Patrick O'Farrell, 'Australia' in Corish, *Ir. catholicism*, vi, fasc. 6. Fr T. J. Linane has compiled a biographical register of all nineteenth-century priests. It is in process of publication in *Footprints: Quarterly Journal of the Melbourne Historical Commission* (1971–   ). Part of the biographical list has been published separately in two volumes by T. J. Linane, *From Abel to Zundalovich* (Armadale, Vic., [1979]).

[3] Ronald Fogarty, *Catholic education in Australia, 1806–1950* (Melbourne, 1969), pp 264–75. There is a very substantial literature on the histories of Irish teaching orders in Australia: references to work published up to 1984 may be found in the bibliography of O'Farrell, *Catholic church and community*. However, the extent of formative Irish influences within the catholic school system may not have been as considerable as has been usually assumed; this is the conclusion of Louise A. Mazzaroli, 'The Irish in New South Wales and Queensland, 1884–1914' (Ph.D. thesis, University of New South Wales, 1980). For instance, in the teaching of history, catholic schools conformed to the state syllabus, which was English and Australian history. Little Irish history was taught. See Patrick O'Farrell, 'Teaching history, as seen in the Australian catholic church: a survey of attitudes, 1892–1947' in *University of Newcastle Historical Journal*, iii, no. 2 (Feb. 1976), pp 3–16.

ate identity, their claim to recognition and status, and their avenue to social betterment and self-esteem—in *this* world. The increasingly intransigent and triumphalist tone of the church from the 1880s and its eagerness to enter sectarian battle reflect the aggressive self-confidence of a self-made community rising rapidly in the world, no longer willing to accept an inferior role. This was linked with the remarkable success of the catholic education system, the greatest achievement of Australian catholicism. Refusing from the 1860s to accept the state's secular education proposals, catholics began to build their own separate system. It was an endeavour that moulded their character. If it meant a sacrificial drain on their financial resources, it proved they had such resources, and was an enormous source of pride. It both welded them together and set them apart.

The thoroughly Irish character of Australian catholicism bears the marks of deliberate contrivance by clerics, beginning with John McEncroe, who arrived in 1832. Despite the Irish birth or derivation of Australia's catholics, many forces were working against Irishness in religion. One was the English Benedictine hierarchy in Sydney, but the strongest was a feeling among many of the laity that anything too Irish or too catholic would offend the protestant majority, and thus hinder their own social acceptance and advancement. There is ample evidence that contradicts the Irish clerical assertion, made loudly from the 1850s, that the Australian laity, being Irish, wanted an Irish episcopacy and clergy. Indeed the balance of evidence indicates that the drive towards banishment of the Benedictines (ousted finally in 1883) and their replacement by an Irish clerical authority—Irish clerical imperialism—is related not to the existence of vigorous and widespread Irish piety, but to the reverse, widespread apathy and indifference.[1] To use the words of Bishop Murray of Maitland in 1870, it was in order 'to root out of this land that fatal indifference to religion which is the curse of this country'[2] that Irish clergy and bishops set out to impose on Australia an imitation of Irish religious culture. The basic proposition, still being proclaimed vigorously by Archbishop Mannix in the 1920s,[3] was that to cultivate an Irish atmosphere was to cultivate true religion.

Irish nationalism was another matter. In Ireland, nationalism was often in tension or conflict with the church. In Britain's colonies it was no asset and often a liability in the church's relationship with its environment. To maintain a balance where catholics would be Irish for religious purposes and British-Australian for political and social purposes was a feat beyond the capacity (and sometimes the inclinations) of most clerics, and certainly beyond the comprehension or ready tolerance of many in the general Australian community. The Irish subculture in Australia was a phenomenon imposed by the clergy from

[1] See above, p. 667, n. 1. For the Irish campaign against Benedictine authority in Sydney, see T. L. Suttor, *Hierarchy and democracy in Australia, 1788–1870* (Melbourne, 1965).

[2] James Murray to Mgr Tobias Kirby, 6 Sept. 1870 (Irish College, Rome, Archives).

[3] *Tribune*, 20 Mar. 1924, quoted in Patrick and Deirdre O'Farrell, *Documents in Australian catholic history* (2 vols, London, 1969), ii, 219.

above, rather than a natural growth from below. The major influx of Irish migrants had eased by the 1870s.[1] By that time the Irish-born proportion of Australia's population had begun a rapid decline, and by the 1880s their actual numbers were declining. Yet the period when the Irish-Australian subculture flourished came later, from the 1880s to the 1930s. It was substantially of clerical manufacture.

The Irish clerical campaign to gain control of the Australian catholic church reached its most aggressively strident in the 1850s and 1860s, linking catholicism with Irishness, and provoking public hostility to both. This hostility stemmed first from the gradually developing pressure of Irish catholics towards improving their religious and socio-economic position. However, such pressure was diffused, and related to the success of individuals, not expressed in any unanimous or concerted action in the public sphere: the lack of political agreement or solidarity among Irish catholics in Australia was apparent from the first elections in New South Wales in 1843.[2] This did not, however, prevent hostile critics maintaining that the Irish were an organised and clerically disciplined pressure group, subversive of the public good. In the 1860s, local fears were inflated by a sympathetic hysteria prompted by fenian activities in Britain. Though a tiny fenian organisation existed in Australia and New Zealand in the 1870s,[3] there appears to be no evidence of its existence in March 1868 when the Irishman O'Farrell attempted to assassinate the duke of Edinburgh.[4]

This attempt was seized on as evidence of a specific fenian revolutionary plot and general indication of the disloyalty of the Irish. Politicians, notably Henry Parkes and the New South Wales premier James Martin, exploited the extraordinary fear and panic that gripped the colonies in order to split the community and to focus its fears and hatreds on the Irish and the catholic church. The attempted assassination, and its political exploitation, aroused bitter, corrosive, and enduring sectarian animosity throughout Australia, much of it expressed in anti-Irish forms: 'No Irish need apply' became a familiar addendum to advertisements for job vacancies. Speaking to the electors of Mudgee in January 1872, Henry Parkes gave a typical summation of the anti-Irish image: they were a disruptive alien tribe; they imported their national grievances to disturb Australia, acting in politics as an irrational and irresponsible political bloc under clerical dictation, failing to become true

---

[1] A. J. Rose, 'Irish migration to Australia in the twentieth century' in *Ir. Geography*, iv, no. 1 (1959), p. 79. See also Fitzpatrick, above, p. 671, n. 3.

[2] See J. M. O'Brien, 'Catholics and politics in New South Wales, 1835–1870' (M.A. thesis, Newcastle, N.S.W., 1972); O'Brien, 'W. A. Duncan, the "Irish question" and the N.S.W. elections of 1843' in *Journal of the Australian Catholic Historical Society*, iv, pt 1 (1972), pp 40–57.

[3] *Devoy's post-bag*, i, 130, 181–5, 197–9.

[4] For detailed discussion of this incident see Mark Lyons, 'Aspects of sectarianism in New South Wales, c.1880' (Ph.D. thesis, Australian National University, 1972), and Brian McKinlay, *The first royal tour, 1867–1868* (Adelaide, 1970).

Australian colonists; and in any case their numbers among immigrants were excessive and disproportionate.[1]

Were Parkes's allegations justified? Generally, no. Statistically, Irish immigration was not disproportionate. The Irish did not act in political concert, but (and this was crucial in sustaining the public impression that they did) some Irish activists believed and demanded loudly that they should. These doctrinaire Irish grouped around the Sydney *Freeman's Journal*, founded by Archdeacon McEncroe in 1850. Their central conviction was that the O'Connell model of disciplined Irish catholic unity, allied with the forces of religion, pursuing a policy of aggressive confrontation to any opposition, was the only appropriate political exemplar for Irish catholics in Australia.[2] But the *Freeman's Journal* was constantly bemoaning the fact that Irish catholics would not act thus. Local issues and personalities, and economic interests, counted much more in the politics of Australia's Irish catholics than their being Irish or catholic. However, the Irish doctrinaires, a small minority, were forever proclaiming themselves to be *the* Irish in Australia. Sometimes this had a coercive effect on Irish moderates, arousing them, through guilt rather than desire, to support more aggressive or more Irish policies, and always the clamour of the doctrinaires served to convince those disposed to think ill of the Irish that they were correct in doing so.

Was it true, as Parkes claimed in 1872, that Irishmen had not learnt to be Australian colonists? History proved Parkes wrong. True, some found integration easy, some found it difficult, a very few almost impossible. In the 1850s and 1860s some rural Irish 'built farms and communities that seemed oddly out of place in the Victorian landscape ... and bespoke an ethos radically different from the one which dominated the colony of Victoria'.[3] But generally, assimilate they did, if sometimes slowly, both in the sense of accepting and identfying with their Australian environment, and in the sense of mixing with non-Irish neighbours. It is significant that when Irishmen set up social organisations proclaiming their nationality—St Patrick's societies, Hibernian associations, Celtic clubs—membership was never large, nor exclusive in any abnormal way. Such organisations, and they were neither many nor powerful, were merely another aspect of the diverse and often home-country-oriented colonial social activity of that time.*

[1] *Freeman's Journal* (Sydney), 13 Jan. 1872.

[2] For the policies of the *Freeman's Journal* see Waldersee, *Catholic society*; O'Brien, 'Catholics and politics'; T. L. Suttor, *Hierarchy and democracy in Australia, 1788-1870* (Melbourne, 1965); Gregory Haines, 'The *Freeman's Journal*, 1857-1860: criticism within the catholic church' in *Journal of the Australian Catholic Historical Society*, iv, pt 1 (1972), pp 80-96.

[3] Neil Coughlan, 'The coming of the Irish to Victoria' in *Historical Studies*, xii, no. 45 (Oct. 1965), p. 86.

* The period covered by this chapter is examined in greater detail in Patrick O'Farrell, *The Irish in Australia* (Sydney, 1987), which has an extensive bibliography.

CHAPTER XXXI

The Irish in North America, 1776–1845

DAVID NOEL DOYLE

SINCE the 1770s, the major developments in Irish political and cultural history cannot be adequately portrayed without consideration of the role of great numbers of Irishmen in the New World. The Volunteers, the United Irishmen, and the movements for catholic emancipation and repeal had their American dimensions: a stimulus in the first instance, a problematic resource in the latter three. The United States became a refuge for radicals in 1848 as well as in 1798, and Ontario became a frontier of opportunity for Orangeism after the suppressions of 1825 and 1836. Later, fenianism, the land league, and the Gaelic League are more certainly clearly dependent on Irish-American impetus and support, while catholic growth after 1850, home rule politics, the literary revival, Sinn Fein, and the war of independence were at least partially financed and encouraged from the United States.

It is now possible to describe the principal Irish-American communities from 1840 to 1920 with some accuracy and attention to their regional variations, and thereby to illuminate the special strengths and difficulties of their tributary part in Irish development. For the seventy years before 1840, however, the evidence is more impressionistic: fewer sources survive, and the first censuses to record immigrants' country of birth with any accuracy came in 1842 (Ontario), 1845 (New York State), 1850 (United States), and 1871 (Canada)—although careful extrapolation from nomenclature has yielded results for the United States in 1790.

From an economic historian's viewpoint, to emphasise only the political and the cultural effects of emigrant feedback is to turn the story inside out, for even before the famine, Ireland contributed a third of all migration to the United States: between 1815 and 1845 certainly 420,000 and possibly as many as 500,000 people. Another contribution to the United States came through British North America: the Scotswoman Frances Wright reported in 1819 that servants 'in the Atlantic cities where servants must generally be sought ... are, for the most part, stragglers from the crowd of emigrants poured into the St Lawrence',[1] although the cities involved, New York and Philadelphia, were themselves important entry-points. Taking the perspective of a full century, it can be estimated from the statistical reports compiled by American, British, and Irish authorities, including extrapolations made for the years before 1834 and for 1846–55, when these series prove least complete, that between 1820 and 1920 from 4.3 to 4.9 million Irish emigrants went to the United States. (Moreover, a significant part of Connacht's mid-century population, in addition to recorded emigrants, disappears if births are compared with deaths and known migration figures, confirming the recognised failure of the authorities to catch all migration from the west, particularly that to North America via Scottish ports.) Thus Irish emigrants to the United States in that century numbered at least 5 million, or one-sixth of all European emigrants (about 29.8 million)—roundly fifteen times more than Ireland's share of Europe's population should warrant.[2] Although only a quarter or less of these had arrived in the United States by 1851, two-thirds of the 1,120,000 going direct to British North America in the period 1815–1920 had arrived by that year. As stated, large numbers of the Canadian Irish later (often with little delay) reemigrated to the United States: 920,000 Irish arrivals to British North America between 1815 and 1861 produced a total of only 286,000 Irish-born in the Canadian censuses of 1861. Indeed the Irish-born and their offspring constituted probably the second largest ethnic ingredient, after French Canadians, in Canada's 1.97 million migrants to the United States from 1820 to 1920—a migration even less reliably chronicled by officials than the transatlantic one.[3] Also, Irish came from Australia to America: almost half of San Francisco's Irish-born in 1852 had come from there. Even more considerable were those of Irish birth or parentage who came to industrial America after training in the mills and mines of Lancashire, Staffordshire, south Wales, and central Scotland. These identified with Irish-American communities, especially in Massachusetts, Pennsylvania, and Illinois. Allowing for shortcomings in the basic official sources, such as failure to count returnees and reentrants, allowing too for those who died within their first six months after arrival, especially many in 1846–50, the immigrant base of Irish America, 1820–1920, cannot have been less than five million, and may

[1] Frances Wright, *Views of society and manners in America*, ed. Paul Barker (Cambridge, Mass., 1963), p. 238.
[2] Kerby A. Miller, *Emigrants and exiles: Ireland and the Irish exodus to North America* (Oxford and New York, 1985), pp 193–9, 291–3, 346–53, 569–71; Cormac Ó Gráda, 'A note on nineteenth-century Irish emigration statistics' in *Population Studies*, xxix (1975), pp 143–9: D. H. Akenson, *The Irish in Ontario* (Montreal, 1984), pp 9–15, 28–32; *Historical statistics of the United States to 1970* (Washington, D.C., 1973), series C, 89–92.
[3] J. A. King, 'Genealogy, history and Irish immigration' in *Canadian Journal of Irish Studies*, x, no. 1 (1984), pp 41–50; Kathleen Neils Conzen, *Immigrant Milwaukee, 1836–1860* (Cambridge, Mass., 1976), fig. 5, pp 40, 41–2; D. H. Akenson, *Being had: historians, evidence, and the Irish in North America* (Port Credit, Ont., 1985), pp 52–9. The U.S. recorded land crossings from Canada only since 1893.

have been as many as five and a half million; more if Irish Canada is added. This is the stuff of true drama, as their return letters show.[1]

Unsurprisingly, this migration is widely interpreted as a demographic adjustment, which allowed Ireland's high levels of fertility to coexist with limited expansion in agriculture and a fairly sustained decline in industry. It also changed the ratio of protestants to catholics in Ireland: indeed, differential migration had probably been doing this from at least the 1770s, but the absence of reliable figures before 1861 makes the impact of the years 1770–1834, when protestants clearly made up a majority of mass migration, difficult to assess.[2] More importantly and popularly, the emigration was an epic involving more active participants than any other conscious mass-movement in Irish history, although strangely it has found neither Irish nor Irish-American literary figures equal to its scope—unlike the Scandinavian, Italian, German, and Jewish migrations—perhaps because it cut too deep. For it was an epic that emptied countrysides, separated families, scattered talent, vivacity, and ability,[3] spread Irish Christianity and its divisions, and introduced myriads of country people to the strains and opportunities of a vast commercialised society.

In American terms, the migration can be seen as a huge importation of man-power, skills, and consumers during the formative century 1770–1870; a transfer that was neither marginal nor indispensable but substantial, which declined proportionately as further Irish migrants were overshadowed by continental Europeans. The quality of the transfer is difficult to evaluate, as immigrants found when confronted by native Americans' complaints about the tax costs of imported poverty, but the youthfulness of the newcomers made its credit value unanswerable. From indentures of the 1740s and 1770s, from the ships' passenger lists of the Napoleonic period, and from the unpublished pre-famine American returns and the published post-famine British and Irish ones, the youthfulness of the emigrants is clear, and indeed increased as time went on. The proportion of emigrants aged fifteen to twenty-four rose from 37 per cent in 1803–5 to 45 per cent in 1847–8, and to 57 per cent in 1881. Together with those aged twenty-five to thirty-four, the migration was rarely less than 65 per cent and usually from 70 to 85 per cent composed of those with the bulk of their productive years ahead of them and the costs of their rearing and education complete.[4] In pre-famine years, family migration was not un-

[1] Patrick Blessing, 'Irish emigration to the United States, 1800–1920: an overview' in P. J. Drudy (ed.), *The Irish in America (Irish Studies 4)* (Cambridge, 1985), table 2:1, p. 14; D. H. Akenson, *The Irish in Ontario* (Montreal, 1984), pp 9–15, 28–32; D. H. Akenson, *Being had: historians, evidence, and the Irish in North America* (Port Credit, Ont., 1985), pp 52–4, 89.

[2] Jacques Verrière, *La population de l'Irlande* (Paris, 1979), pp 280, 392, table III-21, p. 442; R. E. Kennedy, jr, *The Irish: emigration, marriage, and fertility* (Berkeley, Cal., 1975), pp 15–18, 110–38, 173; Adams, *Ir. emigration to New World*, pp 190–92.

[3] Mokyr, *Why Ire. starved*, pp 247–52.

[4] Cormac Ó Gráda, 'Across the briny ocean: some thoughts on pre-famine emigration to America' in T. M. Devine and David Dickson (ed.), *Ireland and Scotland, 1600–1850: parallels and contrasts in economic and social development* (Edinburgh, 1983), table 1, p. 123; Mokyr, *Why Ire. starved*,

common, usually consisting of two or three members (presumably a young couple and a child), as during the first two years of the famine. Even then unaccompanied emigrants were a considerable percentage, and from 1848 onwards they were a growing majority, as indeed they may have always been—if poorer remigration from British North America could be properly studied.[1]

There is little evidence of sustained large-scale unemployment among the emigrants (apart from seasonal joblessness among construction workers), except during the major recessions of 1818–21, 1837–43, 1873–7, 1883–5, and 1891–7, and during the labour gluts in special sectors, such as casual labour, in the famine and pre-famine years, 1847–55. Emigration from Ireland to the United States was sensitive to the downturns in opportunity; for example, it fell from 75,000 in 1873 to 12,000 in 1877, as earlier it had fallen from 30,000 in 1836 to 12,500 in 1838. This suggests a process of rational preparation and massive feedback of information from forerunners, which the surviving letters demonstrate but scarcely measure.[2] It underlines what should be evident: America absorbed virtually all the labour Ireland could send, 1847–55 excepted, and during recessions the majority of the Irish remained in employment. This contrasts with the long-term quasi-employment characteristic of Irish experience in Glasgow, Merseyside, or Salford, and especially in Dublin, Cork, and Galway. The emigrants' distribution confirms this: contrary to the anguished complaints of Irish visitors like Francis Wyse, Canon John O'Hanlon, and John Francis Maguire, among many others, there was no overconcentration in seaboard slums. Again, apart from a short period (1847–51), immigrants spread in almost exact proportion to the incidence of expanding economic opportunities; their preference, for example, for the north-eastern and mid-western states reflected the development of transport, trade, commercial temperate farming, and manufacturing there.[3] In short, the volume, periodic variation, and age-structure of the migration, and the ensuing employment and distribution patterns of those who went, show the coherence of the overall movement, which responded to the development of the host economy. Individual misfortunes and nationalist dismay should not obscure this, nor should the special features of the famine decade and its aftermath, which unquestionably furnished thousands of images of overwhelming wretchedness,

tables 8.1, p. 234, and 8.3, p. 242; Kerby A. Miller, *Emigrants and exiles* (Oxford and New York, 1985), table 11, p. 581.

[1] Ó Gráda, op. cit., tables, 2, 3, and 6A, pp 124–6; A. Gibbs Mitchell, 'Irish family patterns: nineteenth-century Ireland, and Lowell, Massachusetts' (Ph.D. thesis, Boston, 1976), tables 16–18, pp 165–9.

[2] Nicholas Nolan, 'The Irish emigration: a study in demography' (Ph.D. thesis, N.U.I. (U.C.D.), 1935), pp 196–8, 220ff; *Historical statistics of the United States to 1970*, series C-92 correlated to series N-111-17, U-187-9, and V-20-30.

[3] Patrick Blessing, 'Irish emigration to the United States, 1800–1920: an overview' in P. J. Drudy (ed.), *The Irish in America* (Cambridge, 1985), pp 21–3; Morton D. Winsberg, 'Irish settlement in the United States, 1850–1980' in *Éire-Ireland*, xx, no. 1 (spring 1985), pp 7–14; David Ward, *Cities and immigrants* (New York, 1971), pp 3–83.

be permitted to disguise the prosaic power of a mass migration that had begun before it, and would have continued, even accelerated, without it. Finally, in this calculus of effects, it is being established that, from at least 1875, Irish-American fertility patterns in states such as Massachusetts compensated for a decline in middle-class native American fertility, although by 1910–11 these differentials were more marked in rural areas and small towns than in the cities.[1] Here the behaviour of the American Irish contrasted with that of the Irish in Britain.

American historians are again demonstrating the role of the Irish as a potent force in the creation of popular and representative politics and a variegated culture. As participants in the revolution and in state constitution making, as voters and small politicians during the years 1790–1816 (usually on the more radical side of the Jeffersonian Republicans), as rebels against the newly respectable National Republicanism (and thereby supporting Jackson's new Democratic Republicans to 1836), the Irish helped to transform a politics of deference based on religious tests, closed candidate selection, restricted franchises, and unequal electoral districts. Then they divided: the protestants and their descendants became first Whigs, then Republicans; the majority, the catholic Irish, remained associated with the now less progressive, but yet assertively popular, Democratic party, which they slowly forged into an instrument of immigrant-stock power in local and metropolitan government. As generally poorer immigrants—including presbyterian, anglican, or catholic—they joined those Americans who opposed the merchant-responsive protestant establishment, which exerted disproportionate power from about 1824 on standards of civil acceptability. That such an establishment was informal, identified more often with the losing Whig cause than the triumphant Democratic one, did not incline the Irish to accept its pretensions, although both sides believed in the need for a virtuous republic, for a natural-law base for legislation, equity, and jurisprudence, and for the moral and patriotic foundation of education. Social barriers—disdain on one side, resentment on the other—rather than opposed ideas or simple class antagonisms, probably accounted for the Irish catholics joining with the anti-establishment Jacksonians. The recent historiographical fashion for multi-ethnic pluralism can generate but a minor rainbow of special effects, apart from blacks, free or enslaved, for the years 1775–1890; but this rainbow everywhere refracts specific characteristics and dispostions among the Irish, as among the Germans, the major white minorities. These were primarily ethno-cultural and religious, linking classes in a shared politics.[2] The sharper class distinctions, however,

[1] United States, Senate, *Reports of the immigration commission*, vol. xxviii, *Fecundity of immigrant women* (61 Congress, 2nd session, doc. no. 282) (Washington, 1911), pp 733 ff, especially tables 36 and 37, pp 806–7, 808–9; A. Gibbs Mitchell, 'Irish family patterns' (Ph.D. thesis, Boston, 1976), pp 313–14; Hasia R. Diner, *Erin's daughters in America* (Baltimore, 1983), p. 54 and p. 168, n. 17; Joellen M. Vinyard, *The Irish on the urban frontier: nineteenth-century Detroit* (New York, 1976), tables A-38, A-39, pp 409–10.

[*See opposite page for n. 2*]

developing with the simultaneous coming of the factory system and vast numbers of catholic Irish, further influenced their status and subculture. Ironically, catholic Irish could thus find outlets in a protestant Irish tradition of seeking popular rights. In short, a truly post-revolutionary party had to promote outsiders and small men; the catholic choice had been determined by a pre-existing presbyterian logic.

FROM an Irish-American standpoint, the emigration and its early results were only the beginning of a protean history, not the least important parts of which were a tenacious sentiment of descent and a remarkable continuity of institutional association, based ultimately on huge and ever-reinforced numbers.[1] English and German emigration to the United States was as numerous and continuous as the Irish, from the days of indentured servants, through the mid-nineteenth-century arrivals of hundreds of thousands of skilled workers and farmers, to the early twentieth-century mass migrations from the cities of northern England and the Rhineland to Chicago and Cleveland. But English and German migration was not linked to such unchanging emphasis on group identification as was the Irish. With the English, assimilation came easily and spelt rapid social mobility; with the Germans, assimilation meant the loss of their language, which was the core of their subculture in America. In both cases, therefore, strong group identity rarely survived the second generation, and often did not survive the first. With the Irish, new arrivals interacted with the Americanised and the American-born in such a way that assimilation in manners, livelihood, and education neither opened all doors to social acceptance and career advancement nor snapped the links forged by churchgoing and pride of ancestry between the poor and the better-off or those men born in Ireland and those born in the United States. A common outlook and appearance, however imponderable, survived the loss of Irish accents and customs, and even survived American birth: Governor George Clinton of New York (1739–1812) was known as the 'Old Irishman' though born in the state, of 1720s Longford immigrant parents.

There is perhaps no need to presume the continued existence of a complex subculture, based on insulation from the modernising and individualising host society, in order to explain Irish-American continuities. Some immigrants could indeed have agreed with their mid-century fellow countryman in New York city who confessed: 'we are a primitive people wandering wildly in a strange

[1] Lee Benson, *The concept of Jacksonian Democracy* (Princeton, 1961); Ronald Formisano, *The birth of mass political parties: Michigan, 1827–1861* (Princeton, 1971); Michael Holt, *Forging a majority: Pittsburgh, 1848–1860* (New Haven, 1969); Paul Kleppner, *The cross of culture: a social analysis of midwestern politics, 1850–1900* (New York, 1970).

[1] R. A. Burchell, 'The historiography of the American Irish' in *Immigrants and Minorities*, i (1982), pp 281–305; United States Bureau of the Census, *Statistical abstract, 1981* (Washington, 1982), table 42, p. 35; Michael F. Funchion (ed.), *Irish American voluntary organisations* (Westport, Conn., 1983).

land, the nineteenth century';[1] but young people adapted rapidly, for such comments can be balanced by many on the ease with which young Irish people became American in accent and outlook. In addition, the general identification with the Irish tradition, even among the American-born, extends beyond those most sensitive to the clash of cultures. This is especially true in the institutional continuity that was sustained by the successful: the Charitable Irish Society of Boston (1737), the Friendly Sons of St Patrick of Philadelphia (1771), the Friendly Sons of St Patrick (1784), and the Shamrock Society (c. 1812) of New York, the Hibernian Societies of Charleston (1803), Baltimore (1816), and New Orleans (1817), and the Erin Society of St Louis (1819) may each have deserved the tart comment of the New York *Freeman's Journal* on the Friendly Sons, that it was by 1863 'a sort of Irish "What-is-it?"'.[2] But they could function charitably as well as convivially, comprehensively as well as exclusively, and first institutionalised the message that one might be successful, monied, American, non-sectarian, even second- or third-generation, and yet organise as Irish without partisan political purpose. Legitimate Irishness was thus pioneered by the least alienated in America; much later did it become an instrument of either the uprooted, or the upwardly mobile.[3]

Yet, in search of Irish-American consciousness, Irish-American historians exaggerate its importance. Millions can be identified as Irish in the census schedules, parish registers, press obituaries, and voter rolls. Often, however, such origins played little part in their subjects' immediate lives. The father of writer and diplomat Maurice Francis Egan, who came from Tipperary in the 1820s, though with romantic feelings about the old Irish brigade in France, withdrew from the Democrats over Copperheadism; opposed Irish-American nationalism and Irish separatism; distrusted his convert American wife's forceful catholic spirituality; was enthusiastic above all about the development of machinery; and of his Irish home recollected only the picture 'of a small running river half choked by water cresses'.[4] Although he took an Irish-American weekly newspaper, he was not pleased when his son made his first career in the catholic press. Such complicated personalities were doubtless more common and typical than an emphasis on strictly Irish-American or census documents might indicate.

This emphasises the greatest problem of assessing Irish-Americans' influence on Ireland. They were not a country, a single caste, a general class, an establishment, a set of statistical certainties, or a predictable pattern of behaviour: they were a populace scattered and distended by a vast geography— within states as well as throughout the union—frequently changing home and

---

[1] Kerby A. Miller, *Emigrants and exiles* (Oxford and New York, 1985), p. 326.
[2] Funchion, op. cit., pp 69–74, 138–41, 141–5, 249–61; Robert Ernst, *Immigrant life in New York City, 1825–1863* (New York, 1949), p. 32.
[3] Cf. Miller, op. cit., pp 328–9; Dale Light, 'Irish-American organisation' in P. J. Drudy (ed.), *The Irish in America* (Cambridge, 1985), pp 120–35.
[4] M. F. Egan, *Recollections of a happy life* (London, 1924), p. 56.

home town, immersed in a workaday world, and preoccupied with raising families. Waves of young newcomers washed afresh into them yearly, and seasoned men sought ever wider opportunities. Such changes eventually produced discernible shifts of collective character; from the rudimentary disorganisation of the Pennsylvania frontier in the 1740s to the settled 'Scotch-Irish' farmer communities of the revolution, and to the more eclectic but still largely protestant and protestant-led minority in a nationalist young nation (c.1815); from the quiet, widely spread, Munster and south Ulster people, seeking assimilation in labouring, farming, and in the smaller cities (c. 1835), to the pathetic post-famine crowds of the eastern cities' tenements (c. 1855), and thence to the mature urban Irish-American society of 1880–1920, which mirrored the social patterns of the wider metropolis. Yet such shifts, so useful to scholarship, distort the continuing accumulations and dispersals and hide the multitudinous relations between the separate layers of experience: at the most simple, for example, they ignore the tendency of newcomers to seek their American relatives, regardless of their politics, culture, or place of birth.[1]

Amid such change the precarious and transient quality of much Irish-American life seems natural, even within the skeletal continuities of clubs and societies. It is the sustained interest of small groups in overcoming this that is all the more remarkable; and particularly the determination of a few to direct the variable 'Irishness' of their people beyond local concerns to the affairs of Ireland. Familiarity with the sources compels admiration for the sheer amount of work and journeying required. Neither the homesick patriotism of the unsuccessful nor the respectable ambitions of the resolutely American *and* Irish could alone have overcome the centrifugal fragmentation begun by the decision to leave Ireland and accelerated on arrival in America. Irish-America was an almost formless quantity that was the product of emigration, remigration, and the labour market, and purposeful Irish-American communities had to be made. Fortunately, the opportunities for work that America gave to newcomers, however unstable, helped organisers because they concentrated the Irish in towns, along canal and rail routes, and in manufacturing districts. Also, the resolve of churchmen to gather, identify, and minister to their flocks united for one purpose those whom others would unite for another purpose—indeed, clarified the very milieu in which contacts could be made.[2]

The scale, nevertheless, of the migration, the size of the Irish communities, the size of the Irish element in the American population, and the energies devoted to their organisation contrast strangely with the scope of the return contribution to Irish development. Distance, difference, and inefficiency conspired to thwart many of the emigrants' efforts for their homeland, and to

---

[1] J. A. Dunlevy and H. A. Gemery, 'British-Irish settlement patterns in the U.S.: the role of family and friends' in *Scottish Journal of Political Economy*, xxiv (1977), pp 257–63.

[2] Sheridan Gilley, 'The Roman Catholic church and the nineteenth-century Irish diaspora' in *Jn. Ecc. Hist.*, xxxv (1984), pp 188–207; Murray W. Nicholson, 'The role of religion in Irish North American studies' in *Ethnic Forum*, iv (1984), pp 64–77.

redirect them towards a mastery of American circumstances. Distance was probably most important, for the Atlantic passage took forty to forty-four days in the 1840s, at best thirty-five in the 1850s by sail, and ten or twelve days by steam thenceforward. Journeys between Liverpool and central or south-western Ireland have to be added. In 1850 Iowa, Wisconsin, Chicago, and central Illinois were about two weeks by rail, steamboat, and canal from New York and Philadelphia; St Louis was eight days up river from New Orleans, and Pittsburgh and Cincinnati were a week from Philadelphia.[1] After the civil war, and the completion of the railway grid, although the west coast was twelve days, midwestern centres were only two or three days away from the eastern ports—one reason why Parnell and Davitt could enjoy more effective liaison with Irish-Americans than had O'Connell. Differences also sprang from separate situations, and in 1916–21, often separate nationality: successively men as diverse as Henry Flood, Edward Newenham, Archibald Hamilton Rowan, Daniel O'Connell, James Stephens, C. S. Parnell, James Larkin, and Eamon de Valera found themselves at odds with their American Irish sympathisers. The more informed Irish-Americans, by background and news, had a good grasp of Irish affairs, and in fact did not 'see their way clearly' to simple solutions;[2] hence their poignant reliance on the dominant movement in contemporary Ireland. Irish leaders rarely had as good a grasp of the American situation, but used Irish-Americans as a source of money and support, especially the more uncritical and excitable element, whom they thereby inevitably disappointed. Irishmen did, of course, have a better grasp of what was practicable at home than the more impatient in America, and even the best expatriates, from MacNeven in the 1820s to McGarrity in 1916–21, had been 'out of things' for ten years or more.

BEFORE and during the American revolution, Ulster-Americans were the predominant minority, apart from slaves, especially in the nine colonies south of New England, outnumbering other Irish, Scots, and Germans. As a cohesive group, strengthened by their struggles to control the presbyterian church and to assert their right to representation in the colonial assemblies,[3] they largely dominated the radical patriot cause in Pennsylvania, Delaware, and the valley of Virginia in 1776. Elsewhere, less organised, more hesitant, and generally poorer, they mobilised in the revolution's defence following the British invasions of New York in 1776 and 1777, and of the Carolinas in 1780–81.[4] After the

[1] Kerby A. Miller, 'Emigrants and exiles' (Ph.D. thesis, University of California, Berkeley, 1976); ch. XI, table XII, 'Voyage length', pp 677–80; Rev. John O'Hanlon, *The Irish emigrant's guide*, ed. E. J. Maguire (New York, 1976), pp 79–91.

[2] J. F. Maguire, *The Irish in America* (London, 1868; reprint, New York, 1969), p. 609.

[3] Elizabeth I. Nybakken, 'New light on the old side: Irish influences on colonial presbyterianism' in *Journal of American History*, lxviii (1982), pp 813–32; W. L. Bockelman and O. S. Ireland, 'The internal revolution in Pennsylvania: an ethno-religious interpretation' in *Pennsylvania History*, xli (1974), pp 125–59.

[4] David Noel Doyle, *Ireland, Irishmen, and revolutionary America, 1760–1820* (Dublin, 1981), pp 109–37.

war, their power and status were enhanced by their military success and by the political liberality of the confederated states.

The period between the revolution and the election to the presidency in 1828 of Andrew Jackson (frontier-born son of south Antrim parents) was important, for it saw the formal emergence of an Irish-American community, with a discernible outlook, politics, and church life. By 1828 the slow fulfilment of the agenda of adult male equality and political participation, proclaimed in the declaration of independence, provided the context of this advance, as did the now rapid attainments of Ulster-Americans. Little is known of the social support of the new Irish leaders: all estimates of numbers, both of immigrants and of Irish stock, have been questioned, revised, and questioned again; even their significance has been questioned, because there was a widespread tendency among the Ulster-Americans to identify wholly with the new nation.[1] Nor can newcomers be precisely related to the large pre-revolutionary communities, although the natural links between the heavy migrations of the early 1770s and the later 1780s cannot be denied; for Ulster-Americans, the war of independence was only a punctuation mark in a cumulative process, as the civil war would be for Munstermen in the 1860s. After 1828 came an era of mass migration, strong native American reaction, a growing preponderance of catholic immigrants, and a discernibly catholic politics in the United States as in Ireland, so that ambiguities disappear over the next decade. At stake in America as in Ireland was the question: whose traditions were to shape the chief elements of Irishness? Yet the changing answer was largely supplied in terms of the inertias of settlement.

Before 1828, with religious freedom guaranteed under the first amendment (1791), and numbers limited, general assimilation and intra-Irish harmony were practicable, so that what became of Irishness was a tangential matter, not—as at home—the substance of conflict, power, and livelihood. Although the eirenic disposition of their lawyers, merchants, and politicians did not reflect the realities of catholic and protestant life, yet most immigrants looked up to those whose achievements made them both respectably American and self-respectingly Irish: especially the revolutionary survivors, Thomas McKean (1734–1817), governor of Pennsylvania 1799–1809, and George Clinton (1739–1812), governor of New York 1777–95 and 1801–4.[2] But the leadership of the newcomers fell to once radical immigrants, newly successful in America: the publisher Mathew Carey in Philadelphia, the former United Irishmen Thomas Addis Emmet, William Sampson, and William James MacNeven in New York, and others. Indeed, among these, George Cuming opposed the Clintonians in New York, and John Binns and James Reynolds

[1] M. A. Jones, 'The Scotch-Irish: post-revolutionary migration' in Stephan Thernstrom (ed.), *Harvard encyclopaedia of American ethnic groups* (Cambridge, Mass., 1980), pp 902–3; Kerby A. Miller, *Emigrants and exiles* (Oxford and New York, 1985), pp 169–97; Doyle, op. cit., pp 186–7, 220–23.

[2] John M. Coleman, *Thomas McKean* (Rockaway, N.J., 1975); L. K. Caldwell, 'George Clinton—democratic administrator' in *New York History*, xxxii (1951), pp 134–56.

led anti-McKean factions in Philadelphia, both struggles suggesting a breach between established American-born beneficiaries of the revolution and the newcomers, despite a common enthusiasm for Thomas Jefferson (although the back-country Ulster-Americans in Pennsylvania, led by Ulster-born veterans of 1776, also opposed McKean).[1] Yet it remains true that 'what is striking about the group consciousness of this period . . . is that immigrants from every part of Ireland shared a sense of fellow feeling',[2] while a real Ulster-American continuity provided a context for loyalty to both new and old that transcended generational factions and the tensions between well-off and poor.

In 1790, from 14 to 17 per cent of the white population of the United States were of identifiable Irish extraction: from 440,000 to 517,000 out of a population of 3.17 million whites. The majority, upwards of 350,000, were of Scotch-Irish descent, with an unknown percentage actually Irish-born. The rest were of 'native' Irish and some of Anglo-Irish origin. Scholars, though disagreeing about details, broadly agree that around 10 per cent of early white Americans were Scotch-Irish, and 4 to 5 per cent of partly 'native' Irish stock.[3] Bulk migration, including many women, had enabled the former to reproduce themselves as a distinct people; regional concentration, rural isolation, common mores, and presbyterian organisation had ensured their coherence as a group for several generations, as had the prejudice and partial disfranchisement that they suffered before 1776. Afterwards, only a minority remained presbyterian (for many had been lost through frontier schisms and lack of ministers), although that church's organisation kept pace with their distribution.[4] The total Scotch-Irish population of 1790 raises doubts about the standard figure of 300,000 pre-revolutionary Scotch-Irish immigrants, even of the approximate figure of 120,000 for 1753–75. Ships' tonnages were routinely exaggerated for purposes of advertising and consequently passenger numbers have been inflated by historians.[5] High fertility in distinctive back-country areas may account better for the Ulster-America of the 1770s, and throw light on its enthusiastic Americanism, and on the tendency of its plainer members to leave the educated kirk.

[1] Doyle, op. cit., pp 192–200, 214–18; Maurice J. Bric, 'The Irish and the evolution of the "New Politics" in America' in P. J. Drudy (ed.), *The Irish in America* (Cambridge, 1985), pp 149–61.

[2] M. A. Jones, 'Ulster emigration, 1783–1815' in E. R. R. Green (ed.), *Essays in Scotch-Irish history* (London, 1969), p. 67.

[3] Forrest McDonald and Ellen S. McDonald, 'The ethnic origins of the American people, 1790' in *William & Mary Quart.*, 3rd ser., xxxviii (1980), pp 179–99; [Thomas L. Purvis, Donald H. Akenson, and Forrest and Ellen McDonald], 'The population of the United States, 1790: a symposium' in *William & Mary Quart.*, 3rd ser., xli (1984), pp 85–135; calculations from ibid., table II, p. 98 (Purvis) and independently in Doyle, op. cit., pp 71–6.

[4] Elizabeth I. Nybakken, 'New light on the old side' in *Journal of American History*, lxviii (1982), pp 829–34; L. J. Cappon, *Atlas of early American history: the revolutionary era, 1760–1790* (Princeton, 1976), pp 24, 36–9, 66, 71.

[5] Contrast tonnages provided for the same vessels in R. J. Dickson, *Ulster emigration to colonial America, 1718–1775* (London, 1966), pp 229–79, and Audrey Lockhart, *Emigration from Ireland to the North American colonies, 1660–1775* (New York, 1976), pp 175–208 (from advertisements), with those in John McCusker, 'Ships registered at the port of Philadelphia before 1776', MS (1970) at the Historical Society of Pennsylvania, Philadelphia, based on first registrations there.

The catholic Irish almost wholly had come as indentured servants in fewer, more crowded, sailings, numbering at the very most not more than 100,000, including many catholic servants from Ulster. They did not create a distinct community, for they were accompanied by few women, and catholicism was proscribed almost everywhere outside Pennsylvania. In 1757 practising Irish catholics numbered less than 400 in south-eastern Pennsylvania; in 1790 there were only 6,000 catholics, largely German, in the same state.[1] Yet the population with catholic Irish names then numbered as many as 43,000 in Pennsylvania and as many as 184,000 in the nation as a whole. This 'hidden Ireland' confirms Michael J. O'Brien's classic defence of a pre-revolutionary Irish immigration apart from the Scotch-Irish;[2] but it was hidden precisely because it was intermarried and absorbed into the general population. Outside Philadelphia and a few Maryland counties, this Irish tradition was dissipated into little more than an anti-British bias favouring a new nationality, as both the revolutionary muster rolls and the cases of Matthew Lyon, Mathew Thornton, and General John Sullivan suggest[3]—a pattern analogous to Australia before the 1850s, except that the Ulster-Americans provided the main impetus to such 'ex-servant' emotions in America.

Between 1782 and 1828 emigration was uneven, but its volume before 1803 startled observers and was put down to the new nation's prestige (its economic pull did not intensify until the 1820s). Maldwyn Jones argues that 100,000 emigrated from Ireland to the United States in the period 1783–1815.[4] Dublin Castle and opposition newspapers argued about the numbers, but reliable statistics are hard to come by. Robert Stephenson reported a heavy flow from Munster in 1784, 'a circumstance not much known before the present time'.[5] While the indentured servant trade declined gradually (a shipload of 300 from Cork in 1811 seemed unusual), American records confirm the overall increase in free migration in the 1790s. Fear of its scale, and consequent attempts to redirect the flow to British North America, caused Westminster in 1803, 1805, and 1816 to impose low passenger-per-ton ratios on American-bound vessels, while favouring the Canadian trade expressly in 1817.[6] This effectively doubled fares to the United States compared with Canada and deflected poorer migrants northwards. Although Malthusian and political anxieties led to the

---

[1] James F. Connelly (ed.), *The history of the archdiocese of Philadelphia* (Philadelphia, 1976), pp 35, 58.

[2] M. J. O'Brien, *Irish settlers in America: a consolidation of articles from the Journal of the American Irish Historical Society* (2 vols, Baltimore, 1979); McDonald, 'Ethnic origins', p. 197, and Purvis, 'The population of the U.S., 1790', table II, p. 98 (see above, p. 692, n. 3); calculations mine.

[3] Aleine Austin, *Matthew Lyon* (University Park, Pa., 1981); Charles P. Whittemore, 'John Sullivan: luckless Irishman' in George A. Billias (ed.), *Washington's generals* (New York, 1964), pp 137–62.

[4] M. A. Jones, 'Ulster emigration, 1783–1815' in E. R. R. Green (ed.), *Essays in Scotch-Irish history*, (London, 1969), p. 49.

[5] Stephenson to Orde, 7 June 1784 (N.L.I., Bolton papers, MS 15827/3).

[6] MacDonagh, *Pattern of govt growth*, pp 54–65; H. J. M. Johnston, *British emigration policy, 1815–1830* (Oxford, 1972), pp 2, 25–6, 119.

repeal of the differentials in 1823 and 1827, new fares still favoured British North America, so that a pattern persisted until 1838 whereby the better-off Ulster presbyterians went to Philadelphia, and poorer catholics to Quebec, St John (New Brunswick), and later to New York.[1] British North America, however, was sought only as a transit base by the poor; apart from Newfoundland, government assistance was necessary for them to begin land settlement there.

Government policy contracted and redirected emigration after 1803; new policies encouraged its heavy resumption via Canada after 1816, and directly to the United States by 1826. The decay of the Irish economy and concurrent boom in North America after 1815, especially when the 1819–22 banking crisis ended, was the real stimulus. However, readiness to emigrate, most usual in those under thirty, seems to have accompanied the spread of English between 1780 and 1830 through much of Munster, the west midlands, and south Ulster.[2] These trends account for the characteristics of those leaving from 1815 to 1845. Emigrants from Ulster and north Leinster, who had under the 1803–5 acts consisted mainly of the more prosperous, now became more typical of the area's social and religious structure, except that the very poor did not go. Evidence from Cavan suggests an atypical level of literacy in the labourers' and small farmers' families whose sons emigrated.[3] The destruction of the weaving and spinning economy in south and west Ulster made subsistence more precarious as farmers hired fewer labourers in order to profit from cross-channel markets. But Cork and the south-east, gradually taking in Limerick and the south midlands, matched Ulster by the 1830s, with a similar outward flow of the better labourers, and of distressed weavers, millers, artisans, and farmers, but especially of the sons of literate small farmers and cottiers. In pre-famine Ireland such people, whether from north or south, had some self-esteem and position.[4] Evidence from New York suggests that many attained a level of social mobility unusual by the standards of nineteenth-century Irish immigrants, most of whom came with little capital or useful skills.[5] In their first year, only the best connected and educated could avoid the stigma of being poor Irish (as

[1] Nicholas Nolan, 'The Irish emigration: a study in demography' (Ph.D. thesis, N.U.I. (U.C.D.), 1935), pp 119–24; Adams, *Ir. emigration to New World*, pp 143–5, 156, 161; Cormac Ó Gráda, 'Across the briny ocean' in T. M. Devine and David Dickson (ed.), *Ireland and Scotland, 1600–1850* (Edinburgh, 1983), table 7, p. 127.

[2] Cf. maps 1–5 in Garret Fitzgerald, 'Estimates for baronies of minimum level of Irish-speaking amongst successive decennial cohorts, 1771–1781 to 1861–1871' in *R.I.A. Proc.*, lxxxiv (1984), sect. C, pp 117–55, with those in S. H. Cousens, 'The regional variations in emigration from Ireland between 1821 and 1841' in *Transactions and papers of the Institute of British Geographers*, xxxvii (1965), figs 2–4, pp 19–22.

[3] Kevin O'Neill, *Family and farm in pre-famine Ireland: the parish of Killashandra* (Madison, Wis., 1985), pp 121–2, 169–70.

[4] Ó Gráda, op. cit., pp 120, 121–2, tables 3, 4, and 6B, pp 125, 127; Joel Mokyr and Cormac Ó Gráda, 'Emigration and poverty in pre-famine Ireland' in *Working Paper No. 1, Centre for Economic Research, U.C.D.* (Dublin, 1982), pp 23–31, 39–40; Kerby A. Miller, *Emigrants and exiles* (Oxford and New York, 1985), pp 193–223.

[5] Elizabeth M. O'Connell, '"The best poor man's country in the world": Irish immigrants in New York in the early nineteenth century' in *Historian* [New York], viii (1977), pp 37–47.

New York City council complained of Newry arrivals in 1796). Contrasts between past and present status may well have accounted for the assertiveness of Irish communities after 1800 and explain why the rhetoric of equality attracted them.

These years also saw a basic shift in the American regions associated with the Irish. The 1790 census had confirmed the impressionistic geography of Ulster-American settlement and politics in the back country. Central and western Pennsylvania, western Maryland, the ridge-and-valley country of Virginia, and the Carolinas' piedmont and contiguous Georgia had populations that were half and more than half of Irish stock, giving those states, as a whole, Scots-Irish and largely post-catholic Irish ingredients ranging from 15 per cent to 25 per cent.[1] They had spread west to the new states of Kentucky (admitted to the union in 1792) and Tennessee (admitted 1796), favourite resorts of would-be clerks and businessmen going out direct from Ulster to join American cousins. But between 1790 and 1820, the Irish element in Kentucky's population dropped from one-third to one-quarter.[2] The loss of control in the 1760s of American presbyterianism by Irish Old Side ministers (whiggish and anti-revivalist) had hastened the tendency of Ulster-Americans to become baptists and methodists, and the erosion of the distinct regional community. The larger numbers of newer presbyterian immigrants did not establish a church structure similar to that of the 1740s, or to that of their catholic contemporaries, nor did anti-Irish prejudice drive them together. Ironically, religious and political factionalism seem to have thrived as hallmarks of their now ready acceptance as Americans,[3] which has made their collective story difficult to establish.

The areas of Irish visibility shifted to the eastern cities and surrounding towns. Catholic parish life was established between 1775 and 1790; in New York, Boston, Albany, Alexandria, New Castle (Delaware), and Charleston; to the first diocese, Baltimore, erected in 1789, were added Boston, New York, Philadelphia, and Bardstown (Kentucky) in 1808. The paid clergy (not always happy choices) and bishops (usually better) were almost all Irish by birth or descent, reflecting a reality that Elizabeth Seton (canonised 1975), whose father had given his life for fever-stricken Irish immigrants in 1801, candidly admitted meant a sharp fall into poverty and vulgarity when she became a catholic in 1805.[4] Already by the 1770s one-quarter of Irish servants were indentured to urban masters; by 1815-18, the work force of Du Pont's gunpowder works,

[1] Purvis *et al.*, 'The population of the United States, 1790', table II, p. 98 (see above, p. 692, n. 3); Doyle, op. cit., app. 1, p. 75.
[2] Thomas L. Purvis, 'The ethnic descent of Kentucky's early population' in *The Register of the Kentucky Historical Society*, lxxx (1982), table III, p. 263, and p. 266.
[3] W. L. Fisk, 'The Associate Reformed Church in the old Northwest' in *Journal of Presbyterian History*, xlvi (1968), pp 157–74; W. W. McKinney, *Early Pittsburgh presbyterianism, 1758–1839* (Pittsburgh, 1938).
[4] Joseph I. Dirvin, *Mrs Seton: foundress of the American Sisters of Charity* (new ed., New York, 1975), pp 170–71; Theodore Roemer, *The catholic church in the United States* (St Louis, 1950), pp 79 ff, 399–412.

south of Philadelphia, was an Ulster catholic one.[1] In 1790 Mathew Carey founded an emigrant aid society in Philadelphia and Dr Robert Hogan founded another in New York in 1814. Craftsmen, displaced in Ireland by rising costs before 1815 and unemployment thereafter, found a market for their strength if not their skills. The demand for diggers, hauliers, heavers, warehousemen, dockers, and carters grew as rapidly as the entrepôts of the new commerce.

If the 'Old Irish' merchants kept up the amicable interdenominational Irishness of the 1780s in their various Hibernian societies, tensions among the poor led to riots: by poor protestant Irish against established mercantile catholics in Philadelphia in 1799; by poor catholics against Orange parades in New York in 1824. These tensions broke up the St Tammany Society of Philadelphia (which in 1783 had toasted Irish independence), when too many catholics and Irish-speakers joined for comfort. Yet these two cities were exceptional, with the Irish constituting one-fifth of around 100,000 inhabitants in each by 1820. Elsewhere the Irish were as yet knots of people in small sea and river ports, and market towns; or they were farmers and labourers in a vast countryside. Hence the 'American' quality of their life in these years, and the mixed and liberal character of much of their organisation and politics.

As America's buoyant economy gave livelihoods to the Irish, so too did the optimism of American popular politics give a stimulus to the dying Irish radicalism of the 1790s. The Federalists, architects of the constitution of 1787 and of its consolidation in the 1790s, mistrusted democracy and social equality, interpreted republicanism as the right of the propertied to representation, disliked the French revolution and the United Irishmen, favoured Anglo-American understanding and trade, believed in national development under the joint guidance of business and government, and were homogenous, protestant, and pre-revolutionary in origin. The Jeffersonian or Democratic Republicans favoured extending the franchise, spoke of egalitarianism, stood for states' rights against federal power, sentimentalised French and Irish radicals, were anti-British, argued for decentralised economic growth, and believed that elites should be reborn continuously and without privilege from the people—broadly understood—whom all elites must serve. Ulster-Americans had either opposed the constitution before its ratification, like William Findley of Pennsylvania,[2] or later joined Jefferson in being disillusioned with the Federalist view of it, like Thomas McKean—the latter in spite of a sober anti-jacobinism.

Naturally, Irish newcomers who were poor, or radical, or both, favoured the Jeffersonians, especially their extreme factions. This tendency was strength-

[1] Doyle, op. cit., pp 96–7; Dennis Clark, *The Irish relations* (Rutherford, N.J., 1982), pp 47–8.
[2] Callista Schramm, 'William Findley in Pennsylvania politics' in *Western Pennsylvania Historical Magazine*, xx (1937), pp 31–40; Robert G. Crist, *Robert Whitehill and the struggle for civil rights* (Lemoyne, Pa., 1958).

ened by four sets of grievances: restrictions on free speech and freedom of the press; impediments to free immigration and easy naturalisation; the existence of religious tests and establishments; and the prevalence of restricted franchises and unequal electoral districts. Quite consistently, the 'high' Federalists sought to restrain the right of opposition in time of diplomatic crisis; and one of the first victims of the consequent sedition law was the Wicklow-born congressman from Vermont, Matthew Lyon. Led by John Jay and Rufus King, they also sought to restrict the naturalisation of foreigners, raising the residence requirement from James Madison's two years in 1790 to fourteen years in 1798, and linking this to their threatened deportation of United Irish radicals.[1] Federalist areas, such as New England, New York, and the Carolinas, made it more difficult to become naturalised, or to acquire citizenship—even to immigrate—than did states under Jeffersonian control. The catholic Irish inherited this grievance from the presbyterians, and local regulations annoyed them until the 1850s.[2] Religious tests, linked to federalist tradition, likewise irritated: the congregational establishment survived in Connecticut until 1818 and in Massachusetts until 1833; public office was restricted to protestants in New Hampshire until 1876, in North Carolina until 1835, and in New Jersey until 1844.[3] John Jay had secured an oath requiring the abjuration of foreign ecclesiastical authority as a condition of citizenship in New York in 1777 (repealed in 1806). By contrast, the four states of strongest Scotch-Irish presence, Virginia, Maryland, Delaware, and Pennsylvania, had abolished such disabilities during the revolution, apart from wartime anti-anglican and anti-pacifist oaths in Pennsylvania. Ulster-Americans supported similar change in the Carolinas, Georgia, and New York, and liberal constitutions in the new states of Tennessee and Kentucky. From Virginia southward, they had joined baptists, liberal anglicans, and deists in a continuation of the earlier post-revolutionary movement to ensure that anglicanism was not restored as an established church. In all this, incoming catholics adopted the Scotch-Irish ethos. Finally, the Jeffersonian movement for full male suffrage, the abolition of property qualifications for office, and equitable electoral districts (anticipated in Pennsylvania's wartime constitution) embodied semi-permanent Ulster-American objectives (where these had not been achieved), and likewise attracted the immigrants.[4]

During the period of the first 'Americanisation' from 1800 to the mid-1820s, under successive Republican administrations, many of these grievances were

[1] Maurice J. Bric, 'The Irish and the evolution of the "New Politics"' in P. J. Drudy (ed.), *The Irish in America* (Cambridge, 1985), pp 153–4, 156–7.

[2] 'Admission of immigrants under state laws, 1788–1882' in Edith Abbott, *Immigration: select documents and case records* (Chicago, 1924; reprint, New York, 1969), pp 102–80; T. C. Grattan, *Civilized America* (2 vols, London, 1859), ii, 15–25.

[3] F. X. Curran, *Catholics in colonial law* (Chicago, 1963), pp 112, 115, 116, 120, 122, 124.

[4] Kirk H. Porter, *A history of suffrage in the United States* (Chicago, 1918; reprint, New York, 1971), pp 20–46, 112–34.

removed, consolidating that party's appeal to the Irish. Local rivalries and minor appointments likewise secured their loyalty—a task made easier by their sentimental identification with American-born Irish presbyterians such as Robert Smith (1757–1842) to whom high office could safely be given. Prominent exceptions, such as James McHenry, President John Adams's Ballymena-born secretary of war, and the catholic merchant federalists of the ports, such as Thomas FitzSimons, could not stop the convergence of immigrants and Ulster-Americans in the Republican camp. (Nor could the belated sympathies for Ireland of younger and more pragmatic Federalists after 1800.) By 1824, the *National Gazette* listed seven Irish-Americans, of both stocks, one Irish-born, in the house of representatives, all Republicans.[1] But by that time the respectability of the party under James Monroe and John Quincy Adams, and its inclination to resurrect a federalist view of government and economy, was forcing most of the Irish towards its more populist faction led by Andrew Jackson, soon to emerge as the Democratic party. Jackson was to carry four of the seven Irish-American congressmen of 1824 when he won the election in 1828. The history of the United Irish émigrés in politics, who became Jacksonians, has to be located in this tradition. Their great achievement was incorporating the discontents of new, largely catholic, immigrants into the ordered politics of the Jeffersonian and later Democratic parties; in creating a common Irish consciousness that—despite factions—placed Ulster-American connections, achievements, and objectives at the service of their successors. The war of 1812 had offered an emotive outlet for this pan-Irish unity of purpose.[2]

Admittedly, even by 1820, with the foundation of the Orange Order in the United States, this unity had begun to decay into a partnership of tradition and convenience. William Sampson and Thomas Addis Emmet, indeed, took up catholic emancipation, and branches of the Friends of Ireland, O'Connell's American auxiliary, flourished in several Ulster-American centres: Savannah, Huntsville, Natchez, and Charleston.[3] The Democratic Republicans championed O'Connell and defended the right of the Irish in America to organise in his support, a right the followers of John Quincy Adams tended to deny. Assisted by his Belfast-born cousin, Thomas Suffern, Jackson had the route to Irish hearts, though wiser heads, such as Mathew Carey, Robert Walsh of the *National Gazette*, and MacNeven from 1834, opposed his demagoguery. On the other hand, O'Connell rejected MacNeven's suggestion that he should use the

[1] Jeremiah O'Brien (Maine), George Casseday (New Jersey), Samuel McKean (Pennsylvania), Louis McLane (Delaware), Henry Connor (North Carolina), Henry Conway (Arkansas), and Patrick Farrelly (Pennsylvania): see *Biographical directory of the American congress, 1774–1961* (Washington, D.C., 1961), pp 672, 730, 732, 876, 1303, 1308, 1398–9.
[2] 'John Rhea' in *Dictionary of American biography*, xv [viii, pt 1], pp 524–5; supporting areas were largely Scotch-Irish, see Marshall Smelser, *The Democratic Republicans, 1801–1815* (New York, 1968), map, p. 217.
[3] Thomas F. Moriarty, 'The Irish-American response to catholic emancipation' in *Catholic Historical Review*, lxvi (1980), pp 356, 360, 364, 366, and n. 83, p. 371.

Catholic Association to seek a federal solution to Anglo–Irish relations; his followers using instead the threat of the American Irish to warn Britain that if emancipation were delayed 'the violent party would have triumphed over the moderate; the American would have gained over the British'[1]—a picture that exaggerated the weary aspirations of distant, now moderate, and fairly poor auxiliaries.

These episodes, nevertheless, presaged the beginning of a more distinctly catholic 'Irish-America', noticeable particularly in the composition of the Friends of Ireland, most of whose active twenty-four branches were in the port cities. They also suggested that residual Irish protestant politics in America were by now artificial and somewhat manipulative. The journalists of the protestant Irish supporters of Jefferson—William Duane, Thomas Branagan, John D. Burk, David McKeehan, and Joseph Charless—had, like their contemporaries Carey and Walsh, written consciously for American audiences.[2] With the appearance in New York of O'Connor's *Shamrock* in 1810, and the *Truth Teller* in 1825, as well as various newspapers in Philadelphia, all directed at catholic and Irish readers, the creation of a distinctive Irish-American opinion was begun.[3] If it helped bishops to win their battles against American-born traders who sought uncanonical control over parish life as trustees of church property (the immigrants sometimes backing the churchmen),[4] this opinion also underlined the end of the earlier interdenominational informality and the beginning of an organised Irish-America. It was thus ironic that Andrew Jackson's accession (1829), partly a result of this older partnership, coincided with catholic emancipation in Ireland, which was symptomatic of the passing of such a partnership on both sides of the Atlantic. Increasingly the catholics sought security in a new group-consciousness, realising that the only reliable supporters of their difficult religious commitments and burdensome social predicament were themselves. Yet this realism was made possible only by the cultural diversity, religious freedom, and political rights pioneered for all Irishmen by Ulster-Americans and United Irishmen as prelude to their own happy assimilation into a republican society. Strangely too, the paradox of getting catholic emancipation by mass politics in a Europe where catholicism was afraid of revolutionary democracy was not a problem in the United States. Indeed the New York Irish, who in 1821 had welcomed the extension of the state franchise only slightly beyond 'forty-shilling renters' but had to wait until 1837 for full rights in local elections, had a better grasp of the link between mass

[1] Ibid., quoting Wyse, *Catholic Association*, i, 320.
[2] Joseph I. Shulim, *John Daly Burk, Irish revolutionist* (Philadelphia, 1964); David Kaser, *Joseph Charless, printer in the Western Country* (Philadelphia, 1963).
[3] W. L. Joyce, *Editors and ethnicity: a history of the Irish-American press, 1848–1883* (New York, 1976), pp 49–50.
[4] Walter Cox, *A short sketch of the present state of the catholic church in New York in a letter to the right reverend Bishop Connolly* (New York, 1819), pp 10–16; Patrick Carey, *People, priests, and prelates* (Notre Dame, Ind., 1987), chs 6 and 7.

politics and religious rights than did those at home: thus they protested against the disfranchisement that accompanied emancipation in Ireland.[1]

EVERY distinctive aspect of Irish-America was discernible before the great famine. Elements present before 1828 had by 1845 been amplified in a growing and conscious society. Outside British North America, the fertile and ambiguous overlap with the Ulster tradition now largely disappeared. Irish and American historians and Victorian commentators have argued that the famine produced a uniquely Irish society overseas through the scale and character of the ensuing migration. They assumed that a flow along earlier lines would have been more naturally assimilated. The reality of the Irish in both the United States and British North America from 1829 to 1845 suggests otherwise.

Direct migration to the United States after 1829 fell below 10,000 only once, in 1838. If we accept reliable indications that just over half of Irish migrants bound for British North America later travelled south, then total emigration to the United States rose continuously from about 29,000 annually in 1830–40 to 50,000 annually in 1841–4.[2] These years saw the real shift to mass migration, with no real evidence for W. B. Adams's belief that the turning point was around 1834–5. Instead the increase in emigration during the American recession of 1837–43 reversed normal patterns and shows how the exodus from crisis-ridden Ireland, with a decade of momentum behind it, defied its usual sensitivity to United States business cycles. In 1843 the wholesale price index fell to 75, its lowest point in the nineteenth century, yet immigration increased to over 45,000 in 1844. (In 1819 a fall in the index to 125 had sharply curbed emigration, as would the depressions of the 1870s, 1890s, and 1930s.)

The mechanics of migration also changed during these years. The organised passenger business dated back to the 1750s in Ulster, Dublin, and Cork, proliferating in the 1770s. As late as 1830, it remained haphazard, with no scheduled services, with sailings delayed until complements were filled, and with rudimentary regard for the health and comfort of the travellers. A sharp decline in Irish–American trade after 1815 meant that return journeys from the States were often in ballast. From the 1820s, North American shippers concentrated their cotton, flaxseed, and even Canadian timber imports through Liverpool; low-volume return cargoes could be cheaply filled out with passengers, so that by 1834, 80 per cent, and by 1845 92.6 per cent, of Irish emigrants to the United States went from Liverpool.[3] Only the Derry–Philadelphia connection survived this vast redirection, apart from direct

[1] Thomas F. Moriarty, 'The Irish-American response to catholic emancipation' in *Catholic Historical Review*, lxvi (1980), p. 369.

[2] Adams, *Ir. emigration to New World*, pp 197–200, app., pp 413–15; Helen I. Cowan, *British emigration to British North America* (rev. ed., Toronto, 1961), pp 187, 190–91, 195–8, app. B, tables II and IV, pp 289, 293; *Historical statistics of the United States to 1970*, series C 89–92.

[3] Adams, *Ir. emigration to New World*, p. 204; *Census Ire., 1851*, pt vi, *General report, appendix*, table XVIII, p. cii [2134], H.C. 1856, xxxi, 106.

Irish–Canadian routes, used in 1842 by 80.6 per cent of Quebec-bound emigrants, and in 1845 by 80 per cent of *all* Canada-bound emigrants.[1] New York replaced Philadelphia as the terminus of most Liverpool sailings, with protean consequences, not least being the emergence of both Liverpool and New York as the dominant Irish centres in northern England and North America. New York, with a vigorous middle class, and largely free of the strong protestant Irish communities that characterised Philadelphia, became the virtual capital of the now less diversified American-Irish, while the two cities' links allowed easy remigration of industrially trained Irishmen from Lancashire to America's factory regions.

British policy increasingly favoured emigration as a solution to Ireland's problems. Fear that she would 'deluge Great Britain with poverty and wretchedness and gradually ... equalise the state of the English and Irish peasantry' was strongly felt, since it was assumed that 'two different rates of wages and two different conditions of the labouring classes cannot possibly coexist'.[2] But such lessons from neither Malthus nor Ricardo could prompt general schemes of state-funded removal. Pilot schemes in 1823 and 1825, planned by Robert Wilmot Horton, under-secretary of state for war and the colonies, and implemented by Peter Robinson, brought 2,600 people from disturbed north Cork to Peterborough in Ontario. But the cost of £53,000 and unsatisfactory results won few friends in parliament, while as a venture of the 'protestant' party in Irish affairs it found no wide favour in Ireland. Parliamentary select committees of 1825 and 1826–7, which endorsed mass emigration, but on the *laissez-faire* principle, helped change restrictive passenger–tonnage ratios, and led to official, if informal, promotion of a climate of emigration, including the establishment of a board of emigration in 1831 to collect information and encourage emigration to British possessions.[3] Worries about British livelihood, Irish stability, and the peopling of the empire suggested partial deregulation of the emigrant trade and its redirection to British North America, but the immediate and irreversible result was a greater flow to the United States.

Nationalist opinion reluctantly followed the government. In 1829, the Catholic Association petitioned against a revival of colonisation by Horton, but in 1843 O'Connell joined others in establishing a Catholic Emigration Society.[4] Rejecting the view of Nassau William Senior and George Nicholls that emigration was a general panacea, they saw it now as a vital auxiliary relief; ironically, this had been the view of Malthus himself in 1816–17. Between 1831 and 1834,

---

[1] Ibid., Cowan, op. cit., table IV, pp 291–3; I have assumed that nine-tenths of Liverpool, and one-fifth of Glasgow–Greenock, embarkees were Irish.

[2] Third report of the select committee on emigration from the United Kingdom, 1827, quoted in Adams, *Ir. emigration to New World*, p. 284.

[3] Above, p. 121; H. J. M. Johnston, *British emigration policy, 1815–1830* (Oxford, 1972), pp 91–128; Cowan, op. cit., pp 87–93, 97–8; MacDonagh, *Pattern of govt growth*, pp 66, 77, 79–80; Adams, *Ir. emigration to New World*, pp 240–333.

[4] *Nation*, 6 May 1843, p. 466; cf. above, pp 586, 598.

booklets urging emigration were published in Dublin and Westport. The poor inquiry foreshadowed the introduction of an Irish poor law, and many landlords came to prefer supporting the emigration of their poorer tenants, to supporting the tenants by a costly poor rate. James Grattan apart, they favoured Horton's last appeal in 1829, and several now began private schemes, notably Lord Egremont's settlement of 1,800 Clare tenants in Canada before 1839. O'Connell helped such men incorporate a Canadian colonisation company in 1835.[1]

Migration to the United Kingdom made many familiar with sea crossings. It is estimated that 254,000 went permanently to Britain in 1820–41 (probably an underestimate); in 1841 at least 57,651 went by steam packets, chiefly as migratory harvesters, and largely via Liverpool.[2] To move further afield was natural as opportunities became known. Likewise the heavy recruitment of Irish into the British army and navy constituted another pool of potential emigrants: Irish fathers made no provision for demobilised soldiers, whose way thereafter was in the wider world. Again, Britain's public works, especially canals, begun many years before North America's, provided a mechanism whereby Irish countrymen could acquire marketable skills. Thus many of the blasters, artisans, contractors, and labourers who in 1825–6 built the Providence–Worcester canal were professional 'canalers' of small farmer and artisan backgrounds in Cork, Tipperary, and south-east Ireland, trained in building English canals, often after service in the Napoleonic wars. Canal finishing involved brickwork and timberwork, which led many into brickmaking and laying, masonry work, lumbering, and carpentry. Tyrone Power's harrowing descriptions of those digging the canal from Lake Pontchartrain to New Basin near New Orleans in 1834 should not obscure the steps and skills by which youths of 'middling' background used such works towards settlement and improved condition.[3]

Many of these projects got under way just as mass migration to North America began. A transport revolution laid the foundation of the continent's full-scale commercialisation: 'the annihilation of distance' as men called it. The Erie canal, first envisaged by Christopher Colles of Kilkenny, trained on the Inistioge canal, was begun in 1817 with American workers to link the Atlantic with the Great Lakes via the Hudson river, and finished in 1825 by huge Irish gangs. Their Irish bosses and subcontractors then bid for sections of the hundred or so other canals under construction by 1826. By the late 1820s, the 350-mile Erie canal spread about 50,000 Irish-born men across upstate New York, with a middle class of brewers, salt-makers, and merchants in the canal

---

[1] Cowan, op. cit., p. 127.

[2] Lynn Hollen Lees, *Exiles of Erin* (Manchester, 1979), p. 36; Nicholas Nolan, 'The Irish emigration: a study in demography' (Ph.D. thesis, N.U.I. (U.C.D.), 1935), pp 77–8, 96–8, 110; Mokyr, *Why Ire. starved*, p. 230.

[3] [William Grattan] Tyrone Power, *Impressions of America during the years 1833, 1834, and 1835* (2 vols, London, 1836), ii, 238–9.

ports of Buffalo, Rochester, Syracuse, and Albany.[1] Ex-canalers acquired land or permanent jobs along the 452-mile Wabash and Erie route as it was completed from Toledo (Ohio) to Evansville (Indiana) between 1832 and 1856, and along the Illinois and Michigan route from 1838 to 1848, with its nascent outport at Chicago.[2] Yet underpayment, the truck system, periodic layoffs, accident and disease, shanty housing, employers' abuse of whiskey rations, and permanent overstrain did produce a subculture of impoverished canalers who could never rise to such security. Others preferred road making. An 'Irish brigade', 1,000 strong, worked the Pennsylvania sections (built 1811–18) of the vast national road linking Maryland and Illinois. Advantageous settlement resulted where canals and roads opened new or partly empty countryside, as in upper New York, Illinois, or mid-Pennsylvania, but when canals such as the Chesapeake and Ohio canal (built 1828–50) crossed settled areas, tensions between canalers and settlers were high, and the former settled less frequently. Unlike Canada or the United Kingdom, railroad building also overlapped for a generation with canals in the United States: the Baltimore and Ohio, Memphis and Charleston, and Mohawk and Hudson lines, all begun 1828–9, provided further construction opportunities. These outlets lasted as line followed line into the 1890s. Here concurrent settlement awaited explicit company promotion as initiated by the Illinois Central Rail Road during the 1850s. Canada likewise built a competing series of canals to outflank the Erie system, to render the St Lawrence navigable, and to facilitate imperial defence. The Welland, Lachine, and Rideau canals (c. 1829–33) also depended upon Irish labour, as did a new system of government roads in Upper Canada. Indeed, it was here that the deliberate tying of land grants to construction work was pioneered— informally from the late 1820s, by legislation from 1841.

Yet public works, whether as means or as end, tended to concentrate immigrants in the United States and not in British North America, for, as the imperial emigration commissioners admitted, 'Canada does not possess a tithe of the capital necessary for their employment'.[3] Hence Ulster anglicans with some means settled somewhat disproportionately in Upper Canada (Ontario), while rather more presbyterians and catholics tended southwards.[4] This, rather than inducements to the former to build up an imperial interest on a protestant basis, perhaps accounts for the patterns of chosen settlement. The several

---

[1] Thomas Mooney, Nine years in America (Dublin, 1850), pp 98–105; George Potter, To the golden door: the story of the Irish in Ireland and America (Boston and Toronto, 1960), pp 184–7; W. E. Rowley, 'The Irish aristocracy of Albany, 1788–1878' in New York History, lii (1971), pp 275–304.

[2] Elfrieda Lang, 'Irishmen in northern Indiana before 1850' in Mid-America, xxxvi (1954), pp 190–98.

[3] Colonial land and emigration commission, 1850, quoted in Cowan, op. cit., p. 199 (a retrospect).

[4] Cormac Ó Gráda, 'Across the briny ocean' in T. M. Devine and David Dickson (ed.), Ireland and Scotland, 1600–1850 (Edinburgh, 1983), table 7, p. 127; D. H. Akenson, The Irish in Ontario (Montreal, 1984), pp 23–6, 224–6, 263–7, 390–93; C. J. Houston and W. J. Smyth, The sash Canada wore: a historical geography of the Orange Order in Canada (Toronto, 1980), pp 31–2, 93–6.

groups, nevertheless, interacted everywhere, not least on construction works. By the 1830s, the Irish conditions prompting mass movement of equal numbers of Ulstermen and Munstermen found expression in new tensions when they met in North America.

As many as 450,000 Ulster emigrants entered North America between 1800 and 1845. Between 1803 and 1819 they accounted for 65 per cent and possibly 75 per cent of the total Irish immigration, although after 1820 they fell to 60 per cent of Canadian arrivals and 40 per cent of American.[1] But total numbers were always increasing, and this new Ulster migration, which by 1845 was twice that of the entire eighteenth century, left many traces, most visibly in Ontario and Pennsylvania, although these were not microcosms of the whole. Emigrant letters, usually presbyterian, reveal poor, earnest, ambitious youths moving from job to job to better themselves.[2] Yet Ulster emigrants can be found in the less skilled jobs, which did not require literacy: half the Ulster workers on Canada's Rideau canal in 1829 were illiterate, and many of the labourers of the Chesapeake & Ohio and the Wabash & Erie canals were 'Far Downs' (*Fear an Dúin* or *Fear aduain*, County Down man or stranger, the Munster term for northerners). After 1815 migration became more frequent in all areas and social groups in Ulster. By 1830, most emigrants would have had some schooling even from those counties, such as Cavan and Londonderry, which had relatively low levels of literacy before 1834. Likewise, the percentage of all emigrants who were artisans, textile workers, professional people, and farmers with capital and families fell. Such farmers alone fell from 44 per cent of arrivals in the United States in 1819–20 (admitting that the poor were deterred in that year by financial crisis) to 15.8 per cent in New York, 1820–45.[3] In short, the Ulster migration still influenced the whole Irish migration, though it no longer shaped it.

The Ulster migration had more to do with transferring the sharp rivalries of early nineteenth-century Ireland to North America than the rising nationalism of Munster emigrants. Heavy numbers from Cavan, Monaghan, and Armagh, where protestants and catholics coexisted in large numbers in a contracting economy, sharpened craft competition in Philadelphia and competition for land in Ontario. However, the canal gang combats in 1834 and later in Ohio and Maryland show that regional factions were often non-religious: Munstermen anticipated scholarship by seeing catholics from Longford (which had the highest pre-famine emigration rate) as 'Far Downs', products of the northern migration zone. More predictable distinctions appeared among the literate leadership: one-third of 1,116 known members of the Boston Repeal Associa-

[1] Ó Gráda, op. cit., tables 5A and 5B, p. 126; Adams, *Ir. emigration to New World*, pp 120–21, 420–25, calculated against total flows; see above, pp 693, 700.
[2] Kerby A. Miller, *Emigrants and exiles* (Oxford and New York, 1985), pp 263–8; P.R.O.N.I.: Brice Black letters, 1821–8 (T3633); Wray letters, 1817–22 (T1727); Cooke letters, 1824–30 (T3592); John McBride letters, 1819–27 (T2613); McClorg letters, 1819–37 (T1227).
[3] Ó Gráda, op. cit., table 3, p. 125.

tion were from Ulster, chiefly from its catholic south and west.[1] The Ancient Order of Hibernians, established in St James's Church in New York in early 1836, was authorised by twelve signatories, all resident in Ulster, north Connacht, and north Leinster, and presumably Defenders. Among the Ulster protestants the Orange Order was established in New York (*c.* 1820), the Gideonite society (1829) and Orange Association (*c.* 1830) in Philadelphia, and in Boston the Irish Protestant Association (*c.* 1835). As with the Hibernians, a constructive outlet for Ulster traditions lay in reinforcing orthodoxy. After the congregational–presbyterian plan of union in 1800, a combination of New York's excited 'new measures' and New England's liberal emphasis on human benevolence and will threatened the Westminster confession. Princeton University then reestablished Old School presbyterianism with support from both ministers and kirk sessions from the so-called Pittsburgh–Philadelphia axis. Just as Irish catholic immigrants helped their bishops against fractious trustees, so new Ulster immigrants, many influenced by Henry Cooke's revival, made possible a successful redefinition of orthodoxy against American experimentalism, though this split the church from 1837 (informally from 1828).[2]

Those with small capital might purchase farms in settled Scotch-Irish areas. In the woodlands of the Great Lakes basin, farms could be pioneered over several years for a minimum of $500, a sum within the reach of those who brought £20 to £50 or saved their first year's wages. Ulster protestant group-settlements developed here, as at Tyrone in upstate New York, Lima and Koshkonong in southern Wisconsin, and in Allen County, Indiana, with some ranging outside this region, as those who pioneered Staggers Point in north-east Texas. But individual farm acquisition seems to have been more usual. The most concentrated settlement was on the north-west side of Lakes Ontario and Erie, amid the rolling post-glacial topography of Upper Canada, with its rich woodland soils.

Nicholas Davin's later designation of 'the Irish period' in Canadian history (1824–54)[3] was well based and threw much light on the belief of most Victorian Irishmen that the Irish could prosper in the empire and that their preference was for a 'Canadian' (imperial) rather than 'American' (republican) model for Anglo-Irish agreement. Here, too, strong intra-Irish differences invigorated, rather than paralysed, their shared polity. From 120,000 to 134,000 Irish-born and their offspring lived in Ontario in 1842, over one-quarter of its population and twice as numerous as either the English, Scottish, or American elements. Two-thirds were protestant, largely from Ulster. In 1851–61, three-quarters of the Irish-born were rural dwellers, both catholic and protestant, although later catholic newcomers did settle disproportionately in towns. Settling in a

[1] Calculated from table x in Oscar Handlin, *Boston's immigrants 1790–1880* (2nd rev. ed., New York, 1972), p. 247.

[2] M. W. Armstrong and others, *The presbyterian enterprise* (Philadelphia, 1956), pp 146–71.

[3] Nicholas Flood Davin, *The Irishman in Canada* (Toronto, 1877; reprint, Shannon, 1970), pp 582, 589.

common zone, twenty to sixty miles inland from the developed lakeshore area, the two groups took separate but contiguous blocks in each township, sometimes deliberately 'lined out' as in Mono and Emily. In County Armagh, population densities varied from 383 to 453 per square mile from 1821 to 1851, but in Ontario similar community tensions persisted although there was plenty of land (the population density was only 30 per square mile). Ulster protestants and southern Irish, however, used the same techniques of farming, but gradually learnt Canadian innovations. Better initial land grants may explain the view of the former that they were better farmers, a view unshared by Davin and unsupported by the evidence.[1]

The Irish were prominent in politics, although their share of power was not commensurate with their numbers. They shared a common outlook and created a viable party by the 1820s (which survived and even linked the coming of separate Orange and Green organisations), in spite of being busy settling new farms, divided by religion, and grateful for their land. As earlier in the United States, this coalition had its roots in a common antagonism towards an established ruling party, unresponsive, if not hostile, to their claims, and controlled by the high-tory 'family compact'. The opposition was inspired and organised by an immigrant anglican Irish connection and their offspring, with roots in the Volunteer politics of Munster and in a whiggish Irish patriotism, not unsympathetic to Great Britain, that had opposed both union and rebellion at home. Its progenitor was Robert Baldwin, editor of the *Cork Volunteer Journal*, who came to Ontario in 1799 with his son, Dr William Baldwin, effective founder of the group; others were William's Canadian-born son, Robert Baldwin; Robert Baldwin Sullivan, a nephew from Bandon; Cork-born Connell Baldwin, a catholic, and cousin of William Baldwin and of Daniel O'Connell; and their immigrant kinsmen, Joseph and William Willcocks, who established the first opposition paper in 1807. By the 1820s this group took the view that only responsible government could prevent executive reaction from playing into the hands of the radical 'American' party, a view similar to that of Robert Baldwin senior on Irish affairs in the 1790s.[2]

By contrast, Orangeism in Upper Canada, led by Wexford-born Ogle Gowan and other southern Irish protestants, grew rapidly in the Irish settlements, numbering 154 lodges with about 14,000 members by 1834. The need for society and mutual aid in the outback, the absence of old ties, and traditional religious and political motives encouraged its growth. Neither the first

[1] D. H. Akenson, *The Irish in Ontario* (Montreal, 1984), pp 14–28, 139–282; William J. Smyth, 'The Irish in mid-nineteenth-century Ontario' in *Ulster Folklife*, xxiii (1977), pp 97–106; John Mannion, *Irish settlements in eastern Canada* (Toronto, 1974), pp 15–18, 40–43, 74–86, 106–16, 159–74; Davin, op. cit., pp 245, 309, 359–60. There were also 43,942 Irish-born in Lower Canada (Quebec) in 1844: see Patrick M. Redmond, *Irish life in rural Quebec: a history of Frampton* (Montreal, 1981).

[2] H. H. Guest, 'Upper Canada's first political party' in *Ontario History*, liv (1963), pp 296 ff; Graeme Patterson, 'Whiggery, nationality, and the Upper Canadian reform tradition' in *Canadian Historical Review*, lvi (1975), pp 25–44.

American settlers nor the 'family compact', much less the liberal Irish reformers, had time for so divisive a loyalism. But the Order, encouraged from London, helped Orangemen to get the better lands through official connections, drew in Ulster settlers, and emboldened the 'blazers' who 'lined off' catholic districts.[1] Yet Ogle Gowan shared the Baldwins' antipathy to both the 'family compact' and the democratic radicals, and their desire for responsible government. Together, their loose 'Orange and Green' partnership temporarily abandoned reform to outflank both extremes, and then joined to raise troops to quell the revolt of William Lyon Mackenzie in 1837. As Lt-col. Charles Grey wrote to his father, Lord Grey, 'there was not a single instance of an Irishman being suspected. . . . Protestant and catholic were equally loyal.'[2] Perhaps these shifts reflect successful local drives for power by the incoming protestant Irish in a fluid society where both organised self-advancement and a façade of tolerance were not inconsistent.[3]

Robert Baldwin converted Lord Durham to the idea of responsible government during his term as governor-general; but Durham's proposal that French Lower Canada be united with Upper Canada (enacted in 1840)[4] changed Orange politics and divided the Irish. Gowan sought to exclude Quebec's catholics from power and joined the older tories through the United Empire Association, until he accepted John Macdonald's need for conservative Francophone support, and split the Orange Order.[5] But most Irish, including many Ulster presbyterians, believing in responsible government and the voluntary principle in education, also accepted Baldwin's reform party's championing of Quebecois rights within the framework of the union. Indeed Irish-born merchants in Montreal, such as Thomas Holmes and Francis Hincks, provided important links, since most non-Irish English-speakers in Quebec were tory, whereas through the nineteenth century most Quebec Irish identified with provincial rights. In 1847 Robert Baldwin, Hincks, and Louis Lafontaine won 57 seats in the united assembly of the former provinces of Upper and Lower Canada, compared with the tories' 27; and effective responsible government, including Quebec influence, came on their forming a government in February 1848. Hincks, noted for his broad sympathies, succeeded Baldwin as chief minister in 1851 and held office until 1854. The intra-Irish appeal of reform politics and their impact on Ireland await study; but the clarity was blurred by the rival impulses in Orangeism, which in the early 1840s sought the formation of a mounted police to disarm Irish canalers and an inquiry into public contracts that benefited Irish catholic businessmen.[6] Yet

---

[1] C. J. Houston and W. J. Smyth, *The sash Canada wore* (Toronto, 1980), pp 15–36, 86, 112–13, 127–31, 141.
[2] Lt-col. Charles Grey to Earl Grey, 11 Aug. 1838 (William Ormsby (ed.), *Crisis in the Canadas, 1838–39: the Grey journals and letters* (Toronto, 1964), p. 98).
[3] D. H. Akenson, *The Irish in Ontario* (Montreal, 1984), pp 169–97.
[4] 3 & 4 Vict., c. 35 (23 July 1840).   [5] Houston and Smyth, op. cit., p. 147.
[6] Davin, op. cit., pp 491–3, 520–21.

the character of some newer immigrants, such as the Bytown (now Ottawa) timber workers under Peter Aylen, who fought a 'Shiners war' to gain local power, caused even the settled catholic Irish to distance themselves unheroically from their rowdier fellows.[1] As in the United States, their place in reform politics partly depended on deferring to protestant leadership, and intra-Irish cooperation only partially survived the coming of mass catholic politics among O'Connellite immigrants and the Quebecois after 1840. In the more remote Maritime Provinces, less threatened by American or French-Canadian interests, Irish-born editors and politicians, such as Lawrence O'Connor Doyle and Edward Whelan, more safely organised the Irish in the reform interest against the local 'family compacts', and—like the Baldwins—combined this with support for repeal at home.[2] Enough of these traditions survived to entice Thomas D'Arcy Magee north from the United States in 1857, to keep most Canadian-Irish out of fenianism and assist the birth of confederation in 1867. Ontario did, nevertheless, suggest that even a modest catholic use of representative politics could provoke a tory realignment among some Ulster protestants.

Indeed, even in Pennsylvania there were vertical combinations of Ulster immigrants. In mill villages south of Philadelphia, Samuel Riddle from Belfast and Bernard McCready employed large numbers of protestant newcomers at Rockdale; while at Kellyville and Cobb's Crook, Dennis Kelly from Donegal built catholic settlements around his mills.[3] Yet a common interest in securing protection for textiles united them all in favour of Henry Clay's American system (of which Mathew Carey was one of the theorists), and delayed and partly averted the intra-Irish conflicts that partisan rhetoric and new interests increasingly caused between protestants and catholics in New York as in Ontario. Whether these movements can be separated from the sharper distinctions in Ireland in the 1820s is questionable. In Canada Sir Richard Bonnycastle distinguished old settlers, including catholics ('by no means the worst') from newcomers, 'Orangemen . . . who defy the pope and are loyal to the backbone' and 'repealers, sure of immediate wealth' who 'kick up a deuce of a row; for two shillings and sixpence is paid for a day's labour, . . . a hopeless week's fortune in Ireland'.[4] Suggestively, he linked the new tensions with economic, religious, and political changes. Renewal and revivalism were then transatlantic forces among both catholics and protestants. The elements that

---

[1] Michael S. Cross, 'The Shiners' war: social violence in the Ottawa valley in the 1830s' in *Canadian Historical Review*, liv (1973), pp 1–26; Ruth Bleasdale, 'Class conflict on the canals of Upper Canada in the 1840s' in *Labour/Le Travailleur*, vii (1981), pp 9–39.

[2] *Dictionary of Canadian Biography*, ix (1861–70), pp 224–7, 828–35; *Nation* (Dublin), 25 Feb. 1843, pp 317–18.

[3] A. F. C. Wallace, *Rockdale: the growth of an American village in the early industrial revolution* (New York, 1980), pp 37, 40, 43–4, 98–101; Dennis Clark, 'Kellyville: immigrant enterprise' in *Pennsylvania History*, xxxix (1972), pp 40–49.

[4] Quoted in Davin, op. cit., p. 401.

produced the self-conscious 'Scotch-Irish' after the famine were already under way by 1840.

Apart from Ulster, catholics came from two distinct regions before 1845. Between 5 and 22 per cent of the 1801–21 birth cohorts emigrated or migrated from Sligo, Leitrim, Roscommon, Longford (with the highest percentage), and Louth. Likewise 2.5 per cent of the same generation emigrated from County Cork and surrounding areas, except Kerry. Most left between 1821 and 1841, not all for North America (though but few to other Irish counties).[1] All came from areas that strongly supported Daniel O'Connell and were troubled by agrarian disturbances. Canniness, organisation, and a predisposition to regard livelihoods (however simplistically) as threatened by protestant power made such people less amenable to gentlemanly 'Old Irish' direction. Experience in North America confirmed their outlook; yet charting their movements is difficult, for only in Newfoundland were they numerous enough to shape politics. In 1811–16 and 1825–33 two waves of small farmers' sons, fishermen-farmers, and cottiers from Wexford, Waterford, and Tipperary intermarried with existing Irish settlers to produce by 1836 a catholic population of 27,322, compared with 30,766 protestants of largely English descent. From 1784 to 1893 the see of St John's was held by Irish-born bishops; the Irish gained many seats on the governor's council and in the assembly after the 1832 reform. An attempt to upset the 1832 reform in 1842 by Lord Stanley prompted Daniel O'Connell to warn Bishop Michael Fleming of a bid 'to transfer all power to the aristocracy or monopoly party'.[2]

Almost three thousand miles south-west, in Matamoros in Mexico, an Irish merchant community was established by 1829, pointing to extensive, although thin, settlement along the gulf coast. From the 1750s, men from south-eastern Ireland, often connected with continental trade or armed service, found their way to French Louisiana. Spanish control was consolidated after 1769 by Meath-born governor Alexander O'Reilly, who favoured established and new Irish families against the Voltairean creoles. Merchants such as John Fitzpatrick, Oliver Pollock, John Mullanphy, and the Forstalls built a network for the Irish who came to St Louis and New Orleans after the United States's acquisition of Louisiana in 1803.[3] Four such Gulf merchants, John McGloin, James McMullen, James Power, and James Hewetson, received *empresario* (colonisation) grants from Mexico in 1828 for two vast areas between the Neuces and San Antonio rivers. The first two brought Irish-Americans to their San Patricio colony; the latter two, between 1829 and 1834, brought Wexford

---

[1] S. H. Cousens, 'The regional variations in emigration from Ireland between 1821 and 1841' in *Transactions and Papers of the Institute of British Geographers*, xxxvii (1965), figs 2 and 3, pp 19, 20.

[2] O'Connell to Fleming, 2 June 1842 (*O'Connell corr.*, vii, 162–3); John F. Mannion (ed.), *The peopling of Newfoundland* (St John's, 1977), pp 7–10; Arthur P. Monahan, 'Canada' in Corish, *Ir. catholicism*, vi, fasc. 3, pp 2–8.

[3] G. C. Din, 'Spain's immigration policy in Louisiana' in *Southwestern Historical Quarterly*, lxxvi (1973), pp 255–76; E. F. Niehaus, *The Irish in New Orleans, 1800–1860* (New York, 1976), pp 3–22.

settlers direct to their Refugio colony. These colonists supported Texan independence, fighting in the battles of Goliad and Coleto Creek. Climate and distance deterred many from following them, but like the Newfoundland Irish, they preserved in isolation the social and spiritual discipline of rural south-east Ireland.[1] Other knots of Irish in the gulf region were too scattered to cohere (the presence or absence of priests determining survival or disappearance). Paradoxically, the Old Irish merchants of New Orleans, St Louis, Natchez, and Mobile, unusual in being largely catholic, ensured that in a pseudo-aristocratic South catholics lacked neither respect nor polished leadership, even as the plainer immigrants were ushering the church away from creole forms toward ordinary, even plebeian forms more suited to the American era.[2]

Irish cattle farming was skilfully transferred to the hot, dry bluestem prairies and mesquite savannahs of southern Texas and to the moist cool shores of eastern Newfoundland.[3] While most Irish went into cities and towns, more settled on the land than is usually supposed, entering as always the growth sectors of the American economy. In 1820, 72 per cent of adult Americans were engaged in agriculture; by 1860, this had fallen to 59 per cent, but actual numbers had tripled to 6.2 million.[4] It was a farmers' age, as the new transport networks linked expanding acreages and growing markets. Contemporary letters and settlement patterns show that many ante-bellum immigrants sought farms, if only after trying other things. Success came most often in developing zones, changing by decade: in central Pennsylvania and upstate New York in the 1820s and 1830s, in Illinois, Michigan, Iowa, and Wisconsin in the 1840s, and in Kansas, Nebraska, and Minnesota in 1855–75. In 1835 Tyrone Power noted that almost everywhere 'the provident amongst the exiles ... form an important portion of the freemen of the soil'.[5] There were 50,000 Irish-born catholics in the scattered parishes of the Albany area in 1845, and as many in the Buffalo area; both areas were erected into dioceses in 1847. In 1834, Bishop Francis Kenrick worried that only five places outside Philadelphia enjoyed permanent catholic services; by 1845, five-sixths of his seventy-seven churches were outside the city (apart from those erected into the Pittsburgh diocese in 1843), in mill villages as well as rural townships. Some group-farm colonies were set up, as in the Bombay, Java, and Hogansburg townships in New York after 1825–9.

As with Ulstermen, the settlement then shifted to the Great Lakes–Mississippi basin. In 1850 Irish settlers owned one-third of Dubuque County,

[1] John B. Flannery, *The Irish Texans* (Austin, 1980), pp 31–89.

[2] Dennis Clark, 'The South's Irish catholics: a case of cultural confinement' in R. M. Miller and J. L. Wakelyn (ed.), *Catholics in the Old South* (Macon, Ga., 1983), pp 195–210.

[3] Ada L. K. Newton, 'The Anglo-Irish [*recte* English-speaking Irish] house of the Rio Grande' in *Pioneer America*, v (1973), pp 33–8; John Mannion, *Irish settlements in Eastern Canada* (Toronto, 1974), pp 27–8, 63, 66–8, 73, 170.

[4] *Historical statistics of the United States to 1970*, series D 75–84, p. 134.

[5] Tyrone Power, *Impressions of America during the years 1833, 1834, and 1835* (2 vols, London, 1836), ii, 348.

Iowa, establishing townships such as the neighbouring Garryowen. In 1850 there were but ten Irish paupers in the 'canal belt' crossing Indiana diagonally, and 53 per cent of 1,776 Irish-born household heads were farmers. In such areas, 'the proportion of successful farmers among [the Irish] is as high as among the natives and English stock'.[1] Wisconsin evidence confirms the view of Thomas Mooney that agriculture held the best that America then offered the Irish. In 1847–8 Rev. John O'Hanlon, chaplain to established farmer communities in Missouri, was worried at the ignorance, aimlessness, and dejection of the less prepared, but noticed the success of others in wheat, maize, and stock production. To James Hack Tuke and Charles Casey, the efficient and well liked Irish farmers did much to dispel the stigmas of prejudice.[2]

Deforestation rivalled public works in providing mobile manual work and a distribution grid for settlement. It took thirty-two days to clear one acre of forest. Over a hundred million acres were cleared between 1800 and 1850, another 40 million acres in the 1850s, preceding the spread of farming from western New York to western Wisconsin. Many farmers employed woodsmen for land clearance, but timber companies used more. Well into the 1850s America built itself with timber and heated itself with wood. Irish lumbermen, many first trained in Canada, had a better entrée into local habits, society, and farm practices than did segregated canalers, and they followed the trade until they had enough to take a forest farm. Others went into timber-milling or building. From Maine to Michigan, they provided much of the folk culture of American lumbering and helped to incline its politics—virulently Jacksonian—towards a melodrama of 'sweats' against 'wits'.[3] Taken together, a much higher proportion than W. B. Adams's conjectured 10 per cent of pre-famine immigrants worked on the land as farmers, labourers, jobbing or market-gardeners, dairymen, cattlemen, and lumbermen. Census takers' insistence on recording but one occupation per person (as in Ireland) obscured the full picture of the immigrant rural economy. Only in the South did several attempts to replace slaves with cheaper Irish labour fail: the Irish rejected the loss of status entailed.[4]

These patterns frustrate any attempt to see the American-Irish as a tight proletarian corollary to the rise of North American capitalism. Yet the shift from Ireland caught tens of thousands in an exploited, if fluid, dependence.

[1] Joseph Schaefer, *Social history of American agriculture* (New York, 1936), p. 212.

[2] Merle Curti and others, *The making of an American community* (Stanford, 1969), pp 93–4, 177, 182–7, 191, 196; Thomas Mooney, *Nine years in America* (Dublin, 1850), pp 19, 37, 40; J. H. Tuke, *A visit to Connaught in the autumn of 1847* (2nd ed., London, 1848), pp 13, 43–4; Charles Casey, *Two years on a farm of Uncle Sam* (London, 1852), pp 222–4, 241.

[3] Michael Williams, 'Clearing the United States forests: the pivotal years' in *Journal of Historical Geography*, viii (1982), pp 12–28; James A. King, *The Irish lumberman-farmer* (Lafayette, Cal., 1982), pp 65–8, 114–25; Lee Benson, *The concept of Jacksonian Democracy* (Princeton, 1961), pp 203–5.

[4] U. B. Phillips, *Life and labor in the Old South* (Boston, 1963), pp 253–4; Sir Charles Lyell, *Travels in North America* (2 vols, London, 1845), i, 131.

Already the Irish were fragmented by place, task, and status, quite apart from religious differences, and many newcomers were at a disadvantage in a country of strenuous men on the make. The very successes of some sharpened the contrasts between them and the failures, and obscured, even among radical theorists, the engines of such relative debasement: past poverty and its habits, harsh and debasing early labour, low pay and loneliness, and the high cost of family maintenance. While pointing this out, Irish commentators conceded that most Americans judged men by success, and not by nationality.[1] They did not pretend that foresight, industry, and initiative were tricks; they shared the century's respect for them, but instead argued that the poorer Irish should not be abused or underpaid simply for not having them. Indeed, precisely because the overall American view of the Irish was good, failure to concede their specific economic handicaps led to easy acquiescence in their condition, whereby after 1830 the majority seem 'to toil without ceasing . . ., but a very limited proportion . . . ever reach to mediocrity, much less to affluence or station'.[2] While the 'respectable portion are more respected than the natives of any other country and amalgamate soonest with the Americans . . ., the lowest orders generally bear a bad character, particularly in New York'.[3] Inundated with three-quarters of the Irish arriving after 1830, that city made such problems especially visible and presaged the post-famine years. Thomas Mooney believed it had 80,000 Irish in 1843 out of a population of 400,000. Philadelphia, though displaced as the first Irish city of America, also reflected such problems, though less sharply: in 1833 Mathew Carey believed that a quarter of its inhabitants were poor, and that these were largely Irish.[4]

In both cities the Irish unwittingly facilitated the shift from independent workshops with well paid craftsmen to large concentrations of employees in both out-work and factories. Those who examined this in the early 1840s urged their fellow countrymen to acquire skills that could not be degraded by technical change, but here native Americans were well established as cabinet-makers, ships' carpenters, machinists, metal workers, and quality tailors, leaving the Irish to mass employment in textiles, construction, haulage, docking, and (in Massachusetts) shoe-making. Entrepreneurs found that rationalised piece-work, by ignoring distinctions between masters and journeymen, led to success in the wider markets created by canals, roads, and the railways. In reply, workers created America's first large-scale labour movement, leading to the world's first working men's parties, in New York City and Philadelphia in 1828–9. Their defeat revived earlier tactics of using city-wide unions to secure better wages and hours by strikes and to gain the ten-hour day by seeking

[1] Patrick O'Reilly, *Advice and guide to emigrants going to the United States of America* (Dublin, 1834), pp 12–14, 20–21, 44; Rev. John O'Hanlon, *The Irish emigrant's guide*, ed. E. J. Maguire (New York, 1976), pp 216–24; Francis Wyse, *America* (3 vols, London, 1846), iii, 3, 26–32.

[2] Francis Wyse, op. cit., iii, 31; cf. below, pp 723–4.

[3] Walter Myler, *Reminiscences of a trans-Atlantic traveller, 1831–2* (Dublin, 1835), pp 20–21.

[4] Mathew Carey, *Appeal to the wealthy of the land* (Philadelphia, 1833), p. 7.

pledges of support from local politicians. The first phase was almost wholly unconnected with the Irish and the second included some leaders of Irish extraction (such as John Commerford, John Farrel, and Thomas Hogan) in organising the inter-city National Trades Union in 1834, but usually the incoming Irish, unfamiliar with past patterns, and notably less interested in their own crafts as such, took what they could and accepted the new 'boss' system as the norm. Farrel led the Irish weavers of Kensington to join Philadelphia's General Trades' Union in 1835–6, but the recession of 1837–43 broke this early alliance and religious loyalties reasserted themselves, as feared by labour leaders.[1] The riots of 1844 were a serious setback for such attempts to unionise the Irish and to control the paradox of the Irish weakening traditional labour even as they invigorated management and output. Afterwards union leaders drew in their horns, restricted the membership of their unions, and left the unskilled Irish to informal, and often violent, activity.

Outside the trade unions, there was increasing organisation before the 1840s. The catholic population, now largely Irish, doubled from about 300,000 to 660,000 between 1830 and 1840, and rose to about 1,100,000 by 1845.[2] New York city, which erected only four parishes between 1785 and 1829, added seven for the Irish between 1833 and 1845 (as well as four German and one French). Philadelphia's loss of primacy is shown by the fact that it erected none from 1834 to 1839, but six from 1839 to 1845. But such parochial provision lagged behind immigration. By contrast, dioceses were erected boldly, following the full pre-famine dispersal. To Charleston, Richmond, and Cincinnati (1820–21) were added St Louis and New Orleans in 1826, Mobile in 1829, Detroit, Vincennes, Dubuque, Natchez, and Nashville in 1833–7, and Chicago, Milwaukee, Little Rock, Pittsburgh, and Hartford in 1843.[3] Only Little Rock seems inexplicable in terms of Irish settlement.

More than organisation was involved. When in 1829 the first provincial council was convened at Baltimore, the dominant personalities were not Irish: for example, James Whitfield, archbishop of Baltimore, who presided, was English; apart from an Irish bishop in Philadelphia, the other sees were held by French, Italians, and Americans. Whitfield wished Rome to know of his opposition to 'warm-headed' Irish colleagues, with 'strong Irish predilections in favour of Irish bishops and Irish discipline for the U. States'.[4] But within a few years the most populous sees had ignored his advice: the scholarly and prudent Dubliner Francis Kenrick was in effect bishop of Philadelphia from

[1] David Montgomery, 'The shuttle and the cross: weavers and artisans in the Kensington riots of 1844' in *Journal of Social History*, v (1972), pp 417–21.
[2] Gerald Shaughnessy, *Has the immigrant kept the faith?* (New York, 1925; reprint, 1969), p. 125; R. F. Hueston, *The catholic press and nativism, 1840–1860* (New York, 1976), p. 34.
[3] Theodore Roemer, *The catholic church in the United States* (St Louis, 1950), pp 151–2, 164–5, 182–5, 209–10.
[4] Whitfield to Nicholas Wiseman (rector of English College, Rome), 6 June 1833 (Thomas T. McAvoy, *A history of the catholic church in the United States* (Notre Dame, Ind., 1969), p. 130).

1830 to 1851; the dynamic and imprudent Ulsterman John Hughes was coadjutor of New York from 1838 to 1842 and archbishop from 1842 to 1864; John Purcell became bishop of Cincinnati in 1833 (serving until 1883), his early years there being energetic and able; William Quarter, born in King's County, was first bishop of the Chicago diocese between 1843 and 1848; John England continued in Charleston until 1842, its three lone parishes signs that the Irish were flowing elsewhere; Michael O'Connor went to Pittsburgh as its first bishop in 1843. Thus by the famine the major centres of Irish presence and future growth were under Irish bishops long resident in America and familiar with its ways, yet at ease with their immigrant fellow countrymen.[1] It was a timely alteration.

These bishops in turn accelerated the creation of a distinct Irish-American culture that was urban and catholic. The press supports this: early Irish journals had been chiefly political, but between 1836 and 1845 explicitly catholic periodicals increased from six to fifteen, notably Patrick Donahoe's Boston *Pilot* (1838), the White brothers' New York *Freeman's Journal* (1840), and Bishop O'Connor's Pittsburgh *Catholic* (1844). Kenrick and Purcell put their brothers, who were priests, in charge of the Philadelphia *Catholic Herald* (founded 1833) and Cincinnati *Catholic Telegraph* (founded 1831). The journals were 'calculated to explain our doctrines, protect our feelings, and increase our devotion',[2] as the bishops wrote in 1833, the second object being extended to include O'Connellite nationalism and American aspirations after the narrowly religious papers had failed. At the same time, the catholic school system was launched; twenty or so parish schools in New York City and Philadelphia reached at most a third of the children of Irish parents, with only 5,000 pupils or 8 per cent of total school enrolments in New York in 1840—a low proportion, yet one not equalled again until 1880.[3] Irish-born bishops, zealous for press and schools, coordinated their efforts at five provincial councils between 1829 and 1843 to attain them. If not general, the response of a minority community was considerable, suggesting much common agreement on the need for specific, distinctive, and costly initiatives. Open opposition to such schools increased their Irish appeal after 1843–4 and clarified the adjustments necessary between catholic, protestant, and secular views of education.

Other indications of Irish solidarity emerged, but without the permanence of catholic organisation. In each city, humdrum Irish clubs, armed militias, mutual-aid groups, cultural societies, and emigrant assistance charities now paralleled the exclusive societies of the 'Old Irish'. Boston, New York, and New Orleans had units of Montgomery Guards in the 1830s, named after the

---

[1] E.g. Patrick O'Kelly, *Advice and guide to emigrants. . .* (Dublin, 1834), pp 7, 37.

[2] Peter Guilday (ed.), *The national pastorals of the American hierarchy, 1792–1919* (Washington, D.C., 1923), p. 68.

[3] Jay Dolan, *The immigrant church: New York's Irish and German catholics, 1815–1865* (Baltimore, 1975), p. 105; Diane Ravitch, *The great school wars: New York City, 1805–1973* (New York, 1974), p. 405; James F. Connelly (ed.), *The history of the archdiocese of Philadelphia* (Philadelphia, 1976), p. 171.

County-Dublin-born hero of 1775; these cities created or revived Hibernian or Shamrock benevolent societies between 1839 and 1844 as the recession changed priorities; Boston's Hibernian Lyceum, Hartford's Hibernian Institute, and New York's Carroll Club served the bookish; the Irish in New York city also created provident and temperance societies. Indeed, the Boston Irish organised an Irish Temperance Society in 1836, two years before Fr Mathew's in Cork. Among all these, only the Irish Emigrant Aid Society, founded by Archbishop Hughes in 1841, the Irish Emigrants' Society of 1844 (later the Emigrant Savings Bank), and the Ancient Order of Hibernians of 1836 survived—all linked to church circles in New York city. Much else failed, such as a movement for catholic adult education. The young Thomas D'Arcy McGee, returning from Boston to Ireland in 1845, concluded that much organisation was born of a false sense of inferiority that fled from improvement, and failed because Irishmen were 'too independent with each other, and not sufficiently so with other classes'.[1] Yet the extension of prejudice drove immigrants with gifts of leadership and education to work with their fellow Irishmen; whereas before 1835 visitors like Tyrone Power and Walter Myler assumed that prejudice existed against only the poorer Irish, afterwards even suave sojourners such as Thomas Colley Grattan and Francis Wyse noted that all Irishmen now encountered some dislike.[2] As yet, the conditions to produce Irish organisations that were not linked to religion had not fully developed.

For churchmen, editors, and laymen saw the new country in a more optimistic light before 1840 than at any time until the 1890s. To Alexis de Tocqueville, catholics were the most republican and democratic group in politics, but the most deferential in doctrine. Though fearing a certain Pelagian self-reliance in its culture, Francis Kenrick assumed this in his seven-volume application (1839–43) of Ligourian theology to American circumstance.[3] As a lower-class religious minority, catholics had much to gain from republican institutions and the separation of church and state. To de Tocqueville, the religious principle moderated the race for comfort, and joined together men divided by an obsessive individuality. Roman Catholicism—certain, clear, and equal in its criteria of salvation—best performed these functions, for it was beyond the reach of pantheism and chaotic subjectivity, in a society of equals bent on self-improvement.[4] Less boldly, most catholics experienced a natural connection between faith, everyday life, and politics, if few shared Bishop John England's enthusiasm for America as a field for evangelisation.[5] Common and

[1] George Potter, *To the golden door* (Boston and Toronto, 1960), p. 434.

[2] Walter Myler, *Reminiscences of a trans-Atlantic traveller, 1831-2* (Dublin, 1835), p. 21; Francis Wyse, *America* (3 vols, London, 1846), iii, 3–4, 33, 201; T. C. Grattan, *Civilized America* (2 vols, London, 1859), ii, 27–8.

[3] Michael Moran, 'The writings of Francis Patrick Kenrick, archbishop of Baltimore' in *Records of the American Catholic Historical Society*, xli (1930), p. 245.

[4] Alexis de Tocqueville, *Democracy in America*, ed. J. P. Mayer (New York, 1969), pp 287–90, 445–51.

[5] Patrick Carey, *An immigrant bishop* (Yonkers, 1982), p. 146.

statute law, popular custom, and personal and property rights were largely congruent with catholic ideas; jurists upheld a generalised Christianity as the civic religion of the republic, and a 'common sense' natural law as the basis of constitutional and legal reasoning. Popular morality in the northern states respected feminine virtue and asserted family values to a degree that astounded continental Europeans and reassured the Irish, even if men's restless ambition did weaken the substance of social and family life. Waves of popular anti-catholicism, still limited, broke as much on the decencies of American protest-ants as on the example of the settled Irish: in 1836 Maria Monk's fabricated *Awful disclosures* evoked an immediate and carefully researched rebuttal from William Stone, editor of New York's *Commercial Appeal* (though it did go on to sell 300,000 copies by 1860, becoming the '*Uncle Tom's cabin* of Know Nothingism').[1] If Charlestown's Ursuline convent was burnt down in 1834 by New England working men, hundreds of other churches and schools were built without opposition, even with encouragement. Andrew Jackson, attuned to such currents, safely made Roger B. Taney (legal adviser to the catholic hierarchy) attorney general in 1831, and Martin Van Buren promoted him to the chief-justiceship in 1837. Indeed, ordinary Irishmen tended to overlook the protestant context of American law, custom, and behaviour (as continental European visitors did not). They thus ascribed reaction against them to evangelical revival alone, failing to see the latter's intimate connections with American culture. Likewise, they overestimated the future convergence between American culture and catholic beliefs: the Boston *Pilot* prophesied in 1843 that 'catholicism will obtain an ascendancy over all the minds in the land ...', while the Cincinnati *Catholic Telegraph* asserted that by 1885 that city would be 'a little Rome in the west'.[2] Thus the very optimism of the 1830s fostered impolitic expectations, soon sharply reversed, and also emboldened catholics to an extent that made the older mediating role of Irish protestants awkward, though hardly superfluous.

The impact of American politics had similar effects. Grasped in an initial mood of cheerful—at times ructious—participation, party activities brought home the Irish presence to others, and by causing reaction played into the hands of those who wanted to win over various constituencies by anti-Irish rhetoric.[3] They also taught the Irish that—like it or not—their secular fortunes, too, were collective as well as individual. Irish-American nationalism pre-supposed these lessons; the expansion of church and community networks was aided by the rise of an Irish-American politics, with voting power used for local advantages. Party managers, especially Democrats, mobilised Irish catholic

[1] Ray Allen Billington, *The protestant crusade, 1800–1860* (Chicago, 1964), pp 99–107.
[2] *Pilot*, 16 Sept. 1843, and *Catholic Telegraph*, 30 Dec. 1843, quoted in R. F. Hueston, *The catholic press and nativism, 1840–1860* (New York, 1976), pp 38–9.
[3] Blarney O'Democrat [pseud.], *The Irish-office-hunter-oniad* (New York, 1838) [Library of Congress]; T. C. Grattan, op. cit., ii, 7–8, 29–32; Francis J. Grund, *Aristocracy in America* [1839] (New York, 1959), pp 50–51.

voters more readily, if subordinately, when close elections and high turnouts (reaching 78 per cent of those eligible by 1840) drove competing parties to secure every possible follower. To the attractions of the 1820s—franchise extension, abolition of religious tests, easy naturalisation, the cult of the 'Irish-American' Jackson—were added Working Men's Party reforms belatedly espoused by the Democrats: mechanics' lien laws, free public education, the ten-hour day on public works, and the abolition of imprisonment for debt; all important to poorer men.[1] The long resistance of the New England and the southern seaboard states to granting full civic rights for foreign-born, unpropertied, catholic, and migratory males kept the earlier slights and issues alive, for the Irish were often all four. Moreover, the anti-elitist and anti-monopoly rhetoric of the Jacksonians, especially when aimed at the Second Bank of the United States, renewed such resentments, and had an appeal for newcomers, attracted by O'Connell's attacks at home on the tory establishment and his efforts to break the power of the Bank of Ireland by establishing rival commercial, agricultural, and provincial banks. The new-style electioneering, with mass meetings, barnstorming, canvassing, and demagoguery appealed to immigrants who regarded politics as an outlet for participatory enthusiasm rather than as an object of systematic calculations (a Jacksonian spokesman believed the Irish correct but unattractive in their politics).[2] Local manœuvrings suggest that many did understand the stakes and strengthened the drift to the Democrats. In upstate New York, transplanted New Englanders grasped successfully at the opportunities of the region, but Irish competition was close. The former embraced the 'free grace' principle of revivalism, a general-access Calvinism, and the 'fair field and no favour' economic ideal, turning first to political anti-freemasonry (linked there with anti-catholicism) and thence to the Whig party. Ulster protestant immigrants, and more slowly the settled Ulster-Americans of Ulster and Orange Counties, found this new politics congenial.[3] The counter-coalition of poorer farmers, unrevived protestants, old New Yorker families, private bankers, freethinkers, lumbermen, and Irish catholics formed logically enough. The Democrat Martin Van Buren opposed Irish enfranchisement in 1821, supported it in 1826, and won catholic support as a result. In New York city, the old Irish merchant community and unrevived protestants drew newcomers to the Democrats and gave various minor offices to catholics by 1843, as well as the leading positions in the older Friendly Sons of St Patrick. But in the city, too, anti-catholicism was an ingredient in politics by 1835–6.[4] In short, a natural differentiation of communities in a helter-skelter world of

[1] Lee Benson, *The concept of Jacksonian Democracy* (Princeton, 1961), pp 33–5; Edward Pessen, *Most uncommon Jacksonians* (Albany, 1967), pp 9–33.
[2] Francis J. Grund, *The Americans* (2 vols, London, 1837), i, 96–8.
[3] Benson, op. cit., pp 136–9, 167–8, 183, 185.
[4] Walter Myler, *Reminiscences of a trans-Atlantic traveller, 1831–2* (Dublin, 1835), pp 88–9; Louis Dow Scisco, *Political nativism in New York State* (New York, 1901; reprint, 1968), pp 20–30.

rapid development produced a normal enough differentiation of voting patterns, and hence the emergence of a catholic Irish-American politics.

The schools question accelerated this; although the Democrats refused to support denominational schools, they benefited from the demand for them, being seen as more neutral than the rival Whigs, at least by the Irish. Catholics had two aims: to create parochial schools where they could and to make the public schools more acceptable by depriving them of specific protestant management, content, and tone. Any neat protestant–catholic division (much less agreement) was precluded by the complexity of the jurisdictions involved, by the varied and changing values of their residents, by the prohibition of public aid to religious schools as such, and by the huge numbers of children of Irish catholics attending public schools from poverty or preference. Catholics allied with less established protestants to secure non-denominational schools (as indeed they did also in Ontario in the 1820s);[1] this was another factor drawing them to the Democrats. Whigs, and later Republicans, tended to be more sympathetic to the popular feeling that believed a broadly evangelical curriculum to be American without being a formal establishment of religion. Strangely, yet logically, the first major crisis came when New York's Whigs, wishing to redress their over-reliance on such support, offered to create special public schools catering for minority convictions. Though sincere, Governor William Seward sought gains among the state's 120,000, largely Irish, catholics. Archbishop John Hughes in turn sought funds from the state assembly and the New York city council for his parochial schools, since few catholics could afford their fees, but both refused his request. Seward then replaced the city's protestant Public Schools Society with an elective school board responsive to catholics. The Democrats refused to back any aid schemes, yet held the Irish vote by patronage and tradition, while Hughes ran sufficient of his own candidates to irritate both parties. Affronted by these manœuvres, nativists organised their first major party and captured the city council in 1844, with strong immigrant Orange support.[2]

Seward and Hughes held that minority rights in a free republic ought to be given the fullest recognition, but failed to see that, for many Americans whose culture was inextricably bound to protestantism, such objectivity could seem 'a preconceived determination ... to put down the whole protestant religion as being sectarian', as the nativist party manifesto put it.[3] Thereafter, the new school board did indeed veer towards the secular moralism of Horace Mann, doctrinaire secretary of the Massachusetts school board (1837–48), but politicians saw to it that teaching appointments reflected local realities, aiding over 80 per cent of the city's children to attend common schools during the next half-

[1] Franklin A. Walker, *Catholic education and politics in Upper Canada* (Toronto, 1964).

[2] Vincent Lannie, *Public money and parochial education: Bishop Hughes, Governor Seward, and the New York school controversy* (Cleveland, 1968); Diane Ravitch, *The great school wars* (New York, 1974), pp 3–76; Scisco, op. cit., pp 39–46; Hueston, op. cit., pp 52–66.

[3] Scisco, op. cit., p. 41.

century. Such intangible results persuaded the hierarchy of the need for parochial schools by their first plenary council in 1851, and caused them to make such provision mandatory in every parish by the third plenary council in 1884, although never obligatory for all catholic children.[1]

In Philadelphia, where the schools issue was scarcely raised by catholics, severe riots followed in the wake of New York's disputes. In 1834 Pennsylvania had abolished its education system, provided by a protestant body, and replaced it with neutral public schools that attracted most catholics, as Bishop Francis Kenrick's seminary rector, Dr Edward Barron, wrote to Paul Cullen. Kenrick did not object to the common reading of the King James Bible in them, nor did he seek state aid, but on 12 November 1842 and 12 March 1844 he did request the city's school board to allow optional use of the Douai version of the Bible on request.[2] The American Protestant Association (to which most ministers belonged) and the local nativist party represented this as a full-scale threat to Bible education for American children. When they met on 3 May 1844 in Kensington, an Irish district, rioting broke out. During the next six days, nativists and Orangemen invaded the district, burning sixty catholic Irish houses and two churches; twelve nativists died in an attack on the Hibernian volunteer firehouse. In July, rioting was renewed in the Southwark district, the St Philip Neri's church was attacked, and at least thirteen were killed in clashes with state militia. Although almost all the dead were native Americans, these incidents made a deep impression on Philadelphia's Irish parishes (the German ones had been unmolested). In New York, plans for mass agitation were called off when Archbishop Hughes warned that the city would be burnt if a single church were attacked. Clearly, combustible men, rather than the progress of events, made Philadelphia the flash-point over schools. Heavy Irish immigration, bringing with it job rivalry and sectarian tension, too few police, the established pattern of anti-abolitionist violence (countenanced by the propertied in the 1830s), crude press and stage propaganda, the breakdown of trades unions, the strategies of nativists, exaggerated rumours from New York, and the failure of political leaders to cope, all explained the outbreaks.[3] They had the good effect, however, of discrediting nativism for a decade. In New York, the Whigs had contained the nativists by 'ticket-fusion'. In Philadelphia, nativism had mushroomed as the party of nationality, protestant piety, temperance, craft-exclusiveness, and anti-Irishism, while the Whigs were split on how

[1] Harold Buetow, *Of singular benefit* (New York, 1970), pp 146–54.
[2] Hugh J. Nolan, 'Francis Patrick Kenrick: first coadjutor-bishop' in James F. Connelly (ed.), *The history of the archdiocese of Philadelphia* (Philadelphia, 1976), pp 171–2, 174–5, and 177–86 *passim*; Vincent Lannie and Bernard Diethorn, 'For the honor and glory of God: the Philadelphia Bible riots of 1840' [*recte* 1844]' in *History of Education Quarterly*, viii (1968), pp 46, 55–7, 68–9, and 44–105 *passim*.
[3] 'A protestant and native Philadelphian' in *The truth unveiled. . . . the terrible riots in Philadelphia on May 6th, 7th, and 8th, A.D. 1844* (Philadelphia, 1844); Michael Feldberg, *The Philadelphia riots of 1844* (Westport, Conn., 1975); David Montgomery, 'The shuttle and the cross: weavers and artisans in the Kensington riots of 1844' in *Journal of Social History*, v (1972), pp 411–46.

to conciliate these forces and retain such Irish support as they had. The general collapse of nativism now indicated how positive, if limited, were pre-famine American views of the Irish; these had to change before so narrow a movement could revive. But opposition in New York and the riot in Philadelphia dispelled optimisim, and caused the Irish to regard political friendliness towards catholic schools, or at least neutrality, as one yardstick of their own acceptance—more so than their children's attendance might suggest.

The extension of the repeal movement to America was the most direct and immediate re-creation of matters Irish in America in these years. From the 1780s to the 1820s, American presbyterians supported Irish patriots and émigré radicals from motives of New World liberalism as well as Old World memory or descent. Between 1850 and 1921, such movements, even when they did not, like fenianism and Clan na Gael, originate in America, were led and supported by residents long Americanised and by the American-born Irish. By contrast, repeal had virtually no support from older Ulster-American communities, and drew little impetus from long-established catholic Americans. Instead, it began in 1840 among the Boston Irish, whose community was 'as yet but infantine', employed generally 'in manual labour . . . with the exception of those who keep little groceries, groggeries, boarding-houses, and the like'—yet 'sensitively alive to the sufferings of their fellow countrymen'.[1] This repeal view was confirmed by the British consul there, the Anglo-Irishman Thomas Colley Grattan: not 'the historical names' (Emmet, O'Connor, and MacNeven), but 'the obscure inhabitants of Boston . . . [with] such patronymics as McHugh, McGinniskin, and Murphy . . . and others of no note or position',[2] created the movement on Monday 12 October 1840 in Boylston Hall, Boston, six months after its beginnings in Dublin. Apart from Patrick Donohoe, editor of the *Pilot*, and his deputy, it was run by a fish-packer, a coal-dealer, and a hack-driver. The contrast with repeal's patrician leadership in Ireland may illuminate O'Connell's reserve about such auxiliaries. If at first the plainer Irish acted spontaneously, others came in by mid-December as the movement spread through the New England mill towns to Philadelphia and New York city. In the latter city Tammany, the local Democratic organisation, lent its hall, and Robert Emmet (Thomas Addis's son) presided until O'Connell criticised the men of 1798. The next year the Atlantic ports south as far as Baltimore, and the towns along the canals and rivers, formed branches.

The delegates to the first National Repeal Convention in Philadelphia (February 1842) included 'a cross section of the substantial catholic Irish population . . . merchants, traders, shopkeepers, doctors, lawyers, journalists, and public works contractors',[3] suggesting a natural cohesion and need for leadership by men of some means in the new Irish communities. Yet, incom-

[1] Thomas Mooney, *Nine years in America* (Dublin, 1850), p. 118.
[2] T. C. Grattan, *Civilized America* (2 vols, London, 1859), ii, 44.
[3] George Potter, *To the golden door* (Boston and Toronto, 1960), pp 396–8.

prehensibly, they failed to set up a permanent organisation. Support for repeal, educational freedom for catholics, and the status of Irish-Americans were the chief concerns. So obvious an avenue to otherwise scattered voters could not be ignored: in September 1843, the second National Repeal Convention met in the Broadway Tabernacle, New York city, with President John Tyler's son, Robert, presiding—a somewhat complicating coup, for the Tylers were a power in search of a constituency. The father, the republic's first vice-president to succeed to the presidency (on the death of William Harrison in 1841) was an ex-Democrat, now deserted by the Whigs, and, like his son but unlike the Irish majority, he was pro-slavery and fiscally orthodox in his views. The Irish could not yet afford to ignore such support; for, as they realised, only outsiders for the 1844 presidential nominations such as John Tyler, R. M. Johnson, and Lewis Cass endorsed repeal;[1] insiders James Polk, Henry Clay, and George Dallas discreetly remained silent (though Dallas's patrons, the ex-president Andrew Jackson and the historian George Bancroft, did favour some settlement). The second convention harvested the enthusiasm of the 'repeal year', but was shadowed by a growing realisation that Peel would suppress the movement in Ireland. This gave an opening to those who wished to discuss physical force, but the five-man governing directory shrewdly interpreted physical force to mean monetary contribution, and Dr Edmund Bailey O'Callaghan, historian of the state of New York, spoke eloquently on moral force from his experience as an exiled veteran of Louis Papineau's 1837-8 *émeute* in Lower Canada. With 405 delegates, large sums to spend, mass support, and much American sympathy, its wise leaders were attuned to O'Connell's mind, and deserved better from him.

It was not the question of slavery as much as misinformation based on mis-understanding that separated O'Connell from these recent emigrants. He used the slavery question partly to distance himself from a movement he wrongly believed to be based on United Irish traditions. Thomas Mooney—mercurial, occasionally brilliant, O'Connell's self-appointed agent in America since early 1841, and his erstwhile banking rival—was an accurate observer of Irish-Americans' social exigencies, but an unreliable reporter of their politics. He probably did more for repeal than his reputation suggests, certainly more than Thomas D'Arcy McGee, who arrived a year later to help in Boston. But Mooney split the New York movement and compromised the Boston society by placing guns on its table. Reporting meetings back to the *Nation* in Dublin, he exaggerated their radicalism, coyly decrying the danger of 'ill-concerted insurrectionary attack' while urging the example of 1776, on his own account, if repeal were thwarted.[2] At Mullaghmast, on 1 October 1843, O'Connell

[1] Francis Wyse, *America* (3 vols, London, 1846), iii, 40–41; 'Letter from America IV' in *Nation*, 22 Apr. 1843, p. 444.

[2] 'Letter from America IV' in *Nation*, 22 Apr. 1843, p. 444, and 'Letter from America XVI' in ibid., 14 Oct. 1843, p. 842; on Mooney, G. L. Barrow, 'Justice for Thomas Mooney' in *Dublin Hist. Rec.*, xxiv (1970), pp 173–88; Mooney, op. cit.

revealed how closely his desire to conciliate Britain by denouncing American belligerence was linked to his use of anti-slavery:

I denounce the slavery of the negro in America. I pronounce it an injustice against man, and a sin in its operation against the eternal God. . . . Let that cry go to America. My friends, I want nothing for the Irish but their country, and I think the Irish are competent to obtain their own country for themselves. I like to have the sympathy of every good man everywhere, but I want not armed support or physical strength from any country. . . . I want not the support of America; I have physical support about me to achieve any change; but you know well that it is not my plan.[1]

As he spoke, his followers distributed the latest repeal address of the pro-slavery Robert Tyler. In Britain, anti-slavery rhetoric was the then usual mode of reprobating America, given the friction between Britain and the United States in Texas, Oregon, and Maine; it was dear to the hearts of O'Connell's British allies, such as Lord Morpeth; it was conventional, because emancipation was already achieved in the British empire; and the transatlantic anti-slavery connection, notably the quakers of New York and Dublin, kept up more pressure on O'Connell than did Irish-Americans.

O'Connell's abolitionism placed grave strains on America's repealers. At the first national meeting in 1842, his 'Address of the people of Ireland to their countrymen and countrywomen in America', signed by 60,000 and just received made loyalty to him inconsistent with loyalty to the Democrats, who were determined to keep the issue out of federal politics. After some heat, they resolved to 'avoid domestic American controversies'.[2] Taking evidence of their anti-abolitionism to mean they were pro-slavery, O'Connell then in May 1843 threatened to disown Irish-American support. Only the prestige of the 'repeal year' revived many of the split associations in America. Once again, the slavery question was excluded from the second convention in September 1843. When O'Connell returned to the matter, a few days after Clontarf, he showed a better grasp of their position: he asked that Irish-Americans should no longer defend slavery, and should work to end the slave trade in Washington D.C., to repeal the rule prohibiting congressional debates on slavery, to promote voluntary manumission and the rights of free blacks, and to efface Irish racism.[3] His appeal was unquestionably sincere, yet its timing and motivation, at least partly for political uses, weakened its appeal. In 1840 James G. Birney (son of Ulster parents) received only 7,059 votes, or 0.3 per cent of the total, as an anti-slavery presidential candidate. To weigh down the Irish in America with emancipationism, much less abolitionism, in 1841–3, would have been to jeopardise their acceptability in America; their small leverage was among the pro-slavery Democrats, and they rivalled abolitionists as targets of northern mob violence

---

[1] *Nation*, 7 Oct. 1843, p. 829.
[2] Potter, op. cit., pp 396–8.
[3] *Nation*, 14 Oct. 1843, pp 844–5.

between 1835 and 1843. O'Connell scarcely grasped this; as a master politician he should have done.

Repeal helped fuel nativist reaction during these years. But it also caused leading Americans, from John Quincy Adams to Andrew Jackson, to argue that one might agitate for freedom in the Old World, despite the Monroe docrine, stopping short of practical intervention[1]—a stand later applied to the European insurrections in 1848. Indeed, repeal arguments may have helped shape 'American mission' ideology in the 'Young America' movement of the time, especially that of its theorist John L. Sullivan. Repeal also brought the Irish question into American politics for the first time. For the Irish community, as Thomas Colley Grattan observed, it marked a movement for greater group esteem. In America, more than in Ireland, it inaugurated the appropriation of democracy (in the strict sense) by 'obscure inhabitants'.[2]

On the eve of the famine, the themes and structures of Irish-America were all in place. Already New York and Philadelphia knew overcrowding and division, although the Irish were dispersed wherever opportunity suggested: Thomas Mooney could point to established leaders in almost every northern and western town. The lessons of organisation in a country where so much was achieved by voluntary cooperation were being learnt by repealers, trade unionists, churchmen, educators, and businessmen—if more easily put into effect where people were congregated than (as was then more usual) where they were scattered. Very substantial contributions to education were made by protestant immigrants, especially in Maryland, Virginia, Kentucky, and Tennessee, building on an eighteenth-century pattern begun by Francis Alison and others. John Oliver, Alexander McCaine, and Samuel Knox each founded academies in Baltimore by 1821, the last planning a free national system of education through to a federal university. In the west, adherents of a 'family craft' approach divided from those favouring a 'state craft' one, along lines of greater or lesser doctrinal commitment. Non-immigrant Ulster-Americans continued their tradition of establishing colleges, academies, and reformed curricula for primary schools, which strongly emphasised 'the evidence of Christianity', graded developments, and American material; William McGuffey was only the most influential. Incoming Irishmen could always find a township to give them the ill-paid and ill-regarded job of teaching literacy and numeracy to farm children in draughty, stove-warmed cabins. The catholic contribution too had begun in more organised ways.[3]

The ambivalent attitudes of Americans towards Irishmen invited already an effort at self-explanation and self-improvement, which had a broadening effect. Americans were affable towards the Irishman's livelier aspects, simplifying him

[1] Andrew Jackson to Thomas Mooney, 23 May 1842 (Francis Wyse, op. cit., iii, 45–7).
[2] T. C. Grattan, *Civilized America* (2 vols, London, 1859), ii, 3–11, 45.
[3] Harold Buetow, *Of singular benefit* (New York, 1970), pp 114ff, and the many articles on Irish pioneer educators listed in Barbara A. Braun, *Richard J. Purcell, 1887–1950: a bio-bibliography* (Washington, D.C., 1955).

as warm, droll, friendly, brave, familiar, and impertinent, if rarely villainous, but dismissed him as lazy, passive, and insecure. Oddly, they did not notice his political and religious character, except during group conflict; perhaps he was not meant to be so complex, or perhaps historians exaggerate grand themes in the lives of ordinary people.[1] Employers thought highly of him; the wealthy distanced themselves from him; those of recent, unstable position slighted him; New Englanders disdained him; but most Americans from New York south-ward and westwards took him as he was, more or less; even evangelical sermons and novels sought a Gothic unfamiliarity of terrain for their anti-Roman themes, for the Irishman was too homely to furnish such overwrought imagination.[2] The very doubt, widely held and honoured, that catholicism could coexist with the psychology and institutions of free men, helped ensure that it would do so. Only armed nativism, grosser exploitation, and the cholera, which last devastated Irish settlements in 1832,[3] had no beneficial effects, other than to prepare the Irish for their recurrence. The majority of Americans accepted it as natural that Irishmen should come among them, a vital prepara-tion for the famine influx. The Ulster-American tradition had prepared the Irish to identify closely with the constitutions and people of the new land. Interdenominational amity, if damaged by politicised evangelicalism and electoral violence, still survived; survived even the launching of Orangeism in the 1820s, and its revival in New York as the Berean Order in 1844–5.

Hundreds of thousands of newer immigrants had found their feet by 1845. Family solidarity was already vital: in May and June 1844, 41 per cent of Irish arrivals came to New York with passages prepaid. Knowledge of America was already diffused among them: only 5 per cent of these 10,668 arrivals stayed in New York city.[4] The Irish Emigration Society founded in 1841, although poorly financed by comparison with the repeal movement, did much useful work before merging its services with those of the state commissioners of emigration, established (partly at the prompting of the Irish Emigration Society and Arch-bishop John Hughes) in 1847 in time for the great migration.[5] The St Vincent de Paul Society, with so vital a future in urban America in the absence of welfare systems, was nowhere established except in St Louis (1845) and New York city (1846). Coming from Paris, it appealed only slowly to rural, family-conscious Irishmen, until they learnt its urban potential; it was introduced by priests and

---

[1] Dale T. Knobel, 'A vocabulary of ethnic perception: content analysis of the American stage Irishman' in *Journal of American Studies*, xv (1981), pp 45–71.
[2] Sir Charles Lyell, *A second visit to the United States* [1845–6] (2 vols, New York, 1849), ii, 187; Francis J. Grund, *The Americans* (2 vols, London, 1837), i, 90–96; Mooney, op. cit., p. 88; Stephen G. Bolger, *The Irish character in American fiction, 1830–1860* (New York, 1976), pp 122–51 and *passim*.
[3] Charles E. Rosenberg, *The cholera years* (Chicago, 1962), pp 24, 37, 55–7, 61–4.
[4] Richard J. Purcell, 'The Irish Emigrant Society of New York City' in *Studies*, xxvii (1938), p. 593.
[5] Ibid., pp 581–2, 594, 596; Oliver MacDonagh, 'The Irish famine emigration to the United States' in *Perspectives in American History*, x (1976), p. 394.

laity of European education or background such as Bryan Mullanphy. Most important, the economy began a slow recovery in 1844, accelerating after 1849 with an inflow of British capital and the export of California gold to pay for the trade deficit. This started a railway boom; the recovery spread to Canada by 1850 and, apart from a short-lived panic in 1857–8, a long cycle of economic expansion continued effectively to the mid-1870s. Non-agricultural employment began to expand more rapidly than population, from 1.7 million jobs in 1840 to 4.3 million in 1860. Despite the real tragedy of the famine years, the capacity of the United States to absorb two million Irish immigrants, and the existence of a viable subculture in America to ground those that came in some real familiarity and spiritual comfort, ensured that the tragedy was far less horrific than otherwise might have been.

CHAPTER XXXII

Ireland *c*.1870

W. E. VAUGHAN

THE years 1869–70 were one of those short periods when Ireland played an apparently important part in British politics, comparable with 1829, 1846, 1881, and 1886. Admittedly the land act of 1870 did not do as much as the land act of 1881, and the church act was hardly as important as the catholic relief act; nor did Irish questions bring down a government as in 1846 and 1886; but together, the church act and the land act were as substantial as the municipal reform act of 1840, the most important of O'Connell's legislative achievements after 1829, and more substantial than Peel's three Irish measures in 1844 and 1845. For one thing, the church act and the land act affected greater interests and more people than any legislation since the union: almost half a million yearly tenancies were changed; the tenant right of Ulster, sometimes valued at £20 million, was turned into a legal asset; property, estimated by Gladstone to be worth £16 million, was taken away from the Irish church; 667,998 protestant episcopalians and 497,648 presbyterians had to bestir themselves to support their clergy without any assistance from the state; Maynooth's parliamentary grant was converted into an endowment that put the college's finances forever beyond the cavilling of zealous protestants in parliament. The church act, like the constabulary act of 1836, the land purchase acts, the congested districts act, and the local government act of 1898, was one of those changes made by parliament that became fundamental and permanent, surviving even the establishment of self-government in 1921–2, for whatever the shortcomings of Gladstone's policy, there was never any prospect that another church would be established in place of the Irish church. (An unexpected result of the church act was the fact that many tenants indirectly became mortgagees of their landlords, for the three disendowed churches invested much of their compensation money in Irish land.)

Although the reconstruction of the Church of Ireland and the passage of the land act engaged the attention of many during 1870, there was much besides. The outbreak of war between France and Prussia on 19 July stirred up great excitement: bands played the 'Marseillaise' before the French consulate at 37 Lower Gardiner Street; meetings gathered in small Ulster villages and passed resolutions supporting the king of Prussia; newspapers supplemented news of the war with articles on earlier wars, with protestants and tories generally taking an anti-French stand, and catholics, liberals, and nationalists taking a pro-French stand. When the news of the battle of Sedan spread in early September, there were pro-French meetings in Wexford, Athlone, Mallow, Killarney, Limerick, Killaloe, and Youghal. Although the land bill received a lot of attention from February until July, and the war absorbed attention from the end of July, distracting attention even from the promulgation of the dogma of papal infallibility on 18 July, the newspapers had some time for other matters. The deaths of Maclise and his friend Dickens were noted (Dickens had visited Dublin in 1869); the execution of Laurence and Margaret Sheils in Tullamore was reported in detail (it was the first execution in Ireland to take place within a prison under the Capital Punishment Amendment Act); the kidnapping of Lord and Lady Muncaster, and the murder of some of their companions near Athens, which occurred in spite of the British government's attempts to offer the brigands a ransom, a free pardon, and a passage on a British warship to Malta, was recounted with remarkable sang-froid; the Mordaunt divorce case, which at least had some Irish interest through the appearance of Lord Cole as a co-respondent, and the strange behaviour of Lord Arthur Pelham-Clinton, titillated the palates of those who relished scandal in high places. The return of Irish emigrants from Algeria, some of whom were admitted to Whitechapel workhouse in September 1870, reminded the public of Marshal MacMahon's unlucky attempt to establish an Irish colony (to be known as Saint-Patrice) in Algeria. Jostling with these and many others was the report of the meeting in Bilton's hotel on 19 May when Isaac Butt launched the home rule movement. Ireland was a surprisingly open country, not only in the sense that it avidly received news from abroad, but also because knowledge of Ireland was more copious and more widely disseminated than ever before. The great official compilations—the decennial censuses, the agricultural statistics, and the reports of the registrar general—were matched by an outpouring of pamphlets, special reports, and travellers' descriptions in the late 1860s. The minutiae of landlord and tenant relations, of the established church, and of crime and disorder were matched by descriptions of country houses, and hotels such as Hunter's Hotel near Wicklow, whose civil landlord and beautiful setting won the hearts of many travellers.

THE disestablishment of the Irish church was Gladstone's first great Irish measure. In his speech on 1 March 1869 he outlined the bill that he himself had prepared with assistance from, among others, Chichester Fortescue and Archdeacon Stopford. His aims were comprehensive. 'So long as that establishment lives,' he told the house, 'painful and bitter memories of ascendancy can never be effaced.'[1] His hope was that this 'long continued controversy' should be put away 'out of sight, out of hearing, out of mind if it may be'.[2] In a speech that

---

[1] *Hansard 3*, cxciv, 414 (1 Mar. 1869). [2] Ibid., 417–18.

lasted over three hours he outlined his plans for compensating existing interests including Maynooth and the presbyterians, for managing church property after disestablishment, for the government of the church, and for the disposal of the remaining property when all claims had been settled. On the latter point he was firm: 'It is written that the money is to be applied to Irish purposes; and it is written that it is to be applied to purposes not ecclesiastical.'[1] The bill was a masterly exercise in the constitutional dismantling of a great and complicated vested interest. From 1 January 1871 the church's corporate property was to be transferred to commissioners, the Irish bishops were to leave the lords, and ecclesiastical law 'except in so far as [it] relates to matrimonial causes and matters shall cease to exist as law'.[2] From the property of the church—tithe-rentcharge, lands, and investments—the commissioners were to compensate the clergy, presbyterian ministers, patrons of livings, the Presbyterian Widows Fund Association, Maynooth, vergers, sextons, schoolmasters, parish clerks, and others such as the professors of Assembly's college in Belfast. In addition, the church was to receive compensation for private endowments received since 1660. The commissioners were to raise the money by selling tithe-rentcharge at twenty-two and a half years' purchase, by selling church lands, and by selling back to the church, on very favourable terms, its glebes and glebe houses. They were also empowered to borrow from the national debt commissioners to enable them to pay compensation immediately. Perhaps the most interesting part of these arrangements was the fact that sitting tenants could buy their holdings, if they could raise one-quarter of their purchase price. The terms of compensation varied. Bishops, dignitaries, beneficed clergymen, permanent curates, ministers, and professors were to receive life annuities based on their incomes; the clergy of the Church of Ireland were to be assessed according to their incomes on 1 January 1870, and the presbyterians according to what they had received from the *regium donum* during the financial year 1868–9. Maynooth and the presbyterian widows were to receive fourteen years' purchase of what they had received during 1868–9. Temporary curates were to receive gratuities that were not to exceed £200; slightly different arrangements were made for lay patrons, and the crown gave up its rights for nothing. Most importantly, the commissioners were empowered to convert annuities into lump sums, which were to be handed over to the church and the presbyterian authorities. The church was to be incorporated; arrangements were made for the disposal of churchyards and ruined churches, and for the upkeep of churches that were considered 'national' monuments (the church was to receive grants for twelve of these, and ruins such as Cashel were to be taken over by the commissioners of works). Much of the legislation regulating

[1] *Hansard 3*, cxciv, 455.
[2] Clause 21 of *A bill to put an end to the establishment of the Church of Ireland, and to make provision in respect of the temporalities thereof, and in respect of the Royal College of Maynooth*, H.C. 1868–9 (bill 27), iii, 85.

Maynooth was to be repealed.[1] Between the passing of the act and 1 January 1871 vacancies in the church could be filled but those appointed were not to receive compensation. Finally clause 59 specified the purposes for which the surplus would be used: the support of infirmaries, hospitals, lunatic asylums, industrial schools, and trained nurses and midwives.

In work of this kind Gladstone was in his most congenial element, mastering the nice calculations on which his predictions were based, revelling in the clarity of his policy, describing the theological position of the church in the early seventeenth century, and expatiating on the good works of Dean Swift, whom he saw as a sort of ecclesiastical Robinson Crusoe stranded at Laracor. Between 24 March and 31 May he guided the bill through the commons without suffering major hostile amendments; he successfully resisted opposition to the compensation for Maynooth, which was arguably much more generous than that given to the church and which arguably contradicted the preamble of the act by devoting money to religious purposes ('The final division on the pricking point [of Maynooth] with a majority of 107 was the most creditable (I think) that I have ever known');[2] he resisted the argument that he had exaggerated the value of tithe-rentcharge; he dealt with the distractions caused by the egregious lord mayor of Cork. Opinion in Ireland, except among the clerical dispossessed and their supporters, was favourable, and the liberals disappointed their opponents by not repeating the confusion of 1866. The most important change in the bill, which grew from 63 clauses to 71, was in the compensation for temporary curates, who were now to receive £25 for every year they had served and could receive up to £600. Otherwise the changes were trifling: archbishops, bishops, and deans, for example, were allowed to keep their titles and precedence after 1 January 1871.

The bill received its first reading in the lords on 1 June. The bill's opponents had high hopes of what the lords would do; and even if they were disappointed by the lords' failure to reject the bill during the debate on its second reading, which began on 14 June, they were not disappointed by the Gilbertian exuberance with which their lordships fell to amending it. Nor were they disappointed by the oratory, for the speech of William Connor Magee on 15 June was quite equal to Gladstone's on 1 March. The bill, according to Magee, was not a violation of the coronation oath, or of the act of union, or an attack on private property, although he warned that 'corporate property is always the first to be attacked in all great democratic revolutions', and revolutions begin with sacrilege and go on to communism.[3] An endowed church was merely 'an ecclesiastical firm' with which the state contracts 'to do its duty of religious teaching'.[4] The only question was which firm was better? If parliament thought that

[1] Below, p. 735.
[2] H. C. G. Matthew (ed.), *The Gladstone diaries* (9 vols, Oxford, 1968–86), vii, 64–5.
[3] *Hansard 3*, cxcvi, 1855 (15 June 1869).
[4] Ibid., 1858.

catholic priests could do the job better than protestant clergymen, why not endow them? But according to Magee, the people of England and Scotland did not think they would do the job better, for they 'are so deeply convinced of the inequality of these two religions that, whilst they could endure the endowment of the one, nothing would induce them to listen to a proposal for the endowment of the other'.[1] 'It appears to me', said Magee, 'that to treat equally things that are unequal, is not justice, but the very greatest injustice.'[2] But Magee did not confine himself to high-flown statements of principle, for he relieved his feelings, somewhat unfairly, by accusing Gladstone of meanness: 'Throughout its provisions this bill is characterised by a hard and niggardly spirit. I am surprised by the injustice and impolicy of the measure, but I am still more astonished at its intense shabbiness.'[3] Somewhat less unfairly, he administered a rebuke to 'some members of the English church, admirable vicars and other dignitaries, all full of a generous anxiety to bestow on their reverend brethren in Ireland that measure of apostolic poverty which they show no particular affection for themselves'.[4] Gladstone relieved his feelings by reading *Phineas Finn* and Thomas à Kempis and deploring in his diary the 'sad work in the lords' on 6 July when the heavily amended bill came out of committee.[5]

The bill received its third reading in the lords on 12 July, an inauspicious day given the circumstances. Altogether the lords' amendments affected almost every major group of clauses. Some were relatively trivial: for example, archdeacons were added to those dignitaries in clause 13 who were allowed to retain their precedence and titles for life. Others were not trivial but did not greatly change the bill: the date of disestablishment was postponed from 1 January to 1 May 1871, which, if the weather had been seasonable, would have removed some of the lugubriousness from Mrs Alexander's hymn.[6] Another, to clause 20, which had changed the status of ecclesiastical law, provided that no changes made in the articles, doctrines, rites, and discipline of the church after disestablishment 'shall be binding on any ecclesiastical person' who dissented within six months.[7] The lords also rewrote the preamble of the bill, making it possible for parliament in the future to devote some of the church's property to religious objects. (They also struck out most of clause 68 (formerly clause 59), in which Gladstone had enumerated the objects on which the surplus should be spent.) These two changes, combined with the amendment to clause 27, allowing the commissioners to provide houses for priests and ministers, altered

---

[1] *Hansard 3*, cxcvi, 1859.
[2] Ibid., 1858.
[3] Ibid., 1874.
[4] Ibid., 1865.
[5] Matthew, op. cit., p. 92.
[6] 'Dimly dawns the New Year on a churchless nation, / Ammon and Amalek tread our borders down.' Quoted in Eleanor Alexander (ed.), *Primate Alexander, archbishop of Armagh, a memoir* (London, 1913), p. 183.
[7] For the lords' amendments see under the appropriate clauses in *A bill [as amended by the lords] intituled 'An act to put an end to the establishment of the Church of Ireland, and to make provision in respect of the temporalities thereof, and in respect of the Royal College of Maynooth*, H.C. 1868–9 (bill 209), iii, 191.

the whole tenor of the bill by allowing for concurrent endowment, and were the most likely cause of a conflict between the two houses.

In practical terms, however, the most important amendments were those that tried to change the terms of the church's disendowment by adding to its compensation. Seven of those were estimated by William Neilson Hancock to add £2,803,881 to the church's compensation.[1] The most important was Lord Carnarvon's amendment to clause 23, proposing to give the church a straightforward fourteen years' purchase for all life interests, regardless of the actuarial prospects of individual clergymen. This was a shrewd blow to Gladstone's calculations. First, it would have added, according to Hancock, £1,221,750 to what the clergy would get under clause 23. (Commutators' lives were eventually estimated to be worth only 11.4 years' purchase, so Carnarvon proposed to add about 23 per cent.) Secondly, the proposal was plausible since it put the church on the same footing as Maynooth, whose compensation of fourteen years' purchase was left untouched by the lords. The second biggest change was to clause 15, giving an extra £519,150 to curates by increasing the number of 'temporary' curates. A third amendment tidied up the means by which the church would be compensated for private endowments under clause 29: the strange, and contentious, choice of 1660 was abandoned, and the church was given a lump sum of £500,000. (Hancock calculated that this added £212,957 to the church's compensation.) The remaining four amendments accounted for smaller sums: an amendment to clause 14 would have increased the annuities of the clergy by reducing the deductions to be made from their regular incomes (£254,450 added); an amendment to clause 27, proposing to give glebe houses and glebes free of charge to the church, added £153,289; an amendment to clause 29, proposing to allow the church to keep all glebe land granted by the crown since 1559, would have added £422,285; finally, a further amendment to clause 14 relating to visitation fees would have added £20,000.

The cabinet was prepared to make some concessions to prevent a constitutional crisis and to save itself the difficulty of having to devote the next session to introducing a new bill. They accepted the payment of a lump sum of £500,000 for private endowments; they refused Carnarvon's amendment giving fourteen years' purchase but offered a 7 per cent bonus to commutators (this added about £420,000, or about one-third of what Carnarvon proposed). Otherwise, they stood firm, especially on concurrent endowment, the disposal of the surplus, and the date of disestablishment, and the commons removed most of the lords' amendments on 15 and 16 July. Between 16 and 22 July negotiations involving the government, Lord Cairns, Disraeli, Archbishop Tait, and the dean of Windsor narrowed the area of disagreement to the preamble and clause 68 on the disposal of the surplus, to the date of disestablishment, the terms of commutation, curates, and glebes. The government compromised on the first by leaving the question open; they were also prepared to give way on

[1] P. M. H. Bell, *Disestablishment in Ireland and Wales* (London, 1969), pp 358-9.

the second, but the opposition seemed indifferent, so 1 January 1871 remained. By 22 July the strain had caused Gladstone to be laid up, but Cairns produced three proposals that finally closed the gap between the government and the tories: first, the curates should get an extra £380,000; secondly, the bonus for commutators should be increased from 7 per cent to 12 per cent (adding £300,000 to the £420,000 already conceded); thirdly, the church should be allowed to buy back the glebes on easier terms than those proposed in clause 27, saving the church some £140,000. On the first and second points Gladstone, negotiating through Lord Granville, refused to yield but eventually gave way on the second. (Cairns, however, gained one small point: the bonus of 12 per cent was to be paid when three-quarters of the annuitants agreed to commute, and not four-fifths as proposed by the bill.) The news of the agreement was brought to Gladstone on his sofa, and that evening the lords accepted the compromise, abandoning the curates, the glebes, and glebe houses, and leaving badly housed priests and ministers to their own devices. The next day, 23 July, the commons accepted the compromise and the bill received the royal assent on 26 July.

As a legislative achievement, the church act was an admirable example of constructive dismantling. A great grievance was removed, but little real damage was done to the important interests of those concerned; indeed, in some respects all affected were left stronger, or at any rate, potentially stronger. The Church of Ireland was left free from state control, but with a corporate structure, the representative church body and the general synod, that it used with skill; it was left, too, with a substantial endowment, for by 1880 it had received £8,327,302 from the commissioners of the church temporalities, which invested at 4 per cent would have yielded an income rather larger than the corporate income of the university of Cambridge and its colleges. Unfortunately for the church, however, much of this capital had to be used to pay annuities, but even by 1895 some £4,000,000 remained, which combined with other funds gave the church an invested capital of £6,952,000. The church was lucky, too, because none of its really rich bishops died in the uneasy period between 26 July 1869 and 1 January 1871; only Kilmore showed an inconvenient tendency to episcopal mortality; but better Kilmore than the rich and relatively youthful bishop of Derry and Raphoe, whose compensation came to a staggering £111,367. 19s. 1d. Maynooth was left free, except in the neglected matter of its statutes, and its compensation of £372,331, if invested at 4 per cent, would have left it as well off as some of the more substantial Cambridge colleges, such as Pembroke or Gonville and Caius. The presbyterians had always been free and well organised, and by 1880 received £764,688 in lieu of the *regium donum*, of which £621,082 was commuted.

The main administrative shortcoming of the act was its expensiveness, leaving rather less for 'Irish purposes' than Gladstone had expected. Gladstone had assumed that the church's property was worth £16 million and that compensation would cost £8,650,000; in fact compensation to all interests, including lay patrons, came to £11,537,936 by 1880. Only part of this discrepancy of nearly three million was caused by the lords' amendments (about £1.3 million); the rest suggest that Gladstone and William Neilson Hancock were the victims of their own optimism. They underestimated, for example, the cost, even before paying the 12 per cent bonus, of compensating bishops, incumbents, and curates by some £1.9 million. More serious, however, for 'Irish interests' was the apparently unforeseen cost of turning the complicated property of the church into cash, especially tithe-rentcharges, which were over-valued at twenty-two and a half years' purchase. As a result the commissioners had to borrow £9 million from the commissioners of the national debt, and by 1880 this had cost them (and 'Irish interests') £2,296,000 in interest. As an exercise in constitutional expropriation, however, the act was a triumph of legislative and administrative skill. On the whole its most important shortcomings were of a wider kind, unconnected with its construction. It did not, however one defines fenianism, 'draw a line between the fenians and the people of Ireland, & . . . make the people of Ireland indisposed to cross it'.[1] Nor did it really clear up relations between the state and the religious denominations in Ireland.

THE church act dealt with a number of limited and specific problems—the property and status of the established church, the parliamentary grants received by Maynooth and presbyterian ministers. It did not establish a new system of relations between church and state, or between the different denominations. After 1869 Ireland was unique in the United Kingdom in having no formal connection between the state and organised religion. There was even an insouciance about the niceties of ecclesiastical precedence that had preoccupied some legislators in 1869, for the royal warrant regulating the precedence of protestant and catholic bishops was not issued immediately. The freedom from state supervision enjoyed by the different denominations in Ireland was unusual in Europe (although it was not in north America and in Australia and New Zealand), for nearly all European countries in 1870 had ministries of public worship or ecclesiastical affairs, whose degree of supervision varied, but whose very name was as familiar a part of departmental nomenclature as ministries of foreign affairs, or war, or marine. In 'catholic' countries, such as Austria, Bavaria, France, and Spain, a connection between the state and the church existed, nor was it considered unlikely that those countries would intervene in the Vatican council. Even in countries that were not 'catholic', control was not unknown, even of groups whose religion was different from that which dominated the state. In Prussia, for example, the government appointed catholic priests and bishops, whom it also paid, except in the Rhenish provinces where church-state relations were regulated by a

[1] H. C. G. Matthew, *The Gladstone diaries* (9 vols, Oxford, 1968–86), vii, 45.

concordat made during the pontificate of Pius VII (1800–23). In Russia (readers of Irish newspapers learned in December 1869) the Jews were allowed for the first time to build a synagogue; it is worth noting, too, that the Russian government had refused to allow its catholic bishops to attend the Vatican council. In Switzerland the new federal constitution of 1874 not only reenacted the old law expelling the Jesuits, but also regulated the erection of catholic dioceses and the creation of new monasteries. Some Irish catholics gloried in their freedom. Myles O'Reilly, for example, was pleased that catholics were 'free to teach, to publish, to form what religious associations, to found and endow what institutions we please', and that 'no royal exsequatur is required before papal bulls or decrees can be published in this country; no minister of the sovereign can forbid our bishops to publish a papal encyclical letter. . . . That no permission from the civil governor is needed to build or endow a church, a convent, or an asylum.' O'Reilly had little enthusiasm for the position of the catholic church in certain continental countries: 'May not our example also teach that our cold and rugged northern freedom is as favourable to the catholic church, as the so-called paternal care of kings, who trammel its action, while they load it with oppressive favours.'[1]

Even a cursory glance at Irish newspapers, however, suggests that there was much that could have been regulated, even within an entirely voluntary system. The O'Keeffe case in 1871–3 showed that it was almost impossible to separate church and state and that there was an embarrassing lack of clearly enunciated principles that could be applied to religious affairs. On the one hand, Fr Robert O'Keeffe was dismissed from the management of Callan national school by the commissioners of education and from his workhouse chaplaincy by the poor law commissioners because his bishop suspended him, demonstrating that government boards would enforce episcopal decrees, even though Fr O'Keeffe's offence was that he had sued his bishop in the queen's courts! On the other hand, Fr O'Keeffe was able to take Cardinal Cullen to court with no more regard for his dignity than if he had been the offending treasurer of a badly run benefit society. At least the O'Keeffe case was important in that it raised important problems, revealing not so much a conflict of jurisdictions as the absence of any active ecclesiastical courts in the catholic church in Ireland. There were, however, many quarrels that were merely disedifying. In 1863 near Kilconnell, County Galway, for example, there was a quarrel between the rector and parish priest about the burial of the station master of Woodlawn, who was the protestant partner in a mixed marriage. The priest claimed that he had baptised and anointed the station master on his death bed, and

having thus transferred him to his own church, he expressed his intention of attending his funeral, and reading the Roman Catholic burial service over his remains. Mr [H. R.]

[1] Myles O'Reilly, *Progress of catholicity in Ireland in the nineteenth century. Being a paper read before the Catholic Congress of Mechlin, Sept. 1863* (Dublin, 1865), pp 13, 29.

Fleming [the rector], a man of zeal and nerve, expressed his determination to attend also, and read the service of the protestant church. . . . To do the people justice, they behaved very well under such exciting circumstances. Mr Fleming was rudely jostled once or twice, and in the copious sprinkling of holy water the rev. gentleman got more than his share of it, but he remained last upon the ground; and it is stated that though the priest ordered his people to put on their hats when he retired, many of them remained uncovered till the protestant service was over.[1]

Part of the problem was the survival of remnants of the penal laws that had escaped the repealing statutes. Until 1870, for example, it was a criminal offence for a catholic priest to perform a marriage between a catholic and a protestant, and priests were occasionally prosecuted. (Section 38 of the Matrimonial Causes and Marriage Law (Ireland) Amendment Act, 1870,[2] allowed catholic clergymen to perform mixed marriages, although it was stipulated that it must be done in a church 'with open doors'.) Even Gladstone in 1869 failed to repeal section 4 of the act that founded Maynooth,[3] which required that all by-laws, rules, regulations, and statutes proposed by the college trustees should have the approval of the lord lieutenant. (A bill introduced in July 1871 received only a first reading in the commons.) Part of the problem was caused by new enactments, which either confirmed old restrictions or invented new ones. The catholic relief act of 1829, for example, made it illegal for judicial and civil officers to attend catholic services in their robes of office; admitting persons to the religious orders became a misdemeanour; catholic clergy could not wear their religious habits outside their chapels. Many restrictions were brought in either in the heat of the moment, like the ecclesiastical titles act, or to make concessions to catholics more palatable to protestants. The strange practical results were often not foreseen. Maziere Brady, for example, told a select committee of a monument to a catholic bishop of Meath that had its inscription in Latin in order to avoid contravening the ecclesiastical titles act. Even well meant measures could lead to embarrassment. The charitable donations and bequests act[4] was as prosaic a statute as any connected with Sir Robert Peel, but its sixteenth section insisted that religious bequests had to be made three months before the testator's death. When Archbishop Cullen arrived in Armagh in 1850 he found that his predecessor's will was invalid because it was made only the day before he died; the archbishop's house and the seminary passed to William Crolly's heir-at-law, who was minor and therefore unable to transfer his property to the new archbishop.

Although a competent parliamentary draftsman might have done much to rid Ireland of petty legal disputes, the problem was more complicated than that. While the state made grants to schools managed by the churches, employed chaplains in prisons and workhouses, and in the army and navy, there was bound to be some friction, even if there was no established

[1] *Annual Reg., 1863*, pp 75–6.
[2] 33 & 34 Vict., c. 110 (10 Aug. 1870).
[3] 35 George III, c. 21 (5 June 1795).
[4] 7 & 8 Vict., c. 97 (9 Aug. 1844).

church. It is surprising, for example, how politicians who argued so vehemently against concurrent endowment in 1869 could accept the national school system. Nor was it easy to see how the boundary between the churches and the state could be defined. The state in 1871 dismissed a particular clique of clerical servants, no longer expecting the senior ones to act as legislators or the junior ones to cure souls in their parishes, just as from time to time it disbanded regiments and decommissioned ships of war. That was not, however, the end of the matter, for it still employed clergymen to teach and to perform marriages. The matrimonial causes act—brought in because the church act abolished the church courts—set up a secular court to deal with matrimonial disputes (although it did not grant divorces); in addition, the state also took upon itself the power to define those groups that it recognised as churches, for section 37, which recognised thirteen protestant organisations and the Religious Society of Friends, looks very like article 44 of the Irish constitution, except of course in one very important detail.

Part of the problem was the physical difficulty of restraining outbursts of sectarian exuberance, of which the riots in Belfast in August 1864 and the affair of William Johnston in 1867 were among the most recent examples. Neither the ordinary law nor the party processions acts of 1850 and 1860 prevented provocative behaviour and sectarian clashes.[1] The former was frequently used by northern magistrates, especially in Belfast, but without effecting a change in popular manners. In 1870, for example, the Belfast police court fined John Kerr 40s. for cursing the pope, George Murray the same amount for cursing the pope and the pope's granny, and Teresa Brown the same amount for the ecumenical gesture of naming her two cats Orange Bill and Papist Kate. The party processions acts were in theory a powerful restraint on party displays. The act of 1850 made it a criminal offence to persist in parading with firearms, or carrying any banner, emblem, flag or symbol, or playing music, or singing songs, 'which may be calculated or tend to provoke animosity between different classes of her majesty's subjects'. The act of 1860 made it illegal to display party flags on buildings, or to discharge cannon or firearms in 'any public street, road, or place'. Unfortunately neither legislative restraint nor freedom seemed to work: the affray at Dolly's Brae in 1849 took place when there was no party processions act in force; the affray at Derrymacash, near Lisburn, in 1860 took place in spite of the act of 1850. At best the act of 1850 persuaded the more sedate Orange lodges to meet in demesnes or to parade around fields, or to march without sashes, bands, or arms. It did not, however, prevent illegal marches; in 1870, for example, according to the R.M.s' reports 12,000 Orangemen marched through Lisburn 'playing party tunes, carrying flags, and wearing sashes' and there were meetings in Rathfriland and Newry that 'were in every instance bold violations of the party processions act'.[2] Only legislation that

[1] 13 Vict., c. 2 (12 Mar. 1850), and 23 & 24 Vict., c. 141 (28 Aug. 1860).
[2] S.P.O., O.P. 1870/7.

combined draconian severity with almost supernatural foresight could have anticipated all the contingencies created by the ingenuity and exuberance of Orangemen and their opponents. In 1849 the Orangemen at Dolly's Brae appeared to be in the wrong because they took the long road home; at Derrymacash in 1860 they were in the wrong when they took the shortest road home. The difficulty of defining party tunes and symbols, of cajoling recalcitrant juries, of curing the sudden, temporary, and inexplicable fits of blindness suffered by magistrates was beyond the wisdom of parliament.

Some politicians, particularly tories, were quick enough to try to transform these irritants into unguents. In 1867, for example, Lord Naas introduced a bill allowing an officeholder to attend any place of worship in 'the robe, gown, or other peculiar habit of his office, or with the ensign or insignia of or belonging to the same, without incurring any forfeiture of office or penalty for such attendance'.[1] (The *Catholic Directory* noted that on 5 January 1868 Sir William Carroll, lord mayor of Dublin, and 'several members of the town council attended in state at the celebration of high mass in the cathedral, Marlborough Street. The chief magistrate was received at the principal entrance of the church by the lord cardinal. Owing to the penal enactments, of the recent repeal of which this auspicious incident is one of the first fruits, no similar event had been witnessed in Dublin for nearly two centuries.')[2] The same act made it possible for catholics to become lord chancellors of Ireland, which opened the way for Thomas O'Hagan in 1868. The tories met catholic susceptibilities more indirectly by discouraging attempts to extend the divorce act of 1857 to Ireland. The act applied only to England and Wales, leaving Ireland with the church courts, which could grant only judicial separations and annulments, and divorce by private act of parliament, which was expensive and unavailable to wives 'except in cases of aggravated enormity'.[3] To remedy this, some Irish liberal peers tried to introduce a bill allowing Irish residents to take their cases to the English court, but the tory government of Lord Derby, conscious of the electoral good that conciliating catholics in a small way would produce, opposed these efforts.

Catholics seem to have appreciated small official gestures. The *Catholic Directory* was pleased in 1867 when Cardinal Cullen appeared in his cardinal's robes and red cap at the lord mayor's banquet:

It was the first time that ever a cardinal met the lord lieutenant in the Dublin Mansion House. It was certainly startling to see 'a prince of the church' whom the penal code was designed to annihilate, ascending the dais next to the lord lieutenant, having on his arm

---

[1] 30 & 31 Vict., c. 75 (12 Aug. 1867).
[2] *Catholic directory, almanac, and registry of Ireland, England, and Scotland . . . 1869* (Dublin, 1869), p. 293.
[3] *First report of the commissioners appointed by her majesty to enquire into the law of divorce, and more particularly into the mode of obtaining divorces à vinculo matrimonii*, p. 11 [1604], H.C. 1852–3, xl, 263.

Lady Rachel Butler, sister to Earl Russell, and chatting pleasantly with Lady Abercorn, in a room which was once the very temple of protestant ascendancy.[1]

Satisfaction was even more deeply felt in the following year when Cullen dined 'by special invitation' with the prince of Wales in Dublin castle and 'his eminence was placed next immediately after royalty, and everything due to his rank was freely and cordially accorded to it'.[2]

Although it is tempting to see Ireland as a country peculiarly plagued by disputes about mixed marriages, the religion of foundlings, the use of grave-yards, and party processions, the temptation must be resisted. Throughout Europe similar quarrels, often on a grander scale, were taking place. The clergy of the established church no doubt felt aggrieved after 1869, but they had suffered surgery at the hands of a compassionate expert compared with the financial butchery suffered by the catholic church in the kingdom of Italy. It is doubtful if any Irish case, even the evictions at Partry carried out by Bishop Plunket, achieved the international notoriety of the Mortara case, which provoked not only public agitation all over Europe but also made Cavour, Napoleon III, and Franz Josef intercede with Pius IX. Even the affair at Kilconnell can be matched, in rather grander circumstances, by Pius IX's prohibition in 1870 of the requiem mass in the Ara Coeli that the Comte de Montalembert was entitled to as a Roman patrician. Tension between govern-ments and clergy in Ireland, except possibly in the 1820s and early 1850s, rarely reached the levels achieved in Prussia during the Cologne mixed-marriage dispute or during the *Kulturkampf*. Whatever unease was felt by catholic bishops in dealing with the government, they knew that they were less likely to see the inside of a prison, except on a pastoral visit, than their Prussian fellows. Fr Clune may have come close to death at the hands of the military in 1852, but there was little chance that Cardinal Cullen would emulate Archbishop Darboy and exchange his red hat for a martyr's crown.

IN 1871 catholics were by far the largest denomination in Ireland, accounting for just over three-quarters of the population; the second biggest denomina-tion, the Church of Ireland, accounted for only 12 per cent, and presbyterians for 9 per cent. The number of methodists was small, just under 1 per cent, and they were outnumbered by a miscellaneous collection of 'other' denomina-tions, which included small groups such as the unitarians (9,373), the Religious Society of Friends (3,814), the Plymouth Brethren (578), the Jews (285), the congregationalists (162), and the Mormons (33). The different denominations were distributed over the whole country, and the bigger ones had systems of government that were national in scope. Even the most protestant county, Antrim, included 55,640 catholics (24 per cent), and the most catholic county, Clare, where catholics were 98 per cent, had 3,424 non-catholics, of which the Church of Ireland's 3,027 was the biggest group; but there were also 220

---

[1] *Catholic directory . . . 1868*, p. 345.   [2] Ibid., *1869*, p. 305.

presbyterians and 64 methodists. There were, however, considerable geographical concentrations, of which the province of Ulster was the most remarkable, for it contained 60 per cent of the country's Church of Ireland population and 96 per cent of its presbyterians. (Although the Church of Ireland was the biggest protestant denomination in Ireland, it came second to presbyterianism in Ulster.) Within Ulster the pattern varied from county to county. Antrim, Down, and Belfast had the largest protestant majorities; in Armagh and Londonderry protestants accounted for just over half of the population. The most catholic counties were Donegal, Cavan, and Monaghan. Tyrone and Fermanagh had catholic majorities that resembled the protestant majorities in Armagh and Londonderry. The concentration of protestants outside Ulster varied: Leinster was the most protestant and Connacht the least protestant province. Counties outside Ulster ranged from Clare, where protestants were 2 per cent, to County Dublin where they were nearly 30 per cent, Dublin city (21 per cent), and Wicklow (19 per cent). Indeed it is worth noting that protestants were as important in percentage terms and in numbers in Dublin and Wicklow as they were in Cavan, Monaghan, and Donegal.

County percentages, however, can be misleading (and were often meant to be). For one thing, counties varied greatly in size: County Down was three times as big as Fermanagh (there were more catholics in Belfast, where they accounted for only 32 per cent, than in Fermanagh where they were over half). Also, within counties there were variations: north Down and north Armagh were more protestant than south Down and south Armagh. North Fermanagh was more protestant than south Fermanagh, and although protestants were a minority in the county they could scrape together enough strength to return a unionist for the northern division from 1886 on. Tyrone was even more baffling, with west Tyrone having large protestant communities. Even within apparently homogenous districts there were variations. In the parish of Magheracross, for example, in north Fermanagh, protestants accounted for 65 per cent of the population, which was higher than in the county as a whole. But an analysis of the townlands in Magheracross shows that protestants and catholics varied even within the parish, the former being present in all its townlands but ranging from 100 per cent in one townland to a mere 10 per cent in another. In so far as there was a pattern, protestants tended to be concentrated most strongly to the south and west of the village of Ballinamallard, and catholics to the north and east, on the higher ground; but there were exceptions to this, for strongly protestant and catholic townlands lay beside each other, especially in the south and east of the parish.[1] Protestants and catholics throughout much of Ulster, therefore, lived in circumstances that imposed on individuals a series of overlapping identities; a protestant farmer, living in the north-east of the parish of Magheracross, was in a minority in his immediate locality, in a majority in the parish, in a minority in the county, and so on.

[1] Below, p. 801.

Simple county percentages are also misleading because they give an erroneous impression of protestant strength in Ulster. Looked at from one point of view, from Cork, for example, protestants dominated only two of the nine counties, assuming that the town of Belfast was denied the dignity of an existence independent of Antrim and Down. Yet that did not really reflect their strength; for one thing, their strength in the population of the whole province was increasing, reaching just over 51 per cent in 1871 (they were 49 per cent in 1861) and 56 per cent in 1911. The peculiar concentration of Ulster protestants in the north-east of the province gave them a strength that they would not have had if they had been evenly distributed throughout the nine counties. Concentration around Belfast made organisation easy, provided a viable base for newspapers, and brought all the different denominations together where they could resolve their differences. The small protestant communities in Fermanagh, Tyrone, and Monaghan were connected by tentacles of protestant settlement with this core that made them a part of a substantial whole rather than isolated communities. The catholics were in the opposite position although their numbers were not substantially smaller than the protestants'. There was no core of catholic influence in the province; where their numbers were greatest, in Donegal, Cavan, and Monaghan, they were scattered rather than concentrated; where they were concentrated, in Belfast, they were vastly outnumbered.

Protestants and catholics were also distributed differently among occupations. In 1871 catholics were 77 per cent of the population, but their representation varied from 30 per cent of barristers to 89 per cent of fishmongers. They were apparently well represented at the top of the social scale among the landlords, accounting for 38 per cent in 1871. It is doubtful, however, if they owned 38 per cent of the land. In the late eighteenth century they owned about 5 per cent[1] and it is unlikely that this fell in the nineteenth century, because catholics purchased land in the encumbered estates court, and there were some remarkable recruitments of catholic strength through the conversion of landlords like Lord Dunraven and Lord Granard. It is unlikely, however, that their share had increased to 38 per cent by 1871. (It is possible, too, that the 1871 figure included the owners of house-rents and small estates. Many of the purchasers under the encumbered estates courts bought small parcels of land; Cardinal Cullen bought three houses in 1856 in Lower Exchange Street in Dublin for £330.) There were of course large catholic landlords such as the earl of Fingall (9,589 acres), the earl of Kenmare (118,606 acres), and the earl of Dunraven (15,467 acres). It is doubtful, nevertheless, if catholics' estates were even half as large as protestants', and 15 per cent is probably closer to the truth than 38 per cent. At the bottom of the social scale catholics accounted for 87 per cent of general labourers, 90 per cent of outdoor labourers, and 86 per cent of indoor labourers. Both of these measures show that while catholics were under-

[1] Above, iv, 13.

represented at the top and over-represented at the bottom of the social pyramid, they had reached, or rather surprisingly retained, a foothold at the very top, and were not concentrated at the very bottom. Whatever else protestant ascendancy meant it did not mean that lowly occupations were a catholic monopoly and landed wealth a protestant one. (Presbyterians, for example, accounted for only 6 per cent of landlords in 1871.)

In the middle ranks catholics were more comfortably represented than at the extremes. They accounted, for example, for 78 per cent of farmers. As in the case of landlords, it is doubtful if they farmed 78 per cent of the land, but the difference between their numbers and acreage was less than in the case of the landlords, for there were many large farmers like Edward Delany of Woodtown, near Dunshaughlin, who farmed 500 acres in the 1870s. It is unlikely, therefore, that catholics occupied less than 65 per cent of the land. The difference between protestant and catholic farmers was probably greater in the north than in the south. In the parish of Magheracross, in County Fermanagh, catholic farms were smaller than protestant ones, with the former being valued at about £10 and the latter at £17. On the estates of the earl of Gosford in County Armagh, however, the difference was not as great; the biggest farms were held by presbyterians, paying on average rents of £16; next came the Church of Ireland tenants, paying just over £10, closely followed by catholics, paying just under £10. (The smallest farmers were 'others', paying about £8.)

Among the professions and better-paid occupations the pattern varied: catholics were under-represented among doctors (34 per cent), barristers (30 per cent), solicitors (37 per cent), and clergymen (49 per cent). They were better represented among policemen (70 per cent), schoolteachers (61 per cent), and civil servants (50 per cent), but they were not so well represented among some of the other 'new' professions such as civil engineers (34 per cent), photographers (41 per cent), authors, editors, and writers (48 per cent), and architects (34 per cent). They were also under-represented among the 'financial' professions such as merchants (42 per cent), bankers (27 per cent), auctioneers (54 per cent), and accountants (50 per cent). But they were over-represented in the retail trades, such as publicans and hotelkeepers (79 per cent), shopkeepers (83 per cent), butchers (88 per cent), fishmongers (89 per cent), bakers (82 per cent). Among the skilled manual trades the pattern varied; they were over-represented among engine drivers (78 per cent), pilots (83 per cent), wheelwrights (86 per cent), masons (83 per cent), tailors (90 per cent), and shoemakers (78 per cent); they were under-represented among printers (54 per cent), bricklayers (67 per cent), plumbers (66 per cent), and cabinet makers (58 per cent). They were just about adequately represented among carpenters (74 per cent) and coachmakers (76 per cent).

The effect of this erratic distribution on the division of wealth in the country is roughly indicated by the following table, which is based on Baxter's figures and on figures from the 1871 census.[1] This table shows the great bulk of catholic incomes came from the lower categories, where catholics were well or over-represented; in the higher categories protestants, who accounted for less than one-quarter of the population, enjoyed about three-quarters of the wealth. The effects of this on the general distribution of wealth among the two populations, however, were not as drastic as has been argued.[2] Per capita incomes, for example, seem to have been closer to each other than the concentration of great wealth in protestant hands would lead one to expect; indeed, among the

Catholic and protestant shares of gross income, 1867

categories	protestants (£)	catholics (£)
rents	11,731,373 [85]	2,070,242 [15]
farming profits	1,031,346 [35]	1,915,356 [65]
government stock	762,254 [66]	392,676 [34]
professions & profits	3,482,125 [66]	1,793,822 [34]
salaries	661,625 [51]	635,679 [49]
total (schedules A–E)	17,668,723 [72]	6,807,775 [28]
under £100	3,109,600 [23]	10,410,400 [77]
skilled workers	1,012,500 [27]	2,737,500 [73]
lower skilled	3,561,360 [22]	12,626,640 [78]
agricultural & unskilled	2,187,720 [12]	16,043,280 [88]
total lower incomes	9,871,180 [19]	41,817,820 [81]
total incomes	27,539,903 [36]	48,625,595 [64]
per capita incomes (£)	21.83	11.71

The figures in square brackets give the percentage shares allocated to protestants and catholics.

[1] Below, p. 779. Instead of using Baxter's figures for large and middling incomes, the amounts assessed under the income tax schedules were used. The catholic share of incomes under £100, and of higher skilled, lower skilled, and unskilled incomes is relatively easy to calculate by using the census to adjust Baxter's figures. The larger incomes are more difficult and the problem was solved by making some arbitrary estimates; 15 per cent for rents is only a rough guess and may be too high; 65 per cent for farming profits is a better guess and may be a little low; 34 per cent for government stock is based on the catholics' share of profits and professional incomes; 34 per cent for profits and professional incomes is based on the numbers of catholic barristers, solicitors, doctors, merchants, and bankers in the census, and may be too high; and 49 per cent for salaries is based on the catholics who were civil servants, priests, law clerks, civil engineers, and accountants.

[2] Cf. Emmet Larkin, *The historical dimensions of Irish catholicism* (Washington, D.C., 1984), p. 47.

lower incomes, the protestant average is only slightly higher than the catholic one, and the median incomes in both populations were not as far apart as one would expect: the median catholic was at the top of the unskilled and agricultural category or just at the bottom of the lower skilled; the median protestant was rather better off, occurring just about the middle of the lower skilled category—a humble enough position given the concentration of protestants at the very top of the social scale. It is worth noting, too, that the difference between the two populations was caused by about 12 per cent of incomes, or about £9 million, most of which was accounted for by rents.

THE major denominations had much in common: from 1 January 1871 they were all voluntary associations; they were combatative, or at least assertive; they maintained elaborate clerical establishments, and buildings that were meant to catch the eye by their size or to impress by their modesty; they believed in infallibility, although they disagreed about its location and scope; they were not averse to using worldly power to advance spiritual values—in 1870, for example, the parish priest in Mullingar persuaded a landlord to evict a pimp. By the 1860s trends that were long in existence were showing results: greater clerical discipline in the catholic church and less absenteeism and pluralism in the Church of Ireland; more regular attendance at church and chapel, and greater lay involvement in religious affairs; the merging of traditional Christian morality with Victorian respectability. There were, however, limits to all of these. First, clerical discipline was not as complete as it might have been: Cardinal Cullen and Archbishop Trench might have agreed, for example, that Fr Lavelle was as big a nuisance as Rev. Tresham Dames Gregg. Secondly, religious observance was neither as strict nor as elaborate as many clergymen would have wished. In a police report in 1870 on the custom of ringing the angelus an R.M. in Westmeath claimed that 'not one in five hundred catholics at fair or market, anxiously following their occupations, ever think of uncovering at the sound of the bell'.[1] In the parish of Magheracross in 1870, there were over 1200 members of the Church of Ireland, and on average 300 attended morning prayer on Sundays; but only 35 attended evening prayer, and only 30 received communion on Easter Sunday; furthermore, although there were 180 Church of Ireland children in the parish's day schools, only 110 attended Sunday school. In higher circles less than perfection prevailed. Even in the newly restored St Patrick's cathedral clerical absenteeism persisted, for at a service on a holiday

Of the ten or twelve clergymen whose duty it is to attend the daily service, there was one solitary representative, who is both a minor canon and a vicar choral. Neither dean nor sub-dean was there, and the only other clergyman who attended was a prebendary. Only three singing men were present, in place of twelve vicars choral. The surplices of the

[1] S.P.O., R.P. 1870/3725.

boys of the choir were untidy, and seemed as though their washing was paid for by the ecclesiastical commissioners.[1]

Respectability, too, had its limits. Sunday observance was probably better than it had been thirty years before, especially in those catholic dioceses where bishops closed public houses; there were probably more carriages and top-hats to be seen on Sunday mornings; but public misbehaviour persisted, for in 1870 96,116 men and women were convicted at the petty sessions of drunkenness, and the police recorded the existence of 563 brothels throughout the country.

The most apparent characteristic of Irish Christians was their fear of each other. For protestants 'the pope was the perpetual bugbear—a great devouring "beast", which threatened to swallow up all our institutions, not excepting the throne, and to gulp down first of all the Irish protestant establishment, which would render the rest an easy prey'.[2] For catholics the threat was less defined, but only because their opponents had no pope. Cardinal Cullen's evidence to the Powis commission on national education began from premises that few Christians would have denied: religious training was a necessary consequence of the fall of man; catholics were obliged to submit to many rules that 'if not taught to practise and respect them at an early age, they will scarcely ever bring themselves to observe them when life is more advanced'. Many would have agreed that 'at the present time there is a great tendency to materialism, to the promotion of everything affecting the interests of this world, and there is a great neglect at the same time of everything supernatural, of everything relating to the world to come'.[3] When, however, he came to the actual problem of mixed schools his words would have produced less agreement: if catholic children 'are constantly with protestant children as companions or playmates, they will begin to think that one religion is as good as another. . . . Thus, a general system of indifference will be introduced, or a system of contentions and disputes.'[4] Even in the teaching of secular subjects, he thought that 'it is practically impossible that a teacher of one religion can instruct the children of another religion without producing an effect upon them. . . . If the protestant teacher be a respectable man, if he be looked up to, and esteemed by, the children, they will persuade themselves that everything he holds is right.'[5] There seemed to be little common ground, except a wish for exclusiveness from the cradle to the grave, with separate schools, separate benefit societies, separate festivals, separate hospitals, and separate graveyards. Protestants feared catholic ascendancy and believed in the existence of a legislative programme that included, at a conservative estimate, the abolition not only of the established church but also of Trinity College, the queen's colleges, the

[1] *Clerical Journal*, quoted in James Godkin, *Ireland and her churches* (London, 1867), p. 163.
[2] Ibid., p. 110.
[3] *Royal commission of inquiry into primary education (Ireland)*, iv, *containing the evidence taken before the commissioners from 24 Nov. 1868 to 29 May 1869*, p. 1177 [C 6-III], H.C. 1870, xxviii, pt iv, p. 405.
[4] Ibid., p. 1179.　　　　　　　　　　　　　　　　　　　　　　[5] Ibid., p. 1183.

Hibernian Military Academy, the endowed schools, the coronation oath, and the protestant succession. Catholics who agreed with Cardinal Cullen seemed to fear that catholic faith was a fragile plant that would be ruined by the blast of protestantism. Superficially at least there was only one meeting point: a fear of 'rationalism'. Cullen, for example, told the Powis commission of 'a history of modern rationalism written by Mr Lecky ... a work in which nearly all the chief doctrines of the catholic church are impugned with great art and great plausibility, and almost everything of a supernatural character in Christianity is assailed'.[1] Protestant fears were vaguer, for 'the twin sisters of Ritualism and Rationalism' were seen as allies of Rome on her rapid march 'towards the goal of her long-coveted ascendancy'.[2] Neither Cardinal Cullen nor devout protestants had much to fear from rationalists, for only six were recorded in the 1871 census; indeed, rationalists, freethinkers, materialists, and atheists could not muster more than a few score. Whatever divided people in Ireland, they had one thing in common: nearly all professed some religious affiliation, for only 1,044 refused to state their religion in 1871.

It is relatively easy to demonstrate the unease caused by these contending sovereignties, but it is not easy to demonstrate the ordinary, everyday compromises that tempered them, for in the nature of things neighbourliness, self-interest, and a penchant for the quiet life did not find systematic exposition before parliamentary inquiries. The affair at Kilconnell, for example, was mitigated by the fact that the catholics present remained uncovered while the protestant service was being read.[3] In 1860 when Fermanagh's first catholic high sheriff met the robustly protestant grand jury, there was a 'strife of courtesy and Christian kindness' between them.[4] Clergymen in northern parishes occasionally were bold enough to defy their parishioners by removing Orange flags from their churches. (Magee modestly referred, during his speech to the lords, to his own efforts to remove flags when he was rector of Enniskillen.) In 1868 there were 76 catholic students in Trinity, and in 1869 461 in Queen's College, Galway, 94 in Cork, and 18 in Belfast, in spite of the 'grievous and intrinsic dangers' for catholics that the synod of Thurles saw in those institutions.[5] An analysis of tenant right sales in the parish of Magherarcross suggests that catholics and protestants sold land to each other.[6] More important, there was some degree of cooperation, willing and otherwise, in politics. In Ulster from 1868 to 1880 the success of the liberals was based on an alliance between presbyterians and catholics; in southern constituencies protestant liberals, such as Lord Otho Fitzgerald (County Kildare, 1865–74),

---

[1] Ibid., 1178.

[2] Fielding Ould, *Our British constitution, and its position at the present crisis* (London, 1867), p. 1.

[3] Above, pp 734–5.

[4] Larcom papers (T.C.D., MS 1710/41).

[5] Quoted in Emmet Larkin, *The making of the Roman Catholic church in Ireland, 1850–1860* (Chapel Hill, 1980), p. 35.

[6] Above, p. 739.

were returned, and more remarkably some protestant tories, such as Arthur MacMorrough Kavanagh (County Wexford, 1866–8, and County Carlow, 1868–80). The identification of toryism and protestantism was by no means complete, for John Pope Hennessy (M.P. for King's County, 1859–65, and County Wexford, 1866) was a catholic tory.

GLADSTONE'S speech on 15 February 1870 introducing the land bill was not one of his great speeches, reflecting perhaps the fact that the real battles had already been fought in the cabinet.[1] It had few flashes of oratory (some of his best touches came later, such as his reference to Landseer's lions in Trafalgar Square), and little of the impressive mastery of detail that characterised his budget speeches. He contented himself with enumerating the grievances of the tenants: the withdrawal of customary privileges, 'the lavish and pitiless use of notices to quit', evictions, and rents that absorbed the value of improvements. 'We cannot name a point in which the relation of landlord and tenant in Ireland and in Great Britain are the same, except only in what may be called the abstract and general idea.' Relations between landlords and tenants in Ireland were peculiar because they were embittered by memories of conquest, by differences in religion and politics, by landlords' absenteeism, and by their failure to provide capital and to give leases, so that the tenant has no right 'in anything which he has put into the soil'. (Irish landlords listening were no doubt gratified to hear that they were unlike British landlords because they did not have to discharge an 'immense mass of public duties'.) The most interesting point of comparison between Britain and Ireland in Gladstone's list, however, was his belief that holding by contract was unfamiliar in Ireland, because 'the old Irish ideas and customs were never supplanted except by the rude hand of violence and by laws written in the statute book, but never entering into the heart of the Irish people'.[2]

He was particularly weak in explaining why he had taken up the question in 1870. He denied that there had been continuous progress during the last twenty years. 'Between 1849 and 1860 there was a great and general increase in the rate of wages throughout Ireland', but 'since 1860 that rate of wages has not generally advanced'; he admitted that evictions had been fewer since 1860 but contended that 'some of the most indefensible, nay, some of the most guilty of evictions, have occurred between the two dates to which I have referred'; between 1860 and 1868 pasturage had increased by about 560,000 acres and the number dependent on the poor law from 170,000 to 289,000. He tried to strengthen his argument by claiming that neither the poor law, nor emigration ('another word for banishment'), nor the encumbered estates acts had worked; 'notwithstanding all these things, I doubt whether at this moment, so far as the

---

[1] E. D. Steele, *Irish land and British politics. Tenant right and nationality 1865–70* (Cambridge, 1974), pp 200–54.

[2] *Hansard 3*, cxcix, 339–40, 355 (15 Feb. 1870).

law is concerned, the condition of the Irish peasant is materially better, or even better at all, than it was before the mitigation of the penal laws'.[1]

The gravamen of his case was that insecurity of tenure was 'the great mischief'. To remedy this, he proposed to legalise the Ulster custom and similar customs outside Ulster; to establish a scale of damages for eviction; and to give tenants compensation for improvements 'irrespective of the claim for damages by eviction'. He rejected the idea of turning existing rents into perpetuities because landlords would have to be compensated 'for the loss of their chances in the future', either 'by our old familiar friend, the consolidated fund', or by 'an immediate increase of the rents now payable in Ireland'. He was determined that the landlords should not be allowed to become mere *rentiers*, like 'fundholders, entitled to apply on a certain day from year to year for a certain sum of money'. 'Are you prepared,' he asked, 'to absolve them from their duties with regard to the land?' He did, however, allow the courts, when awarding compensation for eviction, to consider the level of the rent, for 'of late years especially there may have grown up in certain cases contracts for rent of a character most extravagant, which it is totally impossible for the tenant to pay and at the same time to live upon his holding'. His speech ended on an optimistic note: 'There is, as I believe, a huge fund of national wealth in the soil, as yet undeveloped.'[2]

His arguments were at least debatable. English methodists and Scottish free churchmen would have not agreed that there were no differences of politics and religion between landlords and tenants in Britain. Protestant tenants in Ulster (who were better treated in his bill than southern tenants) could hardly have agreed that they were on bad terms with their landlords because of confiscation. Officials in Dublin castle, familiar with police reports of complicated transactions between tenants and money-lenders, involving sub-lettings that resembled the more dignified mortgages of landlords, would not have agreed that Irishmen were unfamiliar with freedom of contract, although justices listening to cases between farmers and labourers about unpaid wages and petty tyranny might have agreed that contract did not always work. He was right when he said that some dramatic evictions had taken place since 1860, if he meant John George Adair's eviction of forty-seven families at Derryveagh in 1861, and William Scully's attempt to remove the Ballycohey tenants in 1868; but these were isolated incidents and could not be compared with the famine evictions. His reference to the 'lavish and pitiless use of notices to quit'[3] was almost certainly a reference to the third earl of Leitrim, who was alleged to have them printed on the backs of his rent-receipts; but it is impossible to calculate how many other landlords did this, for there were no statistics of notices to quit. His argument about prosperity was too simple. He was right when he said that wages had increased less rapidly after 1860, but he would have been wiser to have alluded to the agricultural depression of the early 1860s, which was what

[1] Ibid., 341, 345–6.   [2] Ibid., 350–51, 371, 379, 385.   [3] Ibid., 355.

mattered to farmers. That, however, would have been an argument for legislating in 1863 or 1864, but not for legislating in 1870 when prosperity was at an unprecedented height. (His choice of 1860 as a turning-point was probably caused by his concern not to disown Edward Cardwell, his secretary for war, who had tried to solve the land question in 1860.)

Much of Gladstone's speech must be seen as a parade of subaltern arguments, marshalled to support his determination to give the tenants security of tenure. But why did his policy need such support? Almost fifty years ago J. L. Hammond in his *Gladstone and the Irish nation* pointed out that Gladstone was handicapped in 1870 by not having the findings of a royal commission to support his case. But Gladstone and parliament were not without detailed, contemporary information. Apart from a small library of pamphlets, most notably George Campbell's *The Irish land* (published in 1869) and William O'Connor Morris's *Letters on the land question of Ireland* (published in 1870), there was an official report, compiled by the Irish poor law inspectors and published as a parliamentary paper in 1870, which supplemented the reports of special committees already published in 1865 and 1867. The real problem was not lack of information but the presumed existence of a 'monster evil' that was as elusive as the Cheshire cat, whose acquaintance the public had made in 1865. In all of this material there was no evidence of widespread, intolerable tyranny; there was indeed a sense of insecurity amng tenants; there were examples of harsh landlords, often long dead, but not forgotten; notices to quit were served, but there was no evidence that they rained down like snowflakes, or even like autumnal leaves in Vallambrosa; it was not even clear that most landlords did not help their tenants with improvements. Estate papers and official statistics support this picture: evictions were not frequent; rents, far from absorbing the value of tenants' improvements, did not even keep up with agricultural prices; between 1841 and 1871 76,855 new second-class houses were enumerated by the census commissioners, which suggests that house-building went on at about the same rate in 1841–71 as it did between 1871 and 1881. Not surprisingly Gladstone was cautious about discussing tenants' discontent; he could not plausibly argue that he was weaning them away from fenianism, because very few of them were fenians, and agrarian outrages had fallen to a very low figure in the mid-1860s. He confined himself to referring in dismissive terms to the wave of disorder that had broken out in the winter of 1869, which some of his critics blamed on his election speeches: 'I cannot, for one moment, be surprised that, in some cases where ... hope has been revived, it has in the minds of some been such as to exhibit elements of a riotous exuberance.'[1]

What was there to reform? Were tenants' grievances so great that principle and policy justified giving them rights enjoyed by no other class in the United Kingdom or, indeed, enjoyed by tenants anywhere in Europe? As Gladstone read the reports of the poor law inspectors it must have occurred to him that his

[1] *Hansard 3*, cxcix, 349, 369.

upas tree was at best a dwarf alpine, if not a bonsai? There were facts, however, that could be grasped. The fact that yearly tenants had no right to compensation for their buildings, drains, roads, and fences was a weakness and there were cases of tenants being robbed by unscrupulous landlords. Compensation for improvements was straightforward enough, and many Irish landlords, including Lord Mayo (chief secretary, 1866–8), who had introduced a compensation bill in 1867, were in favour of changing the law. The problem here was not the principle, but the practice, and on the whole, Gladstone's solution was one of the simplest ever proposed, even if it was limited by a mass of qualifications. The one accusation against Irish landlords that had a sound foundation was their failure to invest a large proportion of their rents in their estates; but there was little in Gladstone's bill to encourage them, and the passage of the bill itself may have discouraged them. Legalising the Ulster custom was more complicated; its existence and smooth working might have been adduced as reasons for leaving it alone; certainly, after 1870 it would have been hard to argue that the custom's natural symbiosis was not damaged by the litigation caused by sections 1 and 15 of the land act. (Gladstone was as alive to the difficulties of legalising tenant right as anyone who ever studied that elusive custom; he told Lord Clarendon in September 1869: 'I have puzzled & puzzled over it & cannot for the life of me see how it is to be legalised without being essentially changed. It is like trying in algebra to solve a problem of two unknown quantities with only one equation.')[1] To prevent a repetition of the Derryveagh evictions would be a good thing. Yet Gladstone did not mention them in his speech, although Lord Palmerston, no sentimentalist in his attitude to Irish tenants, had condemned them in 1861. (Perhaps he felt uneasy at his own silence in the commons debate on Derryveagh in 1861, when he was chancellor of the exchequer?)

There was no doubt that the bill addressed itself successfully to problems like Derryveagh and Ballycohey and produced quite an effective compromise solution. But such evictions were not the most common problem. The simultaneous eviction of forty-seven tenants who had paid their rents was a rare event after the early 1850s. The most common victim of eviction was the tenant who could not pay his rent, and the bill gave him nothing except compensation for improvements, whose value would almost certainly be absorbed by the landlord's counter-claim for arrears. There was, however, a fact that either could not be grasped, or if grasped could not easily be explained, for there was a sense in which tenants were insecure and probably discontented. Since rents lagged behind agricultural prices, tenants naturally felt uneasy about rent increases that would absorb some at least of their prosperity; they also felt uneasy about competition for land, although few farms were let by auction; but most importantly, tenants who could not sell their interest, or tenant right, in their farms could not capitalise their temporary good fortune; nor could they

[1] H. C. G. Matthew (ed.), *The Gladstone diaries* (9 vols, Oxford, 1968–86), vii, 137.

easily borrow on its security. What faced Gladstone, therefore, was not a crisis of poverty and tyranny but a crisis of prosperity. Even if he fully grasped the problem, there was little he could do about it, once he abandoned the idea of extending the Ulster custom to the whole of Ireland. The strange thing about the speech, however, was not its analysis of landlord–tenant relations but its concentration on the plight of agricultural labourers: it was mainly labourers who peopled the workhouses, it was labourers who emigrated, and it was labourers who suffered from the rising price of food. Gladstone recognised this last point, admitting that the cost of subsistence had gone up, which 'is a great boon to the Irish farmer, but to the labourer or the man who is the buyer rather than a grower of produce such a change represents a condition, not of increase, but of stinted and narrowed circumstances'.[1]

After four days of debate, the bill had a triumphant second reading on 11 March, when a well attended house divided 442 to 11. The majority included a remarkable range of Irish opinion: Ulster tory landlords such as William Verner (County Armagh, 1868–73), and Lt-col. W. B. Forde (County Down, 1857–74); the Orangeman William Johnston (Belfast, 1868–78); southern tory landlords such as Arthur MacMorrough Kavanagh (County Carlow, 1868–80); and liberals in all their diverse manifestations, such as the O'Conor Don (Roscommon, 1860–80) and the O'Donoghue (Tralee, 1865–85), as well as veterans of the early 1850s such as John Francis Maguire (Cork city, 1865–72) and George Henry Moore (County Kilkenny, 1868–70), and large landlords such as H. A. Herbert (County Kerry, 1868–80) and Lord Castlerosse (County Kerry, 1852–72) who inherited the earldom of Kenmare and 118,606 acres in 1871. (Many of the liberals who supported the bill were returned as home rulers in 1874, although there were exceptions: Capt. Edward Saunderson (County Cavan, 1865–74) became leader of the Ulster unionists, H. A. Herbert survived as a liberal in 1874, and the O'Donoghue postponed his conversion until 1880). The eleven who opposed the second reading were mainly Irish M.P.s, the best known of whom were Sir John Gray (Kilkenny city, 1865–75) and Phillip Callan (Dundalk, 1868–80). Gray's opposition was remarkable in view of Maguire and Moore's support, for Gladstone's bill did not go as far as their own bill in 1857.

In committee, however, the bill came near to disaster when William Fowler's amendment, proposing that holdings valued at more than £50 should be excluded from compensation for disturbance, was only narrowly defeated on 7 April by 250 to 218. The most important changes made in the commons were in the amount of compensation to be awarded in clause 3 for disturbance: first the scale was made more complicated, which reduced the amount given to the larger holdings; secondly, a ceiling of £250 was placed on compensation; thirdly, existing holdings (but not future ones) valued at over £100 were excluded; fourthly, compensation for disturbance was to last only to 1891 'and

---

[1] *Hansard 3*, cxcix, 342 (15 Feb. 1870).

thereafter until parliament shall otherwise determine'.[1] In the lords, efforts were made to reduce the amount of compensation given to all but the very smallest tenants and to make the granting of a lease for twenty-one years, instead of thirty-one years, sufficient to exclude new lettings from compensation for disturbance. Neither of these was accepted by the government. The most important amendment made by the lords was to clause 8, which allowed the courts to decide on 'special grounds' that a tenant ejected for non-payment of rent could be compensated for disturbance. The lords deleted the lines conferring this power, but eventually they accepted ejectment for non-payment of 'exorbitant' rents as disturbance. Unfortunately this removed a discretionary power that might have been valuable in the agricultural crisis of 1879. Another small change provided that clause 3 would become inoperative in 1891 unless it was explicitly renewed by parliament. The lords did not make much of a fight and there was no risk of a conflict between the two houses such as that of the previous summer. Only Lord Salisbury came close to emulating Magee when he attacked the fundamental assumption on which the bill was based:

Is it come to this, then, that we are to compensate anyone who loses his employment, the loss of which would expose him to the workhouse or America? Are you prepared to accept that proposition in its breadth—to apply it to all the circumstances of life, and to all parts of her majesty's dominions? We have had great distress recently in the east end of London. We have had dockyard labourers living on the very verge of their resources. . . . Would you be prepared to entertain a measure forcing their employers to give them seven years' wages as compensation upon dismissing them?[2]

The bill received its third reading in the lords on 8 July and became law on 1 August, becoming effective immediately in all its provisions, unlike the church act of the previous year.

THE aim of Gladstone's act was to protect tenants from capricious eviction by giving them rights that penalised evicting landlords.[3] These rights were conferred on most agricultural tenants who were in possession on 1 August 1870, but the law also prevented existing and future tenants—with important exceptions—from contracting out of the act. By limiting the freedom of contract of tenants whose holdings were valued under £50 per year, they were put in the same legal position as lunatics, minors, and expectant heirs—until 1891 in the case of 'disturbance', and for ever in the case of improvements. The act was a complicated measure running to seventy-three sections; it did not enunciate any great principle or intention; it had none of the rhetoric of the Gettysburg address; it did not even rise to the portentousness of section 3 of

[1] A bill [as amended in committee, and on consideration of bill as amended] to amend the law relating to the occupation and ownership of land in Ireland, H.C. 1870 (bill 145), ii, 333.

[2] Hansard 3, ccii, 80 (14 June 1870).

[3] 33 & 34 Vict., c. 46 (1 Aug. 1870).

Deasy's act.[1] Most of the sections made changes that were either routine, or ancillary to sections 1–15, which were the most important: sections 16–25 laid down how disputes between landlords and tenants would be settled; sections 26–56 regulated the powers of limited owners, the sale of land to tenants, and powers of the Board of Works to make loans to landlords and tenants; probably section 44, which allowed the board of works to lend two-thirds of the purchase price of their farms, repayable over thirty-five years by annuities of 5 per cent, was the most important of these. Sections 57–73 were supplemental and miscellaneous provisions, of which the most interesting was perhaps section 58, which obliged landlords to put a stamp worth 2s. 6d. on notices to quit. Narrowing down the important part of the act to sections 1–15, however, merely circumscribes the area of complexity. Sections 1–4 were undoubtedly the most important. The first two legalised the Ulster tenant right custom and any custom in the rest of the country 'which in all essential particulars corresponds with the Ulster tenant right custom'. Section 3 allowed tenants who were 'disturbed' by their landlords to claim compensation based on a sliding scale of values, which gave the smallest holdings and those paying the highest rents the most compensation. Section 4 gave tenants, whether 'disturbed' or leaving voluntarily, the right to compensation for improvements made before and after the passing of the act. Of the remaining eleven sections, sections 7 and 9 were probably the most important. The former allowed tenants who did not come under sections 1–3 to claim compensation for money given 'with the express or implied consent of the landlord on account of his . . . coming into his holding.' The latter attempted to define 'disturbance' and to protect small tenants whose rents were 'exorbitant'.

The act bristled with difficulties and complexities. Sections 1 and 2 were vague and did not attempt to define tenant right, even in the most general way. Section 4, on improvements, contained nine major limitations on the right to compensation. Section 3, probably the most remarkable legislative measure passed by the eighth parliament of Queen Victoria, provided a scale of compensation but did not make it clear how the courts were to be guided by it; it also allowed tenants in a higher class to claim under a lower class, in order to protect those at the extreme ends of each class. No doubt, this was skilful contrivance, but even the most clear-minded solicitors must have found it difficult to explain to their clients. Distinctions between different kinds of tenancies were made, but some did not apply uniformly throughout the act. The most important distinction was that made between tenants who could claim for tenant right and those who could not, because the former had the option of claiming under sections 3, 4, and 7, as well as under sections 1 and 2; in other words, Ulster tenants could take as their minimum the best that was available to others. Also, a distinction was made between tenants evicted for arrears and those evicted on notice to quit: the latter could claim under sections 3, 4, and 7, but the former could not

[1] 23 & 24 Vict., c. 154 (28 Aug. 1860); see above, pp 458–63.

claim under section 3. Leaseholders and yearly tenants, existing tenants and new tenants, big tenants and small tenants were treated differently. All existing yearly tenants could claim for improvements; but new tenants, entering after 1 August 1870, could be made to contract out of the act if their holdings were valued at £50 or more. The same distinction was made for claims for disturbance. The treatment of large holdings whose value exceeded £100 was also varied: they could not claim for disturbance but they could claim for improvements; when they claimed for improvements, however, they did not, like their smaller fellows, enjoy the benefit of section 5, which provided that 'all improvements . . . shall, until the contrary is proved, be deemed to have been made by the tenant or his predecesors in title'. The distinctions between existing leaseholders and new ones were equally sharp: existing leaseholders whose terms were for longer than a year could not claim for disturbance, but new leaseholders, created after 1 August 1870, could—if their lease was for less than thirty-one years. When claiming for improvements leaseholders faced further complexities: the rights of existing ones depended on the length of their leases, those for thirty-one years and upwards getting less than those with shorter leases. New leaseholders were even more complicated, for those whose holdings were valued at £50 or more could be made to contract out of the act, and the rights of those under £50 again depended on the length of their leases.

Behind this mass of legal distinctions there were principles that were clear enough: leases and written agreements must be given more protection from legislative interference than yearly tenancies because it was assumed that they had been entered into deliberately and freely; improvements were more important than compensation for disturbance; big tenants were given less protection than small tenants because it was assumed that they were able to look after themselves; landlords should be encouraged to give thirty-one year leases in order to free themselves from section 3 and part of section 4. The great intention of the act, to confer an inalienable status on small yearly tenants, was clear but fearsomely qualified. Nowhere were the restrictions more daunting than in section 3, and sections 9 and 14, which attempted to define it. Most important, a tenant evicted for non-payment of rent could not claim for disturbance. Nor could a tenant claim for disturbance if he subdivided or sub-let his holding or unreasonably refused to allow his landlord to enter his holding to hunt or shoot, to cut turf, or to make roads or drains. Even if a tenant succeeded in getting compensation, the landlord could make deductions for arrears of rent and taxes and for 'deterioration'. Likewise, the right to compensation for improvements was narrow; all future improvements were eligible but those made before 1870 were limited to permanent buildings and the reclamation of waste land; other improvements were eligible only if they were made within the twenty years before the claim was made. Furthermore, when giving compensation the courts were to 'take into consideration the time during which [the] tenant may have enjoyed the advantage of such improvements'.

Section 15, which excluded holdings in demesnes and townparks from any compensation, even for tenant right under section 1, was a further irritating restriction.

In spite of its limitations, however, the land act of 1870 was a remarkable change, whose significance should not be diminished by comparing it with the act of 1881, or even with the land purchase acts. If it is seen against a background of actual estate management, or even against the prejudices of a parliament dominated by property owners, it represented a drastic change in the rights of property. By giving hundreds of thousands of farmers a right to compensation for disturbance, it conferred on them a right that was not generally enjoyed by the rest of the population until well into the twentieth century when workers were given the right to redundancy payments. It could be argued that the landlords had no right to their estates, but it could hardly be argued with any consistency that the tenants were their moral heirs. As Gladstone said, 'the occupiers of land in Ireland, though they of themselves constitute something near a moiety of the people of the country, yet are not the whole people'.[1] If land is seen as a vast engine for the production of food, having an intrinsic value independent of the labour and capital used by its cultivators, it obviously belongs to everyone or to no one; its disposal, therefore, poses some nice questions. A partial solution to the problem, which can only work because it assumes that the population of a country is morally sovereign, is to impose all of the taxes on the land. Mathematically this would have worked nicely in 1870 for the total revenue of Ireland was within a couple of millions of its rental. It is doubtful, however, if it would have found many supporters, even among treasury officials.

Gladstone argued that there were precedents for limiting freedom of contract, pointing to the regulation of emigrant ships and the factory acts as examples. He was, of course, right, and modesty perhaps prevented him from pointing to the 'parliamentary' trains. But the act of 1870 was not just a prohibition or restriction, it also conferred a right to compensation that would have been unthinkable in the cotton mills or coal mines of Britain. Even before the passing of the land act, tenants were in a relatively privileged position in Irish society: they had the use of land; they had some property in the form of livestock; they could not just be thrown out without ceremony like agricultural labourers; many of them were better-off than industrial workers. Tenants were certainly better-off than agricultural labourers, who were a sort of submerged class in post-famine Ireland, attracting little comment from those who so feelingly described the plight of tenants. 'I may now, perhaps, be asked what we have done for the Irish labourer,' said Mr Gladstone in his speech introducing the land bill; his answer was as *laissez-faire* as even the most strict follower of Adam Smith could have wished: 'the only great boon ... which it is in the power of the legislature to give to the agricultural labourer in Ireland is to

[1] *Hansard 3*, cxcix, 352 (15 Feb. 1870).

increase the demand for his labour'.[1] The legal position of labourers was a precarious one: they could be employed by the day and frequently were; indeed irregularity of employment was their major grievance in 1870. If, however, they were bound by contract to their masters, they could suffer something more than dismissal for bad behaviour. Until 1867 servants' breaches of contract and misconduct could be punished with imprisonment; the master and servant act of 1867[2] made breach of contract a civil wrong but retained imprisonment for circumstances of 'an aggravated character'. Irish masters and servants seem to have gone into court more frequently than those in Britain; in 1854 and 1855 almost one-third of the United Kingdom's convictions for breach of contract were in Ireland; convictions under the new act were just as frequent, for between 1868 and 1872 Ireland had one-third of the United Kingdom's convictions. A typical case was heard at the petty sessions in Lisnaskea in 1873: a farmer named Wilson complained 'that Thomas Montray, his hired servant, was insubordinate, disobedient, and refused to do his work at Lisnaskea on Tuesday, 31 December 1872';[3] the court sentenced Montray to one month's imprisonment. Servants could sue employers and occasionally employers were convicted or made to pay damages: at Ballymena petty sessions in January 1870 William Hood was sued for not paying his servant's wages; there had been no agreement, but the bench urged Hood, 'as a matter of generosity' to give something; but Hood refused: 'He was like smoke to mine eyes and vinegar to my teeth; and I will not violate my conscience by paying him a single penny.'[4] The plight of agricultural labourers, therefore, was greater than that of the tenants and might have merited more attention.

As an incursion into the actual running of estates, the land act was important. From 1 August 1870 it became more difficult for landlords to change the terms of existing yearly tenancies. Existing rents could not be changed except by the agreement of both parties, or by the landlord evicting the tenant; but if the tenant were evicted, he might receive as much as seven times the existing rent in compensation for disturbance. In other words, a landlord would need a rent increase of about 40 per cent to make such an operation cover its costs, and a much larger one to make it profitable. Managing estates was essentially a matter of overcoming obstacles. Legal changes before 1870, such as the civil bill act of 1851,[5] tended to make it easier for landlords to evict, but the land act reversed that trend. Any obstacle in the way of the landlord gave the tenant not only greater security of tenure, but the improved prospect that his rent would not be increased. After 1870 the value of agricultural output increased steadily

---

[1] Ibid., 383.

[2] 30 & 31 Vict., c. 141 (20 Aug. 1867).

[3] *First report of the commissioners appointed to inquire into the working of the master and servant act, 1867, and the criminal law amendment act, 34 & 35 Vict. c. 32, and for other purposes, together with minutes of evidence*, p. 34 [C 1094], H.C. 1874, xxiv, 424.

[4] *Ballymena Observer*, 22 Jan. 1870.

[5] 14 & 15 Vict., c. 57 (1 Aug. 1851).

until 1876. This increase, and the increase that took place in the late 1860s, should have led to a round of rent increases, but rents increased hardly at all on most estates after 1870, and the gap between output and rent became greater than it had been before. It is impossible to prove that this stagnation was entirely due to the land act; it may be that landlords suffered a loss of nerve that had nothing to do with the details of the act; it may be that the new prosperity did not last long enough for landlords to take advantage of it. While there is evidence for both of these arguments, it can also be argued that the act played its part. On an estate in Clare, for example, leases made in the 1850s began to expire in the early 1870s. These leaseholders could not claim for disturbance under section 3 and some of them suffered large increases; a tenant who had leased a farm for twenty-one years in 1854 at a rent of £33 was given a new lease for thirty-two years in 1875 at a rent of £50, an increase of 50 per cent. (A survey of the estate noted that this 'tenant has improved his farm more than any of the others. . . . House . . . in good repair. Office thatched and good.') The agent noted that on another farm, held on a thirty-one-year lease with seventeen years still to run, there was 'an exceedingly low rent. If the lands were now to be relet, double the yearly rent could be obtained.'[1] The fortunes of the lease-holders on this estate who were unprotected by section 3 of the land act were so different from the mass of tenants who were protected that they suggest that the act gave more protection against rent increases in practice than it did in theory.

How different was Gladstone's act from earlier land bills? It went much further than the tories' bill of 1867, introduced by the chief secretary, Lord Naas, and the solicitor general, which allowed tenants compensation for future improvements, even if they were made without the landlords' consent, but which allowed nothing for disturbance. The idea of disturbance was a fairly familiar one: it appeared as early as 1848 in a bill introduced by Sharman Crawford and the repeal member for Roscommon, Valentine Blake, which allowed the tenant to sell his tenant right or to be compensated 'for any loss or injury he may sustain by dispossession from the premises, in as ample a manner as such tenant would receive compensation for lands taken for public purposes under [8 Vict., c. 18]'.[2] It appeared again in bills introduced in 1866 and 1867, but only as a general formula, and Gladstone's contribution was to produce a sliding-scale of actual monetary values. Gladstone did not, of course, make any arrangements to allow the courts to adjust rents, except in section 9, which dealt with 'exorbitant' rents. In that respect the act gave less than had been proposed by Sharman Crawford's bill in 1848, Mr Serjeant Shee's bill in November 1852, and D. J. Rearden and Michael Bass's bill in July 1868. It must be remembered, however, that by legalising the tenant right custom he did establish rudimentary rent adjustment of a kind for about one-third of the

---

[1] Survey of the estate of the Westropp family in the counties of Clare and Limerick, 1871–7, Robert L. Brown agent (N.L.I., MS 5397, pp 75, 69).
[2] *A bill to secure the rights of outgoing tenants in Ireland*, p. 3, H.C. 1847–8 (bill 155), iv, 553.

tenants. The Ulster custom was not the three Fs as was often argued by its advocates, but its essence was the fact that tenants could sell their 'interest', which was not only improvements but the difference between the rents they paid and the real value of their land. The relationship between rents and tenant right was not a matter of rules or principles; it could not in fact be easily explained or explicitly stated; it was really a subterfuge, concealing a dynamic and irreconcilable conflict, which worked so long as landlords had considerable reserves of power that they used moderately. Yet when the courts came to deal with tenant right claims they had to define fair rents. In 1872, for example, a tenant in Armagh, threatened with eviction because she would not agree to pay a rent increase of 27 per cent, claimed in the county court that her tenant right was worth £700; her counsel, Isaac Butt, 'asked the chairman to fix the rent at a fair sum', having produced a valuator who claimed that the old rent was adequate. The chairman, who agreed that 'the issue to be decided was whether the demand of the landlord was reasonable', decided that the rent should not be increased and awarded the tenant £300, which was almost twenty times the old rent.[1]

It is interesting, however, to speculate on what would have happened if these bills had become law; Shee's bill defined a fair rent as 'the landlord's just proportion of the money value of the gross produce (according to the market value of such produce)';[2] Rearden and Bass's bill in 1868 allowed valuers to fix rents every twenty-one years, allowing the landlord 'any increase which may have taken place in the market or selling value of such land'.[3] It is almost certain that Crawford's 1848 bill would have led to many rent reductions because of the famine, although his definition of fair rent was a capacious one as 'the rent for which one year with another the premises might be reasonably expected to let to a solvent tenant'.[4] If Shee's bill had become law in 1853, however, it would have come into effect just as prices were rising and it might have had less effect than Crawford's. But what would have happened in the 1870s under Rearden and Bass's bill, which allowed the landlord a 'natural increase'? Prices had been rising steadily and outpacing rents; when a new tenement valuation was proposed in 1876 the prices on which it was based were much higher than those used in the 1850s; calculations made under the Trinity College Dublin Leasing and Perpetuity Act, 1851, a system of statutory rent-fixing that had been imposed on the college estates, showed that rents should have increased by about 50 per cent between 1852 and 1870.[5] It is possible,

[1] Carraher v. Bond, I.L.T. digest 1872, pp 19–20.
[2] A bill to provide for the better securing of and regulating the custom of tenant right as practised in the province of Ulster, and to secure compensation to improving tenants who may not make claim under the said custom, and to limit the power of eviction in certain cases, p. 4, H.C. 1852–3 (bill 25), vii, 340.
[3] A bill to amend the law relating to the tenure and improvement of land, and to facilitate and promote the sale and purchase of land and tenants' interests, and the reclamation of waste lands in Ireland, p. 7, H.C. 1867–8 (bill 244), v, 251.
[4] A bill to secure the rights of outgoing tenants in Ireland, p. 4, H.C. 1847–8 (bill 155), iv, 554.
[5] 14 & 15 Vict., c. cxxviii (1 Aug. 1851).

therefore, that the valuers might have actually increased rents under this bill; it is highly unlikely that there would have been big reductions. It is possible that Gladstone's act was more effective from the tenants' point of view than Rearden and Bass's would have been. By providing no mechanism for adjusting rents it prevented statutory increases, and by making it difficult to increase rents it held back natural increases.

The weakness of Gladstone's act was the scale of values in section 3 and its exclusion of tenants evicted for arrears. The maximum sum awarded, seven times the rent for tenants whose holdings were valued at £10 and under, seemed generous, especially when it is remembered that dismissed labourers got nothing (on the other hand, clergymen of the disestablished Irish church got, on average, thirteen times the amount of their incomes); but seven years' purchase did not represent the tenant right value of most holdings and was not enough to allow an evicted tenant to buy another farm. The fact that the compensation was based on the rent meant that the scale worked in the opposite way to tenant right: it benefited the tenant who paid a high rent but deprived the moderately rented tenant of a valuable property. The failure to be generous to insolvent tenants was perhaps one of the weakest parts of the act. Some protection was given to solvent tenants, and after 1870 neither John George Adair nor William Scully could have carried out their peculiar transactions without financial risk; but, as the crisis of 1879 was to show, insolvent tenants were vulnerable. Indeed, from the early 1850s to 1882 insolvent tenants were the most common victims of eviction. The simplest solution would have been to extend section 3 to tenants evicted for arrears, as was proposed in the compensation for disturbance bill, rejected by the house of lords in August 1880; that would have had the additional advantage of putting southern tenants on the same footing as those in Ulster. Another possibility that would not admittedly have appealed to Gladstone, although it might have appealed to Bismarck, was compulsory insurance of rents, financed by contributions from landlords and tenants.

ONE of the strangest books published in 1870 was Patrick Lavelle's *The Irish landlord since the revolution, with notices of ancient and modern land tenures in various countries*, which ranged over modern and ancient Europe, as well as over Irish history, to demonstrate the wickedness of landlordism and the virtue of security of tenure.[1] Lavelle was a crank, but more thoughtful men turned to European land systems for inspiration in putting forward schemes in Ireland. H. D. Hutton advocated the Prussian model in his *The Prussian land tenure reforms and a farmer proprietary for Ireland*, where he drew attention to the rent banks.[2] Belgium was not infrequently referred to as a model, and such was the influence of foreign parallels that the government systematically collected

---

[1] Dublin, 1870.
[2] Dublin and London, 1867.

information on practically every country in Europe and the near east, which was published in three volumes of parliamentary papers in 1870–72.[1]

How peculiar was the Irish land system? Large estates were not uncommon in Europe, especially in Austria-Hungary, Italy, and Spain, and even in France; systems of tenure were not, superficially at least, all that different, certainly in terms of security for the occupiers. The *métayers* in Piedmont and Lombardy, for example, held by the year and could be dismissed with six months' notice to quit; in the Roman states when land was let, it was let by competition and not by valuation. The amount given by *métayers* to landowners seems large by Irish standards: about half of their produce in Piedmont and one-third in parts of the papal states. (The Irish farmers invited to the colony of Saint-Patrice in Algeria by Marshal MacMahon would have been expected to hand over half of their produce annually.)

These estates would at least have been recognisable in Ireland; but much more mysterious was Prussia, so frequently held up as a peasant elysium created by the Stein-Hardenberg reforms. Prussia was indeed a country of peasant proprietors; but it was also a country of large estates. Admittedly the estates were not as big as those in Ireland; in 1870, for example, it was estimated that scarcely 100 Prussian landowners had 2,000 acres and more, 'whilst the owners of 10,000 acres can almost be counted on one's fingers'.[2] (In Ireland there were 2,000 estates of more than 2,000 acres, and owners of 10,000 acres and over numbered about 400.) Although Prussian estates were small, they accounted for a large proportion of the country, and combined with the crown estates, they accounted for almost half of the area of Posen, Silesia, and Upper Lusatia, leaving just over half for the peasant proprietors. These estates were, for the most part, untenanted, and were managed as large farms under the direct supervision of the owner or his manager. The labourers who worked on them had no security of tenure. In Silesia, for example, landowners did not build cottages or give labourers land 'by any other arrangement but one of the most transitory character', for 'there is a latent feeling in existence that a long occupation of self-contained premises, or of small farms, may be invoked at some future period as conferring a title to permanency and to further limitations of the rights of property'.[3] The peasant proprietors were no more openhanded, for they bought up houses and knocked them down 'merely to prevent the possibility of the next lodgers in them becoming chargeable to the commune and a burthen to the rates'.[3] About half of rural workers were landless labourers who slightly outnumbered peasant proprietors. In some parts at least their conditions were not wretched; in Danzig, for example, they ate meat two or three times a week; nevertheless, throughout north-east Germany, 'the

---

[1] *Reports from her majesty's representatives respecting the tenure of land in the several countries of Europe, 1869*, pt i [C 66], H.C. 1870, lxvii, 1; pt ii [C 75], ibid., 549; pt iii [C 271], H.C. 1871, lxvii, 749; pt iv [C 426], ibid., 809; pt v [C 572], H.C. 1872, lxii, 695.

[2] Ibid., pt i, p. 355.　　　　　　　　　　　　　　　　　[3] Ibid., pt ii, pp 132–3.

agricultural labourer lives and dies a mere day labourer. He knows he cannot change his lot.'[1] Tenants did exist, especially on the crown estates where their relations with the treasury were regulated by covenants; but these have a familiar ring for anyone acquainted with Ireland: 'The conditions of these covenants are so severe upon the tenants that they would hardly venture to accept them if they did not know that these are equitably and humanely interpreted by the treasury.'[2] Landless labourers in Germany, therefore, were not much different from landless labourers in Ireland. The peasants who owned land were obviously better off than yearly tenants in Ireland; but they had their problems, which to some extent emanated from their ownership of land. In Posen, for example, 'Hebrew money-lenders are to be found in small towns ready to lend at a rate of interest beyond that which agricultural improvements can repay, and many a peasant who has been tempted to have recourse to this sort of expensive credit, ends by disposing of his freehold.'[3] Statistics of forced sales for debt between 1858 and 1867 show that they were more frequent than evictions in Ireland.

Other countries were less like Ireland. In Finland most of the land was owned by peasants and the crown, but tenancies did exist. Tenants could be served with notice to quit, and they had no right to remain in occupation even if they paid their rents; eviction was not easy but 'it is a very common practice amongst peasants who are proprietors, in order to evade the great delay and trouble of eviction, to take by force the windows and doors out of the tenant's house; this procedure, when carried out in winter, has frequently the desired result.'[4] Belgium was a land of small landowners. According to Fr Lavelle, 'if we pass from Prussia to Belgium, we find a rural prosperity and independence not less striking than in the larger state. *Fixity of tenure* and small farms of from five to ten acres form the rule; and we have it on the authority of the *Encyclopedia Britannica* that "no country in Europe provides from its soil so great a quantity of sustenance".'[5] Lavelle was, however, only partly right; the holdings of Belgian landowners were very small, smaller on average than that of the average Irish tenant, and two-thirds of the productive land was in the hands of tenants. In other words, small tenants rented land from small landlords. Of Belgium's 572,000 farmers, only 21 per cent owned all the land they worked, and 38 per cent owned only part of their land, while 41 per cent rented all the land they worked. The number of farmers who owned land was impressive, but the pattern was not as simple as it seemed to many in Ireland. In Belgium a large number of peasant proprietors had turned themselves into small landlords. When Gladstone introduced the land bill he rejected the possibility of allowing Irish tenants to turn themselves into petty landlords for that 'would

---

[1] *Reports from her majesty's representatives respecting the tenure of land in the several countries of Europe, 1869*, pt i, p. 361.
[2] Ibid., pt ii, p. 134.
[3] Ibid., pt ii, p. 186.
[4] Ibid., pt ii, p. 255.
[5] Lavelle, op. cit., p. 81.

soon generate the very mischiefs which you proposed to extinguish'.[1] Whether Belgium suffered from these mischiefs is not clear, although there was an outbreak of disorder between 1836 and 1842 when there were eleven assassinations. What is clear, however, is that Belgian landlords had a power of eviction that would have made Irish landlords envious: in the Pays de Waes, for example, a notice to quit delivered by a *huissier* on the day before Christmas eve came into effect immediately, 'and from the moment that the notice has been served the tenant may not set foot on the land'.[2]

BEFORE parliament settled down to serious consideration of the land bill, the chief secretary, Chichester Fortescue, introduced a peace preservation bill, which became law on 4 April. The act,[3] which was intended to remain in force only until 1 August 1871, but was later amended and continued until 1880, was an extension of earlier acts, which empowered the lord lieutenant to make disturbed or 'proclaimed' districts pay for the upkeep of extra police and which made the carrying of arms without licences in such districts illegal. The new act, however, added to these restrictions and extended the powers of the lord lieutenant, justices, and police in proclaimed districts: the lord lieutenant could confiscate newspapers carrying seditious or treasonable matter, and close public houses; the police could arrest strangers, and persons found out at night 'under suspicious circumstances'; justices could punish persons refusing to give evidence about felonies and misdemeanours, and issue warrants for the searching of houses of those suspected of writing threatening letters. The control of firearms was increased: holders of game licences had to have licences to carry arms, and it was necessary to have special licences for revolvers. Finally, grand juries could compensate the victims of agrarian outrages. This act was hardly the 'monstrous engine of tyranny and despotism',[4] that its critics claimed it to be: it did not suspend habeas corpus or trial by jury; it did not set up military courts, or limit freedom of association and speech, except in the case of seditious newspapers; it did not impose curfews or make citizens carry identity cards.

The act did, however, draw the attention of parliament to the problem of disorder in Ireland, which had increased during the winter of 1869–70, and coming so soon after the suspension of habeas corpus, which had lasted from February 1866 to March 1869, it helped to create an impression of endemic disorder in Ireland. There was much to confirm this impression. 'Coercion' acts, similar to the peace preservation act, had been passed regularly since 1847; Ireland had an elaborate peace-keeping force that was unique in the

---

[1] *Hansard 3*, cxcix, 353 (15 Feb. 1870).

[2] *Reports from her majesty's representatives respecting the tenure of land in the several countries of Europe, 1869*, pt i, p. 123 [C 66], H.C. 1870, lxvii, 131.

[3] 33 Vict., c. 9 (4 Apr. 1870).

[4] John Blunden, *The coercion acts (Ireland). A speech delivered before a meeting of the home government association, 24 June 1873* (Dublin, 1873), p. 5.

United Kingdom, for it was centrally controlled, and armed, well-drilled, and numerous. Certain events in Ireland also helped; the 'battle' of Ballycohey in August 1868, for example, when William Scully was wounded while serving ejectment processes, and his bailiff and a policeman killed. The impression was reinforced by the publication of such books as William Steuart Trench's *Realities of Irish life*,[1] a well-written, inaccurate book, whose stories, alive with consenting adults gliding smoothly to their different consummations, have more in common with John Cleland than with Sir Walter Scott. (It took Gladstone nearly three weeks to read it in 1869, which does not suggest that he was carried along by its flow of narrative.) But the impression was misleading in many respects. The police force was indeed elaborate, and probably too big for mere routine law enforcement. On the basis of population, there were twice as many police in Ireland as in England and Wales; on the other hand, the population was scattered over an area half the size of England, so population on its own is probably not a fair measure. Although the government valued the Royal Irish Constabulary as it existed in 1870, using it as a sort of civil service, it is doubtful if they would have invented it, given the task of producing a new force. The constabulary, after thirty years existence, was the product of history, rather than of 1870.

The 'coercion' acts were never regarded as permanent. While their frequent renewal gives an impression of continuous disorder, it might equally be seen as a sign of parliament's optimism and high regard for the rights of the subject. During the period 1847 to 1865, the crime and outrage act of 1847 (called the peace preservation act from 1856) was renewed ten times, usually for one year, or at most two years (in 1858 and 1860). More serious were the suspensions of habeas corpus in 1848–9 and 1866–9; but again, the frequent renewals (five separate acts were passed during the later period) suggest the exceptional nature of this measure, which was essentially used against political conspiracy until the Westmeath act.[2] (One suspects that the existence of habeas corpus rather than its suspension would have impressed continental policemen.) The coercion acts passed between 1847 and 1875 can be seen as the first original post-union trend in coercion, distinguished by combining different types of powers, and different from the insurrection acts inherited from the Irish parliament, which culminated in the unused act of 1835.[3] From the mid-1820s, however, special legislation of this kind became a distinguishing feature of Ireland, for previously Great Britain had employed very similar legislation, and had usually set a fashion for Ireland to follow. This change created an anomaly. Within the union permanent repressive measures for Ireland were almost unthinkable. Thus Ireland was distinguished by a succession of exceptional and temporary measures, usually attended by controversy, and perhaps less

[1] London, 1868.
[2] 34 & 35 Vict., c. 25 (16 June 1871).
[3] 5 & 6 Will. IV, c. 48 (31 Aug. 1835).

effective for being temporary. It was only in 1885–7 that a serious attempt was made to grapple with this, which included the proposals of Spencer and others for a general strengthening of the criminal law in the whole United Kingdom (to get rid of the objection to 'exceptional' legislation) and the passing of Balfour's crimes act[1] (to get rid of the disadvantages of 'temporary' legislation). Nor were the contents of the crime and outrage acts, and even of the peace preservation act of 1870, remarkable. It does not, certainly in retrospect, seem particularly tyrannical to make localities pay for some of the cost of their own squabbling; or to allow the police to arrest suspicious characters found wandering at night; or to search houses for evidence of threatening letters; or to allow the highest official in the land to close public houses.

The regulation of firearms seems to have been spasmodic and limited to 'proclaimed' districts, which was surprising in a country that was supposed to be plagued with violent crime. An act of 1843 made it necessary to have a licence, licensed arms were marked, and lists of licensees were made; the import and distribution of arms and gunpowder were regulated.[2] The act was allowed to expire in 1845, and in 1847 the inspector general complained that the police had 'no legitimate means' of ascertaining how many stands of arms were imported.[3] The crime and outrage act of 1847 made it illegal 'to carry or have, within the district specified in any such proclamation, elsewhere than in his or her own dwelling house, any gun, pistol, or other firearm';[4] but this applied only to proclaimed districts, and Orangemen, for example, were able to march armed (as they did at Dolly's Brae on 12 July 1849) outside proclaimed districts, until the passing of the party processions act in 1850.[5] In 1870 control was tightened: revolvers had to be specially licensed, and an excise act, which covered the whole United Kingdom, obliged 'every person who shall use or carry a gun elsewhere than in a dwelling house or the curtilage thereof' to buy a licence.[6] Control, therefore, depended on exceptional legislation that had to be renewed; it did not apply to the whole country, for even in the 1870s the whole country was not proclaimed; even in proclaimed districts before 1870 it was possible to have unlicensed firearms in a dwelling house. The excise act of 1870 made it relatively expensive for poor men to have firearms, but it was a fiscal measure, and not a system of restricting the possession of arms, like the fire-arms act of 1920, which allowed the police to issue firearms certificates.[7] For a country that was supposed to be plagued by disorder, the control of arms was poor, to put it mildly. In 1869, a London postman was able to hire a revolver in a surgical instrument maker's shop in the Tottenham Court Road, and go to Ireland for the weekend to shoot his father's landlord, without apparently committing any offence until he opened fire. Ireland was not exceptional in

---

[1] 50 & 51 Vict., c. 20 (19 July 1887).
[3] P.R.O., H.O., 45/1695, 28 Jan. 1847.
[5] 13 Vict., c. 2 (12 Mar. 1850).
[7] 10 & 11 Geo. V, c. 43 (16 Aug. 1920).

[2] 6 & 7 Vict., c. 74 (22 Aug. 1843).
[4] 11 Vict., c. 2 (20 Dec. 1847), sect. 9.
[6] 33 & 34 Vict., c. 57 (9 Aug. 1870), sect. 7.

Europe either in its restrictions or its freedoms. Even in the late 1880s, there were no regulations prohibiting the carrying of firearms in Denmark, Norway and Sweden, Switzerland, and Servia; there were regulations, however, in France, Italy, Spain, Portugal, Bulgaria, and Greece; in Hungary all parliamentary electors could carry arms without a licence, but in Austria a permit (issued only 'to persons of irreproachable character') was necessary, except 'for those who in accordance with the national costumes of some parts of the monarchy are required to carry arms forming part of such dress'.[1]

The most important fact qualifying the picture of Ireland as a crime-ridden country was not the caution of its special repressive legislation, but its crime statistics. Since the early 1850s serious crime had fallen faster than the population. In 1850 there had been 10,639 outrages reported to the constabulary office, including 139 homicides; in 1870 the total was 4,351, including 77 homicides. Neither of these years, however, are good measures of what had been achieved in the previous generation: 1870 was a particularly bad year, measured by the standards of the 1860s, and 1850 was marked by the great wave of criminality that had begun in 1846, arising out of the famine. The first post-famine year whose total resembled that of the pre-famine years was 1853, when 5,452 outrages were reported; thereafter, the total fell steadily year after year with some interruptions, in 1862 for example, until 1866 when it fell to 1,964. (Homicides fell from 119 to 51 in the same period.) A comparison of indictable offences in Ireland and England and Wales in 1870 shows that Ireland had, on the basis of population, only about two-thirds as much serious crime as England and Wales. The Irish committed far fewer offences against property, but slightly more offences against human life than the English. The striking contrast, however, occurred with assaults and malicious offences against property: the Irish committed five times as many common assaults, five times as many assaults on police officers, and six times as many malicious offences against property as the English, if the comparison is based on population. The Irish also were five times more likely to commit breaches of the peace, but these were a very small fraction of the whole. On the credit side, the Irish were much less likely than the English to commit suicide, sodomy, bestiality, bigamy, and rape.

Crime statistics are difficult to interpret. Practices of definition varied even within the same jurisdiction; the comprehensiveness of reporting varied, and there was a 'dark figure' that eluded even the most vigilant police forces; the attention of the police was directed and distracted by pressure from the public, magistrates, and the government. The high propensity of the Irish to assault police officers, for example, may be explained by the provocativeness of the police, or the turbulence of the public; but it certainly owed something to the fact that there were more policemen to assault. Only murder and attempted

[1] *Reports respecting laws in European countries as to the carrying of firearms by private persons*, p. 2 [C 5819], H.C. 1889, lxxvi, 444.

murder stand out as reliable enough to admit rough comparisons between countries, and even they are not infallible. Although murder is difficult to conceal, or to invent, it is not unreasonable to assume that the 'dark figure' was lower in Denmark than it was in Servia. But comparing serious crimes against human life in Ireland and England suggests that there was little difference between the two countries, which made Ireland one of the safest places in Europe. Jean-Claude Chesnais in his *Histoire de la violence*[1] takes statistics of convictions for homicide in 1880 as a measure of violence. England, Scotland, Germany, and France had the fewest, with England having less than half as many as France; the southern European countries were much worse, for the best of them, Roumania, had nine times as many as England, and the worst, Servia, eighteen times as many.

THE main responsibility for policing the country fell on the Royal Irish Constabulary and the Dublin Metropolitan Police. The former numbered almost 13,000 in 1870 and the latter just over 1,000; the former, commanded by an inspector general and three assistant inspectors general, was paid for almost entirely by the treasury, and operated throughout the whole country; the latter, commanded by two commissioners, was a completely separate force, confined in its operations to the Dublin metropolitan area, and paid for by a police tax, a hackney carriage tax, drivers' and pawnbrokers's licences, and fines from the police courts. At first sight, Ireland seems to have been a well policed country; on the basis of population she had twice as many police as England and Wales; the number of police actually increased since the 1840s, although the population had fallen. If anything the area outside Dublin was more highly policed than the city itself: the Dublin metropolitan police bore roughly the same relation to population as the constabulary, but the thousand men of the D.M.P. had to cope with more indictable offences than the whole of the R.I.C. The cost of maintaining the two police forces was about a million pounds in 1870, making it more expensive than the cost of relieving over 200,000 paupers (£668,202), the cost of teaching almost a million children in the national schools (£373,950), the cost of the civil service and public buildings (£483,023), and the cost of the established church (£582,000). It was, however, much cheaper to maintain a policeman than a soldier, costing just about half as much; and since the cost of maintaining a prisoner was about half the cost of maintaining a policeman, the prevention of crime, as opposed to its detection, was a useful contribution to public economy.

Not only did the police detect criminals, they were also responsible for a wide range of activities that might have been more appropriately, but hardly more cheaply or efficiently, discharged by the civil service and local officials. Their most obvious contribution to government was their collection of statistics, for the decennial censuses (from 1841), and for the agricultural

[1] *Histoire de la violence en occident de 1800 à nos jours* (Paris, 1981), p. 64.

statistics (annually from 1847). A measure of their efficiency as collectors and compilers of statistics can be gained by comparing the agricultural statistics with the judicial statistics that were produced annually by court officials from 1863. The former were complete and comprehensive from their first year of publication; in spite of the efforts of William Neilson Hancock, the latter took years to establish a complete coverage of all courts, although it was easier to enumerate court cases than to enumerate livestock. The police did not, however, undertake the registration of births, deaths, and marriages, which became compulsory from 1864, although the inspector general, Sir Henry Brownrigg, had argued before a parliamentary committee that they were well qualified to do so. The censuses and the agricultural statistics, however, were only the most copious and routine of their compilations. They also collected annual statistics on evictions, loan funds, and emigration; occasionally, in emergencies, they collected information for the government: in 1861 on turf and 'symptoms of apprehension' among 'the poorer class of peasantry'.[1] Most important, however, was their constant reporting to Dublin castle on matters other than crime and sedition, which included such diverse matters as the eligibility of the Queenstown yacht club to be granted the title 'royal', the number of policemen who went off to join the papal army, the wages of agricultural labourers, and the management of the third earl of Leitrim's estates in County Donegal.

The circulars and general orders issued by the inspector general reveal an enormous range of activities that went far beyond the suppression of crime. The police played a part in protecting public monuments;[2] they enforced the nuisances act,[3] the poaching prevention act,[4] the dogs regulation act,[5] the chimney sweepers regulation act,[6] and the sale of poisons act;[7] they restrained the exuberance of beggars, enforced certain sections of the refreshment houses act,[8] inspected weights and measures,[9] prevented the hawking of spirits,[10] the illegal growth of tobacco, cock-fighting,[11] and illegal 'pugilistic encounters'. Their most invidious duty, however, was probably the suppression of illegal distillation, which they had taken over from the revenue police in 1857. As in the case of births, deaths, and marriages, the constabulary were anxious to take over this task. 'We know every man who raises an acre or half an acre of oats or barley,' the inspector general, Sir Duncan McGregor, told a select committee in 1854.[12] The duty was discharged with vigour. In 1860 constables were warned that the recent increase in spirits duty would encourage illicit distillation and they were to watch coopers, workers in tin, and sellers of molasses, but the

[1] P.R.O., H.O. 184/113, 10 Sept. 1861.
[2] 24 & 25 Vict., c. 97, sect. 39 (6 Aug. 1861).
[3] 11 & 12 Vict., c. 123 (4 Sept. 1848).
[4] 25 & 26 Vict., c. 114 (7 Aug. 1861).
[5] 28 Vict., c. 50 (19 June 1865).
[6] 33 & 34 Vict., c. 26 (14 July 1870).
[7] 27 & 28 Vict., c. 37 (30 June 1864).
[8] 23 & 24 Vict., c. 107 (28 Aug. 1860).
[9] 14 & 15 Vict., c. 92 (7 Aug. 1851).
[10] 23 & 24 Vict., c. 114 (28 Aug. 1860).
[11] 12 & 13 Vict., c. 92 (1 Aug. 1849).
[12] *Report from the select committee of the house of lords, appointed to consider the consequences of extending the functions of the constabulary in Ireland to the suppression or prevention of illicit distillation; together with the minutes of evidence, and an appendix and index*, p. 153, H.C. 1854 (53), x, 159.

police found it difficult 'to enforce a law which was not directed against a moral offence',[1] for even respectable citizens refused to help. The police complained in 1860, for example, that the coast guards would not lend them boats to raid islands off the coast. (When Edward Cardwell (chief secretary 1859–61) complained to the admiralty, he was told that the lords commissioners believed that the coast guards were 'lowered in the estimation of the country people and the service injured by employment of their boats on the duty referred to'.[2]) The police's great administrative achievement of the 1860s, however, was the prevention of the spread of foot-and-mouth disease, an achievement whose monetary value probably far exceeded the cost of maintaining the constabulary for two or three years. Not only the government imposed miscellaneous duties on the police: ordinary citizens often applied to them for information or 'characters', a practice that was frowned on by the inspector general; in 1850 he forbade them to give character references unless required by the courts and in 1864 they were forbidden to answer queries about the character, respectability, or 'money value' of persons in their districts. Most remarkably, the constabulary seem to have issued certificates for passports, for in 1864 they were forbidden to issue them 'to any but persons of known respectability'.[3]

A modest revolution in public behaviour seems to have taken place in the 1850s and 1860s, as the police enforced a series of laws that went far beyond traditional Christian morality or the fundamental exigencies of preventing murder, thieving, and fighting. In 1851 the summary jurisdiction act set new standards for behaviour on the roads. It became an offence to leave a cart unharnessed on a public road, to leave stones, dung, timber, or turf 'so as to cause danger', to have dogs unmuzzled or unlogged within fifty yards of a public road, to carry loads that projected more than two feet beyond the wheels of a cart, to allow swine to wander on the roads, to sell livestock on the roads, and to fly a kite from the road. Furthermore, the act, continuing a process of labelling that had begun with the census, the ordnance survey, and tenement valuation, required that all carts should display their owners' names 'in legible letters not less than one inch in height'.[4] This was hardly a draconian or intrusive act, but it was part of a trend that continued and culminated in the public health act of 1878, which was intrusive. It became illegal to keep swine in a house 'so as to be a nuisance to any person'; to have a wake for anyone who died of a dangerous, infectious disease; not to remove manure when ordered to do so by a justice; not to disinfect houses whose inhabitants had infectious diseases.[5] Most remarkable of all was section 147, which made it compulsory to have all children under fourteen vaccinated. (A further act in 1879 made vaccination compulsory within three months of birth.)[6] These acts were part of a process that went further than carts and vaccination. In 1862 the police were

[1] Ibid.   [2] P.R.O., C.O. 906/11, 21 May 1860, p. 44.
[3] Ibid., H.O. 184/113, circular 148.   [4] 14 & 15 Vict., c. 92 (7 Aug. 1851).
[5] 41 & 42 Vict., c. 52 (8 Aug. 1878).   [6] 42 & 43 Vict., c. 70 (15 Aug. 1879).

given powers to search suspected poachers on the public road;[1] in 1863 the compulsory registration of births, deaths, and marriages was established;[2] in 1865 dogs had to be licensed;[3] in 1868 railways companies were forbidden to put on special trains for prize fights;[4] and in 1878 the regulation of public houses culminated in the imposition of Sunday closing in rural areas.[5]

The police seem to have dealt with petty offences, including these new ones, with a thoroughness that was a function either of their numbers or of their fine organisation; in April 1867, for example, less than a month after the fenian rebellion, a general order of the inspector general reminded the constabulary that it was not enforcing the dogs regulation act satisfactorily. The most impressive measure of their zeal was the number of prosecutions brought before the petty sessions. In 1870 214,406 offences were prosecuted, which was twice as many as in England and Wales on the basis of population. The impressive starkness of this figure can only be fully grasped when it is understood that most of those prosecuted were men who were of previous good character. In other words, it seems that most of the male, adult population appeared before the petty sessions once a decade. By 1870, therefore, the petty sessions impinged on the lives of ordinary men almost as much as the confessional and the national school, if less frequently and persistently. The three most common offences were drunkenness and being drunk and disorderly (45 per cent), infractions of the ways acts (18 per cent), and common assaults (16 per cent). Compared with England and Wales, there were in Ireland more than three times as many prosecutions for drunkenness and being drunk and disorderly, more than five times as many prosecutions for offences against the ways acts, and more than twice as many prosecutions for common assault. Although the remaining offences account for only 21 per cent, they also offer a remarkable contrast with England and Wales: the Irish were prosecuted more frequently than the English for infractions of laws against false weights and measures, prostitution, vagrancy, and nuisances, and for infractions of the fishery acts, the master and servant act, the licenced victuallers and beer acts, the Lord's day act, and the cattle plague orders. They were prosecuted less frequently than the English for breaches of the factory acts, the pawnbrokers acts, the chimney sweepers act, and the game acts. This does not necessarily mean that the Irish were more prone than the English to give false measures, to prostitution, vagrancy, and desecration of the sabbath; or less prone to usury and poaching; it suggests rather that the police were more likely to prosecute for certain offences, especially those connected with drunkenness, brawling, and slovenly behaviour on the roads, which because of their public nature were more likely to come to the notice of a numerous and ubiquitous constabulary.

[1] 25 & 26 Vict., c. 114 (7 Aug. 1852).
[2] 26 Vict., c. 11 (20 Apr. 1863); 26 & 27 Vict., c. 90 (28 July 1863).
[3] 28 & 29 Vict., c. 50 (19 June 1865).
[4] 31 & 32 Vict., c. 119, sect. 21 (31 July 1868).
[5] 41 & 42 Vict., c. 72 (16 Aug. 1878).

How effective were the Royal Irish Constabulary and the Dublin Metropolitan Police? They did not fail to elicit praise, especially from visitors to Ireland: 'a more moral and better behaved body there is not';[1] 'they are as smart and clean, lithe and soldier-like, as the severest sergeant could desire';[2] they were the pioneers of civilisation, 'universally distinguished by their spruce, tidy appearance';[3] 'they are tall, broad-shouldered, handsome'.[4] Their reputation spread outside Ireland; in 1882 the Dutch government asked for a memorandum on the organisation of the police in Ireland; many officers in the British county forces had been Irish policemen, such as Valentine Goold, the chief constable of Somerset; when Sierra Leone was looking for a chief police officer, the inspector general was asked to find a candidate. Praise also came from more knowledgeable observers than travellers; Michael O'Shaughnessy, the chairman of the quarter sessions in County Clare, told Sir Robert Peel (chief secretary 1861–5): 'I have seen hostility give way to popularity; distrust and suspicion changed into respect and confidence.'[5]

They could take some credit for the fall in serious crime that had taken place since the early 1850s, especially the decline of such characteristically Irish crimes as faction fighting. They were not, however, exclusively responsible, for emigration, prosperity, greater literacy, and more rigorous clerical control also played a part. The reputation of the constabulary reached its zenith in September 1867 when it was given the title 'royal'. Yet this honour, usually bestowed on learned societies and yacht clubs, concealed many difficulties in the work of suppressing crime. To some extent, the fenian crisis had saved the constabulary from an attack that had been gathering strength since the early 1860s, especially since the assassination of three landlords within a few months of each other in 1862 provoked a wave of criticism from grand juries. (Valentine Goold added his voice to the chorus, suggesting that head constables should be used as detectives and the whole force more dispersed. Brownrigg was particularly annoyed by Goold's suggestions: 'Were I not aware that he formerly served as a junior sub-inspector in the force, I should have concluded that they emanated from an utter stranger to the country. ... Upon [a] former occasion, Mr Goold's suggestions were accompanied by an application ... for the post of assistant inspector general.')[6] The main criticism was that the constabulary were handicapped in detecting criminals by their military character, which was emphasised by their re-equipment with the long Enfield rifle after the French invasion scare of 1859 (and the issue of a drill manual calculated to enable them to act as a military force). There was a detective body known as the 'disposables', but they were ordinary constables who took up clandestine duties for a

[1] James Bury, *Pickings up in Ireland. By an Englishman* (London, 1859), p. 32.
[2] S. Reynolds Hole, *A little tour of Ireland* (3rd ed., London, 1896), p. 37.
[3] Lord John Manners, *Notes of an Irish tour* (London, 1849), p. 39.
[4] [W. H. Richardson], *Notes of a tour in the north and north-west of Ireland, August 1880* (Leicester, 1880), p. 28.
[5] P.R.O., H.O. 45/7648, 14 Mar. 1864.   [6] Ibid., 15 July 1862.

short period; their critics said they were useless because they were easily recognised by their height and military bearing; some, however, seem to have fallen into the other extreme, for the home secretary, Sir George Grey, was told that 'not long ago a disposable man in Tipperary was arrested by the local constabulary of the county as a suspicious character'.[1] Brownrigg, the inspector general, took these criticisms seriously and tried to answer them in his *Examination of some recent allegations concerning the constabulary force of Ireland* ... in 1864;[2] but soon other events distracted attention from the weaknesses of the constabulary by revealing their strengths.

The fenian rising, however, was hardly suppressed before another, and more revealing, crisis began: during 1868 two landlords were murdered, as well as a bailiff and a policeman at the 'battle' of Ballycohey. The trouble continued between 1869 and 1871, when two bailiffs, a process server, and caretaker were murdered; sixteen landlords and their servants were fired at, including some socially prominent victims, such as J. A. Nicholson, J.P., Richard Warburton, J.P. and high sheriff of Queen's County, Captain T. E. Lambert, J.P., and Rev. James Crofton, rector of Dunleer. This trouble was particularly alarming, for it arose from an apparently intractable conspiracy in Westmeath and from a wave of agrarian disorder that affected many counties, especially Mayo, in the winter of 1869–70. The authorities responded firmly. In 1870 the peace preservation act was passed, and in 1871 the Westmeath act,[3] which allowed the lord lieutenant to imprison Ribbon suspects without trial. Discipline in the force was improved. General orders and circulars from headquarters in 1868 noted that 'there has appeared a general want of knowledge, on the part of county and sub-inspectors, of the regulations bearing on their practical ... duties';[4] that constables were 'exceedingly defective in their replies to such questions about what to do on hearing of serious crime'.[5] By 1869 there were signs of improvement for a general inspection showed that sub-inspectors' performance was 'very gratifying', although constables were still 'generally deficient'; the inspector general was, morever, vexed to find that 'in but few districts ... the names of suspicious characters and their descriptions are known'.[6] Colonel John Stewart Wood, who had succeeded Brownrigg in 1865, grasped the problem of providing detectives, which had bothered Brownrigg, who was afraid of ruining the force by unleashing on the public a parcel of ill-controlled *mouchards* and *agents provocateurs*. In a memorandum in April 1869 Stewart Wood argued that 'it cannot be concealed that, while the constabulary force of Ireland are generally held to be, as a body, the best police force in the world ... yet it is widely felt, and with too much truth, that it fails to a great extent in the detection of certain classes of serious offenders'.[7] To remedy this the treasury

---

[1] P.R.O., H.O. 45/648, 26 Mar. 1864.   [2] Dublin, 1864.
[3] 34 & 35 Vict., c. 25 (16 June 1871).
[4] P.R.O., H.O. 184/114, general order no. 62, 1 July 1868.
[5] Ibid., memorandum 14 Mar. 1868.   [6] Ibid., memorandum IV, 2 Oct. 1869.
[7] Ibid., memorandum III, 1 Apr. 1869.

approved in December 1869 the Irish government's proposal to appoint a detective director for the R.I.C. Yet the old obsession with the military bearing and esprit de corps of the force persisted; in October 1869 the inspector general noted that 'officers are deficient in the manner of saluting with the sword' and belts were not cleaned with good blacking.[1]

During this crisis police officers insisted that generally the constabulary had a good record in bringing criminals to justice; but in dealing with agrarian crime, it was admitted, they faced peculiar difficulties. J. C. Rutherford, R.M., in a report in 1870 argued that 'the detection of crime and the procuring of any reliable evidence will always be extremely difficult, as long as the people are dissatisfied with the laws, especially those relating to land'.[2] Agrarian crime certainly attracted more attention than ordinary crime, although it formed only a small percentage of the total; when it is analysed, furthermore, it appears that the constabulary defined as agrarian a wide range of offences that did not involve landlords or their servants, such as family disputes about inheritance, and rows between neighbouring tenants and between tenants and sub-tenants. The proportion of serious crime caused by landlord and tenant disputes therefore was small. An analysis of the causes of homicides, made by the police in 1876, for example, showed that out of 106 cases only 5 were caused by disputes between landlords and tenants, and that was more than was usual throughout the decades after the famine. The most common causes of homicides were 'casual' quarrels (23) and drunken brawls (27), which together accounted for almost half; next in importance were family disputes (10) and occasions for the protection of property or the enforcement of legal rights (9). Disputes between landlords and tenants had to jostle at the bottom with party fights (6), criminal negligence (6), rows between tenants about land (4), 'immorality' (4), and poaching affrays (3).

As a means of preventing crime the temperance movement seemed to have greater potential than the land act of 1870. When considering the constabulary's record of detection it is tempting to discount agrarian crime as being too small to make an impression on their record as a whole, even if it is admitted that they failed to deal with it. It would be wrong, moreover, to assume that they did not deal successfully with it. They endured some embarrassing failures: threatening letters, the most common agrarian crime, were by their nature difficult to trace back to their perpetrators, and caused the constabulary much trouble; they failed to find those who fired at William Scully at Ballycohey, and ten years later they failed to bring the assassins of Lord Leitrim to the gallows. But they had successes, as the records of capital sentences in the 1850s and 1860s grimly illustrate. There was not the exact numerical correspondence that the *lex talionis* required, but there was enough to suggest that attempting to shoot a landlord was a dangerous business. In 1862, for example, when three

---

[1] Ibid., memorandum IV, dated 2 Oct. 1869.
[2] S.P.O., R.P. 1870/2757, report of J. C. Rutherford.

landlords were murdered within months of each other, the police succeeded in prosecuting Thomas Beckham, the murderer of Francis Fitzgerald; they also demonstrated the speed of nineteenth-century justice, for the murder, and Beckham's arrest, conviction, and hanging occurred within a nine-week period. As far as indictable crime as a whole was concerned they did not perform as well as the chairman of the quarter sessions in Meath claimed, for it was not true that 'in all instances of ordinary crime such as private murders and assaults, casual riots, larcenies etc., which are all unconnected with dangerous confederacies in Ireland, the crimes are made amenable to the law'.[1] It is difficult to compare detection and conviction rates in Ireland and England, but a rough comparison suggests that the Irish police, including the D.M.P., did rather better than the English: for every conviction by a jury in England, there were four indictable crimes; in Ireland there were three.

Attacks on landlords received a disproportionate amount of official attention, for fairly obvious reasons: landlords were often public figures, at least in their own counties; their violent escapades were occasionally attended by scandalous or eccentric circumstances; their opponents, the advocates of tenant right, practised a sort of moral entrepreneurship by arguing that land reform would prevent crime. But there was a deeper reason, not always clear to the public: friction arising from disputes between landlords who were justices, and police officers, resident magistrates, and ultimately the government, which for most of the period between 1846 and 1874 was whig or liberal. A centralised police force, working according to strict rules, affected the position of the justices: they ceased to be the source of law and order in their localities; they were under constant scrutiny; they did not control the constabulary, or even greatly influence the distribution of its patronage; they could do relatively little to influence the course of justice. If, for example, the 200,000 offences annually brought before the petty sessions had been matters for bargaining, favouritism, and revenge, the landlords would have controlled a mighty engine for generating power in their localities. As it was the landlords and the constabulary were frequently, like eccentric water and bureaucratic oil, immiscible. Disputes were common and acrimonious, involving high-spirited, cantankerous justices on the one hand, and officious, self-confident constabulary officers and R.M.s on the other. In 1864 in County Fermanagh, for example, Henry Mervyn D'Arcy Irvine was furious when a very severe sentence he had imposed on a poteen-maker was reduced through the recommendation of the inspector general. 'I will not lend myself to be any party in making the office of judge secondary to that of the police,' he protested; but he went further, and accused the lord lieutenant of ruling the country through the police, complained of police tyranny, and pointed out that it was only by 'the mere sufferance of the magistrates and gentry' that

[1] Larcom papers (N.L.I., MS 7619, no. 21).

Dublin Castle existed at all.[1] He was removed from the commission of the peace.

THE coming into effect of the church and land acts coincided with the establishment of the home government association. As the land bill was passing through its final stages, Isaac Butt was writing *Irish federalism! Its meaning, its objects, and its hopes*. Much of Butt's case against the union rested on the inadequacy of British legislation for Ireland. Irish bills, according to Butt, were dealt with at the end of the session or 'when the grey dawn of the morning is struggling through the stained glass windows of the commons hall'; if Irish M.P.s tried to divide the house, they were thwarted by 'a number of apparitions [that] glide along the corridors from the library, or emerge from the subterranean recesses of the smoking room'. The effect on Irish acts of parliament was that 'there is not one of them which does not contain some extension of the power of some centralising board, some attack upon the principle of local government, some new power to the police, or some violation of public freedom'. Butt's inspiration was the British North America act, which established a confederation of Ontario, Quebec, New Brunswick, and Nova Scotia. Under Butt's scheme, which resembled Gladstone's bill in 1886, Ireland would have controlled all her domestic affairs, including the railways, and the post office; the imperial parliament would have been left with the army and navy, India, and foreign affairs. The pamphlet is measured in tone and rarely strikes a harsh note. Butt was severe on what he called 'the most ignoble system of police despotism in Europe', which had given neither peace nor even 'a well administered police tyranny';[2] but that exceptional outburst was the old tory coming out in him, and in his dislike of the police he was probably as close to that other old Ulster tory, Henry Mervyn D'Arcy Irvine, who was removed from the commission of the peace in 1864, as to his new-found friends in the national movement. Butt certainly underestimated the problems of establishing a federal system in the British Isles, especially the problem of re-organising finance; his proposal, for example, that imperial charges of over £50 million could be raised by succession, legacy, and stamp duties was unrealistic, for these raised only £9 million in 1870–71. He probably also underestimated the difficulties of confederation in British North America, which were less intractable than in an old, established unitary state, where wealth and power were well concentrated, but nevertheless considerable; he was silent, for example, on the fact that the British North America act split the former Canada, which had been united since 1840, and that Newfoundland and Prince Edward Island were reluctant to join.

[1] *Copy of all correspondence between Mr Henry Mervyn D'Arcy Irvine, a justice of the peace in Ireland, and her majesty's government relative to the police etc.*, pp 3, 6, H.L. 1865 (76), xvii, 103, 106.
[2] Isaac Butt, *Irish federalism! Its meaning, its objects, and its hopes* (2nd ed., London and Dublin, 1870), pp 65, 77–9.

How well founded were Butt's criticisms of the way Ireland was governed? It would be hard to sustain the argument that Irish legislation was bad, if only because so much of it survived for a long time, like, for example, the Public Records (Ireland) Act, 1867. Parliament's output of legislation for Ireland was in itself impressive; in 1867, for example, which was not a particularly busy year in Irish affairs, twenty-seven Irish acts were passed, which accounted for nearly 20 per cent of the whole legislative output. (In 1927 the oireachtas passed only forty acts, in spite of the fact that the scope of legislation had greatly increased during the previous half century.) Butt had more substance in his claim that Irish legislation was dealt with late at night; in 1867 almost one-third of the divisions that occurred after midnight were related to Irish business, but these related only to a very small part of Ireland's parliamentary business. They certainly did not arise out of repressive legislation, for the major piece of repressive legislation in that session, the act suspending habeas corpus, did not cause any post-midnight divisions. In fact the subjects that caused post-midnight divisions were a mixture of the routine and the controversial: a bridges bill, a bill regulating the court of chancery, and a proposal to set up a select committee to examine the working of the ecclesiastical titles act. If Irish debates were dull and badly attended that was the fault of Irish M.P.s as much as of anyone (those interested in colonial affairs and India might have said the same about the state of the house when they were discussed). Indeed, general slackness in the house was common and provoked reproofs from serious official men including Palmerston and Gladstone. (Even in the hectic 1869 session Gladstone had to remind one of his Irish supporters, Lord Otho Fitzgerald, who was controller of the household, that it was his duty to attend debates regularly. Fitzgerald's excuse was that the late hours had been 'too much' for him.[1])

The tendency of legislation was hardly as draconian as Butt alleged. Most obvious were the crime and outrage acts, the suspension of habeas corpus, the party processions act, and the party emblems act, but the importance of these can be exaggerated.[2] The period from 1846 to 1867 was not one of great legislative advance, certainly not when compared with the 1830s or with Gladstone's first ministry. Legislation was often controversial, like the divorce act of 1857, but it was only occasionally fundamental like the reform act of 1867. Ireland's legislation, therefore, was of a piece with all domestic legislation in that it was dull, routine, and petty, being frequently inspired by nothing grander than the modest routine needs of the government. Butt was closer to the truth when he complained of the centralising tendencies of the Irish government, for Ireland did indeed have a more centralised government than the rest of the United Kingdom: the police were controlled by the central government, lay magistrates were supervised and reprimanded by the government's resident magis-

---

[1] Quoted in H. C. G. Matthew (ed.), *The Gladstone diaries* (9 vols, Oxford, 1968–86), vii, 110.
[2] Above, pp 761–4.

trates; the national school system was controlled from Dublin. Apart from the poor law boards, and the town commissions, and some of the bigger towns, local elected government did not exist.

Yet it is difficult to dismiss Dublin Castle during the under-secretaryship of Thomas Larcom as either tyrannical or incompetent. What stands out from the files of the chief secretary's office is not a conspiracy against liberty, but a high regard for law and a sharp awareness of the limits of executive authority. There were indeed blunders; the escape of Stephens from Richmond jail in November 1865, for example, was embarrassing; there were failures, such as the failure of the police to identify those involved in the attack on William Scully in August 1868; there were noisy squabbles with magistrates, such as Lord Leitrim; there was the inability of the government to enforce its will on certain occasions—it could not prevent, for example, policemen going off to join the papal army. There were however, corresponding successes. There was the enormous quantity of information amassed and published, such as the decennial censuses, and the agricultural statistics. There was the improved performance of magistrates, who had to abandon their connections with the Orange order when they were placed on the commission. There was too the fact that certain aspects of Irish government enjoyed an international celebrity: the school books of the national commissioners were widely used outside Ireland, and the prison experiments of Sir Walter Crofton were admired by Italian parliamentarians. In the 1860s, however, the Irish government scored one of its most impressive achievements when it saved Ireland from the cattle plague by using the legislative power of the Irish privy council and the strength of the constabulary to enforce a 'Prussian' policy of slaughtering sick animals and isolating infected areas. England and Scotland were not so fortunate in fighting the cattle plague because the quarter sessions, with some exceptions, did not have the strengths of the Irish executive. Even the handling of the fenians was an improvement on what had happened on previous occasions. There was none of the nervousness of 1848, although there was a certain amount of meretricious, music-hall fear (the home office, for example, was seriously worried that the sewers of Buckingham Palace would be infiltrated); there were no massacres or bloody assizes; engagements between insurgents and the forces of the crown were not particularly spectacular, but they were at least more gratifying to the *amour propre* of both parties than the affair at Ballingarry in 1848. Perhaps the worst miscalculation in relation to the fenians, except possibly the hanging of Allen, Larkin, and O'Brien in 1867, was the conferring of the title 'royal' on the Irish constabulary, breaking one of the first rules of police-management, which is that policemen thrive best when they are criticised. Dublin Castle was not a perfect instrument of government; it was slow to innovate (except possibly in the use of photography in law enforcement); it disliked politicians of high and low degree ('Who would govern Ireland', wrote Larcom, 'must have patience, with a wholesome disregard to cuckoos and parrots, whether in parliament or the press');[1] it would have preferred a country without general elections, newspapers, or turbulent eccentrics. But its power was limited: its highest officials were responsible to the house of commons; but far more importantly, they were servants of a state that was as parsimonious of legislative time as it was of money; its lowest officials, even a sub-constable, knew that his most routine report would be read by the lord lieutenant and that his least prudent actions might land him before the petty sessions.

It is doubtful if a self-governing Ireland would have been very different. There might, of course, have been more rather than less of the sort of legislation that Butt disliked. Assuming that an Irish parliament would have been dominated by the landed interest, shopkeepers, lawyers, northern industrialists, it is highly unlikely that it would have introduced protection. Even if local government had been made more democratic, and the powers of the J.P.s reduced or abolished, it is doubtful if a native government would have reduced the Castle. Indeed, it is arguable that the abolition of J.P.s would have increased rather than reduced bureaucratic growth, for experience suggested that the only alternative to the gentry was professional lawyers acting as magistrates. It is also unlikely that anyone—priests, clergy, or politicians— would have dared to get rid of a centralised constabulary. As for legislative innovation, the main changes would have been the repeal of the ecclesiastical titles act and the party processions act, some form of tenant right, local government reform, and concessions to the Roman Catholic priesthood on questions such as denominational education and support for a catholic university. (It is highly doubtful if there would have been any attempt to restore a religious establishment.) Finally, it is hard to resist the conclusion that more would have been spent on public works. The performance of an independent Irish state would probably have resembled that of the general synod of the Church of Ireland. The big issues, like the Athanasian creed, and the powers of bishops, would have been dealt with quickly and deftly; the small issues, like the problem of having too many clergymen in Cork and too few in Belfast, would have baffled the best minds. All this assumes the smooth transfer of power from Westminster to Irish politicians and their ability to keep the country together; at the very least, the problems would have been as great as those faced by upper and lower Canada after 1840.

Although Irish affairs received more than their fair share of parliamentary time in 1869 and 1870, it is puzzling why they did not receive more throughout the 1850s and 1860s. Ireland had 105 of the 658 seats in the commons, and Irish whigs and tories were substantial groups within the larger political groups; compared with influential groups such as the Peelites, the Irish were substantial in numbers. Yet the Irish made little headway in any important way. They held none of the great offices of state, especially under the whigs and liberals,

[1] Larcom papers (N.L.I., MS 7619).

when they were found mainly among the Robeys and the Rattlers; under the three short-lived tory ministries, Irishmen at least dominated Dublin Castle, and in Disraeli's first ministry an Irishman, Lord Cairns, was lord chancellor of Great Britain. Gladstone, who was so deeply committed to Irish legislation, did not rely heavily on Irishmen: his ministry contained only five Irishmen, apart from the Irish law officers and lord chancellor: Chichester Fortescue (chief secretary, with a seat in the cabinet); Lord Dufferin, chancellor of the duchy of Lancaster, but not in the cabinet; Lord Lansdowne, who as a junior lord of the treasury fulfilled the role ordained for Irish politicians by Trollope; William Monsell, M.P. for County Limerick, who was under-secretary for the colonies; and Sir Colman O'Loghlen, who was judge advocate-general. The Irish were perhaps more prominent in the senior household appointments: the earl of Bessborough was lord steward, Lord Otho Fitzgerald was controller of the household, Viscount Castlerosse was vice-chamberlain, and the earl of Cork was master of the buckhounds. The fact that the Irish were better represented in the decorative than in the efficient part of Gladstone's administration seems to sum up their official achievements in the years before 1870, for at most they were grandly subaltern, virtually monopolising the order of St Patrick, and occupying those offices that only Irishmen could respectably fill (Irish law offices and lieutenancies of counties), and occasionally a colonial governor-ship, and very occasionally something really splendid like the Indian vice-royalty, to which the earl of Mayo was appointed in 1868. In one respect, however, the Irish did fairly well, for they seem to have been able to muster that combination of distinction, indigence, and political influence that secured civil list pensions. In 1861 Irish recipients had 9 per cent of the civil list pensions, and the list included at various times in the 1850s and 1860s Mary Ellen Banim (£50), William Carleton (£200), John O'Donovan (£50), Sir William Rowan Hamilton (£200), Rev. Edward Hincks (£100), Bessy Moore (£100 'in consideration of the literary merits of her husband'), and Fr Theobald Mathew (£300).

The reasons for the relative impotence of the Irish are complicated. Partly it was a lack of leadership, for neither George Henry Moore nor the O'Donoghue could impose their will on a cohesive group of followers; partly it was lack of first-rate 'official' ability: Lord Naas and Lord Dufferin had remarkable careers but neither was in the first rank of official men. Partly it was that the Irish were on the wrong side in party politics, generally returning a majority of whigs or liberals. But between 1846 and 1866 the whigs enjoyed a fairly easy dominance of British politics, and were less dependent on the Irish than they would have been if the tories had been able to win at least one general election after 1846. Partly too it must be admitted that many of those who were in political life were satisfied with the existing order. Yet a part of the United Kingdom as distinctive as Ireland—strongly rural and catholic, declining in population, and only two generations away from quasi-autonomy—might have been more manageable if it had enjoyed some compensating privilege, or some peculiar access to the centre of power. In some ways the United Kingdom was too equally ruled in essentials, especially when so many inessential trappings of local distinctiveness survived. By 1870 taxation was almost uniform;[1] access to the empire was so free that it was not a privilege; Irish farmers and distillers enjoyed no palpable advantage over foreign producers. There were some who appreciated and took advantage of what was available. In 1870, for example, Trinity and the queen's colleges had seven successful candidates in the Indian civil service examinations, which compared well with the eight from Oxford, Cambridge, and London, but not so well with the eleven from the Scottish universities. Fr O'Connor appreciated the providential nature of the British empire in spreading 'the faith of the Irish people' throughout the world, for

under the 'Union Jack', on which the crosses of St George and St Andrew are blended, but so blended as to prevent any Christian symbol being recognised (a fit emblem of the effect of the union of jarring sects, each professing to proclaim Christianity, but between them only obscuring and obstructing it)—the Irishman, too, is borne to the distant colony.[2]

When Gladstone resolved that the balance of the church's property should be devoted to Irish purposes he was weightily conscious of conferring a boon; but only a former chancellor of the exchequer, who had done so much to rearrange the fiscal burdens of the United Kingdom, was likely to appreciate fully the generosity of that boon. To say that Ireland had sunk to the status of colony is not only to use loosely a term that contemporaries used precisely (a colony was actually defined by act of parliament),[3] but also to ignore the relatively privileged position of the British colonies in north America, south Africa, and Australia, which did not have to contribute to the upkeep of the British army and navy. To say that Ireland was like a wife or a daughter in the Victorian household is hardly precise enough, given the variety of models available. Was she Mrs Proudie? Or Mrs Gamp? ('Leave the bottle on the chimley-piece, and don't ask me to take none, but let me put my lips to it when I am so dispoged'?) Or perhaps Mrs Bardell, with Gladstone devilling for Dodson & Fogg?

WHETHER Ireland remained part of the United Kingdom, or became independent, by 1870 she had shrunk relatively compared with Britain. In 1867 Robert Baxter estimated that the national income of the United Kingdom was

---

[1] Below, pp 785–90.

[2] M. O'Connor, 'The destiny of the Irish race' in *I.E.R.*, i (Oct. 1865), p. 72.

[3] 28 Vict. c. 14 (7 Apr. 1865): 'The term "colony" includes any plantation, island, or other possession, within her majesty's dominions, exclusive of the United Kingdom of Great Britain and Ireland, and of the islands being dependencies thereof, and exclusive of India.'

£814 million.[1] Ireland's share was modest, £78 million, which was only slightly greater than Scotland's, although Scotland had a much smaller population. Baxter, basing his calculations on income tax returns, found that Ireland's national income was distributed as follows.

Gross income of Ireland, 1867

no.	categories	incomes	amount (£)
I	large incomes:		
	(a) £5,000 and over	400 [.01]	4,985,000 [6.4]
	(b) £1,000 to £5,000	2,700 [0.1]	5,379,000 [6.9]
II	middle incomes:		
	£300 to £1000	14,400 [0.6]	7,347,000 [9.4]
III	small incomes:		
	(a) £100 to £300	78,500 [3.2]	8,527,000 [10.9]
	(b) under £100	338,000 [13.5]	13,520,000 [17.3]
total I–III		434,000 [17.4]	39,758,000 [51.0]
IV	skilled workers	85,000 [3.4]	3,750,000 [4.8]
V	lower skilled	710,000 [28.5]	16,188,000 [20.8]
VI	agricultural & unskilled	1,259,000 [50.6]	18,231,000 [23.4]
total IV–VI		2,054,000 [82.6]	38,169,000 [49.0]
total I–VI		2,488,000	77,927,000

The figures in square brackets give the categories as percentages of the totals.

Baxter's calculations show a society of remarkable contrasts. A very small group of rich people, less than 20,000, received almost one-quarter of the national income; the handful of very rich people at the very top of the hierarchy earned more than the 85,000 skilled workers in category IV. Nearly four-fifths of the population were in the two poorest categories, but between them they received just over 40 per cent of the national income. The average income of the poorest category, about £15 a year, was very small compared with the incomes in the first two categories; but it was also small compared with the average income of £44 a year received by the skilled workers in category IV. The recipient of a typically large income, about £12,500, could buy the labour of 284 skilled workers every year, or the labour of 833 unskilled workers. Yet Ireland seems to have been less unequally divided than England and Scotland, where the top two categories received almost 40 per cent of national income,

[1] R. Dudley Baxter, *National income. The United Kingdom. Read before the Statistical Society of London, 21 Jan. 1868* (London, 1868), p. 60.

which was more than the 23 per cent received by the same categories in Ireland. The picture is less clear when Ireland is compared with other countries. The top 20 per cent in Ireland, roughly categories I–III, received 51 per cent of national income; in Prussia the top 20 per cent received 63 per cent, but in Saxony only 48 per cent. The top 5 per cent in Ireland received at least 35 per cent, compared with 26 per cent in Prussia, 34 per cent in Saxony, and 37 per cent in Denmark.

In 1867 Ireland's national income was only 10 per cent of the United Kingdom's, although her population was 17 per cent. According to Baxter the average income in England was £68 a year and £53 in Scotland; in Ireland it was only £31, or less than half of the combined British average. It is possible, however, that Baxter underestimated Irish national income because he relied on income tax statistics. Under schedule C, income from government stock, for example, Ireland was credited with only 3 per cent of the United Kingdom's total; yet she accounted for 6 per cent of all income tax assessments. It seems that most assessments of Irish residents' holdings of government stock were made in London and not credited to Ireland in the published statistics; it is not unreasonable, therefore, to add at least a million to Baxter's total for Ireland. More seriously, however, Baxter underestimated the value of agriculture in the Irish economy. It is possible to reconstruct how he dealt with agricultural incomes; he included rents and farming profits (about £12.5 million) in categories I–II; he included in small incomes under £100 two-thirds of the farmers, allowing only £40 a head, which amounted to £11 million; in category VI he put the remainder of the farmers and agricultural labourers, whose gross incomes amounted to about £13.8 million. When these are added, they come to only £37 million, which was about £5 million less than the value of agricultural output in 1870. If Baxter's estimates are increased by including these items, Ireland's per capita income goes up to just about half the British figure. As a region of the British Isles, Ireland was not impressively advanced, in spite of the previous twenty years' progress. Yet the relative position of Ireland within the United Kingdom was only slightly worse than that of the mid-western and southern states in the U.S.A., when compared with the northern states; in 1856, for example, incomes in the southern states were only 55 per cent of those in the north.

How did Ireland compare with other European countries? Economic historians have established a basis for comparing the main European countries with each other in 1870. Britain was at the top of the league, followed by Belgium, where incomes were about 80 per cent of Britain's; next came Denmark, France, Germany, the Netherlands, and Switzerland, at about 60 per cent of the British level; Italy came eighth, with incomes that were just over half of the British level. Ireland fits in at this point, coming ninth in the European league, ahead of Norway and Austria (49 per cent), Finland and Spain (43 per cent), Sweden (39 per cent), Hungary (38 per cent), Greece

(35 per cent), and Russia (28 per cent). Portugal's statistics were so defective that no estimate could be made of her national income in 1870.

In 1870 Ireland was enjoying a period of prosperity that had its beginnings in the early 1850s, started apparently by the Crimean war and sustained by buoyant livestock prices. Admittedly, it had been interrupted in the early 1860s, causing some alarmed discussion of the 'supposed decline of Irish prosperity'; but recovery had begun in 1864, and the mid-1860s were particularly prosperous, especially for livestock farmers, for Ireland escaped not only from the worst ravages of fenian fever, but also from the 'mouth and foot' disease that attacked cattle in Britain. Whether the absence of the latter abated the fury of the former is not clear; but the agency that defeated both was at least identifiable, and if the Irish constabulary were over-praised for their prowess in March 1867, their importance in eradicating the cattle plague by 'Prussian' methods was as great as it was unrecognised. Agriculture accounted for only half of national income, but its prosperity affected the profits of bankers, shopkeepers, builders, and lawyers: bank deposits increased steadily, the consumption of tea, sugar, and tobacco increased more rapidly in Ireland than in Britain, and between 1841 and 1881 158,000 new houses of the second class were constructed, of which 102,000 were in rural districts. It is not surprising, therefore, that the profits of businesses and professions assessed under schedule D of the income tax increased by 65 per cent between 1854 and 1870, suggesting that those who supplied farmers with goods and services did as well as agriculture as a whole. Within the agricultural community, however, there were differences of fortune: farmers did best, partly because rents lagged behind agricultural output and partly because wages just kept up with rising prices.

The prosperity had its limitations. First, emigration continued at levels that neutralised the natural increase of the population, and by 1871 the population had fallen to two-thirds of its size in 1841. Secondly, there was chronic poverty among farm labourers and small farmers, especially in the west, and in towns and cities. Thirdly, some industries continued to decline; distilling, for example, declined because sales at home as well as exports to Britain fell, although the Scottish distillers increased their output between the early 1850s and 1870. Fourthly, strong regional difficulties persisted, in spite of rising incomes. If housing is taken as a measure of wealth and poverty, in 1841 Ulster and Leinster were the most prosperous of the four provinces, with Munster a good third, and Connacht a bad fourth; by 1881 the order had not changed, and Connacht still lagged behind, although it must be admitted that Munster had closed the gap between itself and the two most prosperous provinces. If the counties are ranked according to the quality of their housing in 1841 and 1881 and their order compared in the two years, it appears that little changed. Kildare and Londonderry slipped a little, but only Clare, Leitrim, and Tipperary substantially improved their ranks. Mayo and Kerry were worst in 1841 and 1881; Down, Dublin, Kilkenny, and Wicklow were best in both years.

A comparison of Down and Mayo in 1881 gives an impression of the difference between the richest and poorest counties: over half of the rural population in Down lived in second-class houses (good farmhouses with five to eight rooms), while less than one-fifth did so in Mayo. Yet in the intervening years, the rate of house-building in the poorer counties had been remarkable. The six leaders were the counties with the worst housing in 1841: Kerry, Mayo, Sligo, Leitrim, Roscommon, and Galway, combined, doubled their number of second-class houses.

The difference between Ulster and the other provinces was commented on frequently in 1869 and 1870. In a speech on the land question in the Free Trade Hall in 1869 Sir John Gray, editor and proprietor of the *Freeman's Journal*, argued that

if all Ireland were brought to the same crop and food-producing condition as Ulster, where the small farms abounded, and security for the tenant was the rule, the gross produce of the country would be raised from £30,000,000 to £42,141,000 a year.[1]

Peter MacLagan, M.P. for Linlithgowshire, believed that farming was better in Ulster and that rents were higher there than in the rest of Ireland; George Campbell, whose book on the land question influenced Gladstone, thought there was 'a wide distinction between the careful, pushing, moderately skilful Ulster farmer and the unthrifty, wasteful, unskilful man of the south, the typical Irishman'.[2] Even the less prosperous parts of Ulster were compared favourably with neighbouring counties of Leinster and Connacht: County Fermanagh, according to William O'Connor Morris, was not a wealthy county, but 'contrasted with Connacht, it is another world'.[3] The contrast between Dublin and Belfast was even more striking than that between rural Ulster and the rest of Ireland. In addition to the eulogies of contemporaries there were sound statistical sources for the contrast; by 1870, for example, not only had the population of Belfast begun to approach that of Dublin (it did not exceed it until 1891), but its wealth, as assessed for income tax, had begun to mark it out as a substantial provincial centre, ahead of Cork, and approaching Dublin. The most striking difference between the town and the city, however, was the quality of their housing: half of Dublin's population lived in execrable conditions, defined as fourth-class accommodation by the census commissioners; in Belfast two-thirds of the population lived in the much better second-class accommodation and hardly any, just under 2 per cent, lived in fourth-class accommodation. The contrast between the industrial town, with its huge linen industry, which had reached its peak by 1870, and its shipbuilding that would carry it to even greater heights in the late nineteenth century, and the old,

---

[1] Sir John Gray, *The Irish land question speech of Sir John Gray, delivered in the Free Trade Hall, Manchester, on 18 October 1869* (London and Dublin, 1869), p. 34.
[2] George Campbell, *The Irish land* (London and Dublin, 1869), p. 55.
[3] William O'Connor Morris, *Letters on the land question of Ireland* (London, 1870), p. 240.

decaying capital, relying on the civil service and legal profession, supplemented by brewing and distilling, is perhaps a little strained but is at least straightforward.

The contrast between rural Ulster and the rest of Ireland, however, is not so clear when it is looked at closely; contemporaries' opinions must be treated with caution. First, it was not easy to find a measure of wealth that is entirely satisfactory; secondly, there was a tendentious element in comparisons between Ulster and the rest of Ireland. During the home rule debates the prosperity of Ulster had a clear polemical relevance; but even in 1870, and even in the hands of Sir John Gray, it had a polemical role, for Gray was at pains to emphasise the beneficial effects of tenant right, whose legalisation offered an apparently effective and conservative solution to the land question. There was, too, a tendency among British observers of Irish affairs to ride their peculiar hobby horses. Peter MacLagan, for example, was sure that he could identify the racial origins of Ulster farmers:

The orchards, and general neatness about the doors, and the tidiness and substantial comfort within, show us the descendants of the English settlers; the want of order and neatness about the offices, and the rough comfort within, disclose the Scotch origin of others; while the slovenliness about the doors, and the dirt and discomfort in the house, distinguish the descendants of the native Irish.[1]

It is difficult to assess the accuracy of such statements, and tempting to dismiss them as prejudiced and exaggerated. A survey of the state of farms on the Gosford estate in County Armagh, for example, does not support MacLagan's opinions. The appearance of farms and the state of their buildings were classified as very good, good, middling, bad, and very bad. When these descriptions are given a numerical value, with five representing very good and one very bad, presbyterians scored 3.4, the Church of Ireland 3.1, catholics 2.9, and 'others' 2. In fact, therefore, the rough comfort of the presbyterians put them ahead of the neat and tidy descendants of the English settlers, but more importantly the descendants of the native Irish came rather close to most of their protestant neighbours, and ahead of the 'others'. There was not much difference between the three major denominations, and all three were just about 'middling'.

Applying the simple measure of second-class housing in rural districts shows that Ulster and Leinster were about the same in 1870 and not all that much better than Munster. The distinctive province was not, therefore, Ulster, but Connacht, which was well behind the other three. Comparing Ulster with the rest of Ireland must inevitably be to the disadvantage of 'the rest of Ireland', if that includes Connacht. Comparing individual counties with each other, and using a wider range of measures than second-class housing, including the

[1] Peter MacLagan, *Land culture and land tenure in Ireland. The results of observations during a recent tour in Ireland* (Edinburgh, London, and Dublin, 1869), pp 7–8.

tenement valuation, areas under tillage, and average size of farms, as well as measures of fourth-class housing, produces a more complex result. If the thirty-two counties are ranked according to these measures, six of the Ulster counties come in the first half of the thirty-two, but they are there with Leinster counties such as Dublin (first), Carlow (third equal), and Kilkenny (fifth), and Munster counties such as Waterford (tenth) and Tipperary (sixteenth). Three of the Ulster counties, Tyrone, Cavan, and Donegal, are in the second sixteen, with Longford, Louth, Limerick, and Clare, and with all of the counties of Connacht. In fact the pattern that emerges is an east–west one, and not a north–south one, with some puzzling exceptions. Kildare, Louth, and Meath, for example, are not typical of 'eastern' counties, coming further down than the quality of their soil would suggest; Meath, for example, was the second most fertile county in Ireland, if fertility was measured by tenement valuation; yet its housing was bad, coming twenty-eighth out of the thirty-two for second-class houses and thirtieth for fourth-class. Kildare, Limerick, and Louth present the same picture of good soil and poor housing, but not so extremely as Meath. There were counties that presented the opposite picture: Fermanagh, for example, came nineteenth in fertility but sixth in housing. Wicklow was even more dramatic: it was twenty-fifth in fertility, but best in housing.

THE revenue of the central government in Ireland in the fiscal year 1869–70 was over £7 million; local government and the poor law added another £2.7 million; if tithes, amounting to £364,000, which were not strictly speaking a tax but a public burden nevertheless, are added, the burden on the Irish taxpayer was about £10.4 million, or £1. 18s. a head of the population and 13 per cent of Ireland's gross income as estimated by Robert Baxter, which was a small burden measured by modern standards.

Revenue of the central government 1869—70

	£
customs	2,049,374
excise	3,601,981
income tax	613,113
post office	336,081
estate duties	271,565
stamps	236,824
crown lands	42,000
miscellaneous	180,120
total	7,331,058

The main sources of revenue were taxes that fell on consumption (customs and excise) and those that fell directly on the better-off (income tax, stamp duties, and estate duties). The other sources were relatively small, including the post office, fines, and the crown estates. There were no state lotteries, as in the papal states and Denmark; no state monopolies, as in France and Italy, except the post office; no national domain, as in Portugal, and no poll-tax, as in Turkey, Roumania, and Servia, except on dogs, which were obliged to have a licence costing 4s. from 1865. The smallness of the income tax, which fell on rents and farming profits (schedules A and B) as well as on government securities, profits, and salaries (schedules C, D, E), was most remarkable; levied at 5d. in the pound on incomes over £100 a year it was very small by later standards, although it was much higher than its victims or Mr Gladstone, who first imposed it on Ireland in 1853, would have wished. The main sources of local revenue were grand jury cess, poor law rates, and town taxes, which were direct taxes on land and houses, amounting in 1870 to about a fifth of the rental of the country. There was a fairly clear distinction between local taxes and national taxes: roads, bridges, courthouses, asylums, infirmaries, and the upkeep of paupers were paid for mainly from direct taxes on land and houses; imperial expenditure—the servicing of the national debt, the upkeep of the army and navy, the civil service, and the crown—fell largely on indirect taxes. The local authorities did not raise revenue from indirect taxes and the central government for the most part did not tax land and houses.

Although landed property bore an impressive share of public burdens, it remains true that the main burden fell on consumption, especially through excise duty on alcohol. Again, the rates appear low by modern standards, although measured against the lowest of contemporary incomes they were high: 10s. on a gallon of whiskey represented more than a week's wages for a farm labourer. Customs duties, the other great source of revenue, fell on tea, sugar, tobacco, and imported wines and spirits. The main burden fell on tea and sugar, which together accounted for nearly one-half of the customs duties paid in Ireland. The burden of the state, therefore, fell not only on landlords and tenants, but on tea-drinkers, smokers, and topers as well.

The revenue of Ireland and her contribution to imperial taxation were an important preoccupation of politicians at different times in the nineteenth century. The act of union made complicated provisions for Ireland's contribution to imperial expenditure; famine relief raised in its most tragic form the issue of how far the central government should bear local burdens; the first two home rule bills made arrangements for Ireland's contribution to imperial expenditure. The extension of the income tax to Ireland in 1853 and the increase in the excise duties on spirits seems to have caused discontent that expressed itself formally before a parliamentary committee in 1864 when Joseph Fisher and John Blake Dillon, relying on complicated historical arguments based on article 7 of the act of union, claimed that Ireland was grossly over-taxed. Fisher's case was particularly arresting, for he claimed that between 1821 and 1861 Ireland had been over-taxed by the sum of £144,997,939.[1] Two other arguments were advanced to give extra weight to this estimate; first, figures supplied by the chief clerk of the exchequer, H. W. Chisholm, showed that Ireland's revenue had increased far more rapidly than Great Britain's between 1853 and 1863; secondly, it was pointed out that Sir Robert Peel, who was regarded as a paragon of financial toughness, had not extended the income tax to Ireland in 1843 when it was reimposed in Britain, for he believed that Ireland already contributed enough to the treasury.

How strong was Ireland's case? The problem was a complicated one, for the statistics were slippery and the appropriate amount that any part of the United Kingdom should have contributed to imperial expenditure was imponderable. The amount in dispute, however, was not negligible, even if Fisher's historical estimate is not fully accepted. Fisher assumed that Ireland should pay one-fifteenth of the United Kingdom's revenue; in 1869–70 she actually paid one-tenth; the difference, therefore, was about £2 million, a large sum by contemporary standards. Part of the problem was to measure Ireland's true revenue as opposed to her collected revenue. Excise on whiskey, for example, collected in Dublin, might ultimately be paid by drinkers in London; similarly, customs on tea and sugar, collected in London, might ultimately be paid by tea-drinkers in Donegal. Payments under schedule C of the income tax, on government and India stock, underestimated Ireland's share because many payments on behalf of Irish residents were made directly in London. Retrospective calculations of Ireland's true revenue, published in 1894,[2] suggest, however, that true and collected revenue were close to each other in 1869–70, the difference being a mere £95,274. The difference had been much greater in the past; the difference in 1859–60, for example, had been £602,430, which if it had been known in 1864 would have strengthened Fisher's case.

The discovery of Ireland's true revenue only partially solves the problem of assessing Ireland's fiscal capacity. The Irish were much poorer than the British, earning only about half as much on average; Ireland had 17 per cent of the United Kingdom's population but it would have been unreasonable to have expected her share of taxation to have been 17 per cent, although it is worth remembering that a substantial fraction of the German empire's taxation was imposed on the member states according to the size of their populations. On the other hand, Hungary, which accounted for almost half of the population of Austria-Hungary, bore only 30 per cent of imperial expenditure. Even to assume that Ireland's share should correspond to her share of the United Kingdom's national income, just under 10 per cent, made only a rough allow-

[1] *Report from the select committee appointed to consider the taxation of Ireland, and how far it is in accordance with the provisions of the act of union, or just in reference to the resources of the country; together with the proceedings of the committee, minutes of evidence, and appendix*, p. 328, H.C. 1864 (513), xv, 364.

[2] For retrospective calculations for the period 1819 to 1899 see *Return 'relating to imperial revenue (collection and expenditure) for the year ending 31 Mar. 1899'*, H.C. 1899 (318), li, 227.

ance for the exigencies of her poorer population. That Ireland should have contributed to imperial taxation on the basis of her representation in the house of commons would have been utterly unrealistic, although the argument that representation should coincide with revenue might have found many supporters among Scottish and English M.P.s. (In 1886 Robert Giffen objected to Ireland having any representation in the British parliament because her contribution to imperial taxation was so small.) Baxter thought that schedule D of the income tax, levied in trades and professions, was 'the gauge of the prosperity of the nation';[1] by that standard, which is unfortunately not completely appropriate to a country where landed wealth was so important, Ireland should have paid only one twenty-fifth of the United Kingdom's revenue. Even Fisher would not have gone that far. In 1886 Gladstone thought that legacy and succession duties were a fair test of taxable capacity; if that test is applied to Ireland in 1870 she was certainly over-taxed. In practice Ireland contributed to imperial taxation just slightly less than her share of the United Kingdom's national income would have suggested as appropriate; the share of her national income taken by taxation was the same as that taken in Britain.

Irish taxpayers as individuals were not unfairly taxed, for rates were uniform throughout the United Kingdom since 1853, except possibly on land, which was probably more lightly taxed in Ireland; furthermore, Ireland was not subject to a whole range of taxes imposed in Britain, such as the land tax, house duty, and 'assessed' taxes, which together brought in nearly £3 million in 1869–70 and which might have raised as much as £300,000 if they had been imposed on Ireland. If the principle that individuals should be uniformly taxed is not accepted as fair, it is very difficult to find any other principle that was unobjectionable within a unitary state; if, for instance, Irish taxes had been reduced, the better-off citizens would have benefited at the expense of the less well-off in Britain and Ireland. To some extent the problem of Ireland's taxation was merely a regional reflection of the bias of British taxation as a whole, which weighed relatively heavily on the lower classes. According to Walter Bagehot a small shopkeeper or clerk who was rich enough to pay income tax 'was perhaps the only severely taxed man in the country'.[2] Baxter thought that the 'manual labour class' was more heavily taxed than the upper and middle classes; in Ireland the manual labour class accounted for 49 per cent of incomes, compared with only 39 per cent in England and Wales. It is also clear that revenue was generated by the fact that the Irish seemed to like goods that paid customs and excise, 'the common luxuries of the poor': by 1870 they consumed almost as much tea, sugar, and tobacco as the English and Scots, and rather more spirits, in spite of their much lower incomes. (The Irish were not the

---

[1] R. Dudley Baxter, *National income. The United Kingdom. Paper read before the Statistical Society of London, 21 Jan. 1868* (London, 1868), p. 26.
[2] Walter Bagehot, *The English constitution* (introduction by R. H. S. Crossman, London, 1973), p. 271.

heaviest drinkers in the United Kingdom, but their tendency to drink whiskey rather than beer meant that they were more highly taxed.) At least the common necessities of the poor were not taxed by 1870 and the Irish did not have to pay a salt tax like the French. What seems to have happened between the early 1850s and 1870 was that Ireland lost her relatively privileged position in the British fiscal system; the extension of income tax to Ireland, and the imposition of uniform rates of spirit duty closed the gap between Britain and Ireland; in addition, increasing prosperity in Ireland caused these sources of revenue to increase more sharply than in Britain. Consequently Fisher and Dillon in the 1860s and Sir Joseph McKenna in the 1870s had some substance in their arguments; but they were lamenting the loss of a palpable regional privilege rather than the imposition of an intrinsically unfair system of taxation.

Another aspect of fiscal relations between Britain and Ireland was the amount spent on Irish services such as the judiciary, the police, and the national schools, and the amount retained by the exchequer for imperial services. Expenditure, however, is even more difficult to reconstruct than revenue, for individual items are scattered through the financial amounts, and retrospective calculations made in the 1890s, while useful as a check, do not give individual items. The following table is an attempt to reconstruct government expenditure in 1869–70, using the financial accounts and the retrospective calculations made in the 1890s.

Expenditure of the central government 1869–70

	£
lord lieutenant, government departments, and public buildings	483,838
collection of taxes	256,900
law courts, police, and prisons	1,465,743
education	445,721
post office	285,920
total Irish services	2,938,122
contribution to imperial services	4,392,936

These figures would have evoked different responses from contemporaries. John Blake Dillon would have pointed to the large 'surplus' of £4.4 million retained for imperial services; Isaac Butt might have pointed out that none of the self-governing colonies contributed so much to imperial defence, or to their own defence. Charles Kickham might have pointed out that every inhabitant of Ireland paid £1 a year for the upkeep of forces that held Ireland in subjection and for the servicing of a national debt created by wars to defeat the French, to enslave American colonists, and to keep the Russians out of the Mediterranean. The chief clerk of the exchequer, H. W. Chisholm, would have pointed to certain privileges enjoyed by Ireland but denied to the rest of the United Kingdom: the Irish police were paid for by the treasury and not by local taxpayers as in Britain; the amount given to the national schools was almost as much as that given to schools in the whole of Britain; Dublin tradesmen enjoyed the amenities of a viceregal court (the home office could have produced a petition from the licensed vintners of Dublin in 1861, praying for the retention of the lord-lieutenancy). The chief clerk might also have pointed out that until 1870 the Royal College of St Patrick and Irish presbyterian ministers received a parliamentary grant more than three times as large as that received by ministers of the Scottish church. (Gladstone deftly removed this anomaly in 1869 by making the revenues of the Irish church bear the cost of compensating Maynooth and the presbyterian ministers.) If these palpable advantages had not been enough, the chief clerk might have gone on to argue that the contribution to imperial services was effectively a transfer payment within Ireland rather than an imperial tribute. The income tax returns under schedule C showed, for example, that Irish residents owned government and India stock worth £1 million a year; in fact, they probably owned much more, so an actual income of £1.5 million was probably nearer the truth. There was, too, the financial advantage of having 26,000 soldiers of the regular army stationed in Ireland, or 14 per cent of the British army. While it is doubtful if 14 per cent of the cost of the army was spent in Ireland, it is unlikely that less than one million and a half was spent here—a benefit more warmly appreciated in Fermoy than in Mullinahone. If income from government securities and the cost of the army are deducted from Ireland's imperial contribution, Ireland's net contribution was about one million and a half, which was a very useful sum, making Ireland a more useful imperial asset than British North America but much less useful than India.

Irishmen who were policemen, national schoolteachers, priests, presbyterian ministers, government stockholders, and army contractors might have been impressed by these amounts (the police certainly had every reason to be impressed since increases in their wages and salaries in the 1860s increased the cost of maintaining the constabulary). Other Irishmen, apart from fenians and stern critics of public extravagance, might have been less impressed. Scholars, for example, might not have thought that Ireland was privileged, for the grants given to the Royal Irish Academy (£1,684) and the National Gallery of Ireland (£2,240) compared unfavourably with those given to the British Museum (£113,203), and the National Gallery (£15,978). On the other hand, Dublin doctors worked in hospitals that received a parliamentary grant of £19,045. An Irishman in none of these categories, Gladstone's 'humblest Irishman', for example, might have wondered, if he had ever looked at the annual financial accounts, why his whiskey and tobacco and his wife's tea and sugar were taxed to pay for such exotic items as the hereditary pensions paid to the heirs of William Penn (£4,000), to Mary Anne Forster, late housekeeper of the Irish house of lords (£18. 0s. 10d.), and to the heirs of the duke of Schomberg (£2,160).

The taxation question was not as simple as it appeared. Any Irish state, whether independent or not, would have had to maintain the police, judges, national schools, and public buildings, although it is possible that James Stephens, initially at least, would have been willing to rule Ireland as prince-president for rather less than the £20,000 received by the lord lieutenant. If the fenians had established a peaceful, frugal republic, run on Gladstonian principles, and without an army, navy, and national debt, Irish people would have been about a pound a head better off. None of this was very likely if only because any regime established by revolution would have incurred obligations that would have increased expenditure. It is doubtful, moreover, if law enforcement in an independent Ireland would have been less than under the union. It was highly unlikely that any successor government in Ireland, even an independent republic, could have renounced Ireland's share of the British national debt; for one thing, the British could have confiscated the portion of the debt held by Irish residents; at the very least, therefore, a new Irish state would have been forced to take on at least one-twentieth of the existing debt, which would have made it one of the least indebted states in Europe, although more burdened than Norway, Sweden, Belgium, and Switzerland. Secondly, any renunciation of its debt obligations would have made it very difficult for the new Irish state to borrow in its own right; Portugal, for example, renounced part of its debt on two occasions and was obliged to pay untypically high interest on its new loans in the late 1860s.

It was usual for successor states in Europe to take over the debts of their predecessors; Prussia made arrangements to secure the debts of Hanover, Hasse-Cassel, Schleswig-Holstein, Nassau, and Hamburg when it annexed them; similarly, the kingdom of Italy took over the debts of Lombardy, Emilia, Tuscany, and the kingdom of Naples, as well as part of the pope's debt; in 1868 Hungary took over 30 per cent of the existing debt of the empire. There was also the problem that new regimes seemed to be more expensive than their predecessors, mainly because of the struggle to achieve independence. The Italian debt, for example, almost quadrupled between 1861 and 1870 in spite of the government selling its tobacco monopoly to the French as well as disposing of its railways and much state property; yet the Italians had been lucky in their struggle for independence, having persuaded outsiders to do most of the heavy, structural work for them. The Prussians at first seemed to manage rather better; by 1869 their debt was one of the smallest in Europe, comparable with those of Sweden, Norway, and Switzerland, in spite of the wars against

Denmark and Austria. The war against France was fought very cheaply, for the sums spent were not, in 1870 and 1871, much greater than the revenue of the central government in Ireland; in addition, the enormous indemnity imposed on France enabled the new empire to pay off much of its debt in the early 1870s. Yet in spite of making the French pay for the war, Germany's expenditure on its armed forces increased rapidly in the decades after 1871: by 1880 German expenditure on arms was much greater than Britain's and by 1901 was greater than the combined cost of the British national debt, army, and navy. If by some strange destiny Ireland had become part of the German empire she would have been contributing about £5 million to the empire in 1901 (as well as free military service by all males), which would have compared very unfavourably with the £1.7 million she actually contributed to the upkeep of the British empire at that time.

A federal arrangement would, of course, have been established on fiscal principles that protected the exchequer's interests; indeed, the burden that Gladstone proposed to impose on Ireland was greater than what she actually paid in the 1890s. It is unlikely that a home rule parliament would have run Ireland more cheaply than the treasury. In 1886, for example, it was proposed that not only should the R.I.C. and D.M.P. continue in existence at an annual cost to the Irish taxpayer of one million pounds, but local police forces were to be established as well. The cost of law enforcement, therefore, would have increased by at least 50 per cent, if the new forces were to be effective. Whatever the shortcomings of the union it was probably the cheapest regime available in the 1870s. As it was, the costs of central government were lower in Ireland than in Spain, Italy, and Portugal, which were poorer than she was or almost as poor; she was, however, more highly taxed than Norway and Sweden, which were about the same in wealth, and more highly taxed than Switzerland, which was better off; she was almost as highly taxed as Belgium, which was the second most prosperous country in Europe.

How important was Ireland to Britain? In 1886 Robert Giffen did not rate Ireland highly as an imperial asset; 'as a partner with so rich a state as Great Britain, Ireland must ... be considered strictly as entirely insignificant. It hardly counts one way or the other.'[1] In his article in the *Nineteenth Century* he argued that Ireland had shrunk since the 1840s when her population was almost one-third of the United Kingdom's; British investment in Ireland was negligible compared with an investment of £300 million in India and Australia; the cost of keeping 24,400 soldiers in Ireland was a burden on Britain, which he put at £3 million; trade with Ireland would continue even after separation, 'except through Ireland falling into anarchy'.[2] Even the strategic danger of an independent Ireland did not impress him: it was now relatively cheap to keep

[1] Robert Giffen, 'The economic value of Ireland to Great Britain', in *Nineteenth Century*, xix (Mar. 1886), pp 329–45.
[2] Ibid., p. 340.

'negative' military possession of Ireland, and Dublin and Belfast were no more convenient bases for an enemy than Antwerp, Cadiz, and Hamburg. Yet an imperial contribution of over four millions in 1870 was not negligible, although its loss would hardly have led to the disintegration of the empire; at most it might have added a few pence to the income tax.

From the early 1860s Ireland was declining as a source of revenue. Ireland was not as valuable as India in the 1860s, for Britain controlled the whole of the Indian government's revenue, which was almost as big as that of the United Kingdom; in addition, a fifth of that revenue was spent in Britain, making India, therefore, much more important than Ireland as a market for compulsory invisible exports. Retrospective calculations made in the 1890s showed that Ireland's imperial contribution was £5.4 million in 1859–60; by 1870 it had fallen to £4.5 million and by 1889–90 to £2.7 million. The shrinkage is easily accounted for: the cost of Irish services increased more rapidly than revenue. If home rule had been established in 1886 the exchequer would have been better off, for Gladstone's imperial contribution of £3.2 million would have exceeded the actual contribution in the 1890s, which fell to £1.7 million in 1899. By 1914, however, something almost unthinkable in the nineteenth century had occurred: Ireland's revenue fell short of the cost of her services by £1.2 million. (In the same year Scotland's imperial contribution was £11.2 million and that of England and Wales £95.8 million.) The turning-point had come in 1909 when a surplus of £583,000 turned into a deficit of £2,357,500, the introduction of old-age pensions having converted Ireland from a declining asset to a liability. By 1912, when the third home rule bill was introduced, Ireland was worth getting rid of, even on the comparatively generous terms contemplated in sections 14–26 of the bill. During the first world war, however, Ireland's imperial contribution increased dramatically and between 1915 and 1921 she contributed the enormous sum, by nineteenth-century standards, of £83 million.

Ireland in the mid-nineteenth century was certainly more useful than Canada, or Natal, or New South Wales, which contributed nothing to the upkeep of the British army and navy, or to the servicing of the national debt. Indeed, it was even suggested in 1870 by T. E. Cliffe Leslie that British Columbia should be ceded to the United States in order to weaken the influence of American fenians. Charles Dilke was even more scathing about Canada:

> She draws from us some three millions annually for her defence, she makes no contribution towards the cost; she relies mainly on us to defend a frontier of 4,000 miles, and she excludes our goods by prohibitive duties at her ports.[1]

Gladstone also admitted that

[1] Charles Dilke, *Greater Britain: a record of travels in English-speaking countries during 1866 and 1867* (London, 1868), ii, 149.

it is really the false position in which we are placed by an indefensible frontier in British North America, and the consciousness of weakness thence resulting which has made poor J. Bull content to exhibit to the Americans a submissiveness such as he has never to my knowledge shown to any other people on earth.[1]

Ireland was also a recruiting ground for the army, for 25 per cent of the N.C.O.s, corporals, and privates of the regular army were Irishmen in 1872. (In the 1870s the possibility of recruiting from the white colonial armies was discussed, but it is doubtful if anyone, even the most optimistic, foresaw the scale of the dominions' contribution during the first world war.) Given that Britain relied on a volunteer, regular army, which was expensive compared with the conscript armies of the Continent, any addition to the supply of recruits kept costs down. The existence of the R.I.C., on the other hand, deprived the army of thousands of recruits, who might otherwise have come into the military market. It is doubtful if Ireland added much to the cost of imperial defence. The size of the Royal Navy was determined by the size of other European navies and not by the length of coastline it had to guard. During the invasion scares of the 1860s Ireland did not appear prominently in defence calculations: of the £11,850,000 proposed to be spent on coastal fortification only £120,000 was to be spent on Cork, although the commission on defence appreciated the importance of Cork 'as an advanced position clear of the Channel, where a fleet might wait orders with the certainty of not being delayed by westerly gales'.[2] Also, it is doubtful if the British army, especially after 1870, could have been smaller than it was, even if Ireland had not to be garrisoned. The main problem for the Horse Guards was the size of the army in Ireland, for it is difficult to establish whether its size was determined by the need to repel invasion, or by the need to aid the police (increasingly rare after the 1840s), or by the availability of convenient accommodation. In the event of a war with France, a garrison of 26,000 might have been too small but in a war with Russia it would have been too big. After the battle of Sedan, moreover, fear of Britain's old, vainglorious enemy was not immediately replaced by a fear of Germany; indeed, in the 1870s the most likely enemy was Russia, and in ordinary circumstances a war between Britain and Russia would not be fought in the north Atlantic. In a lecture to the United Services Institution in 1878 on 'the security of these islands' Major-general Collinson hardly mentioned Ireland, implying that Ireland was not a major concern of British strategists. According to Collinson foreign plans of invasion 'have had one main idea in common, that of landing the main body of the invaders as nearly as practicable to London';[3] at most, Ireland would be subject only to a diversionary attack. A strong, united, hostile

[1] H. C. G. Matthew (ed.), *The Gladstone diaries* (9 vols, Oxford, 1868–86), vii, 48.

[2] *Report of the commissioners appointed to consider the defences of the United Kingdom; together with the minutes of evidence and appendix; also correspondence relating to a site for an internal arsenal*, p. lv [2682], H.C. 1860, xxii, 485.

[3] Major-general T. B. Collinson, 'On the present facilities for the invasion of England, and for the defence thereof' in *Journal of the Royal United Service Institution*, xxi, no. 89 (1878), p. 7.

Ireland, supported by the Irish in Britain, would no doubt have been a nuisance; but it is doubtful if it could have acted effectively with a Continental power against Britain as long as the Royal Navy dominated the north Atlantic. At most Britain would have had to spend another £11 million on fortifying her west coast, as she had fortified her south coast in the 1860s.

The taxation of Ireland was debated in parliament in 1864, 1867, 1875, 1877, 1882, and 1886; but the debates were not particularly spirited: in 1867 McKenna's motion was withdrawn, in 1875 his motion was negatived without a division, and the house was counted out when he called for a committee of inquiry in 1882. Yet the question was an important one, even before Gladstone brought it to the fore in 1886. A reduction in taxation would have been as useful to Ireland as a reduction in rents, and more widely felt; the sums involved were far greater than the annual income of the Irish church; to have accepted something less than home rule in exchange for escaping from imperial burdens, while enjoying gratuitously the protection of the Royal Navy, would have been a considerable achievement. To have turned Ireland into a fiscal Isle of Man, whose central government was cheaper than Sweden's, might have been the summit of political ambition; but the subject was more complicated and less exciting than its rivals. Irish politicians did not even try to exploit the contribution Ireland made to imperial taxation in the nineteenth century. At the very least she contributed one-twentieth of the revenue that maintained the greatest empire of the day; in return she might have insisted on some direct share in its patronage, such as the king of Bavaria enjoyed in the German army after 1870. At the very least, when separation was discussed, the possibility of dividing the spoils might have been hinted at.

IN 1870 there was no Irishman or Irishwoman of European standing, comparable with O'Connell and Wellington a generation before. Irishmen who were to distinguish themselves in the second half of Victoria's reign were still unknown to the public: Parnell was playing cricket; Wilde had just left Portora to go up to Trinity; Davitt admittedly became well known in July 1870, but not in a way that suggested an enduring reputation. When *Vanity Fair* began publishing its famous portraits in 1869 an Irish subject did not appear in the first twenty, although politicians connected with Ireland did (Gladstone, Cardwell, Clarendon, and Russell). When an Irishman did appear it was William Connor Magee, the bishop of Peterborough, included because of his great speech in the lords against disestablishment, rather than for his achievements as a scholar or ecclesiastic. In Magee's wake, however, Irishmen came thick and fast: Lord Cairns, Chichester Fortescue, the first duke of Abercorn, and Lord Dufferin appeared in the next thirty portraits. (The first Irishman to appear prominently in *Vanity Fair* was not the subject of a portrait but an advertiser: John McGee, who claimed to be the inventor and sole maker of an Irish frieze coat, known as the 'Ulster'.) There were, of course, many Irishmen well known outside their native country: Lord Lawrence, who had been viceroy of India, 1863–9; Cardinal Cullen, one of the very few subjects of Queen Victoria to be made a cardinal, and a distinguished leader of the pro-infallibility party in the Vatican council; Sir Benjamin Lee Guinness, whose great work of restoration had just transformed St Patrick's cathedral into a fine nineteenth-century building and whose name appeared in print as frequently as that of Gladstone's, had died in May 1868; Daniel Maclise, whose reputation in his own day as a painter was as great and as unenduring as Moore's reputation as a poet, died in April 1870, a few months before his friend, Dickens.

The roll-call of Irish genius in the first three-quarters of the nineteenth century is disappointing compared with the eighteenth and twentieth centuries, especially if politicians and soldiers are excluded. Even allowing for changing tastes it is doubtful if Moore, for example, will ever adjust the balance by regaining his nineteenth-century position; only if Havelock Ellis's example is followed, and Charlotte and Emily Brontë are counted as Irish, does the harvest of genius compare with that of Berkeley, Goldsmith, and Burke in the eighteenth century and Yeats, Joyce, and Walton in the twentieth. The urge to dwell on the origins of great men was common among contemporaries. (In Queen's College, Galway, in 1870, for example, candidates taking the paper in metaphysics were invited to discuss the proposition that 'Ireland may claim the distinction of having produced three philosophers, each of whom formed an epoch in the history of thought'.)[1] Its sources were complicated, springing from national *amour propre* (especially among the Scots), from anti-Copernican tendencies in provincial towns, and in the case of Francis Galton, whose *English men of science: their nature and nurture* was published in 1874, from an interest in eugenics. The habit was encouraged by the compilation of those great and characteristically Victorian works of reference such as the *Dictionary of national biography* and by the ceremonial incidents of a long reign and the ending of a great century. Arthur Conan Doyle's article 'On the geographical distribution of British intellect' appeared in the *Nineteenth Century* in the year after the queen's golden jubilee and A. H. H. Maclean's *Where we get our best men* appeared in the last year of the century; the genre reached its climax in 1904 when Havelock Ellis's *A study of British genius* appeared. Two years later D. J. O'Donoghue's *The geographical distribution of Irish ability* appeared as a reply to Ellis and showed that the Irish were less fair-minded than Dr Johnson had found them in the eighteenth century.

The subject of Irish genius is perhaps more curious than substantial, revealing more about Victorian preoccupations with race and religion than about social mobility. As a source of national stereotypes it was probably influential; Maclean found, for example, that the Irish were most distinguished in the law, on the stage, and in government, diplomacy, and religion,

---

[1] *The report of the president of Queen's College, Galway for the years ending 31 Mar. 1869 and 1870*, p. 71 [C 323], H.C. 1871, xxiii, 993.

and least distinguished in medicine, art, and engineering; Ellis was struck by the fact that 'among . . . eminent women more than one in four is Irish'.[1] The subject also reveals that while the Victorians were preoccupied with national origins and characteristics, they were also careless about rigorous ascriptions of identity, using the terms British and English indiscriminately, in spite of Scots susceptibility on that matter. (Not that the Scots were consistent, for Robert Louis Stevenson, on one occasion at least, was content to be described as an Englishman.) Even someone as definitely Irish as Cardinal Cullen was considered British enough by his English contemporaries for them to place his portrait, according to Bishop Ullathorne, among those of the British cardinals in the English College at Rome.

Of those who tried to quantify the origins of eminent Victorians, Francis Galton was probably the most generous to the Irish, although his method of selection was heavily and admittedly biased towards scientists connected with London, for he implied that over 10 per cent of eminent scientists were either Anglo-Irish, Scots-Irish, or 'pure' Irish, which compared with 10 per cent 'pure' Scots, 50 per cent English, and 10 per cent Anglo-Welsh. In ascribing his scientists to particular towns, Galton was also generous to Ireland: Dublin, Belfast, and Cork combined were credited with six, compared with London's twenty-one, Edinburgh and Glasgow's seven, and Birmingham, Liverpool, and Manchester's five. Unfortunately Galton did not explain what he meant by Anglo-Irish, Scots-Irish, and 'pure' Irish, but it is not unreasonable to infer from his work that the Anglo-Irish included the third and fourth earls of Rosse and John Tyndall, that the Scots-Irish included Sir William Thomson, and the 'pure' Irish Sir Robert Kane. (If Galton had made his study in the 1890s it is possible that he would have added the Parsons family to his great scientific dynasties like the Darwins, since Sir Charles Parsons, 'the most original British engineer since James Watt',[2] had added his reputation to that of his father and brother.)

Arthur Conan Doyle—not improperly, considering his background—was generous to Ireland in his article in 1888, ascribing 11 per cent of his '1150 names which cannot be set aside' to Ireland, although this put Ireland after England (72 per cent) and Scotland (14 per cent).[3] On the basis of population, however, Doyle showed that Ireland came well behind England and that Scotland was twice as productive as Ireland. He balanced this, however, by being complimentary to Dublin: 'The lowlands of Scotland, Aberdeenshire, Dublin, Hampshire, Suffolk, London, Devonshire, Gloucestershire, and Berkshire, are, in the order named, the divisions of the kingdom which during the last twenty or thirty years produced the most plentiful crop of distinguished

[1] Havelock Ellis, *A study of British genius* (London, 1904), p. 29.

[2] *D.N.B. concise*, pt ii, p. 335.

[3] Arthur Conan Doyle, 'On the geographical distribution of British intellect' in *Nineteenth Century*, xxiv (Aug. 1888), p. 184.

citizens.'[1] He was also complimentary about individuals: Lecky was one of the three great successors of Carlyle, and Tyndall was put on the same level as Darwin, Owen, and Hooker. Within Ireland, Doyle put Dublin ahead of everywhere else (with Lord Wolseley, Boucicault, Balfe, and Lecky); second was Munster (Maclise, McGinn, General Butler, Sir Hugh Gough, and Sir Bernard Burke), with Ulster coming only third (with Sir William Thomson, Carleton, Allingham, Sir James Emerson Tennent, and Lord Dufferin)—'the intellectual standard in Munster is, man for man, higher than that of Ulster, which is contrary to the generally received opinion'. Leinster, excluding Dublin, came fourth (with Parnell, Percy Fitzgerald, and Tyndall), and Connacht with only seven of the 1150 celebrities was 'the mental nadir' of the United Kingdom coming after even Wales and Cornwall.[2]

A. H. H. Maclean, who tried to hide his Scots origins behind a pseudonym, was less generous to Ireland than Doyle, ascribing only 8 per cent of his 'eminent men' to Ireland, putting it well behind England (57 per cent) and Scotland (14 per cent) but ahead of Wales (2 per cent). From his 'eminent men' Maclean chose one hundred 'preeminent' men ('the greatest of our great men') and here Ireland did better, being credited with 15 per cent, coming second after England (51 per cent), but ahead of Scotland (14 per cent) and Wales (2 per cent), showing that the Irish were 'more than twice as successful in producing "preeminent" men as in supplying "eminent" men'.[3] Also, Maclean admitted that Dublin was a notable cradle of eminent men, coming third equal with Glasgow, after London and Edinburgh and before Liverpool and Aberdeen. Cork was seventh, which put it ahead of much larger cities such as Manchester (tenth) and Birmingham (eleventh). On the basis of population, however, the order changed considerably with Aberdeen first, Edinburgh and Newcastle second and third, and Dublin fourth equal with Bristol, Glasgow, London, and Plymouth. Maclean also identified the universities of his eminent men, finding that Oxford accounted for 35 per cent and Cambridge 31 per cent; Dublin came fifth with only 6 per cent, being slightly behind Edinburgh and London, but ahead of Glasgow, Aberdeen, and St Andrews; Belfast came next, ahead of Durham and Owens College.

Ellis was in some ways the most interesting of those who studied British ability; first, he considered women more seriously than the others, including fifty-five in his population of 1,030; secondly, he covered the whole of British history and not just the reign of Queen Victoria, which probably accounts for the small Irish share of only 6 per cent, the smallest credited to the Irish. 'The Irish', according to Ellis, 'have been seriously hampered by geographical and to some extent by linguistic barriers, as well as by unfortunate political circumstances, in contributing their due share to British civilisation.' But he was

[1] Ibid., p. 195.　　　　　　　　　　　　　　　　　　　[2] Ibid., pp 193, 195.
[3] A. H. H. M[aclean], *Where do we get our best men. Some statistics showing their nationalities, counties, towns, schools, universities, and other antecedents: 1837–97* (London, 1900), p. 6.

optimistic, for 'certainly with the advent of modern times the Irish contribution tends to reach a larger proportion'. There is some substance in D. J. O'Donoghue's complaint that Ellis's method of selection worked against the Irish. His composers did not include John Field and his generals did not include Wellington; his scientists, who numbered 120, included only Tyndall, who 'it may be noted . . . was of original English origin'. The only distinction he attributed to the Irish was among actors and actresses where 'the relative preponderance of the Irish is enormous'.[1] On the other hand he regarded Charlotte Brontë as Irish, which might in the opinion of some outweigh the omission of Hogan and Foley.

If the five estimates of Irish ability are combined (taking Maclean's eminent and preeminent men as two estimates), the Irish accounted for 10 per cent of British ability. Measured against population this was not impressive for in 1841 Ireland accounted for 31 per cent of the United Kingdom's population and for 17 per cent in 1871. Maclean, who went into the relationship between population and ability, put Ireland behind Scotland, England and Wales: the Scots had 57 per cent more eminent men than their population warranted; the English were just about proportionate to their population; the Welsh produced only half as many as they should have, and the Irish only a third. (The Jews and the Aberdonians were the most prolific groups in the country, producing five times the national average of eminent men.)

Was Ireland's poor record due to bias in the compilation of the *D.N.B.*, and the way in which it was used by Ellis, as O'Donoghue claimed? Certainly Ellis's selection of subjects whose biographies occupied three or more pages probably did work against the Irish, although Ellis tried to correct this when he discovered that he had not included Jane Austen in his first selection because her entry did not run to three pages. At first sight, it seems unlikely that the compilers of the *D.N.B.* seriously neglected Ireland; Jack Cade, for example, was described as an Irishman, which was at best a doubtful compliment; Irish surnames from O'Beirne to O'Dugan accounted for nearly 1 per cent of the whole work, which almost certainly exceeds their percentage of the population; the Fitzgeralds alone accounted for forty pages of volume xix. The bias of the *D.N.B.* was not necessarily an anti-Irish one, but arose from a failure to deal adequately with certain kinds of achievement; neither Edward J. Harland nor Gustav Wilhelm Wolff, for example, were included. A sample, taken from all sixty-three volumes, showed that 18 per cent of those born between 1800 and 1870 had some connection with Ireland, which suggests at first sight that something was wrong with the way Ellis and the others made their selections rather than with the *D.N.B.* But several of the group making up the 18 per cent must be excluded because they had no real connection with Ireland, even applying the rather loose taxonomic standards of Victorians. First, there are those who had a family link with Ireland but were not born there: Thomas Lovell Beddoes

[1] Havelock Ellis, *A study of British genius* (London, 1904), pp 24–5, 67, 75.

was a nephew of Maria Edgeworth but seems to have had no connection with Ireland; Albert Denison was the third son of the Marquis Conyngham but devoted his life to Anglo-Saxon archaeology; George Errington, the titular archbishop of Trebizond, had an Irish mother but made his career in England and Rome and had as little connection with Ireland as with his archdiocese. In this group also comes Ned Kelly, who was Irish in a way that these were not, but was not born in Ireland, and in any case, is a dubious candidate for a place in a roll-call of Irish ability. Secondly, there were those born in Ireland but whose careers or backgrounds were not Irish; the most tantalising in this group is Maria Dolores Eliza Rosanna Gilbert, known as Lola Montez, who was born in Limerick and contracted in County Meath what was probably her only legal and valid marriage; yet she must be excluded, although it is a pity to have to exclude what is almost certainly the only Limerick-born woman who captivated a king of Bavaria. Thirdly, there were those who were not born in Ireland but whose careers bound them to the country where they spent most of their lives. Alexander Thom was born in Morayshire and came to Dublin when he was only twenty; it is tempting to regard his great directory, whose 'superiority to its predecessors was due to the incorporation for the first time in a directory of a mass of valuable and skilfully arranged statistics relating to Ireland',[1] as an Irish achievement but strict fairness demands his exclusion when comparing Ireland with the rest of the United Kindom. When these three groups are removed, the Irish account for 11 per cent of *D.N.B.* subjects born between 1800 and 1870, which is rather better than the share given to them by Maclean and about the same as the estimates of Doyle and Galton.

There seems to be little doubt, therefore, that the Irish, on the basis of population, were under-represented among Victorian worthies. It is debateable, however, if population is a fair measure of potential; more important is wealth, in spite of Victorians' obsession with self-made men. In 1870 incomes liable to pay income tax in Ireland accounted for only 6 per cent of those in the United Kingdom; even if a wider measure of wealth is taken, and smaller incomes just below those liable for income tax are included, Irish upper- and middle-class incomes accounted for only 8 per cent of the United Kingdom total. By this measure, Ireland appears to have performed relatively well. (The difference in wealth may account, for example, for the fact that Maclean found that only 5 per cent of his self-made men were Irish.) Differences in wealth, however, do not explain the differences between Ireland and Scotland, for upper- and middle-class incomes were about the same in both countries in 1870. One difference between Ireland and Scotland that may have been important was the number of university places available, for Scotland had more than Ireland; in 1870, for example, Edinburgh and Glasgow on their own had as many students as Trinity and the three Queen's colleges. Another possibility is that Ireland had fewer clerical families than either Scotland or England; Ireland was

[1] *D.N.B.*, lvi, 145.

relatively well endowed with clergymen, but about half of them were priests, whose presbyteries could not in the nature of things be nurseries of talent like the manses of Scotland or the vicarages of England. Ireland in fact had only 9 per cent of the United Kingdom's marriageable clergymen. It is possible, too, that the Irish tended to take up careers that did not lead to eminence. In 1871 20 per cent of the officers in the regular army were Irish, but whatever opportunities for advancement a military career offered, it did not, in this most peaceful of reigns when General William Booth was probably better known outside Britain than General Gordon, produce many great generals. In one field of martial distinction, the winning of V.C.s, the Irish did well; for almost a third of those who won V.C.s during the Crimean war were Irishmen, including the first sailor to win the V.C. (C. D. Lucas from Armagh) and the first soldier (Luke O'Connor from Roscommon). 23-XII-15

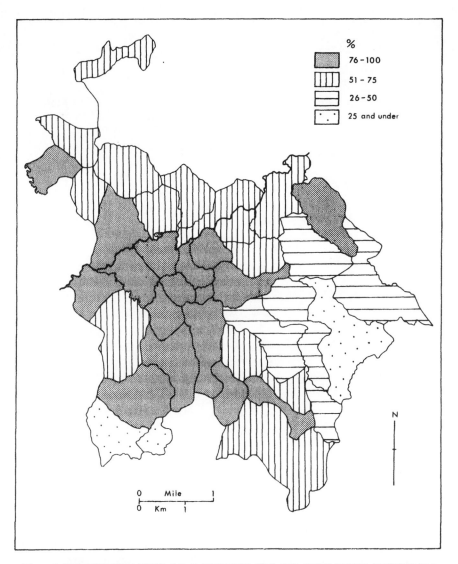

Map 18 PROTESTANTS AS A PERCENTAGE OF POPULATION IN
CERTAIN TOWNLANDS OF THE PARISH OF MAGHERACROSS,
CO. FERMANAGH, by W. E. Vaughan

General valulation of rateable property in Ireland . . . union of Enniskillen (Dublin, 1862), pp 228–41; ibid.,
union of Irvinestown (Dublin, 1862), pp 107–13.

INDEX

All persons of rank are indexed primarily under the family name, cross references being given from the title.

The following abbreviations are used:

abp	archbishop	L.L.	lord lieutenant
bp	bishop	n.	note
C.S.	chief secretary	P.	protestant
L.C.	lord chancellor	R.C.	Roman Catholic

1. (a) 'The union!' by Thomas Rowlandson, 1801

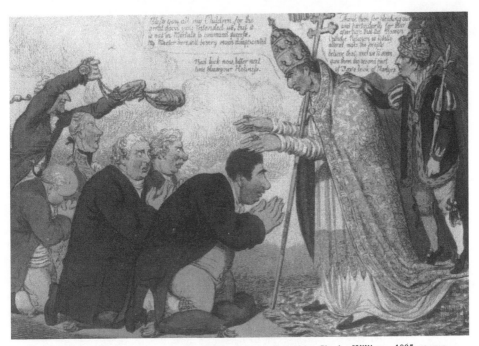

(b) 'The catholic petitioners, recieving [sic] the papal benediction' by Charles Williams, 1805; at rear Grattan, with censers; left to right, Derby, Moira, Norfolk, Sheridan, Fox, Pius VII, and his 'master' Napoleon

2. (a) 'A new Irish jaunting car ...' by Robert Cruikshank, 1819

(b) 'Pat's comment on steam carriages' by 'A. Sharpshooter', 1829

(b) 'The valentine' by 'Phiz', from Dickens, *Pickwick papers*; note placard on mantelshelf

3. (a) 'The major [Sirr] trying a charity sermon', 1810

4. (*a*) George IV landing at Howth, 12 Aug. 1821

(*b*) The Dublin–Kingstown railway at Blackrock, 1834

5. (a) 'An excellent royal extinguisher'; Wellesley (lord lieutenant 1821–8) suppresses orangemen

(b) 'Dissolution of the Association' by William Heath; Wellington (P.M. 1829) attempts to anticipate 'marriage' (catholic relief)

6. O'Connell and his supporters, 1829, by William Harvey: (a) 'A sketch of the great agi-tater' (b) 'An independant [sic] freeholder rejoicing at the triumph of the man of the peo[ple]'

7. (a) 'The three and the deuce' by 'HB' (John Doyle); left to right, John Lawless, O'Connell, and Richard Lalor Shiel

(b) 'The pas d'extase; or, ministerial fascination' by John Leech (*Punch*, 31 May 1845): Peel and O'Connell

8. (a) Belfast, from the lough, by Andrew Nicholl, 1833

(b) Donnybrook fair, by Benjamin Clayton, 1833

9. (a) 'Burning the effigy of Lundy in Derry', artist unknown, c.1830

(b) Protestant missionary settlement, Achill, Co. Mayo, lithograph by A. Fussell

10. (a) 'A Connemara cabin' by F. W. Topham, 1846

(b) Dublin entrance to the demesne of Markree, Co. Sligo, by Francis Goodwin, 1835

11. (a) Alexander's mills near Milford, Co. Carlow, by William Harvey, 1841

(b) Bianconi cars, by William Harvey, 1841

12. Illustrations by Daniel Maclise to *Moore's Irish melodies* (London, 1846)

(b) Lady Morgan, by Daniel Maclise, 1835

13. (a) 'The balance of public favor' probably by 'HB' (John Doyle): Moore prevails over Scott, 1827

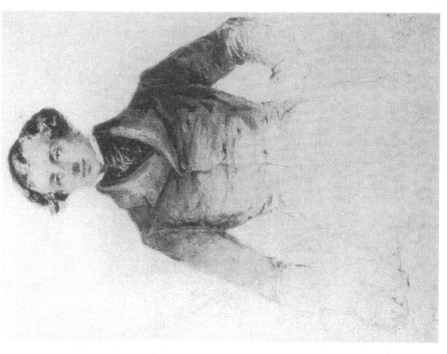

(b) Thomas Francis Meagher, by Edward Hayes

14. (a) **Rev**. Henry Cooke, D.D., by Sir Daniel McNee

15. Constabulary of Ireland: (*a*) an ideal view, *c.* 1836 (*b*) practical duty, 1848

17. (*a*) Funeral at Shepperton lakes, near Skibbereen, Co. Cork, by James Mahony, early 1847

(*b*) Funeral procession of O'Connell in Westmoreland Street and College Green, Dublin, 5 Aug. 1847

18. (*a*) Procession of bishops and clergy at the synod of Thurles, 25 Aug. 1850

(*b*) 'Which is the martyr?', by John Leech (*Punch*, 20 Sept. 1851)

19. 'The emigration agents' office. —The passage money paid', 1851

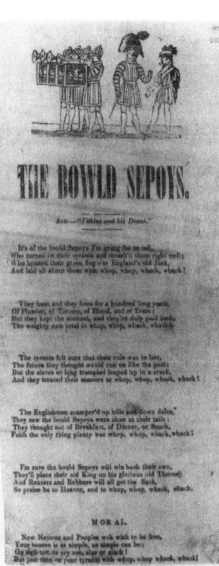

20. Ballads, 1854–7

THE GALLANT ESCAPE OF
PAT M'CARTHY
FROM THE RUSSIANS.

Good people all, both great and small,
  I pray you'll pay attention ;
I'll sing to you a verse or two,
  So mark what I will mention.
I make no doubt, you heard about
  The soldier Pat M'Carthy,
And how he served the Russians out,
  Will make you laugh quite hearty.

CHORUS.

Hurrah ! my boys, with warlike joys ;
  Come, let us all be hearty ;
Fill up the glass, and let it pass,
  And drink to bold M'Carthy.

It was on the glorious battle day,
  The Russians had him taken ;
But like an Irishman so gay,
  Poor Pat was not mistaken,
For there and then, the three great men
  As onwards they were crawling,
He snapt his gun, and showed them fun,
  And sent the Russians sprawling.

It was life and death to draw his breath,
  While he was in their clutches ;
He ran the chance and made them dance
  Like Billy goats on crutches ;
He shot one down upon the ground,
  With just two ounce of powder,
He gave the other a mortal wound,
  That flattened him like a flounder.
              (stretched,
When Pat had both the Russians
  He scampered back so cunning,
The third ran off to Menschikoff,
  And swore the d——l was coming.

Lord Raglan saw the scarlet coat
  Come off so brave and handy ;
He gave to Pat a five pound-note,
  To drink his health in brandy.

M'Carthy made the Russians rue,
  He gave them such a licking ;
The Frenchmen cried out, *mon Dieu !*
  Well done, my gallant chicken,
When Emperor Nick he heard the trick,
  He did not laugh so hearty ;
Like a Russian Bear he wept & swore
  The d——l was in M'Carthy.

You lads and lasses think on him
  Who made the Russians snivel ;
He beat the three right manfully,
  And sent them to the d——l ;
With courage bold, as I am told,
  He walloped them most hearty ;
The Russians will remember still
  The name of Pat M'Carthy.

A British soldier will not yield ;
  His ground he will maintain it.
And when he goes on the battle field,
  To charge them with the bayonet.
The Queen of England may delight,
  And make herself quite hearty,
While she has got such men to fight
  As gallant Pat M'Carthy.

Printed at HALY'S,
86, HANOVER STREET,
CORK.

21. Title-pages: (a) (b) (c) (d) four new Irish journals (e) (f) translations of George Salmon, *A treatise on conic sections* (Dublin, 1847)

22. (a) 'Hibernia lamenting the death of [Dan] Donnelly her favourite champion', c.1820

(b) Master M'Garth, winner of the Waterloo Cup in 1868, 1869, and 1871, with his trainer

23. (a) Assembly of the 72-inch telescope at Birr castle, 1845; lithotint by W. Bevan from drawing by Henrietta M. Crompton

(b) John Hampton's 'Erin go bragh' balloon at Kensington, 1851

24. (*a*) Killyleagh castle, Co. Down, from the south-east, 1833

(*b*) Killyleagh castle from the south-west after refurbishment in 1847–51, Charles Lanyon and partners
architects

25. (*a*) Gold-workings near Woodenbridge, Co. Wicklow, 1841, by Andrew Nicholl

(*b*) Design for proposed new Carlisle Bridge, Dublin, by G. G. Page of London and Richard Turner of Hammersmith iron works, Dublin, 1862

26. (*a*) Carlow union workhouse, George Wilkinson architect, 1841

(*b*) Design for constabulary barrack, J. H. Owen architect, 1870

27. (*a*) Enniscorthy national school, J. H. Owen architect, 1861

(*b*) Queen's College, Cork, during the visit of Queen Victoria and Prince Albert, 3 Aug. 1849; lithograph
by W. Scraggs from drawing by N. M. Cummins

28. Ulster Hall, Belfast, W. J. Barre architect, 1861; lithograph by J. H. Connor

29. (a) Main hall, Dublin International Exhibition, 1865, photograph by William England

(b) 'The 78th Highlanders testing the strength of the galleries, Dublin International Exhibition'

30. (a) Crozier memorial, Banbridge, Co. Down; W. J. Barre architect, J. R. Kirk sculptor, 1862

(b) 'Boy at a stream', J. H. Foley sculptor, 1851

(c) Pulpit, Dublin castle chapel, by John Hardman & Co., 1860

(d) Detail of Caledon column, Caledon, Co. Tyrone; William Murray architect, Thomas Kirk (probably) sculptor, 1840

(b) Sir Thomas Larcom

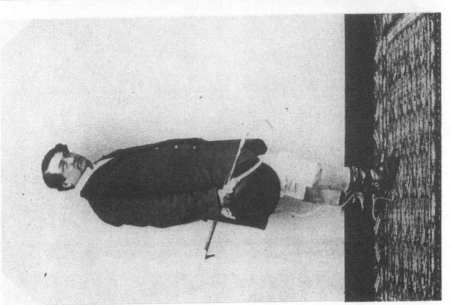

31. (a) Lord Naas

32. Fenian suspects, 1866–8: (*a*) Morgan Burke (*b*) Thomas Gallagher (*c*) J. C. Bright alias James Burns (*d*) Robert Halligan (*e*) Octavi Fariola (*f*) James Lamb

33. Fenian suspects: (*a*) William Hogan (*b*) Robert F. Stowell (*c*) Francis McClelland (*d*) James McCaffrey
Fenian convict: James O'Connor (*e*) before and (*f*) after conviction

(a)

(b)

(c)

34. Cartoons by 'Ape' (Carlo Pellegrini), *Vanity Fair*, 1869: (*a*) Edward Cardwell (*b*) Bishop Magee (*c*) Lord Cairns

(b)

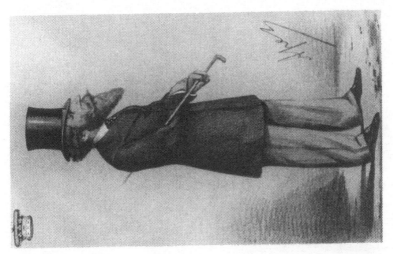

(c)

(a)

35. Cartoons by 'Ape', *Vanity Fair*, 1869–70: (*a*) Chichester Fortescue (*b*) Duke of Abercorn (*c*) Sir Robert Peel

36.   Installation of the prince of Wales as a knight of St Patrick, 14 Apr. 1868, by M. A. Hayes

NATIONAL SCHOOL !

"BIG BOGEY" IN IRELAND.

(b) '"Big bogey" in Ireland' by John Tenniel (*Punch*, 18 Sept. 1869); Cardinal
Cullen discourages interdenominational education

THE CHANGELING.

37. (a) 'The changeling' by John Tenniel (*Punch*, 17 July 1869); Archbishop
A. C. Tait, Bright, and Gladstone

(a)

(b)

(c)

38. (a) 'Captain Rock's banditti swearing in a new member', 1824 Westmeath Ribbon suspects, 1871: (b) James Gilchrist (c) James Melia